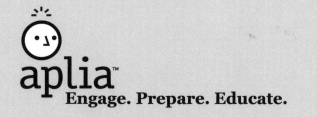

aplia™

Engage. Prepare. Educate.

This edition offers you the chance to use Aplia™, an online, interactive tool that ensures you review fundamental grammar and mechanics and understand concepts presented in *Business Communication: Process and Product, 6e.* Aplia improves learning by increasing student effort and engagement. Using Aplia can be *just that easy.*

If you choose to use Aplia™*, you'll be able to take advantage of many of these benefits:

- Chapter-specific assignments that help you read and understand the text

- Instant detailed feedback on every question

- Grammar and mechanics tutorials that help you practice key writing skills so that your instructors spend less time reviewing and more time teaching advanced writing concepts

- Access to a full ebook version of *Business Communication: Process and Product, 6e*

For more details about using Aplia with *Business Communication: Process and Product, 6e,* **visit www.aplia.com/cengage**

* Aplia is not automatically included with the Sixth Edition. If you would like more information, student pricing, or to see a demo, please contact Aplia at 888.858.7305 or email info@aplia.com.

Business Communication

Process & Product

Sixth Edition

Mary Ellen Guffey

Professor Emerita of Business

Los Angeles Pierce College

SOUTH-WESTERN
CENGAGE Learning

Australia • Brazil • Japan • Korea • Mexico • Singapore • Spain • United Kingdom • United States

Business Communication: Process and Product, 6e
Mary Ellen Guffey

VP/Editorial Director: Jack W. Calhoun

Publisher: Melissa S. Acuña

Acquisitions Editor: Erin Joyner

Sr. Developmental Editor: Mary Draper

Marketing Manager: Mike Aliscad

Sr. Content Project Manager: Tamborah Moore

Manager, Editorial Media: John Barans

Managing Technology Project Manager: Pam Wallace

Technology Project Manager: John Rich

Marketing Communications Manager: Sarah Greber

Sr. Manufacturing Coordinator: Diane Gibbons

Production House: LEAP Publishing Services, Inc.

Compositor: ICC Macmillan Inc.

Art Director: Stacy Jenkins Shirley

Cover and Internal Designer: Craig Ramsdell

Cover Image: © Getty Images

Photography Manager: Deanna Ettinger

Photo Researcher: Terri Miller

For product information and technology assistance, contact us at
Cengage Learning Academic Resource Center, 1-800-423-0563

For permission to use material from this text or product,
submit all requests online at **www.cengage.com/permissions**
Further permissions questions can be emailed to
permissionrequest@cengage.com

Library of Congress Control Number: 2007939610
Package ISBN 13: 978-0-324-54290-5
Package ISBN 10: 0-324-54290-9

Book only ISBN 13: 978-0-324-57867-6
Book only ISBN 10: 0-324-57867-9

South-Western Cengage Learning
5191 Natorp Boulevard
Mason, OH 45040
USA

Cengage Learning products are represented in Canada by
Nelson Education, Ltd.

For your course and learning solutions, visit **academic.cengage.com**
Purchase any of our products at your local college store or at our
preferred online store **www.ichapters.com**

Printed in the United States of America
2 3 4 5 6 7 11 10 09 08

Dear Business Communication
Students:

As the workplace becomes
more complex with advances in
technology and globalization, you
face a challenging future. You need
better intercultural, technology, and
communication skills than ever before.

The Sixth Edition of *Business
Communication: Process and
Product* focuses on preparing you for
careers in an increasingly digital and
global workplace with instructional
materials that provide training as efficiently and
easily as possible. Check out the following features:

- **Expanded coverage of communication technology.** This edition discusses
blogs, instant messaging, wikis, videoconferencing, PowerPoint "decks," and
other communication tools so that you are prepared for today's digital workplace.

- **Increased emphasis on intercultural communication.** More model
documents, more discussion material, and more end-of-chapter activities focus
on techniques for improving intercultural communication to prepare you for
interacting in the global environment.

- **Strengthened coverage of "soft skills" and ethics.** The Sixth Edition boosts
coverage of teamwork, listening, nonverbal, speech, and etiquette skills—all of
which are frequently mentioned in job ads. This edition also adds "Ethics Checks"
to generate discussion of practical classroom and workplace ethical dilemmas.

- **New employment interviewing chapter!** Tips on what to do before, during,
and after an employment interview will help you ace employment interviews.

- **New Web site for students and instructors!** Every student with a new book
has access to the new Web site with chapter reviews, flash cards, diagnostic
quizzes, and many self-directed learning opportunities that extend the textbook
and classroom experience.

- **New easy grammar review!** Completely redesigned grammar/mechanics
exercises in every chapter present a structured review to guide you through all
the rules.

In the preface that follows, we illustrate key features of the Sixth Edition to introduce
you to the process of successful business communication and the conversion of that
process into powerful products. As always, I welcome your comments and suggestions
as you use the No. 1 business communication book in this country and abroad,
Business Communication: Process and Product, 6e.

Cordially,

Mary Ellen Guffey

Guffey... It's Just That Easy

Market-leading and student-oriented, *Business Communication: Process and Product, 6e,* continues to give you the most current and authoritative coverage of communication technology and business communication concepts. Award-winning author Mary Ellen Guffey provides unparalleled student and instructor resources to help you learn business communication concepts. With the book's 3-x-3 writing process, coverage of recent trends and technologies in business communication, and an unmatched ancillary package, you will find that business communication can be *just that easy.*

Communicating at Work Part 1

Wireless Giant Qualcomm Thrives on E-Mail

If you own a cellular telephone, you have probably heard of Qualcomm Incorporated. Founded in 1985, the San Diego–based company is a global leader in developing and delivering innovative wireless products and solutions. Today, hundreds of millions of people worldwide use mobile phones and other wireless services based on Qualcomm's solutions.

Qualcomm prides itself on its positive work environment and excellent employee benefits, which keep employee turnover low. The company consistently earns high rankings on lists such as *Fortune's* 100 Best Companies to Work For and Most Admired Companies, *Industry Week's* 50 Top Manufacturers, and *Business Ethics'* 100 Best Corporate Citizens. [1]

Like most technology companies, Qualcomm considers e-mail its primary form of communication, both internally for employees and externally to vendors and customers. "Qualcomm has had e-mail since day one and is very e-mail centric," says Norm Fjeldheim, senior vice president and chief information officer, who oversees all aspects of Qualcomm's information technology. "Other forms of electronic media, such as instant messaging, are becoming popular as well." [2] Qualcomm employees can now access their e-mail at home or on the road, using their cell phones, other wireless devices, or laptop computers.

Fjeldheim consolidates all of his correspondence in his e-mail inbox. He receives 100 to 300 e-mails daily but has become efficient and effective at handling his messages. "I prefer e-mail and don't suffer from e-mail overload," he says. "E-mail is, to a large degree, how I know what is going on within the company and my department. I tell my employees they can't send me too much e-mail. If they wonder whether to send me an e-mail, I tell them to send it, and I will figure out whether it's of interest to me." [3] His e-mail inbox serves as his to-do list. After reading a message, he leaves action items in his inbox until he completes the task.

Then he moves the e-mail to an appropriate folder. Special filters either reject suspect e-mails or move them to a spam folder.

http://www.qualcomm.com

Critical Thinking

- Why has e-mail become such an important form of business communication? How has it changed the ways employees interact with each other, with vendors, and with customers?
- What are some of the disadvantages of using e-mail in business correspondence, and what practices can you recommend to counteract these drawbacks?
- What strategies does Mr. Fjeldheim use to manage the heavy volume of e-mail he receives?

Applying the Writing Process to E-Mail Messages and Memos

Like most businesses today, Qualcomm relies on e-mail for many of its internal communication needs. In times past, messages among company insiders took the form of hard-copy memorandums. Today, however, e-mail is the communication channel of choice. It has been hailed as one of the greatest productivity tools of our time. [4]

A primary function of e-mail is exchanging messages within organizations. Such internal communication has taken on increasing importance today. Organizations are downsizing, flattening chains of command, forming work teams, and empowering rank-and-file employees. Given more power in making decisions, employees find that they need more information. They must collect, exchange, and evaluate information about the products and services they offer. Management also needs input from employees to respond rapidly to local and global market changes. This growing demand for information means an increasing use of e-mail, although hard-copy memos are still written.

Developing skill in writing e-mail messages and memos brings you two important benefits. First, well-written documents are likely to achieve their goals. They create goodwill by being cautious, caring, and clear. They do not intentionally or unintentionally foment ill feelings. Second, well-written internal messages enhance your image within the organization. Individuals identified as competent, professional writers are noticed and rewarded; most often, they are the ones promoted into management positions.

This chapter focuses on routine e-mail messages and memos. These straightforward messages open with the main idea because their topics are not sensitive and require little

LEARNING OBJECTIVE 1
Discuss how the 3-x-3 writing process helps you produce effective e-mail messages and memos.

E-mail is the communication channel of choice for exchanging information within organizations.

Mail Messages and Memos

171

of words. Asian language characters are much more complex than the Western alphabet; therefore, Asians are said to have a higher competence in the discrimination of visual patterns.

Time Orientation. North Americans consider time a precious commodity to be conserved. They correlate time with productivity, efficiency, and money. Keeping people waiting for business appointments wastes time and is also rude.

In other cultures time may be perceived as an unlimited and never-ending resource to be enjoyed. A North American businessperson, for example, was kept waiting two hours past a scheduled appointment time in South America. She wasn't offended, though, because she was familiar with Hispanics' more relaxed concept of time.

Although Asians are punctual, their need for deliberation and contemplation sometimes clashes with an American's desire for speedy decisions. They do not like to be rushed. A Japanese businessperson considering the purchase of American appliances, for example, asked for five minutes to consider the seller's proposal. The potential buyer crossed his arms, sat back, and closed his eyes in concentration. A scant 18 seconds later, the American resumed his sales pitch to the obvious bewilderment of the Japanese buyer.[33]

As you can see, high-context cultures differ from low-context cultures in many dimensions. These differences can be significant for companies engaging in international business. One of the places where international business is expanding most rapidly is on the World Wide Web. Web sites give companies of all sizes global reach and the immediate ability to interact with customers all over the world. In the face of fierce competition, the most successful Web sites are built by communicators who fully understand the powerful effects of high- and low-context cultures, as discussed in the accompanying Tech Talk.

North Americans tend to correlate time with productivity, efficiency, and money.

Asians tend to need time for deliberation and contemplation.

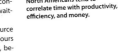

Tech Talk

Going Global With a Culturally Customized Web Site

Early Web sites were almost always in English and meant for Americans. As online access grows around the world, however, companies are reassessing their sites. What should companies do when they decide to go global on the Web?

- **Learn the local lingo.** Other countries have developed their own Web jargon and iconography. *Home page* is "pagina inicial" (initial page) in Spanish and "page d'accueil" (welcome page) in French. Experts warn against simply translating English words page by page. Hiring a proficient translator or working with a local developer is a better idea.
- **Check icons.** American Web surfers easily recognize the mailbox, but in Europe a more universal icon would be an envelope. Test images with local residents.
- **Relax restrictions on consistency.** Allow flexibility to meet local tastes. For example, McDonald's main site greets visitors with the golden arches and a Ronald McDonald-red background. The Japanese site, though, displays softer colors, which are more pleasing in this Asian culture.
- **Keep the message simple.** Whether in English or the local language, use simple, easily translated words. Avoid slang, jargon, acronyms, or ambiguous expressions.
- **Customize Web content for high-context cultures.** For high-context cultures (such as those of Japan and China), Web sites often include images and wording reflecting politeness, flowery language, use of indirect expressions (*perhaps, probably, somewhat*), ... they may include animated images (including

cartoon characters), a soft-sell approach, and appeals to harmony.[34]
- **Customize Web content for low-context cultures.** Web sites in low-context cultures (such as those of the United States and Germany) use more aggressive promotions, discounts, and an emphasis on product advantages using explicit comparisons. They include superlative expressions (*We're No. 1, the world's largest, we lead the market*). Low-context Web sites often identify return policies, guarantees, and purchase conditions.[35]

Career Application
Using Google, locate the Web sites of two high-context companies such as convenience store 7-Eleven Japan (**http://www.sej.co.jp**) or Excite (**http://friends.excite.co.jp/friends**). View the sites in Japanese as well as in English with Google's machine translation feature. (If these URLs change, use Google to search for *www.sej. co.jp* and *Friends Excite Company Japan*.) Then examine the Web sites of two low-context companies such as 7-Eleven U.S. (**http://www.7-eleven.com**) and IBM U.S. (**http://www.ibm.com/us**). View opening and internal pages. How are the suggestions mentioned here reflected in these sites? Do you see subtle differences in Web sites from low- and high-context cultures? Do you think international Web sites might be showing signs of homogenization?

Reshaping the World of Work
...tically as a result of innovative software, superfast wireless ... that allow workers to share information, work from remote ... or away from the office. We're seeing a gradual progression from ... calendaring, to deeper functionality, such as remote database ...-based collaborative applications. Becoming familiar with ...ologies can help you be successful in today's digital workplace.

...phony: VoIP
...ditional phone ...lows callers to ...inating long-distance and local telephone charges. Higher-end VoIP systems now support unified voice mail, e-mail, click-to-call capabilities, and softphones (phones using computer networking). Free or low-cost Internet telephony sites, such as the popular Skype, are also increasingly used by businesses.

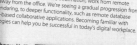

Multifunctional Printers
Stand-alone copiers, fax machines, scanners, and printers have been replaced with multifunctional devices. Offices are transitioning from a "print and distribute" environment to a "distribute and print" environment. Security measures include pass codes and even biometric thumbprint scanning to make sure data streams are not captured, interrupted, or edited.

Open Offices
Widespread use of laptop computers, wireless technology, and VoIP have led to more fluid, flexible, and open workspaces. Smaller computers and flat-screen monitors enable designers to save space with boomerang-shaped workstations and cockpit-style work surfaces rather than space-hogging corner work areas. Smaller breakout areas for impromptu meetings are taking over some cubicle space, and digital databases are replacing file cabinets.

Handheld Wireless Devices
A new generation of lightweight, handheld devices provide phone, e-mail, Web browsing, and calendar options anywhere there's a wireless network. Devices such as the BlackBerry and the Palm Treo now allow you to tap into corporate databases and intranets from remote locations. You can check customers' files, complete orders, and send out receipts without returning to the office.

Company Intranets
To share insider information, many companies provide their own protected Web sites called intranets. An intranet may handle company e-mail, announcements, an employee directory, a policy handbook, frequently asked questions, personnel forms and data, employee discussion forums, shared documents, and other employee information.

Voice Recognition
Computers equipped with voice recognition software enable users to dictate up to 160 words a minute with accurate transcription. Voice recognition is particularly helpful to disabled workers and to professionals with heavy dictation loads, such as physicians and attorneys. Users can create documents, enter data, compose and send e-mails, browse the Web, and control the desktop—all by voice.

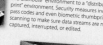

Electronic Presentations
Business presentations in PowerPoint can be projected from a laptop or PDA or posted online. Sophisticated presentations may include animations, sound effects, digital photos, video clips, or hyperlinks to Internet sites. In some industries, PowerPoint slides ("decks") are replacing or supplementing traditional hard-copy reports.

Reshaping: © Creatas / Photolibrary Group / Index Stock Imagery; Telephone: © Jochen Tack / Alamy; Open Offices: © Ablestock / Dynamic Graphics / Jupiterimages; Multifunctional Printer: © Apply Pictures / Alamy; Handheld Wireless: © AP IMAGES; Voice Recognition: © TOSHIFUMI KITAMURA / AFP / Getty images; Company Intranet: © Yent Miller / E-Visual Communications, Inc.; Electronic Presentation: © Image Source / Alamy

Learning With Guffey...
It's Just That Easy

You will find multiple resources with this new edition to help make learning business communication easier. From the famous 3-x-3 writing process to new end-of-chapter activities, Guffey has updated tools and created new ways to keep you interested and engaged. With all of these options, learning can be *just that easy.*

- **Most Current Coverage.** The Sixth Edition presents the very latest in communication technology. Expanded coverage of employment communication and intercultural communication give you the broad base of knowledge you need to succeed in today's digital workplace.

- **Web-based Resources.** The textbook, WebTutor™, and Web site are integrated to give you a variety of alternatives for studying and reinforcing your understanding of chapter topics.

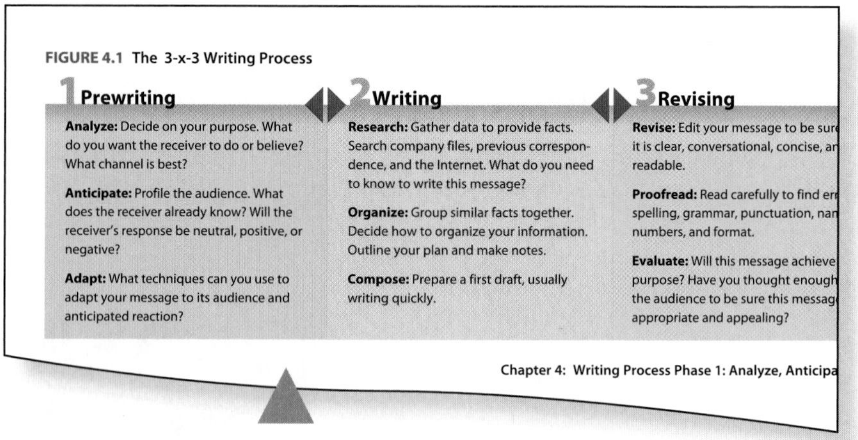

FIGURE 4.1 The 3-x-3 Writing Process

1 Prewriting

Analyze: Decide on your purpose. What do you want the receiver to do or believe? What channel is best?

Anticipate: Profile the audience. What does the receiver already know? Will the receiver's response be neutral, positive, or negative?

Adapt: What techniques can you use to adapt your message to its audience and anticipated reaction?

2 Writing

Research: Gather data to provide facts. Search company files, previous correspondence, and the Internet. What do you need to know to write this message?

Organize: Group similar facts together. Decide how to organize your information. Outline your plan and make notes.

Compose: Prepare a first draft, usually writing quickly.

3 Revising

Revise: Edit your message to be sure it is clear, conversational, concise, and readable.

Proofread: Read carefully to find errors in spelling, grammar, punctuation, names, numbers, and format.

Evaluate: Will this message achieve its purpose? Have you thought enough about the audience to be sure this message is appropriate and appealing?

Chapter 4: Writing Process Phase 1: Analyze, Anticipate

- **3-x-3 Writing Process.** Guffey's 3-x-3 writing process provides you with a solid, three-step strategy for developing effective communication.

- ***NEW* Online Student Interactive Resources.** The newly designed Guffey Web site, **www.meguffey.com**, is an online study assistant that features self-teaching grammar/mechanics review, PowerPoint® slides, chapter review quizzes, Documents for Analysis, and additional resources to enhance learning.

- **Three-part Case Studies.** Most students learn best from real-world examples, and these unique, three-part case studies from high-profile companies reinforce learning.

"I was impressed with the descriptions of new technologies (email, blogs, wikis, etc.) that the chapter described. Many students have used these technologies only informally and it is important for them to envision how they could be used professionally."

GEN FREESE, HARRISBURG AREA COMMUNITY COLLEGE

- **Independent Grammar Review.** Located at the newly designed Guffey Web site, **www.meguffey.com**, the Personal Language Trainer provides you with a simple, interactive tool to help improve grammar and mechanics skills outside of class.

Expose their teeth. Exposing one's teeth is not only immodest but also aggressive. Although current cultural behavior may sometimes seem silly and illogical, nearly all serious rules and values originate in deep-seated beliefs. Rules about exposing teeth or how close to stand are linked to values about sexuality, aggression, modesty, and respect. Acknowledging the inherent logic of a culture is extremely important when learning to accept behavior that differs from one's own cultural behavior.

Marketers of Crest toothpaste face numerous challenges in communicating the value of their brand across cultures—especially Chinese culture. China's citizens traditionally have ignored toothpaste products, choosing instead to freshen up the mouth with green tea. An estimated 57 percent of rural Chinese residents have never brushed their teeth. Though China is currently experiencing a beauty boom, decades ago the country frowned upon personal care products. *How might understanding the characteristics of culture help marketers sell toothpaste to China's over one billion people?*

NEW Photo Essays. These vivid photos with intriguing stories demonstrate real-world applicability of business communication concepts.

NEW Ethics Checks challenge you to consider realistic business scenarios and choose the most appropriate action.

Ethics Check

Trapped by Consumer Debt
Capital One offers multiple credit cards to subprime borrowers and rakes in huge profits from charging high interest and late fees. Some consumer advocates see Cap One's approach as unethical because it traps low-income borrowers in a cycle of debt. Do you agree?

Investment Informat

Writers describing the sale of s protect investors. Any messag must be free from misleading Massachusetts inadvertently After going bankrupt, the com been deceived. A software co that revealed problems in a ne sued, charging that managers prices artificially high. Experie poor timing may provoke litig

Safety Information

Writers describing potentially from physical harm but also arising from product liability

erous
written

BEN & JERRY'S
VERMONT'S FINEST • ICE CREAM & FROZEN YOGURT™

January 18, 2009

Ms. Jennifer Ball
1401 Churchville Lane
Bel Air, MD 21014

Dear Jennifer:

We're delighted to hear of your Ben & Jerry's Club at Franklin Middle School and to send the items you request.

Your club sounds as though it resembles its parent in many ways. We, too, can't seem to control our growth; and we, too, get a little out of control on Friday afternoons. Moreover, the simplicity of your club rules mirrors the philosophy of our cofounder, who says, "If it's not fun, why do it?"

Enclosed are the following items:

- A list of all flavors available in pints. If you can't find these flavors at your grocer's, I'm sending you some "ballots" for your club's use in encouraging your grocer to stock your favorites.
- The latest issue of Ben & Jerry's "Chunk Mail." We're also putting you on our mailing list so that your club will receive our Chunk Mail newsletter regularly.

We hope, Jennifer, that you'll soon tour our plant here in Vermont. Then, you can be on an equal footing with your prez and sport one of our tour buttons. This seems only appropriate for the consensus-building, decision-making model you are pioneering in your Ben & Jerry's Club!

Sincerely,

Personalizes reply and builds goodwill with reference to writer's letter

Uses receiver's name to make letter sound conversational and personal

Opens directly with response to customer's request

Itemizes and explains enclosures requested by customer

Ties in cordial closing with more references to customer's letter

Model Documents with Callouts. Fully formatted model documents demonstrate communication concepts in action. Extensive marginal notes allow you to actually see and understand strategies highlighted in the text.

- **NEW End-of-Chapter Activities and Cases.** The Sixth Edition has the most complete, descriptive, understandable, and relevant activities and cases on the market. Approximately half of the activities are new or refreshed in the Sixth Edition.

- **NEW Technology Options including Aplia™.** (See more about the new technology for the Sixth Edition on the next page!)

Aplia™ With Guffey...
It's Just That Easy

This edition offers you the chance to use Aplia™, an online, interactive tool that ensures you review fundamental grammar and mechanics and understand concepts presented in *Business Communication: Process and Product, 6e.* Aplia improves learning by increasing student effort and engagement. Using Aplia can be *just that easy.*

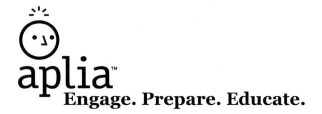

Engage. Prepare. Educate.

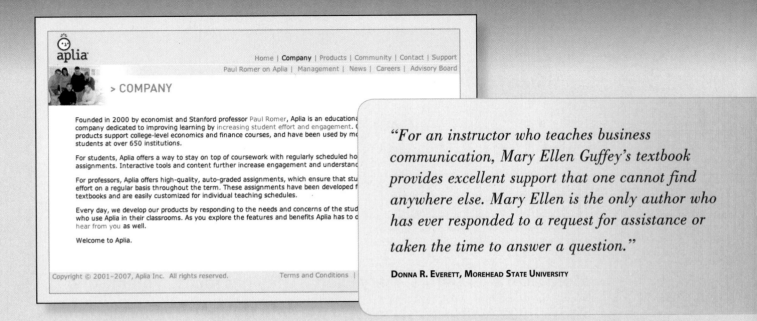

Founded in 2000 by economist and Stanford professor Paul Romer, Aplia is an educational company dedicated to improving learning by increasing student effort and engagement. products support college-level economics and finance courses, and have been used by students at over 650 institutions.

For students, Aplia offers a way to stay on top of coursework with regularly scheduled ho assignments. Interactive tools and content further increase engagement and understand

For professors, Aplia offers high-quality, auto-graded assignments, which ensure that stu effort on a regular basis throughout the term. These assignments have been developed f textbooks and are easily customized for individual teaching schedules.

Every day, we develop our products by responding to the needs and concerns of the stud who use Aplia in their classrooms. As you explore the features and benefits Aplia has to c hear from you as well.

Welcome to Aplia.

"For an instructor who teaches business communication, Mary Ellen Guffey's textbook provides excellent support that one cannot find anywhere else. Mary Ellen is the only author who has ever responded to a request for assistance or taken the time to answer a question."

DONNA R. EVERETT, MOREHEAD STATE UNIVERSITY

If you choose to use Aplia™*, you'll be able to take advantage of many of these benefits:

- Chapter-specific assignments that help you read and understand the text

- Instant detailed feedback on every question

- Grammar and mechanics tutorials that help you practice key writing skills so that your instructors spend less time reviewing and more time teaching advanced writing concepts

- Access to a full ebook version of *Business Communication: Process and Product, 6e*

For more details about using Aplia with *Business Communication: Process and Product, 6e*, visit www.aplia.com/cengage

* Aplia is not automatically included with the Sixth Edition. If you would like more information, student pricing, or to see a demo, please contact Aplia at 888.858.7305 or email info@aplia.com.

Technology With Guffey...
It's Just That Easy

More than ever before, Mary Ellen Guffey has focused on making technology components easy to use with *Business Communication: Process and Product, 6e.* In addition to tried-and-true products like WebTutor™ and Aplia™, a brand new student Web site houses numerous resources to help with teaching and learning. These choices show that using technology can be *just that easy.*

Brand NEW Student Support Web site — **www.meguffey.com** gives you one convenient place to find the support you need. You can study with resources such as self-teaching grammar/mechanics review, PowerPoint slides, chapter review quizzes, Documents for Analysis, and much more.

Positive Team Behavior

Team players

- set rules, abide by them
- analyze tasks, define problems
- contribute information and ideas
- show interest, listen actively
- encourage members to participate
- synthesize points of agreement

23480502 Comstock Images Jupite

Mary Ellen Guffey, *Business Communication: Process and Pr*

Triple-Option PowerPoint® Lecture System. The Triple Option system includes three versions of the PowerPoint slides: (1) a special student version with less detailed coverage of topics, (2) an enhanced instructor version with enrichment items and expanded coverage, and (3) a multimedia version for instructors.

Building Workplace Skills Videos. This video library includes seven high-quality videos to introduce and reinforce text-specific concepts such as intercultural communication, the changing workplace, the writing process, e-mail, the job search, and interviewing. The Sixth Edition features two brand-new videos!

Bridging the Gap Videos. These video cases take you inside real companies allowing you to apply your understanding of business communication concepts to actual business situations. Most videos conclude with a series of discussion questions and an application activity. The companies featured in this video library include Cold Stone Creamery, The Little Guys, Yahoo, Ben & Jerry's, Hard Rock Café, and BuyCostumes.com.

Guffey... It's Just That Easy

What's new in *Business Communication: Process and Product, 6e*

Chapter 1 — Communicating in Today's Workplace

- Revised all learning objectives and correlating content to relate to AACSB competencies to ensure that institutions meet current standards.

- Added new coverage of business ethics with sections on copyright law and whistleblowing so that students are equipped to use practical tools when they meet ethical dilemmas in the workplace.

- Enhanced the focus on ethics with new Ethics Checks, brief scenarios confronting students with moral questions in business.

- Examined every sentence and reference to ensure clarity and currency.

- Conducted research in hundreds of online and print articles and books to extract the latest information resulting in over 30 new endnotes, ensuring that students and instructors have the most up-to-date and best-researched textbook on the market.

- Strengthened students' competitive edge with new coverage of business etiquette to help them succeed in an increasingly rude workplace.

- Added coverage of instant and text messaging as business tools.

Chapter 2 — Developing Team, Listening, and Etiquette Skills

- Combined teamwork, listening, nonverbal, and etiquette skills into one chapter to focus on the soft skills that are so often mentioned in job advertisements.

- Emphasized the importance of soft skills in today's increasingly interconnected, collaborative, and competitive workplace.

- Focused on positive and negative team behaviors with specific examples to help readers improve their teamwork skills.

- Added 11-point checklist to help readers participate actively and productively in meetings.

- Added up-to-date discussion of voice conferencing, videoconferencing, Web conferencing, instant messaging, blogs, and wikis so that students are able to work effectively in today's digital workplace.

- Streamlined discussion of listening to focus on ten keys to building active listening skills.

- Added coverage of professionalism and business etiquette skills because employers are more likely to hire and promote one who is courteous and professional.

- Added Figure 2.9 with specific examples of professional and unprofessional speech habits, e-mail, Internet, voice mail, telephone, and cell phone use.

Chapter 3 — Communicating Across Cultures

- Updated Wal-Mart opening case study with current information.

- Researched hundreds of articles to find interesting, relevant examples illustrating the universality of globalization and its effect on U.S. businesses.

- Strengthened coverage of technology advancements so that readers understand that high-speed, high-capacity, and low-cost communications have made geographical location virtually irrelevant in many business activities.

- Added Tech Talk box titled "Going Global With a Culturally Customized Web Site" to show readers how Web sites can be adapted for high- and low-context cultures.

- Added model documents showing an ineffective intercultural letter along with an improved version so that students can readily see differences in cultural adaptation.

- Presented latest information on bribery laws, including Sarbanes-Oxley Act.

- Developed entertaining new text-specific video titled "Intercultural Communication at Work" to illustrate difficulties and generate lively discussion involving intercultural issues.

Chapter 4 — Writing Process Phase 1: Analyze, Anticipate, Adapt

- Presented new opening case study featuring Suze Orman, personal finance guru.

- Added "persuasive" to discussion of business writing basics.

- Expanded discussion of writing with teams so that students will be better able to collaborate digitally in today's workplace. Added discussion of online collaboration tools.

- Added blogs, instant messaging, and wikis to discussion of communication channels, thus making readers aware of the many current forms of workplace communication.

- Added new section on being conversational but professional so that students can transition more easily from student life to projecting professionalism in their business careers.

Chapter 5 — Writing Process Phase 2: Research, Organize, Compose

- Updated Gap Inc. opening case study with current information about popular clothing retailer Gap Inc.

- Added Writing Improvement Exercises to reinforce specific techniques taught in chapter.

- Strengthened all reinforcement exercises with new material.

- Added new Paragraph Organization exercise at reviewer's request so that students have additional practice items to try out their skills.

Chapter 6 — Writing Process 3: Revise, Proofread, Evaluate

- Updated Taco Bell opening case study with current information and relevant critical thinking questions.

- Added new Career Coach box focused on showing how to calculate the Fog Index to determine readability. Encouraged students to do their own calculation of readability, rather than use the word processing program, so that they better understand what increases reading level.

- Included additional Document for Analysis (making a total of four) in response to reviewer requests.

- Revised Instructor Manual discussion material so that teachers can cite specific writing faults in Documents for Analysis.

- Revised all Writing for Improvement Exercises so that they proceed from simple to complex. Rewrote many items so that they focus on only one fault, thus improving student comprehension, confidence, and learning.

Chapter 7 — E-Mail Messages and Memos

- Presented new opening case study highlighting wireless giant QualComm.

- Updated discussion of e-mail formatting to help readers see the latest conventions in greetings and closings.

- Added new figure illustrating bad and good e-mail messages that show common mistakes and how to remedy them.

- Totally revised Tech Talk box, "How to Avoid Getting Fired Over Your Internet Use" to warn readers of latest dangers involved in workplace e-mail, blogging, and Web use.

- Introduced new Tech Talk box on instant messaging so that readers learn how to use it safely and effectively on the job.

- Strengthened discussion of typical e-mail messages by focusing on four typical business categories: request messages, response messages, procedural messages, and confirmation messages.

- Updated all e-mail model documents to show appropriate greetings and complete signature blocks.

- Provided more activities that are stimulating but short enough to be completed in class. Also added more intercultural activities.

Chapter 8 — Positive Letters and Messages

- Updated the Ben & Jerry's opening case study with current information for the discussion material and for the application assignment.

- Emphasized the power of business letters by highlighting instances when they must be written, despite the popularity of e-mail.

- Changed all model document letter formats to full block style so that students always see the most popular style. Revised model letters to ensure that they (a) illustrated proper use of titles for senders and receivers and (b) contained appropriate contact information in the closings.
- Deleted the coverage of order letters and letters of recommendation because so few are written today.

Chapter 9 — Persuasive and Marketing Messages

- Reorganized entire chapter to put more emphasis on persuasive organizational messages flowing upward and downward because this is a major form of persuasion for businesspeople.
- Revised all learning objectives and correlating content to relate to AACSB competencies to ensure that institutions meet current standards.
- Added new author interview and case study with the CEO of a nonprofit organization because many students will be entering the world of nonprofits.
- Added new model documents with extensive marginal notes so that students actually see and understand strategies highlighted in the text.
- Strengthened students' awareness of what is legal and what is not legal in sales letters so that writers can avoid some of the pitfalls in marketing messages.
- Introduced new coverage including model document showing high- and low-context persuasive techniques to help readers be more sensitive and effective in intercultural and global business transactions.

Chapter 10 — Negative Messages

- Presented a new opening case study featuring Southwest Airlines and its successful strategies for handling bad news to its customers. Included new "Apply Your Skills at Southwest" writing assignment.
- Provided many new examples of bad-news business situations so that students understand how necessary it is to be able to write effective messages that deliver disappointing news.
- Helped readers by providing model verbiage and more examples of apologies, empathy, and alternatives appropriate for bad-news messages.
- Expanded coverage of explanations and reasons in bad-news messages so that readers have more models of appropriate language.
- Updated information about delivering bad news in other cultures.
- Added new information about credit refusals so that business communicators understand their legal obligations.
- Prepared new video writing assignment delivering bad news to a BuyCostumes customer so that students develop skills in realistic business applications.

Chapter 11 — Business Report Basics

- Simplified and streamlined the organization of Chapters 11, 12, and 13 so that each stage of the report-writing process is more distinct and clearly defined for students and instructors in these three chapters.
- Strengthened the emphasis on ethics with two Ethics Checks and new activities that present ethical problems and dilemmas in business.
- Helped students avoid plagiarism with a yet more detailed discussion of the mechanics of proper paraphrasing and citing.
- Expanded the discussion of new trends in report writing including digital formats and PowerPoint decks so that students understand how new technologies are affecting the way business reports are written and delivered.

Chapter 12 — Informal Business Reports

- Provided new, up-to-date examples and cases including Starbucks, Nokia, Nissan, and other high-profile companies.
- Added discussion of decision matrices along with two new end-of-chapter activities to help students practice using this important decision-making tool.
- Increased the coverage of intercultural issues in the research activities at the end of the chapter to expand student awareness and appreciation of globalization.
- Updated model documents and presented a new feasibility report that demonstrates how to apply textbook writing suggestions.
- Updated and added several new self-contained research topics complete with data allowing students to forgo research and instead focus on the analysis of the information provided for them.

Chapter 13 — Proposals and Formal Reports

- Introduced AACSB standards for business communication to student learning objectives.
- Provided a new three-part case study "Communication in Process" that focuses on proposal writing at aerospace giant Raytheon to demonstrate to students a complex team-writing process.
- Presented a new long report in APA documentation style to provide a realistic writing sample and to model correct formatting of formal reports.
- Added an end-of-chapter activity designed to help students pursue their entrepreneurial bent with a proposal-writing task.
- Created new, current end-of-chapter activities to help students practice their report-writing skills.

Chapter 14 — Business Presentations

- Streamlined the organization of the chapter to include general tips for oral presentations, guidelines for multimedia presentations, suggestions for adapting to cross-cultural audiences, strategies for team presentations, and principles of telephone and voicemail self-presentation.
- Updated the coverage of multimedia presentations to reflect the continuing trend toward wider use of technology in today's business presentations.
- Added a detailed discussion of team-based written and oral presentations to assist instructors and students in managing group projects successfully.
- Included an extensive section discussing effective communication by telephone and voicemail to ensure that students learn to present themselves in a positive light.
- Increased the coverage of speaking to international and cross-cultural audiences to prepare students for a progressively more global economy.
- Created new self-contained multimedia end-of-chapter activities to help students hone their presentation skills without the need for further research.

Chapter 15 — The Job Search, Résumés, and Cover Letters

- Provided new opening case study featuring workplace expert Liz Ryan with many job tips for job searching in an online environment.
- Updated all job search coverage so that students have the latest information for conducting a successful job search.
- Emphasized the need to create a customized résumé for every job application and every organization.
- Revised all résumés to include a Summary of Qualifications because today's recruiters look for this information first.
- Advised readers to prepare three résumés: a print-based traditional presentation résumé, a scannable résumé, and a plain-text résumé for electronic submissions so that they are prepared for today's digital workplaces.
- Provided specific advice on preparing and submitting plain-text résumés to help readers know how to function in today's digital job-search environment.
- Created an entertaining new text-specific video illustrating the job search that focuses on good and bad techniques as well as a convincing ethical dilemma.

Chapter 16 — Interviewing and Following Up

- Presented an entirely new chapter on interviewing so that students understand the interviewing process and know what to expect at every step of this life-changing experience.
- Provided helpful advice on what to do before, during, and after an interview to enable job hunters to overcome anxiety and project the confidence necessary to ace important employment interviews.
- Increased the confidence and reduced the fear of job hunters by explaining that an interview is a two-way street: both the interviewer and the interviewee must be satisfied. This realization makes job hunters recognize their power and helps them feel less intimidated.
- Explained how to research target companies, how to prepare success stories, and how to practice answers to typical interview questions.
- Gave tips on how to send positive nonverbal messages, fight fear, and use good techniques in answering interview questions.
- Described how to close an interview positively and ask meaningful questions.

Guffey...
It's Just That Easy

"Your textbook is the standard for all textbooks to meet. You are indeed on the cutting edge in coverage, presentation, and variety. I tell my students that this textbook is not one to sell back because they are investing in a handbook demonstrating all possible communication models in the best organized text on the market."

CYNTHIA H. MAYFIELD
YORK TECHNICAL COLLEGE

Brief Contents

Appreciation for Support   xxiii
About the Author   xxvi

Unit 1 Communication Foundations   1

1   Communicating in Today's Workplace   2
2   Developing Team, Listening, and Etiquette Skills   33
3   Communicating Across Cultures   69

Unit 2 The 3-x-3 Writing Process   99

4   Writing Process Phase 1: Analyze, Anticipate, Adapt   100
5   Writing Process Phase 2: Research, Organize, Compose   123
6   Writing Process Phase 3: Revise, Proofread, Evaluate   148

Unit 3 Business Correspondence   169

7   E-Mail Messages and Memos   170
8   Positive Letters and Messages   200
9   Persuasive and Marketing Messages   233
10 Negative Messages   273

Unit 4 Reports, Proposals, and Presentations   309

11 Business Report Basics   310
12 Informal Business Reports   351
13 Proposals and Formal Reports   393
14 Business Presentations   424

Unit 5 Employment Communication   461

15 The Job Search, Résumés, and Cover Letters   462
16 Interviewing and Following Up   500

Appendices

A   Grammar and Mechanics Guide   A-1
B   Document Format Guide   B-1
C   Documentation Guide   C-1
D   Correction Symbols   D-1

End Matter

Key to C.L.U.E. Review Exercises   Key-1
Glossary   G-1
Notes   N-1
Acknowledgments   ACK-1
Index   I-1

Contents

Appreciation for Support   xxiii
About the Author   xxvi

Unit 1 Communication Foundations   1

Chapter 1 Communicating in Today's Workplace   2

Communicating in Today's Workplace: A Great Communicator Heads Sears and Kmart   3
Building Your Career Success With Communication Skills   3
Thriving as a Knowledge Worker in the Information Age   4
Career Coach: Sharpening Your Skills for Critical Thinking, Problem Solving, and Decision Making   6
Factors Affecting You in Today's Workplace   7
Understanding the Process of Communication   12
Overcoming Interpersonal Communication Barriers   14
Communicating in Organizations   15
Improving the Flow of Information in Organizations   18
Communicating at Work: Sears Holdings   22
Examining Business Communication Ethics   22
Communicating at Work: Applying Your Skills at Sears Holdings   26

Summary of Learning Objectives   26
Chapter Review   28
Critical Thinking   28
Activities   28
Video Resources   31
Grammar and Mechanics Skills With C.L.U.E.   32

Chapter 2 Developing Team, Listening, and Etiquette Skills   33

Communicating at Work: Teamwork Drives Toyota to Success   34
Recognizing the Importance of Soft Skills in Today's Workplace   34
Preparing to Work With Groups and Teams   35
Tech Talk: How to Form and Participate in Effective Virtual Teams   37
Ethical Insights: Ethical Responsibilities of Group Members and Leaders   41
Checklist: Developing Team Effectiveness   42
Communicating at Work: Toyota   43
Planning and Participating in Productive Meetings   43
Checklist: Planning and Participating in Productive Meetings   47
Using Technology to Facilitate Collaboration   48
Listening in the Workplace   50
Career Coach: Listening to Nonnative Speakers in the Workplace   53
Checklist: Improving Listening   54
Communicating Through Nonverbal Messages   55
Career Coach: Perils of Casual Apparel in the Workplace   58
Checklist: Techniques for Improving Nonverbal Communication Skills in the Workplace   59
Developing a Competitive Edge With Professionalism and Business Etiquette Skills   60
Communicating at Work: Applying Your Skills at Toyota   62

Summary of Learning Objectives 62
Chapter Review 64
Critical Thinking 64
Activities 64
Video Resources 68
Grammar and Mechanics Skills C.L.U.E. Review 2 68

Chapter 3 Communicating Across Cultures 69

Communicating at Work: Mighty Wal-Mart Woos Famously Finicky Japanese Consumers 70
Recognizing the Increasing Importance of Intercultural Communication 70
Understanding Culture 73
Tech Talk: Going Global With a Culturally Customized Web Site 77
Achieving Intercultural Proficiency 78
Ethical Insights: Firm Lands in Hot Water for Caving in to Cultural Prejudices 78
Communicating at Work: Wal-Mart 80
Improving Communication in Intercultural Environments 80
Checklist: Improving Intercultural Proficiency and Communication 86
Coping With Intercultural Ethics 86
Capitalizing on Workforce Diversity 89
Career Coach: He Said, She Said: Gender Talk and Gender Tension 91
Communicating at Work: Applying Your Skills at Wal-Mart 93

Summary of Learning Objectives 93
Chapter Review 94
Critical Thinking 94
Activities 95
Video Resources 98
Grammar and Mechanics C.L.U.E. Review 3 98

Unit 2 The 3-x-3 Writing Process 99

Chapter 4 Writing Process Phase 1: Analyze, Anticipate, Adapt 100

Communicating at Work: Suze Orman Preaches Financial Freedom in Simple Language 101
Approaching the Writing Process Systematically 101
Tech Talk: Using Technology to Edit and Revise Collaborative Documents 106
Writing Process Phase 1: Analyze 106
Writing Process Phase 1: Anticipate 108
Writing Process Phase 1: Adapt 109
Communicating at Work: Suze Orman Preaches Financial Freedom in Simple Language 112
Checklist: Adapting a Message to Its Audience 116
Adapting to Legal and Ethical Responsibilities 116
Communicating at Work: Applying Your Skills With Suze Orman 118

Summary of Learning Objectives 119
Chapter Review 120
Critical Thinking 120
Activities 120
Writing Improvement Exercises 121
Video Resources 122
Grammar and Mechanics C.L.U.E. Review 4 122

Chapter 5 Writing Process Phase 2: Research, Organize, Compose 123

Communicating at Work: Once the Height of Hip, Gap Struggles to Stop Sagging Sales 124
Writing Process Phase 2: Research 124
Writing Process Phase 2: Organize 127

Communicating at Work: Gap Inc.   *133*

Writing Process Phase 2: Compose   134

Tech Talk: Seven Ways Computers Can Help You Create Better Written Messages, Oral Presentations, and Web Pages   *134*

Checklist: Composing Sentences and Paragraphs   141

Communicating at Work: Applying Your Skills at Gap Inc.   *141*

Summary of Learning Objectives   142
Chapter Review   142
Critical Thinking   143
Activities   143
Writing Improvement Exercises   145
Video Resources   146
Grammar and Mechanics C.L.U.E. Review 5   147

Chapter 6 Writing Process Phase 3: Revise, Proofread, Evaluate   148

Communicating at Work: Taco Bell Seeks New Menu to Lure Customers   *149*

Writing Process Phase 3: Revise   149

Revising for Clarity   150

Revising for Conversational Tone   151

Revising for Conciseness   151

Revising for Vigor and Directness   153

Revising for Readability   154

Checklist: Revising Messages   156

Career Coach: Applying the Fog Index to Determine Readability   *157*

Writing Process Phase 3: Proofread   157

Communicating at Work: Taco Bell   *158*

Tech Talk: Using Spell Checkers and Grammar/Style Checkers Wisely   *159*

Writing Process Phase 3: Evaluate   160

Communicating at Work: Applying Your Skills at Taco Bell   *160*

Summary of Learning Objectives   162
Chapter Review   162
Critical Thinking   163
Activities   163
Video Resources   167
Grammar and Mechanics C.L.U.E. Review 6   167

Unit 3 Business Correspondence   169

Chapter 7 E-Mail Messages and Memos   170

Communicating at Work: Wireless Giant Qualcomm Thrives on E-Mail   *171*

Applying the Writing Process to E-Mail Messages and Memos   171

Structuring and Formatting E-Mail Messages and Memos   173

Using E-Mail Smartly and Safely   178

Tech Talk: How to Avoid Getting Fired Over Your Internet Use   *180*

Tech Talk: Beyond E-Mail: Instant Messaging Becomes Workplace Communication Tool   *183*

Writing Typical E-Mail Messages and Memos   184

Communicating at Work: Wireless Giant Qualcomm Thrives on E-Mail   *184*

Checklist: Writing Typical E-Mail Messages and Memos   191

Communicating at Work: Applying Your Skills at Qualcomm   *191*

Summary of Learning Objectives   192
Chapter Review   193
Critical Thinking   193
Activities   193

Video Resources   199
Grammar and Mechanics C.L.U.E. Review 7   199

Chapter 8 Positive Letters and Messages   200

Communicating at Work: Ben & Jerry's Uses Positive Letters to Sweeten Relations With Customers   201
Understanding the Power of Business Letters and the Process of Writing   201
Analyzing the Structure of Business Letters   204
Analyzing the Characteristics of Good Business Letters   205
Direct Requests for Information or Action   206
Direct Claims   208
Direct Replies   210
Checklist: Writing Direct Requests   210
Adjustments   214
Goodwill Messages   217
Communicating at Work: Ben & Jerry's   218
Checklist: Positive Reply Letters   218
Checklist: Goodwill Messages   222
International Messages   222
Communicating at Work: Applying Your Skills at Ben & Jerry's   223

Summary of Learning Objectives   224
Chapter Review   225
Critical Thinking   225
Activities   225
Video Resources   232
Grammar and Mechanics C.L.U.E. Review 8   232

Chapter 9 Persuasive and Marketing Messages   233

Communicating at Work: Hands on Miami   234
Understanding Persuasion and How to Use It Effectively and Ethically   234
Applying the 3-x-3 Writing Process to Persuasive Messages   237
Blending Four Major Elements in Successful Persuasive Messages   239
Ethical Insights: What's Fair in Persuasion? Avoiding Common Logical Fallacies   241
Communicating at Work: Hands on Miami   242
Writing Persuasive Messages Requesting Favors and Actions   242
Checklist: Requesting Favors and Actions   244
Writing Persuasive Messages Within Organizations   244
Checklist: Writing Persuasive Messages Within Organizations   248
Writing Persuasive Claim and Complaint Letters   248
Planning and Composing Effective Sales and Marketing Messages   249
Ethical Insights: What's Legal and What's Not in Sales Letters   254
Comparing Persuasion in High- and Low-Context Cultures   255
Checklist: Sales Messages   255
Developing Persuasive Press Releases   259
Communicating at Work: Applying Your Skills at Hands on Miami   261

Summary of Learning Objectives   261
Chapter Review   263
Critical Thinking   263
Activities   263
Video Resources   272
Grammar and Mechanics C.L.U.E. Review 9   272

Chapter 10 Negative Messages   273

Communicating at Work: Passengers LUV Southwest Airlines—Even When Flights Are Late   274
Strategies for Delivering Bad News   274
Techniques for Delivering Bad News Sensitively   278
Refusing Typical Requests   283
Tech Talk: Using Technology to Personalize Form Letters   286
Checklist: Refusing Typical Requests   288
Delivering Bad News to Customers   288
Checklist: Delivering Bad News to Customers   293
Delivering Bad News Within Organizations   293
Communicating at Work: Southwest Airlines   294
Checklist: Delivering Bad News Within Organizations   295
Presenting Bad News in Other Cultures   297
Communicating at Work: Applying Your Skills at Southwest Airlines   298

Summary of Learning Objectives   299
Chapter Review   300
Critical Thinking   300
Activities   300
Video Resources   308
Grammar and Mechanics C.L.U.E. Review 10   308

Unit 4 Reports, Proposals, and Presentations   309

Chapter 11 Business Report Basics   310

Communicating at Work: BzzAgent Supports Women's Right to One True Fit   311
Understanding Report Basics   311
Applying the 3-x-3 Writing Process to Reports   317
Communicating at Work: BzzAgent   322
Gathering Information From Secondary Sources   322
Tech Talk: Managing Your Electronic Research Data Like a Pro   329
Gathering Information From Primary Sources   330
Documenting Data   334
Illustrating Data   337
Ethical Insights: Making Ethical Charts and Graphics   343
Communicating at Work: Applying Your Skills at BzzAgent   344

Summary of Learning Objectives   344
Chapter Review   346
Critical Thinking   346
Activities   346
Grammar and Mechanics C.L.U.E. Review 11   350

Chapter 12 Informal Business Reports   351

Communicating at Work: Starbucks: More Than Just Beans   352
Interpreting Data   352
Drawing Conclusions and Making Recommendations   357
Organizing Data   361
Writing Informational Reports   365
Career Coach: Ten Tips for Designing Better Documents   366
Checklist: Writing Informational Reports   370
Writing Short Analytical Reports   371
Communicating at Work: Starbucks: More Than Just Beans   372
Checklist: Writing Analytical Reports   382
Communicating at Work: Applying Your Skills at Starbucks   382

Summary of Learning Objectives 383
Chapter Review 384
Critical Thinking 384
Activities 384
Grammar and Mechanics C.L.U.E. Review 12 392

Chapter 13 Proposals and Formal Reports 393

Communicating at Work: Winning New Business at Raytheon 394
Preparing Formal and Informal Proposals 394
Checklist: Writing Proposals 400
Communicating at Work: Winning New Business at Raytheon 400
Preparing an Effective Business Plan 401
Writing Formal Reports 402
Final Writing Tips 406
Checklist: Preparing Formal Reports 418
Communicating at Work: Applying Your Skills at Raytheon 419

Summary of Learning Objectives 419
Chapter Review 420
Critical Thinking 420
Activities 420
Grammar and Mechanics C.L.U.E. Review 13 423

Chapter 14 Business Presentations 424

Communicating at Work: Walt Disney Imagineering Sells Tokyo Disneyland on Winnie the Pooh 425
Preparing Effective Oral Presentations 425
Organizing the Content for a Powerful Impact 427
Career Coach: Nine Techniques for Gaining and Keeping Audience Attention 429
Building Audience Rapport Like a Pro 431
Planning Visual Aids and Multimedia Presentations 433
Designing an Impressive Multimedia Presentation 435
Polishing Your Delivery and Following Up 444
Career Coach: How to Avoid Stage Fright 446
Organizing Team-Based Written and Oral Presentations 448
Communicating at Work: Walt Disney Imagineering 450
Adapting Presentations to International and Cross-Cultural Audiences 450
Improving Telephone and Voice Mail Skills 451
Checklist: Preparing and Organizing Oral Presentations 452
Communicating at Work: Applying Your Skills at Walt Disney Imagineering 455

Summary of Learning Objectives 455
Chapter Review 456
Critical Thinking 457
Activities 457
Video Resources 460
Grammar and Mechanics C.L.U.E. Review 14 460

Unit 5 Employment Communication 461

Chapter 15 The Job Search, Résumés, and Cover Letters 462

Communicating at Work: Workplace Expert Liz Ryan Shares Job-Search Tips 463
Preparing for Employment 463
Conducting a Successful Job Search 466
Career Coach: Network Your Way to a Job in the Hidden Market 469
Creating a Customized Résumé 469

Organizing Your Information Into Effective Résumé Categories 471
Communicating at Work: Workplace Expert Liz Ryan Shares Job-Search Tips 475
Optimizing Your Résumé for Today's Technologies 476
Applying the Final Touches to Your Résumé 486
Checklist: Preparing for Employment and Submitting a Customized Résumé 488
Ethical Insights: Are Inflated Résumés Worth the Risk? 489
Creating a Customized Cover Letter 489
Checklist: Preparing and Sending a Customized Cover Letter 495
Communicating at Work: Applying Your Skills With Liz Ryan 496

Summary of Learning Objectives 496
Chapter Review 497
Critical Thinking 497
Activities 497
Video Resources 499
Grammar and Mechanics C.L.U.E. Review 15 499

Chapter 16 Interviewing and Following Up 500

Communicating at Work: Googling for Jobs 501
The Job Interview: Understanding Its Importance, Purposes, and Types 501
Career Coach: Ensuring That You Pass the All-Important Telephone Screening Interview 502
Before the Interview 503
During the Interview 506
Answering Typical Interview Questions 507
Communicating at Work: Googling for Jobs 509
Career Coach: Let's Talk Money: Salary Negotiation Dos and Don'ts 511
Closing the Interview 514
After the Interview 515
Other Employment Documents and Follow-Up Messages 517
Checklist: Performing Effectively Before, During, and After a Job Interview 518
Communicating at Work: Applying Your Skills at Google 521

Summary of Learning Objectives 521
Chapter Review 522
Critical Thinking 523
Activities 523
Video Resources 525
Grammar and Mechanics C.L.U.E. Review 16 525

Appendices

Appendix A: Grammar and Mechanics Guide A-1
Appendix B: Document Format Guide B-1
Appendix C: Documentation Guide C-1
Appendix D: Correction Symbols D-1

End Matter

Key to C.L.U.E. Review Exercises Key-1
Glossary G-1
Notes N-1
Acknowledgments ACK-1
Index I-1

Appreciation for Support

No successful textbook reaches a No. 1 position without a great deal of help. I am exceedingly grateful to the reviewers and other experts who contributed their pedagogic and academic expertise in shaping *Business Communication: Process and Product.*

In addition to these friends and colleagues, sincere thanks go to PWS Kent and Wadsworth for laying the foundation for the first editions. In helping maintain its top position with subsequent editions, I extend sincere thanks to many professionals at South-Western and Cengage, including Jack Calhoun, vice president/editorial director; Ed Moura, president; Melissa Acuna, editor in chief; Erin Joyner, acquisitions editor; Mike Aliscad, marketing manager; Tamborah Moore, production editor; John Rich, technology project manager, and especially to Mary Draper, my exceptional and highly valued senior developmental editor.

My heartfelt appreciation also goes to Dana Loewy, Fullerton Community College; Carolyn Seefer, Diablo Community College; and James Dubinsky, Virginia Technical University, for sharing their expertise in developing specific topics and outstanding support materials.

Finally, I express profound gratitude to my husband, Dr. George R. Guffey, emeritus professor of English, University of California, Los Angeles, for supplying extraordinary computer and language expertise, as well as love, strength, and wisdom.

Mary Ellen Guffey
meguffey@westwords.com

Deepest Thanks to Reviewers of This Edition

Cathie Bishop, Parkland College
Elizabeth Bowers, Orange Coast College and Golden West College
Domenic Bruni, University of Wisconsin Oshkosh
Linda Di Desidero, University of Maryland University College
John Donnellan, University of Texas at Austin
J. Yellowless Douglas, University of Florida
Donna R. Everett, Morehead State University
Gwendolyn Bowie Ewing, Southwest Tennessee Community College
Peggy B. Fisher, Ball State University
Gen Freese, Harrisburg Area Community College
Bill Hargrave, University of West Georgia
Kathy Jesiolowski, Milwaukee Area Technical College
Cheryl L. Kane, University of North Carolina Charlotte
Carolyn E. Kerr, University of Pittsburgh
Sonia Khatchadourian, University of Wisconsin-Milwaukee
Gary E. Lacefield, University of Texas at Arlington
Kristie J. Loescher, The University of Texas at Austin

Anna Maheshwari, Schoolcraft College
Leon Markowicz, Lebanon Valley College
Cynthia H. Mayfield, York Technical College
Beryl C. McEwen, North Carolina A&T State University
Marya McFadden, California State University Northridge
Nancy McGee, Davenport University
Smita Jain Oxford, University of Mary Washington
Shara Toursh Pavlow, University of Miami
Ed Peters, University of Texas at Arlington
Melinda Phillabaum, Indiana University
Richard David Ramsey, Southeastern Louisiana University
Betty Jane Robbins, University of Oklahoma
Jean Anna Sellers, Fort Hays State University
Jan Starnes, The University of Texas at Austin
Deborah Von Spreecken, Anoka-Ramsey Community College
Carol Smith White, Georgia State University
Debbie J. Williams, Abilene Christian University
Karen Zempel, Bryant and Stratton College

Grateful Thanks to Previous Reviewers

Janet G. Adams, Minnesota State University, Mankato
Leslie Adams, Houston Baptist University
Kehinde A. Adesina, Contra Costa College
Asberine Parnell Alford, Suffolk Community College
Virginia Allen, Joliet Junior College
Cynthia Anderson, Youngstown State University
Linda Landis Andrews, University of Illinois, Chicago
Vanessa D. Arnold, University of Mississippi
Lois J. Bachman, Community College of Philadelphia
Rebecca Barksdale, University of Central Florida
Sandra Berill, Arkansas State University
Teresa L. Beyer, Sinclair Community College
Cathie Bishop, Parkland College
Randi Blank, Indiana University
Martha E. Bradshaw, Southeastern Louisiana Univ.
Bernadine Branchaw, Western Michigan University
Maryanne Brandenburg, Indiana University of Pennsylvania
Charles P. Bretan, Northwood University
Paula E. Brown, Northern Illinois University
Vivian R. Brown, Loredo Community College
Phyllis C. Bunn, Delta State University
Mary Ann Burris, Pueblo Community College
Roosevelt D. Butler, College of New Jersey
Jane Campanizzi-Mook, Franklin University
James F. Carey, Onondaga Community College
Leila Chambers, Cuesta College
Patricia H. Chapman, University of South Carolina
Judie C. Cochran, Grand Canyon Unviersity
Randy E. Cone, University of New Orleans
James Conley, Eastern Michigan University
Billie Miller Cooper, Cosumnes River College
Linda W. Cooper, Macon State College
Jane G. Corbly, Sinclair Community College
Martha Cross, Delta State University
Linda Cunningham, Salt Lake Community College
Guy Devitt, Herkimer County Community College
Bertha Du-Babcock, City University of Hong Kong
Dubinsky, Virginia Tech
Dorothy Drayton, Texas Southern University
Kay Durden, University of Tennessee
Anna Easton, Indiana University
Lorena B. Edwards, Belmont University
Donald E. English, Texas A&M University
Margaret Erthal, Southern Illinois University
Terry M. Frame, University of South Carolina
Kerry J. Gambrill, Florida Community College
Judith L. Graham, Holyoke Community College
Carolyn G. Gray, The University of Texas, Austin
Diane Gruber, Arizona State University West
David Hamilton, Bemidji State University
Paul Hegele, Elgin Community College
Susan A. Heller, Reading Area Community College
Rovena L. Hillsman, California State University, Sacramento
Kenneth Hoffman, Emporia State University
Shirley Houston, University of Nebraska
Warren B. Humphrey, University of Central Florida
Robert G. Insley, University of North Texas

Edna Jellesed, Lane Community College
Glen J. Jenewein, Portland Community College
Carolyn Spillers Jewell, Pembroke State University
Pamela R. Johnson, California State University, Chico
Eric Johnstone, Montana State University
Diana K. Kanoy, Central Florida Community College
Tina S. Kazan, University of Illinois, Chicago
Margaret S. Kilcoyne, Northwestern State University
G. Scott King, Sinclair Community College
Suzanne P. Krissler, Orange County Com. College
Linda L. Labin, Husson College
Richard Lacy, California State University, Fresno
Suzanne Lambert, Broward Community College
Marilyn L. Lammers, California State University, Northridge
Lorita S. Langdon, Columbus State Community College
Joyce N. Larsen, Front Range Community College
Barbara Lea, West Valley College
Claire E. Legowski, North Dakota State University
Mary E. Leslie, Grossmont College
Kathy Lynn Lewis-Adler, University of North Alabama
Mary Jean Lush, Delta State University
Sonia Maasik, University of California, Los Angeles
Bruce MacBeth, Clarion University of Pennsylvania
Georgia E. Mackh, Cabrillo College
Andrew Madson, Milwaukee Area Technical College
Maureen L. Margolies, University of Cincinnati
Thomas A. Marshall II, Robert Morris College
Jeanette Martin, University of Mississippi
John F. Mastriani, El Paso Community College
Susan Smith McClaren, Mt. Hood Community College
Diana McKowen, Indiana University
Mary C. Miller, Ashland University
Marci Mitchell, South Texas Community College
Nancy B. Moody, Sinclair Community College
Danne Moore, Shawnee State University
Wayne A. Moore, Indiana University of Pennsylvania
Paul W. Murphey, Southwest Wisconsin Technical College
Lin Nassar, Oakland Community College
Beverly H. Nelson, University of New Orleans
Matt Newby, Heald College
John P. Nightingale, Eastern Michigan University
Ed Nagelhout, University of Nevada
Jeanne E. Newhall, Middlesex Community College
Alexa B. North, State University of West Georgia
Rosemary Olds, Des Moines Area Community College
James S. O'Rourke IV, University of Notre Dame
Janice Rowan, Rowan University
Calvin R. Parks, Northern Illinois University
Pamela A. Patey, Riverside Community College
William Peirce, Prince George's Community College and
     University of Maryland University College
Joan Policano, Onondaga Community College
Paula J. Pomerenke, Illinois State University
Karen Sterkel Powell, Colorado State University
Gloria Power, Delgado Community College
Richard P. Profozich, Prince George's Community College
Carolyn Mae Rainey, Southeast Missouri State University

Richard G. Raspen, Wilkes University
Virginia L. Reynolds, Cleveland State University
Ruth D. Richardson, University of North Alabama
Joseph H. Roach, Middlesex County College
Terry D. Roach, Arkansas State University
Betty Jane Robbins, University of Oklahoma
Linda Sarlo, Rock Valley College
Christine A. Saxild, Mt. Senario College
Joseph Schaffner, State University of New York at Alfred
Annette Schley, North Seattle Community College
Betty L. Schroeder, Northern Illinois University
Carolyn M. Seefer, Diablo Valley Community College
Marilyn Simonson, Lakewood Community College
Sue C. Smith, Palm Beach Community Collage
Kathleen M. Sole, University of Phoenix
Charles L. Snowden, Sinclair Community College
Gayle A. Sobolik, California State University, Fresno
Jeanette Spender, Arkansas State University
Judy Steiner-Williams, Indiana University
Ted D. Stoddard, Brigham Young University
Susan Switzer, Central Michigan University

Roni Szeliga, Gateway Technical College
Leslie S. Talley, University of Central Florida
Barbara P. Thompson, Columbus State Community College
Sally J. Tiffany, Milwaukee Area Technical College
Lori M. Townsend, Niagara County Community College
Mary L. Tucker, Ohio University
Richard F. Tyler, Anne Arundel Community College
Deborah Valentine, Emory University
Doris A. Van Horn Christopher, California State University, Los Angeles
David Victor, Eastern Michigan University
Lois Ann Wagner, Southwest Wisconsin Technical College
John L. Waltman, Eastern Michigan University
Marion Webb, Cleveland State University
Beverly A. Westbrook, Delta College
Carol M. Williams, Pima County Community College
Jane D. Williams, J. Sargeant Reynolds Community College
Rosemary B. Wilson, Washtenaw Community College
Beverly C. Wise, State University of New York, Morrisville
William E. Worth, Georgia State University
Myron D. Yeager, Chapman University

About the Author

A dedicated professional, Mary Ellen Guffey has taught business communication and business English topics for over thirty years. She received a bachelor's degree, *summa cum laude*, from Bowling Green State University; a master's degree from the University of Illinois, and a doctorate in business and economic education from the University of California, Los Angeles (UCLA). She has taught at the University of Illinois, Santa Monica College, and Los Angeles Pierce College.

Now recognized as the world's leading business communication author, Dr. Guffey corresponds with instructors around the globe who are using her books. She is the author of the award-winning *Business Communication: Process and Product,* the leading business communication textbook in this country and abroad. She has also written *Business English,* which serves more students than any other book in its field; *Essentials of College English* (with Carolyn M. Seefer), and *Essentials of Business Communication,* the leading text/workbook in its market. *Essentials of Business Communication* recently received an award of excellence from the Text and Academic Authors Association. The Canadian editions of her books are bestsellers in that country; one was named Book of the Year by Nelson Canada. A new Asian edition of *Essentials of Business Communication* now serves South Asia, India, and Australia.

Dr. Guffey is active professionally, serving on the review board of the *Business Communication Quarterly* of the Association for Business Communication, participating in all national meetings, and sponsoring business communication awards.

A teacher's teacher and leader in the field, Dr. Guffey acts as a partner and mentor to hundreds of business communication instructors nationally and internationally. Her workshops, seminars, teleconferences, newsletters, articles, teaching materials, and Web sites help novice and veteran business communication instructors achieve effective results in their courses. She maintains comprehensive Web sites for students and instructors. Her online newsletters are used by thousands of instructors in this country and around the world.

Unit 1

Communication Foundations

Chapter 1
Communicating in Today's Workplace

Chapter 2
Developing Team, Listening, and Etiquette Skills

Chapter 3
Communicating Across Cultures

© George Doyle & Ciaran Griffin / Stockbyte / Getty Images

Chapter 1

Communicating in Today's Workplace

After studying this chapter, you should be able to

1 Understand the importance of communication skills in relation to career success; and explain the need for thinking critically, taking charge of your career, and strengthening your communication skills.

2 Recognize significant changes in today's workplace and how these changes increase the need for excellent communication skills.

3 Analyze the process of communication and how to engage it effectively.

4 Recognize barriers to interpersonal communication and examine specific strategies for overcoming those barriers.

5 Analyze the internal and external functions of communication in organizations as well as compare the advantages and disadvantages of oral and written communication.

6 Examine critically the flow of communication in organizations including barriers and methods for overcoming those barriers.

7 Understand the ethical goals of a business communicator and tools for doing the right thing.

© Glowimages / Getty Images

Communicating in Today's Workplace Part 1

A Great Communicator Heads Sears and Kmart

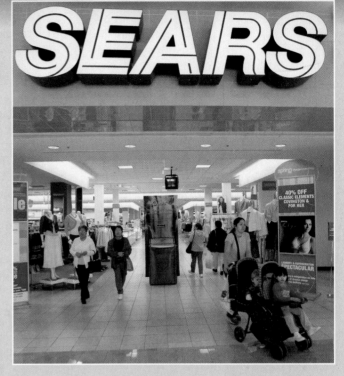

"Our worst stores are dungeons," exclaimed Aylwin B. Lewis, the new chief executive of Sears Holdings Corporation, as he addressed Kmart managers at a dinner meeting. "Well, who wants to work in a dungeon? Who wants to shop in a dungeon?"[1] A gifted speaker and communicator, Lewis was demonstrating one of the skills for which he is best known—inspiring the troops with stirring oratory. It was this and other communication skills that paved the way for his journey through the ranks to become the highest-ranking African-American executive in the U.S. retail industry.

Two massive but troubled retail giants, Sears Roebuck and Kmart, merged to become Sears Holdings. It all started when financier Edward S. Lampert gained control of Kmart at a bargain price as it sank into bankruptcy. Next he snapped up a struggling Sears, thus creating the nation's third-largest retailer with 3,800 stores in the United States and Canada. Lampert then needed an executive to steer the newly formed colossus, and he tapped veteran fast-food restaurant executive Aylwin Lewis.

The son of a factory porter, Lewis paid for his education at the University of Houston by cleaning rugs full time. "I was a typical commuter student," he recalled. He earned dual degrees in literature and business management. "I wanted to get a soft degree that I thought I would use," he explained. "But I wanted a hard degree to understand the world."[2] His business degree honed his business skills, and his literature degree taught him how to do research and how to write. That training, he said, was instrumental in his career success.[3] His speaking skills, developed through church recitations as a boy, made him stand out as a manager. His writing skills led the way to executive promotions.

To pay for graduate school, he worked at Jack in the Box, a fast-food restaurant. "I fell in love with the notion of serving customers," he recalled. "Even as an assistant manager, I liked doing the hiring, the ordering, overseeing the food quality. I loved being a leader."[4] After earning an MBA, he went on to a 25-year career rising through the Jack in the Box ranks and into management positions at Yum Brands, the world's largest restaurant company with holdings that included Taco Bell, Pizza Hut, KFC, Long John Silver's, and A&W All-American Food restaurants.

Asked about his key to climbing the ladder of success, Lewis replied: "I'm a learner. . . . I would have been dead meat leaving the restaurant industry coming to the retail industry if I didn't have the aptitude to say, 'I'm a student of life and I have to learn every day.'"[5] You will learn more about this case study on page 22.

Critical Thinking
- What do you think Aylwin Lewis meant when he referred to a "soft degree" and a "hard degree"?
- What skills do you think businesspeople need to succeed in today's workplace?
- Why do you think it is important today to be willing to continue learning every day?

http://www.searsholdings.com

© Justin Sullivan / Getty Images

Building Your Career Success With Communication Skills

Developing excellent communication skills is extremely important to your career success, whether you are already working or are about to enter today's workplace. Aylwin B. Lewis, CEO of Sears Holdings, which owns both Sears Roebuck and Kmart, found that his speaking and writing skills were crucial as he rose from assistant manager at Jack in the Box to his position as chief of the nation's third-largest retailer. In this chapter you will learn about the importance of communication skills, the changing world of work, the process of communication and its barriers, and ethical challenges facing businesspeople today. Each section covers the latest information about an issue. It also provides tips and suggestions that will help you function successfully in today's dynamic workplace.

LEARNING OBJECTIVE 1
Understand the importance of communication skills in relation to career success; and explain the need for thinking critically, taking charge of your career, and strengthening your communication skills.

The Importance of Communication Skills in Today's Workplace

Employer surveys show that communication skills are critical to effective job placement, performance, career advancement, and organizational success.[6] In making hiring decisions, employers often rank communication skills among the most-requested items. Many

Communication skills are critical to your job placement, performance, career advancement, and organizational success.

Aylwin Lewis, CEO of Sears Holdings, had much experience in fast-food restaurants before being picked to head the giant Sears and Kmart chains. Industry observers thought he might be out of his element in moving to retailing. Although he acknowledged a steep learning curve, Lewis welcomed the challenge. "Leadership skills, communication skills, culture-building skills," he said, "those are all very transferable." These skills are also learnable. Asked if being an African-American role model was a burden, he responded that his goal was to make it easier for the next generation to achieve the American dream. He encourages young people to expect to reach jobs like his. Success is easier to attain, however, if one builds a solid foundation with communication and leadership skills acquired early on. His undergraduate degrees in English and business management helped him rise through the ranks. But he admits that he expects to continue learning every day on the job.

© AP IMAGES

NOTE: Because this is a well-researched textbook, you will find small superscript numbers in the text. These announce information sources. Full citations begin on page N-1 near the end of the book. This edition uses a modified American Psychological Association (APA) format that provides superscripts leading to full citations in the Notes section.

job advertisements specifically ask for excellent oral and written communication skills. In a poll of recruiters, oral and written communication skills were by a large margin the top skill set sought.[7] In another poll, executives were asked what they looked for in a job candidate. The top choices were teamwork skills, critical thinking, analytical reasoning skills, and oral and written communication skills.[8]

When we discuss *communication skills,* we generally mean reading, listening, nonverbal, speaking, and writing skills. In this book we focus on listening, nonverbal, speaking, and writing skills. Chapters are devoted to each of those skills. Special attention is given to writing skills because they are difficult to develop and increasingly significant.

Writing Skills Are More Important Than Ever

Writing skills are particularly important today because technology enables us to transmit messages more rapidly, more often, and to greater numbers of people than ever before. Writing skills are also significant because many people work together but are not physically together. They stay connected through spoken and written messages. Writing skills, which were always a career advantage, are now a necessity.[9] They can be your ticket to work—or your ticket out the door, according to a business executive responding to a recent survey. This survey of 120 American corporations, by the National Commission on Writing, a panel established by the College Board, found that two thirds of salaried employees have some writing responsibility. Yet, about one third of them do not meet the writing requirements for their positions.[10]

"Businesses are crying out—they need to have people who write better," said Gaston Caperton, executive and College Board president. The ability to write opens doors to professional employment. People who cannot write and communicate clearly will not be hired. If already working, they are unlikely to last long enough to be considered for promotion. Writing is a marker of high-skill, high-wage, professional work, according to Bob Kerrey, president of New School University in New York and chair of the National Commission on Writing. If you can't express yourself clearly, he says, you limit your opportunities for many positions.[11]

How important is writing to your income? A *Fortune* magazine article reported this finding: "Among people with a two- or four-year college degree, those in the highest 20 percent in writing ability earn, on average, more than three times what those with the worst writing skills make."[12] One corporate president explained that many people climbing the corporate ladder are good. When he faced a hard choice between candidates, he used writing ability as the deciding factor. He said that sometimes writing is the only skill that separates a candidate from the competition.

Communication Skills Must Be Learned

You are not born with the abilities to read, listen, speak, and write effectively. These skills must be learned. Thriving in the demanding work world depends on many factors, some of which you cannot control. But one factor that you do control is how well you communicate. The goals of this book and this course are to teach you basic business communication skills, such as how to write a memo or letter and how to make a presentation. You will also learn additional powerful communication skills, as summarized in Figure 1.1. This book and this course may well be the most important in your entire college curriculum because they will equip you with the skills most needed in today's dynamic workplace.

Thriving as a Knowledge Worker in the Information Age

Knowledge workers deal with symbols, such as words, figures, and data.

The U.S. economy is based on information and knowledge. Physical labor, raw materials, and capital are no longer the key ingredients in the creation of wealth. Tomorrow's wealth depends on the development and exchange of knowledge. Individuals in the workforce

FIGURE 1.1 How This Book and Course Can Help You Build Communication Skills

This business communication book and this course will help you

- Apply a universal process to solve communication problems throughout your career.
- Learn writing techniques and organizational strategies to compose clear, concise, and purposeful business messages.
- Master effective presentation skills to get your ideas across to large and small groups.
- Learn to be a valuable team player.
- Work productively with the Internet and digital communication technologies.
- Value diversity so that you can function with sensitivity in intercultural work environments.
- Develop tools for meeting ethically challenging situations.
- Land the job of your dreams with invaluable job-search, résumé-writing, and interviewing tips.

offer their knowledge, not their muscles. *Knowledge workers,* said management guru Peter Drucker, get paid for their education and their ability to learn.[13] Microsoft uses the term *information workers* to describe those who work with technology.[14] Regardless of the terminology, knowledge and information workers engage in mind work. They deal with symbols: words, figures, and data. Most recent estimates suggest that knowledge workers outnumber other workers in North America by at least a four-to-one margin.[15]

Some U.S. knowledge workers worry over a new threat—the outsourcing of their jobs to skilled workers in India and China. Outsourcing overseas is a reality, and jobs that can be condensed to a set of rules are likely to go first—either to workers abroad or to computers. However, this country almost certainly will not run out of jobs.[16] Although we cannot predict the kinds of jobs that will be available, they will undoubtedly require brainpower and education. As existing jobs give way to shifts in technology and competition, the economy will adjust, as it has always done in the past. New jobs requiring new skills and talents will emerge.[17]

What Does This Mean for You?

As a knowledge and information worker, you can expect to be generating, processing, and exchanging information. Whether you work in the new economy of *e-commerce* (Internet-based businesses) or the old economy of *bricks-and-mortar* companies, nearly three out of four jobs will involve some form of mind work. Jobs that require thinking, brainpower, and decision-making skills are likely to remain plentiful. To be successful in these jobs, you will need to be able to think critically, make decisions, and communicate those decisions.

Knowledge workers generate, process, and exchange information.

Learning to Think Critically

Management and employees will be working together in such areas as product development, quality control, and customer satisfaction. Whether you are an executive or subordinate, you will be asked to think creatively and critically. Even in factory production lines, workers are part of the knowledge culture. "One of the secrets of Toyota's success," said Takis Athanasopoulos, chief executive of the Japanese carmaker's European operations, "is that the company encourages every worker, no matter how far down the production line, to consider himself a knowledge worker and to think creatively about improving his particular corner of the organization."[18]

Thinking creatively and critically means having opinions that are backed by reasons and evidence. When your boss or team leader says, "What do you think we ought to do?" you want to be able to supply good ideas. The Career Coach box on page 6 provides a five-point critical thinking plan to help you solve problems and make decisions. But having a plan is not enough. You also need chances to try the plan out and get feedback from colleagues and your boss (your instructor, for the time being). At the end of each chapter, you will find activities and problems that will help you develop and apply your critical-thinking skills.

Thinking critically means having opinions that are backed by reasons and evidence.

Taking Charge of Your Career

In the new world of work, you can look forward to constant training to acquire new skills that will help you keep up with evolving technologies and procedures. You can also expect to be exercising greater control over your career. Many workers today will not find nine-to-five

Spotlight on Communicators

"We are entering an age where intangible assets like expertise, intelligence, speed, agility, imagination, maneuverability, networks, passion, responsiveness and innovation—all facets of 'knowledge'— become more important than the tangibles of traditional balance-sheet perspectives," contends Oren Harari, management expert, futurist, and prolific author.

© Professor of Management, University of San Francisco

Sharpening Your Skills for Critical Thinking, Problem Solving, and Decision Making

Gone are the days when management expected workers to check their brains at the door and do only as told. As a knowledge worker, you will be expected to use your brains in thinking critically. You will be solving problems and making decisions. Much of this book is devoted to helping you learn to solve problems and communicate those decisions to management, fellow workers, clients, the government, and the public.

Faced with a problem or an issue, most of us do a lot of worrying before separating the issues or making a decision. All that worrying can become directed thinking by channeling it into the following procedure.

1. **Identify and clarify the problem.** Your first task is to recognize that a problem exists. Some problems are big and unmistakable, such as failure of an air-freight delivery service to get packages to customers on time. Other problems may be continuing annoyances, such as regularly running out of toner for an office copy machine. The first step in reaching a solution is pinpointing the problem area.

2. **Gather information.** Learn more about the problem situation. Look for possible causes and solutions. This step may mean checking files, calling suppliers, or brainstorming with fellow workers. The air-freight delivery service, for example, would investigate the tracking systems of the commercial airlines carrying its packages to determine what went wrong.

3. **Evaluate the evidence.** Where did the information come from? Does it represent various points of view? What biases could be expected from each source? How accurate is the information gathered? Is it fact or opinion? For example, it is a fact that packages are missing; it is an opinion that they are merely lost and will turn up eventually.

4. **Consider alternatives and implications.** Draw conclusions from the gathered evidence and pose solutions. Then weigh the advantages and disadvantages of each alternative. What are the costs, benefits, and consequences? What are the obstacles, and how can they be handled? Most important, what solution best serves your goals and those of your organization? Here's where your creativity is especially important.

5. **Choose the best alternative and test it.** Select an alternative and try it out to see if it meets your expectations. If it does, implement your decision. If it doesn't, rethink your alternatives. The freight company decided to give its unhappy customers free delivery service to make up for the lost packages and downtime. Be sure to continue monitoring and adjusting the solution to ensure its effectiveness over time.

Career Application

As the owner of a popular local McDonald's franchise, you recognize a problem. Customers are unhappy with the multiple lines for service. They don't seem to know where to stand to be next served. Tempers flare when aggressive customers cut in line, and other customers spend so much time protecting their places in line that they fail to study the menu. Then they don't know what to order when they approach the counter. As a franchise owner, you would like to solve this problem. How would the steps discussed here be helpful in approaching this problem?

Icon: © Getty Images

Constantly changing technologies and work procedures mean continual training for employees.

jobs, predictable pay increases, lifetime security, and even conventional workplaces. Don't presume that companies will provide you with a clearly defined career path or planned developmental experiences. In the private sector you can expect to work for multiple employers, moving back and forth between work and education and between work and family responsibilities.[19] Whether you are currently employed or about to enter the constantly changing work world, you must be willing to continuously learn new skills that supplement the strong foundation of basic skills you are acquiring in college. The most successful businesspeople, such as Aylwin Lewis at Sears Holdings, are willing to become lifelong learners.

Strengthening Your Communication Skills

This book, this course, and your instructor can help you develop the skills you need to succeed in today's challenging workplace.

This book is filled with model documents, practice exercises, procedures, tips, strategies, suggestions, summaries, and checklists—all meant to ensure that you develop the superior communication skills that are so vital to your success as a businessperson today.

Remember, communication skills are not inherent; they must be learned. Remember, too, to take advantage of the unique opportunity you now have. You have an expert who is willing to work with you to help improve your writing, speaking, and other communication skills. Many organizations pay thousands of dollars to communication coaches and trainers to teach employees the very skills that you are learning in this course. Your instructor is your coach. Take advantage of this opportunity, and get your money's worth! With this book as your guide and your instructor as your coach, you will find that this course, as we mentioned earlier, could very well be the most important in your entire college curriculum.

Factors Affecting You in Today's Workplace

Today's workplace is undergoing profound changes. As a businessperson and especially as a business communicator, you will undoubtedly be affected by many transformations. Some of the most significant changes include global competition, flattened management hierarchies, and team-based projects. Other changes reflect our constantly evolving information technology, new work environments, a diverse workforce, and the emergence of a knowledge-based economy. The following overview of this new world of work reveals how excellent communication skills are key to your success.

LEARNING OBJECTIVE 2
Recognize significant changes in today's workplace and how these changes increase the need for excellent communication skills.

Many of the changes in the new world of work make communication skills a key to your success.

Heightened Global Competition

Small, medium, and large companies increasingly find themselves competing in global rather than local markets. Improved systems of telecommunication, advanced forms of transportation, and saturated local markets—all of these developments have encouraged companies to move beyond familiar territories to emerging markets around the world. Wal-Mart courts shoppers in China with exotic fruits and live seafood.[20] PepsiCo fights Coca-Cola for new customers in India. FedEx learns the ropes in South America, and McDonald's feeds hungry Russians at Pushkin Square, its busiest restaurant in the world.[21]

Doing business in far-flung countries means dealing with people who may be very different from you. They may have different religions, engage in different customs, live different lifestyles, and rely on different approaches in business. Now add the complications of multiple time zones, vast distances between offices, and different languages. No wonder global communicators can blunder. Take, for example, the failure of Nike's "Just Do It" campaign in China. It emphasized individualistic youthful irreverence, which violates the culture of collectivist China. Nike replaced those ads with a 10-second spot featuring a schoolkid impressing classmates by spinning the globe on his finger. The ad expresses playfulness and daring without rebellion.[22]

Communication is more complicated with people who have different religions, customs, and lifestyles.

Successful communication in these new markets requires developing new skills and attitudes. These include cultural knowledge and sensitivity, flexibility, and patience. Because these skills and attitudes may be difficult to achieve, you will receive special communication training to help you deal with intercultural business transactions.

Flattened Management Hierarchies

In response to intense global competition and other pressures, businesses have for years been cutting costs and flattening their management hierarchies. This flattening means that fewer layers of managers separate decision makers from line workers. In traditional companies, information flows through many levels of managers. In flat organizations, however, where the lines of communication are shorter, decision makers can react more quickly to market changes. Some time ago, toymaker Mattel transformed itself from an "out-of-control money loser" by tightening its organization and cutting six layers from its organizational hierarchy. As a result, when its Matchbox developers came up with a smashing idea for a toy firehouse that required no assembly, the idea could be rushed into production. It didn't languish in the pipeline, drowning in multiple layers of management. Like many restructured organizations, Mattel got rid of "silos" that slice the company up vertically into separate divisions for marketing, operations, production, and human resources. Restructured companies organize work with horizontal teams that allow different areas to interact more efficiently.

Progressive organizations are in the midst of changing from "command and control" to "coordination and cultivation" management styles. This means that work is organized to let people use their own talents more wisely.[23] But today's flatter organizations also bring greater communication challenges. In the past, authoritarian and hierarchical management structures did not require that every employee be a skilled communicator. Managers simply passed along messages to the next level. Today, however, frontline employees as well as managers participate in decision making. Nearly everyone is a writer and a communicator. Businesspeople prepare their own messages; secretaries no longer "clean up" their bosses' writing.

Flatter organizations demand that every employee be a skilled communicator.

Expanded Team-Based Management

Along with flatter chains of command, companies are expanding team-based operations to increase employee involvement in decision making and to improve communication. Nearly

80 percent of employees in all industries have adopted some form of self-directed teams or quality circles. At the Frito-Lay plant in Lubbock, Texas, workers formerly loaded bags of potato chips into cartons. Now organized into work teams, they are responsible for everything from potato processing to equipment maintenance. They even interview new-hires and make quality control decisions.[24] At Cigna Corporation, a huge national insurance company, three organizational layers were flattened and teams were formed to reduce backups in processing customer claims. The formation of these teams forced technology specialists to communicate constantly with business specialists. Suddenly, computer programmers had to do more than code and debug; they had to listen, interpret, and explain. All members of the team had to analyze problems and negotiate solutions.[25]

When companies form cross-functional teams, individuals must work together and share information. Working relationships can become strained when individuals don't share the same background, knowledge, or training. Some companies must hire communication coaches to help existing teams get along. They work to develop interpersonal, negotiation, and collaboration techniques. But companies would prefer to hire new workers who already possess these skills. That is why so many advertisements for new employees say "must possess good communication skills."

Workers on teams need strong communication skills to collaborate and work together effectively.

Ethics Check

Too Connected?

Office workers use smart phones, e-mail, voicemail, and text messaging. Many are literally always on call and feel overwhelmed. What are the limits of connectedness? Is it fair to dodge an unpleasant call by sending it to voice mail or to delay answering certain e-mail messages?

Innovative Communication Technologies

New electronic technologies are dramatically affecting the way workers communicate. We now exchange information and stay in touch by using e-mail, instant messaging, text messaging, PDAs, fax, voice mail, wireless networking, cell phones, powerful laptop computers, and satellite communications. Through teleconferencing and videoconferencing, we can conduct meetings with associates around the world. We're also seeing the rapid development of social software such as weblogs, wikis (multiuser weblogs), and peer-to-peer tools, all of which make it easier for workers to communicate online almost instantaneously. Interactive software enables dozens or even hundreds of users to collaborate on projects. What's more, no self-respecting businessperson today would make a presentation without using sophisticated presentation software. We rely heavily on the Internet and the Web for collecting information, serving customers, and selling products and services. Figure 1.2, on pages 10–11, illustrates many new technologies you will meet in today's workplace.

To use these new resources most effectively, you, as a skilled business communicator, must develop a tool kit of new communication skills. You will want to know how to select the best communication channel, how to use each channel safely and effectively, and how to use online search tools efficiently. All of these topics will be covered in coming chapters.

As digital technology continues to network people around the globe, businesses are increasingly turning to videoconferencing as the ultimate collaboration tool. Whether through basic Web-cam devices or across ultra-high definition video, videoconferencing enables businesspeople to forgo travel yet work with people half a world away—as if they were officemates. *What advantages does videoconferencing have relative to other innovative communication technologies, and how is digital communication contributing to the emergence of the new workplace?*

© Ron Chapple / Thinkstock Images / Jupiterimages

New Work Environments

Today's work environments are also changing. Instead of individual offices and cubicles, companies are encouraging open offices with flexible workstations, shared conference rooms, and boomerang-shaped desks that save space. Thanks largely to advances in communication and mobile technologies, millions of workers no longer work nine-to-five jobs that confine them to offices. They have flexible working arrangements so that they can work at home or on the road. One out of every ten employees now telecommutes full or part time.[26] Moreover, many workers are part of virtual teams that complete projects without ever meeting each other. Tools such as e-mail, instant and text messaging, file sharing, conferencing software, and wireless networking make it easy for employees to collaborate or complete their work in the office, at home, or on the road.

As more and more employees work separately, communication skills become even more important. Staying connected involves sending messages, most of which are written. This means that your writing skills will constantly be on display.

Workers today are collaborating, telecommuting, working in open offices, and serving on virtual teams, all of which demand excellent communication skills.

Increasingly Diverse Workforce

Changes in today's work environments include more than innovative technology, team management, and different work environments. The U.S. workforce is becoming increasingly diverse. As shown in Figure 1.3, the white non-Hispanic population of the United States is expected to drop from 79 percent in 1980 to 64 percent in 2020. Hispanics will climb from 6 percent to 17 percent, African Americans will increase from 12 percent to 13 percent, and Asians will rise from 2 percent to 6 percent.[27] In addition to increasing numbers of minorities, the workforce will see a big jump in older workers. By 2020 the number of workers aged 55 and older will grow to 20 percent.[28] As a result of these and other demographic trends, businesses must create a work environment that values and supports all people.

Communicating with workers who differ in race, ethnicity, gender, and age requires new attitudes and skills.

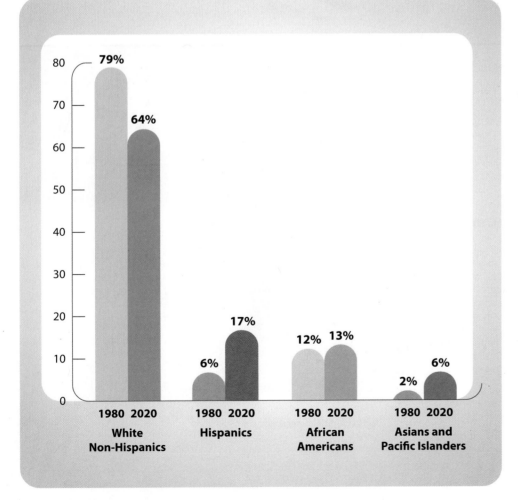

FIGURE 1.3 Racial and Ethnic Makeup of U.S. Population, 1980 to 2020

FIGURE 1.2 Communication and Collaborative Technologies

Communication Technologies: Reshaping the World of Work

Today's workplace is changing dramatically as a result of innovative software, superfast wireless networks, and numerous technologies that allow workers to share information, work from remote locations, and be more productive in or away from the office. We're seeing a gradual progression from basic capabilities, such as e-mail and calendaring, to deeper functionality, such as remote database access, multifunctional devices, and Web-based collaborative applications. Becoming familiar with modern office and collaboration technologies can help you be successful in today's digital workplace.

Telephony: VoIP

Savvy businesses are switching from traditional phone service to Voice over Internet Protocol (VoIP). This technology allows callers to communicate using a broadband Internet connection, thus eliminating long-distance and local telephone charges. Higher-end VoIP systems now support unified voice mail, e-mail, click-to-call capabilities, and softphones (phones using computer networking). Free or low-cost Internet telephony sites, such as the popular Skype, are also increasingly used by businesses.

Multifunctional Printers

Stand-alone copiers, fax machines, scanners, and printers have been replaced with multifunctional devices. Offices are transitioning from a "print and distribute" environment to a "distribute and print" environment. Security measures include pass codes and even biometric thumbprint scanning to make sure data streams are not captured, interrupted, or edited.

Open Offices

Widespread use of laptop computers, wireless technology, and VoIP have led to more fluid, flexible, and open workspaces. Smaller computers and flat-screen monitors enable designers to save space with boomerang-shaped workstations and cockpit-style work surfaces rather than space-hogging corner work areas. Smaller breakout areas for impromptu meetings are taking over some cubicle space, and digital databases are replacing file cabinets.

Handheld Wireless Devices

A new generation of lightweight, handheld devices provide phone, e-mail, Web browsing, and calendar options anywhere there's a wireless network. Devices such as the Black-Berry and the Palm Treo now allow you to tap into corporate databases and intranets from remote locations. You can check customers' files, complete orders, and send out receipts without returning to the office.

Company Intranets

To share insider information, many companies provide their own protected Web sites called intranets. An intranet may handle company e-mail, announcements, an employee directory, a policy handbook, frequently asked questions, personnel forms and data, employee discussion forums, shared documents, and other employee information.

Voice Recognition

Computers equipped with voice recognition software enable users to dictate up to 160 words a minute with accurate transcription. Voice recognition is particularly helpful to disabled workers and to professionals with heavy dictation loads, such as physicians and attorneys. Users can create documents, enter data, compose and send e-mails, browse the Web, and control the desktop—all by voice.

Electronic Presentations

Business presentations in PowerPoint can be projected from a laptop or PDA or posted online. Sophisticated presentations may include animations, sound effects, digital photos, video clips, or hyperlinks to Internet sites. In some industries, PowerPoint slides ("decks") are replacing or supplementing traditional hard-copy reports.

Reshaping- © Creatas / Photolibrary Group / Index Stock Imagery; Telephony- © Jochen Tack / Alamy; Open Offices- © Ablestock / Dynamic Graphics / Jupiterimages; Multifunctional Printer- © Apply Pictures / Alamy; Handheld Wireless- © AP IMAGES; Voice Recognition- © TOSHIFUMI KITAMURA / AFP / Getty Images; Company Intranet- © Terri Miller / E-Visual Communications, Inc.; Electronic Presentation- © Image Source / Alamy

Chapter 1: Communicating in Today's Workplace

Collaboration Technologies: Rethinking the Way We Work Together

Global competition, expanding markets, and the ever-increasing pace of business accelerate the development of exciting collaboration tools. New tools make it possible to work together without being together. Your colleagues may be down the hall, across the country, or around the world. With today's tools, you can exchange ideas, solve problems, develop products, forecast future performance, and complete team projects any time of the day or night and anywhere in the world. Blogs and wikis, part of the so-called Web 2.0 era, are social tools that create multidirectional conversations among customers and employees. Web 2.0 moves Web applications from "read only" to "read-write," thus enabling greater participation and collaboration.

Blogs, Podcasts, and Wikis

A *blog* is a Web site with journal entries usually written by one person with comments added by others. Businesses use blogs to keep customers and employees informed and to receive feedback. Company developments can be posted, updated, and categorized for easy cross-referencing. When the writer adds audio, the blog becomes a *podcast*. A *wiki* is a Web site that allows multiple users to collaboratively create and edit pages. Information gets lost in e-mails, but blogs and wikis provide an easy way to communicate and keep track of what's said.

Voice Conferencing

Telephone "bridges" allow two or more callers from any location to share the same call. *Voice conferencing* (also called *audioconferencing*, *teleconferencing*, or just plain *conference calling*) enables people to collaborate by telephone. Communicators at both ends use enhanced speakerphones to talk and be heard simultaneously.

Videoconferencing

Videoconferencing allows participants to meet in special conference rooms equipped with cameras and television screens. Groups see each other and interact in real time although they may be far apart. Faster computers, rapid Internet connections, and better cameras now enable 2 to 200 participants to sit at their own PCs and share applications, spreadsheets, presentations, and photos.

Web Conferencing

With services such as GoToMeeting, WebEx, or Microsoft LiveMeeting, all you need are a PC and an Internet connection to hold a meeting (*webinar*) with customers or colleagues in real time. Although the functions are constantly evolving, Web conferencing currently incorporates screen sharing, chats, slide presentations, text messaging, and application sharing.

Presence Technology

Presence technology makes it possible to locate and identify a computing device as soon as users connect to the network. This technology is an integral part of communication devices including cell phones, laptop computers, PDAs, pagers, and GPS devices. Collaboration is possible wherever and whenever users are online.

Video Phones

Using advanced video compression technology, video phones transmit real-time audio and video so that communicators can see each other as they collaborate. With a video phone, people can videoconference anywhere in the world over a broadband IP (Internet Protocol) connection without a computer or a television screen.

Communicating in this diverse work environment requires new attitudes and skills. Acquiring these new employment skills is certainly worth the effort because of the benefits diversity brings to consumers, work teams, and business organizations. A diverse staff is better able to read trends and respond to the increasingly diverse customer base in local and world markets. In the workplace, diversity also makes good business sense. Teams made up of people with various experiences are more likely to create the products that consumers demand. Customers also want to deal with companies that respect their values. They are more likely to say, "If you are a company whose ads do not include me, or whose workforce does not include me, I will not buy from you." Learning to cooperate and communicate successfully with diverse coworkers should be a major priority for all businesspeople.

Understanding the Process of Communication

Because communication is a central factor in the emerging knowledge economy and a major consideration for anyone entering today's workforce, we need to look more closely at the total process of communication. Just what is communication? For our purposes communication is the *transmission of information and meaning from one individual or group to another.* The crucial element in this definition is *meaning.* Communication has as its central objective the transmission of meaning. The process of communication is successful only when the receiver understands an idea as the sender intended it. Both parties must agree not only on the information transmitted but also on the meaning of that information. How does an idea travel from one person to another? Despite what you may have seen in futuristic science fiction movies, we can't just glance at another person and transfer meaning directly from mind to mind. We engage in a sensitive process of communication, discussed here and depicted in Figure 1.4.

Sender Has Idea

The communication process had five steps: idea formation, message encoding, message transmission, message decoding, and feedback.

The process of communication begins when the person with whom the message originates—the *sender*—has an idea. The form of the idea will be influenced by complex factors surrounding the sender: mood, frame of reference, background, culture, and physical makeup, as well as the context of the situation and many other factors. The way you greet people on campus or on the job, for example, depends a lot on how you feel, whom you are addressing

FIGURE 1.4 The Communication Process

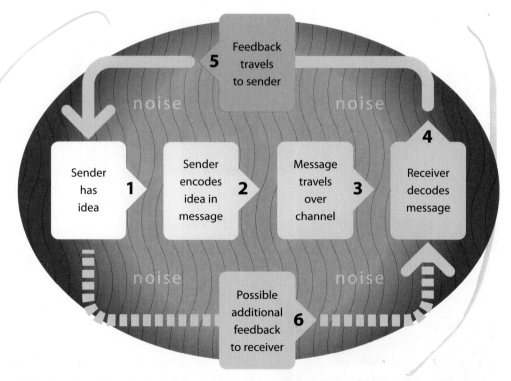

Note: A more comprehensive model of the communication process is available in the instructor's PowerPoint program.

Chapter 1: Communicating in Today's Workplace

(a classmate, a professor, a colleague, or your boss), and what your culture has trained you to say ("Good morning," "Hey," "Hi," "Howdy," or "How ya doing?").

The form of the idea, whether a simple greeting or a complex idea, is shaped by assumptions based on the sender's experiences. A manager sending an e-mail announcement to employees assumes they will be receptive, whereas direct-mail advertisers assume that receivers will give only a quick glance to their message. The ability to accurately predict how a message will affect its receiver and skill in adapting that message to its receiver are key factors in successful communication.

Predicting the effect of a message and adapting the message to a receiver are key factors in successful communication.

Sender Encodes Idea in Message

The next step in the communication process involves *encoding*. This means converting the idea into words or gestures that will convey meaning. A major problem in communicating any message verbally is that words have different meanings for different people. When misunderstandings result from missed meanings, it is called *bypassing*. Recognizing how easy it is to be misunderstood, skilled communicators choose familiar words with concrete meanings on which both senders and receivers agree. In selecting proper symbols, senders must be alert to the receiver's communication skills, attitudes, background, experiences, and culture: How will the selected words affect the receiver? In Great Britain, for example, a Dr. Pepper cola promotion failed miserably because American managers had not done their homework. They had to change their "I'm a Pepper" slogan after learning that *pepper* is British slang for *prostitute*.[29] Because the sender initiates a communication transaction, he or she has primary responsibility for its success or failure. Choosing appropriate words or symbols is critical to a successful message.

Encoding involves converting an idea into words or gestures that convey meaning.

Message Travels Over Channel

The medium over which the message is physically transmitted is the *channel*. Messages may be delivered by computer, telephone, cell phone, letter, memorandum, report, announcement, picture, spoken word, fax, Web page, or through some other channel. Because communication channels deliver both verbal and nonverbal messages, senders must choose the channel and shape the message carefully. A company may use its annual report, for example, as a channel to deliver many messages to stockholders. The verbal message lies in the report's financial and organizational news. Nonverbal messages, though, are conveyed by the report's appearance (showy versus bland), layout (ample white space versus tightly packed columns of print), and tone (conversational versus formal).

Channels are the media—computer, telephone, fax, cell phone, letter, report, and so on—that transmit messages.

Anything that interrupts the transmission of a message in the communication process is called *noise*. Channel noise ranges from static that disrupts a telephone conversation to typographical and spelling errors in a letter or e-mail message. Such errors damage the credibility of the sender. Channel noise might even include the annoyance a receiver feels when the sender chooses an improper medium for sending a message, such as announcing a loan rejection via postcard or firing an employee by e-mail.

Receiver Decodes Message

The individual for whom the message is intended is the *receiver*. Translating the message from its symbol form into meaning involves *decoding*. Only when the receiver understands the meaning intended by the sender—that is, successfully decodes the message—does communication take place. Such success, however, is difficult to achieve because no two people share the same life experiences and because many barriers can disrupt the process.

Decoding involves translating the message from symbol form into meaning.

Decoding can be disrupted internally by the receiver's lack of attention to or bias against the sender. It can be disrupted externally by loud sounds or illegible words. Decoding can also be sidetracked by semantic obstacles, such as misunderstood words or emotional reactions to certain terms. A memo that refers to all the women in an office as "girls" or "chicks," for example, may disturb its receivers so much that they fail to comprehend the total message.

Feedback Travels to Sender

The verbal and nonverbal responses of the receiver create *feedback*, a vital part of the communication process. Feedback helps the sender know that the message was received and understood. If, as a receiver, you hear the message "How are you," your feedback might consist of words ("I'm fine") or body language (a smile or a wave of the hand). Although the receiver may respond with additional feedback to the sender (thus creating a new act of communication), we'll concentrate here on the initial message flowing to the receiver and the resulting feedback.

Asking questions encourages feedback that clarifies communication.

Senders can encourage feedback by asking questions such as, *Am I making myself clear?* and *Is there anything you don't understand?* Senders can further improve feedback by timing the delivery appropriately and by providing only as much information as the receiver can handle. Receivers can improve the process by paraphrasing the sender's message with comments, such as, *Let me try to explain that in my own words.* The best feedback is descriptive rather than evaluative. For example, here's a descriptive response: *I understand you want to launch a used golf ball business.* Here's an evaluative response: *Your business ideas are always goofy.* An evaluative response is judgmental and doesn't tell the sender whether the receiver actually understood the message.

Overcoming Interpersonal Communication Barriers

LEARNING OBJECTIVE 4
Recognize barriers to interpersonal communication and examine specific strategies for overcoming those barriers.

The communication process is successful only when the receiver understands the message as intended by the sender. It sounds quite simple. Yet it is not. How many times have you thought that you delivered a clear message, only to learn later that your intentions were totally misunderstood? Most messages that we send reach their destination, but many are only partially understood.

Obstacles That Create Misunderstanding

Barriers to successful communication include bypassing, differing frames of reference, lack of language or listening skills, emotional interference, and physical distractions.

You can improve your chances of communicating successfully by learning to recognize barriers that are known to disrupt the process. The most significant barriers for individuals are bypassing, differing frames of reference, lack of language skill, and distractions.

Bypassing. One of the biggest barriers to clear communication involves words. Each of us attaches a little bundle of meanings to every word, and these meanings are not always similar. *Bypassing* happens when people miss each other with their meanings.[30] Let's say your boss asks you to "help" with a large customer mailing. When you arrive to do your share, you learn that you are expected to do the whole mailing yourself. You and your boss attached different meanings to the word *help*. Bypassing can lead to major miscommunication because people assume that meanings are contained in words. Actually, meanings are in people. For communication to be successful, the receiver and sender must attach the same symbolic meanings to their words.

Miscommunication often results when the sender's frame of reference differs markedly from the receiver's.

Differing Frames of Reference. Another barrier to clear communication is your *frame of reference*. Everything you see and feel in the world is translated through your individual frame of reference. Your unique frame is formed by a combination of your experiences, education, culture, expectations, personality, and other elements. As a result, you bring your own biases and expectations to any communication situation. Because your frame of reference is totally different from everyone else's, you will never see things exactly as others do. American managers eager to reach an agreement with a Chinese parts supplier, for example, were disappointed with the slow negotiations process. The Chinese managers, on the other hand, were pleased that so much time had been taken to build personal relationships with the American managers. Wise business communicators strive to prevent miscommunication by being alert to both their own frames of reference and those of others. You will learn more about communicating across cultures in Chapter 3.

Lack of Language Skill. No matter how extraordinary the idea, it won't be understood or fully appreciated unless the communicators involved have good language skills. Each individual needs an adequate vocabulary, a command of basic punctuation and grammar, and skill in written and oral expression. Moreover, poor listening skills can prevent us from hearing oral messages clearly and thus responding properly.

Distractions. Other barriers include emotional interference, physical distractions, and digital interruptions. Shaping an intelligent message is difficult when one is feeling joy, fear, resentment, hostility, sadness, or some other strong emotion. To reduce the influence of emotions on communication, both senders and receivers should focus on the content of the message and try to remain objective. Physical distractions such as faulty acoustics, noisy surroundings, or a poor cell phone connection can disrupt oral communication. Similarly, sloppy appearance, poor printing, careless formatting, and typographical or spelling errors can disrupt written messages. What's more, technology doesn't seem to be helping. Knowledge workers are increasingly distracted by multitasking, information overload, conflicting demands, and being constantly available digitally. Clear communication requires focusing on what is important and shutting out interruptions.[31]

Overcoming Communication Obstacles

Careful communicators can conquer barriers in a number of ways. Half the battle in communicating successfully is recognizing that the entire process is sensitive and susceptible to breakdown. Like a defensive driver anticipating problems on the road, a good communicator anticipates problems in encoding, transmitting, and decoding a message. Effective communicators also focus on the receiver's environment and frame of reference. They ask themselves questions such as, *How is that individual likely to react to my message?* or *Does the receiver know as much about the subject as I do?*

Misunderstandings are less likely if you arrange your ideas logically and use words precisely. Mark Twain was right when he said, "The difference between an almost-right word and the right word is like the difference between lightning and the lightning bug." But communicating is more than expressing yourself well. A large part of successful communication is listening. Management advisor Peter Drucker observed that "too many executives think they are wonderful with people because they talk well. They don't realize that being wonderful with people means listening well."[32]

Effective communicators create an environment for useful feedback. In oral communication this means asking questions such as, *Do you understand?* and *What questions do you have?* as well as encouraging listeners to repeat instructions or paraphrase ideas. As a listener it means providing feedback that describes rather than evaluates. In written communication it means asking questions and providing access: *Do you have my phone numbers in case you have questions?* or *Here's my e-mail address so that you can give me your response immediately.*

To overcome obstacles, communicators must anticipate problems in encoding, transmitting, and decoding.

Good communicators ask questions to stimulate feedback.

Communicating in Organizations

Until now, you've probably been thinking about the communication you do personally. But business communicators must also be concerned with the bigger picture, and that involves sharing information in organizations. On the job you will be sharing information by communicating internally and externally.

Internal and External Functions

Internal communication includes exchanging ideas and messages with superiors, co-workers, and subordinates. When those messages must be written, you will probably choose e-mail (see Figure 1.5). When you are communicating externally with customers, suppliers, the government, and the public, you may send letters on company stationery (see the American Airlines letter in Figure 1.5 on page 16).

Some of the functions of internal communication are to issue and clarify procedures and policies, inform management of progress, develop new products and services, persuade employees or management to make changes or improvements, coordinate activities, and evaluate and reward employees. External functions involve answering inquiries about products or services, persuading customers to buy products or services, clarifying supplier specifications, issuing credit, collecting bills, responding to government agencies, and promoting a positive image of the organization.

In all of these tasks, employees and managers use a number of communication skills: reading, listening, speaking, and writing. As college students and workers, you probably realize that you need to raise these skills to the proficiency level required for success in today's knowledge society. This book and this course will provide you with practical advice on how to do just that.

LEARNING OBJECTIVE 5
Analyze the internal and external functions of communication in organizations as well as compare the advantages and disadvantages of oral and written communication.

Internal communication often consists of e-mail, memos, and voice messages; external communication generally consists of letters.

FIGURE 1.5 Internal and External Forms of Communication

AmericanAirlines®

EXECUTIVE OFFICE

March 4, 2009

Ms. Christie Bonner
1792 Southern Avenue
Mesa, AZ 85202

Dear Ms. Bonner:

Congratulations for taking steps to overcome your fear of flying! Your eloquent words are testimony to the effectiveness of our AAir Born program; and more important, they underline how liberating the experience can be. I know the door is now open for you to enjoy many satisfying travel experiences.

Probably the most pleasant part of my responsibilities at American is receiving compliments from our customers about the service provided by our employees. I have passed along your kind words about those individuals who made such a difference to you in realizing your dream of flight. We appreciate the opportunity to recognize their fine performance.

On behalf of all of us associated with the AAir Born program, thank you very much, Ms. Bonner. We look forward to welcoming you aboard again soon.

Sincerely,

Janice Moore

Janice Moore
Staff Supervisor

Letters on company stationery communicate with outsiders. Notice how this one builds a solid relationship between American Airlines and a satisfied customer.

E-mail messages and printed memorandums typically deliver messages within organizations. They use a standardized format and are direct and concise.

File Edit Mailbox Message Transfer Special Tools Window Help

B *I* U | Send

To: Frederick Estrada <festrada@aa.com>
From: Kimberly Mosrati <kmosrati@aa.com>
Subject: News Release About Nashville Crew Base
Cc:
Bcc:
Attached: News_Release.txt

Fred,

As an attachment I'm sending a draft of the news release announcing the Nashville crew base. Please look it over and make any needed changes. We tried to keep it short and to the point. Captain Michael Koleda has agreed to do the media conference late Tuesday morning since your schedule is so tight.

Because *Flagship News* is close to its deadline and would like to run a brief story on the announcement, I'll need your response by August 12. Thanks for your help!

Kim
Kimberly Mosrati
Corporate Communications
E-mail: kmosrati@aa.com
Telephone: (254) 225-3490
FAX: (254) 225-5891

FIGURE 1.6 Functions of Business Communication

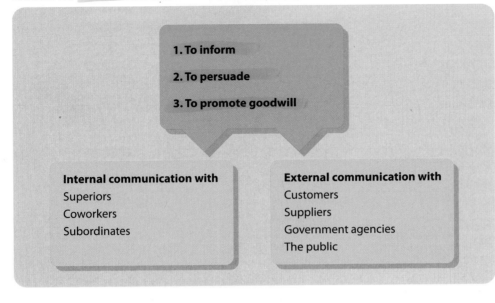

1. To inform
2. To persuade
3. To promote goodwill

Internal communication with
Superiors
Coworkers
Subordinates

External communication with
Customers
Suppliers
Government agencies
The public

Now look back over the preceding discussion of internal and external functions of communication in organizations. Although there appear to be a large number of diverse business communication functions, they can be summarized in three simple categories, as Figure 1.6 shows: (a) to inform, (b) to persuade, and/or (c) to promote goodwill.

Organizational communication has three basic functions: to inform, to persuade, and to promote goodwill.

Emphasis on Interactive, Mobile, and Instant Communication

The flattening of organizations coupled with the development of sophisticated information technology has greatly changed the way we communicate internally and externally. We are seeing a major shift away from one-sided, slow forms of communication, such as memos and letters to more interactive, fast-results communication. Speeding up the flow of communication are technologies such as e-mail, instant messaging (IM), text messaging, smart phones, voice mail, cell phones, and wireless fidelity ("Wi-Fi") networks. Wi-Fi lets mobile workers connect to the Internet at ultrafast speeds without cables.

Communication media are changing from one-sided, slow forms to more interactive, fast-results forms of communication.

Illiana Raveh can't imagine her life without instant and text messaging. An employee at a New York brokerage firm, Illiana uses IM to talk simultaneously with clients, colleagues, and friends. With IM, she can carry on six conversations at once, which helps her get her job done and serve clients better. *Instant messaging* is a type of communications service that allows you to create a private chat room to communicate in real time over the Internet. Typically, the instant messaging system alerts you when someone on your private list is online. *Text messaging* involves sending short text messages usually to a wireless device such as a cell phone or PDA.

Other forms of interactive communication include intranets (company versions of the Internet), Web sites, video transmission, and videoconferencing. You will be learning more about these forms of communication in coming chapters. Despite the range of interactive technologies, communicators are still working with two basic forms of communication: oral and written. Each has advantages and disadvantages.

Oral Communication

Nearly everyone agrees that the best way to exchange information is orally in face-to-face conversations or meetings. Oral communication has many advantages. For one thing, it minimizes misunderstandings because communicators can immediately ask questions to clarify uncertainties. For another, it enables communicators to see each other's facial expressions and hear voice inflections, further improving the process. Oral communication is also an efficient way to develop consensus when many people must be consulted. Finally, most of us enjoy face-to-face interpersonal communication because it is easy, feels warm and natural, and promotes friendships.

Oral communication minimizes miscommunication but provides no written record.

The main disadvantages of oral communication are that it produces no written record, sometimes wastes time, and may be inconvenient. When individuals meet face-to-face or speak on the telephone, someone's work has to be interrupted. And how many of us are

FIGURE 1.7 Forms of Organizational Communication

	Forms	Advantages	Disadvantages
Oral Communication	Phone call	Immediate feedback	No permanent record
	Conversation	Nonverbal clues	Expression may be careless or imprecise
	Interview	Warm feeling	May be inappropriate for formal or complex ideas
	Meeting	Forceful impact	
	Conference	Multiple input	
Written Communication	Announcement	Permanent record	Leaves paper trail
	E-mail, memo, fax	Convenience	Requires skill
	Letter	Economy	Requires effort
	Report, proposal	Careful message	Lacks verbal cues
	Newsletter	Easy distribution	Seems impersonal
	PowerPoint presentation		
	Résumé		

able to limit a conversation to just business? Nevertheless, oral communication has many advantages. The forms and advantages of both oral and written communication are summarized in Figure 1.7.

Written Communication

Written communication provides a permanent record but lacks immediate feedback.

Written communication is impersonal in the sense that two communicators cannot see or hear each other and cannot provide immediate feedback. Most forms of business communication—including e-mail, announcements, memos, faxes, letters, newsletters, reports, proposals, manuals, presentations, and résumés—fall into this category.

Organizations rely on written communication for many reasons. It provides a permanent record, a necessity in these times of increasing litigation and extensive government regulation. Writing out an idea instead of delivering it orally enables communicators to develop an organized, well-considered message. Written documents are also convenient. They can be composed and read when the schedules of both communicators permit, and they can be reviewed if necessary.

Written messages have drawbacks, of course. They require careful preparation. Words spoken in conversation may soon be forgotten, but words committed to hard or soft copy become a public record—and sometimes an embarrassing or dangerous one. E-mail and text-messaging records, even deleted ones, have often become "smoking guns" in court cases, revealing insider information that was never meant for public consumption.[33]

Written messages demand good writing skills, which can be developed through training.

Another drawback to written messages is that they are more difficult to prepare. They demand good writing skills, and we are not born with these skills. But writing proficiency can be learned. Because as much as 90 percent of all business transactions may involve written messages and because writing skills are so important to your business success, you will be receiving special instruction in becoming a good writer.

Improving the Flow of Information in Organizations

LEARNING OBJECTIVE 6
Examine critically the flow of communication in organizations including barriers and methods for overcoming those barriers.

Information within organizations flows through formal and informal communication channels. A free exchange of information helps organizations respond rapidly to changing markets, boost efficiency and productivity, build employee morale, serve the public, and take full advantage of the ideas of today's knowledge workers. Barriers, however, can obstruct the flow of communication, as summarized in Figure 1.8.

Formal Channels

Formal communication channels follow an organization's chain of command.

Formal channels of communication generally follow an organization's hierarchy of command, as shown in Figure 1.9. Information about policies and procedures originates with

FIGURE 1.8 Barriers Block the Flow of Communication in Organizations

executives and flows down through managers to supervisors and finally to lower-level employees. Many organizations have formulated official communication policies that encourage regular open communication, suggest means for achieving it, and spell out responsibilities. Official information among workers typically flows through formal channels in three directions: downward, upward, and horizontally.

Downward Flow. Information flowing downward generally moves from decision makers, including the CEO and managers, through the chain of command to workers. This information includes job plans, policies, and procedures. Managers also provide feedback about employee performance and instill a sense of mission in achieving the organization's goals.

> Job plans, policies, instructions, feedback, and procedures flow downward from managers to employees.

Obstacles to Downward Information Flow. One obstacle that can impede the downward flow of information is distortion resulting from long lines of communication. If, for example, the CEO in Figure 1.9 wanted to change an accounting procedure, she or he

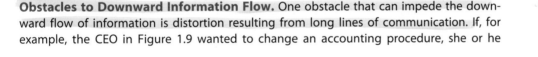

FIGURE 1.9 Formal Communication Channels

would probably not send a memo directly to the cost accountants who would implement the change. Instead, the CEO would relay the idea through proper formal channels—from the vice president for finance, to the accounting manager, to the senior accountant, and so on—until the message reached the affected employees. Obviously, the longer the lines of communication, the greater the chance that a message will be distorted.

Improving Downward Information Flow. To improve communication and to compete more effectively, many of today's companies have restructured and reengineered themselves into smaller operating units and work teams. Rather than being bogged down with long communication chains, management speaks directly to team leaders, thus speeding up the entire process. Management is also improving the downward flow of information through newsletters, announcements, meetings, videos, blogs, webcasts, and company intranets. Instead of hoarding information at the top, today's managers recognize the importance of letting workers know how well the company is doing and what new projects are planned.

Upward Flow. Information flowing upward provides feedback from nonmanagement employees to management. Subordinate employees describe progress in completing tasks, report roadblocks encountered, and suggest methods for improving efficiency. Channels for upward communication include phone messages, e-mail, memos, reports, departmental meetings, and suggestion systems. Ideally, the heaviest flow of information should be upward with information being fed steadily to decision makers. Figure 1.10 summarizes the three directions of information flow within organizations.

Obstacles to Upward Information Flow. A number of obstacles can interrupt the upward flow of communication. Employees who distrust their employers are less likely to communicate openly. Employees cease trusting managers if they feel they are being tricked, manipulated, criticized, or treated unfairly. Unfortunately, some employees today no longer have a strong trusting attitude toward employers. Downsizing, cost-cutting measures, the use of temporary workers, discrimination and harassment suits, outrageous compensation packages for chief executives, and many other factors have lessened the feelings of trust and pride that employees once felt toward their employers and their jobs. Other obstacles include fear of reprisal for honest communication, lack of adequate communication skills, and differing frames of reference. Imperfect communication results when individuals are not using words or symbols with similar meanings, when they cannot express their ideas clearly, or when they come from different backgrounds.

Improving Upward Information Flow. To improve the upward flow of communication, some companies are (a) hiring communication coaches to train employees, (b) asking employees to report customer complaints, (c) encouraging regular meetings with staff, (d) providing a trusting, nonthreatening environment in which employees can comfortably share their observations and ideas with management, and (e) offering incentive programs that

FIGURE 1.10 Organizational Information Flows in Three Directions

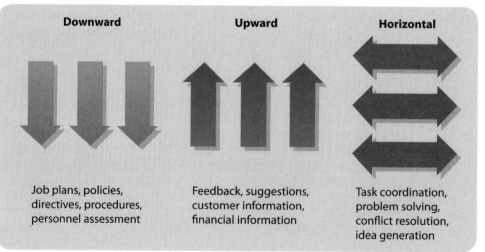

Downward	Upward	Horizontal
Job plans, policies, directives, procedures, personnel assessment	Feedback, suggestions, customer information, financial information	Task coordination, problem solving, conflict resolution, idea generation

Feedback from employees forms the upward flow of communication in most organizations.

encourage employees to collect and share valuable feedback. Companies are also building trust by setting up hotlines for anonymous feedback to management and by installing *ombudsman* programs. An *ombudsman* is a mediator who hears employee complaints, investigates, and seeks to resolve problems fairly.

Horizontal Flow. Lateral channels transmit information horizontally among workers at the same level, such as between the training supervisor and maintenance supervisor in Figure 1.9. These channels enable individuals to coordinate tasks, share information, solve problems, and resolve conflicts. Horizontal communication takes place through personal contact, telephone, e-mail, memos, voice mail, and meetings. Most traditional organizations have few established regular channels for the horizontal exchange of information. Restructured companies with flattened hierarchies and team-based management, however, have discovered that when employees combine their knowledge with that of other employees, they can do their jobs better. Much information in these organizations travels horizontally among team members.[34]

Workers coordinate tasks, share information, solve problems, and resolve conflicts through horizontal communication.

Obstacles to Horizontal Information Flow. Obstacles to the horizontal flow of communication, as well as to upward and downward flow, include poor communication skills, prejudice, ego involvement, and turf wars. Some employees avoid sharing information if doing so might endanger their status or chances for promotion within the organization. Competition within units and an uneven reward system may also prevent workers from freely sharing information.

Improving Horizontal Information Flow. To improve horizontal communication, companies are (a) training employees in teamwork and communication techniques, (b) establishing reward systems based on team achievement rather than individual achievement, and (c) encouraging full participation in team functions. However, employees must also realize that they are personally responsible for making themselves heard, for really understanding what other people say, and for getting the information they need. Developing those business communication skills is exactly what this book and this course will do for you.

Informal Channels

Not all information within an organization travels through formal channels. The *grapevine* is an informal channel of communication that carries organizationally relevant gossip.[35] This informal but powerful channel functions through social relationships in which individuals talk about work when they are having lunch, working out, golfing, carpooling, and, more recently, blogging. One writer called blogs "the grapevine on steroids."[36]

Researchers studying communication flow within organizations know that the grapevine can be a powerful, pervasive source of information. In some organizations it can account for as much as two thirds of an employee's information. Is this bad? Well, yes and no. The grapevine can be a fairly accurate and speedy source of organization information. Studies have demonstrated accuracy ratings of nearly 80 percent for many grapevine transmissions.[37] However, grapevine information is often incomplete because it travels in headlines: "Vice President Sacked" or "Jerk on the Fourth Floor Promoted." When employees obtain most of their company news from the grapevine, management is not releasing sufficient information through formal channels. Managers can influence the grapevine by (a) respecting employees' desire to know, (b) increasing the amount of information delivered through formal channels, (c) sharing bad as well as good news, (d) monitoring the grapevine, and (e) acting promptly to correct misinformation.[38]

The truth is that most employees want to know what's going on. In fact, one study found that regardless of how much information organization members reported receiving, they wanted more.[39] Many companies today have moved away from a rigid authoritarian management structure in which only managers were allowed to see vital information, such as product success and profit figures. Employees who know the latest buzz feel like important members of the team.[40] Through formal lines of communication, smart companies are keeping employees informed. Thus, the grapevine is reduced to carrying gossip about who's dating whom and what restaurant is cool for lunch.

Ethics Check

Office Grapevine
Like a game of "telephone," the grapevine can distort the original message because the news travels through many mouths and ears at the office. Knowing this, can you safely share with even a trusted colleague something that you would not comfortably discuss with everyone?

Communicating at Work Part 2

Sears Holdings

In taking over as CEO of both Sears Roebuck and Kmart, Aylwin Lewis faced many obstacles. Chief among them was combining two retail giants, resurrecting famous brand names (such as Kenmore, Diehard, Craftsman, Lands' End, and Martha Stewart), and finding ways to exploit newfound connections between the two chains.

Since the merger, Lewis has worked tirelessly to establish the framework for a new culture. He and his staff have restructured work flows to enable store employees to spend less time in back rooms and more time interacting with customers. In another move, Lewis required all 3,800 Sears headquarters employees to spend at least a day working in a store, which many had never done. Practicing what he preached, Lewis made frequent store visits, announced and unannounced. Sometimes he even worked alongside clerks. Other times he watched and listened, asking managers what they needed to improve store operations.[41]

Lewis realizes that both Sears and Kmart need to be turned around. Thus far, he says, "we have improved dramatically in terms of housekeeping standards, uniform standards, and presentation standards. I'm proud of that stuff, but at the same time we're still not best-in-class."[42] Lewis faces the daunting task of breathing new life into Kmart and Sears, two down-at-the-heels chains having trouble competing with Target and Wal-Mart. "Make no mistake," he told managers. "We have to change."

© Justin Sullivan / Getty Images

Critical Thinking
- In communicating the changes he wants to make at Sears and Kmart, should CEO Aylwin Lewis use formal or informal channels of communication? Give examples of each.
- In the midst of many organizational changes at Sears and Kmart, what kinds of messages do you think will be traveling downward, upward, and horizontally?
- What kinds of barriers block the flow of communication in any organization undergoing massive changes?

Examining Business Communication Ethics

LEARNING OBJECTIVE 7
Understand the ethical goals of a business communicator and tools for doing the right thing.

As a business communicator, you should understand basic ethical principles so that you can make logical decisions when faced with dilemmas in the workplace. Professionals in any field must deal with moral dilemmas on the job. However, just being a moral person and having sound personal ethics may not be sufficient to handle the ethical issues that you may face in the workplace. Consider the following ethical dilemmas:

E-mail message. You accidentally receive a message outlining your company's restructuring plan. You see that your coworker's job will be eliminated. He and his wife are about to purchase a new home. Should you tell him that his job is in danger?

Customer letter. You are writing a letter to a customer who is irate over a mistake you made. Should you blame it on a computer glitch, point the finger at another department, or take the blame and risk losing this customer's goodwill and possibly your job?

Progress report. Should you write a report that ignores problems in a project, as your boss asks? Your boss controls your performance evaluation.

Sales report. Should you inflate sales figures so that your team can meet its quarterly goal? Your team leader strongly urges you to do so, and you receive a healthy bonus if your team meets its goal.

Presentation. You are rushing to prepare a presentation. On the Web you find perfect wording and great graphics. Should you lift the graphics and wording but change a few words? You figure that if it is on the Web, it must be in the public domain.

Proposal. Your company urgently needs a revenue-producing project. Should you submit a proposal that unrealistically suggests a short completion schedule to ensure that you get the job?

Résumé. Should you inflate your grade-point average or give yourself more experience or a higher job title than your experience warrants to make your résumé more attractive? The job market is very competitive.

On the job you will face many dilemmas, and you will want to react ethically. But what is ethical behavior? Ethics author Mary E. Guy defined ethics as "that behavior which is the *right* thing to do, given the circumstances."[43] Determining the right thing to do, however, is not always an easy task. No solid rules guide us. For some people, following the law is enough. Anything legal must be ethical. Most people, however, believe that ethical standards rise to a higher level. What are those standards? Although many ethical dilemmas have no "right" answer, one solution is often better than another. In deciding on that solution, keep in mind the goals of ethical business communicators.

Goals of Ethical Business Communicators

Taking ethics into consideration can be painful in the short term. But in the long term, ethical behavior makes sense and pays off. Dealing honestly with colleagues and customers develops trust and builds stronger relationships. Many businesses today recognize that ethical practices make good business sense. Ethical companies endure less litigation, less resentment, and less government regulation. The following guidelines can help you set specific ethical goals. Although the following goals hardly constitute a formal code of conduct, they will help you maintain a high ethical standard.

Abiding by the Law. Know the laws in your field and follow them. Particularly important for business communicators are issues of copyright law. Under the concept of *fair use,* individuals have limited rights to use copyrighted material without requiring permission. To be safe, one should assume that anything produced privately after 1989—including words, charts, graphs, photos, music—is copyrighted. By the way, don't assume that Internet items are in the "public domain" and free to be used. Internet items are also covered by copyright laws. If you are in accounting, financial management, investing, or corporate management, you should be aware of the restrictions set forth by the Sarbanes-Oxley Act, officially known as the 'Public Company Accounting Reform and Investor Protection Act of 2002.' Whatever your field, become familiar with its regulations.

Telling the Truth. Ethical business communicators do not intentionally make statements that are untrue or deceptive. We become aware of dishonesty in business when violators break laws, notably in advertising, packaging, and marketing. The Federal Trade Commission, for example, charged Stouffer Foods with misrepresentation for its claim that Lean Cuisine entrees always contain less than 1 gram of sodium. In a fine-print footnote, careful consumers learn that 1 gram is equivalent to 1,000 milligrams, which is the commonly used unit of measurement for sodium.[44] The FTC also has cracked down on the makers of exercise equipment, such as Abflex, because three minutes a day on the "ab" machine doesn't come close to producing a "washboard stomach," as the manufacturer claimed.[45] You will learn more about what is legal in sales promotions in Chapter 9.

Labeling Opinions. Sensitive communicators know the difference between facts and opinions. Facts are verifiable and often are quantifiable; opinions are beliefs held with confidence but without substantiation. It is a fact, for example, that women are starting businesses at two times the rate of men.[46] It is an opinion, though, that the so-called "glass ceiling" has held women back in business organizations with the result that women are forced to start their own businesses. It is a fact that many companies are developing teams as tools to achieve management objectives. It is an opinion that teams are more effective in solving problems than individuals. Stating opinions as if they were facts is unethical.

Being Objective. Ethical business communicators recognize their own biases and strive to keep them from distorting a message. Suppose you are asked to investigate laptop computers and write a report recommending a brand for your office. As you visit stores, you discover that an old high school friend is selling Brand X. Because you always liked this individual and have faith in his judgment, you may be inclined to tilt your recommendation in his direction. However, it is unethical to misrepresent the facts in your report or to put a spin on your arguments based on friendship. To be ethical, you could note in your report that you have known the person for ten years and that you respect his opinion. In this way, you have disclosed your relationship as well as the reasons for your decision. Honest reporting means presenting the whole picture and relating all facts fairly.

Communicating Clearly. Ethical business communicators feel an obligation to write clearly so that receivers understand easily and quickly. Some states have even passed "Plain English" laws that require businesses to write policies, warranties, and contracts in language comprehensible to average readers. Plain English means short sentences, simple words, and clear organization. Communicators who intentionally obscure their meaning with long sentences and difficult words are being unethical.

Using Inclusive Language. Strive to use language that includes rather than excludes. Do not use expressions that discriminate against individuals or groups on the basis of their sex, ethnicity, disability, or age. Language is discriminatory when it stereotypes, insults, or excludes people. You will learn more about how to use inclusive, bias-free language in Chapter 4.

Giving Credit. Ethical communicators give credit for ideas by (a) referring to originators' names within the text; (b) using quotation marks; and (c) documenting sources with endnotes, footnotes, or internal references. You will learn how to do this in Chapter 12 and Appendix C. Don't suggest that you did all the work on a project if you had help. In school or on the job, stealing ideas, words, graphics, or any other original material is unethical.

Members of the International Association of Business Communicators have developed a code of ethics with 12 guidelines (articles) that spell out criteria for determining what is right and wrong for members of its organization. You can see the IABC Code of Ethics for Professional Communicators at **http://www.iabc.com/about/code.htm.**

Tools for Doing the Right Thing

In composing messages or engaging in other activities on the job, business communicators can't help being torn by conflicting loyalties. Do we tell the truth and risk our jobs? Do we show loyalty to friends even if it means bending the rules? Should we be tactful or totally honest? Is it our duty to make a profit or to be socially responsible? Acting ethically means doing the right thing given the circumstances. Each set of circumstances requires analyzing issues, evaluating choices, and acting responsibly.

> "Plain English" laws require simple, understandable language in policies, contracts, warranties, and other documents.

Scandal erupted when Hewlett-Packard board member George Keyworth was caught leaking confidential information to newspapers about HP's corporate strategy. The business scandal widened when it was revealed that methods used to uncover the leaks at the iconic American company included "pretexting"—illegal data mining of phone records—as well as the tracking of e-mails and instant messages. Investigations forced Keyworth's resignation and led to the high-profile indictment of Patricia Dunn, the company's influential former chairwoman. *What ethics tools can help business leaders do the right thing?*

© Mark Wilson / Getty Images

Resolving ethical issues is never easy, but the task can be made less difficult if you know how to identify key issues. The following questions may be helpful.

- **Is the action you are considering legal?** No matter who asks you to do it or how important you feel the result will be, avoid anything that is prohibited by law. Giving a kickback to a buyer for a large order is illegal, even if you suspect that others in your field do it and you know that without the kickback you will lose the sale.

- **How would you see the problem if you were on the opposite side?** Looking at all sides of an issue helps you gain perspective. Consider the issue of mandatory drug testing among employees. From management's viewpoint such testing could stop drug abuse, improve job performance, and lower health insurance premiums. From the employees' viewpoint mandatory testing reflects a lack of trust of employees and constitutes an invasion of privacy. By weighing both sides of the issue, you can arrive at a more equitable solution.

Business communicators can help resolve ethical issues through self-examination.

- **What are alternate solutions?** Consider all dimensions of other options. Would the alternative be more ethical? Under the circumstances, is the alternative feasible? Can an alternate solution be implemented with a minimum of disruption and with a good possibility of success? Let's say you wrote a report about testing a new product, but your boss changed the report to distort the findings. Should you go to the head of the company and reveal that the report is inaccurate? A more tactful alternative would be to approach your boss and ask whether you misunderstood the report's findings or whether an error might have been made.

- **Can you discuss the problem with someone whose advice you trust?** Suppose you feel ethically bound to report accurate information to a client even though your manager has ordered you not to do so. Talking about your dilemma with a coworker or with a colleague in your field might give you helpful insights and lead to possible alternatives.

Discussing an ethical problem with a coworker or colleague might lead to helpful alternatives.

- **How would you feel if your family, friends, employer, or coworkers learned of your action?** If the thought of revealing your action publicly produces cold sweats, your choice is probably unwise. Losing the faith of your friends or the confidence of your customers is not worth whatever short-term gains might be realized.

Perhaps the best advice in ethical matters is contained in the Golden Rule: Do unto others as you would have others do unto you. The ultimate solution to all ethics problems is treating others fairly and doing what is right to achieve what is good. In succeeding chapters you will find additional discussions of ethical questions as they relate to relevant topics.

Whistleblowing: Ethical and Legal Responsibilities

In a perfect world, you would work only for organizations that recognize that good ethics is good business. Wrongdoing, however, does occur in business, as newspaper headlines continually remind us. What if you find yourself in a situation in which you feel that someone in your organization is acting illegally or immorally? When you agree to be hired by an organization, you are agreeing to be loyal to that organization—as long as the organization is not involved in serious wrongdoing. If you do detect serious lapses, do you blow the whistle or protect your job by minding your own business?

Whistleblowing in the workplace is defined as "the reporting, by employees or ex-employees, of wrongdoing such as fraud, malpractice, mismanagement, breach of health and safety law, or any other illegal or unethical act, either on the part of management or by fellow employees."[47] The Sarbanes-Oxley Act institutes significant protections for whistleblowers. However, many workers are still reluctant to report unethical activities.[48] Sometimes it is a difficult judgment call. As an internal auditor, you might look at the numbers and decide that your company is charging the government appropriately. You could, however, look at the numbers differently and decide that your company is seriously overcharging the government. Figures can be interpreted differently.

If you do decide that something is amiss, how can you go about blowing the whistle legally and ethically? First, be certain that you have your facts straight. Don't rely on gossip or

Communicating at Work Your Turn

Applying Your Skills at Sears Holdings

In combining Sears Roebuck and Kmart, CEO Aylwin Lewis recognized that he needed to develop potential leaders in the company to assist in carrying out his mission to transform the troubled retailers.

In rising to the top, Lewis developed his own leadership qualities, including speaking and listening skills. Once a month he listens on the store complaint line and actually answers customer complaints for an hour. Listening to employees is also important. "I gave a speech once about nine years ago," he explained, "and a comment came back from someone at the company that I gave four closings and that it was really long. Since then, if I have 30 minutes to speak, I give them a 22-minute speech. I used to write my speeches out completely and memorize them. Now I put an outline together and address key points, more of a conversation." [49]

Lewis is called a great communicator, and his oratory skills attest to that. But he is also recognized as a skilled people person with a knack for making others comfortable while motivating them to improve. [50] Coworkers in the restaurant business began to call him "Coach." Relying on his oratory, coaching, and leadership skills, Lewis faces a momentous task in conveying his vision to restore luster to Sears Roebuck and Kmart, two struggling retail chains.

© Justin Sullivan / Getty Images

Your Task

As an intern at Sears Holdings, you are part of a leadership training group. In your training, your manager asks you and fellow interns to prepare a list of communication skills that you think are important to leadership success. What skills are important for initial hiring? How can these skills be identified among applicants? What skills are important for promotion? Are they the same? Why? Your intern manager also wants to know whether you think communication and leadership skills can be taught on the job. In teams of three to five, discuss these questions. Summarize your conclusions and (a) appoint one team representative to report to the class or (b) write individual memos or e-mails describing your conclusions. (See Chapter 7 and Appendix B for tips on writing memos.)

---

speculation. Second, try to correct the matter inside the company. Instead of going outside, speak to your supervisor, if at all possible. You may be able to talk with someone else whom you trust and decide on a course of action.

All whistleblowers must weigh the personal risks involved. If you decide that you can't change a situation or if you disagree with a company policy, consider changing jobs.

Summary of Learning Objectives

1 **Understand the importance of communication skills in relation to career success; and explain the need for thinking critically, taking charge of your career, and strengthening your communication skills.** Communication skills are critical to job placement, performance, career advancement, and organizational success. These skills include reading, listening, speaking, and writing. They are not inherent; they must be learned. Writing skills are particularly important because messages today travel more rapidly, more often, and to greater numbers of people than ever before. In today's dynamic workplace you can expect to be a knowledge worker; that is, you will deal with words, figures, and data. You must learn to think critically and develop opinions backed by reasons and evidence. Because technologies and procedures are constantly evolving, you must be flexible and willing to engage in lifelong learning. You should expect to take charge of your career as you work for multiple employers. The most important foundation skill for knowledge workers is the ability to communicate. You can improve your skills by studying the principles, processes, and products of communication provided in this book and in this course.

2 **Recognize significant changes in today's workplace and how these changes increase the need for excellent communication skills.** The workplace is undergoing profound changes, such as the emergence of heightened global competition, flattened management hierarchies, expanded team-based management, innovative communication technologies, new work environments, and an increasingly diverse workforce. Nearly all of these changes require that businesspeople have strong communication skills to be able to make decisions, exchange information, and stay connected with remote colleagues.

3 **Analyze the process of communication and how to engage it effectively.** The sender encodes (selects) words or symbols to express an idea. The message is sent verbally over a channel (such as a letter, e-mail message, or telephone call) or is expressed nonverbally, perhaps with gestures or body language. "Noise"—such as loud sounds, misspelled words, or other distractions—may interfere with the transmission. The receiver decodes (interprets) the message and attempts to make sense of it. The receiver responds with feedback, informing the sender of the effectiveness of the message. The objective of communication is the transmission of meaning so that a receiver understands a message as intended by the sender.

4 **Recognize barriers to interpersonal communication and examine specific strategies for overcoming those barriers.** *Bypassing* causes miscommunication because people have different meanings for the words they use. One's *frame of reference* creates a filter through which all ideas are screened, sometimes causing distortion and lack of objectivity. *Weak language skills* as well as *poor listening skills* impair communication efforts. *Emotional interference*—joy, fear, anger, and so forth—hampers the sending and receiving of messages. *Physical distractions*—noisy surroundings, faulty acoustics, and so forth—can disrupt oral communication. Multitasking, information overload, and being constantly available digitally also make it difficult to focus. You can reduce or overcome many interpersonal communication barriers if you (a) realize that the communication process is imperfect, (b) adapt your message to the receiver, (c) improve your language and listening skills, (d) question your preconceptions, (e) plan for feedback, (f) focus on what is important, and (g) shut out interruptions.

5 **Analyze the internal and external functions of communication in organizations as well as compare the advantages and disadvantages of oral and written communication.** Internal functions of communication include issuing and clarifying procedures and policies, informing management of progress, persuading others to make changes or improvements, and interacting with employees. External functions of communication include answering inquiries about products or services, persuading customers to buy products or services, clarifying supplier specifications, and so forth. Oral, face-to-face communication is most effective, but written communication is often more expedient.

6 **Examine critically the flow of communication in organizations including barriers and methods for overcoming those barriers.** Formal channels of communication follow an organization's hierarchy of command. Information flows downward from management to workers. Long lines of communication tend to distort information. Many organizations are improving the downward flow of communication through newsletters, announcements, meetings, videos, and company intranets. Information flows upward from employees to management, thus providing vital feedback for decision makers. Obstacles include mistrust, fear of reprisal for honest communication, lack of adequate communication skills, and differing frames of reference. To improve upward flow, companies are improving relations with staff, offering incentive programs that encourage employees to share valuable feedback, and investing in communication training programs. Horizontal communication is among workers at the same level. Obstacles include poor communication skills, prejudice, ego involvement, competition, and turf wars. Techniques for overcoming the obstacles include (a) training employees in communication and teamwork techniques, (b) establishing reward systems, and (c) encouraging full participation in team functions. Informal channels of communication, such as the grapevine, deliver unofficial news—both personal and organizational—among friends and coworkers.

7 **Understand the ethical goals of a business communicator and tools for doing the right thing.** The goals of ethical business communicators include abiding by the law, telling the truth, labeling opinions, being objective, communicating clearly, using inclusive language, and giving credit. When faced with a difficult decision, the following questions serve as valuable tools in guiding you to do the right thing: (a) Is the action you are considering legal? (b) How would you see the problem if you were on the opposite side? (c) What are alternate solutions? (d) Can you discuss the problem with someone whose advice you trust? (e) How would you feel if your family, friends, employer, or coworkers learned of your action? If faced with serious wrongdoing on the job, ethical business communicators may be forced to become whistleblowers.

Chapter Review

1. Why are writing skills more important than ever in today's workplace? (Obj. 1)

2. Are communication skills inborn or must they be learned? (Obj. 1)

3. Who are knowledge workers? Why are they hired? (Obj. 1)

4. Name five factors that are creating significant changes in today's workplace. (Obj. 2)

5. What electronic tools enable workers to complete tasks in remote locations? Why are communication skills increasingly important? (Obj. 2)

6. Define *communication* and explain its most critical factor. (Obj. 3)

7. Describe the five steps in the process of communication. (Obj. 3)

8. Describe four interpersonal communication barriers that can create misunderstanding. (Obj. 4)

9. What are the three main functions of organizational communication? (Obj. 5)

10. Compare the advantages and disadvantages of oral, face-to-face communication. (Obj. 5)

11. Compare formal and informal channels of communication within organizations. Which is more valuable to employees? (Obj. 6)

12. Who is generally involved and what information is typically carried in downward, upward, and horizontal communication channels? (Obj. 6)

13. What are seven goals of ethical business communicators? (Obj. 7)

14. When you are faced with a difficult ethical decision, what questions should you ask yourself? (Obj. 7)

15. What is whistleblowing? How can one engage in it legally and ethically? (Obj. 7)

Critical Thinking

1. Why should you, as a business student and communicator, strive to improve your communication skills; and why is it difficult or impossible to do so on your own? (Obj. 1)

2. Recall a time when you experienced a problem as a result of poor communication. What were the causes of and possible remedies for the problem? (Objs. 3, 4)

3. Critics complain that e-mail is reducing the amount of face-to-face communication at work and this is bad for business. Do you agree or disagree? (Objs. 3–5)

4. How are the rules of ethical behavior that govern businesses different from those that govern your personal behavior? (Obj. 7)

5. **Ethical Issue:** Suppose your superior asked you to alter year-end financial data, and you knew that if you didn't you might lose your job. What would you do if it were a small amount? A large amount? (Obj. 7)

Activities

1.1 Online Communication Skills Assessment: How Do You Rate? (Objs. 1–3)

Web

This course can help you dramatically improve your business communication skills. How much do you need to improve? This assessment exercise enables you to evaluate your skills with specific standards in four critical communication skill areas: writing, reading, speaking, and listening. How well you communicate will be an important factor in your future career—particularly if you are promoted into management, as many college graduates are.

Your Task. Either here or online at **www.meguffey.com**, select a number from 1 (indicating low ability) to 5 (indicating high ability) that best reflects your perception of yourself. Be honest in rating yourself. Think about how others would rate you. When you finish, see a rating of your skills. Complete this assessment online to see your results automatically!

Writing Skills

	Low				High
1. Possess basic spelling, grammar, and punctuation skills	1	2	3	4	5
2. Am familiar with proper e-mail, memo, letter, and report formats for business documents	1	2	3	4	5
3. Can analyze a writing problem and quickly outline a plan for solving the problem	1	2	3	4	5
4. Am able to organize data coherently and logically	1	2	3	4	5
5. Can evaluate a document to determine its probable success	1	2	3	4	5

Reading Skills

	Low				High
1. Am familiar with specialized vocabulary in my field as well as general vocabulary	1	2	3	4	5
2. Can concentrate despite distractions	1	2	3	4	5
3. Am willing to look up definitions whenever necessary	1	2	3	4	5
4. Am able to move from recreational to serious reading	1	2	3	4	5
5. Can read and comprehend college-level material	1	2	3	4	5

Speaking Skills

1. Feel at ease in speaking with friends	1	2	3	4	5
2. Feel at ease in speaking before a group of people	1	2	3	4	5
3. Can adapt my presentation to the audience	1	2	3	4	5
4. Am confident in pronouncing and using words correctly	1	2	3	4	5
5. Sense that I have credibility when I make a presentation	1	2	3	4	5

Listening Skills

1. Spend at least half the time listening during conversations	1	2	3	4	5
2. Am able to concentrate on a speaker's words despite distractions	1	2	3	4	5
3. Can summarize a speaker's ideas and anticipate what's coming during pauses	1	2	3	4	5
4. Provide proper feedback such as nodding, paraphrasing, and asking questions	1	2	3	4	5

5. Listen with the expectation of gaining new ideas
   and information   1 2 3 4 5

Total your score in each section. How do you rate?

    22–24 Excellent! You have indicated that you have exceptional communication skills.

    18–21 Your score is above average, but you could improve your skills.

    14–17 Your score suggests that you have much room for improvement.

    10–13 You recognize that you need serious study, practice, and follow-up reinforcement.

Where are you strongest and weakest? Are you satisfied with your present skills? The first step to improvement is recognition of a need. The second step is making a commitment to improve. The third step is following through, and this course will help you do that.

1.2 Collaborating on the Opening Case Study (Objs. 1–5)

Team **Web**

Each chapter contains a three-part case study of a well-known company. To help you develop collaboration and speaking skills as well as to learn about the target company and apply the chapter concepts, your instructor may ask you to do the following.

Your Task. Individually or as part of a three-student team during your course, work on one of the 16 case studies in the textbook. Answer the questions posed in all parts of the case study, look for additional information in articles or Web sites, complete the application assignment, and then make a five- to ten-minute presentation to the class with your findings and reactions.

1.3 Getting to Know You (Objs. 1, 2)

E-Mail

Your instructor wants to know more about you, your motivation for taking this course, your career goals, and your writing skills.

Your Task. Send an e-mail or write a memo of introduction to your instructor. See Appendix B for memo formats and Chapter 7 for tips on preparing an e-mail message. In your message include the following:

a. Your reasons for taking this class
b. Your career goals (both temporary and long-term)
c. A brief description of your employment, if any, and your favorite activities
d. An assessment and discussion of your current communication skills, including your strengths and weaknesses

1.4 Small-Group Presentation: Getting to Know Each Other (Objs. 1, 2)

Team

Many business organizations today use teams to accomplish their goals. To help you develop speaking, listening, and teamwork skills, your instructor may assign team projects. One of the first jobs in any team is selecting members and becoming acquainted.

Your Task. Your instructor will divide your class into small groups or teams. At your instructor's direction, either (a) interview another group member and introduce that person to the group or (b) introduce yourself to the group. Think of this as an informal interview for a team assignment or for a job. You will want to make notes from which to speak. Your introduction should include information such as the following:

a. Where did you grow up?
b. What work and extracurricular activities have you engaged in?
c. What are your interests and talents? What are you good at doing?

d. What have you achieved?
e. How familiar are you with various computer technologies?
f. What are your professional and personal goals? Where do you expect to be five years from now?

To develop listening skills, team members should practice good listening techniques (see Chapter 2) and take notes. They should be prepared to discuss three important facts as well as remember details about each speaker.

1.5 Communication Skills: Analyzing the Want Ads (Obj. 1)

Team **Web**

What do employers request when they list job openings in your field?

Your Task. Individually or in teams, check the listings at an online job board. Visit a job board such as Monster, College Recruiter, Career Builder, or Yahoo! Top Jobs. Use your favorite search engine to locate their sites. Follow the instructions to search job categories and locations. Study the jobs listed. Find five or more job listings in your field. If possible, print the results of your search. If you cannot print, make notes on what you find. Study the skills requested. How often do the ads mention communication, teamwork, and computer skills? What tasks do the ads mention? Discuss your findings with your team members. Prepare a list of the most frequently requested skills. Your instructor may ask you to submit your findings and/or report to the class. If you are not satisfied with the job selection at this site, choose another job board.

1.6 Workplace Writing: Separating Myths From Facts (Obj. 1)

Today's knowledge workers are doing more writing on the job than ever before. Flattened management hierarchies, heightened global competition, expanded team-based management, and heavy reliance on e-mail have all contributed to more written messages.

Your Task. In teams or in class, discuss the following statements. Are they myths or facts?

a. Because I'm in a technical field, I will work with numbers, not words.
b. Secretaries will clean up my writing problems.
c. Technical writers do most of the real writing on the job.
d. Computers can fix any of my writing mistakes.
e. I can use form letters for most messages.

1.7 Communication Skills: CompUSA Suddenly Needs Writers (Objs. 1–3)

Team

"One misspelled word and customers begin to doubt the validity of the information they are getting," warns Mary Jo Lichtenberg. She's director of training, quality, and career development at CompUSA, in Plano, Texas. One of her big problems is training service agents with weak communication skills. "Just because agents understand technically how to troubleshoot computers or pieces of software and can walk customers through solutions extremely well over the telephone doesn't mean they can do the same in writing," she complains. "The skill set for phone does not necessarily translate to the skill set needed for writing e-mail." With more than 200 superstores, CompUSA is a leading retailer and reseller of computer hardware and software. As more and more of its customers choose e-mail and Web chat sessions to obtain service and support, CompUSA service reps are doing more writing.[51]

Your Task. In teams, discuss what communication skills are necessary for service agents troubleshooting computers and software at CompUSA. How are the skill sets different for answering phones and for writing e-mail responses? What suggestions could you make to Lichtenberg as director of training?

1.8 Communication Process: Avoiding Misunderstanding (Obj. 3)

Communication is not successful unless the receiver understands the message as the sender meant it.

Your Task. Analyze the following examples of communication failures. What went wrong?

a. The editor of Salt Lake City's *Deseret News* told his staff to "change the picture" of film icon James Dean, who had a cigarette dangling from his lips. The staff thought that the editor wanted the cigarette digitally removed from the picture, which they did. When published, the altered picture drew considerable criticism. The editor later explained that he had expected the staff to find a new picture.

b. Team leader Tyson said to team member Alicia, "I could really use your help in answering these customer inquiries." Later Alicia was resentful when she found that he expected her to answer all the inquiries herself.

c. A supervisor issued the following announcement: "Effective immediately the charge for copying services in Repro will be raised 5 to 8 cents each." Receivers scratched their heads.

d. A China Airways flight, operating in zero visibility, crashed into the side of a mountain shortly after takeoff. The pilot's last words were "What does *pull up* mean?"

e. Skiers in an Austrian hotel saw the following sign in English: "Not to perambulate the corridors in the hours of repose in the boots of ascension."

f. The following statements actually appeared in letters of application for an advertised job opening. One applicant wrote, "Enclosed is my résumé in response to Sunday's New York Times." Another wrote, "Enclosed is my résumé in response to my search for an editorial/creative position." Still another wrote, "My experience in the production of newsletters, magazines, directories, and online data bases puts me head and shoulders above the crowd of applicants you have no doubtedly been inundated with."

1.9 Miscommunication in Organizations: Understanding the Boss (Objs. 3–6)

` Team `

Sales representative Tim Perez was underperforming. However, the vice president was unaware of this. At a busy sales reception where all of the sales reps were milling about, the CEO pulled the vice president aside and said, "Why is Perez still a sales rep?" The vice president assumed the CEO wanted Perez promoted. Unwilling to question the CEO, the vice president soon thereafter sent down orders to promote Perez. Later, when the CEO learned what had happened, he "came out of his chair like a Saturn rocket." He meant to say, "Why is that guy still on the payroll?"[52]

Your Task. In teams, discuss the factors contributing to this miscommunication. What went wrong in the process of communication? What role did feedback play?

1.10 Differing Frames of Reference: E-Mail Cross-Cultural Misunderstanding (Obj. 4)

` Intercultural `

A cultural misunderstanding nearly derailed an Indo-Japanese bridge-building project. An Indian firm sent a detailed list of technical questions to its Japanese counterpart. The Indian engineers panicked when they received no reply. They wondered what had happened. Was the deal off? A week later, the Japanese engineers responded. Unlike in India or in the United States, the Japanese encourage input from everyone involved in a project. The queries probably went to the heads of different departments so that a complete picture could be presented in the response. In the United States and in India, businesspeople expect an immediate response of some sort from e-mails.[53]

Your Task. Discuss how differing frames of reference affected this misunderstanding. How could such misunderstandings be averted?

1.11 Document for Analysis: Barriers to Communication (Objs. 3–5)

The following memo is from an exasperated manager to her staff. Obviously, this manager has no secretary to clean up her writing.

Your Task. Comment on the memo's effectiveness, tone, and potential barriers to communication. Your instructor may ask you to revise the memo, improving its tone, grammar, and organization.

```
DATE:     Current
TO:       All Employees
FROM:     Albertina Sindaha, Operations Manager
SUBJECT:  Cleanup!
```

You were all suppose to clean up your work areas last Friday, but that didn't happen. A few people cleaned their desks, but no one pitched in to clean the common areas, and you all saw what a mess they were in!

So we're going to try again. As you know, we don't have a big enough custodial budget anymore. Everyone must clean up himself. This Friday I want to see action in the copy machine area, things like emptying waste baskets and you should organize paper and toner supplies. The lunch room is a disaster area. You must do something about the counters, the refrigerator, the sinks, and the coffee machine. And any food left in the refrigerator on Friday afternoon should be thrown out because it stinks by Monday. Finally, the office supply shelves should be straightened.

If you can't do a better job this Friday, I will have to assign individuals to a specific cleaning schedule. Which I don't want to do. But you may force me to.

1.12 Information Flow: What's the Latest Buzz? (Obj. 6)

All organizations provide information to the public and to members through official channels. But information also flows through unofficial channels.

Your Task. Consider an organization to which you belong or a business where you've worked. How did members learn what was going on in the organization? What kind of information flowed through formal channels? What were those channels? What kind of information was delivered through informal channels? Was the grapevine as accurate as official channels? What barriers obstructed the flow of information? How could the flow be improved?

1.13 Workplace Ethics: Where Do You Stand? (Obj. 7)

` Ethics `

How do your ethics compare with those of workers across the country?

Your Task. Answer *yes* or *no* to each item in the following *Wall Street Journal* workplace ethics quiz.[54] Be prepared to discuss your responses in class. At the end of this chapter you can see how others responded to this quiz.

1. Is it wrong to use company e-mail for personal reasons?
2. Is it wrong to use office equipment to help your children or spouse do schoolwork?
3. Is it wrong to play computer games on office equipment during the workday?
4. Is it wrong to use office equipment to do Internet shopping?

5. Is it unethical to blame an error you made on a technological glitch?
6. Is it unethical to visit pornographic Web sites using office equipment?
7. Is a $50 gift to a boss unacceptable?
8. Is a $50 gift FROM the boss unacceptable?
9. Is it OK to take a $200 pair of football tickets from a supplier?
10. Is it OK to accept a $75 prize won at a raffle at a supplier's conference?

1.14 Does White-Collar Crime Pay? (Obj. 7)

`Ethics`   `Web`

You've been asked to participate in a panel discussing white-collar crime. Some people argue that executives seldom serve prison time for white-collar crime. You think that high-profile people have actually been sentenced to prison.

Your Task. Using the Web or a campus database, look for ammunition for your position. Try to find at least five examples of individuals who have been sentenced for corporate wrongdoing. What did they do, and what penalty did they receive? Be sure to document your sources, including author, title, publication, date, and page. If you wish to expand your topic, examine companies that have paid fines, suffered bad press, or been forced into bankruptcy for corporate malfeasance. Remember to choose good search terms to return good results. Try *white-collar crime* and *corporate scandals*, along with other search terms. Discuss your findings in class or in a memo to your instructor. Can you draw any conclusions from your findings?

1.15 Ethical Dilemmas: Applying Tools for Doing the Right Thing (Obj. 7)

`Ethics`

As a business communicator, you may face various ethical dilemmas in your career. Many factors can determine your choice of an action to take.

Your Task. Study the seven dilemmas appearing on page 22 [e-mail message, customer letter, progress report, etc.]. Select four of them and apply the Tools for Doing the Right Thing on page 25 in choosing an appropriate action. In a memo to your instructor or in a team discussion, explain the action you would take for each dilemma. Analyze your response to each question (Is the action you are considering legal? How would you see the problem if you were on the opposite side? And so forth).

1.16 Developing Critical Thinking and Consumer Skills: A Victim of Identity Theft Wants Your Help (Obj. 1)

`Consumer`

Your friend Lisa Williams, whose banking experience consisted mainly of ATM use, knew something was wrong when a Citibank debt consolidation representative called her. Lisa was astounded to learn that she had an overdue credit card balance of $4,600. Impossible! she thought. She didn't even own a Citibank credit card! Unfortunately, Lisa is one of more than 27 million Americans who have been victimized by fraud or identity theft in the past five years.[55]

Your Task. Lisa asks you to help her through this mess. Using the critical-thinking steps outlined in this chapter and listed here, decide on a problem-solving strategy. At the same time, learn more about identity theft for your own protection. To find information, search the Web or use a campus database. Answer the following questions in a class discussion or in a memo to your instructor. (See Chapter 7 and Appendix B for information about writing memos.)

1. **Identify and clarify the problem.** How do banks issue credit cards? What information is needed? How is it verified? How do identity thieves get your personal information?

© Andersen Ross / Digital Vision / Getty Images

2. **Gather information.** Should Lisa ask Citibank for its application record for this fraudulent card? How can you learn more about identity theft in general?
3. **Evaluate the evidence.** Should Lisa investigate this herself or involve the police? Should she go to credit bureaus (Experian, Equifax, and TransUnion) and ask for their help in clearing her credit record?
4. **Consider alternatives and implications.** What actions can a victim of identity theft take?
5. **Choose and implement the best alternative.** What should Lisa do first, and what follow-up actions should she take? How can people reduce the chances of identity theft?

Video Resources

Video Library 1. *Building Workplace Skills* presents five videos that introduce and reinforce concepts in selected chapters. These excellent tools ease the learning load by demonstrating chapter-specific material to strengthen your comprehension and retention of key ideas.

The recommended video for this chapter is *Communication Foundations,* which illustrates how strong communication skills can help you advance your career in today's challenging world of work. Be prepared to discuss critical-thinking questions your instructor may provide.

Responses to the *Wall Street Journal* Workplace Ethics Quiz in Activity 1.13

1. Thirty-four percent said using company e-mail for personal reasons is wrong.
2. Thirty-seven percent said using office equipment to help your children or spouse do schoolwork is wrong.
3. Forty-nine percent said playing computer games at work is wrong.
4. Fifty-four percent said using office equipment to do Internet shopping is wrong.
5. Sixty-one percent said blaming your own error on faulty technology is unethical.
6. Eighty-seven percent said visiting pornographic Web sites using office equipment is unethical.
7. Thirty-five percent said making a $50 gift to a boss is unacceptable.
8. Thirty-five percent said accepting a $50 gift from the boss is unacceptable.
9. Seventy percent said accepting a $200 pair of football tickets from a supplier is unacceptable.
10. Forty percent said accepting a $75 prize won at a raffle at a supplier's conference is unacceptable.

Grammar and Mechanics Skills With C.L.U.E.

Each chapter includes an exercise based on Appendix A: Grammar and Mechanics: Competent Language Usage Essentials (C.L.U.E.). This appendix is a business communicator's condensed guide to language usage, covering 50 of the most used and abused language elements. It also includes a list of frequently misspelled words as well as a list of confusing words. The first ten exercises presented with each chapter will systematically focus on specific grammar/mechanics guidelines. The last six chapter exercises will cover all the guidelines plus spelling and confusing words.

Sentence Structure

Study sentence structure in Guides 1–3 of Appendix A beginning on page A-2. Each of the following sentences has one sentence fault. On a sheet of paper, write a correct version and identify which guide is violated. Avoid adding new phrases or rewriting sentences in your own words. You may need to change or delete one or more words. However, your goal is to correct the sentence with as few marks as possible. When finished, compare your responses with the key beginning on page Key-1.

1. To succeed as a knowledge worker in today's digital workplace. You need highly developed communication skills.

2. Companies are looking for individuals with strong writing and grammar skills. Because employees spend at least 50 percent of their time processing documents.

3. Businesses are cutting costs they are eliminating many layers of management.

4. Knowledge workers may be distracted by multitasking, however, clear communication requires shutting out interruptions.

5. Face-to-face conversations have many advantages. Even though they produce no written record and sometimes waste time.

6. The grapevine can be a major source of information, it is also fairly reliable.

7. Knowledge workers must be critical thinkers they must be able to make decisions and communicate those decisions.

8. Management uses many methods to distribute information downward; Such as newsletters, announcements, meetings, videos, and company intranets.

9. Ethical companies experience less litigation, they also receive less resentment and less government regulation.

10. Horizontal communication starts with coworkers downward communication starts with decision makers.

#1. fragment

#2. fragment turn sentence around

#3 : however,

#4

#5

#6

#7

#8

#9

#10

#8 downward; such as

Chapter 2

Developing Team, Listening, and Etiquette Skills

OBJECTIVES

After studying this chapter, you should be able to

1 Recognize the importance of soft skills and teamwork in today's workplace.

2 Understand how to contribute positively to team performance, including resolving workplace conflicts, avoiding groupthink, and reaching group decisions.

3 Plan and participate in productive meetings.

4 Explain the usefulness of collaborative technologies such as voice conferencing, videoconferencing, Web conferencing, instant messaging, blogs, and wikis.

5 Describe and implement active listening techniques.

6 Understand the forms of nonverbal communication and how they can be used to advance your career.

7 Develop a competitive edge with professionalism and business etiquette skills.

Communicating at Work Part 1

Teamwork Drives Toyota to Success

How does an international corporation that sells cars to customers in more than 170 countries manage employees in its 580 different companies around the world? For Toyota Motor Corporation, the answer is a strong corporate culture that provides a consistent basis for its operations worldwide. Called "The Toyota Way," these guiding principles are a major factor in driving Toyota to No. 3 in revenue, No. 2 in vehicles produced, and No. 1 in profitability among major automobile manufacturers.

Toyota is also one of the world's most admired companies—not only for the quality of its vehicles but also for its commitment to its people and the environment. From its Lexus luxury line to the new youth-oriented Scion brand and its eco-friendly hybrid vehicles, Toyota sets the bar high.

Associates (employees) are at the core of The Toyota Way, which focuses on respect for people, and *kaizen*, or continuous improvement. Its 14 principles emphasize self-motivation, employee involvement, teamwork, and consensus decision making. Because associates may not be familiar with the skills required for effective teamwork, Toyota devotes considerable resources to education and training in this area. Toyota encourages its employees, from top managers to assembly plant workers, to collaborate and take proactive steps to improve productivity and solve problems.[1] Instead of bureaucracy and supervisory control over workers, team members take responsibility for and pride in their efforts. "'Can I prevent it, can I predict it, can I see it?' That's the mentality we're always reinforcing to the staff," said Ray Tanguay, president of Toyota Motor Manufacturing Canada.[2]

Even a company dedicated to collaboration can run unto problems implementing effective work teams, however. At Toyota's North American Parts Center California, 400 workers process and ship about 250,000 parts a day to U.S. regional centers. This center was conceived as a team-based facility. Unfortunately, it opened before team training was complete. Under pressure to ship parts on time, managers reverted to a more traditional bureaucratic structure, with 13 supervisors calling the shots for large work units. "Our focus shifted to doing

everything necessary to process and ship our customers' orders," said Joe Kane, NAPCC's national customer support financial administration manager.[3] The Center's associates, who had been promised a team-oriented work environment, were unhappy—and criticized management for not following through.[4] You will learn more about this case on page 43.

Critical Thinking

- How does Toyota's consistent corporate culture and emphasis on teamwork throughout its global operations contribute to its success?

- What types of barriers to listening and collaboration might arise on an international design team that must conduct its meetings using e-mail, teleconferencing, and other technologies?

- Why do you think it was easier for North American Parts Center California to deliver parts on time using a traditional bureaucratic structure than the promised team environment?

http://www.toyota.com

Recognizing the Importance of Soft Skills in Today's Workplace

LEARNING OBJECTIVE 1

Recognize the importance of soft skills and teamwork in today's workplace.

Toyota is among the many companies expecting employees to possess team and other soft skills. When you look for a job, employers will typically want to know about four key areas: education, experience, hard skills, and soft skills. Hard skills refer to the technical skills in your field. Soft skills, however, are increasingly important in our knowledge-based economy. These include both oral and written communication skills, which you learned about in Chapter 1. Soft skills also include other competencies such as listening proficiency, nonverbal behavior, and etiquette expertise. Employers want team players who can work together efficiently and productively. They want managers and employees who are comfortable with diverse coworkers, who can listen actively to customers and colleagues, who can make eye contact, who display good workplace manners, and who possess a host of other interpersonal skills. These skills are immensely important not only to be hired but also to be promoted.

Soft skills—including team, listening, nonverbal, and etiquette skills—are key in hiring and promotion processes.

Hiring managers expect you to have technical expertise in your field. A good résumé and interview may get you in the door. However, your long-term success is greatly influenced by your ability to communicate with your boss, coworkers, and customers as well as your ability to work as an effective and contributing team member. Even in technical fields such as accounting and finance, employers are looking for soft skills. Based on a survey of international accounting executives, *CA Magazine* concluded that "the future is bright for the next generation of accounting and finance professionals provided they are armed with such soft skills as the ability to communicate, deal with change, and work in a team setting."[5] A survey of chief financial officers revealed that a majority believed that communication skills carry a greater importance today than in the past.[6] Increasingly, finance professionals must be able to interact with the entire organization and explain terms without using financial jargon.

Employers want team players who can work together productively. If you look at current online or newspaper want ads, chances are you will find requirements such as the following:

- Proven team skills to help deliver on-time, on-budget results

- Strong verbal and written communication skills as well as excellent presentation skills

- Excellent interpersonal, organizational, and teamwork skills

- Required competencies: interpersonal and team skills plus well-developed communication skills

- Good people skills and superior teamwork abilities

This chapter focuses on developing team, listening, nonverbal, and etiquette skills. These are some of the soft skills that employers seek in today's increasingly interconnected and competitive environments. You will learn many tips and techniques for becoming a good team member as well as how to expand and perfect your listening, nonverbal, and etiquette skills.

> **Employment advertisements frequently mention team, communication, and people skills.**

Preparing to Work With Groups and Teams

As we discussed in Chapter 1, the workplace and economy are changing. In response to intense global competition, businesses are being forced to rethink and restructure their operations. They must find new and faster ways to develop advanced products and bring them to market efficiently and profitably.[7] Many are turning to teams to innovate, share knowledge, and solve problems. The reasoning behind this thrust is that many heads are better than one.

As a result, today's workplace is teeming with teams. You might find yourself a part of a work team, project team, customer support team, supplier team, design team, planning team, functional team, or cross-functional team. You might be assigned to a committee, task force, steering group, quality control circle, flat team, hierarchical team, advisory team, action team, or some other group. All of these teams are being formed to accomplish specific goals.

Why Form Groups and Teams?

Businesses are constantly looking for ways to do jobs better at less cost. They are forming teams for the following reasons:

- **Better decisions.** Decisions are generally more accurate and effective because group and team members contribute different expertise and perspectives.

- **Faster response.** When action is necessary to respond to competition or to solve a problem, small groups and teams can act rapidly.

- **Increased productivity.** Because they are often closer to the action and to the customer, team members can see opportunities for improving efficiencies.

- **Greater "buy-in."** Decisions arrived at jointly are usually better received because members are committed to the solution and are more willing to support it.

- **Less resistance to change.** People who have input into decisions are less hostile, aggressive, and resistant to change.

- **Improved employee morale.** Personal satisfaction and job morale increase when teams are successful.

- **Reduced risks.** Responsibility for a decision is diffused, thus carrying less risk for any individual.

> **Organizations are forming teams for better decisions, faster response, increased productivity, greater "buy-in," less resistance to change, improved morale, and reduced risks.**

Despite the current popularity of teams, however, they are not a panacea for all workplace problems. Some critics complain that they are the latest in a succession of management

> **Some companies rejected teams because they slowed decisions, shielded workers from responsibility, and reduced productivity.**

Spotlight on Communicators

As head of the team producing Boeing's new 787 aircraft model, Mike Bair put together a team of suppliers and engineers from the United States, Europe, Japan, and Korea. "The mix of people and knowledge is turning out to be a powerful tool," he said, in creating a better aircraft design and more efficient manufacturing process. "In school, teaming is a called cheating, but we're encouraging our people to find other people's ideas and then improve on them." Working together means team meetings at all hours of the day and night to accommodate colleagues in different time zones.

fads. Others charge that teams are a screen behind which management intensifies its control over labor.[8] Companies such as Ford, Levi-Strauss, Honda, and GM's Saturn plant retreated from teams, finding that they slowed decision making, shielded workers from responsibility, and created morale and productivity problems.[9] Yet, in most models of future organizations, teams, not individuals, function as the primary performance unit.

Examples of Effective Teams

Teams can be effective in solving problems and in developing new products. Take, for example, the creation of Red Baron's "Stuffed Pizza Slices." Featuring a one-of-a-kind triangular, vented design, the product delivers taste, convenience, and style. But coming up with an innovative new hit required a cross-functional team with representatives from product development, packaging, purchasing, and operations. The entire team worked to shape an idea into a hit product using existing machinery.[10]

German auto manufacturer BMW likes to "throw together" designers, engineers, and marketing experts to work intensively on a team project. Ten team members, for example, working in an old bank building in London, collaborated on the redesign of the Rolls-Royce Phantom. The result was a best-selling superluxury automobile that remained true to the Rolls heritage. But the new model had twenty-first century lines with BMW's technological muscle under the hood.[11]

The *Democrat,* the only newspaper in Tallahassee, Florida, found that its advertisements were riddled with errors. In one instance, a sloppy ad arrived by fax. It was unreadable, looking as if a rat had crossed the page. Yet, it found its way into print even after passing through the hands of seven employees. No one felt responsible for making it right. They just passed it along. The editor decided to appoint a special team of workers charged with eliminating all errors in advertisements. It took the name ELITE, standing for "ELIminate The Errors." A year later, under ELITE's leadership, advertising accuracy was greatly improved. It reached 99 percent and stayed there.[12]

Virtual Teams

Virtual teams are groups of people who work interdependently with a shared purpose across space, time, and organization boundaries using technology.

Many organizations are creating *virtual teams.* These are groups of people who work interdependently with a shared purpose across space, time, and organization boundaries using technology.[13] The author of this textbook, for example, works in her office in Santa Barbara, California. Her developmental editor is located in Kentucky, the production editor is in Minnesota, and the publisher is in Ohio. Important parts of the marketing team are in Singapore and Canada. Although they work in different time zones and rarely see each other, team members use e-mail and teleconferencing to exchange ideas, make decisions, and stay connected.

Virtual teams may be local or global. At Best Buy's corporate headquarters in Richfield, Minnesota, certain employees are allowed to work anywhere and anytime—as long as they successfully complete their assignments on time. They can decide how, when, and where they work.[14] Although few other organizations are engaging in such a radical restructuring of work, many workers today complete their tasks from remote locations, thus creating local virtual teams. Hyundai Motors exemplifies virtual teaming at the global level. For its vehicles, Hyundai completes engineering in Korea, research in Tokyo and Germany, styling in California, engine calibration and testing in Michigan, and heat testing in the California desert.[15] Members of its virtual teams coordinate their work and complete their tasks across time and geographic zones. Work is increasingly viewed as what you do rather than a place you go.

In some organizations, remote coworkers may be permanent employees from the same office or may be specialists called together for temporary projects. Regardless of the assignment, virtual teams can benefit from shared views and skills. However, not all teams automatically work well together and are productive. The suggestions in the accompanying Tech Talk box offer helpful strategies for avoiding pitfalls.

Tech Talk

How to Form and Participate in Effective Virtual Teams

Virtual team members must overcome many obstacles not faced by intact groups. The following recommendations help members form virtual teams and interact effectively.

- **Select team members carefully.** Choose team members who are self-starters, good communicators, and experts in areas needed by the team.
- **Invest in beginnings.** If possible, meet face-to-face to work out procedures and to bond. Spending time together initially expedites reaching consensus about goals, tasks, and procedures.
- **Redefine "we."** Encourage behavior that reflects unity, such as including one another in decisions and sharing information. Consider having a team photograph taken and made into something used frequently such as a mouse pad or computer wallpaper.
- **Get the maximum benefit from technology.** Make use of speakerphones, collaborative software, e-mail, teleconferencing, videoconferencing, blogs, and wikis. But be sure that members are well trained in their use.
- **Concentrate on building credibility and trust.** Encourage team members to pay close attention to the way others perceive them. Acting consistently, fulfilling promises, considering other members' schedules, and responding promptly to e-mail and voice messages help build credibility and trust.
- **Establish responsibilities.** Identify expectations and responsibilities for each member. Make rules about e-mail response time and sharing information with all team members.
- **Keep track of information.** Capture information and decisions in a shared database, such as a wiki. Make sure all messages define expected actions, responsibilities, and time lines. Track to-do items and follow up as necessary. Expect messages to be more formal than in traditional same-time/same-place teams.
- **Avoid misinterpreting messages.** Because it is easy to misunderstand e-mail messages, be careful about responding quickly and negatively. Always take time to question your reactions.

Career Application

Why do you think increasing numbers of employees are joining virtual teams? What are the advantages and disadvantages for employees and for employers?

Icon: © Getty Images

Four Phases of Team Development

Small groups and teams may be formed to complete single tasks or to function as permanent ongoing bodies. Regardless of their purpose, successful teams normally go through predictable phases as they develop. In this section we will discuss four phases of team development. You will learn how team members can perform positively or negatively in achieving the group's goals. You will also study the role of conflict and how to apply a six-step plan for resolving conflict.

When groups are formed, they generally evolve through four phases, as identified by psychologist B. A. Tuckman. These phases are *forming*, *storming*, *norming*, and *performing*. Some groups get lucky and move quickly from forming to performing. But most struggle through disruptive, although ultimately constructive, team-building stages.

Successful teams generally go through four phases: forming, storming, norming, and performing.

Forming. During the first stage individuals get to know each other. They often are overly polite and feel a bit awkward. As they search for similarities and attempt to bond, they begin to develop trust in each other. Members will discuss fundamental topics such as why the team is necessary, who "owns" the team, whether membership is mandatory, how large it should be, and what talents members can contribute. A leader functions primarily as a traffic director. Groups and teams should resist the efforts of some members to dash through the first stages and race to the performing stage. Moving slowly through the stages is necessary in building a cohesive, productive unit.

Storming. During the second phase, members define their roles and responsibilities, decide how to reach their goals, and iron out the rules governing how they interact. Unfortunately, this stage often produces conflict, resulting in *storming*. A good leader, however, should step in to set limits, control the chaos, and offer suggestions. The leader will be most successful if she or he acts like a coach rather than a cop. Teams composed of dissimilar personality types may take longer to progress through the storming phase. Tempers may flare, sleep may be lost, leaders may be deposed. But most often the storm passes, and a cohesive group emerges.

FIGURE 2.1 Why Teams Fail: Typical Problems, Symptoms, and Solutions

Problems	Symptoms	Solutions
Confused goals	People don't know what they're supposed to do	Clarify team purpose and expected outcomes
Mismatched needs	People with private agendas working at cross-purposes	Get hidden agendas on the table by asking what people personally want from the team
Unresolved roles	Team members are uncertain about what their jobs are	Inform team members what is expected of them
Senseless procedures	The team is at the mercy of an employee handbook from hell	Throw away the book and develop procedures that make sense
Bad leadership	Leader is tentative, inconsistent, or foolish	Leader must learn to serve the team and keep its vision alive or give up the role
Antiteam culture	The organization is not committed to the idea of teams	Team for the right reasons or don't team at all; never force people onto a team
Poor feedback	Performance is not being measured; team members are groping in the dark	Create a system of free flow of useful information from all team members

Adapted from H. A. Robbins and M. Finley, *Why Teams Don't Work.* Reprinted with permission of Peterson's.

In the norming stage, tensions subside, roles are clarified, and information flows among team members.

Norming. Once the sun returns to the sky, teams and groups enter the *norming* stage. Tension subsides, roles are clarified, and information begins to flow among members. The group periodically checks its agenda to remind itself of its progress toward its goals. People are careful not to shake the hard-won camaraderie and formation of a single-minded purpose. Formal leadership is unnecessary because everyone takes on leadership functions. Important data are shared with the entire group, and mutual interdependence becomes typical. The group or team begins to move smoothly in one direction. Members make sure that procedures are in place to resolve future conflicts.

Performing. In Tuckman's team growth model, some groups never reach the final stage of *performing*. Problems that may cause them to fail are shown in Figure 2.1. For those that survive the first three phases, however, the final stage is gratifying. Group members have established routines and a shared language. They develop loyalty and a willingness to resolve all problems. A "can-do" mentality pervades as they progress toward their goal. Fights are clean, and members continue working together without grudges. Best of all, information flows freely, deadlines are met, and production exceeds expectations.

Analyzing Positive and Negative Team Behavior

LEARNING OBJECTIVE 2
Understand how to contribute positively to team performance, including resolving workplace conflicts, avoiding groupthink, and reaching group decisions.

Team members who are committed to achieving the group's purpose contribute by displaying positive behavior. How can you be a good team member? The most effective groups have members who are willing to establish rules and abide by those rules. Effective team members are able to analyze tasks and define problems so that they can work toward solutions. They offer information and try out their ideas on the group to stimulate discussion. They show interest in others' ideas by listening actively. Helpful team members also seek to involve silent members. They help to resolve differences, and they encourage a warm supportive climate by praising and agreeing with others. When they sense that agreement is near, they review significant points and move the group toward its goal by synthesizing points of understanding.

Negative team behavior includes insulting, criticizing, aggressing against others, wasting time, and refusing to participate.

Not all groups, however, have members who contribute positively. Negative behavior is shown by those who constantly put down the ideas and suggestions of others. They insult, criticize, and aggress against others. They waste the group's time with unnecessary recounting of personal achievements or irrelevant topics. The team joker distracts the group with excessive joke telling, inappropriate comments, and disruptive antics. Also disturbing are team members who withdraw and refuse to be drawn out. They have nothing to say, either for or against ideas being considered. To be a productive and welcome member of a group, be prepared to perform the positive tasks described in Figure 2.2. Avoid the negative behaviors.

FIGURE 2.2 Positive and Negative Team Behaviors

Positive Team Behaviors	Negative Team Behaviors
Setting rules and abiding by them	Blocking the ideas and suggestions of others
Analyzing tasks and defining problems	Insulting and criticizing others
Contributing information and ideas	Wasting the group's time
Showing interest by listening actively	Making inappropriate jokes and comments
Encouraging members to participate	Failing to stay on task
Synthesizing points of agreement	Withdrawing, failing to participate

Six-Step Procedure for Dealing With Conflict

Conflict is a normal part of every workplace and every team. Although the word alone is enough to make your heart begin to thump, conflict is not always negative. When managed properly, conflict can improve decision making, clarify values, increase group cohesiveness, stimulate creativity, decrease tensions, and undermine dissatisfaction. Unresolved conflict, however, can destroy productivity and seriously reduce morale. You will be better prepared to resolve workplace conflict if you are able to implement the following six-step procedure for dealing with conflict.[16]

Following an effective six-step procedure can help resolve conflicts through collaboration and cooperation.

1. **Listen.** To be sure you understand the problem, listen carefully. If the other person doesn't seem to be listening to you, you need to set the example and be the first to listen.

2. **Understand the other's point of view.** Once you listen, it is much easier to understand the other's position. Show your understanding by asking questions and paraphrasing. This will also verify what you think the other person means.

3. **Show a concern for the relationship.** By focusing on the problem, not the person, you can build, maintain, and even improve the relationship. Show an understanding of the other person's situation and needs. Show an overall willingness to come to an agreement.

4. **Look for common ground.** Identify your interests and help the other person identify his or her interests. Learn what you have in common, and look for a solution to which both of you can agree.

5. **Invent new problem-solving options.** Spend time identifying the interests of both sides. Then brainstorm to invent new ways to solve the problem. Be open to new options.

6. **Reach an agreement based on what's fair.** Seek to determine a standard of fairness that is acceptable to both sides. Then weigh the possible solutions, and choose the best option.

Avoiding Groupthink

Conflict is normal in team interactions, and successful teams are able to resolve it using the methods you just learned. But some teams avoid conflict. They smooth things over and in doing so may fall victim to *groupthink*. This is a term coined by theorist Irving Janis to describe faulty decision-making processes by team members who are overly eager to agree with one another. Several conditions can lead to groupthink: team members with similar backgrounds, a lack of systematic procedures, a demand for a quick decision, and a strong leader who favors a specific decision. Symptoms of groupthink include pressures placed on any member who argues against the group's mutual beliefs, self-censorship of thoughts that stray from the group's agreement, collective efforts to rationalize, and an unquestioned belief in the group's moral authority. Teams suffering from groupthink fail to check alternatives, are biased in collecting and evaluating information, and ignore the risks of the preferred choice. They may also neglect to work out a contingency plan in case the preferred choice fails.[17]

Groupthink means that team members agree without examining alternatives or considering contingency plans.

Teamwork is essential to the success of any organization. However, group situations can stifle individual creativity, cloud decision making, and limit problem solving. A recent study published in the *Journal of Consumer Research* found that whether the task involves identifying alternative soft drink brands or brainstorming with coworkers, groups fixate on similar ideas and tend to produce fewer alternatives than do individuals working alone. *What premeeting preparation could help teams reduce groupthink and increase the effectiveness of decision making?*

Effective teams avoid groupthink by striving for team diversity—in age, gender, background, experience, and training. They encourage open discussion, search for relevant information, evaluate many alternatives, consider how a decision will be implemented, and plan for contingencies in case the decision doesn't work out.

Reaching Group Decisions

The way teams reach decisions greatly affects the morale and commitment of the team, as well as the implementation of any team decision. In U.S. culture the majority usually rules, but other methods, five of which are discussed here, may be more effective. As you study these methods, think about which would be best for routine decisions and which would be best for dealing with emergencies.

Although time-consuming, consensus decisions generally produce the most team commitment.

- **Majority.** Group members vote and a majority wins. This method results in a quick decision but may leave an alienated minority uncommitted to implementation.

- **Consensus.** Discussion continues until all team members have aired their opinions and, ultimately, agree. This method is time-consuming; but it produces creative, high-quality discussion and generally elicits commitment by all members to implement the decision.

- **Minority.** Typically, a subcommittee investigates and makes a recommendation for action. This method is useful when the full group cannot get together to make a decision or when time is short.

- **Averaging.** Members haggle, bargain, wheedle, and negotiate to reach a middle position, which often requires compromise. With this method, the opinions of the least knowledgeable members may cancel the opinions of the most knowledgeable.

- **Authority rule with discussion.** The leader, boss, or manager listens to team members' ideas, but the final decision is his or hers. This method encourages lively discussion and results in participatory decision making. However, team members must have good communication skills. This method also requires a leader who is willing to make decisions.

Ethics Check

Lazy Team Members, Anyone?
Teamwork is a staple in college classes today and usually works well for students and their instructors. However, occasionally a rogue member will take advantage of a group and barely collaborate. How do you deal with a student who does sloppy work, misses team meetings, and fails to respond to calls or e-mail?

Characteristics of Successful Teams

The use of teams has been called the solution to many ills in the current workplace.[18] Someone even observed that as an acronym TEAM means "Together, Everyone Achieves More."[19]

Chapter 2: Developing Team, Listening, and Etiquette Skills

Many teams, however, do not work well together. In fact, some teams can actually increase frustration, lower productivity, and create employee dissatisfaction. Experts who have studied team workings and decisions have discovered that effective teams share some or all of the following characteristics.

Small Size, Diverse Makeup. Teams may range from 2 to 25 members, although 4 or 5 is optimum for many projects. Larger groups have trouble interacting constructively, much less agreeing on actions.[20] For the most creative decisions, teams generally have male and female members who differ in age, ethnicity, social background, training, and experience. Members should bring complementary skills to a team. Paul Fireman, founder of sports shoe manufacturer Reebok, wisely remarked, "If you put five centers on the basketball court, you're going to lose the game. You need, we all need, people of different strengths and talents—and that means, among other things, people of different backgrounds."[21] The key business advantage of diversity is the ability to view a project and its context from multiple perspectives. Many of us tend to think that everyone in the world is like us because we know only our own experience.[22] Teams with members from different ethnicities and cultures can look at projects beyond the limited view of one culture. Many organizations are finding that diverse teams can produce innovative solutions with broader applications than homogeneous teams can.

Small, diverse teams often produce more creative solutions with broader applications than homogeneous teams do.

Agreement on Purpose. An effective team begins with a purpose. For example, when Magic Johnson Theatres was developing its first theater, it hired a team whose sole purpose was to help Magic Johnson Theatres move rapidly through the arduous state permit application process. Even the task of obtaining a license for the site's popcorn machine was surprisingly difficult.[23] Xerox scientists who invented personal computing developed their team purpose after the chairman of Xerox called for an "architecture of information." A team at Sealed Air Corporation developed its purpose when management instructed it to cut waste and reduce downtime.[24] Working from a general purpose to specific goals typically requires a huge investment of time and effort. Meaningful discussions, however, motivate team members to "buy into" the project.

Ethical Insights

Ethical Responsibilities of Group Members and Leaders

When people form a group or a team to achieve a purpose, they agree to give up some of their individual sovereignty for the good of the group. They become interdependent and assume responsibilities to one another and to the group. Here are important ethical responsibilities for members to follow:

- **Determine to do your best.** When you commit to the group process, you are obligated to offer your skills freely. Don't hold back, perhaps fearing that you will be repeatedly targeted because you have skills to offer. If the group project is worth doing, it is worth the best effort you can offer.
- **Decide to behave with the group's good in mind.** You may find it necessary to set aside your personal goals in favor of the group's goals. Decide to keep an open mind and to listen to evidence and arguments objectively. Strive to evaluate information carefully, even though it may contradict your own views or thwart your personal agendas.
- **Make a commitment to fair play.** Group problem solving is a cooperative, not a competitive, event. Decide that you cannot grind your private ax at the expense of the group project.
- **Expect to give and receive a fair hearing.** When you speak, others should give you a fair hearing. You have a right to expect them to listen carefully, provide you with candid feedback, strive to understand what you say, and treat your ideas seriously. Listeners do not have to agree with you, of course. However, all speakers have a right to a fair hearing.
- **Be willing to take on a participant/ analyst role.** As a group member, it is your responsibility to pay attention, evaluate what is happening, analyze what you learn, and help make decisions.
- **As a leader, be ready to model appropriate team behavior.** It is a leader's responsibility to coach team members in skills and teamwork, to acknowledge achievement and effort, to share knowledge, and to periodically remind members of the team's missions and goals.

Career Application

Assume you are a member of a campus committee to organize a celebrity auction to raise funds for a local homeless shelter. Your friend Marika is committee chair, but she is carrying a heavy course load and is also working part time. As a result, she has taken no action. You call her, but she is evasive when you try to pin her down about committee plans. What should you do?

Icon: © Getty Images

Agreement on Procedures. The best teams develop procedures to guide them. They set up intermediate goals with deadlines. They assign roles and tasks, requiring all members to contribute equivalent amounts of real work. They decide how they will reach decisions using one of the strategies discussed earlier. Procedures are continually evaluated to ensure movement toward the attainment of the team's goals.

Ability to Confront Conflict. Poorly functioning teams avoid conflict, preferring sulking, gossiping, or bickering. A better plan is to acknowledge conflict and address the root of the problem openly using the six-step plan outlined earlier. Although it may feel emotionally risky, direct confrontation saves time and enhances team commitment in the long run. To be constructive, however, confrontation must be task oriented, not person oriented. An open airing of differences, in which all team members have a chance to speak their minds, should center on the strengths and weaknesses of the different positions and ideas—not on personalities. After hearing all sides, team members must negotiate a fair settlement, no matter how long it takes. Good decisions are based on consensus: all members agree.

Good teams exchange information freely and collaborate rather than compete.

Use of Good Communication Techniques. The best teams exchange information and contribute ideas freely in an informal environment. Team members speak clearly and concisely, avoiding generalities. They encourage feedback. Listeners become actively involved, read body language, and ask clarifying questions before responding. Tactful, constructive disagreement is encouraged. Although a team's task is taken seriously, successful teams are able to inject humor into their interactions.

Ability to Collaborate Rather Than Compete. Effective team members are genuinely interested in achieving team goals instead of receiving individual recognition. They contribute ideas and feedback unselfishly. They monitor team progress, including what's going right, what's going wrong, and what to do about it. They celebrate individual and team accomplishments.

Checklist

Developing Team Effectiveness

✓ **Establish small teams.** Smaller teams are thought to function more efficiently and more effectively than larger teams.

✓ **Encourage diversity.** Innovative teams typically include members who differ in age, gender, ethnicity, and background. Team members should possess technical expertise, problem-solving skills, and interpersonal skills.

✓ **Determine the purpose, procedures, and roles.** Members must understand the task at hand and what is expected of them. Teams function best when operating procedures are ironed out early and each member has a specific role.

✓ **Acknowledge and manage conflict.** Conflict is productive when it motivates a team to search for new ideas, increase participation, delay premature decisions, or discuss disagreements. Keep conflict centered on issues rather than on people.

✓ **Cultivate good communication skills.** Effective team members are willing and able to articulate ideas clearly and concisely, recognize nonverbal cues, and listen actively.

✓ **Advance an environment of open communication.** Teams are most productive when members trust each other and feel free to discuss all viewpoints openly in an informal atmosphere.

✓ **Encourage collaboration and discourage competition.** Sharing information in a cooperative effort to achieve the team purpose must be more important than competing with other members for individual achievement.

✓ **Share leadership.** Members with the most expertise should lead at various times during the project's evolution.

✓ **Create a sense of fairness in making decisions.** Effective teams resolve issues without forcing members into a win–lose situation.

✓ **Lighten up.** The most successful teams take their task seriously, but they are also able to laugh at themselves and interject humor to enliven team proceedings.

✓ **Continually assess performance.** Teams should establish checkpoints along the way to determine whether they are meeting their objectives and adjust procedures if progress is unsatisfactory.

Chapter 2: Developing Team, Listening, and Etiquette Skills

Communicating at Work Part 2

Toyota

In response to worker complaints, Toyota's North American Parts Center's management formed a special cross-functional team, Leadership 2000, to plan and execute its restructuring and team-building effort. Associates in the 13 original work units created their own autonomous teams of seven to ten members. After taking inventories to identify their strengths and skills, associates attended special sessions to review the findings. By learning how their own abilities complemented other member's strengths, associates became more effective team members. For example, a team leader might call on an associate with good listening skills to help settle a difference of opinions, while another with good focus might assist with goal setting. Team leaders are chosen for their ability to facilitate rather than dictate. Although management selects team leaders, associates have a say as well, casting votes to indicate their preferences.

The results of the Leadership 2000 initiative were impressive: Productivity rose 6 percent in the first year after restructuring. Teams have more control to handle issues as they arise and to search for ways to improve productivity even more. One team leader said, before teams were established, "We never had . . . the ability to get together for five minutes and either solve the problem or raise it as an issue to deal with later."[25]

Critical Thinking

- Why do you think that management at the North American Parts Center California was willing to undertake the difficult transition to teams, when it would have been easier to stay with the line manager system?
- What were the advantages of choosing a cross-functional team with members from different areas to guide the structural changes at the Center?
- How might a newly formed team in the parts receiving unit move through the four stages of team development? What types of listening skills would help the team succeed?

Acceptance of Ethical Responsibilities. Teams as a whole have ethical responsibilities to their members, to their larger organizations, and to society. Members have a number of specific responsibilities to each other, as described in the Ethical Insights box on page 41. As a whole, teams have a responsibility to represent the organization's view and respect its privileged information. They should not discuss with outsiders any sensitive issues without permission. In addition, teams have a broader obligation to avoid advocating actions that would endanger members of society at large.

Shared Leadership. Effective teams often have no formal leader. Instead, leadership rotates to those with the appropriate expertise as the team evolves and moves from one phase to another. Many teams operate under a democratic approach. This approach can achieve buy-in to team decisions, boost morale, and create fewer hurt feelings and less resentment. But in times of crisis, a strong team member may need to step up as leader.

Planning and Participating in Productive Meetings

As businesses become more team oriented and management becomes more participatory, people are attending more meetings than ever. A recent study revealed that 53 percent of Americans spend one to eight hours each week attending meetings.[26] Yet, meetings are almost universally disliked. Typical comments include, "We have too many of them," "They don't accomplish anything," and "What a waste of time!" In spite of employee reluctance, meetings are not going to go away. Our task, then, as business communicators is to learn how to make them more efficient, satisfying, and productive.

Meetings, by the way, consist of three or more people who gather to pool information, solicit feedback, clarify policy, seek consensus, and solve problems. But meetings have another important purpose for you. They represent opportunities. Because they are a prime tool for developing staff, they are career-critical. "If you can't orchestrate a meeting, you're of little use to the corporation," said Morris Schechtman, head of a leadership training firm.[27] *The Wall Street Journal* concurred: "The inability to run effective meetings can torpedo a

LEARNING OBJECTIVE 3
Plan and participate in productive meetings.

Meetings enable three or more people to pool information and solve problems, but they also represent great opportunities for you to distinguish yourself and advance your career.

career."[28] Why are meetings so important to your career? At meetings, judgments are formed and careers are made. Therefore, instead of treating them as thieves of your valuable time, try to see them as golden opportunities to demonstrate your leadership, communication, and problem-solving skills. So that you can make the most of these opportunities, here are techniques for planning and conducting successful meetings.

Deciding Whether a Meeting Is Necessary

No meeting should be called unless the topic is important, can't wait, and requires an exchange of ideas. If the flow of information is strictly one way and no immediate feedback will result, then don't schedule a meeting. For example, if people are merely being advised or informed, send an e-mail, text message, memo, or letter. Leave a telephone or voice mail message, but don't call a costly meeting. Remember, the real expense of a meeting is the lost productivity of all the people attending. To decide whether the purpose of the meeting is valid, it is a good idea to consult the key people who will be attending. Ask them what outcomes are desired and how to achieve those goals. This consultation also sets a collaborative tone and encourages full participation.

Selecting Participants

The number of meeting participants is determined by the purpose of the meeting, as shown in Figure 2.3. If the meeting purpose is motivational, such as an awards ceremony for sales reps of cosmetics giant Avon, then the number of participants is unlimited. But to make decisions, according to studies at 3M Corporation, the best number is five or fewer participants.[29] Ideally, those attending should be people who will make the decision and people with information necessary to make the decision. Also attending should be people who will be responsible for implementing the decision and representatives of groups who will benefit from the decision. Let's say, for example, that the CEO of sportswear manufacturer Timberland is strongly committed to community service. He wants his company to participate more fully in community service. So he might meet with managers, employee representatives, and community leaders to decide how his employees could volunteer to refurbish a school, build affordable housing, or volunteer at a clinic.[30]

Distributing Advance Information

At least two days in advance of a meeting, distribute an agenda of topics to be discussed. Also include any reports or materials that participants should read in advance. For continuing groups, you might also include a copy of the minutes of the previous meeting. To keep meetings productive, limit the number of agenda items. Remember, the narrower the focus, the greater the chances for success. A good agenda, as illustrated in Figure 2.4, covers the following information:

- Date and place of meeting
- Start time and end time
- Brief description of each topic, in order of priority, including the names of individuals who are responsible for performing some action
- Proposed allotment of time for each topic
- Any premeeting preparation expected of participants

Getting the Meeting Started

To avoid wasting time and irritating attendees, always start meetings on time—even if some participants are missing. Waiting for latecomers causes resentment and sets a bad precedent.

FIGURE 2.3 Meeting Purpose and Number of Participants

Purpose	Ideal Size
Intensive problem solving	5 or fewer
Problem identification	10 or fewer
Information reviews and presentations	30 or fewer
Motivational	Unlimited

FIGURE 2.4 Typical Meeting Agenda

AGENDA

Quantum Travel International
Staff Meeting
September 4, 2009
10 to 11 A.M.
Conference Room

I. Call to order; roll call

II. Approval of agenda

III. Approval of minutes from previous meeting

	Person	Proposed Time
IV. Committee reports		
A. Web site update	Jared	5 minutes
B. Tour packages	LaKisha	10 minutes
V. Old business		
A. Equipment maintenance	John	5 minutes
B. Client escrow accounts	Alicia	5 minutes
C. Internal newsletter	Adrienne	5 minutes
VI. New business		
A. New accounts	Garth	5 minutes
B. Pricing policy for Asian trips	Minh	15 minutes

VII. Announcements

VIII. Chair's summary, adjournment

For the same reasons, don't give a quick recap to anyone who arrives late. At the appointed time, open the meeting with a three- to five-minute introduction that includes the following:

- Goal and length of the meeting

- Background of topics or problems

- Possible solutions and constraints

- Tentative agenda

- Ground rules to be followed

A typical set of ground rules might include arriving on time, communicating openly, being supportive, listening carefully, participating fully, confronting conflict frankly, and following the agenda. More formal groups follow parliamentary procedures based on Robert's Rules. After establishing basic ground rules, the leader should ask if participants agree thus far. The next step is to assign one attendee to take minutes and one to act as a recorder. The recorder stands at a flipchart or whiteboard and lists the main ideas being discussed and agreements reached.

Moving the Meeting Along

Successful leaders keep the meeting moving by avoiding issues that sidetrack the group.

After the preliminaries, the leader should say as little as possible. Like a talk show host, an effective leader makes "sure that each panel member gets some air time while no one member steals the show."[31] Remember that the purpose of a meeting is to exchange views, not to hear one person, even the leader, do all the talking. If the group has one member who monopolizes, the leader might say, "Thanks, Kurt, for that perspective, but please hold your next point while we hear how Ann would respond to that." This technique also encourages quieter participants to speak up.

To avoid allowing digressions to sidetrack the group, try generating a "Parking Lot" list. This is a list of important but divergent issues that should be discussed at a later time. Another way to handle digressions is to say, "Folks, we are getting off track here. Forgive me for pressing on, but I need to bring us back to the central issue of. . . ."[32] It is important to adhere to the agenda and the time schedule. Equally important, when the group seems to have reached a consensus, is to summarize the group's position and check to see whether everyone agrees.

Participating Actively and Productively

To benefit from meetings, arrive early, be prepared, contribute positively and respectfully, stay calm, give credit to others, don't use your cell phone or laptop, help summarize, express your views in the meeting (not after), and complete your assignments.

Meetings are an opportunity for you to showcase your abilities and boost your career. To get the most out of the meetings you attend, try these techniques:[33]

- **Arrive early.** You show respect and look well organized by arriving a little early.

- **Come prepared.** Bring the agenda and any distributed materials. Study the topics and be ready with questions, comments, and good ideas.

- **Bring a positive attitude.** Use positive body language; speak energetically.

- **Contribute respectfully.** Wait your turn to speak; raise your hand to be recognized.

- **Wait for others to finish.** Show respect and good manners by not interrupting.

- **Keep your voice calm and pleasant, yet energetic.** Avoid showing anger as this focuses attention on your behavior rather than on your ideas.

- **Give credit to others.** Gain allies and enhance your credibility by recognizing others in front of peers and superiors.

- **Put the cell phone and laptop away.** Focus your attention on the meeting, not on answering e-mail or working on your computer.

- **Help summarize.** Assist the meeting leader by reviewing points you have noted.

Conferencing firm WebEx Communications Inc. is finding new ways to make meetings more productive—even long after they have ended. Whereas conventional meeting follow-up revolves around handwritten notes, individual memories, and typed minutes, WebEx conferencing software enables businesses to record and archive entire group sessions for future retrieval. *How might computer-based meeting archive systems lead to higher productivity and greater openness in organizations?*

© Peter Cade / Iconica / Getty Images

Chapter 2: Developing Team, Listening, and Etiquette Skills

- **Express your views IN the meeting.** Build trust by not holding postmeeting "sidebars" with criticism and judgments.
- **Follow up.** Send the signal that you are efficient and caring by completing the actions assigned to you.

Handling Conflict in Meetings

As you learned earlier, conflict is natural and even desirable. But it can cause awkwardness and uneasiness. In meetings, conflict typically develops when people feel unheard or misunderstood. If two people are in conflict, the best approach is to encourage each to make a complete case while group members give their full attention. Let each one question the other. Then, the leader should summarize what was said, and the group should offer comments. The group may modify a recommendation or suggest alternatives before reaching consensus on a direction to follow.

When a conflict develops between two members, allow each to make a complete case before the group.

Ending and Following Up

End the meeting at the agreed time. The leader should summarize what has been decided, who is going to do what, and by what time. It may be necessary to ask people to volunteer to take responsibility for completing action items agreed to in the meeting. No one should leave the meeting without a full understanding of what was accomplished. One effective technique that encourages full participation is "once around the table." Everyone is asked to summarize briefly his or her interpretation of what was decided and what happens next. Of course, this closure technique works best with smaller groups. The leader should conclude by asking the group to set a time for the next meeting. He or she should also assure the group that a report will follow and thank participants for attending.

Effective meetings end with a summary of accomplishments with a follow-up reminding participants of their assigned tasks.

If minutes were taken, they should be distributed within a couple of days after the meeting. It is up to the leader to see that what was decided at the meeting is accomplished. The leader may need to call people to remind them of their assignments and also to volunteer to help them if necessary.

Meetings are a necessary evil for today's team-oriented workplace. The following checklist can help you use them effectively and perhaps accelerate your career.

Checklist

Planning and Participating in Productive Meetings

Before the Meeting

✓ **Consider alternatives.** Unless a topic is important and pressing, avoid calling a meeting. Perhaps an e-mail message, telephone call, or announcement would serve the purpose as well.

✓ **Invite the right people.** To make decisions, invite those people who have information and authority to make the decision and implement it.

✓ **Distribute an agenda.** Prepare and distribute an agenda that includes the date and place of meeting, the starting and ending time, a brief description of each topic, the names of people responsible for any action, and a proposed time allotment for each topic.

During the Meeting

✓ **Start on time and introduce the agenda.** Discuss the goal and length of the meeting, provide background of topics for discussion, suggest possible solutions and constraints, propose a tentative agenda, and clarify the ground rules for the meeting.

✓ **Appoint a secretary and a recorder.** Ask one attendee to make a record of the proceedings, and ask another person to record discussion topics on a flipchart or whiteboard.

✓ **Encourage balanced participation.** Strive to be sure that all participants' views are heard and that no one monopolizes the discussion. Avoid digressions by steering the group back to the topics on the agenda.

✓ **Confront conflict frankly.** Encourage people who disagree to explain their positions completely. Then restate each position and ask for group comments. The group may modify a recommendation or suggest alternatives before agreeing on a plan of action.

✓ **Summarize along the way.** When the group seems to reach a consensus, summarize and see whether everyone agrees.

Ending the Meeting and Following Up

✓ **Review meeting decisions.** At the end of the meeting, summarize what has been decided, discuss action items, and establish a schedule for completion.

✓ **Distribute minutes of meeting.** A few days after the meeting, arrange to have the secretary distribute the minutes.

✓ **Remind people of action items.** Follow up by calling people to see whether they are completing the actions recommended at the meeting.

Using Technology to Facilitate Collaboration

LEARNING OBJECTIVE 4

Explain the usefulness of collaborative technologies such as voice conferencing, videoconferencing, Web conferencing, instant messaging, blogs, and wikis.

A number of constantly evolving technologies enable people to collaborate on projects without meeting face-to-face. Everyone agrees that live meetings are best to exchange ideas, brainstorm, build consensus, and develop personal relationships. But collaboration tools are becoming increasingly effective and more popular for a number of reasons. Collaboration tools make it possible for people to work together when they can't be together. These tools are fast, convenient, and can save big bucks in travel costs. For example, when Hewlett-Packard was moving its inkjet cartridge manufacturing line from Oregon to a plant in Singapore, it estimated that using videoconferences saved about six months in project time. Managers also avoided 45 trans-Pacific trips.[34]

E-mail is still a major communication channel for online collaboration. Because e-mail is the first tool most people learn to use, they are often reluctant to move away from e-mail to embrace more effective collaboration tools. Collaborators today have a number of efficient tools including voice conferencing, videoconferencing, Web conferencing, instant messaging, blogs, and wikis. You may already have used many of the following tools.

Voice Conferencing

Voice conferencing enables collaborators to confer with each other by telephone.

Among the simplest collaboration tools is *voice conferencing* (also called *audioconferencing, teleconferencing, conference calling,* or *phone conferencing*). One or more people in a work area use an enhanced speakerphone to confer with others by telephone. Voice conferencing enables people at both ends to speak and be heard simultaneously. Thanks to cell phones, people can even participate in a teleconference from an airplane or the beach. Although voice conferencing is not as glitzy as other collaboration tools, it is the mainstay of the entire teleconferencing industry. Because it is simple and effective, more people use it than any other of the collaboration meeting tools.

Videoconferencing

Videoconferencing combines video, audio, and software to connect collaborators in real time.

If meeting participants need to see each other or share documents, they may use *videoconferencing*. This tool combines video, audio, and communications networking technologies for real-time interaction. Participants generally meet in special conference rooms equipped with cameras and screens for transmitting images and documents. A new generation of videoconference systems, although pricey, is the next best thing to being there. These high-end *telepresence* systems with broadcast-quality cameras and a row of 50- to 65-inch plasma screens can cost as much as $1 million.[35] They are used by scientists, researchers, and top executives for collaboration. More conventional videoconference rooms may cost $5,000 to $80,000 a room. Whether using high- or low-end conferencing tools, participants do not have to journey to distant meetings. Organizations reduce travel expenses, travel time, and employee fatigue.

Web Conferencing

Web conferencing enables collaborators to use their computers in sharing documents, data, and slide shows.

Participants can take part in "real life" meetings from the comfort of their offices. Web conferencing is similar to videoconferencing but may work with or without the transmission of pictures of the participants. Attendees use their computers to access an online virtual meeting room where they can present PowerPoint slides or share spreadsheets or Word documents, just as they might do in a face-to-face meeting. They can even demonstrate products and make changes in real time during a meeting.

GoToMeeting, a reasonably priced commercial conferencing tool, enables you to launch meetings by sending instant messages to attendees, who click on an embedded link to join the group. Participants are generally connected to a phone conference call. On their computers, attendees see the presenter's desktop and all the actions performed there—from viewing Web pages to stepping through a presentation. They can participate with each other using instant messaging in a chat window. WebEx offers a richer Web conferencing tool, including white boarding and other advanced functions.

Skype, a virtually free conferencing tool popular with students and expatriates, is also used by businesspeople. It allows conferencing with or without a camera. All that is needed is a laptop, a headset with a microphone, and a Web camera. Constantly evolving, Web

FIGURE 2.5 Web Conferencing in Practice

Here's how SideKick Enterprises sets up a virtual meeting to design a new athletic shoe.

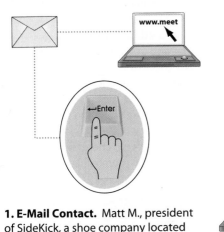

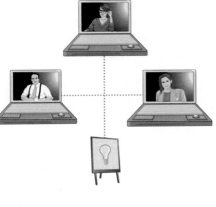

2. Virtual Meeting. When the Web conference begins, participants see live videos of each other's faces on their computer screens. They look at photos of athletic shoes, share ideas, sketch designs on a shared "virtual whiteboard," and review contract terms.

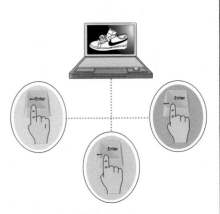

1. E-Mail Contact. Matt M., president of SideKick, a shoe company located in Los Angeles, sends an e-mail to Lisa G., chief designer at NYConcepts, located in New York, to discuss a new athletic shoe. The e-mail includes a date for the meeting and a link to launch the session.

3. Design Collaboration. NYConcepts designers and SideKick managers use peer-to-peer software that allows them to share spaces on each other's computers. The software enables them to take turns modifying the designs, and it also tracks all the changes.

conferencing is changing the way businesspeople work together. Figure 2.5 shows how shoe manufacturer SideKick used Web conferencing to meet virtually and design a new athletic shoe.

Instant Messaging (IM)

Once used almost exclusively by teenagers, instant messaging (IM) is now increasingly accepted as a communication tool in the workplace. In our fast-paced world, many business communicators find that even e-mail is not swift enough. Instead, they rely on instant messaging to deliver messages immediately and directly to the receiver's desktop. Minor matters can be cleared up instantly. Group discussions can be easily initiated with three or more participants. Perhaps the most useful feature of this software tool is the concept of *presence*—awareness of the availability of the recipient. Colleagues may use IM to see whether someone is available for incoming calls or to have a quick online chat. Instant messaging is especially useful for back-and-forth online conversations, such as a customer communicating with a tech support person to solve a problem. Businesses use instant messaging to communicate with customers, colleagues, and vendors down the hall or across the world.

> Instant messaging is useful for immediate online conversations.

Blogs

As you learned earlier (see Figure 1.2 in Chapter 1), *blogs* are a type of interactive online journal that allows collaborators to share information in one central location. A blog is a one-to-many form of communication. That is, one person speaks to an audience who can comment on, but not change, the content. Blogs are especially helpful for cross-departmental teams and when new members must get up to speed quickly. A team leader's blog can provide all project information at one central location, usually on the company's intranet. The leader can update an entire team on progress, goals, and deadlines.

Blogs reduce time spent in unnecessary meetings by allowing minor matters to be handled online. Background and preparatory information can be circulated before virtual or face-to-face meetings. Unlike e-mail messages, blogs are Web-based documents. They can be archived and searched by category, name, title, project, special interest, or authority. As a result, information remains stored, categorized, and accessible—even if the knowledge worker who posted the blog leaves the organization. Most companies use blogs behind corporate firewalls to protect company information.

> Blogs are interactive online journals with information that team members can see and comment on.

Wikis

A *wiki* is a collaborative Web site that enables anyone with access to add, change, or delete information. Content can be edited more easily than in a blog. A wiki is a many-to-many form of communication, whereas blogs are a one-to-many form of communication. Blogs resemble a personal broadcasting system, whereas wikis blend many voices to produce a forum. Like blogs, wiki documents can be digitally stored, categorized, and searched. Because of their ease of use, wikis are a natural when many people are working together and updating information.

As a manager of a bank's security department, Edward Williams set up a wiki for the bank's customer support personnel. It carries the latest news on phishing scams and computer viruses aimed at online banking customers. "Our support workers can easily add information to the wiki while they are working with the customer, which allows us to connect the dots and make a complete picture of a new threat very quickly—something that wasn't really possible with a database solution," said Williams.[36] He expects everyone in the bank to check the security wiki once a day. Companies usually set up wikis on an intranet behind corporate firewalls.

Listening in the Workplace

"No one ever listened himself out of a job," observed President Calvin Coolidge many years ago. His words are even more significant today as employers become increasingly aware that listening is a critical employee and management skill. Listening skills are part of the soft skills that employers seek when looking for well-rounded candidates who can be hired and promoted.

But, you may be thinking, everyone knows how to listen. Most of us believe that listening is an automatic response to noise. We do it without thinking. Perhaps that explains why so many of us are poor listeners. In this chapter we explore the importance of listening, the kinds of listening required in the workplace, and how to become a better listener. Although many of the tips for improving your listening skills will be effective in your personal life, our discussion centers primarily on workplace and employment needs.

As you learned earlier, workers are doing more communicating than ever before, largely because of the Internet, team environments, global competition, and emphasis on customer service. A vital ingredient in every successful workplace is high-quality communication. And three quarters of high-quality communication involves listening.[37]

Listening skills are important for career success, organization effectiveness, and worker satisfaction. Numerous studies and experts report that good listeners make good managers and that good listeners advance more rapidly in their organizations.[38] Studies of Fortune 500 companies report that soft skills such as listening, writing, and speaking are most likely to determine hiring and career success.[39] Listening is especially important in the workplace because we spend so much time doing it. Most workers spend 30 to 45 percent of their communication time listening,[40] whereas executives spend 60 to 70 percent of their communication time listening.[41]

Poor Listening Habits

Although executives and workers devote the bulk of their communication time to listening, research suggests that they are not very good at it. In fact, most of us are poor listeners. Some estimates indicate that only half of the oral messages heard in a day are completely understood.[42] Experts say that we listen at only 25 percent efficiency. In other words, we ignore, forget, distort, or misunderstand 75 percent of everything we hear.

Poor listening habits may result from several factors. Lack of training is one significant reason. Few schools give as much emphasis to listening as they do to the development of reading, speaking, and writing skills. In addition, our listening skills may be less than perfect because of the large number of competing sounds and stimuli in our lives that interfere with concentration. Finally, we are inefficient listeners because we are able to process speech much faster than others can speak. While most speakers talk at about 125 to 250 words per minute, listeners can think at 1,000 to 3,000 words per minute.[43] The resulting lag time fosters daydreaming, which clearly reduces listening efficiency.

Types of Workplace Listening

In an employment environment, you can expect to be involved in many types of listening. These include listening to superiors, listening to fellow colleagues and team members, and listening to customers. If you are an entry-level employee, you will probably be most concerned with listening to superiors. But you also must develop skills for listening to colleagues and team members. As you advance in your career and enter the ranks of management, you will need skills for listening to subordinates. Finally, the entire organization must listen to customers to compete in today's service-oriented economy.

Listening to Superiors. On the job one of your most important tasks will be listening to instructions, assignments, and explanations about how to do your work. You will be listening to learn and to comprehend. To focus totally on the speaker, be sure you are not distracted by noisy surroundings or other tasks. Don't take phone calls, and don't try to complete another job while listening with one ear. Show your interest by leaning forward and striving for good eye contact.

Above all, take notes. Don't rely on your memory. Details are easy to forget. Taking selective notes also conveys to the speaker your seriousness about hearing accurately and completely. Don't interrupt. When the speaker finishes, paraphrase the instructions in your own words. Ask pertinent questions in a nonthreatening manner. And don't be afraid to ask "dumb" questions, if it means you won't have to do a job twice. Avoid criticizing or arguing when you are listening to a superior. Your goals should be to hear accurately and to convey an image of competence.

Listening to Colleagues and Teammates. Much of your listening will result from interactions with fellow workers and teammates. In these exchanges two kinds of listening are important. *Critical listening* enables you to judge and evaluate what you are hearing. You will be listening to decide whether the speaker's message is fact, fiction, or opinion. You will also be listening to decide whether an argument is based on logic or emotion. Critical listening requires an effort on your part. You must remain objective, particularly when you disagree with what you are hearing. Control your tendency to prejudge. Let the speaker have a chance to complete the message before you evaluate it. *Discriminative listening* is necessary when you must understand and remember. It means you must identify main ideas, understand a logical argument, and recognize the purpose of the message.

Listening to superiors involves hearing instructions, assignments, and explanations of work procedures.

Good listening techniques include taking notes, not interrupting, and paraphrasing.

Listening to colleagues and teammates involves critical listening and discriminative listening.

FIGURE 2.6 Listening to Customers: Comparing Untrained and Trained Listeners

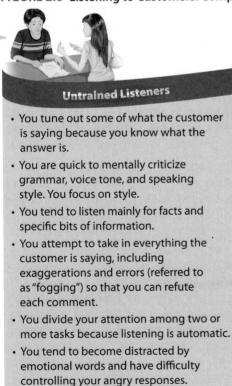

Untrained Listeners	Trained Listeners
• You tune out some of what the customer is saying because you know what the answer is.	• You defer judgement. You listen for the customer's feelings and assess the situation.
• You are quick to mentally criticize grammar, voice tone, and speaking style. You focus on style.	• You pay most attention to content, not to appearances, form, or other surface issues.
• You tend to listen mainly for facts and specific bits of information.	• You listen completely, trying to really understand every nuance. This enthralls speakers.
• You attempt to take in everything the customer is saying, including exaggerations and errors (referred to as "fogging") so that you can refute each comment.	• You listen primarily for the main idea and avoid replying to everything, especially sidetracking issues.
• You divide your attention among two or more tasks because listening is automatic.	• You do one thing at a time, realizing that listening is a full-time job.
• You tend to become distracted by emotional words and have difficulty controlling your angry responses.	• You control your anger and refuse to fight fire with fire.
• You interrupt the customer.	• You are silent for a few seconds after a customer finishes to be sure the thought is completed.
• You give few, if any, verbal responses.	• You give affirming statements and invite additional comments.

Listening to Customers. As the U.S. economy becomes increasingly service oriented, the new management mantra has become "customers rule." Yet, despite 50 years of talk about customer service, the concept of "customer-centric" business is still in its infancy.[44] Many organizations are just learning that listening to customers results in increased sales and profitability as well as improved customer acquisition and retention. The simple truth is that consumers feel better about companies that value their opinions. Listening is an acknowledgment of caring and is a potent retention tool. Customers want to be cared about; by doing so, companies fulfill a powerful human need.

How can organizations improve their customer listening techniques? Because employees are the eyes and ears of the organization, smart companies begin by hiring employees who genuinely care about customers. Listening organizations also train their employees to listen actively and to ask gentle, probing questions to ensure clear understanding. As you can see in Figure 2.6, on page 51, employees trained in listening techniques are far more likely to elicit customer feedback and promote goodwill than untrained employees are.

Improving Workplace Listening

Listening on the job is more difficult than listening in college classes where experienced professors present well-organized lectures and repeat important points. Workplace listening is more challenging because information is often exchanged casually. It may be disorganized, unclear, and cluttered with extraneous facts. Moreover, your fellow workers are usually friends. Because they are familiar with one another, they may not be as polite and respectful as they are with strangers. Friends tend to interrupt, jump to conclusions, and take each other for granted.

Listening in groups or listening to nonnative speakers further complicates the listening process. In groups, more than one person talks at once, and topics change rapidly. Group members are monitoring both verbal and nonverbal messages to learn what relates to their group roles. Listening to nonnative speakers often creates special challenges. The accompanying Career Coach box offers suggestions for improving communication between native and nonnative speakers. Chapter 3 presents more suggestions for communicating across cultures.

Ten Keys to Building Powerful Listening Skills

Despite the complexities and challenges of workplace listening, good listeners on the job must remember that their goal is to listen carefully and to *understand* what is being said so that they can do their work well. The following recommendations can help you improve your workplace listening effectiveness.

1. **Control external and internal distractions.** Move to an area where you can hear without conflicting noises or conversations. Block out surrounding physical distractions. Internally, try to focus totally on the speaker. If other projects are on your mind, put them on the back burner temporarily. When you are emotionally charged, whether angry or extremely happy, it is a good idea to postpone any serious listening.

2. **Become actively involved.** Show that you are listening closely by leaning forward and maintaining eye contact with the speaker. Don't fidget or try to complete another task at the same time you are listening. Listen to more than the spoken words. How are they said? What implied meaning, reasoning, and feelings do you hear behind the spoken words? Does the speaker's body language (eye contact, posture, movements) support or contradict the main message?

3. **Separate facts from opinions.** Facts are truths known to exist; for example, *Microsoft is located in Redmond, Washington.* Opinions are statements of personal judgments or preferences; for example, *Microsoft stock is always a good investment.* Some opinions are easy to recognize because speakers preface them with statements such as, *I think, It seems to me,* and *As far as I'm concerned.*[45] Often, however, listeners must evaluate assertions to decide their validity. Good listeners consider whether speakers are credible and speaking within their areas of competence. They do not automatically accept assertions as facts.

Spotlight on Communicators

Celebrated talk show host Oprah Winfrey owes much of her success to the artful application of the simple process of listening and responding. "Communicating with people is how I always developed any kind of value about myself," said the most successful female entertainer in the world. On her show, she is able to block out external distractions, become actively involved, listen empathically without interrupting, paraphrase her guests' ideas, and ask clarifying questions to draw out deep meanings and issues that underlie their everyday lives.

© Evan Agostini / Getty Images

Chapter 2: Developing Team, Listening, and Etiquette Skills

4. **Identify important facts.** Speakers on the job often intersperse critical information with casual conversation. Unrelated topics pop up—ball scores, a customer's weird request, a computer glitch, the boss's extravagant new SUV. Your task is to select what's important and register it mentally. What step is next in your project? Who does what? What is your role?

5. **Avoid interrupting.** While someone else has the floor, do not interrupt with a quick reply or opinion. And don't show nonverbal disagreement such as negative head shaking, rolling eyes, sarcastic snorting, or audible sighs. Good listeners let speakers have their say. Interruptions are not only impolite, but they also prevent you from hearing the speaker's complete thought. Listeners who interrupt with their opinions sidetrack discussions and cause hard feelings.

6. **Ask clarifying questions.** Good listeners wait for the proper moment and then ask questions that do not attack the speaker. Instead of saying, "But I don't understand how you can say that," a good listener seeks clarification with questions such as, "Please help me understand by explaining more about. . . ." Because questions can put you in the driver's seat, think about them in advance. Use open questions (those without set answers) to draw out feelings, motivations, ideas, and suggestions. Use closed fact-finding questions to identify key factors in a discussion.[46] By the way, don't ask a question unless you are ready to be quiet and listen to the answer.

> You listen better when you refrain from interrupting, ask clarifying questions, paraphrase, capitalize on lag time, take notes, and observe gender differences.

CAREER COACH

Listening to Nonnative Speakers in the Workplace

Many workplaces today involve interaction between native and nonnative English speakers. As immigration increases and as local businesses expand into global markets, the chances are good that you will at times be listening to speakers for whom English is a second language. Although many speakers have studied English and comprehend it, they may have difficulty speaking it. Why? Vowels and consonants are pronounced differently. Learning the inflection and sentence patterns of English is difficult when they conflict with the speaker's native tongue. Most "errors" in pronunciation occur in meaningful patterns traced to their home languages.

Moreover, nonnative speakers are intimidated by the fluency of native speakers; therefore, they don't try to become fluent. They worry about using incorrect verb forms and tenses. They may be trying to translate thoughts from their own language word for word into the foreign language. Often, they spend so long thinking about how to express a thought that the conversation moves on. Many worry about being judged negatively and losing face. What can native speakers do to become better listeners when nonnatives speak?

- **Avoid negative judgment of accented speech.** Many nonnative speakers of English speak an articulate, insightful, and complex variety of English. Their speech may retain remnants of their native language. But don't assume that a nonnative speaker struggling with pronunciation is unintelligent. Instead, imagine how difficult it would be for you to learn that person's language.
- **Be patient.** Americans are notoriously poor listeners. Strive to overcome the need to hurry a conversation along. Give nonnative speakers time to express their thoughts.

- **Don't finish sentences.** Allow nonnative speakers to choose their words and complete their sentences without volunteering your help. You may find that they are saying something quite different from what you expected.
- **Don't correct grammar and pronunciation.** Although you are trying to "help" a nonnative speaker, it is better to focus on what's being expressed and forget about teaching English. As one company caller said, "If I could speak better English, I would already be doing it."
- **Don't pretend to understand.** It is perfectly all right to tell a speaker that you are having a little difficulty understanding him or her.
- **Practice listening to many varieties of English.** Improving your skill at comprehending many accents as well as native dialects (for example, Southern, Western, and Northeastern) can be a valuable skill in today's diverse and intercultural workplace.

Career Application
In a class forum, discuss these questions: How do you think nonnative speakers feel when they must converse with native speakers in a work environment? For nonnative speakers, what is most frustrating in conversation? For native speakers, what is awkward or frustrating in talking with nonnative speakers? What embarrassing moments have you experienced as a result of mispronunciations or misunderstandings? What suggestions can native and nonnative speakers make for improving communication?

7. **Paraphrase to increase understanding.** To make sure you understand a speaker, rephrase and summarize a message in your own words. Be objective and nonjudgmental. Remember, your goal is to understand what the speaker has said—not to show how mindless the speaker's words sound when parroted. Remember, too, that other workplace listeners will also benefit from a clear summary of what was said.

8. **Capitalize on lag time.** While you are waiting for a speaker's next idea, use the time to review what the speaker is saying. Separate the central idea, key points, and details. Sometimes you may have to supply the organization. Use lag time to silently rephrase and summarize the speaker's message. Another effective trick for keeping your mind from drifting is to try to guess what a speaker's next point will be. Most important, keep your mind focused on the speaker and his or her ideas—not on all the other work waiting for you.

9. **Take notes to ensure retention.** Do not trust your memory. A wise person once said that he'd rather have a short pencil than a long memory. If you have a hallway conversation with a colleague and don't have a pencil handy, make a mental note of the important items. Then write them down as soon as possible. Even with seemingly easily remembered facts or instructions, jot them down to ease your mind and also to be sure you understand them correctly. Two weeks later you will be glad you did. Be sure you have a good place to store notes of various projects, such as file folders, notebooks, or computer files.

10. **Be aware of gender differences.** Men tend to listen for facts, whereas women tend to perceive listening as an opportunity to connect with the other person on a personal level.[47] Men tend to use interrupting behavior to control conversations, while women generally interrupt to communicate assent, to elaborate on an idea of another group member, or to participate in the topic of conversation. Women listeners tend to be attentive, provide steady eye contact, remain stationary, and nod their heads.[48] Male listeners are less attentive, provide sporadic eye contact, and move around. Being aware of these tendencies will make you a more sensitive and knowledgeable listener. To learn more about gender differences in communication, see the Career Coach box in Chapter 3.

Checklist

Improving Listening

✓ **Stop talking.** Accept the role of listener by concentrating on the speaker's words, not on what your response will be.

✓ **Work hard at listening.** Become actively involved; expect to learn something.

✓ **Block out competing thoughts.** Concentrate on the message. Don't allow yourself to daydream during lag time.

✓ **Control the listening environment.** Move to a quiet area where you won't be interrupted by telephone calls or visitors. Check to be certain that listeners can hear speakers.

✓ **Maintain an open mind.** Know your biases and try to correct for them. Be tolerant of less-abled and different-looking speakers. Provide verbal and nonverbal feedback. Encourage the speaker with comments such as, "Yes," "I see," "OK," and "Uh huh," and ask polite questions. Look alert by leaning forward.

✓ **Paraphrase the speaker's ideas.** Silently repeat the message in your own words, sort out the main points, and identify supporting details. In conversation sum up the main points to confirm what was said.

✓ **Listen between the lines.** Observe nonverbal cues and interpret the feelings of the speaker: What is really being said?

✓ **Distinguish between facts and opinions.** Know the difference between factual statements and opinions stated as assertions.

✓ **Capitalize on lag time.** Use spare moments to organize, review, anticipate, challenge, and weigh the evidence.

✓ **Use memory devices.** If the information is important, develop acronyms, links, or rhymes to help you remember.

✓ **Take selective notes.** If you are hearing instructions or important data, record the major points; then, revise your notes immediately or verify them with the speaker.

Communicating Through Nonverbal Messages

Understanding messages often involves more than merely listening to spoken words. Nonverbal cues also carry powerful meanings. Nonverbal communication includes all unwritten and unspoken messages, both intentional and unintentional. Eye contact, facial expression, body movements, space, time, distance, appearance—all of these nonverbal cues influence the way a message is interpreted, or decoded, by the receiver. Many of the nonverbal messages that we send are used intentionally to accompany spoken words. When Stacy pounds her desk and shouts "This computer just crashed again!" we interpret the loudness of her voice and the act of slamming her fist as intentional emphasis of her words. But people can also communicate nonverbally even when they don't intend to. What's more, not all messages accompany words. When Jeff hangs on to the rostrum and barely looks at the audience during his presentation, he sends a nonverbal message of fear and lack of confidence.

Because nonverbal communication is an important tool for you to use and control in the workplace, you need to learn more about its functions and forms.

LEARNING OBJECTIVE 6
Understand the forms of nonverbal communication and how they can be used to advance your career.

Functions of Nonverbal Communication

Nonverbal communication helps to convey meaning in at least five ways. As you become more aware of the following functions of nonverbal communication, you will be better able to use these silent codes to your advantage in the workplace.

- **To complement and illustrate.** Nonverbal messages can amplify, modify, or provide details for a verbal message. For example, in describing the size of a cell phone, a speaker holds his fingers apart 5 inches. In pumping up sales reps, the manager jams his fist into the opposite hand to indicate the strong effort required.

- **To reinforce and accentuate.** Skilled speakers raise their voices to convey important ideas, but they whisper to suggest secrecy. A grimace forecasts painful news, whereas a big smile intensifies good news. A neat, well-equipped office reinforces a message of professionalism.

- **To replace and substitute.** Many gestures substitute for words: nodding your head for "yes," giving a V for victory, making a thumbs-up sign for approval, and shrugging your shoulders for "I don't know" or "I don't care." In fact, a complex set of gestures totally replaces spoken words in sign language.

- **To control and regulate.** Nonverbal messages are important regulators in conversation. Shifts in eye contact, slight head movements, changes in posture, raising of eyebrows, nodding of the head, and voice inflection—all of these cues tell speakers when to continue, to repeat, to elaborate, to hurry up, or to finish.

- **To contradict.** To be sarcastic, a speaker might hold his nose while stating that your new perfume is wonderful. During one presidential debate, a candidate was seriously attacking his opponent's "fuzzy" math. The other candidate smiled and winked at the audience. His body language contradicted the attack being made by his opponent. In the workplace, individuals may send contradictory messages with words or actions. The boss, for example, says he wants to promote Kevin, but he fails to submit the necessary recommendation.

Communicators use nonverbal cues to complement and illustrate, to reinforce and accentuate, to replace and substitute, and to control and regulate.

In the workplace people may not be aware that they are sending contradictory messages. Researchers have found that when verbal and nonverbal messages contradict each other, listeners tend to believe and act on the nonverbal message. How would you interpret the following?

- Brenda assures her boss that she has enough time to complete her assigned research, but she misses two deadlines.

Spotlight on Communicators

Some cultures are better at listening and interpreting nonverbal messages than others, says Robert Rosen, psychologist, cross-cultural consultant, and author of *Global Literacies*. In their high-context, nonverbal culture, the Japanese, for example, have developed a special skill for listening deeply. Germans, on the other hand, are better at verbal clues. Westerners in general, Rosen contends, are good verbal communicators. Easterners are good at the nonverbal. The challenge is to learn the skill of the other.

© Courtesy of Healthy Companies International

- Tyler protests that he's not really angry but slams the door when he leaves a group meeting.
- Kyoko claims she's not nervous about a team presentation, but her brow is furrowed and she perspires profusely.

The nonverbal messages in these situations speak louder than the words uttered. In one experiment speakers delivered a positive message but averted their eyes as they spoke. Listeners perceived the overall message to be negative. Moreover, listeners thought that gaze aversion suggested nonaffection, superficiality, lack of trust, and nonreceptivity.[49] The lesson to be learned here is that effective communicators must be certain that all their nonverbal messages reinforce their spoken words and their professional goals. To make sure that you're on the right track to nonverbal communication competency, let's look more carefully at the specific forms of nonverbal communication.

Forms of Nonverbal Communication

Instead of conveying meaning with words, nonverbal messages carry their meaning in a number of different forms ranging from facial expressions to body language and even clothes. Each of us sends and receives thousands of nonverbal messages daily in our business and personal lives. Although the following discussion covers all forms of nonverbal communication, we will be especially concerned with workplace applications. As you learn about the messages sent by eye contact, facial expressions, posture, gestures, as well as the use of time, space, territory, and appearance—think about how you can use these nonverbal cues positively in your career.

Eye Contact. The eyes have been called the "windows to the soul." Even if communicators can't look directly into the soul, they consider the eyes to be the most accurate predictor of a speaker's true feelings and attitudes. Most of us cannot look another person straight in the eyes and lie. As a result, we tend to believe people who look directly at us. We have less confidence in and actually distrust those who cannot maintain eye contact. Sustained eye contact suggests trust and admiration; brief eye contact signifies fear or stress. Prolonged eye contact, however, can be intrusive and intimidating. One successful CEO says that he can tell from people's eyes whether they are focused, receptive, or distant. He also notes the frequency of eye blinks when judging a person's honesty.[50]

Good eye contact enables the message sender to determine whether a receiver is paying attention, showing respect, responding favorably, or feeling distress. From the receiver's perspective good eye contact reveals the speaker's sincerity, confidence, and truthfulness. Because eye contact is a learned skill, however, you must be respectful of people who do not maintain it. You must also remember that nonverbal cues, including eye contact, have different meanings in various cultures. Chapter 3 presents more information about the cultural influence of nonverbal cues.

Facial Expression. The expression on a communicator's face can be almost as revealing of emotion as the eyes. Researchers estimate that the human face can display over 250,000 expressions.[51] Although a few people can control these expressions and maintain a "poker face" when they want to hide their feelings, most of us display our emotions openly. Raising or lowering the eyebrows, squinting the eyes, swallowing nervously, clenching the jaw, smiling broadly—these voluntary and involuntary facial expressions supplement or entirely replace verbal messages. In the workplace, maintaining a pleasant expression with frequent smiles promotes harmony.

Posture and Gestures. An individual's general posture can convey anything from high status and self-confidence to shyness and submissiveness. Leaning toward a speaker suggests attraction and interest; pulling away or shrinking back denotes fear, distrust, anxiety, or disgust. Similarly, gestures can communicate entire thoughts via simple movements. But remember that these nonverbal cues may have vastly different meanings in different cultures. An individual who signals success by forming the thumb and forefinger into a circle would be in deep trouble in Germany or parts of South America. The harmless OK sign is actually an obscene reference in those areas.[52]

In the workplace you can make a good impression by controlling your posture and gestures. When speaking, make sure your upper body is aligned with the person to whom you're talking. Erect posture sends a message of confidence, competence, diligence, and strength. During the Microsoft antitrust trial, CEO Bill Gates slouched in his chair and rocked back and forth as he pondered questions and responded. Body language experts thought his childlike, rhythmic rocking did not help his case.[53] Women are advised to avoid tilting their heads to the side when making an important point. This gesture diminishes the main thrust of the message.[54]

Time. How we structure and use time tells observers about our personality and attitudes. For example, when Maritza Perez, a banking executive, gives a visitor a prolonged interview, she signals her respect for, interest in, and approval of the visitor or the topic being discussed. By sharing her valuable time, she sends a clear nonverbal message. Likewise, when David Ing twice arrives late for a meeting, it could mean that the meeting has low priority to David, that he is a self-centered person, or that he has little self-discipline. These are assumptions that typical Americans might make. In other cultures and regions, though, punctuality is viewed differently. In the workplace you can send positive nonverbal messages by being on time for meetings and appointments, staying on task during meetings, and giving ample time to appropriate projects and individuals.

Being on time sends a positive nonverbal message in North American workplaces.

Space. How we arrange things in the space around us tells something about ourselves and our objectives. Whether the space is a dorm room, an office, or a department, people reveal themselves in the design and grouping of furniture within that space. Generally, the more formal the arrangement, the more formal and closed the communication environment. An executive who seats visitors in a row of chairs across from his desk sends a message of aloofness and desire for separation. A team leader who arranges chairs informally in a circle rather than in straight rows or a rectangular pattern conveys her desire for a more open, egalitarian exchange of ideas. A manager who creates an open office space with few partitions separating workers' desks seeks to encourage an unrestricted flow of communication and work among areas.

The way an office is arranged can send nonverbal messages about the openness of its occupant.

Territory. Each of us has certain areas that we feel are our own territory, whether it is a specific spot or just the space around us. Your father may have a favorite chair in which he is most comfortable, a cook might not tolerate intruders in her kitchen, and veteran employees may feel that certain work areas and tools belong to them. We all maintain zones of privacy in which we feel comfortable. Figure 2.7 categorizes the four zones of social interaction among Americans, as formulated by anthropologist Edward T. Hall. Notice that we North Americans are a bit standoffish; only intimate friends and family may stand closer than about 1½ feet. If someone violates that territory, we feel uncomfortable and defensive and may step back to reestablish our space. A classic episode in the *Seinfeld* TV program aptly described a close-talker as a "space invader."[55] In the workplace be aware of the territorial needs of others and don't invade their space.

FIGURE 2.7 Four Space Zones for Social Interaction

Intimate Zone
(1 to 1½ feet)

Personal Zone
(1½ to 4 feet)

Social Zone
(4 to 12 feet)

Public Zone
(12 or more feet)

Your appearance and the appearance of your documents convey nonverbal messages.

Appearance of Business Documents.

The way a letter, memo, or report looks can have either a positive or a negative effect on the receiver. Envelopes through their postage, stationery, and printing can suggest routine, important, or junk mail. Letters and reports can look neat, professional, well organized, and attractive—or just the opposite. Sloppy, hurriedly written documents convey negative nonverbal messages regarding both the content and the sender. Among the worst offenders are e-mail messages.

Although they seem like conversation, e-mails are business documents that create a permanent record and often a bad impression. Sending an e-mail message full of errors conveys a damaging nonverbal message. It says that the writer doesn't care enough about this message to take the time to make it read well or look good. The receiver immediately doubts the credibility of the sender. How much faith can you put in someone who can't spell, capitalize, or punctuate and won't make the effort to communicate clearly?

In succeeding chapters you will learn how to create documents that send positive nonverbal messages through their appearance, format, organization, readability, and correctness.

Viewers judge a person's status, credibility, personality, and potential on the nonverbal message sent by that person's appearance.

Appearance of People.

The way you look—your clothing, grooming, and posture—telegraphs an instant nonverbal message about you. Based on what they see, viewers make quick judgments about your status, credibility, personality, and potential. Business communicators who look the part are more likely to be successful in working with superiors, colleagues, and customers. Because appearance is such a powerful force in business, some aspiring professionals are turning for help to image consultants (who charge up to $500 an hour!).

What do image consultants say? They suggest investing in appropriate, professional-looking clothing and accessories. Remember that quality is more important than quantity. Avoid flashy garments, clunky jewelry, garish makeup, and overpowering colognes. Pay

CAREER COACH

Perils of Casual Apparel in the Workplace

Your choice of work clothes sends a strong nonverbal message about you. It also affects the way you work. Some surveys suggest that the pendulum is swinging back to more conservative attire in the workplace,[56] although employers and employees have mixed feelings about what to wear to work.

WHAT CRITICS ARE SAYING

Some employers oppose casual dress because, in their opinion, too many workers push the boundaries of what is acceptable. They contend that absenteeism, tardiness, and flirtatious behavior have increased since dress-down policies began to be implemented. Relaxed dress codes also lead to reduced productivity and lax behavior. Image counselor Judith Rasband claimed that the general casualization of America has resulted in an overall decline in civility. "Manners break down, you begin to feel down, and you're not as effective," she said.[57] Others fear that the authority and credibility of casually attired executives, particularly females and minorities, are undermined.[58] Moreover, customers are often turned off by casually attired employees.[59]

WHAT SUPPORTERS ARE SAYING

Supporters argue that comfortable clothes and relaxed working environments lift employee morale, increase employee creativity, and improve internal communication. Employees appreciate reduced clothing-related expenses, while employers use casual dress as a recruitment and retention tool. Because employees seem to love casual dress, nine out of ten employers have adopted casual-dress days for at least part of the workweek—even if it is just on Fridays during the summer.

WHAT EMPLOYEES NEED TO KNOW

The following suggestions, gleaned from surveys and articles about casual-dress trends in the workplace, can help future and current employees avoid casual-dress blunders.

- For job interviews, dress conservatively or call ahead to ask the interviewer or the receptionist what is appropriate.
- Find out what your company allows. Ask whether a dress-down policy is available. Observe what others are wearing on casual-dress days.
- If your company has no casual-dress policy, volunteer to work with management to develop relevant guidelines, including illustrations of suitable casual attire.
- Avoid wearing the following items: T-shirts, sandals, flip-flops, sockless shoes, backless dresses, tank tops, shorts, miniskirts, spandex, athletic shoes, hiking boots, baseball caps, and visors.[60]
- When meeting customers, dress as well as or better than they do.

Career Application

In small groups or in your full class, debate the following proposition: *Resolved: That business casual dress be made the dress standard throughout the United States.* Think of arguments beyond those presented here. Your instructor will provide details for arranging the debate.

FIGURE 2.8 Sending Positive Nonverbal Signals in the Workplace

Eye contact	Maintain direct but not prolonged eye contact.
Facial expression	Express warmth with frequent smiles.
Posture	Convey self-confidence with erect stance.
Gestures	Suggest accessibility with open-palm gestures.
Time	Be on time; use time judiciously.
Space	Maintain neat, functional work areas.
Territory	Use closeness to show warmth and to reduce status differences.
Business documents	Produce careful, neat, professional, well-organized messages.
Appearance	Be well groomed, neat, and appropriately dressed.

© Jon Feingersh / Blend Images / Getty Images

attention to good grooming, including a neat hairstyle, body cleanliness, polished shoes, and clean nails. Project confidence in your posture, both standing and sitting.

One of the latest fashion rages is body art in the form of tattoos. Once seen primarily on bikers and sailors, inked images such as butterflies, bluebirds, spiders, and angels increasingly adorn the bodies of those who seek to be glamorous. Think twice, however, before displaying "tatts" at work. They may make a person feel distinctive and slightly daring, but they could derail a professional career.

A less risky trend is the movement toward one or more days per week of casual dress at work. Be aware, though, that casual clothes change the image you project and also may affect your work style. See the Career Coach box on page 58 regarding the pros and cons of casual apparel.

In the preceding discussion of nonverbal communication, you learned that each of us gives and responds to thousands of nonverbal messages daily in our personal and work lives. You can harness the power of silent messages by reviewing Figure 2.8 and by studying the tips in the following checklist.

Checklist

Techniques for Improving Nonverbal Communication Skills in the Workplace

✓ **Establish and maintain eye contact.** Remember that in the United States and Canada appropriate eye contact signals interest, attentiveness, strength, and credibility.

✓ **Use posture to show interest.** Encourage communication interaction by leaning forward, sitting or standing erect, and looking alert.

✓ **Reduce or eliminate physical barriers.** Move out from behind a desk or lectern; arrange meeting chairs in a circle.

✓ **Improve your decoding skills.** Watch facial expressions and body language to understand the complete verbal and nonverbal message being communicated.

✓ **Probe for more information.** When you perceive nonverbal cues that contradict verbal meanings, politely seek additional clues (*I'm not sure I understand, Please tell me more about . . .*, or *Do you mean that . . .*).

✓ **Avoid assigning nonverbal meanings out of context.** Make nonverbal assessments only when you understand a situation or a culture.

✓ **Associate with people from diverse cultures.** Learn about other cultures to widen your knowledge and tolerance of intercultural nonverbal messages.

✓ **Appreciate the power of appearance.** Keep in mind that the appearance of your business documents, your business space, and yourself send immediate positive or negative messages to others.

✓ **Observe yourself on videotape.** Ensure that your verbal and nonverbal messages are in sync by taping and evaluating yourself making a presentation.

✓ **Enlist friends and family.** Ask friends and family members to monitor your conscious and unconscious body movements and gestures to help you become a more effective communicator.

Developing a Competitive Edge With Professionalism and Business Etiquette Skills

Good manners and a businesslike, professional demeanor are among the soft skills that employers seek in job candidates. Employers are far more likely to hire and promote someone who is courteous and professional than one who lacks these skills and traits. But can you really learn how to be courteous, civil, and professional? Of course! This section gives you a few pointers.

Professionalism Leads to Success

Projecting and maintaining a professional image is key to getting hired and being promoted.

Not everyone who seeks a job is aware of the employer's expectations. Some new-hires have no idea that excessive absenteeism or tardiness are grounds for termination. Others are surprised to learn that they are expected to devote their full attention to their duties when on the job. One young man wanted to read *Harry Potter* novels when things got slow. Many employees don't realize that they are sabotaging their careers when they sprinkle their conversation with *like, you know,* and uptalk (making declarative statements sound like questions). Projecting and maintaining a professional image can make a real difference in helping you obtain the job of your dreams. Once you get that job, you are more likely to be taken seriously and much more likely to be promoted if you look and sound professional. Do not send the wrong message with unwitting or unprofessional behavior. Figure 2.9 reviews six areas you will want to check to be sure you are projecting professionalism.

FIGURE 2.9 Projecting Professionalism When You Communicate

	Unprofessional	Professional
Speech habits	Speaking in *uptalk,* a singsong speech pattern that has a rising inflection making sentences sound like questions; using *like* to fill in mindless chatter, substituting *go* for *said,* relying on slang, or letting profanity slip into your conversation.	Recognizing that your credibility can be seriously damaged by sounding uneducated, crude, or adolescent.
E-mail	Writing messages with incomplete sentences, misspelled words, exclamation points, IM slang, and senseless chatting. Sloppy, careless messages send a nonverbal message that you don't care, don't know, or aren't smart enough to know what is correct.	Employers like to see subjects, verbs, and punctuation marks. They don't recognize IM abbreviations. Call it crazy, but they value conciseness and correct spelling, even in brief e-mail messages.
Internet	Using an e-mail address such as *hotbabe@hotmail.com, supasnugglykitty@yahoo.com,* or *buffedguy@aol.com.*	An e-mail address should include your name or a relevant, positive, businesslike expression. It should not sound cute or like a chat room nickname.
Voice mail	An outgoing message with strident background music, weird sounds, or a joke message.	An outgoing message that states your name or phone number and provides instructions for leaving a message.
Telephone	Soap operas, thunderous music, or a TV football game playing noisily in the background when you answer the phone.	A quiet background when you answer the telephone, especially if you are expecting a prospective employer's call.
Cell and smart phones	Taking or placing calls during business meetings or during conversations with fellow employees; raising your voice (cell yell) or engaging in cell calls when others must reluctantly overhear; using a PDA during meetings.	Turning off phone and message notification, both audible and vibrate, during meetings; using your cell only when conversations can be private.

Gaining an Etiquette Edge

Etiquette, civility, and goodwill efforts may seem out of place in today's fast-paced, high-tech offices. However, an awareness of courtesy and etiquette can give you a competitive edge in the job market. When two candidates have equal qualifications, the one who appears to be more polished and professional is more likely to be hired and promoted.

Being courteous and well-mannered gives you a competitive edge in being hired and promoted.

As workloads increase and face-to-face meetings decline, bad manners and incivility are becoming alarmingly common in the American workplace.[61] One survey showed that 71 percent of workers said they had been insulted, demeaned, ignored, or otherwise treated discourteously by their coworkers and superiors.[62] Employers, of course, suffer from the resulting drop in productivity and exodus of talent. Employees, too, suffer. They worry about incidents, think about changing jobs, and cut back their efforts on the job. It is not hard to understand why employers are looking for people who are courteous, polite, respectful, and well-mannered.

Good manners convey a positive image of an organization. People like to do business with those who show respect and treat others civilly. Most of us also like to work in a pleasant environment. Considering how much time is spent at work, you realize that it makes sense that people prefer an agreeable environment to one that is rude and uncivil.

Etiquette is more about attitude than about formal rules of behavior. That attitude is a desire to show others consideration and respect. It includes a desire to make others feel comfortable. You don't have to become an etiquette nut, but you might need to polish your social competencies a little to be an effective businessperson today. Here are a few simple pointers:

Etiquette involves a desire to show others consideration and respect.

- **Use polite words.** Be generous with words and phrases such as *please, thank you,* and *you're welcome.*

- **Express sincere appreciation and praise.** Tell coworkers how much you appreciate their efforts. Remember that written thank-you notes are even better than saying thanks.

- **Be selective in sharing personal information.** Avoid talking about health concerns, personal relationships, or finances in the office.

- **Don't put people down.** If you have a reputation for criticizing people, your coworkers will begin to wonder what you are saying behind their backs.

- **Respect coworkers' space.** Turn down the ringer on your business phone, minimize the use of speakerphones, and turn your personal cell phone down or off during business hours. Avoid wearing heavy perfumes or bringing strong-smelling food.

- **Rise above others' rudeness.** Don't use profanity or participate in questionable joke telling.

- **Be considerate when sharing space and equipment with others.** Clean up after yourself.

- **Choose the high road in conflict.** Avoid letting discussions degenerate into shouting matches. Keep a calm voice tone and focus on the work rather than on personality differences.

- **Disagree agreeably.** You may not agree with everyone, but you should respect their opinions.

Look for *Dr. Guffey's Guide to Business Etiquette and Workplace Manners* at **www.meguffey .com.** You will find the author's tips on topics such as networking manners, coping with cubicles, managers' manners, business gifts, dealing with angry customers, and gender-free etiquette.

Communicating at Work Your Turn

Applying Your Skills at Toyota

While its peers are losing ground, Toyota continues to grow and could soon be the world's largest and most profitable automotive manufacturer. As it opens assembly plants in diverse locations such as the Czech Republic and China, it faces challenges in educating new associates about The Toyota Way. "The people element is of huge importance to us," says Sarah Fisher, Toyota's human resources director in the United Kingdom. "The strength of our staff is related to the core values of the organization, which is translated into The Toyota Way. There's a real emphasis on teamwork and being a learning organization."

Fisher was responsible for implementing The Toyota Way in the UK. All staff members received a printed brochure explaining The Toyota Way. Senior managers attended the Toyota Institute for training in how to integrate The Toyota Way into the workplace and to present the program to their employees.[63]

Your Task

As a member of Sarah Fisher's implementation team, you attended the Toyota Institute and learned how to conduct training sessions

in The Toyota Way. Now it is your turn to train other managers to introduce The Toyota Way. You will be holding a series of meetings for these managers. One of the most important skills for team leaders and members is staging successful meetings. Prepare a bulleted list outlining guidelines for effective meetings. Because managers will be conducting the meetings, focus on the tasks of team leaders. Summarize how a team leader should prepare for team meetings, conduct meetings, and follow up after meetings. Your list should have at least 15 bulleted items. (See page 154 in Chapter 6 for instructions on making numbered and bulleted lists.)

Summary of Learning Objectives

1 **Recognize the importance of soft skills and teamwork in today's workplace.** Employers seek workers who have strong communication, team, listening, nonverbal, and etiquette skills. Team skills are especially important because many organizations are forming teams in today's competitive, fast-paced, global economy. Virtual teams are groups of people who work independently with a shared purpose across space, time, and organization boundaries using technology. Teams typically go through four stages of development: forming, storming, norming, and performing. Some teams never reach the performing stage; however, when they do, information flows freely, deadlines are met, and production exceeds expectations.

2 **Understand how to contribute positively to team performance, including resolving workplace conflicts, avoiding groupthink, and reaching group decisions.** Team members can contribute positively if they abide by team rules, analyze tasks in problem solving, offer ideas, stimulate discussion, listen actively, show interest in others' ideas, praise others, and move the group toward its goal. In resolving conflict, team members should listen, understand the other's point of view, show a concern for the relationship, look for common ground, invent new problem-solving options, and reach an agreement that is fair. Open discussion of conflict prevents *groupthink,* a condition that leads to faulty decisions. Methods for reaching group decisions include majority, consensus, minority, averaging, and authority rule with discussion. Successful teams are small, diverse, and able to agree on their purpose, procedures, and method of conflict resolution. They use good communication techniques, collaborate rather than compete, accept ethical responsibilities, and share leadership.

3 **Plan and participate in productive meetings.** Effective meetings are called only when urgent two-way communication is necessary. Leaders should limit participation to those directly involved. Leaders should start the meeting on time and keep the discussion on track. Conflict should be confronted openly by letting each person present his or her views fully before having the group decide which direction to take. Leaders should summarize what was said, end the meeting on time, and distribute minutes afterwards. To participate actively, attendees should arrive early, come prepared, bring a positive attitude, and contribute respectfully. They should wait for others to finish, use calm and pleasant voices, give credit to others, avoid using cell phones and laptops, help summarize the discussion, express views IN the meeting (not afterward), and follow up by completing assigned actions.

4 **Explain the usefulness of collaborative technologies such as voice conferencing, videoconferencing, Web conferencing, instant messaging, blogs, and wikis.** *Voice conferencing* enables one or more people in a work area to use an enhanced speakerphone to confer with others by telephone. *Videoconferencing* combines video, audio, and communications networking technologies for real-time interaction in special viewing rooms. *Web conferencing* enables participants to stay in their offices using their computers while presenting slides and sharing documents in a virtual real-time meeting. Participants can talk to each other through a conference call. *Instant messaging* is useful for fast back-and-forth online conversations. *Blogs* are a type of interactive online journal that allows collaborators to share information in one central location. Because blogs are Web-based documents, they can be archived and searched, thus making information permanently accessible. *Wikis* are collaborative Web sites that enable anyone with access to add, change, or delete information.

5 **Describe and implement active listening techniques.** Experts say that we listen at only 25 percent efficiency. While listening to superiors on the job, take selective notes, avoid interrupting, ask pertinent questions, and paraphrase what you hear. When listening to colleagues and teammates, listen critically to recognize facts and listen discriminately to identify main ideas and to understand logical arguments. When listening to customers, defer judgment, pay attention to content rather than form, listen completely, control emotions, give affirming statements, and invite additional comments. Keys to building powerful listening skills include controlling external and internal distractions, becoming actively involved, separating facts from opinions, identifying important facts, refraining from interrupting, asking clarifying questions, paraphrasing, taking advantage of lag time, taking notes to ensure retention, and being aware of gender differences.

6 **Understand the forms of nonverbal communication and how they can be used to advance your career.** Nonverbal communication includes all unwritten and unspoken messages, both intentional and unintentional. Nonverbal communication takes many forms including eye contract, facial expressions, posture and gestures, as well as the use of time, space, and territory. To improve your nonverbal skills, establish and maintain eye contact, use posture to show interest, reduce or eliminate physical barriers, improve your decoding skills, probe for more information, avoid assigning nonverbal meanings out of context, associate with people from diverse cultures, appreciate the power of appearance, observe yourself on videotape, and enlist friends and family to monitor your conscious and unconscious body movements and gestures.

7 **Develop a competitive edge with professionalism and business etiquette skills.** You are more likely to be hired and promoted if you project professionalism in the workplace. This includes avoiding speech habits that make you sound uneducated, crude, or adolescent. Professionalism also is reflected in careful e-mail messages, a businesslike e-mail address, as well as good voice mail, cell phone, and telephone manners. To gain a competitive etiquette edge, use polite words, express sincere appreciation and praise, be selective in sharing personal information with work colleagues, avoid criticizing people, respect coworkers' space, rise above others' rudeness, be considerate when sharing space, choose the high road in conflict, and disagree agreeably.

Chapter Review

1. List five "soft" skills requested by employers, and explain why these skills are important in today's workplace. (Obj. 1)

2. What are the four phases of team development? Is it best to move through the stages quickly? Why or why not? (Obj. 1)

3. Compare and contrast positive and negative team behavior. (Obj. 2)

4. What is *groupthink?* (Obj. 2)

5. Why are team decisions based on consensus generally better than decisions reached by majority rule? (Obj. 2)

6. When groups or teams meet, what are seven ground rules they should begin with? (Obj. 3)

7. List five behaviors you consider most important in participating actively in organizational meetings. (Obj. 3)

8. How is videoconferencing different from Web conferencing? (Obj. 4)

9. What are blogs and wikis, how do they differ, and why are they valuable to collaborators? (Obj. 4)

10. According to experts, we ignore, forget, distort, or misunderstand 75 percent of everything we hear. Why are we such poor listeners? (Obj. 5)

11. What are ten techniques for improving workplace listening? Be prepared to describe each. (Obj. 5)

12. List five functions of nonverbal communication. Provide an original example of each. (Obj. 6)

13. List ten techniques for improving nonverbal communication skills in the workplace. Be prepared to discuss each. (Obj. 6)

14. Compare and contrast examples of professional and unprofessional behavior in regard to workplace speech habits and e-mail. (Obj. 7)

15. What five specific behaviors do you think would be most important in giving you an etiquette edge in your business career? (Obj. 7)

Critical Thinking

1. Evaluate the following statement: "Technical proficiency has never been enough for professionals to grow beyond the staff level."[64] Do you agree or disagree, and why? (Obj. 1)

2. Compare and contrast the advantages and disadvantages of using teams in today's workplace. (Obj. 2)

3. Why do executives and managers spend more time listening than do workers? (Obj. 5)

4. What arguments could you give for or against the idea that body language is a science with principles that can be interpreted accurately by specialists? (Obj. 6)

5. **Ethical Issue:** Tim, a member of your workplace team, talks too much, hogs the limelight, and frequently strays from the target topic. In an important meeting he announces, "Hey, I want you all to listen up. I've got this cool new idea, and you're gonna love it!" Is it unethical for you to tune Tim out based on your past experience with his digressions? You want to sigh deeply and shout, "Not again!" You're inclined to slump in your chair, slam your notebook down on the table, and stop taking notes.
What is your ethical responsibility? What nonverbal message should you send?

Activities

2.1 Soft Skills: Checking Job Ads (Obj. 1)

> Web

What soft skills do employers request when they list job openings in your field?

Your Task. Check job listings in your field at an online job board. Visit a job board such as Monster, College Recruiter, Career Builder, or Yahoo Top Jobs. Follow the instructions to search job categories and locations. Study many job listings in your field. Then prepare a list of the most frequently requested soft skills in your field. Next to each item on the list, indicate how well you think you would qualify for the skill or trait mentioned. Your instructor may ask you to submit your findings and/or report to the class. If you are not satisfied with the job selection at any job site, choose another job board.

2.2 Going It Alone or Making It a Team Effort at Timberland (Obj. 2)

He introduces himself as a New Hampshire bootmaker, but Timberland CEO Jeffrey B. Swartz is much more. Although he heads a fast-rising company that produces boots and sportswear, he is strongly committed to civic responsibility and employee involvement.

Fortune magazine consistently ranks Timberland as one of the 100 best companies to work for in America. With the zeal of a missionary, the enthusiastic, fast-talking Swartz travels extensively, preaching the power of volunteerism among the 200 Timberland stores and factories.[65]

Your Task. Let's say that you work for Timberland, and Swartz asks you to organize an extensive volunteer program using Timberland employees. The program involves much planning and cooperation to be successful. You are flattered that he respects you and thinks that you are capable of completing the task. But you think that a team could do a better job than an individual. What arguments would you use to convince him that a team could work better than a single person?

2.3 Reaching Group Decisions: Which Method? (Obj. 2)

> Team

Your Task. In small groups decide which decision strategy is best for the following situations:

a. Company employees numbering 900 or more must decide whether to adopt a floating holiday plan proposed by management or stay with the current plan. An up-or-down vote is required.

b. The owner of your company is meeting with all managers to decide which departments will be allowed to move into a new facility.

c. Appointed by management, an employee team is charged with making recommendations regarding casual Fridays. Management feels that too many employees are abusing the privilege.

d. The owner of your company is meeting with all managers to decide which departments will be allowed to move into a new facility.

e. Members of a business club must decide which members will become officers.

f. An employee committee of three members (two supervisors and the manager) must decide on promotions within a department.

g. The human resources department of a large company must work with employees to hammer out a new benefits package within its budget.

h. A group of town officials and volunteers must decide how to organize a town Web site. Only a few members have technical expertise.

2.4 Resolving Workplace Conflicts: Apply a Plan (Obj. 2)

Team

Although conflict is a normal part of every workplace, if unresolved, it can create hard feelings and reduce productivity.

Your Task. Analyze the following scenarios. In teams, discuss each scenario and apply the six-step procedure for dealing with conflict described in this chapter. Choose two of the scenarios to role-play, with two of your team members taking roles.

a. A company policy manual is posted and updated at the company intranet, an internal Web site. Employees must sign that they have read and understand the manual. A conflict arises when one team member insists that employees should sign electronically. Another team member thinks that a paper form should be signed by employees so that better records may be kept.

b. Domino's Pizza adopted new uniforms, called "Domino's Gear." The new outfits include colorful polo shirts with side vents so that the shirts could be worn tucked in or out. Crewneck shirts, page-boy hats, and denim caps provided a number of options to employees. Considered a perk, the new uniforms were immediately worn by all employees at the company-owned Domino's units. Owners of two franchised units, however, preferred the old uniforms with traditional polo shirts and khakis. What's more, the old uniforms required no new investment in clothing.

c. Two management team members disagree on a new company e-mail policy. One wants to ban personal e-mail totally. The other thinks that an outright ban is impossible to implement. He is more concerned with limiting Internet misuse, including visits to online game, pornography, and shopping sites. The management team members agree that they need an e-mail policy, but they disagree on what to allow and what to prohibit.

d. A manager and his assistant plan to attend a conference together at a resort location. Six weeks before the conference, the company announces a cutback and limits conference support to only one person. The assistant, who has developed a presentation specifically for the conference, feels that he should be the one to attend. Travel arrangements must be made immediately.

e. Customer service rep Jackie comes to work one morning and finds Alexa sitting at Workstation 2. Although the customer service reps have no special workstation assigned to them, Jackie has the longest seniority and has always assumed that Workstation 2 was hers. Other workstations were available, but the supervisor told Alexa to use Workstation 2 that morning because she didn't know that Jackie would be coming in. When Jackie arrives and sees her workstation occupied, she becomes angry and demands that Alexa vacate "her" station.

2.5 Groupthink: Are We a Bit Overeager? (Obj. 2)

You are a member of the Community Service Committee, which is part of the Business Newcomers Club in your town. Your committee must decide what local cause to support with funds earned at the Newcomers' annual celebrity auction. Matt, the committee chair, suggested that the group support a local literacy program. His aunt is literacy coordinator at the Davis Outreach Center, and he knows that the group would be delighted with any contribution. Sanjaya said that she favors any cause that is educational. Eric announced that he had to leave for an appointment in five minutes. Mona described an article she read in the newspaper about surprisingly large numbers of people who are functionally illiterate. Jared said that he thought they ought to consider other causes such as the homeless center, but Matt dismissed the idea saying, "The homeless already receive lots of funding. Besides, our contribution could make a real difference with the literacy program." The other members of the committee persuaded Jared to agree with them. The committee voted unanimously to support the literacy program.

Your Task. In class discussion, answer the following questions:

a. What aspects of groupthink were at work in this committee?

b. What conditions contribute to groupthink?

c. What can groups do to avoid groupthink?

2.6 Lessons in Teamwork: What We Can Learn From Geese (Objs. 1, 2)

Team

When geese fly in formation, we can't help but look up and marvel at their beauty. But their behavior also represents successful teamwork patterns that have evolved over the ages.

Your Task. In small groups discuss what teamwork lesson might be learned from each of the following:

a. The V formation helps each follower goose derive energy from the flowfield generated by the goose immediately ahead. Every bird experiences lower drag and needs less energy to maintain its speed.

b. Whenever a goose gets out of formation, it tries to get back into formation.

c. When the lead goose gets tired, it rotates back into formation and another goose flies at the head.

d. The geese flying in the rear of the formation honk, apparently to encourage those up front to keep up their speed.

e. When a goose gets sick or wounded and falls, two geese fall out and stay with it until it revives or dies. Then they catch up or join another flock.[66]

2.7 Evaluating Meetings: Effective or Ineffective? (Obj. 3)

Now that you have studied how to plan and participate in productive meetings, you should be able to judge whether meetings are successful and why.

Your Task. Attend a structured meeting of a college, social, business, or other organization. Compare the way the meeting is conducted with the suggestions presented in this chapter. Why did the meeting succeed or fail? In class discussion or in a memo (see Chapter 7) to your instructor, discuss your analysis.

2.8 Blogging: Enhancing Team Communication (Obj. 4)

Team

Companies, including McDonald's, are using blogs to improve internal communications with employees. "Blogs are a way to bring knowledge together," said Dave Weick, chief information officer at McDonald's, who distributes blog access to thousands of employees. Employee communication blogs are gaining popularity because they are easy to set up and inexpensive to run. They generate honest communication, enhance collaboration, and help nurture team building. Assume you have started a blog to share and distribute information about a team project with ten team members.

Your Task. In class teams, discuss how you would you respond to each of the following situations:

a. Adam uses the blog to share personal information instead of communicating information about the team project.
b. Tamika is not participating and has not posted any comments.
c. Jon's comments include insults to other team members.
d. Several team members do not understand how to use the blog.

2.9 Blogging: Establishing Ethical Guidelines (Obj. 4)

Ethics   **Team**   **Web**

Many corporations encourage their employees to participate in external blogs to connect with customers and industry partners, develop relationships with potential customers, and build teamwork among employees. Sun Microsystems, which has a publicly accessible blog site with 1,300 employee blogs at **http://www.blogs.sun.com**, encourages employees to engage customers in technical conversations about Sun products. They consider this blog a valuable medium for exchanging product information and building brand loyalty. Companies can also use blogs to track market trends, collect feedback on its products, and trigger ideas for new products or services. The film distributor Netflix entered a working partnership with a blogger who was attracting 100,000 customers a month with his postings about online movie-rental companies. Netflix used his suggestions to expand its offerings with a new service called Profiles.

This wave of new corporate blogs, however, comes with risks. Employees may reveal confidential company information or embarrassing facts about themselves or colleagues. For example, Mark Jen was fired from Google for sharing in his blog inappropriate comments about the company's financial performance and future products. He also complained about Google's employee benefits while in his first ten days on the job. Other companies have fired employees for similar activities. Microsoft booted a contractor for posting pictures of Apple Macintosh computers at a company office. To safeguard private company information, many companies are developing blogging guidelines for their employees to follow.

Your Task. As a corporate communication intern for a popular producer of consumer products, you have been given a task. Your boss, Meredith Mancuso, knows that you are in college and aware of digital communication. She asks you to help her. The company encourages employees to participate in an external blog that connects them with customers and industry partners. Because the public has access to this site, your company wants to protect confidential information and present a professional image to the public. Ms. Mancuso asks you to develop a list of blogging guidelines for employees to follow. Use the Web or an online database to find information. Submit at least six potential blogging guidelines in a memo to Ms. Mancuso.

2.10 Rating Your Listening Skills (Obj. 5)

You can learn whether your listening skills are excellent or deficient by completing a brief quiz.

Your Task. Take "Dr. Guffey's Listening Quiz" at **www.meguffey.com.** What two listening behaviors do you think you need to work on the most?

2.11 Listening: Recognizing Good Habits (Obj. 5)

You've probably never paid much attention to listening. But now that you have studied it, you have become more conscious of both good and bad listening behavior.

Your Task. For one week focus on the listening behavior of people around you—at work, at school, at home. Make a list of five good listening habits that you see and five bad habits. Identify the situation and participants for each item on your list. Who is the best listener you know? What makes that person a good listener? Be prepared to discuss your responses in class, with your team, or in a memo to your instructor.

2.12 Listening: Skills Required in Different Careers (Obj. 5)

Team

Do the listening skills and behaviors of individuals differ depending on their careers?

Your Task. Your instructor will divide you into teams and give each team a role to discuss, such as business executive, teacher, physician, police officer, attorney, accountant, administrative assistant, mentor, or team leader. Create a list of verbal and nonverbal cues that a member of this profession would display to indicate that he or she is listening. Would the cues and behavior change if the person were trying to listen discriminatively versus critically? How?

2.13 Listening: Tips for Active Involvement (Obj. 5)

"Just because you're talking doesn't mean I'm listening," asserted communication consultant Harvey McChesney III.[67] You decide to use his quotation as the opening in a talk about active listening that you must give before your Toastmasters group.

Your Task. Prepare a list of eight to ten active listening tips appropriate for someone going into your field (such as management, marketing, law enforcement, accounting, corporate communication, and so forth). Include sentences that could serve as a transition from the opening quotation to your list.

2.14 Nonverbal Communication: Recognizing Functions (Obj. 6)

Most of us use nonverbal cues and react to them unconsciously. We seldom think about the functions they serve.

Your Task. To become more aware of the functions of nonverbal communication, keep a log for one week. Observe how nonverbal communication is used by friends, family, instructors, coworkers, managers, politicians, newsmakers, businesses, and others. For each of the five functions of nonverbal communication identified in this chapter, list examples illustrating that function. For example, under "To reinforce and accentuate," you might list a friend who whispers a message to you, thus suggesting that it is a secret. Under "To control and regulate," you might list the steady gaze of your instructor who has targeted a student not paying attention. Train yourself to become more observant, and begin making notes in your log. How many examples can you name for each of the five functions? Be prepared to submit your list or discuss it in class.

2.15 Nonverbal Communication: How to Be More Influential (Obj. 6)

Assume you've just been hired into a prestigious job and you want to make a good impression. You also want very much to become influential in the organization.

Your Task. When you attend meetings, what nonverbal behaviors and signals can you send that will make a good impression as well as improve your influence? In interacting with colleagues, what nonverbal behavior will make you more impressive and influential?

2.16 Nonverbal Communication: Body Language (Obj. 6)

Your Task. What attitudes do the following body movements suggest to you? Do these movements always mean the same thing? What part does context play in your interpretations?

a. Whistling, wringing hands
b. Bowed posture, twiddling thumbs
c. Steepled hands, sprawling position
d. Rubbing hand through hair
e. Open hands, unbuttoned coat
f. Wringing hands, tugging ears

2.17 Nonverbal Communication: Universal Sign for "I Goofed" (Obj. 6)

Team

In an effort to promote tranquility on the highways and reduce road rage, motorists submitted the following suggestions. They were sent to a newspaper columnist who asked for a universal nonverbal signal admitting that a driver had "goofed."[68]

Your Task. In small groups consider the pros and cons for each of the following gestures intended as an apology when a driver makes a mistake. Why would some fail?

a. Lower your head slightly and bonk yourself on the forehead with the side of your closed fist. The message is clear: "I'm stupid. I shouldn't have done that."
b. Make a temple with your hands, as if you were praying.
c. Move the index finger of your right hand back and forth across your neck—as if you were cutting your throat.
d. Flash the well-known peace sign. Hold up the index and middle fingers of one hand, making a V, as in *victory*.
e. Place the flat of your hands against your cheeks, as children do when they've made a mistake.
f. Clasp your hand over your mouth, raise your brows, and shrug your shoulders.
g. Use your knuckles to knock on the side of your head. Translation: "Oops! Engage brain."
h. Place your right hand high on your chest and pat a few times, like a basketball player who drops a pass or a football player who makes a bad throw. This says, "I'll take the blame."
i. Place your right fist over the middle of your chest and move it in a circular motion. This is universal sign language for "I'm sorry."
j. Open your window and tap the top of your car roof with your hand.
k. Smile and raise both arms, palms outward, which is a universal gesture for surrender or forgiveness.
l. Use the military salute, which is simple and shows respect.
m. Flash your biggest smile, point at yourself with your right thumb and move your head from left to right, as if to say, "I can't believe I did that."

2.18 Verbal vs. Nonverbal Signals (Obj. 6)

To show the power of nonverbal cues, the president of a large East Coast consulting company uses the following demonstration with new employees. Raising his right hand, he touches his pointer finger to his thumb to form a circle. Then he asks new employees in the session to do likewise. When everyone has a finger-thumb circle formed, the president tells each person to touch that circle to his or her chin. But as he says this, he touches his own finger-thumb circle to his cheek. What happens? You guessed it! About 80 percent of the group follow what they see the president do rather than following what they hear.[69]

Your Task. Try this same demonstration with several of your friends, family members, or work colleagues. Which is more effective—verbal or nonverbal signals? What conclusion could you draw from this demonstration? Do you think that nonverbal signals are always more meaningful than verbal ones? What other factors in the communication process might determine whether verbal or nonverbal signals were more important?

2.19 Nonverbal Communication: Signals Sent by Business Casual Dress (Obj. 6)

Team

Although many employers allow casual dress, not all employers and customers are happy with the results. To learn more about the implementation, acceptance, and effects of casual-dress programs, select one of the following activities, all of which involve some form of interviewing.

Your Task

a. In teams, gather information from human resources directors to determine which companies allow business casual dress, how often, and under what specific conditions. The information may be collected by personal interviews, by e-mail, or by telephone.
b. In teams, conduct inquiring-reporter interviews. Ask individuals in the community how they react to casual dress in the workplace. Develop a set of standard interview questions.
c. In teams, visit local businesses on both business casual days and on traditional business dress days. Compare and contrast the effects of business dress standards on such factors as the projected image of the company, the nature of the interactions with customers and with fellow employees, the morale of employees, and the productivity of employees. What generalizations can you draw from your findings?

2.20 Body Art: An Angel on Her Arm at Work (Obj. 6)

Nearly 30 percent of American adults now display one or more tattoos, according to a report of the American Academy of Dermatology.[70] However, many people still consider body art edgy or rebellious.

Your Task. Your friend and fellow office worker Avalon proudly shows you an angel tattoo she just got on her upper arm. She wants to know whether you think she may display it at work. What advice would a career-conscious, ambitious person give to a friend?

2.21 Nonverbal Communication: Defining "Business Casual" (Obj. 6)

Team **Web**

Although many business organizations are adopting business casual dress, most people cannot define the term. Your boss asks your internship team to use the Web to find out exactly what "business casual" means.

Your Task. Using a good search engine such as Google, explore the Web for *business casual dress code*. A few Web sites actually try to define the term and give examples of appropriate clothing. Visit several sites and decide whether they are reliable enough to use as sources of accurate information. Print several relevant pages. Get together with your team and compare notes. Then write a memo to your boss explaining what men and women should and shouldn't wear on business casual days.

2.22 Nonverbal Communication Around the World (Obj. 6)

Intercultural   Web

Gestures play an important role when people communicate. Because culture shapes the meaning of gestures, miscommunication and misunderstanding can easily result in international situations.

Your Task. Use the Web to research the meanings of selected gestures. Make a list of ten gestures (other than those discussed in the text) that have different meanings in different countries. Consider the fingertip kiss, nose thumb, eyelid pull, nose tap, head shake, and other gestures. How are the meanings different in other countries?

© John Foxx / Stockbyte / Getty Images

2.23 Guide to Business Etiquette and Workplace Manners: Sharpening Your Skills (Obj. 7)

Business communicators feel more confident and make better impressions when they are aware of current business etiquette and proper workplace manners. But how do you know the right thing to do? You can gauge your current level of knowledge and sharpen your etiquette skills with a little effort.

Your Task. At **www.meguffey.com** find "Dr. Guffey's Guide to Business Etiquette and Workplace Manners." Take the preview test and then study the 17 business etiquette topics presented. Your instructor may give you one or more posttests to learn whether you fully understand the implications of the workplace manners discussed.

2.24 Web Conferencing: What's Available? (Obj. 4)

Consumer   Web

Your company wants to use a Web conferencing service to enable remote employees to hold meetings without traveling to be with each other. These employees need to share documents and Power-Point slides, but they do not have to see each other. Your boss asks you to investigate services and costs.

Your Task. Using the Web, locate three Web conference vendors and check services and costs. (With your instructor's approval and direction, you might sign up for a free demonstration.) Deliver your findings in class discussion or in a short memo (see Chapter 7) addressed to your boss, Darrell Johnson.

Video Resources

Building Workplace Skills Video Library 2
Understanding Teamwork at Cold Stone Creamery
Inside Cold Stone Creamery, the fast-growing ice cream specialty chain, you see that teamwork permeates every facet of Cold Stone's corporate culture. After you watch the video, be prepared to discuss these questions:

a. How is the term *team* defined in this video? Can you offer a definition that is more specific?

b. What six different kinds of teams were mentioned in the Cold Stone Creamery video? Can you provide examples of these teams based on companies with which you are familiar?

c. What characteristics make for effective teams? In your experience with teams, do you agree or disagree?

Grammar and Mechanics C.L.U.E. Review 2

Verbs

Review Guides 4–10 in Appendix A: Grammar and Mechanics Guide (Competent Language Usage Essentials), beginning on page A-3. On a separate sheet, revise the following sentences to correct any errors in verbs. For each error that you locate, write the guide number that reflects this usage. If a sentence is correct, write C. When you finish, check your answers on page Key-1.

Example: I wish I was the vice president for just one day.
Revision: I wish I **were** the vice president for jut one day. [Guide 5]

1. Our team leader said she seen the computer the day before it was stolen.

2. One of the most frequently requested employment skills are writing proficiency.

3. If I was the team leader, I would have gone to the training meeting.

4. Better decisions and faster response time explains why many companies are using teams.

5. Either the team leader or the manager are going to announce the vacation schedule.

6. Conflict and dissension is normal and should be expected in team interactions.

7. Everything in the meeting minutes and the company records are open to public view.

8. We should have a decision soon because the committee are meeting today.

9. If we had taken more time, we could have written a better report.

10. The appearance of letters, memos, and e-mail messages have either a positive or negative effect on receivers.

Chapter 3

Communicating Across Cultures

OBJECTIVES

After studying this chapter, you should be able to

1 Understand three significant trends related to the increasing importance of intercultural communication for business communicators.

2 Define *culture,* describe five noteworthy cultural characteristics, and compare and contrast five key dimensions of culture including high and low context.

3 Explain the effects of ethnocentrism, tolerance, and patience in achieving intercultural proficiency.

4 Identify techniques for improving nonverbal and oral communication in intercultural environments.

5 Identify techniques for improving written messages to intercultural audiences.

6 Discuss intercultural ethics, including business practices abroad, bribery, prevailing customs, and methods for coping.

7 Explain the challenges of, dividends of, and techniques for capitalizing on workforce diversity including being sensitive to racial and gender issues.

1/30/10
Mishawaka

© C Squared Studios / Photodisc / Getty Images

Communicating at Work Part 1

Mighty Wal-Mart Woos Famously Finicky Japanese Consumers

It's 8:15 a.m. and 50 managers of the Seiyu supermarket in Japan are performing the Wal-Mart morning ritual. "Give me an S!" shouts a Japanese boss. The resounding "S!" reverberates through the second floor headquarters. The chant is repeated until the group spells "S-E-I-Y-U." "Who's No. 1?" bellows the cheerleading boss. "Customers!" boom the Japanese managers as they punch the air with their fists.[1]

Routines like this boost employee morale in the United States. If they work here, they must work in Japan, figures Wal-Mart. Seiyu employees are learning Wal-Mart routines because Wal-Mart has purchased and is revamping the Seiyu food and clothing chain to gain a foothold in Japan. Since joining with Seiyu, however, Wal-Mart has lost over $1 billion, and sales are sluggish.[2] The giant retailer has already pulled out of South Korea and Germany, where shoppers failed to warm up to the Wal-Mart way.

Why expand into Japan, where consumers are notoriously fickle?[3] Expanding its international market is a primary push for Wal-Mart because sales growth is declining at home. With fewer new stores opening in the United States, global expansion is a must for Wal-Mart. The Japanese market is especially attractive because it is the second largest economy in the world, and its consumers are Asia's richest. What's more, Japanese consumers are becoming more price conscious, and discounting is increasingly appealing.

Although hugely successful in the United States, Wal-Mart must overcome significant distribution, location, and cultural barriers to become profitable in Japan. Costly real estate and cramped space make it difficult to build the big stores common in the United States. In addition to restricted space, its hallmark "everyday low prices" strategy is confusing to local shoppers accustomed to poring over newspaper ads and scurrying around town for the best buys.

Equally disturbing is the resistance of employees to sell the Wal-Mart way. For one thing, they balk at the "10-foot rule," which

encourages them to offer assistance to any customer within 10 feet. To overcome these hurdles, workers are receiving a heavy dose of "culture training." They're being taught to be more outspoken, upbeat, and goal oriented. You will learn more about this case on page 80.

Critical Thinking

- What domestic and global changes are taking place that encourage the international expansion of companies such as Wal-Mart?
- What other U.S. businesses can you name that have merged with foreign companies or expanded to become multinational in scope? Have you heard of any notable successes or failures?
- Should multinational companies impose their local culture on employees in other countries?

http://www.wal-mart.com

Recognizing the Increasing Importance of Intercultural Communication

LEARNING OBJECTIVE 1
Understand three significant trends related to the increasing importance of intercultural communication for business communicators.

The "global village" predicted many years ago is increasingly a reality. To succeed in this global village, business communicators will want to become more aware of their own culture and how it differs from others. In this chapter you will learn basic characteristics and dimensions of culture, as well as how to achieve intercultural proficiency. We will focus on techniques for improving nonverbal, oral, and written messages to intercultural audiences. You will study intercultural ethics and techniques for capitalizing on workforce diversity at home.

National and even local businesses now peddle their products across borders and seek customers in diverse foreign markets. Especially in North America, this movement toward a global economy has swelled to a torrent. To better compete, many organizations form multinational alliances, such as that between Wal-Mart, the U.S. super discounter, and Seiyu, Japan's fifth-largest food and retail chain. But many expanding companies stumble when they are forced to confront obstacles never before encountered.

Significant obstacles involve misunderstandings and contrary views resulting from intercultural differences. You may face such intercultural differences in your current or future jobs. Your employers, fellow workers, or clients could very well be from other countries.

Learning how culture affects behavior helps you reduce friction and misunderstandings.

You may travel abroad for your employer or on your own. Learning more about the powerful effect that culture has on behavior will help you reduce friction and misunderstanding in your dealings with people from other cultures. Before examining strategies for helping you surmount intercultural obstacles, let's take a closer look at three significant trends: (a) the globalization of markets, (b) technological advancements, and (c) an intercultural workforce.

Globalization of Markets

Doing business beyond borders is now commonplace. Frito-Lay pushes its potato chips in China.[4] Finnish cell phone maker Nokia promotes its mobile phones in the world's fastest-growing markets of India and China. Newell Rubbermaid offers stylish Pyrex cookware to European chefs, and McDonald's and Starbucks serve customers around the world.

Not only are market borders blurring, but acquisitions, mergers, alliances, and buyouts are obscuring the nationality of many companies. Bridgestone/Firestone is owned by a Japanese conglomerate; Sylvania is controlled by German lighting giant OSRAM; and former premier U.S. textile maker Dan River is now owned by an Indian company.[5] Two thirds of Colgate-Palmolive's employees work outside North America, and Nike is raking in more revenue overseas than in the United States. Procter & Gamble now has 3 billion customers worldwide and plans to add 1 billion more by 2010, primarily by expanding into developing markets.[6] What's more, 7-Eleven is the highest-grossing retailer in Japan and has nearly twice as many outlets there as it has in the United States.[7]

To be successful in this interdependent global village, American companies are increasingly finding it necessary to adapt to other cultures. In China, Frito-Lay had to accommodate yin and yang, the Chinese philosophy that nature and life must balance opposing elements. Chinese consider fried foods to be hot and avoid them in summer because two "hots" don't balance. They prefer "cool" snacks in summer; therefore, Frito-Lay created "cool lemon" potato chips dotted with lime specks and mint. The yellow, lemon-scented chips are delivered in a package with breezy-blue skies and rolling green grass.[8]

In promoting its shoes and apparel to kids from Rome to Rio De Janeiro, Nike features Brazilian soccer star Ronaldo, rather than a U.S. basketball star.[9] To sell its laundry products in Europe, Unilever learned that Germans demand a product that is gentle on lakes and rivers. Spaniards wanted cheaper products that get shirts white and soft, and Greeks preferred small packages that were cheap and easy to carry home.[10] To push ketchup in Japan, H. J. Heinz had to overcome a cultural resistance to sweet flavors. Thus, it offered Japanese homemakers cooking lessons instructing them how to use the sugary red sauce on omelets, sausages, and pasta.[11] Domino's Pizza catered to the Japanese by adding squid to its pizza toppings.[12]

When upscale sandwich chain New York NY Fresh Deli opened a franchise in Dubai, it had to replace all salad dressings that contained vinegar. Considered a spirit, vinegar and other alcoholic beverages can be served only in hotels and to non-Muslims.[13] In Taiwan, Dunkin' Donuts catered to local palates with flavors such as pineapple, sweet potato, and green apple.[14]

Why are the businesses of America and other countries rushing to expand around the world? What is causing this dash toward globalization of markets and blurring of national identities? Many companies, such as Wal-Mart, are increasingly looking overseas as domestic markets mature. They can no longer expect double-digit sales growth at home. Another significant factor is the passage of favorable trade agreements. The General Agreement on Tariffs and Trade (GATT) promotes open trade globally, and the North American Free Trade Agreement (NAFTA) expands free trade among Canada, the United States, and Mexico. NAFTA creates the largest and richest free-trade region on earth. In addition, the opening of Eastern Europe and the shift away from communism in Russia further expanded world markets. In Asia, China's admission to the World Trade Organization unlocked its economy and suddenly provided access to a huge population.

Beyond favorable trade agreements, other changes fuel globalization. Parts of the world formerly considered underdeveloped now boast robust middle classes. These consumers crave everything from cola to smart phones and high-definition TVs. What's more, countries such as China and India have become less paranoid about foreign investment and free trade. Rules and red tape previously prevented many companies from doing

National boundaries mean less as businesses expand through acquisitions, mergers, alliances, and buyouts.

American companies in global markets must adapt to other cultures.

Favorable trade agreements, declining domestic markets, and middle-class growth fuel the expansion of global markets.

business at home, much less abroad. Of paramount importance in explaining the explosive growth of global markets is the development of new transportation and information technologies.

Technological Advancements

Advancements in transportation and information technologies contribute to global interconnectivity.

Amazing new transportation and information technologies are major contributors to the development of our global interconnectivity. Supersonic planes now carry goods and passengers to other continents overnight. As a result, produce shoppers in Japan can choose from the finest artichokes, avocados, and apples only hours after they were picked in California. Americans enjoy bouquets of tulips, roses, and exotic lilies soon after harvesting in Holland and Colombia. In fact, 70 percent of the cut flowers in the United States now come from Colombia in South America. Many of us remember when asparagus and strawberries could be enjoyed only in early summer. Today we expect to see these items and other fruits and vegetables in our markets nearly year-round. Continent-hopping planes are so fast and reliable that most of the world is rapidly becoming an open market.

The Internet and the Web are changing the way we live, the way we do business, and the way we communicate. Advancements in communication and transportation have made markets and jobs more accessible. They've also made the world of business more efficient and more globally interdependent. High-speed, high-capacity, and relatively low-cost communications have opened new global opportunities and have made geographical location virtually irrelevant for many activities and services. Workers have access to company records, software programs, and colleagues whether they're working at home, in the office, or at the beach. As discussed in Chapters 1 and 2, technology is making a huge difference in the workplace. Wikis, blogs, wireless devices, and intranets streamline business processes and improve access to critical company information.

The Internet permits instantaneous oral and written communication across time zones and continents. Managers in Miami or Milwaukee can use high-speed data systems to swap marketing plans instantly with their counterparts in Milan or Munich. IBM relies on 5,000 programmers in India to solve intricate computer problems and return the solutions overnight via digital transmission.[15] Employees at Procter & Gamble send their payroll questions to back-office service centers in England, Costa Rica, or Manila.[16] Fashion designers at Liz Claiborne can snap a digital photo of a garment and immediately transmit the image to manufacturers in Hong Kong and Djakarta, Indonesia.[17] They can even include a video clip to show a tricky alteration.

Intercultural Workforce

Immigration makes intercultural communication skills increasingly necessary.

As world commerce mingles more and more, another trend gives intercultural communication increasing importance: people are on the move. Lured by the prospects of peace, prosperity, education, or a fresh start, persons from many cultures are moving to countries promising to fulfill their dreams. For generations the two most popular destinations have been the United States and Canada.

Because of increases in immigration, foreign-born persons are an ever-growing portion of the total U.S. population. Over the next 50 years, the population of the United States is expected to grow by nearly 50 percent, from about 275 million in the year 2000 to an estimated 394 million people in 2050. Two thirds of that increase will be the result of net immigration.[18] Estimates also suggest that immigrants will account for half of all new U.S. workers in the years ahead.[19]

Learning to adapt to an intercultural workforce and multinational companies is an important requirement for business communicators.

This influx of immigrants is reshaping American and Canadian societies. Earlier immigrants were thought to be part of a "melting pot" of ethnic groups. Today, they are more like a "tossed salad" or "spicy stew," with each group contributing its own unique flavor. Instead of the exception, cultural diversity is increasingly the norm. As we seek to accommodate multiethnic neighborhoods, multinational companies, and an intercultural workforce, we can expect some changes to happen smoothly. Other changes will involve conflict and resentment, especially for people losing their positions of power and privilege. Learning to accommodate and manage intercultural change is an important part of the education of any business communicator.

Understanding Culture

Every country or region within a country has a unique common heritage, joint experience, or shared learning. This shared background produces the culture of a region, country, or society. For our purposes, *culture* may be defined as the complex system of values, traits, morals, and customs shared by a society. Culture teaches people how to behave, and it conditions their reactions. The important thing to remember is that culture is a powerful operating force that conditions the way we think and behave. The purpose of this chapter is to broaden your view of culture and open your mind to flexible attitudes so that you can avoid frustration when cultural adjustment is necessary.

LEARNING OBJECTIVE 2
Define culture, describe five noteworthy cultural characteristics, and compare and contrast five key dimensions of culture including high and low context.

Characteristics of Culture

Culture is shaped by attitudes learned in childhood and later internalized in adulthood. As we enter this current period of globalization and interculturalism, we should expect to make adjustments and adopt new attitudes. Adjustment and accommodation will be easier if we understand some basic characteristics of culture.

Understanding basic characteristics of culture helps us make adjustments and accommodations.

Culture Is Learned. Rules, values, and attitudes of a culture are not inherent. They are learned and passed down from generation to generation. For example, in many Middle Eastern and some Asian cultures, same-sex people may walk hand-in-hand in the street, but opposite-sex people may not do so. In Arab cultures conversations are often held in close proximity, sometimes nose to nose. But in Western cultures if a person stands too close, one may react as if violated: "He was all over me like a rash." Cultural rules of behavior learned from your family and society are conditioned from early childhood.

Cultures Are Inherently Logical. The rules in any culture originated to reinforce that culture's values and beliefs. They act as normative forces. For example, in Japan the original Barbie doll was a failure for many reasons, one of which was her toothy smile.[20] This is a country where women cover their mouths with their hands when they laugh so as not to expose their teeth. Exposing one's teeth is not only immodest but also aggressive. Although current cultural behavior may sometimes seem silly and illogical, nearly all serious rules and values originate in deep-seated beliefs. Rules about exposing teeth or how close to stand are linked to values about sexuality, aggression, modesty, and respect. Acknowledging the inherent logic of a culture is extremely important when learning to accept behavior that differs from one's own cultural behavior.

© AP IMAGES

Marketers of Crest toothpaste face numerous challenges in communicating the value of their brand across cultures—especially Chinese culture. China's citizens traditionally have ignored toothpaste products, choosing instead to freshen up the mouth with green tea. An estimated 57 percent of rural Chinese residents have never brushed their teeth. Though China is currently experiencing a beauty boom, decades ago the country frowned upon personal care products. *How might understanding the characteristics of culture help marketers sell toothpaste to China's over one billion people?*

Culture determines our sense
of who we are and our sense of
community.

Culture Is the Basis of Self-Identity and Community.
Culture is the basis for how we tell the world who we are and what we believe. People build their identities through cultural overlays to their primary culture. North Americans, for example, make choices in education, career, place of employment, and life partner. Each of these choices brings with it a set of rules, manners, ceremonies, beliefs, language, and values. They add to one's total cultural outlook, and they represent major expressions of a person's self-identity.

Culture Combines the Visible and Invisible.
To outsiders, the way we act—those things that we do in daily life and work—are the most visible parts of our culture. In Japan, for instance, harmony with the environment is important. Thus, when attending a flower show, a woman would wear a dress with pastel rather than primary colors to avoid detracting from the beauty of the flowers. In India people avoid stepping on ants or insects because they believe in reincarnation and are careful about all forms of life. These practices are outward symbols of deeper values that are invisible but that pervade everything we think and do.

Culture Is Dynamic.
Over time, cultures will change. Changes are caused by advancements in technology and communication, as discussed earlier. Change is also caused by events such as migration, natural disasters, and wars. The American Civil War, for instance, produced far-reaching cultural changes for both the North and the South. Another major event in this country was the exodus of people living on farms. When families moved to cities, major changes occurred in the way family members interacted. Attitudes, behaviors, and beliefs change in open societies more quickly than in closed societies.

About Stereotypes, Prototypes, Prejudices, and Generalizations

Most experts recognize that it is impossible to talk about cultures without using mental categories, representations, and generalizations to describe groups. These categories are sometimes considered *stereotypes*. Because the term *stereotype* has a negative meaning, intercultural authors Varner and Beamer suggested that we distinguish between *stereotype* and *prototype*.

A *stereotype* is an oversimplified behavioral pattern applied uncritically to groups. The term was used originally by printers to describe identical type set in two frames, hence *stereotype*. Stereotypes are fixed and rigid. Although they may be exaggerated and overgeneralized beliefs when applied to groups of people, stereotypes are not always entirely false.[21] Often they contain a grain of truth. When a stereotype develops into a rigid attitude and when it is based on erroneous beliefs or preconceptions, then it should be called a *prejudice*.

Varner and Beamer recommended using the term *prototype* to describe "mental representations based on general characteristics that are not fixed and rigid, but rather are open to new definitions."[22] Prototypes, then, are dynamic and change with fresh experience. Prototypes based on objective observations usually have a considerable amount of truth in them. That is why they can be helpful in studying culture. For example, Latin businesspeople often talk about their families before getting down to business. This prototype is generally accurate, but it may not universally apply and it may change over time.

Some people object to making any generalizations about cultures whatever. It is wise to remember, however, that whenever we are confronted with something new and unfamiliar, we naturally strive to categorize the data in order to make sense out of it. In categorizing these new data, we are making generalizations. Significant intellectual discourse is impossible without generalizations. In fact, science itself would be impossible without generalizations, for what are scientific laws but valid generalizations? Much of what we teach in college courses could be called generalizations. Being able to draw generalizations from masses of data is a sign of intelligence and learning. Unfounded generalizations about people and cultures, of course, can lead to bias and prejudice. But for our purposes, when we discuss cultures, it is important to be able to make generalizations and describe cultural prototypes.

Dimensions of Culture

The more you know about culture in general and your own culture in particular, the better able you will be to adapt to an intercultural perspective. A typical North American has habits and beliefs similar to those of other members of Western, technologically advanced societies. In our limited space in this book, it is impossible to cover fully the infinite facets of culture. But we can outline some key dimensions of culture and look at them from different views.

Ethics Check

Cultural Change: From the Dinner Table to the Drive-Through
The advent of mass mobility by automobile in the 1950s and increasing numbers of women joining the workforce have led to the dramatic rise of the fast-food industry. Middle-class families no longer gathered around the dinner table but became used to snacking on the go. Now many critics blame the fast-food franchises for making us fat. Are these businesses responsible for Americans' expanding waistlines?

Stereotypes are oversimplified behavioral patterns applied uncritically to groups; prototypes describe general characteristics that are dynamic and may change.

FIGURE 3.1 Comparing Low- and High-Context Cultures

Low Context	High Context
Tend to prefer direct verbal interaction	Tend to prefer indirect verbal interaction
Tend to understand meaning at one level only	Tend to understand meanings embedded at many sociocultural levels
Are generally less proficient in reading nonverbal cues	Are generally more proficient in reading nonverbal cues
Value individualism	Value group membership
Rely more on logic	Rely more on context and feeling
Employ linear logic	Employ spiral logic
Say *no* directly	Talk around point; avoid saying *no*
Communicate in highly structured messages, provide details, stress literal meanings, give authority to written information	Communicate in simple, sometimes ambiguous, messages; understand visual messages readily

Low-Context Cultures ←————————————————————————————→ High-Context Cultures

German · North American · French · Spanish · Greek · Chinese

German-Swiss · Scandinavian · English · Italian · Mexican · Arab · Japanese

So that you will better understand your culture and how it contrasts with other cultures, we will describe five key dimensions of culture: context, individualism, formality, communication style, and time orientation.

Context.

Context is probably the most important cultural dimension and also the most difficult to define. It is a concept developed by cultural anthropologist Edward T. Hall. In his model, context refers to the stimuli, environment, or ambience surrounding an event. Communicators in low-context cultures (such as those in North America, Scandinavia, and Germany) depend little on the context of a situation to convey their meaning. They assume that listeners know very little and must be told practically everything. In high-context cultures (such as those in Japan, China, and Arab countries), the listener is already "contexted" and does not need to be given much background information.[23] To identify low- and high-context countries, Hall arranged them on a continuum, as shown in Figure 3.1.

Low-context cultures tend to be logical, analytical, and action oriented. Business communicators stress clearly articulated messages that they consider to be objective, professional, and efficient. High-context cultures are more likely to be intuitive and contemplative. Communicators in high-context cultures pay attention to more than the words spoken. They emphasize interpersonal relationships, nonverbal expression, physical setting, and social setting. For example, a Japanese communicator might say *yes* when he really means *no*. From the context of the situation, the Japanese speaker would indicate whether *yes* really meant *yes* or whether it meant *no*. The context, tone, time taken to answer, facial expression, and body cues would convey the meaning of *yes*.[24] Thus, in high-context cultures, communication cues are transmitted by posture, voice inflection, gestures, and facial expression. Establishing relationships is an important part of communicating and interacting.

In terms of thinking patterns, low-context communicators tend to use *linear logic*. They proceed from Point A to Point B to Point C and finally arrive at a conclusion. High-context communicators, however, may use *spiral logic*, circling around a topic indirectly and looking at it from many tangential or divergent viewpoints. A conclusion may be implied but not argued directly. For a concise summary of important differences between low- and high-context cultures, see Figure 3.1.

Individualism.

An attitude of independence and freedom from control characterizes individualism. Members of low-context cultures, particularly Americans, tend to value individualism. They believe that initiative and self-assertion result in personal achievement. They believe in individual action and personal responsibility, and they desire a large degree of freedom in their personal lives.

Low-context cultures (such as those in North America and Western Europe) depend less on the environment of a situation to convey meaning than do high-context cultures (such as those in Japan, China, and Arab countries).

People in low-context cultures tend to be logical, analytical, and action oriented.

Members of many low-context cultures value independence and freedom from control.

Members of high-context cultures are more collectivist. They emphasize membership in organizations, groups, and teams; they encourage acceptance of group values, duties, and decisions. They typically resist independence because it fosters competition and confrontation instead of consensus. In group-oriented cultures such as those in many Asian societies, for example, self-assertion and individual decision making are discouraged. "The nail that sticks up gets pounded down" is a common Japanese saying.[25] Business decisions are often made by all who have competence in the matter under discussion. Similarly, in China managers also focus on the group rather than on the individual, preferring a "consultative" management style over an autocratic style.[26]

Many cultures, of course, are quite complex and cannot be characterized as totally individualistic or group oriented. For example, European Americans are generally quite individualistic, whereas African Americans are less so, and Latin Americans are closer to the group-centered dimension.[27]

Formality. People in some cultures place less emphasis on tradition, ceremony, and social rules than do members of other cultures. Americans, for example, dress casually and are soon on a first-name basis with others. Their lack of formality is often characterized by directness. In business dealings Americans come to the point immediately; indirectness, they feel, wastes time, a valuable commodity in American culture.

This informality and directness may be confusing abroad. In Mexico, for instance, a typical business meeting begins with handshakes, coffee, and an expansive conversation about the weather, sports, and other light topics. An invitation to "get down to business" might offend a Mexican executive.[28] In Japan signing documents and exchanging business cards are important rituals. In Europe first names are never used without invitation. In Arab, South American, and Asian cultures, a feeling of friendship and kinship must be established before business can be transacted.

In Western cultures people are more relaxed about social status and the appearance of power.[29] Deference is not generally paid to individuals merely because of their wealth, position, seniority, or age. In many Asian cultures, however, these characteristics are important and must be respected. Wal-Mart, facing many hurdles in breaking into the Japanese market, admits having difficulty training local employees to speak up to their bosses. In their culture lower-level employees do not question management. Deference and respect are paid to authority and power. Recognizing this cultural pattern, Marriott Hotel managers learned to avoid placing a lower-level Japanese employee on a floor above a higher-level executive from the same company.

Communication Style. People in low- and high-context cultures tend to communicate differently with words. To Americans and Germans, words are very important, especially in contracts and negotiations. People in high-context cultures, on the other hand, place more emphasis on the surrounding context than on the words describing a negotiation. A Greek may see a contract as a formal statement announcing the intention to build a business for the future. The Japanese may treat contracts as statements of intention, and they assume changes will be made as a project develops. Mexicans may treat contracts as artistic exercises of what might be accomplished in an ideal world. They do not necessarily expect contracts to apply consistently in the real world. An Arab may be insulted by merely mentioning a contract; a person's word is more binding.[30]

North Americans tend to take words literally, whereas Latins enjoy plays on words; and Arabs and South Americans sometimes speak with extravagant or poetic figures of speech that may be misinterpreted if taken literally. Nigerians prefer a quiet, clear form of expression; and Germans tend to be direct but understated.[31]

In communication style North Americans value straightforwardness, are suspicious of evasiveness, and distrust people who might have a "hidden agenda" or who "play their cards too close to the chest."[32] North Americans also tend to be uncomfortable with silence and impatient with delays. Some Asian businesspeople have learned that the longer they drag out negotiations, the more concessions impatient North Americans are likely to make.

Tradition, ceremony, and social rules are more important in some cultures than in others.

Words are used differently by people in low- and high-context cultures.

North Americans value a direct, straightforward communication style.

Chapter 3: Communicating Across Cultures

Western cultures have developed languages that use letters describing the *sounds* of words. But Asian languages are based on pictographical characters representing the *meanings* of words. Asian language characters are much more complex than the Western alphabet; therefore, Asians are said to have a higher competence in the discrimination of visual patterns.

Time Orientation. North Americans consider time a precious commodity to be conserved. They correlate time with productivity, efficiency, and money. Keeping people waiting for business appointments wastes time and is also rude.

In other cultures time may be perceived as an unlimited and never-ending resource to be enjoyed. A North American businessperson, for example, was kept waiting two hours past a scheduled appointment time in South America. She wasn't offended, though, because she was familiar with Hispanics' more relaxed concept of time.

Although Asians are punctual, their need for deliberation and contemplation sometimes clashes with an American's desire for speedy decisions. They do not like to be rushed. A Japanese businessperson considering the purchase of American appliances, for example, asked for five minutes to consider the seller's proposal. The potential buyer crossed his arms, sat back, and closed his eyes in concentration. A scant 18 seconds later, the American resumed his sales pitch to the obvious bewilderment of the Japanese buyer.[33]

As you can see, high-context cultures differ from low-context cultures in many dimensions. These differences can be significant for companies engaging in international business. One of the places where international business is expanding most rapidly is on the World Wide Web. Web sites give companies of all sizes global reach and the immediate ability to interact with customers all over the world. In the face of fierce competition, the most successful Web sites are built by communicators who fully understand the powerful effects of high- and low-context cultures, as discussed in the accompanying Tech Talk.

North Americans tend to correlate time with productivity, efficiency, and money.

Asians tend to need time for deliberation and contemplation.

Tech Talk

Going Global With a Culturally Customized Web Site

Early Web sites were almost always in English and meant for Americans. As online access grows around the world, however, companies are reassessing their sites. What should companies do when they decide to go global on the Web?

- **Learn the local lingo.** Other countries have developed their own Web jargon and iconography. *Home page* is "pagina inicial" (initial page) in Spanish and "page d'accueil" (welcome page) in French. Experts warn against simply translating English words page by page. Hiring a proficient translator or working with a local developer is a better idea.
- **Check icons.** American Web surfers easily recognize the mailbox, but in Europe a more universal icon would be an envelope. Test images with local residents.
- **Relax restrictions on consistency.** Allow flexibility to meet local tastes. For example, McDonald's main site greets visitors with the golden arches and a Ronald McDonald-red background. The Japanese site, though, displays softer colors, which are more pleasing in this Asian culture.
- **Keep the message simple.** Whether in English or the local language, use simple, easily translated words. Avoid slang, jargon, acronyms, or ambiguous expressions.
- **Customize Web content for high-context cultures.** For high-context cultures (such as those of Japan and China), Web sites often include images and wording reflecting politeness, flowery language, use of indirect expressions (*perhaps, probably, somewhat*), and overall humility. They may include animated images (including

cartoon characters), a soft-sell approach, and appeals to harmony.[34]
- **Customize Web content for low-context cultures.** Web sites in low-context cultures (such as those of the United States and Germany) use more aggressive promotions, discounts, and an emphasis on product advantages using explicit comparisons. They include superlative expressions (*We're No. 1, the world's largest, we lead the market*). Low-context Web sites often identify return policies, guarantees, and purchase conditions.[35]

Career Application
Using Google, locate the Web sites of two high-context companies such as convenience store 7-Eleven Japan (**http://www.sej.co.jp**) or Excite (**http://friends.excite.co.jp/friends**). View the sites in Japanese as well as in English with Google's machine translation feature. (If these URLs change, use Google to search for *www.sej .co.jp* and *Friends Excite Company Japan*.) Then examine the Web sites of two low-context companies such as 7-Eleven U.S. (**http://www.7-eleven.com**) and IBM U.S. (**http://www.ibm.com/us**). View opening and internal pages. How are the suggestions mentioned here reflected in these sites? Do you see subtle differences in Web sites from low- and high-context cultures? Do you think international Web sites might be showing signs of homogenization?

Achieving Intercultural Proficiency

LEARNING OBJECTIVE 3
Explain the effects of ethnocentrism, tolerance, and patience in achieving intercultural proficiency.

Being aware of your own culture and how it contrasts with others is an important first step in achieving intercultural proficiency. Another step involves recognizing barriers to intercultural accommodation and striving to overcome them. Some of these barriers occur quite naturally and require a conscious effort to surmount. You might be thinking, why bother? Probably the most important reasons for becoming interculturally competent are that your personal life will be more satisfying and your work life will be more productive, gratifying, and effective.

Avoiding Ethnocentrism

Ethnocentrism, the belief in the superiority of one's own race, tends to cause us to judge others by our own values.

The belief in the superiority of one's own race is known as *ethnocentrism*, a natural attitude inherent in all cultures. If you were raised in North America, many of the dimensions of culture described previously probably seem "right" to you. For example, it is only logical to think that time is money and you should not waste it. Everyone knows that, right? That is why an American businessperson in an Arab or Asian country might feel irritated at time spent over coffee or other social rituals before any "real" business is transacted. In these cultures, however, time is viewed differently. Moreover, personal relationships must be established and nurtured before credible negotiations may proceed.

Ethnocentrism causes us to judge others by our own values. We expect others to react as we would, and they expect us to behave as they would. Misunderstandings naturally result. A North American who wants to set a deadline for completion of negotiations is considered pushy by an Arab. That same Arab, who prefers a handshake to a written contract, is seen as naïve and possibly untrustworthy by a North American. These ethnocentric reactions can be reduced through knowledge of other cultures and the development of increased intercultural sensitivity.

Consider the dilemma of the international consulting firm of Burns & McCallister, described in the accompanying Ethical Insights box. In refusing to send women to negotiate in certain countries, the company enraged some women's rights groups. But was Burns & McCallister actually respecting the cultures of those countries?

Ethical Insights

Firm Lands in Hot Water for Caving in to Cultural Prejudices

At one time the international management consulting firm of Burns & McCallister found itself in cultural hot water. The problem? Although the company had earned kudos for its fair treatment of women in this country, it declined to send female partners to negotiate contracts in certain countries.

Silent Women. In some cultures women may work in clerical positions, but they are not allowed to speak in a meeting of men. Contacts with clients must be through male partners or account executives. Japan, for example, has a two-track hiring system with women represented in only 3 percent of all professional positions. Other women in the workforce are uniformed office ladies who do the filing and serve tea. One American businesswoman said that when she finished a presentation in Japan, the men in the audience would ask who her boss was. She eventually hired a man to go along with her because merely having a man by her side, even a virtual dummy, increased her sales significantly.[36]

Company Justification. In defense of its ban on sending women to negotiate in certain cultures, the head of Burns & McCallister said: "Look, we're about as progressive a firm as you will find. But the reality of international business is that if we try to use women, we don't get the job. It is not a policy on all foreign accounts. We've just identified certain cultures in which women will not

be able to successfully land or work on accounts. This restriction does not interfere with their career track."

Women's Rights. The National Organization for Women (NOW) argued that Burns & McCallister should apply its American standards throughout the world. Since women are not restricted here, they should not be restricted abroad. Our culture treats women fairly, and other cultures should recognize and respect that treatment. Unless Burns & McCallister stands up for its principles, change can never be expected.

Career Application
Organize a debate or class discussion focused on these questions. On what grounds do you support or oppose the position of Burns & McCallister to prohibit women from negotiating contracts in certain cultures? Should U.S. businesses impose their cultural values abroad? Should Burns & McCallister sacrifice potential business to advance a high moral position? If the career advancement of women within the firm is not affected by the policy, should women care? Do you agree with NOW that change cannot occur unless Burns & McCallister takes a stand?

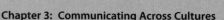

Bridging the Gap

Developing cultural competence often involves changing attitudes. Remember that culture is learned. Through exposure to other cultures and through training, such as you are receiving in this course, you can learn new attitudes and behaviors that help bridge gaps between cultures.

Tolerance. One desirable attitude in achieving intercultural proficiency is that of *tolerance.* Closed-minded people cannot look beyond their own ethnocentrism. But as global markets expand and as our own society becomes increasingly multiethnic, tolerance becomes especially significant. Some job descriptions now include statements such as, "Must be able to interact with ethnically diverse personnel."

To improve tolerance, you will want to practice *empathy.* This means trying to see the world through another's eyes. It means being less judgmental and more eager to seek common ground. For example, one of the most ambitious cross-cultural business projects ever attempted joined Siemens AG, the giant German technology firm, with Toshiba Corporation of Japan and IBM. Scientists from each country worked at the IBM facility on the Hudson River in New York State to develop a revolutionary computer memory chip. All sides devoted extra effort to overcome communication and other problems.

The Siemens employees had been briefed on America's "hamburger style of management." When American managers must criticize subordinates, they generally start with small talk, such as "How's the family?" That, according to the Germans, is the bun on the top of the hamburger. Then they slip in the meat, which is the criticism. They end with encouraging words, which is the bun on the bottom. "With Germans," said a Siemens cross-cultural trainer, "all you get is the meat. And with the Japanese, it's all the soft stuff—you have to *smell* the meat."[37] Along the continuum of high-context, low-context cultures, you can see that the Germans are more direct, the Americans are less direct, and the Japanese are very subtle.

Recognizing these cultural differences enabled the scientists to work together with greater tolerance. They also sought common ground when trying to solve disagreements, such as one involving workspace. The Toshiba researchers were accustomed to working in big crowded areas like classrooms where constant supervision and interaction took place. But IBMers worked in small isolated offices. The solution was to knock out some walls for cooperative work areas while also retaining smaller offices for those who wanted them. Instead of passing judgment and telling the Japanese that solitary workspaces are the best way for serious thinkers to concentrate, the Americans acknowledged the difference in work cultures and sought common ground. Accepting cultural differences and adapting to them with tolerance and empathy often results in a harmonious compromise.

Saving Face. In business transactions North Americans often assume that economic factors are the primary motivators of people. It is wise to remember, though, that strong cultural influences are also at work. *Saving face*, for example, is important in many parts of the world. *Face* refers to the image a person holds in his or her social network. Positive comments raise a person's social standing, but negative comments lower it.

People in low-context cultures are less concerned with face. Germans and North Americans, for instance, value honesty and directness; they generally come right to the point and "tell it like it is." Mexicans, Asians, and members of other high-context cultures, on the other hand, are more concerned with preserving social harmony and saving face. They are indirect and go to great lengths to avoid giving offense by saying *no.* The Japanese, in fact, have 16 different ways to avoid an outright *no.* The empathic listener recognizes the language of refusal and pushes no further.

Patience. Being tolerant also involves patience. If a foreigner is struggling to express an idea in English, Americans must avoid the temptation to finish the sentence and provide the word that they presume is wanted. When we put words into their mouths, our foreign friends often smile and agree out of politeness, but our words may in fact not express their thoughts. Remaining silent is another means of exhibiting tolerance. Instead of filling every lapse in conversation, North Americans, for example, should recognize that in Asian cultures people deliberately use periods of silence for reflection and contemplation.

Because culture is learned, you can learn new attitudes and behaviors through training.

Ethics Check

Culture Clash: Huffing Over Puffing
California, where only 15 percent of adults smoke, passed the world's strictest antismoking laws, banning tobacco use in public places, even beaches and parks. However, in many countries smoking is widespread and tolerated as it may occur in 30 to 60 percent of the population. When abroad, how should business travelers react to this potential culture clash?

Saving face may require indirectness to respect the feelings and dignity of others.

Tolerance sometimes involves being patient and silent.

Communicating at Work Part 2

Wal-Mart

As part of its audacious expansion plan, Wal-Mart sought to introduce discounting strategies in Japan. It joined with Seiyu, Japan's fifth-largest supermarket chain. This local partner promised to help Wal-Mart navigate Japan's dense supplier network as well as provide expensive real estate. But cultural differences may thwart Wal-Mart's expansion hopes.

"Our biggest challenge," said Seiyu President Masao Kiuchi, "is that Japanese people think if it is too cheap, the quality is bad."[38] What's more, they don't understand Wal-Mart's everyday low prices. Most Japanese shoppers are accustomed to weekly advertised bargains. Housewives are addicted to scouring the newspapers for sales and then scurrying around town for the best deals. Wal-Mart, on the other hand, shuns so-called "sales" and features overall low prices every day. Shoppers are also having trouble understanding some of Wal-Mart's jargon, such as "rollbacks."[39]

Teaching employees to sell the Wal-Mart way presents another hurdle. Instead of relying on their hunches, store managers must learn to use laptop computers and spreadsheets to analyze sales and inventory. Company trainers are also trying to teach employees to be more aggressive about approaching customers. One manager explained that the 10-foot rule is difficult for Japanese to apply because they are a very restrained people. In regard to directing employees, Japanese managers balk at the Wal-Mart practice of continually praising coworkers. As one reporter remarked, "Backslapping compliments are rare in a country where workers are taught to be humble and bosses often command respect through intimidation."[40] Unlike American employees, Japanese workers are timid about speaking up to managers and supervisors.

© Fuminori Sato / The New York Times / Redux

Critical Thinking

- How do Japanese and Americans differ on key dimensions of culture as described in this chapter?
- Is it realistic for Wal-Mart's trainers to expect Japanese managers and employees to perform exactly like American workers? Why or why not?
- How can Wal-Mart and other multinational companies overcome the cultural barriers they face when expanding into other countries?

Improving Communication in Intercultural Environments

LEARNING OBJECTIVE 4
Identify techniques for improving nonverbal and oral communication in intercultural environments.

Thus far we've discussed the increasing importance of intercultural proficiency as a result of globalization of markets, increasing migration, and technological advancements. We have described characteristics and dimensions of cultures, and we have talked about avoiding ethnocentrism. Our goal was to motivate you to unlock the opportunities offered by intercultural proficiency. Remember, the key to future business success may very well lie in finding ways to work harmoniously with people from different cultures.

Enhancing Nonverbal Communication in Intercultural Environments

Understanding nonverbal messages is particularly difficult when cultures differ.

Verbal skills in another culture can generally be mastered if one studies hard enough. But nonverbal skills are much more difficult to learn. Nonverbal behavior includes the areas described in Chapter 2, such as eye contact, facial expression, posture, gestures, and the use of time, space, and territory. The messages sent by body language and the way we arrange time and space have always been open to interpretation. Does a raised eyebrow mean that your boss doubts your statement or just that she is seriously considering it? Does that closed door to an office mean that your coworker is angry or just that he is working on a project that requires concentration? Deciphering nonverbal communication is difficult for people who are culturally similar, and it is even more troublesome when cultures differ.

In Western cultures, for example, people perceive silence as a negative trait. It suggests rejection, unhappiness, depression, regret, embarrassment, or ignorance. The English expression, "The silence was deafening," conveys its feeling of oppression. However, the Japanese admire silence and consider it a key to success. A Japanese proverb says, "Those who know do not speak; those who speak do not know." Silence is equated with respect and wisdom.[41]

Gestures can create different reactions in intercultural environments.

Although nonverbal behavior is ambiguous within cultures and even more problematic between cultures, it nevertheless conveys meaning. If you've ever had to talk with someone who does not share your language, you probably learned quickly to use gestures to convey basic messages. Because gestures can create very different reactions in different cultures,

80

Chapter 3: Communicating Across Cultures

one must be careful in using and interpreting them. In some societies it is extremely bad form to point one's finger, as in giving directions. Other hand gestures can also cause trouble. The thumbs-up symbol may be used to indicate approval in North America, but in Iran and Ghana it is a vulgar gesture.

As businesspeople increasingly interact with their counterparts from other cultures, they will become more aware of these differences. Some behaviors are easy to warn against, such as touching people from the Middle East with the left hand (because it is considered unclean and is used for personal hygiene). We are also warned not to touch anyone's head (even children) in Thailand, as the head is considered sacred. Numerous lists of cultural dos and don'ts have been compiled. However, learning all the nuances of nonverbal behavior in other cultures is impossible; such lists are merely the tip of the cultural iceberg.

Although we cannot ever hope to understand fully the nuances of meaning transmitted by nonverbal behavior in various cultures, we can grow more tolerant, more flexible, and eventually, more competent. An important part of achieving nonverbal competence is becoming more aware of our own nonverbal behaviors and their meanings. Much of our nonverbal behavior is learned in early childhood from our families and from society, and it is largely unconscious. Once we become more aware of the meaning of our own gestures, posture, eye gaze, and so on, we will become more alert and more sensitive to variations in other cultures. Striving to associate with people from different cultures can further broaden our intercultural competence.

Becoming more aware of your own use of nonverbal cues can make you more sensitive to variations in other cultures.

Techniques for Achieving Intercultural Competence

In improving effectiveness and achieving intercultural competence, one expert, M. R. Hammer, suggested that three processes or attitudes are effective. *Descriptiveness* refers to the use of concrete and specific feedback. As you learned in Chapter 1 in regard to the process of communication, descriptive feedback is more effective than judgmental feedback. For example, using objective terms to describe the modest attire of Muslim women is more effective than describing it as unfeminine or motivated by oppressive and unequal treatment of females. A second attitude is what Hammer called *nonjudgmentalism*. This attitude goes a long way in preventing defensive reactions from communicators. Most important in achieving effective communication is *supportiveness.* This attitude requires us to support others positively with head nods, eye contact, facial expression, and physical proximity.[42]

Descriptiveness, nonjudgmentalism, and supportiveness all help you broaden your intercultural competence.

From a practical standpoint, when interacting with businesspeople in other cultures, it is always wise to follow their lead. If they avoid intense eye contact, don't stare. If no one is putting his or her elbows on a table, don't be the first to do so. Until you are knowledgeable about the meaning of gestures, it is probably a good idea to keep yours to a minimum. Learning the words for *please, yes,* and *thank you,* some of which are shown in Figure 3.2, is even better than relying on gestures.[43] Achieving intercultural competence in regard to nonverbal behavior may never be totally attained, but sensitivity, nonjudgmentalism, and tolerance go a long way toward improving interactions.

Keep your gestures to a minimum, or follow the lead of native businesspeople.

Enhancing Oral Communication in Intercultural Environments

Although it is best to speak a foreign language fluently, many of us lack that skill. Fortunately, global business transactions are increasingly conducted in English. English has become the language of technology, the language of Hollywood, and the language to know in global business even for traditionally non-English-speaking countries. English is so dominant in business that when Koreans go to China, English is the language they use to conduct business.[44] However, the level of proficiency may be limited among those for whom it is a second language. Americans abroad make a big mistake in thinking that people who speak English always understand what is being said. Comprehension can be fairly superficial. The following suggestions are helpful for situations in which one or both communicators may be using English as a second language.

Don't assume that speakers of English as a second language understand everything you say.

- **Learn foreign phrases.** In conversations, even when English is used, foreign nationals appreciate it when you learn greetings and a few phrases in their language. See Figure 3.2 for a list of basic expressions in some of the world's major languages. Practice the phrases phonetically so that you will be understood.

FIGURE 3.2 Basic Expressions in Other Languages

Country	Good Morning	Please	Thank You	Yes	No	Goodbye
Arabic	saBAH al-khayr	minFUDlak	shookRAAN	NAA-am	LAA	MAA-a salAAMuh
French	Bonjour [bohnzhoor]	S'il vous plaît [see voo pleh]	Merci (beaucoup) [mare-see (bo-coo)]	Oui [weeh]	Non [nonh]	Au revoir [oh vwar]
German	Guten morgen [Goo-ten more-gen]	Bitte [Bitt-eh]	Danke [Dahnk-eh]	Ja [Yah]	Nein [Nine]	Auf Wiedersehen [auwf vee-dur-zain]
Italian	Buon giorno [Bwon jorno]	Per favore/ per piacere	Grazie (tante)	Si	No	ArrivederLa (Arrivederci, informal)
Japanese	Ohayoo [Ohio (go-ZAI-mahss) or simply Ohio]	oh-NEH-ga-ee she-mahss (when requesting)	Arigato [Ah-ree-GAH-tow (go-ZAI-mahss)]	High, so-dess	Ee-yeh	Sayonara
Norwegian	God morgen [Goo morn]	Vaer sa snill [var so snill]	Takk [tahk]	Ja [yah]	Nei [nay]	Adjo [adieu]
Russian	Do'braye oo-tra	Pa-JAH-loos-tah	Spa-SEE-bah	Dah	N'yet	DasviDANya
Spanish	Buenos dias [BWEH-nos DEE-ahs]	Con permiso [Con pair-ME-soh], Por favor [Pohr fah-VOHR]	Gracias [GRAH-seeahs]	Sí [SEEH]	No [NOH]	Adiós

Use simple English and avoid puns, sports references, slang, and jargon when communicating with people for whom English is a second language.

- **Use simple English.** Speak in short sentences (under 20 words) with familiar short words. For example, use *old* rather than *obsolete* and *rich* rather than *luxurious* or *sumptuous*. Eliminate puns, sports and military references, slang, and jargon (special business terms). Be especially alert to idiomatic expressions that can't be translated, such as *burn the midnight oil* and *under the weather*.

- **Speak slowly and enunciate clearly.** Avoid fast speech, but don't raise your voice. Overpunctuate with pauses and full stops. Always write numbers for all to see.

- **Observe eye messages.** Be alert to a glazed expression or wandering eyes—these tell you the listener is lost.

- **Encourage accurate feedback.** Ask probing questions, and encourage the listener to paraphrase what you say. Do not assume that a *yes*, a nod, or a smile indicates comprehension.

To improve communication with those for whom English is a second language, speak slowly, enunciate clearly, observe eye messages, encourage feedback, check for comprehension, accept blame, don't interrupt, remember to smile, and follow up important conversations in writing.

- **Check frequently for comprehension.** Avoid waiting until you finish a long explanation to request feedback. Instead, make one point at a time, pausing to check for comprehension. Do not proceed to B until A has been grasped.

- **Accept blame.** If a misunderstanding results, graciously accept the blame for not making your meaning clear.

- **Listen without interrupting.** Curb your desire to finish sentences or to fill out ideas for the speaker. Keep in mind that North Americans abroad are often accused of listening too little and talking too much.

- **Smile when appropriate.** Roger Axtell, international behavior expert, calls the smile the single most understood and most useful form of communication in either personal or business transactions.[45] In some cultures, however, excessive smiling may seem insincere.[46]

- **Follow up in writing.** After conversations or oral negotiations, confirm the results and agreements with follow-up letters. For proposals and contracts, engage a translator to prepare copies in the local language.

Enhancing Effectiveness in Written Messages to Intercultural Audiences

In sending letters and other documents to businesspeople in other cultures, try to adapt your writing style and tone appropriately. For example, in cultures where formality and tradition are important, be scrupulously polite. Don't even think of sharing the latest joke. Humor translates very poorly and can cause misunderstanding and negative reactions. Familiarize yourself with accepted channels of communication. Are letters, e-mail, and faxes common? Would a direct or indirect organizational pattern be more effective? What's more, forget about trying to cut through "red tape." In some cultures "red tape" is appreciated. The following suggestions, coupled with the earlier guidelines, can help you prepare successful written messages for intercultural audiences.

LEARNING OBJECTIVE 5
Identify techniques for improving written messages to intercultural audiences.

- **Consider local styles.** Learn how documents are formatted and addressed in the intended reader's country. Decide whether to use your organization's preferred format or adjust to local styles.

- **Observe titles and rank.** Use last names, titles, and other signals of rank and status. Send messages to higher-status people and avoid sending copies to lower-rank people.

- **Use short sentences and short paragraphs.** Sentences with fewer than 20 words and paragraphs with fewer than 8 lines are most readable.

- **Avoid ambiguous expressions.** Include relative pronouns (*that, which, who*) for clarity in introducing clauses. Stay away from contractions (especially ones like *Here's the problem*). Avoid idioms and figurative clichés (*once in a blue moon*), slang (*my presentation really bombed*), acronyms (*ASAP,* for *as soon as possible*), abbreviations (*DBA,* for *doing business as*) jargon (*input, bottom line*), and sports references (*play ball, slam dunk, ballpark figure*). Use action-specific verbs (*purchase a printer* rather than *get a printer*).

- **Strive for clarity.** Avoid words that have many meanings (the word *light* has 18 different meanings!). If necessary, clarify words that may be confusing. Replace two-word verbs with clear single words (*return* instead of *bring back; delay* instead of *put off; maintain* instead of *keep up*).

- **Use correct grammar.** Be careful of misplaced modifiers, dangling participles, and sentence fragments. Use conventional punctuation.

- **Cite numbers carefully.** For international trade it is a good idea to learn and use the metric system. In citing numbers use figures (*15*) instead of spelling them out (*fifteen*). Always convert dollar figures into local currency. Avoid using figures to express the month of the year. In North America, for example, March 5, 2009, might be written as 3/5/09, whereas in Europe the same date might appear as 5.3.09. See Figure 3.3 for additional guidelines on data formats.

- **Accommodate the reader in organization, tone, and style.** Organize your message to appeal to the reader. For example, use the indirect strategy for high-context audiences.

To improve written messages, consider local formats, use short sentences and short paragraphs, avoid ambiguous expressions, strive for clarity, use correct grammar, cite numbers carefully, and accommodate readers in organization, tone, and style.

FIGURE 3.3 Typical Data Formats

	United States	United Kingdom	France	Germany	Portugal
Dates	May 15, 2009 5/15/06	15th May 2009 15/5/09	15 mai 2009 15.05.09	15. Mai 2009 15.5.09	09.05.15
Time	10:32 p.m.	10:32 pm	22.32 22 h 32	22:32 Uhr 22.32	22H32m
Currency	$123.45 US$123.45	£123.45 GB£123.45	123F45 123,45F 123.45 euros	DM 123,45 123,45 DM 123.45 euros	123$45 ESC 123.45 123.45 euros
Large numbers	1,234,567.89	1,234,567.89	1.234.567,89 1 234 567	1.234.567,89	1.234.567,89
Phone numbers	(205) 555-1234 205.555.1234	(081) 987 1234 0255 871234	(15) 61-87-12-34 (15) 61.87.12.34	(089) 2 61 12 34	056-212 34 056 45 12 34

FIGURE 3.4 Ineffective Intercultural Letter

Organic Herbal Products

1540 North Third Street
Coeur d'Alene, Idaho 83814

(208) 638-9842
www.organicproducts.com

April 24, 2009

Confuses first and last names; Chinese family names are listed before given names

Mr. Zhao Shanyuan
Eastern Chinese Medicine Export Company
24#1 Longxing Central Road
Huaihua City, Hunan Province
People's Republic of China

Dear Mr. Shanyuan:

Begins informally with slang (*cruising, blown away*)

While cruising the Web, I spotted your site and was totally blown away by your organic herbal products! Just what I'm looking for! If your herbs are half as good as they sound, and if they can get by U.S. customs, I am definitely interested.

Uses overly casual tone throughout and may offend reader by suggesting that products are inferior

Uses ambiguous expression (*really into*), idiom (*pounding down the doors*), figurative cliché (*cash in on craze*)

People in this country are really into Chinese herbs. They're pounding down the doors to get some of the products you show at your Web site. Before I place an order and cash in on this craze, though, I need more information. For one thing, do your herbs and herbal products meet U.S. regulations? What I want to know is if they qualify as food supplements? Another important matter has to do with herbs as legal supplements. Are they? We also need a phytosanitary certificate to import bulk herbs into this country. Can you do that? One more thing. I don't want to put the cart before the horse, so maybe I should try out a small trial order to test the market in my country.

Fails to organize questions into clear format

Includes unclear contraction (*you'll*), acronym (*ASAP*), and unclear date (*6/15*)

If you'll get back to me ASAP, preferably before 6/15, I might do an order. And if everything sounds on the up and up, I might even get over to see you in Huaihua City in the fall.

Uses imprecise expression (*might do an order*) and slang (*on the up and up*)

Caio!

Richard M. Demarjian

Richard M. Demarjian

Closes with *Caio*, which is slang for "stinking" in Singapore

An Intercultural Letter That Misses the Mark

Figure 3.4 illustrates an ineffective intercultural message. The writer uses a casual, breezy tone in a message to a Chinese company when a formal tone would be more appropriate. In addition, the letter includes slang and ambiguous expressions that would almost surely confuse readers for whom English is a second language. Readers may misunderstand expressions such as *cruising the Web, totally blown away, pounding down the doors, cash in on this craze,* and *put the horse before the cart.*

Notice in the effective version of the letter in Figure 3.5 that the writer starts off correctly by addressing the letter to Mr. Zhao. It is often hard for Americans to know whether a Chinese name is the family or given name. In many parts of the world the family name is spoken and written first. Before writing, check to be sure you know the family name. In this letter, the given name is *Shanyuan* and the family name is *Zhao.*

FIGURE 3.5 Effective Intercultural Letter

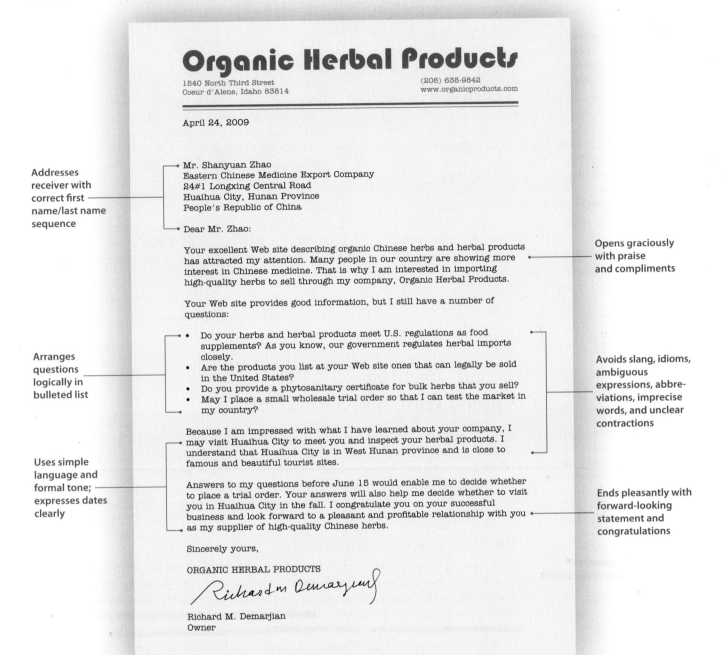

Addresses receiver with correct first name/last name sequence

Opens graciously with praise and compliments

Arranges questions logically in bulleted list

Avoids slang, idioms, ambiguous expressions, abbreviations, imprecise words, and unclear contractions

Uses simple language and formal tone; expresses dates clearly

Ends pleasantly with forward-looking statement and congratulations

In the effective version, the writer adopts a formal but pleasant, polite tone, striving for complete sentences and correct grammar. The effective letter avoids slang (*on the up and up*), idioms, imprecise words (*I might do an order*), unclear abbreviations (*ASAP*), and confusing dates (*6/15*). To further aid comprehension, the writer organizes the letter into a bulleted list with clear questions. Notice, too, that the writer uses simple language throughout. The writer also ends with compliments and wishes for a profitable relationship. Businesspeople in high-context countries, such as China, place great importance on building relationships.

As the world economies continue to intermingle and globalization spreads, more businesspeople are adopting Western ways. Although Japanese writers may open letters with a seasonable greeting (*Cherry trees will soon be blooming*), it is unnecessary for a U.S. correspondent to do so.[47]

The following checklist summarizes suggestions for improving communication with intercultural audiences.

Effective intercultural messages use a pleasant, polite tone that avoids slang, idioms, imprecise words, unclear abbreviations, and confusing dates.

Checklist

Improving Intercultural Proficiency and Communication

✓ **Study your own culture.** Learn about your customs, biases, and views and how they differ from those in other societies. This knowledge can help you better understand, appreciate, and accept the values and behavior of other cultures.

✓ **Learn about other cultures.** Education can help you alter cultural misconceptions, reduce fears, and minimize misunderstandings. Knowledge of other cultures opens your eyes and teaches you to expect differences. Such knowledge also enriches your life.

✓ **Curb ethnocentrism.** Avoid judging others by your personal views. Get over the view that the other cultures are incorrect, defective, or primitive. Try to develop an open mind-set.

✓ **Avoid judgmentalism.** Strive to accept other behavior as different, rather than as right or wrong. Try not to be defensive in justifying your culture. Strive for objectivity.

✓ **Seek common ground.** When cultures clash, look for solutions that respect both cultures. Be flexible in developing compromises.

✓ **Observe nonverbal cues in your culture.** Become more alert to the meanings of eye contact, facial expression, posture, gestures, and the use of time, space, and territory. How do they differ in other cultures?

✓ **Use plain English.** Speak and write in short sentences using simple words and standard English. Eliminate puns, slang, jargon, acronyms, abbreviations, and any words that cannot be easily translated.

✓ **Encourage accurate feedback.** In conversations ask probing questions and listen attentively without interrupting. Do not assume that a *yes* or a smile indicates assent or comprehension.

✓ **Adapt to local preferences.** Shape your writing to reflect the reader's document styles, if appropriate. Express currency in local figures. Write out months of the year for clarity.

Coping With Intercultural Ethics

LEARNING OBJECTIVE 6
Discuss intercultural ethics, including business practices abroad, bribery, prevailing customs, and methods for coping.

A perplexing problem faces conscientious organizations and individuals who do business around the world. Whose values, culture, and, ultimately, laws do you follow? Do you heed the customs of your country or those of the country where you are engaged in business? Some observers claim that when American businesspeople venture abroad, they're wandering into an ethical no-man's land, a murky world of payola where transactions often demand a gratuity to oil the wheels of business.[48]

Business Practices Abroad

When Americans conduct business abroad, their ethics are put to the test.

As companies do more and more business around the globe, their assumptions about ethics are put to the test. Businesspeople may face simple questions regarding the appropriate amount of money to spend on a business gift or the legitimacy of payments to agents and distributors to "expedite" business. They may also encounter out-and-out bribery, child-labor abuse, environment mistreatment, and unscrupulous business practices. In the post-Enron era, the ethics of U.S. businesses are increasingly being scrutinized. Those who violate the law or company policy can land in big trouble. But what ethical standards do these companies follow when they do business abroad?

Today most companies that are active in global markets have ethical codes of conduct. These codes are public documents and can usually be found on company Web sites. They are an accepted part of governance. The growing sophistication of these codes results in ethics training programs that often include complicated hypothetical questions. Ethics trainers teach employees to solve problems by reconciling legal requirements, company policies, and conflicting cultural norms.[49]

Businesses in other countries are also adopting ethics codes and helping employees live up to the standards. In Mexico, where the World Bank estimates that corruption costs nearly 10 percent of the nation's gross domestic product, one food processing company cracked down on "mordidas" (bribes). The company adopted an ethics code forbidding drivers to pay bribes when their trucks were impounded—even though perishable food would go bad. Federal police officers eventually learned that they would receive no bribes, and they stopped impounding the company's trucks. Over time, the company saved more than $100 million because it was no longer paying off officials.[50]

Not all countries, of course, are corrupt. Transparency International, a Berlin-based watchdog group, compiled a ranking of corruption in many countries. Based on polls and surveys of businesspeople and journalists, the index shown in Figure 3.6 presents a look at the perceptions of corruption. Gauging corruption precisely is impossible. But this graph reflects the feelings of individuals doing business in the countries shown. Of the countries selected for this graph, the least corrupt are Finland, New Zealand, Denmark, Sweden, and Switzerland. The most corrupt were Haiti, Iraq, Bangladesh, Pakistan, and Nigeria. The United States ranked between Ireland and Spain, in the top half.

The least corrupt countries are Finland, New Zealand, Denmark, and Sweden.

FIGURE 3.6 Corruption Perceptions Index

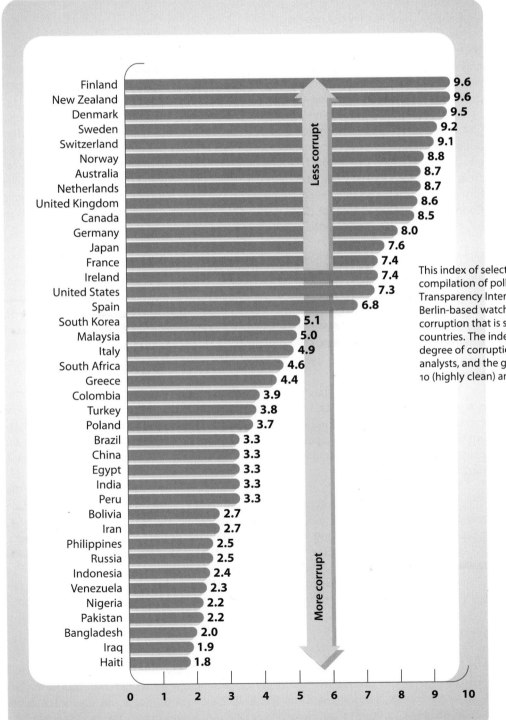

This index of selected countries represents a compilation of polls and surveys put together by Transparency International. The purpose of this Berlin-based watchdog organization is curbing the corruption that is stunting the development of poor countries. The index relates to perceptions of the degree of corruption as seen by businesspeople, risk analysts, and the general public. It ranges between 10 (highly clean) and 0 (highly corrupt).

Laws Forbidding Bribery

The United States leads the global fight against corruption.

The United States is not highest on the index of least corruptible countries. However, it has taken the global lead in fighting corruption. Three decades ago the U.S. government passed the Foreign Corrupt Practices Act of 1977. It prohibits payments to foreign officials for the purpose of obtaining or retaining business. But the law applied only to U.S. companies. Therefore, they were at a decided disadvantage when competing against less scrupulous companies from other nations. U.S. companies complained that they lost billions of dollars in contracts every year because they refused to bribe their way to success.

Most other industrialized countries looked the other way when their corporations used bribes. They considered the "greasing of palms" just a cost of doing business in certain cultures. Until 1999 German corporations were even allowed to deduct bribes as a business expense—as long as they got receipts.

In the United States bribery is a criminal offense, and corporate officials found guilty are fined and sent to jail. The Sarbanes-Oxley Act of 2002 is a new tool in the anticorruption battle. It forbids off-the-book bribes. However, American law does permit payments that may ease the way for routine government actions, such as expediting a visa request. Such payments are reportedly capped at about $500.[51]

More attention is now being paid to the problem of global corruption. With increased global interdependence, corruption is increasingly seen as costly as well as unethical. It has been estimated that moving from a relatively "clean" government like that of Singapore to one as corrupt as Mexico's would have the same effect on foreign direct investment as an increase in the corporate tax rate of 50 percent.[52] Many of the world's industrialized countries formally agreed in 1999 to a new global treaty promoted by the Organization for Economic Cooperation and Development (OECD). This treaty bans the practice of bribery of foreign government officials. Today, bribery is illegal almost everywhere in the world.[53]

Whose Ethics Should Prevail?

Although world leaders agree that bribery of officials is wrong, they do not agree on other ethical behavior.

Although world leaders seem to agree that bribery of officials is wrong, many other shady areas persist. Drawing the lines of ethical behavior here at home is hard enough. When faced with a cultural filter, the picture becomes even murkier. Most people agree that mistreating children is wrong. But in some countries, child labor is not only condoned, it is considered necessary for a family to subsist. Although most countries want to respect the environment, they might also sanction the use of DDT because crops would be consumed by insects without it.

In some cultures "grease" payments to customs officials may be part of their earnings—not blackmail. In parts of Africa a "family" celebration at the conclusion of a business deal includes a party for which you are asked to pay. This payment is a sign of friendship and lasting business relationship, not a personal payoff. In some Third World countries, requests for assistance in developing technologies or reducing hunger may become part of a business package.[54]

Gifts may be a sign of gratitude and hospitality, but they also suggest future obligation.

The exchanging of gifts is another tricky subject. In many non-Western cultures, the gift exchange tradition has become a business ritual. Gifts are not only a sign of gratitude and hospitality, but they also generate a future obligation and trust. Americans, of course, become uneasy when gift giving seems to move beyond normal courtesy and friendliness. If it even remotely suggests influence peddling, they back off. Many companies suggest $50 as a top limit for gifts.

Whose ethics should prevail across borders? Unfortunately, no clear-cut answers can be found. Americans are sometimes criticized for being ethical "fanatics," wishing to impose their "moralistic" views on the world. Also criticized are ethical "relativists," who contend that no absolute values exist.[55]

Making Ethical Decisions Across Borders

Finding practical solutions to ethical problems is most important.

Instead of trying to distinguish "good ethics" and "bad ethics," perhaps the best plan is to look for practical solutions to the cultural challenges of global business interaction. Following are suggestions that acknowledge different values but also respect the need for moral initiative.[56]

- **Broaden your view.** Become more sensitive to the values and customs of other cultures. Look especially at what they consider moral, traditional, practical, and effective.

- **Avoid reflex judgments.** Don't automatically judge the business customs of others as immoral, corrupt, or unworkable. Assume they are legitimate and workable until proved otherwise.

- **Find alternatives.** Instead of caving in to government payoffs, perhaps offer nonmonetary public service benefits, technical expertise, or additional customer service.

- **Refuse business if options violate your basic values.** If an action seriously breaches your own code of ethics or that of your firm, give up the transaction.

- **Work in the fresh air.** Conduct all relations and negotiations as openly as possible.

- **Don't rationalize shady decisions.** Avoid agreeing to actions that cause you to say, *This isn't* really *illegal or immoral, This is in the company's best interest,* or *No one will find out.*

- **Resist legalistic strategies.** Don't use tactics that are legally safe but ethically questionable. For example, don't call *agents* (who are accountable to employers) *distributors* (who are not).

Businesspeople abroad can choose many alternatives that acknowledge different values but also respect the need for moral initiative.

When faced with an intercultural ethical dilemma, you can apply the same five-question test you learned in Chapter 1. Even in another culture, these questions can guide you to the best decision.

1. Is the action you are considering legal?

2. How would you see the problem if you were on the opposite side?

3. What are alternate solutions?

4. Can you discuss the problem with someone whose advice you trust?

5. How would you feel if your family, friends, employer, or coworkers learned of your action?

Capitalizing on Workforce Diversity

LEARNING OBJECTIVE 7
Explain the challenges of, dividends of, and techniques for capitalizing on workforce diversity including being sensitive to racial and gender issues.

At the same time that North American businesspeople are interacting with people from around the world, the domestic workforce is becoming more diverse. This diversity has many dimensions—race, ethnicity, age, religion, gender, national origin, physical ability, and countless other qualities. No longer, say the experts, will the workplace be predominantly Anglo oriented or male. As discussed in Chapter 1, by 2020 many groups now considered minorities (African Americans, Hispanics, Asians, Native Americans) are projected to become 36 percent of the U.S. population. By 2050 these same groups are expected to surge to 47 percent of the U.S. population.[57] Women will become nearly 50 percent of the workforce. Moreover, it is estimated that the share of the population over 65 will jump dramatically from 13 percent now to 20 percent in 2050. Trends suggest that many of these older people will remain in the workforce. Because of technological advances, more physically challenged people are also joining the workforce.

Dividends of Diversity

As society and the workforce become more diverse, successful interaction and communication among the various identity groups bring distinct challenges and dividends in three areas.

A diverse workforce benefits consumers, work teams, and business organizations.

Consumers. A diverse staff is better able to read trends and respond to the increasingly diverse customer base in local and world markets. Diverse consumers now want specialized goods and services tailored to their needs. Teams made up of people with different experiences are better able to create products that these markets require. Consumers also want to deal with companies that respect their values and reflect themselves. "We find that more and more of our clients are demanding that our partners and staff—involved in

With her own television show, doll series, talking kitchen, and line of backpacks, Nickelodeon character Dora the Explorer is the hottest licensing property in the $22 billion toy industry. Tops among a growing list of bilingual toys, the Spanglish-speaking Dora is wildly popular among Hispanic and non-Hispanic children. *How might a diverse workforce benefit businesses that develop multicultural products for global markets?*

securing new business as well as delivering the work—reflect diversity within their organizations," said Toni Riccardi. She represents PricewaterhouseCoopers, the world's largest accounting firm.[58] Sharing this view is Theo Fletcher, vice president of security, compliance, and diversity at IBM's Integrated Supply Chain Group. He said, "It is important that we have a supply base that looks like our employee base and that looks like the market we are trying to attract."[59]

Work Teams. As you learned in Chapter 2, employees today work in teams. Team members with different backgrounds may come up with more creative and effective problem-solving techniques than homogeneous teams. At Procter & Gamble a senior marketing executive hit the nail on the head when he said, "I don't know how you can effectively market to the melting pot that this country represents without a workforce and vendors who have a gut-level understanding of the needs and wants of all of these market segments . . . . When we started getting a more diverse workforce, we started getting richer [marketing] plans, because they came up with things that white males were simply not going to come up with on their own."[60] At PepsiCo, work teams created new products inspired by diversity efforts. Those products included guacamole-flavored Doritos chips and Gatorade Xtremo aimed at Hispanics, as well as Mountain Dew Code Red, which appeals to African Americans. One Pepsi executive said that companies that "figure out the diversity challenge first will clearly have a competitive advantage."[61]

Spotlight on Communicators

"In the past five years, I've realized that customers are the most powerful arbiters of workplace diversity," said J. T. (Ted) Childs Jr. As former vice president, global workforce diversity for IBM Corporation, Childs strived to shift the conversation away from affirmative action and toward the marketplace. Ultimately, he said, promoting diversity is good for business. "More than ever, your customers need to be able to look into your company and see people like themselves."

Business Organizations. Companies that set aside time and resources to cultivate and capitalize on diversity will suffer fewer discrimination lawsuits, fewer union clashes, and less government regulatory action. Most important, though, is the growing realization among organizations that diversity is a critical bottom-line business strategy to improve employee relationships and to increase productivity. Developing a diverse staff that can work together cooperatively is one of the biggest challenges facing business organizations today.

Chapter 3: Communicating Across Cultures

Divisiveness of Diversity

Diversity can be a positive force within organizations. But all too often it can also cause divisiveness, discontent, and clashes. Many of the identity groups, the so-called workforce "disenfranchised," have legitimate gripes.

Women complain of the *glass ceiling*, that invisible barrier of attitudes, prejudices, and "old boy networks" blocking them from reaching important corporate positions. Some women feel that they are the victims of sexual harassment, unequal wages, sexism, and even their style of communication. See the accompanying Career Coach box to learn more about gender talk and gender tension. On the other hand, men, too, have gender issues. One manager described gender discrimination in his office: "My boss was a woman and was very verbal about the opportunities for women to advance in my company. I have often felt she gave much more attention to the women in the office than the men."[62]

Older employees feel that the deck is stacked in favor of younger employees. Minorities complain that they are discriminated against in hiring, retention, wages, and promotions. Physically challenged individuals feel that their limitations should not hold them back, and they fear that their potential is often prejudged. Individuals with different religions feel uncomfortable working alongside each other. A Jew, for example, may be stressed if he has to help train a Palestinian. Similarly, a manager confessed, "I am half Jewish on my father's side. Very often someone will make a comment about Jews and I am always faced with the decision of speaking up or not."[63]

Diversity can cause divisiveness, discontent, and clashes.

The glass ceiling is an invisible barrier of attitudes, prejudices, and "old boy networks" that blocks women from reaching important positions.

CAREER COACH

He Said, She Said: Gender Talk and Gender Tension

Has the infiltration of gender rhetoric done great damage to the workplace? Are men and women throwing rotten tomatoes at each other as a result of misunderstandings caused by stereotypes of "masculine" and "feminine" attitudes? Deborah Tannen's book *You Just Don't Understand: Women and Men in Conversation*, as well as John Grey's *Men Are From Mars, Women Are From Venus*, caused an avalanche of discussion (and some hostility) by comparing the communication styles of men and women. Gender theorists suggest that one reason women can't climb above the glass ceiling is that their communication style is less authoritative than that of men. Here are some of their observations (greatly simplified):[64]

	Women	Men
Object of talk	Establish rapport, make connections, negotiate inclusive relationships	Preserve independence, maintain status, exhibit skill and knowledge
Listening behavior	Attentive, steady eye contact; remain stationary; nod head	Less attentive, sporadic eye contact; move around
Pauses	Frequent pauses, giving chance for others to take turns	Infrequent pauses; interrupt each other to take turns
Small talk	Personal disclosure	Impersonal topics
Focus	Details first, pulled together at end	Big picture
Gestures	Small, confined	Expansive
Method	Questions; apologies; "we" statements; hesitant, indirect, soft speech	Assertions; "I" statements; clear, loud, take-charge speech

Career Application

In small groups or in a class discussion, consider these questions: Do men and women have different communication styles? Which style is more appropriate for today's team-based management? Do we need a kind of communicative affirmative action to give more recognition to women's ways of talking? Should training be given to men and women encouraging the interchangeable use of these styles depending on the situation?

Spotlight on Communicators

In striving to regain Avon's lead in global cosmetics, CEO Andrea Jung had to reorganize the company's total management structure. After years of double-digit growth, Avon's success story turned ugly in 2005 with dramatically reduced revenues. Jung was forced to trim seven layers of management and focus on market-by-market performance. With 70 percent of sales coming from outside the United States, Jung understands how important it is to encourage diversity as well as to avoid groupthink in management decisions. "I have to work harder to bring out the conflict in people because it's my tendency to get everyone to agree. But sometimes conflict is good," she confessed. "You lose a lot of time thinking that people agree and then the issues don't come up. It's important to get them out on the table and work through them."

Tips for Improving Communication Among Diverse Workplace Audiences

Integrating all this diversity into one seamless workforce is a formidable task and a vital one. Harnessed effectively, diversity can enhance productivity and propel a company to success well into the twenty-first century. Mismanaged, it can become a tremendous drain on a company's time and resources. How companies deal with diversity will make all the difference in how they compete in an increasingly global environment. This means that organizations must do more than just pay lip service to these issues. Harmony and acceptance do not happen automatically when people who are dissimilar work together. The following suggestions can help you and your organization find ways to improve communication and interaction.

- **Seek training.** Especially if an organization is experiencing diversity problems, awareness-raising sessions may be helpful. Spend time reading and learning about workforce diversity and how it can benefit organizations. Look upon diversity as an opportunity, not a threat. Intercultural communication, team building, and conflict resolution are skills that can be learned in diversity training programs.

A diverse workforce may reduce productivity unless trained to value differences.

- **Understand the value of differences.** Diversity makes an organization innovative and creative. Sameness fosters an absence of critical thinking called "groupthink," which you learned about in Chapter 2. Case studies, for example, of the *Challenger* shuttle disaster suggest that groupthink prevented alternatives from being considered. Even smart people working collectively can make dumb decisions if they do not see different perspectives.[65] Diversity in problem-solving groups encourages independent and creative thinking.

Don't expect all workers to think or act alike.

- **Don't expect conformity.** Gone are the days when businesses could say, "This is our culture. Conform or leave."[66] Paul Fireman, former CEO of Reebok, stressed seeking people who have new and different stories to tell. "And then you have to make real room for them, you have to learn to listen, to listen closely, to their stories. It accomplishes next to nothing to employ those who are different from us if the condition of their employment is that they become the same as us. For it is their differences that enrich us, expand us, provide us the competitive edge."[67]

- **Learn about your cultural self.** Begin to think of yourself as a product of your culture, and understand that your culture is just one among many. Try to stand outside and look at yourself. Do you see any reflex reactions and automatic thought patterns that are a result of your upbringing? These may be invisible to you until challenged by difference. Remember, your culture was designed to help you succeed and survive in a certain environment. Be sure to keep what works and yet be ready to adapt as environments change.

- **Make fewer assumptions.** Be careful of seemingly insignificant, innocent workplace assumptions. For example, don't assume that everyone wants to observe the holidays with a Christmas party and a decorated tree. Celebrating only Christian holidays in December and January excludes those who honor Hanukkah, Kwanzaa, and the Lunar New Year. Moreover, in workplace discussions don't assume that everyone is married or wants to be or is even heterosexual, for that matter. For invitations, avoid phrases such as *managers and their wives*. *Spouses* or *partners* is more inclusive. Valuing diversity means making fewer assumptions that everyone is like you or wants to be like you.

In times of conflict, look for areas of agreement and build on similarities.

- **Build on similarities.** Look for areas in which you and others not like you can agree or at least share opinions. Be prepared to consider issues from many perspectives, all of which may be valid. Accept that there is room for different points of view to coexist peacefully. Although you can always find differences, it is much harder to find similarities. Look for common ground in shared experiences, mutual goals, and similar values. Concentrate on your objective even when you may disagree on how to reach it.[68]

Communicating at Work Your Turn

Applying Your Skills at Wal-Mart

As part of the U.S. team working with Wal-Mart's Seiyu supermarket chain, you face a big problem. At home Wal-Mart refuses to advertise sales or bargains on specific items. Everyday low prices at Wal-Mart already undercut competitors' prices on nearly all items. After all, the concept of everyday low prices is the bedrock of Wal-Mart's success. In Japan, however, Seiyu's managers contend that Wal-Mart must follow the lead of other local supermarkets and promote sales so that housewives will be enticed to shop at Seiyu. Some members of your team are adamant in demanding that Seiyu discontinue the practice of stuffing mailboxes with circulars publicizing twice-a-week sales.

Although the American management team holds the power and ultimately makes decisions, it resists imposing its will on Seiyu's managers. It is concerned with saving face for them. Yet,

the American managers feel strongly that they should implement the same selling strategies that have worked so well at home.

Your Task

Within your team, discuss and evaluate possible options regarding the promotion of "sales" and distributing circulars twice a week. Select the best option. Your team may be asked to explain its decision to the class or to write an individual summary of the pros and cons of each option. Be prepared to support your choice.

Summary of Learning Objectives

1 **Understand three significant trends related to the increasing importance of intercultural communication for business communicators.** Three trends are working together to crystallize the growing need for developing intercultural proficiencies and improved communication techniques. First, the globalization of markets means that you can expect to be doing business with people from around the world. Second, technological advancements in transportation and information are making the world smaller and more intertwined. Third, more and more immigrants from other cultures are settling in North America, thus changing the complexion of the workforce. Successful interaction requires awareness, tolerance, and accommodation.

2 **Define *culture*, describe five noteworthy cultural characteristics, and compare and contrast five key dimensions of culture including high and low context.** *Culture* is the complex system of values, traits, morals, and customs shared by a society. Significant characteristics of culture include the following: (a) culture is learned, (b) cultures are inherently logical, (c) culture is the basis of self-identity and community, (d) culture combines the visible and invisible, and (e) culture is dynamic. Members of low-context cultures (such as those in North America, Scandinavia, and Germany) depend on words to express meaning, whereas members of high-context cultures (such as those in Japan, China, and Arab countries) rely more on context (social setting, a person's history, status, and position) to communicate meaning. Other key dimensions of culture include individualism, degree of formality, communication style, and time orientation.

3 **Explain the effects of ethnocentrism, tolerance, and patience in achieving intercultural proficiency.** *Ethnocentrism* refers to an individual's feeling that the culture you belong to is superior to all others and holds all truths. To function effectively in a global economy, we must acquire knowledge of other cultures and be willing to change our attitudes. Developing tolerance often involves practicing *empathy*, which means trying to see the world through another's eyes. Saving face and promoting social harmony are important in many parts of the world. Moving beyond narrow ethnocentric views often requires tolerance and patience.

4 **Identify techniques for improving nonverbal and oral communication in intercultural environments.** We can minimize nonverbal miscommunication by recognizing that meanings conveyed by eye contact, posture, and gestures are largely culture dependent. Nonverbal messages are also sent by the use of time, space, and territory. Becoming aware of your own nonverbal behavior and what it conveys is the first step in broadening your intercultural competence. In improving oral messages, you can learn foreign phrases, use simple English, speak slowly and enunciate clearly, observe eye messages, encourage accurate feedback, check for comprehension, accept blame, listen without interrupting, smile, and follow up important conversations in writing.

5 Identify techniques for improving written messages to intercultural audiences. To improve written messages, adopt local formats, observe titles and rank, use short sentences and short paragraphs, avoid ambiguous expressions, strive for clarity, use correct grammar, and cite numbers carefully. Also try to accommodate the reader in organization, tone, and style.

6 Discuss intercultural ethics, including business practices abroad, bribery, prevailing customs, and methods for coping. In doing business abroad, businesspeople should expect to find differing views about ethical practices. Although deciding whose ethics should prevail is tricky, the following techniques are helpful. Broaden your understanding of values and customs in other cultures, and avoid reflex judgments regarding the morality or corruptness of actions. Look for alternative solutions, refuse business if the options violate your basic values, and conduct all relations as openly as possible. Don't rationalize shady decisions. Resist legalistic strategies, and apply a five-question ethics test when faced with a perplexing ethical dilemma.

7 Explain the challenges of, dividends of, and techniques for capitalizing on workforce diversity including being sensitive to racial and gender issues. Having a diverse workforce can benefit consumers, work teams, and business organizations. However, diversity can also cause divisiveness among various identity groups. Business communicators should be aware of and sensitive to differences in the communication techniques of men and women. To promote harmony and communication in diverse workplaces, many organizations develop diversity training programs. As an individual, you must understand and accept the value of differences. Don't expect conformity, and create zero tolerance for bias and prejudice. Learn about your cultural self, make fewer assumptions, and seek common ground when disagreements arise.

Chapter Review

1. Why are domestic companies such as Wal-Mart expanding into overseas markets, and what developments have made such globalization possible? (Obj. 1)

2. Why is geographical location virtually irrelevant for many activities and services today? (Obj. 1)

3. What is culture and how is culture learned? (Obj. 2)

4. Describe five major dimensions of culture. (Obj. 2)

5. Briefly, contrast high- and low-context cultures. (Obj. 2)

6. How do the words *backward, advanced, primitive,* and *sophisticated* relate to *ethnocentrism*? (Obj. 3)

7. How is a *stereotype* different from a *prototype*? (Obj. 3)

8. When interacting with people who do not use your language, why is it important to learn the words for *please, yes,* and *thank you* rather than relying on gestures? (Obj. 4)

9. Name three processes that are effective in achieving competence in dealing with nonverbal messages in other cultures. (Obj. 4)

10. Describe five specific ways you can improve oral communication with someone who speaks another language. (Obj. 4)

11. Describe five specific ways you can improve written communication with someone who speaks another language. (Obj. 5)

12. Why do major companies today hire ethics trainers and create codes of ethics? (Obj. 6)

13. List seven techniques for making ethical decisions across borders. (Obj. 6)

14. Name three groups that benefit from workforce diversity and explain why. (Obj. 7)

15. Describe six tips for improving communication among diverse workplace audiences. (Obj. 7)

Critical Thinking

1. English is becoming the world's business language because the United States is a dominant military and trading force. Why should Americans bother to learn about other cultures? (Objs. 1, 2, and 7)

2. Cultural expert John Engle complained that his American students resist references to cultural generalizations. He asserted, "Thoughtful generalizations are the heart of intercultural communication, allowing us to discuss meaningfully the complex

web of forces acting upon individuals that we call culture." Do you agree or disagree? Why? (Objs. 2, 3)

3. "You can't be a hamburger kind of guy and expect to get along in most cultures," said Frank Brown, a former U.S. business executive and current dean of an international business school south of Paris.[69] What does this statement mean? Do you agree? (Objs. 2, 3)

4. Some economists and management scholars argue that statements such as "diversity is an economic asset" or "diversity is a new strategic imperative" are unproved and perhaps unprovable assertions. Should social responsibility or market forces determine whether an organization strives to create a diverse workforce? Why? (Obj. 7)

5. Aylwin B. Lewis, CEO of Sears Holdings (featured in the Chapter 1 case study), downplays the significance of becoming one of the highest-ranking African Americans in corporate America. When asked about his feelings toward his position, he said, "The notion that I could have a job like this shows us how far we have come in America. The fact that you had to ask the question shows us how far we have to go." What do you think he meant by his response?[70] (Obj. 7)

6. **Ethical Issue:** In many countries government officials are not well paid, and "tips" (called "bribes" in the United States) are a way of compensating them. If such payments are not considered wrong in those countries, should you pay them as a means of accomplishing your business? (Objs. 2, 6)

Activities

3.1 Global Interactions: What We Can Learn When Things Go Wrong (Objs. 1–3)

Intercultural

As business organizations become increasingly global in their structure and marketing, they face communication problems resulting from cultural misunderstandings.

Your Task. Based on what you have learned in this chapter, describe several broad principles that could be applied in helping the individuals involved understand what went wrong in the following events. What suggestions could you make for remedying the problems involved?

a. An advertising agency manager, new to his post in Japan, gathered his team for an old-fashioned brainstorming session in the boardroom. A big presentation loomed, and he expected creative ideas from his staff. Instead, he was met with silence. What went wrong? How could he coax ideas from his staff?[71]

b. J. Bernard van Lierop, a businessperson from Salem, New Hampshire, guided a group of Japanese to a Wisconsin hospital on a business trip. The hospital director threw a handful of his business cards on a table for the Japanese to pick up. "It's so American to dispense with this formality," said Mr. van Lierop.[72] Why might the Japanese be offended?

c. China banned a Nike TV commercial featuring U.S. basketball star LeBron James, who was shown in a video game setting defeating a cartoon kung fu master and a pair of dragons.[73]

d. The employees of a large U.S. pharmaceutical firm became angry over the e-mail messages they received from the firm's employees in Spain. The messages weren't offensive. Generally, these routine messages just explained ongoing projects. What riled the Americans was this: every Spanish message was copied to the hierarchy within its division. The Americans could not understand why e-mail messages had to be sent to people who had little or nothing to do with the issues being discussed. But this was accepted practice in Spain.[74]

e. As China moves from a planned to a market economy, professionals suffer the same signs of job stress experienced in Western countries. Multinational companies have long offered counseling to their expatriate managers. But locals frowned on any form of psychological therapy. Recently, China's largest bank hired Chestnut Global Partners to offer employee counseling services. Chestnut learned immediately that it could not talk about such issues as conflict management. Instead, Chestnut stressed workplace harmony. Chestnut also found that Chinese workers refused one-on-one counseling.[75] They preferred group sessions or online counseling. What cultural elements were at work here?

3.2 Learning to Cope With International Time (Objs. 1–5)

Web

Assume you are a virtual assistant working from your home. As part of your job, you schedule webcasts, online chats, and teleconference calls for businesspeople who are conducting business around the world.

Your Task. To broaden your knowledge of time zones, respond to the following:

a. What does the abbreviation UTC indicate? (Use Google and search for *UTC definition*.)

b. Internationally, time is shown with a 24-hour clock (sometimes called "military time"). What time does 13.00 indicate? (Use Google; search for *24-hour clock*.) How is a 12-hour clock different from a 24-hour clock? With which are you most familiar?

c. You must schedule a teleconference for a businessperson in Indianapolis, Indiana, who wants to talk with a person in Osaka, Japan. What are the best business hours (between 8 and 5) for them to talk? (Many Web sites provide time zone converters. For example, try **http://www.timeanddate.com**. Click **Meeting Planner**. Follow the instructions for selecting a day and locations.)

d. What are the best business hours for an online chat between an executive in Atlanta and a vendor in Singapore? Your instructor may select other cities for you to search.

3.3 Global Economy (Obj. 1)

Intercultural

Fred Smith, CEO of Federal Express, said, "It is an inescapable fact that the U.S. economy is becoming much more like the European and Asian economies, entirely tied to global trade."

Your Task. Read your local newspapers for a week and peruse national news periodicals (*Time, Newsweek, BusinessWeek, U.S. News, The Wall Street Journal*, and so forth) for articles that support this assertion. Your instructor may ask you to (a) report on many articles or (b) select one article to summarize. Report your findings orally or in a memo to your instructor. This topic could be expanded into a long report for Chapters 13 or 14.

3.4 Cross-Cultural Gap at Resort Hotel in Thailand (Objs. 1–4)

Intercultural   **Team**

The Laguna Beach Resort Hotel in Phuket, Thailand, nestled between a tropical lagoon and the sparkling Andaman Sea, is one of the most beautiful resorts in the world. (You can take a virtual tour by using Google and searching for *Laguna Beach Resort Phuket*.) When Brett Peel arrived as the director of the hotel's kitchen, he thought he had landed in paradise. Only on the job six weeks, he

© mediacolor's / Alamy

began wondering why his Thai staff would answer *yes* even when they didn't understand what he had said. Other foreign managers discovered that junior staff managers rarely spoke up and never expressed an opinion contrary to those of senior executives. What's more, guests with a complaint thought that Thai employees were not taking them seriously because the Thais smiled at even the worst complaints. Thais also did not seem to understand deadlines or urgent requests.[76]

Your Task. In teams decide how you would respond to the following. If you were the director of this hotel, would you implement a training program for employees? If so, would you train only foreign managers, or would you include local Thai employees as well? What topics should a training program include? Would your goal be to introduce Western ways to the Thais? At least 90 percent of the hotel guests are non-Thai.

3.5 From Waterloo, Wisconsin, Trek Bicycles Goes Global (Objs. 1, 3, and 7)

Intercultural

In winning his sixth Tour de France, the world's most grueling bicycle race, Lance Armstrong brought international prestige to Waterloo, Wisconsin. That is the home of Trek Bicycle, manufacturer of the superlightweight carbon bikes Armstrong has ridden to victory over the years. The small town of Waterloo (population 2,888) is about the last place you would expect to find the world's largest specialty bicycle maker. Trek started its global business in a red barn smack in the middle of Wisconsin farm country. It employs 1,500 people in Waterloo and serves 2,000 stores in the United States alone and 4,000 dealers worldwide in 65 countries. Nearly 50 percent of the sales of the high-tech bicycles come from international markets. Future sales abroad look promising as Trek expands into Chinese and Indian markets. In Asia, bicycles are a major means of transportation. To accommodate domestic and international consumers, Trek maintains a busy Web site at **http://www.trekbikes.com**.

Like many companies, Trek encountered problems in conducting intercultural transactions. For example, in Mexico, cargo was often pilfered while awaiting customs clearance. Distributors in Germany were offended by catalogs featuring pictures of Betty Boop, a cartoon character that decorated Allied bombers during World War II. In Singapore a buyer balked at a green bike helmet, explaining that when a man wears green on his head it means his wife is unfaithful. In Germany, Trek had to redesign its packaging to reduce waste and meet environmental requirements. Actually, the changes required in Germany helped to bolster the company's overall image of environmental sensitivity.

Your Task. Based on principles you studied in this chapter, name several lessons that other entrepreneurs can learn from Trek's international experiences.[77]

3.6 Interpreting Intercultural Proverbs (Objs. 2, 3)

Intercultural

Proverbs, which tell truths with metaphors and simplicity, often reveal fundamental values held by a culture.

Your Task. Discuss the following proverbs and explain how they relate to some of the cultural values you studied in this chapter. What additional proverbs can you cite, and what do they mean?

North American proverbs
>An ounce or prevention is worth a pound of cure.
>The squeaking wheel gets the grease.
>A bird in the hand is worth two in the bush.
>He who holds the gold makes the rules.

Japanese proverbs
>A wise man hears one and understands ten.
>The pheasant would have lived but for its cry.
>The nail that sticks up gets pounded down.

German proverbs
>No one is either rich or poor who has not helped himself to be so.
>He who is afraid of doing too much always does too little.

3.7 Negotiating Traps (Objs. 2–5)

Intercultural

Businesspeople often have difficulty reaching agreement on the terms of contracts, proposals, and anything that involves bargaining. They have even more difficulty when the negotiators are from different cultures.

Your Task. Discuss the causes and implications of the following common mistakes made by North Americans in their negotiations with foreigners.

a. Assuming that a final agreement is set in stone
b. Lacking patience and insisting that matters progress more quickly than the pace preferred by the locals
c. Thinking that an interpreter is always completely accurate
d. Believing that individuals who speak English understand every nuance of your meaning
e. Ignoring or misunderstanding the significance of rank

3.8 Hearing Greetings in Other Countries (Obj. 4)

Intercultural

When meeting people from other countries, you will feel more comfortable if you know the greeting procedure and recognize how the greeting sounds.

Your Task. Visit the Aquent site at **http://www.businessoftouch.com**. (If this URL doesn't work, use Google to search for *Business of Touch*.) Watch and listen to the animated tutorials.

a. How do people greet each other in Australia, India, Japan, Korea, Netherlands, and Spain?
b. In what countries is it important to keep a certain distance from the person you are greeting?
c. In what countries is a kiss appropriate?

3.9 Analyzing a Problem International Letter (Obj. 5)

Intercultural

American writers sometimes forget that people in other countries, even if they understand English, are not aware of the meanings of certain words and phrases.

Interactive Learning @ www.meguffey.com

Your Task. Study the following letter[78] to be sent by a U.S. firm to a potential supplier in another country. Identify specific weaknesses that may cause troubles for intercultural readers.

Dear Hoshi:

Because of the on-again/off-again haggling with one of our subcontractors, we have been putting off writing to you. We were royally turned off by their shoddy merchandise, the excuses they made up, and the way they put down some of our customers. Since we have our good name to keep up, we have decided to take the bull by the horns and see if you would be interested in bidding on the contract for spare parts.

By playing ball with us, your products are sure to score big. So please give it your best shot and fire off your price list ASAP. We will need it by 3/8 if you are to be in the running.

Yours,

3.10 Talking Turkey: Avoiding Ambiguous Expressions (Obj. 5)

Intercultural

When a German firm received a message from an American firm saying that it was "time to talk turkey," it was puzzled but decided to reply in Turkish, as requested.

Your Task. Assume you are a businessperson engaged in exporting and importing. As such, you are in constant communication with suppliers and customers around the world. In messages sent abroad, what kinds of ambiguous expressions should you avoid? In teams or individually, list three to five original examples of idioms, slang, acronyms, sports references, abbreviations, jargon, and two-word verbs.

3.11 *Baksheesh, Mordida,* and *Kumshah:* Making Grease Payments Abroad (Obj. 6)

Ethics **Intercultural**

In the Middle East, bribes are called *baksheesh*. In Mexico, they are *mordida*; and in Southeast Asia, *kumshah*. Although it takes place in many parts of the world, bribery is not officially sanctioned by any country. In the United States the Foreign Corrupt Practices Act prohibits giving anything of value to a foreign official in an effort to win or retain business. However, this law does allow payments that may be necessary to expedite or secure "routine governmental action." For instance, a company could make small payments to obtain permits and licenses or to process visas or work orders. Also allowed are payments to secure telephone service and power and water supplies, as well as payments for the loading and unloading of cargo.

Your Task. In light of what you have learned in this chapter, how should you act in the following situations? Are the actions legal or illegal?[79]

a. Your company is moving toward final agreement on a contract in Pakistan to sell farm equipment. As the contract is prepared, officials ask that a large amount be included to enable the government to update its agriculture research. The extra amount is to be paid in cash to the three officials you have worked with. Should your company pay?

b. You have been negotiating with a government official in Niger regarding an airplane maintenance contract. The official asks to use your Diner's Club card to charge $2,028 in airplane tickets as a honeymoon present. Should you do it to win the contract?

c. You are trying to collect an overdue payment of $163,000 on a shipment of milk powder to the Dominican Republic. A senior government official asks for $20,000 as a collection service fee. Should you pay?

d. Your company is in the business of arranging hunting trips to East Africa. You are encouraged to give guns and travel allowances to officials in a wildlife agency that has authority to issue licenses to hunt big game. The officials have agreed to keep the gifts quiet. Should you make the gifts?

e. Your firm has just moved you to Malaysia, and your furniture is sitting on the dock. Cargo handlers won't unload it until you or your company pays off each local dock worker. Should you pay?

f. In Mexico your firm has been working hard to earn lucrative contracts with the national oil company, Pemex. One government official has hinted elaborately that his son would like to do marketing studies for your company. Should you hire the son?

3.12 Investigating Gifts, Gratuities, and Entertainment Limits (Obj. 7)

Ethics **Intercultural**

You are one of a group of interns at a large company. As part of your training, your director asks your team to investigate the codes of conduct of other companies. In particular, the manager asks you to find comparison information on gifts, gratuities, and kickbacks.

Your Task. Search the Web for sections in codes of conduct that relate to gifts, gratuities, entertainment, and kickbacks. From three companies or organizations (such as BlueCross BlueShield, 3M Corporation, or a university), investigate specific restrictions. What do these organizations allow and restrict? Prepare a list summarizing your findings in your own words.

3.13 Diversity Role-Playing: Hey, We're All Clones! (Obj. 7)

Reebok International, the athletic footwear and apparel company, swelled from a $12-million-a-year company to a $3 billion footwear powerhouse in less than a decade. "When we were growing very, very fast, all we did was bring another friend into work the next day," recalled Sharon Cohen, Reebok vice president. "Everybody hired nine of their friends. Well, it happened that nine white people hired nine of their friends, so guess what? They were white, all about the same age. And then we looked up and said, 'Wait a minute. We don't like the way it looks here.'"[80] Assume you are a manager for a successful, fast-growing company like Reebok. One day you look around and notice that everyone looks alike.

Your Task. Pair off with a classmate to role-play a discussion in which you strive to convince another manager that your organization would be better if it were more diverse. The other manager (your classmate), however, is satisfied with the status quo. Suggest advantages for diversifying the staff. The opposing manager argues for homogeneity.

3.14 What Makes a "Best" Company for Minorities? (Obj. 7)

In its ranking of the "50 Best Companies for Minorities," *Fortune* listed the following suggestions for fostering diversity: [81]

- Make an effort to hire, retain, and promote minorities.
- Interact with outside minority communities.
- Hold management accountable for diversity efforts.

- Create a culture where people of color and other minorities feel that they belong.
- Match a diverse workforce with diversity in an organization's management ranks and on its board.

Your Task. Assume you are the individual in Activity 3.13 who believes your organization would be better if it were more diverse. Because of your interest in this area, your boss says he'd like you to give a three- to five-minute informational presentation at the next board meeting. Your assignment is to provide insights on what the leading companies for minority employees are doing. You decide to prepare your comments based on *Fortune* magazine's list of the 50 best companies for minorities, using as your outline the previous bulleted list. You plan to provide examples of each means of fostering diversity. Your instructor may ask you to give your presentation to the entire class or to small groups.

3.15 Locating Diversity Training Consultants (Obj. 7)

`E-Mail` `Web`

Management thought it was doing the right thing in diversifying its staff. But now signs of friction are appearing. Staff meetings are longer, and conflicts have arisen in solving problems. Some of the new people say they aren't taken seriously and that they are expected to blend in and become just like everybody else. A discrimination suit was filed in one department.

Your Task. CEO William Somers asks you, a human resources officer, to present suggestions for overcoming this staff problem. Make a list of several suggestions, based on what you have learned in this chapter. In addition, go to the Web and locate three individuals, teams, or firms who you think might be possibilities for developing a diversity training program for your company. Prepare a memo or an e-mail to Mr. Somers outlining your suggestions and listing your recommendations for possible diversity training consultants. Describe the areas of expertise of each potential consultant.

3.16 Consumer: Could You Become a Victim to Cross-Border Fraud?

`Consumer` `E-Mail` `Team` `Web`

Exciting advancements in trade and technology have given consumers unprecedented access to new products, services, information, and markets. But they have also exposed large numbers of consumers to scams and fraud. Pyramid and lottery schemes, travel- and credit-related ploys, and high-tech scams such as modem and Web-page hijacking now plague consumers. Business communicators must be especially alert to cross-border fraud because operators strike quickly and then disappear.

Your Task. To arm yourself against cross-border fraud, use the Web to learn about the latest scams and what you can do if victimized. Individually, search for answers to the questions listed here. Then in teams discuss your findings. Individually or in teams, use e-mail to report your findings to your instructor.

a. What are six kinds of cross-border fraud that have been reported? Explain each.
b. What should you do before ordering from a Web site?
c. What should you do to resolve your complaint if something goes wrong?

Video Resources

Video Library 1. The recommended video for this chapter is *Intercultural Communication at Work*. After watching this video, be prepared to identify the intercultural conflicts that are illustrated and to suggest ways to avoid them.

Grammar and Mechanics C.L.U.E. Review 3

Pronouns

Review Guides 11–18 about pronoun usage in Appendix A: Grammar and Mechanics Guide (Competent Language Usage Essentials), beginning on page A-6. On a separate sheet, revise the following sentences to correct errors in pronouns. For each error that you locate, write the guide number that reflects this usage. Some sentences may have two errors. If the sentence is correct, write *C*. When you finish, check your answers on page Key-1.

Example: We hope that him and her will both be promoted.
Revision: We hope that he and she will both be promoted. [Guide 12]

1. Forward the e-mail to the manager and I so that he and I can study it.

2. Just between you and I, a new salary schedule will soon be announced.

3. The software and it's documentation are difficult to understand.

4. My friend and me could find all of the reports except yours.

5. Tamara and I want all applications sent to her or myself.

6. Every employee should see their performance review in a timely manner.

7. Please deliver the printer supplies to whomever ordered them.

8. Most applications arrived on time, but your's and her's were not received.

9. Because of our outstanding sales, the company gave bonuses to Dario and me.

10. Whom did you say left messages for Jennifer and me?

Interactive Learning @ www.meguffey.com

Unit 2

The 3-x-3 Writing Process

Chapter 4
Writing Process Phase 1:
Analyze, Anticipate,
Adapt

Chapter 5
Writing Process Phase 2:
Research, Organize,
Compose

Chapter 6
Writing Process Phase 3:
Revise, Proofread,
Evaluate

Chapter 4

Writing Process Phase 1: Analyze, Anticipate, Adapt

OBJECTIVES

After studying this chapter, you should be able to

1 Identify four basic principles of business writing, summarize the 3-x-3 writing process, and explain how a writing process helps a writer.

2 Explain how the writing process may be altered and how it is affected by team-written projects requiring collaboration.

3 Clarify what is involved in analyzing a writing task and selecting a communication channel.

4 Analyze the process of anticipating and profiling three typical audiences for business messages: colleagues, decision makers, and customers.

5 Effectively apply audience benefits, the "you" view, bias-free language, a conversational but professional tone, positive expression, courtesy, simple language, and precise words.

6 Summarize the legal and ethical responsibilities of business communicators in the areas of investments, safety, marketing, human resources, and copyright law.

© Tom Grill / Corbis

Communicating at Work Part 1

Suze Orman Preaches Financial Freedom in Simple Language

Personal finance guru Suze Orman has a mission. She wants to change the way people think, act, and talk about money. One of the most widely read financial authorities of our time, she has written seven best-selling financial guidance books. But she is probably best known for her television programs including specials for PBS, the syndicated *Financial Freedom Hour* on QVC network, and an advice show on CNBC. She is also a columnist for *O*, Oprah Winfrey's magazine, and for Yahoo's personal finance site.

Orman's advice is largely for people who are drowning in debt. "Sweetheart," she says to a caller, "burn those credit cards!" She delivers her gospel of financial freedom with an animated conviction and high-energy style that have become her hallmark.[1] In her books and magazine articles, she speaks with the same assurance. "Having talked to literally tens of thousands of people, I can say that what is good for America . . . . is not having credit card debt, not leasing a car, and not having mortgage debt. This is not good for a human being. It's just not!"[2]

Orman knows what it is like to be in debt. After graduating with a degree in sociology, she worked for seven years as a waitress at the Buttercup Bakery in Berkeley, California. With a $50,000 loan from her customers, she intended to finance her own restaurant. Because of bad advice from an investment firm, she lost her $50,000 within four months. However, "she made it all up and then some after the firm hired her as its only female broker."[3]

As a broker, she developed her financial planning skills and built a reputation for honesty and ethical advice. Her books and articles combine emotional and spiritual observations about money and how to avoid the financial problems that caused pain for her family as she was growing up. *The Money Book for the Young, Fabulous and Broke* directs financial advice at young people early in their working lives.

She admits that her message is not new. "It's not the material that I know, but how I communicate the material I know that sets me apart."[4] Orman's advice is practical and cuts through much confusing, contradictory financial information. One of her greatest strengths is breaking complex ideas into easy-to-understand segments. Like

many great communicators, she knows her audience, shapes her message accordingly, and uses simple language.

Critical Thinking
- Whether one is writing a book, making a speech, or composing a business letter, why is it important to anticipate the audience for the message?
- What does writing an effective financial help book have in common with writing an effective business message?
- Why is it important to follow a writing process?

http://www.suzeorman.com

Approaching the Writing Process Systematically

As you approach any writing task or presentation, the task seems easier if you have a systematic process to follow. When financial expert Suze Orman starts a writing assignment, she focuses totally on the task at hand. She takes no phone calls, answers no e-mail, and allows no interruptions. In delivering a convincing message, she employs many of the writing techniques you are about to learn. This chapter presents business writing basics, the 3-x-3 writing process, team writing, and specific tips in Phase 1 of the writing process.

LEARNING OBJECTIVE 1
Identify four basic principles of business writing, summarize the 3-x-3 writing process, and explain how a writing process helps a writer.

Business Writing Basics

Business writing differs from other writing you may have done. In preparing high school or college compositions and term papers, you probably focused on discussing your feelings or displaying your knowledge. Professors wanted to see your thought processes, and they wanted assurance that you had internalized the subject matter. You may have had to meet a minimum word count. Business writers, however, have different goals. For business messages and oral presentations, your writing should be:

- **Purposeful.** You will be writing to solve problems and convey information. You will have a definite purpose to fulfill in each message.

- **Persuasive.** You want your audience to believe and accept your message.

Business writing is purposeful, persuasive, economical, and reader oriented.

- **Economical.** You will try to present ideas clearly but concisely. Length is not rewarded.

- **Reader oriented.** You will concentrate on looking at a problem from the reader's perspective instead of seeing it from your own.

Business writers seek to express rather than impress.

These distinctions actually ease the writer's task. In writing most business documents, you won't be searching your imagination for creative topic ideas. You won't be stretching your ideas to make them appear longer. One writing consultant complained that newly hired graduates entering industry seem to think that quantity enhances quality.[5] Wrong! Get over the notion that longer is better. Conciseness is what counts in business. Furthermore, you won't be trying to dazzle readers with your extensive knowledge, powerful vocabulary, or graceful phrasing. The goal in business writing is to *express* rather than *impress*. You will be striving to get your ideas across naturally, simply, and clearly. At the same time, you want to be persuasive and convincing.

In many ways business writing is easier than academic writing, yet it still requires hard work, especially from beginners. But following a process, studying models, and practicing the craft can make nearly anyone a successful business writer and speaker. This book provides all three components: process, products (models), and practice. First, you will focus on the process of writing business messages.

The 3-x-3 Writing Process

The phases of the 3-x-3 writing process are prewriting, writing, and revising.

This book divides the writing process into three distinct phases, as shown in Figure 4.1, with each phase further divided into three major activities. This 3-x-3 process provides you with a systematic plan for developing all your business communications—from simple memos and informational reports to corporate proposals and presentations.

The time spent on each phase varies with the deadline, purpose, and audience for the message. Let's consider how the 3-x-3 writing process might work in a typical business situation. Suppose you must write a letter to a department store buyer about a jeans order that your company cannot fill. The first phase prepares you to write and involves analyzing, anticipating, and adapting. In analyzing the situation, you decide to focus your letter on retaining the order. That can best be done by persuading the buyer to accept a different jeans model. You anticipate that the buyer will be disappointed that the original model is unavailable. What's more, she will probably be reluctant to switch to a different model. Thus, you must find ways to adapt your message to reduce her reluctance and convince her to switch.

The second phase involves researching, organizing, and then composing the message. To collect facts for this letter, you would probably investigate the buyer's past purchases. You would check to see what jeans you have in stock that she might accept as a substitute. You might do some brainstorming or consult your colleagues for their suggestions about how to retain this order. Then, you would organize your information into a loose outline and decide on a strategy or plan for revealing your information most effectively. Equipped with a plan, you are ready to compose the first draft of the letter.

FIGURE 4.1 The 3-x-3 Writing Process

1 Prewriting	**2 Writing**	**3 Revising**
Analyze: Decide on your purpose. What do you want the receiver to do or believe? What channel is best?	**Research:** Gather data to provide facts. Search company files, previous correspondence, and the Internet. What do you need to know to write this message?	**Revise:** Edit your message to be sure it is clear, conversational, concise, and readable.
Anticipate: Profile the audience. What does the receiver already know? Will the receiver's response be neutral, positive, or negative?	**Organize:** Group similar facts together. Decide how to organize your information. Outline your plan and make notes.	**Proofread:** Read carefully to find errors in spelling, grammar, punctuation, names, numbers, and format.
Adapt: What techniques can you use to adapt your message to its audience and anticipated reaction?	**Compose:** Prepare a first draft, usually writing quickly.	**Evaluate:** Will this message achieve your purpose? Have you thought enough about the audience to be sure this message is appropriate and appealing?

The third phase of the writing process involves revising, proofreading, and evaluating your letter. After writing the first draft, you will revise the message for clarity, conciseness, tone, and readability. You will proofread carefully to ensure correct spelling, grammar, punctuation, and format. Finally, you will evaluate the message to see whether it accomplishes your goal.

Adapting and Altering the Writing Process

Although the diagram in Figure 4.1 shows the three phases equally, the time you spend on each varies. Moreover, the process is not always linear.

LEARNING OBJECTIVE 2
Explain how the writing process may be altered and how it is affected by team-written projects requiring collaboration.

Scheduling the Process. One expert gives these rough estimates for scheduling a writing project: 25 percent worrying and planning (Phase 1), 25 percent writing (Phase 2), 45 percent revising, and 5 percent proofreading (Phase 3). These are rough guides, yet you can see that good writers spend most of their time revising. Much depends, of course, on your project, its importance, and your familiarity with it. What's critical to remember, though, is that revising is a major component of the writing process.

In the writing process, revising takes the most time.

This process may seem a bit complicated for the daily messages and oral presentations that many businesspeople prepare. Does this same process apply to e-mails, memos, and short letters? How do collaborators and modern computer technologies affect the process?

Although good writers proceed through each phase of the writing process, some steps may be compressed for short, routine messages. Brief everyday documents enlist the 3-x-3 process, but many of the steps are performed quickly, without prolonged deliberation. For example, prewriting may take the form of a few moments of reflection. The writing phase may consist of looking in the files quickly, jotting a few notes in the margin of the original document, and composing at your computer. Revising might consist of reading a printout, double-checking the spelling and grammar, and making a few changes. Longer, more involved documents—such as persuasive memos, sales letters, management reports, proposals, and résumés—require more attention to all parts of the process.

Recursive Nature of the Process. One other point about the 3-x-3 writing process needs clarification. It may appear that you perform one step and progress to the next, always following a linear order. Most business writing, however, is not that rigid. Although writers perform the tasks described, the steps may be rearranged, abbreviated, or repeated. Some writers revise every sentence and paragraph as they go. Many find that new ideas occur after they've begun to write, causing them to back up, alter the organization, and rethink their plan. Thus, the 3-x-3 writing process is more nearly recursive than linear. It sometimes curves backward before moving forward.

Steps in the writing process may be rearranged, shortened, or repeated.

You should expect to follow the 3-x-3 process closely as you begin developing your business communication skills. With experience, though, you will become like other good writers and presenters who alter, compress, and rearrange the steps as needed.

Writing in Teams

As you learned in Chapter 2, many of today's workers will work in teams to deliver services, develop products, and complete projects. It is almost assumed that today's progressive organizations will employ teams in some capacity to achieve their objectives. Because much of a team's work involves writing, you can expect to be putting your writing skills to work as part of a team.

When Are Team-Written Documents Necessary? Collaboration on team-written documents is necessary for projects that (a) are big, (b) have short deadlines, and (c) require the expertise or consensus of many people. Businesspeople sometimes collaborate on short documents, such as memos, letters, information briefs, procedures, and policies. But more often, teams work together on big documents and presentations.

Team-written documents are necessary for big projects that have short deadlines and that require the efforts of many people.

Why Are Team Documents Better? Team-written documents and presentations are standard in most organizations because collaboration has many advantages. Most important,

Team-written documents and presentations produce better products.

collaboration usually produces a better product because many heads are better than one. In addition, team members and organizations benefit from team processes. Working together helps socialize members. They learn more about the organization's values and procedures. They are able to break down functional barriers, and they improve both formal and informal chains of communication. Additionally, they "buy into" a project when they are part of its development. Members of effective teams are eager to implement their recommendations.

Teams generally work closely in Phase 1, work separately in Phase 2, and synthesize their drafts in Phase 3.

How Are Team Documents Divided?
With big writing projects, teams may not actually function together for each phase of the writing process. Typically, team members gather at the beginning to brainstorm. They iron out answers to questions about the purpose, audience, content, organization, and design of their document or presentation. They develop procedures for team functioning, as you learned in Chapter 2. Then, they often assign segments of the project to individual members. Thus, teams work together closely in Phase 1 (prewriting) of the writing process. However, members generally work separately in Phase 2 (writing), when they conduct research, organize their findings, and compose a first draft. During Phase 3 (revising) teams may work together to synthesize their drafts and offer suggestions for revision. They might assign one person the task of preparing the final document and another the job of proofreading. The revision and evaluation phase might be repeated several times before the final product is ready for presentation.

What Online Collaboration Tools Support Team Writing?
One of the most frustrating tasks for teams is writing shared documents. Keeping the different versions straight and recognizing who made what comment can be confusing. Fortunately, many online collaboration tools are constantly being developed and improved. They range from simple to complex, inexpensive to expensive, locally installed to remotely hosted, commercial to open source, and large to small. Online collaboration tools are especially necessary when team members are not physically in the same location. But even when members are nearby, they may find it necessary to use online collaboration tools, such as the following:[6]

- **E-mail.** Despite its many drawbacks, e-mail remains a popular tool for online asynchronous (intermittent data transmission) collaboration.

Team writing and collaboration have never been easier, thanks to the wiki. Named after the Hawaiian word for "quick" and popularized by online encyclopedia Wikipedia, wikis enable teams to create and edit shared documents using a simple Web browser. Businesses from Nokia to Motorola are using popular enterprise-class wikis like Atlassian and Socialtext, and about half of all companies will use online collaboration tools within the next year. *What are the pros and cons of using wikis?*

© Purestock / Getty Images

Chapter 4: Writing Process Phase 1: Analyze, Anticipate, Adapt

- **Mailing lists.** With the right software, mailing lists can be archived online, providing a threaded listing of posts and full-text searching.

- **Discussion boards.** Participants can upload documents to the board instead of sending large files to everyone.

- **Instant messaging.** Because it ensures immediate availability, instant messaging is gaining acceptance. It allows members to clear up minor matters immediately, and it is helpful in initiating a quick group discussion.

- **Groupware and portals.** Groupware and portals usually involve expensive software featuring online discussion areas, document and file-sharing areas, integrated calendaring, and collaborative authoring tools.

- **Blogs and wikis.** Blogs, discussed in Chapter 2, are helpful in spreading ideas quickly. Wikis are good tools for building a knowledge repository that can be edited by participants.

In writing shared documents, teams may use e-mail, mailing lists, discussion boards, instant messaging, groupware, portals, blogs, and wikis.

What Tools Work Well for Student Collaboration? Student groups collaborating on assignments may find three tools helpful. Google Docs & Spreadsheets is a free Web-based word processing and spreadsheet program that keeps documents current and lets team members update files from their own computers. A second free collaborative writing tool is Writeboard. Check out either of these free tools by searching Google. A third option, which is part of Microsoft Word, provides a number of tools that enable team members to track changes and insert comments while editing one team document. The accompanying Tech Talk box discusses these tools, and Figure 4.2 illustrates how they work.

In Figure 4.2 team members' comments appear in callout balloons with different colors. Deleted items appear in red balloons.

FIGURE 4.2 Team-Written Document Showing Word Collaboration Tools

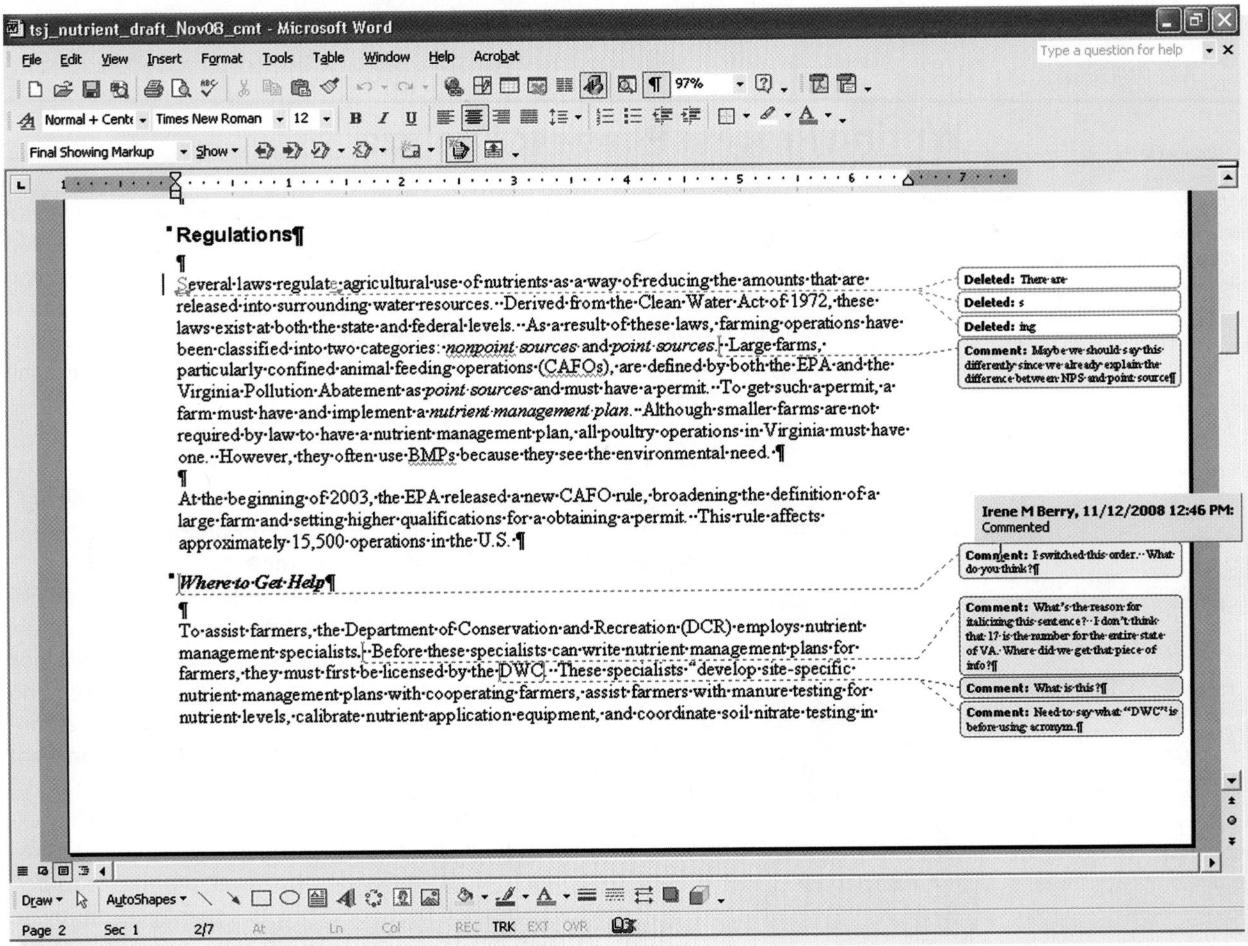

TechTalk

Using Technology to Edit and Revise Collaborative Documents

Collaborative writing and editing projects are challenging. Fortunately, Microsoft Word offers many useful tools to help team members edit and share documents electronically. Two simple but useful editing tools are **Highlight** and **Font Color**. These tools, which are found on the **Formatting** toolbar, enable reviewers to point out errors and explain problematic passages through the use of contrast. However, some projects may require more advanced editing tools such as **Track Changes** and **Insert Comments**.

Track Changes. To suggest specific editing changes to other team members, **Track Changes** is handy. The revised wording is visible on screen, and deletions show up in callout balloons that appear in the right-hand margin (see Figure 4.2). Suggested revisions offered by different team members are identified and dated. The original writer may accept or reject these changes. In recent versions of Word, you will find **Track Changes** on the **Tools** menu.

Insert Comments. Probably the most useful editing tool is **Insert Comments**, also shown in Figure 4.2. This tool allows users to point out problematic passages or errors, ask or answer questions, and share ideas without changing or adding text. When more than one person adds comments, the comments appear in different colors and are identified by the individual writer's name and a date/time stamp. To use this tool in newer versions of Word, each reviewer must click **Tools**, **Options**, and fill in the **User Information** section. In older versions of Word, this collaborative tool was called **Annotation**. To facilitate adding, reviewing, editing, or deleting comments, Word now provides a special toolbar. You can activate it by using the **View** pull-down menu (click **Toolbars** and **Reviewing**). On the **Reviewing** toolbar, click **New Comment**. Then type your comment, which can be seen in the web or print layout view (click **View** and **Print Layout** or **Web Layout**).

Completing a Document. When a document is finished, be sure to accept or reject all changes on the **Reviewing** toolbar, a step that removes the tracking information.

Career Application

Organize into groups of three. Using the latest version of Word, copy and respond to the Document for Analysis in Activity 4.1. Set up a round-robin e-mail file exchange so that each member responds to the other group members' documents by using the **Comment** feature of Word to offer advice or suggestions for improvement. Submit a printout of the document with group comments, as well as a final edited document.

Writing Process Phase 1: Analyze

Whether you're working with a team, composing by yourself, or preparing an oral presentation, the result of your efforts can be greatly improved by following the steps outlined in the 3-x-3 writing process. Not only are you more likely to get your message across, but you will also feel less anxious and your writing will progress more quickly. The remainder of this chapter focuses on the prewriting phase of composition: analyzing, anticipating, and adapting. In this phase you will first need to identify the purpose of the message and select the best channel or form in which to deliver it.

Identifying the Purpose

As you begin to compose a message, ask yourself two important questions: (a) Why am I sending this message? and (b) What do I hope to achieve? Your responses will determine how you organize and present your information.

Your message may have primary and secondary purposes. For college work your primary purpose may be merely to complete the assignment; secondary purposes might be to make yourself look good and to get a good grade. The primary purposes for sending business messages are typically to inform and to persuade. A secondary purpose is to promote goodwill: you and your organization want to look good in the eyes of your audience.

Most business messages do nothing more than *inform*. They explain procedures, announce meetings, answer questions, and transmit findings. Some business messages, however, are meant to *persuade*. These messages sell products, convince managers, motivate employees, and win over customers. Informative messages are developed differently than persuasive messages.

Spotlight on Communicators

Danny O'Neill, president of The Roasterie, a Kansas City coffee retailer, begins each writing session by analyzing his task and thinking about his audience. "Half of my preparation when writing memos is anticipating hurdles and predicting how my employees will react." For example, in a memo on the importance of collecting accounts receivable, he anticipated that some employees might not make this their top priority. Thus, his memo clearly stated that "if we don't collect the money, nothing else matters."

© Courtesy of Danny O'Neill

FIGURE 4.3 Choosing Communication Channels

Channel	Best Use
Blog	When one person needs to present digital information easily so that it is available to others.
E-mail	When you need feedback but not immediately. Lack of security makes it problematic for personal, emotional, or private messages.
Face-to-face conversation	When you need a rich, interactive medium. Useful for delivering persuasive, bad news, and personal messages.
Face-to-face group meeting	When group decisions and consensus are important. Inefficient for merely distributing information.
Fax	When your message must cross time zones or international boundaries, when a written record is significant, or when speed is important.
Instant message	When you are online and need a quick response. Useful for determining whether someone is available for a phone conversation.
Letter	When a written record or formality is required, especially with customers, the government, suppliers, or others outside an organization.
Memo	When you want a written record to clearly explain policies, discuss procedures, or collect information within an organization.
Phone call	When you must deliver or gather information quickly, when nonverbal cues are unimportant, and when you cannot meet in person.
Report or proposal	When you are delivering complex data internally or externally.
Voice mail message	When you wish to leave important or routine information that the receiver can respond to when convenient.
Video- or teleconference	When group consensus and interaction are important but members are geographically dispersed.
Wiki	When digital information must be made available to others. Useful for collaboration because participants can easily add, remove, and edit content.

Selecting the Best Channel

After identifying the purpose of your message, you need to select the most appropriate communication channel. As you learned in Chapter 1, some information is most efficiently and effectively delivered orally. Other messages should be written, and still others are best delivered electronically. A number of channels are available, as summarized in Figure 4.3. Whether to set up a meeting, send a message electronically, or write a report depends on some of the following factors: (a) importance of the message, (b) amount and speed of feedback required, (c) necessity of a permanent record, (d) cost of the channel, (e) degree of formality desired, and (f) confidentiality and sensitivity of the message.

© Steven Brahms / Bloomberg News / Landov

RadioShack Corp. caused a stir when management at the electronics retailer used e-mail to notify 400 employees of their dismissal from the company. "The work force reduction notification is currently in progress," the e-mail reported. "Unfortunately your position is one that has been eliminated." Management experts expressed dismay over the event, questioning whether electronic notification was proper for announcing layoffs. *What communication channels are the most appropriate for delivering bad news to employees?*

Selecting the best channel for your message is a more complex task than in the past. Business communicators today have many speedy channels, but those channels are not always appropriate for serious messages that require careful organization and strategic tactics. In Chapter 7 we will talk more about electronic communication channels.

Writing Process Phase 1: Anticipate

LEARNING OBJECTIVE 4
Analyze the process of anticipating and profiling three typical audiences for business messages: colleagues, decision makers, and customers.

Early in the writing process you should anticipate the audience for your message. What is the reader like? In a college setting, your audience is often your instructor. To get a good grade, you tailor your writing to fit the expectations of that instructor. In your business writing, you may or may not actually know the audience for a message. However, you can usually imagine many characteristics of the intended audience for a message. Picturing a typical reader is important in guiding what you write. One copywriter at Lands' End, the catalog company, pictures his sister-in-law whenever he writes product descriptions for the catalog. You can be sure he is not going to include big words, analytical reasoning, and footnotes, as one might do in academic writing. Picturing your audience helps you decide what to emphasize, how to be convincing, and what words and tone to use.

Anticipating and Analyzing Three Typical Audiences

Most readers of your business messages will fit into one of the following groups: colleagues, decision makers, and customers. In communicating with these audiences, you will adjust your tone, style, and content to accommodate the expectations and needs of these groups. Although you will learn much more about writing to these groups in subsequent chapters, we present a overview here.

Most business messages will be addressed to colleagues, decision makers, or customers.

Writing to Colleagues. Messages for colleagues may be the easiest to write. You usually know these coworkers and what to expect. They generally prefer specific information, simple language, and an informal tone. If they are familiar with the subject, colleagues may not require extensive background information. Remember, however, that your message may be read by others who are less familiar with the subject. A few sentences of background could fill in secondary readers.

Writing to Superiors and Decision Makers. Messages to superiors and decision makers require careful forethought and anticipation. What do they need to know to make a decision? How formal should you be? Most superiors and decision makers prefer concise, direct messages. Background information is important particularly if readers are unfamiliar with the topic. Because information provided to decision makers is critical, it requires a communication channel that provides a permanent record. The message should be well organized and may include informative headings for easy reference. The tone is professional and serious.

Writing to Customers and General Audiences. Messages to customers and general audiences should use simple language and maintain an informal tone. In visualizing them, remember what the Lands' End catalog writer does. He visualizes his sister-in-law and writes to her. Messages should create goodwill for the writer and the organization. A friendly but professional tone is important. Include examples, headings, and lists to help readers understand. However, don't obscure the message with too much data. Include only as much information as is necessary to clarify the topic. You will learn more about these writing techniques shortly.

Visualizing and anticipating your audience is a pivotal step in the writing process. The questions in Figure 4.4 will help you profile your audience. How much time you devote to answering these questions depends greatly on your message and its context. An analytical report that you compose for management or an oral presentation before a big group would, of course, demand considerable audience anticipation. On the other hand, an e-mail to a coworker or a letter

Spotlight on Communicators

Warren Buffett, the second richest man in the United States and one of the most successful investors of all time, offers advice on how to improve your messages by profiling your audience and responding to that profile. When writing annual reports, he pretends that he's talking to his sisters. "I have no trouble picturing them. Though highly intelligent, they are not experts in accounting or finance. They will understand plain English but jargon may puzzle them. . . . No sisters to write to? Borrow mine. Just begin with 'Dear Doris and Bertie,'" he suggested.

© DENNIS VAN TINE / Landov

FIGURE 4.4 Asking the Right Questions to Profile Your Audience

Primary Audience	Secondary Audience
Who is my primary reader or listener?	Who might see or hear this message after the primary audience?
What is my personal and professional relationship with that person?	How do these people differ from the primary audience?
What position does the person hold in the organization?	How must I reshape my message to make it understandable and acceptable to others to whom it might be forwarded?
How much does that person know about the subject?	
What do I know about that person's education, beliefs, culture, and attitudes?	
Should I expect a neutral, positive, or negative response to my message?	

to a familiar supplier might require only a few moments of planning. No matter how short your message, though, spend some time thinking about the audience so that you can tailor your words to your readers or listeners.

Responding to the Profile

Anticipating your audience helps you make decisions about shaping the message. You will discover what kind of language is appropriate, whether you are free to use specialized technical terms, whether you should explain everything, and so on. You will decide whether your tone should be formal or informal, and you will select the most desirable channel. Imagining whether the receiver is likely to be neutral, positive, or negative will help you determine how to organize your message.

By profiling your audience before writing, you can identify the appropriate tone, language, and channel.

Another result of profiling your audience will be recognizing whether a secondary audience is possible. For example, let's say you start to write an e-mail message to your supervisor describing a problem you're having. Halfway through the message you realize that your supervisor will probably forward this message to her boss, the vice president. She will not want to summarize what you said; instead she will take the easy route and merely forward your e-mail. When you realize that the vice president will probably see your message, you decide to back up and use a more formal tone. You remove your inquiry about your supervisor's family, you reduce your complaints, and you tone down your language about why things went wrong. Instead, you provide more background information, and you are more specific in identifying items that the vice president might not recognize. Analyzing the task and anticipating the audience assist you in adapting your message so that it will accomplish what you intend.

Writing Process Phase 1: Adapt

After analyzing your purpose and anticipating your audience, you must convey your purpose to that audience. Adaptation is the process of creating a message that suits your audience.

LEARNING OBJECTIVE 5
Effectively apply audience benefits, the "you" view, bias-free language, a conversational but professional tone, positive expression, courtesy, simple language, and precise words.

One important aspect of adaptation is *tone*. Conveyed largely by the words in a message, tone reflects how a receiver feels upon reading or hearing a message. For example, think how you would react to these statements:

> *You must return the form by 5 p.m.*
> *Would you please return the form by 5 p.m.*

The wording of the first message establishes an aggressive or negative tone—no one likes being told what to do. The second message is reworded in a friendlier, more positive manner. Poorly chosen words may sound demeaning, condescending, discourteous, pretentious, or demanding. Notice in the Lands' End letter in Figure 4.5 that the writer achieves a courteous and warm tone. The letter responds to a customer's concern about the changing merchandise mix available in Lands' End catalogs. The customer also wanted to receive fewer catalogs. The writer explains the company's expanded merchandise line and reassures the customer that Lands' End has not abandoned its emphasis on classic styles.

FIGURE 4.5 Customer Response Letter

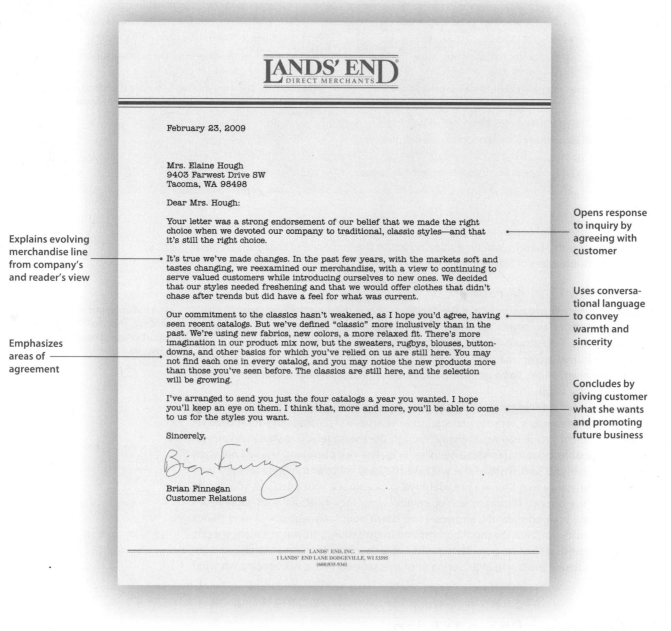

LANDS' END
DIRECT MERCHANTS

February 23, 2009

Mrs. Elaine Hough
9403 Farwest Drive SW
Tacoma, WA 98498

Dear Mrs. Hough:

Your letter was a strong endorsement of our belief that we made the right choice when we devoted our company to traditional, classic styles—and that it's still the right choice.

It's true we've made changes. In the past few years, with the markets soft and tastes changing, we reexamined our merchandise, with a view to continuing to serve valued customers while introducing ourselves to new ones. We decided that our styles needed freshening and that we would offer clothes that didn't chase after trends but did have a feel for what was current.

Our commitment to the classics hasn't weakened, as I hope you'd agree, having seen recent catalogs. But we've defined "classic" more inclusively than in the past. We're using new fabrics, new colors, a more relaxed fit. There's more imagination in our product mix now, but the sweaters, rugbys, blouses, button-downs, and other basics for which you've relied on us are still here. You may not find each one in every catalog, and you may notice the new products more than those you've seen before. The classics are still here, and the selection will be growing.

I've arranged to send you just the four catalogs a year you wanted. I hope you'll keep an eye on them. I think that, more and more, you'll be able to come to us for the styles you want.

Sincerely,

Brian Finnegan
Customer Relations

LANDS' END, INC.
1 LANDS' END LANE DODGEVILLE, WI 53595
(608)935-9341

Explains evolving merchandise line from company's and reader's view

Emphasizes areas of agreement

Opens response to inquiry by agreeing with customer

Uses conversational language to convey warmth and sincerity

Concludes by giving customer what she wants and promoting future business

---

Skilled communicators create effective messages by using a number of adaptive techniques, some of which are unconscious. These include spotlighting audience benefits; cultivating a "you" view; and avoiding gender, racial, age, and disability bias. Additional adaptive techniques include being conversational but professional, being positive, showing courtesy, using familiar words, and choosing precise words.

Spotlighting Audience Benefits

Empathic communicators envision the receiver and focus on benefits to that person.

Focusing on the audience sounds like a modern idea, but actually one of America's early statesmen and authors recognized this fundamental writing principle over 200 years ago. In describing effective writing, Ben Franklin observed, "To be good, it ought to have a tendency to benefit the reader."[7] These wise words have become a fundamental guideline for today's business communicators. Expanding on Franklin's counsel, a contemporary communication consultant gives this solid advice to his business clients: "Always stress the benefit to the readers of whatever it is you're trying to get them to do. If you can show *them* how you're going to save them frustration or help them meet their goals, you have the makings of a powerful message."[8]

Empathy means being able to understand another's situation, feelings, and motives.

Adapting your message to the receiver's needs means putting yourself in that person's shoes. It is called *empathy*. Empathic senders think about how a receiver will decode a message.

They try to give something to the receiver, solve the receiver's problems, save the receiver's money, or just understand the feelings and position of that person. Which of the following messages are more appealing to the receiver?

Sender Focus	Audience Focus
To enable us to update our stockholder records, we ask that the enclosed card be returned.	So that you may promptly receive dividend checks and information related to your shares, please return the enclosed card.
Our warranty becomes effective only when we receive an owner's registration.	Your warranty begins working for you as soon as you return your owner's registration.
We offer a DVD language course that we have complete faith in.	The sooner you order the DVD language program, the sooner the rewards will be yours.
The Human Resources Department requires that every employee complete an online questionnaire immediately so that we can allocate our training resource funds.	You can be one of the first employees to sign up for the new career development program. Complete the online questionnaire and send it immediately.

Cultivating the "You" View

Notice how many of the previous receiver-focused messages included the word *you*. In concentrating on receiver benefits, skilled communicators naturally develop the "you" view. They emphasize second-person pronouns (*you, your*) instead of first-person pronouns (*I/we, us, our*). Whether your goal is to inform, persuade, or promote goodwill, the catchiest words you can use are *you* and *your*. Compare the following examples.

Effective communicators develop the "you" view in a sincere, not manipulative or critical, tone.

"I/We" View	"You" View
I have granted you permission to attend the communication seminar.	You may attend the seminar to improve your communication skills.
We have shipped your order by UPS, and we are sure it will arrive in time for the sales promotion on January 15.	Your order will be delivered by UPS in time for your sales promotion on January 15.
I'm asking all of our employees to respond to the attached survey about working conditions.	Because your ideas count, please complete the attached survey about working conditions.

Your goal is to focus on the reader. But second-person pronouns can be overused and misused. Readers appreciate genuine interest; on the other hand, they resent obvious attempts at manipulation. The authors of some sales messages, for example, are guilty of overkill when they include *you* dozens of times in a direct mail promotion. Furthermore, the word can sometimes create the wrong impression. Consider this statement: *You cannot return merchandise until you receive written approval. You* appears twice, but the reader feels singled out for criticism. In the following version the message is less personal and more positive: *Customers may return merchandise with written approval.* In short, avoid using *you* for general statements that suggest blame and could cause ill will.

Avoid overusing you or including it when it suggests blame.

In recognizing the value of the "you" view, however, writers do not have to sterilize their writing and avoid any first-person pronouns or words that show their feelings. Skilled communicators are able to convey sincerity, warmth, and enthusiasm by the words they choose. Don't be afraid to use phrases such as *I'm happy* or *We're delighted,* if you truly are.

When speaking face to face, communicators show sincerity and warmth with nonverbal cues such as a smile and pleasant voice tone. In letters, memos, and e-mail messages, however, only expressive words and phrases can show these feelings. These phrases suggest hidden messages that say to readers and customers "You are important, I hear you, and I'm honestly trying to please you." Mary Kay Ash, one of the most successful cosmetics entrepreneurs of all times, gave her salespeople wise advice. She had them imagine that any person they were addressing wore a sign saying "Make me feel important."

Spotlight on Communicators

Voted the greatest minority entrepreneur in American history, John H. Johnson was a master at profiling potential customers and cultivating the "you" view. He always focused on what they wanted rather than on what he wanted. His emphasis on the "you" view helped him build *Ebony* and *Jet* magazines, along with *Fashion Fair Cosmetics*, into multimillion-dollar businesses. In explaining his customer approach, he said, "I want to know where they came from, what are their interests, [and] what can I talk to them about." He worked to establish rapport with people by learning their interests.

© AP IMAGES

Communicating at Work Part 2

Suze Orman Preaches Financial Freedom in Simple Language

America's most listened-to personal finance expert, Suze Orman, appears on TV, makes personal appearances, prepares magazine columns, and has written seven best-selling books. One might expect her to be a master multitasker, taking on many jobs at once and juggling all of them perfectly. Wrong, way wrong! When Orman starts a writing task, she focuses on that task only and allows no interruptions. "I came to this conclusion after watching the way race-horses win," she explained. "They come out of the gate with blinders on and go for the finish line." That's how she writes. "All I care about is what I do, and I do absolutely nothing else while I am doing it."[9] Trying to complete more than one task at the same time ends in the "absolute ruination" of any project, she contended. "When I'm writing, I don't answer phones. I don't care what else is going on."[10]

Her total focus enables her to target her advice to specific audiences. She seems to really care about people and is nonjudgmental towards those who have dug themselves into terrible financial trouble. Although much financial information is contradictory and confusing, she offers practical advice in simple, positive language. She explains the reasoning behind her advice and encourages others to learn to make their own financial decisions wisely.

© AP IMAGES

Critical Thinking

- When writing, what are the advantages and disadvantages to multitasking?
- Suze Orman is known for using simple, familiar language to express complex ideas. Does a business writer lose credibility when using this kind of language?
- Why does it make sense for a business writer to express ideas positively instead of negatively?

Using Bias-Free Language

Sensitive communicators avoid gender, racial, ethnic, age, and disability biases.

In adapting a message to its audience, be sure your language is sensitive and bias-free. Few writers set out to be offensive. Sometimes, though, we all say things that we never thought might be hurtful. The real problem is that we don't think about the words that stereotype groups of people, such as *the boys in the mail room* or *the girls in the front office*. Be cautious about expressions that might be biased in terms of gender, race, ethnicity, age, and disability.

Avoiding Gender Bias. You can defuse gender time bombs by replacing words that exclude or stereotype women (sometimes called *sexist language*) with neutral, inclusive expressions. The following examples show how sexist terms and phrases can be replaced with neutral ones.

Gender Biased	Improved
female doctor, woman attorney, cleaning woman	doctor, attorney, cleaner
waiter/waitress, authoress, stewardess	server, author, cabin attendant
mankind, man-hour, man-made	humanity, working hours, artificial
office girls	office workers
the doctor . . . he	doctors . . . they
the teacher . . . she	teachers . . . they
executives and their wives	executives and their spouses
foreman, flagman, workman	lead workers, flagger, worker
businessman, salesman	businessperson, sales representative
Each worker had his picture taken.	Each worker had a picture taken.
	All workers had their pictures taken.
	Each worker had his or her picture taken.

Generally, you can avoid gender-biased language by leaving out the words *man* or *woman*, by using plural nouns and pronouns, or by changing to a gender-free word (*person* or *representative*). Avoid the "his or her" option whenever possible. It is wordy and conspicuous. With a little effort, you can usually find a construction that is graceful, grammatical, and unself-conscious.

Avoiding Racial or Ethnic Bias. You need indicate racial or ethnic identification only if the context demands it.

Chapter 4: Writing Process Phase 1: Analyze, Anticipate, Adapt

Racially or Ethnically Biased

An Indian accountant was hired.

James Lee, an African American, applied.

Improved

An accountant was hired.

James Lee applied.

Avoiding Age Bias.
Specify age only if it is relevant, and avoid expressions that are demeaning or subjective.

Age Biased

The law applied to old people.

Sally Kay, 55, was transferred.

a spry old gentleman

a little old lady

Improved

The law applied to people over 65.

Sally Kay was transferred.

a man

a woman

Avoiding Disability Bias.
Unless relevant, do not refer to an individual's disability. When necessary, use terms that do not stigmatize disabled individuals.

Disability Biased

afflicted with, suffering from, crippled by

defect, disease

confined to a wheelchair

Improved

has

condition

uses a wheelchair

The preceding examples give you a quick look at a few problem expressions. The real key to bias-free communication, though, lies in your awareness and commitment. Be on the lookout to be sure that your messages do not exclude, stereotype, or offend people.

Being Conversational but Professional

Most instant messages, e-mail messages, business letters, memos, and reports replace conversation. Thus, they are most effective when they convey an informal, conversational tone instead of a formal, pretentious tone. Workplace messages should not, however, become so casual that they sound low-level and unprofessional.

Instant messaging (IM) enables coworkers to have informal, spontaneous conversations. Some companies have accepted IM as a serious workplace tool. With the increasing use of instant messaging and e-mail, however, a major problem has developed. Sloppy, unprofessional expression appears in many workplace messages. You will learn more about the dangers of e-mail in Chapter 7. At this point, though, we are focusing on the tone of the language.

To project a professional image, you must sound educated and mature. Overuse of expressions such as *totally awesome, you know,* and *like,* as well as reliance on needless abbreviations (*BTW* for *by the way*), makes a businessperson sound like a teenager. Professional messages do not include IM abbreviations, slang, sentence fragments, and chitchat. We urge you to strive for a warm, conversational tone that avoids low-level diction. Levels of diction, as shown in Figure 4.6, range from unprofessional to formal.

Your goal is a warm, friendly tone that sounds professional. Although some writers are too casual, others are overly formal. To impress readers, they use big words, long sentences,

Strive for conversational expression, but remember to be professional.

A professional image involves sounding educated and mature.

Avoid both extremes: sounding too informal and sounding too formal.

FIGURE 4.6 Levels of Diction

Unprofessional (low-level diction)	Conversational (mid-level diction)	Formal (high-level diction)
badmouth	criticize	denigrate
guts	nerve	courage
pecking order	line of command	dominance hierarchy
ticked off	upset	provoked
rat on	inform	betray
rip off	steal	expropriate
Sentence example: If we just hang in there, we can snag the contract.	**Sentence example:** If we don't get discouraged, we can win the contract.	**Sentence example:** If the principals persevere, they can secure the contract.

legal terminology, and third-person constructions. Stay away from expressions such as *the undersigned, the writer,* and *the affected party.* You will sound more friendly with familiar pronouns such as *I, we,* and *you.* Study the following examples to see how to achieve a professional, yet conversational tone:

Unprofessional	Improved
Hey, boss, GR8 news! Firewall now installed!! BTW, check with me b4 announcing it.	Mr. Smith, our new firewall software is now installed. Please check with me before announcing it.

Unprofessional	Improved
Look, dude, this report is totally bogus. And the figures don't look kosher. Show me some real stats. Got sources?	Because the figures in this report seem inaccurate, please submit the source statistics.

Overly Formal	Conversational
All employees are herewith instructed to return the appropriately designated contracts to the undersigned.	Please return your contracts to me.

Overly Formal	Conversational
Pertaining to your order, we must verify the sizes that your organization requires prior to consignment of your order to our shipper.	We will send your order as soon as we confirm the sizes you need.

Expressing Yourself Positively

Negative expressions can be rephrased to sound positive.

Certain negative words create ill will because they appear to blame or accuse readers. For example, opening a letter to a customer with *You claim that* suggests that you don't believe the customer. Other loaded words that can get you in trouble are *complaint, criticism, defective, failed, mistake,* and *neglected.* Often the writer is unconscious of the effect of these words. To avoid angry reactions, restrict negative words and try to find positive ways to express ideas. You provide more options to the reader when you tell what can be done instead of what can't be done.

Positive language creates goodwill and gives more options to readers.

Negative	Positive
You failed to include your credit card number so we can't mail your order.	We will mail your order as soon as we receive your credit card number.
Your letter of May 2 claims that you returned a defective headset.	Your May 2 letter describes a headset you returned.
You cannot park in Lot H until April 1.	You may park in Lot H starting April 1.
You won't be sorry that . . .	You will be happy that . . .
Without the aid of top management, the problem can't be solved.	With the aid of top management, the problem can be solved.
Do you have any complaints?	Can you suggest ways for us to improve?

Being Courteous

Even when you are justifiably angry, courteous language is the best way to achieve your goals.

Maintaining a courteous tone involves not just guarding against rudeness, but also avoiding words that sound demanding or preachy. Expressions like *you should, you must,* and *you have to* cause people to instinctively react with *Oh, yeah?* One remedy is to turn these demands into rhetorical questions that begin with *Will you please. . . .* Giving reasons for a request also softens the tone.

Less Courteous	More Courteous
You must complete this report before Friday.	Will you please complete the report by Friday.
You should organize a car pool in this department.	Organizing a car pool will reduce your transportation costs and help preserve the environment.

Even when you feel justified in displaying anger, remember that losing your temper or being sarcastic will seldom accomplish your goals as a business communicator to inform, to persuade, and to create goodwill. When you are irritated, frustrated, or infuriated, keep cool and try to defuse the situation. Concentrate on the real problem. What must be done to solve it?

You May Be Thinking This	Better to Say This
This is the second time I've written. Can't you get anything right?	Please credit my account for $843. My latest statement shows that the error noted in my letter of June 2 has not been corrected.
Am I the only one who can read the operating manual?	Let's review the operating manual together so that you can get your documents to print correctly next time.
Hey, don't blame me! I'm not the promoter who took off with the funds.	Please accept our sincere apologies and two complimentary tickets to our next event. Let me try to explain why we had to substitute performers.

In dealing with customers in telephone conversations, use polite phrases such as *It was a pleasure speaking with you, I would be happy to assist you with that,* and *Thank you for being so patient.*

Simplifying Your Language

In adapting your message to your audience, whenever possible use short, familiar words that you think they will recognize. Don't, however, avoid a big word that conveys your idea efficiently and is appropriate for the audience. Your goal is to shun pompous and pretentious language. Instead, use "GO" words. If you mean *begin,* don't say *commence* or *initiate.* If you mean *pay,* don't write *compensate.* By substituting everyday, familiar words for unfamiliar ones, as shown here, you help your audience comprehend your ideas quickly.

Unfamiliar	Familiar
commensurate	equal
interrogate	question
materialize	appear
obfuscate	confuse
remuneration	pay, salary
terminate	end

At the same time, be selective in your use of jargon. *Jargon* describes technical or specialized terms within a field. These terms enable insiders to communicate complex ideas briefly, but to outsiders they mean nothing. Human resources professionals, for example, know precisely what's meant by *cafeteria plan* (a benefits option program), but most of us would be thinking about lunch. Geologists refer to *plate tectonics,* and physicians discuss *metastatic carcinomas.* These terms mean little to most of us. Use specialized language only when the audience will understand it. In addition, don't forget to consider secondary audiences: Will those potential readers understand any technical terms used?

Using Precise, Vigorous Words

Strong verbs and concrete nouns give readers more information and keep them interested. Don't overlook the thesaurus (or the thesaurus program on your computer) for expanding your word choices and vocabulary. Whenever possible, use specific words as shown here.

Using familiar but precise language helps receivers understand.

Imprecise, Dull	More Precise
a change in profits	a 25 percent hike in profits a 10 percent plunge in profits
to say	to promise, confess, understand to allege, assert, assume, judge
to think about	to identify, diagnose, analyze to probe, examine, inspect

By reviewing the tips in the following checklist, you can master the steps of writing preparation. As you review these tips, remember the three basics of prewriting: analyzing, anticipating, and adapting.

Checklist

Adapting a Message to Its Audience

✓ **Identify the message purpose.** Ask yourself why you are communicating and what you hope to achieve. Look for primary and secondary purposes.

✓ **Select the most appropriate form.** Determine whether you need a permanent record or whether the message is too sensitive to put in writing.

✓ **Profile the audience.** Identify your relationship with the reader and your knowledge about that individual or group. Assess how much the receiver knows about the subject.

✓ **Focus on audience benefits.** Phrase your statements from the readers' viewpoint, not the writer's. Concentrate on the "you" view (*Your order will arrive, You can enjoy, Your ideas count*).

✓ **Avoid gender and racial bias.** Use bias-free words (*businessperson* instead of *businessman; working hours* instead of *man-hours*). Omit ethnic identification unless the context demands it.

✓ **Avoid age and disability bias.** Include age only if relevant. Avoid potentially demeaning expressions (*spry old gentleman*), and use terms that do not stigmatize disabled people (*he is disabled* instead of *he is a cripple* or *he has a handicap*).

✓ **Be conversational but professional.** Strive for a warm, friendly tone that is not overly formal or familiar. Avoid slang and low-level diction.

✓ **Express ideas positively rather than negatively.** Instead of *Your order can't be shipped before June 1*, say *Your order can be shipped June 1*.

✓ **Use short, familiar words.** Use technical terms and big words only if they are appropriate for the audience (*end* not *terminate, required* not *mandatory*).

✓ **Search for precise, vigorous words.** Use a thesaurus if necessary to find strong verbs and concrete nouns (*announces* instead of *says, brokerage* instead of *business*).

Adapting to Legal and Ethical Responsibilities

LEARNING OBJECTIVE 6
Summarize the legal and ethical responsibilities of business communicators in the areas of investments, safety, marketing, human resources, and copyright law.

One of your primary responsibilities in writing for an organization or for yourself is to avoid language that may land you in court. Another responsibility is to be ethical. Both of these concerns revolve around the use and abuse of language. You can protect yourself and avoid litigation by knowing what's legal and by adapting your language accordingly. Be especially careful when your messages involve investments, safety, marketing, human resources, and copyright law.

Investment Information

Writers describing the sale of stocks or financial services must follow specific laws written to protect investors. Any messages—including e-mails, letters, newsletters, and pamphlets—must be free from misleading information, exaggerations, or half-truths. One company in Massachusetts inadvertently violated the law by declaring that it was "recession-proof." After going bankrupt, the company was sued by angry stockholders claiming that they had been deceived. A software company caused a flurry of lawsuits by withholding information that revealed problems in a new version of one of its most popular programs. Stockholders sued, charging that managers had deliberately concealed the bad news, thus keeping stock prices artificially high. Experienced financial writers know that careless language and even poor timing may provoke litigation.

Ethics Check

Trapped by Consumer Debt
Capital One offers multiple credit cards to subprime borrowers and rakes in huge profits from charging high interest and late fees. Some consumer advocates see Cap One's approach as unethical because it traps low-income borrowers in a cycle of debt. Do you agree?

Warnings on dangerous products must be written especially clearly.

Safety Information

Writers describing potentially dangerous products worry not only about protecting people from physical harm but also about being sued. During the past three decades, litigation arising from product liability has been one of the most active areas of tort law (tort law involves wrongful civil acts other than breach of contract). Manufacturers are obligated to warn consumers of any risks in their products. These warnings must do more than suggest danger; they must also clearly tell people how to use the product safely. In writing warnings, concentrate on major points. Omit anything that is not critical. In the work area describe a potential problem and tell how to solve it. For example, *Lead dust is harmful and gets on your clothes. Change your clothes before leaving work.*

Clearly written safety messages use easy-to-understand words, such as *doctor* instead of *physician, clean* instead of *sanitary,* and *burn* instead of *incinerate.* Technical terms are defined; for example, *Asbestos is a carcinogen (something that causes cancer)*. Effective safety messages also include highlighting techniques such as headings and bullets. In coming chapters you will learn more about these techniques for improving readability.

Marketing Information

Sales and marketing messages are illegal if they falsely advertise prices, performance capability, quality, or other product characteristics. Marketing messages must not deceive the buyer in any way. A Southern California entrepreneur, for example, promoted a Band-Aid-like device, Le Patch, as "a dramatic breakthrough in weight control technology." When worn around the waist, Le Patch was supposed to reduce appetite. The claims, however, could not be proved; and the promoter was charged with misrepresenting the product. Sellers of services must also be cautious about the language they use to describe what they will do. Letters, reports, and proposals that describe services to be performed are interpreted as contracts in court. Therefore, language must not promise more than intended. In Chapter 9 on page 254 you will learn more about what's legal and what's not in sales letters. Here are some dangerous words (and recommended alternatives) that have created misunderstandings leading to lawsuits.[11]

Dangerous Word	Court Interpretation	Recommended Alternative
inspect	to examine critically, to investigate and test officially, to scrutinize	to review, to study, to tour the facility
determine	to come to a decision, to decide; to resolve	to evaluate, to assess, to analyze
assure	to render safe, to make secure, to give confidence, to cause to feel certain	to facilitate, to provide further confidence, to enhance the reliability of

Sales and marketing messages must not make claims that can't be verified.

Human Resources Information

The vast number of lawsuits relating to employment makes this a treacherous area for business communicators. In evaluating employees in the workplace, avoid making unsubstantiated negative comments. It is also unwise to assess traits (*she is unreliable*) because doing so requires subjective judgment. Concentrate instead on specific incidents (*in the last month she missed four work days and was late three times*). Defamation lawsuits have become so common that some companies no longer provide letters of recommendation for former employees. To be safe, give recommendations only when the former employee authorizes the recommendation and when you can say something positive. Stick to job-related information.

The safest employment recommendations contain positive, job-related information.

Statements in employee handbooks also require careful wording, because a court might rule that such statements are "implied contracts." Consider the following handbook remark: "We at Hotstuff, Inc., show our appreciation for hard work and team spirit by rewarding everyone who performs well." This seemingly harmless statement could make it difficult to fire an employee because of the implied employment promise.[12] Companies are warned to avoid promissory phrases in writing job advertisements, application forms, and offer letters. Phrases that suggest permanent employment and guaranteed job security can be interpreted as contracts.[13]

In statements to existing and prospective employees, companies must recognize that oral comments may trigger lawsuits. A Minnesota television news anchor won damages when she gave up her job search because her station manager promised to extensively market her in a leading role. But he failed to follow through. A Vermont engineer won his case of negligent misrepresentation when he was not told that the defense project for which he was hired faced a potential cutback. Companies are warned to require employees to sign employment agreements indicating that all terms of employment orally agreed upon must be made in writing to be valid.[14]

In adapting messages to meet today's litigious business environment, be sensitive to the rights of others and to your own rights. The key elements in this adaptation process are awareness of laws, sensitivity to interpretations, and careful use of language.

Copyright Information

The Copyright Act of 1976 protects authors—literary, dramatic, and artistic—of published and unpublished works. The word *copyright* refers to "the right to copy," and a key provision is *fair use*.

Under fair use, individuals have limited use of copyrighted material without requiring permission. These uses are for criticism, comment, news reporting, teaching, scholarship, and research. Unfortunately, the distinctions between fair use and infringement are not clearly defined.

Courts use four factors to determine fair use: the purpose of the use, the nature of the work, the amount used, and the effect on the potential market for the work.

Four-Factor Test to Assess Fair Use.

What is fair use? Actually, it is a shadowy territory with vague and often disputed boundaries—now even more so with the addition of cyberspace. Here are four factors that courts use as a test in deciding disputes over fair use:

- **Purpose and character of the use, particularly whether for profit.** Courts are more likely to allow fair use for nonprofit educational purposes than for commercial ventures.

- **Nature of the copyrighted work.** When information is necessary for public good—such as medical news—courts are more likely to support fair use.

- **Amount and substantiality of portion used.** Copying a 200-word passage from a 200,000-word book might be allowed but not 200 words from a 1,000-word article or a substantial part of a shorter work. A total of 300 words is mistakenly thought by many to be an acceptable limit for fair use, but courts have NOT upheld this figure. Don't rely on it.

- **Effect of the use on the potential market for or value of the copyrighted work.** If use of the work may interfere with the author's potential profit from the original, fair use copying would not be allowed.

Writers can avoid violating copyright law by assuming that everything is copyrighted and not in the public domain.

How to Avoid Copyright Infringement.

Whenever you borrow words, charts, graphs, photos, music, or anything created privately, be sure you know what is legal and acceptable. The following guidelines will help:

- **Assume that everything is copyrighted.** Nearly everything created privately and originally after 1989 is copyrighted and protected whether or not it has a copyright notice.

- **Realize that Internet items are NOT in the "public domain."** Nothing modern is in the "public domain" (free to be used by anyone) unless the owner explicitly says so.

- **Observe fair-use restrictions.** Be aware of the four-factor test. Avoid appropriating large amounts of outside material.

- **Ask for permission.** You are always safe if you obtain permission. Write to the source, identify the material you wish to include, and explain where it will be used. Expect to pay for permission.

- **Don't assume that a footnote is all that is needed.** Including a footnote to a source prevents plagiarism but not copyright infringement. Anything copied beyond the boundaries of fair use requires permission. You will learn more about citation methods and ways to avoid plagiarism in Chapter 12.

For more information about *copyright law, fair use, public domain,* and *work for hire,* you can search the Web with these key words.

Communicating at Work Your Turn

Applying Your Skills With Suze Orman

Assume you are applying for a job as research assistant at the Suze Orman Financial Group. All applicants must submit a writing sample.

Your Task
Compose a one-page memo discussing why so many college students are in debt. You should also provide tips to students who want to avoid getting into college-related debt. As a writing sample, your memo will be judged on its clear expression, simple language, and precise words. Address your memo to Melissa M., who is a recruiter hired by Suze Orman to screen applicants. See Chapter 7 for information about preparing memos.

© AP IMAGES

Chapter 4: Writing Process Phase 1: Analyze, Anticipate, Adapt

Summary of Learning Objectives

1 **Identify four basic principles of business writing, summarize the 3-x-3 writing process, and explain how a writing process helps a writer.** Business writing differs from academic writing in that it strives to solve business problems. It is also economical, persuasive, and reader oriented. Phase 1 of the 3-x-3 writing process (prewriting) involves analyzing the message, anticipating the audience, and considering ways to adapt the message to the audience. Phase 2 (writing) involves researching the topic, organizing the material, and composing the message. Phase 3 (revising) includes proofreading and evaluating the message. A writing process helps a writer by providing a systematic plan describing what to do in creating messages.

2 **Explain how the writing process may be altered and how it is affected by team-written projects requiring collaboration.** The writing process may be compressed for short messages; steps in the process may be rearranged. Team writing, which is necessary for large projects or when wide expertise is necessary, alters the writing process. Teams often work together in brainstorming and working out their procedures and assignments. Then individual members write their portions of the report or presentation during Phase 2. During Phase 3 (revising) teams may work together to combine their drafts. Teams use online collaboration tools such as e-mail, mailing lists, discussion boards, instant messaging, groupware, portals, blogs, and wikis.

3 **Clarify what is involved in analyzing a writing task and selecting a communication channel.** Communicators must decide why they are delivering a message and what they hope to achieve. Although many messages only inform, some must also persuade. After identifying the purpose of a message, communicators must choose the most appropriate channel. That choice depends on the importance of the message, the amount and speed of feedback required, the need for a permanent record, the cost of the channel, and the degree of formality desired.

4 **Analyze the process of anticipating and profiling three typical audiences for business messages: colleagues, decision makers, and customers.** A good communicator tries to envision the audience for a message. What does the receiver know about the topic? How well does the receiver know the sender? What is known about the receiver's education, beliefs, culture, and attitudes? Will the response to the message be positive, neutral, or negative? Is the secondary audience different from the primary audience? How should a document be changed if it will be read by additional readers? Messages to colleagues, decision makers, and customers require different strategies, tones, and techniques.

5 **Effectively apply audience benefits, the "you" view, bias-free language, a conversational but professional tone, positive expression, courtesy, simple language, and precise words.** Skilled communicators strive to emphasize audience benefits in business messages. They look at a message from the receiver's perspective applying the "you" view. They select sensitive language that avoids gender, racial, ethnic, age, and disability biases. They convey a conversational but professional tone, state ideas positively, and show courtesy. To improve readability, they use short, familiar, and precise words.

6 **Summarize the legal and ethical responsibilities of business communicators in the areas of investments, safety, marketing, human resources, and copyright law.** In writing about investments, communicators must avoid misleading information, exaggerations, and half-truths. Safety information, including warnings, must tell people clearly how to use a product safely and motivate them to do so. In addition to being honest, marketing information must not promise more than intended. Communicators in the area of human resources must use careful wording (particularly in employment recommendations and employee handbooks) to avoid potential lawsuits. They must also avoid oral promises that can result in lawsuits. In publication, one must be mindful of copyright laws. Assume that everything is copyrighted, even items borrowed from the Internet. Know the implications and limitations of *fair use*.

Chapter Review

1. In what ways is business writing different from academic writing? (Obj. 1)

2. Describe the components in each stage of the 3-x-3 writing process. (Obj. 1)

3. Approximately how much time is spent in each phase of the writing process? (Obj. 2)

4. What are the advantages and disadvantages of team-written documents? (Obj. 2)

5. List five factors to consider when selecting a communication channel. (Obj. 3)

6. Why should you visualize or profile your audience before composing a message? (Obj. 4)

7. What is meant by "audience benefits"? (Obj. 5)

8. When is the "you" view appropriate, and when is it inappropriate? (Obj. 5)

9. What is bias-free language? Give original examples. (Obj. 5)

10. Name replacements for the following gender-biased terms: *waitress, stewardess, foreman.* (Obj. 5)

11. Revise the following expression to show more courtesy: *For the last time, I'm warning all staff members that they must use virus-protection software—or else!* (Obj. 5)

12. What is *jargon*, and when is it appropriate for business writing? (Obj. 5)

13. What's wrong with using words such as *commence, mandate,* and *interrogate*? (Obj. 5)

14. Under copyright law, what does *fair use* mean? (Obj. 6)

15. What kinds of works are protected by copyright laws? (Obj. 6)

Critical Thinking

1. Business communicators are encouraged to profile or visualize the audience for their messages. How is this possible if you don't really know the people who will receive a sales letter or who will hear your business presentation? (Obj. 4)

2. How can the 3-x-3 writing process help the writer of a business report as well as the writer of an oral presentation? (Obj. 1)

3. If adapting your tone to the receiving audience and developing audience benefits are so important, why do we see so much writing that does not reflect these suggestions? (Objs. 3–5)

4. Discuss the following statement: "The English language is a landmine—it is filled with terms that are easily misinterpreted as derogatory and others that are blatantly insulting. . . . Being fair and objective is not enough; employers must also appear to be so."[15] (Obj. 5)

5. **Ethical Issue:** Peter Whitney, an employee at Wells Fargo, launched an Internet blog to chat about his life, his friends, and his job. After criticizing some of his coworkers in his blog, he was fired from his job handling mail and the front desk. Whitney said, "There needs to be clearer guidelines. Some people go to a bar and complain about workers. I decided to do it online. Some people say I deserve what happened, but it was really harsh. It was unfair."[16] Do you agree or disagree, and why?

Activities

4.1 Document for Analysis: Weak Internal Memo (Obj. 5)

Team

Your Task. Study the following memo, which is based on an actual document sent to employees. How can you apply what you learned in this chapter to improving this memo? Revise the memo to make it more courteous, positive, and precise. Focus on developing the "you" view and using familiar language. Remove any gender-biased references. Consider revising this memo as a collaboration project using Word's **Comment** feature.

TO: All Employees Using HP 5000 Computers

It has recently come to my attention that a computer security problem exists within our organization. I understand that the problem is twofold in nature:

a. You have been sharing computer passwords.

b. You are using automatic logon procedures.

Henceforth, you are prohibited from sharing passwords for security reasons that should be axiomatic. We also must forbid you to use automatic logon files because they empower anyone to have access to our entire computer system and all company data.

Enclosed please find a form that you must sign and return to the aforementioned individual, indicating your acknowledgment of and acquiescence to the procedures described here. Any computer user whose signed form is not returned will have his personal password invalidated.

4.2 Selecting Communication Channels (Obj. 3)

Your Task. Using Figure 4.3, suggest the best communication channels for the following messages. Assume that all channels shown are available. Be prepared to explain your choices.

a. You want to know what team members are available immediately for a quick teleconference meeting. They are all workaholics and stuck to their computers.

b. As a manager during a company reorganization, you must tell nine workers that their employment is being terminated.

c. You need to know whether Thomas in Reprographics can produce a rush job for you in two days.

d. Members of your product development team need a central location where each one can see general information about the job as well as add comments for others to see.

e. A prospective client in Italy wants price quotes for a number of your products—pronto!

f. As assistant to the vice president, you are to investigate the possibility of developing internship programs with several nearby colleges and universities.

g. You must respond to a notice from the Internal Revenue Service insisting that you did not pay the correct amount for last quarter's employer's taxes.

Interactive Learning @ www.meguffey.com

4.3 Analyzing Audiences (Obj. 4)

Your Task. Using the questions in Figure 4.4, write a brief analysis of the audience for each of the following communication tasks.

a. A cover letter for a job that you saw advertised in a local newspaper. You are confident that your qualifications match the job description.
b. An e-mail memo to your district sales manager describing your visit to a new customer who demands special discounts.
c. An e-mail memo to your boss persuading her to allow you to attend a computer class that will require you to leave work early two days a week for ten weeks.
d. An unsolicited sales letter to a targeted group of executives promoting part-time ownership in a corporate jet plane.
e. A letter from the municipal water department explaining that the tap water may taste and smell bad; however, it poses no threats to health.

4.4 Copyright Confusion: Myths and Facts (Obj. 6)

Ethics

Your Task. You overheard the following statements as a group of college students discussed copyright issues.[17] Which of these statements do you think are true and which are false?

a. If it doesn't have a copyright notice, it's not copyrighted.
b. If I don't charge for it, it's not a violation.
c. If it's posted to Usenet, it's in the public domain.
d. My posting was just fair use.
e. If you don't defend your copyright, you lose it.
f. If I make up my own stories, but base them on another work, my new work belongs to me.
g. They can't get me; defendants in court have powerful rights!
h. Copyright violation isn't a crime or anything, is it?
i. It doesn't hurt anybody. In fact, it's free advertising.
j. They e-mailed me a copy, so I can post it.

Writing Improvement Exercises

4.5 Audience Benefits and the "You" View (Obj. 5)

Your Task. Revise the following sentences to emphasize the audience's perspective and the "you" view.

a. We regret to announce that the bookstore will distribute free iPods only to students in classes in which the instructor has requested these devices as learning tools.
b. Our safety policy forbids us from renting power equipment to anyone who cannot demonstrate proficiency in its use.
c. To prevent us from possibly losing large sums of money in stolen identity schemes, our bank now requires verification of any large check presented for immediate payment.
d. So that we may bring our customer records up-to-date and eliminate the expense of duplicate mailings, we are asking you to complete and return the enclosed card.
e. For just $159 per person, we have arranged a two-night getaway package to Orlando that includes hotel accommodations, Pleasure Island tickets, and complimentary breakfasts.
f. We find it necessary to request all employees to complete the enclosed questionnaire so that we may develop a master schedule for summer vacations.
g. To enable us to continue our policy of selling name brands at discount prices, we can give store credit but we cannot give cash refunds on returned merchandise.

4.6 Bias-Free Language (Obj. 5)

Your Task. Revise the following sentences to reduce gender, racial, ethnic, age, and disability stereotypes.

a. Every employee must wear his photo ID on the job.
b. Media Moguls hired Sheena Love, an African American, for the position of project manager.
c. A skilled assistant proofreads her boss's documents and catches any errors he makes.
d. Theaters in the multiplex offer discounts for old people.
e. The conference will include special excursions for the wives of executives.
f. Serving on the panel are a lady veternarian, a female doctor, two businessmen, and an Indian CPA.
g. Because Sarah is confined to a wheelchair, she uses the elevator.

4.7 Conversational but Professional (Obj. 5)

Your Task. Revise the following statements to make the tone conversational yet professional.

a. As per your recent request, the undersigned is happy to inform you that we are sending you forthwith the brochures you requested.
b. Pursuant to your letter of the 12th, please be advised that your shipment was sent June 9.
c. BTW, Amy was pretty ticked off because the manager accused her of ripping off office supplies.
d. Hey, Sam! Look, I need you to pound on Lisa so we can drop this budget thingy in her lap.
e. Kindly be informed that your vehicle has been determined to require corrective work.
f. He didn't have the guts to badmouth her 2 her face.
g. The undersigned respectfully reminds affected individuals that employees desirous of changing their health plans must do so before December 30.

4.8 Positive and Courteous Expression (Obj. 5)

Your Task. Revise the following statements to make them more positive.

a. It is impossible for the contractor to complete the footings until the soil is no longer soggy.
b. We must withhold authorizing payment of your consultant's fees because the Legal Committee claims your work is not completed.
c. In the complaint that you sent in your July 2 letter, you claim that our representative was hostile and refused to help you.
d. Plans for the new health center cannot move forward without full community support.
e. This is the last time I'm writing to try to get you to record my January 6 payment of $500 to my account. Anyone who can read can see from the attached documents that I've tried to explain this to you before.
f. Although you apparently failed to read the operator's manual, we are sending you a replacement blade for your food processor. Next time read page 18 carefully so that you will know how to attach this blade.
g. Customers are ineligible for the 10 percent discount unless they show their membership cards.

4.9 Familiar Words (Obj. 5)

Your Task. Revise the following sentences to avoid unfamiliar words.

a. The salary we are offering is commensurate with other managers' remuneration.
b. To expedite ratification of this agreement, we urge you to vote in the affirmative.

c. In a dialogue with the manager, I learned that you plan to terminate our contract.

d. Did the braking problem materialize subsequent to our recall effort?

e. Pursuant to your invitation, we will interrogate our agent.

4.10 Precise Words (Obj. 5)

Your Task. From the choices in parentheses, select the most precise, vigorous words.

a. When replying to e-mail, (*bring in, include, put*) enough of the old message for (*someone, the person, the recipient*) to recognize the original note.

b. For a (*hard, long, complicated*) e-mail message, (*make, create, have*) the note in your word processing program.

c. If an e-mail (*thing, catch, glitch*) interferes while writing, you can easily (*get, have, retrieve*) your message.

d. We plan to (*acknowledge, publicize, applaud*) the work of exemplary employees.

For the following sentences provide more precise alternatives for the italicized words.

e. In her e-mail memo she said that she would (a) *change* overtime hours in order to (b) *fix* the budget.

f. Our new manager (a) *said* that only (b) *the right kind of* applicants should apply.

g. After (a) *reading* the report, I decided it was (b) *bad*.

4.11 Legal Language (Obj. 6)

Your Task. To avoid possible litigation, revise the italicized words in the following sentences taken from proposals.

a. We have *inspected* the hydraulic system and will send a complete report.

b. Our goal is to *assure* completion of the project on schedule.

c. We will *determine* the amount of stress for each supporting column.

4.12 Communicating Mortgage Information: Tired of Paying Rent

`Consumer`   `Web`

Your best friends, Nadia and Mark, are definitely tired of paying rent. One Sunday they saw an "Open House" sign and stopped to see the home that was for sale. They fell in love with the red brick home, but they quickly realized that purchasing a home required more cash and more knowledge than they had. They knew nothing about home mortgages. Because they think you are a whiz at computer searching, they ask you to help them get educated.

© Diane Macdonald / Stockbyte / Getty Images

Your Task. Using a search tool such as Google, locate Web sites with home mortgage tips. Sort through the commercial clutter until you find answers to these questions:

a. What are the advantages and disadvantages of the main types of mortgages?

b. What does a mortgage payment consist of? Explain PITI.

c. How much down payment will Nadia and Mark need?

d. What is prequalification?

e. What are some general tips for new home buyers seeking a mortgage?

After collecting the information, think about the best way to present it to Nadia and Mark. How much do they already know about this subject? How detailed should you make your explanations? What channel of communication would be best? Will they want a written record? Be prepared to discuss your findings and analysis in class, in teams, or in a memo to your instructor.

Video Resources

Video Library 1

The 3-x-3 Writing Process Develops Fluent Workplace Skills
Your instructor may show you a video that steps you through the writing process in a workplace environment. It shows all three phases of the writing process so that you can see how it guides the development of a complete message. This video illustrates concepts in Chapters 4, 5, and 6.

Grammar and Mechanics C.L.U.E. Review 4

Adjectives and Adverbs

Review Guides 19–20 about adjectives and adverbs in Appendix A: Grammar and Mechanics Guide (Competent Language Usage Essentials), beginning on page A-9. On a separate sheet, revise the following sentences to correct errors in adjectives and adverbs. For each error that you locate, write the guide number that reflects this usage. Some sentences may have two errors. If a sentence is correct, write *C*. When you finish, check your answers on page Key-1.

1. Andrea expected to do good on the writing exam because she had studied.

2. Most businesspeople agree that face to face meetings are better than videoconferences.

3. The newly redecorated office no longer had wall to wall carpeting.

4. If one receives on the job criticism, it is best to accept it as constructive help.

5. Locally-installed online collaboration tools are easy-to-use and inexpensive.

6. After the technician left, the printer worked smooth.

7. The nineteen year old applicant did well in her interview and finished the writing exam more quicker than expected.

8. Business writers strive to use easy to understand language and familiar words.

9. The manager told us office workers not to take the CEO's harsh words personal.

10. Clearly-written safety messages use short words that are quickly understood.

Chapter 5

Writing Process Phase 2: Research, Organize, Compose

OBJECTIVES

After studying this chapter, you should be able to

1. Apply Phase 2 of the 3-x-3 writing process, which begins with formal and informal methods for researching data and generating ideas.

2. Explain how to organize data into lists and alphanumeric or decimal outlines.

3. Compare direct and indirect patterns for organizing ideas.

4. Compose the first draft of a message, focusing on effective sentences including techniques for emphasizing important ideas, avoiding misplaced modifiers, and using active and passive voice successfully.

5. Compose effective paragraphs using three classic paragraph plans as well as applying techniques for achieving paragraph coherence.

Communicating at Work Part 1

Once the Height of Hip, Gap Struggles to Stop Sagging Sales

It all started in the summer of 1969. Gap Inc. opened its first store, offering Levi's, records, and tapes to college kids in San Francisco. From a humble start, it grew to become one of the world's largest specialty retailers. However, after spectacular growth, Gap fell from favor. Critics accused it of making every bad move a retailer could. Besides major misses in fashion, the company failed to differentiate among its three major brands—Banana Republic, Gap, and Old Navy—and it opened too many stores.

The company that had pioneered the casual cool look with fitted jeans, khakis, and simple T-shirts lost its fashion compass. "The Gap doesn't seem hip any longer," said one shopper. "They're too preppy and sterile."[1] Another young shopper said, "Gap seems to be stuck in the '90s. I always think of it as the clothes my parents wear."[2] Once the king of casual but classic clothing, Gap has been stung by retailing upstarts that woo young people with trendy fashions at affordable prices. Retailers such as Zara, Mango, Hot Topic, and Hollister are snagging customers with hip styles and competitive pricing.

At its zenith in 1994, Gap launched Old Navy as a fun fashion label with good prices and street-chic attitude. Emphasizing humor and mass appeal, Old Navy gave shoppers music and bright colors while promoting a quirky image. But these days, some are saying that Old Navy is old hat.[3] It has lost its cult status and its aura of campy fashion. In attempting to right the sinking ship, Old Navy overcorrected and "skewed too far toward value," said a Gap spokesperson.[4] That is, it went overboard with inexpensive fashions.

Further compounding their woes, both Gap and Old Navy have saturated the market. Gap has 1,338 stores and Old Navy has 1,008 stores in the United States and Canada.[5] They are almost as ubiquitous as Starbucks. In the fashion business, bigness is not necessarily a plus. With stores in nearly every shopping center, Gap has overexposed the brand. Customers are staying away because its styles no longer seem unique or special.

© Dimas Ardian / Stringer / Getty Images

Under new management, Gap Inc. is working to improve its merchandise mix, reduce inventories, halt capital spending, and enhance its online presence. Ultimately, though, Gap must find a way to lure its customers back.

Critical Thinking

- In what ways would research (gathering information) be important to Gap and Old Navy in getting their customers back?
- Why is it important for Gap managers, as well as other business communicators, to gather all necessary information before making management decisions?
- What techniques can business communicators at Gap and other companies use to generate ideas for new products as well as to improve business processes?

http://www.gap.com

Writing Process Phase 2: Research

LEARNING OBJECTIVE 1

Apply Phase 2 of the 3-x-3 writing process, which begins with formal and informal methods for researching data and generating ideas.

Before beginning to write, writers conduct formal or informal research to collect information or generate ideas.

Business communicators at Gap and Old Navy face daily challenges that require data collection, idea generation, and concept organization. Before they can make decisions and convey those decisions in written messages or presentations, they must gather information and organize that information. These activities are part of the second phase of the 3-x-3 writing process. You will recall that the 3-x-3 writing process, as reviewed in Figure 5.1, involves three phases. This chapter focuses on the second phase of the process: researching, organizing, and composing.

No smart businessperson would begin writing a message before collecting all the needed information. We call this collection process *research,* a rather formal-sounding term. For simple documents, though, the procedure can be quite informal. Research is necessary before beginning to write because the information you collect helps shape the message. Discovering significant data after a message is half completed often means starting over and reorganizing. To avoid frustration and inaccurate messages, collect information that answers a primary question:

- What does the receiver need to know about this topic?

When the message involves action, search for answers to secondary questions:

- What is the receiver to do?
- How is the receiver to do it?
- When must the receiver do it?
- What happens if the receiver doesn't do it?

As consumers increasingly turn to the Internet to shop, recommend products, and rate businesses on their customer service, management teams are turning to a new kind of research to inform business decisions—online "buzz-tracking." Research firms like Nielsen BuzzMetrics and Brandimensions traverse millions of fan sites, blogs, and chat rooms to analyze user feedback and spot consumer trends. *How can buzz-tracking research help communication professionals develop more effective written messages and presentations?*

© IT Stock Free / Jupiterimages

As noted in the photo caption above, more and more consumer research is conducted electronically. Because methods for collecting information continue to evolve, you will have many research sources available before you begin a writing project. Whenever your communication problem requires more information than you have in your head or at your fingertips, you must conduct research. This research may be formal or informal.

Formal Research Methods

Long reports and complex business problems generally require some use of formal research methods. Let us say you are part of the management team at Gap Inc. and you want to evaluate several locations for the placement of a new Old Navy store. Or, let us assume you must write a term paper for a college class. Both tasks require more data than you have in your head or at your fingertips. To conduct formal research, you could:

- **Access electronically.** Like other facets of life, the research process has been changed considerably by the computer. Most businesspeople begin any research process by seeing what they can find electronically. Much of the current printed material in libraries is available from the Internet, databases, or CDs that can be accessed by computer.

FIGURE 5.1 Guffey's 3-x-3 Writing Process

1 Prewriting

Analyze: Decide on the purpose of your message. What do you want the receiver to do or believe? What communication channel is best?

Anticipate: Profile the audience. What does the receiver already know? Will the receiver's response be neutral, positive, or negative?

Adapt: What writing techniques and strategies can you use to adapt your message to its audience? How can you shape the message to achieve your purpose?

2 Writing

Research: Gather background data to provide facts. Search company files, previous correspondence, and the Internet. What do you need to know to write this message?

Organize: Group similar information together. Decide whether to organize your information directly or indirectly. Outline your plan and make notes.

Compose: Prepare a first draft, usually writing quickly. Remember that you will be revising it to improve its readability and impact.

3 Revising

Revise: Edit your message to be sure it is clear, conversational, concise, and readable. Look for ways to highlight important information. Consider bullets, lists, and headings to help the reader understand related points.

Proofread: Read carefully to find and correct errors in spelling, grammar, punctuation, names, numbers, and format.

Evaluate: Will this message achieve your purpose? Have you thought enough about the audience to be sure this message is appropriate and appealing?

Database providers such as ABI/INFORM and Business Source Premier (EBSCO) enable you to search millions of magazine, newspaper, and journal articles. The Internet also provides a wealth of information from public records, public and private organizations, and many other sources. You will learn more about using the Internet and other electronic information resources in Chapter 11.

- **Search manually.** If you need background or supplementary information, you will probably conduct manual research in public or college libraries. These traditional resources include periodical indexes for lists of newspaper, magazine, and journal articles, along with the card catalog for books. Other manual sources are book indexes, encyclopedias, reference books, handbooks, dictionaries, directories, and almanacs.

- **Investigate primary sources.** To develop firsthand, primary information for a project, go directly to the source. In searching for locations for Old Navy stores, you might travel to possible sites and check them out. If you need information about how many shoppers pass by a location or visit a shopping center, you might conduct a traffic count. To learn more about specific shoppers who might become Old Navy customers, you could use questionnaires, interviews, or focus groups. Formal research includes scientific sampling methods that enable investigators to make accurate judgments and valid predictions.

- **Experiment scientifically.** Another source of primary data is experimentation. Instead of merely asking for the target audience's opinion, scientific researchers present choices with controlled variables. Assume, for example, that the management team at Gap wants to know at what price and under what circumstances consumers would purchase jeans from the Gap instead of from Abercrombie & Fitch. Instead of jeans, let us say that management wants to study the time of year and type of weather conditions that motivate consumers to begin purchasing sweaters, jackets, and cold-weather gear. The results of such experimentation would provide valuable data for managerial decision making.

Because formal research techniques are particularly necessary for reports, you will study resources and techniques more extensively in Unit 4.

Informal Research Methods

Most routine tasks—such as composing e-mail messages, memos, letters, informational reports, and oral presentations—require data that you can collect informally. For some projects, though, you rely more on your own ideas instead of—or in addition to—researching existing facts. Here are some techniques for collecting informal data and for generating ideas:

- **Look in the files.** Before asking others for help, see what you can find yourself. For many routine messages you can often find previous documents in digital or paper files to help you with content and format.

- **Talk with your boss.** Get information from the individual making the assignment. What does that person know about the topic? What slant should you take? What other sources would he or she suggest?

- **Interview the target audience.** Consider talking with individuals at whom the message is aimed. They can provide clarifying information that tells you what they want to know and how you should shape your remarks. Suggestions for conducting more formal interviews are presented in Chapter 11.

- **Conduct an informal survey.** Gather unscientific but helpful information via questionnaires, telephone surveys, or online surveys. In preparing a memo report predicting the success of a proposed fitness center, for example, circulate a questionnaire asking for employee reactions.

Generating Ideas by Brainstorming

One popular method for generating ideas is brainstorming. We should point out, however, that some critics argue that brainstorming groups "produce fewer and poorer quality ideas than the same number of individuals working alone."[6] Proponents agree that, when done poorly, brainstorming is a waste of time. When done properly, however, brainstorming is quite effective in unleashing ideas and creative energy.[7] Here are suggestions for productive group brainstorming:

- Define the problem and create an agenda that outlines the topics to be covered.

- Establish time limits, remembering that short sessions are best.

- Set a quota, such as a minimum of 100 ideas. The goal is quantity, not quality.

- Require every participant to contribute ideas, accept the ideas of others, or improve on ideas.

- Encourage wild, "out of the box" thinking. Allow no one to criticize or evaluate ideas.

- Write ideas on flipcharts or on sheets of paper hung around the room.

- Organize and classify the ideas, retaining the best. Consider using cluster diagrams, discussed shortly.

Collecting Information and Generating Ideas on the Job

Assume that you work in the corporate offices of Gap Inc. and that you have been given the task of developing a college recruiting brochure for all Gap stores. You think this is a great idea because Gap Inc. has thousands of stores, and many college students don't know about the exciting career opportunities and benefits it offers. You know right away that you want the brochure to be colorful, exciting, concise, youthfully oriented, lightweight (because it has to be carried to college campuses), and easily updated. Beyond that, you realize that you need ideas from others on how to develop this recruiting brochure.

To collect data for this project, you decide to use both formal and informal research methods. You study recruiting brochures from other companies. You talk with college students about information they would like to see in a brochure. You conduct more formal research among recently hired employees and among Gap division presidents and executives to learn what they think a recruiting brochure should include. Working with an outside consultant, you prepare a questionnaire to use in personal interviews with employees and executives. The interviews include some open-ended questions such as, *How did you start with the company?* The questionnaire also asks specific questions about career paths, degree requirements, personality traits desired, and so forth.

Next you ask five or six fellow employees and team members to help brainstorm ideas for the brochure. In a spirited session, your team comes up the cluster diagram shown in Figure 5.2 on page 128. The ideas range from the cost of the brochure to career development programs and your company's appealing location in the San Francisco Bay area.

From the jumble of ideas in the initial cluster diagram, you see that you can organize most of the information into three main categories relating to the brochure—Development, Form, and Content. You eliminate, simplify, and consolidate some ideas and add other new ideas. Then you organize the ideas into subclusters, shown in Figure 5.3 on page 129. This set of subclusters could form the basis for an outline, which we will talk about shortly. Or you could make another set of subclusters, further outlining the categories.

> To develop ideas for a recruiting brochure, use both formal and informal research.

Writing Process Phase 2: Organize

Well-organized messages group similar ideas together. These groups of ideas are then sequenced in a way that helps the reader understand relationships and accept the writer's views. Unorganized messages proceed free-form, jumping from one thought to another. They look like the jumbled ideas in our Figure 5.2 cluster diagram. Such messages fail to emphasize important points. Puzzled readers can't see how the pieces fit together, and they become frustrated and irritated. Many communication experts regard poor organization as the greatest failing of business writers. Two simple techniques can help you organize data: the scratch list and the outline.

> **LEARNING OBJECTIVE 2**
> *Explain how to organize data into lists and alphanumeric or decimal outlines.*

FIGURE 5.2 Creating Cluster Diagram to Generate Ideas for Old Navy/Gap Recruiting Brochure

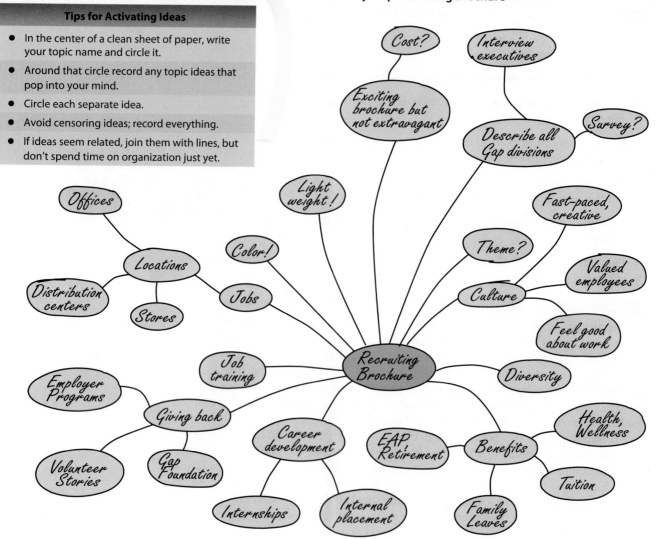

Tips for Activating Ideas

- In the center of a clean sheet of paper, write your topic name and circle it.
- Around that circle record any topic ideas that pop into your mind.
- Circle each separate idea.
- Avoid censoring ideas; record everything.
- If ideas seem related, join them with lines, but don't spend time on organization just yet.

Using Lists and Outlines to Organize Ideas

Two techniques for organizing data are a scratch list and an outline.

In developing simple messages, some writers make a quick scratch list of the topics they wish to cover. Writers often jot this scratch list in the margin of the letter or memo to which they are responding (the majority of business messages are written in response to other documents). These writers then compose a message at their computers directly from the scratch list.

Most writers, though, need to organize their ideas—especially if the project is complex—into a hierarchy, such as an outline. The beauty of preparing an outline is that it gives you a chance to organize your thinking before you get bogged down in word choice and sentence structure. Figure 5.4 shows two outline formats: alphanumeric and decimal. The familiar alphanumeric format uses Roman numerals, letters, and numbers to show major and minor ideas. The decimal format, which takes a little getting used to, has the advantage of showing how every item at every level relates to the whole. Both outlining formats force you to focus on the topic, identify major ideas, and support those ideas with details, illustrations, or evidence.

Spotlight on Communicators

"Writing skills in the business world are no longer simply an advantage— they are a necessity," says Max Messmer, CEO of Robert Half International, the world's first and largest specialized staffing firm. At the heart of effective writing, he contends, is the ability to organize a series of thoughts. He advises taking the time to prioritize and record the key points you want to make. You can do this by using either a formal outline or an informal list.

Chapter 5: Writing Process Phase 2: Research, Organize, Compose

FIGURE 5.3 Organizing Ideas From Cluster Diagram Into Subclusters

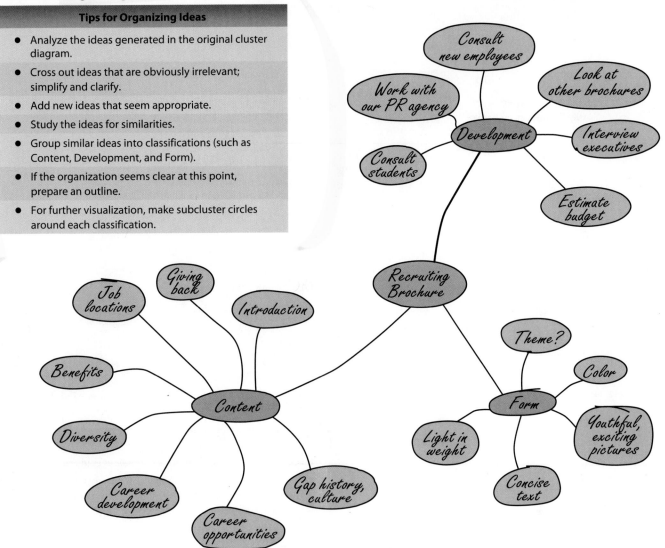

Tips for Organizing Ideas

- Analyze the ideas generated in the original cluster diagram.
- Cross out ideas that are obviously irrelevant; simplify and clarify.
- Add new ideas that seem appropriate.
- Study the ideas for similarities.
- Group similar ideas into classifications (such as Content, Development, and Form).
- If the organization seems clear at this point, prepare an outline.
- For further visualization, make subcluster circles around each classification.

The hardest part of outlining is grouping ideas into components or categories—ideally three to five in number. These categories are very important because they will become the major headings in your report. If you have more than five components, look for ways to combine smaller segments into broader topics. The following example shows how a portion of the Gap recruiting brochure subclusters (Figure 5.3) can be organized into an alphanumeric outline.[8]

Grouping ideas into categories is the hardest part of outlining.

I. Introduction

  A. Brief history of Gap Inc.

    1. Founding

    2. Milestones

  B. Corporate culture

    1. Fast-paced, creative, upbeat attitude

    2. Value diversity, employees

    3. Value social responsibility

II. Careers

  A. Opportunities

    1. Internships

    2. Management trainee programs

    3. MBA programs

  B. Development

    1. Internal promotion

    2. Job training

Alphanumeric outlines show major and minor ideas; decimal outlines show how ideas relate to one another.

FIGURE 5.4 Two Outlining Formats

Format for Alphanumeric Outline	Format for Decimal Outline
Title: Major Idea, Purpose	Title: Major Idea, Purpose

Format for Alphanumeric Outline

I. First major component
   A. First subpoint
      1. Detail, illustration, evidence
      2. Detail, illustration, evidence
   B. Second subpoint
      1.
      2.

II. Second major component
   A. First subpoint
      1.
      2.
   B. Second subpoint
      1.
      2.

III. Third major component
   A.
      1.
      2.
   B.
      1.
      2.

(This method is simple and familiar.)

Format for Decimal Outline

1.0. First major component
   1.1. First subpoint
      1.1.1. Detail, illustration, evidence
      1.1.2. Detail, illustration, evidence
   1.2. Second subpoint
      1.2.1.
      1.2.2.

2.0. Second major component
   2.1. First subpoint
      2.1.1.
      2.1.2.
   2.2. Second subpoint
      2.2.1.
      2.2.2.

3.0. Third major component
   3.1.
      3.1.1.
      3.1.2.
   3.2.
      3.2.1.
      3.2.2.

(This method relates every item to the overall outline.)

Tips for Making Outlines

- Define the main topic (purpose of message) in the title.
- Divide the main topic into major components or classifications (preferably three to five). If necessary, combine small components into one larger category.
- Break the components into subpoints.
- Don't put a single item under a major component; if you have only one subpoint, integrate it with the main item above it or reorganize.
- Strive to make each component exclusive (no overlapping).
- Use details, illustrations, and evidence to support subpoints.

Every major category in an outline should have at least two subcategories.

In making outlines, you should divide each major category into at least two subcategories. These categories are then fleshed out with examples, details, statistics, case histories, and other data. In moving from major point to subpoint, you are progressing from large, abstract concepts to small, concrete ideas. Each subpoint could be further subdivided with more specific illustrations if you desired. You can determine the appropriate amount of detail by considering what your audience (primary and secondary) already knows about the topic and how much persuading you must do.

How you group ideas into components depends on your topic and your channel of communication. Business documents usually contain typical components arranged in traditional patterns, as shown in Figure 5.5.

Thus far, you've seen how to collect information, generate ideas, and prepare an outline. How you order the information in your outline, though, depends on what pattern or strategy you choose.

Chapter 5: Writing Process Phase 2: Research, Organize, Compose

FIGURE 5.5 Typical Major Components in Business Outlines

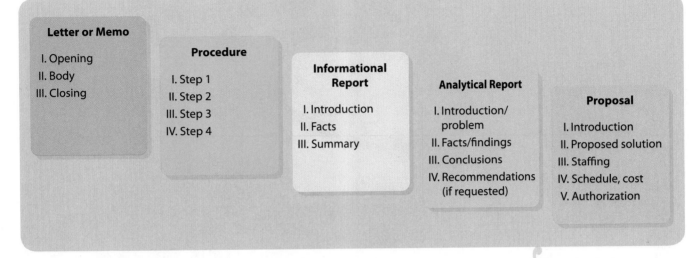

Letter or Memo

I. Opening
II. Body
III. Closing

Procedure

I. Step 1
II. Step 2
III. Step 3
IV. Step 4

Informational Report

I. Introduction
II. Facts
III. Summary

Analytical Report

I. Introduction/ problem
II. Facts/findings
III. Conclusions
IV. Recommendations (if requested)

Proposal

I. Introduction
II. Proposed solution
III. Staffing
IV. Schedule, cost
V. Authorization

Organizing Ideas Into Patterns

Two organizational patterns provide plans of action for typical business messages: the direct pattern and the indirect pattern. The primary difference between the two patterns is where the main idea is placed. In the direct pattern the main idea comes first, followed by details, explanation, or evidence. In the indirect pattern the main idea follows the details, explanation, and evidence. The pattern you select is determined by how you expect the audience to react to the message, as shown in Figure 5.6.

Direct Pattern for Receptive Audiences

In preparing to write any message, you need to anticipate the audience's reaction to your ideas and frame your message accordingly. When you expect the reader to be pleased, mildly interested, or, at worst, neutral—use the direct pattern. That is, put your main point—the purpose of your message—in the first or second sentence. Dianna Booher, renowned writing consultant, pointed out that typical readers begin any message by saying, "So what am I

LEARNING OBJECTIVE 3
Compare direct and indirect patterns for organizing ideas.

Business messages typically follow either the (a) direct pattern, with the main idea first, or (b) the indirect pattern, with the main idea following explanation and evidence.

FIGURE 5.6 Audience Response Determines Pattern of Organization

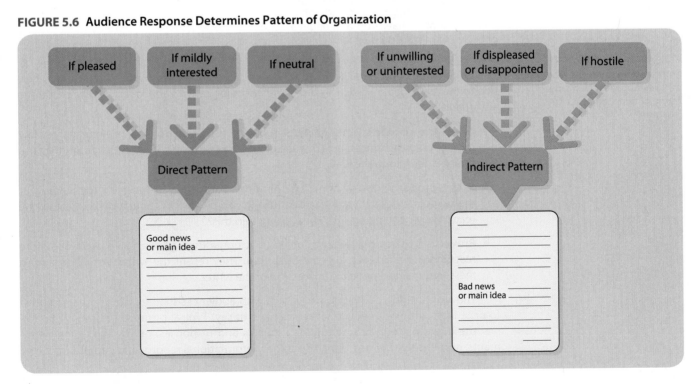

If pleased

If mildly interested

If neutral

If unwilling or uninterested

If displeased or disappointed

If hostile

Direct Pattern

Indirect Pattern

Good news or main idea

Bad news or main idea

Pet owners throughout North America panicked when a broad pet-food recall by Menu Foods, Inc., revealed that the company's cuts-and-gravy style brands had been tainted with a toxic chemical. The U.S. Food and Drug Administration linked thousands of pet illnesses, kidney failures, and even deaths to the company's contaminated products. *How do negative events affect the way business communicators organize their written communications to customers, retailers, and other stakeholders?*

supposed to do with this information?" In business writing you have to say, "Reader, here is my point!"[9] As quickly as possible, tell why you are writing. Compare the direct and indirect patterns in the following memo openings. Notice how long it takes to get to the main idea in the indirect opening.

Indirect Opening

Our company has been concerned with attracting better-qualified prospective job candidates. For this reason, the Management Council has been gathering information about an internship program for college students. After considerable investigation, we have voted to begin a pilot program starting next fall.

Direct Opening

The Management Council has voted to begin a college internship pilot program next fall.

Frontloading saves the reader's time, establishes the proper frame of mind, and prevents frustration.

Explanations and details should follow the direct opening. What's important is getting to the main idea quickly. This direct method, also called *frontloading*, has at least three advantages:

- **Saves the reader's time.** Many of today's businesspeople can devote only a few moments to each message. Messages that take too long to get to the point may lose their readers along the way.

- **Sets a proper frame of mind.** Learning the purpose up front helps the reader put the subsequent details and explanations in perspective. Without a clear opening, the reader may be thinking, "Why am I being told this?"

- **Prevents frustration.** Readers forced to struggle through excessive verbiage before reaching the main idea become frustrated. They resent the writer. Poorly organized messages create a negative impression of the writer.

This frontloading technique works best with audiences that are likely to be receptive to or at least not disagree with what you have to say. Typical business messages that follow the direct pattern include routine requests and responses, orders and acknowledgments, nonsensitive memos, e-mail messages, informational reports, and informational oral presentations. All these tasks have one element in common: none has a sensitive subject that will upset the reader.

Indirect Pattern for Unreceptive Audiences

When you expect the audience to be uninterested, unwilling, displeased, or perhaps even hostile, the indirect pattern is more appropriate. In this pattern you don't reveal the main idea until after you have offered explanation and evidence. This approach works well with three kinds of messages: (a) bad news, (b) ideas that require persuasion, and (c) sensitive news, especially when being transmitted to superiors. The indirect pattern has these benefits:

- **Respects the feelings of the audience.** Bad news is always painful, but the trauma can be lessened when the receiver is prepared for it.

- **Facilitates a fair hearing.** Messages that may upset the reader are more likely to be read when the main idea is delayed. Beginning immediately with a piece of bad news or a persuasive request, for example, may cause the receiver to stop reading or listening.

- **Minimizes a negative reaction.** A reader's overall reaction to a negative message is generally improved if the news is delivered gently.

Typical business messages that could be developed indirectly include letters and memos that refuse requests, deny claims, and disapprove credit. Persuasive requests, sales letters, sensitive messages, and some reports and oral presentations also benefit from the indirect strategy. You will learn more about how to use the indirect pattern in Chapters 9 and 10.

In summary, business messages may be organized directly, with the main idea first, or indirectly, with the main idea delayed. Although these two patterns cover many communication problems, they should be considered neither universal nor inviolate. Every business transaction is distinct. Some messages are mixed: part good news, part bad; part goodwill, part persuasion. In upcoming chapters you will practice applying the direct and indirect patterns in typical situations. Then, you will have the skills and confidence to evaluate communication problems and vary these patterns depending on the goals you wish to achieve.

Communicating at Work Part 2

Gap Inc.

Rebuilding its customer base and correcting its fashion missteps are major initiatives at Gap and its offspring, Old Navy. At the same time the stores must be ever watchful that their garments are not made in sweatshops. Stiff competition and consumer demand for low prices have forced many U.S. apparel manufacturers to shift production offshore. Some of that production ends up in sweatshops, such as those found in Cambodia, Bangladesh, and Honduras. The worst sweatshops use child labor and demand 80-hour workweeks without overtime pay. Bosses routinely shout at workers and may send them home for talking on the job. Workers earn as little as 29 cents an hour.

Like other major apparel manufacturers, Gap Inc. strives to control working conditions with factory-monitoring and labor-standards programs. Around the world Gap Inc. has more than 90 employees whose sole focus is working to improve conditions in the factories that make its clothing. In one year these employees conducted 4,438 inspections at 2,118 garment factories around the world.[10] When a problem is found, Gap takes action. It works with contractors and factories to improve practices and conditions. If conditions don't improve, it stops using errant contractors.[11] Enforcing its standards worldwide requires an ongoing effort. When complaints from human rights activists and others arrive, Gap Inc. must investigate and respond to each inquiry.

© Dimas Ardian / Stringer / Getty Images

Critical Thinking
- When a business communicator responds to an inquiry, such as a letter about human rights violations among contractors, is "research" necessary?
- What are the differences between formal and informal research?
- What are the advantages and disadvantages of brainstorming with groups?

Writing Process Phase 2: Compose

When composing the first draft, some writers prefer to write quickly; others are more deliberate.

Once you've researched your topic, organized the data, and selected a pattern of organization, you're ready to begin composing. Most writers expect to use their computers for composition, but many are unaware of all the ways a computer can help create better written messages, oral presentations, and Web pages. See the accompanying Tech Talk box to learn how you can take full advantage of your computer.

Even with a computer, some writers have trouble getting started, especially if they haven't completed the preparatory work. Organizing your ideas and working from an outline are very helpful in overcoming writer's block. Composition is also easier if you have a quiet environment in which to concentrate. Businesspeople with messages to compose set aside a given time and allow no calls, visitors, or other interruptions. This is a good technique for students as well.

As you begin composing, think about what style fits you best. Some experts suggest that you write quickly (*sprint writing*). Get your thoughts down now and refine them in later versions.[12] As you take up each idea, imagine that you are talking to the reader. Don't let yourself get bogged down. If you can't think of the right word, insert a substitute or type "find perfect word later." Sprint writing works well for some writers, but others prefer to move more slowly and think through their ideas more deliberately. Whether you are a sprint or a deliberate writer, keep in mind that you are writing the first draft. You will have time later to revise and polish your sentences.

Tech Talk

Seven Ways Computers Can Help You Create Better Written Messages, Oral Presentations, and Web Pages

Although computers can't actually do the writing for you, they provide powerful tools that make the composition process easier and the results more professional. Here are seven ways your computer can help you improve your written documents, oral presentations, and even Web pages.

1. **Fighting writer's block.** Because word processors enable ideas to flow almost effortlessly from your brain to a screen, you can expect fewer delays resulting from writer's block. You can compose rapidly, and you can experiment with structure and phrasing, later retaining and polishing your most promising thoughts.
2. **Collecting information electronically.** As a knowledge worker in an information economy, you must find information quickly. Much of the world's information is now accessible in databases or on the Web. You will learn more about these exciting electronic resources in Unit 4.
3. **Outlining and organizing ideas.** Most word processors include some form of "outliner," a feature that enables you to divide a topic into a hierarchical order with main points and subpoints. Your computer keeps track of the levels of ideas automatically so that you can easily add, cut, or rearrange points in the outline.
4. **Improving correctness and precision.** Nearly all word processing programs today provide features that catch and correct spelling and typographical errors. Grammar checkers detect many errors in capitalization, word use (such as *it's, its*), double negatives, verb use, subject–verb agreement, sentence structure, number agreement, number style, and other writing faults. But the errors are merely highlighted—not corrected. You have to do that.

5. **Adding graphics for emphasis.** Your letters, memos, and reports may be improved by the addition of graphs and artwork to clarify and illustrate data. You can import charts, diagrams, and illustrations created in database, spreadsheet, graphics, or draw-and-paint programs. Clip art is available to symbolize or illustrate ideas.
6. **Designing and producing professional-looking documents, presentations, and Web pages.** Most software now includes a large selection of scalable fonts (for different character sizes and styles), italics, boldface, symbols, and styling techniques to aid you in producing consistent formatting and professional-looking results. Presentation software enables you to incorporate showy slide effects, color, sound, pictures, and even movies into your talks for management or customers. Web document builders also help you design and construct Web pages.
7. **Using collaborative software for team writing.** Special programs with commenting and revision features, described in Chapter 4, allow you to make changes and to identify each team member's editing.

Career Application

Individually or in teams, identify specific software programs that perform the tasks described here. Prepare a table naming each program, its major functions, and its advantages and disadvantages for business writers in your field.

Creating Effective Sentences

As you create your first draft, you will be working at the sentence level of composition. Although you've used sentences all your life, you may be unaware of how they can be shaped and arranged to express your ideas most effectively. First, let's review some basic sentence elements.

Complete sentences have subjects and verbs and make sense.

SUBJECT | VERB

The manager of Information Technology sent an e-mail to all employees.

> **Sentences must have subjects and verbs and must make sense.**

Clauses and phrases, the key building blocks of sentences, are related groups of words. Clauses have subjects and verbs; phrases do not.

PHRASE | PHRASE

The manager of Information Technology sent an e-mail to all employees.

> **Clauses have subjects and verbs, but phrases do not.**

PHRASE | PHRASE

By reading carefully, we learned about the latest computer viruses.

CLAUSE | CLAUSE

Because he is experienced, Adam can repair most computer problems.

CLAUSE | CLAUSE

When we have technology problems, we call a technician in our support group.

Clauses may be divided into two groups: independent and dependent. Independent clauses are grammatically complete. Dependent clauses depend for their meaning on independent clauses. In the two preceding examples the clauses beginning with *Because* and *When* are dependent. Dependent clauses are often introduced by words such as *if, when, because,* and *as.*

> **Independent clauses may stand alone; dependent clauses cannot stand alone.**

INDEPENDENT CLAUSE

Adam solves our technology problems.

DEPENDENT CLAUSE | INDEPENDENT CLAUSE

When employees need help, Adam solves our technology problems.

By learning to distinguish phrases, independent clauses, and dependent clauses, you will be able to punctuate sentences correctly and avoid three basic sentence faults: the fragment, the run-on sentence, and the comma splice. In Guide 1, Appendix A, we examine these writing problems in greater detail. For now, however, let us look at some ways to make your sentences more readable.

Preferring Short Sentences. Because your goal is to communicate clearly, you should strive for sentences that average 20 words. Some sentences will be shorter; some will be longer. The American Press Institute reports that reader comprehension drops off markedly as sentences become longer.[13] Thus, in crafting your sentences, think about the relationship between sentence length and comprehension:

> **Effective sentences are short and stress important ideas.**

Sentence Length	Comprehension Rate
8 words	100%
15 words	90%
19 words	80%
28 words	50%

> **Sentences of 20 or fewer words are easiest to understand.**

Instead of stringing together clauses with *and, but,* and *however,* break some of those complex sentences into separate segments. Business readers want to grasp ideas immediately. They can do that best when thoughts are separated into short sentences. On the other hand, too many monotonous short sentences will sound "grammar schoolish" and may bore or even annoy the reader. Strive for a balance between longer sentences and shorter ones. Your computer probably can point out long sentences and give you an average sentence length.

Emphasize an important idea by using vivid words, labeling the main idea, placing the idea first or last in a sentence, or making it the sentence subject.

Emphasizing Important Ideas.

You can stress prominent ideas mechanically by underscoring, italicizing, or boldfacing. We will discuss these graphic highlighting devices shortly. You can also emphasize important ideas with five stylistic devices.

- **Use vivid words.** Vivid words are emphatic because the reader can picture ideas clearly.

  General

  One business uses personal selling techniques.

  Vivid

  Avon uses face-to-face selling techniques.

- **Label the main idea.** If an idea is significant, tell the reader:

  Unlabeled

  Explore the possibility of leasing a site, but also hire a consultant.

  Labeled

  Explore the possibility of leasing a site; but, *most important,* hire a consultant.

- **Place the important idea first or last in the sentence.** Ideas have less competition from surrounding words when they appear first or last in a sentence. Observe how the date of the meeting can be emphasized:

  Unemphatic

  All production and administrative personnel will meet on May 23, at which time we will announce a new plan of salary incentives.

  Emphatic

  On May 23 all personnel will meet to learn about salary incentives.

- **Place the important idea in a simple sentence or in an independent clause.** Don't dilute the effect of the idea by making it share the spotlight with other words and clauses.

  Unemphatic

  Although you are the first trainee that we have hired for this program, we have interviewed many candidates and expect to expand the program in the future. (Main idea lost in introductory dependent clause.)

  Emphatic

  You are the first trainee that we have hired for this program. (Simple sentence contains main idea.)

- **Make sure the important idea is the sentence subject.** You will learn more about active and passive voice shortly, but at this point just focus on making the important idea the subject.

  Unemphatic

  The environmental report was written by Koshi. (De-emphasizes *Koshi;* emphasizes the report.)

  Emphatic

  Koshi wrote the environmental report. (Emphasizes *Koshi.*)

In active-voice sentences, the subject is the doer; in passive-voice sentences, the subject is acted upon.

Managing Active and Passive Voice.

In sentences with active-voice verbs, the subject is the doer of the action. In passive-voice sentences the subject is acted upon.

Passive-Voice Verb

The tax return *was completed* before the April 15 deadline. (The subject, *tax return,* is acted upon.)

Active-Voice Verb

Marcelo *completed* his tax return before the April 15 deadline. (The subject, *Marcelo,* is the doer of the action.)

In the first sentence, the passive-voice verb emphasizes the tax return. In the second sentence, the active-voice verb emphasizes Marcelo. Active-voice sentences are more direct because they reveal the performer immediately. They are easier to understand and shorter. Most business writing should be in the active voice.

Passive-voice verbs, however, are useful in certain instances. In sentences with passive-voice verbs, the doer of the action may be revealed or left unknown. In business writing, as well as in personal interactions, some situations demand tact and sensitivity. Instead of using a direct approach with active-voice verbs, we may prefer the indirectness that passive-voice verbs allow. Rather than making a blunt announcement with an active-voice verb (*Wendy made a major error in the estimate*), we can soften the sentence with a passive construction (*A major error was made in the estimate*).

Here's a summary of the best uses of active- and passive-voice verbs:

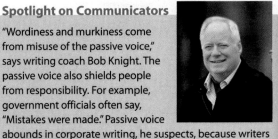
- **Use the active voice for most business writing.** *Our company gives drug tests to all applicants.*

- **Use the passive voice to emphasize an action or the recipient of the action.** *Drug tests are given to all applicants.*

- **Use the passive voice to de-emphasize negative news.** *Your monitor cannot be repaired.*

- **Use the passive voice to conceal the doer of an action.** *A major error was made in the estimate.*

> Passive-voice sentences are useful for tact and to direct attention to actions instead of people.

How can you tell whether a verb is in the active or passive voice? Identify the subject of the sentence and decide whether the subject is doing the acting or whether it is being acted upon. For example, in the sentence *An appointment was made for January 1*, the subject is *appointment*. The subject is being acted upon; therefore, the verb (*was made*) is in the passive voice. Another clue in identifying passive-voice verbs is that they generally include a *to be* helping verb, such as *is, are, was, were, being,* or *been.*

Avoiding Dangling and Misplaced Modifiers.

For clarity, modifiers must be close to the words they describe or limit. A dangling modifier describes or limits a word or words that are missing from the sentence. A misplaced modifier occurs when the word or phrase it describes is not close enough to be clear. In both instances, the solution is to move the modifier closer to the word(s) it describes or limits. Introductory verbal phrases are particularly dangerous; be sure to follow them immediately with the words they logically describe or modify.

> Modifiers must be close to the words they describe or limit.

Dangling Modifier	Improved
After working nine hours, the report was finally finished. (*Did the report work nine hours? The introductory verbal phrase must be followed by a logical subject.*)	After working nine hours, we finally finished the report.
Driving through Malibu Canyon, the ocean suddenly came into view. (*Is the ocean driving through Malibu Canyon?*)	As we drove through Malibu Canyon, the ocean suddenly came into view.
Speaking before the large audience, Luke's knees began to knock. (*Are Luke's knees making a speech?*)	Speaking before the large audience, Luke felt his knees begin to knock.

Try this trick for detecting and remedying these dangling modifiers. Ask the question *Who?* or *What?* after any introductory phrase. The words immediately following should tell the reader *who* or *what* is performing the action. Try the *who?* test on the previous danglers and on the following misplaced modifiers.

Misplaced Modifier

Seeing her error too late, the envelope was immediately resealed by Luna. (*Did the envelope see the error?*)

A wart appeared on my left hand that I want removed. (*Is the left hand to be removed?*)

The busy recruiter interviewed only candidates who had excellent computer skills in the morning. (*Were the candidates skilled only in the morning?*)

Improved

Seeing her error too late, Luna immediately resealed the envelope.

A wart that I want removed appeared on my left hand.

In the morning the busy recruiter interviewed only candidates who had excellent computer skills.

Drafting Meaningful Paragraphs

LEARNING OBJECTIVE 5
Compose effective paragraphs using three classic paragraph plans as well as applying techniques for achieving paragraph coherence.

Effective paragraphs focus on one topic, link ideas to build coherence, and use transitional devices to enhance coherence.

From composing sentences, we progress to paragraphs. A paragraph is one or more sentences designated as a separate thought group. To avoid muddled paragraphs, writers should be able to recognize basic paragraph elements, conventional sentence patterns, and ways to organize sentences into one of three classic paragraph patterns. They must also be able to polish their paragraphs by linking sentences and using transitional expressions.

Well-constructed paragraphs discuss only one topic. They reveal the primary idea in a main sentence that usually, but not always, appears first. Paragraphs may be composed of three kinds of sentences:

> **Main sentence:** *expresses the primary idea of the paragraph.*

> **Supporting sentence:** *illustrates, explains, or strengthens the primary idea.*

> **Limiting sentence:** *opposes the primary idea by suggesting a negative or contrasting thought; may precede or follow the main sentence.*

These sentences may be arranged in three classic paragraph plans: direct, pivoting, and indirect.

Using the Direct Paragraph Plan to Define, Classify, Illustrate, or Describe.
Paragraphs arranged in the direct plan begin with the main sentence, followed by supporting sentences. Most business messages use this paragraph plan because it clarifies the subject immediately. This plan is useful whenever you must define (a new product or procedure), classify (parts of a whole), illustrate (an idea), or describe (a process). Start with the main sentence; then strengthen and amplify that idea with supporting ideas, as shown here:

Main Sentence	<u>A social audit is a report on the social performance of a company.</u>
Supporting Sentences	Such an audit may be conducted by the company itself or by outsiders who evaluate the company's efforts to produce safe products, engage in socially responsible activities, and protect the environment. Many companies publish the results of their social audits in their annual reports. Ben & Jerry's Homemade, for example, devotes a major portion of its annual report to its social audit. The report discusses Ben & Jerry's efforts to support environmental restoration. Moreover, it describes workplace safety, employment equality, and peace programs.

You can alter the direct plan by adding a limiting sentence if necessary. Be sure, though, that you follow with sentences that return to the main idea and support it, as shown here:

Main Sentence	<u>Flexible work scheduling could immediately increase productivity and enhance employee satisfaction in our entire organization.</u>
Limiting Sentence	<u>Such scheduling, however, is impossible for all employees.</u>
Supporting Sentences	Managers would be required to maintain their regular hours. For many other employees, though, flexible scheduling permits extra time to manage family responsibilities. Feeling less stress, employees are able to focus their attention better at work; hence they become more relaxed and more productive.

Using the Pivoting Paragraph Plan to Compare and Contrast.

Paragraphs arranged in the pivoting plan start with a limiting sentence that offers a contrasting or negative idea before delivering the main sentence. Notice in the following example how two limiting sentences about drawbacks to foreign service careers open the paragraph; only then do the main and supporting sentences describing rewards in foreign service appear. The pivoting plan is especially useful for comparing and contrasting ideas. In using the pivoting plan, be sure you emphasize the turn in direction with an obvious *but* or *however*.

The pivoting paragraph pattern is appropriate when comparing and contrasting.

Limiting Sentences	Foreign service careers are certainly not for everyone. Many representatives are stationed in remote countries where harsh climates, health hazards, security risks, and other discomforts exist.
Main Sentence	However, careers in the foreign service offer special rewards for the special people who qualify.
Supporting Sentences	Foreign service employees enjoy the pride and satisfaction of representing the United States abroad. They enjoy frequent travel, enriching cultural and social experiences in living abroad, and action-oriented work.

Using the Indirect Paragraph Plan to Explain and Persuade.

Paragraphs arranged in the indirect plan start with the supporting sentences and conclude with the main sentence. This useful plan enables you to build a rationale, a foundation of reasons, before hitting the audience with a big idea—possibly one that is bad news. It enables you to explain your reasons and then in the final sentence draw a conclusion from them. In the following example, the vice president of a large accounting firm begins by describing the trend toward casual dress and concludes with a recommendation that his firm change its dress code. This indirect plan works well for describing causes followed by an effect.

The indirect paragraph pattern is appropriate when delivering bad news.

| **Supporting Sentences** | According to a recent poll, more than half of all white-collar workers are now dressing casually at work. Many high-tech engineers and professional specialists have given up suits and ties, favoring khakis and sweaters instead. In our own business our consultants say they stand out like "sore thumbs" because they are attired in traditional buttoned-down styles, while the businesspeople they visit are usually wearing comfortable, casual clothing. |
| **Main Sentence** | Therefore, I recommend that we establish an optional "business casual" policy allowing consultants to dress casually, if they wish, as they perform their duties both in and out of the office. |

You will learn more techniques for applying direct and indirect writing strategies when you prepare letters, memos, e-mail messages, reports, and presentations in later chapters.

Linking Ideas to Build Coherence

Paragraphs are coherent when ideas are linked, that is, when one idea leads logically to the next. Well-written paragraphs take the reader through a number of steps. When the author skips from Step 1 to Step 3 and forgets Step 2, the reader is lost. You can use several techniques to keep the reader in step with your ideas.

Coherent paragraphs link ideas by sustaining the main idea, using pronouns, dovetailing sentences, and using transitional expressions.

Sustaining the Key Idea.

Repeating a key expression or using a similar one helps sustain a key idea. In the following example, notice that the repetition of *guest* and *VIP* connects ideas.

Our philosophy holds that every customer is really a guest. *All new employees to our theme parks are trained to treat* guests *as* VIPs. *These* VIPs *are never told what they can or cannot do.*

Using Pronouns.

Familiar pronouns, such as *we, they, he, she,* and *it,* help build continuity, as do demonstrative pronouns, such as *this, that, these,* and *those.* These words confirm that something under discussion is still being discussed. However, be careful with such pronouns. They often need a noun with them to make their meaning absolutely clear. In the following example notice how confusing *this* becomes if the word *training* is omitted.

Using pronouns strategically helps build coherence and continuity.

All new park employees receive a two-week orientation. They learn that every staffer has a vital role in preparing for the show. This training includes how to maintain enthusiasm.

FIGURE 5.7 Transitional Expressions to Build Coherence

To Add or Strengthen	To Show Time or Order	To Clarify	To Show Cause and Effect	To Contradict	To Contrast
additionally	after	for example	accordingly	actually	as opposed to
accordingly	before	for instance	as a result	but	at the same time
again	earlier	I mean	consequently	however	by contrast
also	finally	in other words	for this reason	in fact	conversely
besides	first	put another way	hence	instead	on the contrary
indeed	meanwhile	that is	so	rather	on the other hand
likewise	next	this means	therefore	still	similarly
moreover	now	thus	thus	though	
further	previously			yet	
furthermore	then ·				

Dovetailing sentences means connecting ending and beginning ideas.

Dovetailing Sentences.
Sentences are "dovetailed" when an idea at the end of one connects with an idea at the beginning of the next. Dovetailing of sentences is especially helpful with dense, difficult topics. It is also helpful with ordinary paragraphs, such as the following.

> *New hosts and hostesses learn about the theme park and its* facilities. *These* facilities *include telephones, food services, bathrooms, and attractions, as well as the location of offices. Knowledge of administrative* offices *and the internal workings of the company, such as who's who in administration, ensures that staffers will be able to* serve guests *fully.* Serving guests, *of course, is our No. 1 priority.*

Transitional expressions help readers anticipate what's coming, reduce uncertainty, and speed comprehension.

Showing Connections With Transitional Expressions.
Transitional expressions are another excellent device for showing connections and achieving paragraph coherence. These words, some of which are shown in Figure 5.7, act as verbal road signs to readers and listeners. Transitional expressions enable the receiver to anticipate what's coming, reduce uncertainty, and speed up comprehension. They signal that a train of thought is moving forward, being developed, possibly detouring, or ending. Transitions are especially helpful in persuasive writing.

As Figure 5.7 shows, transitions can add or strengthen a thought, show time or order, clarify ideas, show cause and effect, contradict thoughts, and contrast ideas. Thus, you must be careful to select the best transition for your purpose. Look back at the examples of direct, pivoting, and indirect paragraphs to see how transitional expressions and other devices build paragraph coherence. Remember that coherence in communication rarely happens spontaneously; it requires effort and skill.

Paragraphs with eight or fewer printed lines are inviting and readable.

Composing Short Paragraphs for Readability.
Although no rule regulates the length of paragraphs, business writers recognize that short paragraphs are more attractive and readable than longer ones. Paragraphs with eight or fewer lines look inviting. Long, solid chunks of print appear formidable. If a topic can't be covered in eight or fewer printed lines (not sentences), consider breaking it up into smaller segments.

The following checklist summarizes the key points of composing a first draft.

Checklist

Composing Sentences and Paragraphs

For Effective Sentences

✓ **Control sentence length.** Use longer sentences occasionally, but rely primarily on short and medium-length sentences.

✓ **Emphasize important ideas.** Place main ideas at the beginning of short sentences for emphasis.

✓ **Apply active- and passive-voice verbs carefully.** Use active-voice verbs (*She sent the e-mail* instead of *The e-mail was sent by her*) most frequently; they immediately identify the doer. Use passive-voice verbs to be tactful, to emphasize an action, or to conceal the performer.

✓ **Eliminate misplaced modifiers.** Be sure that introductory verbal phrases are followed by the words that can logically be modified. To check the placement of modifiers, ask *Who?* or *What?* after such phrases.

For Meaningful Paragraphs

✓ **Develop one idea.** Use main, supporting, and limiting sentences to develop a single idea within each paragraph.

✓ **Use the direct plan.** Start most paragraphs with the main sentence followed by supporting sentences. This direct plan is useful in defining, classifying, illustrating, and describing.

✓ **Use the pivoting plan.** To compare and contrast ideas, start with a limiting sentence; then, present the main sentence followed by supporting sentences.

✓ **Use the indirect plan.** To explain reasons or causes first, start with supporting sentences. Build to the conclusion with the main sentence at the end of the paragraph.

✓ **Build coherence by linking sentences.** Hold ideas together by repeating key words, using pronouns, and dovetailing sentences (beginning one sentence with an idea from the end of the previous sentence).

✓ **Provide road signs with transitional expressions.** Use verbal signals to help the audience know where the idea is going. Words and phrases such as *moreover, accordingly, as a result,* and *thus* function as idea pointers.

✓ **Limit paragraph length.** Remember that paragraphs with eight or fewer printed lines look inviting. Consider breaking up longer paragraphs if necessary.

Communicating at Work Your Turn

Applying Your Skills at Gap Inc.

The management team at Gap Inc. is struggling to regain its premier position in retailing. As part of a focus group, you and your team have been asked to brainstorm ideas that will help turn around its fortunes. Your team members are to visit a Gap or Old Navy store and take notes on store appearance, merchandise selection, and customer service. Team members should also look at the Gap Web site to learn about its sense of social responsibility.

Your Task

Form teams of four or five people. Discuss your task and decide on a goal. Make assignments. Who will investigate Gap's Web site? Who will visit stores? Who will lead the brainstorming session? Hold a 10-minute brainstorming session following the suggestions in this chapter for generating ideas. What could be changed to attract more

customers in your age group to Gap and Old Navy? Set a quota of at least 50 suggestions. Take notes on all suggestions. After 10 minutes, organize and classify the ideas, retaining the best. Prepare a cluster diagram. Organize the cluster diagram into an outline, and submit your cluster diagram and outline to your instructor. Your instructor may ask for individual or team submissions.

Summary of Learning Objectives

1 **Apply Phase 2 of the 3-x-3 writing process, which begins with formal and informal methods for researching data and generating ideas.** The second phase of the writing process includes researching, organizing, and writing. Researching means collecting information using formal or informal techniques. Formal research for long reports and complex problems may involve searching electronically or manually, as well as conducting interviews, surveys, focus groups, and experiments. Informal research for routine tasks may include looking in company files, talking with your boss, interviewing the target audience, conducting informal surveys, brainstorming for ideas, and creating cluster diagrams.

2 **Explain how to organize data into lists and alphanumeric or decimal outlines.** One method for organizing data in simple messages is to list the main topics to be discussed. Organizing more complex messages usually requires an outline. To prepare an outline, divide the main topic into three to five major components. Break the components into subpoints consisting of details, illustrations, and evidence. For an alphanumeric outline arrange items using Roman numerals (I, II), capital letters (A, B), and numbers (1, 2). For a decimal outline show the ordering of ideas with decimals (1., 1.1, 1.1.1).

3 **Compare direct and indirect patterns for organizing ideas.** The direct pattern places the main idea first. This pattern is useful when audiences will be pleased, mildly interested, or neutral. It saves the reader's time, sets the proper frame of mind, and prevents reader frustration. The indirect pattern places the main idea after explanations. This pattern is useful for audiences that will be unwilling, displeased, or hostile. It respects the feelings of the audience, encourages a fair hearing, and minimizes negative reactions.

4 **Compose the first draft of a message, focusing on effective sentences including techniques for emphasizing important ideas, avoiding misplaced modifiers, and using active and passive voice successfully.** Compose the first draft of a message in a quiet environment where you won't be interrupted. Compose quickly but plan to revise. Understand the difference between clauses and phrases so that you can write complete sentences. Remember that sentences are most effective when they are short (20 or fewer words). A main idea may be emphasized by making it the sentence subject, placing it first, and removing competing ideas. Effective sentences use active-voice verbs, although passive-voice verbs may be necessary for tact or de-emphasis. Effective sentences avoid dangling and misplaced modifiers.

5 **Compose effective paragraphs using three classic paragraph plans as well as applying techniques for achieving paragraph coherence.** Typical paragraphs follow one of three plans. Direct paragraphs (main sentence followed by supporting sentences) are useful to define, classify, illustrate, and describe. Pivoting paragraphs (limiting sentence followed by main sentence and supporting sentences) are useful to compare and contrast. Indirect paragraphs (supporting sentences followed by main sentence) build a rationale and foundation of ideas before presenting the main idea. Paragraphs are more coherent when the writer links ideas by (a) sustaining a key thought, (b) using pronouns effectively, (c) dovetailing sentences, and (d) employing transitional expressions.

Chapter Review

1. What are the three main activities involved in the second phase of the 3-x-3 writing process? (Obj. 1)

2. What are four primary methods used for conducting formal research? (Obj. 1)

3. Name seven specific techniques for a productive group "brainstorming" session. (Obj. 1)

4. How is an alphanumeric outline different from a decimal outline? (Obj. 2)

5. How are the main headings in an outline used when writing a report? (Obj. 2)

6. Distinguish between the direct and indirect patterns of organization for typical business messages. (Obj. 3)

7. Why should most messages be "frontloaded"? (Obj. 3)

8. Name three business messages that should be frontloaded and three that should not be frontloaded. (Obj. 3)

Chapter 5: Writing Process Phase 2: Research, Organize, Compose

9. Why should writers plan for revision? How can they do it? (Obj. 4)

10. Name three ways to emphasize important ideas in sentences. (Obj. 4)

11. When should business writers use active-voice sentences? Passive-voice sentences? Give an original example of each. (Obj. 4)

12. Give an original example of a dangling or misplaced modifier. Why are introductory verbal phrases dangerous? (Obj. 4)

13. Describe three kinds of sentences used to develop ideas in paragraphs. (Obj. 5)

14. Describe three paragraph plans. Identify the uses for each. (Obj. 5)

15. What is coherence, and how is it achieved? (Obj. 5)

Critical Thinking

1. Why is cluster diagramming considered an intuitive process whereas outlining is considered an analytical process? (Obj. 1)

2. In what ways do you imagine that writing on the job differs from the writing you do in your academic studies? Consider process as well as product. (Obj. 1)

3. What are the advantages and disadvantages to "sprint writing"? (Obj. 4)

4. Why are short sentences and short paragraphs appropriate for business communication? (Objs. 4, 5)

5. **Ethical Issue:** Discuss the ethics of the indirect pattern of organization. Is it manipulative to delay the presentation of the main idea in a message?

Activities

5.1 Document for Analysis (Objs. 3–5)

The following interoffice memo is hard to read. It suffers from numerous writing faults discussed in this chapter.

Your Task. First, read the memo to see whether you can understand what the writer requests from all Southeast Division employees. Then, discuss why this memo is so hard to read. How long are the sentences? How many passive-voice constructions can you locate? How effective is the paragraphing? Can you spot four dangling or misplaced modifiers? In the next activity you will improve the organization of this message. (Superscript numbers in the following sentences are provided to help you identify problem sentences.)

TO: All Southeast Division Employees

[1]Personal computers and all the software to support these computers are appearing on many desks of Southeast Division employees. [2]After giving the matter considerable attention, it has been determined by the Systems Development Department (SDD) that more control should be exerted in coordinating the purchase of hardware and software to improve compatibility throughout the division so that a library of resources may be developed. [3]Therefore, a plan has been developed by SDD that should be followed in making all future equipment selections and purchases. [4]To make the best possible choice, SDD should be contacted as you begin your search because questions about personal computers, word processing programs, hardware, and software can be answered by our knowledgeable staff, who can also provide you with invaluable assistance in making the best choice for your needs at the best possible cost.

[5]After your computer and its software arrive, all your future software purchases should be channeled through SDD. [6]To actually make your initial purchase, a written proposal and a purchase request form must be presented to SDD for approval. [7]A need for the purchase must be established; benefits that you expect to derive resulting from its purchase must be analyzed and presented, and

an itemized statement of all costs must be submitted. [8]By following these new procedures, coordinated purchasing benefits will be realized by all employees. [9]I may be reached at Ext. 466 if you have any questions.

5.2 Organizing Data (Obj. 2)

The interoffice memo in Activity 5.1 is hard to read and hard to follow. One of its biggest problems is organization.

Your Task. Use either a cluster diagram or an outline to organize the garbled message in Activity 5.1. Beyond the opening and closing of the message, what are the three main points the writer is trying to make? Should this message use the direct pattern or the indirect pattern? Your instructor may ask you to discuss how this entire message could be revised or to actually rewrite it.

5.3 Collaborative Brainstorming (Obj. 1)

Team

Brainstorming can be a productive method for generating problem-solving ideas. You can improve your brainstorming skills through practice.

Your Task. In teams of four or five, analyze a problem on your campus such as the following: unavailable classes, unrealistic degree requirements, lack of student intern programs, poor parking facilities, inadequate registration process, lack of diversity among students on campus, and so forth. Use brainstorming techniques to generate ideas that clarify the problem and explore its solutions. Each team member should prepare a cluster diagram to record the ideas generated. Either individually or as a team, organize the ideas into an outline with three to five main points and numerous subpoints. Assume that your ideas will become part of a letter to be sent to an appropriate campus official or to your campus newspaper discussing the problem and your solution. Remember, however, your role as a student. Be polite, positive, and constructive—not negative, hostile, or aggressive.

5.4 Individual Brainstorming (Objs. 1, 2)

E-Mail

Brainstorming techniques can work for individuals as well as groups. Assume that your boss or department chair wants you to submit a short report analyzing a problem.

Your Task. Analyze a problem that exists where you work or go to school, such as long lines at the copy or fax machines, overuse of express mail services, understaffing during peak customer service hours, poor scheduling of employees, inappropriate cell phone use, an inferior or inflexible benefits package, outdated office or other equipment, or one of the campus problems discussed in Activity 5.3. Select a problem about which you have some knowledge. Prepare a cluster diagram to develop ideas. Then, organize the ideas into an outline with three to five main points and numerous subpoints. Be polite, positive, and constructive. E-mail the outline to your boss (your instructor). Include an introduction (such as, *Here is the outline you requested in regard to . . .*). Include a closing that offers to share your cluster diagram if your boss would like to see it.

5.5 Brainstorming Tips for Productive Sessions (Obj. 1)

Web

Casandra M., your supervisor at Gap Inc., has been asked to lead a brainstorming group in an effort to generate new ideas for the company's product line. Although Casandra knows a great deal about the company and its products, she doesn't know much about brainstorming. She asks you to research the topic quickly and give her a concise guide on how to brainstorm. One other thing—Casandra doesn't want to read a lot of articles. She wants you to outline tips for productive brainstorming.

Your Task. Conduct an Internet or database keyword search for *brainstorming tips*. Locate a number of articles with helpful tips. Prepare an outline that tells how to (a) prepare for a brainstorming session, (b) conduct the session, and (c) follow up after the meeting. Submit your outline in a memo or an e-mail message to your supervisor (your instructor).

5.6 Collecting Primary Information: Research Interviewing (Obj. 1)

Team

In your follow-up meeting with Casandra M. from Activity 5.5, she asks you to complete one more task in preparation for the brainstorming session. She needs further insight in defining the problem and creating an agenda for the outline of topics to be covered in the brainstorming session. She asks you to conduct informal interviews of Gap and Old Navy shoppers.

Your Task. Form five-member class groups. Two members of each group, if possible, should be familiar with Gap and Old Navy. Decide who will role-play the interviewer and the two interviewees (those most familiar with Gap and Old Navy), and who will act as recorder and group spokesperson. If your group has fewer than five members, some will have to fill more than one role. The interviewer asks both interviewees the same three questions outlined below. The recorder takes notes, and the group spokesperson summarizes the group's research results during the class discussion. Use the following interview questions:

a. During your last two visits to Gap or Old Navy, were there any products you expected the two stores to carry but couldn't find?

b. Can you think of any seasonal products you would like Gap or Old Navy to carry? Specifically, identify products for winter, spring, summer, and fall.

c. If you were in charge of Gap or Old Navy's product lines, what three changes would you make to the existing product lines? What three totally new product lines would you want to create?

As a team or individually, prepare an outline that summarizes the information gathered from the in-class interviews.

5.7 Outlining (Obj. 2)

Web designers at Gap Inc. are complaining about their assignment to develop Web pages describing Gap's employment benefits. Although Gap Inc. offers one of the most comprehensive benefits packages around, the jumble of information has the Web designers totally confused.

The benefits programs include health and wellness benefits covering medical, dental, and vision care. To promote peace of mind among employees and their eligible dependents, Gap offers life insurance, disability insurance, accidental death and dismemberment insurance, and protection against business travel accidents. Another health benefit is a special health care flexible spending account.

Gap Inc. also offers a service that allows employees to speak with a registered nurse 24 hours a day, seven days a week. It is called NurseLine. To prepare for the future, Gap offers a 401(k) plan plus a separate employee stock purchase option. As a "helping hand" to employees, it provides an employee assistance program (EAP) called Life Resources. This is a confidential service that provides counseling resources to help employees and their families cope with personal problems. Gap also offers home loans, moving and relocation assistance, and travel assistance. One special benefit aimed at career development is the tuition reimbursement plan. Gap also encourages employees to develop their careers through its internal placement program.

Your Task. As part of the human resources staff at Gap Inc., you've been asked to make sense of the preceding information so that your Web designers can build it into a coherent presentation. Arrange the benefits information into a simple outline with five major headings and a title.

5.8 Collaborative Career Info (Objs. 3–5)

Team

One of the best ways to learn about the skills required in your field is to interview individuals working in that field.

Your Task. Divide into teams of three to five people who have similar majors. Work together to compose an inquiry letter requesting career information from someone in your field. Include questions about technical and general courses to take, possible starting salaries, good companies to apply to, technical skills required, necessary interpersonal skills, computer tools currently used, and tips for getting started in the field. Although this is a small project, your team can work more harmoniously if you apply some of the suggestions from Chapter 2. For example, appoint a meeting leader, recorder, and evaluator.

5.9 Brainstorming: Are Ethics Programs Helpful? (Obj. 1)

Ethics   **Team**   **Web**

In the wake of the Enron collapse and other corporate scandals, more companies are hiring ethics officers—sometimes called ethics "cops." Companies are also investing in expensive interactive Web-based ethics training. You have been named to a team to discuss ethics compliance in your company, a large firm with thousands of employees. It has no current program. Other companies have ethics codes, conflicts-of-interest policies, ethics officers, training programs, and hotlines. Some authorities, however, say that ethics

Interactive Learning @ www.meguffey.com

failures are usually not the result of ignorance of laws or regulations.[14] A variety of pressures may cause ethics lapses.

Your Task. Your boss, the Human Resources vice president, wants to learn more about employee feelings in regard to ethics programs. In teams, brainstorm to find reactions to these questions. What kinds of ethical dilemmas do typical entry-level and midlevel managerial employees face? Do you think ethics codes help employees be more ethical? What conditions might force employees to steal, lie, or break the rules? Can ethics be taught? What kind of workplace ethics program would you personally find helpful? Before your brainstorming session, you might want to investigate the topic of ethics programs on the Web. Record your ideas during the session. Then organize the best ones into an outline to be presented to Rita Romano, Human Resources vice president.

5.10 Researching, Brainstorming, and Organizing: Student Loans (Objs. 1–3)

`Consumer` `Team` `Web`

Sarah was all smiles when she graduated and got that degree in her hand. Soon, however, she began to worry about her student loans. Student debt has risen 58 percent in the last decade, according to the College Board, a New York–based college testing and information firm. One study showed that about one third of all recent graduates are unprepared to make their first student loan payment.[15]

Your Task. In teams collect information about student debt. Who has it? How much debt does an average student carry? How do most students repay their loans? What strategies are proposed for helping students avoid, reduce, and repay educational loans? As a group, discuss your findings. Brainstorm for additional strategies. Then organize your findings into an outline with a title, an introduction, and recommendations for helping current students avoid, reduce, and repay their student loans. Submit your outline to your instructor.

© Mike Watson Images / Corbis

Writing Improvement Exercises

5.11 Sentence Elements (Obj. 4)

Your Task. Identify the following groups of words using these abbreviations: independent clause (IC), dependent clause (DC), or phrase(s) (P). For clauses, circle the subject.

a. if your degree is in accounting.

b. you can expect a starting salary of $45,000

c. in the first six months on the job

d. when you are performing multiple tasks requiring your undivided attention

e. your brain can become overloaded

f. of the key components to increasing personal energy

g. because multitasking is a skill that can be learned

h. to do in a more efficient manner with less stress

5.12 Active and Passive Voice (Obj. 4)

Your Task. On a separate sheet, convert the verbs in the following sentences from passive voice to active voice. Notice that you shift the emphasis in the sentence by using passive voice. Be ready to discuss what is effective and ineffective about using passive voice.
Passive voice: Employees are encouraged by the company to participate in volunteer programs.
Active voice: The company encourages employees to participate in volunteer programs.

a. The first digital camera was introduced by Kodak back in 1996.

b. Digital imaging was not ignored by Kodak executives, but it was not taken seriously.

c. Every new Ford vehicle is transported from the factory floor to the dealer's lot by UPS.

d. Repair of your computer cannot be authorized because the warranty period has expired.

e. An all-Hispanic supermercado was built in Houston by the giant grocer Kroger.

Now convert the following active-voice verbs to passive-voice verbs. Notice how you can de-emphasize the doer if desired. Be ready to discuss which version is more effective.
Active voice: We accept returned merchandise only when customers provide a sales receipt.
Passive voice: Returned merchandise is accepted only when a sales receipt is provided.

f. We cannot give you a cash refund for merchandise that you purchased 90 or more days ago.

g. St. Elizabeth's Hospital does not admit patients who are uninsured.

h. Jeremy Jones made a significant costing error in the distributed annual report.

i. Our company provides café-style restaurants for employees in corporate buildings.

j. General Dynamics established interoffice shuttles to improve its transportation system.

5.13 Dangling and Misplaced Modifiers (Obj. 4)

Your Task. On a separate sheet, revise the following sentences to correct any dangling or misplaced modifiers. Add subjects as needed, but retain the introductory phrases. Mark C if correct.

a. To find a good job, your résumé must be targeted to the desired position.

b. Skilled at designing brochures, the contract was awarded to ExpoArts.

c. Ignoring the warning prompt on the screen, the computer was turned off resulting in the loss of data.

d. Using a number of creative search terms, the Web site was finally found.

e. By working as a temporary employee, your chance of permanent employment is greatly improved.

f. Acting as team leader, the meeting was organized and led by Matt.

g. To prevent head injuries, wear a helmet when cycling. *(Tricky!)*

h. The presidential candidate announced her intention to run for national office in her hometown of Pleasantville, New Jersey.

5.14 Transitional Expressions (Obj. 5)

Your Task. Insert transitions to improve the flow of ideas (coherence) in the following paragraphs. Consider transitions such as *consequently, for example, however, on the contrary, moreover,* and *therefore.*

a. The phrase "a good excuse" falsely implies a difference between good and bad excuses. All excuses are bad. They are unacceptable. A reason is a legitimate, truthful account of a situation.

b. We recognize that giving your time to important causes is just as important as giving your money. We've created several programs that make it easy and rewarding for our employees to get involved.

c. Our database file includes all customer contact information. It provides space for name, address, phone, e-mail, and other vital information. It has an area for comments, a feature that comes in handy and helps us keep our records up-to-date.

d. No one likes to turn out poor products. We began highlighting recurring problems. Employees make a special effort to be more careful in doing their work right the first time. Their work does not have to be returned to them for corrections.

5.15 Paragraph Organization (Obj. 5)

Your Task. The following poorly organized paragraphs follow the indirect plan. Decide what the main idea is in each paragraph. Then revise each paragraph so that it is organized directly. Improve coherence by using the techniques described in this chapter.

a. Logos, business stationery, business cards, Web sites, and PowerPoint presentations would benefit from a polished professional image. Small businesses should consider investing in a graphic designer for important visual communications. Professional graphic designers can be helpful to both large and small businesses. Large corporations have the resources to hire graphic designers to help with key projects. These projects might include corporate brochures and annual reports.

b. Many of our customers limp through their business workdays despite problems with their disk drives, printers, and peripherals. We cannot service their disk drives, printers, and peripherals. These customers are unable to go without this equipment long enough for the repair. We've learned that there are two times when we can get to that equipment. We can do our repairs in the middle of the night or on Sunday. All of our staff of technicians now work every Sunday. Please authorize additional funds for my department to hire technicians for night and weekend service hours.

c. Air express is one of the ways SturdyBilt power mowers and chain saws may be delivered. Air express promises two-day delivery but at a considerable cost. The cheapest method is for retailers to pick up shipments themselves at our nearest distribution center. We have distribution centers in St. Louis, Phoenix, and Los Angeles. Another option involves having our trucks deliver the shipment from our distribution center to the retailer's door for an additional fee. These are the options SturdyBilt provides for the retailers purchasing our products.

5.16 Sentence Length (Obj. 4)

Your Task. Break the following sentences into shorter sentences. Use appropriate transitional expressions.

a. If firms have a substantial investment in original research or development of new products, they should consider protecting those products with patents, although all patents eventually expire and what were once trade secrets can become common knowledge in the industry.

b. As soon as consumers recognize a name associated with a product or service, that name is entitled to legal protection as a trademark; in fact, consumers may even create a trademark where none existed or create a second trademark by using a nickname as a source indicator, such as the name "Coke," which was legally protected even before it had ever been used by the company.

c. Although no magic formula exists for picking a good trademark name, firms should avoid picking the first name that pops into someone's head; moreover, they should be aware that unique and arbitrary marks are best, whereas descriptive terms such as "car" or "TV repair" are useless, and surnames and geographic names are weak because they lack distinction and exclusivity.

Video Resources

Video Library 1

Mastering Guffey's 3-x-3 Writing Process

If you didn't see the video *Mastering Guffey's 3-x-3 Writing Process* when you studied Chapter 4, your instructor may show it with this chapter. It shows all three phases of the writing process so that you can see how it guides the development of a complete message. This video illustrates concepts in Chapters 4, 5, and 6.

Interactive Learning @ www.meguffey.com

Grammar and Mechanics C.L.U.E. Review 5

Commas

Review Guides 21–26 about commas in Appendix A: Grammar and Mechanics Guide (Competent Language Usage Essentials), beginning on page A-9. On a separate sheet, revise the following sentences to correct errors in comma usage. For each error that you locate, write the guide number and abbreviation that reflects this usage. The more you recognize the reasons, the better you will learn these punctuation guidelines. If a sentence is correct, write C. When you finish, check your answers on page Key-2.

Guide 21, CmSer
(Comma series)

Guide 24, CmDate (Comma, dates, addresses, geographical names, etc.)

Guide 22, CmIntr
(Comma introductory)

Guide 25, CmIn (Comma, internal sentence interrupters)

Guide 23, CmConj
(Comma conjunction)

Example: When we use company e-mail we know our messages are monitored.

Revision: When we use company e-mail, we know our messages are monitored. [Guide 22, CmIntr]

1. Informal research methods include looking in the files, talking with your boss and interviewing the target audience.

2. When you prepare to write any message you need to anticipate the audience's reaction.

3. By learning to distinguish between dependent and independent clauses you will be able to avoid serious sentence faults.

4. Some business messages require sensitivity and writers may prefer to use passive-voice instead of active-voice verbs.

5. We hired Davida Rivera who was the applicant with the best qualifications as our new marketing manager.

6. Our business was incorporated on August 1, 2003 in Phoenix Arizona.

7. The new business by the way is flourishing and is expected to show a profit soon.

8. After he graduates Dustin plans to move to Atlanta and find work there.

9. Last fall our company introduced policies regulating the use of cell phones instant messaging and e-mail on the job.

10. The problem with many company telecommunication policies is that the policies are self-policing and never enforced.

Chapter 6

Writing Process Phase 3: Revise, Proofread, Evaluate

OBJECTIVES

After studying this chapter, you should be able to

1 Apply Phase 3 of the 3-x-3 writing process, which begins with techniques to make a message clear and conversational.

2 Describe and be able to apply specific revision tactics that make a message concise.

3 Describe and be able to apply revision techniques that make a message vigorous and direct.

4 Discuss and be able to apply revision strategies that improve readability.

5 Recognize proofreading problem areas, and be able to list techniques for proofreading both routine and complex documents.

6 Evaluate a message to judge its success.

Communicating at Work Part 1

Taco Bell Seeks New Menu to Lure Customers

Mexican fast-food favorite Taco Bell has been through some bad times. An *E. coli* outbreak linked to its restaurants in five states followed by a widely distributed video of rats cavorting after hours in one of its New York outlets caused Taco Bell's business to sink temporarily. In time, it overcame the bad publicity; and customers returned to its tacos, burritos, and tostadas. Taco Bell realized, however, that it had to build its customer base by improving its image and its menu.

Taco Bell is owned by the world's largest fast-food operator, Yum Brands Inc., which also operates KFC and Pizza Hut.[1] Although Taco Bell is the most successful of Yum's fast-food chains, it must compete for customers with McDonald's, Burger King, and Wendy's as well as with trendy upstarts Baja Fresh, Chipotle, and Qdoba. Despite the competition, Taco Bell holds a 78 percent share of the Mexican fast-food market.

In overcoming its bad image, Taco Bell had to put the "yum" back into Yum Brands.[2] Even before the *E. coli* outbreak and rat romp, Yum officials had unveiled a revitalization plan aimed at expanding its market share. One portion of the plan unveiled new breakfast products such as a sausage and bacon "Grilled Stuft" burrito; a Southwest sausage burrito; an egg, bacon, and cheese burrito; and cinnamon "Toastadas."[3]

Another part of Taco Bell's revitalization scheme looked beyond breakfast fare. Emil Brolick, president of brand building at Yum, suggested that Taco Bell had higher aspirations. "[W]e believe we have a unique opportunity because while all the sandwich players are trying to one-up each other in the same game, we're going to play a different game."[4] His interest lies in unique flavors and better products.

In the increasingly crowded fast-food market, customers are slowly but surely shifting away from the traditional burger and chicken fast foods.[5] One food industry executive said, "Burgers are your dad's food, and Mexican is the choice of the new generation."[6] Poised to capitalize on this movement, Taco Bell remains keenly aware that (a) it sells a quasi-Mexican food, and (b) its customers are changing. Although its products cannot veer too far from what

appeals to the masses, Taco Bell must also compete with new Mexican restaurants emphasizing low-fat items and fresh ingredients.

A recently hired culinary product manager is charged with the task of coming up with menu suggestions and communicating them to management. You'll learn more about this case on page 158.

Critical Thinking
- When new ideas must be generated and sold to management, what role does communication skill play in the process?
- Do you think the Taco Bell culinary product manager will be making an oral or a written presentation of new menu ideas?
- Why is a writing process helpful in developing a presentation of new ideas?

http://www.tacobell.com

Writing Process Phase 3: Revise

The final phase of the 3-x-3 writing process focuses on revising, proofreading, and evaluating. Revising means improving the content and sentence structure of your message. Proofreading involves correcting its grammar, spelling, punctuation, format, and mechanics. Evaluating is the process of analyzing whether your message achieved its purpose. One would not expect people in the restaurant business to require these kinds of skills. However, the new culinary product manager at Taco Bell—and many other similar businesspeople—realize that bright ideas are worth little unless they can be communicated effectively to fellow workers and to management. In the communication process, the techniques of revision can often mean the difference between the acceptance or rejection of ideas.

Although the composition process differs for individuals and situations, this final phase should occupy a significant share of the total time you spend on a message. As you learned earlier, some experts recommend devoting about half the total composition time to revising and proofreading.[7]

Rarely is the first or even second version of a message satisfactory. Only amateurs expect writing perfection on the first try. The revision stage is your chance to make sure your message says what you mean. Many professional writers compose the first draft quickly without worrying about language, precision, or correctness. Then they revise and polish extensively. Other writers, however, prefer to revise as they go—particularly for shorter business documents.

Important messages—such as those you send to management or to customers or turn in to instructors for grades—deserve careful revision and proofreading. When you finish a

LEARNING OBJECTIVE 1
Apply Phase 3 of the 3-x-3 writing process, which begins with techniques to make a message clear and conversational.

Because few writers can produce a satisfactory copy on the first attempt, revision is an important step in the writing process.

© Joe Raedle / Staff / Getty Images

Communicating in clear, simple language is an uphill battle for some firms. That's why plain-language advocate Christopher Balmford founded Cleardocs.com, a document management company that helps law firms, accountancies, and other highly technical businesses communicate clearly and effectively with clients. Cleardocs' online technology turns complex documents into market-focused plain language, transforming elaborate or technical letters and reports into easily understandable written communications. *What types of businesses have difficulty producing simple, conversational messages, and why?*

first draft, plan for a cooling-off period. Put the document aside and return to it after a break, preferably after 24 hours or longer.

Whether you revise immediately or after a break, you'll want to examine your message critically. You should be especially concerned with ways to improve its clarity, conciseness, vigor, and readability.

Revising for Clarity

The goal of business writing is to *express* rather than *impress*.

One of the first revision tasks is assessing the clarity of your message. A clear message is one that is immediately understood. To achieve clarity, resist the urge to show off or be fancy. Remember that your goal is not to impress a reader. Instead, the goal of business writing is to *express*, not *impress*. This involves keeping it simple and conversational.

Why do some communicators fail to craft simple, direct messages? Following are several reasons:

To achieve clarity, remember to KISS: Keep It Short and Simple!

- Untrained executives and professionals worry that plain messages don't sound important.

- Subordinates fear that plain talk won't impress the boss.

- Unskilled writers create foggy messages because they haven't learned how to communicate clearly.

- Unethical writers intentionally obscure a message to hide the truth.

Whatever the cause, you can eliminate the fog by applying the familiar KISS formula: Keep It Short and Simple! One way to achieve clear writing is to use active-voice sentences that avoid foggy, indirect, and pompous language.

Spotlight on Communicators

Former Secretary of State Colin Powell believes that effective leaders apply the KISS principle in keeping things simple. They articulate vivid, overarching goals and values. Their visions and priorities are lean and compelling, not cluttered and buzz-word-laden. One of Secretary Powell's favorite quotations illustrates his conviction: "Great leaders are almost always great simplifiers, who can cut through argument, debate and doubt, to offer a solution everybody can understand."

Foggy	**Clear**
Employees have not been made sufficiently aware of the potentially adverse consequences involved regarding these chemicals.	Warn your employees about these chemicals.

Foggy	Clear
To be sure of obtaining optimal results, it is essential that you give your employees the implements that are necessary for completion of the job.	To get the best results, give employees the tools they need to do the job.

Revising for Conversational Tone

Clarity is further enhanced by language that sounds like conversation. This doesn't mean that your letters and memos should be chatty or familiar. Rather, you should strive to sound professional, as discussed in Chapter 4. To sound conversational, avoid legal terminology, technical words, and third-person constructions (*the undersigned, the writer*). Business messages should sound warm and friendly—not stuffy and formal. To sound friendly, include occasional contractions (*can't, doesn't*) and first-person pronouns (*I/we*). This warmth is appropriate in all but the most formal business reports. You can determine whether your writing is conversational by trying the kitchen test. If it wouldn't sound natural in your kitchen, it probably needs revision. Note how the following formal sentences were revised to pass the kitchen test.

Strive to achieve a conversational, professional tone without sounding chatty, familiar, or stilted.

Formal	Conversational
As per your verbal instruction, steps will be undertaken immediately to investigate our billing problem.	At your suggestion I'm investigating your billing immediately.
Further notification will follow.	I'll keep you informed.
Our organization takes this opportunity to inform you that your account is being credited in the aforementioned sum.	We are crediting your account for $78.

Revising for Conciseness

In revising, make certain that a message makes its point in the fewest possible words. Messages without flabby phrases and redundancies are easier to comprehend and more emphatic because main points stand out. Efficient messages also save the reader valuable time.

Concise writing, however, is not easy. As one expert copyeditor observed, "Trim sentences, like trim bodies, usually require far more effort than flabby ones."[8] To turn out slim sentences and lean messages, you do not have to be brusque, rude, or simple-minded. Instead, you must take time in the revision stage to "trim the fat." Before you can do that, you must learn to recognize it. Locating and excising wordiness involves eliminating (a) fillers, (b) long lead-ins, (c) redundancies, (d) compound prepositions, and (e) empty words.

LEARNING OBJECTIVE 2
Describe and be able to apply specific revision tactics that make a message concise.

Short messages require more effort than long, flabby ones.

Removing Fillers

Avoid fillers that fatten sentences with excess words. Beginning an idea with *There is* usually indicates that writers are spinning their wheels until they decide where the sentence is going. Used correctly, *there* indicates a specific place (*I placed the box there*). Used as fillers, *there* and occasionally *it* merely take up space. Most, but not all, sentences can be revised so that these fillers are unnecessary.

Wordy	Concise
There are three vice presidents who report directly to the president.	Three vice presidents report directly to president.
It is the client who should make application for a license.	The client should apply for a license.

Deleting Long Lead-Ins

Delete unnecessary introductory words. The meat of the sentence often follows the words *that* and *because*. In addition, many long lead-ins say what is obvious.

Long lead-ins delay getting to the "meat" of the sentence.

Wordy	Concise
I am sending this announcement to let you all know that the office will be closed Monday.	The office will be closed Monday.
This is to inform you that you can redeem travel awards at our Web site.	You can redeem travel awards at our Web site.
I am writing this letter because Dr. Marcia Howard suggested that your organization was hiring trainees.	Dr. Marcia Howard suggested that your organization was hiring trainees.

Eliminating Redundancies

Redundancies convey the same meaning more than once.

Expressions that repeat meaning or include unnecessary words are redundant. To say *unexpected surprise* is like saying "surprise surprise" because *unexpected* carries the same meaning as *surprise*. Excessive adjectives, adverbs, and phrases often create redundancies and wordiness. Redundancies do not add emphasis, as some people think. Instead, they identify a writer as inexperienced. Which word in each of the following expressions creates the redundancy?

Redundancies to Avoid

advance warning	exactly identical	perfectly clear
alter or change	few in number	personal opinion
assemble together	free and clear	potential opportunity
basic fundamentals	grateful thanks	positively certain
collect together	great majority	proposed plan
consensus of opinion	integral part	serious interest
contributing factor	last and final	refer back
dollar amount	midway between	true facts
each and every	new changes	visible to the eye
end result	past history	unexpected surprise

Reducing Compound Prepositions

Wordy prepositional phrases can be shortened to single words.

Single words can often replace wordy prepositional phrases. In the following examples notice how the shorter forms say the same thing but more efficiently.

Wordy Compound Preposition	Shorter Form
as to whether or not	whether
at a later date	later
at this point in time	now
at such time, at which time	when
by means of, in accordance with	by
despite the fact that	although
due to the fact that, inasmuch as, in view of the fact that	because
for the amount of	for
in advance of, prior to	before
subsequent to	after
the manner in which	how
until such time as	until

Purging Empty Words

Familiar phrases roll off the tongue easily, but many contain expendable parts. Be alert to these empty words and phrases: *case, degree, the fact that, factor, instance, nature,* and

Chapter 6: Writing Process Phase 3: Revise, Proofread, Evaluate

quality. Notice how much better the following sentences sound when we remove all the empty words:

> ~~In the case of~~ USA Today, ~~the newspaper~~ *improved its readability.*

> *Because of* ~~the degree of~~ *active participation by our sales reps, profits soared.*

> *We are aware* ~~of the fact~~ *that many managers need assistance.*

> *Except for* ~~the instance of~~ *Toyota, Japanese imports sagged.*

> *She chose a career in a field that was analytical* ~~in nature~~*. (Or, She chose a career in an analytical field.)*

> *Student writing in that class is excellent* ~~in quality~~*.*

Also avoid saying the obvious. In the following examples notice how many unnecessary words we can omit through revision:

> ~~When it arrived~~*, I cashed your check immediately. (Announcing the check's arrival is unnecessary. That fact is assumed in its cashing.)*

> ~~We need printer cartridges; therefore~~*, please send me two dozen laser cartridges. (The first clause is obvious.)*

Finally, look carefully at clauses beginning with *that, which,* and *who.* They can often be shortened without loss of clarity. Search for phrases, such as *it appears that.* Such phrases can be reduced to a single adjective or adverb, such as *apparently.*

>   *successful*
> *Changing the name of a* ^ *company* ~~that is successful~~ *is always risky.*

> *All employees* ~~who are among those~~ *completing the course will be reimbursed.*

>   *final*
> *Our* ^ *proposal,* ~~which was~~ *slightly altered* ~~in its final form~~*, won approval.*

>   *weekly*
> *We plan to schedule* ^ *meetings* ~~on a weekly basis~~*.*

Good writers avoid saying what is obvious.

Revising for Vigor and Directness

Much business writing has been criticized as lifeless, cautious, and just plain boring.[9] This boredom results not so much from content as from wordiness and dull, trite expressions. You have already studied ways to improve clarity and conciseness. You can also reduce wordiness and improve vigor by (a) kicking the noun habit and (b) dumping trite business phrases.

LEARNING OBJECTIVE 3
Describe and be able to apply revision techniques that make a message vigorous and direct.

Kicking the Noun Habit

Some writers become addicted to nouns, needlessly transforming verbs into nouns (*we make a recommendation of* instead of *we recommend*). This bad habit increases sentence length, drains verb strength, slows the reader, and muddies the thought. Notice how efficient, clean, and forceful the following verbs sound compared with their noun phrase counterparts.

Noun conversion lengthens sentences, saps the force of the verb, and muddies the message.

Wordy Noun Phrase	Verb
conduct a discussion of	discuss
create a reduction in	reduce
engage in the preparation of	prepare
give consideration to	consider
make an assumption of	assume
make a discovery of	discover
perform an analysis of	analyze
reach a conclusion about	conclude
take action on	act

Dumping Trite Business Phrases

To sound "businesslike," many writers repeat the same stale expressions that other writers have used over the years. Your writing will sound fresher and more vigorous if you eliminate these phrases or find more original ways to convey the idea.

Train yourself not to use these trite business expressions.

Trite Phrase	Improved Version
as per your request	as you request
pursuant to your request	at your request
enclosed please find	enclosed is
every effort will be made	we'll try
in accordance with your wishes	as you wish
in receipt of	have received
please do not hesitate to	please
thank you in advance	thank you
under separate cover	separately
with reference to	about

Revising for Readability

LEARNING OBJECTIVE 4
Discuss and be able to apply revision strategies that improve readability.

To help receivers anticipate and comprehend ideas quickly, a number of graphic highlighting techniques are helpful. You can use (a) parallelism, which involves balanced writing; (b) lists and bullets, which facilitate quick comprehension; (c) headings, which make important points more visible; and (d) other highlighting techniques to improve readability.

Developing Parallelism for Balance

Parallelism means matching nouns with nouns, verbs with verbs, phrases with phrases, and so on.

As you revise, be certain that you express similar ideas in balanced or parallel construction. For example, the phrase *clearly, concisely, and correctly* is parallel because all the words end in *-ly*. To express the list as *clearly, concisely, and with correctness* is jarring because the last item is not what the receiver expects. Instead of an adverb, the series ends with a noun. To achieve parallelism, match nouns with nouns, verbs with verbs, phrases with phrases, and clauses with clauses. Avoid mixing active-voice verbs with passive-voice verbs.

Not Parallel

The policy affected all vendors, suppliers, and those involved with consulting.

Good managers analyze a problem, collect data, and alternatives are evaluated.

Improved

The policy affected all vendors, suppliers, and consultants.
(Series matches nouns.)

Good managers analyze a problem, collect data, and evaluate alternatives.
(Series matches verb forms.)

Using Numbered and Bulleted Lists for Quick Comprehension

Numbered and bulleted lists improve readability by making important ideas stand out.

One of the best ways to ensure rapid comprehension of ideas is through the use of numbered or bulleted lists. Ideas formerly buried within sentences or paragraphs stand out when listed. Readers not only understand your message more rapidly and easily but also consider you efficient and well organized. Lists provide high "skim value." This means that readers use lists to read quickly and grasp main ideas. By breaking up complex information into smaller chunks, lists improve readability, comprehension, and retention. They also force the writer to organize ideas and write efficiently. Use numbered lists for items that represent a sequence or reflect a numbering system. Use bulleted lists to highlight items that don't necessarily show a chronology.

not in APA no bullets

Chapter 6: Writing Process Phase 3: Revise, Proofread, Evaluate

Numbered List

Our recruiters follow these steps in hiring applicants:

1. Examine the application.
2. Interview the applicant.
3. Check the applicant's references.

Bulleted List

To attract upscale customers, we feature

- Quality fashions
- Personalized service
- A generous return policy

Improve the skim value of a message by adding high-visibility vertical lists.

In listing items vertically, capitalize the word at the beginning of each line. Add end punctuation only if the listed items are complete sentences. Also be sure to use parallel construction. Notice in the numbered list that each item begins with a verb. In the bulleted list each item follows an adjective/noun sequence. In Chapter 7 you will learn more about using lists to improve readability in e-mail messages and memos. Be careful, however, not to overuse the list format. One writing expert warned that too many lists make messages look like grocery lists.[10]

Adding Headings for Visual Impact

Headings are an important tool for highlighting information and improving readability. They encourage the writer to organize carefully so that similar material is grouped together. Headings help the reader separate major ideas from details. Moreover, they enable a busy reader to skim familiar or less important information. They also provide a quick preview or review. Headings appear most often in reports, which you'll study in greater detail in Unit 4. But main headings, subheadings, and category headings can also improve readability in e-mail messages, memos, and letters. Here, they are used with bullets to summarize categories:

Headings help writers to organize information and enable readers to absorb important ideas.

Category Headings
Our company focuses on the following areas in the employment process:

- **Attracting applicants.** We advertise for qualified applicants, and we also encourage current employees to recommend good people.

- **Interviewing applicants.** Our specialized interviews include simulated customer encounters as well as scrutiny by supervisors.

- **Checking references.** We investigate every applicant thoroughly, including conversations with former employers and all listed references.

Improving Readability With Other Graphic Techniques

Vertical lists and headings are favorite tools for improving readability. Other graphic techniques can also focus attention. To highlight individual words, use CAPITAL letters, <u>underlining</u>, **bold** type, or *italics*. Be careful with these techniques, though, because readers may feel they are being shouted at.

One final technique to enhance comprehension is blank space. Space is especially important in e-mail messages when formatting techniques don't always work. Grouping ideas under capitalized headings with blank space preceding the heading can greatly improve readability.

The following chapters supply additional ideas for grouping ideas, spotlighting data, and designing documents for maximum readability. Although highlighting techniques can improve readability, they can also clutter a message if overdone. Many of these techniques, such as listing items vertically, also require more space, so use them judiciously.

Graphic techniques such as capital letters, underlining, bold type, italics, and blank space spotlight ideas. But don't overdo it!

Measuring Readability

Formulas can measure how easy or difficult a message is to read. Two well-known formulas are Robert Gunning's Fog Index and the Flesch-Kincaid Index. Both measure word and sentence length to

Spotlight on Communicators

Arthur Levitt, former chair of the U.S. Securities and Exchange Commission, is said to have been the most activist chair in the SEC's history. As a champion of "plain English," he was instrumental in requiring that disclosure documents written for investors be readable. To improve their readability, he advocated using the active voice, familiar words, and graphic techniques. He recommended emphasizing important ideas with boldface, graphics, headings, lists, and color. All of these techniques can vastly improve the readability of business writing.

© AP IMAGES

Costly Writing

Bad writing can be expensive: A Philadelphia lawyer was charged with malpractice to the tune of $6.6 million for drafting a poor commercial lease. The judge in Los Angeles said the draft was "inartfully written and done so in a confusing fashion, which lends itself to ambiguities and disagreements." Can you think of other situations when writing can be deliberately or accidentally misleading and cost money?

determine readability. The longer a sentence is, the more difficult it is to read. If you are using a current version of Microsoft Word, the software will calculate a readability score for any passage you highlight. Word shows a "reading ease" score as well as the Flesch-Kincaid grade-level score. A score of 10, for example, means that the passage can be easily read by a person with ten years of schooling.

The foggier a message is, the higher its reading level is. Magazines and newspapers that strive for wide readership keep their readability between levels 8 and 12. (*USA Today* is 10.6, *The New York Times* is 12.6,[11] and *People* magazine ranges between 8.4 and 11.2.) By occasionally calculating the Fog Index of your writing, you can ensure that you stay within the 8 to 12 range. Remember that long words—those over two syllables—and long sentences make your writing foggy. To calculate your own Fog Index, see the Career Coach Box on page 157.

Readability formulas, however, don't always tell the full story. They cannot measure how complex the content is, whether the topic is appropriate for the audience, whether the message was designed attractively, or whether the vocabulary is at the right level for the audience. Readability tests would not reflect whether a document contains gender, class, or cultural bias. Readability scores would not reveal whether the material appears in a form and font style that is effectively presented. One might also guess that interest and prior reader knowledge are important in determining whether a document is readable and understandable.

Although readability formulas provide a rough estimate, those based solely on word and sentence counts fail to measure meaningfulness. Even short words (such as *skew, onus,* and *wane*) can cause trouble if readers don't recognize them. More important than length are a word's familiarity and meaningfulness to the reader. In Chapter 4 you learned to adapt your writing to the audience by selecting familiar words. Other techniques that can improve readability include well-organized paragraphs, transitions to connect ideas, headings, and lists.

The task of revision, summarized in the following checklist, is hard work. It demands objectivity and a willingness to cut, cut, cut. Though painful, the process is also gratifying. It's a great feeling when you realize your finished message is clear, concise, and readable.

Checklist

Revising Messages

✓ **Keep the message simple.** Express ideas directly. Don't show off or use fancy language.

✓ **Be conversational.** Include occasional contractions (*hasn't, don't*) and first-person pronouns (*I/we*). Use natural-sounding language.

✓ **Avoid opening fillers and long lead-ins.** Omit sentence fillers such as *there is* and long lead-ins such as *this is to inform you that*.

✓ **Shun redundancies.** Eliminate words that repeat meanings, such as *mutual cooperation*. Watch for repetitive adjectives, adverbs, and phrases.

✓ **Tighten your writing.** Check phrases that include *case, degree, the fact that, factor,* and other words and phrases that unnecessarily increase wordiness. Avoid saying the obvious.

✓ **Don't convert verbs to nouns.** Keep your writing vigorous by avoiding the noun habit (*analyze* not *make an analysis of*).

✓ **Avoid trite phrases.** Keep your writing fresh, direct, and contemporary by skipping such expressions as *enclosed please find* and *pursuant to your request*.

✓ **Strive for parallelism.** Help receivers anticipate and comprehend your message by using balanced writing (*planning, drafting, and constructing* not *planning, drafting, and construction*).

✓ **Highlight important ideas.** Use bullets, lists, headings, capital letters, underlining, boldface, italics, and blank space to spotlight ideas and organization.

✓ **Consider readability.** Strive to keep the reading level of a message between Grades 8 and 12. Remember that short, familiar words and short sentences help readers comprehend.

CAREER COACH

Applying the Fog Index to Determine Readability

One way to calculate the "readability" of a document is by applying the Gunning Fog Index. Here's how you can figure it manually for the business letter shown here.

1. **Select the passage.** Choose a continuous passage of between 100 and 130 words.
2. **Count the total words.** Count numbers, dates, and abbreviations as separate words. Our business letter sample has 110 words.
3. **Count the sentences.** Count all independent clauses separately. For example, *He applied, and he was hired* counts as two sentences. Our sample has seven sentences, marked with superscript numbers.
4. **Find the average sentence length.** Divide the total number of words by the number of sentences (110 divided by 7 equals 16 words).
5. **Count the number of long words.** A word is long if it has three or more syllables. Exclude (a) capitalized words, (b) compound words formed from short words (*nevertheless*), and (c) verbs made into three syllables by the addition of *-ed* or *-es* (*located, finances*). In our sample the long words are underlined.
6. **Find the percentage of long words.** Divide the number of long words by the number of total words (10 divided by 110 equals .09 or 9 percent).
7. **Add the results.** Add the average sentence length (16) and the percentage of long words (9). The result is 25.
8. **Multiply.** Multiply by 0.4 (25 times 0.4 equals 10). The reading level of this letter is 10.

Dear Mrs. Lawrence:

[1]Yes, I can meet with you Thursday, April 3, at 10 a.m. to discuss <u>possible</u> ways to finance the purchase of a new home in San Diego. [2]Before we meet, though, you might like to <u>consider</u> two <u>possible</u> plans.

[3]The first plan finances your purchase with a swing loan, which has a fixed <u>interest</u> rate for a short <u>period</u> of time. [4]A second plan requires you to <u>refinance</u> your present <u>residence</u>. [5]We have located five programs from three <u>different</u> <u>institutions</u> that would do this. [6]Enclosed is a <u>summary</u> of these five plans. [7]I look forward to seeing you Thursday to find a way for you to own a home in San Diego.

Sincerely,

The reading level of this short letter is 10. This level indicates that the reader needs ten years of schooling to understand the letter. Your goal should be to keep your writing between the levels of 8 and 12. Two factors that most influence reading level are sentence length and word length.

Career Application

Compare the reading levels of several publications. Calculate the Fog Index for short passages from your local newspapers, a business document (letter, memo, report), an insurance policy, or two of your college textbooks. Discuss in class the appropriateness of the reading levels for each document.

Writing Process Phase 3: Proofread

Once you have the message in its final form, it's time to proofread. Don't proofread earlier because you may waste time checking items that eventually are changed or omitted. Proofreading is especially difficult because most of us read what we thought we wrote. That's why it's important to look for specific problem areas.

LEARNING OBJECTIVE 5
Recognize proofreading problem areas, and be able to list techniques for proofreading both routine and complex documents.

What to Watch for in Proofreading

Spelling. Now's the time to consult the dictionary. Is *recommend* spelled with one or two *c*'s? Do you mean *affect* or *effect*? Use your computer spell checker, but don't rely on it totally.

Proofreading before a document is completed is generally a waste of time.

Grammar. Locate sentence subjects; do their verbs agree with them? Do pronouns agree with their antecedents? Review the grammar and mechanics principles in Appendix A if necessary. Use your computer's grammar checker, but be suspicious, as explained in the Tech Talk box on page 159.

Punctuation. Make sure that introductory clauses are followed by commas. In compound sentences put commas before coordinating conjunctions (*and, or, but, nor*). Double-check your use of semicolons and colons.

Names and Numbers. Compare all names and numbers with their sources because inaccuracies are not always visible. Especially verify the spelling of the names of individuals receiving the message. Most of us immediately dislike someone who misspells our name.

Spotlight on Communicators

Pulitzer Prize–winning *Washington Post* columnist William Raspberry frequently promotes the value of language skills in relation to career success: "Misused words, haphazard sentences, failed subject–verb agreement can distract people from our ideas and get them concentrating on our inadequacies. Good English, carefully spoken and written, can open more doors than a college degree. Bad English can slam doors we don't even know about."

Communicating at Work Part 2

Taco Bell

The newly hired culinary product manager at Taco Bell has her job cut out for her. Management expects her to anticipate trends in Mexican foods and improve restaurant menus. Part of the challenge is recognizing trends that consumers haven't even picked up yet and then working these trends into restaurant products. In her words, "We want to kick it up a notch, but we still have to deliver to mainstream consumers." She needs to read the market and then create innovative menu ideas. The new chef is eager to incorporate some of the rich, complex flavors of authentic Mexican cuisine. But she must do it in ways that are acceptable to fast-food customers. Although she has excellent culinary references, the new chef has not been trained in communication. She has plenty of ideas to put into a memo or a presentation. Her job now depends on how well she can communicate these ideas to management.

© Joe Raedle / Staff / Getty Images

Critical Thinking
- Based on what you learned in this chapter, what specific advice can you give about keeping a message clear? Should a business message be conversational?
- Why is conciseness important, and what techniques can be used to achieve it?
- Would you advise the culinary chef to be direct with her ideas? What advice can you give for improving the directness and readability of a business message?

Format. Be sure that your document looks balanced on the page. Compare its parts and format with those of standard documents shown in Appendix B. If you indent paragraphs, be certain that all are indented.

How to Proofread Routine Documents

Routine documents require a light proofreading.

Most routine documents require a light proofreading. If you read on screen, use the down arrow to reveal one line at a time. This focuses your attention at the bottom of the screen. A safer proofreading method, however, is reading from a printed copy. Regardless of which method you use, look for typos and misspellings. Search for easily confused words, such as *to* for *too* and *then* for *than*. Read for missing words and inconsistencies. For handwritten or printed messages, use standard proofreading marks, shown in Figure 6.1, to indicate changes.

Most proofreaders use these standard marks to indicate revisions.

FIGURE 6.1 Proofreading Marks

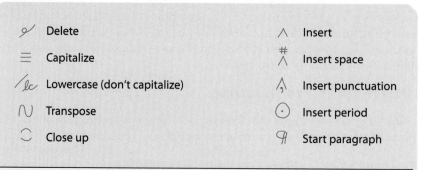

ℒ	Delete	∧	Insert
≡	Capitalize	# ∧	Insert space
ℓc	Lowercase (don't capitalize)	⟨	Insert punctuation
∩	Transpose	⊙	Insert period
⌒	Close up	¶	Start paragraph

Marked Copy

~~This is to inform you that~~ beginning september 1 the doors leading to the West side of the building will have alarms. Because ~~of the fact that~~ these exits doors also function as fire exits they can not actually be locked consequently we are installing alarms. Please utilize use the east side exists to avoid setting off the ear-piercing alarms.

Tech Talk

Using Spell Checkers and Grammar/Style Checkers Wisely

Spell-checking and grammar-checking software are two useful tools that can save you from many embarrassing errors. They can also greatly enhance your revision techniques—if you know how to use them wisely.

SPELL CHECKERS

Although some writers dismiss spell checkers as an annoyance, most of us are only too happy to have our typos and misspelled words detected. If you are using Microsoft Word, you need to set the options to **Check spelling as you type**. (Use the **Tools** menu, click **Options**. On the **Spelling & Grammar** tab, choose **Check spelling as you type** and **Always suggest corrections**.) When you see a wavy red line under a word, you are being notified that the highlighted word is not in the computer's dictionary. Right-click for a list of suggested replacements and other actions.

Spell checkers are indeed wonderful, but they are far from perfect. If you mistype a word, the spell checker is not sure what you meant and the suggested replacements may be way off target. What's more, a spell checker cannot know when you type *form* that you meant *from*. Lesson: Don't rely totally on spell checkers to find all typos and spelling errors.

GRAMMAR AND STYLE CHECKERS

Like spell checkers, today's grammar and style checkers are amazingly sophisticated. Microsoft Word marks faults in capitalization, possessives, plurals, punctuation, subject–verb agreement, and gender-specific words, as well as misused words, double negatives, fragments, wordiness, and many other problems.

How does a grammar checker work? Say you typed the sentence, *The office and its equipment is for sale*. You would see a wavy green line appear under *is*. Click **F7** or **Tools**, and a box identifies the subject–verb agreement error and suggests the verb *are* as a correction. When you click **Change**, the error is corrected. You can set grammar and style options in the **Grammar Settings** dialog box (**Tools** menu, **Options** command, **Spelling & Grammar** tab, and **Settings**).

Before you decide that a grammar checker will solve all your writing problems, think again. Even Word's highly developed software misses plenty of errors, and it also mismarks some correct expressions.

Career Application

Study the spelling and grammar/style settings on your computer. Decide which settings are most useful to you. As you prepare written messages for this class, analyze the suggestions made by your spell checker and grammar checker. For one or two documents, list the spelling, grammar, and style corrections suggested by Word. How many were valid?

How to Proofread Complex Documents

Long, complex, or important documents demand more careful proofreading. Apply the previous suggestions but also add the following techniques:

- Print a copy, preferably double-spaced, and set it aside for at least a day. You'll be more alert after a breather.

- Allow adequate time to proofread carefully. A common excuse for sloppy proofreading is lack of time.

- Be prepared to find errors. One student confessed, "I can find other people's errors, but I can't seem to locate my own." Psychologically, we don't expect to find errors, and we don't want to find them. You can overcome this obstacle by anticipating errors and congratulating, not criticizing, yourself each time you find one.

- Read the message at least twice—once for word meanings and once for grammar and mechanics. For very long documents (book chapters, long articles, or reports), read a third time to verify consistency in formatting.

- Reduce your reading speed. Concentrate on individual words rather than ideas.

- For documents that must be perfect, enlist a proofreading buddy. Have someone read the message aloud. Spell names and difficult words, note capitalization, and read punctuation.

- Use standard proofreading marks, shown in Figure 6.1, to indicate changes.

Many of us struggle with proofreading our own writing because we are seeing the same information over and over. We tend to see what we expect to see as our eyes race over the words without looking at each one carefully. We tend to know what is coming next and glide over it. To change the appearance of what you are reading, you might print it on a different colored paper or change the font. If you are proofing on screen, enlarge the page view or change the background color of the screen.

Ethics Check

Overly Helpful
Students may visit writing centers where they receive useful advice and help. However, some well-meaning tutors take over, revising documents until they don't resemble the original student work. Instructors worry that the resulting documents amount to cheating. Yet in the workplace today, writers must collaborate, and drafts go through multiple revisions. Individual authorship is often not relevant. How much revision is acceptable in a college setting? How much in the workplace?

Writing Process Phase 3: Evaluate

LEARNING OBJECTIVE 6
Evaluate a message to judge its success.

As part of applying finishing touches, take a moment to evaluate your writing. Remember that everything you write, whether for yourself or for someone else, takes the place of a personal appearance. If you were meeting in person, you would be certain to dress appropriately and professionally. The same standard applies to your writing. Evaluate what you have written to be certain that it attracts the reader's attention. Is it polished and clear enough to convince the reader that you are worth listening to? How successful will this message be? Does it say what you want it to? Will it achieve your purpose? How will you know whether it succeeds?

A good way to evaluate messages is through feedback.

As you learned in Chapter 1, the best way to judge the success of your communication is through feedback. For this reason, you should encourage the receiver to respond to your message. This feedback will tell you how to modify future efforts to improve your communication technique.

Your instructor will also be evaluating some of your writing. Although any criticism is painful, try not to be defensive. Look on these comments as valuable advice tailored to your specific writing weaknesses—and strengths. Many businesses today spend thousands of dollars bringing in communication consultants to improve employee writing skills. You are getting the same training in this course. Take advantage of this chance—one of the few you may have—to improve your skills. The best way to improve your skills, of course, is through instruction, practice, and evaluation.

In this class you have all three elements: instruction in the writing process, practice materials, and someone willing to guide and evaluate your efforts. Those three elements are the reasons this book and this course may be the most valuable in your entire curriculum. Because it's almost impossible to improve your communication skills alone, take advantage of this opportunity.

Communicating at Work Your Turn

Applying Your Skills at Taco Bell

Upgrading the menu at Taco Bell is an exciting challenge for the new culinary product manager. In response to management's request, she comes up with terrific ideas for capitalizing on eating trends and converting them to mainstream tastes. She has been asked to submit a memo summarizing her longer report, which will be presented at a management meeting next week.

Although the new culinary product manager has exceptional talent in cuisine, she realizes that her writing skills are not as well developed as her cooking skills. She comes to the corporate communication department and shows your boss the first draft of her memo. Your boss is a nice guy; and, as a favor, he revises the first two paragraphs, as shown in Figure 6.2.

Your Task

Your boss, the head of corporate communication, has many important tasks to oversee. Thus, he hands the product manager's memo

© Joe Raedle / Staff / Getty Images

to you, his assistant, and tells you to finish cleaning it up. He adds, "Her ideas are right on target, but the main points are totally lost in wordy sentences and solid paragraphs. Revise this and concentrate on conciseness, parallelism, and readability. Don't you think some bulleted lists would help this memo a lot?" Revise the remaining four paragraphs of the memo using the techniques you learned in this chapter. Type a copy of the complete memo to submit to your boss (your instructor).

FIGURE 6.2 Partially Revised First Draft

DATE: August 13, 2009

TO: Executive Council

FROM: Tiffany Tushner, Culinary Product Manager

SUBJECT: ~~TRENDS~~ Fast-Food Trends and Menu Options

[annotation: Improves subject line]

At
As per your request, ~~the writer is~~ I am submitting ~~herewith~~ the following ideas
~~that are~~ based on ~~her personal~~ my observation and research ~~in regard to~~ about eating
trends in ~~relation to restaurants that serve~~ (fast-food.) ~~As you suggested, I~~
~~am also offering~~ below is a rough outline of possible concepts to upgrade Taco
Bell's menu. ~~This is to inform you that~~ this memo ~~represents a summary of~~ summarizes
the findings ~~deduced from my longer report~~ to be presented at our next
meeting.

[annotation left: Revises trite expression and uses first-person pronoun]

[annotation right: Eliminates long lead-in (This is to inform you)]

popular
Mexican cuisine is increasingly ~~experiencing popularity~~ from coast to coast,
not only in fast-food restaurants but also in ~~establishments that are~~ (upscale.)
firsthand
From my experience ~~that I gained first-hand~~ as a chef and from current
observed
~~reading and~~ research, I have ~~made an observation of~~ numerous eating
as
trends. ~~In the discussion~~ below are four ~~(4)~~ that ~~I feel~~ are of ~~serious~~ interest
in ~~view of the fact that we~~ are rethinking ~~the~~ Taco Bell menu.

[annotation left: Eliminates wordiness]

[annotation left: Changes noun phrase into forceful verb]

[annotation left: Eliminates compound prepositional phrase (in view of the fact that)]

[annotation right: Changes "that" clauses into adjectives]

[annotation right: Eliminates redundancy (serious interest)]

Current Eating Trends

Spices are important. Consumers are appreciating more highly spiced foods.
Spicy Thai and other ethnic dishes are growing in popularity. Freshness is
another trend. As consumers become more knowledgeable and as more discrimination is available to them, they are demanding ingredients that are
fresher. Higher prices represent a trend also. Consumers are willing to pay
more for fresh and wholesome meals that are also tasty. Last but not least,
a final trend includes big appetites. Other fast-food restaurants are cashing
in on sandwiches that are satisfying, such as the Whopper, the Big Mac, and
the Big Jack. In this respect, teenagers are our prime targets.

[annotation right: Needs bulleted list with headings to highlight main points]

Given the increasing degree of acceptance of Mexican cuisine and the rich
array of flavors and textures in Mexican cuisine, we find that we have
many possibilities for the expansion of our menu. Despite the fact that my
full report contains a number of additional trends and menu ideas, I will
concentrate below on four significant concepts.

[annotation left: Must reduce wordy phrases throughout]

New Menu Concepts

First, I am of the opinion that we should add **More Grilled Items** . Offer spicy
chicken marinated in lime juice or chipotle-rubbed ahi tuna served with cran-
berry mango salsa. A second idea involves **Larger-Portion Sandwiches**.
Consider a "Machaca Taco," an oversized taco featuring shredded beef.
Another possibility is "Mad Mex," a wild burrito served with a smoky rojo
sauce. Third, concentrate on **Higher Quality, More Expensive Dishes**.
Consider churrascos, made with prime beef tenderloin basted with a South
American pesto sauce. Lastly, we should consider a **Self-Serve Salsa Bar**. In
relation to this, we could offer exotic fresh salsas with bold flavors and
textures.

[annotation left: Revise wordy phrase (of the opinion)]

[annotation left: Needs bulleted or numbered list with headings to improve readability]

[annotation left: Must convert noun phrase (have a discussion) and eliminate empty words]

I would be more than happy to have a discussion of these ideas with you in
greater detail and to have a demonstration of them in the kitchen. Thanks for
this opportunity to work with you in the expansion of our menu in a move to
ensure that Taco Bell remains tops in Mexican cuisine.

Summary of Learning Objectives

1 **Apply Phase 3 of the 3-x-3 writing process, which begins with techniques to make a message clear and conversational.** The final phase of the writing process involves editing, revising, and evaluating. Revising for clarity means using active-voice sentences and simple words while avoiding confusing negative expressions. Clarity is further enhanced by language that sounds conversational, including occasional contractions and first-person pronouns (*I/we*).

2 **Describe and be able to apply specific revision tactics that make a message concise.** Concise messages make their points in the fewest possible words. Revising for conciseness involves excluding opening fillers (*There are*), redundancies (*basic essentials*), and compound prepositions (*by means of, due to the fact that*).

3 **Describe and be able to apply revision techniques that make a message vigorous and direct.** Writers can achieve vigor in messages by revising wordy phrases that needlessly convert verbs into nouns. For example, instead of *we conducted a discussion of*, write *we discussed*. To make writing more direct, good writers replace trite business phrases, such as *please do not hesitate to*, with similar expressions, such as *please*.

4 **Discuss and be able to apply revision strategies that improve readability.** One revision technique that improves readability is the use of balanced constructions (parallelism). For example, *collecting, analyzing, and illustrating data* is balanced and easy to read. *Collecting, analysis of, and illustration of data* is more difficult to read because it is unbalanced. Parallelism involves matching nouns with nouns, verbs with verbs, phrases with phrases, and clauses with clauses. Other techniques that improve readability are bullets and lists for quick comprehension, headings for visual impact, and graphic techniques such as capital letters, underlining, italics, and bold print to highlight and order ideas. Readability can be measured by formulas that count long words and sentence length.

5 **Recognize proofreading problem areas, and be able to list techniques for proofreading both routine and complex documents.** Proofreaders must be especially alert to spelling, grammar, punctuation, names, numbers, and document format. Routine documents may be proofread immediately after completion. They may be read line by line on the computer screen or, better yet, from a printed draft copy. More complex documents, however, should be proofread after a breather. To do a good job, you must read from a printed copy, allow adequate time, reduce your reading speed, and read the document at least three times—for word meanings, for grammar and mechanics, and for formatting.

6 **Evaluate a message to judge its success.** Encourage feedback from the receiver so that you can determine whether your communication achieved its goal. Try to welcome any advice from your instructor on how to improve your writing skills. Both techniques contribute to helping you evaluate the success of a message.

Chapter Review

1. How does revising differ from proofreading? (Obj. 1)

2. Should business writers avoid contractions? Why? (Obj. 1)

3. What is a redundancy? Give an example. Why should writers avoid redundancies? (Obj. 2)

4. Why should communicators avoid openings such as *there is*? (Obj. 2)

5. What shorter forms could be substituted for the expressions *at a later time, due to the fact that,* and *subsequent to*? (Obj. 2)

6. Why should a writer avoid the opening *I am sending this e-mail because we have just hired a new manager, and I would like to introduce her*? (Obj. 2)

7. Why should a writer avoid an expression such as *Our staff will immediately perform an analysis of the contract*? (Obj. 3)

8. What's wrong with businesslike expressions such as *as per your request* and *every effort will be made*? (Obj. 3)

9. What is parallelism, and how can you achieve it? (Obj. 4)

10. What is high "skim value," and how can you achieve it? (Obj. 4)

11. What factors determine whether you should use bulleted or numbered items in a list? (Obj. 4)

12. Name five specific items to check in proofreading. Be ready to discuss methods you find useful in spotting these errors. (Obj. 5)

13. In proofreading, what major psychological problem do you face in finding errors? How can you overcome this barrier? (Obj. 5)

14. List four or more effective techniques for proofreading complex documents. (Obj. 5)

15. How can you overcome defensiveness when your writing is criticized constructively? (Obj. 6)

Critical Thinking

1. Why is the last phase of the writing process so important? (Obj. 1)

2. Would you agree or disagree with the following statement by writing expert William Zinsser? "Plain talk will not be easily achieved in corporate America. Too much vanity is on the line." (Objs. 1, 2)

3. Because business writing should have high "skim value," why not write everything in bulleted lists? (Objs. 2, 4)

4. Why should the proofreading process for routine documents differ from that for complex documents? (Objs. 4, 5)

5. **Ethical Issue:** What advice would you give in this ethical dilemma? Lisa is serving as interim editor of the company newsletter. She receives an article written by the company president describing, in abstract and pompous language, the company's goals for the coming year. Lisa thinks the article will need considerable revising to make it readable. Attached to the president's article are complimentary comments by two of the company vice presidents. What action should Lisa take?

Activities

6.1 Document for Analysis: Poorly Written E-Mail Message (Objs. 1–5)

The following message suffers from a number of weaknesses discussed in this chapter.

Your Task. Study the message and analyze its weaknesses. In teams or in a class discussion, list at least five specific weaknesses. Then, revise to avoid long lead-ins, fillers, redundancies, wordy compound prepositions, verbs converted to nouns, trite expressions, and general wordiness. Look for four points that could function as bullet points with category headings. Revise at a computer or on paper using standard proofreading marks.

TO: Jodi Jameson <jjameson@datamine.com>
FROM: Fausto Amato <famato@datamine.com>
DATE: March 20, 2009
SUBJECT: Avoiding a PowerPoint Slumber Party

Jodi,

I am writing this message because, pursuant to your request, I attended a seminar about the use of PowerPoint in business talks. You suggested that there might be PowerPoint tips that I would learn that we could share with other staff members, many of whom create PowerPoint presentations. The speaker, Melissa Frieden, made some very good points on the subject of PowerPoint. There were several points of an important nature that are useful in avoiding a PowerPoint slumber party. Our staff members should give consideration to the following:

Create first the message, not the slide. Only after preparing the entire script should you think about how to make an illustration of it.

You should prepare slides with short lines. Your slides should have only four to six words per line. Short lines act as an encouragement to people to listen to you and not read the slide.

Don't put each and every thing on the slide. If you put too much on the slide, your audience will be reading Item C while you are still talking about Item A. As a last and final point, she suggested that presenters think in terms of headlines. What is the main point? What does it mean to the audience?

Please let me know whether you want me to elaborate and expand on these points subsequent to the next staff meeting.

Fausto

6.2 Document for Analysis: Poorly Written Response Letter (Objs. 1–5)

The following letter suffers from a number of weaknesses discussed in this chapter.

Your Task. Study the letter and analyze its weaknesses. In teams or in a class discussion, list at least five specific weaknesses. Then, revise to avoid long lead-ins, fillers, redundancies, wordy compound prepositions, verbs converted to nouns, trite expressions, and general wordiness. Revise at a computer or on paper using standard proofreading marks.

Current date

Mr. Anthony Burciaga
Salt Lake Systems, Inc.
5342 South Temple
Salt Lake City, UT 84111

Dear Mr. Burciaga

We have received your request for information. As per your request, the undersigned is transmitting to you the attached documents with regard to the improvement of security in your business. To ensure the improvement of your after-hours security, you should initially make a decision with regard to exactly what you contemplate must have protection. You are, in all probability, apprehensive not only about your electronic equipment and paraphernalia but also about your company records, information, and data.

Due to the fact that we feel you will want to obtain protection for both your equipment and data, we will make suggestions for taking a number of judicious steps to inhibit crime. First and foremost, we make a recommendation that you install defensive lighting. A consultant for lighting, currently on our staff, can design both outside and inside lighting, which brings me to my second point. Exhibit security signs, because of the fact that nonprofessional thieves are often as not deterred by posted signs on windows and doors.

As my last and final recommendation, you should install space alarms, which are sensors that look down over the areas that are to receive protection, and activate bells or additional lights, thus scaring off intruders.

After reading the materials that are attached, please call me to initiate a verbal discussion regarding protection of your business.

Sincerely,

6.3 Document for Analysis: Poorly Written Response (Objs. 1–5)

The following letter suffers from a number of weaknesses discussed in this chapter.

Your Task. Study the letter and analyze its faults. In teams or in a class discussion, list at least five specific weaknesses. Then, revise to avoid long lead-ins, fillers, redundancies, wordy compound prepositions, verbs converted to nouns, trite expressions, and general wordiness. Revise at a computer or on paper using standard proofreading marks.

Current date

Ms. Dara Greene
Spector Telecom Center
6250 West Central Texas Expressway
Killeen, TX 76549

Dear Ms. Greene:

I am writing to thank you for your interest in employee leasing through Enterprise Staffing Services. Small businesses like yours can, at this point in time, enjoy powerful personnel tools previously available only to firms that were larger.

The employee leasing concept allows you to outsource personnel duties so that you can focus on the basic fundamentals of running your business. There are many administrative burdens that you can reduce such as monthly payroll, quarterly taxes, and records related to personnel matters. There is also expert guidance available in the areas of human resources, compliance, and matters of a safety nature. In view of the fact that we have extensive experience, your employer liability can be reduced by a significant degree. You can be assured that the undersigned, as well as our entire staff, will assemble together a plan that will save you time and money as well as protect you from employee hassles and employer liability.

Whether or not you offer no benefits or a full benefits package, Enterprise Staffing Services can make an analysis of your needs and help you return back to the basics of running your business and improvement in profits. Please allow me to call you to arrange a time to meet and talk about your specific needs.

Cordially,

6.4 Document for Analysis: Weak E-Mail Message (Objs. 1–5)

The following e-mail message suffers from a number of weaknesses discussed in this chapter.

Your Task. Analyze the faults in the message. In teams or in a class discussion, list at least five specific weaknesses. Then, revise to avoid long lead-ins, fillers, redundancies, wordy compound prepositions, verbs converted to nouns, trite expressions, and general wordiness. In this message consider using two bulleted lists and headings to improve readability. Revise at a computer or use standard proofreading marks to show corrections.

TO: LaTasha Mack, Senior Marketing Manager <lmack@scott.com>
FROM: Ted Gonzalez, Vice President <tgonzalez@scott.com>
DATE: August 16, 2009
SUBJECT: IMPROVING SAFETY AND SECURITY FOR TELECOMMUTERS

This e-mail is to inform you that due to the fact that telecommuting is becoming increasingly popular, your help is needed to develop better safety and security information for your telecommuters.

To aid you in educating and training your telecommuters, a complete guide for managers is now available. There are structured agreements that specify space, equipment, and how you should schedule employees. Please discuss the recommendations that follow for a home workspace as well as recommendations for security with any of your staff members who may be making a consideration of telecommuting.

Home Workspace Recommendations
In regard to the home workspace, employees should create a space that is free and clear of traffic and distractions. They should make the home workspace as comfortable as possible but also provide sufficient space for computer, printer, and for a fax. For security reasons the home workspace should be off limits to family and also to friends. Be sure to provide proper lighting and telephone service.

In regard to the matter of information security and personal security, tell your telecommuters that they should remember that a home office is an extension of the company office. They must be careful and vigilant about avoiding computer viruses and the protection of company information. On the same topic of information security, they should positively be sure to back up information that is important and it should be stored in a safe place

Interactive Learning @ www.meguffey.com

that is off site. We do not recommend at-home meetings for telecommuters. By the same token, postal boxes are suggested rather than giving out home addresses. Smoke detectors should be installed in home work areas.

These are just a few of our recommendations. At this point in time, you will find a complete guide for telecommuters at our Web site for our company. We urge you to read it carefully as soon as possible. Please do not hesitate to call Human Resources if you have questions.

6.5 Writing Improvement Exercise: Removing Fillers (Obj. 2)

Your Task. Revise the following sentences to avoid fillers.

a. There are many businesses that are considering strict e-mail policies.

b. It is the CEO who must give her approval to the plan.

c. The manager said that there are too many employees who are taking long breaks.

d. There are four major fast-food companies that are considering ways to expand their breakfast menus.

6.6 Writing Improvement Exercise: Deleting Long Lead-Ins (Obj. 2)

Your Task. Revise the following sentences to avoid long lead-ins.

a. This message is to let you know that I received your e-mail and its attachments.

b. This memo is to notify everyone that the manager prefers weekly meetings.

c. I am writing this letter to let you know that your homeowners' coverage will soon expire.

d. This is to inform you that the loss of laptops endangers company security.

6.7 Writing Improvement Exercise: Eliminating Redundancies (Obj. 2)

Your Task. Revise the following sentences to avoid redundancies.

a. We will let you know the dollar amount of the remodeling charges.

b. The office walls were painted beige in color.

c. Team members asked to return back to the office.

d. The proposal is so complete that we need not alter or change a thing.

e. A great majority of investors favored the proposed new changes.

6.8 Writing Improvement Exercise: Reducing Wordy Compound Prepositions (Obj. 2)

Your Task. Revise the following sentences to avoid wordy compound prepositions.

a. We were unsure as to whether or not to reveal the actual costs.

b. Despite the fact that we lost the contract, we feel good about the future.

c. Please investigate the manner in which the contract was awarded.

d. At a later date we will revise the contract inasmuch as the law has changed.

e. You have full use of the funds until such time as the contract changes.

6.9 Writing Improvement Exercise: Purging Empty Words (Obj. 2)

Your Task. Revise the following to eliminate empty words and saying the obvious.

a. Our next meeting is scheduled in the month of July.

b. We plan to meet at 10 a.m. in the morning.

c. Because of the surprising degree of enthusiasm, the company expanded its free gift program.

d. Our supply has become very low; therefore, please send us 100 CD-R disks.

e. Are you aware of the fact that deleted files may be recovered from digital media?

6.10 Writing Improvement Exercise: Kicking the Noun Habit (Obj. 3)

Your Task. Revise the following to avoid converting verbs into nouns.

a. The homeowner came to the realization that her asking price was too high.

b. Customers show a preference for rich colors.

c. Management conducted an investigation into efforts for staff reduction.

d. Insurance representatives placed the damage assessment at $1,000.

e. The CEO must first give his approval to the plan.

6.11 Writing Improvement Exercise: Dumping Trite Business Phrases (Obj. 3)

Your Task. Revise the following to avoid trite business phrases.

a. Pursuant to your request, we are correcting your balance due.

b. We have, in accordance with your wishes, credited your account.

c. In the future every effort will be made to send a printed invoice.

d. Enclosed please find the invoice for your recent order.

6.12 Writing Improvement Exercise: Revising for Overall Conciseness (Objs. 1, 2)

Your Task. Revise the following to be simple, clear, concise, and conversational.

a. Please be advised that it is our intention to make every effort to deliver your order by the date of your request, December 1.

b. There is an e-mail policy within our organization that makes a statement that management may access and monitor the e-mail activity of each and every employee.

c. Due to the fact that e-mail is a valuable tool in business, we in management are pleased to make e-mail available to all employees who are authorized to use it.

d. Whether or not we make a continuation of the sales campaign is dependent upon its success in the city of St. Louis.

e. It is our suggestion that you do not attempt to move forward until you seek and obtain approval of the plan from the team leader prior to beginning this project.

6.13 Writing Improvement Exercise: Developing Parallelism (Obj. 4)

Your Task. Revise the following sentences to improve parallelism. If elements cannot be balanced fluently, use appropriate subordination.

a. Your goal should be to write business messages that are concise, clear, and written with courteousness.

b. Ensuring equal opportunities, the removal of barriers, and elimination of age discrimination are our objectives.

c. The market for industrial goods includes manufacturers, contractors, wholesalers, and those concerned with the retail function.

d. To improve your listening skills, you should stop talking, your surroundings should be controlled, be listening for main points, and an open mind must be kept.

e. For this position we assess oral and written communication skills, how well individuals solve problems, whether they can work with teams, and we are also interested in interpersonal skills, such as cultural awareness and sensitivity.

6.14 Writing Improvement Exercise: Lists, Bullets, and Headings (Obj. 4)

Your Task. Revise the following sentences and paragraphs using techniques presented in this chapter. Improve parallel construction and reduce wordiness if necessary.

a. Revise using a bulleted list.
Yellin Resources specializes in preemployement background reports. Among our background reports are ones that include professional reference interviews, criminal reports, driving records, employment verification, and credit reports.

b. Revise using a numbered list.
In writing to customers granting approval for loans, you should follow four steps that include announcing that loan approval has been granted. Then you should specify the terms and limits. Next you should remind the reader of the importance of making payments that are timely. Finally, a phone number should be provided for assistance.

c. Revise using a bulleted list.
The American Automobile Association makes a provision of the following tips for safe driving. You should start your drive well rested. You should wear sunglasses in bright sunshine. To provide exercise breaks, plan to stop every two hours. Be sure not to drink alcohol or take cold and allergy medications before you drive.

d. Revise using bulleted items with category headings.
Our attorney made a recommendation that we consider several things to avoid litigation in regard to sexual harassment. The first thing he suggested was that we should take steps regarding the establishment of an unequivocal written policy prohibiting sexual harassment within our organization. The second thing we should do is make sure training sessions are held for supervisors regarding a proper work environment. Finally, some kind of official procedure for employees to lodge complaints is necessary. This procedure should include investigation of complaints.

6.15 Writing Improvement Exercise: Proofreading (Obj. 5)

Your Task. Use proofreading marks to mark spelling, grammar, punctuation, capitalization, and other errors in the following sentences.

a. One of the beautyes of e-mail, is that it enables you to comunicate quick and easy with colleagues, and customers around theGlobe.

b. English maybe the International Language of commerce but that does not mean that every readr will have a trouble-free experience with message writen in english.

c. Be especially carful with dates. For example A message that reads "Our video conference begins at 6 p.m. on 7/8/09" would mean July 8, 2009, to americans.

d. To europeans the time and date would be written as follows: "The video conference will begin at 18:00 on 8 July 2009.

e. Because europeans use a twenty-four-hour military clock be sure to write int'l messages in that format.

f. To avoid confusion give metric measurments followed by there american equivalents. For Example, "The office is 10 kilometers (6.2 miles from the TrainStation.

6.16 Computing the Fog Index (Obj. 4)

Your Task. As an in-class project or for homework, do the following:

a. Compute the Fog Index for Activity 6.2 (Document for Analysis) **before** you revise it.

b. Revise the letter reducing its length and improving its readability. Eliminate redundancies, wordiness, and trite expressions. Use simple, clear words. Shorten sentences.

c. Prepare a clean copy of the revised letter.

d. After revision, calculate the Fog Index.

e. Compare the before and after versions and discuss their readability.

6.17 Learning About Writing Techniques in Your Field (Objs. 1–6)

How much writing is required by people working in your career area? The best way to learn about on-the-job writing is to talk with someone who has a job similar to the one you hope to have one day.

Your Task. Interview someone in your field of study. Your instructor may ask you to present your findings orally or in a written report. Ask questions such as these: *What kind of writing do you do? What kind of planning do you do before writing? Where do you get information? Do you brainstorm? Make lists? Do you compose with pen and paper, a computer, or a dictating machine? How many e-mail messages do you typically write in a day? How long does it take you to compose a routine one- or two-page memo or letter? Do you revise? How often? Do you have a preferred method for proofreading? When you have questions about grammar and mechanics, what or whom do you consult? Does anyone read your drafts and make suggestions? Can you describe your entire composition process? Do you ever work with others to produce a document? How does this process work? What makes writing easier or harder for you? Have your writing methods and skills changed since you left school?*

6.18 Searching for Deadwood (Obj. 2)

Team   Web

Many writers and speakers are unaware of "deadwood" phrases they use. Some of these are redundancies, compound prepositions, or trite business phrases.

Your Task. Using your favorite Web browser, locate two or three sites devoted to deadwood phrases. Your instructor may ask you to (a) submit a list of ten deadwood phrases (and their preferred substitutes) not mentioned in this textbook, or (b) work in teams to prepare a comprehensive "Dictionary of Deadwood Phrases," including as many as you can find. Be sure to include a preferred substitute.

6.19 Conciseness Is Hard Work (Objs. 2, 3)

Just as most people are unmotivated to read wordy documents, most are unmotivated to listen to wordy speakers. Effective communicators work to eliminate "rambling" in both their written and spoken words.

Abraham Lincoln expressed the relationship between conciseness and hard work with his reply to the question, "How long does it take you to prepare a speech?" "Two weeks for a 20-minute speech," he replied. "One week for a 40-minute speech; and I can give a rambling, two-hour talk right now." Rambling takes little thought and effort; conciseness takes a great deal of both.

Your Task. For a 24-hour period, think about conciseness violations in spoken words. Consider violations in five areas you studied in this chapter: (a) fillers, (b) long lead-ins, (c) redundancies, (d) compound prepositions, and (e) empty words. Identify the source of the violation using descriptors such as *friend, family member, coworker, boss, instructor, actor in TV sitcom, interviewer or interviewee on a radio or TV talk show,* and so forth. Include the communication medium for each example (telephone, conversation, radio, television, etc.). Be prepared to share the results of this activity during a class discussion.

6.20 Communicating With a Nonnative English Speaker

Intercultural   **Web**

In the three chapters devoted to the writing process, most of the advice focuses on communicating clearly and concisely. As the world becomes more globally connected, businesspeople may be increasingly communicating with nonnative speakers and writers. Assume that you have been asked to present a talk to businesspeople in your area. What additional advice would you give to speakers and writers in communicating with nonnative English speakers?

Your Task. Search the Web for advice in communicating with nonnative English speakers. Prepare a list of ten suggestions not mentioned in this chapter. Select those that you think are most important and significant.

6.21 How Plain Is the English in Your Apartment Lease? (Objs. 1–4)

E-Mail   **Ethics**   **Consumer**   **Team**

Have you read your apartment lease carefully? Did you understand it? Many students—and their friends and family members—are intimidated, frustrated, or just plain lost when they try to comprehend an apartment lease.

Your Task. Locate an apartment lease—yours, a friend's, or a family member's. In teams, analyze its format and readability. What size is the paper? How large are the margins? Is the type large or small? How much white space appears on the page? Are paragraphs and sentences long or short? Does the lease contain legalese or obscure language? What makes it difficult to understand? In an e-mail message to your instructor, summarize your team's reaction to the lease. Your instructor may ask you to revise sections or the entire lease to make it more readable. In class discuss how ethical it is for an apartment owner to expect a renter to read and comprehend a lease while sitting in the rental office.

Video Resources

Two sets of videos accompany this edition of Guffey's *Business Communication: Process and Product.*

Video Library 1. *Building Workplace Skills* presents seven videos that introduce and reinforce concepts in selected chapters.

Video Library 2. *Bridging the Gap* presents six videos transporting viewers inside high-profile companies. The recommended video for this chapter is *Writing Skills: The Little Guys.* The Little Guys Home Electronics specializes in selling and installing home theater equipment. In just 12 years, it has grown from a start-up company to an established business with annual sales of more than $10 million. The owners—Dave and Evie Wexler and Paul Gerrity—describe their goals, motivations, and experiences in making their business successful.

As you watch this video, look for (a) good business practices that helped the owners launch a successful business, (b) characteristics of successful entrepreneurs, and (c) reasons some small businesses remain successful whereas others fail.

Your Task. After watching the video, assume that you have been asked to summarize reasons for the success of The Little Guys. Building on what you have learned in this writing process chapter, compose a bulleted list with ten or more items. Use this opening sentence: *The Little Guys Home Electronics business succeeded because the owners did the following.* Add a title to your list.

Grammar and Mechanics C.L.U.E. Review 6

Semicolons, Colons

Review Guides 27–30 about semicolons and colons in Appendix A: Grammar and Mechanics Guide (Competent Language Usage Essentials), beginning on page A-12. On a separate sheet, revise the following sentences to correct errors in semicolon and colon usage. Do not start new sentences. For each error that you locate, write the guide number that reflects this usage. The more you recognize the reasons, the better you will learn these punctuation guidelines. If a sentence is correct, write C. When you finish, check your answers on page Key-2.

Example: Engineers produced a snazzy new product, however it had no exciting name.

Revision: Engineers produced a snazzy new product; however, it had no exciting name. [Guide 27]

1. Companies find it difficult to name new products consequently they often hire specialists.

2. New product names must be interesting however most of the best are already taken.

3. Naming is a costly endeavor, fees may range up to $70,000 for a global name.

4. Expanding markets are in Paris France Beijing China and Dubai City United Arab Emirates.

5. In regard to naming a fashion product, Jasmine Frank said "If I am launching a new fashion label, the task becomes very difficult. I have to find a name that communicates the creative style that the brand is to embody."

6. For a new unisex perfume, Ferrari considered the following names Declaration, Serenity, and Earth.

7. Naming is not a problem for a small company however it is a big problem for global brands.

8. The companies we hired to generate a name were Genesis, Cartier, and Emerging.

9. Attending the conference were James Harper, marketing director, Reva Cruz, product manager, and Cheryl Chang, vice president.

10. Distribution of goods has become global therefore names have to be registered in many countries.

Interactive Learning @ www.meguffey.com   Chapter 6: Writing Process Phase 3: Revise, Proofread, Evaluate   167

Unit 3

Business Correspondence

Chapter 7
E-Mail Messages and Memos

Chapter 8
Positive Letters and Goodwill Messages

Chapter 9
Persuasive and Sales Messages

Chapter 10
Negative Messages

© Ryan McVay / Photodisc / Getty Images

Chapter 7

E-Mail Messages and Memos

Communicating at Work Part 1

Wireless Giant Qualcomm Thrives on E-Mail

If you own a cellular telephone, you have probably heard of Qualcomm Incorporated. Founded in 1985, the San Diego–based company is a global leader in developing and delivering innovative wireless products and solutions. Today, hundreds of millions of people worldwide use mobile phones and other wireless services based on Qualcomm's solutions.

Qualcomm prides itself on its positive work environment and excellent employee benefits, which keep employee turnover low. The company consistently earns high rankings on lists such as *Fortune*'s 100 Best Companies to Work For and Most Admired Companies, *Industry Week*'s 50 Top Manufacturers, and *Business Ethics*' 100 Best Corporate Citizens.[1]

Like most technology companies, Qualcomm considers e-mail its primary form of communication, both internally for employees and externally to vendors and customers. "Qualcomm has had e-mail since day one and is very e-mail centric," says Norm Fjeldheim, senior vice president and chief information officer, who oversees all aspects of Qualcomm's information technology. "Other forms of electronic media, such as instant messaging, are becoming popular as well."[2] Qualcomm employees can now access their e-mail at home or on the road, using their cell phones, other wireless devices, or laptop computers.

Fjeldheim consolidates all of his correspondence in his e-mail inbox. He receives 100 to 300 e-mails daily but has become efficient and effective at handling his messages. "I prefer e-mail and don't suffer from e-mail overload," he says. "E-mail is, to a large degree, how I know what is going on within the company and my department. I tell my employees they can't send me too much e-mail. If they wonder whether to send me an e-mail, I tell them to send it, and I will figure out whether it's of interest to me."[3] His e-mail inbox serves as his to-do list. After reading a message, he leaves action items in his inbox until he completes the task.

Then he moves the e-mail to an appropriate folder. Special filters either reject suspect e-mails or move them to a spam folder.

Critical Thinking

- Why has e-mail become such an important form of business communication? How has it changed the ways employees interact with each other, with vendors, and with customers?
- What are some of the disadvantages of using e-mail in business correspondence, and what practices can you recommend to counteract these drawbacks?
- What strategies does Mr. Fjeldheim use to manage the heavy volume of e-mail he receives?

http://www.qualcomm.com

Applying the Writing Process to E-Mail Messages and Memos

Like most businesses today, Qualcomm relies on e-mail for many of its internal communication needs. In times past, messages among company insiders took the form of hard-copy memorandums. Today, however, e-mail is the communication channel of choice. It has been hailed as one of the greatest productivity tools of our time.[4]

A primary function of e-mail is exchanging messages within organizations. Such internal communication has taken on increasing importance today. Organizations are downsizing, flattening chains of command, forming work teams, and empowering rank-and-file employees. Given more power in making decisions, employees find that they need more information. They must collect, exchange, and evaluate information about the products and services they offer. Management also needs input from employees to respond rapidly to local and global market changes. This growing demand for information means an increasing use of e-mail, although hard-copy memos are still written.

Developing skill in writing e-mail messages and memos brings you two important benefits. First, well-written documents are likely to achieve their goals. They create goodwill by being cautious, caring, and clear. They do not intentionally or unintentionally foment ill feelings. Second, well-written internal messages enhance your image within the organization. Individuals identified as competent, professional writers are noticed and rewarded; most often, they are the ones promoted into management positions.

This chapter focuses on routine e-mail messages and memos. These straightforward messages open with the main idea because their topics are not sensitive and require little

LEARNING OBJECTIVE 1
Discuss how the 3-x-3 writing process helps you produce effective e-mail messages and memos.

E-mail is the communication channel of choice for exchanging information within organizations.

persuasion. You will study the writing process as well as the structure and format of e-mail messages and memos. Because e-mail is such a new and powerful channel of communication, we will devote special attention to composing effective e-mail messages and reading and responding to e-mail professionally. Finally, you will learn to write request, response, procedural, and confirmation memos and e-mail messages.

Careful writing takes time—especially at first. By following a systematic plan and practicing your skill, you can speed up your efforts and greatly improve the product. Bear in mind, moreover, that the effort you make to improve your communication skills can pay big dividends. Frequently, your speaking and writing abilities determine how much influence you will have in your organization. As with other writing tasks, e-mail and memo writing follows the 3-x-3 writing process.

Phase 1: Analysis, Anticipation, and Adaptation

Before writing, ask questions that help you analyze, anticipate, and adapt your message.

In Phase 1, prewriting, you will need to spend some time analyzing your task. It's amazing how many of us are ready to put our pens or computers into gear before engaging our minds. Before writing, ask yourself these important questions:

- **Do I really need to write this e-mail or memo?** A phone call or a quick visit to a nearby coworker might solve the problem—and save the time and expense of a written message. On the other hand, some written messages are needed to provide a permanent record or to show a well-conceived plan.

- **Should I send an e-mail or a hard-copy memo?** It's tempting to use e-mail for all your correspondence. A phone call or face-to-face visit, however, is a better channel choice if you need to (a) convey enthusiasm, warmth, or other emotion; (b) supply a context; or (c) smooth over disagreements.

- **Why am I writing?** Know why you are writing and what you hope to achieve. This will help you recognize what the important points are and where to place them.

- **How will the reader react?** Visualize the reader and the effect your message will have. In writing e-mail messages, imagine that you are sitting and talking with your reader. Avoid speaking bluntly, failing to explain, or ignoring your reader's needs. Consider ways to shape the message to benefit the reader. Also remember that your message may very well be forwarded to someone else.

- **How can I save my reader's time?** Think of ways that you can make your message easier to comprehend at a glance. Use bullets, asterisks, lists, headings, and white space, discussed in Chapter 6, to improve readability.

Phase 2: Research, Organization, and Composition

Gather background information; organize it into an outline; compose your message; and revise for clarity, correctness, and feedback.

In Phase 2, writing, you will first want to check the files, gather documentation, and prepare your message. Make an outline of the points you wish to cover. For short messages jot down notes on the document you are answering or make a scratch list at your computer. As you compose your message, avoid amassing huge blocks of text. No one wants to read endless lines of type. Instead, group related information into paragraphs, preferably short ones. Paragraphs separated by white space look inviting. Be sure each paragraph begins with the main point and is backed up by details. If you bury your main point in the middle of a paragraph, the reader may miss it. Be sure to prepare for revision, because excellence is rarely achieved on the first effort.

Phase 3: Revision, Proofreading, and Evaluation

Phase 3, revising, involves putting the final touches on your message. Careful and caring writers will ask a number of questions as they do the following:

- **Revise for clarity.** Viewed from the receiver's perspective, are the ideas clear? Do they need more explanation? If the memo is passed on to others, will they need further explanation? Consider having a colleague critique your message if it is an important one.

- **Proofread for correctness.** Are the sentences complete and punctuated properly? Did you overlook any typos or misspelled words? Remember to use your spell checker and grammar checker to proofread your message before sending it.

- **Plan for feedback.** How will you know whether this message is successful? You can improve feedback by asking questions (such as *Are you comfortable with these suggestions?* or *What do you think?*). Remember to make it easy for the receiver to respond.

Structuring and Formatting E-Mail Messages and Memos

LEARNING OBJECTIVE 2
Analyze the structure and formatting of e-mail messages and memos.

Because e-mail messages and memos are standard forms of communication within organizations, they will probably become your most common business communication channel. These messages perform critical tasks such as informing employees, giving directions, outlining procedures, requesting data, supplying responses, and confirming decisions. They usually follow similar structure and formatting.

The Four Parts of E-Mail Messages and Memos

Whether electronic or hard copy, routine memos generally contain four parts: (a) an informative subject line that summarizes the message; (b) an opening that reveals the main idea immediately; (c) a body that explains and justifies the main idea; and (d) a closing that presents action information, summarizes the message, or offers a closing thought. Remember that routine messages deliver good news or standard information.

Subject Line.
In e-mails and memos an informative subject line is mandatory. It summarizes the central idea, thus providing quick identification for reading and for filing. In e-mail messages, subject lines are essential. Busy readers glance at a subject line and decide when and whether to read the message. Those without subject lines are automatically deleted.

What does it take to get your message read? For one thing, stay away from meaningless or dangerous words. A sure way to get your message deleted or ignored is to use a one-word heading such as *Issue, Problem, Important,* or *Help.* Including a word such as *Free* is dangerous because it may trigger spam filters. Try to make your subject line "talk" by including a verb. Explain the purpose of the message and how it relates to the reader (*Need You to Showcase Two Items at Our Next Trade Show* rather than *Trade Show*). Finally, update your

Subject lines summarize the purpose of the message in abbreviated form.

© AP IMAGES

Has Starbucks lost its soul? That's the claim made by Starbucks founder Howard Schultz in an e-mail to top management. According to Schultz, the coffee company's chain-oriented growth has watered down the Starbucks experience, turned the brand into a commodity, and created a "sterile cookie-cutter" atmosphere in the stores. After lamenting numerous changes, including the disappearance of Starbucks' traditional Italian espresso makers, Shultz's memo closes: "Let's get back to the core…and do the things necessary to once again differentiate Starbucks from all others." *What makes this an effective closing?*

subject line to reflect the current message (*Staff Meeting Rescheduled for May 12* rather than *Re: Re: Staff Meeting*). Remember that a subject line is usually written in an abbreviated style, often without articles (*a, an, the*). It need not be a complete sentence, and it does not end with a period.

Opening. Most e-mails and memos cover nonsensitive information that can be handled in a straightforward manner. Begin by frontloading; that is, reveal the main idea immediately. Even though the purpose of the memo or e-mail is summarized in the subject line, that purpose should be restated—and amplified—in the first sentence. As you learned in Chapters 5 and 6, busy readers want to know immediately why they are reading a message. Notice how the following indirect opener can be improved by frontloading.

Most e-mails and memos open directly by revealing the main idea immediately.

Indirect Opening

For the past six months the Human Resources Development Department has been considering changes in our employees' benefit plan.

Direct Opening

Please review the following proposal regarding employees' benefits, and let me know by May 20 if you approve these changes.

Body. The body provides more information about the reason for writing. It explains and discusses the subject logically. Good e-mail messages and memos generally discuss only one topic. Limiting the topic helps the receiver act on the subject and file it appropriately. A writer who, for example, describes a computer printer problem and also requests permission to attend a conference runs a 50 percent failure risk. The reader may respond to the printer problem but delay or forget about the conference request.

The body explains one topic and is designed for easy comprehension.

Design your data for easy comprehension by using numbered lists, headings, tables, and other graphic highlighting techniques, as introduced in Chapter 6. Compare the following versions of the same message. Notice how the graphic devices of bullets, columns, headings, and white space make the main points easier to comprehend.

Hard-to-Read Paragraph Version
Effective immediately are the following air travel guidelines. Between now and December 31, only account executives may take company-approved trips. These individuals will be allowed to take a maximum of two trips, and they are to travel economy or budget class only.

Improved Version With Graphic Highlighting
Effective immediately are the following air travel guidelines:

- Who may travel: Account executives only

- How many trips: A maximum of two trips

- By when: Between now and December 31

- Air class: Economy or budget class only

Closing. Generally end with (a) action information, dates, or deadlines; (b) a summary of the message; or (c) a closing thought. Here again the value of thinking through the message before actually writing it becomes apparent. The closing is where readers look for deadlines and action language. An effective memo or e-mail closing might be, *Please submit your report by June 15 so that we can have your data before our July planning session.*

Messages should close with (a) action information including dates and deadlines, (b) a summary, or (c) a closing thought.

In more complex messages a summary of main points may be an appropriate closing. If no action request is made and a closing summary is unnecessary, you might end with a simple concluding thought (*I'm glad to answer your questions* or *This sounds like a useful project*). You needn't close messages to coworkers with goodwill statements such as those found in letters to customers or clients. However, some closing thought is often necessary to prevent a feeling of abruptness. Closings can show gratitude or encourage feedback with remarks such as *I sincerely appreciate your help* or *What are your ideas on this proposal?* Other closings look forward to what's next, such as *How would you like to proceed?* Avoid closing with overused expressions such as *Please let me know if I may be of further assistance.* This ending sounds mechanical and insincere.

Developing a Complete Message. Now let us follow the development of an e-mail message to see how we can apply the ideas just discussed. Figure 7.1 on page 176 shows the first draft of an e-mail message written by Jeff Fritsch to his boss, Sara Watts. Although it contained solid information, the message was so wordy and dense that the main points were submerged.

After writing the first draft, Jeff realized that he needed to reorganize his message into an opening, body, and closing. What's more, he desperately needed to improve the readability. In studying what he had written, he realized that he was talking about two main problems. He also discovered that he could present a three-part solution. These ideas didn't occur to him until he had written the first draft. Only in the revision stage was he able to see that he was talking about two separate problems as well as a three-part solution. The revision process can help you think through a problem and clarify a solution.

Revision helps you think through a problem, clarify a solution, and express it clearly.

In the revised version, Jeff was more aware of the subject line, opening, body, and closing. He used an informative subject line and opened directly by explaining why he was writing. His opening also outlined the two main problems so that his reader understood the background of the following recommendations. In the body of his message, Jeff identified three corrective actions, and he highlighted them with bullets for improved readability. Notice, too, that Jeff closed his message with a deadline and a reference to the next action to be taken.

Formatting E-Mail Messages

Although e-mail is a new communication channel, people are beginning to agree on specific formatting and usage conventions. The following suggestions identify current formatting standards. Always check with your organization, however, to observe its practices.

Guide Words. Following the guide word *To,* some writers insert just the recipient's electronic address, such as *swatts@morris.com.* Other writers prefer to include the receiver's full name plus the electronic address, as shown in Figure 7.2 on page 177. By including full names in the *To* and *From* slots, both receivers and senders are better able to identify the message. By the way, the order of *Date, To, From, Subject,* and other guide words varies depending on your e-mail program and whether you are sending or receiving the message.

E-mails contain guide words, optional greetings, and a concise and easy-to-read message.

Most e-mail programs automatically add the current date after *Date.* On the *Cc* line (which stands for *carbon copy* or *courtesy copy*), you can type the address of anyone who is to receive a copy of the message. Remember, though, to send copies only to those people directly involved with the message. Most e-mail programs also include a line for *Bcc* (*blind carbon copy*). This sends a copy without the addressee's knowledge. Many savvy writers today use *Bcc* for the names and addresses of a list of receivers, a technique that avoids revealing the addresses to the entire group. On the subject line, identify the subject of the memo. Be sure to include enough information to be clear and compelling.

Ethics Check

Hiding Blind Copies
Some workers use *Bcc* (*blind carbon copy*) to copy their friends and colleagues on e-mail when they do not want the recipient to know that a third party will also read the message. Based on the "netiquette" discussed in this chapter, do you believe that hiding copies from the recipient is harmless and acceptable?

Greeting. Begin your message with a friendly greeting such as the following:

Greetings are important to show friendliness and to indicate the beginning of the message.

Hi, Rudy,
Greetings, Amy,
Leslie,

Thank you, Haley,
Dear Mr. Cotter, Dear Chris Cotter,
Dear Leslie,

In addition to being friendly, a greeting provides a visual cue marking the beginning of the message. Many messages are transmitted or forwarded with such long headers that finding the beginning of the message can be difficult. A greeting helps, as shown in Figure 7.2.

FIGURE 7.1 Revising an E-Mail Message That Responds

1 Prewriting

Analyze: The purpose of this memo is to describe database problems and recommend solutions.

Anticipate: The audience is the writer's boss, who is familiar with the topic and who appreciates brevity.

Adapt: Because the reader requested this message, the direct pattern is most appropriate.

2 Writing

Research: Gather data documenting the customer database and how to use Access software.

Organize: Announce recommendations and summarize problems. In the body, list the three actions for solving the problem. In the closing, describe reader benefits, provide a deadline, and specify the next action.

Compose: Prepare the first draft.

3 Revising

Revise: Highlight the two main problems and the three recommendations. Use asterisks, caps, and headings to improve readability. Make the bulleted ideas parallel.

Proofread: Double-check to see whether *database* is one word or two. Use spell checker.

Evaluate: Does this e-mail supply concise information the boss wants in an easy-to-read format?

DRAFT

To: Sara Watts <swatts@morris.com>
From: Jeff Fritsch <jfritsch@morris.com>
Subject: Problems

This is in response to your recent inquiry about our customer database. Your message of February 18 said that you wanted to know how to deal with the database problems.

I can tell you that the biggest problem is that it contains a lot of outdated information, including customers who haven't purchased anything in five or more years. Another problem is that the old database is not compatible with the new Access software that is being used by our mailing service, and this makes it difficult to merge files. I think I can solve both problems, however, by starting a new database. This would be the place where we put the names of all new customers. And we would have it keyed using Access software. The problem with outdated information could be solved by finding out if the customers in our old database wish to continue receiving our newsletter and product announcements. Finally, we would rekey the name of all active customers in the new database.

Jeff

- Uses meaningless subject line
- Fails to reveal purpose quickly
- Buries two problems and three-part solution in huge paragraph
- Forgets to conclude with next action and end date

REVISION

File Edit Mailbox Message Transfer Special Tools Window Help

B *I* U | | | | | | | | | | | | | | | Send

To: Sara Watts <swatts@morris.com>
From: Jeffrey Fritsch <jfritsch@morris.com>
Subject: Improving Our Customer Database

Sara,

As you requested, I am submitting my recommendations for improving our customer database. The database has two major problems. First, it contains many names of individuals who have not made purchases in five or more years. Second, the format is not compatible with the new Access software used by our mailing service.

The following three procedures, however, should solve both problems:

- **Start a new database.** Effective immediately enter the names of all new customers in a new database using Access software.
- **Determine the status of customers in our old database.** Send out a mailing asking whether recipients want to continue receiving our newsletter and product announcements.
- **Rekey or scan the names of active customers.** Enter the names of all responding customers in our new database so that we have only one active database.

These changes will enable you, as team leader, to request mailings that go only to active customers. Please let me know by February 25 whether you think these recommendations are workable. If so, I will investigate costs.

All the best,

Jeff

Jeffrey Fritsch
Senior Technician
Information Technology
Mail: jfritsch@morris.com
Phone: (813) 480-3920
Fax: (813) 480-2981

- Informative subject line summarizes purpose
- Opening states purpose concisely and highlights two problems
- Body organizes main points for readability
- Closing includes key benefit, deadline, and next action
- Signature block provides full contact information

FIGURE 7.2 Formatting an E-Mail Request

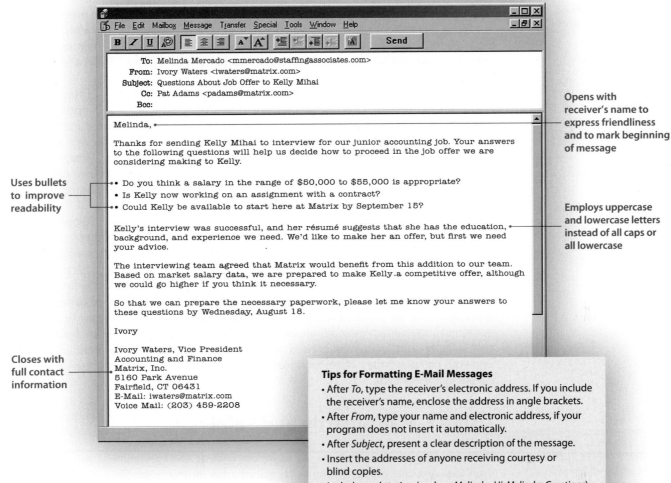

Opens with receiver's name to express friendliness and to mark beginning of message

Uses bullets to improve readability

Employs uppercase and lowercase letters instead of all caps or all lowercase

Closes with full contact information

To: Melinda Mercado <mmercado@staffingassociates.com>
From: Ivory Waters <iwaters@matrix.com>
Subject: Questions About Job Offer to Kelly Mihai
Cc: Pat Adams <padams@matrix.com>
Bcc:

Melinda,

Thanks for sending Kelly Mihai to interview for our junior accounting job. Your answers to the following questions will help us decide how to proceed in the job offer we are considering making to Kelly.

• Do you think a salary in the range of $50,000 to $55,000 is appropriate?
• Is Kelly now working on an assignment with a contract?
• Could Kelly be available to start here at Matrix by September 15?

Kelly's interview was successful, and her résumé suggests that she has the education, background, and experience we need. We'd like to make her an offer, but first we need your advice.

The interviewing team agreed that Matrix would benefit from this addition to our team. Based on market salary data, we are prepared to make Kelly a competitive offer, although we could go higher if you think it necessary.

So that we can prepare the necessary paperwork, please let me know your answers to these questions by Wednesday, August 18.

Ivory

Ivory Waters, Vice President
Accounting and Finance
Matrix, Inc.
5160 Park Avenue
Fairfield, CT 06431
E-Mail: iwaters@matrix.com
Voice Mail: (203) 459-2208

Tips for Formatting E-Mail Messages
• After *To*, type the receiver's electronic address. If you include the receiver's name, enclose the address in angle brackets.
• After *From*, type your name and electronic address, if your program does not insert it automatically.
• After *Subject*, present a clear description of the message.
• Insert the addresses of anyone receiving courtesy or blind copies.
• Include a salutation (such as *Melinda; Hi, Melinda; Greetings*), especially in messages to outsiders.
• Double-space (press *Enter*) between paragraphs.
• Do not type in all caps or in all lowercase letters.
• Include full contact information in the signature block.

Body. When typing the body of an e-mail message, use standard caps and lowercase characters—never all uppercase or all lowercase characters. Cover just one topic, and try to keep the total message under three screens in length. To assist you, many e-mail programs have basic text-editing features, such as cut, copy, paste, and word-wrap.

Complimentary Closing and Signature Block. In closing your message, you may elect to sign off with a complimentary closing such as *Cheers, All the best,* or *Many thanks.* Such a closing is optional. However, providing your name is mandatory. It is also smart to include full contact information as part of your signature block. Some writers prepare a number of "signatures" on their mail programs, depending on what information they want to reveal. They can choose a complete signature with all their contact information, or they can use a brief version. See Figure 7.2 for a complete signature.

E-mail messages are most helpful when they conclude with the writer's full contact information.

Formatting Hard-Copy Memos

Hard-copy memorandums deliver information within organizations. Although e-mail is more often used, hard-copy memos are still useful for important internal messages that require a permanent record or formality. For example, changes in procedures, official instructions, and organization reports are often prepared as hard-copy memos. Because e-mail is new and still evolving, we examined its formatting carefully in the previous paragraphs.

Hard-copy memos require less instruction because formatting is fairly standardized. Some offices use memo forms imprinted with the organization name and, optionally, the department or division names. Although the design and arrangement of memo forms vary, they usually include the basic elements of *Date, To, From,* and *Subject.* Large organizations may include other identifying headings, such as *File Number, Floor, Extension, Location,* and *Distribution.* Many business writers store memo formats in their computers and call them up when preparing memos. The guide words are then printed with the message.

If no printed or stored computer forms are available, memos may be typed on plain paper, as shown in Figure 7.3. You may type the word *Memorandum* 1.5 inches from the top edge. If you decide not to include the word *Memorandum,* start with the dateline, which appears 2 inches from the top edge. Align all the fill-in information two spaces after the longest guide word (usually *Subject*). Leave two blank lines between the last line of the heading and the first line of the memo. Single-space within paragraphs and double-space between paragraphs. Memos are generally formatted with side margins of 1 to 1.25 inches, or they may conform to the printed memo form. Do not justify the right margins. Research has shown that "ragged-right" margins in printed messages are easier to read. Memorandums do not end with complimentary closes or signatures. Instead, writers sign their initials after their names in the *From* line.

Using E-Mail Smartly and Safely

Early e-mail users were encouraged to ignore stylistic and grammatical considerations. They thought that "words on the fly" required little editing or proofing. Correspondents used emoticons (such as sideways happy faces) to express their emotions. Some e-mail today is still quick and dirty. As this communication channel continues to mature, however, messages are becoming more proper and more professional. Today it is estimated that more than 85 billion e-mails are sent each day worldwide.[5] E-mail is twice as likely as the telephone to be used to communicate at work. We have become so dependent on e-mail that 53 percent of people using it at work say that their productivity drops when they are away from it.[6]

Wise e-mail business communicators are aware of the importance as well as the dangers of e-mail as a communication channel. They know that their messages can travel, intentionally or unintentionally, long distances. A quickly drafted note may end up in the boss's mailbox or be forwarded to an enemy's box. Making matters worse, computers—like elephants and spurned lovers—never forget. Even erased messages can remain on multiple servers that are backed up by companies or Internet service providers. Increasingly, e-mail has turned into the "smoking gun" uncovered by prosecutors to prove indelicate or even illegal intentions.[7]

E-mail has become the corporate equivalent of DNA evidence. Like forgotten land mines, damaging e-mails have been dug up to prove a prosecutor's case. A classic case of damaging e-mail involved an antitrust suit against Microsoft. Bill Gates squirmed when the court heard his e-mail in which he asked, "How much do we need to pay you to screw Netscape?" Writers simply forget that their e-mail messages are permanent and searchable and can be forwarded as easily to a thousand people as to just one.[8] Another observer noted that e-mail is like an electronic truth serum.[9] Writers blurt out thoughts without thinking. For these reasons, e-mail represents a number of dangers, both to employees and to employers, as discussed in the accompanying Tech Talk box.

FIGURE 7.3 Hard-Copy Memo That Responds to Request

Aligns all heading words with those following SUBJECT

Leaves side margins of 1.25 inches

Omits a closing and signature

↓ 1.5 inches

MEMORANDUM

↓ 2 blank lines

DATE: November 11, 2009
↓ 1 blank line
TO: Stephanie Sato, President, Hollywood Audience Services
↓ 1 blank line
FROM: Sundance Richardson, Special Events Manager *SR*
↓ 1 blank line
SUBJECT: Improving Web Site Information

↓ 1 or 2 blank lines

In response to your request for ideas to improve our Web site, I am submitting the following suggestions. Because interest in our audience member, seat-filler, and usher services is growing constantly, we must use our Web site more strategically. Here are three suggestions.

First, our Web site should explain our purpose. We specialize in providing customized and responsive audiences for studio productions and award shows. The Web site should distinguish between audience members and seat-fillers. Audience members have a seat for the entire taping of a TV show. Seat-fillers sit in the empty seats of celebrity presenters or performers so that the front section does not look empty to the home audience.

Second, I suggest that our Web designer include a listing such as the following so that readers recognize the events and services we provide:

Event	Audience Members Provided Last Year	Seat-Fillers and Ushers Provided Last Year
Daytime Emmy Awards	53	15
Grammy Awards	34	17
Golden Globe Awards	29	22
Screen Actor's Guild Award	33	16
Family Television Awards	62	20
Soul Train Music Awards	48	14
Selected TV shows	669	57

Third, our Web site should provide answers to commonly asked questions such as the following:

• Do audience members or seat-fillers have to pay to attend the event?
• How often do seat-fillers have to move around?
• Will seat-fillers be on television?

Our Web site can be more informative and boost our business if we implement some of these ideas. Are you free to talk about these suggestions at 10 a.m. on Tuesday, November 19?

Includes initials after printed name and title

Provides ragged line endings— not justified

Uses headings, columns, bold, and white space to highlight information

Tips for Formatting Hard-Copy Memos
• On plain paper, type *MEMORANDUM* 1.5 inches from the top. Leave two blank lines after this heading.
• Set one tab to align entries evenly after *Subject*.
• Leave one or two blank lines after the subject line.
• Single-space all but the shortest memos. Double-space between paragraphs.
• Use 1.25-inch side margins.
• For a two-page memo, use a second-page heading with the addressee's name, page number, and date.
• Handwrite your initials after your typed name.
• Place bulleted or numbered lists flush left or indent them 0.5 inch.

Tech Talk

How to Avoid Getting Fired Over Your Internet Use

As advances in computer technology continue to change the way we work and play, Internet use on and off the job has become a danger zone for employees and employers. Misuse costs employers millions of dollars in lost productivity and litigation, and it can cost employees their jobs. A survey by the American Management Association revealed that 26 percent of employers fired employees for e-mail misuse. In addition, 2 percent terminated employees for instant messenger chat, and another 2 percent for posting offensive blog content from a company or even a home computer.[10]

Recreational activities, as well as unintentional but careless miscues, can gobble up precious network resources and waste valuable work time. Even more important is concern over lawsuits. Companies must maintain a workplace free of harassment. If employees download pornography, transmit sexually explicit jokes, or use inappropriate screen savers, the work environment can become "poisoned" and employers may be sued.

Here are some employee dos and don'ts to keep you out of trouble:

- **Do learn your company's rules.** One employee knew that her employer restricted personal use of work computers, but she believed it focused on Web surfing, not e-mail. She was stunned when her agency fired her after finding 418 personal e-mail messages on her PC.[11]
- **Do minimize sending personal e-mails from work.** Even if your company allows personal use, keep it to a minimum.

- **Do be careful when blogging.** A Canadian blogger lost his job for an entry that read, "Getting to blog for three hours while being paid: priceless."[12]
- **Don't send, download, or exhibit pornography, sexually explicit jokes, or inappropriate screen savers.** Anything that might "poison" the work environment is prohibited.
- **Don't open attachments sent by e-mail.** Attachments with executable files or video files may carry viruses, spyware, or other "malware" (malicious programs).
- **Don't download free software and utilities to company machines.** Employees can unwittingly introduce viruses.
- **Don't store your music library and photos on a company machine (or server), and don't watch streaming videos.** Capturing precious company bandwidth for personal use is a sure way to be shown the door.

Career Application

What additional Internet behavior could get employees fired? Do employees deserve broad Internet access on the job—if they are responsible? Should employers block access to Web sites? If so, what kind?

Getting Started

Because e-mail is now a mainstream communication channel, messages should be well organized, carefully composed, and grammatically correct.

Despite its dangers and limitations, e-mail has become a mainstream channel of communication. That's why it's important to take the time to organize your thoughts, compose carefully, and be concerned with correct grammar and punctuation. The following pointers will help you get off to a good start in using e-mail smartly and safely.

- **Consider composing offline.** Especially for important messages, think about using your word processing program to write offline. Then upload your message to the e-mail network. This avoids "self-destructing" (losing all your writing through some glitch or pressing the wrong key) when working online.

- **Get the address right.** E-mail addresses are sometimes complex, often illogical, and always unforgiving. Omit one character or misread the letter *l* for the number 1, and your message bounces. Solution: Use your electronic address book for people you write to frequently. Double-check every address that you key in manually. Also be sure that you don't reply to a group of receivers when you intend to answer only one.

- **Avoid misleading subject lines.** As discussed earlier, make sure your subject line is relevant and helpful. Generic tags such as *Hi!* and *Important!* may cause your message to be deleted before it is opened.

- **Apply the top-of-screen test.** When readers open your message and look at the first screen, will they see what is most significant? Your subject line and first paragraph should convey your purpose.

An internal strategy dispute at Yahoo inadvertently turned public when an executive-level e-mail titled "The Peanut Butter Manifesto" was forwarded to news media. The memo's amusing subject line reflected the author's view that Yahoo had spread itself thin by chasing Web trends haphazardly and without a cohesive vision. The body of the memo proposed a radical reorganization of the Internet services giant, including the elimination of up to 20 percent of Yahoo's workforce. *What precautions should communicators exercise before sending potentially charged e-mail messages?*

Content, Tone, and Correctness

Although e-mail seems as casual as a telephone call, it definitely is not. Because it produces a permanent record, think carefully about what you say and how you say it.

- **Be concise.** Don't burden readers with unnecessary information. Remember that monitors are small and typefaces are often difficult to read. Organize your ideas tightly.

- **Don't send anything you wouldn't want published.** Because e-mail seems like a telephone call or a person-to-person conversation, writers sometimes send sensitive, confidential, inflammatory, or potentially embarrassing messages. Beware! E-mail creates a permanent record that does not go away even when deleted. Every message is a corporate communication that can be used against you or your employer. Don't write anything that you wouldn't want your boss, your family, or a judge to read.

- **Don't use e-mail to avoid contact.** E-mail is inappropriate for breaking bad news or for resolving arguments. For example, it's improper to fire a person by e-mail. It is also not a good channel for dealing with conflict with supervisors, subordinates, or others. If there's any possibility of hurt feelings, pick up the telephone or pay the person a visit.

- **Care about correctness.** People are still judged by their writing, whether electronic or paper-based. Sloppy e-mail messages (with missing apostrophes, haphazard spelling, and stream-of-consciousness writing) make readers work too hard. They resent not only the information but also the writer.

- **Care about tone.** Your words and writing style affect the reader. Avoid sounding curt, negative, or domineering.

- **Resist humor and tongue-in-cheek comments.** Without the nonverbal cues conveyed by your face and your voice, humor can easily be misunderstood.

Avoid sending sensitive, confidential, inflammatory, or potentially embarrassing messages because e-mail is not private.

Spotlight on Communicators

"To avoid misunderstandings when sending e-mail messages, consider how the recipient will react to your message," says Liz Hughes, former executive director of OfficeTeam, a leading administrative staffing service and current manager of field leadership training for Robert Half International, OfficeTeam's parent company. "If you use terse or abbreviated language, for example, you may appear angry. If your style is too informal, you may seem unprofessional," adds Hughes. Written communication is particularly dangerous because you are not present to correct misunderstandings. Hughes points out that written communication tends to amplify emotions, so be sure to reread the message and check its tone before you send it. Never compose any message while you are upset.

Netiquette

Although e-mail is a new communication channel, a number of rules of polite online interaction are emerging.

Don't send blanket copies or spam, reduce attachments, and use identifying labels if appropriate.

- **Limit any tendency to send blanket copies.** Send copies only to people who really need to see a message. It is unnecessary to document every business decision and action with an electronic paper trail.

- **Never send "spam."** Sending unsolicited advertisements ("spam") either by fax or e-mail is illegal in the United States.

- **Consider using identifying labels.** When appropriate, add one of the following labels to the subject line: *Action* (action required, please respond); *FYI* (for your information, no response needed); *Re* (this is a reply to another message); *Urgent* (please respond immediately); *REQ* (required).

- **Use capital letters only for emphasis or for titles.** Avoid writing entire messages in all caps, which is like SHOUTING.

- **Don't forward without permission.** Obtain approval before forwarding a message.

- **Reduce attachments.** Because attachments may carry viruses, some receivers won't open them. Consider including short attachments within an e-mail message. If you must send a longer attachment, announce it.

Reading and Replying to E-Mail

The following tips can save you time and frustration when reading and answering messages:

Skim all messages before responding, paste in relevant sections, revise the subject if the topic changes, provide a clear first sentence, and never respond when angry.

- **Scan all messages in your inbox before replying to each individually.** Because subsequent messages often affect the way you respond, skim all messages first (especially all those from the same individual).

- **Print only when necessary.** Generally, read and answer most messages online without saving or printing. Use folders to archive messages on special topics. Print only those messages that are complex, controversial, or involve significant decisions and follow-up.

- **Acknowledge receipt.** If you can't reply immediately, tell when you can (*Will respond Friday*).

- **Don't automatically return the sender's message.** When replying, cut and paste the relevant parts. Avoid irritating your recipients by returning the entire "thread" (sequence of messages) on a topic.

- **Revise the subject line if the topic changes.** When replying or continuing an e-mail exchange, revise the subject line as the topic changes.

- **Provide a clear, complete first sentence.** Avoid fragments such as *That's fine with me* or *Sounds good!* Busy respondents forget what was said in earlier messages, so be sure to fill in the context and your perspective when responding.

- **Never respond when you are angry.** Always allow some time to cool off before shooting off a response to an upsetting message. You often come up with different and better alternatives after thinking about what was said. If possible, iron out differences in person.

Personal Use

Remember that office computers are meant for work-related communication.

Spotlight on Communicators

Barbara Hemphill, author of *Taming the Paper Tiger at Work*, helps major corporations increase their productivity and efficiency. When it comes to reading and replying to e-mail, she recommends the FAT™ System: F stands for *File*, A for *Act*, and T for *Toss*. If you need more than two minutes to reply, *File* the message in a folder with a reminder in your calendar system. If you can reply in two minutes, then *Act*. If you aren't sure you need the message, *Toss* it. Unlike using a paper wastebasket, you can retrieve deleted messages in most e-mail systems. Her Web site with more efficiency tips is at **http://www.productiveenvironment.com**

Courtesy of Barbara Hemphill

- **Don't use company computers for personal matters.** Unless your company specifically allows it, never use your employer's computers for personal messages, personal shopping, or entertainment.
- **Assume that all e-mail is monitored.** Employers legally have the right to monitor e-mail, and many do.

Other Smart E-Mail Practices

Depending on your messages and audience, the following tips promote effective electronic communication.

- **Improve the readability of longer messages with graphic highlighting.** When a message requires several screens, help the reader with headings, bulleted listings, side headings, and perhaps an introductory summary that describes what will follow. Although these techniques lengthen a message, they shorten reading time.

- **Consider cultural differences.** When using this borderless tool, be especially clear and precise in your language. Remember that figurative clichés (*pull up stakes, playing second fiddle,*) sports references (*hit a home run, play by the rules*) and slang (*cool, stoked*) cause confusion abroad.

- **Double-check before hitting the Send button.** Have you included everything? Avoid the necessity of sending a second message, which makes you look careless. Use spell-check and reread for fluency before sending. Checking your incoming messages before sending is also a good idea, especially if several people are involved in a rapid-fire exchange. This helps avoid "passing"—sending out a message that might be altered depending on an incoming note.

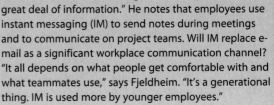
Design your messages to enhance readability, and double-check before sending.

Tech Talk

Beyond E-Mail: Instant Messaging Becomes Workplace Communication Tool

Making its way from teen bedrooms to office boardrooms, instant messaging is becoming a permanent and powerful communication tool.

WHY IS IM SUCH A HIT?

In today's fast-paced world, instant messaging (IM) offers numerous benefits. Its major attraction is real-time communication with colleagues anywhere in the world—so long as a cell phone signal or a Wi-Fi connection is available. IM is a convenient alternative to the telephone and may even replace e-mail. It has been available for years to desktop computer users, but it is now moving rapidly to mobile phones and handheld devices that can text message. Because people can share information immediately and make decisions quickly, the impact of IM on business communication has been dramatic. Group online chat—such as that now available with Skype, the voice over Internet protocol powerhouse—makes it possible to conduct instant online chats with coworkers on far-flung project teams.

WHY IS IM BANNED IN SOME COMPANIES?

However, instant communication has its drawbacks. Many find IM disruptive and stressful. They want time to think before answering. Others say that IM is one more intrusion in a crazy world of multitasking that dilutes focus and reduces efficiency. A bigger worry is that IM opens the door to huge security risks unless businesses invest in professional IM software that sits behind a firewall and logs all communication. The First National Bank of Bosque County in Valley Mills, Texas, banned IM because of the risk of information leaving the institution without approval.

HOW CAN YOU USE IM SAFELY ON THE JOB?

Before using IM on the job, check with your supervisor for approval. Find out whether your company has an Internet policy with rules about using IM. If you do use it, make sure your messaging relates to business and that you don't send anything you wouldn't want to see in print.

Career Application

How could IM be useful in your career field? Does IM produce a permanent record? Do you think that common abbreviations such as *lol* or *imho* as well as all lowercase writing are acceptable in text messages for business? Will the use of shorthand abbreviations as well as creative spelling negatively affect future writing skills?

- **Use instant messaging professionally to expand your communication channel choices.** As more knowledge workers turn to instant messaging on the job, be sure you are using it effectively as a business tool. Take a look at the accompanying Tech Talk box to learn more about this emerging channel.

Writers of e-mail are sometimes tempted to take shortcuts. Figure 7.4 illustrates bad and good e-mail messages so that you can avoid the confusing shortcuts.

Writing Typical E-Mail Messages and Memos

Thus far in this chapter, we have reviewed the writing process, analyzed the structure and format of e-mail messages and memos, and presented a number of techniques for using e-mail smartly and safely. Now we are going to apply those techniques to four categories of typical messages that you can expect to be writing as a business communicator: (a) request messages, (b) response messages, (c) procedural messages, and (d) confirmation messages.

Request Messages

LEARNING OBJECTIVE 4
Write e-mail messages and memos that make requests.

Writing Plan for Request
Opening: Make direct request.
Body: Explain and justify your request.
Closing: Include end date and reason.

When requesting routine information or action within an organization, the direct approach works best. If your request requires persuasion, you should use an indirect approach, which will be presented in Chapter 9. Most routine requests, however, require little persuasion. This means that you can spend less effort on developing the "you" attitude and reader benefits.

Begin directly by stating the request without first providing elaborate explanations and justifications. Remember that readers are usually thinking, *Why me? Why am I receiving this?* Readers can understand the explanation better once they know what you are requesting. If you are seeking answers to questions, you have three options for opening the message: (a) ask the most important question first, followed by an explanation and then the other questions; (b) use a polite command (*Please answer the following questions regarding...*); or (c) introduce the questions with a brief statement (*Your answers to the following questions will help us...*).

Communicating at Work Part 2

Wireless Giant Qualcomm Thrives on E-Mail

Because e-mail has become a standard channel for workplace communication, most companies have developed appropriate use policies. The primary reason for these policies is fear of lawsuits and financial risks, especially from e-mail that involves proprietary or confidential information.[13] A recent survey indicated that 80 percent of companies have an e-mail policy, but only half of these companies follow up with employee training or education.[14]

Qualcomm's policy covers all forms of electronic media, from e-mail, instant messages, and Internet browsing to electronic documents and pictures on computers. Newly hired employees receive this policy along with other corporate policies to read and sign. The policy is posted on the company's intranet, and Senior Vice President and Chief Information Officer Norm Fjeldheim sends out reminders a few times a year. It focuses on protecting intellectual property, including information, ideas, or other intangibles such as trade secrets, marketing materials, and customer lists.

As Fjeldheim explains, "It's a pretty common-sense policy: Don't steal, download music videos files from other sites, don't hack into unauthorized sites, don't leave your laptop lying around, don't send confidential company information, and so forth. Employees should not use e-media in any format that would offend someone. Forwarding an e-mail that is potentially offensive violates our policy. We don't monitor the policy; it is self-policing." Management reviews any reported infractions, and the Human Resources and Legal Departments determine the appropriate action to take, on a case-by-case basis.

However, Qualcomm records (logs) all activity and maintains a record of e-media to use for any investigations. "Logging is common," explains Fjeldheim. "Some companies take a more aggressive approach and block Web sites, monitoring and blocking e-mail for content. We monitor certain types of electronic transmissions, including outgoing files, for intellectual property breaches and certain types of download activity."[15]

Critical Thinking
- Why should a company have a written policy for appropriate use of electronic media? What types of rules should it include?
- What departments should participate in the development, implementation, and enforcement of a corporate e-media policy, and why?
- Do you think it is ethical for a company to log, or record, employee use of electronic media, and why?

© AP IMAGES

FIGURE 7.4 Bad and Good E-Mail Messages

Bad E-Mail Subject	Good E-Mail Subject	Tips
To: Peyton Moss **From:** Gina Jones **Subject:** Need Help!	**To:** Peyton Moss **From:** Gina Jones **Subject:** Need Help in Writing Job Placement Ad	**Expand subject with more information.**

Bad E-Mail Response	Good E-Mail Response	Tips
To: Peyton Moss **From:** Gina Jones **Subject:** Re: Re: Re: Advertising Our Job Opening Yes, I agree totally!	**To:** Peyton Moss **From:** Gina Jones **Subject:** Re: Re: Re: Advertising Our Job Opening Yes, I agree that our first choice should be an online listing at Monster.com.	**Provide context to orient reader, which is especially helpful in messages with many replies and multiperson conversations.**

Bad E-Mail Instructions	Good E-Mail Instructions	Tips
To: Haley Krebs, Brandon Kim, Nicole Sanchez **From:** Gina Jones **Subject:** Relocation Options Ready for Your Analysis Please analyze the four possible relocation sites recommended by our consultants in the attached file. Your written reactions by May 1 will enable us to make a presentation to management by the middle of the month	**To:** Haley Krebs, Brandon Kim, Nicole Sanchez **From:** Gina Jones **Subject:** Relocation Options Ready for Your Analysis Please analyze the four possible relocation sites recommended by our consultants in the attached file. Your written reactions by May 1 will enable us to make a presentation to management by the middle of the month. HALEY: DECISION NEEDED. Check the footage available for office space in each option. BRANDON: FYI, if we move forward, your project will be delayed. NICOLE: PLEASE CONFIRM. Do these four locations meet all the specifications you submitted?	**Send general message to coworkers but include individual action requests to be sure everyone understands specific assignment or ramifications of message.**

Bad Use of Bcc	Good E-Mails	Tips
To: Peyton Moss **From:** Gina Jones **Subject:** Conference Thursday at 2 p.m. **Bcc:** Sabrina Please attend the conference tomorrow (Thursday) at 2 p.m.	**To:** Peyton Moss **From:** Gina Jones **Subject:** Conference Thursday at 2 p.m. Peyton, please attend the conference tomorrow (Thursday) at 2 p.m. **To:** Sabrina **From:** Gina **Subject:** Reserve Conference Room Thursday at 2 p.m. Please reserve the conference room for Peyton and me tomorrow (Thursday) at 2 p.m.	**Send two messages because naming someone in a "bcc" may not sufficiently explain why that person is being copied.**

FIGURE 7.5 E-Mail Message That Makes a Request

1 Prewriting

Analyze: The purpose of this e-mail is to solicit feedback regarding a casual-dress policy.

Anticipate: The message is going to a subordinate who is busy but probably eager to be consulted in this policy matter.

Adapt: Use a direct approach beginning with the most important question. Strive for a positive, professional tone rather than an autocratic, authoritative tone.

2 Writing

Research: Collect secondary information about dress-down days in other organizations. Collect primary information by talking with company managers.

Organize: Begin with the main idea followed by a brief explanation and questions. Conclude with an end date and a reason.

Compose: Prepare the first draft remembering that the receiver is busy and appreciates brevity.

3 Revising

Revise: Rewrite questions to ensure that they are parallel and readable.

Proofread: Decide whether to hyphenate *casual-dress policy* and *dress-down days*. Be sure commas follow introductory clauses. Check question marks.

Evaluate: Does this memo encourage participatory management? Will the receiver be able to answer the questions and respond easily?

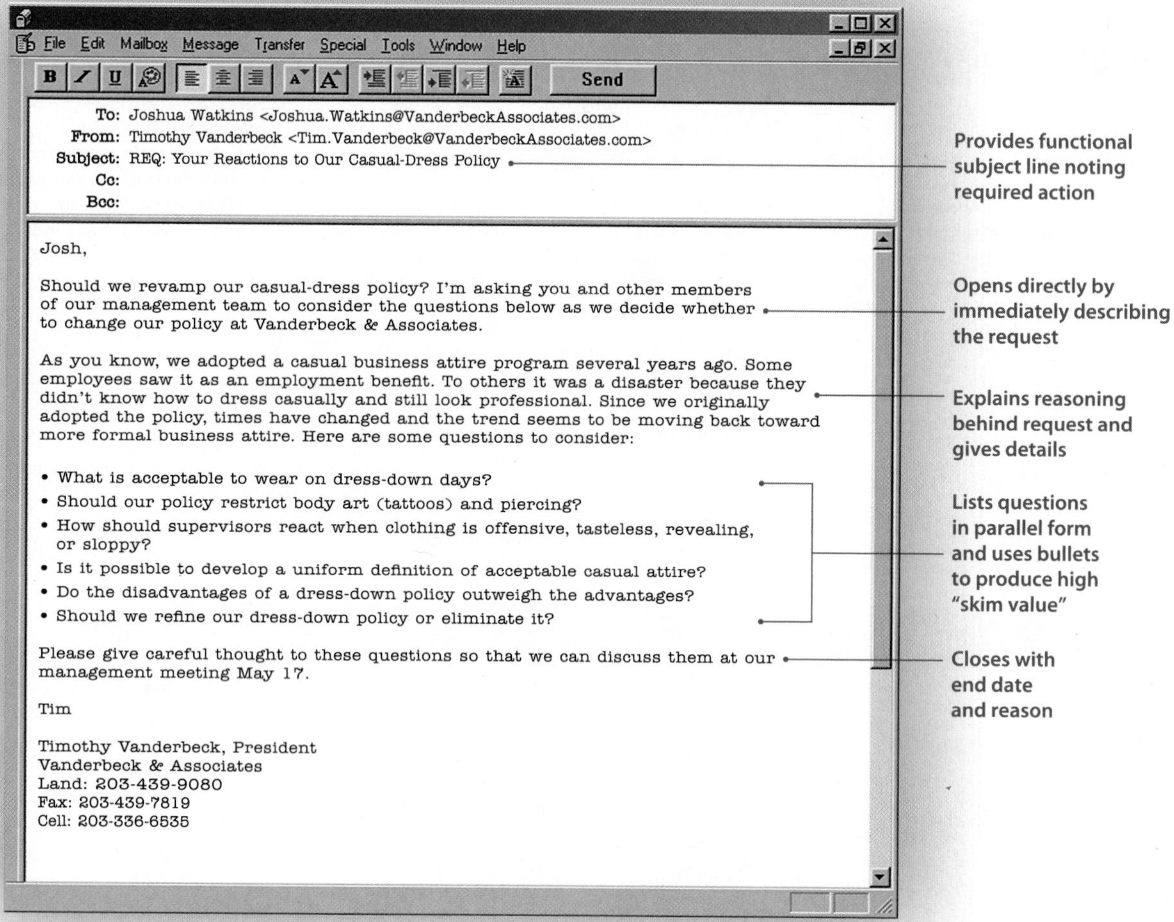

```
File  Edit  Mailbox  Message  Transfer  Special  Tools  Window  Help

B  I  U ...                                          Send

     To: Joshua Watkins <Joshua.Watkins@VanderbeckAssociates.com>
   From: Timothy Vanderbeck <Tim.Vanderbeck@VanderbeckAssociates.com>
 Subject: REQ: Your Reactions to Our Casual-Dress Policy
     Cc:
    Bcc:
```

Josh,

Should we revamp our casual-dress policy? I'm asking you and other members of our management team to consider the questions below as we decide whether to change our policy at Vanderbeck & Associates.

As you know, we adopted a casual business attire program several years ago. Some employees saw it as an employment benefit. To others it was a disaster because they didn't know how to dress casually and still look professional. Since we originally adopted the policy, times have changed and the trend seems to be moving back toward more formal business attire. Here are some questions to consider:

- What is acceptable to wear on dress-down days?
- Should our policy restrict body art (tattoos) and piercing?
- How should supervisors react when clothing is offensive, tasteless, revealing, or sloppy?
- Is it possible to develop a uniform definition of acceptable casual attire?
- Do the disadvantages of a dress-down policy outweigh the advantages?
- Should we refine our dress-down policy or eliminate it?

Please give careful thought to these questions so that we can discuss them at our management meeting May 17.

Tim

Timothy Vanderbeck, President
Vanderbeck & Associates
Land: 203-439-9080
Fax: 203-439-7819
Cell: 203-336-6535

Callouts:
- Provides functional subject line noting required action
- Opens directly by immediately describing the request
- Explains reasoning behind request and gives details
- Lists questions in parallel form and uses bullets to produce high "skim value"
- Closes with end date and reason

In the body of your message, explain and justify your request. When you must ask many questions, list them, being careful to phrase them similarly. Be courteous and friendly. In the closing include an end date (with a reason, if possible) to promote a quick response.

The e-mail message shown in Figure 7.5 requests information. In the subject line the writer alerts the receiver immediately that this is a request with a required action. The message opens with a polite command followed by a brief explanation. Notice that the questions are highlighted with bullets to provide the high "skim value" that is important in business messages. The reader can quickly see what is being asked. The message concludes with an end date and a reason. Providing an end date helps the reader know how to plan a response so that action is completed by the date given. A specific end date also helps the receiver save time when later referring to the request and looking for a completion date. Expressions such as *do it whenever you can* or *complete at as soon as possible* make little impression on procrastinators or very busy people. Establishing specific completion dates prompts receivers to enter these dates on their calendars to serve as reminders.

Another example of a request message appears in Figure 7.2 on page 177. This e-mail requests information about an appropriate salary for a junior accountant. Because this e-mail is traveling outside the organization, it opens with a brief explanation and introduction to the following list of bulleted questions. It concludes with an end date and reason (*So that we can prepare the necessary paperwork, please let me know your answers to these questions by Wednesday, August 18*).

Response Messages

Much business correspondence reacts or responds to previous messages. When responding to an e-mail, memo, or other document, be sure to follow the 3-x-3 writing process. Analyze your purpose and audience, collect whatever information is necessary, and organize your thoughts. Make a brief outline of the points you plan to cover.

The opening should summarize the main information from your reply. The body provides additional information and details in a readable format. The closing provides a concluding remark, summary, or offer of further assistance.

Writers sometimes fall into bad habits in responding to messages. Here are some trite and long-winded openers that are best avoided:

> *In response to your message of the 15th* . . . (States the obvious.)
> *I have before me your memo of the 15th in which you* . . . (Unnecessarily identifies the location of the previous message.)
> *Pursuant to your request of the 15th* . . . (Sounds old-fashioned.)
> *This is to inform you that* . . . (Delays getting to the point.)

Instead of falling into the trap of using one of the preceding shopworn openings, start directly by responding to the writer's request. If you agree to the request, show your cheerful compliance immediately. Consider these good-news openers:

> *Yes, we will be glad to* . . . (Sends message of approval by opening with "Yes.")
> *Here are answers to the questions you asked about* . . . (Sounds straightforward, business-like, and professional.)
> *You are right in seeking advice about* . . . (Opens with two words that every reader enjoys seeing and hearing.)
> *We are happy to assist you in* . . . (Shows writer's helpful nature and goodwill.)
> *As you requested, I am submitting* . . . (Gets right to the point.)

After a direct and empathic opener, provide the information requested in a logical and coherent order. If you are answering a number of questions, arrange your answers in the order of the questions.

To improve readability, use graphic highlighting techniques when appropriate. In the hard-copy memo response shown in Figure 7.3 on page 179, columns and headings helped the reader quickly recognize Hollywood events and the number of audience members, seat-fillers, and ushers provided. In the e-mail response shown in Figure 7.1 on page 176, bullets and category headings make three suggested procedures stand out. Although columns and bullets require more space than paragraph format, these graphic highlighting techniques vastly improve readability and comprehension. Other ways to improve readability include using familiar words, short sentences, short paragraphs, and active-voice verbs. When alternatives exist, make them clear.

Procedural Messages

Messages that explain procedures generally flow downward from management to employees. They usually relate to the daily operation of an organization. In writing these messages, you have one primary function: conveying your idea so clearly that no further explanation

Writing Plan for Response
Opening: Summarize response facts.
Body: Provide details in readable form.
Closing: Offer concluding remark, summary, or further assistance.

Direct opening statements can also be cheerful and empathic.

(return message, telephone call, or personal visit) is necessary. Written procedures and instructions are most effective if you follow these guidelines:

- **List the steps of the procedure in order.** Be sure you proceed forward in time without backtracking.

- **Begin each step with an active verb in the command mode.** For example, *Write a job description,* rather than *You should write a job description.*

- **Treat each step of the procedure in a separate, simple instruction.** For example, *Cut the cord* rather than *Cut the cord and remove a half-inch of insulation from the wire.*

Writing Plan for Procedural Message
Opening: Announce procedure.
Body: Explain need. List numbered steps in order.
Closing: Reinforce benefits and provide source of further information.

Be particularly careful about clarity and readability. Figure 7.6 shows the first draft of a hard-copy memo written by Troy Bell. His memo was meant to announce a new procedure for employees to follow in advertising open positions. However, the tone was negative, the explanation of the problem rambled, and the new procedure was unclear. Notice, too, that Troy's first draft told readers what they *shouldn't* do (*Do not submit advertisements for new employees directly to an Internet job bank or a newspaper*). More helpful is to tell readers what they *should* do. Finally, Troy's memos closed with a threat instead of showing readers how this new procedure will help them.

In the revision, Troy improved the tone considerably. The subject line contains a *please,* which is always pleasant to see even if one is giving an order. The subject line also includes a verb and specifies the purpose of the memo. Instead of expressing his ideas with negative words and threats, Troy revised his message to explain objectively and concisely what went wrong.

Troy realized that his original explanation of the new procedure was vague. Messages explaining procedures are most readable when the instructions are broken down into numbered steps listed chronologically. Each step in the revised version begins with an action verb in the command mode: *Write, Bring, Let,* and *Pick up.* Forcing all the steps in a procedure into command language is sometimes difficult. Troy struggled, but by trying out different wording, he finally found verbs that worked.

Procedures and instructions are often written in numbered steps using command language (*Do this; don't do that*).

Why should you go to so much trouble to make lists and achieve parallelism? Because readers can comprehend what you have said much more quickly. Parallel language also makes you look professional and efficient.

In writing procedure messages, be careful of tone. Today's managers and team leaders seek employee participation and cooperation. These goals can't be achieved, though, if the writer sounds like a dictator or an autocrat. Avoid making accusations and fixing blame. Rather, explain changes, give reasons, and, if possible, suggest benefits to the reader.

A special online supplement at www.meguffey.com site teaches you how to write instructions and provides hot links to real companies.

The writing of instructions and procedures is so important that we have developed a special bonus online supplement providing you with more examples and information. This online supplement extends your textbook with in-depth material including links to real businesses to show you examples of well-written procedures and instructions. You can find it at **www.meguffey.com.** Look for "How to Write Instructions."

Confirmation Messages

LEARNING OBJECTIVE 7
Write e-mail messages and memos that confirm oral decisions, directives, and discussions.

Confirmation messages—also called *to-file reports* or *incident reports*—record oral decisions, directives, discussions, and IM messages. They create a concise, permanent record that could be important in the future. Because individuals may forget, alter, or retract oral commitments, smart communicators establish a written record of significant happenings. In some companies, any time a dollar figure is discussed with a client in an instant message, the writer has to document it in a formal memo.[16] Such records are unnecessary, of course, for minor events. The confirmation e-mail message shown in Figure 7.7 reviews the significant points of a sales agreement discussed in a telephone conversation. When you write to confirm an oral agreement, remember these tips:

- Include the names and titles of involved individuals.

- Itemize major issues or points concisely.

- Request feedback about unclear or inaccurate points.

FIGURE 7.6 Memo That Describes a New Procedure

DRAFT

TO: Ruth DiSilvestro, Manager
FROM: Troy Bell, Human Resources
SUBJECT: Job Advertisement Misunderstanding •————————

We had no idea last month when we implemented new hiring procedures that •
major problems would result. Due to the fact that every department is now
placing Internet advertisements for new-hires individually, the difficulties
occurred. This cannot continue. Perhaps we did not make it clear at that
time, but all newly hired employees who are hired for a position should be
requested through this office.

Do not submit your advertisements for new employees directly to an Internet •
job bank or a newspaper. After writing them, they should be brought to
Human Resources, where they will be centralized. You should discuss each
ad with one of our counselors. Then we will place the ad at an appropriate
Internet site or other publication. If you do not follow these guidelines, chaos
will result. You may pick up applicant folders from us the day after the •
closing date in an ad.

Vague, negative subject line

Fails to pinpoint main idea in opening

New procedure is hard to follow

Uses threats instead of showing benefits to reader

REVISION

DATE: January 5, 2009

TO: Ruth DiSilvestro, Manager

FROM: Troy Bell, Human Resources *TB*

SUBJECT: New Job Advertisement Procedure to Fill Openings Faster •————

You can fill your department job openings faster and more efficiently with a
new procedure that will become effective today.

A major problem resulted from the change in hiring procedures implemented
last month. Each department was placing job advertisements for new-hires
individually, when all such requests should be centralized in this office. To •
process applications more quickly and efficiently, please follow this new
procedure:

• 1. Write an advertisement for a position in your department.

2. Bring the ad to Human Resources and discuss it with one of our counselors.

3. Let Human Resources place the ad at an appropriate Internet job bank or
     submit it to a newspaper.

• 4. Pick up applicant folders from Human Resources the day following the
      closing date provided in the ad.

Following these guidelines will save you work and will also enable Human
Resources to help you fill your openings more quickly. Call Ann Edmonds at •
Ext. 2505 if you have questions about this procedure.

Informative, courteous, upbeat subject line

Summarizes main idea concisely

Explains why change in procedures is necessary

Lists easy-to-follow steps; starts each with a verb

Closes by reinforcing benefits to reader

FIGURE 7.7 E-Mail That Confirms Oral Discussion

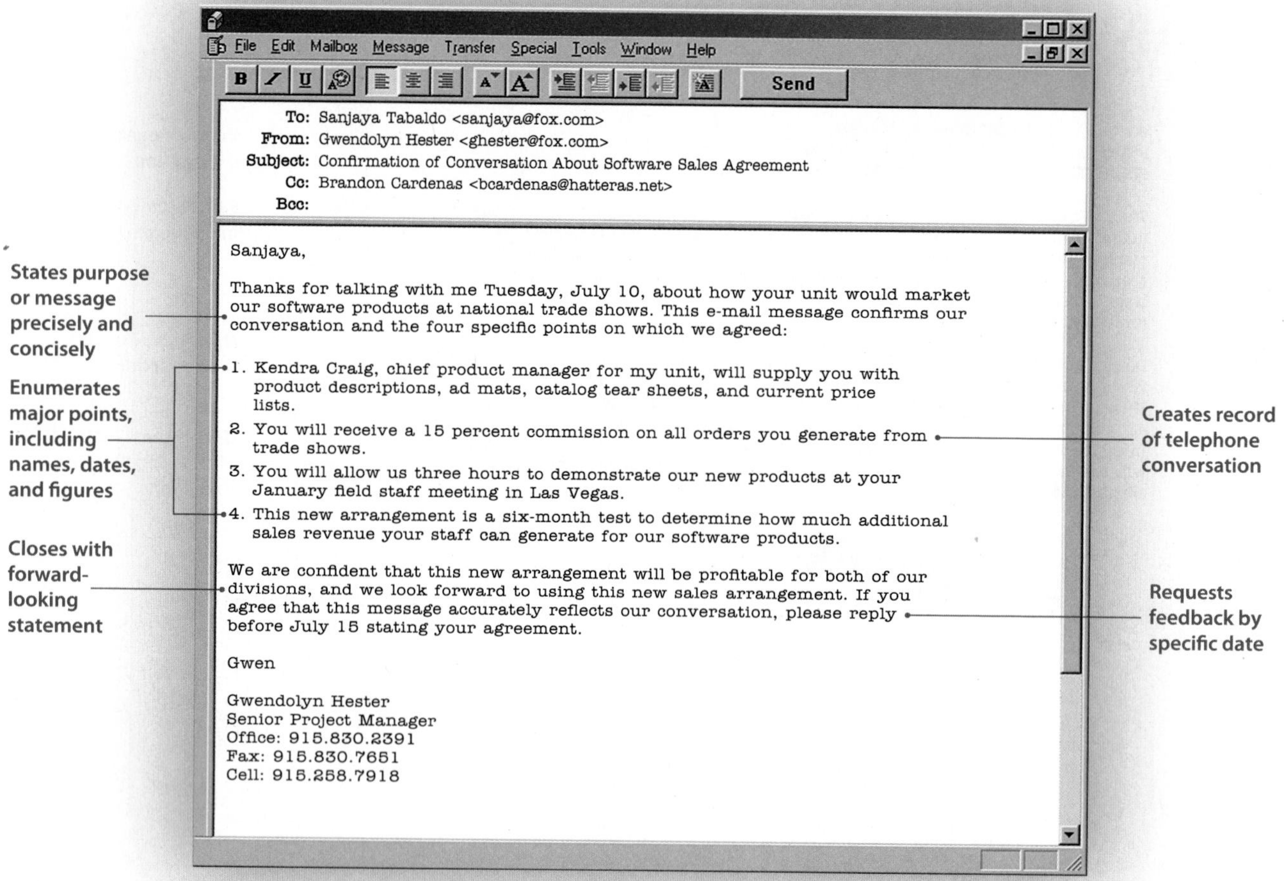

```
To:       Sanjaya Tabaldo <sanjaya@fox.com>
From:     Gwendolyn Hester <ghester@fox.com>
Subject:  Confirmation of Conversation About Software Sales Agreement
Cc:       Brandon Cardenas <bcardenas@hatteras.net>
Bcc:
```

Sanjaya,

Thanks for talking with me Tuesday, July 10, about how your unit would market our software products at national trade shows. This e-mail message confirms our conversation and the four specific points on which we agreed:

1. Kendra Craig, chief product manager for my unit, will supply you with product descriptions, ad mats, catalog tear sheets, and current price lists.
2. You will receive a 15 percent commission on all orders you generate from trade shows.
3. You will allow us three hours to demonstrate our new products at your January field staff meeting in Las Vegas.
4. This new arrangement is a six-month test to determine how much additional sales revenue your staff can generate for our software products.

We are confident that this new arrangement will be profitable for both of our divisions, and we look forward to using this new sales arrangement. If you agree that this message accurately reflects our conversation, please reply before July 15 stating your agreement.

Gwen

Gwendolyn Hester
Senior Project Manager
Office: 915.830.2391
Fax: 915.830.7651
Cell: 915.258.7918

Annotations (left margin):
- States purpose or message precisely and concisely
- Enumerates major points, including names, dates, and figures
- Closes with forward-looking statement

Annotations (right margin):
- Creates record of telephone conversation
- Requests feedback by specific date

Writing Plan for Confirmation Message
Opening: Explain reason for writing.
Body: Identify names, titles, and major issues.
Closing: Request feedback about unclear or inaccurate points.

Confirmation messages can save employees from being misunderstood or blamed unfairly.

Another type of confirmation message simply verifies the receipt of materials or a change of schedule. It is brief and often kept on file to explain your role in a project. For example, suppose you are coordinating an interdepartmental budget report. Carla Ramos from Human Resources calls to let you know that her portion of the report will be a week late. To confirm, you would send Carla the following one-sentence message: *This message verifies our telephone conversation of November 5 in which you said that your portion of the budget report will be submitted November 14 instead of November 7*. Be sure to print a copy if you are using e-mail. Notice that the tone is objective, not accusatory. However, if you are later asked why your project is running late (and you probably will be), you will have a record of the explanation. In fact, you might want to send a copy to your superior in case intervention is necessary.

Some critics complain that too many "cover-your-tail" messages are written, thus creating excessive and unnecessary paperwork. However, legitimate messages that confirm and clarify events have saved many thoughtful workers from being misunderstood or blamed unfairly.

Sometimes taken lightly, e-mail messages and office memos, like other business documents, should be written carefully. Once they leave the author's hands, they are essentially published. They can't be retrieved, corrected, or revised. Review the following checklist for tips in writing typical e-mail messages and memos that accomplish what you intend.

Checklist

Writing Typical E-Mail Messages and Memos

Subject Line

✓ **Summarize the central idea**. Express concisely what the message is about and how it relates to the reader.

✓ **Include labels if appropriate**. Labels such as *FYI* (for your information) and *REQ* (required) help receivers recognize how to respond.

✓ **Avoid empty or dangerous words**. Don't write one-word subject lines such as *Help*, *Problem*, or *Free*.

Opening

✓ **State the purpose for writing**. Include the same information that is in the subject line, but expand it.

✓ **Highlight questions**. If you are requesting information, begin with the most important question, use a polite command (*Please answer the following questions about . . .*), or introduce your request courteously.

✓ **Supply information directly**. If responding to a request, give the reader the requested information immediately in the opening. Explain later.

Body

✓ **Explain details**. Arrange information logically. For complex topics use separate paragraphs developed coherently.

✓ **Enhance readability**. Use short sentences, short paragraphs, and parallel construction for similar ideas.

✓ **Supply graphic highlighting**. If appropriate, provide bulleted or numbered lists, columns, tables, or other graphic devices to improve readability and comprehension.

✓ **Be cautious**. Remember that memos and e-mail messages often travel far beyond their intended audiences.

Closing

✓ **Request action**. If appropriate, state specifically what you want the reader to do. Include a deadline, with reasons, if possible.

✓ **Summarize the memo or provide a closing thought**. For long memos provide a summary of the important points. If neither an action request nor a summary is necessary, end with a closing thought.

✓ **Avoid cliché endings**. Use fresh remarks rather than overused expressions such as *If you have additional questions, please do not hesitate to call* or *Thank you for your cooperation*.

Communicating at Work Your Turn

Applying Your Skills at Qualcomm

Because Qualcomm Vice President Norm Fjeldheim relies heavily on e-mail, he offers his employees guidelines for writing effective e-mail messages. "Good writing practices apply to e-mail as well as to other documents," he says. "Often people don't compose e-mail messages as carefully as other documents. I have to dig through the e-mail to find out what they are trying to say. Get to the point. Give me the executive summary first. Then provide the supporting detail. If I want it, I can read it. Otherwise, I can skip it."

He doesn't like to scroll down. "I tell my staff, 'If you can't make your point in the first window, then I am probably not going to read past that point and I will come back to it later.' So if you need a fast response, tell me right up front."

"You can use a slightly different writing style for e-mail than for report writing," Fjeldheim explains. "Your goal is to get your point across—which means it needs to be read. The easier you can make it to read, the better. But you also need to know your audience. If you are sending an e-mail to an engineer, include more technical information. An executive wants a succinct, to-the-point message. If you provide too much information, the person won't read it."

Formatting—color, fonts, indenting, boldface, and italic—can make e-mail more readable. Fjeldheim reminds his employees, however, that formatting for formatting's sake is not the answer. Some people prefer plain text to formatting. Again, it is important to know

what the recipient likes. "Don't overdo formatting. It should help the reader," he advises. "I had an employee who used asterisks in front of his replies so that *he* could easily identify his responses. But it made it very difficult for *me* to read. 'It's not about making it easy for you, it's about making it easy for me to read,' I told him."

Your Task

Your boss, Mr. Fjeldheim, has been invited to make a presentation to a college management class. The suggested topic is "How to Write E-Mail Messages That Impress the Boss and Keep You Out of Trouble." He asks you, his assistant, to prepare a list of at least ten well-organized points that he can make. Focus primarily on the writing tips you have learned from Mr. Fjeldheim, but add information you think is important. In an e-mail message to Mr. Fjeldheim, list your points.

Summary of Learning Objectives

1 **Discuss how the 3-x-3 writing process helps you produce effective e-mail messages and memos.** Guffey's 3-x-3 writing process helps you analyze your purpose and audience before writing. E-mail and memos are appropriate for routine business messages, but they shouldn't be used if you need to convey enthusiasm, warmth, or some other emotion; if you need to supply a context; or if you need to smooth over a disagreement. The 3-x-3 process helps you decide how the reader will react and makes you consider how you can save the reader's time. Before writing routine e-mails and memos, collect information and organize your thoughts into a brief outline. After composing the first draft, revise for clarity, proofread for correctness, and plan for feedback.

2 **Analyze the structure and formatting of e-mail messages and memos.** Direct (nonsensitive) e-mails and memos begin with a subject line that summarizes the central idea. The opening repeats that idea and amplifies it. The body explains and provides more information. The closing includes (a) action information, dates, and deadlines; (b) a summary of the memo; and/or (c) a closing thought. E-mail messages should be formatted with a meaningful subject line, a greeting, a single-spaced body that is typed with a combination of upper- and lowercase letters, and a closing "signature" that includes contact information. Hard-copy memos are formatted similarly but without a greeting or closing. Writers place their initials next to their names on the *From* line.

3 **Describe smart e-mail practices, including getting started; content, tone, and correctness; netiquette; reading and replying to e-mail; personal use; and other practices.** Careful e-mail users compose offline, get the address right, avoid misleading subject lines, and apply the top-of-the-screen test. They write concisely and don't send anything they wouldn't want published. They don't use e-mail to avoid contact. They care about correctness, resist humor, never send spam, use identifying labels when appropriate, and use attachments sparingly. In reading and responding, they employ a number of efficient practices such as scanning all incoming messages, limiting printing, and revising the subject line as the message thread changes. They don't use company computers for personal use unless specifically allowed to do so, and they realize that e-mail may be monitored. They strive to improve readability through design, they consider cultural differences, and they double-check before hitting the **Send** button.

4 **Write e-mail messages and memos that make requests.** Nonsensitive messages that request information or action open directly by stating the purpose immediately. If you are asking many questions, begin with the most important question, use a polite command (*Please answer the following questions*), or introduce the questions with a brief statement. The body of the message explains and justifies the request. It may list questions. The closing may summarize the request and include an end date—with a reason, if possible.

5 **Write e-mail messages and memos that respond.** Messages that reply to requests open with information the reader most wants to learn, summarizing the main information. The opening should avoid tired expressions such as *Pursuant to your request of the 15th.* The body provides details and explanation. It should use graphic highlighting tools such as bullets, headings, and columns to improve readability. The closing may summarize the important points or offer further assistance.

6 **Write e-mail messages and memos that explain procedures.** Messages that explain procedures usually begin by announcing the procedure. The body explains the need for the procedure and outlines the procedural steps. Procedures should enumerate steps in command language (*Do this, don't do that*) and should be written in parallel form. Each step in the procedure should be treated separately and stated simply. A message outlining a new procedure should close by providing a source for further information if questions arise.

7 **Write e-mail messages and memos that confirm oral decisions, directives, and discussions.** Sometimes called "to-file reports" or "incident reports," confirmation messages create a permanent record of oral decisions, directives, and discussions. They may also confirm the receipt of materials or a change of schedule. Confirmation messages should include the names and titles of involved individuals and the major issues involved. They should conclude with a request for feedback about unclear or inaccurate points.

Chapter Review

1. Why has the writing of e-mail messages and memos taken on increasing importance today? (Obj. 1)

2. List and briefly describe the four parts of typical e-mail messages and memos. (Obj. 2)

3. Compare and contrast the structure and formatting of e-mail messages and memos. (Obj. 2)

4. What are some of the dangers of e-mail for employees in the workplace? (Obj. 3)

5. Suggest at least ten pointers that you could give to a first-time e-mail user. (Obj. 3)

6. How can you use instant messaging safely on the job? (Obj. 3)

7. Name at least five rules of e-mail etiquette that show respect for others. (Obj. 3)

8. Outline the writing plan for a message that requests routine information or action. (Obj. 4)

9. What is wrong with ending a request memo by asking for compliance *as soon as possible?* (Obj. 4)

10. What is the best way to open a message that responds favorably to a request? (Obj. 5)

11. What is wrong with starting a response message, *This is to inform you that...?* (Obj. 5)

12. Outline a writing plan for a procedural message. (Obj. 6)

13. How should a writer prepare procedures and instructions to make them most understandable? (Obj. 6)

14. What is the purpose of a confirmation e-mail message or memo? What other names could the message be given? (Obj. 7)

15. What three elements should most confirmation e-mail messages and memos include? (Obj. 7)

Critical Thinking

1. Why are lawyers and technology experts warning companies to store, organize, and manage computer data, including e-mail and instant messages, with sharper diligence? (Obj. 3)

2. What factors would help you decide whether to write a memo, send an e-mail, try instant messaging, make a telephone call, leave a voice mail message, or deliver a message in person? (Objs. 1, 2)

3. If you have used both e-mail and instant messaging, do you agree or disagree with the following statement: "I use e-mail because it allows me to research, to rewrite, to send when I'm ready, and to save a paper trail. I don't use instant messaging because it's Return Receipt [message option in e-mail] on steroids. It's an imposition! It's an interruption!"

4. Discuss the ramifications of the following statement: Once a memo, e-mail, instant message, or any other document leaves your hands, you have essentially published it. (Objs. 2–7)

5. **Ethical Issue:** Should employers have the right to monitor all e-mail and instant messages that employees exchange on the job? Present the employer's position and then the employees' position.

Activities

7.1 Document for Analysis: Jumbled Request Memo (Objs. 1–4)

Your Task. Analyze the following poorly written memo, and list its weaknesses. If your instructor directs, revise it.

DATE: March 23, 2009
TO: Lucia Carrera, Manager, Marketing
FROM: Myles Jordan, Vice President, Marketing
SUBJECT: Need Help

In all probability, you probably know that the Marketing Division has the responsibility of planning the fall training conference to be held in Miami. Here are the speakers I have lined up for training sessions. I'm thinking that on Tuesday, October 11, we will have Marley A. Moody. Her scheduled topic is "Using E-Mail and IM Effectively." Jackson J. Huggins said he could speak to our group on October 12 (Wednesday). "Leading Groups and Teams" is the topic for Huggins. The last speaker is Sebastian Estrada, scheduled for Thursday, October 13. His topic is "Database Management." Here are their e-mail addresses—Estrada: Sebastian@toptalent.com. Huggins: jjhuggins@sunbelt.net. Moody: Marley.moody@etc.com.

Lucia, you can help us make this one of the best training sessions ever. I need you to send each of these people an e-mail and confirm the dates and topics. Due to the fact that we must print the schedule soon, I will need this done as soon as possible. Don't hesitate to call if you have any questions.

7.2 Document for Analysis: Poorly Written E-Mail Response (Objs. 1–5)

Your Task. Analyze the following poorly written e-mail message, and list its specific weaknesses. If your instructor directs, revise it.

To: Stella Harris <Stella.Harris@alpha.com>
From: William Durham <William.Durham@alpha.com>
Subject: REPORT
Cc:

Stella,

As you know, I attended the Workplace Issues conference on November 3, as you suggested. The topic was how to prevent workplace violence, and I found it very fascinating. Although we have been fortunate to avoid serious incidents at our company, it's better to be safe than sorry. Since I was the representative from our company and you asked for a report, here it is. Susan Sloan was the presenter, and she made suggestions in three categories, which I will summarize here.

Ms. Sloan cautioned organizations to prescreen job applicants. As a matter of fact, wise companies do not offer employment until after a candidate's background has been checked. Just the mention of a background check is enough to make some candidates withdraw. These candidates, of course, are the ones with something to hide.

A second suggestion was that companies should prepare a good employee handbook that outlines what employees should do when they suspect potential workplace violence. This handbook should include a way for informers to be anonymous.

A third recommendation had to do with recognizing red-flag behavior. This involves having companies train managers to recognize signs of potential workplace violence. What are some of the red flags? One sign is an increasing number of arguments (most of them petty) with coworkers. Another sign is extreme changes in behavior or statements indicating depression over family or financial problems. Another sign is bullying or harassing behavior. Bringing a firearm to work or displaying an extreme fascination with firearms is another sign.

By the way, the next Workplace Issues conference is in January, and the topic is employee e-mail monitoring.

I think that the best recommendation is prescreening job candidates. This is because it is most feasible. If you want me to do more research on prescreening techniques, do not hesitate to let me know. Let me know by November 18 if you want me to make a report at our management meeting, which is scheduled for December 3.

Bill

7.3 Document for Analysis: Poorly Written Procedure E-Mail (Objs. 1, 2, and 6)

Your Task. Analyze the following poorly written e-mail message, and list its specific weaknesses. If your instructor directs, revise it.

To: Faith Benoit <Faith.Benoit @stcc.edu>
From: Mia Murillo <Mia.Murillo@stcc.edu>
Subject: Equipment Repairs
Cc:

We have recently instituted a new procedure for all equipment repairs. Effective immediately, we are no longer using the "Equipment Repair Form" that we formerly used. We want to move everyone to an online database system. These new procedures will help us repair your equipment faster and keep track of it better. You will find the new procedure at http://www.BigWebDesk.net. That's where you log in. You should indicate the kind of repair you need. It may be for AudioVisual, Mac, PC, or Printer. Then you should begin the process of data entry for your specific problem by selecting "Create New Ticket." The new ticket should be printed and attached securely to the equipment.

Should you have questions or trouble, just call Sylvia at Extension 255. You can also write to her at Sylvia.Freeman @stcc.edu. The warehouse truck driver will pick up and deliver your equipment as we have always done in the past.

7.4 Document for Analysis: Poorly Written Confirmation E-Mail (Objs. 1, 2, and 7)

Your Task. Analyze the following poorly written e-mail message, and list its specific weaknesses. If your instructor directs, revise it.

To: Jacob Burgess <jburgess@talent-unlimited.com>
From: Danika Haaland-Ford <dhford@aol.com>
Subject: Your Offer
Cc:

Dear Mr. Burgess,
It was good to talk to you on the telephone yesterday (December 2) after exchanging letters with you and after

reading so much about Bermuda. I was very interested in learning about the commercials you want me to write. As I understand it, Mr. Burgess, you want a total of 240 one-minute radio commercials. These commercials are intended to rejuvenate the slumping tourist industry in Bermuda. You said that these commercials would be broadcast from March 30 through June 30. You said these commercials would be played on three radio stations. These stations are in five major cities on the East Coast. The commercials would be aimed at morning and evening drive time, for drivers who are listening to their radios, and the campaign would be called "Radio Bermuda."

I am sure I can do as you suggested in reminding listeners that Bermuda is less than two hours away. You expect me to bring to these commercials the color and character of the island. You want me to highlight the attractions and the civility of Bermuda, at least as much as can be done in one-minute radio commercials. In my notes I wrote that you also mentioned that I should include references to tree frogs and royal palm trees. Another item you suggested that I include in some of the commercials was special Bermuda food, such as delicacies like shark on toast, conch fritters, and mussel stew.

I wanted to be sure to write these points down so that we both agreed on what we said in our telephone conversation. I am eager to begin working on these commercials immediately, but I would feel better if you looked over these points to see if I have it right. I look forward to working with you.

Danika Haaland-Ford

7.5 Writing Improvement Exercises: Message Openers (Objs. 1–3)

Your Task. Revise the following e-mail and memo openers so that they are more direct.

a. A memo announcing a new procedure: It has come to our attention that increasing numbers of staff members are using instant messaging (IM) in sending business messages. We realize that IM often saves time and gets you fast responses, and we are prepared to continue to allow its use, but we have developed some specific procedures that we want you to use to make sure it is safe as well as efficient.

b. An e-mail message inquiring about software: We are interested in your voice recognition software that we understand allows you to dictate and copy text without touching a keyboard. We are interested in answers to a number of questions, such as the cost for a single-user license and perhaps the availability of a free trial version.

c. An e-mail message announcing a training program: For some time we have been investigating the possibility of conducting in-house leadership training courses for interested staff members.

d. An e-mail message introducing a new manager: This is a message to bring you good news. You will be pleased to learn that our long wait is over. After going without a chief for many weeks, we are finally able to welcome our new manager, Kristi Bostock, who comes to us from our Atlanta office. Please welcome her.

7.6 Writing Improvement Exercises: Opening Paragraphs (Objs. 1, 2)

The following opening paragraphs are wordy and indirect. After reading each paragraph, identify the main idea. Then, write an opening sentence that is more direct.

a. Our management team would like to find additional ways to improve employee motivation through recognition and reward programs. The current programs do not seem to generate an appropriate level of motivation. Because we need input from employees, we will be conducting an extensive study of all employees. But we will begin with focus groups of selected employees, and you have been selected to be part of the first focus group.

b. Customer service is an integral part of our business. That's why I was impressed when three of you came to me to ask if you might attend a seminar called "Customer Satisfaction Strategies." I understand the seminar will take place March 15 and will require you to miss a full day of work. This memo is to inform the staff that Ellen Tucker, Ryan Ho, and Sal Avila will be gone March 15 to attend the conference on customer service and satisfaction.

7.7 Writing Improvement Exercises: Bulleted and Numbered Lists (Obj. 2)

a. Use the following wordy instructions to compose a concise bulleted vertical list with an introductory statement:

To write information for a Web site, there are three important tips to follow. For one thing, you should make the formatting as simple as possible. Another thing you must do is ensure the use of strong visual prompts. Last but not least, you should limit directions that are not needed.

b. Revise the following wordy paragraph into an introduction with a list. Should you use bullets or numbers?

Producing excellent digital prints that equal what you see on your computer monitor is the most frustrating aspect of digital photography. You don't have to be frustrated, however. If you follow three steps, you can improve your prints immensely. I recommend that you first calibrate your screen. You should use the Pantone Spyder to do that. Next you should image edit your photo so that your image looks natural and balanced. The final step involves configuring your printer and using the correct type of paper.

c. Revise the following wordy information into a concise bulleted list with category headings:

Our attorney made a recommendation that we consider several things to avoid litigation in regard to sexual harassment. The first thing he suggested was that we take steps regarding the establishment of an unequivocal written policy prohibiting sexual harassment within our organization. The second thing we should do is make sure training sessions are held for supervisors regarding a proper work environment. Finally, some kind of official procedure for employees to lodge complaints is necessary. This procedure should include investigation of complaints.

7.8 Request Memo: Redesigning the Company Web Site (Obj. 4)

You are part of the newly formed Committee on Web Site Redesign. Its function is to look into the possible redesign of your company Web site. Some managers think that the site is looking a bit dated. The committee delegates you to ask Cole Prewarski, Web master and manager, some questions. The committee wonders whether he has done any usability tests on the current site. The committee wants to know how much a total Web redesign might cost. It also would like to know about the cost of a partial redesign.

Someone wanted to know whether animation, sound, or video could be added and wondered if Cole would recommend doing so. Someone else thought that the timing of a redesign might be important. The committee asks you to add other questions to your memo. Invite Cole to a meeting April 6. Assume that he knows about the committee.

Your Task. Write a hard-copy memo or an e-mail to Cole Prewarski requesting answers to several questions and inviting him to a meeting.

7.9 Request E-Mail: Choosing a Holiday Plan (Obj. 4)

E-Mail

In the past your company offered all employees 11 holidays, starting with New Year's Day in January and proceeding through Christmas Day the following December. Other companies offer similar holiday schedules. In addition, your company has given all employees one floating holiday. That day was determined by a companywide vote. As a result, all employees had the same day off. Now, however, management is considering a new plan that involves a floating holiday that each employee may choose. Selections, however, would be subject to staffing needs within individual departments. If two people wanted the same day, the employee with the most seniority would have the day off.

Your Task. As a member of the Human Resources staff, write an e-mail to employees asking them to choose between continuing the current companywide uniform floating holiday or instituting a new plan for an individual floating holiday. Be sure to establish an end date.

© Bob Daemmrich / PhotoEdit

7.10 Request E-Mail: Should We Plan a Team Retreat? (Obj. 4)

E-Mail

Tiptoeing gingerly across a wobbling jerrybuilt bridge of slender planks stretched between two boxes, the chief financial officer of Wells Fargo completed his task. Cheers greeted Howard Atkins as he reached the other side with a final lunge. His team of senior financial executives applauded their leader, who had made it across the bridge without falling off.

Atkins had pulled together a group of 73 financial executives, risk managers, accountants, and group presidents for team-building exercises on the sun-drenched lawns of a luxury hotel in Sonoma, California. The three-day retreat also provided conventional business meetings with reports and presentations. He credits double-digit gains in Wells Fargo income and earnings in large part to the bank's people programs. "Success is more often than not a function of execution, and execution is really about people, so we invest pretty heavily in our people."

For his company's team-building exercises, Atkins chose low-stress challenges such as balancing on planks, building tents blindfolded, and stepping through complex webs of ropes. But other companies use whitewater rafting, rock walls, treetop rope bridges, and even fire pits as metaphors for the business world.

Your boss at BancFirst saw the news about Wells Fargo and is intrigued. He is understandably dubious about whether team building could result from a retreat. However, he is interested because he believes that the widespread use of electronic technology is reducing personal contact. He asks you to have the Human Resources Department investigate.[17]

Your Task. As assistant to the president, draft an e-mail to Charlotte Evers, manager, Human Resources. Ask her to investigate the possibility of a retreat for BancFirst. Your message should include many questions for her to answer. Include an end date and a reason.

7.11 Request E-Mail or Memo: Smokers vs. Nonsmokers (Obj. 4)

E-Mail

The city of Milwaukee has mandated that employers "shall adopt, implement, and maintain a written smoking policy which shall contain a prohibition against smoking in restrooms and infirmaries." Employers must also "maintain a nonsmoking area of not less than two thirds of the seating capacity in cafeterias, lunchrooms, and employee lounges, and make efforts to work out disputes between smokers and nonsmokers."

Your Task. As Lindsay English, director of Human Resources, write an e-mail or memo to all department managers of Imperial Foods, a large food products company. Announce the new restriction, and tell the managers that you want them to set up departmental committees to mediate any smoking conflicts before complaints surface. Explain why this is a good policy.

7.12 Response E-Mail or Memo: Enforcing Smoking Ban (Obj. 5)

E-Mail

As manager of Accounting Services for Imperial Foods, you must respond to Ms. English's memo in the preceding activity. You could have called Ms. English, but you prefer to have a permanent record of this message. You are having difficulty enforcing the smoking ban in restrooms. Only one men's room serves your floor, and 9 of your 27 male employees are smokers. You have already received complaints, and you see no way to enforce the ban in the restrooms. You have also noticed that smokers are taking longer breaks than other employees. Smokers complain that they need more time because they must walk to an outside area. Smokers are especially unhappy when the weather is cold, rainy, or snowy. Moreover, smokers huddle near the building entrances, creating a negative impression for customers and visitors. Your committee members can find no solutions; in fact, they have become polarized in their meetings to date. You need help from a higher authority.

Your Task. Write an e-mail or memo to Ms. English appealing for solutions. Perhaps she should visit your department.

7.13 Response E-Mail or Memo: Office Romance Off Limits? (Obj. 5)

E-Mail   **Team**   **Web**

Where can you find the hottest singles scene today? Some would say in your workplace. Because people are working long hours and have little time for outside contacts, relationships often develop at work. Estimates suggest that one third to one half of all romances start at work. Your boss is concerned about possible problems resulting from relationships at work. What happens if a relationship between a superior and subordinate results in perceived favoritism? What happens if a relationship results in a nasty breakup? Your boss would like to simply ban all relationships among employees. But that's not

likely to work. He asks you, his assistant, to learn what guidelines could be established regarding office romances.

Your Task. Using professional databases or the Web, look for articles on the topic of workplace romance. From various articles, select four or five suggestions that you could make to your boss in regard to protecting an employer. Why is it necessary for a company to protect itself? Discuss your findings and reactions with your team. Individually or as a group, submit your findings and reactions in a well-organized, easy-to-read e-mail or memo to your boss (your instructor). You may list main points from the articles you research, but use your own words to write the message.

7.14 Response E-Mail or Memo: Rescheduling Interviews to Accommodate a Traveling Boss (Obj. 5)

E-Mail

Your boss, Michael Kaufman, has scheduled three appointments to interview applicants for the position of project manager. All of these appointments are for Thursday, May 5. However, he now must travel to Atlanta that week. He asks you to reschedule all the appointments for one week later. He also wants a brief background summary for each candidate.

Although frustrated, you call each person and are lucky to arrange these times. Saul Salazar, who has been a project manager for nine years with Summit Enterprises, agrees to come at 10:30 a.m. Kaitlyn Grindell, who is a systems analyst and a consultant to many companies, will come at 11:30. Camille Montano, who has an MA degree and six years of experience as senior project coordinator at High Point Industries, will come at 9:30 a.m. You are wondering whether Mr. Kaufman forgot to include Bertha Ho, operations personnel officer, in these interviews. Ms. Ho usually is part of the selection process.

Your Task. Write an e-mail or memo to Mr. Kaufman including all the information he needs.

7.15 Response E-Mail or Memo: Proper Dress for Businesspeople in Saudi Arabia (Obj. 5)

E-Mail   **Intercultural**   **Team**
Web

The Air Force's highest ranking female fighter pilot, Lt. Col. Martha McSally, was unhappy about being required to wear neck-to-toe robes in Saudi Arabia when she was off base. She filed a federal lawsuit seeking to overturn the policy that requires female servicewomen to wear such conservative clothing when they are off base.

After seeing an article about this in the newspaper, your boss began to worry about sending female engineers to Saudi Arabia. Your company has been asked to submit a proposal to develop telecommunications within that country, and some of the company's best staff members are female. If your company wins the contract, it will undoubtedly need women to be in Saudi Arabia to complete the project. Because your boss knows little about the country, he asks you, his assistant, to do some research to find out what is appropriate business dress.

Your Task. Visit two or three Web sites and learn about dress expectations in Saudi Arabia. Is Western-style clothing acceptable for men? For women? Are there any clothing taboos? Should guest workers be expected to dress like natives? In teams discuss your findings. Individually or collectively, prepare a memo or e-mail addressed to LaDane Williams, your boss. Summarize your most significant findings.

 Interactive Learning @ www.meguffey.com

7.16 Response E-Mail: Reaching Consensus Regarding Casual-Dress Policy (Obj. 5)

E-Mail Team

Casual dress in professional offices has been coming under attack. Your boss, Joshua Watkins, received the e-mail shown in Figure 7.5 on page 186. He thinks it would be a good assignment for his group of management trainees to help him respond to that message. He asks your team to research answers to the first five questions in CEO Timothy Vanderbeck's message. He doesn't expect you to answer the final question, but any information you can supply to the first questions would help him shape a response.

Vanderbeck & Associates is a public CPA firm with a staff of 120 CPAs, bookkeepers, managers, and support personnel. Located in downtown Pittsburgh, the plush offices in One Oxford Center overlook the Allegheny River and the North Shore. The firm performs general accounting and audit services as well as tax planning and preparation. Accountants visit clients in the field and also entertain them in the downtown office.

Your Task. Decide whether the entire team will research each question in Figure 7.5 or whether team members will be assigned certain questions. Collect information, discuss it, and reach consensus on what you will report to Mr. Watkins. Write a concise, one-page response from your team. Your goal is to inform, not persuade. Remember that you represent management, not students or employees.

7.17 Procedure Memo: Standardizing Purchase Requests (Obj. 6)

The Purchasing Department handles purchases for a growing family company. Some purchase orders arrive on the proper forms, but others are memos or handwritten notes that are barely legible. The owner wants to establish a standard procedure for submitting purchase requests. The purchase requests must now be downloaded from the company intranet. To provide the fastest service, employees should fill out the purchase request. Employees must include everything: date, quantities, catalog numbers, complete descriptions, complete vendor mailing address and contact information, delivery requirements, and shipping methods (usually f.o.b.). The Purchasing Department should be sent the original, and a copy should be kept. An important step in the new procedure is approval by the budget manager on the request form.

Your Task. As assistant manager in the Purchasing Department, write a hard-copy memo to all employees informing them of the new procedure.

7.18 Procedure E-Mail or Memo: Rules for Cell Phone Use in Sales Reps' Cars (Obj. 6)

E-Mail Team Web

As one of the managers of Futura, a hair care and skin products company, you are alarmed at a newspaper article you just saw. A stockbroker for Smith Barney was making cold calls on his personal cell phone while driving. His car hit and killed a motorcyclist. The brokerage firm was sued and accused of contributing to an accident by encouraging employees to use cell phones while driving. To avoid the risk of paying huge damages awarded by an emotional jury, the brokerage firm offered the victim's family a $500,000 settlement.

You begin to worry, knowing that your company has provided its 75 sales representatives with wireless phones to help them keep in touch with the home base while they are in the field. At the next management meeting, other members agreed that you should draft a message detailing some wireless phone safety rules for your sales reps. On the Web you learned that anyone with a cell phone should get to know its features, including speed dial, automatic memory,

and redial. Another suggestion involved using a hands-free device. Management members decided to purchase these for every sales rep and have the devices available within one month. In positioning the cell phone in a car, it should be within easy reach. It should be where you can grab it without removing your eyes from the road. If you get an incoming call at an inconvenient time, your voice mail should be allowed to pick up the call. You should never talk, of course, during hazardous driving conditions, such as rain, sleet, snow, and ice.

Taking notes or looking up phone numbers is dangerous when driving. You want to warn sales reps not to get into dangerous situations by reading (such as an address book) or writing (such as taking notes) while driving.

The more you think about it, the more you think that sales reps should not use their wireless phones while the car is moving. They really should pull over. But you know that would be hard to enforce.

Your Task. Individually or in teams write a memo or e-mail to Futura sales reps outlining company suggestions (or should they be rules?) for safe wireless phone use in cars. You may wish to check the Web for additional safety ideas. Try to suggest reader benefits in this message. How is safety beneficial to sales reps? The message is from you acting as operations manager.

7.19 Procedure E-Mail or Memo: Revising a Rambling Security Memo (Obj. 6)

E-Mail Web

After a recent frightening experience, your boss, Olivia Solano-Benoit, realized that she must draft a memo about office security. Here's why she's concerned. A senior associate, Lucy Bonner, was working overtime cleaning up overdue reports. At about 9 p.m. she heard the office door open, but the intruder quickly left when he found that someone was in the office. Your boss hurriedly put together the following memo to be distributed to office managers in five branch offices. But she was on her way out of town, and she asked you to revise her draft and have it ready for her approval when she returns. One other thing—she wondered whether you would do online research to find other helpful suggestions. Your boss trusts you to totally revise, if necessary.

Your Task. Conduct a database or Web search to look for reasonable office security suggestions. Study the following memo. Then improve its organization, clarity, conciseness, correctness, and readability. Don't be afraid to do a total overhaul. Bulleted points are a must, and check the correctness, too. Your boss is no Ms. Grammar! Be sure to add an appropriate closing.

```
DATE:      Current
TO:        Branch Managers
FROM:      Olivia Solano-Benoit, Vice President
SUBJECT:   Staying Safe in the Office
```

Office security is a topic we have not talked enough about. I was terrified recently when a senior associate, who was working late, told me she heard the front door of the branch office open and she thought she heard a person enter. When she called out, the person apparently left. This frightening experience reminded me there are several things that each branch can do to improve it's office security. The following are a few simple things, but we will talk more about this at our next quarterly meeting (June 8?). Please come with additional ideas.

If an office worker is here early or late, then it is your responsibility to talk with them about before and after hours security. When someone comes in early it is not smart to open the doors until most of the rest of the staff arrive. Needless to say, employees working overtime should make sure the door is locked and they should not open there office doors after hours to people they don't know, especially if you are in the office alone. Dark offices are especially attractive to thieves with valuable equipment.

Many branches are turning off lights at points of entry and parking areas to conserve energy. Consider changing this policy or installing lights connected to motion detectors, which is an inexpensive (and easy!) way to discourage burglars and intruders. I also think that "cash-free" decals are a good idea because they make thieves realize that not much is in this office to take. These signs may discourage breaking and entering. On the topic of lighting, we want to be sure that doors and windows that are secluded and not visible to neighbors or passersby is illuminated.

We should also beware of displaying any valuable equipment or other things. When people walk by, they should not be able to look in and see expensive equipment. Notebook computers and small portable equipment is particularly vulnerable at night. It should be locked up. In spite of the fact that most of our branches are guarded by FirstAlert, I'm not sure all branches are displaying the decals prominently—especially on windows and doors. We want people to know that our premises are electronically protected.

7.20 How to Write Clear Procedures and Instructions (Obj. 6)

Go to www.meguffey.com and click "Writing Resources." You will find a supplement devoted to writing instructions. It includes colorful examples and links to Web sites with relevant examples of real sets of instructions from business Web sites.

Your Task. Locate "How to Write Instructions" and study all of its sections. Then choose one of the following application activities: A-5, "Revising the Instructions for an Imported Fax Machine," or A-6, "Evaluation: Instructions for Dealing With Car Emergencies." Complete the assignment and submit it to your instructor.

7.21 Confirmation Memo or E-Mail: Did I Hear This Correctly? (Obj. 7)

> E-Mail

At lunch one day you had a stimulating discussion with Jayne Moneysmith, an attorney specializing in employment risk management. You are a manager with a growing brokerage firm that employs more than 250 employees. All employees except top managers are "at will" employees without employment contracts. Your company has an extensive set of procedures and policies regarding sexual harassment. But it has no e-mail policies.

Ms. Moneysmith told you that in certain instances e-mail transmissions can constitute hostile-environment sexual harassment. Although an e-mail message is not a "verbal statement" uttered by an alleged harasser face to face, it can cross the legal line. If the message is severe and adversely affects the receiver's work environment, the message could constitute actionable sexual harassment. Even deleted messages can come back to haunt the company in employment discrimination cases. E-mails leave a "meta data" trail revealing attachments, dates and times of edits and transmissions, file size, conversation threads, and document file paths. These attributes ensure that any inappropriate behavior conducted via an employer's digital technology will leave a permanent record. She said that "at will" employees who send inappropriate messages or pornographic materials can legally be terminated if the circumstances suggest that an outright dismissal is appropriate.[18]

Your Task. You would like to report Ms. Moneysmith's remarks at the next management council meeting. Before you do, however,

you want to be sure that you heard her accurately. Write a memo or e-mail to Ms. Moneysmith condensing and confirming the major points she covered.

7.22 Confirmation Memo: A Change in Vacation Plans (Obj. 6)

As Joel Jordan, senior marketing coordinator, you had a vacation planned for May 1 through May 15. But yesterday your wife suggested changing the dates to April 1 through April 15 so that you and she could visit the Dogwood Festival in Atlanta. You are not crazy about dogwoods, but you would like to visit Atlanta and perhaps keep on going for a quick trip to Florida. Perhaps you could change your vacation dates. Unfortunately, you remember that you are scheduled to represent your company at a Las Vegas trade show April 10 through April 12. But maybe Bridget Harris would fill in for you and make the presentation of the company's newest product, the Blutooth Car Kit, which enables hands-free driver telephoning.

You see your boss, Hal Hernandez, in the hall and decide to ask whether you can change your vacation to April 1 through April 15. To your surprise, he agrees to the new dates. He also assures you that he will ask Bridget Harris to make the presentation and encourage her to give a special trade show demonstration to Exell Corporation, which you believe should be targeted.

Your Task. Back in your office, you begin to worry. What if Hal forgets about your conversation? You can't afford to take that chance. Write a confirmation memo to Hal Hernandez, vice president in Marketing. Because you want your note to show your gratitude, send a hard-copy memo. Summarize the necessary facts and also convey your appreciation. Establish an end date and provide a reason.

7.23 Confirmation E-Mail: Negotiating a Cool Deal With a Chinese Supplier (Obj. 7)

> E-Mail   Intercultural

Your company, Pioneer Cable, seeks a cable assembly supplier in China. A few representatives of Pioneer just had a videoconference with AmRep China, a company specializing in finding Chinese manufacturers for American companies. Terrance Shaw, CEO and son of the owner, has been corresponding with Michael Zhu, who represents AmRep. The videoconference went well, but Mr. Shaw, the owner, wants Terrance to confirm in writing what was discussed. Terrance, better known as "Terry" around the office, is an upbeat, gadget-loving young executive who would rather be using IM than writing e-mail. He manages to put together a rough draft, but he asks you to help him improve it.

Your Task. Revise the following e-mail message to make it more formal, readable, and interculturally acceptable.

To: Michael Zhu <Michael.zhu@AmRep.com>
From: Terrance Shaw <tshaw@pioneercable.com>
Subject: Videoconference Info
Cc:

Hey, Michael, it was great seeing and talking with you and your crew in the September 14 videoconference. Everyone here at Pioneer Cable is totally stoked about having AmRep China hook us up with a Chinese cable assembly supplier. We're sure you'll turn over every stone to find us a terrific supplier!

Because of all the heavy accents, it was a little hard to understand some speakers in our videoconference, so let me go over some things we agreed on. AmRep China is going to look for a cable assembly supplier for Pioneer. Right? You'll make no bones about getting us the best price/quality ratio you can

> Interactive Learning @ www.meguffey.com

possibly manage. This is obviously easier for you to do than for us to do because you will be communicating in Chinese.

Unless I misunderstood, I heard one of your staff say that there would be continuous data feedback on quality control and that your company would provide technical conformance to the specifications that we submit. Is that right? There was also quite a discussion on ISO 9001:2000 standards and procedures, and you said that AmRep would definitely find a supplier that adheres to those standards. This is super important to us. I believe I also heard that AmRep would help us manage production and delivery schedules with our Chinese supplier.

The owner says that we must have confirmation of these points before we can continue our negotiations. Hope to hear from you soon!

Terry
CEO, Pioneer Cable
E-Mail: tshaw@pioneercable.com
Phone: (814) 739-2901
FAX: (814) 739-3445

7.24 Confirmation Memo: Verifying a Job Severance Package (Obj. 6)

You are congratulating yourself on landing a fantastic job. Terrific title. Terrific salary. Terrific boss. You were even smart enough to talk about an exit package during your interview. You had read an article in *The Wall Street Journal* suggesting that the best time to win a generous departure deal is before you accept a position.

Because you knew your skills were in high demand for this position and because you would be giving up a good position, you wanted to know what the typical severance package involved. What would you receive if this job disappeared through a merger or downturn in the economy or similar unforeseen event? The hiring manager told you that the standard severance package includes one week's salary for every year of service, outplacement counseling for up to six months, accrued but unused vacation pay, and extended medical coverage. After a little bargaining, you were able to increase the severance pay to two weeks' salary for each year of service and medical insurance for you and your family up to one year or until you found another position.

Then you begin to worry. You didn't get any of this in writing.

Your Task. You decide to write a confirmation memo outlining the severance package discussed in your interview. *The Wall Street*

Journal says that your memo becomes an enforceable contract. Write a hard-copy memo to Jefferson Walker, operations manager, describing your understanding of what you were promised.[19] If Mr. Walker doesn't agree with any of the details, ask him to respond immediately. Show your enthusiasm for the job, and keep the tone of your message upbeat. Add any necessary details.

7.25 Response Memo or E-Mail: What Is a FICO Credit Rating Score? (Obj. 5)

For years the credit industry hushed up a consumer's credit score. Credit bureaus would reveal a consumer's credit rating only to a lender when an applicant wanted a loan. Customers could not learn their scores unless credit was denied. Now, all that has changed. Using the Internet, consumers can check their credit files and even obtain specific credit scores, which are key factors in obtaining loans, renting property, and protecting against identity theft. Although the three national credit bureaus (Equifax, Experian, and TransUnion) may use different scoring systems, many lenders now mention FICO scores as the favored ranking to estimate the risk involved in an individual's loan application.

Your Task. As an intern in architect Eric Larson's office, you must do some Internet research. Mr. Larson recently had to reject two potentially lucrative house construction jobs because the clients received low FICO scores from their credit bureaus. They could not qualify for construction loans. He wants you to learn exactly what "FICO" means and how this score is determined. Mr. Larson also wants to know how consumers can raise their FICO scores. Go to **http://www.myfico.com** and study its information. (Use a search engine with the term "My Fico" if this URL fails.) Summarize your findings in your own words in a well-organized, concise memo or e-mail addressed to Eric Larson at *elarson@arnet.com*. Use bulleted lists for some of the information.

Video Resources

Video Library 1

Smart E-Mail Messages and Memos Advance Your Career

Watch this chapter-specific video for a demonstration of how to use e-mail skillfully and safely. You will better understand the writing process in relation to composing messages. You will also pick up tips for writing messages that advance your career instead of sinking it.

Grammar and Mechanics C.L.U.E. Review 7

Apostrophes and Other Punctuation

Review Guides 31–38 about apostrophes and other punctuation in Appendix A: Grammar and Mechanics Guide (Competent Language Usage Essentials), beginning on page A-14. On a separate sheet, revise the following sentences to correct errors in the use of apostrophes and other punctuation. For each error that you locate, write the guide number that reflects this usage. The more you recognize the reasons, the better you will learn these punctuation guidelines. If a sentence is correct, write *C*. When you finish, check your answers on page Key-2.

Example: We needed the boss signature before we could mail the report.

Revision: We needed the **boss's** signature before we could mail the report. [Guide 32]

1. All employees cars must display a company parking sticker.

2. Our companys health benefits are available immediately.

3. Will you please send me your latest print catalog.

4. The manager questioned John traveling first class on a recent business trip.

5. Is the bank open until 6 p.m.

6. You must replace the ink cartridge see page 8 in the manual, before printing.

7. Justin wondered whether all sales managers databases needed to be updated.

8. (Direct quotation) Health care costs said the CEO will increase substantially this year.

9. In just two months time, we expect to interview five candidates for the opening.

10. The abbreviation GMT means "Greenwich Mean Time," doesn't it.

Chapter 8

Positive Letters and Messages

OBJECTIVES

After studying this chapter, you should be able to

1. Explain why business letters are important and how the three phases of the 3-x-3 writing process relate to creating successful business letters.

2. Analyze the structure and characteristics of good business letters.

3. Write letters that request information or action.

4. Write letters that make direct claims.

5. Write letters that reply directly.

6. Write letters that make adjustments.

7. Write special messages that convey kindness and goodwill.

8. Modify international letters to accommodate other cultures.

Communicating at Work Part 1

Ben & Jerry's Uses Positive Letters to Sweeten Relations With Customers

America's love affair with numbingly rich ice cream may have finally plateaued. Health and weight worries have apparently cut the break-neck growth of superpremium ice creams. However, Ben & Jerry's Homemade, premier purveyor of the superpremiums, remains one of the country's most visible ice cream companies.

In growing from a 12-flavor miniparlor in Burlington, Vermont, into a Fortune 500 company called a "national treasure," Ben & Jerry's has been showered with publicity. The flood of press notices flowed partly from its rapid ascent and its funky flavor hits such as "Chubby Hubby," "Half Baked Carb Karma," "New York Super Fudge Chunk," "Phish Food," and "Dilbert's World Totally Nuts" (butter almond ice cream with roasted hazelnuts, praline pecans, and white fudge-coated almonds). Of even greater media interest was the New Age business philosophy of founders Ben Cohen and Jerry Greenfield. Unlike most entrepreneurs, their aim was to build a successful business but, at the same time, be a force for social change.

Some time ago Ben and Jerry resigned their symbolic positions as brand icons after the company was purchased by the Anglo-Dutch mega-conglomerate Unilever. Despite the change in ownership, Ben & Jerry's continues to try to operate in a way that improves local and global quality of life. The company strives to balance economic, product, and social goals on the way to a sustainable business.

Although no longer locally owned, Ben & Jerry's is a visible company with a popular national product and a strong social image. It naturally generates a good deal of correspondence. Customer letters typically fall into three categories: (a) "fan" mail, (b) information requests, and (c) claims. Fan mail contains praise and testimonials: "Tried the new Cherry Garcia Frozen Yogurt and . . . I want to go to Vermont and shake your sticky hands." Information requests may involve questions about ingredients or food processing. Some letters inquire about Ben & Jerry's position on milk from cloned cows or eggs from caged chickens. Claim letters generally contain a complaint and require immediate response. Responding to customer

© Lon C. Diehl / Photo Edit

letters in all three categories is a critical element in maintaining customer goodwill and market position for Ben & Jerry's.[1] You will learn more about this case on page 218.

Critical Thinking

- Have you ever written a letter or sent an e-mail to a company? What might motivate you to do so? Would you expect a response?
- If a company such as Ben & Jerry's receives a fan letter complimenting products or service, is it necessary to respond?
- Why is it important for companies to answer claim (complaint) letters immediately?

http://www.benjerry.com

Understanding the Power of Business Letters and the Process of Writing

Letters, such as those sent by Ben & Jerry's to its customers, are a primary channel of communication for delivering messages *outside* an organization. This chapter concentrates on positive, straightforward letters through which we conduct everyday business and convey goodwill to outsiders. Such letters go to suppliers, government agencies, other businesses, and, most important, customers. The letters to customers receive a high priority because these messages encourage product feedback, project a favorable image of the company, and promote future business.

LEARNING OBJECTIVE 1
Explain why business letters are important and how the three phases of the 3-x-3 writing process relate to creating successful business letters.

Publisher Malcolm Forbes understood the power of business letters when he said, "A good business letter can get you a job interview, get you off the hook, or get you money. It's totally asinine to blow your chances of getting *whatever* you want—with a business letter that turns people off instead of turning them on."[2] This chapter teaches you what turns readers on. We will begin by discussing the importance of business letters, reviewing the writing process for business letters, and analyzing the structure and characteristics of letters. Then you will learn to apply this information in writing positive letters that request information, require action, and make straightforward claims. You will also learn to grant claims, comply with requests, and compose goodwill messages. Finally, you will study how to modify your letters to accommodate other cultures.

Why Business Letters Are Still Necessary

Even with the new media available today, a letter remains one of the most powerful and effective ways to get your message across. Although e-mail is incredibly successful for both internal and external communication, many important messages still call for letters. Business letters are necessary when (a) a permanent record is required; (b) confidentiality is paramount; (c) formality and sensitivity are essential; and (d) a persuasive, well-considered presentation is important.

Business Letters Produce a Permanent Record. Many business transactions require a permanent record. Business letters fulfill this function. For example, when a company enters into an agreement with another company, business letters introduce the agreement and record decisions and points of understanding. Although telephone conversations and e-mail messages may be exchanged, important details are generally recorded in business letters that are kept in company files. Business letters deliver contracts, explain terms, exchange ideas, negotiate agreements, answer vendor questions, and maintain customer relations. Business letters are important for any business transaction that requires a permanent written record.

Business Letters Can Be Confidential. Carefree use of e-mail was once a sign of sophistication. Today, however, communicators know how dangerous it is to entrust confidential and sensitive information to digital channels. A writer in *The New York Times* recently said, "Despite the sneering term *snail mail,* plain old letters are the form of long-distance communication least likely to be intercepted, misdirected, forwarded, retrieved, or otherwise inspected by someone you didn't have in mind."[3]

Business Letters Convey Formality and Sensitivity. Business letters presented on company stationery carry a sense of formality and importance not possible with e-mail. They look important. They carry a nonverbal message saying the writer considered the message to be so significant and the receiver so prestigious that the writer cared enough to write a real message. Business letters deliver more information than e-mail because they are written on stationery that usually is printed with company information such as logos, addresses, titles, and contact details.

Business Letters Deliver Persuasive, Well-Considered Messages. When a business communicator must be persuasive and can't do it in person, a business letter is more effective than other communication channels. Letters can persuade people to change their actions, adopt new beliefs, make donations, contribute their time, and try new products. Direct-mail letters remain a powerful tool to promote services and products, boost online and retail traffic, and solicit contributions. Business letters represent deliberate communication. They give you a chance to think through what you want to say, organize your thoughts, and write a well-considered argument. You will learn more about writing persuasive and marketing messages in Chapter 9.

Applying the 3-x-3 Writing Process to Create Successful Letters

In this book we will divide letters into these groups: (a) routine letters communicating straightforward requests, replies, and goodwill messages, covered in this chapter; (b) persuasive messages including sales pitches, covered in Chapter 9; and (c) negative messages delivering refusals and bad news, covered in Chapter 10.

Although routine letters may be short and straightforward, they benefit from attention to the composition process. "At the heart of effective writing is the ability to organize a series of thoughts," says writing expert and executive Max Messmer. Taking the time to think through what you want to achieve and how the audience will react makes writing much easier.[4] Here is a quick review of the 3-x-3 writing process to help you think through its application to routine letters.

Phase 1: Analysis, Anticipation, and Adaptation. Before writing, spend a few moments analyzing your task and audience. Your key goals here are (a) determining your purpose, (b) visualizing the audience, and (c) anticipating the reaction to your message. Too often, letter writers start a message without enough preparation.

Alice Blachly, a veteran letter writer from Ben & Jerry's, realized the problem. She said, "If I'm having trouble with a letter and it's not coming out right, it's almost always because I haven't thought through exactly what I want to say."[5] In the Ben & Jerry's letter shown in

FIGURE 8.1 Ben & Jerry's Reply to Customer Inquiry

1 Prewriting

Analyze: The purpose of this letter is to build goodwill and promote Ben & Jerry's products.

Anticipate: The reader is young, enthusiastic, and eager to hear from Ben & Jerry's. She will appreciate personalized comments.

Adapt: Use short sentences, cheerful thoughts, and plenty of references to the reader and to her club, school, and request.

2 Writing

Research: Reread the customer's letter. Decide which items to enclose and locate them.

Organize: Open directly with a positive response. Explain the enclosed items. Find ways to make the reader feel a special connection with Ben & Jerry's.

Compose: Write the first draft quickly. Realize that revision will improve it.

3 Revising

Revise: Revise the message striving for a warm tone. Use the receiver's name. Edit long paragraphs and add bulleted items.

Proofread: Check the address of the receiver. Decide whether to hyphenate *cofounder* and how to punctuate quotations.

Evaluate: Consider how you would feel if you received this letter.

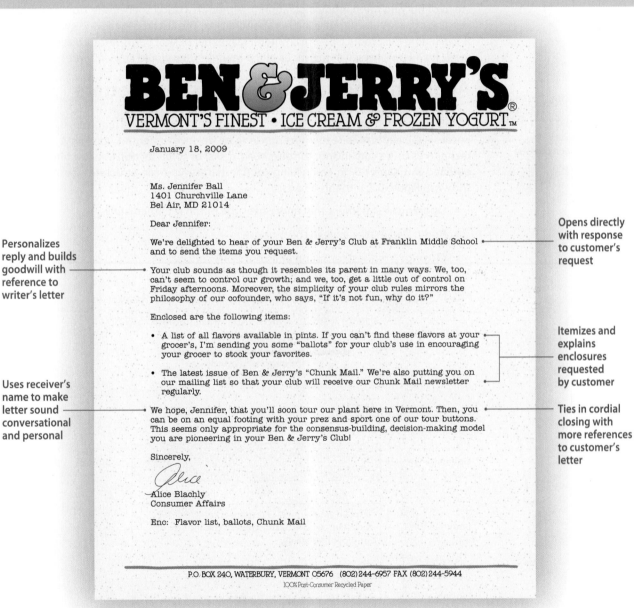

BEN & JERRY'S®
VERMONT'S FINEST • ICE CREAM & FROZEN YOGURT™

January 18, 2009

Ms. Jennifer Ball
1401 Churchville Lane
Bel Air, MD 21014

Dear Jennifer:

[Opens directly with response to customer's request] We're delighted to hear of your Ben & Jerry's Club at Franklin Middle School and to send the items you request.

[Personalizes reply and builds goodwill with reference to writer's letter] Your club sounds as though it resembles its parent in many ways. We, too, can't seem to control our growth; and we, too, get a little out of control on Friday afternoons. Moreover, the simplicity of your club rules mirrors the philosophy of our cofounder, who says, "If it's not fun, why do it?"

Enclosed are the following items:

[Itemizes and explains enclosures requested by customer]
- A list of all flavors available in pints. If you can't find these flavors at your grocer's, I'm sending you some "ballots" for your club's use in encouraging your grocer to stock your favorites.

- The latest issue of Ben & Jerry's "Chunk Mail." We're also putting you on our mailing list so that your club will receive our Chunk Mail newsletter regularly.

[Uses receiver's name to make letter sound conversational and personal] *[Ties in cordial closing with more references to customer's letter]* We hope, Jennifer, that you'll soon tour our plant here in Vermont. Then, you can be on an equal footing with your prez and sport one of our tour buttons. This seems only appropriate for the consensus-building, decision-making model you are pioneering in your Ben & Jerry's Club!

Sincerely,

Alice

Alice Blachly
Consumer Affairs

Enc: Flavor list, ballots, Chunk Mail

P.O. BOX 240, WATERBURY, VERMONT 05676 (802) 244-6957 FAX (802) 244-5944
100% Post-Consumer Recycled Paper

Figure 8.1, Blachly responds to a request from a young Ben & Jerry's customer. Before writing the letter, she thought about the receiver and tried to find a way to personalize what could have been a form letter. Responding to a "fan" letter may seem unnecessary. Research has shown, however, that not responding to a complimentary message may register as rejection.[6]

In Phase 2 of the writing process, gather information, make notes or prepare an outline, and compose the first draft.

Phase 2: Research, Organization, and Composition.

In the second phase, collect information and make a list of the points you wish to cover. For short messages such as an answer to a customer's inquiry, you might jot your notes down on the document you are answering. For longer documents that require formal research, use a cluster diagram or the outlining techniques discussed in Chapter 5. When business letters carry information that won't upset the receiver, you can organize them in the direct manner with the main idea expressed immediately. In Alice Blachly's letter shown in Figure 8.1, she made a scratch outline of the points she wanted to cover before writing.

In Phase 3 of the writing process, revise for clarity, add graphic highlighting if possible, and proofread for correctness.

Phase 3: Revision, Proofreading, and Evaluation.

When you finish the first draft, revise for clarity. The receiver should not have to read the message twice to grasp its meaning. Proofread for correctness. Check for punctuation irregularities, typos, misspelled words, or other mechanical problems. Also be sure to look for ways to create high "skim value." In Figure 8.1 Alice Blachly saw that she could use bullets to highlight two items instead of burying them inside a paragraph. Although a good speller, she wouldn't dream of sending out a letter without using her spell checker. The last step in the 3-x-3 writing process is evaluating the product. Before any letter leaves her desk at Ben & Jerry's, Blachly always re-reads it and puts herself in the shoes of the reader: "How would I feel if I were receiving it?"

Analyzing the Structure of Business Letters

LEARNING OBJECTIVE 2
Analyze the structure and characteristics of good business letters.

The everyday transactions of a business consist mainly of routine requests and responses. Because you expect the reader's response to be positive or neutral, you won't need special techniques to be convincing, to soften bad news, or to be tactful. Use the direct strategy, outlined in Chapter 5. In composing routine letters, you can structure your message, as shown in Figure 8.2, into three parts:

- **Opening:** A statement that announces the purpose immediately
- **Body:** Details that explain the purpose
- **Closing:** A request for action or a courteous conclusion

FIGURE 8.2 Three-Part Structure for Routine Requests and Responses

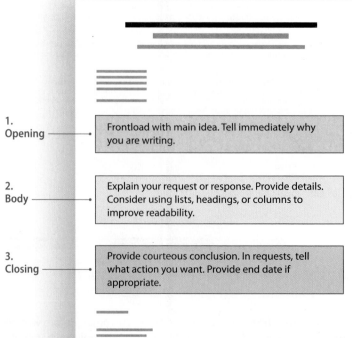

1.
Opening — Frontload with main idea. Tell immediately why you are writing.

2.
Body — Explain your request or response. Provide details. Consider using lists, headings, or columns to improve readability.

3.
Closing — Provide courteous conclusion. In requests, tell what action you want. Provide end date if appropriate.

Frontload in the Opening

You should use the direct strategy for positive, everyday messages. This means developing ideas in a straightforward manner and frontloading the main idea. State immediately why you are writing so that the reader can anticipate and comprehend what follows. Remember, every time a reader begins a message, he or she is thinking, "Why was this sent to me?" "What am I to do?"

Some writers make the mistake of organizing a message as if they were telling a story or solving a problem. They start at the beginning and follow the same sequence in which they thought through the problem. This means reviewing the background, discussing the reasons for action, and then requesting an action. Most business letters, though, are better written "backward." Start with the action desired or the main idea. Don't get bogged down in introductory material, history, justifications, or old-fashioned "business" language. Instead, reveal your purpose immediately. To see the difference, compare the following openers:

Everyday business messages "frontload" by presenting the main idea or purpose immediately.

Indirect Opening

Our company is experiencing difficulty in retaining employees. We also need help in screening job applicants. Our current testing program is unsatisfactory. I understand that you offer employee testing materials, and I have a number of questions to ask.

Direct Opening

Please answer the following questions about your personnel testing materials.

Most simple requests should open immediately with a statement of purpose (*Please answer these questions about . . .*). Occasionally, however, requests may require a sentence or two of explanation or background before the purpose is revealed. What you want to avoid, though, is delaying the purpose of the letter beyond the first paragraph.

Explain in the Body

After a direct opening that tells the reader why you are writing, present details that explain your request or response. This is where your planning pays off, allowing you to structure the information for maximum clarity and readability. Here you should consider using some graphic devices to highlight the details: a numbered or bulleted list, headings, columns, or boldface or italic type.

If you have considerable information, you will want to develop each idea in a separate paragraph with effective transitions to connect them. The important thing to remember is to keep similar ideas together. The biggest problem in business writing is poor organization, and the body of a letter is where that failure becomes apparent.

The body explains the purpose for writing, perhaps using graphic devices to highlight important ideas.

Be Specific and Courteous in the Closing

In the last paragraph of direct letters, readers look for action information: schedules, deadlines, activities to be completed. This is where you tell the reader what to do. If appropriate, include an end date—a date for completion of the action. Giving a reason for establishing the deadline is also a good idea. Research shows that people want to know why they should do something—even if the reason seems obvious. Moreover, people want to be treated courteously (*Please answer these questions before April 1, when we must make a final decision*), not bossed around (*Send this information immediately*).

The closing courteously specifies what the receiver is to do.

Analyzing the Characteristics of Good Business Letters

Although business letters usually deliver straightforward facts, they don't have to sound and look dull or mechanical. At least three characteristics distinguish good business letters: clear content, a tone of goodwill, and correct form.

Clear Content

A clearly written letter separates ideas into paragraphs, uses short sentences and paragraphs, and guides the reader through the ideas with transitional expressions. Moreover, a clear letter

Clear letters feature short sentences and paragraphs, transitional expressions, familiar words, and active-voice verbs.

Spotlight on Communicators

Peggy Foran, a senior vice president at pharmaceutical giant Pfizer Corporation, is known for "pushing the envelope" in practicing good communication with investors. In correspondence, news releases, and proxy statements, Foran insists on clear, basic English. Although accustomed to the dense language of her industry, she admits to confusion. "I do this for a living, and I can't understand a lot of [corporate material] on the first read." She demands clear expression in Pfizer messages. "Transparency is part of our culture. We believe in plain English." To be sure their communication is clear, Pfizer writers are encouraged to put themselves in the shoes of readers, which is good advice for all business communicators.

uses familiar words and active-voice verbs. In other words, it incorporates the writing techniques you studied in Chapters 4, 5, and 6.

But many business letters are not written well. As many as one third of business letters do nothing more than seek clarification of earlier correspondence. Clear letters avoid this problem by answering all the reader's questions or concerns so that no further correspondence is necessary. Some business writers use pretentious, inflated language to make their ideas seem more impressive. You won't sound intelligent, however, if your readers can't understand what you have written. "Being understood the first time through is the most important element of writing for a business audience," said one communication trainer.[7] Clear letters speak the language of the receiver. Analyze your audience and write in words it will understand. This doesn't mean "dumbing down" your remarks. It means taking into consideration what your reader knows about the subject and using appropriate words.

Goodwill Tone

Letters achieve a tone of goodwill by emphasizing a "you" view and reader benefits.

Good letters, however, have to do more than deliver clear messages; they also must build goodwill. Goodwill is a positive feeling the reader has toward an individual or an organization. By analyzing your audience and adapting your message to the reader, your letters can establish an overall tone of goodwill.

To achieve goodwill, look for ways to present the message from the reader's perspective. In other words, emphasize the "you" view and point out benefits to the reader. In addition, be sensitive to words that might suggest gender, racial, age, or disability bias. Finally, frame your ideas positively because they will sound more pleasing and will give more information than negative constructions. For example, which sounds better and gives more information? *We cannot send your order until April 1* or *We can send your order April 1.*

Correct Form

Appropriate letter formats send silent but positive messages.

A business letter conveys silent messages beyond that of its printed words. The letter's appearance and format reflect the writer's carefulness and experience. A short letter bunched at the top of a sheet of paper, for example, looks as though it were prepared in a hurry or by an amateur.

For your letters to make a good impression, you need to select an appropriate format. The block style shown in Figure 8.3 is a popular format. In this style the parts of a letter—dateline, inside address, body, and so on—are set flush left on the page. The letter is arranged on the page so that it is centered and framed by white space. Most letters have margins of 1 to 1 1/2 inches.

Finally, be sure to use ragged-right margins; that is, don't allow your computer to justify the right margin and make all lines end evenly. Unjustified margins improve readability, say experts, by providing visual stops and by making it easier to tell where the next line begins. Although book publishers use justified right margins, as you see on this page, your letters should be ragged right. Study Figure 8.3 for more tips on making your letters look professional. If you have questions about letter forms and formats, see Appendix B.

Direct Requests for Information or Action

LEARNING OBJECTIVE 3
Write letters that request information or action.

The majority of your business letters will involve routine messages organized directly. Before you write any letter, though, consider its costs in terms of your time and workload. Whenever possible, don't write! Instead of asking for information, could you find it yourself? Would a telephone call, e-mail message, instant message, or brief visit to a coworker solve the problem quickly? If not, use the direct pattern to present your request efficiently.

Many of your messages will request information or action. Suppose you have questions about a payroll accounting service your company is considering or you need to ask a customer to supply missing data from an order. If your request involves several questions, you

FIGURE 8.3 Business Letter Formatting—Block Style

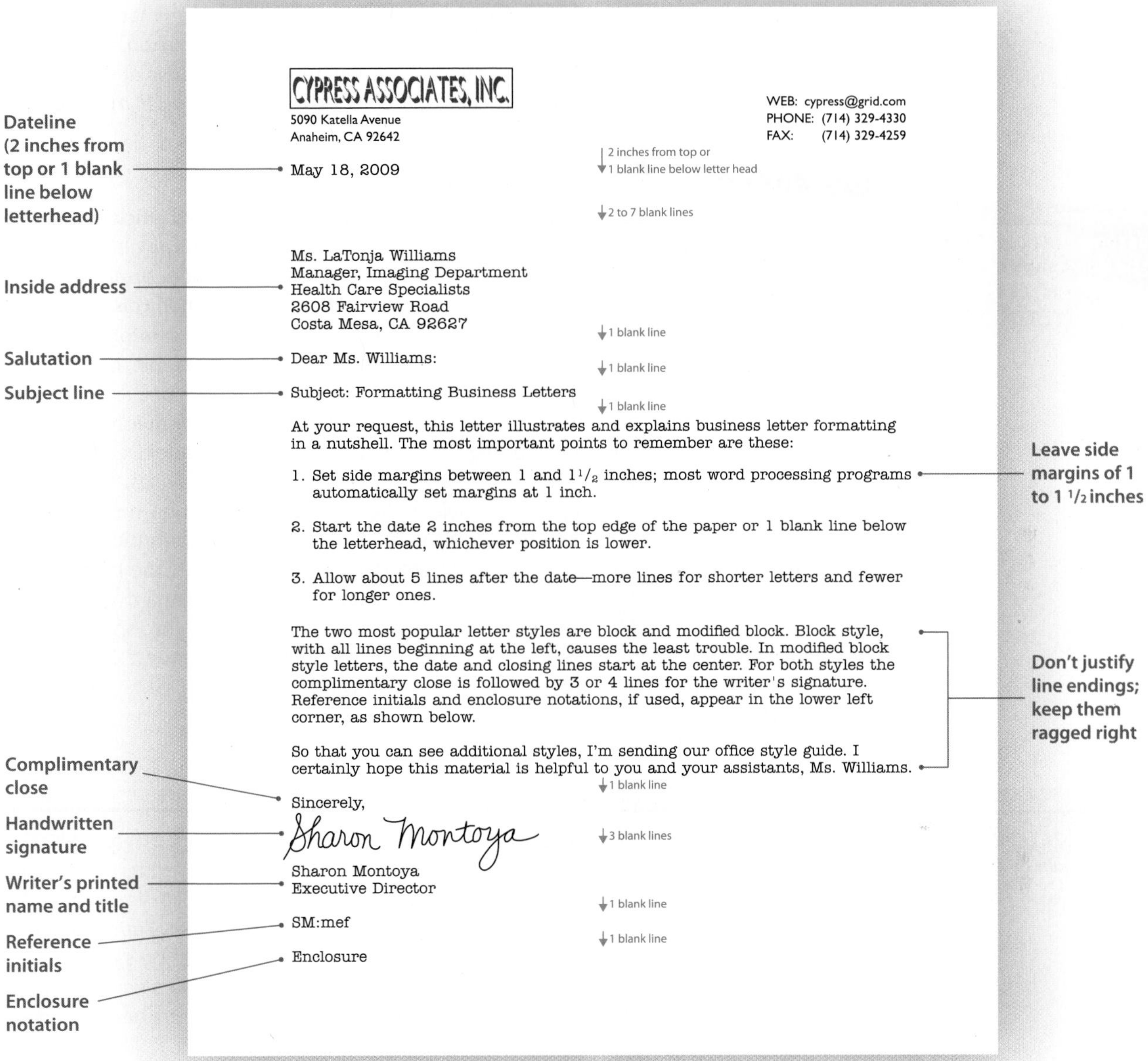

Dateline
(2 inches from top or 1 blank line below letterhead)

Inside address

Salutation

Subject line

Complimentary close

Handwritten signature

Writer's printed name and title

Reference initials

Enclosure notation

CYPRESS ASSOCIATES, INC.
5090 Katella Avenue
Anaheim, CA 92642

WEB: cypress@grid.com
PHONE: (714) 329-4330
FAX: (714) 329-4259

2 inches from top or
1 blank line below letter head

May 18, 2009

2 to 7 blank lines

Ms. LaTonja Williams
Manager, Imaging Department
Health Care Specialists
2608 Fairview Road
Costa Mesa, CA 92627

1 blank line

Dear Ms. Williams:

1 blank line

Subject: Formatting Business Letters

1 blank line

At your request, this letter illustrates and explains business letter formatting in a nutshell. The most important points to remember are these:

1. Set side margins between 1 and 1½ inches; most word processing programs automatically set margins at 1 inch.

2. Start the date 2 inches from the top edge of the paper or 1 blank line below the letterhead, whichever position is lower.

3. Allow about 5 lines after the date—more lines for shorter letters and fewer for longer ones.

The two most popular letter styles are block and modified block. Block style, with all lines beginning at the left, causes the least trouble. In modified block style letters, the date and closing lines start at the center. For both styles the complimentary close is followed by 3 or 4 lines for the writer's signature. Reference initials and enclosure notations, if used, appear in the lower left corner, as shown below.

So that you can see additional styles, I'm sending our office style guide. I certainly hope this material is helpful to you and your assistants, Ms. Williams.

1 blank line

Sincerely,

Sharon Montoya

3 blank lines

Sharon Montoya
Executive Director

1 blank line

SM:mef

1 blank line

Enclosure

Leave side margins of 1 to 1½ inches

Don't justify line endings; keep them ragged right

---

could open with a polite request, such as *Will you please answer the following questions about your payroll service.* Note that although this request sounds like a question, it is actually a disguised command. Because you expect an action rather than a reply, punctuate this polite command with a period instead of a question mark. To avoid this punctuation problem, just omit *Will you* and start with *Please answer.*

Clarify Requests

In the body of your letter, explain your purpose and provide details. If you have questions, express them in parallel form so that you balance them grammatically. To elicit the most information, pose open-ended questions (*What computer lock-down device can you recommend?*) instead of yes-or-no questions (*Do you carry computer lock-down devices?*). If you are asking someone to do something, be sure your tone is polite and undemanding. Remember that your written words cannot be softened by a smile. When possible, focus on benefits to the reader (*To ensure that you receive the exact sweater you want, send us your color choice*).

Questions in direct letters should be parallel (balanced grammatically).

In the closing tell the reader courteously what is to be done. If a date is important, set an end date to take action and explain why. Some careless writers end request letters simply with *Thank you,* forcing the reader to review the contents to determine what is expected and when. You can save the reader time by spelling out the action to be taken. Avoid other overused endings such as *Thank you for your cooperation* (trite), *Thank you in advance for . . .* (trite and presumptuous), and *If you have any questions, do not hesitate to call me* (suggests that you didn't make yourself clear).

Show Appreciation

Request letters maintain a courteous tone, spell out what needs to be done, suggest reader benefits, and make it easy for the reader to respond.

Showing appreciation is always appropriate, but try to do so in a fresh and efficient manner. For example, you could hook your thanks to the end date (*Thanks for returning the questionnaire before May 5, when we will begin tabulation*). You might connect your appreciation to a statement developing reader benefits (*We are grateful for the information you will provide because it will help us serve you better*). You could briefly describe how the information will help you (*I appreciate this information that will enable me to . . .*). When possible, make it easy for the reader to comply with your request (*Note your answers on this sheet and return it in the postage-paid envelope* or *Here is my e-mail address so that you can reach me quickly*).

Analyze the first draft of a direct request letter written by office manager Deana Gomez, shown in Figure 8.4. She wants information about computer security devices, but the first version of her letter is confusing and inefficient. Deana makes a common mistake: starting the message with a description of the problem instead of starting with the main idea. Deana's revision begins more directly. The opening sentence introduces the purpose immediately so that the reader quickly knows why the letter was sent. Deana then provides background information. Most important, she organizes all her requests into specific questions, which are sure to bring a better result than her previous diffuse request. By studying the 3-x-3 writing process outlined in Figure 8.4, you can see the plan Deana followed in improving her letter.

Direct Claims

LEARNING OBJECTIVE 4
Write letters that make direct claims.

In business many things can go wrong—promised shipments are late, warrantied goods fail, or service is disappointing. When you as a customer must write to identify or correct a wrong, the letter is called a *claim*. Straightforward claims are those to which you expect the receiver to agree readily. Even these claims, however, often require a letter. Your first action may be a telephone call or a visit to submit your claim, but you may not be satisfied with the result. Written claims are taken more seriously, and they also establish a record of what happened. Straightforward claims use a direct approach. Claims that require persuasion are presented in Chapter 9.

Open With a Clear Statement

When you, as a customer, have a legitimate claim, you can expect a positive response from a company. Smart businesses want to hear from their customers. They know that retaining a customer is far less costly than recruiting a new customer. That is why you should open a claim letter with a clear statement of the problem or with the action you want the receiver to take. You might expect a replacement, a refund, a new order, credit to your account, correction of a billing error, free repairs, free inspection, or cancellation of an order. When the remedy is obvious, state it immediately (*Please send us 25 Sanyo digital travel alarm clocks to replace the Sanyo analog travel alarm clocks sent in error with our order shipped January 4*). When the remedy is less obvious, you might ask for a change in policy or procedure or simply for an explanation (*Because three of our employees with confirmed reservations were refused rooms September 16 in your hotel, would you please clarify your policy regarding reservations and late arrivals*).

Explain and Justify

In the body of a claim letter, explain the problem and justify your request. Provide the necessary details so that the difficulty can be corrected without further correspondence. Avoid becoming angry or trying to fix blame. Bear in mind that the person reading your letter is seldom responsible for the problem. Instead, state the facts logically, objectively, and

FIGURE 8.4 Direct Request Letter

1 Prewriting

Analyze: The purpose of this letter is to ask specific questions about computer devices.

Anticipate: The audience is expected to be a busy but receptive service representative.

Adapt: Because the reader will react positively, the direct pattern is best.

2 Writing

Research: Determine equipment needs and what questions must be answered.

Organize: Open with a general inquiry. In the body give details; arrange any questions logically. Close by courteously providing a specific deadline.

Compose: Write the first draft.

3 Revising

Revise: Improve the clarity by grouping similar ideas. Improve readability by numbering questions.

Proofread: Look for typos and spelling errors. Check punctuation, placement, and format.

Evaluate: Is this message attractive and easily comprehended?

DRAFT

Dear Mr. Lee:

Our insurance rates will be increased soon if we don't install security devices on our computer equipment. We have considered some local suppliers, but none had exactly what we wanted. — Opens with background information instead of request

We need a device that can be used to secure separate computer components at a workstation including a computer, keyboard, and monitor. We currently own 18 computers, keyboards, and monitors, along with six printers. — Fails to organize information logically

We wonder if professionals are needed to install your security devices. We're also interested in whether the devices can be easily removed when we need to move equipment around. We are, of course, very interested in prices and quantity discounts, if you offer them. Thank you for your attention to this matter. — Ends with cliché; fails to reveal what to do and when

REVISION

EARTH SYSTEMS

Geotechnical Engineers   www.earthsystems.com   (805) 558-8791
4439 Hitchcock Way   Ventura, CA 93105

January 28, 2009

Mr. Adam Lee
Customer Service
Micro Supplies and Software
P.O. Box 648
Fort Atkinson, WI 53538

Dear Mr. Lee: ← Addresses receiver by name

Please provide information and recommendations regarding security equipment to prevent theft of office computers and peripherals. ← Introduces purpose immediately

Our office now has 18 computer workstations and 6 printers that we must secure to desks or counters. Answers to the following questions will help us select the best devices for our purposes:

1.   What device would you recommend that can secure a workstation consisting of a computer, monitor, and keyboard?

2.   What expertise and equipment are required to install and remove the security device?

3.   Do you offer quantity discounts, and if so, how much are they?

← Groups open-ended questions into list for quick comprehension and best feedback

Your response before February 15 will help us meet an April 1 deadline from our insurance carrier for locking down this equipment. Call me at (805) 555-8791 or send an e-mail to dgomez@earthsystems.com. ← Provides end date, reason, and precise contact information

Sincerely,

Deana Gomez

Deana Gomez
Office Manager

unemotionally; let the reader decide on the causes. Include copies of all pertinent documents such as invoices, sales slips, catalog descriptions, and repair records. By the way, be sure to send copies and NOT your originals, which could be lost. When service is involved, cite names of individuals spoken to and dates of calls. Assume that a company honestly wants to satisfy its customers—because most do. When an alternative remedy exists, spell it out (*If you are unable to send 25 Sanyo digital travel alarm clocks immediately, please credit our account now and notify us when they become available*).

Conclude With an Action Request

End a claim letter with a courteous statement that promotes goodwill and summarizes your action request. If appropriate, include an end date (*We realize that mistakes in ordering and shipping sometimes occur. Because we've enjoyed your prompt service in the past, we hope that you will be able to send us the Sanyo digital travel alarm clocks by January 15*). Finally, in making claims, act promptly. Delaying claims makes them appear less important. Delayed claims are also more difficult to verify. By taking the time to put your claim in writing, you indicate your seriousness. A written claim starts a record of the problem, should later action be necessary. Be sure to keep a copy of your letter.

When Keith Krahnke received a statement showing a charge for a three-year service warranty that he did not purchase, he was furious. He called the store but failed to get satisfaction to his complaint. Then he decided to write. You can see the first draft of his direct claim letter in Figure 8.5. This draft gave him a chance to vent his anger, but it accomplished little else. The tone was belligerent, and it assumed that the company intentionally mischarged him. Furthermore, it failed to tell the reader how to remedy the problem. The revision, also shown in Figure 8.5, tempered the tone, described the problem objectively, and provided facts and figures. Most important, it specified exactly what Keith wanted to be done.

Notice in Figure 8.5 that Keith used the personal business letter style, which is appropriate for you to use in writing personal messages. Your return address, but not your name, appears above the date.

To sum up, use the direct pattern with the main idea first when you expect little resistance to letters making requests. The checklist at the bottom of the page reviews the direct strategy for information or action requests and claim letters.

Direct Replies

Often, your messages will reply directly and favorably to requests for information or action. A customer wants information about a product. A supplier asks to arrange a meeting. Another business inquires about one of your procedures or about a former employee. In complying with such requests, you will want to apply the same direct pattern you used in making requests.

Checklist

Writing Direct Requests

Information or Action Request Letters

✓ **Open by stating the main idea.** To elicit information, ask a question or issue a polite command (*Will you please answer the following questions . . .*).

✓ **Explain and justify the request.** In seeking information, use open-ended questions structured in parallel, balanced form.

✓ **Request action in the closing.** Express appreciation, and set an end date if appropriate. Explain how and where to respond. Avoid clichés (*Thank you for your cooperation*).

Direct Claim Letters

✓ **Begin with the purpose.** Present a clear statement of the problem or the action requested—such as a refund, replacement, credit, explanation, or correction of error.

✓ **Explain objectively.** In the body tell the specifics of the claim. Provide copies of necessary documents.

✓ **End by requesting action.** Include an end date if important. Add a pleasant, forward-looking statement. Keep a copy of the letter.

FIGURE 8.5 Direct Claim Letter

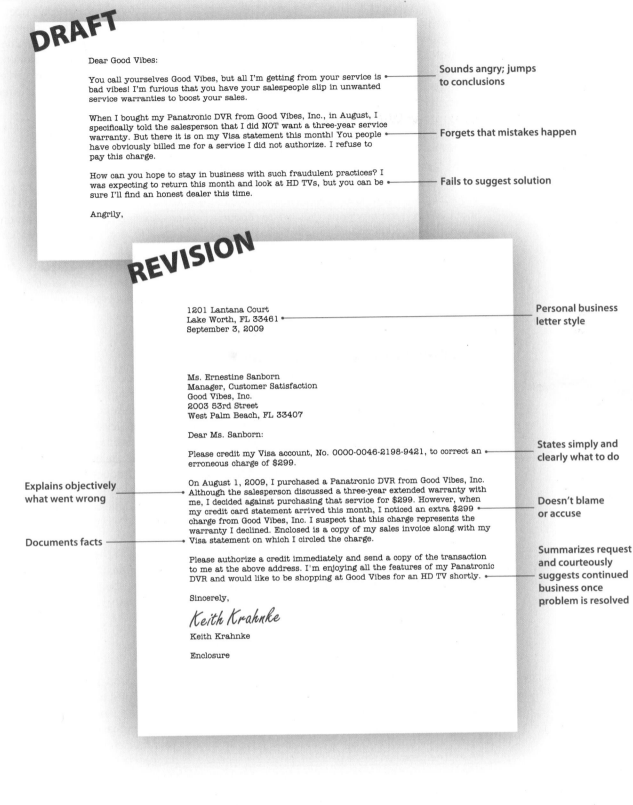

DRAFT

Dear Good Vibes:

You call yourselves Good Vibes, but all I'm getting from your service is bad vibes! I'm furious that you have your salespeople slip in unwanted service warranties to boost your sales.

Sounds angry; jumps to conclusions

When I bought my Panatronic DVR from Good Vibes, Inc., in August, I specifically told the salesperson that I did NOT want a three-year service warranty. But there it is on my Visa statement this month! You people have obviously billed me for a service I did not authorize. I refuse to pay this charge.

Forgets that mistakes happen

How can you hope to stay in business with such fraudulent practices? I was expecting to return this month and look at HD TVs, but you can be sure I'll find an honest dealer this time.

Fails to suggest solution

Angrily,

REVISION

1201 Lantana Court
Lake Worth, FL 33461
September 3, 2009

Personal business letter style

Ms. Ernestine Sanborn
Manager, Customer Satisfaction
Good Vibes, Inc.
2003 53rd Street
West Palm Beach, FL 33407

Dear Ms. Sanborn:

Please credit my Visa account, No. 0000-0046-2198-9421, to correct an erroneous charge of $299.

States simply and clearly what to do

Explains objectively what went wrong

On August 1, 2009, I purchased a Panatronic DVR from Good Vibes, Inc. Although the salesperson discussed a three-year extended warranty with me, I decided against purchasing that service for $299. However, when my credit card statement arrived this month, I noticed an extra $299 charge from Good Vibes, Inc. I suspect that this charge represents the warranty I declined. Enclosed is a copy of my sales invoice along with my Visa statement on which I circled the charge.

Doesn't blame or accuse

Documents facts

Please authorize a credit immediately and send a copy of the transaction to me at the above address. I'm enjoying all the features of my Panatronic DVR and would like to be shopping at Good Vibes for an HD TV shortly.

Summarizes request and courteously suggests continued business once problem is resolved

Sincerely,

Keith Krahnke

Keith Krahnke

Enclosure

The opening of a customer reply letter might contain a subject line, as shown in Figure 8.6. A subject line helps the reader recognize the topic immediately. Usually appearing two lines below the salutation, the subject line refers in abbreviated form to previous correspondence and/or summarizes a message (*Subject: Your July 12 Inquiry About WorkZone Software*). It often omits articles (*a, an, the*), is not a complete sentence, and does not end with a period. Knowledgeable business communicators use a subject line to refer to earlier correspondence so that in the first sentence, the most emphatic spot in a letter, they are free to emphasize the main idea.

Open Directly

In the first sentence of a direct reply letter, deliver the information the reader wants. Avoid wordy, drawn-out openings such as *I have before me your letter of August 5, in which you request information about.* . . . More forceful and more efficient is an opener that answers the inquiry (*Here is the information you wanted about . . .*). When agreeing to a request for action, announce the good news promptly (*Yes, I will be happy to speak to your business communication class on the topic of . . .*).

In the body of your reply, supply explanations and additional information. Because a letter written on company stationery is considered a legally binding contract, be sure to check facts and figures carefully. If a policy or procedure needs authorization, seek approval from a supervisor or executive before writing the letter.

Arrange Information Logically

When answering a group of questions or providing considerable data, arrange the information logically and make it readable by using lists, tables, headings, boldface, italics, or other graphic devices. When customers or prospective customers inquire about products or services, your response should do more than merely supply answers. Try to promote your organization and products. Often, companies have particular products and services they want to spotlight. Thus, when a customer writes about one product, provide helpful information that satisfies the inquiry, but consider using the opportunity to introduce another product as well. Be sure to present the promotional material with attention to the "you" view and to reader benefits (*You can use our standardized tests to free you from time-consuming employment screening*). You will learn more about special techniques for developing marketing and persuasive messages in Chapter 9.

In concluding, make sure you are cordial and personal. Refer to the information provided or to its use. (*The enclosed list summarizes our recommendations. We wish you all the best in redesigning your Web site.*) If further action is required, describe the procedure and help the reader with specifics (*The Small Business Administration publishes a number of helpful booklets. Its Web address is . . .*).

Emphasize the Positive in Mixed Messages

The direct pattern is also appropriate for messages that are mostly good news but may have some negative elements. For example, a return policy has time limits; an airfare may contain holiday restrictions; a speaker can come but not at the time requested; an appliance can be repaired but not replaced. When the message is mixed, emphasize the good news by presenting it first (*Yes, I would be delighted to address your marketing class on the topic of . . .*). Then, explain why a problem exists (*My schedule for the week of October 10 takes me to Washington and Philadelphia, where I am . . .*). Present the bad news in the middle (*Although I cannot meet with your class at that time, perhaps we can schedule a date during the week of . . .*). End the message cordially by returning to the good news (*Thanks for the invitation. I am looking forward to arranging a date in October when I can talk with your students about careers in marketing*).

Your goal is to present the negative news clearly without letting it become the focus of the message. Therefore, you want to spend more time talking about the good news; and by placing the bad news in the middle of the letter, you de-emphasize it. You will study other techniques for presenting bad news in Chapter 10.

FIGURE 8.6 Customer Reply Letter

The Three Phases of the Writing Process

1 Prewriting

Analyze: The purpose of this letter is to provide helpful information and to promote company products.

Anticipate: The reader is the intelligent owner of a small business who needs help with personnel administration.

Adapt: Because the reader requested this data, she will be receptive to the letter. Use the direct pattern.

2 Writing

Research: Gather facts to answer the business owner's questions. Consult brochures and pamphlets.

Organize: Prepare a scratch outline. Plan for a fast, direct opening. Use numbered answers to the business owner's three questions.

Compose: Write the first draft on a computer. Strive for short sentences and paragraphs.

3 Revising

Revise: Eliminate jargon and wordiness. Look for ways to explain how the product fits the reader's needs. Revise for "you" view.

Proofread: Double-check the form of numbers (*July 12, page 6, 8 to 5 PST*).

Evaluate: Does this letter answer the customer's questions and encourage an order?

SONOMA SOFTWARE, INC.

520 Sonoma Parkway
Petaluma, CA 94539
(707) 784-2219
www.sonomasoft.com

July 15, 2009

Mr. Jeffrey M. White
Director, Human Resources
White-Rather Enterprises
1349 Century Boulevard
Wichita Falls, TX 76308

Dear Mr. White:

Subject: Your July 12 Inquiry About WorkZone Software

Yes, we do offer personnel record-keeping software specially designed for small businesses like yours. Here are answers to your three questions about this software:

1. Our WorkZone software provides standard employee forms so that you are always in compliance with current government regulations.

2. You receive an interviewer's guide for structured employee interviews, as well as a scripted format for checking references by telephone.

3. Yes, you can update your employees' records easily without the need for additional software, hardware, or training.

Our WorkZone software was specially designed to provide you with expert forms for interviewing, verifying references, recording attendance, evaluating performance, and tracking the status of your employees. We even provide you with step-by-step instructions and suggested procedures. You can treat your employees as if you had a professional human resources specialist on your staff.

On page 6 of the enclosed pamphlet, you can read about our WorkZone software. To receive a preview copy or to ask questions about its use, just call 1-800-354-5500. Our specialists are eager to help you weekdays from 8 to 5, PST. If you prefer, visit our Web site to receive more information or to place an order.

Sincerely,

Linda DeLorme

Linda DeLorme
Senior Marketing Representative

Enclosure

Callout annotations:

- Puts most important information first
- Lists answers to sender's questions in order asked
- Helps reader find information by citing pages
- Identifies previous correspondence and subject
- Emphasizes "you" view
- Links sales promotion to reader benefits
- Makes it easy to respond

Royal Caribbean International's service reputation ran aground temporarily when a scheduling error sank one couple's plans for a romantic honeymoon cruise. The vacation company's alternate arrangements also went adrift when representatives failed to notify the newlyweds about their rescheduled trip. Although the newlyweds eventually received a $1,700 voucher from Royal Caribbean for a future cruise, the couple was disappointed that Royal Caribbean's initial apology letter wasn't accompanied by a full refund. *What are the key elements of an effective adjustment letter?*

© AP IMAGES

Adjustments

LEARNING OBJECTIVE 6
Write letters that make adjustments.

When a company responds favorably to a customer's claim, the response is called an *adjustment.*

Favorable responses to claims follow the direct pattern; unfavorable responses follow the indirect pattern.

Adjustment letters seek to right wrongs, regain customer confidence, and promote further business.

Even the best-run and best-loved businesses occasionally receive claims or complaints from consumers. When a company receives a claim and decides to respond favorably, the letter is called an *adjustment* letter. Most businesses make adjustments promptly: they replace merchandise, refund money, extend discounts, send coupons, and repair goods. Businesses make favorable adjustments to legitimate claims for two reasons. First, consumers are protected by contractual and tort law for recovery of damages.[8] If, for example, you find an insect in a package of frozen peas, the food processor of that package is bound by contractual law to replace it. If you suffer injury, the processor may be liable for damages. Second, and more obviously, most organizations genuinely want to satisfy their customers and retain their business.

To compete globally and to pump up local markets, most businesses today honestly want to please their customers. Retaining current customers is enormously important. A survey of financial services companies revealed that the average cost to retain a customer was $57. The cost to recruit a new customer was a whopping $279![9]

In responding to customer claims, you must first decide whether to grant the claim. Unless the claim is obviously fraudulent or excessive, you will probably grant it. When you say yes, your adjustment letter will be good news to the reader. Deliver that good news by using the direct pattern. When your response is no, the indirect pattern might be more appropriate. Chapter 10 discusses the indirect pattern for conveying negative news.

You have three goals in adjustment letters:

- Rectifying the wrong, if one exists
- Regaining the confidence of the customer
- Promoting further business

Revealing Good News in the Opening

Instead of beginning with a review of what went wrong, present the good news immediately. When Amy Hopkins responded to the claim of customer Sound Systems, Inc., about a missing shipment, her first draft, shown at the top of Figure 8.7, was angry. No wonder. Sound Systems had apparently provided the wrong shipping address, and the goods were returned. Once Amy and her company decided to send a second shipment and comply with

FIGURE 8.7 Customer Adjustment Letter

Fails to reveal good news immediately and blames customer

Gentlemen:

In response to your recent complaint about a missing shipment, it's very difficult to deliver merchandise when we have been given an erroneous address.

Our investigators looked into your problem shipment and determined that it was sent immediately after we received the order. According to the shipper's records, it was delivered to the warehouse address given on your stationery: 3590 University Avenue, St. Paul, Minnesota 55114.

Creates ugly tone with negative words and sarcasm

Unfortunately, no one at that address would accept delivery, so the shipment was returned to us. I see from your current stationery that your company has a new address. With the proper address, we probably could have delivered this shipment.

Sounds grudging and reluctant in granting claim

Although we feel that it is entirely appropriate to charge you shipping and restocking fees, as is our standard practice on returned goods, in this instance we will waive those fees. We hope this second shipment finally catches up with you at your current address.

Sincerely,

Amy Hopkins

REVISION

EW **ELECTRONIC WAREHOUSE**

930 Abbott Park Place
Providence, RI 02903-5309

Phone: (401) 876-8201
Fax: (401) 876-8345
Web: www.ewarehouse.com

February 21, 2009

Mr. Jeremy Garber, CEO
Sound Systems, Inc.
2293 Second Avenue
St. Paul, MN 55120

Dear Mr. Garber: ●

Uses customer's name in salutation

Subject: Your February 14 Letter About Your Purchase Order

You should receive by February 25 a second shipment of the speakers, DVDs, headphones, and other electronic equipment that you ordered January 20.

Announces good news immediately

The first shipment of this order was delivered January 28 to 3590 University Avenue, St. Paul, Minnesota 55114. When no one at that address would accept the shipment, it was returned to us. Now that I have your letter, I see that the order should have been sent to 2293 Second Avenue, St. Paul, Minnesota 55120. When an order is undeliverable, we usually try to verify the shipping address by telephoning the customer. Somehow the return of this shipment was not caught by our normally painstaking shipping clerks. You can be sure that I will investigate shipping and return procedures with our clerks immediately to see whether we can improve existing methods.

Regains confidence of customer by explaining what happened and by suggesting plans for improvement

Your respect is important to us, Mr. Garber. Although our rock-bottom discount prices have enabled us to build a volume business, we don't want to be so large that we lose touch with valued customers like you. Over the years our customers' respect has made us successful, and we hope that the prompt delivery of this shipment will retain yours. Please call me at (401) 876-8201, Ext. 450, if I can serve you personally.

Closes confidently with genuine appeal for customer's respect

Sincerely,

Amy Hopkins

Amy Hopkins
Distribution Manager

c: David Cole
   Shipping Department

the customer's claim, however, she had to give up the anger. Her goal was to regain the goodwill and the business of this customer. The improved version of her letter announces that a new shipment will arrive shortly.

If you decide to comply with a customer's claim, let the receiver know immediately. Don't begin your letter with a negative statement (*We are very sorry to hear that you are having trouble with your dishwasher*). This approach reminds the reader of the problem and may rekindle the heated emotions or unhappy feelings experienced when the claim was written. Instead, focus on the good news. The following openings for various letters illustrate how to begin a message with good news:

You're right! We agree that the warranty on your American Standard Model UC600 dishwasher should be extended for six months.

You will be receiving shortly a new slim Nokia cell phone to replace the one that shattered when dropped recently.

Please take your portable Admiral microwave oven to A-1 Appliance Service, 200 Orange Street, Pasadena, where it will be repaired at no cost to you.

The enclosed check for $325 demonstrates our desire to satisfy our customers and earn their confidence.

In announcing that you will make an adjustment, be sure to do so without a grudging tone—even if you have reservations about whether the claim is legitimate. Once you decide to comply with the customer's request, do so happily. Avoid halfhearted or reluctant responses (*Although the American Standard dishwasher works well when used properly, we have decided to allow you to take yours to A-1 Appliance Service for repair at our expense*).

Explaining Compliance in the Body

In responding to claims, most organizations sincerely want to correct a wrong. They want to do more than just make the customer happy. They want to stand behind their products and services; they want to do what's right.

Most businesses comply with claims because they want to promote customer goodwill.

In the body of the letter, explain how you are complying with the claim. In all but the most routine claims, you should seek to regain the confidence of the customer. You might reasonably expect that a customer who has experienced difficulty with a product, with delivery, with billing, or with service has lost faith in your organization. Rebuilding that faith is important for future business.

How to rebuild lost confidence depends on the situation and the claim. If procedures need to be revised, explain what changes will be made. If a product has defective parts, tell how the product is being improved. If service is faulty, describe genuine efforts to improve it. Notice in Figure 8.7 that the writer promises to investigate shipping procedures to see whether improvements might prevent future mishaps.

Sometimes the problem is not with the product but with the way it is being used. In other instances customers misunderstand warranties or inadvertently cause delivery and billing mix-ups by supplying incorrect information. Remember that rational and sincere explanations will do much to regain the confidence of unhappy customers.

Because negative words suggest blame and fault, avoid them in letters that attempt to build customer goodwill.

In your explanation avoid emphasizing negative words such as *trouble, regret, misunderstanding, fault, defective, error, inconvenience,* and *unfortunately.* Keep your message positive and upbeat.

Deciding Whether to Apologize

Apologize if it seems natural and appropriate.

Whether to apologize is a debatable issue. Studies of adjustment letters received by consumers show that a majority do contain apologies, either in the opening or in the closing.[10] Attorneys generally discourage apologies fearing that they admit responsibility and will trigger lawsuits. But an analysis of case outcomes indicates that both judges and juries tend to look on apologies favorably. A few states are even passing laws that protect those who apologize.[11] Some business writing experts advise against apologies, contending that they are counterproductive and merely remind the customer of unpleasantness related to the claim. If, however, apologizing seems natural, do so.

People like to hear apologies. It raises their self-esteem, shows the humility of the writer, and acts as a form of "psychological compensation."[12] Don't, however, fall back on the familiar phrase, *I'm sorry for any inconvenience we may have caused*. It sounds mechanical and insincere. Instead, try something like this: *We understand the frustration our delay has caused you, We're sorry you didn't receive better service*, or *You're right to be disappointed*. If you feel that an apology is appropriate, do it early and briefly. You will learn more about delivering apologies in Chapter 10 when we discuss negative messages.

The primary focus of an adjustment letter is on how you are complying with the request, how the problem occurred, and how you are working to prevent its recurrence.

Using Sensitive Language

The language of adjustment letters must be particularly sensitive, because customers are already upset. Here are some don'ts:

- Don't use negative words (*trouble, regret, misunderstanding, fault, error, inconvenience, you claim*).

- Don't blame customers—even when they may be at fault.

- Don't blame individuals or departments within your organization; it's unprofessional.

- Don't make unrealistic promises; you can't guarantee that the situation will never recur.

Avoiding negative language retains customer goodwill, and resale information rebuilds customer confidence.

To regain the confidence of your reader, consider including resale information. Describe a product's features and any special applications that might appeal to the reader. Promote a new product if it seems appropriate.

Showing Confidence in the Closing

End positively by expressing confidence that the problem has been resolved and that continued business relations will result. You might mention the product in a favorable light, suggest a new product, express your appreciation for the customer's business, or anticipate future business. It's often appropriate to refer to the desire to be of service and to satisfy customers. Notice how the following closings illustrate a positive, confident tone:

Close an adjustment letter with appreciation, thanks for past business, a desire to be of service, or the promotion of a new product.

> *You were most helpful in informing us of this situation and permitting us to correct it. We appreciate your thoughtfulness in writing to us.*

> *Thanks for writing. Your satisfaction is important to us. We hope that this refund check convinces you that service to our customers is our No. 1 priority. Our goals are to earn your confidence and continue to justify that confidence with quality products and excellent service.*

> *Your flat panel Inspiron 1200 Notebook will come in handy whether you're working at home or on the road. What's more, you can upgrade to a 17-inch display for only $100. Take a look at the enclosed booklet detailing the big savings for essential technology on a budget. We value your business and look forward to your future orders.*

Although the direct pattern works for many requests and replies, it obviously won't work for every situation. With more practice and experience, you will be able to alter the pattern and apply the writing process to other communication problems.

Goodwill Messages

LEARNING OBJECTIVE 7
Write special messages that convey kindness and goodwill.

Many communicators are intimidated when they must write goodwill messages expressing thanks, recognition, and sympathy. Finding the right words to express feelings is often more difficult than writing ordinary business documents. That is why writers tend to procrastinate when it comes to goodwill messages. Sending a ready-made card or picking up the telephone is easier than writing a message. Remember, though, that the personal sentiments of the sender are always more expressive and more meaningful to readers than are printed cards or oral messages. Taking the time to write gives more importance to our well-wishing. Personal notes also provide a record that can be reread, savored, and treasured.

Communicating at Work Part 2

Ben & Jerry's

Customer letters arriving at Ben & Jerry's got special attention from Alice Blachly, a former consumer affairs coordinator. In responding to fan letters, Blachly prepared handwritten cards or printed letters that promoted good feelings and cemented a long-lasting bond between Ben & Jerry's and its satisfied consumers. To letters with questions, Blachly located the information and responded. For example, a consumer worried that cottonseed oil, formerly contained in the one of the nut-butter portions of an exotic ice cream, might be contaminated by pesticides. Blachly checked with company quality assurance experts and also investigated articles about cottonseed oil before responding. Other consumers wondered about Ben & Jerry's position on using milk from cloned cows and eggs from cage-free growers.

However, letters with consumer complaints, such as *My pint didn't have quite enough cookie dough,* always received top priority. "We have trained our consumers to expect the best," said Blachly, "so they are disappointed when something goes wrong. And we are disappointed, too. We refund the purchase price, and we explain what caused the problem, if we know."

© Lon C. Diehl / Photo Edit

Critical Thinking

- When customers write to Ben & Jerry's for information and the response must contain both positive and negative news, what strategy should the respondent follow?
- If a customer writes to complain about something for which Ben & Jerry's is not responsible (such as ice in frozen yogurt), should the response letter contain an apology? Why or why not?
- Why is letter-writing an important function for a company such as Ben & Jerry's?

In expressing thanks, recognition, or sympathy, you should always do so promptly. These messages are easier to write when the situation is fresh in your mind. They also mean more to the recipient. Don't forget that a prompt thank-you note carries the hidden message that you care and that you consider the event to be important. The best goodwill messages—whether thanks, congratulations, praise, or sympathy—concentrate on the five Ss. Goodwill messages should be

- **Selfless.** Be sure to focus the message solely on the receiver, not the sender. Don't talk about yourself; avoid such comments as *I remember when I. . . .*

- **Specific.** Personalize the message by mentioning specific incidents or characteristics of the receiver. Telling a colleague *Great speech* is much less effective than *Great story about McDonald's marketing in Moscow.* Take care to verify names and other facts.

Let others speak of themselves not just about yourself

Checklist

Positive Reply Letters

Letters That Comply With Requests

✓ **Consider using a subject line.** Identify previous correspondence and the topic of this letter.

✓ **Open directly.** In the first sentence deliver the information the reader wants (*Yes, I can meet with your class* or *Here is the information you requested*). If the message is mixed, present the best news first.

✓ **In the body provide explanations and additional information.** Arrange this information logically, perhaps using a bulleted list, headings, or columns. For prospective customers build your company image and promote your products.

✓ **End with a cordial, personalized statement.** If further action is required, tell the reader how to proceed and give helpful details.

Letters That Make Adjustments

✓ **Open with approval.** Comply with the customer's claim immediately. Avoid sounding grudging or reluctant.

✓ **In the body win back the customer's confidence.** Explain the cause of the problem or describe your ongoing efforts to avoid such difficulties. Focus on your efforts to satisfy customers. Apologize if you feel that you should, but do so early and quickly. Avoid negative words, accusations, and unrealistic promises. Consider including resale and sales promotion information.

✓ **Close positively.** Express appreciation to the customer for writing, extend thanks for past business, anticipate continued patronage, refer to your desire to be of service, and/or mention a new product if it seems appropriate.

- **Sincere.** Let your words show genuine feelings. Rehearse in your mind how you would express the message to the receiver orally. Then transform that conversational language to your written message. Avoid pretentious, formal, or flowery language (*It gives me great pleasure to extend felicitations on the occasion of your firm's twentieth anniversary*).

- **Spontaneous.** Keep the message fresh and enthusiastic. Avoid canned phrases (*Congratulations on your promotion, Good luck in the future*). Strive for directness and naturalness, not creative brilliance.

- **Short.** Although goodwill messages can be as long as needed, try to accomplish your purpose in only a few sentences. What is most important is remembering an individual. Such caring does not require documentation or wordiness. Individuals and business organizations often use special note cards or stationery for brief messages.

Thanks

When someone has done you a favor or when an action merits praise, you need to extend thanks or show appreciation. Letters of appreciation may be written to customers for their orders, to hosts and hostesses for their hospitality, to individuals for kindnesses performed, and especially to customers who complain. After all, complainers are actually providing you with "free consulting reports from the field." Complainers who feel that they were listened to often become the greatest promoters of an organization.[13]

Because the receiver will be pleased to hear from you, you can open directly with the purpose of your message. The letter in Figure 8.8 thanks a speaker who addressed a group of marketing professionals. Although such thank-you notes can be quite short, this one is a little longer because the writer wants to lend importance to the receiver's efforts. Notice that every sentence relates to the receiver and offers enthusiastic praise. By using the receiver's name along with contractions and positive words, the writer makes the letter sound warm and conversational.

Written notes that show appreciation and express thanks are significant to their receivers. In expressing thanks, you generally write a short note on special notepaper or heavy card stock. The following messages provide models for expressing thanks for a gift, for a favor, and for hospitality.

To Express Thanks for a Gift

Thanks, Laura, to you and the other members of the department for honoring me with the elegant Waterford crystal vase at the party celebrating my twentieth anniversary with the company.

The height and shape of the vase are perfect to hold roses and other bouquets from my garden. Each time I fill it, I'll remember your thoughtfulness in choosing this lovely gift for me.

Identify the gift, tell why you appreciate it, and explain how you will use it.

To Send Thanks for a Favor

I sincerely appreciate your filling in for me last week when I was too ill to attend the planning committee meeting for the spring exhibition.

Without your participation much of my preparatory work would have been lost. Knowing that competent and generous individuals like you are part of our team, Mark, is a great comfort. Moreover, counting you as a friend is my very good fortune. I'm grateful to you.

Tell what the favor means using sincere, simple statements.

To Extend Thanks for Hospitality

Jeffrey and I want you to know how much we enjoyed the dinner party for our department that you hosted Saturday evening. Your charming home and warm hospitality, along with the lovely dinner and sinfully delicious chocolate dessert, combined to create a truly memorable evening.

Most of all, though, we appreciate your kindness in cultivating togetherness in our department. Thanks, Jennifer, for being such a special person.

Compliment the fine food, charming surroundings, warm hospitality, excellent host and hostess, and good company.

FIGURE 8.8 Thank-You Letter for a Favor

1 Prewriting

Analyze: The purpose of this letter is to express appreciation to a business executive for presenting a talk before professionals.

Anticipate: The reader will be more interested in personalized comments than in general statements showing gratitude.

Adapt: Because the reader will be pleased, use the direct pattern.

2 Writing

Research: Consult notes taken during the talk.

Organize: Open directly by giving the reason for writing. Express enthusiastic and sincere thanks. In the body provide specifics. Refer to facts and highlights in the talk. Supply sufficient detail to support your sincere compliments. Conclude with appreciation. Be warm and friendly.

Compose: Write the first draft.

3 Revising

Revise: Revise for tone and warmth. Use the reader's name. Include concrete detail but do it concisely. Avoid sounding gushy or phony.

Proofread: Check the spelling of the receiver's name; verify facts. Check the spelling of *gratitude, patience, advice, persistence,* and *grateful*.

Evaluate: Does this letter convey sincere thanks?

International Marketing Association

225 West 17th Street
New York, New York 10029
http://www.ima.com

February 26, 2009

Mr. Michael T. Reese
Marketing Manager
Toys "R" Us, Inc.
One Geoffrey Way
Wayne, NJ 07470-2030

Dear Michael:

Thank you for providing the Manhattan chapter of the IMA with one of the best presentations our group has ever heard. — *Tells purpose and delivers praise*

Personalizes the message by using specifics rather than generalities — Your description of the battle Toys "R" Us waged to begin marketing products in Japan was a genuine eye-opener for many of us. Nine years of preparation establishing connections and securing permissions seems an eternity, but obviously such persistence and patience pay off. We now understand better the need to learn local customs and nurture relationships when dealing in Japan or other Asian countries.

In addition to your good advice, we particularly enjoyed your sense of humor and jokes—as you must have recognized from the uproarious laughter. What a great routine you do on faulty translations! — *Spotlights the reader's talents*

Concludes with compliments and thanks — We're grateful, Michael, for the entertaining and instructive evening you provided our marking professionals.

Cordially

Rosetta H. Johnson

Rosetta H. Johnson
Program Chair, IMA

RHJ:mef

Responding to Goodwill Messages

Should you respond when you receive a congratulatory note or a written pat on the back? By all means! These messages are attempts to connect personally; they are efforts to reach out, to form professional and/or personal bonds. Failing to respond to notes of congratulations and most other goodwill messages is like failing to say "You are welcome" when someone says "Thank you." Responding to such messages is simply the right thing to do. Do avoid, though, minimizing your achievements with comments that suggest you don't really deserve the praise or that the sender is exaggerating your good qualities.

Take the time to respond to any goodwill message you may receive.

To Answer a Congratulatory Note

Thanks for your kind words regarding my award, and thanks, too, for sending me the newspaper clipping. I truly appreciate your thoughtfulness and warm wishes.

To Respond to a Pat on the Back

Your note about my work made me feel good. I'm grateful for your thoughtfulness.

Sympathy

Most of us can bear misfortune and grief more easily when we know that others care. Notes expressing sympathy, though, are probably more difficult to write than any other kind of message. Commercial "In sympathy" cards make the task easier—but they are far less meaningful. Grieving friends want to know what you think—not what Hallmark's card writers think. To help you get started, you can always glance through cards expressing sympathy. They will supply ideas about the kinds of thoughts you might wish to convey in your own words. In writing a sympathy note, (a) refer to the death or misfortune sensitively, using words that show you understand what a crushing blow it is; (b) in the case of a death, praise the deceased in a personal way; (c) offer assistance without going into excessive detail; and (d) end on a reassuring, forward-looking note. Sympathy messages may be typed, although handwriting seems more personal. In either case, use notepaper or personal stationery.

Sympathy notes should refer to the misfortune sensitively and offer assistance.

To Express Condolences

We are deeply saddened, Gayle, to learn of the death of your husband. Warren's kind nature and friendly spirit endeared him to all who knew him. He will be missed.

Although words seem empty in expressing our grief, we want you to know that your friends at QuadCom extend their profound sympathy to you. If we may help you or lighten your load in any way, you have but to call.

We know that the treasured memories of your many happy years together, along with the support of your family and many friends, will provide strength and comfort in the months ahead.

Mention the loss tactfully; recognize good qualities of the deceased; assure the receiver of your concern; offer assistance; and conclude on a positive, reassuring note.

© Andrew Fox / Alamy

Businesses express condolences to bereaved employees in many ways. Flowers, cards, "comfort baskets," and pictures are popular corporate-sympathy gifts that allow coworkers to grieve their loss with caring support from the company. Though such gift ideas are appropriate, a note of personal sympathy from a boss or colleague can be a more meaningful way to console an individual who is coping with misfortune and loss. *What important guidelines should be followed when extending sympathy in a personal letter?*

Checklist

Goodwill Messages

General Guidelines: The Five Ss

✓ **Be selfless.** Discuss the receiver, not the sender.

✓ **Be specific.** Instead of generic statements (*You did a good job*), include special details (*Your marketing strategy to target key customers proved to be outstanding*).

✓ **Be sincere.** Show your honest feelings with conversational, unpretentious language (*We are all very proud of your award*).

✓ **Be spontaneous.** Strive to make the message natural, fresh, and direct. Avoid canned phrases (*If I may be of service, please do not hesitate . . .*).

✓ **Keep the message short.** Remember that, although they may be as long as needed, most goodwill messages are fairly short.

Giving Thanks

✓ **Cover three points in gift thank-yous.** (a) Identify the gift, (b) tell why you appreciate it, and (c) explain how you will use it.

✓ **Be sincere in sending thanks for a favor.** Tell what the favor means to you. Avoid superlatives and gushiness. Maintain credibility with sincere, simple statements.

✓ **Offer praise in expressing thanks for hospitality.** Compliment, as appropriate, the (a) fine food, (b) charming surroundings, (c) warm hospitality, (d) excellent host and hostess, and (e) good company.

Responding to Goodwill Messages

✓ **Respond to congratulations.** Send a brief note expressing your appreciation. Tell how good the message made you feel.

✓ **Accept praise gracefully.** Don't make belittling comments (*I'm not really all that good!*) to reduce awkwardness or embarrassment.

Extending Sympathy

✓ **Refer to the loss or tragedy directly but sensitively.** In the first sentence mention the loss and your personal reaction.

✓ **For deaths, praise the deceased.** Describe positive personal characteristics (*Howard was a forceful but caring leader*).

✓ **Offer assistance.** Suggest your availability, especially if you can do something specific.

✓ **End on a reassuring, positive note.** Perhaps refer to the strength the receiver finds in friends, family, colleagues, or religion.

International Messages

LEARNING OBJECTIVE 8
Modify international letters to accommodate other cultures.

The letter-writing suggestions you've just studied work well for correspondence in this country. You may need, however, to modify the organization, format, and tone of letters going abroad.

American businesspeople appreciate efficiency, straightforwardness, and conciseness in letters. Moreover, American business letters tend to be informal and conversational. Foreign correspondents, however, may look upon such directness and informality as inappropriate, insensitive, and abrasive.[14] Letters in Japan, for example, may begin with deference, humility, and references to nature:

> *The season for cherry blossoms is here with us and everybody is beginning to feel refreshed. We sincerely congratulate you on becoming more prosperous in your business.*[15]

The writers of Chinese letters strive to build relationships. A sales letter might begin with the salutation *Honored Company*, indicating a high level of respect. Figure 9.8 in Chapter 9 illustrates a Chinese persuasive letter, which contains a low-key sales approach. Although American business writers might use high-pressure tactics and direct requests, Chinese writers are more tentative. For example, a Chinese sales letter might say, *I hope you will take a moment to complete and mail the enclosed application*. The verb *hope* reduces the imposition of a direct request. Avoiding pressure tactics results from the cultural need to show respect and preserve harmony. Demonstrating humility, Chinese writers may refer to their own supposedly meager skills.[16] A typical closing in Chinese letters, *wishing good health*, emphasizes the importance of showing respect and developing reciprocal relationships.

Business letters in Germany tend to be informal. Business correspondents, however, generally address each other with honorifics and last names (Sehr geehrter Herr Woerner = Dr. Mr. Woerner), even if they have known each other for years. Letter introductions may refer to past encounters, meetings, or subjects previously discussed.[17] Italian business letters may refer to the receiver's family and children.

Applying Your Skills at Ben & Jerry's

Alice Blachly, customer affairs coordinator at Ben & Jerry's, is overloaded with work. She asks you, her assistant, to help out as she hands you a stack of letters. The top one is from a customer who complains that she didn't get quite enough cookie and chocolate chunks in her last pint. The customer also wants to know why Ben & Jerry's has strayed from its Vermont roots and rural values by setting up dairy operations in Nevada. However, she agrees with Ben & Jerry's strong stand against using milk from cloned cows.

Blachly tells you to explain that, although we work hard and long at it, the chunking equipment for nuts, chocolate, and cookies is as not always as consistent as B & J would like and that you will report the problem of cookie and chocolate chunks to production. She tells you to refund the estimated purchase price for one pint of ice cream. As she walks away, she says that B & J went to Nevada to supply its product to ice cream eaters on the West Coast. "Saves energy costs," she said. "We don't truck milk across the country."

Your Task

Respond to all three of the comments in the letter of Cora Nicol, 246 Falls Overlook Drive, Niagara Falls, NY 14109. Although her complaint was gentle, it is, nevertheless, a complaint that warrants an adjustment. In your response strive to maintain her goodwill and favorable opinion of Ben & Jerry's.

© Lon C. Diehl / Photo Edit

French correspondents would consider it rude to begin a letter with a request before it is explained. French letters typically include an ending with this phrase (or a variation of it): *I wish to assure you* [insert reader's most formal title] *of my most respectful wishes* [followed by the writer's title and signature].[18] Foreign letters are also more likely to include passive-voice constructions *(your letter has been received)*, exaggerated courtesy *(great pleasure, esteemed favor)*, and obvious flattery *(your distinguished firm)*.

Foreign letters may use different formatting techniques. Whereas American business letters are typewritten and single-spaced, in other countries they may be handwritten and single- or double-spaced. Address arrangements vary as well, as shown in the following:

German	Japanese
Herr [title, Mr., on first line]	Ms. Atsuko Takagi [title, name]
Deiter Woerner [name]	5-12 Koyo-cho 4 chome [street, house number]
Fritz-Kalle-Straße 4 [street, house number]	Higashinada-ku [city]
6200 Wiesbaden [postal district, city]	Tokyo 194 [prefecture, postal district]
Germany [country]	Japan [country]

Dates and numbers can be particularly confusing, as shown here:

United States	Some European Countries
June 3, 2006	3rd of June 2006
6/3/06	3.6.06
$5,320.00	US $5.320,00

To be safe, spell out the names of months instead of using figures. Verify sums of money and identify the currency unit.

Because the placement and arrangement of letter addresses and closing lines vary greatly, you should always research local preferences before writing. For important letters going abroad, have someone familiar with local customs read and revise the message. An American graduate student learned this lesson when she wrote a letter, in French, to a Paris museum asking for permission to do research. She received no response. Before writing a second time, she took the letter to her French tutor. "No, no, mademoiselle! It will never do! It must be more respectful. You must be very careful of individuals' titles. Let me show you!" The second letter won the desired permission.

Summary of Learning Objectives

1 **Explain why business letters are important and how the three phases of the 3-x-3 writing process relate to creating successful business letters.** Although many e-mail messages are written today, business letters are necessary when a permanent record is required; when confidentiality is critical; when formality and sensitivity are essential; and when a persuasive, well-considered presentation is important. In Phase 1 of the writing process for straightforward letters, you should determine your purpose, visualize the audience, and anticipate the reaction of the reader to your message. In Phase 2 you should collect information, make an outline of the points to cover, and write the first draft. In Phase 3 you should revise for clarity, proofread for correctness, and look for ways to apply graphic highlighting techniques so that the message has high "skim value." Finally, you should decide whether the message accomplishes its goal.

2 **Analyze the structure and characteristics of good business letters.** Most straightforward business letters include a three-part structure: (a) an opening that announces the purpose immediately, (b) a body with details explaining the purpose, and (c) a closing that includes a request for action or a courteous conclusion. Letters that make requests close by telling what action is desired and establishing a deadline (end date) for that action. Good letters are characterized by clear content, a tone of goodwill, and correct form. Letters carrying positive or neutral messages should be organized directly. That means introducing the main idea (the purpose for writing) immediately in the opening.

3 **Write letters that request information or action.** In a letter requesting information or action, the opening immediately states the purpose of the letter, perhaps asking a question. The body explains and justifies the request. If many questions are asked, express them in parallel form and balance them grammatically. The closing tells the reader courteously what to do and shows appreciation.

4 **Write letters that make direct claims.** When a customer writes to identify and correct a wrong, the message is called a *claim*. A direct claim is one in which the receiver is expected to readily agree. A well-written claim begins by describing the problem clearly or telling what action is to be taken. The body explains and justifies the request without anger or emotion. The closing summarizes the request or action to be taken. It includes an end date, if appropriate, and courteously looks forward to continued business if the problem is resolved. Copies of relevant documents should be enclosed.

5 **Write letters that reply directly.** In a letter that replies directly and complies with a request, a subject line may identify previous correspondence, and the opening immediately delivers the good news. If the message is mixed, the best news comes first. The body explains and provides additional information. The closing is cordial and personalized. If action is necessary, the ending tells the reader how to proceed and gives helpful details.

6 **Write letters that make adjustments.** When a company grants a customer's claim, it is called an *adjustment*. An adjustment letter has three goals: (a) rectifying the wrong, if one exists; (b) regaining the confidence of the customer; and (c) promoting further business. The opening immediately grants the claim without sounding grudging. To regain the confidence of the customer, the body may explain what went wrong and how the problem will be rectified. However, the writer may strive to avoid accepting responsibility for any problems. The closing expresses appreciation, extends thanks for past business, refers to a desire to be of service, and may mention a new product. If an apology is offered, it should be presented early and briefly.

7 **Write special messages that convey kindness and goodwill.** Messages delivering thanks, praise, or sympathy should be selfless, specific, sincere, spontaneous, and short. Gift thank-yous should identify the gift, tell why you appreciate it, and explain how you will use it. Thank-yous for favors should tell, without gushing, what they mean to you. Expressions of sympathy should mention the loss tactfully; recognize good qualities in the deceased (in the case of a death); offer assistance; and conclude on a positive, reassuring note.

8 **Modify international letters to accommodate other cultures.** Letters going to individuals in some areas, such as South Asia and Europe, should probably use a less direct organizational pattern and be more formal in tone. They should also be adapted to appropriate regional letter formats.

Chapter Review

1. Under what conditions is it important to send business letters rather than e-mail messages? (Obj. 1)

2. What three activities should you perform in Phase 1 of the writing process for a business letter? (Obj. 1)

3. Describe the three-part structure of a typical business letter. (Obj. 2)

4. What is "frontloading," and why is it useful in routine business letters? (Obj. 2)

5. Why is it best to write most business letters "backward"? (Obj. 2)

6. What do readers look for in the last paragraph of a letter? (Obj. 2)

7. Why should you avoid writing business letters, and how can you do it? (Obj. 3)

8. What is a claim? When is it straightforward? (Obj. 4)

9. In complying with requests, why is it especially important that all facts are correct on letters written on company stationery? (Obj. 5)

10. What is an adjustment letter? (Obj. 6)

11. What are a writer's three goals in writing adjustment letters? (Obj. 6)

12. Name four things to avoid in adjustment letters. (Obj. 6)

13. Name five characteristics of goodwill messages. (Obj. 7)

14. What are four groups of people to whom business communicators might write letters of appreciation? (Obj. 7)

15. Describe three elements of business letters going abroad that might be modified to accommodate readers from other cultures. (Obj. 8)

Critical Thinking

1. An article in a professional magazine carried this headline: "Is Letter Writing Dead?"[19] How would you respond to such a question? (Obj. 1)

2. In promoting the value of letter-writing, a well-known columnist recently wrote, "To trust confidential information to e-mail is to be a rube."[20] What did he mean? Do you agree? (Obj. 1)

3. Why is it important to regain the confidence of a customer in an adjustment letter? How can it be done? (Obj. 6)

4. How are American business letters different from those written in other countries? Why do you suppose this is so? (Obj. 8)

5. **Ethical Issue:** Assume that you have drafted a letter to a customer in which you apologize for the way the customer's account was fouled up by the Accounting Department. You show the letter to your boss, and she instructs you to remove the apology. It admits responsibility, she says, and the company cannot allow itself to be held liable. You are not an attorney, but you can't see the harm in a simple apology. What should you do? Refer to the section "Tools for Doing the Right Thing" in Chapter 1 to review the five questions you might ask yourself in trying to do the right thing.

Activities

8.1 Writing Improvement Exercise: Direct Openings
(Objs. 1–7)

Your Task. Revise the following openings so that they are more direct. Add information if necessary.

a. Alliance Associates has undertaken a management initiative to pursue an internship program. I have been appointed as the liaison person to conduct research regarding our proposed program. We are fully aware of the benefits of a strong internship program, and our management team is eager to take advantage of some of these benefits. We would be deeply appreciative if you would be kind enough to help us out with answers to a number of specific questions.

b. My name is Justin Wilmot, and I am assistant to the manager of Information Services & Technology at Meredian, Inc. Our company wants to improve its integration of human resources and payroll functions. I understand that you have a software product called HRFocus that might do this, and I need to ask you some questions about it.

c. Your letter of March 4 has been referred to me. Pursuant to your inquiry, I have researched your question in regard to whether or not

we offer our European-style patio umbrella in colors. This unique umbrella is one of our most popular items. Its 10-foot canopy protects you when the sun is directly overhead, but it also swivels and tilts to virtually any angle for continuous sun protection all day long. It comes in two colors: cream and forest green.

d. In regard to your inquiry of June 14, which was originally sent to *Classic Motorcycle Magazine*, I am happy to respond to you. In your letter you ask about the tire choices for the Superbike and Superstock teams competing at the Honda Superbike Classic in Alabama. As you noted, the track temperatures reached above 125 degrees and the asphalt surface had an abrasive effect on tires. With the added heat and reduced grip, nearly all of the riders in the competition selected Dunlop Blue Groove hard compound front and rear tires.

e. I am pleased to receive your inquiry regarding the possibility of my acting as a speaker at the final semester meeting of your business management club on May 2. The topic of online résumés interests me and is one on which I think I could impart helpful information to your members. Therefore, I am responding in the affirmative to your kind invitation.

f. Thank you for your recent order of February 4. We are sure your customers and employees will love the high-quality Color-Block Sweatshirts with an 80/20 cotton/polyester blend that you ordered from our spring catalog. Your order is currently being processed and should leave our warehouse in Iowa in mid-February. We use UPS for all deliveries in southern California. Because you ordered sweatshirts with your logo embroidered in a two-tone combination, your order cannot be shipped until February 18. You should not expect it until about February 20.

8.2 Document for Analysis: Information Request (Obj. 3)

Your Task. Analyze the following poorly written letter, and list its weaknesses. If your instructor directs, revise it using the suggestions you learned in this chapter.

Current date

Planning Facilities Manager
Bellagio Hotel & Casino
3600 South Las Vegas Boulevard
Las Vegas, NV 89109

Dear Sir:

My name is Courtney Lewis, and I was recently hired as the special events manager at my company BareEssentials. I am writing for the purpose of making initial inquiries in regard to our next marketing meeting. Pursuant to this assignment, I would like to find a resort hotel with conference facilities, and we have heard wonderful things about the Bellagio Hotel & Casino.

Our marketing meeting will require banquet facilities where we can all be together, but we will also need at least four meeting rooms that are small in size. Each of these rooms should accommodate about 75. We hope to arrange our conference in the month of November, from the second to the fourth. We expect in the neighborhood of 250 sales associates. Most of our associates will be flying in, so I'm interested in transportation to and from the airport.

Due to the fact that we will be making electronic presentations, does Bellagio have audiovisual equipment and computer facilities for presentations in the meeting rooms? At your Web site I saw something about using your Tuscany Exhibition Kitchen for team-building activities. But I need more information.

Thank you for your cooperation.

Sincerely,

8.3 Document for Analysis: Direct Claim (Obj. 4)

Your Task. Analyze the following poorly written letter, and list its weaknesses. If your instructor directs, revise it using the suggestions you learned in this chapter.

Current date

Mr. Orion Murillo
Manager, Customer Response Center
Western Car Rentals
2259 Weatherford Boulevard
Dallas, TX 74091

Dear Manager Orion Murillo:

This is to inform you that you can't have it both ways. Either you provide customers with cars with full gas tanks or you don't. And if you don't, you shouldn't charge them when they return with empty tanks!

In view of the fact that I picked up a car at the Dallas-Ft. Worth International Airport on June 23 with an empty tank, I had to fill it immediately. Then I drove it until June 26. When I returned the car to Houston, as previously planned, I naturally let the tank go nearly empty, since that is the way I received the car in Dallas-Ft. Worth. But your attendant in Houston charged me to fill the tank—$49.43 (premium gasoline at premium prices)! Although I explained to her that I had received it with an empty tank, she kept telling me that company policy required that she charge for a fill-up. My total bill came to $426.50, which, you must agree, is a lot of money for a rental period of only three days. I have the signed rental agreement and a receipt showing that I paid the full amount and that it included $49.43 for a gas fill-up when I returned the car. Any correspondence should be directed to the undersigned at Impact Group, 402 North Griffin Street, Dallas, TX 74105.

Inasmuch as my company is a new customer and inasmuch as we had hoped to use your agency for our future car rentals because of your competitive rates, I trust that you will give this matter your prompt attention.

Your unhappy customer,

8.4 Document for Analysis: Adjustment (Obj. 6)

Your Task. Analyze the following poorly written letter, and list its weaknesses. If your instructor directs, revise it using the suggestions you learned in this chapter.

Current date

Ms. Sharon Nickels
2459 Drew Street
Clearwater, FL 33765

Dear Ms. Nickels:

Your letter has been referred to me for reply. You claim that the painting recently sent by Manhattan Galleries arrived with sags in the canvas and that you are unwilling to hang it in your company's executive offices.

I have examined your complaint carefully, and, frankly, I find it difficult to believe because we are so careful about shipping, but if what you say is true, I suspect that the shipper may be the source of your problem. We give explicit instructions to our shippers that large paintings must be shipped standing up, not lying down. We also wrap every painting in two layers of convoluted foam and one layer of Perf-Pack foam, which we think should be sufficient to withstand any bumps and scrapes that negligent shipping may cause. We will certainly look into this.

Although it is against our policy, we will in this instance allow you to take this painting to a local framing shop for restretching. We are proud that we can offer fine works of original art at incredibly low prices, and you can be sure that we do not send out sagging canvases.

Sincerely,

8.5 Direct Request: Learning From a Veteran Manager in Your Field (Obj. 3)

You feel fortunate to have found a manager in your field who is willing to talk to you about careers. Your purpose is to learn more about your career area so that you can train for the occupation and also find a job when you finish your schooling. The manager you selected is a busy person, and he will try to work a personal interview into his schedule. But in case he can't meet you in person, he would like to have your questions in letter form so that he could answer them in a telephone conversation if necessary. Seeing the questions arranged in a logical order will also help him be best prepared.

Your Task. Write an information request to a real or fictitious person in a company where you would like to work. If you want to start your own business, write to someone who has done it. Assume that the person has agreed to talk with you, but you haven't set a date. Use your imagination in creating five to eight interview questions. Be sure to show appreciation!

8.6 Direct Request: Wheel Fun Rentals Wants Web Site (Obj. 3)

Team

As the successful co-owners of Wheel Fun Rentals, you and your partner decide that you need a Web site to attract even more business to your resort location. Primarily you rent bicycles and surreys to tourists visiting hotels along the beach. In addition, you carry tandems, pedal go-carts, mountain bikes, slingshot and chopper trikes, other unique bikes, and inline skates. Business is good at your sunny beachside location, but a Web site would provide 24-hour information and attract a wider audience. The trouble is that you don't know anything about creating, hosting, or maintaining a Web site. Your partner has heard of a local company called Xpress Web Design, and you decide to inquire about creating a Web site. You and he prefer to write a letter so that you can work on your questions together and create a unified, orderly presentation.

Your Task. In teams of two or three, prepare an information request with logical questions about designing, hosting, and maintaining a Web site for a small business. You are not expected to create the content of the site. That will come later. Instead you want to ask questions about how a Web site is developed. You know for sure that you want a page that invites resort and hotel operators to feature your fun-filled facilities at their sites, but you don't know how to go about it. Address your letter to John Sebesy, Xpress Web Design, 11040 Pleasant Valley Road, Parma, OH 44130. Be sure to include an end date, a reason, and a way to contact you.

8.7 Information Request: Raising Money by Selling Krispy Kreme Doughnuts (Obj. 3)

You've always loved Krispy Kreme doughnuts, so you were delighted to learn that they are now being sold in a nearby shopping center. You also heard that they can be used in fund-raising events. As chair of the spring fund-raising committee for Little Angels Children's Center, you need to learn more about how Krispy Kreme's fund-raising partnership works. Do you hold a traditional bake sale or what? You wonder how you can make any money if you sell the doughnuts at their regular retail price. You looked at the company's Web site and got basic information. However, you are still unclear

about how certificates work in fund-raising. You also want to know more about Krispy Kreme partnership cards. You left a brief note at the Krispy Kreme Web site, but you didn't get a response. Now you decide to write.

Your Task. Compose a letter asking specific questions about how you can partner with Krispy Kreme in raising funds. Use your return address in a personal business letter style (see Figure 8.5). Send your letter to Customer Relations, Krispy Kreme Doughnut Corporation, P.O. Box 83, Winston-Salem, NC 27103. Decide on a deadline for feedback, and explain how you want Krispy Kreme to respond.

8.8 Direct Request: Las Vegas Calling (Obj. 3)

Your company, Amsoft Technologies, has just had an enormously successful two-year sales period. CEO Ricardo Ulrey has asked you, as marketing manager, to arrange a fabulous conference/retreat. "This will be a giant thank-you gift for all 125 of our engineers, product managers, and salespeople," he said. Warming up to the idea, he said, "I want the company to host a four-day combination sales conference/vacation/retreat at some spectacular location. Let's begin by inquiring at Paris Las Vegas. I hear it's awesome!" You check its Web site and find some general information. However, you decide to write a letter so that you can have a permanent, formal record of all the resorts you investigate. You estimate that your company will require about 100 rooms—preferably with a view of the Strip. You will also need about three conference rooms for one and a half days. You want to know room rates, conference facilities, and entertainment possibilities for families. The CEO gave you two possible times: July 8–12 or August 18–22. You know that these are off-peak times, and you wonder whether you can get a special room rate. You also wonder about the entertainment that will be showing at Paris Las Vegas during these times. One evening the CEO will want to host a banquet for about 250 people. Oh yes, he wants a report from you by March 1.

Your Task: Write a well-organized information request to Ms. Leza Molitoris, Manager, Convention Services, Paris Las Vegas, 281 Paris Drive, Las Vegas, NV 87551. Spell out your needs, conclude with a logical end date, and provide a way to contact you.

8.9 Direct Request: Computer Code of Conduct (Obj. 3)

Web

As an assistant in the campus computer laboratory, you have been asked by your boss to help write a code of conduct for use of the laboratory facilities. This code will spell out what behavior and activities are allowed in your lab. The first thing you are to do is conduct a search of the Internet to see what other college or university computing labs have written as conduct codes.

Your Task. Using at least two search engines, search the Web employing variations of the keywords *computer code of conduct*. Print two or three codes that seem appropriate. Write a letter (or an e-mail message, if your instructor agrees) to the director of an educational computer laboratory asking for further information about its code and its effectiveness. Include at least five significant questions. Attach your printouts to your letter.

8.10 Direct Request: Feeding Finicky Hikers (Obj. 3)

As Samantha Lafayette, manager of a health spa and also an ardent backpacker, you are organizing a group of hikers for a wilderness trip to Canada. One item that must be provided is freeze-dried food for the three-week trip. You are unhappy with the taste and quality of the backpacking food products currently available. You expect to have a group of hikers who are older, affluent, and natural-food enthusiasts. Some are concerned about products containing preservatives, sugar, and additives. Others are on diets restricting carbohydrates, cholesterol, fat, and salt. It is a rather finicky group!

You heard that North Woods Outfitters offers a new line of freeze-dried products. You want to know what they offer and whether they have sufficient variety to serve all the needs of your group. You need to know where their products can be purchased and what the cost range is. You'd also like to try a few of their items before placing a large order. You are interested in production, ingredients, and shelf life.

Your Task. Write an information request letter to Timothy Showalter, North Woods Outfitters, 1350 Austin Bluffs Parkway, Colorado Springs, CO 80933. Be sure to tell him how to respond.

8.11 Direct Claim: Hurricane Arrives Early and Ruins Caribbean Cruise (Obj. 4)

You own a small marketing firm and employ three people. After a very successful year, you decided to reward your employees with a five-day cruise on Carnival's *Sensation*. This luxury liner would visit two tropical islands in the Eastern Caribbean. Each employee could bring a guest, making a total of eight in your party. In addition to acting as a reward, the trip was meant to develop company spirit. You thought that by planning a trip for mid-July, you would miss the hurricane season. That season is usually from mid-August through December. But Hurricane Emily arrived early and struck during the cruise. Both of your ports of call were cancelled. The cruise was not rerouted, and your party was confined to the ship for the entire five days. While on board, you were offered a small nonrefundable shipboard credit for the missed ports. You were also offered a 50 percent discount on a future cruise.

When you departed from Port Canaveral, Florida, skies were overcast, but your happy party was looking looked forward to the charm of Old San Juan, Puerto Rico, and to the delightful mix of French and Dutch cultures in St. Maarten. Sunshine, world-class scuba diving, and tropical delights awaited you. Instead, you ended up confined to a crowded ship with increasingly irritable guests and overworked service personnel. What's more, it rained constantly.

After the cruise you called to ask for a refund of the port charges, since the *Sensation* didn't stop at any ports. On the bill from your travel agent, the port charges were listed at $119 per person, which for a party of eight would add up to $952. A cruise representative said that you shouldn't be concerned about not getting the port charges back because it was a small amount of money. However, you think that it was a large enough amount to complain about.

In speaking to a company representative on the telephone, you said you wanted to invoke "Carnival's Vacation Guarantee." But Jennifer, the cruise representative, replied that Carnival's policy states that passengers who are unhappy with their cruises can get off at the first port. Carnival will pay to fly them home and will refund the unused portion of the cruise. Because your trip didn't stop anywhere, the satisfaction guarantee didn't apply. (To see the guarantee, search the Web for *Carnival's Vacation Guarantee*.)[21]

Your Task. Because your telephone chat with a Carnival representative was unsuccessful, you decide to write a direct claim. Should you demand a full-trip refund ($800 per person) or just ask for a refund of the port charges ($119 per person)? Should you send a letter or an e-mail? Address your message to Angelina M. Juarez, Customer Service, Carnival Cruise Lines, 3655 NW 87th Avenue, Miami, FL 33178-2428 (amrodriquez@carnival.com). Supply any necessary details.

8.12 Direct Claim: Headaches From "No Surprise" Offer (Obj. 4)

As vice president of Breakaway Travel Service, you are upset with Virtuoso Enterprises. Virtuoso is a catalog company that provides imprinted promotional products for companies. Your travel service was looking for something special to offer in promoting its cruise ship travel packages. Virtuoso offered free samples of its promotional merchandise, under its "No Surprise" policy.

You figured, what could you lose? So on February 5 you placed a telephone order for a number of samples. These included an insulated lunch sack, an AM-FM travel radio, a square-ended barrel bag with fanny pack, as well as a deluxe canvas attaché case and two colors of garment-dyed sweatshirts. All items were supposed to be free. You did think it odd that you were asked for your company's MasterCard credit number, but Virtuoso promised to bill you only if you kept the samples.

When the items arrived, you were not pleased, and you returned them all on February 11 (you have a postal receipt showing the return). But your March credit statement showed a charge of $229.13 for the sample items. You called Virtuoso in March and spoke to Rachel, who assured you that a credit would be made on your next statement. However, your April statement showed no credit. You called again and received a similar promise. It's now May and no credit has been made. You decide to write and demand action.

Your Task. Write a claim letter that documents the problem and states the action that you want taken. Add any information you feel is necessary. Address your letter to Ms. Paula Loveday, Customer Services, Virtuoso Enterprises, 420 Ninth Street South, LaCrosse, WI 54602.

8.13 Direct Claim: This Desk Is Going Back (Obj. 4)

As the founder and president of a successful consulting firm, you decided to splurge and purchase a fine executive desk for your own office. You ordered an expensive desk described as "North American white oak embellished with hand-inlaid walnut crossbanding." Although you would not ordinarily purchase large, expensive items by mail, you were impressed by the description of this desk and by the money-back guarantee promised in the catalog.

When the desk arrived, you knew that you had made a mistake. The wood finish was rough, the grain looked splotchy, and many of the drawers would not pull out easily. The advertisement had promised "full suspension, silent ball-bearing drawer slides."

Your Task. Because you are disappointed with the desk, you decide to send it back, taking advantage of the money-back guarantee. Write a claim letter to Patrick Dwiggens, Operations Manager, Premier Wood Products, P.O. Box 528, High Point, NC 27261, asking for your money back. You are not sure whether the freight charges can be refunded, but it is worth a try. Supply any details needed.

8.14 Direct Claim: Backing Out of Project Management Seminar (Obj. 4)

Ace Executive Training Institute offered a seminar titled "Enterprise Project Management Protocol" that sounded terrific. It promised to teach project managers how to estimate work, report status, write work packages, and cope with project conflicts. Because your company often is engaged in large cross-functional projects, it decided to send four key managers to the seminar to be held June 1–2 at the Ace headquarters in Pittsburgh. The fee was $2,200 each, and it was paid in advance. About six weeks before the seminar, you learned

Interactive Learning @ www.meguffey.com

that three of the managers would be tied up in projects that would not be completed in time for them to attend.

Your Task. On your company letterhead, write a claim letter to Addison O'Neill, Registrar, Ace Executive Training Institute, 5000 Forbes Avenue, Pittsburgh, PA 15244. Ask that the seminar fees for three employees be returned because they cannot attend. Give yourself a title and supply any details necessary.

8.15 Direct Claim: A Matter of Mismeasurement (Obj. 4)

As the owner of Custom Designs, you recently completed a living room remodel that required double-glazed, made-to-order oak French doors. You ordered them, by telephone, on April 14 from Capitol Lumber and Hardware. When they arrived on May 18, your carpenter gave you the bad news: the doors were cut too small. Instead of measuring a total of 11 feet 8 inches, the doors measured 11 feet 4 inches. In your carpenter's words, "No way can I stretch those doors to fit these openings!" You waited nearly five weeks for these doors, and your clients wanted them installed immediately. Your carpenter said, "I can rebuild this opening for you, but I'm going to have to charge you for my time." His extra charge came to $376.

You feel that the people at Capitol Lumber should reimburse you for this amount because it was their error. In fact, you actually saved them a bundle of money by not returning the doors. You decide to write to Capitol Lumber and enclose a copy of your carpenter's bill. You wonder whether you should also include a copy of Capitol Lumber's invoice, even though it does not show the exact door measurements. You are a good customer of Capitol Lumber and Hardware, having used their quality doors, windows, and hardware on many other remodeling jobs. You are confident that it will grant this claim.

Your Task. Write a claim letter to Sal Rodriguez, Sales Manager, Capitol Lumber and Hardware, 3568 East Washington Avenue, Indianapolis, IN 46204.

8.16 Direct Claim: The Real Thing (Obj. 4)

Like most consumers, you have probably occasionally been unhappy with service or with products you have used.

Your Task. Select a product or service that has disappointed you. Write a claim letter requesting a refund, replacement, explanation, or whatever seems reasonable. Generally, such letters are addressed to customer service departments. For claims about food products, be sure to include bar-code identification from the package, if possible. Your instructor may ask you to actually mail this letter. Remember that smart companies want to know what their customers think, especially if a product could be improved. Give your ideas for improvement. When you receive a response, share it with your class.

8.17 Direct Reply: So You Want an Internship at the Gap? (Obj. 5)

`Web`

The Gap Inc. headquarters in the San Francisco Bay area is a popular place to work. Many students inquire about summer internships. Although it supplies oodles of information about internships at its Web site, Gap Inc. still receives letters requesting this information. As one of its current summer interns, you have been given a task by your supervisor. She wants you to write a general letter that she can use to reply to requests from college students seeking summer internships. She doesn't have time to answer each one individually, and she doesn't want to tell them all to just go to the Web site. She feels responsible to reply in a way

that builds goodwill for Gap, which also operates Old Navy and Banana Republic.

Your Task. Draft a reply to students seeking summer intern information. Go to the Gap Web site and study its offerings. Prepare a letter that describes the summer intern program, its requirements, and how to apply. Summarize some of the lengthy descriptions from the Web site. Use bulleted lists where appropriate. Since the letter may involve two pages, group similar information under side headings that improve its readability. Although your letter may become a form letter, address your draft to Lisa M. Hernandez, 493 Cesar Court, Walnut Creek, CA 94598.

8.18 Direct Reply: River Rafting on the Web (Obj. 5)

`Web`

As the program chair for the Southern Illinois University Ski Club, you have been asked by the president to investigate river rafting. The Ski Club is an active organization, and its members want to schedule a summer activity. A majority favored rafting. Use a browser to search the Web for relevant information. Select five of the most promising Web sites offering rafting. If possible, print copies of your findings.

Your Task. Summarize your findings in a letter to Brian Krauss, Ski Club president. The next meeting of the Ski Club is May 8, but you think it would be a good idea to discuss your findings with Brian before the meeting. Write to Brian Krauss, SIU Ski Club, 303 Founders Hall, Carbondale, IL 62901.

8.19 Direct Reply: Krispy Kreme Helps Raise Funds (Obj. 5)

`Web`

Despite growing concern for obesity, people still crave yummy doughnuts—especially the oh-so-light yet rich and scrumptious Krispy Kreme creations. As a customer service representative at Krispy Kreme in Winston-Salem, you have received a letter from a customer interested in using your doughnuts as a fund-raising activity for Little Angels Children's Center (see **Activity 8.7**). Although much of the information is at the Web site, you must answer this customer's letter personally.

Your Task. Respond to Mrs. Charity Wofford, 350 Ocean Breeze Drive, Palm Bay, FL 32909. You need to explain the four ways that Krispy Kreme helps organizations raise funds. Use the Krispy Kreme Web site to gather information, but summarize and paraphrase what you find. Compose a letter that not only provides information but also promotes your product. Consider using bullet points and paragraph headings to set off the major points.

8.20 Direct Reply: Tell Me About Your Major (Obj. 5)

A friend in a distant city is considering moving to your area for more education and training in your field. This individual wants to know about your program of study.

Your Task. Write a letter describing a program in your field (or any field you wish to describe). What courses must be taken? Toward what degree, certificate, or employment position does this program lead? Why did you choose it? Would you recommend this program to your friend? How long does it take? Add any information you feel would be helpful.

8.21 Direct Reply: Backpacking Meals for Finicky Eaters (Obj. 5)

As Timothy Showalter, owner of North Woods Outfitters, which produces freeze-dried backpacking foods, you must respond to

Samantha Lafayette (see **Activity 8.10**). You are eager to have Ms. Lafayette sample your new all-natural line of products containing no preservatives, sugar, or additives. You want her to know that you started this company two years ago after you found yourself making custom meals for discerning backpackers who rejected typical camping fare. Some of your menu items are excellent for individuals on restricted diets. Some dinners are cholesterol-, fat-, and salt-free. Others feature low carbs, but she'll have to look at your list to see for herself.

You will send her your complete list of dinner items and the suggested retail prices. You will also send a sample "Saturday Night on the Trail," a four-course meal that comes with fruit candies and elegant appetizers. All your food products are made from choice ingredients in sanitary kitchens that you personally supervise. They are flash frozen in a new vacuum process that you patented. Although your dried foods are meant to last for years, you don't recommend that they be kept beyond 18 months because they may deteriorate. This could happen if a package were punctured or if the products became overheated.

Your Task. Write a response to Samantha Lafayette, Secret Garden Spa, 459 Evergreen Street, Cambridge, MN 55008.

8.22 Adjustment: A Matter of Mismeasurement (Obj. 6)

As Sal Rodriguez, sales manager of Capitol Lumber and Hardware, you have a problem. Your firm manufactures quality precut and custom-built doors and frames. You have received a letter dated May 25 from Candace Olmstead (described in **Activity 8.15**). Ms. Olmstead is an interior designer, and she complains that the oak French doors she recently ordered for a client were made to the wrong dimensions.

Although they were the wrong size, she kept the doors and had them installed because her clients were without outside doors. However, her carpenter charged an extra $376 to install them. She claims that you should reimburse her for this amount, because your company was responsible for the error. You check her June 9 order and find that the order was filled correctly. In a telephone order, Ms. Olmstead requested doors that measured 11 feet 4 inches, and that is what you sent. Now she says that the doors should have been 11 feet 8 inches. Your policy forbids refunds or returns on custom orders. Yet, you remember that in the early part of June you had two new people working the phones taking orders. Possibly they did not hear or record the measurements correctly. You don't know whether to grant this claim or refuse it. But you do know that you must look into the training of telephone order takers and be sure that they verify all custom order measurements. It might also be a good idea to have your craftsmen call a second time to confirm custom measurements.

Ms. Olmstead is a successful interior designer and has provided Capitol Lumber and Hardware with a number of orders. You value her business but aren't sure how to respond.

Your Task. Decide how to treat this claim and then write to Candace Olmstead, Custom Designs, 903 Hazel Dell Parkway, Carmel, IN 46033. In your letter remind her that Capitol Lumber and Hardware has earned a reputation as the manufacturer of the finest wood doors and frames on the market. Your doors feature prime woods, and the craftsmanship is meticulous. The designs of your doors have won awards, and the engineering is ingenious. You have a new line of greenhouse windows that are available in three sizes. Include a brochure describing these windows.

8.23 Adjustment: Backing Out of a Project Management Seminar (Obj. 6)

Ace Executive Training Institute offered a seminar titled "Enterprise Project Management Protocol" for June 1–2 and was delighted to receive reservations from Raintree Manufacturing for four employees to attend (See **Activity 8.14**). But six weeks before the seminar, Ace received a letter from Raintree asking for a refund because three of the four cannot attend. Ace has already hired the instructor and made arrangements for the seminar based on the projected attendance, so it is disappointed to see this cancellation. However, it wants to retain good relations with Raintree in anticipation of future business. It will return the registration fees of $6,600. Because Raintree is having difficulty allowing its employees to get away for training, it may be interested in Ace's AccuVision Training Series with on-site training modules. These modules bring the seminar to the client. They teach team building, situational interaction style, initiative, and analysis/problem solving—right on the client's premises. Your Web site provides all the details.

Your Task. As assistant to Addison O'Neill, registrar, write an adjustment letter to Kit Adkins, Raintree Manufacturing, 491 South Emerald Road, Greenwood, SC 29647. Take advantage of this opportunity to promote your company's on-site programs.

8.24 Adjustment: This Desk Came Back (Obj. 6)

As Patrick Dwiggens, Premier Wood Products, you reply to customer claims, and today you must respond to Stephanie Ahlfeldt (described in **Activity 8.13**). You are unhappy that she is returning the executive desk (Invoice No. T-2873), but your policy is to comply with customer wishes. If she doesn't want to keep the desk, you will certainly return the purchase price plus shipping charges. On occasion, desks are damaged in shipping, and this may explain the marred finish and the sticking drawers.

You want Ms. Ahlfeldt to give Premier Wood Products another chance. After all, your office furniture and other wood products are made from the finest hand-selected woods by master artisans. Because she is apparently furnishing her office, send her another catalog and invite her to look at the traditional conference desk on page 5. This is available with a matching credenza, file cabinets, and accessories.

Your Task. Write an adjustment letter granting the claim of Stephanie Ahlfeldt, President, Ahlfeldt Consulting Services, 258 Mountain View Drive, Fargo, ND 58105. She might be interested in your furniture-leasing plan, which can produce substantial savings. Be sure to promise that you will personally examine any furniture she may order in the future. Add any necessary details.

8.25 Adjustment: No Birds Will Be Harmed (Obj. 6)

You didn't want to do it. But guests were complaining about the pigeons that roost on the Scottsdale Hilton's upper floors and tower.

Pigeon droppings splattered sidewalks, furniture, and people. As the hotel manager, you had to take action. You called an exterminator, who recommended Avitrol. This drug, he promised, would disorient the birds, preventing them from finding their way back to the Hilton. The drugging, however, produced a result you didn't expect: pigeons began dying.

After a story hit the local newspapers, you began to receive complaints. The most vocal came from the Avian Affairs Coalition, a local bird-advocacy group. It said that the pigeons are really Mediterranean rock doves, the original "Dove of Peace" in European history and the same species the Bible said Noah originally released from his ark during the great flood. Activists claimed that Avitrol is a lethal drug causing birds, animals, and even people who ingest as little as 1/600th of a teaspoon to convulse and die lingering deaths of up to two hours.

Repulsed at the pigeon deaths and the bad publicity, you stopped the use of Avitrol immediately. You are now considering installing wires that offer a mild, nonlethal electrical shock. These wires, installed at the Maricopa County Jail in downtown Phoenix for $50,000, keep thousands of pigeons from alighting and could save $1 million in extermination and cleanup costs over the life of the building. You are also considering installing netting that forms a transparent barrier, sealing areas against entry by birds.

Your Task. Respond to Mrs. Deborah Leverette, 24 Canyon Lake Shore Drive, Spring Branch, TX 52319, a recent Scottsdale Hilton guest. She sent a letter condemning the pigeon poisoning and threatening to never return to the hotel unless it changed its policy. Try to regain the confidence of Mrs. Leverette and promote further business.[22]

8.26 Adjustment: Cure for "No Surprise" Headache (Obj. 6)

Virtuoso Enterprises prides itself on its "No Surprise" offer. This means that anything ordered from its catalog of promotional products may be returned for a full refund within two weeks of purchase. The claim from Breakaway Travel Service (see **Activity 8.12**) describes an order placed February 5 and returned February 11. As assistant to Paula Loveday, manager, Customer Services, you check the return files and see that items were received February 16. You speak with service agent Rachel, who agrees with you—the credit of $229.13 should have been granted to Breakaway Travel. She reminds you that a new system for handling credits was implemented in March. Perhaps the Breakaway return slipped through the cracks. Regardless of the reason, you decide to tell accounting to issue the credit immediately.

Your Task. In an adjustment letter, try to regain the confidence and the business of Breakaway Travel Service, 350 Valle Vista Drive, San Luis Obispo, CA 93403. Include a sample imprinted travel mug in a gift box and a Coleman 8-quart jug cooler. You know that you are the most reliable source for the lowest-priced imprinted promotional products in the field, and this travel agency should be able to find something suitable in your catalog. Address your letter to Leila Chambers.

8.27 Thanks for a Favor: Got the Job! (Obj. 7)

Congratulations! You completed your degree and got a terrific job in your field. One of your instructors was especially helpful to you when you were a student. This instructor also wrote an effective letter of recommendation that was instrumental in helping you obtain your job.

Your Task. Write a letter thanking your instructor.

8.28 Thanks for the Hospitality: Holiday Entertaining (Obj. 7)

You and other members of your staff or organization were entertained at an elegant dinner during the winter holiday season.

Your Task. Write a thank-you letter to your boss (supervisor, manager, vice president, president, or chief executive officer) or to the head of an organization to which you belong. Include specific details that will make your letter personal and sincere.

8.29 Sending Good Wishes: Personalizing Group Greeting Cards (Obj. 7)

> Team | Web

When a work colleague has a birthday, gets promoted, or retires, someone generally circulates a group greeting card. In the past it wasn't a big deal. Office colleagues just signed their names and passed the store-bought card along to others. But the current trend is toward personalization with witty, oh-so-clever quips. And that presents a problem. What should you say—or not say? You know that people value special handwritten quips, but you realize that you are not particularly original and you don't have a store of "bon mots" (clever sayings, witticisms). You are tired of the old standbys, such as *This place won't be the same without you* and *You are only as old as you feel*.

Your Task. To be prepared for the next greeting card that lands on your desk at work, you decide to work with some friends to make a list of remarks appropriate for business occasions. Use the Web to research witty sayings appropriate for promotions, birthdays, births, weddings, illnesses, or personal losses. Use a search term such as *birthday sayings, retirement quotes,* or *cool sayings*. You may decide to assign each category (birthday, retirement, promotion, and so forth) to a separate team. Submit the best sayings in a memo to your instructor.

8.30 Responding to Good Wishes: Saying Thank You (Obj. 7)

Your Task. Write a short note thanking a friend who sent you good wishes when you recently completed your degree.

8.31 Extending Sympathy: To a Spouse (Obj. 7)

Your Task. Imagine that a coworker was killed in an automobile accident. Write a letter of sympathy to his or her spouse.

8.32 Consumer Claim: The Check in the Mail Is a Bill (Obj. 4)

> Consumer | Team

Houston chiropractor Brett Downey cashed a $2.50 check last December from Yellow Pages Inc. of Anaheim, California. That is when his troubles began. He thought the check was some kind of refund for overpaying his company's ad in the Southwestern Bell's local telephone book. Like many small business owners and professional people, he takes care of his own bills and does not have time to read everything carefully.

In January he was flabbergasted to receive a bill for $179 from the Anaheim company for registering his Fairview Health Center in its Yellow Pages directory. He called and discovered that by cashing the check, he unknowingly had signed up for a one-year listing on the Internet. Fine print on the back of the check apparently authorized the listing. Representatives of the company insisted that by signing the check, Dr. Downey had accepted their promotional incentive, which starts the billing process. He did, after all, sign the check.[23]

Your Task. In teams or individually, analyze what happened. How many companies do you think have "Yellow Pages" in their names? Does this "Yellow Pages" check offer sound like a scam? What other scams do you know about that involve small businesspeople? Should Dr. Downey contact the Better Business Bureau?

Assume that Dr. Downey has received several billings, and he wants them to stop. He asks you to help him write an appropriate letter to Yellow Pages Inc., P.O. Box 4298, Anaheim, CA 95091. Should he send back the $2.50 from the check he cashed? Use the simplified letter style to avoid a salutation.

Video Resources

Bridging the Gap Video Library 2
Adjustment Letter: Ben & Jerry's
In an exciting inside look, you see managers discussing six factors that determine Ben & Jerry's continuing success. Toward the end of the video, you hear staffers discuss a new packaging material made with unbleached paper. As a socially responsible company, Ben & Jerry's wanted to move away from ice cream packages made from bleached papers. Bleaching requires chlorine, a substance that contains dioxin, which is known to cause cancer, genetic and reproductive defects, and learning disabilities. In producing paper, pulp mills using chlorine are also adding to dioxin contamination of waterways. After much research, Ben & Jerry's found a chlorine-free, unbleached paper board for its packages. That was the good news. The bad news is that the inside of the package is now brown.

Assume you have been hired at Ben & Jerry's to help answer incoming letters. Although you are fairly new, your boss gives you a letter from an unhappy customer. This customer opened a pint of Ben & Jerry's "World's Best Vanilla" and then threw it out. After seeing the brown inner lid, he decided that his pint must have been used for chocolate before it was used for vanilla. Or, he said, "the entire pint has gone bad and somehow turned the sides brown." Whatever the reason, he wasn't taking any chances. He wanted his money back.

Your Task. Write a letter that explains the brown carton, justifies the reason for using it, and retains the customer's business. Address the letter to Mr. Cecil Hamm, 1608 South McKenna, Poteau, OK 74954.

Grammar and Mechanics C.L.U.E. Review 8

Capitalization

Review Guides 39–46 about capitalization in Appendix A: Grammar and Mechanics Guide (Competent Language Usage Essentials), beginning on page A-16. On a separate sheet, revise the following sentences to correct capitalization errors. For each error that you locate, write the guide number that reflects this usage. Sentences may have more than one error. If a sentence is correct, write *C*. When you finish, check your answers on page Key-2.

Example: Once the Management Team and the Union members finally agreed, mayor murphy signed the Agreement.

Revision: Once the **management team** and the **union** members finally agreed, **Mayor Murphy** signed the **agreement**. [Guides 39, 41]

1. All southwest airlines passengers will exit the Plane at gate 14 when they reach ontario international airport.

2. Personal Tax Rates for japanese citizens are low by International standards, according to professor yamaguchi at osaka university.

3. The vice president of the united states said that this country continues to seek middle east peace.

4. My Father, who lives in the midwest, has Skippy Peanut Butter and coca-cola for Breakfast.

5. Our Sales Manager and Director of Marketing both expected to receive Federal funding for the project.

6. Although the Manager recommended purchasing dell computers, our Vice President wanted to wait.

7. Sana Nadir, who heads our customer communication division, has a Master's Degree in social psychology from the university of new mexico.

8. Please consult figure 4.5 in chapter 4 to obtain U.S. census bureau population figures for the pacific northwest.

9. Did you see the article in *businessweek* titled, "The global consequences of using crops for fuel"?

10. Christian plans to take courses in Marketing, Business Law, and English during the Fall.

Chapter 9

Persuasive and Marketing Messages

© TRBfoto / Photodisc / Getty Images

OBJECTIVES

After studying this chapter, you should be able to

1 Define the concept of persuasion, identify effective and ineffective persuasive techniques, and discuss the importance of tone in persuasive messages.

2 Apply the 3-x-3 writing process to persuasive messages.

3 Explain the four major elements in successful persuasive messages and how to blend those elements into effective and ethical business messages.

4 Write messages that request favors and actions.

5 Write persuasive messages within organizations.

6 Write effective claim and complaint letters.

7 Write effective, yet ethical, sales and marketing messages.

8 Compare effective persuasion techniques in high- and low-context cultures.

9 Understand basic patterns and techniques in developing persuasive press releases.

Communicating at Work Part 1

Hands on Miami

"We make a living by what we get, but we make a life by what we give," said Winston Churchill. To Pat Morris, this is a creed to live by.

"For me, it is about trying to make a difference in my community," said Morris, CEO of Hands on Miami, a volunteer organization dedicated to making Miami a better place to live. "Giving to others," said Morris, "often comes back to you many, many times."[1]

Morris helped found Hands on Miami (HOM) to create a user-friendly approach to community service. HOM's new method involves making it easy for volunteers to participate regardless of their hectic schedules. Projects take place outside traditional work hours, and flexible time commitments permit volunteers to serve once a week, once a month, or whenever they can.

Hands on Miami partners with schools, social service organizations, and environmental organizations to offer more than 80 service opportunities each month. This gives thousands of Miamians the chance to make a difference in their community. Volunteers can spend a morning delivering care packages to AIDS patients in a local hospital, an afternoon planting native vegetation to restore natural beauty and ecosystems, or an evening reading bedtime stories to children at an emergency shelter. What's distinctive about HOM's program is that it makes community service accessible to anyone regardless of schedule. Because volunteerism is essential to enriching a community's well-being, most HOM projects are team based and take place in the evenings and on weekends, making it easy for busy people to give back to the community. HOM's hallmark flexible volunteering program has been a resounding success.

In addition to organizing volunteers, HOM acts as a consultant on a fee-for-service basis to design volunteer opportunities to meet a company's particular needs. Carnival Cruise Lines and other local companies often use the expertise of HOM in planning their own volunteer programs. Corporate donors provide further assistance by sponsoring big events such as Hands on Miami Day.

© Jeff Greenberg / PhotoEdit

As CEO, Pat Morris uses persuasion to keep his staff energized, motivated, and organized. He must be persuasive in reaching out to corporate donors to persuade them to send volunteers to participate in Hands on Miami programs. He must also sway corporations to sponsor events with cash contributions. Persuasion is a large part of his leadership role at Hands on Miami.[2] You will learn more about Hands on Miami on page 242.

Critical Thinking

● Pat Morris at Hands on Miami believes firmly in the benefits of volunteering. In his role as CEO, who must he effectively persuade to ensure the success of the organization?
● In your own career, when might you find it necessary to be persuasive?
● In your experience, what techniques are effective or ineffective in persuading others to accept your views?

http://www.handsonmiami.org

Understanding Persuasion and How to Use It Effectively and Ethically

LEARNING OBJECTIVE 1
Define the concept of persuasion, identify effective and ineffective persuasive techniques, and discuss the importance of tone in persuasive messages.

The art of convincing others that your point of view is the right one is a critical business communication skill. At Hands on Miami, CEO Pat Morris must be persuasive in all aspects of his job—in convincing his staff about the importance of their tasks, in winning over corporate sponsors, and in swaying volunteers to support community projects. For all businesspeople, persuasion is a critical skill. However, many of us do it poorly or unconsciously.[3] You have already studied techniques for writing routine request messages that required subtle forms of persuasion. This chapter focuses on messages that require deliberate and skilled persuasion. You will learn what persuasion is and how to apply it effectively when you write requests for favors and action, make claims, and prepare marketing messages. This is one of the most important chapters in the book because much of your success in business depends on how skilled you are at persuading people to believe, accept, and act on what you are saying.

What Is Persuasion?

Persuasion is the ability to use argument or discussion to change beliefs or actions.

Persuasion is defined as the ability to use argument or discussion in attempting to change an individual's beliefs or actions. Parents use persuasion to cajole their kids into doing their

Does "climate change" evoke more positive emotions than "global warming?" Frank Luntz thinks so, and he wrote the book on persuasion—literally. The communication expert's top selling book, *Words That Work,* examines words, phrases, and message strategies that resonate with audiences in the 21st century. Luntz's ground-breaking research, including the use of Instant Response dial technology to gauge the impact of words on live audiences, has aided politicians and guided Fortune 500 clients including American Express and Disney. *When is persuasion ethical, and when is it manipulation and "spin"?*

homework. A team member uses persuasion to convince her technology-averse manager that instant messaging is an excellent tool to keep all team members informed about a project. You might want to persuade your boss to allow you to work at home part of the time. In Figure 9.1 Stacy McPherson, general manager of Oak Park Town Center, uses persuasion in a memo to the mall owner and president. She wants to convince him to restrict the access of unchaperoned teenagers on weekends and evenings.

Some people think that persuasion involves coercion or trickery. They think that you can achieve what you seek only if you twist an arm or deceive someone. Such negative tactics are ineffective and unethical. What's more, these tactics don't truly represent persuasion. To persuade is to present information enabling others to see the benefits of what you are offering, without browbeating or tricking them into agreement.

Successful persuasion depends largely on the reasonableness of your request, your credibility, and your ability to make the request attractive to the receiver. Many techniques can help you be effective in getting your ideas accepted by your fellow workers, superiors, and clients.

Successful persuasion results from a reasonable request, a credible source, and a well-presented argument.

Effective Persuasion Techniques

When you want your ideas to prevail, spend some time thinking about how to present them. Listeners and readers will be more inclined to accept what you are offering if you focus on the following important strategies, which are outlined here and further discussed with illustrations throughout the chapter.

Establish credibility. To be persuasive, you must engender trust. People must believe that you are telling the truth, are experienced, and know what you are talking about. Most of us would not be swayed if a soccer or film star told us how to ease world tensions. If you lack credentials or experience, use testimonials, expert opinion, and research to support your position.

Make a reasonable, precise request. Persuasion is most effective if your request is realistic, doable, and attainable. Don't ask for $100,000 worth of equipment when your department's budget is $5,000. Also be clear about your objective. In one research study, students posed as beggars and asked for money. If they asked for an unspecified amount,

FIGURE 9.1 Persuasive Action Request

MEMO

DATE: April 2, 2009

TO: Antwoine M. Jones, President, Oak Park Associates

FROM: Stacy R. McPherson, General Manager, Oak Park Town Center *S R M*

SUBJECT: Encouraging Adult Shoppers to Return to Oak Park Town Center

Families and adult shoppers have largely disappeared at Oak Park Town Center after 5 p.m. Attendance at our 21-screen cinema has dropped 40 percent, and all five of our anchor stores report slow weekend and evening sales. Families and older consumers seem to be scared off by rowdy teens who congregate and socialize but do not shop. On some weekends, we have expelled up to 750 teens a night.

Restricting Access

It might be wise for Oak Park to follow the lead of other malls facing similar problems. A survey of 1,000 members of the International Council of Shopping Centers found that nearly a third of the respondents had adopted policies that limited access of teenagers. Here are a few examples:

- Mall of America, Bloomington, Minnesota, prohibits unchaperoned teens 17 and under from access after 4 p.m. on weekends.
- Holyoke Mall and Eastfield Mall in Massachusetts restrict teenagers 17 and under from entering after 4 p.m. on Fridays and Saturdays unless escorted by an adult.
- Fairlane Town Center, Dearborn, Michigan, requires teens 17 and under to be escorted by a chaperone after 5 p.m. every evening.

Benefits of Restricted Access

If Oak Park institutes restrictions, we could experience a number of benefits:

- Increased profits by attracting a wider range of customers who spend money
- Less shoplifting
- Fewer disruptive incidents such as fights
- Savings of $5,600 in salaries for seven off-duty police officers currently hired for weekend duty

Winning support for a teen restriction policy at Oak Park would require cooperation from school officials, local civil rights groups, and religious leaders. Considerable effort would be necessary to make our program work, but I am convinced that the benefits are well worth the effort. Please examine the program I have outlined in the attached sheet.

If we don't begin to restrict teenagers, Oak Park will continue to lose adult shoppers, and we may have to expand the number of police officers as the summer approaches. May I talk with you about my plan to return Oak Park to a lively but secure shopping center? I will call you Monday to arrange an appointment.

Attachment

Establishes credibility by citing specific data and examples

Uses careful tone ("it might be wise") in message to a superior

Lists benefits to management including increased profits and monetary savings

Motivates reader by mentioning what could be lost if action is not taken

Gains attention by presenting graphic details of problems

Builds interest and enhances readability with bulleted list and parallel phrasing

Expects community resistance and describes plan to overcome it

---

they received money 44 percent of the time. If they asked for a precise sum (say, $1), they received money 64 percent of the time.[4] Precise requests are more effective.

Tie facts to benefits. Line up solid information to support your view. Use statistics, printed resources, examples, and analogies to help people understand. Remember, however, that information alone rarely changes attitudes. Marketers have pumped huge sums into failed advertising and public relations campaigns that provided facts alone. More important is converting those facts into benefits for the audience, as Stacy did in Figure 9.1.

Recognize the power of loss. Describing the benefits of your proposal is a powerful motivator. Another powerful motivator is the thought of what the other person will lose if he or she doesn't agree. The threat of losing something one already possesses—such as time, money, competitive advantage, profits, reputation—seems to be more likely to motivate people than the idea of gaining that very same thing.[5]

Expect and overcome resistance. When proposing ideas, be prepared for resistance. This may arise in the form of conflicting beliefs, negative attitudes, apathy, skepticism, and opposing loyalties. Recognize any weakness in your proposal and be prepared to

You will be more persuasive if you are credible, make a reasonable request, tie facts to benefits, recognize the power of loss, overcome resistance, share solutions, and are ready to compromise.

counter with well-reasoned arguments and facts. In Figure 9.1, Stacy realized that her proposal to restrict the access of unchaperoned teenagers would require acceptance and cooperation from community groups.

Share solutions and compromise. The process of persuasion may involve being flexible and working out a solution that is acceptable to all concerned. Sharing a solution requires listening to people and developing a new position that incorporates their input. When others' views become part of a solution, they gain a sense of ownership; they "buy in" and are more eager to implement the solution.

The Importance of Tone

Tone is particularly important in persuasion today because the workplace has changed. Gone are the days when managers could simply demand compliance. Today's managers and team leaders strive to generate cooperation and "buy-in" instead of using intimidation, threats, and punishment to gain compliance.[6] Team members no longer accept unquestioned authority. How can persuaders improve the tone of their requests?

- **Avoid sounding preachy or parental.** People don't want to be lectured or instructed in a demeaning manner. No one likes to be treated like a child.

- **Don't pull rank.** Effective persuasion doesn't result from status or authority. People want to be recognized as individuals of worth. Pulling rank may secure compliance but not buy-in.

- **Avoid making threats.** People may comply when threatened, but their compliance may disappear over time. For example, many drivers follow the speed limit only when a patrol car is near. Threats also may result in retaliation, reduced productivity, and low morale.

- **Soften your words when persuading upward.** When you must persuade someone who has more clout than you, use words such as *suggest* and *recommend.* Craft sentences that begin with *It might be a good idea to . . .* Make suggestions without threatening authority.

- **Be enthusiastic.** Convey your passion for an idea through your body language, voice, and words. When you enthusiastically request something to be done, people feel more confident that they can do it.

- **Be positive and likeable.** If people feel positively toward you and perceive you as a friend, they are more likely to agree with you. Use sincere compliments and praise. Describe what a positive impact others have had. Offer to reciprocate, if you are asking a favor.

The tone of effective persuasive business requests invites cooperation; it avoids intimidation, lecturing, and excessive authoritarianism.

Applying the 3-x-3 Writing Process to Persuasive Messages

Persuasion means changing people's views, and that's often a difficult task. Pulling it off demands planning and perception. The 3-x-3 writing process provides you with a helpful structure for laying a foundation for persuasion. Of particular importance here are (a) analyzing the purpose, (b) adapting to the audience, (c) collecting information, and (d) organizing the message.

LEARNING OBJECTIVE 2
Apply the 3-x-3 writing process to persuasive messages.

Analyzing the Purpose

The purpose of a persuasive message is to convert the receiver to your ideas or to motivate action. A message without a clear purpose is doomed. Not only must you know what your purpose is and what response you want, but you must know these things when you start writing your message or planning a presentation. Too often, inexperienced writers reach the end of the first draft of a message before discovering exactly what they want the receiver to do. Then they must start over, giving the request a different "spin" or emphasis. Because your purpose establishes the strategy of the message, determine it first.

Persuasive messages require a careful analysis of the purpose for writing.

Spotlight on Communicators

As CEO of Internet auction giant eBay, Margaret "Meg" Whitman realizes the enormous benefits of adapting to her audience. In making eBay one of the most powerful economic forces on the Internet, Whitman is constantly "listening, adapting, enabling." To know her audience thoroughly, she regularly attends customer conferences and also brings 10 to 20 of eBay's best customers into its offices each month. Her goal is getting to know them and their shopping habits. Understanding your audience is a major part of every successful marketing effort.

Effective persuasive messages focus on audience needs or goals.

Let's say you must convince Rachel, your department manager, that you could be more productive if you could work from home. Before approaching Rachel, know exactly what you want. How much time do you want to work at home? Full time? Part time? On special projects? Do you want Rachel to merely talk about it with you? Do you want her to set a time when you could start? Should you suggest a trial period? By identifying your purpose up front, you can shape the message to point toward it. This planning effort saves considerable rewriting time and produces the most successful persuasive messages.

Adapting to the Audience

While you are considering the purpose of a persuasive message, you also need to concentrate on the receiver. How can you adapt your request to that individual so that your message is heard? Zorba the Greek wisely observed, "You can knock forever on a deaf man's door." A persuasive message is equally futile unless it meets the needs of its audience. In a broad sense, you will be seeking to show how your request helps the receiver achieve some of life's major goals or fulfills key needs: money, power, comfort, confidence, importance, friends, peace of mind, and recognition, to name a few.

On a more practical level, you want to show how your request solves a problem, achieves a personal or work objective, or just makes life easier for your audience. In your request for a flexible work schedule, you could appeal to Rachel's expressed concern for increasing productivity. Your goal is to make the boss look good by granting your request.

To adapt your request to the receiver, consider these questions that receivers will very likely be asking themselves:

Why should I?

What's in it for me?

What's in it for you?

Who cares?

Adapting to your audience means being ready to answer these questions. It means learning about audience members and analyzing why they might resist your proposal. It means searching for ways to connect your purpose with their needs. If completed before you begin writing, such analysis goes a long way toward overcoming resistance and achieving your goal.

Researching and Organizing Data

The key components of a persuasive request are gaining attention, showing the worth of the proposal, overcoming resistance, and motivating action.

Once you've analyzed the audience and considered how to adapt your message to its needs, you are ready to collect data and organize it. You might brainstorm and prepare cluster diagrams to provide a rough outline of ideas. For your request for a flexible work schedule, you might gather information describing how other comparable companies have developed telecommuting programs and how effective they are. You could work out a possible schedule outlining when you would be working at home and when you would be in the office for meetings and face-to-face discussions. You are certain you could complete more work at home, but how can you prove it in your request? To overcome resistance, you might describe your work-at-home office, equipment, and procedures. You could also explain your plan for staying in touch with and being responsive to inquiries and requests.

The next step in a persuasive message is organizing your data into a logical sequence. If you are asking for something that you know will be approved, little persuasion is required. Thus, you would make a direct request, as you studied in Chapters 7 and 8. But when you expect resistance or when you need to educate the receiver, the indirect pattern often works better. The following four-part indirect pattern works well for many persuasive requests:

1. Gain attention

2. Build interest

3. Reduce resistance

4. Motivate action

Blending Four Major Elements in Successful Persuasive Messages

Although the indirect pattern appears to contain separate steps, successful persuasive messages actually blend four steps into a seamless whole. However, the sequence of the elements may change depending on the situation and the emphasis. Regardless of where they are placed, the key elements in persuasive requests are (a) gaining your audience's attention, (b) building interest by convincing your audience that your proposal is worthy, (c) reducing resistance, and (d) motivating action.

Gaining Attention

To grab attention, the opening statement in a persuasive request should be brief, relevant, and engaging. When only mild persuasion is necessary, the opener can be low-key and factual. If, however, your request is substantial and you anticipate strong resistance, provide a thoughtful, provocative opening. Following are some examples.

Successful openers to persuasive requests should be brief, relevant, and engaging.

- **Problem description.** In a recommendation to hire temporary employees: *Last month legal division staff members were forced to work 120 overtime hours, costing us $6,000 and causing considerable employee unhappiness.* With this opener you've presented a capsule of the problem your proposal will help solve.

- **Unexpected statement.** In a memo to encourage employees to attend an optional sensitivity seminar: *Men and women draw the line at decidedly different places in identifying what behavior constitutes sexual harassment.* Note how this opener gets readers thinking immediately.

- **Reader benefit.** In a letter promoting Clear Card, a service that helps employees make credit card purchases without paying interest: *The average employee carries nearly $9,000 in revolving debt and pays $1,800 in interest and late fees. The Clear Card charges zero percent interest. You can't beat it!* Employers immediately see this offer as a benefit it can offer employees.

- **Compliment.** In a letter inviting a business executive to speak: *Because our members admire your success and value your managerial expertise, they want you to be our speaker.* In offering praise or compliments, however, be careful to avoid obvious flattery.

- **Related facts.** In a message to company executives who are considering restricting cell phone use by employee drivers: *A recent study revealed that employers pay an average of $16,500 each time an employee is in a traffic accident.* This relevant fact sets the scene for the interest-building section that follows.

- **Stimulating question.** In a plea for funds to support environmental causes: *What do golden tortoise beetles, bark spiders, flounders, and Arctic foxes have in common?* Readers will be curious to find the answer to this intriguing question. [They all change color depending on their surroundings.]

Building Interest

After capturing attention, a persuasive request must retain that attention and convince the audience that the request is reasonable. To justify your request, be prepared to invest in a few paragraphs of explanation. Persuasive requests are likely to be longer than direct requests because the audience must be convinced rather than simply instructed. You can build interest and conviction through the use of the following:

The body of a persuasive request may require several paragraphs to build interest and reduce resistance.

- Facts, statistics
- Expert opinion
- Direct benefits
- Examples
- Specific details
- Indirect benefits

Showing how your request can benefit the audience directly or indirectly is a key factor in persuasion. If you were asking alumni to contribute money to a college foundation, for example, you might promote *direct benefits* such as listing the donor's name in the college magazine or sending a sweatshirt with the college logo. Another direct benefit is a tax write-off for the contribution. An *indirect benefit* might be feeling good about helping

Spotlight on Communicators

Powerful new viruses and wily hackers are a growing danger to the security of the Internet. But Symantec CEO John W. Thompson gives consumers and corporations a whole arsenal of defenses. Described as a hard-charging but trustworthy leader, Thompson uses both emotional and rational appeals to reduce resistance in crafting Symantec's sales messages. The company makes rational promises assuring users of its real-time analysis by a staff of security experts using cutting-edge technology to monitor cyber-intrusion. Emotionally, it assures users that they can rest easy knowing that it will issue alerts within 15 minutes of virus, worm, and other attack trends before major problems arise.

Persuasive requests reduce resistance by addressing *What if?* questions and establishing credibility.

the college and knowing that students will benefit from the gift. Nearly all charities rely in large part on indirect benefits to promote their causes.

Reducing Resistance

One of the biggest mistakes in persuasive requests is the failure to anticipate and offset audience resistance. How will the receiver object to your request? In brainstorming for clues, try *What if?* scenarios. Let's say you are trying to convince management that the employees' cafeteria should switch from paper and plastic plates and cups to ceramic. What if managers say the change is too expensive? What if they argue that they are careful recyclers of paper and plastic? What if they contend that ceramic dishes would increase cafeteria labor and energy costs tremendously? What if they protest that ceramic is less hygienic? For each of these *What if?* scenarios, you need a counterargument.

Unless you anticipate resistance, you give the receiver an easy opportunity to dismiss your request. Countering this resistance is important, but you must do it with finesse (*Although ceramic dishes cost more at first, they actually save money over time*). You can minimize objections by presenting your counterarguments in sentences that emphasize benefits: *Ceramic dishes may require a little more effort in cleaning, but they bring warmth and graciousness to meals. Most important, they help save the environment by requiring fewer resources and eliminating waste.* However, don't spend too much time on counterarguments, thus making them overly important. Finally, avoid bringing up objections that may never have occurred to the receiver in the first place.

Another factor that reduces resistance is credibility. Receivers are less resistant if your request is reasonable and if you are believable. When the receiver does not know you, you may have to establish your expertise, refer to your credentials, or demonstrate your competence. Even when you are known, you may have to establish your knowledge in a given area. If you are asking your manager for a new laptop computer, you might have to establish your credibility by showing your manager articles about the latest laptops. You could point out that a laptop would enable you to work away from the office while staying in touch by e-mail. Some charities establish their credibility by displaying on their stationery the names of famous people who serve on their boards. The credibility of speakers making presentations is usually outlined by someone who introduces them.

Persuasive requests motivate action by specifying exactly what should be done.

Motivating Action

After gaining attention, building interest, and reducing resistance, you will want to inspire the receiver to act. This is where your planning pays dividends. Knowing exactly what action you favor before you start to write enables you to point your arguments toward this important final paragraph. Here you will make your recommendation as specifically and confidently as possible—without seeming pushy. A proposal from one manager to another might conclude with, *So that we can begin using the employment assessment tests by May 1, please send a return e-mail immediately.* In making a request, don't sound apologetic (*I'm sorry to have to ask you this, but . . .*), and don't supply excuses (*If you can spare the time, . . .*). Compare the following closings for a persuasive memo recommending training seminars in communication skills.

Too General
We are certain we can develop a series of training sessions that will improve the communication skills of your employees.

Too Timid
If you agree that our training proposal has merit, perhaps we could begin the series in June.

Too Pushy
Because we are convinced that you will want to begin improving the skills of your employees immediately, we have scheduled your series to begin in June.

FIGURE 9.2 Components of a Persuasive Message

Gaining Attention	Building Interest	Reducing Resistance	Motivating Action
Summary of problem	Facts, figures	Anticipate objections	Describe specific request
Unexpected statement	Expert opinion	Offer counterarguments	Sound confident
Reader benefit	Examples	Employ *What if?* scenarios	Make action easy to take
Compliment	Specific details	Establish credibility	Offer incentive
Related fact	Direct benefits	Demonstrate competence	Don't provide excuses
Stimulating question	Indirect benefits	Show value of proposal	Repeat main benefit

Effective

You will see decided improvement in the communication skills of your employees. Please call me at 439-2201 by May 1 to give your approval so that training sessions may start in June, as we discussed.

Note how the last opening suggests a specific and easy-to-follow action. It also provides a deadline and a reason for that date. Figure 9.2 summarizes techniques for overcoming resistance and crafting successful persuasive messages.

Being Persuasive and Ethical

Business communicators may be tempted to make their persuasion even more forceful by fudging on the facts, exaggerating a point, omitting something crucial, or providing deceptive emphasis. Consider the case of a manager who sought to persuade employees to accept a change in insurance benefits. His memo emphasized a small perk (easier handling of claims) but de-emphasized a major reduction in total coverage. Some readers missed the main point—as the manager intended. Others recognized the deception, however, and before long the manager's credibility was lost. A persuader is effective only when he or she is believable. If receivers suspect that they are being manipulated or misled or if they find any part of the argument untruthful, the total argument fails. Persuaders can also fall into traps of logic without even being aware of it. Take a look at the accompanying Ethical Insights box to learn about common logical fallacies that you will want to avoid.

Persuasion becomes unethical when facts are distorted, overlooked, or manipulated with an intent to deceive. Of course, persuaders naturally want to put forth their strongest case. But that argument must be based on truth, objectivity, and fairness.

> Ethical business communicators maintain credibility and respect by being honest, fair, and objective.

Ethical Insights

What's Fair in Persuasion? Avoiding Common Logical Fallacies

While being persuasive, we must be careful to remain ethical. In our eagerness to win others over to our views, we may inadvertently overstep the bounds of fair play. Philosophers through the years have pinpointed a number of logical fallacies. Here are three you will want to avoid in your persuasive messages. For an online discussion of many logical fallacies, use a Web search engine to find "Stephen's Guide to the Logical Fallacies."

- **Circular reasoning.** When the support given for a contention merely restates the contention, the reasoning is circular. For example, *Investing in the stock market is dangerous for short-term investors because it is unsafe.* The evidence (*because it is unsafe*) offers no proof. It merely circles back to the original contention. Revision: *Investing in the stock market is dangerous for short-term investors because stock prices fluctuate widely.*
- **Begging the question.** A statement such as *That dishonest CEO should be replaced* begs the question. Merely asserting that the CEO is dishonest is not enough. Be sure to supply solid evidence for such assertions. Revision: *That CEO is dishonest because he*

awards contracts only to his friends. A good manager would require open bidding.
- **Post hoc (*after, thus, because*).** Although two events may have happened in immediate sequence, the first did not necessarily cause the second. For example, *The company switched to team-based management, and its stock price rose immediately afterward.* Switching to teams probably had no effect on the stock price. Revision: *At about the same time the company switched to team-based management, its stock price began to rise, although the two events are probably unrelated.*

Career Application

In teams or in a class discussion, cite examples of how these fallacies could be used in persuasive messages or sales letters. Provide a logical, ethical revision for each.

Communicating at Work Part 2

Hands on Miami

Being good corporate citizens ranks high with many businesses today, and Hands on Miami helps them do just that. Its Corporate Services Program assists businesses in developing community service projects. More and more business organizations today realize that their commitment to social responsibility provides many advantages. In a Points of Light Foundation poll, 90 percent of companies surveyed believed their employer-sponsored community service programs enhanced their public image, boosted employee morale and job satisfaction, helped recruit and retain quality employees, and built better work teams.

Volunteerism gives corporations an edge. Many corporations, however, do not have the staff resources or expertise to develop and manage corporate volunteer efforts. That's where Hands on Miami's Corporate Services Program comes in. Its fee-based consulting services can survey employees about their volunteer interests, develop employee volunteer programs, and design and lead corporate volunteer days. It can also facilitate long-term employee volunteering, train and educate employee volunteers, and track employee volunteer hours.

Hands on Miami helped organize and now serves as advisor to Carnival Cruise Lines' employee volunteer program, the F.U.N. Team (Friends Uniting Neighbors). Their ongoing volunteer activities not only support the community but also improve company pride, teamwork, and leadership skills.

With the assistance of Hands on Miami, Time Warner added a highly successful team-building component to an annual conference

© Jeff Greenberg / PhotoEdit

in Miami. Attendees turned an abandoned courtyard into a garden and painted reading-themed murals at an agency for homeless women and children.

Pat Morris at Hands on Miami knows that its Corporate Services Program can help organizations develop successful employee volunteer initiatives that fit their business climate, employees' interests, and community goals. The problem is persuading more corporations to do it.

Critical Thinking

- Do you agree that corporations derive benefits from sponsoring volunteer programs and encouraging employees to participate?
- Pat Morris must write a letter persuading Miami corporations to use its fee-based Corporate Services Program. What direct benefits could he cite?
- In his persuasive letter, what indirect benefits could Pat Morris cite?

In prompting ethical and truthful persuasion, two factors act as powerful motivators. The first is the desire to preserve your reputation and credibility. Once lost, a good name or reputation is difficult to regain. An equally important force prompting ethical behavior, though, is your opinion of yourself. Glen Senk, president of the retailer Anthropologie, tells a story of a super-saleswoman at his store. She vastly outsold her colleagues on virtually every shift she worked. Senk went to her store one day to watch and realized that the saleswoman would push anything on customers. It didn't matter whether items matched or the clothes looked good. She was fired. "Our customers are our friends," explained Senk. "It's never about the quick sale."[7] Senk was more concerned with preserving the store's reputation and his own self-image than making money.

Writing Persuasive Messages Requesting Favors and Actions

LEARNING OBJECTIVE 4
Write messages that request favors and actions.

The indirect pattern is appropriate for business messages that request favors and actions.

Convincing someone to change a belief or to perform an action when that individual is reluctant requires planning and skill—and sometimes a little luck. If the request is in writing, rather than face-to-face, the task is a bit harder. However, persuasion is often more precise and controlled when you can think through your purpose and prepare a thoughtful message in writing. The indirect pattern gives you an effective structure.

Persuading someone to do something that largely benefits you may not be the easiest task. Fortunately, many individuals and companies are willing to grant requests for time, money, information, special privileges, and cooperation. They grant these favors for a variety of reasons. They may just happen to be interested in your project, or they may see goodwill potential for themselves. Professionals sometimes feel obligated to contribute their time or expertise to "pay their dues." Often, though, businesses and individuals comply because they see that others will benefit from the request.

Figure 9.3 shows a persuasive favor request from Cynde Ferris. Her research firm seeks to persuade other companies to complete a questionnaire revealing salary data. To most organizations, salary information is strictly confidential. What can she do to convince strangers to part with such private information?

FIGURE 9.3 Persuasive Favor Request

1 Prewriting

Analyze: The purpose of this letter is to persuade the reader to complete and return a questionnaire.

Anticipate: Although the reader is busy, she may respond to appeals to her professionalism and to her need for salary data in her own business.

Adapt: Because the reader may be uninterested at first and require persuasion, use the indirect pattern.

2 Writing

Research: Study the receiver's business and find ways to relate this request to company success.

Organize: Gain attention by opening with relevant questions. Build interest by showing how the reader's compliance will help her company and others. Reduce resistance by promising confidentiality and offering free data.

Compose: Prepare a first draft with the intention to revise.

3 Revising

Revise: Revise to show direct and indirect benefits more clearly. Make sure the message is as concise as possible.

Proofread: In the first sentence, spell out "percent" rather than using the symbol. Check the use of all question marks. Start all lines at the left for a block-style letter.

Evaluate: Will this letter convince the reader to complete and return the questionnaire?

A R A I

Anderson Research Associates, Inc.

4208 Congress Avenue
Lake Worth, FL 33461
PH   561-349-2219
FAX   561-349-8967
www.andersonresearch.com

October 14, 2009

Ms. Susan Rivas
Assistant Vice President
Five Star Finance Consultants
1106 Englewood Avenue
Durham, NC 27701

Dear Ms. Rivas:

Poses two short questions related to the reader — Has your company ever lost a valued employee to another organization that offered 20 percent more in salary for the same position? Have you ever added a unique job title but had no idea what compensation the position demanded? — *Gains attention*

Presents reader benefit tied to request explanation; establishes credibility — To remain competitive in hiring and to retain qualified workers, companies rely on survey data showing current salaries. Anderson Research Associates has been collecting business data for a quarter century and has been honored by the American Management Association for its accurate data. We need your help in collecting salary data for today's workers. Information from the enclosed questionnaire will supply companies like yours with such data. — *Builds interest*

Anticipates and counters resistance to confidentiality and time/effort objections — Your information, of course, will be treated confidentially. The questionnaire takes but a few moments to complete, and it can provide substantial dividends for professional organizations that need comparative salary data. — *Reduces resistance*

Offers free salary data as a direct benefit — To show our gratitude for your participation, we will send you comprehensive salary surveys for your industry and your metropolitan area. Not only will you find basic salaries, but you will also learn about bonus and incentive plans, special pay differentials, expense reimbursements, perquisites such as a company car and credit card, and special payments such as beeper pay.

Provides deadline and a final benefit to prompt action — Comparative salary data are impossible to provide without the support of professionals like you. Please complete the questionnaire and return it in the prepaid envelope before November 1, our fall deadline. You will no longer be in the dark about how much your employees earn compared with others in your industry. — *Motivates action*

Sincerely yours,

Cynde Ferris

Cynde Ferris
Director, Survey Research

Enclosures

Checklist

Requesting Favors and Actions

Prewrite

☑ Determine your purpose. Know exactly what you are requesting.

☑ Anticipate the reaction of your audience. Remember that the receiver is thinking *Why should I? What's in it for me? What's in it for you? Who cares?*

Gain Attention

☑ Use the indirect pattern rather than blurting out the request immediately.

☑ Begin with a problem description, unexpected statement, compliment, praise, related facts, stimulating question, or reader benefit to grab attention.

Build Interest

☑ Develop interest by using facts, statistics, examples, testimonials, and specific details.

☑ Establish your credibility, if necessary, by explaining your background and expertise. Use testimonials, expert opinion, or research if necessary.

☑ Support your request by tying facts to direct benefits (increased profits, more efficient operations, better customer relations, saving money, a returned favor) or indirect benefits (improving the community, giving back to the profession, helping the environment).

Reduce Resistance

☑ Anticipate objections to your request and provide counterarguments.

☑ Suggest what might be lost if the request is not granted, but don't make it sound like a threat.

☑ Explain how easy it is to respond to the request.

Motivate Action

☑ Make a precise request that spells out exactly what you want done. Add a deadline date if necessary.

☑ Repeat a benefit, provide additional details, or offer an incentive. Express appreciation.

Persuasive favor requests must gain attention, build interest, establish trust, reduce resistance, and motivate action.

To gain attention, she begins her persuasive favor request by posing two short questions that spotlight the need for salary information. To build interest and establish trust, she mentions that Anderson Research Associates has been collecting business data for a quarter century and has received awards from the American Management Association. Developing credibility is especially important when persuading strangers to do something. Making a reasonable request tied to benefits is also important. Cynde does this by emphasizing the need for current salary information.

To reduce resistance, Cynde promises confidentiality and explains that the questionnaire takes but a few moments to complete. She offers free salary data as a direct benefit. This data may help the receiver learn how its salary scale compares with others in its industry. But Cynde doesn't count on this offer as the only motivator. As an indirect benefit, she appeals to the professionalism of the receiver. She's hoping that the receiver will recognize the value of providing salary data to the entire profession. To motivate action, Cynde closes with a deadline and reminds the reader that her company need not be in the dark about comparative salaries within its industry.

This favor request incorporates many of the techniques that are effective in persuasion: establishing credibility, making a reasonable and precise request, tying facts to benefits, and overcoming resistance.

Writing Persuasive Messages Within Organizations

LEARNING OBJECTIVE 5
Write persuasive messages within organizations.

As discussed in Chapter 1, messages within organizations may move in one of three ways: downward, upward, or horizontally. The strategies and tone employed in these messages depend on the organizational position of the sender and that of the receiver. Let's say you want to persuade your boss to handle orders differently on the company's Web site. Your message would follow the four-part indirect plan. But the tone and content of your message would be different from that of the boss sending a similar persuasive message on the same topic. In this section we will focus on messages flowing downward and messages flowing upward within organizations. Horizontal messages traveling between coworkers are similar to those discussed earlier in requesting favors and actions. Thus, this section focuses only on persuasive downward and upward messages.

Chapter 9: Persuasive and Marketing Messages

Persuasive Messages Flowing Downward

Instructions or directives moving downward from superiors to subordinates usually require little persuasion. Employees expect to be directed in how to perform their jobs. These messages (such as information about procedures, equipment, or customer service) follow the direct pattern, with the purpose immediately stated. However, employees are sometimes asked to volunteer for projects. For example, some organizations ask employees to join programs to stop smoking, lose weight, or start exercising. Organizations may ask employees to participate in capacities outside their work roles—such as spending their free time volunteering for charity projects. In such cases, the four-part indirect pattern provides a helpful structure.

Persuasive requests flowing downward may ask employees to participate in capacities outside their typical work roles.

Messages flowing downward require attention to tone. Warm words and a conversational tone convey a caring attitude. Persuasive requests coming from a trusted superior are more likely to be accepted than requests from a dictatorial executive who may rely on threats and punishments to secure compliance. As mentioned earlier, the proverbial carrot has always been more persuasive than the stick. Managers should avoid sounding preachy or parental. Employees don't want to be treated as children. Because the words *should* and *must* sometimes convey a negative tone, be careful in using them.

Persuasive messages flowing downward should sound conversational, not authoritarian, preachy, or parental.

Figure 9.4 is a memo from Jessica Jeffers, director of Human Resources at a large bank. Her goal is to persuade employees to participate in Hands on Miami Day, a fund-raising and

FIGURE 9.4 Persuasive Organizational Message Flowing Downward

MEMO

DATE: June 10, 2009

TO: All First Federal Staff Members

FROM: Jessica M. Jeffers, Human Resources JMJ

SUBJECT: Serving Our Community and Having Fun at Hands on Miami Day, November 5

Captures attention by describing indirect benefits of volunteering in Miami

Every day in Miami volunteers make our community a better place to live and work. They feed the homeless, provide companionship to the elderly, build low-income housing, restore the natural environment, tutor at-risk children, read to children in shelters, participate in hurricane recovery efforts, and even care for homeless pets! These and other volunteer opportunities will be available on Hands on Miami Day, a fund-raising event that we at First Federal endorse with immense pride.

Gains attention

Develops interest with examples and survey results

In partnership with United Way of Miami-Dade County and with Carnival Cruise Lines, we at First Federal are joining in this day of change for our community. You can be part of the change as 6,000 hands come together to paint, plant, create murals, and clean neighborhoods and beaches. Last year a First Federal team at Hands on Miami Day landscaped and repainted the Miami Beach boardwalk. Afterwards, a survey showed that 86 percent of the volunteers thought the experience was worthwhile and that their efforts made a difference.

Builds interest

Reduces resistance by emphasizing both direct and indirect benefits

To participate, each volunteer pays a registration fee of $20. You may wonder why you should pay to volunteer. Hands on Miami Day is the agency's only fund-raising event, and it supports year-round free services and programs for the entire Miami-Dade community. For your $20, you receive breakfast and an event T-shirt. Best of all, you share in making your community a better place to live and work.

Reduces resistance

Makes it easy to comply with request

In order to provide the best registration process possible, we are excited to work with TeamFootWorks, which has extensive experience managing registration for large-scale community events. Just go to **http://www.TeamFootWorks.com** and request a registration form before October 20.

Prompts action by providing deadline and incentive

You can make a huge difference to your community by volunteering for Hands on Miami Day, November 5. Join the fun and your First Federal colleagues in showing Miami that we value volunteerism that achieves community goals. For every employee who volunteers before October 20, First Federal will contribute $20 to United Way. Sign up now and name the team members you will work with.

Motivates action

community service event that her bank sponsors. In addition to volunteering their services for a day, employees also have to pay $20 to register! You can see that this will be no small persuasion task for Jessica.

Jessica decides to follow the four-part indirect pattern beginning with gaining attention. Notice that she strives to capture attention by describing specific benefits of volunteering in Miami. She explains ways that volunteers make Miami a better place to live and work. Feeding the homeless, providing companionship to the elderly, building low-income housing, restoring the natural environment—all these examples of selfless giving not only gain attention but also suggest indirect benefits to the reader.

The second paragraph of this persuasive message builds interest by listing examples of what volunteers have accomplished during previous Hands on Miami events. Volunteers can expect to join 6,000 other "hands" who paint, plant, create murals, and clean neighborhoods and beaches. To build further interest, the letter includes the results of a survey showing that a vast majority of volunteers thought the experience was worthwhile and that their efforts made a difference. People are more inclined to agree to do something if they know that others have done it in the past and found it beneficial.

To reduce resistance, the third paragraph explains why the $20 fee makes sense. Jessica skillfully combines both direct benefits (free breakfast and an event T-shirt) with indirect benefits (sharing in making the community a better place to live and work).

Good persuasive requests close by making it easy to comply and by finding some way to motivate action. In complying with the request in this message, all the reader has to do is go to a Web site and request a registration form. To motivate action in the closing, Jessica saved a strong indirect benefit. The bank will chip in $20 for every employee who volunteers before the deadline. Readers can see that their participation reaches beyond their individual contribution. Although readers don't benefit directly from the company's contribution to United Way, they can see that others will benefit. This significant indirect benefit along with the direct benefits of having fun and joining colleagues in a community activity combine for a strong persuasive message.

Persuasive Messages Flowing Upward

Another form of persuasion within organizations centers on suggestions made by subordinates. Convincing management to adopt a procedure or invest in a product or new equipment requires skillful communication. Managers are just as resistant to change as others are. Providing evidence is critical when subordinates submit recommendations to their bosses. Be ready to back up your request with facts, figures, and evidence. When selling an idea to management, strive to make a strong dollars-and-cents case.[8] A request that emphasizes how the proposal saves money or benefits the business is more persuasive than one that simply announces a good deal or tells how a plan works.

In describing an idea to your boss, state it confidently and fairly. Don't undermine your suggestions with statements such as *This may sound crazy* or *I know we tried this once before but. . . .* Show that you have thought through the suggestion by describing the risks involved as well as the potential benefits. You may wonder whether you should even mention the downside of a suggestion. Most bosses will be relieved and impressed to know that you have considered the risks as well as the benefits to a proposal.[9] Two-sided arguments are generally more persuasive because they make the source sound credible and fair. Presenting only one side of a proposal reduces its effectiveness because such a proposal seems biased, subjective, and flawed. You can make a stronger argument by acknowledging and neutralizing opposing points of view.

Persuasive messages traveling upward require a special sensitivity to tone. When asking superiors to change views or take action, use words such as *suggest* and *recommend* rather than *you must* and *we should*. Avoid sounding pushy or argumentative. Strive for a conversational, yet professional, tone that conveys warmth, competence, and confidence.

Figure 9.5 shows the draft copy of a persuasive memo that needs revision. Marketing manager Grant Zuckerman wants his boss to authorize the purchase of a second copy machine. Grant was so excited about a good deal that he wrote his memo quickly and didn't spend much time organizing it. Before sending it, though, he reconsidered. Although he thought that his request was reasonable, he realized that his memo failed to present a well-organized "dollars-and-cents" case. He also recognized that if he had spent a little

Successful internal persuasive messages build interest by emphasizing benefits and overcoming resistance.

When selling an idea to management, writers often are successful if they make a strong case for saving money.

FIGURE 9.5 Persuasive Organizational Message Flowing Upward

DRAFT

TO: Elliott Brumner, Vice President

Although you've opposed the purchase of additional copiers in the past, I think I've found a great deal on a copier that's just too good to pass up but we must act before May 1. Copy City has reconditioned copiers that are practically being given away. If we move fast, they will provide many free incentives—like a free copier stand, free starter supplies, free delivery, and free installation.

We must find a way to reduce copier costs in my department. Our current copier can't keep up with our demand. We're sending secretaries or sales reps to Copy Quick for an average of 10,000 copies a month. These copies cost 7 cents a page and waste a lot of time. We're making at least eight trips a week, adding up to a considerable expense in travel time and copy costs.

Please give this matter your immediate attention and get back to me as soon as possible. We don't want to miss this great deal!

Begins poorly with reminder of past negative feelings

Sounds high-pressured

Fails to compare costs and emphasize savings in logical, coherent presentation

Does not request or motivate specific action

REVISION

DATE: April 12, 2009
TO: Elliott Brumner, Vice President
FROM: Grant Zuckerman, Marketing *GZ*
SUBJECT: Saving Time and Money on Copying

Describes topic positively without revealing request

We're losing money on our current copy services and wasting the time of employees as well. Because our Canon copier is in use constantly, we find it increasingly necessary to send major jobs out to Copy Quick. Just take a look at how much we spend each month for outside copy service:

Summarizes problem

Copy Costs: Outside Service

10,000 copies/month made at Copy Quick	$700.00
Salary costs for assistants to make 32 trips to drop off originals and pick up copies	384.00
Total	$1,084.00

Uses headings and columns for easy comparison

When sales reps make the trips, the costs are even greater. Because this expense must be reduced, I've been considering alternatives. New copiers with collating capability and automatic multidrawer paper feeding are very expensive. But reconditioned copiers with all the features we need are available—and at attractive prices and terms. From Copy City we can get a fully remanufactured copier that is guaranteed to work like new. After we make an initial payment of $219, our monthly costs would look like this:

Proves credibility of request with facts and figures

Copy Costs: Remanufactured Copier

Paper supplies for 10,000 copies	$130.00
Toner and copy supplies	95.00
Labor of assistants to make copies	130.00
Monthly financing charge for copier (purchase price of $1,105 amortized at 10% with 29 payments)	34.52
Total	$389.52

As you can see, **a remanufactured copier saves us nearly $700 per month.**

Highlights most important benefit

For a limited time Copy City is offering a free 15-day trial offer, a free copier stand (worth $165), free starter supplies, and free delivery and installation. We have office space available, and my staff is eager to add a second machine.

Provides more benefits

Counters possible resistance

Call me at Ext. 630 if you have questions. This copier is such a good opportunity that I've attached a purchase requisition authorizing the agreement with Copy City. With your approval before May 1, we can have our machine by May 10 and start saving time and nearly $700 every month. Fast action will also take advantage of Copy City's free start-up incentives.

Makes it easy to grant approval

Repeats main benefit with motivation to act quickly

Attachment

Checklist

Writing Persuasive Messages Within Organizations

Prewrite

✓ Know your purpose and be able to state it precisely and concisely. What do you want the receiver to do? Make sure your request is doable and attainable.

✓ Profile the audience. Play *What if?* scenarios to anticipate how the receiver will react to your request. What direct or indirect benefits can you cite?

Gain Attention

✓ Make the reader aware of a problem, use a startling statement, provide a significant fact related to the request, describe possible benefits, ask a stimulating question, or offer compliments and praise.

✓ Establish your credibility but don't pull rank.

Build Interest

✓ Use facts, statistics, examples, and specific details to build a solid foundation for your request.

✓ Strive for a personal but professional tone. Be enthusiastic and positive.

✓ Soften your words when persuading upward. Suggest benefits to the reader.

Reduce Resistance

✓ Recognize any weakness in your proposal and suggest well-reasoned counterarguments and facts.

✓ In requests flowing upward, consider making a strong dollars-and-cents appeal for requests involving budgets.

✓ In requests flowing downward, avoid sounding preachy, parental, or overly authoritarian.

Motivate Action

✓ State a specific request including a deadline if appropriate. Suggest ways to make it effortless and painless for the receiver to respond.

✓ Repeat a major benefit that appeals to the reader.

✓ Include an incentive or reason to act, and express appreciation if appropriate.

---

more time developing his persuasive argument, he would have had a better chance of approval.

Notice that although Grant's revision is longer, it is far more effective. A successful persuasive message will typically take more space than a direct message because proving a case requires evidence. Grant's revised memo includes a subject line that tells the purpose of the memo without disclosing the actual request. By delaying the request until he's had a chance to describe the problem and discuss a solution, Grant prevents the reader's premature rejection.

The strength of this revision, though, is in the clear presentation of comparison figures showing how much money his company could save by purchasing a remanufactured copier. Although the organization pattern is not obvious, the revised memo begins with an attention-getter (frank description of problem), builds interest (with easy-to-read facts and figures), provides benefits, and reduces resistance. Notice that the conclusion tells what action is to be taken, makes it easy to respond, and repeats the main benefit to motivate action.

> **Persuasive messages often are longer than direct messages because proving a case requires evidence.**

Writing Persuasive Claim and Complaint Letters

LEARNING OBJECTIVE 6
Write effective claim and complaint letters.

Persuasive claim letters typically involve damaged products, mistaken billing, inaccurate shipments, warranty problems, return policies, insurance snafus, faulty merchandise, and so on. Generally, the direct pattern is best for requesting straightforward adjustments (see Chapter 8). When you feel your request is justified and will be granted, the direct strategy is most efficient. But if a past request has been refused or ignored or if you anticipate reluctance, then the indirect pattern is appropriate.

In a sense, a claim letter is a complaint letter. Someone is complaining about something that went wrong. Some complaint letters just vent anger. The writers are mad, and they want to tell someone about it. But if the goal is to change something (and why bother to write except to motivate change?), then persuasion is necessary. Effective claim letters make

> **Effective claim and complaint letters make reasonable claims backed by solid evidence.**

a reasonable request, present a logical case with clear facts, and adopt a moderate tone. Anger and emotion are not effective persuaders.

Working for Logical Development

Strive for logical development in a claim letter. You might open with sincere praise, an objective statement of the problem, a point of agreement, or a quick review of what you have done to resolve the problem. Then you can explain precisely what happened or why your claim is legitimate. Don't provide a blow-by-blow chronology of details; just hit the highlights. Be sure to enclose copies of relevant invoices, shipping orders, warranties, and payments. Close with a clear statement of what you want done: refund, replacement, credit to your account, or other action. Be sure to think through the possibilities and make your request reasonable.

Using a Moderate Tone

The tone of the letter is important. Don't suggest that the receiver intentionally deceived you or intentionally created the problem. Rather, appeal to the receiver's sense of responsibility and pride in the company's good name. Calmly express your disappointment in view of your high expectations of the product and of the company. Communicating your feelings without rancor is often your strongest appeal.

Writing an Effective Complaint Letter

Marilyn Easter's letter, shown in Figure 9.6, follows the persuasive pattern as she seeks credit for two VoIP (voice over Internet protocol) systems. Actually, she was quite upset because her company was counting on these new Internet systems to reduce its phone bills. Instead, the handsets produced so much static that incoming and outgoing calls were all but impossible to hear. What's more, she was frustrated that the "Return Merchandise Authorization" form she filled out at the company's Web site seemed to sink into a dark hole in cyberspace. She had reason to be angry! But she resolved to use a moderate tone in writing her complaint letter.

Notice that her tone is objective, rational, and unemotional. She begins with a compliment and explains why her company needs a VoIP system. She provides identifying data and justifies her claim by explaining that installation instructions were carefully followed. Claim letters are particularly effective when writers express their personal disappointment and feelings. Marilyn explains her strong disappointment in view of the promotional statement ensuring a clear signal. She would like to have been more forceful, but she knew that a calm, unemotional tone would be more effective. She wondered whether she should say that she was really ticked off that she had spent hours researching the product. The new system took additional hours to install and troubleshoot. After all that work, she couldn't use it because of the static. Nevertheless, she stuck to the plan of using a positive opening, a well-documented claim, and a request for specific action in the closing.

Planning and Composing Effective Sales and Marketing Messages

Sales and marketing messages use persuasion to promote specific products and services. In our coverage we will be most concerned with sales messages delivered by mail. Many of the concepts you will learn about marketing persuasion, however, can be applied to online, wireless, TV, print, radio, and other media. The best sales messages, whether delivered by e-marketing or direct mail, have much in common. In this section you will study how to apply the 3-x-3 writing process to sales messages. Then you will learn techniques developed by experts to draft effective sales messages, both in print and online.

Direct-Mail Sales Letters

Our main focus in this chapter will be on writing sales letters as part of direct-mail marketing. Traditional sales letters are a powerful means to make sales, generate leads, boost retail traffic, solicit donations, and direct consumers to Web sites. Mail allows a personalized, tangible, three-dimensional message that is less invasive than telephone solicitations and less reviled than unsolicited e-mail.

Claim and complaint messages should adopt a moderate tone, express disappointment, and appeal to the receiver's sense of responsibility.

LEARNING OBJECTIVE 7
Write effective, yet ethical, sales and marketing messages.

FIGURE 9.6 Persuasive Claim (Complaint) Letter

ARTE INTERNATIONAL FURNISHINGS

3256 Riverton Avenue, North Hollywood, CA 91601   http://www.artedemexico.com

February 16, 2009

Customer Service
ZTech Electronics
1005 West McKinley Avenue
Mishawaka, IN 46545

Dear ZTech Customer Service:

Your VoIP Expandable Telephone System came highly recommended and seemed to be the answer to increasingly expensive telephone service. Here at Arte International Furnishings we were looking for a way to reduce our local and long-distance telephone charges. The VoIP system was particularly attractive to us because it offered Internet phone service with unlimited calling to the United States, Canada, and Puerto Rico. Our business in fine furnishings and unique objets d'art requires us to make and receive national and international calls.

Begins with compliment; keeps tone objective, rational, and unemotional

On February 8 we purchased two VoIP systems (SGU #IP7402-2) for our main office here in North Hollywood and for our Las Vegas showroom. Each system came with two cordless handsets and charging docks. Although we followed all the installation instructions, we discovered that an irritating static sound interfered with every incoming and outgoing telephone call.

Provides identifying data and justifies claim

This static is surprising and disappointing because the product description promised the following: "You will experience excellent signal clarity with Frequency Hopping Digital Spread Spectrum (FHDSS) transmission and a frequency of 5.8GHz. Ninety-five channel auto-search ensures a clear signal."

Explains why claim is valid and suggests responsibility of receiver

On February 10 we filled out a Return Merchandise Authorization form at your Web site. However, we are frustrated that we have had no response. We're confident that a manufacturer with your reputation for reliable products and superior customer service will want to resolve this matter quickly.

Expresses disappointment and appeals to receiver's reputation and customer service

Please authorize return of these two systems and credit our account for $377.24, which represents the original cost plus taxes and shipping. Attached is a copy of the invoice with our credit card number.

Tells what action to take

Sincerely,

Marilyn Easter

Marilyn Easter
President

Enclosure

Tips for Making Complaints

- Begin with a compliment, point of agreement, statement of the problem, or brief review of action you have taken to resolve the problem.
- Provide identifying data.
- Prove that your claim is valid; explain why the receiver is responsible.
- Enclose document copies supporting your claim.
- Appeal to the receiver's fairness, ethical and legal responsibilities, and desire for customer satisfaction.
- Describe your feelings and your disappointment.
- Avoid sounding angry, emotional, or irrational.
- Close by telling exactly what you want done.

Professionals who specialize in traditional direct-mail services have made it a science. They analyze a market, develop an effective mailing list, study the product, prepare a sophisticated campaign aimed at a target audience, and motivate the reader to act. You've probably received many direct-mail packages, often called "junk mail." These packages typically contain a sales letter, a brochure, a price list, illustrations of the product, testimonials, and other persuasive appeals.

We are most concerned here with the sales letter: its strategy, organization, and evidence. Because sales letters are generally written by specialists, you may never write one on the job. Why, then, learn how to write a sales letter? In many ways, every letter we create is

Studying marketing messages helps consumers become more perceptive in understanding sales strategies.

a form of sales letter. We sell our ideas, our organizations, and ourselves. Learning the techniques of sales writing will help you be more successful in any communication that requires persuasion and promotion. What's more, you will recognize sales strategies that enable you to become a more perceptive consumer of ideas, products, and services.

Applying the 3-x-3 Writing Process to Sales Messages

Marketing professionals analyze every aspect of a sales message because consumers reject most direct-mail offers. Like the experts, you will want to pay close attention to the preparatory steps of analysis and adaptation before writing the actual message.

Analyzing the Product and Purpose for Writing.

Before sitting down to write a sales letter, you must study the product carefully. What can you learn about its design, construction, raw materials, and manufacturing process? What can you learn about its ease of use, efficiency, durability, and applications? Be sure to consider warranties, service, price, premiums, exclusivity, and special appeals. At the same time, evaluate the competition so that you can compare your product's strengths against the competitor's weaknesses.

> Successful sales messages require research on the product or service offered and an analysis of the purpose for writing.

Now you are ready to identify your central selling points. At Lands' End a central selling point for one marketing campaign was economical custom clothing. The company used a testimonial from a real customer who said that the $49 Lands' End custom dress shirts he bought were better than the $120 shirts he previously purchased from custom shops.[10] Analyzing your product and studying the competition help you determine what to emphasize in your sales letter.

Equally important is determining the specific purpose of your letter. Do you want the reader to call for a free video and brochure? See a demonstration at your Web site? Fill out an order form? Send a credit card authorization? Before you write the first word of your message, know what response you want and what central selling points you will emphasize to achieve that purpose.

Adapting to the Audience.

Blanket mailings sent "cold" to occupants generally produce low responses—typically less than 2 percent. That means that 98 percent of the receivers usually toss direct-mail sales letters right into the trash. But the response rate can be increased dramatically by targeting the audience through selected database mailing lists. These lists can be purchased or compiled. By directing your message to a selected group, you can make certain assumptions about the receivers. Let's say you are selling fitness equipment. A good mailing list might come from subscribers to fitness or exercise magazines. You would expect similar interests, needs, and demographics (age, income, and other characteristics). With this knowledge you can adapt the sales letter to a specific audience.

> Using mailing lists enables writers to tailor messages to targeted audiences.

Crafting a Winning Sales Message

Your primary goal in writing a sales message is to get someone to devote a few moments of attention to it.[11] You may be promoting a product, a service, an idea, or yourself. In each case the most effective messages will (a) gain attention, (b) build interest, (c) reduce resistance, and (d) motivate action. This is the same recipe we studied earlier, but the ingredients are different.

> Openers for sales messages should be brief, honest, relevant, and stimulating.

Gaining Attention.

One of the most critical elements of a sales letter is its opening paragraph. This opener should be short (one to five lines), honest, relevant, and stimulating. Marketing pros have found that eye-catching typographical arrangements or provocative messages, such as the following, can hook a reader's attention:

- **Offer:** *A free trip to Hawaii is just the beginning!*

- **Promise:** *Now you can raise your sales income by 50 percent or even more with the proven techniques found in. . . .*

- **Question:** *Do you yearn for an honest, fulfilling relationship?*

- **Quotation or proverb:** *Necessity is the mother of invention.*

Spotlight on Communicators

In writing winning sales messages, beware of impossible promises, warns Herb Kelleher, cofounder of Southwest Airlines. He believes his company has the quickest baggage delivery in the industry—only eight minutes from jetway to pickup. But when his marketing staff proposed making such a promise in the Southwest promotions, Kelleher balked. On rare occasions Southwest wouldn't be able to deliver, he reasoned, and broken promises are not easily forgotten.

© AP IMAGES

- **Fact:** *The Greenland Eskimos ate more fat than anyone in the world. And yet . . . they had virtually no heart disease.*

- **Product feature:** *Volvo's snazzy new convertible ensures your safety with a roll bar that pops out when the car tips 40 degrees to the side.*

- **Testimonial:** *My name is Sheldon Schulman. I am a practicing medical doctor. I am also a multimillionaire. I didn't make my millions by practicing medicine, though. I made them by investing in my spare time.*

- **Startling statement:** *Let the poor and hungry feed themselves! For just $100 they can.*

- **Personalized action setting:** *It's 4:30 p.m. and you've got to make a decision. You need everybody's opinion, no matter where they are. Before you pick up your phone to call them one at a time, pick up this card: WebEx Teleconference Services.*

Other openings calculated to capture attention might include a solution to a problem, an anecdote, a personalized statement using the receiver's name, or a relevant current event.

Building Interest.

In this phase of your sales message, you should describe clearly the product or service. In simple language emphasize the central selling points that you identified during your prewriting analysis. Those selling points can be developed using rational or emotional appeals.

Rational appeals are associated with reason and intellect. They translate selling points into references to making or saving money, increasing efficiency, or making the best use of resources. In general, rational appeals are appropriate when a product is expensive, long-lasting, or important to health, security, and financial success. Emotional appeals relate to status, ego, and sensual feelings. Appealing to the emotions is sometimes effective when a product is inexpensive, short-lived, or nonessential. Many clever sales messages, however, combine emotional and rational strategies for a dual appeal. Consider these examples:

Rational Appeal
You can buy the things you need and want, pay household bills, and pay off higher-cost loans and credit cards—as soon as you are approved and your Credit-Line account is opened.

Emotional Appeal
Leave the urban bustle behind and escape to sun-soaked Bermuda! To recharge your batteries with an injection of sun and surf, all you need are your bathing suit, a little suntan lotion, and your Credit-Line card.

Dual Appeal
New Credit-Line cardholders are immediately eligible for a $200 travel certificate and additional discounts at fun-filled resorts. Save up to 40 percent while lying on a beach in picturesque, sun-soaked Bermuda, the year-round resort island.

A physical description of your product is not enough, however. Zig Ziglar, thought by some to be America's greatest salesperson, pointed out that no matter how well you know your product, no one is persuaded by cold, hard facts alone. In the end, people buy because of product benefits.[12] Your job is to translate those cold facts into warm feelings and reader benefits. Let's say a sales message promotes a hand cream made with aloe and cocoa butter extracts, along with Vitamin A. Those facts become, *Nature's hand helpers—including soothing aloe and cocoa extracts, along with firming Vitamin A—form invisible gloves that protect your sensitive skin against the hardships of work, harsh detergents, and constant environmental assaults.*

Reducing Resistance.

Marketing pros use a number of techniques to overcome resistance and build desire. When price is an obstacle, consider these suggestions:

- Delay mentioning price until after you've created a desire for the product.

Rational appeals reflect reason and intellect.

Emotional appeals reflect status, ego, and sensual feelings.

Dual appeals combine reason and emotion.

To capture attention in its sales messages for Pampers diapers, Procter & Gamble may show a happy, healthy baby. But the sales copy develops an emotional yet rational appeal as it discusses the development of babies when they get a good night's sleep from having a drier diaper than that sold by the competition. "This is probably the biggest challenge for our advertising—how you move beyond functional advertising to emotional resonance," reports manager Austin Lally. *Why are dual appeal messages especially persuasive to parents of young children?*

- Show the price in small units, such as the price per issue of a magazine.

- Demonstrate how the reader saves money by, for instance, subscribing for two or three years.

- Compare your prices with those of a competitor.

In addition, you need to anticipate other objections and questions the receiver may have. When possible, translate these objections into selling points (*If you are worried about training your staff members on the new software, remember that our offer includes $1,000 worth of on-site one-on-one instruction*). Other techniques to overcome resistance and prove the credibility of the product include the following:

Translate objections into selling points.

- **Testimonials:** *"I never stopped eating, yet I lost 107 pounds."—Tina Rivers, Greenwood, South Carolina.*

- **Names of satisfied users** (with permission, of course): *Enclosed is a partial list of private pilots who enthusiastically subscribe to our service.*

- **Money-back guarantee or warranty:** *We offer the longest warranties in the business—all parts and service on-site for five years!*

- **Free trial or sample:** *We are so confident that you will like our new accounting program that we want you to try it absolutely free.*

- **Performance tests, polls, or awards:** *Our TP-3000 was named Best Web Phone, and Etown.com voted it Cell Phone of the Year.*

Techniques for reducing resistance include testimonials, guarantees, warranties, samples, and performance polls.

Motivating Action.

All the effort put into a sales message goes to waste if the reader fails to act. To make it easy for readers to act, you can provide a reply card, a stamped and preaddressed envelope, a toll-free telephone number, an easy-to-scan Web site, or a promise of a follow-up call. Because readers often need an extra push, consider including additional motivators, such as the following:

- **Offer a gift:** *You will receive a free cell phone with the purchase of any new car.*

Techniques for motivating action include offering a gift or incentive, limiting an offer, and guaranteeing satisfaction.

- **Promise an incentive:** *With every new, paid subscription, we will plant a tree in one of America's Heritage Forests.*

- **Limit the offer:** *Only the first 100 customers receive free checks.*

- **Set a deadline:** *You must act before June 1 to get these low prices.*

- **Guarantee satisfaction:** *We will return your full payment if you are not entirely satisfied— no questions asked.*

The final paragraph of the sales letter carries the punch line. This is where you tell readers what you want them to do and give them reasons for doing it. Most sales letters also include postscripts because they make irresistible reading. Even readers who might skim over or bypass paragraphs are drawn to a P.S. Therefore, use a postscript to reveal your strongest motivator, to add a special inducement for a quick response, or to reemphasize a central selling point.

Although you want to be persuasive in sales letters, you must guard against overstepping legal and ethical boundaries. Information contained in sales letters has landed some writers in hot water. See the accompanying Ethical Insights box to learn how to stay out of trouble.

Ethical Insights

What's Legal and What's Not in Sales Letters

In promoting products and writing sales letters, be careful with the words you choose and the claims you make. How far can you go in praising and selling your product?

- **Puffery.** In a sales letter, you can write, *Hey, we've got something fantastic! It's the very best product on the market!* Called "puffery," such promotional claims are not taken literally by reasonable consumers.
- **Proving your claims.** If you write that three out of four dentists recommend your toothpaste, you'd better have competent and reliable scientific evidence to support the claim. Such a claim goes beyond puffery and requires proof. Vital Basics recently paid a $1 million settlement for claiming that its "Focus Factor" helped improve memory, a claim unsubstantiated by proof, said the Federal Trade Commission.[13]
- **Celebrities.** The unauthorized use of a celebrity's name, likeness, or nickname is not permitted in sales messages. For example, late-night talk-show host Johnny Carson won a case against a portable toilet firm that promoted a "Here's Johnny" toilet. Similarly, film star Dustin Hoffman won millions of dollars for the unauthorized use of a digitally altered photo showing him in an evening gown and Ralph Lauren heels. Even a commercial showing the image of a celebrity such as Tiger Woods on a camera phone is risky.
- **Misleading statements.** You cannot tell people that they are winners or finalists in a sweepstake unless they actually are. American Family Publishers was found guilty of sending letters tricking people into buying magazine subscription in the belief that they had won $1.1 million. Similarly, the Damart clothing

company was reprimanded for sending a mailing with "final reminder" printed in bold, red lettering on the envelope. It referred to a final reminder about an outstanding offer, clearly a deceptive and distressing message.[14] Companies may not misrepresent the nature, characteristics, qualities, or geographic origin of goods or services they are promoting.

- **Unwanted merchandise.** If you enclose unsolicited merchandise with a letter, don't expect the receiver to be required to pay for it or return it. Express Publishing, for example, sent a copy of its *Food & Wine Magazine's Cookbook* with a letter inviting recipients to preview the book. "If you don't want to preview the book, simply return the advance notice card within 14 days." Courts, however, have ruled that recipients are allowed to retain, use, or discard any unsolicited merchandise without paying for it or returning it.

Career Application

Bring to class at least three sales letters or advertisements that may represent issues described here. What examples of puffery can you identify? Are claims substantiated by reliable evidence? What proof is offered? Do any of your examples include names, images, or nicknames of celebrities? How likely is it that the celebrity authorized this use? Have you ever received unwanted merchandise as part of a sales campaign? What were you to do with it?

Putting It All Together. Sales letters are a preferred marketing medium because they can be personalized, directed to target audiences, and filled with a more complete message than other advertising media. But direct mail is expensive. That's why the total sales message is crafted so painstakingly.

Figure 9.7 shows a sales letter addressed to a target group of small business owners. To sell the new magazine *Small Business Monthly,* the letter incorporates all four components of an effective persuasive message. Notice that the personalized action-setting opener places the reader in a familiar situation (getting into an elevator) and draws an analogy between failing to reach the top floor and failing to achieve a business goal. The writer develops a rational central selling point (a magazine that provides valuable information for a growing small business) and repeats this selling point in all the components of the letter. Notice, too, how a testimonial from a small business executive lends support to the sales message, and how the closing pushes for action. Because the price of the magazine is not a selling feature, price is mentioned only on the reply card. This sales letter saves its strongest motivator—a free booklet—for the high-impact P.S. line.

Whether you actually write sales letters on the job or merely receive them, you will better understand their organization and appeals by reviewing this chapter and the tips in the checklist below.

> Because direct mail is an expensive way to advertise, messages should present complete information in a personalized tone for specific audiences.

Comparing Persuasion in High- and Low-Context Cultures

The explosion of global communication, transportation, and marketing, along with the continuing migration of people, has moved all of us closer to a global society. As a business communicator, you can expect to interact with people from different cultures both at home and abroad. To be effective, as discussed in Chapter 3, you must be aware of

LEARNING OBJECTIVE 8
Compare effective persuasion techniques in high- and low-context cultures.

Checklist

Sales Messages

Prewrite

✓ Analyze your product or service. What makes it special? What central selling points should you emphasize? How does it compare with the competition?

✓ Profile your audience. How will this product or service benefit this audience?

✓ Decide what you want the audience to do at the end of your message.

Gain Attention

✓ Describe a product feature, present a testimonial, make a startling statement, or show the reader in an action setting.

✓ Offer something valuable, promise the reader a result, or pose a stimulating question.

✓ Suggest a solution to a problem, offer a relevant anecdote, use the receiver's name, or mention a meaningful current event.

Build Interest

✓ Describe the product or service in terms of what it does for the reader. Connect cold facts with warm feelings and needs.

✓ Use rational appeals if the product or service is expensive, long-lasting, or important to health, security, and financial success. Use emotional appeals to suggest status, ego, or sensual feelings.

✓ Explain how the product or service can save or make money, reduce effort, improve health, produce pleasure, or boost status.

Reduce Resistance

✓ Counter anticipated reluctance with testimonials, money-back guarantees, attractive warranties, trial offers, or free samples.

✓ Build credibility with results of performance tests, polls, or awards.

✓ If price is not a selling feature, describe it in small units *(only 99 cents an issue),* show it as savings, or tell how it compares favorably with that of the competition.

Motivate Action

✓ Close by repeating a central selling point and describing an easy action to be taken.

✓ Prompt the reader to act immediately with a gift, incentive, limited offer, deadline, or guarantee of satisfaction.

✓ Put the strongest motivator in a postscript.

FIGURE 9.7 Sales Letter

1 Prewriting

Analyze: The purpose of this letter is to persuade the reader to return the reply card and subscribe to *Small Business Monthly*.

Anticipate: The targeted audience consists of small-business owners. The central selling point is providing practical business data that will help their business grow.

Adapt: Because readers will be reluctant, use the indirect pattern.

2 Writing

Research: Gather facts to promote your product, including testimonials.

Organize: Gain attention by opening with a personalized action picture. Build interest with an analogy and a description of magazine features. Use a testimonial to reduce resistance. Motivate action with a free booklet and an easy-reply card.

Compose: Prepare first draft for pilot study.

3 Revising

Revise: Use short paragraphs and short sentences. Replace *malfunction* with *glitch*.

Proofread: Indent long quotations on the left and right sides. Italicize or underscore titles of publications. Hyphenate *hard-headed* and *first-of-its-kind*.

Evaluate: Monitor the response rate to this letter to assess its effectiveness.

---

small business monthly
28 North Ferry Road • Waterford, CT 06386

April 15, 2009

Mr. James Wehrley
1608 Montlieu Avenue
High Point, NC 27262

Dear Mr. Wehrley:

(Puts reader into action setting / Gains attention)
You walk into the elevator and push the button for the top floor. The elevator glides upwards. You step back and relax.

But the elevator never reaches the top. A glitch in its electronics prevents it from processing the information it needs to take you to your destination.

(Suggests analogy / Builds interest)
Do you see a similarity between your growing company and this elevator? You're aiming for the top, but a lack of information halts your progress. Now you can put your company into gear and propel it toward success with a new publication—*Small Business Monthly*.

(Emphasizes central selling point)
This first-of-its-kind magazine brings you marketing tips, hard-headed business pointers, opportunities, and inspiration. This is the kind of current information you need today to be where you want to be tomorrow. One executive wrote:

(Uses testimonial for credibility / Reduces resistance)
> As president of a small manufacturing company, I read several top business publications, but I get my "bread and butter" from *Small Business Monthly*. I'm not interested in a lot of "pie in the sky" and theory. I find practical problems and how to solve them in *SBM*.
> —Mitchell M. Perry, Bowling Green, Ohio

Mr. Perry's words are the best recommendation I can offer you to try *SBM*. In less time than you might spend on an average business lunch, you learn the latest in management, operations, finance, taxes, business law, compensation, and advertising.

(Repeats central sales pitch in last sentence / Motivates action)
To evaluate *Small Business Monthly* without cost or obligation, let me send you a free issue. Just initial and return the enclosed card to start receiving a wealth of practical information that could keep your company traveling upward to its goal.

Cordially,

Cheryl Owings

Cheryl Owings
Vice President, Circulation

(Spotlights free offer in P.S. to prompt immediate reply)
P.S. Act before May 15 and I'll send you our valuable booklet *Managing for Success*, revealing more than 100 secrets for helping small businesses grow.

your own culture. In addition, you should learn about other cultures to better understand how to be effective and to avoid confusion and miscommunication. What works in a low-context culture such as the United States may not be as effective in a high-context culture such as China.

Being Persuasive in High-Context Cultures

Countries in Asia, Africa, South America, and much of the Middle East are considered *high context*. As you learned in Chapter 3, high-context cultures generally value group sense rather than individualism. In such cultures, much information is not explicit; that is, it is not transmitted as words in a message. Meaning may be conveyed by clues in the situational context. Advertisements in high-context cultures are often indirect, polite, modest, and ambiguous. Even business messages can be so subtle that the meaning is unclear. Advertisements tend to emphasize harmony and beauty. For example, pictures of butterflies, flowers, nature scenes, and cultural artifacts are often seen on Japanese Web sites. Because of the respect for harmony and politeness, direct comparisons in persuasive messages are considered in bad taste. Nike advertisements in Japan would not mention its superior styling compared to Reebok or another named brand.

High-context countries (Asia, Africa, South America, much of Middle East) prefer indirectness, politeness, soft-sell approach, building relationships, and a collectivist view.

Sales letters, advertisements, Web sites, and other persuasive efforts aimed at high-context cultures may be characterized by the following:

- **Indirectness.** Use of indirect expressions (such as *perhaps, probably, somewhat*). Preference for softened words (*would appreciate* rather than *must* or *expect*). Aversion to blunt hard-sell tactics and long, verbose messages.

- **Politeness.** Expressions of politeness, use of honorifics (*Esteemed* and *Revered Customer*), flowery language, wishful requests (*we hope*), and overall humility.

- **Soft-sell approach.** Use of simple facts without embellishment or superlatives. Web sites may feature entertainment themes to promote products. Emphasis on harmony.

- **Relationship appeal.** Attempts to establish a long-term relationship.

- **Collectivist view.** Emphasis on *we* and *our* rather than on *I* or the "you" view.

Analyzing a High-Context Sales Letter.

Sales letters in high-context cultures definitely aim to be persuasive, but the tone and strategy are different from the techniques discussed thus far in this chapter. A letter from the Xuzhou First Motor Company in China, shown in Figure 9.8, promotes its renovated facilities and new line of motor cars. The formal salutation (*Honored company*) reflects respect for the addressee. The first sentences in the letter (*How are you? You must be very busy with your work at this time of the year*) are quite different from typical U.S. sales letters. These leisurely opening sentences attempt to build a relationship. They signal that the company is interested in more than a quick sales promotion. Although such an opening might be considered naïve in this country, it is seen differently in China. The motor company wants to appear friendly and recognizes that all business dealings proceed more smoothly when the goal is a long-term relationship.

High-context sales letters focus on building credibility and developing long-term relationship.

To establish its credibility, the company points out that it is part of a large national motor car manufacturer. This ensures that readers will respect the company because it is not a small-time facility, lacking the skills, expertise, and automobile models of a big company. To build interest, the letter uses facts and details about its cars (*imported engines, air-conditioning, GPS navigation systems*). The letter touts the features (*powerful engines, fast acceleration, quiet motors, low petrol consumption, spacious seating, reasonable price*). Notice, however, that the letter neither uses superlatives (*the biggest and best GPS system in today's cars!*), nor attempts to focus on benefits to the reader. No effort is made to develop a "you" view; benefits are described in general terms. The entire approach is low-key, rather than focusing on appeals to the reader. Notice, too, that most references are to *our* and *we*, which are appropriate in a collectivist culture.

In reducing resistance, the letter again refers to the motor company's size (*a large enterprise*) and its reputation (*the envy of motor manufacturers*). However, the statements

FIGURE 9.8 Sales Message, High-Context Culture (English translation)

Xuzhou First Motor Company Ltd.

Xuzhou, Jiangsu

Phone: 86-10-6800-1452   Fax: 86-10-6800-1452

Lang Xun Products
Room 2111, International Tower
No. 3, Fuhua Road
Futian District
Shenzhen, Guangdong
China

Opens with respectful salutation

Honored company,

How are you? You must be very busy with your work at this time of the year.

Attempts to build relationship

Establishes credibility and respect

As a branch of No. 1 Motors Group of China, Xuzhou First Motor Company was established in January 1992. It is located in the ancient city of Xuzhou. After many years of hard work and great efforts, our company is putting on a brand new look and a new line of motor cars.

Mentions selling points but does not address the reader directly; no "you" view

Our goal has always been to produce comfortable luxury cars of high standard and good quality. Our engineers have all the expertise in design and manufacturing skills. The cars we produce are equipped with imported engines, air-conditioning, and GPS navigating systems with features including voice prompts for turns and guidance. Our cars are characterized by powerful engines, fast acceleration, quiet motors, low petrol consumption, spacious seating, and reasonable price. Our cars enjoy a strong reputation for their dignity, performance, and quality in Huaihai Economic Zone, and even in the northern and middle parts of China.

Uses low-key sales approach with few superlatives; avoids high-pressure tactics

After a humble beginning, Xuzhou First Motor Company has grown into a large enterprise and is the envy of the motor manufacturers of modern and luxury cars. We are offering various kinds of special prices. If you are interested in our new motor cars, please contact us. We plan to hold a marketing day of our latest models (the specific time for this will be informed later).

Shows politeness by using "please"

We welcome you to come and place an order or hold trade talks with us. We will offer you warm-hearted service. Looking forward to hearing from you soon.

Closes without deadlines, incentives, or postscript; attempts to show respect and harmony

Thank you for your cooperation!

Sales Department
Xuzhou First Motor Company Ltd.
July 15, 2009

寄：廣東省深圳市福田區福華路3號國際大樓2111室 (Receiver's address)

朗訊產品公司 (Receiver's company)

xxx先生 (Receiver's name)

---

are all fairly formal, dignified, polite, and bland. One clear contrast with sales letters in this country and other low-context cultures is the lack of high pressure. Notice that the closing is genteel and friendly (*we welcome you to come and place an order*). Again, it attempts to build a relationship, assuring *warm-hearted service*. This sales letter lacks high-pressure incentives, deadlines, and P.S. statements hammering home important reader benefits. The letter is also fairly short, contrasting with longer sales letters in this country. In low-context cultures, writers tend to use more words to ensure that they can be precise in explaining and persuading.

Being Persuasive in Low-Context Cultures

Countries in Northern Europe, North America, Scandinavia, and Australia are classified as *low context*. As discussed in Chapter 3, low-context cultures tend to be logical, linear, and action oriented. Information is explicit and formalized in written documents. People in low-context cultures use words precisely and expect them to be understood literally. They rely less on the unspoken context and nonverbal clues to convey important messages. They are comfortable with direct, explicit, and confrontational appeals in advertising and persuasion. Sales letters, advertisements, Web sites, and other persuasive efforts within low-context cultures may be characterized by the following:

- **Directness.** Expression of requests may be made directly without attempts to use soft wording. Precision in expression is preferred.

- **Superlatives.** Use of superlatives such as *The lowest price, highest quality, and best customer service on the planet!* Little hesitation to "toot one's own horn." General acceptance of puffery. No expectation of humility or modesty in advertising or sales.

- **Hard-sell approach.** Aggressive promotions, incentives, testimonials, deadlines, and emphasis on product advantages using explicit comparisons with competitors.

- **Short-term goal.** Little attempt to establish long-term relationships. Tendency to develop transitory personal relationships.

- **"You" view.** Emphasis on projecting benefits to an individual, instead of focusing on group perspectives.

As globalization expands and the huge markets of China and India open up, Western business practices may become more dominant even in high-context cultures. We may see more evidence of low-context strategies in sales messages in high-context cultures. Underlying cultural differences, however, will continue to exert considerable influence. Effective business communicators who understand the powerful effect of high- and low-context cultures will always have a distinct advantage.

Low-context sales messages include directness, superlatives, hard-sell, short-term goals, and "you" view.

Developing Persuasive Press Releases

Press (news) releases announce information about your company to the media: new products, new managers, new facilities, participation in community projects, awards given or received, joint ventures, donations, or seminars and demonstrations. Naturally, you hope that this news will be published and provide good publicity for your company. But this kind of largely self-serving information is not always appealing to magazine and newspaper editors or to TV producers. To get them to read beyond the first sentence, try these suggestions:

LEARNING OBJECTIVE 9
Understand basic patterns and techniques in developing persuasive press releases.

- Open with an attention-getting lead or a summary of the important facts.

- Include answers to the five *W*s and one *H* (*who, what, when, where, why,* and *how*) in the article—but not all in the first sentence!

- Appeal to the audience of the target media. Emphasize reader benefits written in the style of the focus publication or newscast.

- Present the most important information early, followed by supporting information. Don't put your best ideas last because they may be chopped off or ignored.

- Make the release visually appealing. Limit the text to one or two double-spaced pages with attractive formatting.

- Look and sound credible—no typos, no imaginative spelling or punctuation, no factual errors.

Effective press releases feature an attention-getting opener, place key information up front, appeal to the target audience, and maintain visual interest.

The most important ingredient of a press release, of course, is *news*. Articles that merely plug products end up in the circular file. The Google press release in Figure 9.9 announced a new search device. Good press releases focus on reader and consumer benefits. The lead in this press release appeals to readers by describing a more comprehensive way to search and view information online. The press release is appealing because of the addition of a quotation from a Google vice president and the inclusion of her photo, thus personalizing the information. By including personal comments, the press release becomes more of a real news story. Newspapers and magazines will be more likely to publish a press release that is both informative and interesting. Many companies provide readily available press information, including releases and photos, on their Web sites.

FIGURE 9.9 Press Release

Provides optional headlines

Places key information up front

Relates to target audience with story and conversational language

Shows key benefits in visually appealing, high-skim format

Uses pound symbols to signal end of release

Opens with attention-getting lead packed with information

Makes optional photo available

Emphasizes central selling points

Supplies means of obtaining additional information

Google™ Press Release

GOOGLE GETS THE MESSAGE, LAUNCHES GMAIL

User Complaint About Existing Services Leads Google to Create Search-Based Webmail

Search Is Number Two Online Activity—E-Mail is Number One; "Heck, Yeah," Say Google Founders

MOUNTAIN VIEW, CALIF.—Amidst rampant media speculation, Google Inc. today announced it is testing a preview release of Gmail—a free search-based webmail service with a storage capacity of up to eight billion bits of information, the equivalent of 500,000 pages of e-mail. Per user.

The inspiration for Gmail came from a Google user complaining about the poor quality of existing e-mail services, recalled Larry Page, Google cofounder and president, Products. "She kvetched about spending all her time filing messages or trying to find them," Page said. "And she has to delete e-mail like crazy to stay under the obligatory four-megabyte limit. So she asked, 'Can't you people fix this?'"

"If a Google user has a problem with e-mail, well, so do we," said Google cofounder and president of Technology, Sergey Brin. "And while developing Gmail was a bit more complicated than we anticipated, we're pleased to be able to offer it to the user who asked for it." Key features of Gmail include the following:

- **Search** Built on Google search technology, Gmail enables people to quickly search every e-mail they've ever sent or received. Using keywords, Gmail users can find what they need, when they need it.

- **Storage** Google believes people should be able to hold onto their mail forever. That's why Gmail comes with 1,000 megabytes (1 gigabyte) of free storage—more than 100 times what most other free webmail services offer.

- **Speed** Gmail makes using e-mail faster and more efficient by eliminating the need to file messages into folders, and by automatically organizing individual e-mails into meaningful "conversations."

Those interested in learning more about Gmail can visit **http://gmail.google.com.**

About Google Inc.
Google's innovative search technologies connect millions of people around the world with information every day. Founded in 1998 by Stanford Ph.D. students Larry Page and Sergey Brin, Google today is a top Web property in all major global markets. For more information, visit **www.google.com** or contact Steve Jones at (859) 240-5000.

# # #

Communicating at Work Your Turn

Applying Your Skills at Hands on Miami

As a communication intern at Hands on Miami, you have been learning the ropes about publicizing and organizing programs. One day Pat Morris sees a newspaper article and says to you, "Listen to this! Did you know that service organizations can earn up to $10 for used print cartridges and up to $20 for recycled cell phones? This sounds like a terrific idea for raising funds for our Community Bridges program. Why don't you do some research and find out more about this. Then I'd like you to draft a message that we could send to Miami businesses letting them know how they can help our programs. This is a good chance for you to try out your persuasion skills!"

In your research you discover that 300 million ink cartridges are discarded every year. You are horrified to learn that the industrial plastics in these cartridges take a thousand years to decompose. You find out that 40,000 tons of plastic could be diverted from landfills every year if ink cartridges were recycled. Your research also reveals that hundreds of thousands of cell phones are no longer being used as new models flood the market. Where do all of those unused cell phones go?

In doing your research, you discover that cartridges and cell phones may be dropped off at recycling centers. They can also be mailed in, or they can even be picked up. The best way for businesses to learn how to do this is to visit **http://www.miamidaderecycling.org** or call 1-800-534-9989 for details.

Morris asks you to focus on raising funds for Community Bridges, one of the flexible calendar programs at Hands on Miami. Volunteers like this program because it is flexible and allows them to choose their hours and be personally involved. Some volunteers provide

food service at the Miami Rescue Mission. Some are part of work crews to clean up Pelican Harbor, and those with carpentry skills enjoy working with Habitat for Humanity. Some volunteers help maintain the Miami Beach Botanical Gardens. One group of business professionals reads bedtime stories at the Salvation Army. Other volunteers care for animals at the humane society. These are just a few of the many volunteer services that make Miami a better place to live and work.

Your Task

In teams or individually, draft a persuasive letter for the signature of Pat Morris. Your letter will go to 50 or more Miami area businesses. Ask the businesses to save used ink cartridges and old cell phones for Hands on Miami. As you compose your letter, follow the plan described in this chapter. You know the benefits that Hands on Miami will enjoy, but what benefits can you cite for the receiver? What incentive or final idea can you use to motivate action? Use your imagination, but stay within reason.

Summary of Learning Objectives

1 **Define the concept of persuasion, identify effective and ineffective persuasive techniques, and discuss the importance of tone in persuasive messages.** Persuasion may be defined as the ability to use argument or discussion to change an individual's beliefs or actions. Effective persuasive techniques include establishing credibility, making a reasonable and precise request, tying facts to benefits, recognizing the power of loss, expecting and overcoming resistance, sharing solutions, and compromising. Persuasion is more effective if one avoids sounding preachy or parental, doesn't pull rank, softens the tone when persuading upward, sounds enthusiastic, and presents a positive and likeable image.

2 **Apply the 3-x-3 writing process to persuasive messages.** The first step in the writing process for a persuasive message is an analysis of the audience and the purpose for writing. Writers must know exactly what they want the receiver to do or think. The second step involves thinking of ways to adapt the message to the audience. Particularly important is shaping the rhetoric of the message to its purpose. This includes expressing the request so that it may benefit the reader. The writer must collect information and organize it into an appropriate strategy. An indirect strategy is probably best if the audience might resist the request.

3 **Explain the four major elements in successful persuasive messages and how to blend those elements into effective and ethical business messages.** The most effective persuasive messages include four major elements: gaining attention, building interest, reducing resistance, and motivating action. Writers gain attention by opening with a problem, unexpected statement, reader benefit, compliment, related fact, stimulating question, or similar device. They build interest with facts, expert opinions, examples, details, and direct and indirect reader benefits. They reduce resistance by anticipating objections and presenting counterarguments. They conclude by motivating a specific action and making it easy for the reader to respond. Skilled communicators avoid distortion, exaggeration, and deception when making persuasive arguments.

4 **Write messages that request favors and actions.** In asking for favors and actions, writers must know exactly what they are requesting. They anticipate the receiver's reaction by asking *What if?* questions. Persuasive requests often begin indirectly with a problem description, unexpected statement, compliment, praise, related facts, stimulating question, or reader benefit. Interest is built with facts, statistics, examples, testimonials, and details. Effective requests include testimonials, expert opinion, and research to establish credibility. Readers tend to respond favorably when requests are tied to direct benefits such as increased profits, more efficient operations, better customer relations, improved employee retention, monetary gain, or a returned favor. Resistance can be reduced by anticipating objections and providing counterarguments. Action is motivated by stating exactly what is to be done and by when.

5 **Write persuasive messages within organizations.** Before writing a persuasive business message, writers should profile the audience, know exactly what the receiver is to do or believe, and anticipate resistance. To gain attention, the writer might make the receiver aware of a problem, use a startling statement, provide a significant fact related to the request, describe possible benefits, ask a stimulating question, or offer compliments and praise. Facts, statistics, examples, and specific details build a foundation for the request. Receivers are interested in direct benefits such as how agreeing to the request will help the receiver solve problems or improve his or her work and career. Recognizing weaknesses in the proposal and offering well-reasoned counterarguments are effective in reducing resistance. In messages flowing downward, avoid sounding preachy, parental, or overly authoritarian. In messages flowing upward, consider making a strong dollars-and-cents appeal for requests involving budgets. Persuasive messages should end with a specific request and a deadline if appropriate.

6 **Write effective claim and complaint letters.** Effective claim letters may begin with a compliment, point of agreement, statement of the problem, or brief review of action taken to resolve the problem. Relevant data, including copies of invoices, shipping orders, warranties, payments, and so forth, document the claim and prove its validity. Claims should explain why the receiver is responsible. They should appeal to the receiver's fairness, ethics, legal responsibilities, and desire for customer satisfaction. Describing feelings and expressing disappointment are effective devices. Messages should avoid sounding angry, emotional, or irrational. Closings should explain exactly what is to be done.

7 **Write effective, yet ethical, sales and marketing messages.** Careful analysis of the product or service is necessary before one composes a sales message. Effective sales messages usually begin with an attention-getting statement that is short, honest, relevant, and stimulating. Simple language describing appropriate appeals builds interest. Testimonials, a money-back guarantee, a free trial, or some other device can reduce resistance. A gift, incentive, deadline, or other device can motivate action.

8 **Compare effective persuasion techniques in high- and low-context cultures.** Sales letters, advertisements, Web sites, and other persuasive efforts aimed at high-context cultures often exhibit by politeness, indirectness, a soft-sell approach, and attempts to establish a long-term client relationship. Persuasive messages in low-context cultures may be characterized by directness, superlatives, and a hard-sell approach.

9 **Understand basic patterns and techniques in developing persuasive press releases.** Press releases usually open with an attention-getting lead or summary of the important facts. They attempt to answer the questions *who, what, when, where, why,* and *how.* They are written carefully to appeal to the audience of the target media. The best press releases present the most important information early, make the release visually appealing, and look and sound credible.

Chapter Review

1. What is persuasion? (Obj. 1)
2. List six general techniques that are effective in persuasion. (Obj. 1)
3. What is the first step in the writing process for a persuasive message, and why is this step important? (Obj. 2)
4. What four questions are receivers of persuasive messages likely to be asking themselves? (Obj. 2)
5. List the four major elements in a persuasive request. (Obj. 3)
6. List effective tools for building interest in a persuasive request. (Obj. 3)
7. Why is a written favor request or action request more effective than a face-to-face request? (Obj. 4)
8. When is persuasion necessary in business messages flowing downward in an organization? (Obj. 5)
9. When might persuasion be necessary in messages flowing upward? (Obj. 5)
10. Describe the most effective tone for a claim or complaint letter. (Obj. 6)
11. What could be included in an effective opening and closing of a claim or complaint letter? (Obj. 6)
12. Name eight or more ways to attract attention in opening a sales message. (Obj. 7)
13. How can a writer motivate action in a sales letter? (Obj. 7)
14. How do persuasive messages in high- and low-context cultures differ? (Obj. 8)
15. List five or more topics that an organization might feature in a press release. (Obj. 9)

Critical Thinking

1. The word *persuasion* turns some people off. What negative connotations can it have? (Obj. 1)
2. How are persuasive requests and sales letters similar and how are they different? (Objs. 4, 7)
3. What are some of the underlying motivations that prompt individuals to agree to requests that do not directly benefit themselves or their organizations? (Obj. 4)
4. Why is it important to know your needs and have documentation when you make requests of superiors? (Obj. 5)
5. **Ethical Issue:** What is puffery, and how can it be justified in marketing messages? Consider the following: Dr. Phil calls himself "America's most trusted relationship counselor." Rush Limbaugh claims to be "America's anchorman." Sony's Cyber-Shot camera advertisement says "Make time stand still."

Activities

9.1 Document for Analysis: Weak Favor Request (Obj. 4)

Your Task. Analyze the following poorly written invitation. List its weaknesses. If your instructor directs, revise the letter. Add appropriate information if needed.

Current date

Mr. Nelson J. Daugherty
Operations Manager
Roxbury Hotels and Restaurants, Inc.
303 Lombard Plaza
Philadelphia, PA 19148

Dear Mr. Daugherty:

Although you are a busy hospitality professional, we would like you to make a presentation to the Washington, DC, chapter of the National Restaurant Alliance. I was asked to write you since I am program chair.

I heard that you made a good presentation at your local chapter recently. I think you gave a talk called "Avoiding the Seven Cardinal Sins in Food Service" or something like that. Whatever it was, I'm sure we would like to hear the same or a similar presentation. All restaurant operators are interested in doing what we can to avoid potential problems involving discrimination, safety at work, how we hire people, etc. As you well know, operating a fast-paced restaurant is frustrating—even on a good day. We are all in a gigantic rush from opening the door early in the morning to shutting it again after the last customer has gone. It's a rat race and easy to fall into the trap with food service faults that push a big operation into trouble.

Enclosed please find a list of questions that our members listed. We would like you to talk about 45 minutes. Our June 10 meeting will be at the Red Sage restaurant in Washington and dinner begins at 7 p.m.

How can we get you to come to Washington? We can offer you a honorarium of $200, and we would pay for your travel expenses. You can expect a large crowd of restaurateurs who are known for hooting and hollering when they hear good stuff! As you can see, we are a rather informal group. Hope you can join us!

Sincerely,

9.2 Document for Analysis: Poor Action Request for Internship (Obj. 4)

Your Task. Analyze the poorly written persuasive request. List its weaknesses. If your instructor directs, revise the letter. Add any information necessary.

4320 Mountlake Terrace Drive
Lynnwood, WA 98250
Current date

Ms. Nancy Ashley, Director
Human Resources Department
Software Enterprises, Inc.
268 Redmond Avenue
Bellevue, WA 98420

Dear Ms. Ashley:

I'm looking for an internship position that will earn me three units of credit. Perhaps I could fill in for employees who are taking vacations or who might be released for training at Software Enterprises, Inc.

I have taken a number of courses, and now I really need some experience. I'm a college senior at Edmonds College, and I have communication and computer skills. I know Word and Excel, and I've had training in letter and report writing. Are these skills that might be useful in one of your departments? Although I can't work in the mornings because that's when I take classes, I am available in the afternoons but I couldn't give you more than 15 hours a week. I need to do this during the next 14 weeks if possible.

I realize that equipment and desk space at your company may not be available for an intern. You may also be worried about insurance, but don't give it a thought. Our college has liability insurance for all interns. I'm sending a copy of my résumé for you to see.

Please let me know about the possibility of an internship.

Sincerely,

9.3 Document for Analysis: Weak Persuasive Memo Flowing Upward (Obj. 5)

Your Task. Analyze the following memo, which suffers from many writing faults. List its weaknesses. If your instructor directs, revise the letter.

DATE: Current
TO: Candace Daly, Vice President, Marketing
FROM: Robert Forsythe, Exhibit Manager
SUBJECT: Trade Booth

Trade shows are a great way for us to meet customers and sell our Life Fitness equipment. But instead of expanding our visits to these trade shows, we continue to cut back the number that we attend. And we send fewer staff members. I know that you've been asking us to find ways to reduce costs, but perhaps we are not going about it right.

With increased airfares and hotel charges, my staff has tried to find ways to live within our very tight budget. Yet, we are being asked to find other ways to reduce our costs. I'm currently thinking ahead to the big Las Vegas trade show coming up in September.

One area where we could make a change is in the gift that we give away. In the past we have presented booth visitors with a nine-color T-shirt that is silk screened and gorgeous. But it comes at a cost of $15 for each and every one of these beauties from a top-name designer. To save money, I suggest that we try a $4 T-shirt made in China, which is reasonably presentable. It's got our name on it, and, after all, folks just use these shirts for workouts. Who cares if it is a fancy silk-screened T-shirt or a functional Chinese one that has "Life Fitness" plastered on the chest? Since we give away 2,000 T-shirts at our largest show, we could save big bucks by dumping the designer shirt. But we have to act quickly. I've enclosed a cheap one for you to see.

Let me know what you think.

9.4 Document for Analysis: Poor Claim Letter (Obj. 6)

Your Task. Analyze the following poorly written claim letter. List its weaknesses. If your instructor directs, revise it.

Current date

Mr. Morgan Monroe
Modern Office Systems
210 Halsted Street
Chicago Heights, IL 60411

Dear Sir:

Recently my company purchased four of your Matrix 500 photocopiers, and we've had nothing but trouble ever since.

Our salesperson, Sheila Feldman, assured us that the Matrix 500 could easily handle our volume of 3,000 copies a day. This seemed strange since the sales brochure said that the Matrix 500 was meant for 500 copies a day. But we believed Ms. Feldman. Big mistake! Our four Matrix copiers are down constantly; we can't go on like this. Because they are still under warranty, they eventually get repaired. But we are losing considerable business in downtime.

Because your Ms. Feldman has been less than helpful, I telephoned the district manager, Marko Santillan. I suggested that we trade in our Matrix 500 copiers (which we got for $2,500 each) on two Matrix 800 models (at $13,500 each). However, Mr. Santillan said he would have to charge 50 percent depreciation on our Matrix 500 copiers. What a rip-off! I think that 20 percent depreciation is more reasonable since we've had the machines only three months. Mr. Santillan said he would get back to me, and I haven't heard from him since.

Now I'm forced to write to your headquarters because I have no faith in either Ms. Feldman or Mr. Santillan, and I need to see some action on these machines. If you understood anything about business, you would see what a sweet deal I'm offering you. I'm willing to stick with your company and purchase your most expensive model—but I can't take such a steep loss on the Matrix 500 copiers. These copiers are relatively new; you should be able to sell them with no trouble. And think of all the money you will save by not having your repair technicians making constant trips to service our underpowered Matrix 500 copiers! Please let me hear from you immediately.

Sincerely yours,

9.5 Sales Letter Analysis (Obj. 7)

Your Task. Select a one- or two-page sales letter received by you or a friend. Study the letter and then answer these questions:

a. What techniques capture the reader's attention?
b. Is the opening effective? Explain.
c. What are the central selling points?
d. Does the letter use rational, emotional, or a combination of appeals? Explain.
e. What reader benefits are suggested?
f. How does the letter build interest in the product or service?
g. How is price handled?

h. How does the letter anticipate reader resistance and offer couter-arguments?
i. What action is the reader to take? How is the action made easy?
j. What motivators spur the reader to act quickly?

9.6 Persuasive Favor/Action Request: Inviting Banquet Speaker (Obj. 4)

As program chair of the Southern Florida University Management Society, you must invite a well-known business writer to speak at your organization's banquet on February 2. The author, Joyce Lain Kennedy, has written many columns and books on careers, focusing recently on Internet job searching. Unfortunately, the SFU Management Society has no budget for speakers. But you saw a recent newspaper item saying that Ms. Kennedy has a winter home in St. Petersburg, so she might consider coming since she is a neighbor and since she has a track record of speaking to student audiences. Two of her recent books are *Résumés for Dummies* and *Cover Letters for Dummies*. She is called the "dean of career columnists."

Your Task. Individually or in teams, apply the four-part plan in persuading Ms. Kennedy to speak. Add any necessary information but keep it within reason. Address your letter to Ms. Joyce Lain Kennedy, 230 73rd Avenue, St. Petersburg, FL 33706.

9.7 Persuasive Favor/Action Request: Asking Beijing to Use Excel (Objs. 4, 8)

Intercultural

Mario Franchini, regional sales manager for a multinational manufacturer, is always in a hurry and doesn't take the time to write careful messages. As his assistant, you sometimes revise messages for him. Today he asks you to look over his message to Zhu Chen, regional sales manager for the company's prosperous branch in Beijing. On his way out the door, Mario says to you, "Please fix up the following memo. Make it sound better!"

> Hi there, Zhu! I know you haven't heard from me 4 a while, so don't hit the panic button! I need you to do me a big favor. I'm going to skip the bull and drive right to the point. I need your sales figures to be submitted in Excel spreadsheets. You could hit a home run by zeroing in on the sales for your region and zapping them to us in a better format. We just can't use the ledger account forms you usually send. They may work for your office in Beijing, but they won't fly here in Seattle. I'm counting on you to come through for me by using Excel in submitting your future sales figures. You already have the software available through our home office intranet. Just download it. You will see it's easy as pie to learn. When you send your next quarterly figures at the end of September, I expect to see them in Excel. Chow!

Your Task. You know that messages to your office from Beijing are usually more formal and often begin with a friendly greeting. You decide to try out your intercultural skills in writing a better favor request. For your boss's signature, revise this message using memo format. After approval, the memo will be faxed.

9.8 Persuasive Favor/Action Request: Borrowing Suits for Interviews (Obj. 4)

You saw an interesting article describing a "Suitable Suits" program at Barnard College. Its College of Career Development kept a closet filled with 21 crisp black suits that students could borrow for job interviews. Students made an appointment with the office and agreed to dry clean the suits before returning them. At Barnard the program was paid for with a grant from Goldman Sachs Group.[15]

You think that a Suitable Suits program is worth exploring with your dean.

Your Task. Write a persuasive letter requesting an appointment with your dean to discuss a Suitable Suits program at your school. You don't have all the answers and you are not sure how such a program would operate, but you think the idea is worth discussing. Can you convince the dean to see you?

9.9 Persuasive Favor/Action Request: A Helping Hand for College Expenses (Obj. 4)

Team

After working a few years, you would like to extend your college education on a part-time basis. You know that your education can benefit your employer, but you can't really afford the fees for tuition and books. You've heard that many companies offer reimbursement for fees and books when employees complete approved courses with a grade of C or higher.

Your Task. In teams discuss the best way to approach an employer whom you wish to persuade to start a tuition/books reimbursement program. How could such a program help the employer? Remember that the most successful requests help receivers see what's in it for them. What objections might your employer raise? How can you counter them? After discussing strategies in teams, write a team memo or individual memos to your boss (for a company where you now work or one with which you are familiar). Persuade her or him to act on your action request.

9.10 Persuasive Favor/Action Request: School Vending Machines Become Weighty Problem (Obj. 4)

Team **Web**

"If I start to get huge, then, yeah, I'll cut out the chips and Coke," says 17-year-old Nicole O'Neill, as she munches sour cream-and-onion-potato chips and drinks a cold can of soda fresh from the snack machine. Most days her lunch comes from a vending machine. The trim high school junior, however, isn't too concerned about how junk food affects her weight or overall health. Although she admits she would prefer a granola bar or fruit, few healthful selections are available from school vending machines.

Vending machines loaded with soft drinks and snacks are increasingly under attack in schools and lunchrooms. Some school boards, however, see them as cash cows. In Gresham, Oregon, the school district is considering a lucrative soft drink contract. If it signs an exclusive 12-year agreement with Coca-Cola to allow vending machines at Gresham High School, the school district will receive $75,000 up front. Then it will receive an additional $75,000 three years later. Commission sales on the 75-cent drinks will bring in an additional $322,000 over the 12-year contract, provided the school sells 67,000 cans and bottles every year. In the past the vending machine payments supported student body activities such as sending students to choir concerts and paying athletic participation fees. Vending machine funds also paid for an electronic reader board in front of the school and a sound system for the gym. The latest contract would bring in $150,000, which is already earmarked for new artificial turf on the school athletic field.

Coca-Cola's vending machines would dispense soft drinks, Fruitopia, Minute Maid juices, Powerade, and Dasani water. The hands-down student favorite, of course, is calorie-laden Coke. Because increasing childhood and adolescent obesity across the nation is a major health concern, the Gresham Parent-Teacher Association (PTA) decided to oppose the contract. The PTA realizes that the school board is heavily influenced by the income generated from the Coca-Cola contract. It wonders what other school districts are doing about their vending machine contracts.

Your Task. As part of a PTA committee, you have been given the task of researching and composing a persuasive but concise (no more than one page) letter addressed to the school board. Use the Web or databases to locate articles that might help you develop arguments, alternatives, and counterarguments. Meet with your team to discuss your findings. Then individually or as a group, write a letter to the Board of Directors, Gresham-Barlow School District, P.O. Box 310, Gresham, OR 97033.

9.11 Persuasive Organizational Message Flowing Upward: We Need GPS Navigators to Keep Hotel Guests on Course (Obj. 5)

Hotel guests often ask for directions to local restaurants or special local sights. But they sometimes get lost or exasperated when they can't find what they seek. Guests also go walking, jogging, or sightseeing and can't find their way back to the hotel.

As the assistant manager at an upscale hotel in your town or area, you saw a newspaper article about the five-star Rosewood hotel chain. It offers use of handheld GPS navigators free at select properties. You have a GPS device in your car, and you know how amazing it is when it can talk you right to your destination. Clearly, your hotel could distinguish itself competitively and be among the first to offer this new perk to guests. Rosewood hotels offering this service include The Carlyle (Manhattan), The Mansion on Turtle Creek (Dallas), and Hotel Crescent Court (Dallas).[16]

You would like to convince your manager to offer this service. On the Web you discover that a Garmin iQue M3 GPS Navigator is just the right size. If a hotel guest is out jogging or sightseeing and loses the way, the guest can hit "home" and the GPS tells the direction back to the hotel from anywhere. The Garmin costs $330, which you think is not excessive. Although your manager is cost-conscious, he loves gadgets. You think that if the GPS device could attract just two guests per month, it would probably be worth it. You like the fact that when hotel guests at Rosewood hotels ask for directions, a concierge can plug in the desired location, hit "go," and the GPS will talk guests through the drive or walk until they arrive.

Your Task. Write a convincing memo to Manager Jeff Joyner. Before writing, decide what you want to ask. Should you ask for a meeting to discuss the proposal? Should you request a trial period in which you try out one or two GPS Navigators? You haven't worked out all of the details of a GPS program, but you think the idea is worth talking about. You will need to gather information about a GPS device that might work for your purpose. Name specific restaurants or local attractions in your memo. What benefits can you suggest for your manager and for the hotel?

9.12 Persuasive Organizational Message Flowing Upward: We Need to Get Organized! (Obj. 5)

E-mail

As the supervisor of administrative support at an architectural engineering firm, you serve five project managers. You find it difficult to keep track of what everybody is doing and where they are working. Mike is in New Orleans, Jason just left for Kansas City, Brian is working on a project in St. Louis, and Andrea is completing a job in Houston. With so many people working on different projects at different places, it is hard to know where people are and what they are doing. Assigning administrative assistants and tracking their work is difficult. You decide that you and your managers need a dry erase board in the office to record projects and their status. Plain dry erase boards are not expensive at Wal-Mart. But can you persuade the managers to accept this new tool? They are largely independent engineers who are not attuned to following office procedures. Moreover, who will keep the board current?

Your Task: Write a convincing e-mail message that persuades managers that your office needs a dry erase board to record weekly projects. Outline the benefits. How can you make it easy for them to "buy in" to using this new tool? Fill in any details from your imagination, but keep the message fairly simple. Address the first e-mail message to *Mike.Kuryia@walters-inc.com*.

9.13 Persuasive Organizational Message Flowing Upward: Telecommuters Want Freedom But Not Too Much (Obj. 5)

E-mail   **Team**   **Web**

James Lush arose from bed in his Connecticut home and looked outside to see a heavy snowstorm creating a fairyland of white. But he felt none of the giddiness that usually accompanies a potential snow day. Such days were a gift from heaven when schools closed, businesses shut down, and the world ground to a halt. As an on-and-off telecommuter for many years, he knew that snow days were a thing of the past. These days, work for James Lush and 23.5 million other American employees is no farther than their home office.[17]

More and more employees are becoming telecommuters. They want to work at home, where they feel they can be more productive and avoid the hassle of driving to work. Some need to telecommute only temporarily, while they take care of family obligations, births, illnesses, or personal problems. Others are highly skilled individuals who can do their work at home as easily as in the office. Businesses definitely see advantages to telecommuting. They don't have to supply office space for workers. What's more, as businesses continue to flatten management structures, bosses no longer have time to micromanage employees. Increasingly, they are leaving workers to their own devices.

But the results have not been totally satisfactory. For one thing, in-house workers resent those who work at home. More important are problems of structure and feedback. Telecommuters don't always have the best work habits, and lack of communication is a major issue. Unless the telecommuter is expert at coordinating projects and leaving instructions, productivity can fizzle. Appreciating the freedom but recognizing that they need guidance, employees are saying, "Push me, but don't leave me out there all alone!"

As human resources manager at your company, you already have 83 employees who are either full- or part-time telecommuters. With increasing numbers asking to work in remote locations, you decide that workers and their managers must receive training on how to do it effectively. You are considering hiring a consultant to train your prospective telecommuters and their managers. Another possibility is developing an in-house training program.

Your Task. As human resources manager, you must convince Victor Vasquez, vice president, that your company needs a training program for all individuals who are currently telecommuting or who plan to do so. Their managers should also receive training. You decide to ask your staff of four to help you gather information. Using the Web, you and your team read several articles on what such training should include. Now you must decide what action you want the vice president to take. Meet with you to discuss a training program? Commit to a budget item for future training? Hire a consultant or agency to come in and conduct training programs? Individually or as a team, write a convincing message that describes the problem, suggests what the training should include, and asks for action by a specific date. Add any reasonable details necessary to build your case.

9.14 Persuasive Organizational Message Flowing Upward: Dear Boss (Obj. 5)

> **E-mail**

In your own work or organization experience, identify a problem for which you have a solution. Should a procedure be altered to improve performance? Would a new or different piece of equipment help you perform your work better? Could some tasks be scheduled more efficiently? Are employees being used most effectively? Could customers be better served by changing something? Do you want to work other hours or perform other tasks? Do you deserve a promotion? Do you have a suggestion to improve profitability?

Your Task. Once you have identified a situation requiring persuasion, write a memo or an e-mail to your boss or organization head. Use actual names and facts. Employ the concepts and techniques in this chapter to help you convince your boss that your idea should prevail. Include concrete examples, anticipate objections, emphasize reader benefits, and end with a specific action to be taken.

9.15 Persuasive Organizational Message Flowing Upward: PDAs Would Lighten Realtors' Load in Historic Charleston (Obj. 5)

> **Team** **Web**

Charleston, South Carolina, one of America's most beautifully preserved architectural and historic treasures, enjoys a booming real estate market. *Forbes* magazine forecasts a 200 percent appreciation for its properties by the year 2009. The Cooper River Bridge project is America's largest construction project, and the entire regional economy glows. Real estate agents have plenty of work showing off new homes as well as beautifully preserved structures from the colonial and antebellum periods. The problem is that agents have to grapple with telephone directory–size books of multiple listings—or run back and forth to their offices as they show home buyers what's on the market.

As a staffer at one of Charleston's top realty agencies, you recently attended an Association of Realtors meeting and talked with fellow agent Bob Drewisch. He showed you his new personal digital assistant (PDA) and said, "Watch this." He accessed listing after listing of homes for sale by his company and others. You couldn't believe your eyes. You saw island properties, historic homes, beachfront condos—all with pictures and complete listing information. In this little device, which could easily fit into a pocket (or purse), you could

© Bob Krist / CORBIS

carry six months' worth of active, pending, and closed listings, along with contact details for agents and other valuable information.

You thought about the size of your multiple listing books and how often you had to trudge back to the office when a home buyer wanted to see a market listing. "Looks terrific," you said to Bob. "But what about new listings? And how much does this thing cost? And I bet it has a steep learning curve." Eager to show off his new toy, Bob demonstrated its user-friendly interface that follows intuitive prompts such as *price, area,* and *number of bedrooms.* He explained that his agency bought the software for $129. For a monthly fee of $19, he downloads updates as often as he likes. In regard to ease of use, Bob said that even his fellow agent Emily, notoriously computer challenged, loved it. None of the staff found it confusing or difficult to operate.

You decide that the agency where you work should provide this service to all 18 full-time staff agents. Assume that multiple listing software is available for the greater Charleston area.

Your Task. With other staff members (your classmates), decide how to approach the agency owner, who is "old school" and shuns most technology. Decide what you want to request. Do you merely want the owner to talk with you about the service? Should you come right out and ask for PDAs and the service for all 18 staff members? Should you expect staff members to provide the hardware (a basic PDA at about $200) and the agency to purchase the service and individual updates for each full-time agent? Or should you ask for the service plus a top-of-the-line device that combines a PDA, phone, GPS (global positioning system), and other capabilities? Learn more about PDA possibilities on the Web. Explore this information with your team. Once you decide on a course of action, what appeals would be most persuasive? Discuss how to handle price in your persuasive argument. Individually or as a group, prepare a persuasive message to George R. Hollings, president, Hollings Carolina Realty. Decide whether you should deliver your persuasive message as a hard-copy memo or an e-mail.[18]

9.16 Persuasive Organizational Message Flowing Upward: Servers Want Mandatory Tipping (Obj. 5)

> **Team**

Centered in the heart of a 2,400-acre Florida paradise, the Bayside Inn Golf and Beach Resort offers gracious hospitality and beautiful accommodations. Its restaurant, Dolphin Watch, overlooks the scenic Choctawhatchee Bay, a perfect place to spy dolphins. As a server in the Dolphin Watch, you enjoy working in this resort setting—except for one thing. You have occasionally been "stiffed" by a patron who left no tip. You know your service is excellent, but some customers just don't get it. They seem to think that tips are optional, a sign of appreciation. For servers, however, tips are 80 percent of their income.

In a recent *New York Times* article, you learned that some restaurants—such as the famous Coach House Restaurant in New York—automatically add a 15 percent tip to the bill. In Santa Monica the Lula restaurant prints "gratuity guidelines" on checks, showing customers what a 15 or 20 percent tip would be. You also know that American Express recently developed a gratuity calculation feature on its terminals. This means that diners don't even have to do the math!

Your Task. Because they know you are studying business communication, your fellow servers have asked you to write a serious letter to Nicholas Ruiz, General Manager, Bayside Inn Golf and Beach Resort, 9300 Emerald Coast Parkway West, Sandestin FL 32550-7268. Persuade him to adopt mandatory tipping guidelines in the restaurant. Talk with fellow servers (your classmates) to develop logical persuasive arguments.

9.17 Persuasive Organizational Messages Flowing Downward: And Now We Want Your Blood! (Obj. 5)

Team

Companies are increasingly asking employees to take on-site blood tests. Because forcing employees to do so would invade their privacy, companies must persuade them to volunteer. Why should companies bother?

Blood tests are part of health risk assessments. Such assessments are considered the first step toward controlling chronic and expensive health problems such as diabetes, obesity, and tobacco addiction. According to American Healthways, employers using blood tests have seen between a $300 and $1,440 decrease in health care costs per participant, depending on what kind of incentive they offer to participants.

Snap-on, a well-known manufacturer of power and hand tools, began offering blood tests as part of a health assessment program a year ago. Although the first-year sign-up was slow, Snap-on saw a 50 percent increase in sign-ups the following year as employees became familiar with the plan. Employees filled out questionnaires on assessing their health risks. Then they received results so that they could see how their blood work compared with their own assessments. Snap-on assured employees that the company would never see the results. The blood tests, conducted by American Healthways, screened for cholesterol, diabetes, hypertension, body fat, liver function, and nicotine. Employers receive only combined data about their employees.

Even though employees were the benefactors of these blood tests, Snap-on had to offer an incentive to urge them to participate. Employees received a $20 monthly discount on health care premiums for agreeing to the full assessment process, including the blood test.

However, another company found that the penalty approach was more effective in encouraging employee participation. Westell Technologies, which makes broadband communication equipment, charged employees 10 percent higher health care premiums if they refused to take the blood tests. This penalty program resulted in 80 percent participation. Regardless of the method used to encourage participation, any on-site blood testing must be voluntary.[19]

Assume you are part of a group of interns at manufacturer Colman International, which employs 900 people. The director of interns, Christine Davis, is also vice president of Human Resources. One day she calls your group together and says, "Listen up! Colman needs employees to take these blood tests and fill out health-risk assessment forms. We know this is a hard sell, but we think it is the right thing to do—not only for employees but also for the company because it will lower our skyrocketing health care costs. So here's what I want you interns to do as a training exercise. Get together and decide what you think is the best way for us to persuade employees to participate. Should we offer incentives or threaten penalties?"

Seeing the blank expressions on your faces, she said, "Oh, you can assume that the company will back whatever decision you make—so long as it's not out of line with what other companies are doing. Once you decide what to do, I want you to prepare a message to employees. Medical staff from American Healthways will be in the human resources training room to conduct the blood tests beginning Monday, November 17, through Friday, November 21. Appointments are available between 7:30 a.m. and 5:30 p.m. Employees may sign up for appointments by e-mailing Christine Davis before November 10 at *cdavis@colman.com* and requesting an appointment time. They will receive a confirmation e-mail stating the date and appointment time.

Your Task. Individually or as a group, prepare two messages. Address one to Christine Davis. Explain what your group decided and justify the rationale for your decisions. Address the second message to Colman employees for the signature of Ms. Davis. Your second message should persuade employees to participate in the program. Remember to anticipate objections to your request. How can these objections be overcome? Should you emphasize benefits to the reader or to the company? What direct and indirect benefits can you name? What is the best communication channel for this message? How can you make it easy for receivers to respond?

9.18 Persuasive Organizational Message Flowing Downward: Reducing Overnight Shipping Costs (Obj. 5)

As office manager of an East Coast software company, write a memo persuading your technicians, engineers, programmers, and other employees to reduce the number of overnight or second-day mail shipments. Your Federal Express and other shipping bills have been sky high, and you feel that staff members are overusing these services.

You think employees should send messages by e-mail or fax. Sending a zipped file as an e-mail attachment costs very little. What's more, a fax costs only about 35 cents a page to most long-distance areas and nothing to local areas. Compare this with $15 to $20 for FedEx service! Whenever possible, staff members should obtain the FedEx account number of the recipient and use it for charging the shipment. If staff members plan ahead and allow enough time, they can use UPS or FedEx ground service, which takes three to five days and is much cheaper. You wonder whether staff members consider whether the recipient is *really* going to use the message as soon as it arrives. Does it justify an overnight shipment? You would like to reduce overnight delivery services voluntarily by 50 percent over the next two months. Unless a sizable reduction occurs, the CEO threatens severe restrictions in the future.

Your Task. Address your memo to all employees. What other ways could employees reduce shipping costs?

9.19 Persuasive Organizational Message Flowing Downward: Supporting Project H.E.L.P. (Obj. 5)

E-mail

As employee relations manager of The Prudential Insurance Company, one of your tasks is to promote Project H.E.L.P. (Higher Education Learning Program), an on-the-job learning opportunity. Project H.E.L.P. is a combined effort of major corporations and the Newark Unified School District. You must recruit 12 employees who will volunteer as instructors for 50 or more students. The students will spend four hours a week at the Prudential Newark facility earning an average of five units of credit a semester.

This semester the students will be serving in the Claims, Word Processing, Corporate Media Services, Marketing, Communications, Library, and Administrative Support departments. Your task is to convince employees in these departments to volunteer. They will be expected to supervise and instruct the students. In return, employees will receive two hours of release time per week to work with the students. The program has been very successful thus far. School officials, students, and employees alike express satisfaction with the experience and the outcomes.

Your Task. Write a persuasive memo or e-mail message with convincing appeals that will bring you 12 volunteers to work with Project H.E.L.P.

9.20 Persuasive Organizational Message Flowing Downward: Revising Miserable Memo (Obj. 5)

The following memo (with names changed) was actually sent.

Your Task. Based on what you have learned in this chapter, improve the memo. Expect the staff to be somewhat resistant because they've never before had meeting restrictions.

```
TO:        All Managers and Employees
FROM:      Nancy Nelson, CEO
SUBJECT:   Scheduling Meetings

Please be reminded that travel in the greater Los
Angeles area is time consuming. In the future we are
asking that you set up meetings that

1. Are of critical importance
2. Consider travel time for the participants
3. Consider phone conferences (or video or e-mail) in
lieu of face-to-face meetings
4. Meetings should be at the location where most of
the participants work and at the most opportune
travel times
5. Traveling together is another way to save time and
resources.

We all have our traffic stories. A recent one is that
a certain manager was asked to attend a one-hour
meeting in Burbank. This required one hour travel in
advance of the meeting, one hour for the meeting, and
two and a half hours of travel through Los Angeles
afterward. This meeting was scheduled for 4 p.m.
Total time consumed by the manager for the one-hour
meeting was four and a half hours.

Thank you for your consideration.
```

9.21 Persuasive Organizational Message Flowing Downward: Curbing Profanity on the Job (Obj. 5)

E-mail   **Web**

As sales manager for a large irrigation parts manufacturer, you are concerned about the use of profanity by your sales associates. Some defend profanity, claiming that it helps them fit in. Your female sales reps have said that it helps relax listeners, drives home a point, and makes them "one of the boys." You have done some research, however, and learned that courts have ruled that profanity can constitute sexual harassment—whether in person or in print. In addition to causing legal problems, profanity on the job projects a negative image of the individual and of the company. Although foul language is heard increasingly on TV and in the movies, you think it is a bad habit and you want to see it curbed on the job.

Your Task. Use the Web or databases to locate articles related to the use of profanity and strategies employed by organizations for dealing with it. One good resource is **http://www.cusscontrol.com**. In small groups or in class, discuss the place of formal and informal language in communication. Prepare a list of reasons people curse and reasons not to do so. Your instructor may ask you to interview employers to learn their reactions to the issue of workplace profanity. As sales manager at Rain City, compose a persuasive e-mail or memo to your sales staff that will encourage them to curb their use of profanity.[20]

© Image Source Pink / Alamy

9.22 Persuasive Claim: Wounded Buffalo and Pygmy Circus Skip Summertime Slam (Obj. 6)

You and your friend bought $75 tickets to the "Summertime Slam" concert featuring Wounded Buffalo and Pygmy Circus. These two high-energy rock bands were to perform at Five Flags Lake Point Park. But when you arrived for the concert July 4, neither the Buffalos nor the Pygmys appeared. Instead, three decidedly not-ready-for-prime-time groups filled in. You had been looking forward to this concert for seven weeks. After the concert started, you and your friend stayed through two acts to see whether the talent might improve. It didn't. You remember seeing newspaper advertisements publicizing the Buffalo/Pygmy performance as recently as the day of the concert. When you left the Five Flags parking lot after your early exit from the concert, you saw a small poster describing a "change in the talent" for the evening's concert.

When you called to demand a refund, you were told that a change had been announced prior to the concert. You were fuming! How could a tiny poster be sufficient to announce a major change in talent! You also learned that Five Flags could not refund your ticket price because you had stayed for the concert. You felt that they should have paid you to sit through the lame performance that was presented! What a scam! They advertised big-name groups and then filled in with three no-name talentless garage bands. Adding insult to injury, they refused to refund the ticket price!

In the heat of your fury, you wrote an angry letter to express your frustration and resentment over your treatment. But, wisely, you didn't mail the letter.

Your Task. Compose a claim letter based on the suggestions in this chapter. Strive for a moderate tone that achieves your goal. Send your letter to Ms. Felicity Meadows, Guest Relations, Five Flags Lake Point Park, P.O. Box 4300, Sandusky, OH 45320.

9.23 Persuasive Claim: Overcharged and Unhappy (Obj. 6)

As regional manager for an electronics parts manufacturer, you and two other employees attended a conference in Nashville. You stayed at the Country Inn because your company recommends that employees use this hotel chain. Generally, your employees have liked their accommodations, and the rates have been within your company's budget.

Now, however, you are unhappy with the charges you see on your company's credit statement from Country Inn. When your department's administrative assistant made the reservations, she was assured that you would receive the weekend rates and that a hot breakfast—in the hotel restaurant, the Atrium—would be included in the rate. You hate those cold sweet rolls and instant coffee "continental" breakfasts, especially when you have to leave early and won't get another meal until afternoon. So you and the other two employees went to the restaurant and ordered a hot meal from the menu.

When you received the credit statement, though, you see a charge for $114 for three champagne buffet breakfasts in the Atrium. You hit the ceiling! For one thing, you didn't have a buffet breakfast and certainly no champagne. The three of you got there so early that no buffet had been set up. You ordered pancakes and sausage, and for this you were billed $35 each. You are outraged! What's worse, your company may charge you personally for exceeding the expected rates.

In looking back at this event, you remembered that other guests on your floor were having a "continental" breakfast in a lounge on your floor. Perhaps that's where the hotel expected all guests on the weekend rate to eat. However, your administrative assistant had specifically asked about this matter when she made the reservations, and she was told that you could order breakfast from the menu at the hotel's restaurant.

Your Task. You want to straighten out this matter, and you can't do it by telephone because you suspect that you will need a written record of this entire mess. Write a claim request to Customer Service, Country Inn, Inc., 428 Church Street, Nashville, TN 37219. Should you include a copy of the credit statement showing the charge?

9.24 Persuasive Claim: Legal Costs for Sharing a Slice of Heaven (Obj. 6)

Originally a shipbuilding village, the town of Mystic, Connecticut, captures the spirit of the nineteenth-century seafaring era. But it is best known for Mystic Pizza, a bustling local pizzeria featured in a movie that launched the film career of Julia Roberts. Today, customers line the sidewalk waiting to taste its pizza, called by some "a slice of Heaven."

Assume that you are the business manager for Mystic Pizza's owners. They were approached by an independent vendor who wants to use the Mystic Pizza name and secret recipes to distribute frozen pizza through grocery and convenience stores. As business manager, you worked with a law firm, Giordano, Murphy, and Associates. This firm was to draw up contracts regarding the use of Mystic Pizza's name and quality standards for the product. When you received the bill from Henry Giordano, you were flabbergasted. It itemized 38 hours of attorney preparation, at $400 per hour, and 55 hours of paralegal assistance, at $100 per hour. The bill also showed $415 for telephone calls, which might be accurate because Mr. Giordano had to talk with the owners, who were vacationing in Italy at the time. You seriously doubt, however, that an experienced attorney would require 38 hours to draw up the contracts in question. When you began checking, you discovered that excellent legal advice could be obtained for $200 an hour.

Your Task. Decide what you want to request, and then write a persuasive request to Henry Giordano, Attorney at Law, Giordano, Murphy, and Associates, 254 Sherborn Street, Boston, MA 02215. Include an end date and a reason for it.

9.25 Persuasive Claim: Botched Print Job (Obj. 6)

As president of Holiday Travel, you delivered a very complex print job to the Jiffy Printers in Brighton, New York. It took almost 15 minutes to explain the particulars of this job to the printer. When you left, you wondered whether all of the instructions would be followed precisely. You even brought in your own special paper, which added to the cost of printing.

When you got the job back (a total of 1,500 sheets of paper) and returned to your office, you discovered a host of problems. One of the pages had 300 copies made on a cheap 20-pound paper. This means that the printer must have run out of your special paper and substituted something else for one of the runs. The printer also made copies of your original photos and graphics, so that all the final prints were run from second-generation prints, which reduced the quality of the graphics enormously. What's more, many of the sheets were poorly or improperly cut. In short, the job was unacceptable.

Because you were desperate to complete the job, you allowed the print shop to repeat the job using its paper supply. When you inquired about the cost, the counter person Don was noncommittal. He said you would have to talk to the owner, who worked in the Rochester shop. The repeat print job turned out fairly well, and you paid the full price of $782. But you are unhappy and Don sensed that Jiffy Printers would not see Holiday Travel again as a customer. He encouraged you to write to the owner and ask for an adjustment.

Your Task. Write a claim letter to Mr. Howard Moscatelli, Jiffy Printers, 3402 South Main Street, Rochester, NY 14634. What is a reasonable claim to make? Do you simply want to register your unhappiness, or do you want a refund? Supply any needed information.

9.26 Sales Letter: Dropping the Pounds at Financial One (Obj. 7)

Web

Obesity in this country is swelling to unprecedented levels with nearly 60 percent of adults overweight. In addition to the risks to individuals, obesity costs American companies $56 billion in lost productivity caused by disability, illness, and death.[21] Companies from Wall Street to the Rust Belt are launching or improving programs to help employees lose weight. Union Pacific Railroad is considering giving out pedometers to track workers around the office, as well as dispensing weight loss drugs. Merrill Lynch sponsors Weight Watchers meetings. Caterpillar instituted the Healthy Balance Program. It promotes long-term behavioral change and healthier lifestyles for Caterpillar workers. Estimates suggest that employers and employees could save $1,200 a year for each person's medical costs if overweight employees shed their excess weight.

As a sales representative for Global Fitness, one of the country's leading fitness operators, you are convinced that your fitness equipment and programs are instrumental in helping people lose weight. With regular exercise at an on-site fitness center, employees lose weight and improve overall health. As employee health improves, absenteeism is reduced and overall productivity increases. What's more, employees love working out before or after work. They make the routine part of their workday, and they often have work buddies who share their fitness regimen.

Although many companies resist spending money to save money, fitness centers need not be large or expensive to be effective. Studies show that moderately sized centers coupled with motivational and training programs yield the greatest success. For just $30,000, Global Fitness will provide exercise equipment including treadmills, elliptical trainers, exercise bikes, multigyms, and weight machines. Their fitness experts will design a fitness room, set up the equipment, and create appropriate programs. Best of all, the one-time cost is usually offset by cost savings within one year of center installation. For additional fees Global can provide fitness consultants for employee fitness assessments. Global specialists will also train employees on the proper use of the equipment and clean and manage the facility—for an extra charge, of course.

Your Task. Use the Web to update your obesity statistics. Then prepare a sales letter addressed to Holly Hadden, Director, Human Resources, Financial One, Inc., 17208 North 32nd Street, Phoenix, AZ 85035. Ask for an appointment to meet with her. Send a brochure detailing the products and services that Global Fitness provides. As an incentive, offer a free fitness assessment for all employees if Financial One installs a fitness facility by December 1.

9.27 Adapting a Sales Letter From Low Context to High Context (Obj. 8)

`Intercultural` `Team`

The following letter, adapted from an Australian sales message, is intended for a low-context culture.[22]

Your Task. In teams, study the following letter. List at least six factors and techniques used in this letter that typify low-context persuasive sales messages. Then discuss how the letter could be changed if it were to appeal to high-context cultures. Your instructor may ask your team to compose a high-context version of the letter.

Dear Mr. Smith,

Since you are one of our important customers who appreciates convenience and value, I am writing to share an opportunity to enjoy both!

For example, would you like to choose $60 worth of Innovations merchandise—absolutely FREE? And could you benefit from a very convenient credit card—one that offers you a free Rewards program, unsurpassed card protection, free PhotoCard, free Purchase Cover, exceptional personal customer service—and is accepted at over 400,000 locations in Australia, more than 14 million establishments worldwide, and gives you cash access at over 341,000 ATMs?

Realistically, how could you pass up these attractive opportunities? They each represent the very practical (and innovative!) reasons for you to apply for a Citibank Visa or MasterCard. Because I feel so confident that you will truly appreciate a Citibank Credit Card, I would like you to have two $30 vouchers for anything in your Innovations catalogue. Use them separately or together. They are valid until 28 February on your choice of items. But you must reply to this very special offer before 28 November.

= = = = = = = = = = [More incentives detailed here]

I hope you will take a moment to complete and mail (or fax) the enclosed application for your Citibank Credit Card today. I'm certain you will enjoy its many benefits—as well as $60 of vouchers for Innovations merchandise with our compliments. Happy shopping!

Yours sincerely,
Judy Powell, Managing Director

P.S. We can only reserve this exclusive offer until 28 November. So apply for your Citibank Visa or MasterCard today. Once you are approved, you will receive $60 of Innovations vouchers shortly after your new card. And for Double Rewards points, use your card on any Innovations purchase until 28 February of next year!

9.28 Sales Letter: Promoting Your Product or Service (Obj. 7)

Identify a situation in your current job or a previous one in which a sales letter is or was needed. Using suggestions from this chapter, write an appropriate sales letter that promotes a product or service. Use actual names, information, and examples. If you have no work experience, imagine a business you'd like to start: word processing, pet grooming, car detailing, tutoring, specialty knitting, balloon decorating, delivery service, child care, gardening, lawn care, or something else. Write a letter selling your product or service to be distributed to your prospective customers. Be sure to tell them how to respond.

9.29 Press Release: Smart Car Introduces EarthShell Biodegradable Dinnerwear (Obj. 9)

`Web`

You have been interviewed for a terrific job in corporate communications at EarthShell. It produces biodegradable packaging materials for traditional food service items. Its clamshell sandwich containers and food wraps are made from potato starch, limestone, and other biodegradable materials that actually decompose like leaves and grass. At this writing, its biggest news is that EarthShell Hidalgo in Mexico has received a significant order from Wal-Mart of Mexico for EarthShell plates and bowls.

You are excited about the possibility of working at EarthShell in Lutherville, Maryland. However, EarthShell wants you to submit a press release as a writing sample. EarthShell features some rather long press releases at its Web site. Many articles about its products have also appeared in periodicals. The EarthShell recruiter wants you to submit a press release that would appeal to the publisher of your local newspaper.

Your Task. Locate EarthShell information on the Web. Read several articles. At its Web site (use a search engine to locate), study its current press releases. Select one event or product that you think would interest your local newspaper. Although you can use the information from current EarthShell press releases, don't copy the exact wording because it will be obvious to EarthShell.

9.30 Press Release: This Is New! (Obj. 9)

Your Task. For a company where you now work or an organization you belong to, identify a product or service that could be publicized. Consider writing a press release announcing a new course at your college, a new president, new equipment, or a campaign to raise funds. Write the press release for your local newspaper.

9.31 Persuasive Claim: Honolulu Country Club Gets Scammed on Phony Toner Phoner (Obj. 7)

`Consumer`

Heather W. was new to her job as administrative assistant at the Waialae Country Club in Honolulu. Alone in the office one morning, she answered a phone call from Rick, who said he was the country club's copier contractor. "Hey, look, babydoll," Rick purred, "the price on the toner you use is about to go way up. I can offer you a great price on this toner if you order right now." Heather knew that the copy machine regularly needed toner, and she thought she should probably go ahead and place the order to save the country club some money. Ten days later two bottles of toner arrived, and Heather was pleased at the perfect timing. The copy machine needed it right away. Three weeks later Maureen, the bookkeeper, called to report a bill from Copy Machine Specialists for $960.43 for two bottles of toner. "What's going on here?" said Maureen. "We don't purchase supplies from this company, and this price is totally off the charts!"[23]

Heather spoke to the manager, Steven Tanaka, who immediately knew what had happened. He blamed himself for not training Heather. "Never, never order anything from a telephone solicitor, no matter how fast-talking or smooth he sounds," warned Steven. He outlined an office policy for future supplies purchases. Only certain people can authorize or finalize a purchase, and purchases require a confirmed price including shipping costs settled in advance. But what to do about this $960.43 bill? The country club had already begun to use the toner, although the current copies were looking faint and streaked.

Your Task. As Steven Tanaka, decide how to respond to this obvious scam. Should you pay the bill? Should you return the unused bottle? Write a persuasive claim to Copy Machine Specialists, 4320 Admiralty Way, Honolulu, HI 96643. Supply any details necessary.

Video Resources

This chapter has two videos with writing assignments.

Bridging the Gap **Video Library 2**

Persuasive Request: Hard Rock Café

This video takes you inside the Hard Rock Café where you learn about changes it has undergone in surviving over 30 years in the rough-and-tumble world of hospitality. One problem involves difficulty in maintaining its well-known logo around the world. As you watch the video, look for references to the changes taking place and the discussion of brand control.

Your Task. As an assistant in the Hard Rock Corporate Identity Division, you have been asked to draft a persuasive message to be sent to the Edinburgh International Comedy Festival. In doing research, you learned that this festival is one of the three largest comedy festivals in the world, alongside Melbourne Madness Festival and Montreal's Just for Laughs Festival. An annual event, the Edinburgh International Comedy Festival takes over this Scotland city each autumn with stand-up comedy, cabaret, theater, street performance, film, television, radio, and visual arts programs. Some of the programs raise funds for charity.

The problem is that the festival is staging some of its events at the Hard Rock Café, and the festival is using outdated Hard Rock logos at their Web site and in print announcements. Your task is to persuade the Edinburgh International Comedy Festival organizers

to stop using the old logos. Explain why it is necessary to use the official Hard Rock logo. Make it easy for them to obtain the official logo at **http://www.hardrock.net.official.logo**. Organizers must also sign the logo usage agreement. Organizers may be resistant because they have invested in announcements and Web designs with the old logo. If they don't comply by June 1, Hard Rock attorneys may begin legal actions. However, you need to present this date without making it sound like a threat. Your boss wants this message to develop goodwill, not motivate antagonism.

Write a persuasive e-mail message to Edinburgh International Comedy Festival organizer Barry Cook at *bcook@edinburghfestival.com*. Add any reasonable details.

Bridging the Gap **Video Library 2**

Innovation, Learning, and Communication: A Study of Yahoo

This video familiarizes you with managers and inside operating strategies at the Internet company Yahoo. After watching the film, assume the role of assistant to John Briggs, senior producer, who appeared in the video. John has just received a letter asking for permission from another film company to use Yahoo offices and personnel in an educational video, similar to the one you just saw.

Briggs wants you to draft a message for him to send to the operations manager, Ceci Lang, asking for permission for VX Studios to film. VX says it needs about 15 hours of filming time and would like to interview four or five managers as well as founders David Filo and Jerry Yang. VX would need to set up its mobile studio van in the parking lot and would need permission to use advertising film clips. Although VX hopes to film in May, it is flexible about the date. John Briggs reminds you that Yahoo has participated in a number of films in the past two years, and some managers are complaining that they can't get their work done.

Your Task. After watching the video, write a persuasive memo or e-mail message to Ceci Lang, operations manager, asking her to allow VX Studios to film at Yahoo. Your message should probably emphasize the value of these projects in enhancing Yahoo's image among future users. Provide any other details you think are necessary to create a convincing request message that will win authorization from Ceci Lang to schedule this filming.

Grammar and Mechanics C.L.U.E. Review 9

Number Use

Review Guides 47–50 about number use in Appendix A: Grammar and Mechanics Guide (Competent Language Usage Essentials), beginning on page A-18. On a separate sheet, revise the following sentences to correct number usage errors. For each error that you locate, write the guide number that reflects this usage. Sentences may have more than one error. If a sentence is correct, write C. When you finish, check your answers on page Key-2.

Example: 25 employees signed up for health insurance.
Revision: **Twenty-five** employees signed up for health insurance.
  [Guide 47]

1. We ordered 3 new computers and 2 printers for our department.
2. 31 candidates applied for the 3 advertised positions.

3. My company paid five hundred dollars for me to attend the 3-day workshop.
4. Our UPS deliveries arrive before 11:00 o'clock a.m.
5. Personal income tax returns must be mailed by April 15th.
6. We earned 7.5% dividends on our two thousand dollar investment.
7. Our company applied for a one hundred thousand dollar loan at six%.
8. A total of 2,000,000 people attended the World's Fair.
9. I bought the item on eBay for one dollar and fifty cents and sold it for fifteen dollars.
10. That store offers a thirty-day customer-satisfaction return policy.

Interactive Learning @ www.meguffey.com

Chapter 10

Negative Messages

OBJECTIVES

After studying this chapter, you should be able to

1 Describe the goals and strategies of business communicators in delivering bad news, including knowing when to use the direct and indirect patterns, applying the writing process, and avoiding legal problems.

2 Explain effective techniques for delivering bad news sensitively.

3 Identify typical requests and describe an effective strategy for refusing such requests.

4 Explain effective techniques for delivering bad news to customers.

5 Explain effective techniques for delivering bad news within organizations.

6 Compare strategies for revealing bad news in other cultures.

© Tom Grill / Corbis

Communicating at Work Part 1

Passengers LUV Southwest Airlines—Even When Flights Are Late

About 25 percent of the nation's 660 million airline passengers experienced flight delays last year. Many criticized the airlines for not providing information about flight status. Southwest Airlines' passengers, however, are less likely to be among the complainers. That is because Southwest takes a proactive approach, giving its customers timely and regular updates—even when the news is bad. An ice storm caused a several-hour delay on a flight leaving St. Louis. Southwest flight attendants and pilots walked through the plane regularly, answering passengers' questions and providing information on connecting flights. Passengers on that flight were pleasantly surprised when vouchers for free round-trip flights arrived a few days later. The vouchers were accompanied by a letter from the airline apologizing for the inconvenience.

Such practices are the norm for Southwest, whose stock symbol is LUV. The Dallas-based discount airline—known for its low fares, lack of frills, and efficient service—has become a powerful brand in a competitive industry since its humble beginnings in 1971. Founders Rollin King and Herb Kelleher had a unique vision for their new company: Get passengers where they want to go, on time, at the lowest price—and make flying fun for both employees and passengers.

Their formula worked. Today, Southwest is the largest carrier in the United States based on domestic departures. It currently operates more than 3,200 flights a day to 63 cities in 32 states. Whereas other airlines are struggling to cut costs and stay alive, Southwest recently reported its 34th profitable year.

Such high standards have won Southwest a spot on *Business-Week's* ranking of the country's 25 best customer-service providers. Southwest consistently ranks lowest of domestic airlines in the number of complaints per passenger—and just as consistently leads the airline industry in customer satisfaction.

Like its peers, however, Southwest has its share of problems. Irate customers complain about lost baggage, weather delays, and canceled flights. The difference is its response strategy. Fred Taylor,

senior manager of proactive customer communications, tracks operating disruptions across the organization. He meets daily with departmental representatives to discuss possible problems and develop strategies to minimize difficulties before they happen. Regardless of his proactive efforts to minimize customer complaints, Taylor still must respond occasionally to disappointed customers.[1] Delivering bad news and responding to customer complaints are major responsibilities of his job. You'll learn more about this case on page 294.

Critical Thinking

- Suppose you applied for a job that you really wanted, but the company hired someone else. To notify you of the bad news, the company sends a letter. Should the letter blurt out the bad news immediately or soften the blow somewhat?
- What are some techniques you could use if you have to deliver bad news in business messages?
- What goals should you try to achieve when you have to give disappointing news to customers, employees, suppliers, or others on behalf of your organization?

http://www.southwest.com

Strategies for Delivering Bad News

LEARNING OBJECTIVE 1

Describe the goals and strategies of business communicators in delivering bad news, including knowing when to use the direct and indirect patterns, applying the writing process, and avoiding legal problems.

Receivers of bad news are less disappointed if they (a) know the reason for the rejection, (b) feel that the news was revealed sensitively, (c) think the matter was treated seriously, and (d) believe the decision was fair.

In all businesses, things sometimes go wrong. At Southwest Airlines, flights are canceled, baggage is lost, and weather diverts flights. In other businesses, goods are not delivered, products fail to perform as expected, service is poor, billing gets fouled up, or customers are misunderstood. You may have to write messages ending business relationships, declining proposals, announcing price increases, refusing requests for donations, terminating employees, turning down invitations, or responding to unhappy customers. You might have to apologize for mistakes in orders, errors in pricing, the rudeness of employees, overlooked appointments, substandard service, pricing errors, faulty accounting, defective products, or jumbled instructions.

Everyone occasionally must deliver bad news. Because bad news disappoints, irritates, and sometimes angers the receiver, such messages must be written carefully. The bad feelings associated with disappointing news can generally be reduced if the receiver (a) knows the reasons for the rejection, (b) feels that the news was revealed sensitively, (c) thinks the matter was treated seriously, and (d) believes that the decision was fair.

In this chapter you will learn when to use the direct pattern and when to use the indirect pattern to deliver bad news. You will study the goals of business communicators in working with bad news, and you will examine three causes for legal concerns. The major focus of this chapter, however, is on developing the indirect strategy and applying it to situations in which you must refuse typical requests, decline invitations, and deliver negative news to employees and customers. You will also learn how other cultures handle bad news.

© AP IMAGES

Ford Motor Company is attempting to jump-start a turnaround in the face of new plant closings, dwindling market share, massive recalls, "junk" credit ratings, and sagging truck sales. The stalled automaker's restructuring effort, dubbed the "Way Forward," will slash up to 30,000 jobs and close 14 North American factories by 2012. News of the layoffs was leaked in a *Time* cover story on former CEO William Ford Jr. and later buried in a press release praising Ford's future models and innovation. *Should businesses use an indirect strategy when announcing layoffs?*

Primary and Secondary Goals in Communicating Bad News

Delivering bad news is not the happiest writing task you may have, but it can be gratifying if you do it effectively. As a business communicator working with bad news, you will have many goals, the most important of which are these:

Primary Goals

- Make the receiver understand the bad news
- Have the receiver accept the bad news
- Maintain a positive image of you and your organization

Secondary Goals

- Reduce bad feelings
- Convey fairness
- Eliminate future correspondence
- Avoid creating legal liability or responsibility for you or your organization

When you communicate bad news, your primary goals are to make the receiver understand and accept the bad news and to maintain a good image of you and your organization.

These are ambitious goals, and we're not always successful in achieving them all. The patterns you're about to learn, however, provide the beginning communicator with strategies and tactics that many writers have found helpful in conveying disappointing news sensitively and safely. With experience, you will be able to vary these patterns and adapt them to your organization's specific writing tasks.

Using the Indirect Pattern to Prepare the Reader

Whereas good news can be revealed quickly, bad news is generally easier to accept when broken gradually. Revealing bad news slowly and indirectly shows sensitivity to your reader. By preparing the reader, you tend to soften the impact. A blunt announcement of disappointing news might cause the receiver to stop reading and toss the message aside. The indirect strategy enables you to keep the reader's attention until you have been able to explain the reasons for the bad news. In fact, the most important part of a bad-news letter is

The indirect pattern softens the impact of bad news by giving reasons and explanations first.

FIGURE 10.1 Four-Part Indirect Pattern for Bad News

Buffer →	Reasons →	Bad News →	Closing →
Open with a neutral but meaningful statement that does not mention the bad news.	Explain the causes of the bad news before disclosing it.	Reveal the bad news without emphasizing it. Provide an alternative or compromise, if possible.	End with a personalized, forward-looking, pleasant statement. Avoid referring to the bad news.

the explanation, which you will learn about shortly. The indirect plan consists of four parts, as shown in Figure 10.1:

- **Buffer.** Introduce the message with a neutral statement that makes the reader continue reading.

- **Reasons.** Explain why the bad news was necessary and that the matter was taken seriously.

- **Bad news.** Provide a clear but understated announcement of the bad news that might include an alternative or a compromise.

- **Closing.** End with a warm, forward-looking statement that might mention good wishes, gifts, or sales promotion.

When to Use the Direct Pattern

Many bad-news letters are best organized indirectly, beginning with a buffer and reasons. The direct pattern, with the bad news first, may be more effective, though, in situations such as the following:

- **When the receiver may overlook the bad news.** Rate increases, changes in service, new policy requirements—these critical messages may require boldness to ensure attention.

- **When organization policy suggests directness.** Some companies expect all internal messages and announcements—even bad news—to be straightforward and presented without frills.

- **When the receiver prefers directness.** Busy managers may prefer directness. If you know that the reader prefers that the facts be presented straightaway, use the direct pattern.

- **When firmness is necessary.** Messages that must demonstrate determination and strength should not use delaying techniques. For example, the last in a series of collection letters that seek payment of overdue accounts may require a direct opener.

- **When the bad news is not damaging.** If the bad news is insignificant (such as a small increase in cost) and doesn't personally affect the receiver, then the direct strategy certainly makes sense.

> The direct pattern is appropriate when the receiver might overlook the bad news, when directness is preferred, when firmness is necessary, and when the bad news is not damaging.

Applying the 3-x-3 Writing Process

Thinking through the entire writing process is especially important in bad-news letters. Not only do you want the receiver to understand and accept the message, but you also want to be careful that your words say only what you intend. Thus, you will want to apply the familiar 3-x-3 writing process to bad-news letters.

> The 3-x-3 writing process is especially important in crafting bad-news messages because of the potential consequences of poorly written messages.

Analysis, Anticipation, and Adaptation.
In Phase 1 (prewriting) you need to analyze the bad news so that you can anticipate its effect on the receiver. If the disappointment will be mild, announce it directly. If the bad news is serious or personal, consider

techniques to reduce the pain. Adapt your words to protect the receiver's ego. Instead of *You neglected to change the oil, causing severe damage to the engine,* switch to the passive voice: *The oil wasn't changed, causing severe damage to the engine.* Choose words that show you respect the reader as a responsible, valuable person.

Research, Organization, and Composition.

In Phase 2 (writing) you can gather information and brainstorm for ideas. Jot down all the reasons you have that explain the bad news. If four or five reasons prompted your negative decision, concentrate on the strongest and safest ones. Avoid presenting any weak reasons; readers may seize on them to reject the entire message. After selecting your best reasons, outline the four parts of the bad-news pattern: buffer, reasons, bad news, closing. Flesh out each section as you compose your first draft.

Revision, Proofreading, and Evaluation.

In Phase 3 (revising) you're ready to switch positions and put yourself into the receiver's shoes. Have you looked at the problem from the receiver's perspective? Is your message too blunt? Too subtle? Does the message make the refusal, denial, or bad-news announcement clear? Prepare the final version, and proofread for format, punctuation, and correctness.

Avoiding Three Causes of Legal Problems

Before we examine the components of a bad-news message, let's look more closely at how you can avoid exposing yourself and your employer to legal liability in writing negative messages. Although we can't always anticipate the consequences of our words, we should be alert to three causes of legal difficulties: (a) abusive language, (b) careless language, and (c) the "good-guy syndrome."

Abusive Language.

Calling people names (such as *deadbeat, crook,* or *quack*) can get you into trouble. *Defamation* is the legal term for any false statement that harms an individual's reputation. When the abusive language is written, it is called *libel*; when spoken, it is *slander*.

To be actionable (likely to result in a lawsuit), abusive language must be (a) false, (b) damaging to one's good name, and (c) "published"—that is, written or spoken within the presence of others. Thus, if you were alone with Jane Doe and accused her of accepting bribes and selling company secrets to competitors, she couldn't sue because the defamation wasn't published. Her reputation was not damaged. However, if anyone heard the words or if they were written, you might be legally liable.

In a new wrinkle, you may now be prosecuted if you transmit a harassing or libelous message by e-mail or on a bulletin board. Such electronic transmissions are considered to be "published." Moreover, a company may incur liability for messages sent through its computer system by employees. That's why many companies are increasing their monitoring of both outgoing and internal messages. "Off-the-cuff, casual e-mail conversations among employees are exactly the type of messages that tend to trigger lawsuits and arm litigators with damaging evidence," says e-mail guru Nancy Flynn.[2] Instant messaging adds another danger for companies. Whether in print or electronically, competent communicators avoid making unproven charges and letting their emotions prompt abusive language.

Abusive language becomes legally actionable when it is false, harmful to the person's good name, and "published."

Careless Language.

As the marketplace becomes increasingly litigious, we must be certain that our words communicate only what we intend. Take the case of a factory worker injured on the job. His attorney subpoenaed company documents and discovered a seemingly harmless letter sent to a group regarding a plant tour. These words appeared in the letter: *Although we are honored at your interest in our company, we cannot give your group a tour of the plant operations as it would be too noisy and dangerous.* The court found in favor of the worker, inferring from the letter that working conditions were indeed hazardous.[3] The letter writer did not intend to convey the impression of dangerous working conditions, but the court accepted that interpretation.

Careless language includes statements that could be damaging or misinterpreted.

The Good-Guy Syndrome.

Most of us hate to have to reveal bad news—that is, to be the bad guy. To make ourselves look better, to make the receiver feel better, and to maintain good relations, we are tempted to make statements that are legally dangerous. Consider the case of a law firm interviewing job candidates. One of the firm's partners was asked to inform a candidate that she was not selected. The partner's letter said, "Although you were by far the most qualified candidate we interviewed, unfortunately, we have decided we do not have a position for a person of your talents at this time." To show that he personally had no reservations about this candidate and to bolster the candidate, the partner offered his own opinion. However, he differed from the majority of the recruiting committee. When the rejected interviewee learned later that the law firm had hired two male attorneys, she sued, charging sexual discrimination. The court found in favor of the rejected candidate. It agreed that a reasonable inference could be made from the partner's letter that she was the "most qualified candidate."[4]

Two important lessons emerge. First, business communicators act as agents of their organizations. Their words, decisions, and opinions are assumed to represent those of the organization. If you want to communicate your personal feelings or opinions, use your home computer or write on plain paper (rather than company letterhead) and sign your name without title or affiliation. Second, volunteering extra information can lead to trouble. Thus, avoid supplying data that could be misused, and avoid making promises that can't be fulfilled. Don't admit or imply responsibility for conditions that caused damage or injury. Even apologies (*We're sorry that a faulty bottle cap caused damage to your carpet*) may suggest liability.

In Chapter 4 we discussed four information areas that generate the most lawsuits: investments, safety, marketing, and human resources. In this chapter we will make specific suggestions for avoiding legal liability in writing responses to claim letters, credit letters, and personnel documents. You may find that in the most critical areas (such as collection letters or hiring/firing messages) your organization provides language guidelines and form letters approved by legal counsel. As the business environment becomes more perilous, we must not only be sensitive to receivers but also keenly aware of risks to ourselves and to the organizations we represent.

Techniques for Delivering Bad News Sensitively

Legal matters aside, let's now study specific techniques for using the indirect pattern in sending bad-news messages. In this pattern the bad news is delayed until after explanations have been given. The four components of the indirect pattern, shown in Figure 10.2, include buffer, reasons, bad news, and closing.

Buffering the Opening

A buffer is a device to reduce shock or pain. To buffer the pain of bad news, begin with a neutral but meaningful statement that makes the reader continue reading. The buffer should be relevant and concise and provide a natural transition to the explanation that follows. The individual situation, of course, will help determine what you should put in the buffer. Avoid trite buffers such as *Thank you for your letter*. Here are some possibilities for opening bad-news messages.

Best News.

Start with the part of the message that represents the best news. For example, a message to workers announced new health-plan rules limiting prescriptions to a 34-day supply and increasing co-payments. With home delivery, however, employees could save up to $24 on each prescription. To emphasize the good news, you might write, *You can now achieve significant savings and avoid trips to the drugstore by having your prescription drugs delivered to your home.*[5]

Compliment.

Praise the receiver's accomplishments, organization, or efforts, but do so with honesty and sincerity. For instance, in a letter declining an invitation to speak, you could write, *The Thalians have my sincere admiration for their fund-raising projects on behalf of hungry children. I am honored that you asked me to speak Friday, November 5.*

FIGURE 10.2 Delivering Bad News Sensitively

Buffer	Reasons	Bad News	Closing
• Best news • Compliment • Appreciation • Agreement • Facts • Understanding • Apology	• Cautious explanation • Reader or other benefits • Company policy explanation • Positive words • Evidence that matter was considered fairly and seriously	• Embedded placement • Passive voice • Implied refusal • Compromise • Alternative	• Forward look • Information about alternative • Good wishes • Freebies • Resale • Sales promotion

Appreciation. Convey thanks to the reader for doing business, for sending something, for conveying confidence in your organization, for expressing feelings, or simply for providing feedback. Suppose you had to draft a letter that refuses employment. You could say, *I appreciated learning about the hospitality management program at Cornell and about your qualifications in our interview last Friday.* Avoid thanking the reader, however, for something you are about to refuse.

Agreement. Make a relevant statement with which both reader and receiver can agree. A letter that rejects a loan application might read, *We both realize how much the export business has been affected by the relative weakness of the dollar in the past two years.*

Facts. Provide objective information that introduces the bad news. For example, in a memo announcing cutbacks in the hours of the employees' cafeteria, you might say, *During the past five years the number of employees eating breakfast in our cafeteria has dropped from 32 percent to 12 percent.*

Understanding. Show that you care about the reader. Notice how in this letter to customers announcing a product defect, the writer expresses concern: *We know that you expect superior performance from all the products you purchase from OfficeCity. That's why we're writing personally about the Exell printer cartridges you recently ordered.*

Apologizing

You learned about making apologies in adjustment letters discussed in Chapter 8. We expand that discussion here because apologies are often part of negative-news messages. The truth is that sincere apologies work. Peter Post, great grandson of famed etiquette expert Emily Post and director of the Emily Post Institute, said that Americans love apologies. They will forgive almost anything if presented with a sincere apology.[6] An apology is defined as an "admission of blameworthiness and regret for an undesirable event."[7] Here are some tips on how to apologize effectively in business messages:

- Apologize to customers if you or your company erred. Apologies cost nothing, and they go a long way in soothing hard feelings. Use good judgment, of course. Don't admit blame if it might prompt a lawsuit.

- Apologize sincerely. People dislike apologies that sound hollow (*We regret that you were inconvenienced* or *We regret that you are disturbed*). Focusing on your regret does not convey sincerity. Explaining what you will do to prevent recurrence of the problem projects sincerity in an apology.

- Accept responsibility. One CEO was criticized for the following weak apology: *I want our customers to know how much I personally*

An apology is an admission of blameworthiness and regret for an undesirable event.

Spotlight on Communicators

When leaders accept blame or apologize, executive coach Marshall Goldsmith believes, it is "one of the most powerful and resonant gestures in the human arsenal—almost as powerful as a declaration of love. If love means, 'I care about you, and I'm happy about it,' then an apology means, 'I hurt you, and I'm sorry about it.'" Named one of the 50 greatest thinkers and business management leaders, Goldsmith explains that the best thing about apologizing is that it forces everyone to let go of the past. In effect, an apology says, I screwed up, I'm sorry, I'll do better. "That's tough for even the most cold-hearted to resist," says Goldsmith.

regret any difficulties you may experience as a result of the unauthorized intrusion into our computer systems. Apology experts faulted this apology because it did not acknowledge responsibility.[8]

Consider these poor and improved apologies:

> **Poor apology:** We regret that you are unhappy with the price of ice cream purchased at one of our scoop shops.

> **Improved apology:** We are genuinely sorry that you were disappointed in the price of ice cream recently purchased at one of our scoop shops. Your opinion is important to us, and we appreciate your giving us the opportunity to look into the problem you describe.

> **Poor apology:** We apologize if anyone was affected.

> **Improved apology:** I apologize for the frustration our delay caused you. As soon as I received your message, I began looking into the cause of the delay and realized that our delivery tracking system must be improved.

> **Poor apology:** We are sorry that mistakes were made in filling your order.

> **Improved apology:** You're right to be concerned. We sincerely apologize for the mistakes we made in filling your order. To prevent recurrence of this problem, we are. . . .

Conveying Empathy

One of the hardest things to do in apologies is to convey sympathy and empathy. As we discussed earlier, *empathy* is the ability to understand and enter into the feelings of another. When ice storms trapped JetBlue Airways passengers on hot planes for hours, CEO Neeleman wrote a letter of apology that sounded as if it came from his heart. He said, *Dear JetBlue Customers: We are sorry and embarrassed. But most of all, we are deeply sorry.* Later in his letter he said, *Words cannot express how truly sorry we are for the anxiety, frustration, and inconvenience that you, your family, friends, and colleagues experienced.*[9] Neeleman put himself into the shoes of his customers and tried to experience their pain.

Here are other examples of ways to express empathy in written messages:

- In writing to an unhappy customer: *We did not intentionally delay the shipment, and we sincerely regret the disappointment and frustration you must have suffered.*

- In laying off employees: *It is with great regret that we must take this step. Rest assured that I will be more than happy to write letters of recommendation for anyone who asks.*

- In responding to a complaint: *I am deeply saddened that our service failure disrupted your sale, and we will do everything in our power to . . . .*

- In showing genuine feelings: *You have every right to be disappointed. I am truly sorry that. . . .*

Presenting the Reasons

The most important part of a bad-news letter is the section that explains why a negative decision is necessary. Without sound reasons for denying a request or refusing a claim, a letter will fail, no matter how cleverly it is organized or written. As part of your planning before writing, you analyzed the problem and decided to refuse a request for specific reasons. Before disclosing the bad news, try to explain those reasons. Providing an explanation reduces feelings of ill will and improves the chances that readers will accept the bad news.

Explaining Clearly. If the reasons are not confidential and if they will not create legal liability, you can be specific: *Growers supplied us with a limited number of patio roses, and our demand this year was twice that of last year.* In responding to a billing error, explain what happened: *After you informed us of an error on your January bill, we investigated the matter and admit the mistake was ours. Until our new automated system is fully online, we are still subject to the frailties of human error. Rest assured that your account has been credited as*

Spotlight on Communicators

Millionaire publisher Malcolm Forbes recognized that being agreeable while disagreeing is truly an art. He advised being positive and "nice." Contrary to the cliché, genuinely nice people most often finish first or very near it. He suggested using the acid test, particularly for a bad-news message. After you finish, read it out loud. You will know whether it sounds natural, positive, and respectful.

© Yvonne Hemsey / Contributor / Getty Images

you will see on your next bill. In refusing a speaking engagement, tell why the date is impossible: *On January 17 we have a board of directors meeting that I must attend.* Don't, however, make unrealistic or dangerous statements in an effort to be the "good guy."

Citing Reader or Other Benefits if Plausible.
Readers are more open to bad news if in some way, even indirectly, it may help them. In refusing a customer's request for free hemming of skirts and slacks, Lands' End wrote: *We tested our ability to hem skirts a few months ago. This process proved to be very time-consuming. We have decided not to offer this service because the additional cost would have increased the selling price of our skirts substantially, and we did not want to impose that cost on all our customers.*[10] Readers also accept bad news more readily if they recognize that someone or something else benefits, such as other workers or the environment: *Although we would like to consider your application, we prefer to fill managerial positions from within.* Avoid trying to show reader benefits, though, if they appear insincere: *To improve our service to you, we're increasing our brokerage fees.*

Readers accept bad news more readily if they see that someone benefits.

Explaining Company Policy.
Readers resent blanket policy statements prohibiting something: *Company policy prevents us from making cash refunds* or *Contract bids may be accepted from local companies only* or *Company policy requires us to promote from within.* Instead of hiding behind company policy, gently explain why the policy makes sense: *We prefer to promote from within because it rewards the loyalty of our employees. In addition, we've found that people familiar with our organization make the quickest contribution to our team effort.* By offering explanations, you demonstrate that you care about readers and are treating them as important individuals.

Choosing Positive Words.
Because the words you use can affect a reader's response, choose carefully. Remember that the objective of the indirect pattern is holding the reader's attention until you've had a chance to explain the reasons justifying the bad news. To keep the reader in a receptive mood, avoid expressions with punitive, demoralizing, or otherwise negative connotations. Stay away from such words as *cannot, claim, denied, error, failure, fault, impossible, mistaken, misunderstand, never, regret, rejected, unable, unwilling, unfortunately,* and *violate.*

Showing That the Matter Was Treated Seriously and Fairly.
In explaining reasons, demonstrate to the reader that you take the matter seriously, have investigated carefully, and are making an unbiased decision. Receivers are more accepting of disappointing news when they feel that their requests have been heard and that they have been treated fairly. In canceling funding for a program, board members provided this explanation: *As you know, the publication of* Urban Artist *was funded by a renewable annual grant from the National Endowment for the Arts. Recent cutbacks in federally sponsored city arts programs have left us with few funds. Because our grant has been discontinued, we have no alternative but to cease publication of* Urban Artist. *You have my assurance that the board has searched long and hard for some other viable funding, but every avenue of recourse has been closed before us. Accordingly, June's issue will be our last.*

Cushioning the Bad News

Although you can't prevent the disappointment that bad news brings, you can reduce the pain somewhat by breaking the news sensitively. Be especially considerate when the reader will suffer personally from the bad news. A number of thoughtful techniques can cushion the blow.

Positioning the Bad News Strategically.
Instead of spotlighting it, sandwich the bad news between other sentences, perhaps among your reasons. Don't let the refusal begin or end a paragraph—the reader's eye will linger on these high-visibility spots. Another technique that reduces shock is putting a painful idea in a subordinate clause: *Although another candidate was hired, we appreciate your interest in our organization and wish you every success in your job search.* Subordinate clauses often begin with words such as *although, as, because, if,* and *since.*

Techniques for cushioning bad news include positioning it strategically, using the passive voice, implying the refusal, and suggesting alternatives or compromises.

Using the Passive Voice. Passive-voice verbs enable you to depersonalize an action. Whereas the active voice focuses attention on a person (*We don't give cash refunds*), the passive voice highlights the action (*Cash refunds are not given because . . .*). Use the passive voice for the bad news. In some instances you can combine passive-voice verbs and a subordinate clause: *Although franchise scoop shop owners cannot be required to lower their ice cream prices, we are happy to pass along your comments for their consideration.*

Accentuating the Positive. As you learned earlier, messages are far more effective when you describe what you can do instead of what you can't do. Rather than *We will no longer allow credit card purchases,* try a more positive appeal: *We are now selling gasoline at discount cash prices.*

Implying the Refusal. It is sometimes possible to avoid a direct statement of refusal. Often, your reasons and explanations leave no doubt that a request has been denied. Explicit refusals may be unnecessary and at times cruel. In this refusal to contribute to a charity, for example, the writer never actually says *no: Because we will soon be moving into new offices in Glendale, all our funds are earmarked for relocation costs. We hope that next year we will be able to support your worthwhile charity.* The danger of an implied refusal, of course, is that it is so subtle that the reader misses it. Be certain that you make the bad news clear, thus preventing the need for further correspondence.

Suggesting a Compromise or an Alternative. A refusal is not so depressing—for the sender or the receiver—if a suitable compromise, substitute, or alternative is available. In denying permission to a group of students to visit a historical private residence, for instance, this writer softens the bad news by proposing an alternative: *Although private tours of the grounds are not given, we do open the house and its gardens for one charitable event in the fall.* You can further reduce the impact of the bad news by refusing to dwell on it. Present it briefly (or imply it), and move on to your closing.

Closing Pleasantly

Closings to bad-news messages might include a forward look, an alternative, good wishes, freebies, and resale or sales promotion information.

After explaining the bad news sensitively, close the message with a pleasant statement that promotes goodwill. The closing should be personalized and may include a forward look, an alternative, good wishes, freebies, resale information, or an off-the-subject remark.

Forward Look. Anticipate future relations or business. A letter that refuses a contract proposal might read: *Thanks for your bid. We look forward to working with your talented staff when future projects demand your special expertise.*

Alternative Follow-Up. If an alternative exists, end your letter with follow-through advice. For example, in a letter rejecting a customer's demand for replacement of landscaping plants, you might say: *I will be happy to give you a free inspection and consultation. Please call 746-8112 to arrange a date for my visit.* In a message to a prospective homebuyer: *Although the lot you saw last week is now sold, we do have two excellent view lots available at a slightly higher price.* In reacting to an Internet misprint: *Please note that our Web site contained an unfortunate misprint offering $850-per-night Bora Bora bungalows at $85. Although we cannot honor that rate, we are offering a special half-price rate of $425 to those who responded.*

Good Wishes. A letter rejecting a job candidate might read: *We appreciate your interest in our company, and we extend to you our best wishes in your search to find the perfect match between your skills and job requirements.*

Freebies. When customers complain—primarily about food products or small consumer items—companies often send coupons, samples, or gifts to restore confidence and to promote future business. In response to a customer's complaint about a frozen dinner, you could write: *Your loyalty and your concern about our frozen entrees are genuinely appreciated. Because we want you to continue enjoying our healthful and convenient dinners, we're enclosing a coupon that you can take to your local market to select your next Green Valley entree.*

Resale or Sales Promotion. When the bad news is not devastating or personal, references to resale information or promotion may be appropriate: *The computer workstations you ordered are unusually popular because of their stain-, heat-, and scratch-resistant finishes. To help you locate hard-to-find accessories for these workstations, we invite you to visit our Web site where our online catalog provides a huge selection of surge suppressors, multiple outlet strips, security devices, and PC tool kits.*

Avoid endings that sound canned, insincere, inappropriate, or self-serving. Don't invite further correspondence (*If you have any questions, do not hesitate . . .*), and don't refer to the bad news. To review these suggestions for delivering bad news sensitively, take another look at Figure 10.2.

Refusing Typical Requests

Every business communicator will occasionally have to say *no* to a request. Depending on how you think the receiver will react to your refusal, you can use the direct or the indirect pattern. If you have any doubt, use the indirect pattern.

LEARNING OBJECTIVE 3
Identify typical requests and describe an effective strategy for refusing such requests.

Rejecting Requests for Favors, Money, Information, and Action

Most of us prefer to be let down gently when we're being refused something we want. That's why the reasons-before-refusal pattern works well when you must turn down requests for favors, money, information, action, and so forth.

The reasons-before-refusal pattern works well when turning down requests for favors, money, information, or action.

Saying *No* to Requests From Outsiders. Requests for contributions to charity are common. Many big and small companies receive requests for contributions of money, time, equipment, and support. Although the causes may be worthy, resources are usually limited. In a letter from Forest Financial Services, shown in Figure 10.3, the company must refuse a request for a donation to a charity. Following the indirect strategy, the letter begins with a buffer acknowledging the request. It also praises the good works of the charity and uses those words as a transition to the second paragraph. In the second paragraph the writer explains why the company cannot donate. Notice that the writer reveals the refusal without actually stating it (*Because of sales declines and organizational downsizing, we're forced to take a much harder look at funding requests that we receive this year.*) This gentle refusal makes it unnecessary to be more blunt in stating the denial.

In some donation refusal letters, the reasons may not be fully explained: *Although we can't provide financial support at this time, we all unanimously agree that the Make-A-Wish Foundation contributes a valuable service to sick children.* The emphasis is on the foundation's good deeds rather than on an explanation for the refusal. In the letter shown in Figure 10.3, the writer felt a connection to the charity. Therefore, he wanted to give a fuller explanation.

If you were required to write frequent refusals, you might prepare a form letter, changing a few variables as needed. See the Tech Talk box on page 286 to learn how you can personalize form letters by using word processing software. The refusal for a donation shown in Figure 10.3 could be adapted, using word processing equipment, to respond to other charity requests.

Refusing Internal Requests. Just as managers must refuse requests from outsiders, they must also occasionally refuse requests from employees. In Figure 10.4 you see the first draft and revision of a message responding to a request from a key manager, Mark Stevenson. He wants permission to attend a conference. However, he can't attend the conference because the timing is bad; he must be present at budget planning meetings scheduled for the same two weeks. Normally, this matter would be discussed in person. However, Mark has been traveling among branch offices, and he just hasn't been in the office recently.

The vice president's first inclination was to send a quickie memo, as shown in Figure 10.4, and "tell it like it is." In revising, the vice president realized that this message was

Internal request refusals focus on explanations and praise, maintaining a positive tone, and offering alternatives.

FIGURE 10.3 Refusing Donation Request

1 Prewriting

Analyze: The purpose of this letter is to reject the request for a monetary donation without causing bad feelings.

Anticipate: The reader is proud of his or her organization and the good work it pursues.

Adapt: The writer should strive to cushion the bad news and explain why it is necessary.

2 Writing

Research: Collect information about the receiver's organization as well as reasons for the refusal.

Organize: Use the indirect strategy. Begin with complimentary comments, present reasons, reveal the bad news gently, and close pleasantly.

Compose: Write the message and consider keeping a copy to serve as a form letter.

3 Revising

Revise: Be sure that the tone of the message is positive and that it suggests that the matter was taken seriously.

Proofread: Check the receiver's name and address to be sure they are accurate. Check the letter's format.

Evaluate: Will this message retain goodwill of the receiver despite its news?

FOREST FINANCIAL SERVICES
3410 Willow Grove Boulevard
Philadelphia, PA 19137
215.593.4400
www.forestfinancial.com

November 14, 2009

Ms. Rachel Brown, Chair
Montgomery County Chapter
National Reye's Syndrome Foundation
342 DeKalb Pike
Blue Bell, PA 19422

Dear Ms. Brown:

We appreciate your letter describing the good work your Montgomery County chapter of the National Reye's Syndrome Foundation is doing in preventing and treating this serious affliction. Your organization is to be commended for its significant achievements resulting from the efforts of dedicated members.

Supporting the good work of your organization and others, although unrelated to our business, is a luxury we have enjoyed in past years. Because of sales declines and organizational downsizing, we're forced to take a much harder look at funding requests that we receive this year. We feel that we must focus our charitable contributions on areas that relate directly to our business.

We're hopeful that the worst days are behind us and that we'll be able to renew our support for worthwhile projects like yours next year.

Sincerely,

Paul Rosenberg

Paul Rosenberg
Vice President

Annotations (left):
- Opens with praise and compliments
- Transitions with repetition of key idea (*good work*)
- Reveals refusal without actually stating it

Annotations (right):
- Doesn't say *yes* or *no*
- Explains sales decline and cutback in gifts
- Closes graciously with forward look

FIGURE 10.4 Refusing an Internal Request

DRAFT

DATE: July 2, 2009

TO: Mark Stevenson
          Manager, Telecommunications

FROM: Ann Wells-Freed   *AWf*
          VP, Management Information Systems

SUBJECT: Conference Request

We can't allow you to attend the conference in September, Mark. Perhaps you didn't know that budget-planning meetings are scheduled for that month. — *Announces the bad news too quickly and painfully*

Your expertise is needed here to help keep our telecommunications network on schedule. Without you, the entire system—which is shaky at best—might fall apart. I'm sorry to have to refuse your request to attend the conference. I know this is small thanks for the fine work you have done for us. Please accept our humble apologies. — *Gives reasons, but includes a dangerous statement*

In the spring I'm sure your work schedule will be lighter, and we can release you to attend a conference at that time. — *Makes a promise that might be difficult to keep*

REVISION

DATE: July 2, 2009

TO: Mark Stevenson
          Manager, Telecommunications

FROM: Ann Wells-Freed   *AWf*
          VP, Management Information Systems

SUBJECT: Request to Attend September Conference

Transition: Uses date to move smoothly from buffer to reasons — The Management Council and I are extremely pleased with the leadership you have provided in setting up live video transmission to our regional offices. Because of your genuine professional commitment, Mark, I can understand your desire to attend the conference of the Telecommunication Specialists of America September 23 to 28 in Atlanta. — *Buffer: Includes sincere praise*

Bad news: Implies refusal — The last two weeks in September have been set aside for budget planning. As you and I know, we have only scratched the surface of our teleconferencing projects for the next five years. Since you are the specialist and we rely heavily on your expertise, we need you here for those planning sessions. — *Reasons: Tells why refusal is necessary*

Closing: Contains realistic alternative — If you are able to attend a similar conference in the spring and if our workloads permit, we will try to send you then. You are a valuable player, Mark, and I am grateful you are on our MIS team.

going to hurt and that it had possible danger areas. Moreover, the memo misses a chance to give Mark positive feedback. An improved version of the memo starts with a buffer that delivers honest praise (*pleased with your leadership* and *your genuine professional commitment*). By the way, don't be stingy with compliments; they cost you nothing. As a philosopher once observed, *We don't live by bread alone. We need buttering up once in a while.* The buffer also includes the date of the meeting, used strategically to connect the reasons that follow. You will recall from Chapter 5 that repetition of a key idea is an effective transitional device to provide smooth flow between components of a message.

The middle paragraph in Figure 10.4 provides reasons for the refusal. Notice that they focus on positive elements: Mark is the specialist; the company relies on his expertise; and everyone will benefit if he passes up the conference. In this section it becomes obvious that the request will be refused. The writer is not forced to say, *No, you may not attend.* The closing suggests a qualified alternative (*if our workloads permit, we will try to send you then*). It also ends positively with gratitude for Mark's contributions to the organization and with another compliment (*you're a valuable player*). The improved version focuses on explanations and praise rather than on refusals and apologies. The success of this message depends on attention to the entire writing process, not just on using a buffer or scattering a few compliments throughout.

In the following Tech Talk, notice how form letters can be individualized by using word-processing technology.

Tech Talk

Using Technology to Personalize Form Letters

If you had to send the same information to 200 or more customers, would you write a personal letter to each? Probably not! Responding to identical requests can be tedious, expensive, and time-consuming. That's why many businesses turn to form letters for messages like these: announcing upcoming sales, responding to requests for product information, and updating customers' accounts.

But your letters don't have to sound or look as if a computer wrote them. Word processing equipment can help you personalize those messages so that receivers feel they are being treated as individuals. Here's how the process works.

First, create a form letter (main document) with the basic text that is the same in every document. Insert codes or "merge fields" at each point where information will vary, for example, for the customer's name and address, item ordered, balance due, or due date. A database contains the recipient list. The main document is then merged with the recipient list to create a personalized letter for each individual. It is usually wise to minimize the variable information within the body of your message to keep the merging operation as simple as possible.

FORM LETTER (MAIN DOCUMENT)
Current date
<<Title>> <<First_Name>> <<Last_Name>>
<<Address 1>>
<<City>>, <<State>> <<Zip_Code>>

Dear <<Title>> <<Last_Name>>:

Thanks for your recent order from our fall catalog.

One item that you requested, <<Item>>, has proved to be very popular this season. Occasionally, we are able to appeal to our manufacturers to make more of a popular item. In this instance, though, our pleas went unanswered.

More than anything, we hate to disappoint customers like you, <<Title>> <<Last_Name>>. We pledge to do better with your future orders.

Sincerely,

Cindy Scott

LIST OF VARIABLE INFORMATION IN DATA SOURCE
<<Title>> Mr.
<<First_Name>> Drew
<<Last_Name>> Jamison
<<Street>> 17924 Dreyfuss Avenue
<<City>> Evansville
<<State>> IN
<<Zip Code>> 47401
<<Item>> No. 8765 Ivory Pullover.

COMPLETED FORM LETTER
Current Date

Mr. Drew Jamison
17924 Dreyfuss Avenue
Evansville, IN 47401

Dear Mr. Jamison:

Thanks for your recent order from our fall catalog.

One item that you requested, No. 8765 Ivory Pullover, has proved to be very popular this season. Occasionally, we are able to appeal to our manufacturers to make more of a popular item. In this instance, though, our pleas went unanswered.

More than anything, we hate to disappoint customers like you, Mr. Jamison. We pledge to do better with your future orders.

Sincerely,

Cindy Scott

Career Application
Bring in a business letter that could be adapted as a form letter. Using it as a guide, prepare a rough draft of the same message indicating the locations of all necessary variables. Then ask someone from your class or your campus computer center to demonstrate how this letter would be set up and merged using word processing software.

Declining Invitations

When we must decline an invitation to speak or attend a program, we generally try to provide a response that says more than *I can't* or *I don't want to*. Unless the reasons are confidential or business secrets, try to explain them. Because responses to invitations are often taken personally, make a special effort to soften the refusal. In the letter shown in Figure 10.5, an accountant must say *no* to the invitation from a friend's son to speak before the young man's college business club. This refusal starts with conviviality and compliments.

The writer then explains why she cannot accept. The refusal is embedded in a long paragraph and de-emphasized in a subordinate clause (*Although your invitation must be declined*). The reader naturally concentrates on the main clause that follows (*I would like to recommend . . .*). If no alternative is available, focus on something positive about the situation (*Although I'm not an expert, I commend your organization for selecting this topic*). Overall, the tone of this refusal is warm, upbeat, and positive.

Compliments can help buffer the impact of request refusals.

FIGURE 10.5 Refusing an Invitation

Opens cordially with praise

Focuses attention on alternative

Reduces impact of refusal by placing it in subordinate clause

Ends positively with compliments and offer of assistance

GALLAGHER, BRACIO, CASAGRANDE, L.L.P.
Certified Public Accountants
942 Lafayette Boulevard
Bridgeport, CT 06604
(203) 435-9800

E-mail: cpa@gbcllp.com   www.gbcllp.com

April 14, 2009

Mr. Tyler Simpson
4208 Aspetuck Avenue
Fairfield, CT 04519

Dear Tyler:

News of your leadership position in Epsilon Phi Delta, the campus business honorary club, fills me with delight and pride. Your father must be proud also of your educational and extracurricular achievements.

You honor me by asking me to speak to your group in the spring about codes of ethics in the accounting field. Because our firm has not yet adopted such a code, we have been investigating the codes developed by other accounting firms. I am decidedly not an expert in this area, but I have met others who are. Although your invitation must be declined, I would like to recommend Dr. Carolyn S. Marshall, who is a member of the ethics subcommittee of the Institute of Internal Auditors. Dr. Marshall is a professor who often addresses groups on the subject of ethics in accounting. I spoke with her about your club, and she indicated that she would be happy to consider your invitation.

It's good to learn that you are guiding your organization toward such constructive and timely program topics. Please call Dr. Marshall at (203) 389-2210 if you would like to arrange for her to address your club.

Sincerely,

Joan F. Gallagher

Joan F. Gallagher, CPA

JFG:mhr

Checklist

Refusing Typical Requests

Prewrite

✓ If the bad news is serious or personal, consider techniques to reduce its pain.

✓ Remember that your primary goal is to make the receiver understand and accept the bad news as well as maintain a positive image of you and your organization.

Begin With a Buffer

✓ Pay a compliment to the reader, show appreciation for something done, or mention some mutual understanding.

✓ Avoid raising false hopes or thanking the reader for something you will refuse.

Provide Reasons

✓ In the body explain why the request must be denied—without revealing the refusal.

✓ Avoid negativity (*unfortunately*, *unwilling*, and *impossible*) and potentially damaging statements.

✓ Show how your decision is fair and perhaps benefits the reader or others, if possible.

Soften the Bad News

✓ Reduce the impact of bad news by using (a) a subordinate clause, (b) the passive voice, (c) a long sentence, or (d) a long paragraph.

✓ Consider implying the refusal, but be certain it is clear.

✓ Suggest an alternative, such as a lower price, a different product, a longer payment period, or a substitute.

Close Pleasantly

✓ Supply more information about an alternative, look forward to future relations, or offer good wishes and compliments.

✓ Maintain a bright, personal tone. Avoid referring to the refusal.

The above checklist reviews the steps in composing letters that refuse typical requests.

Delivering Bad News to Customers

LEARNING OBJECTIVE 4
Explain effective techniques for delivering bad news to customers.

Businesses must occasionally respond to disappointed customers. In Chapter 8 you learned to use the direct strategy in granting claims and making adjustments because these were essentially good-news messages. But in some situations you have little good news to share. Sometimes your company is at fault, in which case an apology is generally in order. Other times the problem is with orders you can't fill, claims you must refuse, or credit you must deny. Messages with bad news for customers generally follow the same pattern as other negative messages. Customer letters, though, differ in one major way: they usually include resale or sales promotion emphasis.

Damage Control: Dealing With Disappointed Customers

When a customer problem arises and the company is at fault, many businesspeople call and apologize, explain what happened, and follow up with a goodwill letter.

All companies occasionally disappoint their customers. Merchandise is not delivered on time, a product fails to perform as expected, service is deficient, charges are erroneous, or customers are misunderstood. All businesses offering products or services must sometimes deal with troublesome situations that cause unhappiness to customers. Whenever possible, these problems should be dealt with immediately and personally. A majority of business professionals strive to control the damage and resolve such problems in the following manner:[11]

- Call the individual involved.

- Describe the problem and apologize.

- Explain why the problem occurred, what you are doing to resolve it, and how you will prevent it from happening again.

- Follow up with a letter that documents the phone call and promotes goodwill.

Dealing with problems immediately is very important in resolving conflict and retaining goodwill. Written correspondence is generally too slow for problems that demand

Taco Bell's management reacted quickly when food poisoning sickened more than 100 customers at locations across New Jersey, New York, and Pennsylvania. As sales at the Mexican-food restaurant chain plummeted, Taco Bell President Greg Creed directed a response towards anxious customers. "We've taken this health issue very seriously and are extremely concerned for all those who are ill," Creed said in a company statement. "We are not willing to take any risk with the public's safety." *How should businesses approach customers in crisis situations?*

immediate attention. But written messages are important (a) when personal contact is impossible, (b) to establish a record of the incident, (c) to formally confirm follow-up procedures, and (d) to promote good relations.

A bad-news follow-up letter is shown in Figure 10.6. Consultant Catherine Martinez found herself in the embarrassing position of explaining why she had given out the name of her client to a salesperson. The client, Alliance Resources International, had hired her firm, Paragon Consulting Associates, to help find an appropriate service for outsourcing its payroll functions. Without realizing it, Catherine had mentioned to a potential vendor (Payroll Services, Inc.) that her client was considering hiring an outside service to handle its payroll. An overeager salesperson from Payroll Services immediately called on Alliance, thus angering the client. The client had hired the consultant to avoid this very kind of intrusion. Alliance did not want to be hounded by vendors selling their payroll services.

When she learned of the problem, the first thing consultant Catherine Martinez did was call her client to explain and apologize. She was careful to control her voice and rate of speaking. A low-pitched, deliberate pace gives the impression that you are thinking clearly, logically, and reasonably—not emotionally and certainly not irrationally. However, she also followed up with the letter shown in Figure 10.6. The letter not only confirms the telephone conversation but also adds the right touch of formality. It sends the nonverbal message that the writer takes the matter seriously and that it is important enough to warrant a written letter.

A written follow-up letter is necessary when personal contact is impossible, to establish a record, to formally confirm follow-up procedures, and to promote good relations.

Handling Problems With Orders

Not all customer orders can be filled as received. Suppliers may be able to send only part of an order or none at all. Substitutions may be necessary, or the delivery date may be delayed. Suppliers may suspect that all or part of the order is a mistake; the customer may actually want something else. In writing to customers about problem orders, it is generally wise to use the direct pattern if the message has some good-news elements. However, when the message is disappointing, the indirect pattern may be more appropriate.

Let's say you represent Live and Learn Toys, a large West Coast toy manufacturer, and you're scrambling for business in a slow year. A big customer, Child Land, calls in August and asks you to hold a block of your best-selling toy, the Space Station. Like most vendors, you

In handling problems with orders, writers use the indirect pattern unless the message has some good-news elements.

FIGURE 10.6 Bad-News Follow-Up Message

PARAGON CONSULTING ASSOCIATES

4350 Camelback Blvd.
Scottsdale, AZ 85255

Voice: (480) 259-0971
Web: www.paaragonassociates.com

May 7, 2009

Mr. Eric Nasserizad
Director, Administrative Operations
Alliance Resources International
538 Maricopa Plaza, Suite 1210
Phoenix, AZ 85008

Dear Mr. Nasserizad:

You have every right to expect complete confidentiality in your transactions •—— **Opens with agreement and apology**
with an independent consultant. As I explained in yesterday's telephone call,
I am very distressed that you were called by a salesperson from Payroll
Services, Inc. This should not have happened, and I apologize to you again for
inadvertently mentioning your company's name in a conversation with a
potential vendor, Payroll Services, Inc.

All clients of Paragon Consulting are assured that their dealings with our
firm are held in the strictest confidence. Because your company's payroll •—— **Explains what caused the problem and how it was resolved**
needs are so individual and because you have so many contract workers, I
was forced to explain how your employees differed from those of other
companies. Revealing your company name was my error, and I take full
responsibility for the lapse. I can assure you that it will not happen again. I •—— **Takes responsibility and promises to prevent recurrence**
have informed Payroll Services that it had no authorization to call you
directly and its actions have forced me to reconsider using its services for
my future clients.

A number of other payroll services offer outstanding programs. I'm sure we
can find the perfect partner to enable you to outsource your payroll
responsibilities, thus allowing your company to focus its financial and human •—— **Closes with forward look**
resources on its core business. I look forward to our next appointment when
you may choose from a number of excellent payroll outsourcing firms.

Sincerely,

PARAGON CONSULTING ASSOCIATES

Catherine Martinez

Catherine Martinez
Partner

Tips for Resolving Problems and Following Up
- Whenever possible, call or see the individual involved.
- Describe the problem and apologize.
- Explain why the problem occurred.
- Take responsibility, if appropriate.
- Explain what you are doing to resolve the problem.
- Explain how it will not happen again.
- Follow up with a letter that documents the personal contact.
- Look forward to positive future relations.

---

require a deposit on large orders. September rolls around, and you still haven't received any money from Child Land. You must now write a tactful letter asking for the deposit—or else you will release the toy to other buyers. The problem, of course, is delivering the bad news without losing the customer's order and goodwill. Another challenge is making sure the reader understands the bad news. An effective letter might begin with a positive statement that also reveals the facts:

> *You were smart to reserve a block of 500 Space Stations, which we have been holding for you since August. As the holidays approach, the demand for all our learning toys, including the Space Station, is rapidly increasing.*

Next, the letter should explain why the payment is needed and what will happen if it is not received:

> Toy stores from Florida to California are asking us to ship these Space Stations. One reason the Space Station is moving out of our warehouses so quickly is its assortment of gizmos that children love, including a land rover vehicle, a shuttle craft, a hover craft, astronauts, and even a robotic arm. As soon as we receive your deposit of $4,000, we will have this popular item on its way to your stores. Without a deposit by September 20, though, we must release this block to other retailers.

The closing makes it easy to respond and motivates action:

> Use the enclosed envelope to send us your check immediately. You can begin showing this fascinating Live and Learn toy in your stores by November 1.

Denying Claims

Customers occasionally want something they're not entitled to or that you can't grant. They may misunderstand warranties or make unreasonable demands. Because these customers are often unhappy with a product or service, they are emotionally involved. Letters that say *no* to emotionally involved receivers will probably be your most challenging communication task. As publisher Malcolm Forbes observed, "To be agreeable while disagreeing—that's an art."[12]

Fortunately, the reasons-before-refusal plan helps you be empathic and artful in breaking bad news. Obviously, in denial letters you will need to adopt the proper tone. Don't blame customers, even if they are at fault. Avoid *you* statements that sound preachy (*You would have known that cash refunds are impossible if you had read your contract*). Use neutral, objective language to explain why the claim must be refused. Consider offering resale information to rebuild the customer's confidence in your products or organization. In Figure 10.7 the writer denies a customer's claim for the difference between the price the customer paid for speakers and the price he saw advertised locally (which would have resulted in a cash refund of $151). Although the catalog service does match any advertised lower price, the price-matching policy applies *only* to exact models. This claim must be rejected because the advertisement the customer submitted showed a different, older speaker model.

The letter to Matthew Tyson opens with a buffer that agrees with a statement in the customer's letter. It repeats the key idea of product confidence as a transition to the second paragraph. Next comes an explanation of the price-matching policy. The writer does not assume that the customer is trying to pull a fast one. Nor does he suggest that the customer is a dummy who didn't read or understand the price-matching policy. The safest path is a neutral explanation of the policy along with precise distinctions between the customer's speakers and the older ones. The writer also gets a chance to resell the customer's speakers and demonstrate what a quality product they are. By the end of the third paragraph, it is evident to the reader that his claim is unjustified.

In denying claims, the reasons-before-refusal pattern sets an empathic tone and buffers the bad news.

Refusing Credit

When customers apply for credit, they must be notified if that application is rejected. The Fair Credit Reporting Act and Equal Credit Opportunity Act state that consumers who are denied loans must receive a notice of "adverse action" explaining the decision.[13] This notification may come directly from the credit-reporting agency, such as Experian, Equifax, or TransUnion. More often, however, the credit agency reports its findings to the business. The business then makes a decision whether to grant credit based on the information supplied.

If you must write a letter to a customer denying credit, you have four goals in conveying the refusal:

Goals when refusing credit include maintaining customer goodwill and avoiding actionable language.

- Avoiding language that causes hard feelings
- Retaining customers on a cash basis
- Preparing for possible future credit without raising false expectations
- Avoiding disclosures that could cause a lawsuit

FIGURE 10.7 Denying a Claim

430 Market Street, San Francisco CA 94230 • phone (415) 450-2100 • fax (415) 455-3260 • http://www.celestial.com

February 19, 2009

Mr. Matthew R. Tyson
5801 Hollywood Boulevard
Pembroke Pines, FL 33025

Dear Mr. Tyson:

Combines agreement with resale → You're right, Mr. Tyson. We do take pride in selling the finest products at rock-bottom prices. The Boze speakers you purchased last month are premier concert hall speakers. They're the only ones we present in our catalog because they're the best. ← **Buffer**

Explains price-matching policy and how reader's purchase is different from lower-priced model → We have such confidence in our products and prices that we offer the price-matching policy you mention in your letter of February 15. That policy guarantees a refund of the price difference if you see one of your purchases offered at a lower price for 30 days after your purchase. To qualify for that refund, customers are asked to send us an advertisement or verifiable proof of the product price and model. As our catalog states, this price-matching policy applies only to exact models with USA warranties. ← **Reasons**

Without actually saying *no*, shows why reader's claim can't be honored → Our Boze AM-5 II speakers sell for $749. You sent us a local advertisement showing a price of $598 for Boze speakers. This advertisement, however, describes an earlier version, the Boze AM-4 model. The AM-5 speakers you received have a wider dynamic range and smoother frequency response than the AM-4 model. Naturally, the improved model you purchased costs a little more than the older AM-4 model that the local advertisement describes. Your speakers have a new three-chamber bass module that virtually eliminates harmonic distortion. Finally, your speakers are 20 percent more compact than the AM-4 model. ← **Implied refusal**

Builds reader's confidence in wisdom of purchase

Continues resale; looks forward to future business → You bought the finest compact speakers on the market, Mr. Tyson. If you haven't installed them yet, you may be interested in ceiling mounts, shown in the enclosed catalog on page 48. For the most up-to-date prices and product information, please see our online catalog at our prize-winning Web site. We value your business and invite your continued comparison shopping. ← **Positive closing**

Sincerely yours,

Rick K. Thalman
Customer Service

mmt
Enclosure

Because credit applicants are likely to continue to do business with an organization even if they are denied credit, you will want to do everything possible to encourage that patronage. Thus, keep the refusal respectful, sensitive, and upbeat. A letter to a customer denying her credit application might begin as follows:

We genuinely appreciate your application of January 12 for a Fashion Express credit account.

To avoid possible litigation, many companies offer no explanation of the reasons for a credit refusal. Instead, they provide the name of the credit-reporting agency and suggest that inquiries be directed to it. In the following example notice the use of passive voice (*credit cannot be extended*) and a long sentence to de-emphasize the bad news:

After we received a report of your current credit record from Experian, it is apparent that credit cannot be extended at this time. To learn more about your record, you may call an Experian credit counselor at (212) 356-0922.

Checklist

Delivering Bad News to Customers

Prewrite

✓ Analyze the situation and anticipate how the reader will react.

✓ Think through the reasons creating the bad news.

✓ Consider alternatives.

Begin Indirectly

✓ Express appreciation, but don't thank the reader for requesting something you are about to refuse.

✓ Show agreement on some point, review facts, or show understanding.

✓ Consider apologizing if your organization was responsible for disappointing the customer.

Provide Reasons

✓ Except in credit denials, justify the bad news with objective reasons.

✓ Explain what went wrong, what you are doing to resolve the problem, and how you will prevent it from happening again.

✓ Avoid blaming the customer or hiding behind company policy.

✓ Look for reader benefits.

Present the Bad News

✓ Decide whether to soften the bad news by using (a) a subordinate clause, (b) the passive voice, (c) a long sentence, or (d) a long paragraph.

✓ Consider implying the bad news rather than stating it overtly.

✓ Offset disappointment by offering gifts, a reduced price, benefits, tokens of appreciation, or something appropriate.

✓ Suggest an alternative if one is possible.

Close Pleasantly

✓ Look forward to future business.

✓ Suggest action on an alternative.

✓ Offer best wishes, refer to gifts, or use resale sensitively.

✓ Don't mention the bad news.

The cordial closing looks forward to the possibility of a future reapplication:

Thanks, Ms. Love, for the confidence you've shown in Fashion Express. We invite you to continue shopping at our stores, and we look forward to your reapplication in the future.

Some businesses do provide reasons explaining credit denials (*Credit cannot be granted because your firm's current and long-term credit obligations are nearly twice as great as your firm's total assets*). They may also provide alternatives, such as deferred billing or cash discounts. When the letter denies a credit application that accompanies an order, the message may contain resale information. The writer tries to convert the order from credit to cash. For example, if a big order cannot be filled on a credit basis, perhaps part of the order could be filled on a cash basis.

Whatever form the bad-news letter takes, it is a good idea to have the message reviewed by legal counsel because of the litigation land mines awaiting unwary communicators in this area. The above checklist provides tips on how to craft effective bad-news letters to customers.

Delivering Bad News Within Organizations

A tactful tone and a reasons-first approach help preserve friendly relations with customers. These same techniques are useful when delivering bad news within organizations. Interpersonal bad news might involve telling the boss that something went wrong or confronting an employee about poor performance. Organizational bad news might involve declining profits, lost contracts, harmful lawsuits, public relations controversies, and changes in policy. Whether you use a direct or an indirect pattern in delivering that news depends primarily on the anticipated reaction of the audience. Generally, bad news is better received when reasons are given first. Within organizations, you may find yourself giving bad news in person or in writing.

LEARNING OBJECTIVE 5
Explain effective techniques for delivering bad news within organizations.

Giving Bad News Personally

Whether you are an employee or a supervisor, you may have the unhappy responsibility of delivering bad news. First, decide whether the negative information is newsworthy. For example, trivial, noncriminal mistakes or one-time bad behaviors are best left alone. However,

Communicating at Work Part 2

Southwest Airlines

For Fred Taylor, Southwest's senior manager of proactive customer communications, delivering bad news and apologizing to customers is all in a day's work. He is the point person when it comes to informing employees of problem situations and providing them with an appropriate response. When Southwest falls short of satisfying its customers, he prepares personal apology letters to passengers—about 20,000 in an average year, covering more than 180 flight disruptions. The letters have his direct phone number, and many include a free flight voucher. As he explained to customers on a recent flight from Phoenix to Albuquerque, the strange odor in the plane was from a defective valve but not dangerous. "Erring on the side of caution, our captain decided to return to Phoenix rather than second-guess the smell that was in the cabin," he wrote. Southwest's apologies even cover circumstances beyond Southwest's control, such as an ice storm that delayed a St. Louis flight. "It's not something we had to do," he says. "It's just something we feel our customers deserve."[14]

Critical Thinking
- What are the advantages to Southwest of its proactive approach to passenger problems?
- How might Fred Taylor use the four-part plan suggested in this chapter to compose his apology letters to passengers?
- Contrast the strategies Taylor would develop to deliver bad news to Southwest's employees and to its passengers.

© AP IMAGES

fraudulent travel claims, consistent hostile behavior, or failing projects must be reported.[15] For example, you might have to tell the boss that the team's computer crashed with all its important files. As a team leader or supervisor, you might be required to confront an underperforming employee. If you know that the news will upset the receiver, the reasons-first strategy is most effective. When the bad news involves one person or a small group nearby, you should generally deliver that news in person. Here are pointers on how to do so tactfully, professionally, and safely:[16]

When delivering bad news within organizations, strive to do so tactfully, professionally, and safely.

- **Gather all the information.** Cool down and have all the facts before marching in on the boss or confronting someone. Remember that every story has two sides.

- **Prepare and rehearse.** Outline what you plan to say so that you are confident, coherent, and dispassionate.

- **Explain: past, present, future.** If you are telling the boss about a problem such as the computer crash, explain what caused the crash, the current situation, and how and when you plan to fix it.

- **Consider taking a partner.** If you fear a "shoot the messenger" reaction, especially from your boss, bring a colleague with you. Each person should have a consistent and credible part in the presentation. If possible, take advantage of your organization's internal resources. To lend credibility to your view, call on auditors, inspectors, or human resources experts.

- **Think about timing.** Don't deliver bad news when someone is already stressed or grumpy. Experts also advise against giving bad news on Friday afternoon when people have the weekend to dwell on it.

- **Be patient with the reaction.** Give the receiver time to vent, think, recover, and act wisely.

Delivering Workplace Bad News

Organizations can sustain employee morale by communicating bad news openly and honestly.

Many of the same techniques used to deliver bad news personally are useful when organizations face a crisis or must deliver bad news in the workplace. Smart organizations involved in a crisis prefer to communicate the news openly to employees, customers, and stockholders. A crisis might involve serious performance problems, a major relocation, massive layoffs, a management shake-up, or public controversy. Instead of letting rumors distort the truth, they explain the organization's side of the story honestly and early. Morale can be destroyed when employees learn of major events affecting their jobs through the grapevine or from news accounts—rather than from management.

When bad news must be delivered to employees, management may want to deliver the news personally. With large groups, however, this is generally impossible. Instead, organizations deliver bad news through hard-copy memos. Organizations are experimenting with other delivery channels such as e-mail, videos, webcasts, and voice mail. Still, hard-copy memos seem to function most effectively because they are more formal and make a permanent record.

The draft of the memo shown in Figure 10.8 announces a substantial increase in the cost of employee health care benefits. However, the memo suffers from many problems. It reveals the jolting news bluntly in the first sentence. Worse, it offers little or no explanation for the steep increase in costs. It also sounds insincere (*We did everything possible . . .*) and arbitrary. In a final miscue, the writer fails to give credit to the company for absorbing previous health cost increases.

Saying *No* to Job Applicants

Being refused a job is one of life's major rejections. Tactless letters intensify the blow (*Unfortunately, you were not among the candidates selected for . . .*).

You can reduce the receiver's disappointment somewhat by using the indirect pattern—with one important variation. In the reasons section it is wise to be vague in explaining why the candidate was not selected. First, giving concrete reasons may be painful to the receiver (*Your grade point average of 2.7 was low compared with the GPAs of other candidates*). Second, and more important, providing extra information may prove fatal in a lawsuit. Hiring and firing decisions generate considerable litigation today. To avoid charges of discrimination or wrongful actions, legal advisors warn organizations to keep employment rejection letters general, simple, and short.

The job refusal letter shown in Figure 10.9 on page 297 is tactful but intentionally vague. It implies that the applicant's qualifications don't match those needed for the position, but the letter doesn't reveal anything specific. The writer could have included this alternate closing: *We wish you every success in finding a position that exactly fits your qualifications.*

The following checklist gives tips on how to communicate bad news within organizations.

Letters that deny applications for employment should be courteous and tactful but free of specifics that could trigger lawsuits.

Checklist

Delivering Bad News Within Organizations

Prewrite
- ✓ Analyze the bad news and anticipate its effect on employees.
- ✓ Decide whether to deliver the bad news in person or in writing.

Start With a Buffer
- ✓ Open with a small bit of good news, praise, appreciation, agreement, understanding, or a discussion of facts leading to the reasons section.
- ✓ If appropriate, consider an apology that conveys empathy.

Discuss Reasons
- ✓ Except in job refusal letters, explain what caused the decision necessitating the bad news.
- ✓ Use objective, nonjudgmental, and nondiscriminatory language.
- ✓ Show that fairness governed the decision.

Reveal the Bad News
- ✓ Make the bad news clear but don't accentuate it.
- ✓ Consider cushioning the bad news by using (a) a subordinate clause, (b) the passive voice, (c) a long sentence, or (d) a long paragraph.
- ✓ Avoid negative language.

Suggest Alternatives
- ✓ If alternatives or compromises are possible, present them.
- ✓ Consider alternate work assignments, extended deadlines, substitute tasks, job relocations, or whatever suits the situation.

Close Harmoniously
- ✓ End on a positive, friendly note. For job refusals, extend good wishes.
- ✓ Maintain a bright, personal tone. Avoid referring to the refusal.

FIGURE 10.8 Announcing Bad News to Employees

1 Prewriting

Analyze: The purpose of this memo is to tell employees that they must share with the company the increasing costs of health care.

Anticipate: The audience will be employees who are unaware of health care costs and, most likely, reluctant to pay more.

Adapt: Because the readers will probably be unhappy and resentful, use the indirect pattern.

2 Writing

Research: Collect facts and statistics that document health care costs.

Organize: Begin with a buffer describing the company's commitment to health benefits. Provide an explanation of health care costs. Announce the bad news. In the closing, focus on the company's major share of the cost.

Compose: Draft the first version with the expectation to revise.

3 Revising

Revise: Remove negativity (*unfortunately, we can't, we were forced, inadvisable, we don't think*). Explain the increase with specifics.

Proofread: Use a semicolon before *however*. Use quotes around *defensive* to show its special sense. Spell out *percent* after *300*.

Evaluate: Is there any other way to help readers accept this bad news?

DRAFT

Beginning January 1 your monthly payment for health care benefits will be increased to $119 (up from $52 last year).

Every year health care costs go up. Although we considered dropping other benefits, Midland decided that the best plan was to keep the present comprehensive package. Unfortunately, we can't do that unless we pass along some of the extra cost to you. Last year the company was forced to absorb the total increase in health care premiums. However, such a plan this year is inadvisable.

We did everything possible to avoid the sharp increase in costs to you this year. A rate schedule describing the increases in payments for your family and dependents is enclosed.

- Hits readers with bad news without any preparation
- Offers no explanation
- Fails to take credit for absorbing previous increases

REVISION

DATE: October 2, 2009

TO: Fellow Employees

FROM: Lawrence R. Romero, President   *LRR*

SUBJECT: Maintaining Quality Health Care

Begins with positive buffer

Health care programs have always been an important part of our commitment to employees at Northern, Inc. We're proud that our total benefits package continues to rank among the best in the country.

Offers reasons costs are rising

Such a comprehensive package does not come cheaply. In the last decade health care costs alone have risen over 300 percent. We're told that several factors fuel the cost spiral: inflation, technology improvements, increased cost of outpatient services, and "defensive" medicine practiced by doctors to prevent lawsuits.

Reveals bad news clearly but embeds it in paragraph

Just two years ago our monthly health care cost for each employee was $515. It rose to $569 last year. We were able to absorb that jump without increasing your contribution. But this year's hike to $639 forces us to ask you to share the increase. To maintain your current health care benefits, you will be paying $119 a month. The enclosed rate schedule describes the costs for families and dependents.

Ends positively by stressing the company's major share of the costs

Northern continues to pay the major portion of your health care program ($520 each month). We think it's a wise investment.

Enclosure

FIGURE 10.9 Saying *No* to Job Candidates

Doesn't indicate good or bad news

To prevent possible lawsuits, gives no explanation

Shows appreciation

Places bad news in dependent clause

Ends with best wishes

Xeradyne Telecom

510 East 74th Street   New York, NY 10021
212.445.9800   www.xeradynetelecom.com

June 7, 2009

Ms. Tracee Porter
245 Mullica Hill Road
Glassboro, NJ 08026

Dear Ms. Porter:

Thanks for letting us review your résumé submitted for our advertised management trainee opening.

We received a number of impressive résumés for this opening. Although another candidate was selected, your interest in our organization is appreciated. So that you may continue your search for a position at another organization, I am writing to you immediately.

With your credentials I am certain you will find a suitable position because you have a great deal to offer. Please accept my best wishes for the future.

Sincerely,

XERADYNE TELECOM

Leonora M. Kirby

Leonora M. Kirby
Director, Human Resources

Presenting Bad News in Other Cultures

To minimize disappointment, Americans generally prefer to present negative messages indirectly. Other cultures may treat bad news differently.

In Germany, for example, business communicators occasionally use buffers but tend to present bad news directly. British writers also tend to be straightforward with bad news, seeing no reason to soften its announcement. In Latin countries the question is not how to organize negative messages but whether to present them at all. It is considered disrespectful and impolite to report bad news to superiors. Thus, reluctant employees may fail to report accurately any negative messages to their bosses.

In Asian cultures, harmony and peace are sought in all relationships. Disrupting the harmony with bad news is avoided. To prevent discord, Japanese communicators use a number of techniques to indicate *no*—without being forced to say it. In conversation they may

LEARNING OBJECTIVE 6
Compare strategies for revealing bad news in other cultures.

Communicating bad news in other cultures may require different strategies.

respond with silence or with a counter question, such as, *Why do you ask?* They may change the subject or tell a white lie to save face for themselves and for the questioner. Sometimes the answer sounds like a qualified *yes: I will do my best, but if I cannot, I hope you will understand.* If the response is *Yes, but . . . ,* or *Yes* followed by an apology, beware. All of these responses should be recognized as *no.*

In China, Westerners often have difficulty understanding the "hints" given by communicators.

I agree might mean *I agree with 15 percent of what you say.*

We might be able to could mean *Not a chance.*

We will consider could mean *WE will, but the real decision maker will not.*

That is a little too much might equate to *That is outrageous.*[17]

Conveying bad news in some cultures is so subtle that literal-minded Americans may misunderstand.

In Thailand the negativism represented by a refusal is completely alien; the word *no* does not exist. In many cultures negative news is offered with such subtlety or in such a positive light that it may be overlooked or misunderstood by literal-minded Americans.

In many high-context cultures, saving face is important. A refusal is a potential loss of face for both parties. To save face, a person who must refuse an invitation to dine out with a business associate might say, *You must be very tired and want to have a quiet evening.*[18] This subtle refusal avoids putting it in words. To understand the meaning of what's really being communicated, we must look beyond an individual's actual words and consider the communication style, the culture, and especially the context.

A recent study showed that business letters conveying bad news in Latin America were quite short and did not employ buffers. This may be a result of the desire to avoid negative news completely, feeling it is discourteous to bring bad news.[19]

Conveying bad news in any culture is tricky and requires sensitivity to and awareness of cultural practices.

Communicating at Work Your Turn

Applying Your Skills at Southwest Airlines

Southwest Airlines, whose motto is "Share the Spirit," is actively involved in the communities it serves. Its high level of participation has earned the company a place on the 100 Best Corporate Citizens list. Employees volunteer in dozens of local events. On a national level, it partners with a wide range of charities, including the Hispanic Association of Colleges and Universities' national educational travel award program, the Ronald McDonald House, Junior Achievement, Read Across America, and Parkland Burn Camp. Through its award-winning Adopt-a-Pilot program, a fifth-grade classroom is paired with a pilot mentor for four weeks. Students correspond with their pilots and track their travels, engaging in aviation-themed science, math, research, writing, history, geography, and career-planning lessons and activities.

With such a high public profile, the airline receives many requests for donations, from monetary contributions and event sponsorships to numerous appeals for free flight tickets from charities holding fund-raising events. Its detailed guidelines for groups seeking donations, published on its Web site, state, *A standard donation is two round-trip passes good for transportation between any two cities Southwest Airlines serves within the continental U.S.* Charities must mail their requests for free tickets to the Charitable

Giving Department at Southwest's Dallas headquarters, which then determines the recipients.[20]

Your Task
Assume that you are an intern in Southwest Airlines, Charitable Giving Department. Your manager hands you a letter from Elizabeth Dunbar, Director, Animal Rescue League of Iowa, 5452 Northeast 22nd Street, Des Moines, IA 50313. This organization never turns away an animal in need, but it has run out of space and desperately needs a new shelter. To build a $6.5 million state-of-the-art facility, it is sponsoring a local raffle. One prize would be ten round-trip tickets anywhere in the United States, and it asks Southwest to provide those tickets. The problem is that the request arrived 30 days before the event and is nonstandard. Deny the request but offer an alternative. You like animals, too!

© AP IMAGES

Summary of Learning Objectives

1 **Describe the goals and strategies of business communicators in delivering bad news, including knowing when to use the direct and indirect patterns, applying the writing process, and avoiding legal problems.** All businesses will occasionally deal with problems. Good communicators have several primary goals in delivering bad news: making the reader understand and accept the bad news and promoting and maintaining a good image of themselves and their organizations. Secondary goals include reducing bad feelings, conveying fairness, eliminating future correspondence, and avoiding legal liability. The indirect pattern involves delaying the bad news until reasons have been presented. The direct pattern reveals the main idea immediately. The direct pattern is preferable when the receiver may overlook the bad news, when the organization policy suggests directness, and for other reasons. Careful communicators will avoid careless and abusive language, which is actionable when it is false, damages a person's reputation, and is "published" (spoken within the presence of others or written). Messages written on company stationery represent that company and can be legally binding.

2 **Explain effective techniques for delivering bad news sensitively.** Begin with a buffer, such as a compliment, appreciation, a point of agreement, objective information, understanding, or some part of the message that represents good news. Then explain the reasons that necessitate the bad news, trying to cite benefits to the reader or others. Choose positive words, and clarify company policy if necessary. Announce the bad news strategically, mentioning a compromise or alternative if possible. Close pleasantly with a forward-looking goodwill statement.

3 **Identify typical requests and describe an effective strategy for refusing such requests.** Typical requests ask for favors, money, information, action, and other items. When the answer will be disappointing, use the reasons-before-refusal pattern. Open with a buffer; provide reasons; announce the refusal sensitively; suggest possible alternatives; and end with a positive, forward-looking comment.

4 **Explain effective techniques for delivering bad news to customers.** When a company disappoints its customers, most organizations (a) call the individual involved, (b) describe the problem and apologize (when the company is to blame), (c) explain why the problem occurred and what is being done to prevent its recurrence, and (d) follow up with a letter that documents the phone call and promotes goodwill. Some organizations also offer gifts or benefits to offset customers' disappointment and to reestablish the business relationship. In denying claims or refusing credit, begin indirectly, provide reasons for the refusal, and close pleasantly, looking forward to future business. When appropriate, resell a product or service.

5 **Explain effective techniques for delivering bad news within organizations.** When delivering bad news personally to a superior, gather all the information, prepare and rehearse, explain what happened and how the problem will be repaired, consider taking a colleague with you, think about timing, and be patient with the reaction. In delivering workplace bad news, use the indirect pattern but be sure to provide clear, convincing reasons that explain the decision. In refusing job applicants, however, keep letters short, general, and tactful.

6 **Compare strategies for revealing bad news in other cultures.** American communicators often prefer to break bad news slowly and indirectly. In other low-context cultures, such as Germany and Britain, however, bad news is revealed directly. In most high-context cultures, such as China and Japan, however, straightforwardness is avoided. In Latin cultures bad news may be totally suppressed. In Asian cultures negativism is avoided and hints may suggest bad news. Subtle meanings must be interpreted carefully.

Chapter Review

1. What are the writer's primary and secondary goals in communicating bad news? (Obj. 1)

2. Describe the four parts of the indirect message pattern. (Obj. 1)

3. Name five situations in which the direct pattern should be used for bad news. (Obj. 1)

4. What is the difference between libel and slander? (Obj. 1)

5. What is a buffer? Name five or more techniques to buffer the opening of a bad-news message. (Obj. 2)

6. What is an apology? When should an apology be offered to customers? (Obj. 2)

7. Name four or more techniques that cushion the delivery of bad news. (Obj. 2)

8. What are some typical requests that big and small businesses must refuse? (Obj. 3)

9. How can form letters be personalized? (Obj. 3)

10. Identify a process used by a majority of business professionals in resolving problems with disappointed customers. (Obj. 4)

11. If you must deny the claim of a customer who is clearly at fault, should you respond by putting the blame squarely on the customer? (Obj. 4)

12. List four goals a writer seeks to achieve in writing messages that deny credit to prospective customers. (Obj. 4)

13. What actions are tactful, professional, and safe when a subordinate must personally deliver upsetting news to a superior? (Obj. 5)

14. What are some channels that large organizations may use when delivering bad news to employees? (Obj. 5)

15. In Latin countries why may employees sometimes fail to report accurately any negative messages to management? (Obj. 6)

Critical Thinking

1. Does bad news travel faster and farther than good news? Why? What implications would this have for companies responding to unhappy customers? (Objs. 1–5)

2. Some people feel that all employee news, good or bad, should be announced directly. Do you agree or disagree? Why? (Objs. 1–5)

3. Consider times when you have been aware that others have used the indirect pattern in writing or speaking to you. How did you react? (Objs. 1–5)

4. When Boeing Aircraft reported that a laptop containing the names, salary information, and social security numbers of 382,000 employees had been stolen from an employee's car, CEO Jim McNerney wrote this e-mail to employees: *I've received many e-mails over the past 24 hours from employees expressing disappointment, frustration, and downright anger about yesterday's announcement of personal information belonging to thousands of employees and retirees being on a stolen computer. I'm just as disappointed as you are about it. I know that many of us feel that this data loss amounts to a betrayal of the trust we place in the company to safeguard our personal information. I certainly do.* Critics have faulted this apology. With what did they find fault? Do you agree?

5. **Ethical Issue:** You work for a large corporation with headquarters in a small town. Recently you received shoddy repair work and a huge bill from a local garage. Your car's transmission has the same problems that it did before you took it in for repair. You know that a complaint letter written on your corporation's stationery would be much more authoritative than one written on plain stationery. Should you use corporation stationery? (Obj. 1)

Activities

10.1 Writing Improvement Exercise: Organizational Patterns (Objs. 1–5)

Your Task. Identify which organizational pattern you would use for the following messages: direct or indirect.

a. A letter from a theme park refusing the request of a visitor who wants free tickets. The visitor was unhappy that he had to wait in line a very long time to ride a new thrill roller coaster.

b. A letter refusing a request by a charitable organization to use your office equipment on the weekend.

c. A memo from the manager denying an employee's request for special parking privileges. The employee works closely with the manager on many projects.

d. An announcement to employees that a financial specialist has canceled a scheduled lunchtime talk and cannot reschedule.

e. A letter to its customers from a bank revealing that one of its offices mislaid a CD containing details including customer addresses, dates of birth, account numbers, and the value of investments.

f. A form letter from an insurance company announcing new policy requirements that many policyholders may resent. If policyholders do not indicate the plan they prefer, they may lose their insurance coverage.

g. The last in a series of letters from a collection agency demanding payment of a long-overdue account. The next step will be hiring an attorney.

h. A letter from a computer company refusing to authorize repair of a customer's computer on which the warranty expired six months ago.

i. A memo from an executive refusing a manager's proposal to economize by purchasing reconditioned computers. The executive and the manager both appreciate efficient, straightforward messages.

j. A letter informing a company that the majority of the company's equipment order will not be available for six weeks.

10.2 Writing Improvement Exercise: Employing Passive-Voice Verbs (Obj. 2)

Your Task. Revise the following sentences to present the bad news with passive-voice verbs.

a. Company policy prevents us from offering health and dental benefits until employees have been on the job for 12 months.

b. We will no longer be accepting credit cards for purchases under $5.

c. Because management now requires more stringent security, we are postponing indefinitely requests for company tours.

d. We do not examine patients until we have verified their insurance coverage.

e. Your car rental insurance coverage does not cover large SUVs.

10.3 Writing Improvement Exercise: Subordinating Bad News (Obj. 2)

Your Task. Revise the following sentences to position the bad news in a subordinate clause. (**Hint:** Consider beginning the clause with *Although*.) Use passive-voice verbs for the bad news.

a. We are sorry to report that we are unable to ship your complete order at this point in time. However, we are able to send two corner workstations now; you should receive them within five days.

b. Unfortunately, we no longer print a complete catalog. However, we now offer all of our catalog choices at our Web site, which is always current.

c. We appreciate your interest in our organization, but we are unable to extend an employment offer to you at this time.

d. State law does not allow smoking within 5 feet of a state building. But the college has set aside 16 outdoor smoking areas.

10.4 Writing Improvement Exercise: Implying Bad News (Obj. 2)

Your Task. Revise the following statements to *imply* the bad news. If possible, use passive-voice verbs and subordinate clauses to further de-emphasize the bad news.

a. We cannot ship our fresh fruit baskets c.o.d. Your order was not accompanied by payment, so we are not shipping it. We have it ready, though, and will rush it to its destination as soon as you call us with your credit card number.

b. Unfortunately, we find it impossible to contribute to the fund-raising campaign this year. At present all the funds of my organization are needed to lease new equipment and offices for our new branch in Richmond. We hope to be able to support this endeavor in the future.

c. Because of the holiday period, all our billboard space was used this month. Therefore, we are sorry to say that we could not give your charitable group free display space. However, next month, after the holidays, we hope to display your message as we promised.

10.5 Writing Improvement Exercise: Evaluating Bad-News Statements (Obj. 2)

Your Task. Discuss the strengths or weaknesses of the following bad-news statements.

a. Although we had hoped to do so earlier, we cannot repaint your offices until January 1.

b. Frankly, we like your résumé, but we were hoping to hire someone a little younger who might be able to stay with us longer.

c. I'm thoroughly disgusted with this entire case, and I will never do business with shyster lawyers like you again.

d. We can assure you that on any return visit to our hotels, you will not be treated so poorly.

e. We must deny your credit application because your record shows a history of late payments, nonpayment, and irregular employment.

f. *In a confidential company memo:* I cannot recommend that we promote this young lady into any position where she will meet the public. Her colorful facial decoration, as part of her religion, may offend our customers.

10.6 Document for Analysis: Request Refusal (Objs. 1–3)

Your Task. Analyze the following letter. List its weaknesses. If your instructor directs, revise it using the suggestions you learned in this chapter.

Current date

Ms. Sheila Trumbo, Owner
Royal Oak Realty, Inc.
743 South Washington
Royal Oak, MI 48067

Dear Ms. Trumbo:

We regret to inform you that we cannot allow you to convert the payments you have been making on your Canon X1000 color copier toward its purchase, much as we would love to do so. We understand that you have been making regular payments for the past 16 months.

Our established company policy prohibits such conversion of leasing monies. Perhaps you have noticed that we offer extremely low leasing and purchase prices. Obviously, these low prices would never be possible if we agreed to many proposals such as yours. Because we are striving to stay in business, we cannot agree to your request asking us to convert all 14 months of rental payments toward the purchase of our popular new equipment.

It is our understanding, Ms. Trumbo, that you have had the Canon X1000 color copier for 16 months, and you claim that it has been reliable and versatile. We would like to tell you about another Canon model—one that is perhaps closer to your limited budget.

Sincerely,

10.7 Document for Analysis: Favor Refusal (Objs. 1–3)

Your Task. Analyze the following poorly written letter, and list its weaknesses. If your instructor directs, revise it using the suggestions you learned in this chapter.

Current date

Mr. Blake Dahlke
Senior Correspondent
Marketing and Management Today
309 Fifth Avenue
New York, NY 10011

Dear Mr. Dahlke:

Your message has been referred to me for response. I understand you are inviting my company to participate in your research for a proposed article about "sales stars who are ascending." Unfortunately, your request involves salaries of young salespeople. As must be apparent to any clear-thinking executive, we cannot accept your invitation to release salary information. Exposing the salaries of our salespeople—regardless of how outstanding they are—would violate their privacy, jeopardize their careers, and reveal insider information. Doing so might even violate the law.

We do, however, have many outstanding young salespeople who command top salaries, and we are proud of their success. Unfortunately, during salary negotiations several years ago we reached an agreement. Both sales staff members and management agreed to keep the terms of individual contracts confidential. We could not possibly reveal specific salaries and commission rates.

Since your article is to focus on star performers, you might be interested in our ranked list of top salespeople for the past five years. As I glance over the list, I see that three of our current top salespeople are under the age of 35. We have a fact sheet about all of our top salespeople, and I will include that sheet.

Perhaps you can include some of this information in your article because we would like to see our company represented.

Cordially,

10.8 Document for Analysis: Refusing a Job Applicant (Objs. 1, 2, and 5)

Your Task. Analyze the following letter. List its weaknesses. If your instructor directs, revise it.

Current date

Mr. Mark Richardson
3290 Lake Shore Drive
Canandaigua, NY 14424

Dear Mr. Richardson:

Mr. Rhodes and I wish to thank you for the pleasure of allowing us to interview you last Thursday. We were delighted to learn about your superb academic record, and we also appreciated your attentiveness in listening to our description of the operations of Zumeriz Technologies.

However, we had many well-qualified applicants who were interested in the advertised position of human resources assistant. As you may have guessed, we were particularly eager to find a minority individual who could help us fill out our Affirmative Action goals. Although you did not fit one of our goal areas, we enjoyed talking with you. We hired a female graduate from the State University of New York who had most of the qualities we sought.

Although we realize that the job market is difficult at this time, you have our heartfelt wishes for good luck in finding precisely what you are looking for.

Sincerely,

10.9 Negative News in Other Cultures (Obj. 6)

Your Task. Interview fellow students or work colleagues who are from other cultures. How is negative news handled in their cultures? How would typical individuals refuse a request for a favor, for example? How would a business refuse credit to customers? How would an individual be turned down for a job? Is directness practiced? Report your findings to the class.

10.10 Request Refusal: Jamba Asks for Juicy Favor (Objs. 1–3)

In an aggressive expansion effort, Jamba Juice became a good customer of your software company. You have enjoyed the business it brought, and you are also quite fond of its products—especially Banana Berry and Mega Mango smoothies. Jamba Inc. is in the midst of expanding its menu with the goal of becoming the Starbucks of the smoothie. "Just as Starbucks defined the category of coffee, Jamba has the opportunity to define the category of the healthy snack," said analyst Brian Moore. One goal of Jamba is to boost the frequency of customer visits by offering some products that are more filling. Then it could attract hungry customers as well as thirsty ones. It was experimenting with adding grains such as oatmeal or nuts such as almonds so that a smoothie packs more substance and could substitute for a meal.

You receive a letter from Joe Wong, your business friend and contact at Jamba Juice. He asks you to do him and Jamba Juice a favor. He wants to set up a juice tasting bar in your company cafeteria to test his new experimental drinks. All the drinks would be free, of course, but employees would have to fill out forms to evaluate each recipe. The details could be worked out later.

Your Task. You definitely support healthy snacks, but you think this idea is terrible. First of all, your company doesn't even have a cafeteria. It has a small lunch room, and employees bring their own food. Secondly, you would be embarrassed to ask your boss to do this favor for Jamba Juice, despite the business it has brought your company. Write a letter that retains good customer relations with Jamba Juice but refuses this request. What reasons can you give, and what alternatives are available? Address your message to Joe Wong, Vice President, Product Development, Jamba Inc., 450 Golden Gate Avenue, San Francisco, 94102.[21]

10.11 Request Refusal: Seven Sins Speaker Says *No* (Objs. 1–3).

As Nelson J. Daugherty, operations manager at Roxbury Hotels and Restaurants, you have been asked to make a presentation to the Washington, DC, chapter of the National Restaurant Alliance (see **Chapter 9, Activity 9.1**). Although you have given this presentation before, you can't be in Washington on June 10. The Roxbury, which you manage in Philadelphia, is hosting a corporate team-building event on that date. Your restaurant will entertain a large group of representatives in town for an AT&T convention, and you will be supervising cooking demonstrations and organizing operations during the event. Maybe you can deliver your presentation some other time.

Your Task. Refuse the invitation but suggest an alternative. Send your letter to Ms. Charlesetta Watson, Program Chair, DC Chapter, National Restaurant Alliance, 980 Ninth Street NW, Washington, DC 20001.

10.12 Request Refusal: Dummies Author Declines (Objs. 1–3)

Joyce Lain Kennedy received a request (see **Chapter 9, Activity 9.6**) asking her to speak at the South California University Management

Interactive Learning @ www.meguffey.com

Society banquet May 5. She is deluged with work as she strives to complete a new e-marketing book with a June 1 deadline. Although she can't spare the time to make this presentation, she doesn't want to dampen the enthusiasm and goodwill that she enjoys from these potentially influential businesspeople. She wonders if this group might consider a substitute speaker, Anderson B. Andrews. He has been a coauthor on some of her books and helps her with research. He's particularly knowledgeable about technology trends.

Your Task. As her assistant, write a refusal letter for the signature of Joyce Lain Kennedy. Address it to Professor Rachel Pierce, Department of Management, South California University, P.O. Box 286, San Diego, CA 92044. Add appropriate information.

10.13 Request Refusal: Thumbs Down on PDAs for Charleston Agents (Objs. 1–3)

George R. Hollings, president of Hollings Carolina Realty, is not keen on using technology to sell real estate. As you learned in **Chapter 9, Activity 9.15**, he was asked to purchase PDAs plus software plus monthly updates for all 18 staff members of his firm. He did the math, and it figures out to be something like $6,000 for the initial investment plus $4,000 per year for updates. That's a lot of money for technology that he's not convinced is needed. He appreciated the tactful, logical, and persuasive memo that he received from a talented agent requesting this PDA support. He wants to respond in writing because he can control exactly what he says and a written response is more forceful. His memo will also make a permanent record of this decision, in case agents make similar requests in the future. The more he ponders the request, the more Mr. Hollings thinks that this kind of investment in software and hardware should be made by agents themselves—not by the agency.

Your Task. Put yourself in the place of Mr. Hollings and write a refusal that retains the goodwill of the agent yet makes it clear that this request cannot be granted.

10.14 Request Refusal: Carnival Rejects Under-21 Crowd (Objs. 1–3)

The world's largest cruise line finds itself in a difficult position. Carnival climbed to the number one spot by promoting fun at sea and pitching its appeal to younger customers who were drawn to on-board discos, swim-up bars, and hassle-free partying. But apparently the partying of high school and college students went too far. Roving bands of teens had virtually taken over some cruises in recent years. Travel agents complained of "drunken, loud behavior," as reported by Mike Driscall, editor of *Cruise Week*.

To crack down, Carnival raised the drinking age from 18 to 21 and required more chaperoning of school groups. But young individual travelers were still unruly and disruptive. Thus, Carnival instituted a new policy, effective immediately. No one under 21 may travel unless accompanied by an adult over 25. Says Vicki Freed, Carnival's vice president for marketing, "We will turn them back at the docks, and they will not get refunds." As Eric Rivera, a Carnival marketing manager, you must respond to the inquiry of Sheryl Kiklas of All-World Travel, a New York travel agency that features special spring- and summer-break packages for college and high school students.

All-World Travel has been one of Carnival's best customers. However, Carnival no longer wants to encourage unaccompanied young people. You must refuse the request of Ms. Kiklas to help set up student tour packages. Carnival discourages even chaperoned tours. Its target market is now families. You must write to All-World Travel and break the bad news. Try to promote fun-filled, carefree

© Don Despain / www.rekindlephoto.com / Alamy

cruises destined for sunny, exotic ports of call that remove guests from the stresses of everyday life. By the way, Carnival attracts more passengers than any other cruise line—over a million people a year from all over the world. Over 98 percent of Carnival's guests say that they were well satisfied.

Your Task. Write your letter to Sheryl Kiklas, All-World Travel Agency, 440 East Broadway, New York, NY 10014. Send her a schedule for spring and summer Caribbean cruises. Tell her you will call during the week of January 5 to help her plan special family tour packages.[22]

10.15 Request Refusal: Excessive Noise Prompts Action (Obj. 4)

Web

As the owner of Peachtree Business Plaza, you must respond to the request of Michael Vazquez, one of the tenants in your three-story office building. Mr. Vazquez, a CPA, demands that you immediately evict a neighboring tenant who plays loud music throughout the day, interfering with Mr. Vazquez' conversations with clients and with his concentration. The noisy tenant, Anthony Chomko, seems to operate an entertainment booking agency and spends long hours in his office. You know you can't evict Mr. Chomko because, as a legal commercial tenant, he is entitled to conduct his business. However, you might consider adding soundproofing, an expense that you would prefer to share with Mr. Chomko and Mr. Vazquez. You might also discuss limiting the time of day that Mr. Chomko could make noise.

Your Task. Before responding to Mr. Vazquez, you decide to find out more about commercial tenancy. Use the Web to search the keywords *commercial eviction*. Then develop a course of action. In writing to Mr. Vazquez, deny his request but retain his goodwill. Tell him how you plan to resolve the problem. Write to Michael Vazquez, CPA, Suite 230, Peachtree Business Plaza, 116 Krog Street, Atlanta, GA 30307. Your instructor may also ask you to write an appropriate message to Mr. Anthony Chomko, Suite 225.

10.16 Claim Denial: Refusing Wounded Buffalo and Pygmy Circus Refund (Obj. 4)

As manager of Promotions and Advertising, Five Flags Lake Point Park, you must respond to a recent letter. Nataleigh Haggard complained that she was "taken" by Five Flags when the park had to substitute performers for Wounded Buffalo and Pygmy Circus "Summertime Slam" performance Sunday, July 4 (see **Chapter 9, Activity 9.23**). Explain to her that the concert was planned by an independent promoter. Your only obligation was to provide the theater facility and advertising. Three days before the event, the promoter left town, taking with him all advance payments from financial backers. As it turned out, many of the artists he had promised to deliver were not even planning to attend.

Left with a messy situation, you decided on Thursday to go ahead with a modified version of the event since you had been advertising it and many would come expecting some kind of talent. At that time you changed your radio advertising to say that for reasons beyond your control, the Wounded Buffalo and Pygmy Circus bands would not be appearing. You described the new talent and posted signs at the entrance and in the parking lot announcing the change. Contrary to Ms. Haggard's claim, no newspaper advertising featuring Wounded Buffalo or the Pigs appeared on the day of the concert (at least you did not pay for any to appear that day). Somehow she must have missed your corrective radio advertising and signs at the entrance. You feel you made a genuine effort to communicate the changed program. In your opinion, most people who attended the concert thought that Five Flags had done everything possible to salvage a rather unfortunate situation.

Ms. Haggard wants a cash refund of $150 (two tickets at $75 each). Five Flags has a no-money-back policy on concerts after the event takes place. If Ms. Haggard had come to the box office before the event started, you could have returned her money. But she stayed to see the concert. She claims that she didn't know anything about the talent change until after the event was well underway. This sounds unlikely, but you don't quarrel with customers. Nevertheless, you can't give her cash back. You already took a loss on this event. But you can give two complimentary passes to Five Flags Lake Point Park.

Your Task. Write a refusal letter to Ms. Nataleigh Haggard, 9684 Middletown Road, Germantown, OH 45327. Invite her and a friend to return as guests under happier circumstances.

10.17 Claim Denial: Airline Loses Passenger's Glasses (Obj. 4)

American Southern Airline (ASA) had an unhappy customer. Leticia Tomlinson flew from Atlanta to Seattle. The flight stopped briefly at Chicago O'Hare, where she got off the plane for half an hour. When she returned to her seat, her $400 prescription reading glasses were gone. She asked the flight attendant where the glasses were, and the attendant said they probably were thrown away since the cleaning crew had come in with big bags and tossed everything in them. Ms. Tomlinson tried to locate the glasses through the airline's lost-and-found service, but she failed. Then she wrote a strong letter to the airline demanding reimbursement for the loss. She felt that it was obvious that she was returning to her seat. The airline, however, knows that an overwhelming number of passengers arriving at hubs switch planes for their connecting flights. The airline does not know who is returning. What's more, flight attendants usually announce that the plane is continuing to another city and that passengers who are returning should take their belongings. Cabin-cleaning crews speed through planes removing newspapers, magazines, leftover foods, and trash. Airlines feel no responsibility for personal items left in cabins.[23]

Your Task. As a staff member of the customer relations department of American Southern Airline, deny the customer's claim but retain her goodwill using techniques learned in this chapter. The airline never refunds cash, but it might consider travel vouchers for the value of the glasses. Remember that apologies cost nothing. Write a claim denial to Mrs. Leticia Tomlinson, 1952 Kanako Lane, Mount Vernon, WA 98273.

10.18 Bad News to Customers: The StairClimber or the LifeStep? (Obj. 4)

You are delighted to receive a large order from Greg Waller at New Bodies Gym. This order includes two Lifecycle Trainers (at $1,295 each), four Pro Abdominal Boards (at $295 each), three Tunturi Muscle Trainers (at $749 each), and three Dual-Action StairClimbers (at $1,545 each).

You could ship immediately except for one problem. The Dual-Action StairClimber is intended for home use, not for gym or club use. Customers like it because they say it is more like scaling a mountain than climbing a flight of stairs. With each step, users exercise their arms to pull or push themselves up. Its special cylinders absorb shock so that no harmful running impact results. However, this model is not what you would recommend for gym use. You feel Mr. Waller should order your premier stairclimber, the LifeStep (at $2,395 each) This unit has sturdier construction and is meant for heavy use. Its sophisticated electronics provide a selection of customer-pleasing programs that challenge muscles progressively with a choice of workouts. It also quickly multiplies workout gains with computer-controlled interval training. Electronic monitors inform users of step height, calories burned, elapsed time, upcoming levels, and adherence to fitness goals. For gym use the LifeStep is clearly better than the StairClimber. The bad news is that the LifeStep is considerably more expensive.

You get no response when you try to telephone Mr. Waller to discuss the problem. Should you ship what you can, or hold the entire order until you learn whether he wants the StairClimber or the LifeStep? Or perhaps you should substitute the LifeStep and send only two of them.

Your Task. Decide what to do and write a letter to Greg Waller, New Bodies Gym, 3402 Copeland Drive, Athens, OH 45701.

10.19 Damage Control for Disappointed Customers: J. Crew Goofs on Cashmere Turtleneck (Obj. 4)

Who wouldn't want a cashmere zip turtleneck sweater for $18? At the J. Crew Web site, many delighted shoppers scrambled to order the bargain cashmere. Unfortunately, the price should have been $218! Before J. Crew officials could correct the mistake, several hundred e-shoppers had bagged the bargain sweater for their digital shopping carts.

When the mistake was discovered, J. Crew immediately sent an e-mail message to the soon-to-be disappointed shoppers. The subject line shouted "Big Mistake!" Emily Woods, chairwoman of J. Crew, began her message with this statement: "I wish we could sell such an amazing sweater for only $18. Our price mistake on your new cashmere zip turtleneck probably went right by you, but rather than charge you such a large difference, I'm writing to alert you that this item has been removed from your recent order."

As an assistant in the communication department at J. Crew, you saw the e-mail message that was sent to customers and you tactfully suggested that the bad news might have been broken differently. Your boss says, "OK, hot stuff. Give it your best shot."

Your Task: Although you have only a portion of the message, analyze the customer bad-news message sent by J. Crew. Using the principles suggested in this chapter, write an improved e-mail message. In the end, J. Crew decided to allow customers who ordered the sweater at $18 to reorder it for $118.80 to $130.80, depending on the size. Customers were given a special Web site to reorder (make up an address). Remember that J. Crew customers are youthful and hip. Keep your message upbeat.[24]

10.20 Damage Control for Disappointed Customers: Worms in Her PowerBars!

Web

In a recent trip to her local grocery store, Kelly Keeler decided for the first time to stock up on PowerBars. These are low-fat, high-carbohydrate energy bars that are touted as a highly nutritious snack food specially formulated to deliver long-lasting energy. Since 1986, PowerBar (**http://www.powerbar.com**) has been dedicated to helping athletes and active people achieve peak performance. It claims to be "the fuel of choice" for top athletes around the world. Kelly is a serious runner and participates in many track meets every year.

On her way to a recent meet, Kelly grabbed a PowerBar and unwrapped it while driving. As she started to take her first bite, she noticed something white and shiny in the corner of the wrapping. An unexpected protein source wriggled out of her energy bar—a worm! Kelly's first inclination was to toss it out the window and never buy another PowerBar. On second thought, though, she decided to tell the company. When she called the toll-free number on the wrapper, Sophie, who answered the phone, was incredibly nice, extremely apologetic, and very informative about what happened. "I'm very sorry you experienced an infested product," said Sophie.

She explained that the infamous Indian meal moth is a pantry pest that causes millions of dollars in damage worldwide. It feeds on grains or grain-based products, such as cereal, flour, dry pasta, crackers, dried fruits, nuts, spices, and pet food. The tiny moth eggs lie dormant for some time or hatch quickly into tiny larvae (worms) that penetrate food wrappers and enter products.

At its manufacturing facilities, PowerBar takes stringent measures to protect against infestation. It inspects incoming grains, supplies proper ventilation, and shields all grain-storage areas with screens to prevent insects from entering. It also uses light traps and electrocuters; these devices eradicate moths with the least environmental impact.

PowerBar President Brian Maxwell makes sure every complaint is followed up immediately with a personal letter. His letters generally tell customers that it is rare for infestations like this to occur. Entomologists say that the worms are not toxic and will not harm humans. Nevertheless, as President Maxwell says, "it is extremely disgusting to find these worms in food."

Your Task. For the signature of Brian Maxwell, PowerBar president, write a bad-news follow-up letter to Kelly Keeler, 932 Opperman Drive, Eagan, MN 55123. Keep the letter informal and personal. Explain how pests get into grain-based products and what you are doing to prevent infestation. You can learn more about the Indian meal moth by searching the Web. In your letter include a brochure titled "Notes About the Indian Meal Moth," along with a kit for Kelly to mail the culprit PowerBar to the company for analysis in Boise, Idaho. Also send a check reimbursing Kelly $26.85 for her purchase.[25]

10.21 Damage Control for Disappointed Customers: Costly SUV Upgrade to a Ford Excursion (Obj. 4)

Steven Chan, a consultant from Oakland, California, was surprised when he picked up his rental car from Budget in Seattle over Easter weekend. He had reserved a full-size car, but the rental agent told him he could upgrade to a Ford Excursion for an additional $25 a day. "She told me it was easy to drive," Mr. Chan reported. "But when I saw it, I realized it was huge—like a tank. You could fit a full-size bed inside."

On his trip Mr. Chan managed to scratch the paint and damage the rear-door step. He didn't worry, though, because he thought the damage would be covered since he had charged the rental on his American Express card. He knew that the company offered backup car rental insurance coverage. To his dismay, he discovered that its car rental coverage excluded large SUVs. "I just assumed they'd cover it," he confessed. He wrote to Budget to complain about not being warned that certain credit cards may not cover damage to large SUVs or luxury cars.

Budget agents always encourage renters to sign up for Budget's own "risk product." But they don't feel that it is their responsibility to study the policies of customers' insurance carriers and explain what may or may not be covered. Moreover, they try to move customers into their rental cars as quickly as possible and avoid lengthy discussions of insurance coverage. Customers who do not purchase insurance are at risk. Mr. Chan does not make any claim against Budget, but he is upset about being "pitched" to upgrade to the larger SUV, which he didn't really want.[26]

Your Task. As a member of the communication staff at Budget, respond to Mr. Chan's complaint. Budget obviously is not going to pay for the SUV repairs, but it does want to salvage his goodwill and future business. Offer him a coupon worth two days' free rental of any full-size sedan. Write to Steven Chan, 5300 Park Ridge, Apt. 4A, Oakland, CA 93578.

10.22 Damage Control for Disappointed Customers: McDonald's Squirms Over McAfrika Protests (Obj. 4)

The McAfrika burger sounded like a terrific new menu sandwich to fast-food giant McDonald's. Made from an authentic African recipe, the pita bread sandwich combined beef, cheese, tomatoes, and salad. But when launched in Norway, it triggered an avalanche of criticism and bad publicity. McDonald's was accused of "extreme insensitivity" in releasing the new sandwich when 12 million people are facing starvation in southern Africa.

Aid agencies trying to raise funds to avert famine in southern Africa were particularly vociferous in their complaints. They said the McAfrika marketing campaign was "insensitive, crass, and ill considered." Linn Aas-Hansen, of Norwegian Church Aid, complained that it was "inappropriate and distasteful to launch a hamburger called McAfrika when large portions of southern Africa are on the verge of starvation." To punctuate their protest, members of the aid group distributed "catastrophe crackers" outside McDonald's restaurants in Oslo. These crackers are protein-rich biscuits given to starving Africans.

Facing a public relations debacle, McDonald's Norway immediately began a damage-control strategy. Spokeswoman Margaret Brusletto apologized, saying that the name of the product and the timing of its launch were unfortunate. She said the company would consider sharing the proceeds from its sales with aid agencies. McDonald's also offered to allow aid agencies to leave collection boxes and fund-raising posters in its Norwegian restaurants that sold the McAfrika sandwich during its promotional sale.

McDonald's head office issued a statement saying, "All of the involved parties are happy with the solution. We hope this will put a wider focus on the important job that these organizations are doing, and McDonald's in Norway is pleased to be able to support this." Although the McAfrika was launched only in Norway, the protest made headlines in the United States and other countries.[27]

Your Task. As a member of the McDonald's corporate communication staff, you are given the task of drafting a letter to be sent to U.S. customers who have written to protest the McAfrika sandwich in Norway and its possible launch in the United States. Most of the letters ask McDonald's to withdraw the offending product, a request you must refuse. Address the letter to Mrs. Janice M. Clark, 35 South Washington, Carthage, IL 62325. Prepare your letter so that it can be sent to others.

10.23 Damage Control for Disappointed Customers: Late Delivery of Printing Order (Obj. 4)

Team

Kevin Kearns, a printing company sales manager, must tell one of his clients that the payroll checks his company ordered are not going to be ready by the date Kearns had promised. The printing company's job scheduler overlooked the job and didn't get the checks into production in time to meet the deadline. As a result, Kearns' client, a major insurance company, is going to miss its pay run.

Kearns meets with internal department heads. They decide on the following plan to remedy the situation: (a) move the check order to the front of the production line; (b) make up for the late production date by shipping some of the checks—enough to meet their client's immediate payroll needs—by air freight; (c) deliver the remaining checks by truck.[28]

Your Task. Form groups of three to four students. Discuss the following issues about how to present the bad news to Andrew Tyra, Kearns' contact person at the insurance company.

a. Should Kearns call Tyra directly or delegate the task to his assistant?

b. When should Tyra be informed of the problem?

c. What is the best procedure for delivering the bad news?

d. What follow-up would you recommend to Kearns?

Be prepared to share your group's responses during a class discussion. Your instructor may ask two students to role-play the presentation of the bad news.

10.24 Credit Refusal: Cash Only at Gold's Gym and Fitness Center (Obj. 4)

As manager of Gold's Gym and Fitness Center, you must refuse the application of Becky Peniccia for an Extended Membership. This is strictly a business decision. You liked Becky very much when she applied, and she seems genuinely interested in fitness and a healthful lifestyle. However, your Extended Membership plan qualifies the member for all your testing, exercise, recreation, yoga, and aerobics programs. This multiservice program is expensive for the club to maintain because of the huge staff required. Applicants must have a solid credit rating to join. To your disappointment, you learned

that Becky's credit rating is decidedly negative. Her credit report indicates that she is delinquent in payments to four businesses, including Desert Athletic Club, your principal competitor.

You do have other programs, including your Drop In and Work Out plan, that offers use of available facilities on a cash basis. This plan enables a member to reserve space on the racquetball and handball courts. The member can also sign up for yoga and exercise classes, space permitting. Since Becky is far in debt, you would feel guilty allowing her to plunge in any more deeply.

Your Task. Refuse Becky Peniccia's credit application, but encourage her cash business. Suggest that she make an inquiry to the credit reporting company Experian to learn about her credit report. She is eligible to receive a free credit report if she mentions this application. Write to Rebecca Peniccia, Box 103, Westgate Hills, 1402 Olive Avenue, Mesa, AZ 85301.

10.25 Credit Refusal: Risky Order for Cool Camera Phones (Obj. 4)

As a CellCity sales manager, you are delighted to land a sizable order for your new T-Mobile Nokia digital video camera phone. This great phone is too cool with its full-color LCD, multimedia player, speakerphone, and voice dialing.

The purchase order comes from Beech Grove Electronics, a retail distributor in Indianapolis. You send the order on to Pat Huckabee, your credit manager, for approval of the credit application attached. To your disappointment, Pat tells you that Beech Grove doesn't qualify for credit. Experian Credit Services reports that credit would be risky for Beech Grove.

Because you think you can be more effective in writing than on the telephone, you decide to write to Beech Grove with the bad news and offer an alternative. Suggest that Beech Grove order a smaller number of the camera phones. If it pays cash, it can receive a 2 percent discount. After Beech Grove has sold these fast-moving units, it can place another cash order through your toll-free order number. With your fast delivery system, its inventory will never be depleted. Beech Grove can get the camera phones it wants now and can replace its inventory almost overnight. Credit Manager Huckabee tells you that your company generally reveals to credit applicants the name of the credit reporting service it used and encourages them to investigate their credit record.

Your Task. Write a credit refusal to Jacob Jackson, Beech Grove Electronics, 3590 Plainfield Road, Indianapolis, IN 46296.

10.26 Bad News to Employees: Company Games Are Not Date Nights (Obj. 5)

E-Mail

As director of Human Resources at Weyerman Paper Company, you received an unusual request. Several employees asked that their spouses or friends be allowed to participate in Weyerman intramural sports teams. Although the teams play only once a week during the season, these employees claim that they can't afford more time away from friends and family. Over 100 employees currently participate in the eight coed volleyball, softball, and tennis teams, which are open to company employees only. The teams were designed to improve employee friendships and to give employees a regular occasion to have fun together.

If nonemployees were to participate, you're afraid that employee interaction would be limited. Although some team members might have fun if spouses or friends were included, you are not so sure all employees would enjoy it. You're not interested in turning intramural sports into "date night." Furthermore, the company would have

Interactive Learning @ www.meguffey.com

to create additional teams if many nonemployees joined, and you don't want the administrative or equipment costs of more teams. Adding teams also would require changes to team rosters and game schedules. This could create a problem for some employees. You do understand the need for social time with friends and families, but guests are welcome as spectators at all intramural games. Besides, the company already sponsors a family holiday party and an annual company picnic.

Your Task. Write an e-mail or hard-copy memo to the staff denying the request of several employees to include nonemployees on Weyerman's intramural sports teams.

10.27 Bad News to Employees: No Go for Tuition Reimbursement (Obj. 5)

Team

Ashley Arnett, a hard-working bank teller, has sent a request asking that the company create a program to reimburse the tuition and book expenses for employees taking college courses (see **Chapter 9, Activity 9.9**). Although some companies have such a program, First Federal has not felt that it could indulge in such an expensive employee perk. Moreover, the CEO is not convinced that companies see any direct benefit from such a program. Employees improve their educational credentials and skills, but what is to keep them from moving that education and skill set to another employer? First Federal has over 200 employees. If even a fraction of them started classes, the company could see a huge bill for the cost of tuition and books. Because the bank is facing stiff competition and its profits are sinking, the expense of such a program is out of the question. In addition, it would involve administration—applications, monitoring, and record keeping. It is just too much of a hassle. When employees were hard to hire and retain, companies had to offer employment perks. But with a soft economy, such inducements are unnecessary.

Your Task. As director of Human Resources, send an individual response to Ashley Arnett. The answer is a definite *no*, but you want to soften the blow and retain the loyalty of this conscientious employee.

10.28 Bad News to Employees: Suit Up or Ship Out (Obj. 5)

During the feverish dot-com boom days, "business casual" became the workplace norm. Like many other companies, Bear Stearns, the sixth largest securities firm in the United States, loosened its dress policies. It allowed employees to come to work in polo shirts, khaki pants, and loafers for two important reasons: It had to compete with Internet companies in a tight employment market, and it wanted to fit in with its casual dot-com customers. But when the dot-com bubble burst and the economy faltered, the casual workplace environment glorified by failed Internet companies fell out of favor.

Managers at Bear Stearns decided to reverse course and cancel the casual dress code that had been in effect for two years. Company spokesperson Elizabeth Ventura said, "Our employees should reflect the professionalism of our business." Some observers felt that relaxed dress codes carried over into relaxed work attitudes.

Particularly in difficult economic times, Bear Stearns believed that every aspect of the business, including dress, should reflect the serious attitude and commitment it had toward relations with clients. After the securities market plunged, Bear Stearns slashed 830 jobs, amounting to 7.5 percent of its workforce. This was the biggest cut in company history, and officials vowed to get serious about regaining market share.

To put into effect its more serious business tone, Bear Stearns decided to return to a formal dress code. For men, suits and ties would be required. For women, dresses, suits with skirts or slacks, or "equivalent attire" would be expected. Although Bear Stearns decided to continue to allow casual dress on Fridays, sports jackets would be required for men.

Despite the policy reversal, company officials downplayed the return to traditional, more formal attire. Spokesperson Ventura noted that the company's legal, administrative, and private client services departments had never adopted the casual-dress code. In addition, she said, "We've always had a formal dress policy for meetings with clients."

To ease the transition, nearby Brooks Brothers Inc., a conservative clothing store, offered a special invitation. On September 20 it would stay open an extra hour to host an evening of wine, cheese, and shopping with discounts of 20 percent for Bear Stearns staffers.[29]

Your Task. As an assistant to John Jones, chairman of the Management and Compensation Committee, you have the challenging task of drafting a message to employees announcing the return to a formal dress code. He realizes that this is going to be a tough sell, but he's hoping that employees will recognize that difficult economic times require serious efforts and sacrifices. In the message to employees, he wants you to tell supervisors that they must speak to employees who fail to adhere to the new guidelines. You ask Mr. Jones whether he wants the message to open directly or indirectly. He says that Bear Stearns generally prefers directness in messages to employees, but he wants you to prepare two versions and he will choose one.

10.29 Is Increased Credit Card Security Worth the Inconvenience? (Obj. 4)

Consumer

Travel writer Arlene Getz was mystified when the sales clerk at a Paris department store refused her credit card. "Sorry," the clerk said, "your credit card is not being accepted. I don't know why." Getz found out soon enough. Her bank had frozen her account because of an "unusual" spending pattern. The problem? "We've never had a charge from you in France before," a bank official told her. The bank didn't seem to remember that Getz had repeatedly used that card in cities ranging from Boston to Tokyo to Cape Town over the past six years, each time without incident.

Getz was a victim of neural-network technology, a tool that is intended to protect credit cardholders from thieves who steal cards and immediately run up huge purchases. This technology tracks spending patterns. If it detects anything unusual—such as a sudden splurge on easy-to-fence items like jewelry—it sets off an alarm. Robert Boxberger, senior vice president of fraud management at Fleet Credit Card Services, says that the system is "geared toward not declining any travel and entertainment expenses, like hotels, restaurants, or car rentals." But somehow it goofed and did not recognize that Arlene Getz was traveling, although she had used her card earlier to rent a car in Paris, a sure sign that she was traveling.

Getz was what the credit card industry calls a false positive–a legitimate cardholder inconvenienced by the hunt for fraudsters. What particularly riled her was finding out that 75 percent of the transactions caught in the neural network turn out to be legitimate. Yet the technology has been immensely successful for credit card companies. Since Visa started using the program, its fraud rate dropped from 15 cents to 6 cents per $100. To avoid inconveniencing cardholders, the company doesn't automatically suspend a card when it suspects fraud. Instead, it telephones the cardholder to verify purchases. Of course, cardholders who are traveling are impossible to reach.

Angry at the inconvenience and embarrassment she experienced, Getz sent a letter to Visa demanding an explanation in writing.

Your Task. As an assistant to the vice president in charge of fraud detection at Visa, you have been asked to draft a letter that can be used to respond to Arlene Getz as well as to other unhappy customers whose cards were wrongly refused by your software. You know that the program has been an overwhelming success. It can, however, inconvenience people, especially when they are traveling. You've heard your boss tell travelers that it is a good idea to touch base with the bank before leaving and take along the card's customer service number (1-800-553-0321). Write a letter that explains what happened, retains the goodwill of the customer, and suggests reader benefits. Address your letter to Ms. Arlene Getz, 68 Riverside Drive, Apt. 35, New York, NY 10025.

Video Resources

Video Library 2
Bad News: BuyCostumes
This video features BuyCostumes, the world's largest online costume and accessories retailer. After watching the video, play the part of a customer service representative.

BuyCostumes is proud of its extensive stock of costumes, its liberal return policy, and its many satisfied customers. But one day a letter arrived with a request that went beyond the company's ability to deliver. The customer said that he had ordered the Gorilla Blinky Eye With Chest costume. This popular gorilla costume comes with a unique gorilla mask, attractive suit with rubber chest, foot covers, and hands. The customer complained that the gorilla costume did not arrive until two days after his Halloween party. He planned an elaborate party with a gorilla theme, and he was extremely unhappy that he did not have his costume. He asks BuyCostumes to reimburse $300 that he spent on theme-related decorations, which he says were useless when he failed to receive his costume.

As a customer service representative, you checked his order and found that it was not received until five days before Halloween, the busiest time of the year for your company. The order was filled the next day, but standard shipping requires three to six business days for delivery. The customer did not order express or premium delivery; his shipping option was marked "Standard."

You showed the letter to the owner, Mr. Getz, who said that this request was ludicrous. However, he wanted to retain the customer's goodwill. Obviously, BuyCostumes was not going to shell out $300 for late delivery of a costume. But Mr. Getz suggested that the company would allow the customer to return the costume (in its original packaging) with a credit for the $134.99 charge. In addition, BuyCostumes would send a coupon for $20 off on the next costume purchase.

Your Task. Mr. Getz asks you to write a letter that retains the goodwill of this customer. Address your bad-news letter to Mr. Christopher King, 3579 Elm Street, Buffalo, NY 14202. Check http://www.buycostumes.com for more company information.

Grammar and Mechanics C.L.U.E. Review 10

Confusing Words and Frequently Misspelled Words

Review the lists of confusing words and frequently misspelled words in Appendix A: Grammar and Mechanics Guide (Competent Language Usage Essentials), beginning on page A-21. On a separate sheet, revise the following sentences to correct word usage errors. Sentences may have more than one error. If a sentence is correct, write **C**. When you finish, check your answers on page Key-3.

Example: Have you allready sent the reccomendation?
Revision: Have you **already** sent the **recommendation?**

1. Good listeners absorb facts rather then interupting with frequent questions.

2. Her principle reason for declining the invitation was her busy calander.

3. The manager was conscience of the navigation problems at the company Web sight.

4. Because Nedra felt overwhelmed by the every day demands of her job, she sought advise from her mentor.

5. Before you procede with the report, check those embarassing statistics.

6. Although we should look into this matter farther, I am not suprised at your report.

7. The judge declared that the comments of there attorneys were irrevelant to the case at hand.

8. Because the property was to difficult to apprise, its value was unrecorded.

9. Jordan hoped to illicit advice from his counselor, but he was disapointed.

10. Is it neccessary to complement fellow team members when they excel?

Unit 4

Reports, Proposals, and Presentations

Chapter 11
Business Report Basics

Chapter 12
Informal Business Reports

Chapter 13
Proposals and Formal Reports

Chapter 14
Business Presentations

© Photodisc / Getty Images

Chapter 11

Business Report Basics

OBJECTIVES

After studying this chapter, you should be able to

1 Describe business report basics, including functions, patterns (indirect or direct), writing style, and formats.

2 Apply the 3-x-3 writing process to business reports to create documents that show an understanding of basic organizational patterns in written communication and a firm grasp of audience and purpose.

3 Understand how to find, evaluate, and use print and electronic sources of secondary data.

4 Comprehend the evolving nature of communication technology: the Web, electronic databases, and other resources for business writers and researchers.

5 Understand how to generate and use primary data while avoiding researcher bias.

6 Recognize the purposes and techniques of documentation in business reports and avoid plagiarism.

7 Illustrate reports with graphics that create meaning and interest; display numeric information in the appropriate graphic form; and show skill in generating, using, and converting data to visual aids.

Communicating at Work Part 1

BzzAgent Supports Women's Right to One True Fit

"Imagine an army of unpaid endorsers . . . telling their friends, family and colleagues about [a] product, who in turn tell their friends, family and colleagues."[1] The impact these unpaid endorsers create is known as *buzz*, a marketing phenomenon consisting of word-of-mouth advertising. Dave Balter, CEO for BzzAgent, is a strong advocate of word-of-mouth advertising. He believed that BzzAgent could help Lee Jeans market a new line of jeans called One True Fit by creating buzz.

Lee Jeans had experimented with word-of-mouth advertising before and had seen the value of creating buzz. The company approached Balter and BzzAgent based on the recommendation of one of its agency executives, who had actually worked as an unpaid BzzAgent for Balter. Their goal was to reach women in the 18- to-34 age bracket, for whom they had designed the One True Fit line.[2] Lee knew that these women, especially those who had just had children, often were unable to find jeans that fit.[3] Lee also believed that reaching this audience might require supplementing its traditional advertising strategies with a more personal approach.

Based on his experience and recent survey data,[4] Balter believed that his company's proprietary software system, the BzzEngine, and his well-prepared "volunteer brand evangelists" would be an ideal way to supplement Lee's current marketing strategies.[5] He thought that Lee's target audience was ideal for his company's word-of-mouth campaign built on goodwill and honesty.

Armed with his knowledge about word-of-mouth advertising and his belief that women in this target audience liked to share their opinions about products,[6] Balter set out to study the target group's reaction to these jeans. He had two goals. First, he had to determine whether his company could commit to the product; he needed to know whether the One True Fit line lived up to its promises. Second,

if it did, he had to show Lee Jeans how his company's system would reach the target audience and add value by generating awareness, delivering credibility, and creating positive buzz about the One True Fit line. You will learn more about this case on page 322.

Critical Thinking

- Do you think an advertising executive such as Dave Balter, who wants to demonstrate the added value his company can provide, should make his pitch orally or in writing?
- In your present work or organization experience, what kinds of reports are you familiar with? What is their purpose and how are they presented?
- Before funding an expensive advertising campaign, what would most companies require?

http://www.bzzagent.com

Understanding Report Basics

Reports are common in North American business. In this low-context culture, our values and attitudes seem to prompt us to write reports. We analyze problems, gather and study the facts, and then assess the alternatives. We pride ourselves on being practical and logical as we apply scientific procedures. When we must persuade a client that our services can add value, as Dave Balter of BzzAgent hoped to do, we generally write a report outlining our case.

Management decisions in many organizations are based on information submitted in the form of reports. Reports help us understand and study systematically the challenges that we encounter in business before we can outline the steps toward solving them. Historian and author David McCullough said it best: "Trying to plan for the future without a sense of the past is like trying to plant cut flowers."[7] Business solutions are unthinkable without a thorough examination of the problems that prompted them.

This chapter examines the functions, patterns, writing style, and formats of typical business reports. It also introduces the report-writing process and discusses methods of collecting, documenting, and illustrating data.

Business reports range from informal half-page trip reports to formal 200-page financial forecasts. Reports may be presented orally in front of a group or electronically on a computer screen. Some reports appear as words on paper in the form of memos and letters. Others are primarily numerical data, such as tax reports or profit-and-loss statements. Increasingly, reports are delivered and presented digitally, for instance, as PDF (portable

LEARNING OBJECTIVE 1
Describe business report basics, including functions, patterns (indirect or direct), writing style, and formats.

digital format) documents or as electronic "slide decks." These files can then be e-mailed, distributed on the company intranet, or posted on the Internet. Hyperlinks tie together content within the document, between associated files, and with Web site sources. Such linking adds depth and flexibility to traditional linear texts. Some reports provide information only; others analyze and make recommendations. Although reports vary greatly in length, content, form, and formality level, they all have one common purpose: *to answer questions and solve problems*.

Effective business reports answer questions and solve problems systematically.

Functions

In terms of what they do, most reports fit into two broad categories: informational reports and analytical reports.

Informational reports present data without comment or recommendations. Analytical reports provide analysis, conclusions, and, if requested, recommendations.

Informational Reports.
Reports that present data without analysis or recommendations are primarily informational. For such reports, writers collect and organize facts, but they do not analyze the facts for readers. A trip report describing an employee's visit to a trade show, for example, presents information. Other reports that present information without analysis involve routine operations, compliance with regulations, and company policies and procedures.

Analytical Reports.
Reports that provide data, analyses, and conclusions are analytical. If requested, writers also supply recommendations. Analytical reports may intend to persuade readers to act or change their beliefs. For example, if you were writing a feasibility report that compares several potential locations for a fast-food restaurant, you might conclude by recommending one site. Your report, an analysis of alternatives and a recommendation, attempts to persuade readers to accept that site.

Organizational Patterns

Like letters and memos, reports may be organized directly or indirectly. The reader's expectations and the content of a report determine its pattern of development, as illustrated in Figure 11.1. In long reports, such as corporate annual reports, some parts may be developed directly whereas other parts are arranged indirectly.

FIGURE 11.1 Audience Analysis and Report Organization

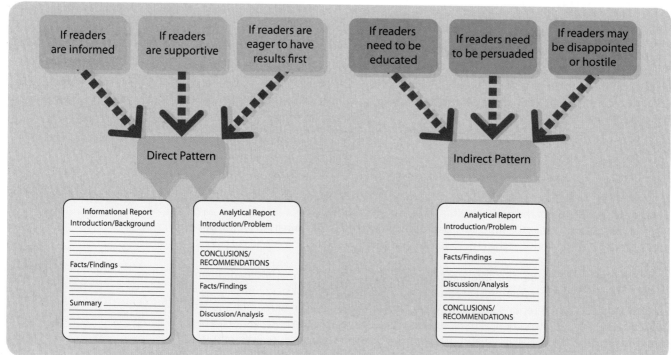

Direct Pattern. When the purpose for writing is presented close to the beginning, the organizational pattern is direct. Informational reports, such as the letter report shown in Figure 11.2, are usually arranged directly. They open with an introduction, which is followed by the facts and a summary. In Figure 11.2 the writer explains a legal services plan using a letter report. The report begins with an introduction. The facts, divided into three subtopics and identified by descriptive headings, follow. The report ends with a summary and a complimentary close.

FIGURE 11.2 Informational Report—Letter Format

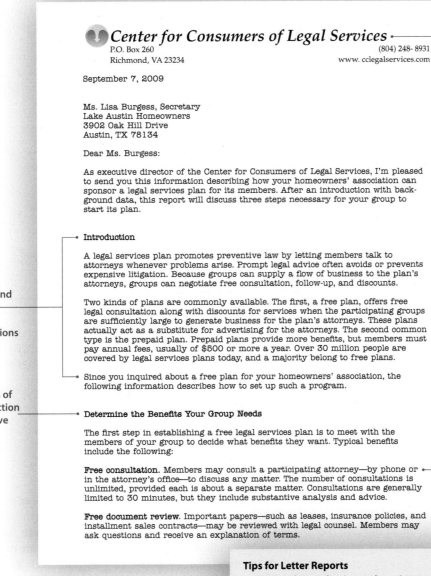

Uses letterhead stationery for an informal report addressed to an outsider

Center for Consumers of Legal Services
P.O. Box 260
Richmond, VA 23234
(804) 248-8931
www.cclegalservices.com

September 7, 2009

Ms. Lisa Burgess, Secretary
Lake Austin Homeowners
3902 Oak Hill Drive
Austin, TX 78134

Dear Ms. Burgess:

As executive director of the Center for Consumers of Legal Services, I'm pleased to send you this information describing how your homeowners' association can sponsor a legal services plan for its members. After an introduction with background data, this report will discuss three steps necessary for your group to start its plan.

Presents introduction and facts without analysis or recommendations

Introduction

A legal services plan promotes preventive law by letting members talk to attorneys whenever problems arise. Prompt legal advice often avoids or prevents expensive litigation. Because groups can supply a flow of business to the plan's attorneys, groups can negotiate free consultation, follow-up, and discounts.

Two kinds of plans are commonly available. The first, a free plan, offers free legal consultation along with discounts for services when the participating groups are sufficiently large to generate business for the plan's attorneys. These plans actually act as a substitute for advertising for the attorneys. The second common type is the prepaid plan. Prepaid plans provide more benefits, but members must pay annual fees, usually of $500 or more a year. Over 30 million people are covered by legal services plans today, and a majority belong to free plans.

Since you inquired about a free plan for your homeowners' association, the following information describes how to set up such a program.

Arranges facts of report into section with descriptive headings

Determine the Benefits Your Group Needs

The first step in establishing a free legal services plan is to meet with the members of your group to decide what benefits they want. Typical benefits include the following:

Free consultation. Members may consult a participating attorney—by phone or in the attorney's office—to discuss any matter. The number of consultations is unlimited, provided each is about a separate matter. Consultations are generally limited to 30 minutes, but they include substantive analysis and advice.

Emphasizes benefits in paragraph headings with boldface type

Free document review. Important papers—such as leases, insurance policies, and installment sales contracts—may be reviewed with legal counsel. Members may ask questions and receive an explanation of terms.

Tips for Letter Reports
- Use letter format for short informal reports sent to outsiders.
- Organize the facts section into logical divisions identified by consistent headings.
- Single-space the body.
- Double-space between paragraphs.
- Leave two blank lines above each side heading.
- Create side margins of 1 to 1¼ inches.
- Add a second-page heading, if necessary, consisting of the addressee's name, the date, and the page number.

FIGURE 11.2 (Continued)

Ms. Lisa Burgess   Page 2   September 7, 2009 •————

Discount on additional services. For more complex matters, participating
attorneys will charge members 75 percent of the attorney's normal fee. However,
some organizations choose to charge a flat fee for commonly needed services.

Select the Attorneys for Your Plan •————

Groups with geographically concentrated memberships have an advantage in
forming legal plans. These groups can limit the number of participating attorneys
and yet provide adequate service. Generally, smaller panels of attorneys are
advantageous.

Assemble a list of candidates, inviting them to apply. The best way to compare
prices is to have candidates submit their fees. Your group can then compare fee
schedules and select the lowest bidder, if price is important. Arrange to interview
attorneys in their offices.

After selecting an attorney or a panel, sign a contract. The contract should include
the reason for the plan, what the attorney agrees to do, what the group agrees to
do, how each side can end the contract, and the signatures of both parties. You
may also wish to include references to malpractice insurance, assurance that the
group will not interfere with the attorney–client relationship, an evaluation form,
a grievance procedure, and responsibility for government filings.

Publicize the Plan to Your Members •————

Members won't use a plan if they don't know about it, and a plan will not be
successful if it is unused. Publicity must be vocal and ongoing. Announce it in
newsletters, meetings, bulletin boards, and flyers.

Persistence is the key. All too frequently, leaders of an organization assume
that a single announcement is all that's needed. They expect members to see the
value of the plan and remember that it's available. Most organization members,
though, are not as involved as the leadership. Therefore, it takes more publicity
than the leadership usually expects in order to reach and maintain the desired
level of awareness.

Summary

A successful free legal services plan involves designing a program, choosing the
attorneys, and publicizing the plan. To learn more about these steps or to order
a $35 how-to manual, call me at (804) 355-9901.

Sincerely,

Richard M Ramos •————

Richard M. Ramos, Esq.
Executive Director

pas

Analytical reports may also be organized directly, especially when readers are supportive of or familiar with the topic. Many busy executives prefer this pattern because it gives
them the results of the report immediately. They don't have to spend time wading through
the facts, findings, discussion, and analyses to get to the two items they are most interested
in—the conclusions and recommendations. Figure 11.3 illustrates such an arrangement.
This analytical memo report describes environmental hazards of a property that a realtor
has just listed. The realtor is familiar with the investigation and eager to find out the recommendations. Therefore, the memo is organized directly. You should be aware, though, that
unless readers are familiar with the topic, they may find the direct pattern confusing. Many
readers prefer the indirect pattern because it seems logical and mirrors the way they solve
problems.

**The indirect pattern works
best for analytical reports that
convey bad news or seek to
persuade.**

Indirect Pattern.   When the conclusions and recommendations, if requested, appear
at the end of the report, the organizational pattern is indirect. Such reports usually begin
with an introduction or description of the problem, followed by facts and interpretations

FIGURE 11.3 Analytical Report—Memo Format

Applies memo format for short, informal internal report

Presents recommendations first (direct pattern) because reader is supportive and familiar with topic

Combines findings and analyses in short report

Atlantic Environmental, Inc.

Interoffice Memo

DATE: March 7, 2009

TO: Kermit Fox, President

FROM: Cynthia M. Rashid, Environmental Engineer   *CMR*

SUBJECT: Investigation of Mountain Park Commercial Site

For Allegheny Realty, Inc., I've completed a preliminary investigation of its Mountain Park property listing. The following recommendations are based on my physical inspection of the site, official records, and interviews with officials and persons knowledgeable about the site.

Recommendations

To reduce its potential environmental liability, Allegheny Realty should take the following steps in regard to its Mountain Park listing:

- Conduct an immediate asbestos survey at the site, including inspection of ceiling insulation material, floor tiles, and insulation around a gas-fired heater vent pipe at 2539 Mountain View Drive.

- Prepare an environmental audit of the generators of hazardous waste currently operating at the site, including Mountain Technology.

- Obtain lids for the dumpsters situated in the parking areas and ensure that the lids are kept closed.

Findings and Analyses

My preliminary assessment of the site and its immediate vicinity revealed rooms with damaged floor tiles on the first and second floors of 2539 Mountain View Drive. Apparently, in recent remodeling efforts, these tiles had been cracked and broken. Examination of the ceiling and attic revealed further possible contamination from asbestos. The insulation for the hot-water tank was in poor condition.

Located on the property is Mountain Technology, a possible hazardous waste generator. Although I could not examine its interior, this company has the potential for producing hazardous material contamination.

In the parking area large dumpsters collect trash and debris from several businesses. These dumpsters were uncovered, thus posing a risk to the general public.

In view of the construction date of the structures on this property, asbestos-containing building materials might be present. Moreover, this property is located in an industrial part of the city, further prompting my recommendation for a thorough investigation. Allegheny Realty can act immediately to eliminate one environmental concern: covering the dumpsters in the parking area.

Uses first paragraph as introduction

Tips for Memo Reports

- Use memo format for most short (ten or fewer pages) informal reports within an organization.
- Leave side margins of 1 to 1¼ inches.
- Sign your initials on the *From* line.
- Use an informal, conversational style.
- For direct analytical reports, put recommendations first.
- For indirect analytical reports, put recommendations last.

---

from the writer. They end with conclusions and recommendations. This pattern is helpful when readers are unfamiliar with the problem. This pattern is also useful when readers must be persuaded or when they may be disappointed in or hostile toward the report's findings. The writer is more likely to retain the reader's interest by first explaining, justifying, and analyzing the facts and then making recommendations. This pattern also seems most rational to readers because it follows the normal thought process: problem, alternatives (facts), solution.

FIGURE 11.4 Report-Writing Styles

	Formal Writing Style	Informal Writing Style
Use	Theses Research studies Controversial or complex reports (especially to outsiders)	Short, routine reports Reports for familiar audiences Noncontroversial reports Most reports for company insiders
Effect	Impression of objectivity, accuracy, professionalism, fairness Distance created between writer and reader	Feeling of warmth, personal involvement, closeness
Characteristics	Absence of first-person pronouns; use of third-person (*the researcher, the writer*) Absence of contractions (*can't, don't*) Use of passive-voice verbs (*the study was conducted*) Complex sentences; long words Absence of humor and figures of speech Reduced use of colorful adjectives and adverbs Elimination of "editorializing" (author's opinions, perceptions)	Use of first-person pronouns (*I, we, me, my, us, our*) Use of contractions Emphasis on active-voice verbs (*I conducted the study*) Shorter sentences; familiar words Occasional use of humor, metaphors Occasional use of colorful speech Acceptance of author's opinions and ideas

Writing Style

Reports can be formal or informal depending on the purpose, audience, and setting.

Like other business messages, reports can range from informal to formal, depending on their purpose, audience, and setting. Research reports from consultants to their clients tend to be rather formal. Such reports must project an impression of objectivity, authority, and impartiality. But a report to your boss describing a trip to a conference would probably be informal.

An office worker once called a grammar hot-line service with this problem: "We've just sent a report to our headquarters, and it was returned with this comment, 'Put it in the third person.' What do they mean?" The hot-line experts explained that management apparently wanted a more formal writing style, using third-person constructions (*the company* or *the researcher* instead of *we* and *I*). Figure 11.4, which compares characteristics of formal and informal report-writing styles, can help you decide which writing style is appropriate for your reports.

Formats

A report's format depends on its length, audience, topic, and purpose.

The format of a report depends on its length, topic, audience, and purpose. After considering these elements, you will probably choose from among the following formats.

Letter Format. Use letter format for short (usually eight or fewer pages) informal reports addressed outside an organization. Prepared on office stationery, a letter report contains a date, inside address, salutation, and complimentary close, as shown in Figure 11.2. Although they may carry information similar to that found in correspondence, letter reports usually are longer and show more careful organization than most letters. They also include headings.

Memo Format. For short informal reports that stay within organizations, the memo format is appropriate. Memo reports begin with essential background information, using standard headings: *Date, To, From,* and *Subject,* as shown in Figure 11.3. Like letter reports, memo reports differ from regular memos in length, use of headings, and deliberate organization.

Manuscript Format. For longer, more formal reports, use the manuscript format. These reports are usually printed on plain paper instead of letterhead stationery or memo forms. They begin with a title followed by systematically displayed headings and subheadings. You will see examples of proposals and formal reports using the manuscript format in Chapter 13.

Printed Forms. Prepared forms are often used for repetitive data, such as monthly sales reports, performance appraisals, merchandise inventories, and personnel and financial reports. Standardized headings on these forms save time for the writer. Preprinted forms also make similar information easy to locate and ensure that all necessary information is provided.

Digital Format. Digital media allow writers to produce and distribute reports in electronic form, not in hard copy. With Adobe Acrobat any report can be converted into a PDF document that retains its format and cannot be changed. In addition, today's communicators can use programs such as PowerPoint to create electronic presentations that often double as a "slide deck." This slide deck concisely displays the content of a report. Such presentations serve not so much for verbal delivery because they are more text heavy than typical PowerPoint slides; rather, they are intended for posting online and e-mailing. When printed out, the stacks of hard-copy slides resemble decks of playing cards. Digital delivery has also changed Microsoft Word documents. This popular program lets users hyperlink multimedia content within the document or with associated text or media files. Thus, such digital documents create a nonlinear reading experience similar to that of browsing Web pages.

Applying the 3-x-3 Writing Process to Reports

LEARNING OBJECTIVE 2
Apply the 3-x-3 writing process to business reports to create documents that show an understanding of basic organizational patterns in written communication and a firm grasp of audience and purpose.

Because business reports are systematic attempts to answer questions and solve problems, the best reports are developed methodically. In earlier chapters the 3-x-3 writing process was helpful in guiding short projects such as e-mails, memos, and letters. That same process is even more necessary in helping you prepare longer projects such as reports and proposals. After all, an extensive project poses a greater organizational challenge than a short one and, therefore, requires a rigorous structure to help readers grasp the message. Let's channel the writing process into seven specific steps:

Step 1: Analyze the problem and purpose.

Step 2: Anticipate the audience and issues.

Step 3: Prepare a work plan.

Step 4: Implement your research strategy.

Step 5: Organize, analyze, interpret, and illustrate the data.

Step 6: Compose the first draft.

Step 7: Revise, proofread, and evaluate.

How much time you spend on each step depends on your report task. A short informational report on a familiar topic might require a brief work plan, little research, and no data analysis. A complex analytical report, on the other hand, might demand a comprehensive work plan, extensive research, and careful data analysis. In this section we will consider the first three steps in the process—analyzing the problem and purpose, anticipating the audience and issues, and preparing a work plan.

The best reports grow out of a seven-step process beginning with analysis and ending with proofreading and evaluation.

To illustrate the planning stages of a report, we will watch Diane Camas develop a report she's preparing for her boss, Mike Rivers, at Mycon Pharmaceutical Laboratories. Mike asked Diane to investigate the problem of transportation for sales representatives. Currently, some Mycon reps visit customers (mostly doctors and hospitals) using company-leased cars. A few reps drive their own cars, receiving reimbursements for use. In three months Mycon's leasing agreement for 14 cars expires, and Mike is considering a major change. Diane's task is to investigate the choices and report her findings to Mike.

Analyzing the Problem and Purpose

The first step in writing a report is understanding the problem or assignment clearly. For complex reports, prepare a written problem statement to clarify the task. In analyzing her report task, Diane had many questions: Is the problem that Mycon is spending too much money on leased cars? Does Mycon wish to invest in owning a fleet of cars? Is Mike unhappy

Before beginning a report, identify the problem to be solved in a clear statement.

with the paperwork involved in reimbursing sales reps when they use their own cars? Does he suspect that reps are submitting inflated mileage figures? Before starting research for the report, Diane talked with Mike to define the problem. She learned several dimensions of the situation and wrote the following statement to clarify the problem—both for herself and for Mike.

> *Problem statement: The leases on all company cars will be expiring in three months. Mycon must decide whether to renew them or develop a new policy regarding transportation for sales reps. Expenses and paperwork for employee-owned cars seem excessive.*

Diane further defined the problem by writing a specific question that she would try to answer in her report:

> *Problem question: What plan should Mycon follow in providing transportation for its sales reps?*

Now Diane was ready to concentrate on the purpose of the report. Again, she had questions: Exactly what did Mike expect? Did he want a comparison of costs for buying and leasing cars? Should she conduct research to pinpoint exact reimbursement costs when employees drive their own cars? Did he want her to do all the legwork, present her findings in a report, and let him make a decision? Or did he want her to evaluate the choices and recommend a course of action? After talking with Mike, Diane was ready to write a simple purpose statement for this assignment.

> *Simple statement of purpose: To recommend a plan that provides sales reps with cars to be used in their calls.*

A simple purpose statement defines the focus of a report.

Preparing a written purpose statement is a good idea because it defines the focus of a report and provides a standard that keeps the project on target. In writing useful purpose statements, choose action verbs telling what you intend to do: *analyze, choose, investigate, compare, justify, evaluate, explain, establish, determine,* and so on. Notice that Diane's statement begins with the action verb *recommend*.

Some reports require only a simple statement of purpose: to investigate expanded teller hours, to select a manager from among four candidates, to describe the position of accounts supervisor. Many assignments, though, demand additional focus to guide the project. An expanded statement of purpose considers three additional factors: scope, significance, and limitations.

Setting boundaries on a project determines its scope.

Scope. What issues or elements will be investigated? The scope statement prepares the audience by clearly defining which problem or problems will be analyzed and solved. To determine the scope, Diane brainstormed with Mike and others to pin down her task. She learned that Mycon currently had enough capital to consider purchasing a fleet of cars outright. Mike also told her that employee satisfaction was almost as important as cost-effectiveness. Moreover, he disclosed his suspicion that employee-owned cars were costing Mycon more than leased cars. Diane had many issues to sort out in setting the boundaries of her report.

Significance. Why is the topic worth investigating at this time? Some topics, after initial examination, turn out to be less important than originally thought. Others involve problems that cannot be solved, making a study useless. For Diane and Mike the problem had significance because Mycon's leasing agreement would expire shortly and decisions had to be made about a new policy for transportation of sales reps.

Limitations. What conditions affect the generalizability and utility of a report's findings? As part of the scope statement, the limitations further narrow the subject by focusing on constraints or exclusions. For this report, Diane realized that her conclusions and recommendations might apply only to reps in her Kansas City sales district. Her findings would probably not be reliable for reps in Seattle, Phoenix, or Atlanta. Another limitation for Diane was time. She had to complete the report in four weeks, thus restricting the thoroughness of her research.

Diane decided to expand her statement of purpose to define the scope, explain the significance of the problem, and describe the limitations of the report.

> *Expanded statement of purpose: The purpose of this report is to recommend a plan that provides sales reps with cars to be used in their calls. The report will compare costs for three plans: outright ownership, leasing, and compensation for employee-owned cars. It will also measure employee reaction to each plan. The report is significant because Mycon's current leasing agreement expires April 1 and an improved plan could reduce costs and paperwork. The study is limited to costs for sales reps in the Kansas City district.*

An expanded purpose statement considers scope, significance, and limitations.

After expanding her statement of purpose, Diane checked it with Mike Rivers to be sure she was on target.

Anticipating the Audience and Issues

After defining the purpose of a report, a writer must think carefully about who will read it. Concentrating solely on a primary reader is a major mistake. Although one individual may have solicited the report, others within the organization may eventually read it, including upper management and people in other departments. A report to an outside client may first be read by someone who is familiar with the problem and then be distributed to others less familiar with the topic. Moreover, candid statements to one audience may be offensive to another audience. Diane could make a major blunder, for instance, if she mentioned Mike's suspicion that sales reps were padding their mileage statements. If the report were made public—as it probably would be to explain a new policy—the sales reps could feel insulted that their integrity was questioned.

As Diane considered her primary and secondary readers, she asked herself these questions:

Report writers must take into account both primary and secondary readers.

- *What do my readers need to know about this topic?*

- *What do they already know?*

- *What is their educational level?*

- *How will they react to this information?*

- *Which sources will they trust?*

- *How can I make this information readable, believable, and memorable?*

Answers to these questions help writers determine how much background material to include, how much detail to add, whether to include jargon, what method of organization and presentation to follow, and what tone to use.

In the planning stages a report writer must also break the major investigative problem into subproblems. This process, sometimes called factoring, identifies issues to be investigated or possible solutions to the main problem. In this case Mycon must figure out the best way to transport sales reps. Each possible "solution" or issue that Diane considers becomes a factor or subproblem to be investigated. Diane came up with three tentative solutions to provide transportation to sales reps: (a) purchase cars outright, (b) lease cars, or (c) compensate employees for using their own cars. These three factors form the outline of Diane's study.

Major report problems should be broken down into subproblems—or factored—to highlight possible solutions.

Diane continued to factor these main points into the following subproblems for investigation:

What plan should Mycon use to transport its sales reps?

I. Should Mycon purchase cars outright?

   A. How much capital would be required?

   B. How much would it cost to insure, operate, and maintain company-owned cars?

   C. Do employees prefer using company-owned cars?

Spotlight on Communicators

A. J. Jamal, who hosted the Comedy Channel TV show *Comic Justice,* attributes his successful career to basic problem-solving skills he learned while working for IBM. "Everybody wonders why I am so businesslike with comedy, and it dawned on me that doing comedy is like troubleshooting a technical problem." Jamal explained that IBM taught its employees to break down a big problem into smaller components and look for solutions to each one. This process, called factoring, is also an important first step in outlining the major issues in any report.

© Pete Mitchell / WireImage / Getty Images

II. Should Mycon lease cars?

   A. What is the best lease price available?

   B. How much would it cost to insure, operate, and maintain leased cars?

   C. Do employees prefer using leased cars?

III. Should Mycon compensate employees for using their own cars?

   A. How much has it cost in the past to compensate employees who used their own cars?

   B. How much paperwork is involved in reporting expenses?

   C. Do employees prefer being compensated for using their own cars?

Each subproblem would probably be further factored into additional subproblems. These issues may be phrased as questions, as Diane's are, or as statements. In factoring a complex problem, prepare an outline showing the initial problem and its breakdown into subproblems. Make sure your divisions are consistent (don't mix issues), exclusive (don't overlap categories), and complete (don't skip significant issues).

Preparing a Work Plan

After analyzing the problem, anticipating the audience, and factoring the problem, you're ready to prepare a work plan. A good work plan includes the following:

- Statement of the problem (based on key background/contextual information)

- Statement of the purpose including scope, significance, and limitations

- Research strategy including a description of potential sources and methods of collecting data

- Tentative outline that factors the problem into manageable chunks

- Work schedule

A work plan outlines the resources, priorities, stages, and schedule of a project.

Preparing a plan encourages you to evaluate your resources, set priorities, outline a course of action, and establish a time schedule. Having a plan keeps you on schedule and provides management a means of measuring your progress.

A work plan gives a complete picture of a project. Because the usefulness and quality of any report rest primarily on its data, you will want to develop a clear research strategy, which includes allocating plenty of time to locate sources of information. For firsthand information you might interview people, prepare a survey, or even conduct a scientific experiment. For secondary information you will probably search printed materials such as books and magazines—in addition to electronic materials on the Internet. Your work plan describes how you expect to generate or collect data. Because data collection is a major part of report writing, the next section of this chapter treats the topic more fully.

Figure 11.5 shows a complete work plan for a proposal that Dave Balter will present to Lee Jeans. This work plan is particularly useful because it outlines the issues to be investigated. Notice that considerable thought and discussion and even some preliminary research are necessary to be able to develop a useful work plan.

Although this tentative outline guides investigation, it does not determine the content or order of the final report. You may, for example, study five possible solutions to a problem. If two prove to be useless, your report may discuss only the three winners. Moreover, you will organize the report to accomplish your goal and satisfy the audience. Remember that a busy executive who is familiar with a topic may prefer to read the conclusions and recommendations before a discussion of the findings. If someone authorizes the report, be sure to review the work plan with that individual (your manager, client, or professor, for example) before proceeding with the project.

Spotlight on Communicators

At Phelps County Bank in Rolla, Missouri, loan department assistant Peggy Laun investigated whether the bank should offer its customers electronic tax filing with the IRS. She saw a problem, conducted research, collected data, evaluated the results, and then concluded that the existing software was not safe and reliable enough. Good research usually begins with a work plan designed to solve a specific problem.

© Mark Katzman / Ferguson & Katzman

FIGURE 11.5 Work Plan for a Formal Report

Statement of Problem

Many women between the ages of 18 and 34 have trouble finding jeans that fit. Lee Jeans hopes to remedy that situation with its One True Fit line. We want to demonstrate to Lee that we can create a word-of-mouth campaign that will help it reach its target audience.

Defines purpose, scope, limits, and significance of report

Statement of Purpose

The purpose of this report is to secure an advertising contract from Lee Jeans. We will examine published accounts about the jeans industry and Lee Jeans in particular. In addition, we will examine published results of Lee's current marketing strategy. We will conduct focus groups of women in our company to generate campaign strategies for our pilot study of 100 BzzAgents. The report will persuade Lee Jeans that word-of-mouth advertising is an effective strategy to reach women in this demographic group and that BzzAgent is the right company to hire. The report is significant because an advertising contract with Lee Jeans would help our company grow significantly in size and stature.

Research Strategy (Sources and Methods of Data Collection)

Describes primary and secondary data

We will gather information about Lee Jeans and the product line by examining published marketing data and conducting focus group surveys of our employees. In addition, we will gather data about the added value of word-of-mouth advertising by examining published accounts and interpreting data from previous marketing campaigns, particularly those with similar age groups. Finally, we will conduct a pilot study of 100 BzzAgents in the target demographic.

Tentative Outline

Factors problem into manageable chunks

I. How effectively has Lee Jeans marketed to the target population (women, ages 18–34)?
   A. Historically, who has typically bought Lee Jeans products? How often? Where?
   B. How effective are the current marketing strategies for the One True Fit line?
II. Is this product a good fit for our marketing strategy and our company?
   A. What do our staff members and our sample survey of BzzAgents say about this product?
   B. How well does our pool of BzzAgents correspond to the target demography in terms of age and geographic distribution?
III. Why should Lee Jeans engage BzzAgent to advertise its One True Fit line?
   A. What are the benefits of word of mouth in general and for this demographic in particular?
   B. What previous campaigns have we engaged in that demonstrate our company's credibility?
   C. What are our marketing strategies, and how well did they work in the pilot study?

Work Schedule

Estimates time needed to complete report tasks

Investigate Lee Jeans and the One True Fit line's current marketing strategy	July 15–25
Test product using focus groups	July 15–22
Create campaign materials for BzzAgents	July 18–31
Run a pilot test with a selected pool of 100 BzzAgents	August 1–21
Evaluate and interpret findings	August 22–25
Compose draft of report	August 26–28
Revise draft	August 28–30
Submit final report	September 1

Tips for Preparing a Work Plan

- Start early; allow plenty of time for brainstorming and preliminary research.
- Describe the problem motivating the report.
- Write a purpose statement that includes the report's scope, significance, and limitations.
- Describe the research strategy including data collection sources and methods.
- Divide the major problem into subproblems stated as questions to be answered.
- Develop a realistic work schedule citing dates for completion of major tasks.
- Review the work plan with whoever authorized the report.

Communicating at Work Part 2

BzzAgent

Companies have long understood that word of mouth is a powerful force, but few companies have figured out how to use it effectively. Dave Balter has an answer: turn his network of up to 50,000 agents into "volunteer brand evangelists." However, to achieve the kind of commitment necessary to influence consumer attitudes and affect the distribution cycle positively, Balter believes that his agents, while passionate, must also be honest. The literature the company sends its agents explains that "the personal nature of a BzzAgent campaign requires honesty in order for agents to maintain credibility."[8]

Thus, for the Lee campaign, one of Balter's first tasks was to determine whether he, his marketing team, and his network of BzzAgents believed in the product. He began by asking Lee to send several pairs of jeans to his Boston headquarters. These jeans were shown to women in the company to learn whether this product would fit within their community. In addition, he began polling his network of agents to learn about the word on the street. Only after Balter and his staff recognized the potential using "volunteer brand evangelism" could he and his company begin work.

In the case of Lee's One True Fit jeans, the response from his staff and agents was extremely favorable, but the campaign still faced obstacles. The marketing team had to take Lee's marketing messages and materials, which focused on sexy models and the tagline of "find your one true fit," and transition them into actual communications that people would generate. This work occurs in what Balter calls a "BzzSession," in which the team breaks down the marketing materials, asking key questions such as, *Who are the targets? What types of people should we talk to about the product?* and *Why would*

people think this product works? Balter calls the answers to these questions "BzzHooks" or "BzzFacts." In this campaign, for example, two such BzzFacts were (a) the jeans do not gap in the back when women sit and (b) the leather patch has been eliminated. Following the BzzSession for Lee, Balter and his staff began to put together a proposal that included the segment of agents he recommended (in this case about 1,000), a suggested trial of the product, a reward structure, and key communication components featuring what he calls BzzTargets, BzzActivities, BzzStories, and BzzFacts.

© Lee Jeans a division of VF Jeanswear Limited Partnership

Critical Thinking

- To secure management backing from Lee, should Dave Balter and his team choose an informational or analytical approach to the proposal? Why?
- Should Balter's proposal be developed directly or indirectly? Why? Should it be written formally or informally?
- What are some of the questions that Balter and his team should ask themselves about their audience before making their presentation or writing their proposal?

Gathering Information From Secondary Sources

LEARNING OBJECTIVE 3
Understand how to find, evaluate, and use print and electronic sources of secondary data.

A report is only as good as its data.

One of the most important steps in the process of writing a report is that of gathering information (research). As the philosopher Goethe once said, "The greater part of all mischief in the world arises from the fact that men do not sufficiently understand their own aims. They have undertaken to build a tower, and spend no more labor on the foundation than would be necessary to erect a hut." Think of your report as a tower. Because a report is only as good as its foundation—the questions you ask and the data you gather to answer those questions—the remainder of this chapter describes the fundamental work of finding, documenting, and illustrating data.

As you analyze a report's purpose and audience and prepare your research strategy, you will identify and assess the data you need to support your argument or explain your topic. As you do, you will answer questions about your objectives and audience: Will the audience need a lot of background or contextual information? Will your readers value or trust statistics, case studies, or expert opinions? Will they want to see data from interviews or surveys? Will summaries of focus groups be useful? Should you rely on organizational data? Figure 11.6 lists five forms of data and provides questions to guide you in making your research accurate and productive.

Primary data come from firsthand experience and observation; secondary data, from reading.

Data fall into two broad categories, primary and secondary. Primary data result from firsthand experience and observation. Secondary data come from reading what others have experienced and observed. Coca-Cola and Pepsi-Cola, for example, produce primary data when they stage taste tests and record the reactions of consumers. These same sets of data become secondary after they have been published and, let's say, a newspaper reporter uses them in an article about soft drinks. Secondary data are easier and cheaper to develop than primary data, which might involve interviewing large groups or sending out questionnaires.

American consumers may see more Smart cars on the road if Congress raises the Corporate Average Fuel Economy (CAFE) standards for U.S. automobiles. Environmental lobbyists distressed over global energy consumption are pressing Detroit's automakers to increase the average fuel efficiency of their vehicle fleets to 35 miles per gallon. Big Three automakers and CAFE opponents like Michigan Senator Carl Levin claim the steep regulation could bankrupt car manufacturers and endanger motorists who drive light-construction minicars. *What forms of data might persuade audiences of automakers' claims?*

We are going to discuss secondary data first because that is where nearly every research project should begin. Often, something has already been written about your topic. Reviewing secondary sources can save time and effort and prevent you from "reinventing the wheel." Most secondary material is available either in print or electronically.

FIGURE 11.6 Gathering and Selecting Report Data

Form of Data	Questions to Ask
Background or historical	How much do my readers know about the problem?
	Has this topic/issue been investigated before?
	Are those sources current, relevant, and/or credible?
	Will I need to add to the available data?
Statistical	What or who is the source?
	How recent are the data?
	How were the figures derived?
	Will these data be useful in this form?
Expert opinion	Who are the experts?
	What are their biases?
	Are their opinions in print?
	Are they available for interviewing?
	Do we have in-house experts?
Individual or group opinion	Whose opinion(s) would the readers value?
	Have surveys or interviews been conducted on this topic?
	If not, do questionnaires or surveys exist that I can modify and/or use?
	Would focus groups provide useful information?
Organizational	What are the proper channels for obtaining in-house data?
	Are permissions required?
	How can I learn about public and private companies?

Print Resources

Print sources are still the most visible part of libraries.

Although we're seeing a steady movement away from print to electronic data, print sources are still the most visible part of most libraries. Much information is available only in print, and you may want to use some of the following print resources.

By the way, if you are an infrequent library user, begin your research by talking with a reference librarian about your project. These librarians won't do your research for you, but they will steer you in the right direction. And they are very accommodating. Several years ago a *Wall Street Journal* poll revealed that librarians are perceived as among the friendliest, most approachable people in the working world. Many librarians help you understand their computer, cataloging, and retrieval systems by providing advice, brochures, handouts, and workshops.

Books. Although quickly outdated, books provide excellent historical, in-depth data. Books can be located through print or online listings.

- **Card catalogs.** A few small public or high school libraries still maintain card catalogs with all books indexed on 3-by-5 cards alphabetized by author, title, and subject.

- **Online catalogs.** Most libraries today have computerized their card catalogs. Some systems are fully automated, thus allowing users to learn not only whether a book is located in the library but also whether it is currently available. Moreover, online catalogs can help you trace and retrieve items from other area libraries if your college doesn't own them.

Books provide historical, in-depth data; periodicals focus on up-to-date information.

Periodicals. Magazines, pamphlets, and journals are called *periodicals* because of their recurrent, or periodic, publication. Journals are compilations of scholarly articles. Articles in journals and other periodicals will be extremely useful because they are concise, limited in scope, current, and can supplement information in books.

- **Print indexes.** Most university libraries now offer online access to *The Readers' Guide to Periodical Literature.* You may still find print copies of this valuable index of general-interest magazine article titles in small libraries. It includes such magazines as *Time, Newsweek, The New Yorker,* and *U.S. News & World Report.* However, business writers today rely almost totally on electronic indexes and databases.

Exploration of secondary sources includes searching both electronic and print periodicals.

- **Electronic indexes.** Online indexes are stored in digital databases. Most libraries now provide such databases to help you locate references, abstracts, and full-text articles from magazines, journals, and newspapers, such as *The New York Times.* When using Web-based online indexes, follow the on-screen instructions or ask for assistance from a librarian. Beginning with a subject search is helpful because it generally turns up more relevant citations than keyword searches—especially when searching for names of people or companies. Once you locate usable references, either print a copy of your findings, save them to a portable flash memory device, or send them to your e-mail address.

Electronic Databases

Most researchers begin by looking in electronic databases.

As a writer of business reports today, you will probably begin your secondary research with electronic resources. Online databases have become the staple of secondary research. Most writers turn to them first because they are fast and easy to use. This means that you can conduct detailed searches without ever leaving your office, home, or dorm room.

A database is a collection of information stored electronically so that it is accessible by computer and is digitally searchable. Databases provide both bibliographic (titles of documents and brief abstracts) and full-text documents. Most researchers prefer full-text documents because they are convenient. Various databases contain a rich array of magazine, newspaper, and journal articles, as well as newsletters, business reports, company profiles, government data, reviews, and directories. The four databases most useful to business writers for general searches are ABI/INFORM (ProQuest), Factiva (Dow Jones), LexisNexis Academic, and Academic Search Elite (EBSCO). Your college library and many businesses probably subscribe to these expensive resources and perhaps to other, more specialized commercial databases. Figure 11.7 shows the ABI/INFORM search menu.

FIGURE 11.7 ABI/INFORM (ProQuest)

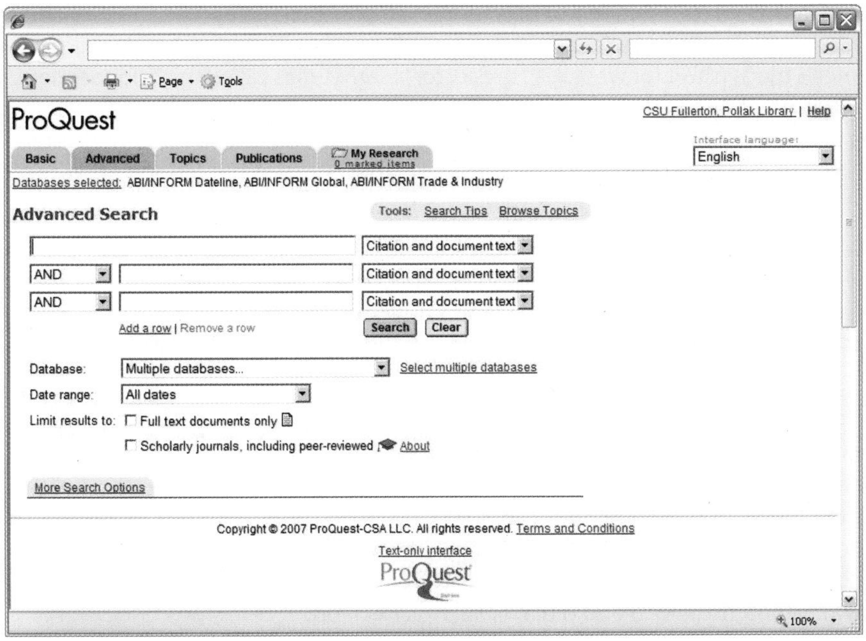

Source: Image published with permission of ProQuest. Further reproduction is prohibited without permission.

Developing a search strategy and narrowing your search can save time. As you develop your strategy, think about the time frame for your search, the language of publication, and the types of materials you will need. Most databases enable you to focus a search easily. For example, if you were researching the corporate accounting scandals that occurred recently and wanted to look at articles published in a specific year, most search tools would enable you to limit your search to that period. All databases and search engines allow you to refine your search and increase the precision of your hits. In addition, for research in international business, don't limit yourself to English-language articles only; some Web sites, most notably AltaVista's Babel Fish, offer rough but free translations. What's more, many organizations overseas present their Web content in multiple languages.

Electronic resources may take time to master. Therefore, before wasting time and retrieving lots of useless material, talk to a university librarian. College and public libraries as well as some employers offer free access to several commercial databases, sparing you the high cost of individual subscriptions.

Commercial databases offer articles, reports, and other full-text information online.

The World Wide Web

If you are like most students today, you probably use the Web every day. You stay in touch with your friends by e-mail and instant messaging, and perhaps exchange text and picture messages using increasingly more capable cellular phones. Chances are you have a personal page on a social-networking site such as MySpace or Facebook, and perhaps you play one of the countless free online games. You have probably looked up directions on MapQuest and may have bid on or sold items on eBay. You are likely to download ring tones for your cell phone and perhaps you obtain your favorite music from iTunes, not some illegal file-sharing site. Your generation is much more likely to follow the news online than in the daily paper or even on TV. In short, you rely on the Internet daily for information and entertainment. You are part of a vast virtual community that, in turn, consists of many smaller communities all over the world. The Web and the Internet as a whole are referred to as a "global village" for a reason.

Understanding the Vastness and Complexity of the Web.
The Web is an amazing resource. It started as a fast, but exclusive network linking scientists, academics, military people, and other "tech heads." In the beginning information traveled purely in text form. Today the Web is user-friendly with multimedia content ranging from digital sound files to vivid images and video files. More important, the Web is considered an ever-expanding democratic medium where anyone can be a publisher and consume most of its boundless content free of charge. Armed with camera phones, average citizens post their

LEARNING OBJECTIVE 4
Comprehend the evolving nature of communication technology: the Web, electronic databases, and other resources for business writers and researchers.

Ethics Check

Web Piracy

As consumers of Web content, we are used to free information at our fingertips. Some have argued that the anonymity of the Web encourages piracy partly because users expect content to be free of charge. What type of information, if any, would you be willing to pay for?

videos on the hugely popular site YouTube and act as virtual reporters. Interest groups of all stripes gather in Usenet communities or newsgroups (digital bulletin boards and discussion forums). They exchange news, opinions, and other information. The fastest-growing sector of the Internet is blogs (short for weblogs); the sector is sometimes called the "blogosphere." These online journals allow users to comment on any imaginable topic or event and post their views instantly. Corporate blogs are also growing as companies begin to understand their marketing potential. In short, the Web is an invaluable resource, but report writers must approach it with caution and sound judgment.

- **Virtual communities.** The Web has fostered virtual communities and encourages teamwork among strangers all over the United States and globally. One such democratic, free-access tool is the wiki. This group communication software enables users to create and change Web pages. The best known perhaps is Wikipedia, a free online reference that can be edited even by a layperson. Behind company firewalls many wikis help technical experts and other specialists to collaborate.

- **Information mobility.** Digital content on the Web has also become more mobile in recent years. Thanks to browser-enabled smartphones and wireless personal digital assistants (PDAs), businesspeople can surf Web pages and write e-mail on the go with devices that fit into their pockets. Similarly, users can listen to podcasts, digital recordings of radio programs, and other audio files on demand. Podcasts are distributed for downloading to an MP3 audio player such as the iPod.

Information on the Web grows and changes constantly and is available on the go with handheld devices.

With nearly three quarters of Americans online[9] and literally trillions of pages of information available on the World Wide Web, odds are that if you have a question, an answer exists online. To a business researcher, the Web offers a wide range of organizational and commercial information. You can expect to find such items as product and service facts, public relations material, mission statements, staff directories, press releases, current company news, government information, selected article reprints, collaborative scientific project reports, and employment information.

Learning to navigate the depths of the Web will enable you to become a critical consumer of its information.

Although a wealth of information is available on the Web, finding exactly what you need can be frustrating and time-consuming. The constantly changing contents of the Web and its lack of organization make it more problematic for research than commercial databases, such as LexisNexis. Moreover, Web content is uneven, and often the quality is questionable. The problem of gathering information is complicated by the fact that the total number of Web sites recently surpassed 100 million, growing at the rate of about 4 million new addresses each month.[10]

To succeed in your search for information and answers, you need to understand the search tools available to you. You also need to understand how to evaluate the information you find.

Search tools such as Google, Yahoo, and MSN help you locate specific Web sites and information.

Identifying Search Tools. Finding what you are looking for on the Web is hopeless without powerful, specialized search tools such as Google, Yahoo, MSN, AOL, and Ask. These search tools can be divided into two types: subject (or Web) directories and search engines. In addition, some search engines specialize in "metasearching." This means they combine several powerful search engines into one (Dogpile). Large search sites such as Yahoo and Google Directory are actually search engines and subject directories combined. Subject directories fall into two categories—commercial ones (e.g., Yahoo, About, and others) and academic ones (e.g., InfoMine). Organized into subject categories, these human-compiled directories contain a collection of links to Internet resources submitted by site creators or evaluators.

Search engines differ in the way they trawl the vast amount of data on the Web. Google uses automated software "spiders" that crawl through the Web at regular intervals to collect and index the information from each location visited. Clusty by Vivísimo not only examines several search engines, but also groups results into topics called clusters. Some search tools (e.g., Ask) use natural language–processing technology to enable you to ask questions to gather information. Both search engines and subject directories will help you find specific information. Figure 11.8 shows Business.com, a search engine and subject directory in one. This resource indexes any imaginable business topic and is very useful to business communicators.

No search engine or directory indexes all Web pages.

Even though search engines such as Google boast about the numbers of items they have indexed—current estimates range from 20 to 24 billion[11]—no single search engine

FIGURE 11.8 Business.com

Source: Courtesy of Business.com.

or directory can come close to indexing all the pages on the Internet. However, if you try a multiple-search site such as Dogpile, you can save much time because its metasearch technology compares the results of at least seven major search engines, eliminates duplicates, and then ranks the best hits.[12] To help you search for data effectively, consider using the search tools listed in Figure 11.9.

Applying Internet Search Strategies and Techniques.

To conduct a thorough search for the information you need, build a (re)search strategy by understanding the tools available.

- **Use two or three search tools.** Begin by conducting a topic search. Use a subject directory such as Yahoo, About, or Open Directory Project. Once you have narrowed your topic, switch to a search engine or metasearch engine.

- **Know your search tool.** When connecting to a search site for the first time, always read the description of its service, including its FAQs (Frequently Asked Questions), Help, and How to Search sections. Often there are special features (e.g., the News, Images, Video, Books, and other categories on Google) that can speed up the search process.

- **Understand case sensitivity.** Generally use lowercase for your searches, unless you are searching for a term that is usually written in upper- and lowercase, such as a person's name.

- **Use nouns as search words and up to six to eight words in a query.** The right key words—and more of them—can narrow the search effectively.

- **Combine keywords into phrases.** Phrases, marked by the use of quotation marks (e.g., "business ethics"), will limit results to specific matches.

- **Omit articles and prepositions.** Known as "stop words," articles and prepositions do not add value to a search. Instead of *request for proposal,* use *proposal request.*

- **Use wildcards.** Most search engines support wildcards, such as asterisks. For example, the search term *cent** will retrieve *cents,* while *cent*** will retrieve both *center* and *centre.*

- **Learn basic Boolean search strategies.** You can save yourself a lot of time and frustration by narrowing your search with the following Boolean operators:

AND   Identifies only documents containing all of the specified words: **employee AND productivity AND morale**

OR   Identifies documents containing at least one of the specified words: **employee OR productivity OR morale**

Web research is often time-consuming and frustrating unless you know special search techniques.

FIGURE 11.9 Web Search Tools for Business Writers

Business Databases (subscription-based, commercial)	Features
ABI/INFORM Complete (ProQuest)	Best database for reliable, scholarly sources; recommended first stop for business students
LexisNexis Academic	Database of over 5,000 newspapers, magazines, etc.; very current; forces users to limit their search to fewer than 1,000 hits
Factiva	Stores over 5,000 periodicals; very current; best with narrow search subject or to add results to other searches (unlimited results)
JSTOR	Scholarly articles; best for historical, not current information
Search Engines (open-access business information)	
Business.com http://www.business.com	Search engine and subject directory/portal in one; features any business-related subject
BRINT BizTech Network http://www.brint.com/interest.html	Huge search portal; business research in information and technology; 20 main business subject categories
CEO Express http://www.ceoexpress.com	Human-selected directories of subjects relevant to business executives and researchers
Google Scholar http://scholar.google.com	Scholarly articles in various disciplines—business, administration, finance, and economics among them
Search Engines (general)	
Google http://www.google.com	Relevance ranking; most popular search site or portal; advanced search options and subject directories
Yahoo http://www.yahoo.com	Search engine and directory; popular free e-mail site; relevance ranking
All the Web http://www.alltheweb.com	Advanced search option; searches for audio and video files
Ask http://www.ask.com	Plain English (natural language) questions
Metasearch Engines (results from several search sites)	
Vivísimo/Clusty http://www.vivisimo.com http://clusty.com	Metasearch function clusters results into categories; offers advanced search options and help
InfoSpace http://www.infospace.com http://dogpile.com http://www.webcrawler.com http://www.metacrawler.com	Metasearch technology; searches Google, Yahoo, MSN Search, Ask, and more; owns other metasearch engines: **Dogpile, WebCrawler, MetaCrawler,** etc.
Search http://www.search.com	Searches Google, Ask, LookSmart, and dozens of other leading search engines
Subject Directories or Portals	
About http://www.about.com	Directory that organizes content from over 1.2 million sites with commentary from 500 "guides," chosen experts on 57,000+ topics
InfoMine http://infomine.ucr.edu	Directory of over 100,000 sites, grouped into nine indexed and annotated categories for scholarly research
Librarian's Internet Index http://lii.org	Over 20,000 entries; maintained by librarians and organized into 14 main topics and nearly 300 related topics

NOT   Excludes documents containing the specified word: **employee productivity NOT morale**

NEAR   Finds documents containing target words or phrases within a specified distance, for instance, within 10 words: **employee NEAR productivity.**

- **Bookmark the best.** To keep track of your favorite Internet sites, save them as bookmarks or favorites.

- **Keep trying.** If a search produces no results, check your spelling. If you are using Boolean operators, check the syntax of your queries. Try synonyms and variations on words. Try to be less specific in your search term. If your search produces too many hits, try to be more specific. Use the Advanced feature of your search engine to narrow your search. Think of words that uniquely identify what you're looking for. Use as many relevant keywords as possible.

- **Repeat your search a week later.** For the best results, return to your search a couple of days or a week later. The same keywords will probably produce additional results. That's because millions of new pages are being added to the Web every day.

Remember, subject directories and search engines vary in their contents, features, selectivity, accuracy, and retrieval technologies. Only through clever cybersearching can you uncover the jewels hidden in the Internet.

Evaluating Web Sources.
Most of us using the Web have a tendency to assume that any information turned up by a search engine has somehow been evaluated as part of a valid selection process. Wrong! The truth is that the Internet is rampant with unreliable sites that reside side by side with reputable sites. Anyone with a computer and an Internet connection can publish anything on the Web. Unlike library-based research, information at many sites has not undergone the editing or scrutiny of scholarly publication procedures. The information we read in journals and most reputable magazines is reviewed, authenticated, and evaluated. That's why we have learned to trust these sources as valid and authoritative.

Information on the Web is much less reliable than data from traditional sources. Wikis, blogs, and discussion forum entries are a case in point. Although they turn up in many Internet searches, they are mostly useless because they are short-lived. They change constantly

Search engines vary in their ability to retrieve data. Learn about their advanced features, and then practice using them.

TechTalk

Managing Your Electronic Research Data Like a Pro

In amassing electronic data, you can easily lose track of Web sites and articles you quoted. To document Web data that may change as well as to manage all of your electronic data, you need a specific plan for saving sources. At the very least, you will want to create a *working bibliography* in which you record the URL of each electronic source and its access date. Here are techniques that can help you build your bibliography as well as manage your electronic data like a pro:

- **Saving sources to disk** has advantages, including being able to open the document in a browser even if you don't have access to the Internet. More important, saving sources to disk or memory stick ensures that you will have access to information that may or may not be available later. Using either the **File** and **Save As** or the **File** and **Save Page As** menu command in your browser, you will be able to store the information permanently. Saving images and other kinds of media can be accomplished with your mouse by either right-clicking or command clicking on the item, followed by a command such as **Save Picture As** or **Save Image As** from a pop-up window.
- **Copying and pasting** information you find on the Web into word processing documents is an easy way to save and store it. Remember to also copy and paste the URL into the file as well, and record the URL in your working bibliography.
- **Printing** pages is a handy way to gather and store information. Doing so enables you to have copies of important data that you can annotate or highlight. Make sure the URL prints with the document (usually on the bottom of the page). If not, write it on the page.

- **Bookmarking favorites** is an option within browsers to enable users to record and store the URLs for important sources. The key to using this option is learning to create folders with names that are relevant and to use names for bookmarks that make sense and are not redundant. If no name is provided, the browser will default to the URL.
- **E-mailing** documents, URLs, or messages to yourself is another useful strategy. Many databases and online magazines permit you to e-mail information and sometimes the entire article to your account. If you combine the copy-and-paste function with e-mail, you can send yourself nearly any information you find on the Web.

Career Application

Use Google or another search engine that supports Boolean searches to investigate a topic such as corporate social responsibility. Explore the same topic using (a) keywords and (b) Boolean operators. Which method produces more relevant hits? Save two relevant sources from each search using two or more of the strategies presented here. Remember to include the URL for each article. In a memo to your instructor, list the bibliographic information from all four sources and explain briefly which method was more productive.

and may disappear fast, so that your source can't be verified. Academic researchers prefer lasting, scholarly sources. Many professors will not allow you to cite from Wikipedia, for example, because this collaborative tool and online reference can be edited by any contributor and is considered to be unreliable. Moreover, citing from an encyclopedia shows poor research skills. Some Web sites exist to propagandize; others want to sell you something. To use the Web meaningfully, you must scrutinize what you find and check who authored and published it. Here are specific questions to ask as you examine a site:

Evaluate the currency, authority, content, and accuracy of Web sites carefully.

- **Currency.** What is the date of the Web page? When was it last updated? Is some of the information obviously out-of-date? If the information is time sensitive and the site has not been updated recently, the site is probably not reliable.

- **Authority.** Who publishes or sponsors this Web page? What makes the presenter an authority? Is information about the author or creator available? Is a contact address available for the presenter? Learn to be skeptical about data and assertions from individuals and organizations whose credentials are not verifiable.

- **Content.** Is the purpose of the page to entertain, inform, convince, or sell? How would you classify this page (e.g., news, personal, advocacy, reference)? Who is the intended audience, based on content, tone, and style? Can you judge the overall value of the content compared with the other resources on this topic? Web presenters with a slanted point of view cannot be counted on for objective data. Be particularly cautious with blogs. They often abound with grandstanding and ranting but lack factual information. Read them side by side with reputable news sources.

- **Accuracy.** Do the facts that are presented seem reliable to you? Do you find errors in spelling, grammar, or usage? Do you see any evidence of bias? Are footnotes provided? If you find numerous errors and if facts are not referenced, you should be alert that the data may be questionable.

Gathering Information From Primary Sources

LEARNING OBJECTIVE 5
Understand how to generate and use primary data while avoiding researcher bias.

Up to this point, we have been talking about secondary data. You should begin nearly every business report assignment by evaluating the available secondary data. However, you will probably need primary data to give a complete picture. Business reports that solve specific current problems typically rely on primary, firsthand data. If, for example, management wants to discover the cause of increased employee turnover in its Seattle office, it must investigate conditions in Seattle by collecting recent information. Providing answers to business problems often means generating primary data through surveys, interviews, observation, or experimentation.

Business reports often rely on primary data from firsthand experience.

Surveys

Surveys yield efficient and economical primary data for reports.

Surveys collect data from groups of people. When companies develop new products, for example, they often survey consumers to learn their needs. The advantages of surveys are that they gather data economically and efficiently. Mailed surveys reach big groups nearby or at great distances. Moreover, people responding to mailed surveys have time to consider their answers, thus improving the accuracy of the data.

Mailed questionnaires, of course, have disadvantages. Most of us rank them with junk mail, so response rates may be no higher than 5 percent. Furthermore, those who do respond may not represent an accurate sample of the overall population, thus invalidating generalizations from the group. Let's say, for example, that an insurance company sends out a questionnaire asking about provisions in a new policy. If only older people respond, the questionnaire data cannot be used to generalize what people in other age groups might think. A final problem with surveys has to do with truthfulness. Some respondents exaggerate their incomes or distort other facts, thus causing the results to be unreliable. Nevertheless, surveys may be the best way to generate data for business and student reports. In preparing print or electronic surveys, consider these pointers:

- **Select the survey population carefully.** Many surveys question a small group of people (a sample) and project the findings to a larger population. Let's say that a survey

In its annual reports FedEx aims to communicate not only the company's financials but also its service pledge, "The Purple Promise." At the heart of The Purple Promise is the trusted relationship FedEx develops with businesses and nonprofit organizations that rely upon the express delivery giant for shipping. The company's annual report features customer success stories, such as FedEx's role in aiding tsunami victims, which capture the reader's attention and put a human face on the firm's detailed financial data. *What primary and secondary sources are commonly used for writing annual reports?*

of your class reveals that the majority prefer Chicago-style pizza. Can you then say with confidence that all students on your campus (or in the nation) prefer Chicago-style pizza? To be able to generalize from a survey, you need to make the sample as large as possible. In addition, you need to determine whether the sample is like the larger population. For important surveys you will want to consult books on or experts in sampling techniques.

- **Explain why the survey is necessary.** In a cover letter or an opening paragraph, describe the need for the survey. Suggest how someone or something other than you will benefit. If appropriate, offer to send recipients a copy of the findings.

- **Consider incentives.** If the survey is long, persuasive techniques may be necessary. Response rates can be increased by offering money (such as a $1 bill), coupons, gift certificates, free books, or other gifts.

- **Limit the number of questions.** Resist the temptation to ask for too much. Request only information you will use. Don't, for example, include demographic questions (income, gender, age, and so forth) unless the information is necessary to evaluate responses.

- **Use questions that produce quantifiable answers.** Check-off, multiple-choice, yes-no, and scale (or rank-order) questions, illustrated in Figure 11.10, provide quantifiable data that are easily tabulated. Responses to open-ended questions (*What should the bookstore do about plastic bags?*) reveal interesting, but difficult-to-quantify, perceptions.[13] To obtain workable data, give interviewees a list of possible responses, as shown in items 5 through 8 of Figure 11.10. For scale and multiple-choice questions, try to present all the possible answer choices. To be safe, add an "Other" or "Don't know" category in case the choices seem insufficient to the respondent. Many surveys use scale questions because they capture degrees of feelings. Typical scale headings are "agree strongly," "agree somewhat," "neutral," "disagree somewhat," and "disagree strongly."

- **Avoid leading or ambiguous questions.** The wording of a question can dramatically affect responses to it.[14] When respondents were asked, "Are we spending too much, too little, or about the right amount on *assistance to the poor?*" [emphasis added],

Effective surveys target appropriate samples and ask a limited number of specific questions.

The way a question is stated influences its response.

FIGURE 11.10 Preparing a Survey

1 Prewriting

Analyze: The purpose is to help the bookstore decide whether it should replace plastic bags with cloth bags for customer purchases.

Anticipate: The audience will be busy students who will be initially uninterested.

Adapt: Because students will be unwilling to participate, the survey must be short and simple. Its purpose must be significant and clear.

2 Writing

Research: Ask students how they would react to cloth bags. Use their answers to form question response choices.

Organize: Open by explaining the survey's purpose and importance. In the body ask clear questions that produce quantifiable answers. Conclude with appreciation and instructions.

Compose: Write the first draft of the questionnaire.

3 Revising

Revise: Try out the questionnaire with a small, representative group. Revise unclear questions.

Proofread: Read for correctness. Be sure that answer choices do not overlap and that they are complete. Provide "other" category if appropriate (as in No. 9).

Evaluate: Is the survey clear, attractive, and easy to complete?

North Shore College Bookstore
STUDENT SURVEY

The North Shore College Bookstore wants to do its part in protecting the environment. Each year we give away 45,000 plastic bags for students to carry off their purchases. We are considering changing from plastic to cloth bags or some other alternative, but we need your views.

Explains need for survey (use cover letter for longer surveys)

Please place checks below to indicate your responses.

Uses groupings that do not overlap (not 9 to 15 and 15 or more)

1. How many units are you presently carrying?
   ___ 15 or more units
   ___ 9 to 14 units
   ___ 8 or fewer units

   ___ Male
   ___ Female

2. How many times have you visited the bookstore this semester?
   ___ 0 times ___ 1 time ___ 2 times ___ 3 times ___ 4 or more times

3. Indicate your concern for the environment.
   ___ Very concerned ___ Concerned ___ Unconcerned

4. To protect the environment, would you be willing to change to another type of bag when buying books?
   ___ Yes
   ___ No

Indicate your feeling about the following alternatives.

	Agree	Undecided	Disagree
For major purchases the bookstore should			
5. Continue to provide plastic bags.	___	___	___
6. Provide no bags; encourage students to bring their own bags.	___	___	___
7. Provide no bags; offer cloth bags at reduced price (about $3).	___	___	___
8. Give a cloth bag with each major purchase, the cost to be included in registration fees.	___	___	___

Uses scale questions to channel responses into quantifiable alternatives, as opposed to open-ended questions

9. Consider another alternative, such as

_____

Allows respondent to add an answer in case choices provided seem insufficient

Please return the completed survey form to your instructor or to the survey box at the North Shore College Bookstore exit. Your opinion counts.

Tells how to return survey form

Thanks for your help!

---

13 percent responded "too much." When the same respondents were asked, "Are we spending too much, too little, or about the right amount on *welfare?*"[emphasis added], 44 percent responded "too much." Because words have different meanings for different people, you must strive to use objective language and pilot test your questions with typical respondents. Stay away from questions that suggest an answer (*Don't you agree that the salaries of CEOs are obscenely high?*). Instead, ask neutral questions (*Do CEOs earn too much, too little, or about the right amount?*). Also avoid queries that really ask two or more things (*Should the salaries of CEOs be reduced or regulated by government legislation?*). Instead, break them into separate questions (*Should the salaries of CEOs be reduced by government legislation? Should the salaries of CEOs be regulated by government legislation?*).

- **Make it easy for respondents to return the survey.** Provide a stamped, return-addressed envelope, a handy collection box, or some other means for respondents to submit the survey.

- **Conduct a pilot study.** Try the questionnaire with a small group so that you can remedy any problems. For example, in the survey shown in Figure 11.10, a pilot study revealed that female students generally favored cloth book bags and were willing to pay for them. Male students opposed purchasing cloth bags. By adding a gender category, researchers could verify this finding. The pilot study also revealed the need to ensure an appropriate representation of male and female students in the survey.

Interviews

Some of the best report information, particularly on topics about which little has been written, comes from individuals. These individuals are usually experts or veterans in their fields. Consider both in-house and outside experts for business reports. Tapping these sources will call for in-person, telephone, or online interviews. To elicit the most useful data, try these techniques:

Interviews with experts yield useful report data, especially when little has been written about a topic.

- **Locate an expert.** Ask managers and individuals whom they consider to be most knowledgeable in their areas. Check membership lists of professional organizations, and consult articles about the topic or related topics. Most people enjoy being experts or at least recommending them. You could also post an inquiry to an Internet newsgroup. An easy way to search newsgroups in a topic area is through the **Browse all groups** category indexed by the popular search tool Google.

- **Prepare for the interview.** Learn about the individual you are interviewing, and make sure you can pronounce his or her name. Research the background and terminology of the topic. Let's say you are interviewing a corporate communication expert about producing an in-house newsletter. You ought to be familiar with terms such as *font* and software such as QuarkXPress and Adobe InDesign. In addition, be prepared by making a list of questions that pinpoint your focus on the topic. Ask the interviewee if you may record the talk.

- **Maintain a professional attitude.** Call before the interview to confirm the arrangements, and then arrive on time. Be prepared to take notes if your recorder fails (and remember to ask permission beforehand if you want to record). Use your body language to convey respect.

- **Make your questions objective and friendly.** Adopt a courteous and respectful attitude. Don't get into a debating match with the interviewee. Remember that you are there to listen, not to talk! Use open-ended, rather than yes-or-no, questions to draw experts out.

- **Watch the time.** Tell interviewees in advance how much time you expect to need for the interview. Don't overstay your appointment.

- **End graciously.** Conclude the interview with a general question, such as "Is there anything you would like to add?" Express your appreciation, and ask permission to telephone later if you need to verify points.

Observation and Experimentation

Some kinds of primary data can be obtained only through firsthand observation and investigation. If you determine that the questions you have require observational data, then you need to plan the observations carefully. One of the most important questions is to ask what or whom you're observing and how often those observations are necessary to provide reliable data. For example, if you want to learn more about an organization's customer service phone service, you probably need to conduct an observation (along with interviews and perhaps even surveys). You will want to answer questions such as, "How long does a typical caller wait before a customer service rep answers the call?" and "Is the service consistent?" Recording observations for 60-minute periods at different times throughout a week will give you a better picture than just observing for an hour on a Friday before a holiday.

When you observe, plan ahead. Arrive early enough to introduce yourself and set up whatever equipment you think is necessary. Make sure that you've received permissions beforehand, particularly if you are recording. In addition, take notes, not only of the events or actions but also of the settings. Changes in environment often have an effect on actions.

Experimentation produces data suggesting causes and effects. Informal experimentation might be as simple as a pretest and posttest in a college course. Did students expand their knowledge as a result of the course? More formal experimentation is undertaken by scientists and professional researchers who control variables to test their effects. Assume, for example, that the Hershey Company wants to test the hypothesis (which is a tentative assumption) that chocolate lifts people out of the doldrums. An experiment testing the hypothesis would separate depressed individuals into two groups: those who ate chocolate (the experimental group) and those who did not (the control group). What effect did chocolate have? Such experiments are not done haphazardly, however. Valid experiments require sophisticated research designs and careful attention to matching the experimental and control groups.

Some of the best report data come from firsthand observation and investigation.

Documenting Data

LEARNING OBJECTIVE 6
Recognize the purposes and techniques of documentation in business reports and avoid plagiarism.

In writing business and other reports, you will often build on the ideas and words of others. In Western culture, whenever you "borrow" the ideas of others, you must give credit to your information sources. This is called *documentation*.

Recognizing the Purposes of Documentation

As a careful writer, you should take pains to properly document report data for the following reasons:

Documenting data lends credibility, protects the writer from charges of plagiarism, and aids the reader.

- **To strengthen your argument.** Including good data from reputable sources will convince readers of your credibility and the logic of your reasoning.

- **To protect yourself against charges of plagiarism.** Acknowledging your sources keeps you honest. Plagiarism, which is illegal and unethical, is the act of using others' ideas without proper documentation.

- **To instruct the reader.** Citing references enables readers to pursue a topic further and make use of the information themselves.

Distinguishing Between Academic Documentation and Business Practices

In the academic world, documentation is critical. Especially in the humanities and sciences, students are taught to cite sources by using quotation marks, parenthetical citations, footnotes, and bibliographies. College term papers require full documentation to demonstrate that a student has become familiar with respected sources and can cite them properly in developing an argument. Giving credit to the author is extremely important. Students who plagiarize risk a failing grade in a class and even expulsion from school.

In the business world, however, documentation is often viewed differently. Business communicators on the job may find that much of what is written does not follow the standards they learned in school.[15] In many instances, individual authorship is unimportant. For example, employees may write for the signature of their bosses. The writer receives no credit. Similarly, team projects turn out documents written by many people, none of whom receives individual credit. Internal business reports, which often include chunks of information from previous reports, also fail to acknowledge sources or give credit. Even information from outside sources may lack proper documentation. Yet, if facts are questioned, business writers must be able to produce their source materials.

Although both internal and external business reports are not as heavily documented as school assignments or term papers, business communication students are well advised to learn proper documentation methods. Your instructor may use a commercial plagiarism detection service such as Turnitin.com, which can cross-reference much of the information on the Web, looking for documents with similar phrasing. The result, an "originality report," will provide the instructor with a clear idea of whether you've been accurate and honest.

Plagiarism of words or ideas is a serious charge and can lead to loss of a job. Famous historians, several high-level journalists, and recently a professor at the University of Cincinnati[16] suffered serious consequences for copying from unnamed sources. You can avoid charges of plagiarism as well as add clarity to your work by knowing what to document and by developing good research habits.

Learning What to Document

When you write reports, especially in college, you are continually dealing with other people's ideas. You are expected to conduct research, synthesize ideas, and build on the work of others. But you are also expected to give proper credit for borrowed material. To avoid plagiarism, you must give credit whenever you use the following:[17]

- Another person's ideas, opinions, examples, or theory
- Any facts, statistics, graphs, and drawings that are not common knowledge
- Quotations of another person's actual spoken or written words
- Paraphrases of another person's spoken or written words

Information that is common knowledge requires no documentation. For example, the statement *The Wall Street Journal is a popular business newspaper* would require no citation. Statements that are not common knowledge, however, must be documented. For example, *Eight of the nation's top 10 fastest growing large cities (100,000 or more population) since Census 2000 lie in the Western states of Arizona, Nevada, and California* would require a citation because most people do not know this fact. Cite sources for proprietary information such as statistics organized and reported by a newspaper or magazine. You probably know to use citations to document direct quotations, but you must also cite ideas that you summarize in your own words.

Developing Good Research Habits

Report writers who are gathering information have two methods available for recording the information they find. The time-honored manual method of notetaking works well because information is recorded on separate cards, which can then be arranged in the order needed to develop a thesis or argument. Today, though, writers rely heavily on electronic researching. Traditional notetaking methods may seem antiquated and laborious in comparison. Let's explore both methods.

Manual Notetaking.
To make sure you know whose ideas you are using, train yourself to take excellent notes. If possible, know what you intend to find before you begin your research so that you won't waste time on unnecessary notes. Here are some pointers on taking good notes.

- Record all major ideas from various sources on separate note cards.

- Include all publication information (author, date, title, and so forth) along with precise quotations.

- Consider using one card color for direct quotes and a different color for your paraphrases and summaries.

- Put the original source material aside when you are summarizing or paraphrasing.

Set up a folder for electronic notes, but be careful not to cut and paste excessively in writing reports.

Electronic Notetaking. Instead of recording facts on note cards, savvy researchers today take advantage of electronic tools, as noted in the earlier Tech Talk box. Beware, though, not to cut-and-paste your way into plagiarism. Here are some pointers on taking good electronic notes:

- Begin your research by setting up a folder on your hard drive. On the go, you can use a storage device such as a USB flash drive, CD-RW, or computer disk to carry your data.

- Create subfolders for major sections, such as introduction, body, and closing.

- When you find facts on the Web or in electronic databases, highlight the material you want to record, copy it, and paste it into a document in an appropriate folder.

- Be sure to include all publication data.

- As discussed in the section on managing research data, consider archiving on a memory stick those Web pages or articles used in your research in case the data must be verified.

Practicing the Fine Art of Paraphrasing

In writing reports and using the ideas of others, you will probably rely heavily on *paraphrasing,* which means restating an original passage in your own words and in your own style. To do a good job of paraphrasing, follow these steps:

Paraphrasing involves putting an original passage into your own words.

- Read the original material intently to comprehend its full meaning.

- Write your own version without looking at the original.

- Avoid repeating the grammatical structure of the original and merely replacing words with synonyms.

- Reread the original to be sure you covered the main points but did not borrow specific language.

To better understand the difference between plagiarizing and paraphrasing, study the following passages. Notice that the writer of the plagiarized version uses the same grammatical construction as the source and often merely replaces words with synonyms. Even the acceptable version, however, requires a reference to the source author.

Source
While the BlackBerry has become standard armor for executives, a few maverick leaders are taking action to reduce e-mail use. . . . The concern, say academics and management thinkers, is misinterpreted messages, as well as the degree to which e-mail has become a substitute for the nuanced conversations that are critical in the workplace.[18]

The plagiarized version uses the same sentence structure as the original and makes few changes other than replacing some words.

Plagiarized Version
Although smartphones are standard among business executives, some pioneering bosses are acting to lower e-mail usage. Business professors and management experts are concerned that messages are misinterpreted and that e-mail substitutes for nuances in conversations that are crucial on the job (Brady, 2006).

The acceptable paraphrase presents ideas from a different perspective and uses a different sentence structure than the original.

Acceptable Paraphrase
E-mail on the go may be the rage in business. However, some executives are rethinking its use, as communication experts warn that e-mail triggers misunderstandings. These specialists believe that e-mail should not replace the more subtle face-to-face interaction needed on the job (Brady, 2006).

Knowing When and How to Quote

On occasion you will want to use the exact words of a source. But beware of overusing quotations. Documents that contain pages of spliced-together quotations suggest that writers have few ideas of their own. Wise writers and speakers use direct quotations for three purposes only:

- To provide objective background data and establish the severity of a problem as seen by experts

- To repeat identical phrasing because of its precision, clarity, or aptness

- To duplicate exact wording before criticizing

Use quotation only to cite experts, to repeat memorable phrasing, or to reproduce exact wording before criticizing.

When you must use a long quotation, try to summarize and introduce it in your own words. Readers want to know the gist of a quotation before they tackle it. For example, to introduce a quotation discussing the shrinking staffs of large companies, you could precede it with your words: *In predicting employment trends, Charles Waller believes the corporation of the future will depend on a small core of full-time employees.* To introduce quotations or paraphrases, use wording such as the following:

According to Waller, ...

Waller argues that . . . .

In his recent study, Waller reported . . . .

Use quotation marks to enclose exact quotations, as shown in the following: "The current image," says Charles Waller, "of a big glass-and-steel corporate headquarters on landscaped grounds directing a worldwide army of tens of thousands of employees may soon be a thing of the past" (2006, p. 51).

Using Citation Formats

You can direct readers to your sources with parenthetical notes inserted into the text and with bibliographies. The most common citation formats are those presented by the Modern Language Association (MLA) and the American Psychological Association (APA). Learn more about how to use these formats in Appendix C.

Illustrating Data

After collecting and interpreting information, you need to consider how best to present it. If your report contains complex data and numbers, you may want to consider using graphics such as tables and charts. These graphics clarify data, create visual interest, and make numerical data meaningful. By simplifying complex ideas and emphasizing key data, well-constructed graphics make key information easier to remember. However, the same data can be shown in many forms, for example, in a chart, table, or graph. That's why you need to recognize how to match the appropriate graphic with your objective and incorporate it into your report.

LEARNING OBJECTIVE 7
Illustrate reports with graphics that create meaning and interest; display numeric information in the appropriate graphic form; and show skill in generating, using, and converting data to visual aids.

Matching Graphics and Objectives

In developing the best graphics, you must decide what data you want to highlight and which graphics are most appropriate to your objectives. Tables? Bar charts? Pie charts? Line charts? Surface charts? Flowcharts? Organization charts? Pictures? Figure 11.11 summarizes appropriate uses for each type of graphic. The following text discusses each visual in more detail.

Effective graphics clarify numerical data and simplify complex ideas.

Tables. Probably the most frequently used graphic in reports is the table. Because a table presents quantitative or verbal information in systematic columns and rows, it can clarify large quantities of data in small spaces. The disadvantage is that tables do not readily display trends. You may have made rough tables to help you organize the raw data collected from questionnaires or interviews. In preparing tables for your readers or listeners, though,

Tables permit the systematic presentation of large amounts of data, whereas charts and graphs enhance visual comparisons.

FIGURE 11.11 Matching Graphics to Objectives

Graphic		Objective
Table	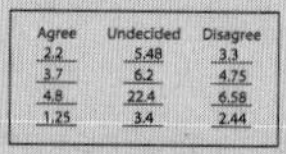	To show exact figures and values
Bar chart		To compare one item with others
Line chart	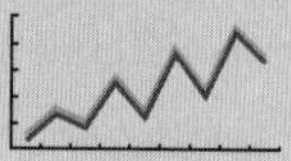	To demonstrate changes in quantitative data over time
Pie chart		To visualize a whole unit and the proportions of its components
Flowchart	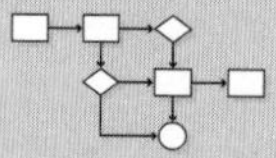	To display a process or procedure
Organization chart	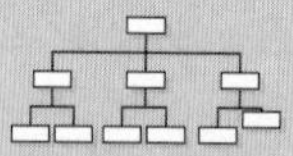	To define a hierarchy of elements
Photograph, map, illustration		To create authenticity, to spotlight a location, and to show an item in use

you will need to pay more attention to clarity and emphasis. Here are tips for making good tables, such as the one in Figure 11.12:

- Place titles and labels at the top of the table.

- Arrange items in a logical order (alphabetical, chronological, geographical, highest to lowest), depending on what you need to emphasize.

- Provide clear headings for the rows and columns.

- Identify the units in which figures are given (percentages, dollars, units per worker hour, and so forth) in the table title, in the column or row heading, with the first item in a column, or in a note at the bottom.

FIGURE 11.12 Table Summarizing Precise Data

Figure 1 MPM ENTERTAINMENT COMPANY Income by Division (in millions of dollars)				
	Theme Parks	Motion Pictures	DVDs & Videos	Total
2005	$15.8	$39.3	$11.2	$66.3
2006	18.1	17.5	15.3	50.9
2007	23.8	21.1	22.7	67.6
2008	32.2	22.0	24.3	78.5
2009 (projected)	35.1	21.0	26.1	82.2

Source: *Industry Profiles* (New York: DataPro, 2008) 225.

- Use *N/A* (not available) for missing data.

- Make long tables easier to read by shading alternate lines or by leaving a blank line after groups of five.

- Place tables as close as possible to the place where they are mentioned in the text.

Figure 11.11 shows how various graphics are effective in serving different purposes. Tables are especially suitable for illustrating exact figures in systematic rows and columns. The table in Figure 11.12 is particularly useful because it presents data about the MPM Entertainment Company over several years, making it easy to compare several divisions. Figures 11.13 through 11.16 highlight some of the data shown in the MPM Entertainment Company table, illustrating vertical, horizontal, grouped, and segmented bar charts, each of which achieves a different effect.

Selecting the appropriate graphic depends on the purpose that it serves.

FIGURE 11.13 Vertical Bar Chart

Figure 1
2008 MPM INCOME BY DIVISION

Source: *Industry Profiles* (New York: DataPro, 2008), 225.

FIGURE 11.14 Horizontal Bar Chart

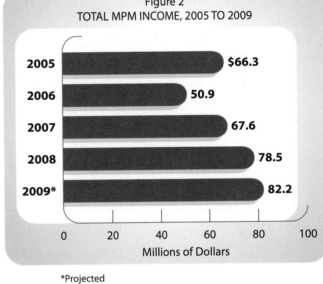

Figure 2
TOTAL MPM INCOME, 2005 TO 2009

*Projected
Source: *Industry Profiles.*

FIGURE 11.15 Grouped Bar Chart

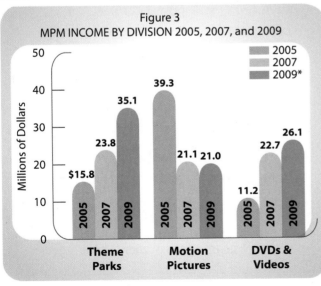

Figure 3
MPM INCOME BY DIVISION 2005, 2007, and 2009

*Projected
Source: *Industry Profiles.*

FIGURE 11.16 Segmented 100% Bar Chart

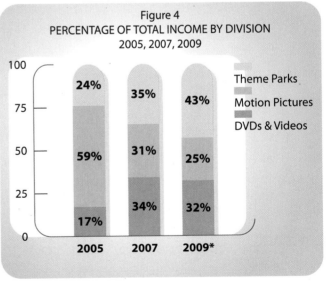

Figure 4
PERCENTAGE OF TOTAL INCOME BY DIVISION
2005, 2007, 2009

*Projected
Source: *Industry Profiles.*

Bar Charts. Although they lack the precision of tables, bar charts enable you to make emphatic visual comparisons by using horizontal or vertical bars of varying lengths. Bar charts are useful to compare related items, illustrate changes in data over time, and show segments as a part of the whole. Note how the varied bar charts present information in differing ways.

Many techniques for constructing tables also hold true for bar charts. Here are a few additional tips:

- Keep the length and width of each bar and segment proportional.

- Include a total figure in the middle of the bar or at its end if the figure helps the reader and does not clutter the chart.

- Start dollar or percentage amounts at zero.

- Place the first bar at some distance (usually half the amount of space between bars) from the *y* axis.

- Avoid showing too much information, thus producing clutter and confusion.

- Place each bar chart as close as possible to the place where it is mentioned in the text.

Line charts illustrate trends and changes in data over time.

Line Charts. The major advantage of line charts is that they show changes over time, thus indicating trends. The vertical axis is typically the dependent variable, and the horizontal axis the independent one. Simple line charts (Figure 11.17) show just one variable. Multiple line charts compare items, such as two or more data sets, using the same variable (Figure 11.18). Segmented line charts (Figure 11.19), also called surface charts, illustrate how the components of a whole change over time. To prepare a line chart, remember these tips:

- Begin with a grid divided into squares.

- Arrange the time component (usually years) horizontally across the bottom; arrange values for the other variable vertically.

- Draw small dots at the intersections to indicate each value at a given year.

- Connect the dots and add color if desired.

- To prepare a segmented (surface) chart, plot the first value (say, DVD and video income) across the bottom; add the next item (say, motion picture income) to the first figures for

FIGURE 11.17 Simple Line Chart

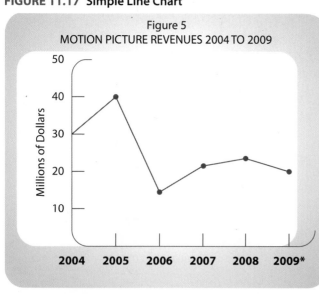

*Projected
Source: *Industry Profiles.*

FIGURE 11.18 Multiple Line Chart

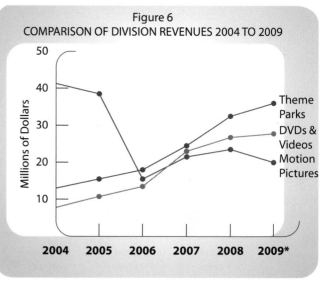

*Projected
Source: *Industry Profiles.*

FIGURE 11.19 Segmented Line (Surface) Chart   **FIGURE 11.20 Pie Chart**

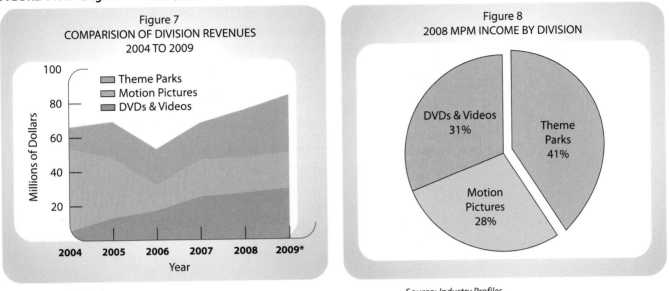

Figure 7
COMPARISION OF DIVISION REVENUES
2004 TO 2009

Theme Parks
Motion Pictures
DVDs & Videos

Millions of Dollars

2004 2005 2006 2007 2008 2009*
Year

*Projected
Source: *Industry Profiles.*

Figure 8
2008 MPM INCOME BY DIVISION

DVDs & Videos
31%

Theme
Parks
41%

Motion
Pictures
28%

Source: *Industry Profiles.*

every increment; for the third item (say, theme park income), add its value to the total for the first two items. The top line indicates the total of the three values.

Pie Charts. Pie, or circle, charts enable readers to see a whole and the proportion of its components, or wedges. Although less flexible than bar or line charts, pie charts are useful in showing percentages, as Figure 11.20 illustrates. They are very effective for lay or nonexpert audiences. Notice that a wedge can be "exploded" or popped out for special emphasis, as seen in Figure 11.20. For the most effective pie charts, follow these suggestions:

Pie charts are most useful in showing the proportion of parts to a whole.

- Make the biggest wedge appear first. Remember that beginning at the 12 o'clock position, computer spreadsheet programs correctly assign the biggest wedge first and arrange the others in order of decreasing size as long as you list the data representing each wedge on the spreadsheet in descending order.

- Include, if possible, the actual percentage or absolute value for each wedge.

- Use four to six segments for best results; if necessary, group small portions into a wedge called "other."

- Draw radii from the center.

- Distinguish wedges with color, shading, or cross-hatching.

- Keep all the labels horizontal.

Flowcharts. Procedures are simplified and clarified by diagramming them in a flowchart, as shown in Figure 11.21. Whether you need to describe the procedure for handling a customer's purchase, highlight steps in solving a problem, or display a problem with a process, flowcharts help the reader visualize the process. Traditional flowcharts use the following symbols:

- Ovals to designate the beginning and end of a process

- Diamonds to designate decision points

- Rectangles to represent major activities or steps

Organization Charts. Many large organizations are so complex that they need charts to show the chain of command, from the boss down to the line managers and employees. Organization charts like the one in Figure 1.9 in Chapter 1 provide such information as who

Organization charts show the line of command and thus the flow of official communication from management to employees.

FIGURE 11.21 Flowchart

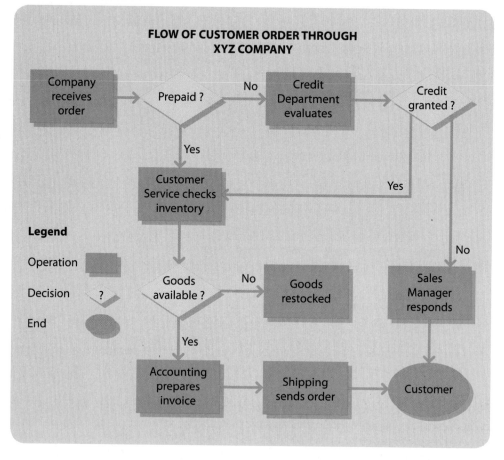

reports to whom, how many subordinates work for each manager (the span of control), and what channels of official communication exist. These charts may illustrate a company's structure, for example, by function, customer, or product. They may also be organized by the work being performed in each job or by the hierarchy of decision making.

Photographs, Maps, and Illustrations. Some business reports include photographs, maps, and illustrations to serve specific purposes. Photos, for example, add authenticity and provide a visual record. An environmental engineer may use photos to document hazardous waste sites. Maps enable report writers to depict activities or concentrations geographically, such as dots indicating sales reps in states across the country. Illustrations and diagrams are useful in indicating how an object looks or operates. A drawing showing the parts of a printer with labels describing their functions, for example, is more instructive than a photograph or verbal description. With today's computer technology, photographs, maps, and illustrations can be scanned directly into business reports, or they can be accessed through hyperlinks within an electronically delivered document.

Computer technology permits photographs, maps, and illustrations to be hyperlinked to content or scanned directly into reports.

Incorporating Graphics in Reports

Used appropriately, graphics make reports more interesting and easier to understand. In putting graphics into your reports, follow these suggestions for best effects:

Effective graphics are accurate and ethical; they do not overuse color or decorations; and they include titles or labels.

- **Evaluate the audience.** Consider the reader, the content, your schedule, and your budget. Graphics take time and can be costly to print in color, so think carefully before deciding how many graphics to use. Six charts in an internal report to an executive may seem like overkill; but in a long technical report to outsiders, six may be too few.

- **Use restraint.** Don't overuse color or decorations. Although color can effectively distinguish bars or segments in charts, too much color can be distracting and confusing.

Remember, too, that colors themselves sometimes convey meaning: reds suggest deficits or negative values; blues suggest calmness and authority; and yellow may suggest warning.

- **Be accurate and ethical.** Double-check all graphics for accuracy of figures and calculations. Be certain that your visuals aren't misleading—either accidentally or intentionally. Manipulation of a chart scale can make trends look steeper and more dramatic than they really are. Moreover, be sure to cite sources when you use someone else's facts. The accompanying Ethical Insights box discusses in more detail how to make ethical charts and graphs.

- **Introduce a graph meaningfully.** Refer to every graphic in the text, and place the graphic close to the point where it is mentioned. Most important, though, help the reader understand the significance of the graphic. You can do this by telling the reader what to look for or by summarizing the main point of the graphic. Don't assume the reader will automatically draw the same conclusions you reached from a set of data. Instead of *The findings are shown in Figure 3,* tell the reader what to look for: *Two thirds*

Graphics should be introduced by statements that help readers interpret them.

Ethical Insights

Making Ethical Charts and Graphics

Business communicators must present graphical data in the same ethical, honest manner required for all other messages. Remember that the information shown in your charts and graphics will be used to inform others or help them make decisions. If this information is not represented accurately, the reader will be incorrectly informed; any decisions based on the data are likely to be faulty. And mistakes in interpreting such information may have serious and long-lasting consequences.

Chart data can be distorted in many ways. Figure 1 shows advertising expenses displayed on an appropriate scale. Figure 2 shows the same information, but the horizontal scale, from 2004 to 2009, has been lengthened. Notice that the data have not changed, but the increases and decreases are smoothed out, so changes in expenses appear to be slight. In Figure 3 the vertical scale is taller and the horizontal scale is shortened, resulting in what appear to be sharp increases and decreases in expenses.

To avoid misrepresenting data, keep the following pointers in mind when designing your graphics:

- Use an appropriate type of chart or graphic for the message you wish to convey.

- Design the chart so that it focuses on the appropriate information.
- Include all relevant or important data; don't arbitrarily leave out necessary information.
- Don't hide critical information by including too much data in one graphic.
- Use appropriate scales with equal intervals for the data you present.

Career Application
Locate one or two graphics in a newspaper, magazine article, or annual report. Analyze the strengths and weaknesses of each graphic. Is the information presented accurately? Select a bar or line chart. Sketch the same chart but change the vertical or horizontal scales on the graphic. How does the message of the chart change?

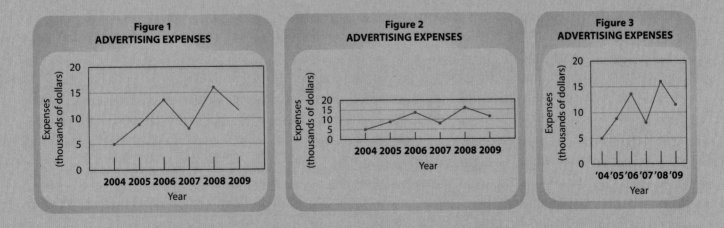

Communicating at Work Your Turn

Applying Your Skills at BzzAgent

© Lee Jeans a division of VF Jeanswear Limited Partnership

Dave Balter and his colleagues at BzzAgent believed in Lee's new product, and they were convinced that their company's method would produce positive results. Their pilot study, which included face-to-face discussions with women in the company, e-mail conversations with their agents, and surveys of those agents, demonstrated that the Lee One True Fit jeans were truly different. One True Fit was, in the language of one of the agents, "the perfect pair of jeans." Another agent wore her new Lee jeans after work and her husband of eight years told her how "great" she looked in the jeans. She bought several new pairs.[19] However, Balter and his staff now had to convince Lee that their services, which cost approximately $85,000 to deploy 1,000 agents for 12 weeks, were worth the investment.

Balter's task was to write a proposal to Lee Jeans' management that outlined the value of his company's system. To write the proposal, his team planned to gather information (a) from studies about various forms of marketing, with an emphasis on word of mouth; (b) from data generated from previous campaigns, particularly those with similar age groups; and (c) from their pilot study. Potential print sources included *Forbes* and *BusinessWeek*, advertising trade journals, business journals, and interviews with potential customers.

Your Task

As writing consultants, you and several of your colleagues have been asked by Dave's team to help write a persuasive proposal that outlines the strategies and predicts the success of the campaign. You've been assigned the task of researching Lee Jeans and gathering general market information about jeans. Using both electronic databases and the Web, put together a short report that lists articles that will be useful for the report writers. Add a short summary of your findings as an introduction. Submit your results in a memo or e-mail message to your instructor.

---

of the responding employees, as shown in Figure 3, favor a flextime schedule. The best introductions for graphics interpret them for readers.

- **Choose an appropriate caption or title style.** Like reports, graphics may use "talking" titles or generic, descriptive titles. "Talking" titles are more persuasive; they tell the reader what to think. Descriptive titles describe the facts more objectively

Talking Title

Average Annual Health Care Costs Per Worker Rise Steeply as Workers Grow Older

Descriptive Title

Average Annual Health Care Costs per Worker as Shown by Age Groups

Summary of Learning Objectives

1 **Describe business report basics, including functions, patterns (indirect or direct), writing style, and formats.** Business reports generally function either as informational reports (without analysis or recommendations) or as analytical reports (with analysis, conclusions, and possibly recommendations). Reports organized directly present the purpose immediately. This pattern is appropriate when the audience is supportive and familiar with the topic. Reports organized indirectly provide the conclusions and recommendations last. This pattern is helpful when the audience is unfamiliar with the problem or when they may be disappointed or hostile. Reports written in a formal style use third-person constructions (*the researcher* instead of *I*), avoid contractions (*do not* instead of *don't*), and may include passive-voice verbs (*the findings were analyzed*). Reports written informally use first-person constructions, contractions, shorter sentences, familiar words, and active-voice verbs. Reports may be formatted as letters, memos, manuscripts, prepared forms, or electronic slides.

2 **Apply the 3-x-3 writing process to business reports to create documents that show an understanding of basic organizational patterns in written communication and a firm grasp of audience and purpose.** Report writers begin by analyzing a problem and writing a problem statement, which may include the scope, significance, and limitations of the project. Writers then analyze the audience and define major issues. They prepare a work plan, including a tentative outline and work schedule. They collect, organize, interpret, and illustrate their data. Then they compose the first draft. Finally, they revise (often many times), proofread, and evaluate.

3 **Understand how to find, evaluate, and use print and electronic sources of secondary data.** Secondary data may be located by searching for books, periodicals, and newspapers through print or electronic indexes. Look for information using electronic databases such as ABI/Inform and LexisNexis. You may also find information on the Internet, but searching for it requires knowledge of search tools and techniques. Popular search tools such as Google, Yahoo, and MSN will help you. Once found, however, information obtained on the Internet should be scrutinized for currency, authority, content, and accuracy.

4 **Comprehend the evolving nature of communication technology: the Web, electronic databases, and other resources for business writers and researchers.** The World Wide Web is used every day by individuals and organizations for business and pleasure. A vast resource, the Web offers a wealth of varied and often uneven secondary data. It is a complex network of information from private citizens, businesses, and other institutions that form a global virtual community. At the same time, these users also announce and advertise their local presence. As a business communicator, you must be aware that information online changes rapidly and is not considered as lasting as scholarly sources. To make the most of Web sites, you must be a critical consumer of the information you retrieve. You need to understand the function of Web search tools and the reliability of the results they present. As an honest researcher, you must keep track of the retrieved data and incorporate them ethically into your documents.

5 **Understand how to generate and use primary data while avoiding researcher bias.** Researchers generate firsthand, primary data through surveys (in-person, print, and online), interviews, observation, and experimentation. Surveys are most economical and efficient for gathering information from large groups of people. Interviews are useful when working with experts in a field. Firsthand observation can produce rich data, but it must be objective. Experimentation produces data suggesting causes and effects. Valid experiments require sophisticated research designs and careful attention to matching the experimental and control groups.

6 **Recognize the purposes and techniques of documentation in business reports and avoid plagiarism.** Documentation means giving credit to information sources. Careful writers document data to strengthen an argument, protect against charges of plagiarism, and instruct readers. Although documentation is less strict in business reports than in academic reports, business writers should learn proper techniques to be able to verify their sources and to avoid charges of plagiarism. Report writers should document others' ideas, facts that are not common knowledge, quotations, and paraphrases. Good notetaking, either manual or electronic, enables writers to give accurate credit to sources. Paraphrasing involves putting another's ideas into your own words. Quotations may be used to provide objective background data, to repeat memorable phrasing, and to duplicate exact wording before criticizing.

7 **Illustrate reports with graphics that create meaning and interest; display numeric information in the appropriate graphic form; and show skill in generating, using, and converting data to visual aids.** Good graphics improve reports by clarifying, simplifying, and emphasizing data. Tables organize precise data into rows and columns. Bar and line charts enable data to be compared visually. Line charts are especially helpful in showing changes over time. Pie charts show a whole and the proportion of its components. Organization charts, pictures, maps, and illustrations serve specific purposes. In choosing or crafting graphics, effective communicators evaluate their audience, purpose, topic, and budget to determine the number and kind of graphics. They write "talking" titles (telling readers what to think about the graphic) or descriptive titles (summarizing the topic objectively). Finally, they work carefully to avoid distorting visual aids.

Chapter Review

1. Explain the difference between informational and analytical reports. (Obj. 1)

2. Describe the direct and indirect patterns of report development. (Obj. 1)

3. Name five common report formats. (Obj. 1)

4. List the seven steps in the report-writing process. (Obj. 2)

5. Identify the questions you should ask to anticipate your audience's reaction. (Obj. 2)

6. Compare primary data and secondary data. Give an original example of each. (Obj. 3)

7. Name at least two of the top four business databases and identify their chief strengths. (Objs. 3, 5)

8. List four major sources of primary information. (Obj. 4)

9. What are the two greatest dangers in preparing and conducting surveys? (Obj. 4)

10. Why are your professors likely to discourage your use of Wikipedia, blogs, and many other sources found on the Web as sources in your reports? (Obj. 5)

11. List two strategies for managing your electronic research data. (Objs. 5, 6)

12. Describe what documentation is, and why it is necessary in reports. (Obj. 6)

13. In what way is documentation of sources in colleges and universities different from business practices? (Obj. 6)

14. Briefly compare the advantages and disadvantages of illustrating data with charts (bar and line) versus tables. (Obj. 7)

15. Name five techniques you can use to ensure that visual aids do not distort graphic information. (Obj. 7)

Critical Thinking

1. Why do businesses spend so much time producing reports, both informational and analytical? Why do they compose long reports when no one seems to have time to read them?

2. When you are engaged in the planning process of a report, what is the advantage of factoring (the process of breaking problems into subproblems)?

3. For long reports, why is a written work plan a wise idea? (Obj. 2)

4. Is information obtained on the Web as reliable as information obtained from journals, newspapers, and magazines? (Obj. 3)

5. Some people say that business reports never contain footnotes. If you were writing your first report for a business and you did considerable research, what would you do about documenting your sources? (Obj. 6)

6. **Ethical Issue:** Your sales team has experienced a sharp decline of revenue after the departure of the two top sellers, and you dread the sales meeting at headquarters where the latest numbers will be crunched and compared to past performance. Your presentation partner suggests that you stretch the time line of your graphic to make the drop in sales revenue look less steep. Should you go along?

Activities

11.1 Report Functions, Writing Styles, and Formats (Obj. 1)

Your Task. For the following reports, (a) name the report's primary function (informational or analytical), (b) recommend a direct or indirect pattern of development, and (c) select a report format (memo, letter, or manuscript).

a. A persuasive proposal from a group of concerned citizens to their city council opposing the conversion of a nearby park and recreational area to a construction zone. A builder wants to pay the city a lot of money to turn the grounds into a gated community and a private golf course.

b. A feasibility report in the leisure industry put together by consultants who compare the potential of a future theme park at two different sites.

c. A report submitted by a sales rep to her manager describing her attendance at a marathon pre-race exhibition, including the reactions of runners to a new low-carbohydrate energy drink.

d. A recommendation report from a special review team (composed of members of the board of directors and staff) to the executive director of a major nonprofit organization to outline the necessary computer and phone system upgrades for the organization's headquarters building.

e. A progress report from a location manager to a Hollywood production company describing safety, fire, and environmental precautions taken for the shooting of a stunt involving blowing up a power boat in the Alamitos Bay marina.

f. A report from a national shipping company telling state authorities how it has improved its safety program so that its trucks now comply with state regulations. The report describes but doesn't interpret the program.

g. A report prepared by an outside consultant examining whether a sports franchise should refurbish its stadium or look to relocate to another city.

11.2 Collaborative Project: Report Portfolio (Obj. 1)

> Team

Your Task. In teams of three or four, collect several corporate annual reports. For each report identify and discuss the following characteristics:

a. Function (informational or analytical)

b. Pattern (primarily direct or indirect)

c. Writing style (formal or informal)

d. Format (memo, letter, manuscript, preprinted form)

e. Effectiveness (clarity, accuracy, expression)

In an informational memo report to your instructor, describe your findings.

11.3 Data Forms and Questions (Obj. 3)

Your Task. In conducting research for the following reports, name at least one form of data you will need and questions you should ask to determine whether that set of data is appropriate (see Figure 11.6).

a. A report on business attire in banking that you must submit to your company's executives who want to issue a formal professional dress code on the job.

b. A report by the Center for Science in the Public Interest investigating the nutritional value of products advertised on afternoon and Saturday television for kids.[20]

c. A report by federal investigators analyzing the causes of a massive Midwest power-grid failure.[21]

d. A report examining the effectiveness of ethics codes in American businesses.

11.4 Problem, Purpose, and Scope Statements (Obj. 2)

Your Task. The following situations require reports. For each situation write (a) a concise problem question, (b) a simple statement of purpose, and (c) a scope statement.

a. Car buyers regularly complain in postpurchase surveys about the persuasive tactics of the so-called "closers," salespeople trained to finalize the deal. Your car dealership wishes to improve customer satisfaction in the stressful price-negotiation process.

b. Last winter a severe ice storm damaged well over 50 percent of the pecan trees lining the main street in the small town of Ardmore. The local university's experts believe that well over 70 percent of the damaged trees will die in the next two years and that this variety is not the best one for providing shade (one of the major reasons for planting them ten years ago).

c. New York enacted strict regulations banning trans fats in restaurant fare. Food processors nationwide are wondering whether they need to make changes too before being forced to switch to nonhydrogenated fats by law. Food and Drug Administration regulations have already changed the definitions of common terms such as *fresh, fat free, low in cholesterol,* and *light.* The Thin Crust Bakery worries that it may have to change its production process and rewrite all its package labels. Thin Crust doesn't know whether to hire a laboratory or a consultant for this project.

d. Customers placing telephone orders for outdoor gear with REI typically order only one or two items. The company wonders whether it can train telephone service reps to motivate customers to increase the number of items ordered per call.

11.5 Problem and Purpose Statements (Obj. 2)

Your Task. Identify a problem in your current job or a previous job, such as inadequate equipment, inefficient procedures, poor customer service, poor product quality, or personnel problems. Assume your boss agrees with your criticism and asks you to prepare a report. Write (a) a two- or three-sentence statement describing the problem, (b) a problem question, and (c) a simple statement of purpose for your report.

11.6 Plagiarism, Paraphrasing, and Citing Sources (Obj. 6)

One of the biggest problems of student writers is paraphrasing secondary sources correctly to avoid plagiarism.

Your Task. For each of the following, read the original passage. Analyze the paraphrased version. List the weaknesses in relation to what you have learned about plagiarism and the use of references. Then write an improved version.

a. Original Passage
The collapse in the cost of computing has made cellular communication economically viable. Worldwide, one in two new phone subscriptions is cellular. The digital revolution in telephony is most advanced in poorer countries because they have been able to skip the outdated technological step of relying on land lines.

Paraphrased Passage
The drop in computing costs now makes cellular communication affordable around the world. In fact, one out of every two new phones is cellular. The digital revolution in cellular telephones is developing faster in poorer countries because they could skip the outdated technological process of using land lines (Henderson 44).

b. Original Passage
Search site Yahoo kept world news prominent on its front page because users feel secure knowing that it is easily accessible, even if they don't often click it. Conspicuous placement also went to entertainment, which draws heavy traffic from people seeking a diversion at work. By contrast, seemingly work-related content such as finance gets ample use in the evening when people pay bills and manage personal portfolios.[22]

Paraphrased Passage
Search giant Yahoo kept news prominent on its portal since its customers feel good knowing it is there, even though they don't read it much. Such noticeable placement was also used for entertainment news that attracts heavy traffic from users searching for a distraction at work. As opposed to that, what may seem work related, such as finance, is much visited at night when people pay their bills and manage their portfolios.

c. Original Passage
Wal-Mart's bid to offer more fashionable apparel was a bid for Target's business. With designer names and fashion flair, Target has made customers comfortable buying dental floss and flirty dresses under one giant, uber-hip roof. ... Wal-Mart found out that though its edgier Metro 7 line for women sold well in several hundred stores, the line's skinny jeans and other higher-style fashions bombed when the company expanded it to all of its stores.[23]

Paraphrased Passage
By offering more fashionable clothes, Wal-Mart was bidding for Target's business. With fashion flair and designer names, Target had attracted customers who would buy dental floss and sexy dresses under one roof. Wal-Mart learned that its hip Metro 7 line for women sold well in hundreds of stores, but the skinny jeans and higher-style clothes misfired when the retailer took them to 3,000 of its stores.

11.7 Factoring and Outlining a Problem (Obj. 2)

Japan Airlines has asked your company, Connections International, to prepare a proposal for a training school for tour operators. JAL wants to know whether Burbank would be a good spot for its school. Burbank interests JAL but only if nearby entertainment facilities can be used for tour training. JAL also needs an advisory committee consisting, if possible, of representatives of the travel community and perhaps executives of other major airlines. The real problem is how to motivate these people to cooperate with JAL.

You've heard that NBC Studios in Burbank offers training seminars, guest speakers, and other resources for tour operators. You

© Kirk Weddle / Photodisc / Getty Images

wonder whether Magic Mountain in Valencia would also be willing to cooperate with the proposed school. And you remember that Griffith Park is nearby and might make a good tour training spot. Before JAL will settle on Burbank as its choice, it wants to know if access to air travel is adequate. JAL's management team is also concerned about available school building space. Moreover, JAL wants to know whether city officials in Burbank would be receptive to this tour training school proposal.

Your Task. To guide your thinking and research, factor this problem into an outline with several areas to investigate. Further divide the problem into subproblems, phrasing each entry as a question. For example, *Should the JAL tour training program be located in Burbank?* (See the work plan model in Figure 11.5.)

11.8 Developing a Work Plan (Obj. 2)

Any long report project requires a structured work plan.

Your Task. Select a report topic from those listed at the ends of Chapters 12 and 13 and at www.meguffey.com. For that report prepare a work plan that includes the following:

a. Statement of the problem

b. Expanded statement of purpose (including scope, limitations, and significance)

c. Research strategy to answer the questions

d. Tentative outline of key questions to answer

e. Work schedule (with projected completion dates)

11.9 Using Secondary Sources (Obj. 3)

Secondary sources can provide quite different information depending on your mode of inquiry.

Your Task. Pick a business-related subject you want to know more about and run it through a search engine such as Google. Compare your results with Dogpile, a metasearch site. Write a short memo or e-mail message to your instructor explaining the differences in the search results. In your message describe what you have learned about the advantages and disadvantages of each search tool.

11.10 Developing Primary Data: Collaborative Survey (Obj. 4)

Team

The dining facilities on campus have again ignited a controversy among students but also faculty and staff. The students are mainly unhappy about what they perceive to be high prices, whereas professors and campus employees seem to want more healthful food choices. The dining facility managers claim their prices are competitive with outside eateries. They also point to a few available low-fat, high-fiber options, such as boxed salads and "lean" sandwiches.

Your Task. You are one of several student representatives on the Campus Food Committee consisting of administrators and Associated Students staff. Associated Students is a for-profit campus organization that runs all dining facilities at the university. At your monthly meeting you are discussing several faculty, staff, and student complaints. The criticism seems to center on food pricing and its healthfulness. In teams of three to five, design a questionnaire to probe the opinions of faculty and staff to be distributed by the campuswide e-mail network or posted on the campus intranet. Learn which specific choices this particular population would like to see in campus cafeterias and how these options should be priced to be considered profitable by administrators. Investigate the price ranges for comparable food items off campus. As a team, write a memo for the Campus Food Committee comparing food choices and their cost on campus and outside. Be sure to consider how the results will be tabulated and interpreted.

Your instructor may ask you to complete this activity as a report assignment after you study Chapter 12. If so, write a report for the Campus Food Committee and be prepared to interpret your survey results. You will also be expected to issue recommendations to the committee.

11.11 Finding Secondary Data: Hot Trends in the Tech Industry (Objs. 3, 5, and 6)

Team

Are you a member of the "thumb generation"? Can you work the keyboard of your cell phone or personal digital assistant faster than most people can speak? The term "thumb generation" was coined in South Korea and Japan and is applied to young people under 25 who furiously finger their handheld devices to text message, e-mail, and complete other electronic functions at lightning speeds.

More technological innovations are coming that are likely to transform our lives. WiMAX is a new wireless super technology that will cover entire cities at cable speeds. New-Field Communication (NFC) takes the Bluetooth technology a step further to connect cell phones and other devices. NFC is touted for its boundless commercial applications enabling Americans soon to complete many sales transactions by cell phone, as is already customary in Korea, Japan, and Finland. These and other trends are described in a *BusinessWeek* article titled "The Future of Tech."[24]

Your Task: You are one of several marketing interns at MarketNet Global, a worldwide e-commerce specialist. Your busy boss, Rick Rivera, wants to know more about the cutting-edge trends described in the *BusinessWeek* article he saw. He is particularly interested in learning whether they might be successfully used in selling and marketing. Individually or as a team, research one or several of these high-tech concepts. Chances are you will not find scholarly articles on these subjects because peer-reviewed publications take years to complete. Instead, rely on the Web and on electronic databases to find up-to-date information. If you use search engines, you will retrieve many forum and discussion board contributions as well. Examine them critically for authority and validity. In teams or individually, write an informative memo to Rick Rivera, complete with a short list of references in MLA or APA documentation style. Explain what each new trend is. Your instructor may ask you to complete this activity as a report assignment after you study Chapter 12. You could use your research to write a short informational memo report describing to Rick Rivera what your sources suggest the new trends may mean for the future of business, specifically e-commerce and online marketing.

11.12 Researching and Evaluating Data: Global Internet Access (Objs. 3, 5, and 7)

Team **Web**

Out of nearly 700 million global Internet users, the United States is the country with the most online visitors in the world, followed by China, Japan, Germany, the United Kingdom, and South Korea, according to ComScore, a global Internet information provider.[25] However, the United States does not even rank among the top 15 countries in average monthly hours spent online. Here much smaller countries rule, namely Israel, Finland, South Korea, the Netherlands, Taiwan, and Sweden. Other data analyzing which nations have the most connected populations suggest that Scandinavians rank high; the tiny country of Iceland is often cited as the top Internet presence per resident. On the opposite side of the spectrum, Internet access is very low in Africa, where less than 1 percent of the population is online. Chip maker AMD and scientists at MIT have independently announced plans to build and distribute low-cost computers to poor children in developing countries.

Your Task: As an entry-level employee at chip maker AMD, you are part of a young team entrusted with the task of researching global Internet use and market saturation with computers. In other words, you are to examine access to computers and the Internet in a given population. Find ComScore's World Metrix data and examine how they were collected. Are they credible? Do other reputable sources reference this survey? Retrieve other statistical information from the Internet or electronic databases that discuss online access and Internet use in relation to population size. How does the focus on absolute numbers as opposed to percentages of the population skew the outcome? What conclusions can be drawn from such information?

Write a memo to the head of the task force at AMD, Corinne Ardeau, about the challenges of interpreting such numeric data. In addition, Ms. Ardeau is looking for volunteers to research attempts by competitors and independent organizations (e.g., the United Nations, other corporations, and universities), to provide basic computing devices to developing countries. Write an informative memo to Ms. Ardeau listing your findings without comments or recommendations. Your instructor may ask you to complete this activity as an analytical report after you study Chapters 12 and 13.

11.13 Researching Data: Target Aims at Charitable Giving (Objs. 3, 6, and 7)

Team **Web**

Lauren Bacall and Robert Redford have both promoted it. And Oprah Winfrey thinks it is so chic that she pronounces its name in mock-French ("Tarjay"). Unlike its big-box competitors, Target is an American discount retailer that appeals to many female shoppers with trendy and edgy but affordable fashions. However, Target is also proud of its positive corporate image. The company has been praised for giving back to the community with higher-than-usual charitable contributions. At 5 percent of pretax earnings, Target's annual donations are more than double the national average among big corporations, in absolute dollars recently as high as $101 million a year. The company gives 5 percent of pretax profits consistently, in fat and in lean times.

This tradition was established six decades ago by Target's founder, George Dayton. Such generosity is more than a public relations move, especially because Target polls its core group of shoppers, 35- to 45-year-old mothers, about their favorite causes. Then it distributes funds to those charities. The company even managed to regain the goodwill of the Salvation Army after driving out its bell ringers citing no-solicitation rules.[26]

Your Task. Select one of the following tasks. (a) As a summer intern at Wal-Mart, you were asked to prepare an informational memo to your boss, Ever Duran, about Target's charitable practices. Wal-Mart is seeking greater community involvement to boost its public image. What types of projects does the Target Corporation fund? What other policies set this company apart from its competitors when it comes to giving back to the community? Write an individual informative memo or one collaborative memo as a team of summer interns. Alternatively, Ever Duran could ask you to write a memo describing how Target handled the Salvation Army controversy and what its actions say about the company's management and its philosophy.

(b) As a team of summer interns for Wal-Mart, research the charitable giving of Target and other major corporations. Prepare an informational memo comparing and contrasting corporate practices. Target ranks fourth behind Wal-Mart, Home Depot, and Lowe's in size. How much of their pretax earnings are these and other big chain stores spending on philanthropy? What types of causes do they embrace and why? Do their policies seem consistent and purposeful over the long term? How do they justify charitable giving to their shareholders?

In each case, compile a bibliography of sources you used. Whenever appropriate, display numbers visually by creating charts, graphs, and tables.

You may want to start by viewing company mission statements and annual reports for discussions of corporate social responsibility, charitable giving, and worthy causes companies support. Then, go to independent sources for a more detached, objective perspective.

11.14 Gathering and Documenting Data: Biotechnology Alters Foods (Obj. 3)

Web

California is home to the nation's most diverse and valuable agricultural industry. Many of its crops are sold in Japanese and European markets where customers are extremely wary of genetically modified foods. Despite that fact, sources in the state capital are reporting that the biotech industry is actively seeking sponsors for a bill in the state legislature that would preempt the right of counties to ban genetically engineered crops. As an intern working for the Organic Consumers Association, the nation's largest public interest group dedicated to a healthy and sustainable food system, your supervisor, Andrea Lopez, asked you to gather data about the dangers of genetically engineered crops. The organization plans to write a report to the state government about this issue.

Your Task. Conduct a keyword search using three search engines on the Web. Select three articles you think would be most pertinent to the organization's argument. Save them using the strategies for managing data, and create a bibliography. Conduct the same keyword search with ABI/INFORM or LexisNexis. Save the three most relevant articles, and add these items to your bibliography. In a short memo to Andrea Lopez, Director of Government Relations, summarize what you've found and describe its value. Attach the bibliography.

11.15 Selecting Graphics (Obj. 7)

Your Task. Identify the best graphics form to illustrate the following data.

a. Figures comparing the costs of cable, DSL, and satellite Internet service in ten major metropolitan areas of the United States for the past ten years (for a congressional investigation)

b. Figures showing the distribution of West Nile Virus in humans by state

c. Figures showing the process of delivering electricity to a metropolitan area

d. Data showing areas in the United States most likely to have earthquakes

e. Figures showing what proportion of every state tax dollar is spent on education, social services, transportation, debt, and other expenses

f. Data showing the academic, administrative, and operation divisions of a college, from the president to department chairs and division managers

g. Figures comparing the sales of PDAs (personal digital assistants), cell phones, and laptop computers over the past five years

h. Percentages showing the causes of forest fires (lightning, 73 percent; arson, 5 percent; campfires, 9 percent; and so on) in the Rocky Mountains

11.16 Evaluating Graphics (Obj. 7)

Your Task. Select four graphics from newspapers or magazines. Look in *The Wall Street Journal, USA Today, BusinessWeek, U.S. News & World Report, Fortune,* or other business news publications. In a memo to your instructor, critique each graphic based on what you have learned in this chapter. What is correctly shown? What is incorrectly shown? How could the graphic be improved?

11.17 Drawing a Bar Chart (Obj. 7)

Your Task. Prepare a bar chart comparing the tax rates of eight industrial countries in the world: Canada, 34 percent; France, 42 percent; Germany, 39 percent; Japan, 26 percent; Netherlands, 48 percent; Sweden, 49 percent; United Kingdom, 37 percent; United States, 28 percent. These figures represent a percentage of the gross domestic product for each country. The sources of the figures are the International Monetary Fund and the Japanese Ministry of Finance. Arrange the entries logically. Write two titles: a talking title and a descriptive title. What should be emphasized in the chart and title?

11.18 Drawing a Line Chart (Obj. 7)

Your Task. Prepare a line chart showing the sales of Sidekick Athletic Shoes, Inc., for these years: 2008, $6.7 million; 2007, $5.4 million; 2006, $3.2 million; 2005, $2.1 million; 2004, $2.6 million; 2003, $3.6 million. In the chart title, highlight the trend you see in the data.

11.19 Studying Graphics in Annual Reports (Obj. 7)

Your Task. In a memo to your instructor, evaluate the use and effectiveness of graphics in three to five corporation annual reports. Critique their readability, clarity, and effectiveness in visualizing data. How were they introduced in the text? What suggestions would you make to improve them?

11.20 Avoiding Huge Credit Card Debt for College Students (Objs. 3, 5, and 6)

`Consumer` `Web`

College students represent a new push for credit card companies. An amazing 56 percent of students carried a credit card in the most recent study of undergraduate card use,[27] and the number undoubtedly continues to skyrocket. Credit cards are a contributing factor when students graduate with an average of $20,000 debt. Because they can't buy cars, rent homes, or purchase insurance, graduates with big credit debt see a bleak future for themselves.

A local newspaper plans to run a self-help story about college credit cards. The editor asks you, a young part-time reporter, to prepare a memo with information that could be turned into an article. The article would be targeted to parents of students who are about to leave for college. What can parents do to help students avoid sinking deeply into credit card debt?

Your Task. Using ABI/INFORM, Factiva, or LexisNexis and the Web, locate basic information about student credit card options. In a memo discuss shared credit cards and other options. Your goal is to be informative, not to reach conclusions or make recommendations. Use one or more of the techniques discussed in this chapter to track your sources. Address your memo to Barbara Hagler, editor.

Grammar and Mechanics C.L.U.E. Review 11

Total Review

The first ten chapters reviewed specific guides from Appendix A: Grammar and Mechanics Guide (Competent Language Usage Essentials). The remaining exercises are total reviews, covering all of the grammar/mechanics guides plus confusing words and frequently misspelled words.

Each of the following sentences has a total of three errors in grammar, punctuation, capitalization, usage, or spelling. On a separate sheet, write a correct version. Avoid adding new phrases, starting new sentences, or rewriting in your own words. When finished, compare your responses with the key beginning on page Key-3.

Example: To succede as a knowledge worker in todays digital workplace you need highly developed communication skills.

Revision: To **succeed** as a knowledge worker in **today's** digital **workplace,** you need highly developed communication skills.

1. Companys are looking for individuals with strong writing and grammer skills, because much time is spent communicating.

2. Permenant employees can expect to spend at least fifty percent of there time processing documents.

3. One organization paid three thousand dollars each for twelve employees to attend a one week workshop in communication training.

4. Although it cost four hundred dollars, my BlackBerry allow my manager and I to stay in touch through e-mail.

5. If you work in a office with open cubicles it's rude to listen to Web radio, streaming audio, or other multimedia, without headphones.

6. Bad news is genrally disappointing, however the negative feelings can be reduced.

7. On June 1st our company President revealed a four million dollar drop in profits, which was bad news for everyone.

8. Most of us prefer to be let down gently, when we're being refused something, that is why the reasons before refusal pattern is effective.

9. If I was you I would begin the bad-news message with a complement, not a blunt rejection.

10. Because of rising health costs our Director of Human Resources announced an increase in everyones contribution.

Chapter 12

Informal Business Reports

OBJECTIVES

After studying this chapter, you should be able to

1 Show skill and accuracy in tabulating information, using statistical techniques, and creating decision matrices to sort and interpret business report data.

2 Draw meaningful conclusions and make practical report recommendations based on prior logical analysis.

3 Organize report data logically and provide cues to aid readers' comprehension.

4 Prepare short informational reports.

5 Prepare short analytical reports that solve business problems.

Communicating at Work Part 1

Starbucks: More Than Just Beans

Howard Schultz returned to Seattle from Italy in 1984 impressed by the espresso bars he had visited in Milan. In no time Schultz set up the first U.S. espresso bar in a downtown Seattle Starbucks store, one of only five Starbucks in existence at the time. Until then, Starbucks had sold only coffee beans, not drinks. Today, Starbucks is the world's largest coffee shop chain, with more than 13,000 retail locations North America, Latin America, Europe, the Middle East, and the Pacific Rim—37 countries in all. The company serves more than 40 million customers weekly and generates more than $7.8 billion in annual sales.

Starbucks' customers love such exotic drinks as its Iced Caramel Macchiato and its Espresso Frappuccino blended coffee. What's more, employees love working there. Who wouldn't, with perks such as health coverage for those who put in 20 or more hours a week and stock options, called "Bean Stock," after one year. Adding to its accolades, Starbucks ranks among the top five in the *Fortune* magazine list of "America's Most Admired Companies" and repeatedly was named among *Fortune's* "100 Best Companies to Work For."

Starbucks is probably best known for bucking traditional retail wisdom. It regularly breaks the retail rule about locating stores so closely that they cannibalize each other's sales. Take Chicago, for example. Starbucks has over 100 shops, and many of them are on the same street. Marshall Fields even has two shops in the same store, one on its lower level and another on its first floor. In metropolitan areas such as London and New York City, you may find over 150 Starbucks outlets within a five-mile radius.

This "being everywhere" approach creates several distinct advantages. Clustered storefronts act as billboards, thus allowing Starbucks to keep its advertising budget to a minimum. Its numerous locations mean that Starbucks intercepts consumers on their way to work, home, or anywhere in between. Moreover, ubiquity builds brand awareness.[1] However, explosive growth and the push

© Pascal Le Segretain / Staff / Getty Images

for efficiency may have led to a "watering down of the Starbucks experience," in the words of Chairman Schultz. Specifically, he worries about the use of automatic espresso machines and flavor-locked packaging. Schultz fears that Starbucks stores "no longer have the soul of the past, and reflect a chain of stores vs. the warm feeling of a neighborhood store."[2] You will learn more about this case on page 372.

Critical Thinking

- What kind of information should Starbucks gather to help it decide how closely to locate its stores?
- How could Howard Schultz test his impression that the intimate communal coffee-drinking experience is fading at Starbucks?
- How can collected information be transmitted to Starbucks' decision makers?

http://www.starbucks.com

Interpreting Data

LEARNING OBJECTIVE 1
Show skill and accuracy in tabulating information, using statistical techniques, and creating decision matrices to sort and interpret business report data.

Interpreting data means sorting, analyzing, combining, and recombining to yield meaningful information.

Starbucks and all other organizations need information to stay abreast of what is happening inside and outside of their firms. Much of that information will be presented to decision makers in the form of reports. This chapter will focus on interpreting and organizing data, drawing conclusions, providing reader cues, and writing informal business reports.

Assume you have collected a mass of information for a report. You may feel overwhelmed as you look at a jumble of printouts, note cards, copies of articles, interview notes, questionnaire results, and statistics. It is a little like being a contractor who allowed suppliers to dump all the building materials for a new house in a monstrous pile. Like the contractor you must sort the jumble of raw material into meaningful, usable groups. Unprocessed data become meaningful information through skillful and accurate sorting, analysis, combination, and recombination. You will be examining each item to see what it means by itself and what it means when connected with other data. You are looking for meanings, relationships, and answers to the research questions posed in your work plan.

Tabulating and Analyzing Responses

Numerical data must be tabulated and analyzed statistically to bring order out of chaos.

If you have collected considerable numerical and other information, you must tabulate and analyze it. Fortunately, several tabulating and statistical techniques can help you create order from the chaos. These techniques simplify, summarize, and classify large amounts of data into meaningful terms. From the condensed data you are more likely to be able to draw valid conclusions and make reasoned recommendations. The most helpful summarizing techniques include tables, statistical concepts (mean, median, and mode), correlations, grids, and decision matrices.

Tables. Numerical data from questionnaires or interviews are usually summarized and simplified in tables. Using systematic columns and rows, tables make quantitative information easier to comprehend. After assembling your data, you will want to prepare preliminary tables to enable you to see what the information means. Here is a table summarizing the response to one question from a campus survey about student parking:

Question: Should student fees be increased to build parking lots?

	Number	Percent	
Strongly agree	76	11.5	} To simplify the table, combine these items.
Agree	255	38.5	
No opinion	22	3.3	
Disagree	107	16.1	} To simplify the table, combine these items.
Strongly disagree	203	30.6	
Total	**663**	**100.0**	

Notice that this preliminary table includes a total number of responses and a percentage for each response. (To calculate a percentage, divide the figure for each response by the total number of responses times 100.) To simplify the data and provide a broad overview, you can join categories. For example, combining "strongly agree" (11.5 percent) and "agree" (38.5 percent) reveals that 50 percent of the respondents supported the proposal to finance new parking lots with increased student fees.

Sometimes data become more meaningful when cross-tabulated. This process allows analysis of two or more variables together. By breaking down our student survey data into male and female responses, shown in the following table, we make an interesting discovery.

Question: Should student fees be increased to build parking lots?

	Total		Male		Female	
	Number	Percent	Number	Percent	Number	Percent
Strongly agree	76	11.5	8	2.2	68	22.0
Agree	255	38.5	54	15.3	201	65.0
No opinion	22	3.3	12	3.4	10	3.2
Disagree	107	16.1	89	25.1	18	5.8
Strongly disagree	203	30.6	191	54.4	12	4.0
Total	**663**	**100.0**	**354**	**100.0**	**309**	**100.0**

Although 50 percent of all student respondents supported the proposal, among females the approval rating was much stronger. Notice that 87 percent of female respondents (combining 22 percent "strongly agree" and 65 percent "agree") endorsed the proposal to increase fees for new parking lots. But among male students, only 17 percent agreed with the proposal. You naturally wonder why such a disparity exists. Are female students more unhappy than male students with the current parking situation? If so, why? Is safety a reason? Are male students more concerned with increased fees than female students are?

By cross-tabulating the findings, you sometimes uncover data that may help answer your problem question or that may prompt you to explore other possibilities. Do not, however, undertake cross-tabulation unless it serves more than mere curiosity. Tables also help you compare multiple data collected from questionnaires and surveys. Figure 12.1 shows, in raw form, responses to several survey items. To convert these data into a more usable form, you need to calculate percentages for each item. Then you can arrange the responses in some rational sequence, such as largest percentage to smallest.

FIGURE 12.1 Converting Survey Data Into Finished Tables

Raw Data From Survey Item

Indicate Your Feelings Toward the Following Proposed
Solutions to the Student Parking Problem on Campus.

	Agree	No opinion	Disagree	
1. Increase student fees to build parking lots	331	22	310	Shows raw figures from which percentages are calculated
2. Limit student parking to satellite lots, providing shuttle buses to campus	52	31	580	
3. Offer incentives to use public transportation	111	29	523	
4. Restrict visitor parking	612	15	36	

Finished Table

Reactions of South Bay College Students to Four
Proposed Solutions to Campus Parking Problem*
Spring 2006
N = 663 students

	Agree	No opinion	Disagree	
Restrict visitor parking	92.3%	2.3%	5.4%	Uses percent sign only at beginning of column
Increase student fees to build parking lots	49.9	3.3	46.8	
Offer incentives to use public transportation	16.7	4.4	78.9	
Limit student parking to satellite lots, providing shuttle buses to campus	7.8	4.7	87.5	Avoids cluttering the table with total figures

Orders items from highest to lowest "Agree" percentages

*Figures may not equal 100 percent because of rounding.

Tips for Converting Raw Data

- Tabulate the responses on a copy of the survey form.
- Calculate percentages (divide the score for an item by the total for all responses to that item; for example, for item 1, divide 331 by 663 times 100).
- Round off figures to one decimal point or to whole numbers.
- Arrange items in a logical order, such as largest to smallest percentage.
- Prepare a table with a title that tells such things as who, what, when, where, and why.
- Include the total number of respondents.

Once the data are displayed in a table, you can more easily draw conclusions. As Figure 12.1 shows, South Bay College students apparently are not interested in public transportation or shuttle buses from satellite lots. They want to park on campus, with restricted visitor parking; and only half are willing to pay for new parking lots.

Three statistical concepts—mean, median, and mode—help you describe data.

The Three Ms: Mean, Median, Mode. Tables help you organize data, and the three Ms help you describe it. These statistical terms—mean, median, and mode—are all occasionally used loosely to mean "average." To be safe, though, you should learn to apply these statistical terms precisely. When people say *average,* they usually intend to indicate the *mean,* or arithmetic average. Let's say that you are studying the estimated starting salaries of graduates from various disciplines, ranging from education to medicine:

Education	$31,000	*Mode (figure occurring most frequently)*
Sociology	31,000	
Humanities	31,000	
Biology	35,000	
Health sciences	40,000	*Median (middle point in continuum)*
Business	46,000	*Mean (arithmetic average)*
Engineering	50,000	
Law	55,000	
Medicine	95,000	

A range of starting salaries becomes more meaningful when one can see a mode, median, and mean.

To find the mean, you simply add up all the salaries and divide by the total number of items ($414,000 ÷ 9 = $46,000). Therefore, the mean salary is $46,000. Means are very useful to indicate central tendencies of figures, but they have one major flaw: extremes at either end cause distortion. Notice that the $95,000 figure makes the mean salary of $46,000 deceptively high. It does not represent a valid average for the group. Because means can be misleading, you should use them only when extreme figures do not distort the result.

The *median* represents the midpoint in a group of figures arranged from lowest to highest (or vice versa). In our list of salaries, the median is $40,000 (health sciences). In other words, half the salaries are above this point and half are below it. The median is useful when extreme figures may warp the mean. Although salaries for medicine distort the mean, the median, at $40,000, is still a representative figure.

The mean is the arithmetic average; the median is the midpoint in a group of figures; the mode is the most frequently occurring figure.

The *mode* is simply the value that occurs most frequently. In our list $31,000 (for education, sociology, and the humanities) represents the mode because it occurs three times. The mode has the advantage of being easily determined—just a quick glance at a list of arranged values reveals it. Although mode is infrequently used by researchers, knowing the mode is useful in some situations. Assume that 7-Eleven sampled its customers to determine what drink size they preferred: 12-ounce, 16-ounce, or Big-Gulp 24-ounce. Finding the mode—the most frequently named figure—makes more sense than calculating the median, which might yield a size that 7-Eleven does not even offer. (To remember the meaning of *mode,* think about fashion; the most frequent response, the mode, is the most fashionable.)

Mean, median, and mode figures are especially helpful when the range of values is also known. Range represents the span between the highest and lowest values. To calculate the range, you simply subtract the lowest figure from the highest. In starting salaries for graduates, the range is $64,000 (95,000 − 31,000). Knowing the range enables readers to put mean and median figures into perspective. This knowledge also prompts researchers to wonder why such a range exists, thus stimulating hunches and further investigation to solve problems.

Correlations. In tabulating and analyzing data, you may see relationships among two or more variables that help explain the findings. If your data for graduates' starting salaries also included years of education, you would doubtless notice that graduates with more years of education received higher salaries. For example, beginning teachers, with four years of education, earn less than beginning physicians, who have completed nine or more years of education. Thus, a correlation may exist between years of education and starting salary.

Correlations between variables suggest possible relationships that will explain research findings.

Intuition suggests correlations that may or may not prove to be accurate. Is there a relationship between studying and good grades? Between new office computers and increased productivity? Between the rise and fall of hemlines and the rise and fall of the stock market (as some newspaper writers have suggested)? If a correlation seems to exist, can we say that one event caused the other? Does studying cause good grades? Does more schooling guarantee increased salary? Although one event may not be said to cause another, the business researcher who sees a correlation begins to ask why and how the two variables are related. In this way, apparent correlations stimulate investigation and present possible solutions to be explored.

FIGURE 12.2 Grid to Analyze Complex Verbal Data About Building Cash Reserves

	Point 1	Point 2	Point 3	Point 4	Overall Reaction
Vice President 1	Disapproves. "Too little, too late."	Strong support. "Best of all points."	Mixed opinion. "Must wait and see market."	Indifferent.	Optimistic, but "hates to delay expansion for six months."
Vice President 2	Disapproves. "Creates credit trap."	Approves.	Strong disapproval.	Approves. "Must improve receivable collections."	Mixed support. "Good self-defense plan."
Vice President 3	Strong disapproval.	Approves. "Key to entire plan."	Indifferent.	Approves, but with "caveats."	"Will work only with sale of unproductive fixed assets."
Vice President 4	Disapproves. "Too risky now."	Strong support. "Start immediately."	Approves, "but may damage image."	Approves. "Benefits far outweigh costs."	Supports plan. Suggests focus on Pacific Rim markets.

In reporting correlations, you should avoid suggesting that a cause-and-effect relationship exists when none can be proved. Only sophisticated research methods can statistically prove cause and effect. Instead, present a correlation as a possible relationship (*The data suggest that beginning salaries are related to years of education*). Cautious statements followed by explanations gain you credibility and allow readers to make their own decisions.

Grids permit analysis of raw verbal data by grouping and classifying.

Grids. Another technique for analyzing raw data—especially verbal data—is the grid. Let's say you have been asked by the CEO to collect opinions from all vice presidents about the CEO's four-point plan to build cash reserves. The grid shown in Figure 12.2 enables you to summarize the vice presidents' reactions to each point. Notice how this complex verbal information is transformed into concise, manageable data; readers can see immediately which points are supported and which are opposed. Imagine how long you could have struggled to comprehend the meaning of this verbal information before plotting it on a grid.

Arranging data in a grid also works for projects such as feasibility studies and yardstick reports that compare many variables. Assume you must recommend a new printer to your manager. To see how four models compare, you could lay out a grid with the names of printer models across the top. Down the left side, you would list such significant variables as price, warranty, service, capacity, compatibility, and specifications. As you fill in the variables for each model, you can see quickly which model has the lowest price, longest warranty, and so forth. *Consumer Reports* often uses grids to show information.

In addition, grids help classify employment data. For example, suppose your boss asks you to recommend one individual from among many job candidates. You could arrange a grid with names across the top and distinguishing characteristics—experience, skills, education, and other employment interests—down the left side. Summarizing each candidate's points offers a helpful tool for drawing conclusions and writing a report.

Decision Matrices. A decision matrix is a special grid that helps managers make the best choice among complex options. Designed to eliminate bias and poor judgment, decision matrices are helpful in many fields. Assume you need to choose the most appropriate laptop computer for your sales representatives. You are most interested in weight, battery life, price, and hard drive size. You want to compare these features in four laptop models. Figure 12.3 shows a simple decision matrix to help you make the choice. In this case, the most important criteria were weight, battery, price, and hard drive size. In Table 1, you evaluate each of these features on a scale of 1 to 5. Because the Dell Inspiron has a good price, you give it a score of 4. However, its weight is less desirable, and you give it a score of 2.

After you have evaluated all of the laptop models in Table 1, you assign relative weights to each feature. You decide to assign a factor of 5 to weight as well as to unit price because these two aspects are of average importance. However, your field sales reps want laptops with batteries that last. Therefore, battery life is twice as important; you assign it a factor of 10. You assign a factor of 7 to the size of the hard drive because this option is slightly

FIGURE 12.3 Decision Matrix Used to Choose a Laptop for Sales Reps

Unweighted Decision Matrix—Table 1

Features:	Weight	Battery Life	Price	Hard Drive	Total
Laptop Options					
Dell Inspiron 1501: 1.8 GHz AMD, 6.2 lbs, 3.5 hrs, $520, 60 GB	2	3	4	2	
Sony VAIO VGN-N320EB: 1.6 GHz Pentium T2060, 6.5 lbs, 4 hrs, $850, 120 GB	1	4	1	5	
Acer Aspire 5570-2609: 1.6 GHz Pentium T2060, 5.3 lbs, 3 hrs, $662, 80 GB	4	2	3	3	
IBM ThinkPad R31: 1.13 GHz Pentium III, 6.2 lbs, 2.9 hrs, $399, 40 GB	2	2	5	1	

Weighted Decision Matrix—Table 2

Features:	Weight	Battery	Price	Hard Drive	Total
Laptop Options Weights:	5	10	5	7	
Dell Inspiron 1501: 1.8 GHz AMD, 6.2 lbs, 3.5 hrs, $520, 60 GB	10	30	20	14	74
Sony VAIO VGN-N320EB: 1.6 GHz Pentium T2060, 6.5 lbs, 4 hrs, $850, 120 GB	5	40	5	35	85
Acer Aspire 5570-2609: 1.6 GHz Pentium T2060, 5.3 lbs, 3 hrs, $662, 80 GB	20	20	15	21	76
IBM ThinkPad R31: 1.13 GHz Pentium III, 6.2 lbs, 2.9 hrs, $399, 40 GB	10	20	25	7	62

Tips for Creating a Decision Matrix

- **Select the most important criteria.** For a laptop computer, the criteria were weight, battery life, price, and size of hard drive.
- **Create a matrix.** List each laptop model (Dell, Sony, and others) down the left side. Place the features across the top of the columns.
- **Evaluate the criteria.** Use a scale of 1 (lowest) to 5 (highest). Rate each feature for each option, as shown in Table 1.
- **Assign relative weights.** Decide how important each feature is and give it a weight.
- **Multiply the scores.** For each feature in Table 1, multiply by the weights in Table 2 and write the score in the box.
- **Total the scores.** The total reveals the best choice.

more important than price, but somewhat less important than battery life. Then you multiply the scores in Table 1 with the weights and total them, as shown in Table 2. According to the weighted matrix and the rating system used, the Sony Vaio should be purchased for the sales reps because it received the highest score of 85 points.

Drawing Conclusions and Making Recommendations

The most widely read portions of a report are the sections devoted to conclusions and recommendations. Knowledgeable readers go straight to the conclusions to see what the report writer thinks the data mean. Because conclusions summarize and explain the findings, they represent the heart of a report.

LEARNING OBJECTIVE 2
Draw meaningful conclusions and make practical report recommendations based on prior logical analysis.

Spotlight on Communicators

As PepsiCo's first female CEO, Indra Nooyi stands among an elite group of women who lead a Fortune 500 company. The Indian–born executive's historic appointment as chief won the plaudits of analysts, even earning Nooyi a No. 1 ranking in *Fortune* magazine's 50 Most Powerful Women in Business. As former president and financial officer at PepsiCo, Nooyi used her expert data analysis skills to direct the food-and-beverage giant toward healthier brands such as Aquafina, Tropicana, and Quaker Oats.

Your value in an organization rises considerably if you can draw conclusions that analyze information logically and show how the data answer questions and solve problems. To tap into a potential $1 billion market for cellular phones in developing countries, Finnish mobile-phone manufacturer Nokia researched the needs of its customers. It created handsets that can withstand the tough living conditions and harsh weather in India and Africa. To reach customers, the company sent vans into rural India. Kai Oistamo, executive vice president and general manager for mobile phones, said: "You have to understand where people live, what the shopping patterns are. You have to work with local means to reach people—even bicycles or rickshaws."[3] Doing research and drawing logical conclusions from data are crucial to business success.

Analyzing Data to Arrive at Conclusions

Conclusions summarize and explain the findings in a report.

Any set of data can produce a variety of meaningful conclusions. Always bear in mind, though, that the audience for a report wants to know how these data relate to the problem being studied. What do the findings mean in terms of solving the original report problem?

For example, the Marriott Corporation recognized a serious problem among its employees. Conflicting home and work requirements seemed to be causing excessive employee turnover and decreased productivity. To learn the extent of the problem and to consider solutions, Marriott surveyed its staff. It learned, among other things, that nearly 35 percent of its employees had children under age twelve, and 15 percent had children under age five. Other findings, shown in Figure 12.4, indicated that one third of its staff with young children took time off because of child-care difficulties. Moreover, many current employees left previous jobs because of work and family conflicts. The survey also showed that managers did not consider child-care or family problems to be appropriate topics for discussion at work.

A sample of possible conclusions that could be drawn from these findings is shown in Figure 12.4. Notice that each conclusion relates to the initial report problem. Although only a few possible findings and conclusions are shown here, you can see that the conclusions try to explain the causes for the home/work conflict among employees. Many report writers would expand the conclusion section by explaining each item and citing supporting evidence. Even for simplified conclusions, such as those shown in Figure 12.4, you will want to itemize each item separately and use parallel construction (balanced sentence structure).

Although your goal is to remain objective, drawing conclusions naturally involves a degree of subjectivity. Your goals, background, and frame of reference all color the inferences you make. When Federal Express, for example, initially expanded its next-day delivery service to Europe, it racked up a staggering loss of $1.2 billion in four years of operation.[4] The facts could not be disputed. But what conclusions could be drawn? The CEO might conclude that the competition was greater than anticipated but that FedEx was making inroads; patience was all that was needed. The board of directors and stockholders, however, might conclude that the competition was too well entrenched and that it was time to pull the plug on an ill-fated operation. All writers interpret findings from their own perspectives, but they should not manipulate them to achieve a preconceived purpose.

Effective report conclusions are objective and bias-free.

You can make your report conclusions more objective if you use consistent evaluation criteria. Let's say you are comparing computers for an office equipment purchase. If you evaluate each by the same criteria (such as price, specifications, service, and warranty), your conclusions are more likely to be bias-free.

You also need to avoid the temptation to sensationalize or exaggerate your findings or conclusions. Be careful of words such as *many, most,* and *all.* Instead of *many of the respondents felt...*, you might more accurately write *some of the respondents....* Examine your motives before drawing conclusions. Do not let preconceptions or wishful thinking color your reasoning.

Preparing Report Recommendations

Conclusions explain a problem; recommendations offer specific suggestions for solving the problem.

Conclusions explain what the problem is, whereas recommendations tell how to solve it. Typically, readers prefer specific, practical recommendations. They want to know exactly how to implement the suggestions. The specificity of your recommendations depends on your authorization. What are you commissioned to do, and what does the reader expect?

In the planning stages of your report project, you anticipate what the reader wants in the report. Your intuition and your knowledge of the audience indicate how far your recommendations should be developed.

In the recommendations section of the Marriott employee survey, shown in Figure 12.4, many of the recommendations are summarized. In the actual report each recommendation could have been backed up with specifics and ideas for implementing them. For example, the child-care resource recommendation would be explained: it provides parents with names of agencies and professionals who specialize in locating child care across the country.

A good report provides practical recommendations that are agreeable to the audience. In the Marriott survey, for example, report researchers knew that the company wanted to

The best recommendations offer practical suggestions that are feasible and agreeable to the audience.

FIGURE 12.4 Report Conclusions and Recommendations

REPORT PROBLEM

Marriott Corporation experienced employee turnover and lowered productivity resulting from conflicting home and work requirements. The hotel conducted a massive survey resulting in some of the following findings.

PARTIAL FINDINGS

1. Nearly 35 percent of employees surveyed have children under age twelve.

2. Nearly 15 percent of employees have children under age five.

3. The average employee with children younger than twelve is absent four days a year and tardy five days because of child-related issues.

4. Within a one-year period, nearly 33 percent of employees who have young children take at least two days off because they can't find a replacement when their child-care plans break down.

5. Nearly 20 percent of employees left a previous employer because of work and family concerns.

6. At least 80 percent of female employees and 78 percent of male employees with young children reported job stress as a result of conflicting work and family roles.

7. Managers perceive family matters to be inappropriate issues for them to discuss at work.

From these and other findings, the following conclusions were drawn.

CONCLUSIONS

1. Home and family responsibilities directly affect job attendance and performance.

2. Time is the crucial issue to balancing work and family issues.

3. Male and female employees reported in nearly equal numbers the difficulties of managing work and family roles.

4. Problems with child-care arrangements increase employees' level of stress and limit their ability to work certain schedules or overtime.

5. A manager supportive of family and personal concerns is central to a good work environment.

Condenses significant findings in numbered statements

Uses conclusion section to present sensible analysis without exaggerating or manipulating data

Explains what findings mean in terms of report problem

Tips for Writing Conclusions
- Interpret and summarize the findings; tell what they mean.
- Relate the conclusions to the report problem.
- Limit the conclusions to the data presented; do not introduce new material.
- Number the conclusions and present them in parallel form.
- Be objective; avoid exaggerating or manipulating the data.
- Use consistent criteria in evaluating options.

FIGURE 12.4 (Continued)

Arranges actions to solve problems from most important to least important

RECOMMENDATIONS

1. Provide managers with training in working with personal and family matters.

2. Institute a flextime policy that allows employees to adapt their work schedules to home responsibilities.

3. Investigate opening a pilot child development center for preschool children of employees at company headquarters.

4. Develop a child-care resource program to provide parents with professional help in locating affordable child care.

5. Offer a child-care discount program to help parents pay for services.

6. Authorize weekly payroll deductions, using tax-free dollars, to pay for child care.

7. Publish a quarterly employee newsletter devoted to family and child-care issues.

Tips for Writing Recommendations
- Make specific suggestions for actions to solve the report problem.
- Prepare practical recommendations that will be agreeable to the audience.
- Avoid conditional words such as *maybe* and *perhaps*.
- Present each suggestion separately as a command beginning with a verb.
- Number the recommendations for improved readability.
- If requested, describe how the recommendations may be implemented.
- When possible, arrange the recommendations in an announced order, such as most important to least important.

help employees cope with conflicts between family and work obligations. Hence, the report's conclusions and recommendations focused on ways to resolve the conflict. If Marriott's goal had been merely to save money by reducing employee absenteeism, the recommendations would have been quite different.

If possible, make each recommendation a command. Note in Figure 12.4 that each recommendation begins with a verb. This structure sounds forceful and confident and helps the reader comprehend the information quickly. Avoid words such as *maybe* and *perhaps;* they suggest conditional statements that reduce the strength of recommendations.

Experienced writers may combine recommendations and conclusions. In short reports writers may omit conclusions and move straight to recommendations. An important point about recommendations is that they include practical suggestions for solving the report problem. Furthermore, they are always the result of prior logical analysis.

Moving From Findings to Recommendations

Recommendations evolve from interpretation of the findings and conclusions. Consider the following examples from the Marriott survey:

Finding
Managers perceive family matters to be inappropriate issues to discuss at work.

Conclusion
Managers are neither willing nor trained to discuss family matters that may cause employees to miss work.

Recommendation
Provide managers with training in recognizing and working with personal and family matters that affect work.

Finding

Within a one-year period, nearly 33 percent of employees who have young children take at least two days off because they can't find a replacement when their child-care plans break down.

Conclusion

Problems with child-care arrangements increase employees' level of stress and limit their ability to work certain schedules or overtime.

Recommendation

Develop a child-care resource program to provide parents with professional help in locating affordable child care.

Organizing Data

LEARNING OBJECTIVE 3
Organize report data logically and provide cues to aid readers' comprehension.

After collecting sets of data, interpreting them, drawing conclusions, and thinking about the recommendations, you are ready to organize the parts of the report into a logical framework. Poorly organized reports lead to frustration. Readers will not understand, remember, or be persuaded. Wise writers know that reports rarely "just organize themselves." Instead, organization must be imposed on the data, and cues must be provided so the reader can follow the logic of the writer.

Informational reports, as you learned in Chapter 11, generally present data without interpretation. As shown in Figure 12.5, informational reports typically consist of three parts: (a) introduction/background, (b) facts/findings, and (c) summary/concluding remarks. Analytical reports, which generally analyze data and draw conclusions, typically contain four parts: (a) introduction/problem, (b) facts/findings, (c) discussion/analysis, and (d) conclusions/recommendations. However, the parts in analytical reports do not always follow the same sequence. For readers who know about the project, are supportive, or are eager to learn the results quickly, the direct method is appropriate. Conclusions and recommendations, if requested, appear up front. For readers who must be educated or persuaded, the indirect method works better. Conclusions/recommendations appear last, after the findings have been presented and analyzed.

Although every report is different, the overall organizational patterns described here typically hold true. The real challenge, though, lies in (a) organizing the facts/findings and discussion/analysis sections and (b) providing reader cues.

The direct pattern is appropriate for informed or receptive readers; the indirect pattern is appropriate when educating or persuading.

Ordering Information Logically

Whether you are writing informational or analytical reports, the data you have collected must be structured coherently. Five common organizational methods are by time, component, importance, criteria, or convention. Regardless of the method you choose, be sure that it helps the reader understand the data. Reader comprehension, not writer convenience, should govern organization. For additional examples of organizational principles, please go to pages 428–430 in Chapter 14.

Organization by time, component, importance, criteria, or convention helps readers comprehend data.

Time. Ordering data by time means establishing a chronology of events. Agendas, minutes of meetings, progress reports, and procedures are usually organized by time. For example, a report describing an eight-week training program would most likely be organized by weeks. A plan for step-by-step improvement of customer service would be organized

FIGURE 12.5 Organizational Patterns for Informational and Analytical Reports

Informational Reports	Analytical Reports	
	Direct Pattern	**Indirect Pattern**
I. Introduction/background	I. Introduction/problem	I. Introduction/problem
II. Facts/findings	II. Conclusions/recommendations	II. Facts/findings
III. Summary/conclusion	III. Facts/findings	III. Discussion/analysis
	IV. Discussion/analysis	IV. Conclusions/recommendations

by steps. A monthly trip report submitted by a sales rep might describe customers visited Week 1, Week 2, and so on. Beware of overusing chronologies (time) as an organizing method for reports, however. Although this method is easy and often mirrors the way data are collected, chronologies—like the sales rep's trip report—tend to be boring, repetitious, and lacking in emphasis. Readers cannot always pick out what is important.

Component. Especially for informational reports, data may be organized by components such as location, geography, division, product, or part. For instance, a report detailing company expansion might divide the plan into West Coast, East Coast, and Midwest expansion. The report could also be organized by divisions: personal products, consumer electronics, and household goods. A report comparing profits among makers of athletic shoes might group the data by company: Nike, Reebok, Adidas, and so forth. Organization by components works best when the classifications already exist.

Organizing by level of importance saves the time of busy readers and increases the odds that key information will be retained.

Importance. Organization by importance involves beginning with the most important item and proceeding to the least important—or vice versa. For example, a report discussing the reasons for declining product sales would present the most important reason first followed by less important ones. The Marriott report describing work/family conflicts might begin by discussing child care, if the writer considered it the most important issue. Using importance to structure findings involves a value judgment. The writer must decide what is most important, always keeping in mind the readers' priorities and expectations. Busy readers appreciate seeing important points first; they may skim or skip other points. On the other hand, building to a climax by moving from least important to most important enables the writer to focus attention at the end. Thus, the reader is more likely to remember the most important item. Of course, the writer also risks losing the attention of the reader along the way.

Criteria. Establishing criteria by which to judge helps writers to treat topics consistently. Let's say your report compares health plans A, B, and C. For each plan you examine the same standards: Criterion 1, cost per employee; Criterion 2, amount of deductible; and Criterion 3, patient benefits. The resulting data could then be organized either by plans or by criteria:

To evaluate choices or plans fairly, apply the same criteria to each.

By Plan	By Criteria
Plan A	Criterion 1
Criterion 1	Plan A
Criterion 2	Plan B
Criterion 3	Plan C
Plan B	Criterion 2
Criterion 1	Plan A
Criterion 2	Plan B
Criterion 3	Plan C
Plan C	Criterion 3
Criterion 1	Plan A
Criterion 2	Plan B
Criterion 3	Plan C

Although you might favor organizing the data by plans (because that is the way you collected the data), the better way is by criteria. When you discuss patient benefits, for example, you would examine all three plans' benefits together. Organizing a report around criteria helps readers make comparisons, instead of forcing them to search through the report for similar data.

Organizing by convention simplifies the organizational task and yields easy-to-follow information.

Convention. Many operational and recurring reports are structured according to convention. That is, they follow a prescribed plan that everyone understands. For example, an automotive parts manufacturer might ask all sales reps to prepare a weekly report with these headings: *Competitive observations* (competitors' price changes, discounts, new products, product problems, distributor changes, product promotions), *Product problems* (quality, performance, needs), and *Customer service problems* (delivery, mailings, correspondence). Management gets exactly the information it needs in an easy-to-read form.

Like operating reports, proposals are often organized conventionally. They might use such groupings as background, problem, proposed solution, staffing, schedule, costs, and authorization. As you might expect, reports following these conventional, prescribed structures greatly simplify the task of organization. Proposals and long reports will be presented in Chapter 13.

Providing Reader Cues

When you finish organizing a report, you probably see a neat outline in your mind: major points, supported by subpoints and details. Readers, however, do not know the material as well as you do; they cannot see your outline. To guide them through the data, you need to provide the equivalent of a map and road signs. For both formal and informal reports, devices such as introductions, transitions, and headings prevent readers from getting lost.

Introduction. One of the best ways to point a reader in the right direction is to provide a report introduction that does three things:

Good openers tell readers what topics will be covered in what order and why.

- Tells the purpose of the report

- Describes the significance of the topic

- Previews the main points and the order in which they will be developed

The following paragraph includes all three elements in introducing a report on computer security:

> *This report examines the security of our current computer operations and presents suggestions for improving security. Lax computer security could mean loss of information, loss of business, and damage to our equipment and systems. Because many former employees released during recent downsizing efforts know our systems, major changes must be made. To improve security, I will present three recommendations: (a) begin using smart cards that limit access to our computer system, (b) alter sign-on and log-off procedures, (c) move central computer operations to a more secure area.*

This opener tells the purpose (examining computer security), describes its significance (loss of information and business, damage to equipment and systems), and outlines how the report is organized (three recommendations). Good openers in effect set up a contract with the reader. The writer promises to cover certain topics in a specified order. Readers expect the writer to fulfill the contract. They want the topics to be developed as promised—using the same wording and presented in the order mentioned. For example, if in your introduction you state that you will discuss the use of *smart cards,* do not change the heading for that section to *access cards.* Remember that the introduction provides a map to a report; switching the names on the map will ensure that readers get lost. To maintain consistency, delay writing the introduction until after you have completed the report. Long, complex reports may require introductions for each section.

Transitions. Expressions such as *on the contrary, at the same time,* and *however* show relationships and help reveal the logical flow of ideas in a report. These transitional expressions enable writers to tell readers where ideas are headed and how they relate. Notice how abrupt the following two sentences sound without a transition: *The Microsoft Zune player offers several technological advances that exceed the capabilities of Apple's iPod devices. The Zune [however] is locked into a clunky online music store that isn't likely to win many fans.*

Transitional expressions inform readers where ideas are headed and how they relate.

The following transitional expressions (see Chapter 5, Figure 5.7 for a complete list) enable you to show readers how you are developing your ideas.

> ***To present additional thoughts:*** *additionally, again, also, moreover, furthermore*
>
> ***To suggest cause and effect:*** *accordingly, as a result, consequently, therefore*
>
> ***To contrast ideas:*** *at the same time, but, however, on the contrary, though, yet*
>
> ***To show time and order:*** *after, before, first, finally, now, previously, then, to conclude*
>
> ***To clarify points:*** *for example, for instance, in other words, that is, thus*

In using these expressions, recognize that they do not have to sit at the head of a sentence. Listen to the rhythm of the sentence, and place the expression where a natural pause occurs. If you are unsure about the placement of a transitional expression, position it at the beginning of the sentence. Used appropriately, transitional expressions serve readers as guides; misused or overused, they can be as distracting and frustrating as too many road signs on a highway.

Headings. Good headings are another structural cue that assists readers in comprehending the organization of a report. They highlight major ideas, allowing busy readers to see the big picture at a glance. Moreover, headings provide resting points for the mind and for the eye, breaking up large chunks of text into manageable and inviting segments.

Report writers may use functional or talking headings. Functional headings (for example, *Background, Findings, Personnel,* and *Production Costs*) describe functions or general topics. They show the outline of a report but provide little insight for readers. Functional headings are useful for routine reports. They are also appropriate for sensitive topics that might provoke emotional reactions. By keeping the headings general, experienced writers hope to minimize reader opposition or response to controversial subjects. Talking headings (for example, *Lack of Space and Cost Compound Campus Parking Problem* or *Survey Shows Support for Parking Fees*) provide more information and interest. Unless carefully written, however, talking headings can fail to reveal the organization of a report. With some planning, though, headings can be both functional and talking, such as *Parking Recommendations: Shuttle and New Structures.*

The best strategy for creating helpful talking headings is to write a few paragraphs first and then generate talking headings that sum up the major point of each paragraph. To create the most effective headings, follow a few basic guidelines:

- **Use appropriate heading levels.** The position and format of a heading indicate its level of importance and relationship to other points. Figure 12.6 illustrates and discusses a commonly used heading format for business reports. For an overview of alphanumeric and decimal outlines, please see pages 129–130.

- **Capitalize and underline carefully.** Most writers use all capital letters (without underlines) for main titles, such as the report, chapter, and unit titles. For first- and second-level headings, they capitalize only the first letter of main words. For additional emphasis, they use a bold font, as shown in Figure 12.6.

- **Try to balance headings within levels.** Although it may not be always possible, attempt to create headings that are grammatically similar at a given level. For example, *Developing Product Teams* and *Presenting Plan to Management* are balanced, but *Development of Product Teams* and *Presenting Plan to Management* are not.

- **For short reports use first-level or first- and second-level headings.** Many business reports contain only one or two levels of headings. For such reports use first-level headings (centered, bolded) and/or second-level headings (flush left, bolded). See Figure 12.6.

- **Include at least one heading per report page.** Headings increase the readability and attractiveness of report pages. Use at least one per page to break up blocks of text.

Mass production of the new 787 Dreamliner requires careful coordination between the Boeing Company and its suppliers. To achieve timely delivery of the lightweight, ultra-fuel-efficient jet airliner, project managers set precise production schedules, making adjustments to accommodate interruptions in the manufacturing process. The job is a team effort: one supplier's failure to deliver parts and materials can delay production for months. *How do informational reports help managers keep projects on schedule?*

© FRANK BRANDMAIER / dpa / Landov

FIGURE 12.6 Levels of Headings in Reports

2-inch top margin

REPORT, CHAPTER, AND PART TITLES

Places major headings in the center

2 blank lines

The title of a report, chapter heading, or major part (such as CONTENTS or NOTES) should be centered in all caps. If the title requires more than one line, arrange it in an inverted triangle with the longest lines at the top. Begin the text a triple space (two blank lines) below the title, as shown here.

2 blank lines

Capitalizes initial letters of main words

First-Level Subheading

1 blank line

Headings indicating the first level of division are centered and bolded. Capitalize the first letter of each main word. Whether a report is single-spaced or double-spaced, most typists triple-space (leaving two blank lines) before and double-space (leaving one blank line) after a first-level subheading.

Does not indent paragraphs because report is single-spaced

1 blank line

Every level of heading should be followed by some text. For example, we could not jump from "First-Level Subheading," shown above, to "Second-Level Subheading," shown below, without some discussion between.

Good writers strive to develop coherency and fluency by ending most sections with a lead-in that introduces the next section. The lead-in consists of a sentence or two announcing the next topic.

2 blank lines

Starts at left margin

Second-Level Subheading

Headings that divide topics introduced by first-level subheadings are bolded and begin at the left margin. Use a triple space above and a double space after a second-level subheading. If a report has only one level of heading, use either first- or second-level subheading style.

Always be sure to divide topics into two or more subheadings. If you have only one subheading, eliminate it and absorb the discussion under the previous major heading. Try to make all headings within a level grammatically equal. For example, all second-level headings might use verb forms (*Preparing*, *Organizing*, and *Composing*) or noun forms (*Preparation*, *Organization*, and *Composition*).

1 blank line

Makes heading part of paragraph

Third-level subheading. Because it is part of the paragraph that follows, a third-level subheading is also called a "paragraph subheading." Capitalize only the first word and proper nouns in the subheading. Bold the subheading and end it with a period. Begin typing the paragraph text immediately following the period, as shown here. Double-space before a paragraph subheading. If the entire report is double-spaced, paragraphs would be indented, including this third-level subheading.

- **Keep headings short but clear.** One-word headings are emphatic but not always clear. For example, the heading *Budget* does not adequately describe figures for a summer project involving student interns for an oil company in Texas. Try to keep your headings brief (no more than eight words), but make sure they are understandable. Experiment with headings that concisely tell who, what, when, where, and why.

Writing Informational Reports

Now that we have covered the basics of gathering, interpreting, and organizing data, we are ready to put it all together into short informational or analytical reports. Informational reports often describe periodic, recurring activities (such as monthly sales or weekly customer calls) as well as situational, nonrecurring events (such as trips, conferences, and progress on special projects). What they have in common is delivering information to readers who do not have to be persuaded. Informational report readers usually are neutral or receptive.

You can expect to write many informational reports as an entry-level or middle-management employee. Because these reports generally deliver nonsensitive data and thus

LEARNING OBJECTIVE 4
Prepare short informational reports.

Informational reports provide data on periodic and situational activities for readers who do not need to be persuaded.

CAREER COACH

Ten Tips for Designing Better Documents

Desktop publishing packages, high-level word processing programs, and advanced printers now make it possible for you to turn out professional-looking documents and promotional materials. The temptation, though, is to overdo it by incorporating too many features in one document. Here are ten tips for applying good sense and good design principles in "publishing" your documents.

- **Analyze your audience.** Sales brochures and promotional letters can be flashy—with color print, oversized type, and fancy borders—to attract attention. But such effects are out of place for most conservative business documents. Also consider whether your readers will be reading painstakingly or merely browsing. Lists and headings help those readers who are in a hurry.
- **Choose an appropriate type size.** For most business memos, letters, and reports, the body text should be 11 to 12 points tall (a point is 1/72 of an inch). Larger type looks amateurish, and smaller type is hard to read.
- **Use a consistent type font.** Although your software may provide a variety of fonts, stay with a single family of type within one document—at least until you become more expert. The most popular fonts are Times Roman and Arial. For emphasis and contrast, you can vary the font size and weight with **bold**, *italic*, ***bold italic***, and other selections.
- **Generally, do not justify right margins.** Textbooks, novels, newspapers, magazines, and other long works are usually set with justified (even) right margins. However, for shorter works ragged-right margins are recommended because such margins add white space and help readers locate the beginnings of new lines. Slower readers find ragged-right copy more legible.
- **Separate paragraphs and sentences appropriately.** In most business documents the first line of a paragraph is preceded by a blank line, but some writers like to indent the first line five spaces from the left margin. To separate sentences, typists have traditionally left two spaces after the period. This spacing is still acceptable, and proponents argue that this practice enhances readability, but most writers now follow printers' standards and leave only one space. Whichever standard you adopt, be sure to maintain it consistently.
- **Design readable headlines.** Presenting headlines and headings in all caps is generally discouraged because solid blocks of capital letters interfere with recognition of word patterns. To further improve readability, select a sans serif typeface (one without cross strokes or embellishment), such as Arial.
- **Strive for an attractive page layout.** In designing title pages or graphics, provide a balance between print and white space. Also consider placing the focal point (something that draws the reader's eye) at the optical center of a page—about three lines above the actual center. Moreover, remember that the average reader scans a page from left to right and top to bottom in a *Z* pattern. Plan your graphics accordingly.
- **Use graphics and clip art with restraint.** Charts, original drawings, photographs, and clip art can be scanned into documents. Use such images, however, only when they are well drawn, relevant, purposeful, and appropriately sized.
- **Avoid amateurish effects.** Many beginning writers, eager to display every graphic device a program offers, produce busy, cluttered documents. Too many typefaces, ruled lines, oversized headlines, and images will overwhelm readers. Strive for simple, clean, and forceful effects.
- **Develop expertise.** Learn to use the desktop publishing features of your current word processing software, or investigate one of the special programs, such as QuarkXPress, Adobe's InDesign, and Corel's Ventura. Although the learning curve for many of these programs is steep, such effort is well spent if you will be producing newsletters, brochures, announcements, visual aids, and promotional literature.

Career Application

Buy or borrow a book or two on designing documents, and select ten tips that you could share with the class. In teams of three or four, analyze the design and layout of three or four annual reports. Evaluate the appropriateness of typeface and type size, white space, headings, and graphics.

---

will not upset the reader, they are organized directly. Often they need little background material or introductory comments because readers are familiar with the topics. Although they are generally conversational and informal, informational reports should not be so casual that the reader struggles to find the important points. Main points must be immediately visible. Headings, lists, bulleted items, and other graphic highlighting, as well as clear organization, enable readers to grasp major ideas immediately. The lessons that you have learned about conciseness, clarity, courtesy, and effective writing in general throughout earlier chapters apply to report writing as well. After all, competent reports can boost your visibility in the company and promote your advancement. The accompanying Career Coach box provides additional pointers on design features and techniques that can improve your reports.

Periodic (Activity) Reports

Most businesses—especially larger ones—require periodic reports (sometimes called *activity reports*) to keep management informed

Spotlight on Communicators

Regular financial reports keep Protocol Telecommunications squeaky clean. Anthony Miranda, president of Protocol, doesn't wait for his bankers or investors to demand his financials. "I want there to be no question at any time that our financial information was misstated or less than fully disclosed." In addition to periodic financial reports, Protocol employees may submit trip and conference reports describing attendance at trade shows or meetings. Such reports identify the event, summarize relevant information acquired, itemize expenses, and suggest how the information may be applied.

Chapter 12: Informal Business Reports

of operations. These recurring reports are written at regular intervals—weekly, monthly, yearly—so that management can monitor and, if necessary, remedy business strategies. Some periodic reports simply contain figures, such as sales volume, number and kind of customer service calls, shipments delivered, accounts payable, and personnel data. More challenging periodic reports require descriptions and discussions of activities. In preparing a narrative description of their activities, employees writing periodic reports usually do the following:

Periodic reports keep management informed of operations and activities.

- Summarize regular activities and events performed during the reporting period

- Describe irregular events deserving the attention of management

- Highlight special needs and problems

Managers naturally want to know that routine activities are progressing normally. They are often more interested, though, in what the competition is doing and in how operations may be affected by unusual events or problems. In companies with open lines of communication, managers expect to be informed of the bad news along with the good news. Joel Rutherford, sales rep for a West Coast sprinkler manufacturer, worked with a group of fellow sales reps and managers to produce the format for the periodic report shown in Figure 12.7. In Joel's words, "We used to write three- and four-page weekly activity reports that, I hate to admit, rambled all over the place. When our managers complained that they were not getting the information they wanted, we sat down together and developed a report form with four categories: (a) activity summary, (b) competition update, (c) product problems and comments, and (d) needs. Then one manager wrote several sample reports that we studied. Now, my reports are shorter and more focused. I try to hit the highlights in covering my daily activities, but I really concentrate on product problems and items that I must have to do a better job. Managers tell us that they need this kind of detailed feedback so that they can respond to the competition and also develop new products that our customers want."

Trip, Convention, and Conference Reports

Employees sent on business trips or to conventions and conferences typically must submit reports when they return. Organizations want to know that their money was well spent in funding the travel. These reports inform management about new procedures, equipment, and laws as well as supply information affecting products, operations, and service.

The hardest parts of writing these reports are selecting the most relevant material and organizing it coherently. Generally, it is best not to use chronological sequencing (*in the morning we did X, at lunch we heard Y, and in the afternoon we did Z*). Instead, you should focus on three to five topics in which your reader will be interested. These items become the body of the report. Then simply add an introduction and closing, and your report is organized. Here is a general outline for trip, conference, and convention reports:

- Begin by identifying the event (exact date, name, and location) and previewing the topics to be discussed.

- Summarize in the body three to five main points that might benefit the reader.

- Itemize your expenses, if requested, on a separate sheet.

- Close by expressing appreciation, suggesting action to be taken, or synthesizing the value of the trip or event.

Trip and conference reports identify the event, summarize three to five main points, itemize expenses separately, and express appreciation or suggest action to be taken.

Jack Horn was recently named employment coordinator in the Human Resources Department of an electronics appliance manufacturer headquartered in central Ohio. Recognizing his lack of experience in interviewing job applicants, he asked permission to attend a one-day conference on the topic. His boss, Elizabeth Greene, encouraged Jack to attend, saying, "We all need to brush up on our interviewing techniques. Come back and tell us what you learned." When he returned, Jack wrote the conference report shown in Figure 12.8. Here is how he described its preparation: "I know my boss values brevity, so I worked hard to make my report no more than a page and a quarter. The conference saturated me with great ideas, far too many to cover in one brief report. So, I decided to discuss

FIGURE 12.7 Periodic (Activity) Report—Memo Format

1 Prewriting

Analyze: The purpose of this report is to inform management of the week's activities, customer reactions, and the rep's needs.

Anticipate: The audience is a manager who wants to be able to pick out the report highlights quickly. His reaction will probably be neutral or positive.

Adapt: Introduce the report data in a direct, straightforward manner.

2 Writing

Research: Verify data for the landscape judging test. Collect facts about competitors. Double-check problems and needs.

Organize: Make lists of items for each of the four report categories. Be sure to distinguish between problems and needs. Emphasize needs.

Compose: Write and print first draft on a computer.

3 Revising

Revise: Look for ways to eliminate wordiness. For greater emphasis use a bulleted list for *Competition Update* and for *Needs*. Make all items parallel.

Proofread: Run spell checker. Adjust white space around headings.

Evaluate: Does this report provide significant data in an easy-to-read format?

Rain Land
Where every drop counts

DATE:	March 15, 2009
TO:	John Greenfield
FROM:	Joel Rutherford
SUBJECT:	Weekly Activity Report

Presents internal informational report in memo format

Activity Summary

Highlights of my activities for the week ending March 14 follow:

Fort Worth. On Thursday and Friday I demonstrated our new Rain Stream drip systems at a vendor fair at Benbrook Farm Supply, where more than 500 people walked through.

Arlington State College. Over the weekend I was a judge for the Texas Landscape Technician test given on the ASC campus. This certification program ensures potential employers that a landscaper is properly trained. Applicants are tested in such areas as irrigation theory, repair, trouble-shooting, installation, and controller programming. The event proved to be very productive. I was able to talk to my distributors and to several important contractors whose crews were taking the tests.

Condenses weekly activity report into topics requested by management

Competition Update

- Toronado can't seem to fill its open sales position in the west Texas territory.
- RainCo tried to steal the Trinity Country Club golf course contract from us by waiting until the job was spec'd our way and then submitting a lower bid. Fortunately, the Trinity people saw through this ploy and awarded us the contract nevertheless.
- Atlas has a real warranty problem with its 500 series in this area. One distributor had over 200 controllers returned in a seven-week period.

Uses bulleted list for high "skim value"

Product Problems, Comments

A contractor in Wichita Falls told me that our Rain Stream No. 250 valves do not hold the adjustment screw in the throttled-down position. Are they designed to do so?

Our Remote Streamer S-100 is generating considerable excitement. Every time I mention it, people come out of the woodwork to request demos. I gave four demos last week and have three more scheduled this week. I'm not sure, though, how quickly these demos will translate into sales.

Needs

- More information on xerigation training.
- Spanish training videos showing our products.
- Spray nozzle to service small planter areas, say 6 to 8 feet.

Summarizes needs in abbreviated, easy-to-read form

---

three topics that would be most useful to our staff. Although I had to be brief, I nonetheless wanted to provide as many details—especially about common interviewing mistakes—as possible. By the third draft, I had compressed my ideas into a manageable size without sacrificing any of the meaning."

FIGURE 12.8 Conference Report—Memo Format

//TriCom
Total HR Services
Interoffice Memo

DATE: April 22, 2009
TO: Elizabeth Greene
FROM: Jack Horn
SUBJECT: Conference on Employment Interviews

I enjoyed attending the "Interviewing People" training conference sponsored by
the National Business Foundation. This one-day meeting, held in Columbus on
April 19, provided excellent advice that will help us strengthen our interviewing
techniques. Although the conference covered many topics, this report
concentrates on three areas: structuring the interview, avoiding common
mistakes, and responding to new legislation.

Identifies topic and previews how the report is organized

Structuring the Interview

Job interviews usually have three parts. The opening establishes a friendly
rapport with introductions, a few polite questions, and an explanation of the
purpose for the interview. The body of the interview consists of questions
controlled by the interviewer. The interviewer has three goals: (a) educating
the applicant about the job, (b) eliciting information about the applicant's
suitability for the job, and (c) promoting goodwill about the organization. In
closing, the interviewer should encourage the applicant to ask questions,
summarize main points, and indicate what actions will follow.

Sets off major topics with centered headings

Avoiding Common Mistakes

Probably the most interesting and practical part of the conference centered on
common mistakes made by interviewers, some of which I summarize here:

1. Not taking notes at each interview. Recording important facts enables you to
   remember the first candidate as easily as you remember the last—and all
   those in between.

2. Not testing the candidate's communication skills. To be able to evaluate a
   candidate's ability to express ideas, ask the individual to explain some
   technical jargon from his or her current position.

3. Having departing employees conduct the interviews for their replacements.
   Departing employees may be unreliable as interviewers because they tend to
   hire candidates not quite as strong as they are.

4. Failing to check references. As many as 45 percent of all résumés may contain
   falsified data. The best way to check references is to network: ask the person
   whose name has been given to suggest the name of another person.

Covers facts that will most interest and help reader

Elizabeth Greene   Page 2   April 22, 2009

Responding to New Legislation

Current federal provisions of the Americans With Disabilities Act prohibit
interviewers from asking candidates—or even their references—about candidates'
disabilities. A question we frequently asked ("Do you have any physical limitations
which would prevent you from performing the job for which you are applying?")
would now break the law. Interviewers must also avoid asking about medical
history; prescription drug use; prior workers' compensation claims; work absenteeism
due to illness; and past treatment for alcoholism, drug use, or mental illness.

Concludes with offer to share information

Sharing This Information

This conference provided me with valuable training that I would like to share with
other department members at a future staff meeting. Let me know when it can
be scheduled.

Progress and Interim Reports

Continuing projects often require progress or interim reports to describe their status. These
reports may be external (advising customers regarding the headway of their projects) or
internal (informing management of the status of activities). Progress reports typically follow
this pattern of development:

Progress and interim reports describe ongoing projects to both internal and external readers.

- Specify in the opening the purpose and nature of the project.

- Provide background information if the audience requires filling in.

- Describe the work completed.

- Explain the work currently in progress, including personnel, activities, methods, and locations.

- Describe current problems and anticipate future problems and possible remedies.

- Discuss future activities and provide the expected completion date.

As a location manager for Eagle Video Productions, Gina Genova frequently writes progress reports, such as the one shown in Figure 12.9. Producers want to be informed of what she is doing, and a phone call does not provide a permanent record. Here is how she described the reasoning behind her progress report: "I usually include background information in my reports because a director does not always know or remember exactly what specifications I was given for a location search. Then I try to hit the high points of what I have completed and what I plan to do next, without getting bogged down in tiny details. Although it would be easier to skip them, I have learned to be up front with any problems that I anticipate. I do not tell how to solve the problems, but I feel duty-bound to at least mention them."

Investigative Reports

Investigative reports provide information without interpretation or recommendations.

Investigative or informational reports deliver data for a specific situation—without offering interpretation or recommendations. These nonrecurring reports are generally arranged in a direct pattern with three segments: introduction, body, and summary. The body—which includes the facts, findings, or discussion—may be organized by time, component, importance, criteria, or convention. What is important is dividing the topic into logical segments, say, three to five areas that are roughly equal and do not overlap.

The subject matter of the report usually suggests the best way to divide or organize it. Beth Givens, an information specialist for a Minneapolis health care consulting firm, was given the task of researching and writing an investigative report for St. John's Hospital. Her assignment: study the award-winning patient-service program at Good Samaritan Hospital and report how it improved its patient satisfaction rating from 6.2 to 7.8 in just one year. Beth collected data and then organized her findings into four parts: management training, employee training, patient services, and follow-up program. Although we do not show Beth's complete report here, you can see a similar informational report in Chapter 11, Figure 11.2.

Whether you are writing a periodic, trip, conference, progress, or investigative report, you will want to review the suggestions found in the following checklist.

Checklist

Writing Informational Reports

Introduction

✓ **Begin directly.** Identify the report and its purpose.

✓ **Provide a preview.** If the report is over a page long, give the reader a brief overview of its organization.

✓ **Supply background data selectively.** When readers are unfamiliar with the topic, briefly fill in the necessary details.

✓ **Divide the topic.** Strive to group the facts or findings into three to five roughly equal segments that do not overlap.

Body

✓ **Arrange the subtopics logically.** Consider organizing by time, component, importance, criteria, or convention.

✓ **Use clear headings.** Supply functional or talking headings (at least one per page) that describe each important section.

✓ **Determine degree of formality.** Use an informal, conversational writing style unless the audience expects a more formal tone.

✓ **Enhance readability with graphic highlighting.** Make liberal use of bullets, numbered and lettered lists, headings, underlined items, and white space.

Summary/Concluding Remarks

✓ **When necessary, summarize the report.** Briefly review the main points and discuss what action will follow.

✓ **Offer a concluding thought.** If relevant, express appreciation or describe your willingness to provide further information.

FIGURE 12.9 Progress Report—Letter Format

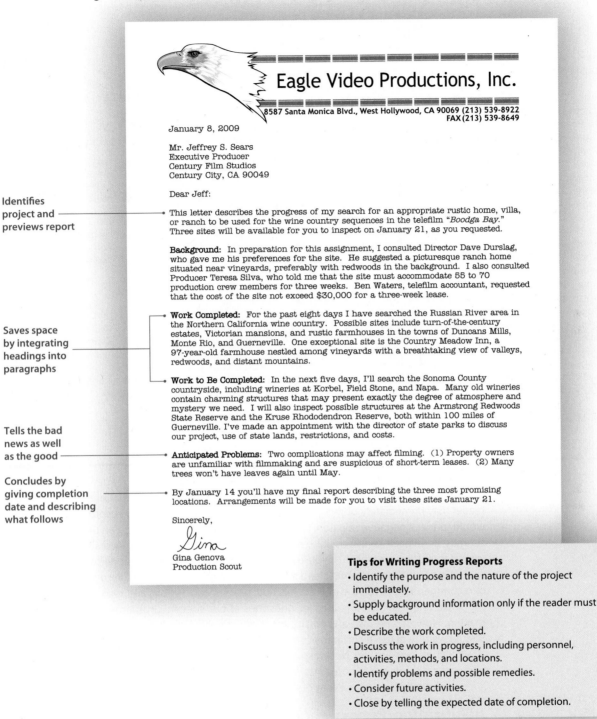

Eagle Video Productions, Inc.

8587 Santa Monica Blvd., West Hollywood, CA 90069 (213) 539-8922
FAX (213) 539-8649

January 8, 2009

Mr. Jeffrey S. Sears
Executive Producer
Century Film Studios
Century City, CA 90049

Dear Jeff:

Identifies project and previews report →
This letter describes the progress of my search for an appropriate rustic home, villa, or ranch to be used for the wine country sequences in the telefilm "*Boodga Bay.*" Three sites will be available for you to inspect on January 21, as you requested.

Background: In preparation for this assignment, I consulted Director Dave Durslag, who gave me his preferences for the site. He suggested a picturesque ranch home situated near vineyards, preferably with redwoods in the background. I also consulted Producer Teresa Silva, who told me that the site must accommodate 55 to 70 production crew members for three weeks. Ben Waters, telefilm accountant, requested that the cost of the site not exceed $30,000 for a three-week lease.

Saves space by integrating headings into paragraphs →
Work Completed: For the past eight days I have searched the Russian River area in the Northern California wine country. Possible sites include turn-of-the-century estates, Victorian mansions, and rustic farmhouses in the towns of Duncans Mills, Monte Rio, and Guerneville. One exceptional site is the Country Meadow Inn, a 97-year-old farmhouse nestled among vineyards with a breathtaking view of valleys, redwoods, and distant mountains.

Work to Be Completed: In the next five days, I'll search the Sonoma County countryside, including wineries at Korbel, Field Stone, and Napa. Many old wineries contain charming structures that may present exactly the degree of atmosphere and mystery we need. I will also inspect possible structures at the Armstrong Redwoods State Reserve and the Kruse Rhododendron Reserve, both within 100 miles of Guerneville. I've made an appointment with the director of state parks to discuss our project, use of state lands, restrictions, and costs.

Tells the bad news as well as the good →
Anticipated Problems: Two complications may affect filming. (1) Property owners are unfamiliar with filmmaking and are suspicious of short-term leases. (2) Many trees won't have leaves again until May.

Concludes by giving completion date and describing what follows →
By January 14 you'll have my final report describing the three most promising locations. Arrangements will be made for you to visit these sites January 21.

Sincerely,

Gina Genova
Production Scout

Tips for Writing Progress Reports

- Identify the purpose and the nature of the project immediately.
- Supply background information only if the reader must be educated.
- Describe the work completed.
- Discuss the work in progress, including personnel, activities, methods, and locations.
- Identify problems and possible remedies.
- Consider future activities.
- Close by telling the expected date of completion.

Writing Short Analytical Reports

Analytical reports differ significantly from informational reports. Although both seek to collect and present data clearly, analytical reports also analyze the data and typically try to persuade the reader to accept the conclusions and act on the recommendations. Informational reports emphasize facts; analytical reports emphasize reasoning and conclusions.

For some readers you may organize analytical reports directly with the conclusions and recommendations near the beginning. Directness is appropriate when the reader has

LEARNING OBJECTIVE 5
Prepare short analytical reports that solve business problems.

Analytical reports present information but emphasize reasoning, conclusions, and recommendations.

Communicating at Work Part 2

Starbucks: More Than Just Beans

Under the leadership of chairman and chief global strategist Howard Schultz, Starbucks plans to expand the number of stores and to pursue many other avenues of growth beyond its core coffeehouse business. Rather than striving to make Starbucks the world's biggest coffee shop chain, Schultz is focusing on turning Starbucks into the most recognizable and respected brand in the world. Even as Starbucks grows, however, Schultz and his team must strive to maintain "the intimacy and personalized feel of every Starbucks encounter." He says Starbucks' biggest challenge is "to get big but stay small."[5]

Pursuing the right growth strategy is not easy, and Starbucks has definitely had some flops. *Joe,* the coffeehouse magazine published jointly with *Time,* lasted only three issues. An Internet venture to sell kitchen products online was announced one day, and the next day the stock fell 28 percent. Five Starbucks Café restaurants that opened a few years ago no longer exist; and the Mazagran, a carbonated coffee beverage developed with PepsiCo, fizzled out.[6]

Although thousands of copycat coffee shops are springing up around the country, none is positioned to overtake the front-running Starbucks. Specialty coffee retailers such as Caribou Coffee—the second-largest nonfranchised coffee chain in the United States—The Coffee Bean & Tea Leaf, and Diedrich Coffee are all much smaller than the market leader. But Starbucks knows that the competition never sleeps. Its biggest rivals in the industry are the low-end and low-cost coffee powerhouses Dunkin' Donuts, Nestlé, and McDonald's. Now, Italian coffee makers such as Illy and

its Espressamente stores are taking on Starbucks in the top market segment. Along with other niche players, Illy wants to rival the American giant on the high end with gourmet premium coffee and very upscale locations.[7] Another way to grow and keep the competition in check is strategic acquisition: over the course of several years, Starbucks bought Torrefazione Italia, Seattle's Best Coffee, and, most recently, Portland's Coffee People as well as 40 company-owned retail stores from Diedrich Coffee.[8] You will learn more about this case on page 382.

Critical Thinking

- How important to Starbucks are the collection, organization, and distribution of up-to-date information regarding food and beverage trends, competition, and product development?
- In what ways could Starbucks use the Internet to monitor its competitors, Caribou Coffee and Illy Caffè?
- What kind of reports might be made to management by employees assigned the task of monitoring Starbucks' competition?

---

confidence in the writer, based on either experience or credentials. Frontloading the recommendations also works when the topic is routine or familiar and the reader is supportive.

Directness can backfire, though. If you announce the recommendations too quickly, the reader may immediately object to a single idea. You may have had no suspicion that this idea would trigger a negative reaction. Once the reader is opposed, changing an unfavorable mindset may be difficult or impossible. A reader may also think you have oversimplified or overlooked something significant if you lay out all the recommendations before explaining how you arrived at them. When you must lead the reader through the process of discovering the solution or recommendation, use the indirect method: present conclusions and recommendations last.

Most analytical reports answer questions about specific problems and aid in decision making. How can we use a Web site most effectively? Should we close the El Paso plant? Should we buy or lease company cars? How can we improve customer service? Three typical analytical reports answer business questions: justification/recommendation reports, feasibility reports, and yardstick reports. Because these reports all solve problems, the categories are not mutually exclusive. What distinguishes them are their goals and organization.

Justification/Recommendation Reports

Justification/recommendation reports follow the direct or indirect pattern depending on the audience and the topic.

Both managers and employees must occasionally write reports that justify or recommend something, such as buying equipment, changing a procedure, hiring an employee, consolidating departments, or investing funds. These reports may also be called *internal proposals* because their persuasive nature is similar to that of external proposals (presented in Chapter 13). Large organizations sometimes prescribe how these reports should be organized; they use forms with conventional headings. When you are free to select an organizational plan yourself, however, let your audience and topic determine your choice of direct or indirect structure.

The direct pattern is appropriate for justification/recommendation reports on nonsensitive topics and for receptive audiences.

Direct Pattern.
For nonsensitive topics and recommendations that will be agreeable to readers, you can organize directly according to the following sequence:

- Identify the problem or need briefly.

This greenhouse at the popular Keukenhof Gardens in Holland became a key point in the justification report of a tour organizer. In supporting this inclusion of the Keukenhof in a proposed itinerary for an American travel company, the writer argued that tourists can never be rained out. In addition to the 70 acres of outdoor gardens, thousands of flowers bloom under glass. *What are the key elements of a persuasive justification report?*

- Announce the recommendation, solution, or action concisely and with action verbs.

- Explain more fully the benefits of the recommendation or steps necessary to solve the problem.

- Include a discussion of pros, cons, and costs.

- Conclude with a summary specifying the recommendation and necessary action.

Here is how Cory Black applied the process in justifying a purchase. Cory is operations manager in charge of a fleet of trucks for a large parcel delivery company in Atlanta. When he heard about a new Goodyear smart tire with an electronic chip, Cory thought his company should give the new tire a try. Because new tires would represent an irregular purchase and because they would require a pilot test, he wrote the justification/recommendation report, shown in Figure 12.10, to his boss. Cory described his report in this way: "As more and more parcel delivery companies crop up, we have to find ways to cut costs so that we can remain competitive. Although more expensive initially, smart tires may solve many of our problems and save us money in the long run. I knew Jim Jordan, operations vice president, would be interested in them, especially in view of the huge Firestone tire fiasco.[9] Because Jim would be most interested in what they could do for us, I concentrated on benefits. In my first draft the benefits were lost in a couple of long paragraphs. Only after I read what I had written did I see that I was really talking about four separate benefits. Then I looked for words to summarize each one as a heading. So that Jim would know exactly what he should do, I concluded with specifics. All he had to do was say 'Go.'"

Indirect Pattern. When a reader may oppose a recommendation or when circumstances suggest caution, do not rush to reveal your recommendation. Consider using the following sequence for an indirect approach to your recommendations:

- Make a general reference to the problem, not to your recommendation, in the subject line.

- Describe the problem or need your recommendation addresses. Use specific examples, supporting statistics, and authoritative quotes to lend credibility to the seriousness of the problem.

- Discuss alternative solutions, beginning with the least likely to succeed.

- Present the most promising alternative (your recommendation) last.

The indirect pattern is appropriate for justification/ recommendation reports on sensitive topics and for potentially unreceptive audiences.

- Show how the advantages of your recommendation outweigh its disadvantages.
- Summarize your recommendation. If appropriate, specify the action it requires.
- Ask for authorization to proceed if necessary.

FIGURE 12.10 Justification/Recommendation Report: Direct Pattern

1 Prewriting

Analyze: The purpose of this report is to persuade the manager to authorize the purchase and pilot testing of smart tires.

Anticipate: The audience is a manager who is familiar with operations but not with this product. He will probably be receptive to the recommendation.

Adapt: Present the report data in a direct, straightforward manner.

2 Writing

Research: Collect data on how smart tires could benefit operations.

Organize: Discuss the problem briefly. Introduce and justify the recommendation by noting its cost-effectiveness and paperwork benefits. Explain the benefits of smart tires. Describe the action to be taken.

Compose: Write and print first draft.

3 Revising

Revise: Revise to break up long paragraphs about benefits. Isolate each benefit in an enumerated list with headings.

Proofread: Double-check all figures. Be sure all headings are parallel.

Evaluate: Does this report make its request concisely but emphatically? Will the reader see immediately what action is required?

DATE: July 19, 2009
TO: Jim Jordan
FROM: Cory Black, Operations Manager
SUBJECT: Goodyear Smart Tires—Pilot Test

Next to fuel, truck tires are our biggest operating cost. Last year we spent $236,000 replacing and retreading tires for 495 trucks. This year the costs will be greater because prices have jumped at least 12 percent and because we've increased our fleet to 550 trucks. Truck tires are an additional burden because they require labor-intensive paperwork to track their warranties, wear, and retread histories. To reduce our long-term costs and to improve our tire tracking system, I recommend that we do the following:

- Purchase 24 Goodyear smart tires.
- Begin a one-year pilot test on six trucks.

How Smart Tires Work

Smart tires have an embedded computer chip that monitors wear, performance, and durability. The chip also creates an electronic fingerprint for positive identification of a tire. By passing a handheld sensor next to the tire, we can learn where and when a tire was made (for warranty and other identification), how much tread it had originally, and its serial number.

How Smart Tires Could Benefit Us

Although smart tires are initially more expensive than other tires, they could help us improve our operations and save us money in four ways:

1. **Retreads.** Goodyear believes that the wear data is so accurate that we should be able to retread every tire three times, instead of our current two times. If that's true, in one year we could save at least $27,000 in new tire costs.
2. **Safety.** Accurate and accessible wear data should reduce the danger of blowouts and flat tires. Last year, drivers reported six blowouts.
3. **Record keeping and maintenance.** Smart tires could reduce our maintenance costs considerably. Currently, we use an electric branding iron to mark serial numbers on new tires. Our biggest headache is manually reading those serial numbers, decoding them, and maintaining records to meet safety regulations. Reading such data electronically could save us thousands of dollars in labor.
4. **Theft protection.** The chip can be used to monitor each tire as it leaves or enters the warehouse or yard, thus discouraging theft.

Summary and Action

Specifically, I recommend that you do the following:
- Authorize the special purchase of 24 Goodyear smart tires at $500 each, plus one electronic sensor at $1,500.
- Approve a one-year pilot test in our Atlanta territory that equips six trucks with smart tires and tracks their performance.

Introduces problem briefly

Presents recommendations immediately

Justifies recommendation by explaining product and benefits

Enumerates items for maximum impact and readability

Explains recommendation in more detail

Specifies action to be taken

Lara Brown, an executive assistant at a large petroleum and mining company in Grand Prairie, Texas, received a challenging research assignment. Her boss, the director of Human Resources, asked her to investigate ways to persuade employees to quit smoking. Here is how she described her task: "We banned smoking many years ago inside our buildings, but we never tried very hard to get smokers to actually kick their habits. My job was to gather information about the problem and how other companies have helped workers stop smoking. The report would go to my boss, but I knew he would pass it along to the management council for approval. If the report were just for my boss, I would put my recommendation right up front, because I'm sure he would support it. But the management council is another story. They need persuasion because of the costs involved—and because some of them are smokers. Therefore, I put the alternative I favored last. To gain credibility, I footnoted my sources. I had enough material for a ten-page report, but I kept it to two pages in keeping with our company report policy."

Lara single-spaced her report, shown in Figure 12.11, because her company prefers this style. Some companies prefer the readability of double spacing. Be sure to check with your organization for its preference before printing out your reports.

> Footnoting sources lends added credibility to justification/recommendation reports.

FIGURE 12.11 Justification/Recommendation Report: Indirect Pattern, MLA Style

DATE: October 11, 2009

TO: Gordon McClure, Director, Human Resources

FROM: Lara Brown, Executive Assistant

SUBJECT: Smoking Cessation Programs for Employees

At your request, I have examined measures that encourage employees to quit smoking. As company records show, approximately 23 percent of our employees still smoke, despite the antismoking and clean-air policies we adopted in 2006. To collect data for this report, I studied professional and government publications; I also inquired at companies and clinics about stop-smoking programs.

Introduces purpose of report, tells method of data collection, and previews organization

This report presents data describing the significance of the problem, three alternative solutions, and a recommendation based on my investigation.

Avoids revealing recommendation immediately

Significance of Problem: Health Care and Productivity Losses

Uses headings that combine function and description

Employees who smoke are costly to any organization. The following statistics show the effects of smoking for workers and for organizations:

• Absenteeism is 40 to 50 percent greater among smoking employees.
• Accidents are two to three times greater among smokers.
• Bronchitis, lung and heart disease, cancer, and early death are more frequent among smokers (Arhelger 15).

Documents data sources for credibility; uses MLA style citing author, date, and page number in the text

Although our clean-air policy prohibits smoking in the building, shop, and office, we have done little to encourage employees to stop smoking. Many workers still go outside to smoke at lunch and breaks. Other companies have been far more proactive in their attempts to stop employee smoking. Many companies have found that persuading employees to stop smoking was a decisive factor in reducing their health insurance premiums. Below is a discussion of three common stop-smoking measures tried by other companies, along with a projected cost factor for each (Rindfleisch 1).

Alternative 1: Literature and Events

Discusses least effective alternative first

The least expensive and easiest stop-smoking measure involves the distribution of literature, such as "The Ten-Step Plan" from Smokefree Enterprises and government pamphlets citing smoking dangers. Some companies have also sponsored events such as the Great American Smoke-Out, a one-day occasion intended to develop group spirit in spurring smokers to quit. "Studies show, however," says one expert, "that literature and company-sponsored events have little permanent effect in helping smokers quit" (Mendel 108).

Cost: Negligible

FIGURE 12.11 (Continued)

Gordon McClure   Page 2   October 11, 2009

Alternative 2: Stop-Smoking Programs Outside the Workplace

Local clinics provide treatment programs in classes at their centers. Here in Houston we have the Smokers' Treatment Center, ACC Motivation Center, and New-Choice Program for Stopping Smoking. These behavior-modification stop-smoking programs are acknowledged to be more effective than literature distribution or incentive programs. However, studies of companies using off-workplace programs show that many employees fail to attend regularly and do not complete the programs.

Cost: $1,200 per employee, three-month individual program •———— Highlights costs for
         (New-Choice Program)   easy comparison
         $900 per employee, three-month group session

Alternative 3: Stop-Smoking Programs at the Workplace

Many clinics offer workplace programs with counselors meeting employees •———— Arranges alternatives
in company conference rooms. These programs have the advantage of   so that most
keeping a firm's employees together so that they develop a group spirit and effective is last
exert pressure on each other to succeed. The most successful programs are
on company premises and also on company time. Employees participating
in such programs had a 72 percent greater success record than employees
attending the same stop-smoking program at an outside clinic (Honda 35).
A disadvantage of this arrangement, of course, is lost work time—amounting
to about two hours a week for three months.

Cost: $900 per employee, three-month program for two hours per
         week release time for three months

Conclusions and Recommendation •———— Summarizes findings
                                            and ends with specific
                                            recommendation

Smokers require discipline, counseling, and professional assistance in kicking the nicotine habit, as explained at the University of Michigan Health System Web site (Guide to Quitting Smoking). Workplace stop-smoking programs on company time are more effective than literature, incentives, and off-workplace programs. If our goal is to reduce health care costs and lead our employees to healthful lives, we should invest in a workplace stop-smoking program with release time for smokers. Although the program temporarily reduces productivity, we can expect to recapture that loss in lower health care premiums and healthier employees.

Therefore, I recommend that we begin a stop-smoking treatment program on •———— Reveals recommendation
company premises with two hours per week of release time for participants   only after discussing all
for three months.   alternatives

Lists all references in MLA style

3

Works Cited

Magazine ———— • Arhelger, Zack. "The End of Smoking." *The World of Business* 5 Nov.
                    2007: 3–8.

Web site ———— • "Guide to Quitting Smoking." *American Cancer Society* 27 Oct. 2008. Retrieved
                    2 July 2009 <http://www.cancer.org/docroot/home/index.asp>.

Journal ———— • Honda, Emeline Maude. "Managing Anti-Smoking Campaigns: The Case for
                    Company Programs.*Management Quarterly*   Mar. 2008: 52–69.

Book ———— • Mendel, I. A. The *Puff Stops Here*. Chicago: Science Publications, 2007.

Database ———— • Rindfleisch, Terry. "Smoke-Free Workplaces Can Help Smokers Quit, Expert
                    Says.*Knight Ridder Tribune Business News* 4 Jan. 2008. Retrieved
                    2 July 2009, ABI/INFORM database.

Feasibility Reports

Feasibility reports examine the practicality and advisability of following a course of action. They answer this question: Will this plan or proposal work? Feasibility reports typically are internal reports written to advise on matters such as consolidating departments, offering a wellness program to employees, or hiring an outside firm to handle a company's accounting or computing operations. These reports may also be written by consultants called in to investigate a problem. The focus in these reports is on the decision: stopping or proceeding with the proposal. Because your role is not to persuade the reader to accept the decision, you will want to present the decision immediately. In writing feasibility reports, consider these suggestions:

- Announce your decision immediately.

- Provide a description of the background and problem necessitating the proposal.

- Discuss the benefits of the proposal.

- Describe the problems that may result.

- Calculate the costs associated with the proposal, if appropriate.

- Show the time frame necessary for implementing the proposal.

Clara H. Damien, human resources director for a large high-tech company in San Jose, California, wrote the feasibility report shown in Figure 12.12. She explained what prompted the report: "Our IT people and reps travel all over the world, both individually and in groups. We also hold large company gatherings in San Jose and in San Francisco. We learned from clients and through observation that some of our highly skilled staff members had poor manners. At the same time we needed to be tactful because no one likes to be scolded, least of all highly competent individuals. Because external consultants charge exorbitant fees, we decided to explore the training of our own corporate etiquette expert. My report is short and sweet, complete with background, benefits, drawbacks, costs, and a schedule for completion."

Yardstick Reports

"Yardstick" reports examine problems with two or more solutions. To evaluate the best solution, the writer establishes criteria by which to compare the alternatives. The criteria then act as a yardstick against which all the alternatives are measured. This yardstick approach is effective when companies establish specifications for equipment purchases, and then compare each manufacturer's product with the established specs. The yardstick approach is also effective when exact specifications cannot be established.

For example, before Nissan Motor Company decided to move its U.S. headquarters from Los Angeles to Franklin, Tennessee, the No. 4 global carmaker evaluated several sites, including Dallas, Texas, and multiple locations in the Nashville, Tennessee, region. For each site, Nissan compared tax incentives, real estate and utility costs, workforce education levels, proximity to its existing plant in Smyrna (Tennessee), and other criteria that would allow the company to save money.[10] The real advantage to yardstick reports is that alternatives can be measured consistently using the same criteria. Reports using a yardstick approach typically are organized this way:

- Begin by describing the problem or need.

- Explain possible solutions and alternatives.

- Establish criteria for comparing the alternatives; tell how the criteria were selected or developed.

- Discuss and evaluate each alternative in terms of the criteria.

- Draw conclusions and make recommendations.

Feasibility reports analyze whether a proposal or plan will work.

A typical feasibility report presents the decision, background information, benefits, problems, costs, and a schedule.

Yardstick reports consider alternative solutions to a problem by establishing criteria against which to weigh options.

FIGURE 12.12 Feasibility Report

DATE: October 24, 2009
TO: Julia Evangeline, VP Personnel
FROM: Clara H. Damien, Human Resources Director C.H.D.
SUBJECT: In-House Business Etiquette Training

Training our own business etiquette expert who would then coach employees in house is a good plan that would help us save money. My report addresses the background, benefits, drawbacks, costs, and time frame needed to execute the plan.

Background: Need to Improve Staff Members' "Soft Skills." We know from anonymous customer surveys and anecdotal evidence that many of our new-hires as well as some veteran staff members may need help with communication and people skills. Some lack basic knowledge of dining, greeting, mingling, and other conventions. After a review of available services and costs, we decided that hiring external etiquette consultants would be too expensive for our purposes. Instead, you asked me to explore the option of training our own expert at the Protocol School of Washington (PSOW).

Benefits: In-House Training Lowers Costs and Offers Flexibility. PSOW trains and certifies corporate etiquette consultants. The school provides all teaching tools, including PowerPoint presentations, displays, and handouts, saving us the time and cost of developing such materials. Our coach could be deployed whenever instruction fits staffing and scheduling needs.

Challenges: Learning Curve and Potential Resistance. The designated future expert will need practice after the intensive training. Some staff members may scoff at an internal training plan and fail to recognize their own deficiencies. We will emphasize the benefit of the training to the participants. Rather than framing the etiquette instruction as remedial or punitive, we will stress the gains the staff can obtain in terms of career advancement and promotions. Furthermore, we must highlight how the success of our company depends on polished and well-groomed employees.

Costs. The only direct costs are the tuition, accommodations, and travel expenses for the employee we choose to send. The Protocol School of Washington charges $5,000 for tuition. Another $2,000 will cover air travel and six nights at the Ritz-Carlton in Tysons Corner, Virginia. For a relatively small investment of approximately $7,000, we will have a certified in-house business etiquette consultant.

Time Frame. Corporate Etiquette and International Protocol Consultant courses are offered four times a year. With your approval, we would select our employee to attend the training course that starts on February 11, 2010. After completing the intensive five-day course, our employee/coach would be ready to start training our employees immediately upon returning.

Outlines organization of the report

Reveals decision immediately

Describes problem and background

Evaluates positive and negative aspects of proposal objectively

Presents costs and schedule; omits unnecessary summary

Ethics Check

Music Labels Vs. Students

Bloomberg News reports that the recording industry is cracking down on the 50 percent of U.S. college students who illegally downloaded 1.3 billion songs and movies last year. Legal downloading cannot offset a 20 percent loss in CD sales. The music industry is sending letters to universities disclosing offenders' e-mail addresses and threatening copyright infringement lawsuits unless individuals pay up to $5,000 to settle such claims. Is this antipiracy campaign fair?

Jenny Gomez, benefits administrator for computer manufacturer CompuTech, was called on to write a report comparing outplacement agencies. These agencies counsel discharged employees and help them find new positions; fees are paid by the former employer. Jenny knew that times were bad for CompuTech and that extensive downsizing would take place in the next two years. Her task was to compare outplacement agencies and recommend one to CompuTech.

After collecting information, Jenny found that her biggest problem was organizing the data and developing a system for making comparisons. All the outplacement agencies she investigated seemed to offer the same basic package of services. Here is how she described her report, shown in Figure 12.13:

"With the information I gathered about three outplacement agencies, I made a big grid listing the names of the agencies across the top. Down the side I listed general categories—such as services, costs, and reputation. Then I filled in the information for each agency. This grid, which began to look like a table, helped me organize all the bits and pieces of information. After studying the grid, I saw that all the information could be grouped into four categories: counseling services, administrative and research assistance, reputation, and costs. I made these the criteria I would use to compare agencies. Next, I divided my grid into two parts, which became Table 1 and Table 2. In writing the report, I could have made each agency a separate heading, followed by a discussion of how it measured up to the criteria. Immediately, though, I saw how repetitious that would become. So I used the criteria as headings and discussed how each agency met each criterion—or failed to meet it. Making a recommendation was easy once I had made the tables and could see how the agencies compared."

Grids are a useful way to organize and compare data for a yardstick report.

FIGURE 12.13 Yardstick Report

DATE: April 28, 2009

TO: Graham T. Burnett, Vice President

FROM: Jenny Gomez, Benefits Administrator

SUBJECT: Selecting Outplacement Services

Here is the report you requested April 1 investigating the possibility of CompuTech's use of outplacement services. It discusses the problem of counseling services for discharged staff and establishes criteria for selecting an outplacement agency. It then evaluates three prospective agencies and presents a recommendation based on that evaluation.

Introduces purpose and gives overview of report organization

Problem: Counseling Discharged Staff

In an effort to reduce costs and increase competitiveness, CompuTech will begin a program of staff reduction that will involve releasing up to 20 percent of our workforce over the next 12 to 24 months. Many of these employees have been with us for ten or more years, and they are not being released for performance faults. These employees deserve a severance package that includes counseling and assistance in finding new careers.

Discusses background briefly because readers already know the problem

Solution and Alternatives: Outplacement Agencies

Numerous outplacement agencies offer discharged employees counseling and assistance in locating new careers. This assistance minimizes not only the negative feelings related to job loss but also the very real possibility of litigation. Potentially expensive lawsuits have been lodged against some companies by unhappy employees who felt they were unfairly released.

In seeking an outplacement agency, we should find one that offers advice to the sponsoring company as well as to dischargees. Frankly, many of our managers need help in conducting termination sessions. The law now requires certain procedures, especially in releasing employees over forty. CompuTech could unwittingly become liable to lawsuits because our managers are uninformed of these procedures. Here in the metropolitan area, I have located three potential outplacement agencies appropriate to serve our needs: Gray & Associates, Right Access, and Careers Plus.

Uses dual headings, giving function and description

Announces solution and the alternatives it presents

Establishing Criteria for Selecting Agency

In order to choose among the three agencies, I established criteria based on professional articles, discussions with officials at other companies using outplacement agencies, and interviews with agencies. Here are the four groups of criteria I used in evaluating the three agencies:

Tells how criteria were selected

1. Counseling services—including job search advice, résumé help, crisis management, corporate counseling, and availability of full-time counselors

2. Administrative and research assistance—including availability of administrative staff, librarian, and personal computers

3. Reputation—based on a telephone survey of former clients and listing with a professional association

4. Costs—for both group programs and executive services

Creates four criteria to use as yardstick in evaluating alternatives

FIGURE 12.13 (Continued)

Vice President Burnett   Page 2   April 28, 2009

Discussion: Evaluating Agencies by Criteria

Each agency was evaluated using the four criteria just described. Data comparing the first three criteria are summarized in Table 1.

Table 1

A COMPARISON OF SERVICES AND REPUTATIONS
FOR THREE LOCAL OUTPLACEMENT AGENCIES

	Gray & Associates	Right Access	Careers Plus
Counseling services			
Résumé advice	Yes	Yes	Yes
Crisis management	Yes	No	Yes
Corporate counseling	Yes	No	No
Full-time counselors	Yes	No	Yes
Administrative, research assistance			
Administrative staff	Yes	Yes	Yes
Librarian, research library	Yes	No	Yes
Personal computers	Yes	No	Yes
Listed by National Association of Career Consultants	Yes	No	Yes
Reputation (telephone survey of former clients)	Excellent	Good	Excellent

Counseling Services

All three agencies offered similar basic counseling services with job-search and résumé advice. They differed, however, in three significant areas.

Right Access does not offer crisis management, a service that puts the discharged employee in contact with a counselor the same day the employee is released. Experts in the field consider this service especially important to help the dischargee begin "bonding" with the counselor immediately. Immediate counseling also helps the dischargee through the most traumatic moments of one of life's great disappointments and helps him or her learn how to break the news to family members. Crisis management can be instrumental in reducing lawsuits because dischargees immediately begin to focus on career planning instead of concentrating on their pain and need for revenge. Moreover, Right Access does not employ full-time counselors; it hires part-timers according to demand. Industry authorities advise against using agencies whose staff members are inexperienced and employed on an "as-needed" basis.

In addition, neither Right Access nor Careers Plus offers regular corporate counseling, which I feel is critical in training our managers to conduct terminal interviews. Careers Plus, however, suggested that it could schedule special workshops if desired.

Administrative and Research Assistance

Both Gray & Associates and Careers Plus offer complete administrative services and personal computers. Dischargees have access to staff and equipment to assist them in their job searches. These agencies also provide research libraries, librarians, and databases of company information to help in securing interviews.

Places table close to spot where it is first mentioned

Summarizes complex data in table for easy reading and reference

Highlights the similarities and differences among the alternatives

Does not repeat obvious data from table

FIGURE 12.13 (Continued)

Discusses objectively how each agency meets criteria

Selects most important data from table to discuss

Gives reasons for making recommendation

Narrows choice to final alternative

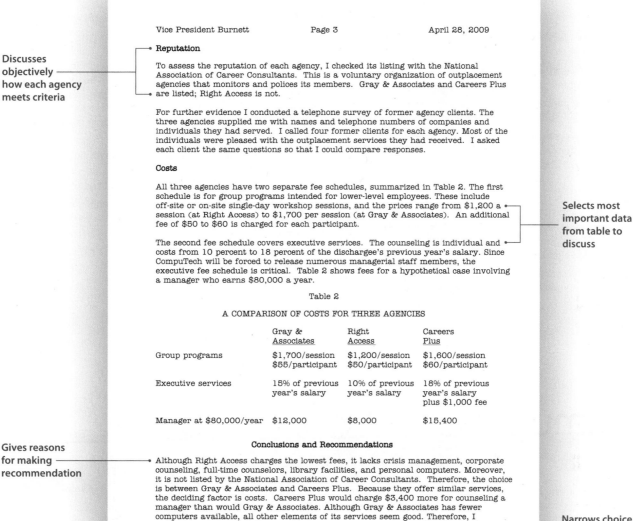

Vice President Burnett   Page 3   April 28, 2009

Reputation

To assess the reputation of each agency, I checked its listing with the National Association of Career Consultants. This is a voluntary organization of outplacement agencies that monitors and polices its members. Gray & Associates and Careers Plus are listed; Right Access is not.

For further evidence I conducted a telephone survey of former agency clients. The three agencies supplied me with names and telephone numbers of companies and individuals they had served. I called four former clients for each agency. Most of the individuals were pleased with the outplacement services they had received. I asked each client the same questions so that I could compare responses.

Costs

All three agencies have two separate fee schedules, summarized in Table 2. The first schedule is for group programs intended for lower-level employees. These include off-site or on-site single-day workshop sessions, and the prices range from $1,200 a session (at Right Access) to $1,700 per session (at Gray & Associates). An additional fee of $50 to $60 is charged for each participant.

The second fee schedule covers executive services. The counseling is individual and costs from 10 percent to 18 percent of the dischargee's previous year's salary. Since CompuTech will be forced to release numerous managerial staff members, the executive fee schedule is critical. Table 2 shows fees for a hypothetical case involving a manager who earns $80,000 a year.

Table 2

A COMPARISON OF COSTS FOR THREE AGENCIES

	Gray & Associates	Right Access	Careers Plus
Group programs	$1,700/session $55/participant	$1,200/session $50/participant	$1,600/session $60/participant
Executive services	15% of previous year's salary	10% of previous year's salary	18% of previous year's salary plus $1,000 fee
Manager at $80,000/year	$12,000	$8,000	$15,400

Conclusions and Recommendations

Although Right Access charges the lowest fees, it lacks crisis management, corporate counseling, full-time counselors, library facilities, and personal computers. Moreover, it is not listed by the National Association of Career Consultants. Therefore, the choice is between Gray & Associates and Careers Plus. Because they offer similar services, the deciding factor is costs. Careers Plus would charge $3,400 more for counseling a manager than would Gray & Associates. Although Gray & Associates has fewer computers available, all other elements of its services seem good. Therefore, I recommend that CompuTech hire Gray & Associates as an outplacement agency to counsel discharged employees.

Checklist

Writing Analytical Reports

Introduction

✓ **Identify the purpose of the report.** Explain why the report is being written.

✓ **Describe the significance of the topic.** Explain why the report is important.

✓ **Preview the organization of the report.** Especially for long reports, explain to the reader how the report will be organized.

✓ **Summarize the conclusions and recommendations for receptive audiences.** Use the direct pattern only if you have the confidence of the reader.

Findings

✓ **Discuss pros and cons.** In recommendation/justification reports evaluate the advantages and disadvantages of each alternative. For unreceptive audiences consider placing the recommended alternative last.

✓ **Establish criteria to evaluate alternatives.** In "yardstick" reports, create criteria to use in measuring each alternative consistently.

✓ **Support the findings with evidence.** Supply facts, statistics, expert opinion, survey data, and other proof from which you can draw logical conclusions.

✓ **Organize the findings for logic and readability.** Arrange the findings around the alternatives or the reasons leading to the conclusion. Use headings, enumerations, lists, tables, and graphics to focus emphasis.

Conclusions/Recommendations

✓ **Draw reasonable conclusions from the findings.** Develop conclusions that answer the research question. Justify the conclusions with highlights from the findings.

✓ **Make recommendations, if asked.** For multiple recommendations prepare a list. Use action verbs. Explain fully the benefits of the recommendation or steps necessary to solve the problem or answer the question.

Communicating at Work Your Turn

Applying Your Skills at Starbucks

One of the most interesting of Starbucks' growth strategies is selling hip music and, more recently, select films and books in its outlets. After disappointing results with its Hear Music Media Bars in 45 Starbucks locations, the specialty coffee retailer is still aiming to become a lifestyle/entertainment enterprise as part of a broader strategy.[11]

Although Starbucks' reliance on downloading and burning custom CDs in an age of MP3 players misfired, the Seattle-based company scored success selling CDs of artists ignored by mainstream media and traditional music stores. CEO Howard Schultz explained Starbucks' expansion into music and other ventures by citing the need to stay on the cutting edge: "The music world is changing, and Starbucks Hear Music will continue to be an innovator in the industry."[12] The bet on music seems to bear fruit. Within two years, CD unit sales at Starbucks grew 200 percent to about 3.6 million CDs sold.

In an unprecedented move, Starbucks established its own Web page on iTunes and offers its very diverse music portfolio online. Moreover, Schultz announced plans to offer MP3 downloading of music in Starbucks stores in the near future. Despite the strategic partnership with Apple's iTunes, Howard Schultz's mention of the MP3 format suggests that he may be keeping his options open to entertain advances from Microsoft. Unlike the popular iPod, the software giant's Zune player uses the MP3 format, but its pricing and security features make its use cumbersome. Apple is the market leader in legal music downloading, but Microsoft may be poised to

grab a portion of that lucrative market share.

Critics fear that the transformation of Starbucks into a lifestyle/entertainment enterprise will corrupt the brand. In contrast, Schultz sees the company's expansion plans as the next step along Starbucks' path toward becoming, yes, the world's biggest brand. He believes that "great retailers recognize that they are in the business of constantly surprising and delighting their customers." He expects this move into music, film, and book selling to do both.[13]

Your Task

As assistant to Howard Schultz, you are asked to form two research teams. One is to study the feasibility of in-store music downloading. The other team must decide whether to recommend Apple or Microsoft to diversify Starbucks' revenue, increase store traffic, and boost sales per customer.

http://www.starbucks.com

Summary of Learning Objectives

1 **Show skill and accuracy in tabulating information, using statistical techniques, and creating decision matrices to sort and interpret business report data.** Report data are more meaningful when sorted into tables or when analyzed by mean (the arithmetic average), median (the midpoint in a group of figures), and mode (the most frequent response). Range represents a span between the highest and lowest figures. Grids help organize complex data into rows and columns. Decision matrices employ a special grid with weights to help decision makers choose objectively among complex options. Accuracy in applying statistical techniques is crucial to gain and maintain credibility with the reader.

2 **Draw meaningful conclusions and make practical report recommendations based on prior logical analysis.** Conclusions tell what the survey data mean—especially in relation to the original report problem. They interpret key findings and may attempt to explain what caused the report problem. They are usually enumerated. In reports that call for recommendations, writers make specific suggestions for actions that can solve the report problem. Recommendations should be feasible, practical, and potentially agreeable to the audience. They should all relate to the initial problem. Recommendations may be combined with conclusions.

3 **Organize report data logically and provide cues to aid readers' comprehension.** Reports may be organized in many ways, including by (a) time (establishing a chronology or history of events), (b) component (discussing a problem by geography, division, or product), (c) importance (arranging data from most important to least important, or vice versa), (d) criteria (comparing items by standards), or (e) convention (using an already established grouping). To help guide the reader through the text, introductions, transitions, and headings serve as cues.

4 **Prepare short informational reports.** Periodic, trip, convention, progress, and investigative reports are examples of typical informational reports. Such reports include an introduction that may preview the report purpose and supply background data if necessary. The body of the report is generally divided into three to five segments that may be organized by time, component, importance, criteria, or convention. The body should include clear headings and may use an informal, conversational style unless the audience expects a more formal tone. The summary or conclusion reviews the main points and discusses what action will follow. The conclusion may offer a final thought, express appreciation, or signal a willingness to provide further information. Like all professional business documents, a clear, concise, well-written report cements the writer's credibility with the audience. Because they are so important, reports require writers to apply all the writing techniques addressed in Chapters 4, 5, and 6.

5 **Prepare short analytical reports that solve business problems.** Typical analytical reports include justification/recommendation reports, feasibility reports, and yardstick reports. Justification/recommendation reports organized directly identify a problem, immediately announce a recommendation or solution, explain and discuss its merits, and summarize the action to be taken. Justification/recommendation reports organized indirectly describe a problem, discuss alternative solutions, prove the superiority of one solution, and ask for authorization to proceed with that solution. Feasibility reports study the advisability of following a course of action. They generally announce the author's proposal immediately. Then they describe the background of, advantages and disadvantages of, costs of, and time frame for implementing the proposal. Yardstick reports compare two or more solutions to a problem by measuring each against a set of established criteria. They usually describe a problem, explain possible solutions, establish criteria for comparing alternatives, evaluate each alternative in terms of the criteria, draw conclusions, and make recommendations. The advantage to yardstick reports is consistency in comparing alternatives. Most reports serve as a basis for decision making in business.

Chapter Review

1. When are tables the most appropriate analytical tool and tabulating technique? What types of data are best presented in tables? (Obj. 1)

2. Calculate the mean, median, and mode for these figures: 3, 4, 4, 4, 10. (Obj. 1)

3. What is data tabulation? Provide an original example. Why is tabulation necessary for a researcher who has collected large amounts of data? (Obj. 1)

4. Why is a decision matrix a valuable managerial tool? (Obj. 1)

5. What are the two most widely read sections of a report? (Obj. 2)

6. How do conclusions differ from recommendations? (Obj. 2)

7. What are the characteristics of the best recommendations? (Obj. 2)

8. Name five methods for organizing report data. Be prepared to discuss each. (Obj. 3)

9. What three devices can report writers use to prevent readers from getting lost in the text? (Obj. 3)

10. How do business writers organize most informational reports, and what can writers assume about the audience? (Obj. 4)

11. Describe periodic reports and what they generally contain. (Obj. 4)

12. What should a progress report include? (Obj. 4)

13. When is the indirect pattern appropriate for justification/recommendation reports? (Obj. 5)

14. What is a feasibility report? Are such reports generally intended for internal or external audiences? (Obj. 5)

15. What is a yardstick report? (Obj. 5)

Critical Thinking

1. What are the best uses of mean, median, and mode? (Obj. 1)

2. Researchers can draw various conclusions from a set of data. How do you know how to shape conclusions and recommendations? (Obj. 2)

3. Why is audience analysis particularly important in making report recommendations? (Obj. 2)

4. Should all reports be organized so that they follow the sequence of investigation—that is, a description of the initial problem, an analysis of the issues, data collection, data analysis, and conclusions? Why or why not? (Obj. 3)

5. What are the major differences between informational and analytical reports? (Objs. 4, 5)

6. **Ethical Issue:** Like other professionals—for instance, physicians, psychotherapists, and lawyers—consultants must follow a professional code of ethics. Consultants may have to issue recommendations that will not be acceptable to the organization that hired them and will pay them. Discuss the risks of "bending" the truth for fear of displeasing or losing a client.

Activities

12.1 Tabulation and Interpretation of Survey Results (Obj. 1)

Team

Your business communication class at South Bay College was asked by the college bookstore manager, Harry Locke, to conduct a survey. Concerned about the environment, Locke wants to learn students' reactions to eliminating plastic bags, of which 45,000 are given away annually by the bookstore. Students answered questions about a number of proposals, resulting in the following raw data:

For major purchases the bookstore should:

	Agree	Undecided	Disagree
1. Continue to provide plastic bags	132	17	411
2. Provide no bags; encourage students to bring their own bags	414	25	121
3. Provide no bags; offer cloth bags at a reduced price (about $3)	357	19	184
4. Give a cloth bag with each major purchase, the cost to be included in registration fees	63	15	482

Your Task. In groups of four or five, do the following:

a. Convert the data into a table (see Figure 12.1) with a descriptive title. Arrange the items in a logical sequence.

b. How could these survey data be cross-tabulated? Would cross-tabulation serve any purpose?

c. Given the conditions of this survey, name at least three conclusions that could be drawn from the data.

d. Prepare three to five recommendations to be submitted to Mr. Locke. How could they be implemented?

e. Role-play a meeting in which the recommendations and implementation plan are presented to Mr. Locke. One student plays the role of Mr. Locke; the remaining students play the role of the presenters.

12.2 Evaluating Conclusions (Obj. 2)

E-Mail

Your Task. Read an in-depth article (800 or more words) in *BusinessWeek, Fortune, Forbes,* or *The Wall Street Journal.* What conclusions does the author draw? Are the conclusions valid, based on the evidence presented? In an e-mail message to your instructor, summarize the main points in the article and analyze the conclusions. What conclusions would you have drawn from the data?

12.3 Distinguishing Between Conclusions and Recommendations (Obj. 2)

A study of red light traffic violations produced the following findings: Red light traffic violations were responsible for more than 25,000 crashes in one state. Crashes from running red lights decreased by 10 percent in areas using camera programs to cite offenders. Two out of seven local governments studied showed a profit from the programs; the others lost money.[14]

Your Task. Based on the preceding facts, indicate whether the following statements are conclusions or recommendations:

a. Red light violations are dangerous offenses.

b. Red light cameras are an effective traffic safety tool.

c. Local governments should be allowed to implement red light camera programs.

d. Although red light camera programs are expensive, they prevent crashes and are, therefore, worthwhile.

e. The city of Centerville should not implement a red light program because of the program's cost.

f. Red light programs are not necessarily profitable for local governments.

12.4 Using Decision Matrices (Objs. 1, 2)

You want to buy a low-cost laptop for your college work and consider price the most important feature.

Your Task. Study Figure 12.3 on page 357 and change the weights in Table 2 to reflect your emphasis on low price, to which you will assign a factor of 10 because it is twice as important to you as unit weight, which receives a factor of 5. The hard drive is likewise secondary to you, so you give it a 5 also. Last, you change battery life to a factor of 7 from 10 because it is less important than price, but more important than unit weight and hard drive size. Calculate the new scores. Which low-budget computer wins this time?

12.5 Buying a Car: Create a Decision Matrix (Objs. 1, 2)

David, an outrigger canoe racer, needs to buy a new car. He wants a vehicle that will carry his disassembled boat and outrigger. At the same time he will need to travel long distances on business. His passion is soft-top sports cars, but he is also concerned about gas mileage. These four criteria are impossible to find in one vehicle.

David has the following choices:

- Station wagon
- SUV with or without a sun roof
- Four-door sedan, a high-miles-per-gallon "family car"
- Sports car, convertible

He wants to consider the following criteria:

- Price
- Ability to carry cargo such as a canoe
- Fuel efficiency
- Comfort over long distances
- Good looks and fun
- Quality build/manufacturer's reputation

Your Task. Follow the steps outlined in Figure 12.3 to determine an assessment scale and to assign a score to each feature. Then, consider which weights are probably most important to David, given his needs. Calculate the totals to find the vehicle that's most suitable for David.

12.6 Organizing Data (Obj. 3)

Your Task. In groups of three to five, discuss how the findings in the following reports could be best organized. Consider these methods: time, component, importance, criteria, and convention.

a. A monthly sales report submitted to the sales manager.

b. A progress report submitted six months into the process of planning the program for your organization's convention.

c. A report comparing three locations for a fast-food company's new restaurant. The report presents data on real estate values, construction costs, traffic patterns, competition, state taxes, labor availability, and population demographics.

d. A report describing the history of the development of dwarf and spur apple trees, starting with the first genetic dwarfs discovered about 100 years ago and progressing to today's grafted varieties on dwarfing rootstocks.

e. An informational brochure for job candidates that describes your company's areas of employment: accounting, finance, information systems, operations management, marketing, production, and computer-aided design.

f. A recommendation report to be submitted to management presenting four building plans to improve access to your building, in compliance with federal regulations. The plans range considerably in feasibility and cost.

g. An informational report describing a company's expansion plans in South America, Europe, Australia, and Southeast Asia.

h. An employee performance appraisal submitted annually.

12.7 Evaluating Headings and Titles (Obj. 3)

Your Task. Identify the following report headings and titles as *functional*, *talking*, or *combination*. Discuss the usefulness and effectiveness of each.

a. Costs

b. Survey Shows Greater Customer Satisfaction

c. Alternatives

d. How to Install a Spam Filter

e. Case History: Focusing on Customer Service

f. Recommendations: Solving Our Applicant Tracking Problem

g. Comparing Costs of Hiring Exempt and Nonexempt Employees

h. Upgrades

12.8 Writing a Survey: Studying Employee Use of Instant Messaging (Obj. 1)

Web

Instant messaging (IM) is a popular way to exchange messages in real time. It offers the convenience of telephone conversations and e-mail. Best of all, it allows employees to contact anyone in the world while retaining a written copy of the conversation—without a whopping telephone bill! But instant messaging is risky for companies. They may lose trade secrets or confidential information over insecure lines. They also may be liable if inappropriate material is exchanged. Moreover, IM opens the door to viruses that can infect a company's entire computer system.

Your boss just read an article stating that 40 percent of companies now use IM for business and up to 90 percent of employees use instant messaging WITHOUT their manager's knowledge or authorization. She asks you to prepare a survey of your 48-member staff to learn how many are using IM. She wants to know what type of IM software they have downloaded, how many hours a day they spend on IM, what the advantages of IM are, and so forth. The goal is not to identify those using or abusing IM. Instead, the goal is to learn when, how, and why employees use instant messaging so that appropriate policies can be designed.

Your Task. Use the Web or an electronic database to learn more about instant messaging. Then prepare a short employee survey (see Figure 11.10). Include an appropriate introduction that explains the survey and encourages a response. Should you ask for names on the survey? How can you encourage employees to return the forms? Your instructor may wish to expand this survey into a report by having you produce fictitious survey results, analyze the findings, draw conclusions, and make recommendations.

12.9 Periodic Report: Filling in the Boss (Obj. 4)

E-Mail

You work hard at your job, but you rarely see your boss. Keeping him or her informed of your activities and accomplishments is difficult.

Your Task. For a job that you currently hold or a previous one, describe your regular activities, discuss irregular events that management should be aware of, and highlight any special needs or problems. Use a memo format in writing a periodic e-mail report to your boss.

12.10 Progress Report: Checking In (Obj. 4)

E-Mail

Students writing a long report described in Chapter 13 must keep their instructors informed of their progress.

Your Task. Write a progress report informing your instructor of your work. Briefly describe the project (its purpose, scope, limitations, and methodology), work completed, work yet to be completed, problems encountered, future activities, and expected completion date. Address the e-mail report to your instructor.

12.11 Investigative Report: Ensuring Fair Employment Practices Abroad (Obj. 4)

Ethics   Intercultural   Web

Nike's image took a big hit a few years ago, when the company became associated with sweatshop conditions in Asian factories that supplied its shoes and apparel. Other sports and garment companies also became targets of criticism and campus boycotts in the United States for their ties to sweatshop labor. Since then, American companies have tried to investigate and end the abuses.

However, oversight is difficult, and Chinese factories dodge the labor auditors sponsored by American retail chains and manufacturers. To complicate matters, China is the largest supplier of American imports, to the tune of $280 billion annually. U.S. consumers have come to expect inexpensive goods—athletic shoes, clothing, and electronic gadgets. The downward price pressure may be prompting the Chinese suppliers to cut corners and to ignore the fair labor regulations of American companies. According to *BusinessWeek,* U.S. corporations are struggling with imposing "Western labor standards on a nation that lacks real labor unions and a meaningful rule of law."[15]

Your Task. Investigate the efforts of the Fair Labor Association, a coalition of 20 retailers and apparel manufacturers, such as Nike, Adidas, Nordstrom, and Eddie Bauer. The problem is not confined to the garment industry; violations also occur in offshore suppliers producing household appliances, computers, and electronics. Explore the types of abuses and the obstacles to reform. Then recommend actions that could make offshore factories play by the rules. You can start by visiting the Fair Labor Association's Web site: **http://www.fairlabor.org/.**

© Digital Vision / Getty Images

12.12 Investigative Report: Exploring a Possible Place to Work (Obj. 4)

Web

You are thinking about taking a job with a Fortune 500 company, and you want to learn as much as possible about the company.

Your Task. Select a Fortune 500 company, and collect information about it on the Web. Visit **http://www.hoovers.com** for basic facts. Then take a look at the company's Web site; check its background, news releases, and annual report. Learn about its major product, service, or emphasis. Find its Fortune 500 ranking, its current stock price (if listed), and its high and low range for the year. Look up its profit-to-earnings ratio. Track its latest marketing plan, promotion, or product. Identify its home office, major officers, and number of employees. In a memo report to your instructor, summarize your research findings. Explain why this company would be a good or bad employment choice.

12.13 Investigative Report: Marketing Abroad (Obj. 4)

Intercultural   Web

You have been asked to prepare a training program for U.S. companies doing business outside the country.

Your Task. Select a country to investigate. Check to see whether your school or library subscribes to *CultureGrams,* an online resource with rich data about the daily lives and cultures of the world's peoples. Collect data from *CultureGrams* files, *CountryWatch,* or from the country's embassy in Washington. Interview on-campus international students. Use the Web to discover data about the country. See **Activity 13.7** and Figure 13.5 in the next chapter for additional ideas on gathering information on intercultural communication. Collect information about formats for written communication, observance of holidays, customary greetings, business ethics, and other topics of interest to businesspeople. Remember that your report should promote business, not tourism. Prepare a memo report addressed to Kelly Johnson, editor for the training program materials.

12.14 Investigative Report: Expanding Operations Abroad (Obj. 4)

Intercultural   Team   Web

You have been asked to brief your boss, Dori Lundy, about the status of women in business, customs, and general business etiquette in a country that may not be friendly to Western businesswomen. Ms. Lundy is planning an international trip to expand her high-tech company.

Your Task. Select a country to investigate that has a culture markedly different from our own, for example, Saudi Arabia, Egypt,

Iran, Japan, or South Korea, but don't forget Italy, Spain, Germany, or the Scandinavian countries. Collect data from *CultureGrams,* to which many libraries subscribe; search *CountryWatch* and other Web sites. Interview international students on campus. See **Activity 13.5** and Figure 13.5 in the next chapter for additional ideas on gathering information on intercultural communication. Collect information about customary greetings, business ethics, dress codes, and other topics of interest to a traveling businesswoman. The purpose of your report is to promote business, not tourism, and to help your boss avoid embarrassment or worse. Prepare a memo report addressed to Dori Lundy, president of Paradigm CompuTech.

12.15 Progress Report: Heading Toward That Degree (Obj. 4)

You have made an agreement with your parents (or spouse, relative, or significant friend) that you would submit a progress report at this time.

Your Task. Prepare a progress report in letter format. Describe your headway toward your educational goal (such as employment, degree, or certificate). List your specific achievements, and outline what you have left to complete.

12.16 Conference or Trip Report: In Your Dreams (Obj. 4)

You have been sent to a meeting, conference, or seminar in an exotic spot at company expense.

Your Task. From a business periodical select an article describing a conference or meeting connected with your major area of study. The article must be at least 500 words long. Assume that you attended the meeting. Prepare a memo report to your supervisor.

12.17 Justification/Recommendation Report: Searching for the Best Philanthropic Project (Obj. 5)

Ethics   Web

Great news! MegaTech, the start-up company where you work, has become enormously successful. Now the owner wants to support some kind of philanthropic program. He does not have time to check out the possibilities, so he asks you, his assistant, to conduct research and report to him and the board of directors.

Your Task. He wants you to investigate the philanthropic projects at 20 high-profile companies of your choice. Visit their Web sites and study programs such as volunteerism, cause-related marketing, matching funds, charitable donations, and so forth. In a recommendation report, discuss five of the best programs and recommend one that can serve as a philanthropic project model for your company.

12.18 Justification/Recommendation Report: Solving a Campus Problem (Obj. 5)

Team

Your Task. In groups of three to five, investigate a problem on your campus, such as inadequate parking, slow registration, limited dining options, poor class schedules, inefficient bookstore, weak job-placement program, unrealistic degree requirements, or lack of internship programs. Within your group develop a solution to the problem. If possible, consult the officials involved to ask for their input in arriving at a feasible solution. Do not attack existing programs; strive for constructive discussion and harmonious improvements. After reviewing the persuasive techniques discussed in Chapter 9, write a group or individual justification/recommendation report. Address your report to the vice president of student affairs or the college president. Copy your instructor.

12.19 Justification/Recommendation Report: Developing an Organizational E-Mail Policy (Obj. 5)

Team   Web

As a manager in a midsized engineering firm, you are aware that members of your department frequently use e-mail and the Internet for private messages, shopping, and games. In addition to the strain on computer facilities, you worry about declining productivity as well as security problems. When you walked by one worker's computer and saw what looked like pornography on the screen, you knew you had to do something. Although workplace privacy is a hot-button issue for unions and employee-rights groups, employers have legitimate reasons for wanting to know what is happening on their computers. A high percentage of lawsuits involve the use and abuse of e-mail. You think that the executive council should establish some kind of e-mail policy. The council is generally receptive to sound suggestions, especially if they are inexpensive. At present no e-mail policy exists, and you fear that the executive council is not fully aware of the dangers. You decide to talk with other managers about the problem and write a justification/recommendation report.

Your Task. In teams discuss the need for an e-mail policy. Using the Web and electronic databases, find information about other firms' use of such policies. Look for examples of companies struggling with lawsuits over e-mail abuse. In your report, should you describe suitable e-mail policies? Should you recommend computer monitoring and surveillance software? Should the policy cover blogging, cell phones, personal digital assistants (PDAs), and instant messaging? Each member of the team should present and support his or her ideas regarding what should be included in the report. Individually or as a team, write a convincing justification/recommendation report to the executive council based on the conclusions you draw from your research and discussion. Decide whether you should be direct or indirect.

12.20 Feasibility Report: International Organization (Obj. 5)

Intercultural

To fulfill a senior project in your department, you have been asked to submit a letter report to the dean evaluating the feasibility of starting an organization of international students on campus.

Your Task. Find out how many international students are on your campus, what nations they represent, how one goes about starting an organization, and whether a faculty sponsor is needed. Assume that you conducted an informal survey of international students. Of the 39 who filled out the survey, 31 said they would be interested in joining.

12.21 Feasibility Report: Improving Employee Fitness (Obj. 5)

Your company is considering ways to promote employee fitness and morale.

Your Task. Select a possible fitness program that seems reasonable for your company. Consider a softball league, bowling teams, basketball league, lunchtime walks, lunchtime fitness speakers and demos, company-sponsored health club membership, a workout room, a fitness center, a fitness director, and so on. Assume that your boss has tentatively agreed to one of the programs and has asked you to write a memo report investigating its feasibility.

12.22 Yardstick Report: Evaluating Equipment (Obj. 5)

You recently complained to your boss that you were unhappy with a piece of equipment that you use (printer, computer, copier, fax, or the like). After some thought, the boss decided you were right and told you to go shopping.

Your Task. Compare at least three manufacturers' models and recommend one. Because the company will be purchasing ten or more units and because several managers must approve the purchase, write a careful report documenting your findings. Establish at least five criteria for comparing the models. Submit a memo report to your boss.

12.23 Yardstick Report: Measuring the Alternatives (Obj. 5)

Your Task. Identify a problem or procedure that must be changed at your work or in an organization you know. Consider challenges such as poor scheduling of employees, outdated equipment, slow order processing, failure to encourage employees to participate fully, restrictive rules, inadequate training, or disappointed customers. Consider several solutions or courses of action (retaining the present status could be one alternative). Develop criteria that you could use to evaluate each alternative. Write a report measuring each alternative by the yardstick you have created. Recommend a course of action to your boss or to the organization head.

12.24 Investigative Report: Check Overdraft Protection —Valuable Service or Consumer Rip-Off? (Obj. 4)

Consumer   **Web**

Bounce-protection programs sound like a terrific service to checking account customers. Also called overdraft privilege and courtesy overdraft, these popular banking programs automatically cover bounced checks. Customers can overdraw up to a certain dollar amount and pay a fee, rather than interest. Commercial banks long ago abandoned the practice of short-term loans. But banks are now encouraging fee-based overdrafts, and the effective interest rate is enormous. On an overdraft of $100 that is outstanding for two weeks, you might pay a $20 fee, which amounts to an annual interest rate of 520 percent![16] Consumers receive the equivalent of an unsecured loan, which they can use if they run short of cash between paydays. Critics complain that the programs charge excessive fees and prey on the poor. They also point out that banks exploit customers by processing the largest checks first, thus draining a checking account faster and bouncing several checks at once. Each overdrawn check, no matter how small, is hit for a separate fee! Yet, fee-based overdraft programs are growing wildly. Banks say that consumers love the service. Critics claim that banks encourage people to overdraw their accounts and then charge them for doing so.[17]

Your Task. First Alert, a consumer advocate organization where you work, has decided to investigate the issue. As a member of its Banking Practices Committee, you are to conduct research and prepare an information report. Use the Web and electronic databases to collect information about programs that permit customers to overdraft for a fee. In your report discuss the problem and present well-organized pro and con arguments. What stance has the Federal Reserve taken? If your instructor asks you to make this an analytical report, draw conclusions and make recommendations to the Federal Reserve. Should it allow banks to avoid credit laws and continue these programs?

Self-Contained Report Activities

No Additional Research Required

12.25 Justification/Recommendation Report: Improving Greenhouse Market's Service * (Obj. 5)

You are a recently hired manager for Greenhouse Market, a high-end fast-food restaurant that has been in business for three years.

* Instructors: See the Instructor's Manual for additional resources.

The restaurant specializes in a wide selection of quality "deli-style" sandwiches, desserts, and coffees. The restaurant's owner, Kate Lilly, tells you that the volume of business, especially at lunch hour, has increased considerably lately.

After your first month on the job, you notice that, because of the increased volume, the method of delivering orders to customers seems to be inadequate. At present, the ordering system consists of the following: (a) the customer's order and table number are recorded by counter staff on a ticket; (b) after the customer pays, the ticket is given to the sandwich makers, who complete the order; (c) one of the counter staff then takes the order to the customer's table. Coffee and desserts are also brought to the customer's table. Additional beverages are located in a refrigerated display case, where customers help themselves. You notice that three counter staff work with one cash register, and two sandwich makers are on duty.

You bring the problem to Kate's attention, and she responds by saying, "As business increases, one must keep up with the times and continually assess ways to do business better." She asks you to help solve the problem by analyzing how similar businesses handle their service during lunch hour. You begin by selecting three fast-food restaurants similar to Greenhouse Market. You observe each restaurant during its lunch hour to determine its serving techniques. You also decide to determine the amount of time it takes for a customer to receive an order relative to Greenhouse Market. Presently, the average time it takes for a customer to receive an order at Greenhouse Market is 4.6 minutes. The following is a rough account of your observations.

The Lame Duck
- Limited menu selection
- Orders are taken using an electronic system that includes the customer's number
- Customers pay immediately
- Customers pick up their orders after their numbers have been called and retrieve their own beverages
- Each sandwich maker is assigned a different task
- Four counter employees at four registers; three sandwich makers
- Average time a customer waits to receive an order: 2.7 minutes

Kimmie's Kitchen
- Limited menu selection
- Order takers call out the menu item as the order is taken
- Tickets are used to inform sandwich makers of extras such as cheese, mayo, etc.
- Counter employees serve beverages
- Customers pay immediately
- Three sandwich makers make each sandwich in assembly-line fashion
- Customers wait at the counter to pick up their orders
- One counter employee at one register; three sandwich makers
- Average time a customer waits to receive an order: 2.3 minutes

Brooklyn New York Bagels
- Limited menu selection
- Tickets are used to record the menu selection; customers pay immediately
- Food and beverages are brought to the customer's table
- Four employees are assigned different tasks: one takes the customer's order, another makes the food, another delivers the order
- Average time a customer waits to receive an order: 3.5 minutes

Your Task. Now it is up to you to sift through the data you have collected and draw conclusions. In a short memo report to Kate Lilly present your findings, discuss your conclusions, and make recommendations. You may want to present the data using visual aids, but you also realize you must emphasize the important findings by presenting them in an easy-to-read list.

12.26 Justification/Recommendation Report: Improving Register Efficiency at CircuitCentral (Obj. 5)

CircuitCentral is a high-volume market-leading retailer of consumer electronics and appliances. It has established a reputation for outstanding customer service, selection, and prices. As a supervisor at one of the store's busiest locations, you must ensure that the checkout and customer service lanes operate efficiently. To make your job easier and to ensure consistency in every store, CircuitCentral has established an action plan to prevent long waiting times at registers.

The plan includes assigning backup cashiers from other departments for each shift. Additionally, remote registers are located in several departments to reduce customer flow at the registers nearest the exit. CircuitCentral's goal is to achieve at least a 35 percent "excellent" response rating from customers. Even the best plans can go awry, however; and this usually happens during holidays such as Thanksgiving, Christmas, Memorial Day, and Labor Day. With the Labor Day weekend only two months away, you want to avoid the occasional gridlock you encountered last Memorial Day.

Customer Survey Data

To gather information from customers, you decide to tabulate responses to questions from comment cards submitted during the last month. You are particularly interested in the time customers spent in the checkout lines. Here are the results of 320 customer comment cards:

Questions on Comment Cards	Responses/Score (5 = excellent, 4 = very good, 3 = good, 2 = fair, 1 = poor)				
	5	4	3	2	1
1. Based on your shopping experience, how would you rate this CircuitCentral store?	112	102	63	29	14
2. Based on your shopping experience, how would you rate the likelihood that you will return to this CircuitCentral store?	166	96	43	8	2
3. How would you rate the likelihood that you would recommend this CircuitCentral store to a friend?	118	88	76	23	15
4. How would you rate your overall satisfaction with register checkout times?	51	80	144	32	13
5. How would you rate your satisfaction with the time spent in line at the customer service counter?	19	38	128	96	39
6. How would you rate the service staff's handling of problems?	26	96	54	129	15

Staff Survey

To gather additional information, you conduct a survey of 20 staff members, including cashiers, customer service representatives, and salespeople. Here are the results of your survey:

Which of the following has caused a delay at a register?

1. Soft tag or CD case removal	64%	
2. Approval or override	86	
3. Register malfunction	3	
4. Incomplete paperwork	7	
5. Product registration	13	(e.g., Internet service providers)
6. Employee error	16	

Figures do not total 100 percent because of multiple answers.

Personal Observations

Finally, you selected ten registers at random (five near the front entrance, three in customer service, and one each in the TV and Digital Imaging departments) and observed them for five minutes, taking notes. You chose Saturday for these observations because of the typically higher volume of business. Following is a summary of your observations:

- During all five of your visits to registers near the front entrance, you noticed that, although a manager was often needed for a check approval or override, which caused delays, employee confusion about procedures and the registers themselves seemed to account for the majority of delays. You also observed five instances in which an employee needed to go to another cash register to remove security devices. Finally, you noticed several customers in line with satellite TV and wireless equipment.
- In both of your visits to the service desk, one employee was operating one of three available registers. For this reason several customers were left waiting in line for service. During one visit, you observed that when a product needed to be certified by a technician before it could be exchanged, the employee had to walk to the technical department to locate a technician, causing further delay.
- During your visits to the TV and Digital Imaging departments, you saw that floor personnel were overwhelmed with customers asking questions about products. In other words, no one

seemed to be available to handle transactions at the open registers. Cheating a bit, you walked over to the kitchen appliance department, where you saw few customers but several employees in the area.

Your Task. After carefully comparing customer and employee perceptions, present your findings in a memo report to Pat Diggins, general manager, CircuitCentral. In your report, include as much information from the tables as possible, but present it in an easy-to-understand way. What conclusions can you draw from your findings? What recommendations will you make to Ms. Diggins to ensure a successful Labor Day weekend?

12.27 Yardstick Report: Comparing Clothing Retailers' Web Sites (Obj. 5)

You work for the Marketing Department of Urban Jungle Apparel, an ascendant specialty retailer offering clothing, accessories, and personal care products for trendy men and women. Although Urban Jungle has a Web presence, it wants to update its site based on what online competitors are doing and what customers think is important about Web sites in general. Currently, Urban Jungle's Web site contains little more than online advertisements about its products and a store locator. You decide to analyze and evaluate SnazzyDuds.com and Zoom2.com, two companies with Web sites in direct competition with Urban Jungle. Your analysis is based on the following criteria: (a) speed, (b) convenience, (c) privacy/security, (d) customer service, (e) design, and (f) sales promotions. You also conduct a survey of 150 shoppers to discover their online shopping habits and preferences. Following are the results of your research.

SnazzyDuds.com

Speed. The pages, including the enlarged pop-up images of clothing items, load fast, and the order process is smooth and uncomplicated.

Convenience. The site is convenient for finding the right size, fit, and care instructions. Nearly any size is available. Additionally, if customers are not satisfied with an item, they may return it free of charge by mail or to any SnazzyDuds store in the United States. One drawback is that SnazzyDuds.com customers may find a product only by looking at images or lists; in other words, the site has no search function for locating a product by item or number.

Privacy/Security. The site is secure, using Secure Sockets Layer (SSL) technology. Purchases up to $50 are covered.

Customer Service. Overall, the service is very good to excellent. Customers may contact customer service via e-mail or use a toll-free service line any time of the day. In an experiment, two calls were made and one e-mail was sent to evaluate customer service. In general, service reps were friendly and helpful, responding politely and quickly to questions about locating products. Additional services include gift wrapping, delivery, and shopping by phone.

Design. The site is very well designed and is user friendly. The home page is uncluttered and without distractions. Customers simply click either the *Men* or *Women* link to access subsequent pages. Once they have chosen a category, customers are linked to a well-organized collection of merchandise.

Promotions. SnazzyDuds.com's "All-Year-Long Sale" section is available to anyone. Although returns cost nothing, free shipping is offered only periodically. Customers who sign up receive e-mail specials twice a month.

Zoom2.com

Speed. The ordering process is slow. Because the site is set up in an illogical fashion with both men's and women's clothing displayed on the same pages, finding an item is time consuming.

Convenience. Zoom2.com has a search-by-item number feature. It also offers care instructions as well as a wide-ranging size chart. If customers are unhappy with an item, they must return it by mail. Zoom2 stores will not accept returns of Web items.

Privacy/Security. The site is secure, using Secure Sockets Layer (SSL) technology. It also promotes itself as a "VeriSign" secure site. Purchases up to $50 are covered.

Customer Service. Service is fair. Customers may contact customer service via e-mail or use a toll-free service line any time of the day for questions. In an experiment, three calls were made and one e-mail was sent to evaluate customer service. Two of the calls required an average of 45 seconds for a rep to reach the phone. Additional services include gift wrapping, delivery, and shopping by phone.

Design. For a first-time customer, the home page is somewhat confusing. It has too many options from which to choose. Beyond the home page, the design improves, with clearly defined categories.

Promotions. Zoom2.com offers a new promotion every week. Repeat customers also receive an e-mail promotion twice a month, which can include free shipping and a percentage off the total purchase.

Consumer Survey

1. Have you ever purchased anything online?   Yes: 39   No: 111

2. If you answered yes to the preceding question, which of the following have you ordered? Please check all that apply.

   Cosmetics: 32   Clothing and accessories: 41

   Flowers: 30   CDs, recorded music: 90

3. How many purchases have you made on the Internet in the past year?

   3–4: 35   5–9: 49   10–24: 42   25 or more: 24

4. What elements of online shopping are most important to you? Please check all that apply.

   Speed: 135   Promotions: 120

   Web design: 60   Security: 105

   Convenience: 105   Customer service: 83

5. What kinds of services do you expect when you shop online? Please check all that apply.

   Free shipping: 140   Sales: 120

   Free return: 90   Promotions: 65

   Your Task. Analyze the data you have available. What data could be presented in graphs or charts? What graphic forms should be used to best illustrate the most important data? In a memo report to your supervisor, Terry O'Donnell, director of marketing, include objective conclusions based on your analysis. Also submit recommendations regarding the steps Urban Jungle should take when upgrading its Web site. If your instructor directs, prepare visual aids to accompany your yardstick report.

12.28 Feasibility Report: Can Rainbow Precision Instruments Afford a Children's Center?[18] (Obj. 5)

> Ethics

Rainbow Precision Instruments (RPI) is a $60 million manufacturer of specialty gauges for the aerospace industry, mainly flight deck or cockpit instruments, located in a small town in the Pacific Northwest. To accommodate its workforce of approximately 55 percent female employees, the company has been operating a state-of-the art Children's Center. More than a child-care center, the facility is an award-winning and well-equipped learning center that covers two shifts, from 7:00 a.m. until 10:30 p.m.

Such innovation and extensive coverage are not cheap. A recent overhaul of the facility cost $150,000, and the annual budget to instruct and care for 145 children reached $300,000. The Children's Center provides a state-certified curriculum taught by professional preschool faculty. The children also receive their meals at the facility. At its inception, the costly investment seemed fully justified. However, the number of employee children started slowly dropping until fewer than 10 percent of enrollees were children of RPI workers. The company responded by opening the Center to surrounding communities, where quality day care is scarce.

Year	2000	2005	2007
Percent of employee children at the Center	55 percent	25 percent	10 percent

Instead of raising the tuition to market levels to recoup some of its investment, RPI continues to subsidize the Center annually with approximately $200,000, not differentiating between Rainbow employees and parents from the local area. The annual tuition is $696 per child.

To make matters worse, RPI has suffered financial setbacks and is currently losing about $2.5 million annually. Finding alternatives for looking after the few remaining company children would seem less expensive than keeping the Center open. RPI has unsuccessfully pursued other options, such as selling the Children's Center or finding an independent operator to run it.

Your Task. From the available evidence, decide whether it is advisable for the company to close the Children's Center or keep it open. If you choose to keep it open, you will need to argue for some substantial changes in company operations. Your memo report will announce the decision, describe the problem, and discuss both the advantages and disadvantages of your proposal. Last, your document will focus on costs and the time frame needed to implement your decision.

12.29 Research Data for Various Report Types: Exploring Alternative Ordering Methods for Gino's Pizza (Obj. 1)

eBuyer Group, a leading consumer and research firm, has been asked to study alternative ordering methods for Gino's Pizza, a 30-unit delivery and takeout chain. Fast-food franchises across the nation have become increasingly interested in using the Internet to supplement traditional takeout and delivery options. In fact, several prominent national pizza chains have already adopted, or are testing, online ordering. Well-known examples include Papa John's, Pizza Hut, and Domino's. Another more recently explored option is interactive television (iTV). Gino Vanilli, CEO of Gino's Pizza, wants to know whether the chain should continue using its conventional phone-ordering/delivery method or adopt one of the two alternatives. The following represents your preliminary research.

The Online Consumer

- Approximately 50 percent of American adults have shopped online (Scarborough Research).
- Currently, about 80 percent of the online population over age 13 shops online (eMarketer).
- Thirteen percent of online shoppers have made food or drink purchases (Ernst & Young).
- By 2010, 85 percent of U.S. homes will be online. Approximately 75 percent will use a computer for access (Strategy Analysis).

- The composition of online shoppers is 56 percent male, 39 percent of whom are between the ages of 18 and 34 (Scarborough Research).

Online Ordering

The most common method involves using an intermediary that accepts orders for the restaurant. For example, Food.Com licenses its ROSY (Restaurant Ordering System) to Papa John's. The intermediary's Web site contains the interactive menus of its client restaurants. After consumers join Food.Com, they are able to access participating restaurants' menus and place orders; then, Food.Com sends the completed order by fax to the restaurant. A percentage of each sale, roughly 3 percent, is billed monthly to the restaurant.

Advantages of Online Ordering

- The intermediary handles most technological aspects of the process.
- The restaurant does not spend as much on computer technology and training.
- Most restaurants already use fax machines to conduct business with suppliers and main offices.
- Capital expenditures are minimal.
- Many pizza takeout and delivery restaurants and chains have created a Web presence.

Disadvantages of Online Ordering

- Because of current technology, ordering by phone takes less time.
- Consumers are still concerned about online security issues.
- One Pizza Hut operator reported receiving 5 Internet orders per day compared with a typical 140 telephone orders.
- The Pizza Time delivery and restaurant chain reported sales expectations of 10 to 12 percent of total sales based on a recent online ordering survey it conducted.

In a recent survey, the Pizza Time delivery and restaurant chain learned that online ordering would account for only 10 to 12 percent of its total sales. This is not significant enough to justify the costs. In addition to the previous information, several Internet-based grocery and food delivery ventures have disappeared (e.g., WebVan, Home Grocer, and Publix Direct) or struggled with expansion and had to downsize to survive (Pink Dot).

The iTV Consumer

- Satellite TV subscribers as of the end of last year totaled 9.39 million (OpenTV.com).
- Approximately 95 percent of U.S. households receive digital TV via a direct-to-home satellite service (OpenTV.com).
- Within three years, 117 million homes worldwide will be receiving digital TV from cable operators, and 145 million households will be receiving it from satellite services (OpenTV.com).
- Approximately 85 percent of homes in the country have cable access (Strategy Analysis).
- Roughly 6 percent of U.S. homes have iTV (Strategy Analysis).

iTV Ordering

iTV can be delivered in a number of ways. TV sets with integrated interactive receivers are on the market. However, trends suggest that some consumers will use iTV through set-top boxes for some time. Set-top boxes, such as those provided by WebTV or DirectTV, are available at local retail stores and have a street price of about $200. The most prominent player in the iTV market is OpenTV. Pizza Hut and Time Warner test marketed ordering by cable TV in Hawaii using digital cable boxes. Domino's teamed with RespondTV, a San Francisco–based software firm, to offer pizza delivery through WebTV. Finally, iTV is popular in Europe, and ordering pizza is one of its most popular uses.

Advantages of iTV

- A significant number of consumers already have cable TV.
- It eliminates the need for the consumer to input name and address repeatedly.
- It creates a secure channel for passing charge account information.
- The interface is intuitive and user friendly.

Disadvantages of iTV

- Conversion to digital cable and satellite TV has been slow.
- Arguments over technical standards have delayed a mass-market rollout in the United States.
- The viability of marketing restaurant food is unproven.
- Costs are relatively high for businesses.

Consumer Survey

Following are the results of a telephone survey obtained from a random sample of Americans from across the nation:

Questions	Yes	No
1. Have you ordered pizza for delivery within the last month?	799	226
2. Would you consider ordering pizza online as opposed to calling?	133	892
3. Would you consider ordering pizza using your television set as opposed to calling?	665	360

Your Task. As a consultant for eBuyer Group, study the preceding information. You have several options for the type of report you could prepare, based on the research data. Choose from among the following options, and address your report to Mr. Gino Vanilli, CEO of Gino's Pizza. Use at least one visual aid.

a. You could write a yardstick report establishing criteria and then comparing and contrasting the various forms of pizza ordering and delivery. You should recommend the most efficient and cost-effective solution. Decide whether to organize the report directly or indirectly.

b. You have heard from a reliable Gino's Pizza company insider that Mr. Vanilli privately strongly favors the iTV option. However, you find this option risky because iTV is still in its infancy and its future reception by consumers seems shaky. Prepare a feasibility report discussing the viability of the iTV option for Gino's Pizza. As an ethical consultant, you are beholden to the truth. If you disagree with the client, you need to find a way to dish out the unpleasant findings gently. If iTV is an appropriate option in your view, then your approach could be direct.

c. Prepare a justification/recommendation report that studies the several ordering options and proposes the most appropriate one for Mr. Vanilli's business. Although you cannot discuss the specific costs of each proposal, you can draw conclusions and make practical recommendations based on the facts presented here. What items are most important to show visually?

Grammar and Mechanics C.L.U.E. Review 12

Total Review

The first ten chapters reviewed specific guides from Appendix A: Grammar and Mechanics Guide (Competent Language Usage Essentials). The remaining exercises are total reviews, covering all of the grammar/mechanics guides plus confusing words and frequently misspelled words.

Each of the following sentences has a total of three errors in grammar, punctuation, capitalization, usage, or spelling. On a separate sheet, write a correct version. Avoid adding new phrases, starting new sentences, or rewriting in your own words. When finished, compare your responses with the key beginning on page Key-3.

Example: After our supervisor and her returned from their meeting at 2:00 p.m. we were able to sort the customers names more quickly.

Revision: After our supervisor and **she** returned from their meeting at **2 p.m.,** we were able to sort the **customers'** names more quickly.

1. Reports are a fact of life in american business consequently business writers must learn to prepare them.

2. Adrians report, which he sent to the manager and I, was distinguished by three characteristics, clear content, good organization, and correct form.

3. 6 members of our team will attend the writers' workshop, therefore, be sure they recieve notices.

4. More then ninety percent of companies now use e-mail. Which explains why we need an e-mail policy.

5. To search the Internet you need a browser such as Microsoft internet explorer.

6. Rachel was offered four hundred dollars to complete Roberts report but she said it was too little.

7. The format of a report is determined by: length, topic audience and purpose.

8. Our latest press release which was written in our Corporate Communication Department announces the opening of 3 Canadian offices.

9. Letter reports usualy has side margins of one and one quarter inches.

10. The CEO and Manager, who had went to a meeting in the West, delivered a report to Jeff and I when they returned.

Interactive Learning @ www.meguffey.com

Chapter 13

Proposals and Formal Reports

OBJECTIVES

After studying this chapter, you should be able to

1 Discuss the general uses and basic components of proposals and grasp their audience and purpose.

2 Discuss formal proposals and how to anticipate a receiver's reaction to your message.

3 Identify the components of typical business plans and ethically create buy-in for your business ideas.

4 Describe the formal report components that precede the introduction as well as elements to include in the introduction and how they further the purpose of your communication.

5 Describe the formal report components that follow the introduction and how they further the purpose of your communication.

6 Specify tips that aid writers of formal reports as they use their analytic skills and reflective thinking skills.

Communicating at Work Part 1

Winning New Business at Raytheon

It was a sunny November morning in Southern California. The director of operations at Raytheon Company's Santa Barbara business unit stood in front of an audience of about 20 engineers and managers—the individuals selected by management to write a proposal for the Aerosol Polarimetry Sensor on the National Polar-Orbiting Operational Environmental Satellite System. He began by telling them, "The request for proposal (RFP) has finally arrived. I know that many of you have been thinking about how to win this contract for more than a year. Now it's time to turn that thinking into words—time to write the proposal!"[1]

He then introduced the proposal volume managers. They would be directing most of the team's writing efforts. Finally, he identified the proposal team's newest member, Dr. Mark Grinyer, a Raytheon proposal specialist who had been asked to write the vitally important executive summary volume. He closed with a final comment, "Remember, everyone, we're on the clock now. We've got less than 60 days to build a winning proposal for almost $100 million in new business."

As Dr. Grinyer listened, he thought, "It'll be a busy holiday season." Such schedules, however, were typical for aerospace industry proposals. Several companies were competing for this contract, and only one proposal would win.

A leading aerospace company, Raytheon is a Fortune 500 giant with about 73,000 employees. Most are technicians, engineers, scientists, and managers involved in high-technology military and government programs. Raytheon's Remote Sensing business unit in Santa Barbara specializes in high-quality electro-optical sensor systems for weather satellites and other space-based vehicles. Their sensors on weather satellites provide images seen on TV every day and enable better weather predictions around the world.

Like most aerospace companies, Raytheon's success depends on its ability to produce winning proposals selling complex systems

that involve many disciplines. High-tech companies use a structured proposal development process. This process enables teams of employees who are neither professional writers nor proposal experts to work together, often under pressing time constraints. Their goal is to develop winning proposals against tough competition.

Critical Thinking
- Why are proposals vitally important to a company like Raytheon?
- How are proposals at Raytheon similar to and different from proposals or long reports written by students?
- How can team members maintain consistency and meet deadlines when writing important, time-constrained, multivolume documents such as this proposal?

http://www.raytheon.com

Preparing Formal and Informal Proposals

LEARNING OBJECTIVE 1
Discuss the general uses and basic components of proposals and grasp their audience and purpose.

Proposals are written offers to solve problems, provide services, or sell equipment. Some proposals are internal, often taking the form of justification and recommendation reports. You learned about these reports in Chapter 12. Most proposals, however, are external, such as those written at Raytheon. They are a critical means of selling equipment and services that generate income for the giant aerospace company.

Because proposals are vital to their success, high-tech companies and defense contractors maintain specialists, like Dr. Mark Grinyer, who do nothing but write proposals. Such proposals typically tell how a problem can be solved, what procedure will be followed, who will do it, how long it will take, and how much it will cost. One proposal expert said that companies today want to be able to compare "apples with apples," and they also want the protection offered by proposals, which are legal contracts.[2]

Government agencies and many companies use requests for proposals (RFPs) to solicit competitive bids on projects.

Proposals may be divided into two categories: solicited and unsolicited. When firms know exactly what they want, they prepare a request for proposal (RFP), specifying their requirements. Government agencies as well as private businesses use RFPs to solicit competitive bids from vendors. Most proposals are solicited, such as that presented by the city of Federal Way, Washington. Its RFP offered $10,000 to the winning consulting firm for promoting tourism in the region.[3] Enterprising companies looking for work might submit unsolicited proposals. For example, a team led by Goldman Sachs submitted an unsolicited proposal for a truck-only toll lanes project on an interstate in Georgia.[4]

FIGURE 13.1 Components of Formal and Informal Proposals

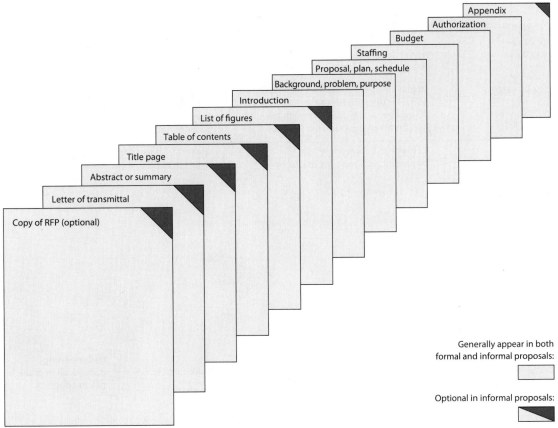

Generally appear in both
formal and informal proposals:

Optional in informal proposals:

Components of Informal Proposals

Informal proposals may be presented in short (two- to four-page) letters. Sometimes called *letter proposals*, they may contain six principal components: introduction, background, proposal, staffing, budget, and authorization request. As you can see in Figure 13.1, both informal and formal proposals contain these six basic parts. Figure 13.2, an informal letter proposal to a Tampa dentist to improve patient satisfaction, illustrates the six parts of letter proposals.

Informal proposals may contain an introduction, background information, the proposal, staffing requirements, a budget, and an authorization request.

Hoku Scientific is a hot new player in the solar energy market. As a maker of space-age photovoltaic installations that provide solar-generated electricity to homes and businesses, the Hawaii-based clean-energy producer is helping create a sustainable world powered by 100 percent renewable energy. Hoku's proposals have led to formal negotiations and million-dollar contracts with Suntech Power Holdings, Sanyo Electric, and Hawaiian Electric Co. What persuasive "hooks" could Hoku include in its proposals to persuade companies to buy its solar components?

© Emilio Ereza / Alamy

FIGURE 13.2 Informal Proposal

1 Prewriting

Analyze: The purpose is to persuade the reader to accept this proposal.

Anticipate: The reader must be convinced that this survey project is worth its hefty price.

Adapt: Because the reader will be resistant at first, use a persuasive approach that emphasizes benefits.

2 Writing

Research: Collect data about the reader's practice and other surveys of patient satisfaction.

Organize: Identify four specific purposes (benefits) of this proposal. Specify the survey plan. Promote the staff, itemize the budget, and ask for approval.

Compose: Prepare for revision by composing at a word processor.

3 Revising

Revise: Revise to emphasize benefits. Improve readability with functional headings and lists. Remove jargon and wordiness.

Proofread: Check spelling of client's name. Verify dates and calculation of budget figures. Recheck all punctuation.

Evaluate: Is this proposal convincing enough to sell the client?

Becker Marketing
MARKET RESEARCH CONSULTANTS

1302 Prudential Drive
Jacksonville, FL 32099
(866) 270-5110
www.beckermarketing.com

March 3, 2009

Peter R. Daltrey, DDS
1015 Oaks Plaza
Tampa, FL 33620

Dear Dr. Daltrey:

Grabs attention with "hook" that focuses on key benefit

Helping you improve your practice is of the highest priority at Becker Marketing. That's why we are pleased to submit the following proposal outlining our plan to help you more effectively meet your patients' needs by analyzing their views about your practice.

Uses opening paragraph in place of introduction

Background and Purpose

We understand that you have been incorporating a total quality management system in your practice. Although you have every reason to believe your patients are pleased with the service you provide, you would like to give them an opportunity to discuss what they like and possibly don't like about your service. Specifically, your purposes are to survey your patients to (a) determine the level of their satisfaction with you and your staff, (b) elicit their suggestions for improvement, (c) learn more about how they discovered you, and (d) compare your "preferred" and "standard" patients.

Identifies four purposes of survey

Announces heart of proposal

Proposed Plan

Based on our experience in conducting many local and national customer satisfaction surveys, Becker Marketing proposes the following plan to you.

Divides total plan into logical segments for easy reading

Survey. We will develop a short but thorough questionnaire probing the data you desire. Although the survey instrument will include both open-ended and closed questions, it will concentrate on the latter. Closed questions enable respondents to answer easily; they also facilitate systematic data analysis. The questionnaire will measure patient reactions to such elements as courtesy, professionalism, accuracy of billing, friendliness, and waiting time. After you approve it, the questionnaire will be sent to a carefully selected sample of 300 patients whom you have separated into groupings of "preferred" and "standard."

Describes procedure for solving problem or achieving goals

Analysis. Data from the survey will be analyzed by demographic segments, such as patient type, age, and gender. Our experienced team of experts, using state-of-the-art computer systems and advanced statistical measures, will study the (a) degree of patient satisfaction, (b) reasons for satisfaction or dissatisfaction, and (c) relationship between responses of your "preferred" and "standard" patients. Moreover, our team will report to you specific suggestions for making patient visits more pleasant.

Report. You will receive a final report with the key findings clearly spelled out, Dr. Daltrey. Our expert staff will also draw conclusions based on these findings. The report will include tables summarizing all responses, broken down into groups of preferred and standard patients.

FIGURE 13.2 (Continued)

Dr. Peter R. Daltrey   Page 2   March 3, 2009

Schedule. With your approval, the following schedule has been arranged for your patient satisfaction survey:

Questionnaire development and mailing	April 1–6
Deadline for returning questionnaires	April 25
Data tabulation and processing	April 25–26
Completion of final report	May 2

Uses past-tense verbs to show that work has already started on the project

Staffing

Promotes credentials and expertise of key people

Becker Marketing is a nationally recognized, experienced consulting firm specializing in survey investigation. I have assigned your customer satisfaction survey to Dr. Ellen Mayo, our director of research. Dr. Mayo was trained at Penn State and has successfully supervised our research program for the past nine years. Before joining Becker, she was a marketing analyst with Procter & Gamble Company. Assisting Dr. Mayo will be a team headed by Gordon Scott, our vice president for operations. Mr. Scott earned a bachelor's degree in computer science and a master's degree in marketing from the University of South Carolina, where he was elected to Phi Delta Mu honor society. Within our organization he supervises our computer-aided telephone interviewing (CATI) system and manages our 30-person professional interviewing staff.

Builds credibility by describing outstanding staff and facilities

Budget

Itemizes costs carefully because a proposal is a contract offer

	Estimated Hours	Rate	Total
Professional and administrative time			
Questionnaire development	3	$150/hr.	$ 450
Questionnaire mailing	4	40/hr.	160
Data processing and tabulation	12	40/hr.	480
Analysis of findings	15	150/hr.	2,250
Preparation of final report	5	150/hr.	750
Mailing costs			
300 copies of questionnaire			150
Postage and envelopes			350
Total costs			$4,590

Authorization

Makes response easy

We are convinced, Dr. Daltrey, that our professionally designed and administered client satisfaction survey will enhance your practice. Becker Marketing can have specific results for you by May 2 if you sign the enclosed duplicate copy of this letter and return it to us with a retainer of $2,300. The prices in this offer are in effect only until July 1.

Closes by repeating key qualifications and main benefits

Provides deadline

Sincerely,

Ann Becker

Ann Becker, PhD
President

AB:las
Enclosure

Introduction. Most proposals begin by briefly explaining the reasons for the proposal and by highlighting the writer's qualifications. To make your introduction more persuasive, you need to provide a "hook," such as the following:

- Hint at extraordinary results with details to be revealed shortly.

- Promise low costs or speedy results.

- Mention a remarkable resource (well-known authority, new computer program, well-trained staff) available exclusively to you.

- Identify a serious problem (worry item) and promise a solution, to be explained later.

- Specify a key issue or benefit that you feel is the heart of the proposal.

Although writers may know what goes into the proposal introduction, many face writer's block before they can get started. When she worked as a proposals manager at Hewlett-Packard, Mary Piecewicz recognized that writer's block was a big problem for sales representatives on a proposal team. They simply didn't know how to get started. Piecewicz offered the following advice: "To conquer writer's block, begin with a bulleted list of what the customer is looking for. This list is like a road map; it gets you started and keeps you headed in the right direction."

In the proposal introduction shown in Figure 13.2, Ann Becker focused on what the customer was looking for. She analyzed the request of the Tampa dentist, Dr. Daltrey, and decided that he was most interested in specific recommendations for improving service to his patients. However, Becker didn't hit on this hook until she had written a first draft and had come back to it later. Indeed, it is often a good idea to put off writing the proposal introduction until after you have completed other parts. In longer proposals the introduction also describes the scope and limitations of the project, as well as outlining the organization of the material to come.

Background, Problem, and Purpose.

The background section identifies the problem and discusses the goals or purposes of the project. In an unsolicited proposal your goal is to convince the reader that a problem exists. Thus, you must present the problem in detail, discussing such factors as monetary losses, failure to comply with government regulations, or loss of customers. In a solicited proposal your aim is to persuade the reader that you understand the problem completely. Therefore, if you are responding to an RFP, this means repeating its language. For example, if the RFP asks for the *design of a maintenance program for wireless communication equipment*, you would use the same language in explaining the purpose of your proposal. This section might include segments entitled *Basic Requirements, Most Critical Tasks,* or *Most Important Secondary Problems.*

Proposal, Plan, and Schedule.

In the proposal section itself, you should discuss your plan for solving the problem. In some proposals this is tricky because you want to disclose enough of your plan to secure the contract without giving away so much information that your services aren't needed. Without specifics, though, your proposal has little chance, so you must decide how much to reveal. Tell what you propose to do and how it will benefit the reader. Remember, too, that a proposal is a sales presentation. Sell your methods, product, and "deliverables"—items that will be left with the client. In this section some writers specify how the project will be managed and how its progress will be audited. Most writers also include a schedule of activities or timetable showing when events will take place.

Staffing.

The staffing section of a proposal describes the credentials and expertise of the project leaders. It may also identify the size and qualifications of the support staff, along with other resources such as computer facilities and special programs for analyzing statistics. The staffing section is a good place to endorse and promote your staff and to demonstrate to the client that your company can do the job. Some firms, like Raytheon, follow industry standards and include staff qualifications in an appendix. Raytheon features the résumés of the major project participants, such as the program manager, the technical director, and team leaders. If key contributors must be replaced in the course of the project, Raytheon commits to providing only individuals with equivalent qualifications. The first rule is to give the clients exactly what they asked for regarding staff qualifications, the number of project participants, and proposal details.

Budget.

A central item in most proposals is the budget, a list of proposed project costs. You need to prepare this section carefully because it represents a contract; you cannot raise the price later—even if your costs increase. You can—and should—protect yourself from rising costs with a deadline for acceptance. In the budget section some writers itemize hours and costs; others present a total sum only. A proposal to install a complex computer system might, for example, contain a detailed line-by-line budget. Similarly, Ann Becker felt that she needed to justify the budget for her firm's patient satisfaction survey, so she itemized the costs, as shown in Figure 13.2. However, the budget included for a proposal to conduct a one-day seminar to improve employee communication skills might be a lump sum only. Your analysis of the project will help you decide what kind of budget to prepare.

Authorization Request.

Informal proposals often close with a request for approval or authorization. In addition, the closing should remind the reader of key benefits and motivate action. It might also include a deadline beyond which the offer is invalid. At Raytheon authorization information can be as simple as naming in the letter of transmittal the company official who would approve the contract resulting from the proposal. However, in most cases, a model contract is sent along that responds to the requirements specified by the RFP. This model contract almost always results in negotiations before the final project contract is awarded.

Special Components of Formal Proposals

Formal proposals differ from informal proposals not in style but in size and format. Formal proposals respond to big projects and may range from 5 to 200 or more pages. To facilitate comprehension and reference, they are organized into many parts, as shown in Figure 13.1. In addition to the six basic components described for informal proposals, formal proposals may contain some or all of the following front and end parts.

LEARNING OBJECTIVE 2
Discuss formal proposals and how to anticipate a receiver's reaction to your message.

Copy of the RFP. A copy of the RFP may be included in the opening parts of a formal proposal. Large organizations may have more than one RFP circulating, and identification is necessary.

Letter of Transmittal. A letter of transmittal, usually bound inside formal proposals, addresses the person who is designated to receive the proposal or who will make the final decision. The letter describes how you learned about the problem or confirms that the proposal responds to the enclosed RFP. This persuasive letter briefly presents the major features and benefits of your proposal. Here, you should assure the reader that you are authorized to make the bid and mention the time limit for which the bid stands. You may also offer to provide additional information and ask for action, if appropriate.

Formal proposals might also contain a copy of the RFP, a letter of transmittal, an abstract, a title page, a table of contents, a list of figures, and an appendix.

Abstract or Executive Summary. An abstract is a brief summary (typically one page) of a proposal's highlights intended for specialists or for technical readers. An executive summary also reviews the proposal's highlights, but it is written for managers and should be less technically oriented. Formal proposals may contain either or both. For more information about writing executive summaries and abstracts, use a search engine such as Google.

An abstract summarizes a proposal's highlights for specialists; an executive summary does so for managers.

Title Page. The title page includes the following items, generally in this order: title of proposal, name of client organization, RFP number or other announcement, date of submission, authors' names, and/or the name of their organization.

Table of Contents. Because most proposals do not contain an index, the table of contents becomes quite important. A table of contents should include all headings and their beginning page numbers. Items that appear before the contents (copy of RFP, letter of transmittal, abstract, and title page) typically are not listed in the contents. However, any appendixes should be listed.

List of Figures. Proposals with many tables and figures often contain a list of figures. This list includes each figure or table title and its page number. If you have just a few figures or tables, however, you may omit this list.

Appendix. Ancillary material of interest to some readers goes in appendixes. Appendix A might include résumés of the principal investigators or testimonial letters. Appendix B might include examples or a listing of previous projects. Other appendixes could include audit procedures, technical graphics, or professional papers cited in the body of the proposal.

Proposals in the past were always paper-based and delivered by mail or special messenger. Today, however, companies increasingly prefer online proposals. Receiving companies may transmit the electronic proposal to all levels of management without ever printing a page, thus appealing to many environmentally conscious organizations.

Well-written proposals win contracts and business for companies and individuals. Many companies depend entirely on proposals to generate their income, so proposal writing is extremely important. The following checklist summarizes important elements to remember in writing proposals.

Spotlight on Communicators

Well-known proposal consultant Dr. Tom Sant advises proposal writers to (a) state the client's key need or problem, (b) spell out why the need must be addressed, (c) present a solution in concrete terms, and (d) fill in the details. Above all, he says, be sure a proposal is client focused rather than product focused. If the price tag is hefty, he suggests highlighting long-term savings and cost-effectiveness.

© Hyde Park Partners

Checklist

Writing Proposals

Introduction

✓ **Indicate the purpose.** Specify why you are making the proposal.

✓ **Develop a persuasive "hook."** Suggest excellent results, low costs, or exclusive resources. Identify a serious problem or name a key issue or benefit.

Background, Problem, Purpose

✓ **Provide necessary background.** Discuss the significance of the proposal and its goals or purposes.

✓ **Introduce the problem.** For unsolicited proposals convince the reader that a problem exists. For solicited proposals show that you fully understand the problem and its ramifications.

Proposal, Plan, Schedule

✓ **Explain the proposal.** Present your plan for solving the problem or meeting the need.

✓ **Discuss plan management and evaluation.** If appropriate, tell how the plan will be implemented and evaluated.

✓ **Outline a timetable.** Furnish a schedule showing what will be done and when.

Staffing

✓ **Promote the qualifications of your staff.** Explain the specific credentials and expertise of the key personnel for the project.

✓ **Mention special resources and equipment.** Show how your support staff and resources are superior to those of the competition.

Budget

✓ **Show project costs.** For most projects itemize costs. Remember, however, that proposals are contracts.

✓ **Include a deadline.** Here or in the conclusion present a date beyond which the bid figures are no longer valid.

Authorization

✓ **Ask for approval.** Make it easy for the reader to authorize the project (for example, *Sign and return the duplicate copy*).

Communicating at Work Part 2

Winning New Business at Raytheon

Raytheon's proposal process adapts the writing process to a team-writing environment. Dr. Mark Grinyer, who was assigned the task of writing the important executive summary, described how he used this process to complete his portion of Raytheon's Aerosol Polarimetry Sensor proposal.

First, he studied the customer's RFP looking for what the client really cared about. Then he talked to proposal team members and read descriptions of the company's offering. He turned this information into persuasive themes, outlines, and visuals, which he organized into ten storyboards (graphic organizers), one for each section of the summary. Proposal team members and a "Pink Team" of company executives reviewed these storyboards and made suggestions for improvement. "They focused on content quality, organization, and accuracy," Dr. Grinyer said.

Using the storyboards, Dr. Grinyer quickly wrote the first draft working section by section. He and his teammates revised the draft until all contributors were satisfied that it effectively addressed the interests of its audience of decision makers. A formal "Red Team" of company executives confirmed this assessment. The proposal was then ready for final corrections, formatting, proofreading, printing, and submission to the customer. "Overall," Dr. Grinyer explained, "the guidance provided by my teammates and reviewers kept me on target throughout the proposal effort."

© Steven E. Frischling / Bloomberg News / Landov

Critical Thinking

- How does Raytheon's proposal process incorporate good writing practices that you can apply to your own work?
- How do you think the different reviewers and their reviews help ensure the success of a proposal effort?
- Why do you think Raytheon puts so much effort into proposal executive summaries?

Preparing an Effective Business Plan

Another form of proposal is a business plan. Let us say you want to start your own business. Unless you can count on the Bank of Mom and Dad, you will need financial backing such as a bank loan or venture capital supplied by investors. A business plan is critical for securing financial support of any kind. Such a plan also ensures that you have done your homework and know what you are doing in launching your business. It provides you with a detailed road map to chart a course to success.

According to the Small Business Administration, most entrepreneurs spend about 400 hours writing a good business plan. The average consultant can do it in about 40 hours.[5] Nevertheless, many budding entrepreneurs prefer to save the cash and do it themselves. Increasingly sophisticated software, such as Business Plan Pro, PlanWrite, and Planmagic, is available for those who have done their research, assembled the relevant data, and just want formatting help. Free shareware can also be found on the Internet.[6]

Components of Typical Business Plans

If you are serious about starting a business, the importance of a comprehensive, thoughtful business plan cannot be overemphasized, says the Small Business Administration. Your business plan is more likely to secure the funds you need if it is carefully written and includes the following elements:

- **Letter of transmittal and/or executive summary with mission statement.** Explain your reason for writing. Provide your name, address, and telephone number, along with contact information for all principals. Include a concise mission statement for your business. Describe your business explaining the reasons it will succeed. Because potential investors will be looking for this mission statement, consider highlighting it with a paragraph heading (*Mission statement*) or use bolding or italics. Some consultants say that you should be able to write your mission statement on the back of a business card. Others think that one or two short paragraphs might be more realistic. To give it special treatment, you could make the mission statement a section of its own following the table of contents. Your executive summary should conclude by introducing the parts of the following plan and asking for support.

- **Table of contents.** List the page numbers and topics included in your plan.

- **Company description.** Identify the form of your business (proprietorship, partnership, or corporation) and its type (merchandising, manufacturing, or service). For existing companies, describe the company's founding, growth, sales, and profit.

- **Product/service description.** In jargon-free language, explain what you are providing, how it will benefit customers, and why it is better than existing products or services. For start-ups, explain why the business will be profitable. Investors aren't always looking for a unique product or service. Instead, they are searching for a concept whose growth potential distinguishes it from others competing for funds.

- **Market analysis.** Discuss market characteristics, trends, projected growth, customer behavior, complementary products and services, and barriers to entry. Identify your customers and how you will attract, hold, and increase your market share. Discuss the strengths and weaknesses of your direct and indirect competitors.

- **Operations and management.** Explain specifically how you will run your business, including location, equipment, personnel, and management. Highlight experienced and well-trained members of the management team and your advisors. Many investors consider this the most important factor in assessing business potential. Can your management team implement this business plan?

- **Financial analysis.** Outline a realistic start-up budget that includes fees for legal/professional services, occupancy, licenses/permits, equipment, insurance, supplies, advertising/promotions, salaries/wages, accounting, income, and utilities. Also present an operating budget that projects costs for personnel, insurance, rent, depreciation, loan payments, salaries, taxes, repairs, and so on. Explain how much money you have, how much you will need to start up, and how much you will need to stay in business.

- **Appendixes.** Provide necessary extras such as managers' résumés, promotional materials, and product photos.

Seeing Sample Business Plans on the Web

Writing a business plan is easier if you can see examples and learn from experts' suggestions. On the Web you will find many sites devoted to business plans. Some sites want to sell you something; others offer free advice. One of the best sites (**http://www.bplans.com**) does try to sell business plans and software. However, in addition to useful advice and blogs from experts, the site also provides over 100 free samples of business plans ranging from aircraft rental to wedding consultant businesses. These simple but helpful plans, provided by Palo Alto Software, Inc., illustrate diverse business start-ups.

At the Small Business Administration (SBA) Web site (**http://www.sba.gov/smallbusinessplanner/**), you will find more business plan advice. In addition to suggestions for writing and using a business plan, the SBA site provides helpful business start-up information about financing, marketing, employees, taxes, and legal matters. The SBA site also provides local resources and tools for the budding entrepreneur.

Writing Formal Reports

Formal reports are similar to formal proposals in length, organization, and serious tone. Instead of making an offer, however, formal reports represent the end product of thorough investigation and analysis. They present ordered information to decision makers in business, industry, government, and education. In many ways formal reports are extended versions of the analytical business reports presented in Chapter 12. Figure 13.3 shows the components of typical formal reports, their normal sequence, and parts that might be omitted in informal reports.

FIGURE 13.3 Components of Formal and Informal Reports

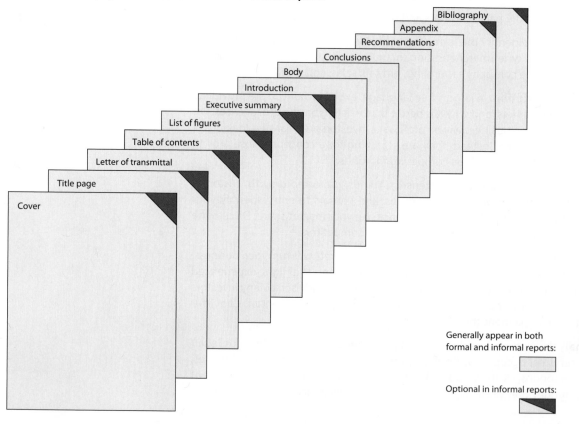

Generally appear in both formal and informal reports:

Optional in informal reports:

Merging two companies is a lengthy process that requires approval from antitrust regulators. When Sirius and XM delivered a proposal for their merger to the Justice Department and the FCC, the satellite radio giants claimed that their union wouldn't constitute a monopoly. The merger proposal attempted to prove that satellite radio was in fair competition with MP3 players, terrestrial radio, digital radio, and cell phones. In what section of a formal report do businesses generally deliver a full written justification of their proposed actions?

Components of Formal Reports

A number of front and end items lengthen formal reports but enhance their professional tone and serve their multiple audiences. Formal reports may be read by many levels of managers, along with technical specialists and financial consultants. Therefore, breaking a long, formal report into small segments makes its information more accessible and easier to understand for all readers. These segments are discussed here and also illustrated in the model report shown later in the chapter (Figure 13.4). This analytical report studies the economic impact of an industrial park on Flagstaff, Arizona, and makes recommendations for increasing the city's future revenues.

Cover. Formal reports are usually enclosed in vinyl or heavy paper binders to protect the pages and to give a professional, finished appearance. Some companies have binders imprinted with their name and logo. The title of the report may appear through a cut-out window or may be applied with an adhesive label. Good stationery and office supply stores usually stock an assortment of report binders and labels.

> Like proposals, formal reports are divided into many segments to make information comprehensible and accessible.

Title Page. A report title page, as illustrated in the Figure 13.4 model report, begins with the name of the report typed in uppercase letters (no underscore and no quotation marks). Next comes *Presented to* (or *Submitted to*) and the name, title, and organization of the individual receiving the report. Lower on the page is *Prepared by* (or *Submitted by*) and the author's name plus any necessary identification. The last item on the title page is the date of submission. All items after the title are typed in a combination of upper- and lowercase letters.

Letter or Memo of Transmittal. Generally written on organization stationery, a letter or memorandum of transmittal introduces a formal report. You will recall that letters are sent to outsiders and memos to insiders. A transmittal letter or memo follows the direct pattern and is usually less formal than the report itself (for example, the letter or memo may use contractions and the first-person pronouns *I* and *we*). The transmittal letter or memo typically (a) announces the topic of the report and tells how it was authorized; (b) briefly describes the project; (c) highlights the report's findings, conclusions, and recommendations, if the reader is expected to be supportive; and (d) closes with appreciation for the assignment, instruction for the reader's follow-up actions, acknowledgment of help from others, or offers of assistance in answering questions. If a report is going to various readers, a special transmittal letter or memo should be prepared for each, anticipating how each reader will use the report.

> A letter or memo of transmittal gives a personalized overview of a formal report.

Table of Contents.   The table of contents shows the headings in the report and their page numbers. It gives an overview of the report topics and helps readers locate them. You should wait to prepare the table of contents until after you've completed the report. For short reports you should include all headings. For longer reports you might want to list only first- and second-level headings. Leaders (spaced or unspaced dots) help guide the eye from the heading to the page number. Items may be indented in outline form or typed flush with the left margin.

List of Figures.   For reports with several figures or illustrations, you may wish to include a list of figures to help readers locate them. This list may appear on the same page as the table of contents, space permitting. For each figure or illustration, include a title and page number. Some writers distinguish between tables and all other illustrations, which are called figures. If you make the distinction, you should prepare separate lists of tables and figures. Because the model report in Figure 13.4 has few illustrations, the writer labeled them all "figures," a method that simplifies numbering.

Executive Summary.   The purpose of an executive summary is to present an overview of a longer report to people who may not have time to read the entire document. Generally, an executive summary is prepared by the author of the report. However, occasionally you may be asked to write an executive summary of a published report or article written by someone else. In either case you will probably do the following:

> An executive summary supplies an overview of a longer report.

- **Summarize key points.** Your goal is to summarize the important points including the purpose of the report; the problem addressed; and the findings, conclusions, and recommendations. You might also summarize the research methods, if they can be stated concisely.

- **Look for strategic words and sentences.** Read the completed report carefully. Pay special attention to the first and last sentences of paragraphs, which often contain summary statements. Look for words that enumerate (*first, next, finally*) and words that express causation (*therefore, as a result*). Also look for words that signal essentials (*basically, central, leading, principal, major*) and words that contrast ideas (*however, consequently*).

- **Prepare an outline with headings.** At a minimum, include headings for the purpose, findings, and conclusions/recommendations. What kernels of information would your reader want to know about these topics?

- **Fill in your outline.** Some writers use their computers to cut and paste important parts of the text. Then they condense with careful editing. Others find it more efficient to create new sentences as they prepare the executive summary.

- **Begin with the purpose.** The easiest way to begin an executive summary is with the words "The purpose of this report is to. . . ." Experienced writers may be more creative.

- **Follow the report sequence.** Present all your information in the order in which it is found in the report.

- **Eliminate nonessential details.** Include only main points. Do not include anything not in the original report. Use minimal technical language.

- **Control the length.** An executive summary is usually no longer than 10 percent of the original document. Thus, a 100-page report might require a 10-page summary. A 10-page report might need only a 1-page summary—or no summary at all. The executive summary for a long report may also include graphics to adequately highlight main points.

To see a representative executive summary, look at Figure 13.4 on page 411. Although it is only one page long, this executive summary includes headings to help the reader see the main divisions immediately. Let your organization's practices guide you in determining the length and form of an executive summary.

Introduction. Formal reports begin with an introduction that sets the scene and announces the subject. Because they contain many parts serving different purposes, formal reports are somewhat redundant. The same information may be included in the letter of transmittal, summary, and introduction. To avoid sounding repetitious, try to present the data slightly differently. However, do not skip the introduction because you've included some of its information elsewhere. You cannot be sure that your reader saw the information earlier. A good report introduction typically covers the following elements, although not necessarily in this order:

The introduction to a formal report describes the background, explains the purpose, and discusses the significance, scope, and organization of the topic.

- **Background.** Describe events leading up to the problem or need.

- **Problem or purpose.** Explain the report topic and specify the problem or need that motivated the report.

- **Significance.** Tell why the topic is important. You may wish to quote experts or cite newspapers, journals, books, and other secondary sources to establish the importance of the topic.

- **Scope.** Clarify the boundaries of the report, defining what will be included or excluded.

- **Organization.** Orient readers by giving them a road map that previews the structure of the report.

Beyond these minimal introductory elements, consider adding any of the following information that is relevant to your readers:

- **Authorization.** Identify who commissioned the report. If no letter of transmittal is included, also tell why, when, by whom, and to whom the report was written.

- **Literature review.** Summarize what other authors and researchers have published on this topic, especially for academic and scientific reports.

- **Sources and methods.** Describe your secondary sources (periodicals, books, databases). Also explain how you collected primary data, including survey size, sample design, and statistical programs used.

- **Definitions of key terms.** Define words that may be unfamiliar to the audience. Also define terms with special meanings, such as *small business* when it specifically means businesses with fewer than 30 employees.

Body. The principal section in a formal report is the body. It discusses, analyzes, interprets, and evaluates the research findings or solution to the initial problem. This is where you show the evidence that justifies your conclusions. Organize the body into main categories following your original outline or using one of the patterns described earlier (such as time, component, importance, criteria, or convention).

Although we refer to this section as the body, it does not carry that heading. Instead, it contains clear headings that explain each major section. Headings may be functional or talking. Functional heads (such as *Results of the Survey, Analysis of Findings,* or *Discussion*) help readers identify the purpose of the section but do not reveal what is in it. Such headings are useful for routine reports or for sensitive topics that may upset readers. Talking heads (for example, *Findings Reveal Revenue and Employment Benefits*) are more informative and interesting, but they do not help readers see the organization of the report. The model report in Figure 13.4 uses combination headings; as the name suggests, they combine functional heads for organizational sections (*Introduction, Conclusions* and *Recommendations*) with talking heads that reveal the content. The headings divide the body into smaller parts.

LEARNING OBJECTIVE 5
Describe the formal report components that follow the introduction and how they further the purpose of your communication.

Conclusions. This important section tells what the findings mean, particularly in terms of solving the original problem. Some writers prefer to intermix their conclusions with the analysis of the findings—instead of presenting the conclusions separately. Other writers place the conclusions before the body so that busy readers can examine the significant information immediately. Still others combine the conclusions and recommendations. Most writers, though, present the conclusions after the body because readers expect this structure. In long reports this section may include a summary of the findings. To improve comprehension, you may present the conclusions in a numbered or bulleted list. See Chapter 12 for more suggestions on drawing conclusions.

Recommendations.

When asked, you should submit recommendations that make precise suggestions for actions to solve the report problem. Recommendations are most helpful when they are practical and reasonable. Naturally, they should evolve from the findings and conclusions. Do not introduce new information in the conclusions or recommendations sections. As with conclusions, the position of recommendations is somewhat flexible. They may be combined with conclusions, or they may be presented before the body, especially when the audience is eager and supportive. Generally, though, in formal reports they come last.

Recommendations require an appropriate introductory sentence, such as *The findings and conclusions in this study support the following recommendations*. When making many recommendations, number them and phrase each as a command, such as *Begin an employee fitness program with a workout room available five days a week*. If appropriate, add information describing how to implement each recommendation. Some reports include a timetable describing the who, what, when, where, and how for putting each recommendation into operation. Chapter 12 provides more information about writing recommendations.

Appendix.

Incidental or supporting materials belong in appendixes at the end of a formal report. These materials are relevant to some readers but not to all. Appendixes may include survey forms, copies of other reports, tables of data, computer printouts, and related correspondence. If additional appendixes are necessary, they would be named *Appendix A, Appendix B*, and so forth.

Works Cited or References.

If you use the MLA (Modern Language Association) referencing format, all sources of information would be listed alphabetically in the "Works Cited." If you use the APA (American Psychological Association) format, your list would be called "References." Regardless of the format, you must include the author, title, publication, date of publication, page number, and other significant data for all ideas or quotations used in your report. For electronic references include the preceding information plus a description of the electronic address or path leading to the citation. Also include the date on which you located the electronic reference. To see electronic and other citations, examine the list of references at the end of Figure 13.4. Appendix C of the text contains additional documentation information.

Final Writing Tips

Formal reports are not undertaken lightly. They involve considerable effort in all three phases of writing, beginning with analysis of the problem and anticipation of the audience (as discussed in Chapter 4). Researching the data, organizing it into a logical presentation, and composing the first draft (Chapter 5) make up the second phase of writing. Revising, proofreading, and evaluating (Chapter 6) are completed in the third phase. Although everyone approaches the writing process somewhat differently, the following tips offer advice in problem areas faced by most formal report writers:

- **Allow sufficient time.** The main reason given by writers who are disappointed with their reports is "I just ran out of time." Develop a realistic timetable and stick to it.

- **Finish data collection.** Do not begin writing until you've collected all the data and drawn the primary conclusions. Starting too early often means backtracking. For reports based on survey data, complete the tables and figures first.

- **Work from a good outline.** A big project such as a formal report needs the order and direction provided by a clear outline, even if the outline has to be revised as the project unfolds.

- **Provide a proper writing environment.** You will need a quiet spot where you can spread out your materials and work without interruption. Formal reports demand blocks of concentration time.

- **Use the features of your computer.** Preparing a report on a word processor enables you to keyboard quickly; revise easily; and check spelling, grammar, and synonyms readily. A word of warning, though: save your document often and print occasionally so that you have a hard copy. Take these precautions to guard against the grief caused by lost files, power outages, and computer malfunctions.

- **Write rapidly; revise later.** Some experts advise writers to record their ideas quickly and save revision until after the first draft is completed. They say that quick writing avoids wasted effort spent in polishing sentences or even sections that may be cut later. Moreover, rapid writing encourages fluency and creativity. However, a quick-and-dirty first draft does not work for everyone. Many business writers prefer a more deliberate writing style, so consider this advice selectively and experiment with the method that works best for you.

- **Save difficult sections.** If some sections are harder to write than others, save them until you've developed confidence and a rhythm working on easier topics.

- **Be consistent in verb tense.** Use past-tense verbs to describe completed actions (for example, *the respondents said* or *the survey showed*). Use present-tense verbs, however, to explain current actions (*the purpose of the report is, this report examines, the table shows,* and so forth). When citing references, use past-tense verbs (*Jones reported that*). Do not switch back and forth between present- and past-tense verbs in describing related data.

- **Generally avoid *I* and *we*.** To make formal reports seem as objective and credible as possible, most writers omit first-person pronouns. This formal style sometimes results in the overuse of passive-voice verbs (for example, *periodicals were consulted* and *the study was conducted*). Look for alternative constructions (*periodicals indicated* and *the study revealed*). It is also possible that your organization may allow first-person pronouns, so check before starting your report.

- **Let the first draft sit.** After completing the first version, put it aside for a day or two. Return to it with the expectation of revising and improving it. Do not be afraid to make major changes.

- **Revise for clarity, coherence, and conciseness.** Read a printed copy out loud. Do the sentences make sense? Do the ideas flow together naturally? Can wordiness and flabbiness be cut out? Make sure that your writing is so clear that a busy manager does not have to reread any part. See Chapter 6 for specific revision suggestions.

- **Proofread the final copy three times.** First, read a printed copy slowly for word meanings and content. Then read the copy again for spelling, punctuation, grammar, and other mechanical errors. Finally, scan the entire report to check its formatting and consistency (page numbering, indenting, spacing, headings, and so forth).

Putting It All Together

Formal reports in business generally aim to study problems and recommend solutions. Sylvia Hernandez, senior research assistant with Del Rio Industrial Consultants, was asked to study the economic impact of a local industrial park on the city of Flagstaff, Arizona, resulting in the formal report shown in Figure 13.4.

The city council hired the consultants to evaluate Coconino Industrial Park and to assess whether future commercial development would stimulate further economic growth. Sylvia Hernandez subdivided the economic impact into three aspects: Revenue, Employment,

Smart report writers allow themselves plenty of time, research thoroughly, and draw up a useful outline.

Ethics Check

Who's to Blame?

If one of your teammates cowriting a formal report with you has been found to have plagiarized a portion of your writing project, typically the instructor will punish the entire group, assuming ownership of the entire team. After all, researchers are expected to deliver a product that they have jointly prepared. Is this approach fair?

Effective formal reports maintain parallelism in verb tenses, avoid first-person pronouns, and use the active voice.

FIGURE 13.4 Model Format Report With APA Citation Style

Title Page

2 inches

Includes report title in all caps with longer line above shorter line

ECONOMIC IMPACT OF COCONINO INDUSTRIAL PARK ON THE CITY OF FLAGSTAFF

Highlights name of report recipient

Presented to
The Flagstaff City Council
Flagstaff, Arizona

Divide blank lines equally to separate the sections

Identifies report writer

Prepared by
Sylvia Hernandez
Senior Research Consultant
Del Rio Industrial Consultants

January 10, 2008

Omits page number

2 inches

The title page is usually arranged in four evenly balanced areas. If the report is to be bound on the left, move the left margin and center point ¼ inch to the right (i.e., set the left margin to 1.25 inches). Notice that no page number appears on the title page, although it counts as page i. In designing the title page, be careful to avoid anything unprofessional—such as too many type fonts, italics, oversized print, and inappropriate graphics. Keep the title page simple and professional.

This model report uses APA documentation style. However, it does not use double-spacing, the recommended format for research papers using APA style. Instead, this model uses single-spacing, which saves space and is more appropriate for business reports.

FIGURE 13.4 (Continued) Letter of Transmittal

DEL RIO INDUSTRIAL CONSULTANTS

110 West Route 66
Flagstaff, Arizona 86001

www.delrio.com
(928) 774-1101

January 12, 2008

City Council
City of Flagstaff
211 West Aspen Avenue
Flagstaff, AZ 86001

Dear Council Members:

The attached report, requested by the Flagstaff City Council in a letter to Goldman-Lyon & Associates dated October 20, describes the economic impact of Coconino Industrial Park on the city of Flagstaff. We believe you will find the results of this study useful in evaluating future development of industrial parks within the city limits.

This study was designed to examine economic impact in three areas:

- Current and projected tax and other revenues accruing to the city from Coconino Industrial Park

- Current and projected employment generated by the park

- Indirect effects on local employment, income, and economic growth

Primary research consisted of interviews with 15 Coconino Industrial Park (CIP) tenants and managers, in addition to a 2007 survey of over 5,000 CIP employees. Secondary research sources included the annual budget of the city of Flagstaff, county and state tax records, government publications, periodicals, books, and online resources. Results of this research, discussed more fully in this report, indicate that Coconino Industrial Park exerts a significant beneficial influence on the Flagstaff metropolitan economy.

We would be pleased to discuss this report and its conclusions with you at your request. My firm and I thank you for your confidence in selecting our company to prepare this comprehensive report.

Sincerely,

Sylvia Hernandez

Sylvia Hernandez
Senior Research Consultant

SMH:mef
Attachment

ii

Annotations (left margin):
- Announces report and identifies authorization
- Gives broad overview of report purposes
- Describes primary and secondary research
- Offers to discuss report; expresses appreciation
- Uses Roman numerals for prefatory pages

A letter or memo of transmittal announces the report topic and explains who authorized it. It briefly describes the project and previews the conclusions, if the reader is supportive. Such messages generally close by expressing appreciation for the assignment, suggesting follow-up actions, acknowledging the help of others, or offering to answer questions. The margins for the transmittal should be the same as for the report, about 1 to 1¼ inches on all sides. The letter should be left-justified. A page number is optional.

FIGURE 13.4 (Continued) Table of Contents and List of Figures

Uses leaders to guide eye from heading to page number

Indents secondary headings to show levels of outline

Includes tables and figures in one list for simplified numbering

TABLE OF CONTENTS

EXECUTIVE SUMMARY iv

INTRODUCTION: COCONINO AND THE LOCAL ECONOMY 1

BACKGROUND: THE ROLE OF CIP IN COMMERCIAL DEVELOPMENT 1

DISCUSSION: REVENUES, EMPLOYMENT, AND INDIRECT BENEFITS 2

    Revenues 2
        Sales and Use Revenues 3
        Other Revenues 3
        Projections 3

    Employment 3
        Distribution 3
        Wages 4
        Projections 5

CONCLUSIONS AND RECOMMENDATIONS 5

REFERENCES 6

LIST OF FIGURES

Figure
1   Revenues Received by the City of Flagstaff From
     Coconino Industrial Park 2
2   Employment Distribution of Industry Groups 4
3   Average Annual Wages by Industry Groups 4

iii

Because the table of contents and the list of figures for this report are small, they are combined on one page. Notice that the titles of major report parts are in all caps, while other headings are a combination of upper- and lowercase letters. This duplicates the style within the report. Advanced word processing capabilities enable you to generate a contents page automatically, including leaders and accurate page numbering—no matter how many times you revise. Notice that the page numbers are right-justified. Multiple-digit page numbers must line up properly (say, the number 9 under the 0 of 10).

FIGURE 13.4 (Continued) Executive Summary

EXECUTIVE SUMMARY

Opens directly with major research findings

The city of Flagstaff can benefit from the development of industrial parks like the Coconino Industrial Park. Both direct and indirect economic benefits result, as shown by this in-depth study conducted by Del Rio Industrial Consultants. The study was authorized by the Flagstaff City Council when Goldman-Lyon & Associates sought the city council's approval for the proposed construction of a G-L industrial park. The city council requested evidence demonstrating that an existing development could actually benefit the city.

Identifies data sources

Our conclusion that the city of Flagstaff benefits from industrial parks is based on data supplied by a survey of 5,000 Coconino Industrial Park employees, personal interviews with managers and tenants of CIP, city and state documents, and professional literature.

Summarizes organization of report

Analysis of the data revealed benefits in three areas:

- **Revenues.** The city of Flagstaff earned nearly $2 million in tax and other revenues from the Coconino Industrial Park in 2006. By 2012 this income is expected to reach $3.4 million (in constant 2006 dollars).

- **Employment.** In 2006 CIP businesses employed a total of 7,035 workers, who earned an average wage of $56,579. By 2012 CIP businesses are expected to employ directly nearly 15,000 employees who will earn salaries totaling over $998 million.

- **Indirect benefits.** Because of the multiplier effect, by 2012 Coconino Industrial Park will directly and indirectly generate a total of 38,362 jobs in the Flagstaff metropolitan area.

Condenses recommendations

On the basis of these findings, it is recommended that development of additional industrial parks be encouraged to stimulate local economic growth. The city would increase its tax revenues significantly, create much-needed jobs, and thus help stimulate the local economy in and around Flagstaff.

iv

For readers who want a quick overview of the report, the executive summary presents its most important elements. Executive summaries focus on the information the reader requires for making a decision related to the issues discussed in the report. The summary may include some or all of the following elements: purpose, scope, research methods, findings, conclusions, and recommendations. Its length depends on the report it summarizes. A 100-page report might require a 10-page summary. Shorter reports may contain one-page summaries, as shown here. Unlike letters of transmittal (which may contain personal pronouns and references to the writer), the executive summary of a long report is formal and impersonal. It uses the same margins as the body of the report. See the discussion of executive summaries in this chapter.

FIGURE 13.4 (Continued) Page 1

INTRODUCTION: COCONINO AND THE LOCAL ECONOMY

This study was designed to analyze the direct and indirect economic impact of Coconino Industrial Park on the city of Flagstaff. Specifically, the study seeks answers to these questions:

Uses a bulleted list for clarity and ease of reading

- What current tax and other revenues result directly from this park? What tax and other revenues may be expected in the future?

Lists three problem questions

- How many and what kinds of jobs are directly attributable to the park? What is the employment picture for the future?

- What indirect effects has Coconino Industrial Park had on local employment, incomes, and economic growth?

BACKGROUND: THE ROLE OF CIP IN COMMERCIAL DEVELOPMENT

Describes authorization for report and background of study

The development firm of Goldman-Lyon & Associates commissioned this study of Coconino Industrial Park at the request of the Flagstaff City Council. Before authorizing the development of a proposed Goldman-Lyon industrial park, the city council requested a study examining the economic effects of an existing park. Members of the city council wanted to determine to what extent industrial parks benefit the local community, and they chose Coconino Industrial Park as an example.

For those who are unfamiliar with it, Coconino Industrial Park is a 400-acre industrial park located in the city of Flagstaff about 4 miles from the center of the city. Most of the area lies within a specially designated area known as Redevelopment Project No. 2, which is under the jurisdiction of the Flagstaff Redevelopment Agency. Planning for the park began in 1994; construction started in 1996.

The original goal for Coconino Industrial Park was development for light industrial users. Land in this area was zoned for uses such as warehousing, research and development, and distribution. Like other communities, Flagstaff was eager to attract light industrial users because such businesses tend to employ a highly educated workforce, are relatively quiet, and do not pollute the environment (Cohen, 2007). The city of Flagstaff recognized the need for light industrial users and widened an adjacent highway to accommodate trucks and facilitate travel by workers and customers coming from Flagstaff.

1

Titles for major parts of a report are centered in all caps. In this model document we show several combination headings. As the name suggests, combination heads are a mix of functional headings, such as *INTRODUCTION, BACKGROUND, DISCUSSION,* and *CONCLUSIONS,* and talking heads that reveal the content. Most business reports would use talking heads or a combination, such as *FINDINGS REVEAL REVENUE* and *EMPLOYMENT BENEFITS.* First-level headings (such as *Revenues* on page 2) are printed with bold upper- and lowercase letters. Second-level headings (such as *Distribution* on page 3) begin at the side, are bolded, and are written in upper- and lowercase letters. See Figure 12.5 for an illustration of heading formats. This business report is shown with single-spacing, although some research reports might be double-spaced. Always check with your organization to learn its preferred style.

FIGURE 13.4 (Continued) Page 2

The park now contains 14 building complexes with over 1.25 million square feet of completed building space. The majority of the buildings are used for offices, research and development, marketing and distribution, or manufacturing. Approximately 50 acres of the original area are yet to be developed.

Provides
specifics
for data
sources

Data for this report came from a 2006 survey of over 5,000 Coconino Industrial Park employees, interviews with 15 CIP tenants and managers, the annual budget of the city of Flagstaff, county and state tax records, current books, articles, journals, and online resources. Projections for future revenues resulted from analysis of past trends and "Estimates of Revenues for Debt Service Coverage, Redevelopment Project Area 2" (Miller, 2006, p. 79).

Uses combination heads

DISCUSSION: REVENUES, EMPLOYMENT, AND INDIRECT BENEFITS

Previews organization of report

The results of this research indicate that major direct and indirect benefits have accrued to the city of Flagstaff and surrounding metropolitan areas as a result of the development of Coconino Industrial Park. The research findings presented here fall into three categories: (a) revenues, (b) employment, and (c) indirect benefits.

Revenues

Coconino Industrial Park contributes a variety of tax and other revenues to the city of Flagstaff, as summarized in Figure 1. Current revenues are shown, along with projections to the year 2012. At a time when the economy is unstable, revenues from an industrial park such as Coconino can become a reliable income stream for the city of Flagstaff.

Places figure close to textual reference

Figure 1

REVENUES RECEIVED BY THE CITY OF FLAGSTAFF
FROM COCONINO INDUSTRIAL PARK

Current Revenues and Projections to 2012

	2007	2012
Sales and use taxes	$ 904,140	$1,335,390
Revenues from licenses	426,265	516,396
Franchise taxes	175,518	229,424
State gas tax receipts	83,768	112,134
Licenses and permits	78,331	112,831
Other revenues	94,039	141,987
Total	$1,762,061	$2,448,162

Source: Arizona State Board of Equalization Bulletin. Phoenix: State Printing Office, 2007, p. 28.

2

Notice that this formal report is single-spaced. Many businesses prefer this space-saving format. However, some organizations prefer double-spacing, especially for preliminary drafts. If you single-space, do not indent paragraphs. If you double-space, do indent the paragraphs. Page numbers may be centered 1 inch from the bottom of the page or placed 1 inch from the upper right corner at the margin. Your word processor can insert page numbers automatically. Strive to leave a minimum of 1 inch for top, bottom, and side margins. References follow the parenthetical citation style (or in-text citation style) of the American Psychological Association (APA). Notice that the author's name, the year of publication, and page number appear in parentheses. The complete bibliographic entry for any in-text citation appears at the end of report in the references section.

FIGURE 13.4 (Continued) Page 3

Sales and Use Revenues

Continues interpreting figures in table

As shown in Figure 1, the city's largest source of revenues from CIP is the sales and use tax. Revenues from this source totaled $904,140 in 2007, according to figures provided by the Arizona State Board of Equalization (2007, p. 28). Sales and use taxes accounted for more than half of the park's total contribution to the city of $1,762,061.

Other Revenues

Other major sources of city revenues from CIP in 2007 included alcohol licenses, motor vehicle in lieu fees, and trailer coach licenses ($426,265); franchise taxes ($175,518); and state gas tax receipts ($83,768). Although not shown in Figure 1, other revenues may be expected from the development of recently acquired property. The U.S. Economic Development Administration has approved a grant worth $975,000 to assist in expanding the current park eastward on an undeveloped parcel purchased last year. Revenues from leasing this property may be sizable.

Projections

Includes description of electronic reference

Total city revenues from CIP will nearly double by 2012, producing an income of $2.45 million. This estimate is based on an annual growth rate of 0.65 percent, as projected by the Bureau of Labor Statistics and reported at the Web site of Infoplease.com ("Economic Outlook," 2007).

Employment

Previews next topic to be discussed

One of the most important factors to consider in the overall effect of an industrial park is employment. In Coconino Industrial Park the distribution, number, and wages of people employed will change considerably in the next six years.

Distribution

A total of 7,035 employees currently work in various industry groups at Coconino Industrial Park. The distribution of employees is shown in Figure 2. The largest number of workers (58 percent) is employed in manufacturing and assembly operations. The next largest category, computer and electronics, employs 24 percent of the workers. Some overlap probably exists because electronics assembly could be included in either group. Employees also work in publishing (9 percent), warehousing and storage (5 percent), and other industries (4 percent).

Although the distribution of employees at Coconino Industrial Park shows a wide range of employment categories, it must be noted that other industrial parks would likely generate an entirely different range of job categories.

3

Only the most important research findings are interpreted and discussed for readers. The depth of discussion depends on the intended length of the report, the goal of the writer, and the expectations of the reader. Because the writer wants this report to be formal in tone, she avoids *I* and *we* in all discussions.

As you type a report, avoid widows and orphans (ending a page with the first line of a paragraph or carrying a single line of a paragraph to a new page). Strive to start and end pages with at least two lines of a paragraph, even if a slightly larger bottom margin results.

FIGURE 13.4 (Continued) Page 4

Pie chart shows proportion of a whole and includes percentage figures for clarity

Places figure close to textual reference

Aligns figures on the right and centers headings over columns

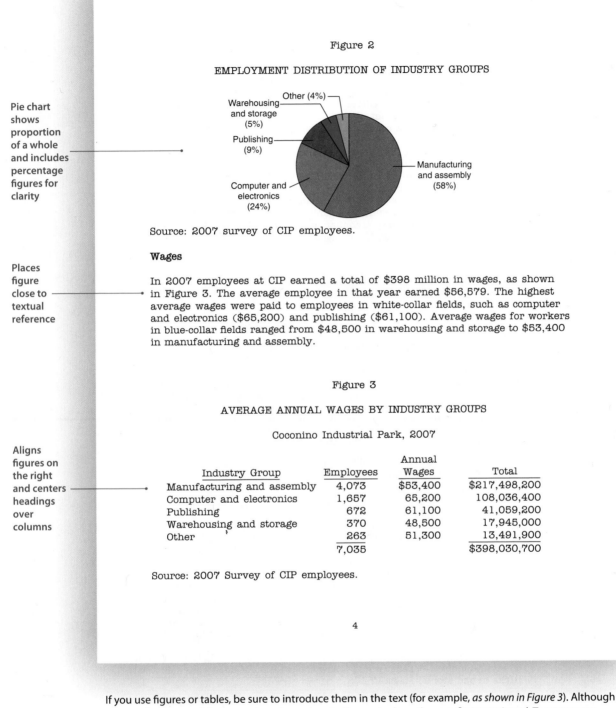

Figure 2

EMPLOYMENT DISTRIBUTION OF INDUSTRY GROUPS

Other (4%)
Warehousing and storage (5%)
Publishing (9%)
Manufacturing and assembly (58%)
Computer and electronics (24%)

Source: 2007 survey of CIP employees.

Wages

In 2007 employees at CIP earned a total of $398 million in wages, as shown in Figure 3. The average employee in that year earned $56,579. The highest average wages were paid to employees in white-collar fields, such as computer and electronics ($65,200) and publishing ($61,100). Average wages for workers in blue-collar fields ranged from $48,500 in warehousing and storage to $53,400 in manufacturing and assembly.

Figure 3

AVERAGE ANNUAL WAGES BY INDUSTRY GROUPS

Coconino Industrial Park, 2007

Industry Group	Employees	Annual Wages	Total
Manufacturing and assembly	4,073	$53,400	$217,498,200
Computer and electronics	1,657	65,200	108,036,400
Publishing	672	61,100	41,059,200
Warehousing and storage	370	48,500	17,945,000
Other	263	51,300	13,491,900
	7,035		$398,030,700

Source: 2007 Survey of CIP employees.

4

If you use figures or tables, be sure to introduce them in the text (for example, *as shown in Figure 3*). Although it is not always possible, try to place them close to the spot where they are first mentioned. To save space, you can print the title of a figure at its side. Because this report contains few tables and figures, the writer named them all "Figures" and numbered them consecutively. Graphics that serve for reference only and aren't discussed in the text belong in the appendix.

FIGURE 13.4 (Continued) Page 5

Clarifies information and tells what it means in relation to original research questions

Projections

By 2012 Coconino Industrial Park is expected to more than double its number of employees, bringing the total to over 15,000 workers. The total payroll in 2012 will also more than double, producing over $998 million (using constant 2007 dollars) in salaries to CIP employees. These projections are based on a 9 percent growth rate (Miller, 2006, p. 78), along with anticipated increased employment as the park reaches its capacity.

Future development in the park will influence employment and payrolls. One CIP project manager stated in an interview that much of the remaining 50 acres is planned for medium-rise office buildings, garden offices, and other structures for commercial, professional, and personal services (I. M. Novak, personal communication, November 30, 2007). Average wages for employees are expected to increase because of an anticipated shift to higher-paying white-collar jobs. Industrial parks often follow a similar pattern of evolution (Badri, 2007). Like many industrial parks, CIP evolved from a warehousing center into a manufacturing complex.

Combines conclusions and recommendations

CONCLUSIONS AND RECOMMENDATIONS

Analysis of tax revenues, employment data, personal interviews, and professional literature leads to the following conclusions and recommendations about the economic impact of Coconino Industrial Park on the city of Flagstaff:

Uses a numbered list for clarity and ease of reading

1. Sales tax and other revenues produced nearly $1.8 million in income to the city of Flagstaff in 2007. By 2012 sales tax and other revenues are expected to produce $2.5 million in city income.

2. CIP currently employs 7,035 employees, the majority of whom are working in manufacturing and assembly. The average employee in 2007 earned $56,579.

3. By 2012 CIP is expected to employ more than 15,000 workers producing a total payroll of over $998 million.

4. Employment trends indicate that by 2012 more CIP employees will be engaged in higher-paying white-collar positions.

On the basis of these findings, we recommend that the Flagstaff City Council authorize the development of additional industrial parks to stimulate local economic growth. The direct and indirect benefits of Coconino Industrial Park strongly suggest that future commercial development would have a positive impact on the Flagstaff community and the surrounding region as population growth and resulting greater purchasing power would trigger higher demand.

As the Coconino example shows, gains in tax revenue, job creation, and other direct and indirect benefits would follow the creation of additional industrial parks in and around Flagstaff.

5

After discussing and interpreting the research findings, the writer articulates what she considers the most important conclusions and recommendations. Longer, more complex reports may have separate sections for conclusions and resulting recommendations. In this report they are combined. Notice that it is unnecessary to start a new page for the conclusions.

FIGURE 13.4 (Continued) Page 6 References

Arranges references in alphabetical order

Brochure ──────────→

Magazine ──────────→

Newspaper retrieved from electronic database ──────────→

Web page ──────────→

Book ──────────→

Article published online ──────────→

Follows American Psychological Association documentation style

REFERENCES

Arizona State Board of Equalization bulletin. (2007). Phoenix: State Printing Office, 26–29.

Badri, M. A. (2007, April 1). Infrastructure, trends, and economic effects of industrial parks. *Industry Week News*, pp. 38–45.

Cohen, A. P. (2007, December 10). Industrial parks invade suburbia. *The New York Times*, p. C1. Retrieved December 15, 2007, from Lexis-Nexis database.

Bureau of Labor Statistics (2007). Economic outlook through 2014. Retrieved November 24, 2007, from http://www.infoplease.com/ipa/A0300371.html

Miller, A. M. (2006). *Redevelopment projects: future prospects*. New York: Rincon Press.

Pearson, S. (2007, June 30). Travel to work characteristics for the 50 largest metropolitan areas by population in the United States. *The Wall Street Journal*. Retrieved December 15, 2007, from http://www.wsj.com/article121504.html

6

On this page the writer lists all references cited in the text as well as others that she examined during her research. The writer lists these citations following the APA referencing style. Notice that all entries are arranged alphabetically. Book and periodical titles are italicized, but they could be underlined. When referring to online items, she shows the full name of the citation and then identifies the URL as well as the date on which she accessed the electronic reference. This references page is shown with single-spacing, which is preferable for business reports. However, APA style recommends double-spacing for research reports, including the references page. APA style also shows "References" in upper- and lowercase letters. However, the writer preferred to use all caps to be consistent with other headings in this business report.

and Indirect Benefits. The report was compiled from survey data as well as from secondary sources that Sylvia researched.

Sylvia's report illustrates many of the points discussed in this chapter. Although it is a good example of the typical report format and style, it should not be viewed as the only way to present a report. Wide variation exists in reports.

The checklist on the next page summarizes the report process and report components in one handy list.

Checklist

Preparing Formal Reports

Report Process

✓ **Analyze the report and purpose.** Develop a problem question (*How is e-mail affecting productivity and security at MegaTech?*) and a purpose statement (*The purpose of this report is to investigate the use of e-mail at MegaTech and recommend policies and procedures that enhance company productivity and security*).

✓ **Anticipate the audience and issues.** Consider primary and secondary audiences. What do they already know? What do they need to know? Divide the major problem into subproblems for investigation.

✓ **Prepare a work plan.** Include problem and purpose statements, as well as a description of the sources and methods of collecting data. Prepare a tentative project outline and work schedule with anticipated dates of completion for all segments of the project.

✓ **Collect data.** Begin by searching secondary sources (electronic databases, books, magazines, journals, newspapers) for information on your topic. Then, if necessary, gather primary data by surveying, interviewing, observing, and experimenting.

✓ **Document data sources.** Prepare note cards or separate sheets of paper citing all references (author, date, source, page, and quotation). Select a documentation format and use it consistently.

✓ **Interpret and organize the data.** Arrange the collected information in tables, grids, or outlines to help you visualize relationships and interpret meanings. Organize the data into an outline (Chapter 5).

✓ **Prepare graphics.** Make tables, charts, graphs, and illustrations—but *only* if they serve a function. Use graphics to help clarify, condense, simplify, or emphasize your data.

✓ **Compose the first draft.** At a computer write the first draft from your outline. Use appropriate headings as well as transitional expressions (such as *however, on the contrary,* and *in addition*) to guide the reader through the report.

✓ **Revise and proofread.** Revise to eliminate wordiness, ambiguity, and redundancy. Look for ways to improve readability, such as bulleted or numbered lists. Proofread three times for (a) word and content meaning, (b) grammar and mechanical errors, and (c) formatting.

✓ **Evaluate the product.** Examine the final report. Will it achieve its purpose? Encourage feedback so that you can learn how to improve future reports.

Report Components

✓ **Title page.** Balance the following lines on the title page: (a) name of the report (in all caps); (b) name, title, and organization of the individual receiving the report; (c) author's name, title, and organization; and (d) date submitted.

✓ **Letter of transmittal.** Announce the report topic and explain who authorized it. Briefly describe the project and preview the conclusions, if the reader is supportive. Close by expressing appreciation for the assignment, suggesting follow-up actions, acknowledging the help of others, or offering to answer questions.

✓ **Table of contents.** Show the beginning page number where each report heading appears in the report. Connect the page numbers and headings with leaders (spaced dots) using your word processing software. In MS Word, for example, pull down the **Format** menu and go to **Tabs**.

✓ **List of illustrations.** Include a list of tables, illustrations, or figures showing the title of the item and its page number. If space permits, put these lists on the same page with the table of contents.

✓ **Executive summary.** Summarize the report purpose, findings, conclusions, and recommendations. Gauge the length of the summary by the length of the report and by your organization's practices.

✓ **Introduction.** Explain the problem motivating the report; describe its background and significance. Clarify the scope and limitations of the report. Optional items include a review of the relevant literature and a description of data sources, methods, and key terms. Close by previewing the report's organization.

✓ **Body.** Discuss, analyze, and interpret the research findings or the proposed solution to the problem. Arrange the findings in logical segments following your outline. Use clear, descriptive headings.

✓ **Conclusions and recommendations.** Explain what the findings mean in relation to the original problem. If asked, make enumerated recommendations that suggest actions for solving the problem.

✓ **Appendix.** Include items of interest to some, but not all, readers, such as a questionnaire or computer printouts. Add graphics that are not discussed directly in the text.

✓ **Works Cited or References.** If footnotes are not provided in the text, list all references in a section called "Works Cited" or "References."

Communicating at Work Your Turn

Applying Your Skills at Raytheon

Proposals and reports are written, often in teams, to accomplish serious business purposes. Both require research and sometimes unavailable resources. Assume that you are an intern at Raytheon working with Dr. Grinyer. He has asked you to help him develop materials to improve Raytheon reports and proposals. He suggests two possible tasks:

1. A short (three to five pages) business report recommending a structured writing process to be used for team-written company documents

2. A memo evaluating several (two to four) proposal consulting companies that might be able to help Raytheon teams write good proposals when the company's proposal specialists are unavailable

Your Task
Select one of the suggested tasks. For Option 1, in a two- or three-person team, plan the required report and have each team member prepare an outline of his or her assigned section. As a team, review and improve the outlines with written comments and annotations. For Option 2, individually research, plan, and write the required one- to two-page memo for your instructor.

© Steven E. Frischling / Bloomberg News / Landov

Summary of Learning Objectives

1 **Discuss the general uses and basic components of proposals and grasp their audience and purpose.** Most informal proposals contain the following: (a) a persuasive introduction that explains the purpose of the proposal and qualifies the writer; (b) background material identifying the problem and project goals; (c) a proposal, plan, or schedule outlining the project; (d) a section describing staff qualifications; (e) a budget showing expected costs; and (f) a request for approval or authorization.

2 **Discuss formal proposals and how to anticipate a receiver's reaction to your message.** Beyond the six components generally contained in informal proposals, formal proposals may include these additional parts: (a) a copy of the RFP (request for proposal), (b) a letter of transmittal, (c) an executive summary, (d) a title page, (e) a table of contents, (f) a list of illustrations, and (g) an appendix.

3 **Identify the components of typical business plans and ethically create buy-in for your business ideas.** Business plans help entrepreneurs secure start-up funding and also provide a road map to follow as a business develops. Typical business plans include the following: letter of transmittal or executive summary, table of contents, company description, product or service description, market analysis, description of operations and management, financial analysis, and appendixes. For start-up businesses seeking financial backing, the product/service description as well as the operations and management analyses are particularly important. They must promote growth potential and promise a management team capable of implementing the business plan.

4 **Describe the formal report components that precede the introduction as well as elements to include in the introduction and how they further the purpose of your communication.** Formal reports may include these beginning components: a vinyl or heavy paper cover, a title page, a letter of transmittal, a table of contents, a list of illustrations, and an executive summary. The introduction to a formal report sets the scene by discussing some or all of the following topics: background material, problem or purpose, significance of the topic, scope and organization of the report, authorization, review of relevant literature, sources and methods, and definitions of key terms.

5 **Describe the formal report components that follow the introduction and how they further the purpose of your communication.** The body of a report discusses, analyzes, interprets, and evaluates the research findings or solution to a problem. The conclusion tells what the findings mean and how they relate to the report's purpose. The recommendations tell how to solve the report problem. The last portions of a formal report are the appendix and references.

6 Specify tips that aid writers of formal reports as they use their analytic skills and reflective thinking skills. Before writing, develop a realistic timetable and collect all necessary data. During the writing process, work from a good outline, work in a quiet place, and use a computer. Also, try to write rapidly, revising later. While writing, use verb tenses consistently, and avoid *I* and *we*. A few days after completing the first draft, revise to improve clarity, coherence, and conciseness. Proofread the final copy three times.

Chapter Review

1. Are proposals internal or external documents? (Obj. 1)
2. What is the difference between solicited and unsolicited proposals? (Obj. 1)
3. What are the six principal components of an informal letter proposal? (Obj. 1)
4. How is a formal proposal different from an informal proposal? (Obj. 2)
5. Why does an entrepreneur need to write a business plan? (Obj. 3)
6. Name eight components of typical business plans. (Obj. 3)
7. What should a business plan mission statement include and how long should it be? (Obj. 3)
8. Why are formal reports written in business? Give an original example of a business-related formal report. (Obj. 4)

9. What is a letter or memorandum of transmittal? (Obj. 4)
10. How long should a typical executive summary be? (Obj. 4)
11. What should be included in the executive summary of a formal report? (Obj. 4)
12. What should be included in the introduction to a formal report? (Obj. 4)
13. What should the writer strive to do in the body of a formal report? (Obj. 5)
14. What is the purpose of references or works cited? (Obj. 5)
15. In your view, what are six of the most important tips for the writer of a formal report? Explain each of your choices. (Obj. 6)

Critical Thinking

1. Why write long, formal reports to busy readers in business, given how much time, effort, and expense such documents devour? (Objs. 4–6)
2. Why are proposals important to many businesses? (Obj. 1)
3. Compare and contrast proposals and business plans. (Objs. 1–3)
4. How do formal reports differ from informal reports? (Objs. 4–6)

5. Discuss the three phases of the writing process in relation to formal reports. What activities take place in each phase? (Objs. 4–6)
6. **Ethical Issue:** How can a team of writers ensure that each member shoulders an equal or fair amount of the work on an extensive writing project, such as a formal proposal or report?

Activities

13.1. Proposals: Solving a Workplace Problem in an Unsolicited Informal Proposal (Obj. 1)

The ability to spot problems before they turn into serious risks is prized by most managers. Draw on your internship and work experience. Can you identify a problem that could be solved with a small to moderate financial investment? Look for issues such as missing lunch or break rooms for staff; badly needed health initiatives such as gyms or sports club memberships; low-gas-mileage, high-emission company vehicles; lack of recycling efforts, and so forth.

Your Task. Discuss with your instructor the workplace problem that you have identified. Make sure you choose a relatively weighty problem that can nevertheless be lessened or eliminated with a minor expenditure. Be sure to include a cost-benefit analysis. Address your unsolicited letter or memo proposal to your current or former boss and copy your instructor.

13.2 Proposals: Think Like an Entrepreneur (Obj. 1)

Perhaps you have fantasized about one day owning your own company, or maybe you have already started a business. Proposals are

offers to a very specific audience whose business you are soliciting. Think of a product or service that you like or know much about. On the Web or in electronic databases, research the market so that you understand going rates, prices, and costs. Search the Small Business Administration's Web site (**http://www.sba.gov/**) for valuable tips on how to launch and manage a business.

Your Task. Choose a product or service you would like to offer to a particular audience, such as a window-cleaning business, an online photography business, a new vehicle on the U.S. market, or a new European hair care line. Discuss products and services as well as target audiences with your instructor. Write a letter proposal promoting your chosen product or service.

13.3 Proposals: Comparing Real Proposals (Objs. 1, 2)

> **Web**

Many new companies with services or products to offer would like to land corporate or government contracts. However, they are intimidated by the proposal (RFP process). You have been asked for help by your friend Mikayla, who has started her own designer uniform company. Her goal is to offer her colorful yet functional uniforms to hospitals and clinics. Before writing a proposal, however, she wants to see examples and learn more about the process.

Your Task. Use the Web to find at least two examples of business proposals. Do not waste time on sites that want to sell templates or books. Find actual examples. Then prepare a memo to Mikayla in which you do the following:

a. Identify two sites with sample business proposals.

b. Outline the parts of each proposal.

c. Compare the strengths and weaknesses of each proposal.

d. Draw conclusions. What can Mikayla learn from these examples?

13.4 Proposals: Medicus Associates Solicits Your Proposal (Obj. 1)

> Team

In university towns, sports medicine is increasingly popular. A new medical clinic, Medicus Associates, is opening its doors in your community. A friend recommended your small business to the administrator of the clinic, and you received a letter asking you to provide information about your service. The new medical clinic specializes in sports medicine, physical therapy, and cardiac rehabilitation services. It is interested in retaining your company, rather than hiring its own employees to perform the service your company offers.

Your Task. Working in teams, first decide what service you will offer. It could be landscaping, uniform supply, laundry of uniforms, general cleaning, computerized no-paper filing systems, online medical supplies, patient transportation, supplemental hospice care, temporary office support, or food service. As a team, develop a letter proposal outlining your plan, staffing, and budget. Use persuasion to show why contracting your services is better than hiring in-house employees. In the proposal letter, request a meeting with the administrative board. In addition to a written proposal, you may be expected to make an oral presentation that includes visual aids and/or handouts. Send your proposal to Dr. Pat Leigh, Director, Medicus Associates. Supply a local address.

13.5 Proposal and Grant Writing: Learning From the Nonprofits (Objs. 1, 2)

> Web

You would like to learn more about writing business proposals and especially about writing grants. Grants are written to solicit funding from institutions, foundations, or the government. You might one day even decide to become a professional grant/proposal writer. However, first you need experience.

Your Task. Volunteer your services for a local nonprofit organization, such as a United Way (**http://national.unitedway.org/**) member agency, an educational institution, or your local religious community. To learn more about writing grants, use a search engine to look up *proposal*. Try categories such as *business proposal writing* and *grant proposal writing*. In the browser window, enclose the search terms in quotation marks. Your instructor may ask you to submit a preliminary memo report outlining ten or more pointers you learn about writing proposals and grants for nonprofit organizations.

13.6 Business Plans: Can Your Team Write a Winning Plan? (Obj. 3)*

> Team   > Web

Business plans at many schools are more than classroom writing exercises. They have won regional, national, and worldwide prizes.

* A complete instructional module for this activity is available at www.meguffey.com.

Although some contests are part of MBA programs, other contests are available for undergraduates. One business plan project at the University of California, Santa Barbara, resulted in the development of a portable oxygen concentrator. Three students wrote a proposal that not only won one of the school's business plan writing contests but also attracted venture capital backing of over $500,000. The trio was challenged to come up with a hypothetical business plan. One of the team members suggested making a portable oxygen device to improve the mobility and quality of life for her grandmother. The students didn't actually make the device—they just outlined the concept. Contest judges recognized the commercial potential and helped bring the device into production.[7]

As part of a business plan project, you and your team are challenged to come up with an idea for a new business or service. For example, you might want to offer a lunch service with fresh sandwiches or salads delivered to office workers' desks. You might propose building a better Web site for an organization. You might want to start a document preparation business that offers production, editing, and printing services. You might have a terrific idea for an existing business to expand with a new product or service.

Your Task. Working in teams, explore entrepreneurial ventures based on your experience and expertise. Conduct team meetings to decide on a product or service, develop a work plan, assign responsibilities, and create a schedule. Your goal is to write a business plan proposal that will convince potential investors (sometimes your own management) that you have an excellent business idea and that you can pull it off. Check out sample business plans on the Web. The two "deliverables" from your project will be your written business plan plus an oral presentation. Your written report should include a cover, transmittal document (letter or memo), title page, table of contents, executive summary, proposal (including introduction, body, and conclusion), appendix items, optional glossary, and sources. In the body of the proposal, be sure to explain your mission and vision, the market, your marketing strategy, operations, and financials. Address your business plan proposal to your instructor.

13.7 Formal Reports: Intercultural Communication (Objs. 4–6)

> Intercultural   > Team

U.S. businesses are expanding into foreign markets with manufacturing plants, sales offices, and branches abroad. Most Americans, however, have little knowledge of or experience with people from other

© DAJ / Getty Images

cultures. To prepare for participation in the global marketplace, you are to collect information for a report focused on an Asian, Latin American, or European country where English is not regularly spoken. Before selecting the country, though, consult your campus international student program for volunteers who are willing to be interviewed. Your instructor may make advance arrangements with international student volunteers.

Your Task. In teams of three to five, collect information about your target country from the library and other sources. Then invite an international student representing your target country to be interviewed by your group. As you conduct primary and secondary research, investigate the topics listed in Figure 13.5. Confirm what you learn in your secondary research by talking with your interviewee. When you complete your research, write a report for the CEO of your company (make up a name and company). Assume that your company plans to expand its operations abroad. Your report should advise the company's executives of the social customs, family life, attitudes, religions, education, and values in the target country. Remember that your company's interests are business oriented; do not dwell on tourist information. Write your report individually or in teams.

13.8 Business Plans: Studying Samples and Selecting the Best (Obj. 3)

> Web

As a member of a group of venture capitalists with money to invest in start-up companies, you must make a choice. Assume your group has received three business plan proposals.

FIGURE 13.5 Intercultural Interview Topics and Questions

Social Customs

1. How do people react to strangers? Are they friendly? Hostile? Reserved?

2. How do people greet each other?

3. What are the appropriate manners when you enter a room? Bow? Nod? Shake hands with everyone?

4. How are names used for introductions? Is it appropriate to inquire about one's occupation or family?

5. What are the attitudes toward touching?

6. How does one express appreciation for an invitation to another's home? Bring a gift? Send flowers? Write a thank-you note? Are any gifts taboo?

7. Are there any customs related to how or where one sits?

8. Are any facial expressions or gestures considered rude?

9. How close do people stand when talking?

10. What is the attitude toward punctuality in social situations? In business situations?

11. What are acceptable eye contact patterns?

12. What gestures indicate agreement? Disagreement?

Family Life

1. What is the basic unit of social organization? Basic family? Extended family?

2. Do women work outside of the home? In what occupations?

Housing, Clothing, and Food

1. Are there differences in the kinds of housing used by different social groups? Differences in location? Differences in furnishings?

2. What occasions require special clothing?

3. Are some types of clothing considered taboo?

4. What is appropriate business attire for men? For women?

5. How many times a day do people eat?

6. What types of places, food, and drink are appropriate for business entertainment? Where is the seat of honor at a table?

Class Structure

1. Into what classes is society organized?

2. Do racial, religious, or economic factors determine social status?

3. Are there any minority groups? What is their social standing?

Political Patterns

1. Are there any immediate threats to the political survival of the country?

2. How is political power manifested?

3. What channels are used for expression of popular opinion?

4. What information media are important?

5. Is it appropriate to talk politics in social situations?

Religion and Folk Beliefs

1. To which religious groups do people belong? Is one predominant?

2. Do religious beliefs influence daily activities?

3. Which places have sacred value? Which objects? Which events?

4. How do religious holidays affect business activities?

Economic Institutions

1. What are the country's principal products?

2. Are workers organized in unions?

3. How are businesses owned? By family units? By large public corporations? By the government?

4. What is the standard work schedule?

5. Is it appropriate to do business by telephone? By computer?

6. How has technology affected business procedures?

7. Is participatory management used?

8. Are there any customs related to exchanging business cards?

9. How is status shown in an organization? Private office? Secretary? Furniture?

10. Are businesspeople expected to socialize before conducting business?

Value Systems

1. Is competitiveness or cooperation more prized?

2. Is thrift or enjoyment of the moment more valued?

3. Is politeness more important than factual honesty?

4. What are the attitudes toward education?

5. Do women own or manage businesses? If so, how are they treated?

6. What are your people's perceptions of Americans? Do Americans offend you? What has been hardest for you to adjust to in America? How could Americans make this adjustment easier for you?

Your Task. Visit either Bplans.com at **http://www.bplans.com** or the Small Business Administration site at **http://www.sba.gov/smallbusinessplanner/**. Search for sample business plans. Browse the list and select three business plans to study. Analyze all parts of each plan. Then, select one that you will recommend for funding. Prepare a memo to your investor group explaining why you think this start-up business will succeed. Also comment on the organization, format, and writing style of the business plan. What are its strengths and weaknesses? Address your memo to your instructor.

13.9 Proposal, Business Plan, and Report Topics (Objs. 1–6)

A list with nearly 100 report topics is available at **www.meguffey.com.** The topics are divided into the following categories: accounting, finance, personnel/human resources, marketing, information systems, management, and general business/education/campus issues. You can collect information for many of these reports by using electronic databases and the Web. Your instructor may assign them as individual or team projects. All involve critical thinking in organizing information, drawing conclusions, and making recommendations. The topics include assignments appropriate for proposals, business plans, and formal reports. Remember that a number of self-contained report activities that require no additional research are provided at the end of Chapter 12.

13.10 Executive Summary: Reviewing Articles (Objs. 5, 6)

Web

Many managers and executives are too rushed to read long journal articles, but they are eager to stay current in their fields. Assume your boss has asked you to help him stay abreast of research in his field. He asks you to submit to him one executive summary every month on an article of interest.

Your Task. In your field of study, select a professional journal, such as the *Journal of Management*. Using ProQuest, Factiva, EBSCO, or some other database, look for articles in your target journal. Select an article that is at least five pages long and is interesting to you. Write an executive summary in a memo format. Include an introduction that might begin with *As you requested, I am submitting this executive summary of* . . . . Identify the author, article name, journal, and date of publication. Explain what the author intended to do in the study or article. Summarize three or four of the most important

findings of the study or article. Use descriptive rather than functional headings. Summarize any recommendations made. Your boss would also like a concluding statement indicating your reaction to the article. Address your memo to Marcus E. Fratelli. Alternatively, your instructor may ask you to e-mail your executive summary in the body of a properly formatted message or as an MS Word attachment in correct memo format.

13.11 Unsolicited Proposal: Thwarting Dorm Room Thievery (Objs. 1, 2)

Consumer   Team

As an enterprising college student, you recognized a problem as soon as you arrived on campus. Dorm rooms filled with pricey digital doodads were very attractive to thieves. Some students move in with more than $3,000 in gear, including laptop computers, flat-screen TVs, digital cameras, MP3 players, video game consoles, PDAs, and DVD players. You solved the problem by buying an extra-large steel footlocker to lock away your valuables. However, shipping the footlocker was expensive (nearly $100), and you had to wait for it to arrive from a catalog company. Your bright idea is to propose to the Associated Student Organization (ASO) that it allow you to offer these steel footlockers to students at a reduced price and with campus delivery. Your footlocker, which you found by searching the Web, is extremely durable and works great as a coffee table, nightstand, or card table. It comes with a smooth interior liner and two compartments.

Your Task. Working individually or with a team, imagine that you have made arrangements with a manufacturer to act as a middleman selling footlockers on your campus at a reduced price. Consult the Web for manufacturers and make up your own figures. However, how can you get the ASO's permission to proceed? Give that organization a cut? Use your imagination in deciding how this plan might work on a college campus. Then prepare an unsolicited proposal to your ASO. Outline the problem and your goals of protecting students' valuables and providing convenience. Check the Web for statistics regarding on-campus burglaries. Such figures should help you develop one or more persuasive "hooks." Then explain your proposal, project possible sales, discuss a timetable, and describe your staffing. Submit your proposal to Billie White, president, Associated Student Organization.

Grammar and Mechanics C.L.U.E. Review 13

Total Review

Each of the following sentences has a total of **three** errors in grammar, punctuation, capitalization, usage, or spelling. On a separate sheet, write a correct version. Avoid adding new phrases, starting new sentences, or rewriting in your own words. When finished, compare your responses with the key beginning on page Key-3.

Example: The following 3 statistical terms frequently describe data, Mean, median, and mode.

Revision: The following **three** statistical terms frequently describe **data: mean,** median, and mode.

1. The format and organization of a proposal is important. If a writer wants to be taken serious.

2. Our team members' prepared 2 proposals for the three million dollar project.

3. Just between you and I, we worked especial hard to develop a "hook" to capture a readers attention.

4. The manager and him realized an item was missing from the April 2nd shipment, consequently, they sent a claim request.

5. Readers of business' reports often turn 1st to the conclusions and recommendations, therefore, these sections must be written carefully.

6. If a proposal is sent to the President or I it should definitely explain the specific credentials and expertise of key personal for the project.

7. Benjamin and her wanted to start there own business, therefore, they wrote a business plan.

8. We invited seventy-five employees to hear 2 experts disberse information about wellness.

9. Memo's usually contain four necessary parts, subject line, opening, body and action closing.

10. Darrin Jizmejian who was recently evaluated, wondered whether his formal report would be presented at the March 13th meeting?

Chapter 14

Business Presentations

OBJECTIVES

After studying this chapter, you should be able to

1 Discuss two important first steps in preparing effective oral presentations.

2 Explain the major elements in organizing the content of a presentation, including the introduction, body, and conclusion.

3 Identify techniques for gaining audience rapport, including (a) using effective imagery, (b) providing verbal signposts, and (c) sending appropriate nonverbal messages.

4 Discuss designing visual aids, handouts, and multimedia presentation materials and using presentation technology competently.

5 Specify delivery techniques for use before, during, and after a presentation, and apply reflective thinking skills.

6 Organize team-based oral presentations and recognize communication tasks in teamwork processes.

7 Explain effective techniques for adapting oral presentations to cross-cultural audiences, and demonstrate multicultural and diversity understanding.

8 List techniques for improving telephone and voice mail skills to project a positive image.

Communicating at Work Part 1

Walt Disney Imagineering Sells Tokyo Disneyland on Winnie the Pooh

Although many new Japanese theme parks have failed, Tokyo Disneyland continues to rank as one of the world's most popular attractions. It received 25 million visitors last year.[1] However, it has felt the pinch of increasing competition and declining attendance during periods of economic slowdown. Like all theme parks, Tokyo Disneyland understood the need to offer fresh attractions and exciting new rides to keep the crowds coming back year after year. In its search for dynamic new ideas to expand its already popular park, Tokyo Disneyland turned to Walt Disney Imagineering.

Generating and implementing new ideas for the Disney theme parks are tasks of Walt Disney Imagineering. This is the research, design, and engineering subsidiary of Walt Disney Attractions. Although Tokyo Disneyland is a Disney theme park and Disney retains creative control of the park, the park is actually owned and operated by the Oriental Land Company. This company makes all financial and investment decisions. Although creative concepts come from Disney Imagineering teams, those ideas are not automatically accepted by theme park owners. Imagineering teams not only have to dream up exciting new concepts for the Tokyo park, but they also have to *sell* the ideas and win the approval of Japanese owners. Millions of dollars in contracts and hundreds of jobs in the United States and in Japan rest on successful presentations to the owners of Tokyo Disneyland.

Jon Georges, former lead show producer for the Tokyo Disneyland Project, was part of a talented Imagineering team that came up with a totally new attraction and restaurant concept for the Disney theme park. Based on Winnie the Pooh and Alice in Wonderland characters, the creative project involved two phases. The first was a theme restaurant called the "Queen of Hearts Banquet Hall." The second was a major ride attraction based on Winnie the Pooh characters. Both concepts required considerable persuasion to win approval.

Traditionally, the Japanese park owners had accepted only attractions that had proved technically successful in other theme parks.

Naturally, they were reluctant to try a restaurant concept and a ride technology that were both brand new. Selling the Japanese on the new concepts required exceptional oral presentations from Jon Georges and the Imagineering team.[2] You will learn more about this case on page 450.

Critical Thinking

- What kinds of oral presentations might you have to make in your chosen career field?
- Why are most people fearful of making presentations?
- How do you think people become effective speakers?

http://imagineering.themedattractions.com/

Preparing Effective Oral Presentations

At some point everyone in business has to sell an idea, and such persuasion is often done in person. Like most of us, Jon Georges, formerly of Walt Disney Imagineering, does not consider himself a professional speaker. He admits that he once was so afraid of public speaking that he started a couple of speech courses as part of his degree program at UCLA but always dropped out. Finally, he took a night class in speaking and began to get over his fears.

Many future businesspeople fail to take advantage of opportunities in college to develop speaking skills. However, such skills often play an important role in a successful career. In fact, the No. 1 predictor of success and upward mobility, according to an AT&T and Stanford University study, is how much you enjoy public speaking and how effective you are at it.[3] Speaking skills are useful at every career stage. You might, for example, have to make a sales pitch before customers or speak to a professional gathering. You might need to describe your company's expansion plans to your banker, or you might need to persuade management to support your proposed marketing strategy. This chapter prepares you to use speaking skills in making oral presentations, whether alone or as part of a team.

For any presentation, you can reduce your fears and lay the foundation for a professional performance by focusing on five areas: preparation, organization, audience rapport, visual aids, and delivery.

LEARNING OBJECTIVE 1
Discuss two important first steps in preparing effective oral presentations.

Knowing Your Purpose

Preparing for an oral presentation means identifying the purpose and knowing the audience.

The most important part of your preparation is deciding what you want to accomplish. Do you want to sell a health care program to a prospective client? Do you want to persuade management to increase the marketing budget? Do you want to inform customer service reps of three important ways to prevent miscommunication? Whether your goal is to persuade or to inform, you must have a clear idea of where you are going. At the end of your presentation, what do you want your listeners to remember or do?

Mark Miller, a loan officer at First Fidelity Trust, faced such questions as he planned a talk for a class in small business management. Mark's former business professor had asked him to return to campus and give the class advice about borrowing money from banks in order to start new businesses. Because Mark knew so much about this topic, he found it difficult to extract a specific purpose statement for his presentation. After much thought he narrowed his purpose to this: *To inform potential entrepreneurs about three important factors that loan officers consider before granting start-up loans to launch small businesses.* His entire presentation focused on ensuring that the class members understood and remembered three principal ideas.

Knowing Your Audience

A second key element in preparation is analyzing your audience, anticipating its reactions, and making appropriate adaptations. Audiences may fall into four categories, as summarized in Figure 14.1. By anticipating your audience, you have a better idea of how to organize your presentation. A friendly audience, for example, will respond to humor and personal experiences. A neutral audience requires an even, controlled delivery style. The talk would probably be filled with facts, statistics, and expert opinions. An uninterested audience that is forced to attend requires a brief presentation. Such an audience might respond best to humor, cartoons, colorful visuals, and startling statistics. A hostile audience demands a calm, controlled delivery style with objective data and expert opinion.

FIGURE 14.1 Succeeding With Four Audience Types

Audience Members	Organizational Pattern	Delivery Style	Supporting Material
Friendly			
They like you and your topic.	Use any pattern. Try something new. Involve the audience.	Be warm, pleasant, and open. Use lots of eye contact and smiles.	Include humor, personal examples, and experiences.
Neutral			
They are calm, rational; their minds are made up, but they think they are objective.	Present both sides of the issue. Use pro/con or problem/solution patterns. Save time for audience questions.	Be controlled. Do nothing showy. Use confident, small gestures.	Use facts, statistics, expert opinion, and comparison and contrast. Avoid humor, personal stories, and flashy visuals.
Uninterested			
They have short attention spans; they may be there against their will.	Be brief—no more than three points. Avoid topical and pro/con patterns that seem lengthy to the audience.	Be dynamic and entertaining. Move around. Use large gestures.	Use humor, cartoons, colorful visuals, powerful quotations, and startling statistics.
	Avoid darkening the room, standing motionless, passing out handouts, using boring visuals, or expecting the audience to participate.		
Hostile			
They want to take charge or to ridicule the speaker; they may be defensive, emotional.	Organize using a noncontroversial pattern, such as a topical, chronological, or geographical strategy.	Be calm and controlled. Speak evenly and slowly.	Include objective data and expert opinion. Avoid anecdotes and humor.
	Avoid a question-and-answer period, if possible; otherwise, use a moderator or accept only written questions.		

Other elements, such as age, gender, education, experience, and the size of the audience will affect your style and message content. Analyze the following questions to help you determine your organizational pattern, delivery style, and supporting material.

Audience analysis issues include size, age, gender, experience, attitude, and expectations.

- *How will this topic appeal to this audience?*

- *How can I relate this information to my listeners' needs?*

- *How can I earn respect so that they accept my message?*

- *What would be most effective in making my point? Facts? Statistics? Personal experiences? Expert opinion? Humor? Cartoons? Graphic illustrations? Demonstrations? Case histories? Analogies?*

- *What measures must I take to ensure that this audience remembers my main points?*

If you have agreed to speak to an audience with which you are unfamiliar, ask for the names of a half dozen people who will be in the audience. Contact them and learn about their backgrounds and expectations for the presentation. This information can help you answer questions about what they want to hear and how deeply you should explore the subject. You will want to thank these people when you start your speech. Doing this kind of homework will impress the audience.

Organizing the Content for a Powerful Impact

Once you have determined your purpose and analyzed the audience, you are ready to collect information and organize it logically. Good organization and intentional repetition are the two most powerful keys to audience comprehension and retention. In fact, many speech experts recommend the following admittedly repetitious, but effective, plan:

LEARNING OBJECTIVE 2
Explain the major elements in organizing the content of a presentation, including the introduction, body, and conclusion.

- **Step 1:** Tell them what you're going to say.

- **Step 2:** Say it.

- **Step 3:** Tell them what you have just said.

In other words, repeat your main points in the introduction, body, and conclusion of your presentation. Although it seems redundant, this strategy works surprisingly well. Let's examine how to construct the three parts of an effective presentation.

Capturing Attention in the Introduction

How many times have you heard a speaker begin with, *It's a pleasure to be here.* Or, *I'm honored to be asked to speak.* Boring openings such as these get speakers off to a dull start. Avoid such banalities by striving to accomplish three goals in the introduction to your presentation:

- Capture listeners' attention and get them involved.

- Identify yourself and establish your credibility.

- Preview your main points.

Attention-grabbing openers include questions, startling facts, jokes, anecdotes, and quotations.

If you are able to appeal to listeners and involve them in your presentation right from the start, you are more likely to hold their attention until the finish. Consider some of the same techniques that you used to open sales letters: a question, a startling fact, a joke, a story, or a quotation. Some speakers achieve involvement by opening with a question or command that requires audience members to raise their hands or stand up. Additional techniques to gain and keep audience attention are presented in the Career Coach box on page 429.

To establish your credibility, you need to describe your position, knowledge, or experience—whatever qualifies you to speak. Try also to connect with your audience. Listeners respond particularly well to speakers who reveal something of themselves and identify with them. A consultant addressing office workers might reminisce about

Spotlight on Communicators

Starbucks' messianic CEO Howard Schultz uses stories to make an emotional connection with his listeners. One of his famous stories describes a trip to Italy that inspired him to transform a Seattle coffee shop into a global brand on his first visit to a Starbucks. "A heady aroma of coffee reached out and drew me in. I stepped inside and saw what looked like a temple for the worship of coffee. . . . It was my Mecca. I had arrived," said Schultz. Intriguing stories told with enthusiasm help capture an audience's attention and get them involved.

© Rebecca Cook / Reuters / Landov

FIGURE 14.2 Oral Presentation Outline

What Makes a Loan Officer Say *Yes*?

I. INTRODUCTION

Captures attention —— A. How many of you expect one day to start your own businesses? How many of you have all the cash available to capitalize that business when you start?

Involves audience —— B. Like you, nearly every entrepreneur needs cash to open a business, and I promise you that by the end of this talk you will have inside information on how to make a loan application that will be successful.

Identifies speaker —— C. As a loan officer at First Fidelity Trust, which specializes in small-business loans, I make decisions on requests from entrepreneurs like you applying for start-up money.
Transition: Your professor invited me here today to tell you how you can improve your chances of getting a loan from us or from any other lender. I have suggestions in three areas: experience, preparation, and projection. —— *Previews three main points*

II. BODY

Establishes main points —— A. First, let's consider experience. You must show that you can hit the ground running.
1. Demonstrate what experience you have in your proposed business.
2. Include your résumé when you submit your business plan.
3. If you have little experience, tell us whom you would hire to supply the skills that you lack.
Transition: In addition to experience, loan officers will want to see that you have researched your venture thoroughly. —— *Develops coherence with planned transitions*

B. My second suggestion, then, involves preparation. Have you done your homework?
1. Talk to local businesspeople, especially those in related fields.
2. Conduct traffic counts or other studies to estimate potential sales.
3. Analyze the strengths and weaknesses of the competition.
Transition: Now that we've discussed preparation, we're ready for my final suggestion.

C. My last tip is the most important one. It involves making a realistic projection of your potential sales, cash flow, and equity.
1. Present detailed monthly cash-flow projections for the first year.
2. Describe *What-if* scenarios indicating both good and bad possibilities.
3. Indicate that you intend to supply at least 25 percent of the initial capital yourself.
Transition: The three major points I've just outlined cover critical points in obtaining start-up loans. Let me review them for you.

III. CONCLUSION

Summarizes main points —— A. Loan officers are most likely to say *yes* to your loan application if you do three things: (1) prove that you can hit the ground running when your business opens; (2) demonstrate that you've researched your proposed business seriously; and (3) project a realistic picture of your sales, cash flow, and equity.

B. Experience, preparation, and projection, then, are the three keys to launching your business with the necessary start-up capital so that you can concentrate on where your customers, not your funds, are coming from. —— *Provides final focus*

---

how she started as an administrative assistant; a CEO might tell a funny story in which the joke is on himself.

After capturing attention and establishing yourself, you will want to preview the main points of your topic, perhaps with a visual aid. You may wish to put off actually writing your introduction, however, until after you have organized the rest of the presentation and crystallized your principal ideas.

Take a look at Mark Miller's introduction, shown in Figure 14.2, to see how he integrated all the elements necessary for a good opening.

Organizing the Body

The best oral presentations focus on a few key ideas.

The biggest problem with most oral presentations is a failure to focus on a few principal ideas. Thus, the body of your short presentation (20 or fewer minutes) should include a limited number of main points, say, two to four. Develop each main point with adequate, but not excessive, explanation and details. Too many details can obscure the main message, so keep your presentation simple and logical. Remember, listeners have no pages to leaf back through should they become confused.

CAREER COACH

Nine Techniques for Gaining and Keeping Audience Attention

Experienced speakers know how to capture the attention of an audience and how to maintain that attention during a presentation. Here are nine proven techniques.

- **A promise.** Begin with a promise that keeps the audience expectant (for example, *By the end of this presentation I will have shown you how you can increase your sales by 50 percent*).
- **Drama.** Open by telling an emotionally moving story or by describing a serious problem that involves the audience. Throughout your talk include other dramatic elements, such as a long pause after a key statement. Change your vocal tone or pitch. Professionals use high-intensity emotions such as anger, joy, sadness, and excitement.
- **Eye contact.** As you begin, command attention by surveying the entire audience to take in all listeners. Give yourself two to five seconds to linger on individuals to avoid fleeting, unconvincing eye contact. Don't just sweep the room and the crowd.
- **Movement.** Leave the lectern area whenever possible. Walk around the conference table or between the aisles of your audience. Try to move toward your audience, especially at the beginning and end of your talk.
- **Questions.** Keep listeners active and involved with rhetorical questions. Ask for a show of hands to get each listener thinking. The response will also give you a quick gauge of audience attention.
- **Demonstrations.** Include a member of the audience in a demonstration (for example, *I'm going to show you exactly how*

to implement our four-step customer courtesy process, but I need a volunteer from the audience to help me).

- **Samples/gimmicks.** If you are promoting a product, consider using items to toss out to the audience or to award as prizes to volunteer participants. You can also pass around product samples or promotional literature. Be careful, though, to maintain control.
- **Visuals.** Give your audience something to look at besides yourself. Use a variety of visual aids in a single session. Also consider writing the concerns expressed by your listeners on a flipchart or on the board as you go along.
- **Self-interest.** Review your entire presentation to ensure that it meets the critical *What's-in-it-for-me?* audience test. Remember that people are most interested in things that benefit them.

Career Application

Watch a lecture series speaker on campus, a department store sales presentation, a TV "infomercial," or some other speaker. Note and analyze specific techniques used to engage and maintain the listener's attention. Which techniques would be most effective in a classroom presentation? Before your boss or work group?

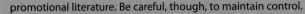

When Mark Miller began planning his presentation, he realized immediately that he could talk for hours on his topic. He also knew that listeners are not good at separating major and minor points. Thus, instead of submerging his listeners in a sea of information, he sorted out a few main ideas. In the banking industry, loan officers generally ask the following three questions of each applicant for a small business loan: (1) Are you ready to "hit the ground running" in starting your business? (2) Have you done your homework? and (3) Have you made realistic projections of potential sales, cash flow, and equity investment? These questions would become his main points, but Mark wanted to streamline them further so that his audience would be sure to remember them. He capsulized the questions in three words: *experience, preparation,* and *projection.* As you can see in Figure 14.2, Mark prepared a sentence outline showing these three main ideas. Each is supported by examples and explanations.

How to organize and sequence main ideas may not be immediately obvious when you begin working on a presentation. The following methods, which review and amplify those discussed in Chapter 12, provide many possible strategies and examples to help you organize a presentation:

- **Chronology.** Example: A presentation describing the history of a problem, organized from the first sign of trouble to the present.

- **Geography/space.** Example: A presentation about the changing diversity of the workforce, organized by regions in the country (East Coast, West Coast, and so forth).

- **Topic/function/conventional grouping.** Example: A report discussing mishandled airline baggage, organized by names of airlines.

- **Comparison/contrast (pro/con).** Example: A report comparing organic farming methods with those of modern industrial farming.

> Main ideas can be organized according to chronology, geography/space, topic/function/conventional grouping, comparison/contrast, journalism pattern, value/size, importance, problem/solution, simple/complex, and best case/worst case.

- **Journalistic pattern (the six Ws).** Example: A report describing how identity thieves can ruin your good name. Organized by *who, what, when, where, why,* and *how.*

- **Value/size.** Example: A report describing fluctuations in housing costs, organized by prices of homes.

- **Importance.** Example: A report describing five reasons that a company should move its headquarters to a specific city, organized from the most important reason to the least important.

- **Problem/solution.** Example: A company faces a problem such as declining sales. A solution such as reducing the staff is offered.

- **Simple/complex.** Example: A report explaining genetic modification of plants such as corn, organized from simple seed production to complex gene introduction.

- **Best case/worst case.** Example: A report analyzing whether two companies should merge, organized by the best-case result (improved market share, profitability, employee morale) opposed to the worst-case result (devalued stock, lost market share, employee malaise).

In the presentation shown in Figure 14.2, Mark arranged the main points by importance, placing the most important point last where it had maximum effect. When organizing any presentation, prepare a little more material than you think you will actually need. Savvy speakers always have something useful in reserve such as an extra handout, transparency, or idea—just in case they finish early. At the same time, most speakers go about 25 percent over the allotted time as opposed to their practice runs at home in front of the mirror. If your speaking time is limited, as it usually is in your classes, aim for less than the limit when rehearsing, so that you don't take time away from the next presenters.

Summarizing in the Conclusion

Effective conclusions summarize main points and allow the speaker to exit gracefully.

Nervous speakers often rush to wrap up their presentations because they can't wait to flee the stage. However, listeners will remember the conclusion more than any other part of a speech. That's why you should spend some time to make it most effective. Strive to achieve three goals:

- Summarize the main themes of the presentation.

- Leave the audience with a specific and memorable "take-away."

- Include a statement that allows you to leave the podium gracefully.

Some speakers end limply with comments such as, *I guess that's about all I have to say* or *That's it.* Such lame statements show little enthusiasm and are not the culmination of the talk that listeners expect. Skilled speakers alert the audience that they are finishing. They use phrases such as, *In conclusion, As I end this presentation,* or, *It's time for me to sum up.* Then they proceed immediately to the conclusion. Audiences become justly irritated with a speaker who announces the conclusion but then digresses with one more story or talks on for ten more minutes.

A straightforward summary should review major points and focus on what you want the listeners to do, think, or remember. You might say, *In bringing my presentation to a close, I will restate my major purpose . . . ,* or, *In summary, my major purpose has been to . . . . In support of my purpose, I have presented three major points. They are (1) . . . , (2) . . . , and (3) . . . .* Notice how Mark Miller, in the conclusion shown in Figure 14.2, summarized his three main points and provided a final focus to listeners.

If you are promoting a recommendation, you might end as follows: *In conclusion, I recommend that we retain Matrixx Marketing to conduct a telemarketing campaign beginning September 1 at a cost of X dollars. To complete this recommendation, I suggest that we (a) finance this campaign from our operations budget, (b) develop a persuasive message describing our new product, and (c) name Lisa Beck to oversee the project.*

A conclusion is akin to a punch line and must be memorable. Think of it as the high point of your presentation, a valuable kernel of information to take away. The valuable kernel of information, or take-away, should tie in with the opening or present a forward-looking idea. Avoid merely rehashing, in the same words, what you said before, but ensure that the audience will take away very specific information or benefits and a positive impression of you and your company. The so-called take-away is the value of the presentation to the audience and the benefit audience members believe they have received. The tension that you built in the early parts of the talk now culminates in the close.

In your conclusion you might want to use an anecdote, an inspiring quotation, or a statement that ties in the opener and offers a new insight. Whatever you choose, be sure to include a closing thought that indicates you are finished. For example, *This concludes my presentation. After investigating many marketing firms, we are convinced that Matrixx is the best for our purposes. Your authorization of my recommendations will mark the beginning of a very successful campaign for our new product. Thank you.*

Building Audience Rapport Like a Pro

Good speakers are adept at building audience rapport. They form a bond with the audience; they entertain as well as inform. How do they do it? Based on observations of successful and unsuccessful speakers, we learn that the good ones use a number of verbal and nonverbal techniques to connect with the audience. Their helpful techniques include providing effective imagery, supplying verbal signposts, and using body language strategically.

LEARNING OBJECTIVE 3
Identify techniques for gaining audience rapport, including (a) using effective imagery, (b) providing verbal signposts, and (c) sending appropriate nonverbal messages.

Effective Imagery

You will lose your audience quickly if you fill your talk with abstractions, generalities, and dry facts. To enliven your presentation and enhance comprehension, try using some of the following techniques. However, beware of exaggeration or distortion. Keep your imagery realistic and credible.

- **Analogies.** A comparison of similar traits between dissimilar things can be effective in explaining and drawing connections. For example, *Product development is similar to the process of conceiving, carrying, and delivering a baby.* Or, *Downsizing or restructuring is similar to an overweight person undergoing a regimen of dieting, habit changing, and exercising.*

Use analogies, metaphors, similes, personal anecdotes, personalized statistics, and worst- and best-case scenarios instead of dry facts.

© AP Images

The Coca-Cola Company, in partnership with the World Wildlife Foundation, launched a $20 million water conservation project to replenish the 76 billion gallons of water it uses annually on beverage products. Representatives meet regularly to explore how the cola giant and its water-guzzling sugar cane suppliers can improve water efficiency and preserve natural resources. One proposal calls for the protection of major rivers, including the Yangtze and Rio Grande. How can Coca-Cola spokespersons build audience rapport during presentations to the World Wildlife Foundation?

- **Metaphors.** A comparison between otherwise dissimilar things without using the words *like* or *as* results in a metaphor. For example, *Our competitor's CEO is a snake when it comes to negotiating.* Or, *My desk is a garbage dump.*

- **Similes.** A comparison that includes the words *like* or *as* is a simile. For example, *Our critics used our background report like a drunk uses a lamppost—for support rather than for illumination.* Or, *She's as happy as someone who just won the lottery.*

- **Personal anecdotes.** Nothing connects you faster or better with your audience than a good personal story. In a talk about e-mail techniques, you could reveal your own blunders that became painful learning experiences. In a talk to potential investors, the founder of a new ethnic magazine might tell a story about growing up without positive ethnic role models.

- **Personalized statistics.** Although often misused, statistics stay with people—particularly when they relate directly to the audience. A speaker discussing job searching might say, *Look around the room. Only three out of five graduates will find a job immediately after graduation.* If possible, simplify and personalize facts. For example, *The sales of Coca-Cola totaled 2 billion cases last year. That means that every man, woman, and child in the United States consumed six full cases of Coke.*

- **Worst- and best-case scenarios.** Hearing the worst that could happen can be effective in driving home a point. For example, *If we do nothing about our computer backup system now, it's just a matter of time before the entire system crashes and we lose all of our customer contact information. Can you imagine starting from scratch in building all of your customer files again? However, if we fix the system now, we can expand our customer files and actually increase sales at the same time.*

Verbal Signposts

Speakers must remember that listeners, unlike readers of a report, cannot control the rate of presentation or flip back through pages to review main points. As a result, listeners get lost easily. Knowledgeable speakers help the audience recognize the organization and main points in an oral message with verbal signposts. They keep listeners on track by including helpful previews, summaries, and transitions, such as these:

- **Previewing**

  The next segment of my talk presents three reasons for . . . .

  Let's now consider the causes of . . . .

- **Summarizing**

  Let me review with you the major problems I have just discussed . . . .

  You see, then, that the most significant factors are . . . .

- **Switching directions**

  Thus far we have talked solely about . . . ; now let's move to . . . .

  I have argued that . . . and . . . , but an alternate view holds that . . . .

You can further improve any oral presentation by including appropriate transitional expressions such as *first, second, next, then, therefore, moreover, on the other hand, on the contrary,* and *in conclusion.* These transitional expressions, which you learned about in Figure 5.7 on page 140, build coherence, lend emphasis, and tell listeners where you are headed. Notice in Mark Miller's outline, in Figure 14.2, the specific transitional elements designed to help listeners recognize each new principal point.

Nonverbal Messages

Although what you say is most important, the nonverbal messages you send can also have a potent effect on how well your audience receives your message. How you look, how you move, and how you speak can make or break your presentation. The following suggestions focus on nonverbal tips to ensure that your verbal message is well-received.

> Knowledgeable speakers provide verbal signposts to indicate when they are previewing, summarizing, or switching directions.

> A speaker's appearance, movement, and speech affect the success of a presentation.

- **Look terrific!** Like it or not, you will be judged by your appearance. For everything but small in-house presentations, be sure you dress professionally. The rule of thumb is that you should dress at least as well as the best-dressed person in the audience.

- **Animate your body.** Be enthusiastic and let your body show it. Emphasize ideas to enhance points about size, number, and direction. Use a variety of gestures, but don't consciously plan them in advance.

- **Speak extemporaneously.** Do not read from notes or a manuscript but speak freely. Use your presentation slides to guide your talk. You will come across as more competent and enthusiastic if you are not glued to your notes or manuscript. Use note cards or a paper outline only if presenting without an electronic slideshow.

- **Punctuate your words.** You can keep your audience interested by varying your tone, volume, pitch, and pace. Use pauses before and after important points. Allow the audience to take in your ideas.

- **Get out from behind the podium.** Avoid being glued to the podium. Movement makes you look natural and comfortable. You might pick a few places in the room to walk to. Even if you must stay close to your visual aids, make a point of leaving them occasionally so that the audience can see your whole body.

- **Vary your facial expression.** Begin with a smile, but change your expressions to correspond with the thoughts you are voicing. You can shake your head to show disagreement, roll your eyes to show disdain, look heavenward for guidance, or wrinkle your brow to show concern or dismay. To see how speakers convey meaning without words, mute the sound on your TV and watch the facial expressions of a talk show personality.

Whenever possible, beginning presenters should have an experienced speaker watch them and give them tips as they rehearse. Your instructor is an important coach who can provide you with invaluable feedback. In the absence of helpers, tape yourself and watch your nonverbal behavior on camera.

Spotlight on Communicators

Cisco is a worldwide leader in networking that transforms how people connect, communicate, and collaborate. When Chairman and CEO John Chambers introduces new Cisco products to a diverse audience made up of analysts, media, and consumers, he captivates his audience using persuasive communication skills. One of his strategies is to use movement and hand gestures to punctuate every sentence, allowing him to work the stage and the crowd. To maintain your listener's attention, strive to be animated in your voice and body.

© Daniel Acker / Bloomberg News / Landov

Planning Visual Aids and Multimedia Presentations

Before you make a business presentation, consider this wise proverb: "Tell me, I forget. Show me, I remember. Involve me, I understand." Your goals as a speaker are to make listeners understand, remember, and act on your ideas. To get them interested and involved, include effective visual aids. Some experts say that we acquire 85 percent of all our knowledge visually. Therefore, an oral presentation that incorporates visual aids is far more likely to be understood and retained than one lacking visual enhancement. Apple's CEO Steve Jobs, for example, uses slides with an absolute minimum of text and relies primarily on images.

Good visual aids have many purposes. They emphasize and clarify main points, thus improving comprehension and retention. They increase audience interest, and they make the presenter appear more professional, better prepared, and more persuasive. Furthermore, research suggests that the use of visual aids may actually shorten meetings.[4] Visual aids are particularly helpful for inexperienced speakers because the audience concentrates on the aid rather than on the speaker. However, experienced speakers work hard at not being eclipsed or upstaged by their slideshows. Good visuals also serve to jog the memory of a speaker, thus improving self-confidence, poise, and delivery.

LEARNING OBJECTIVE 4
Discuss designing visual aids, handouts, and multimedia presentation materials and using presentation technology competently.

Visual aids clarify points, improve comprehension, and aid retention.

Types of Visual Aids

Fortunately for today's speakers, many forms of visual media are available to enhance a presentation. Figure 14.3 describes the pros and cons of a number of visual aids that can guide

FIGURE 14.3 Pros and Cons of Visual Aid Options

Medium	Pros	Cons
Multimedia slides 	Create professional appearance with many color, art, graphic, and font options. Easy to use and transport via removable storage media, Web download, or e-mail attachment. Inexpensive to update.	Present potential incompatibility issues. Require costly projection equipment and practice for smooth delivery. Tempt user to include razzle-dazzle features that may fail to add value.
Transparencies 	Give professional appearance with little practice. Easy to (a) prepare, (b) update and maintain, (c) locate reliable equipment, and (d) limit information shown at one time.	Appear to some as an outdated presentation method. Hold speaker captive to the machine. Provide poor reproduction of photos and some graphics.
Handouts 	Encourage audience participation. Easy to maintain and update. Enhance recall because audience keeps reference material.	Increase risk of unauthorized duplication of speaker's material. Can be difficult to transport. May cause speaker to lose audience's attention.
Flipcharts or whiteboards 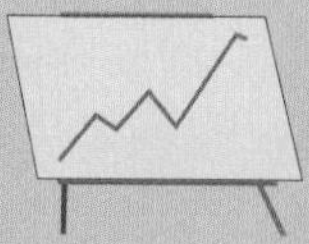	Provide inexpensive option available at most sites. Easy to (a) create, (b) modify on the spot, (c) record comments from the audience, and (d) combine with more high-tech visuals in the same presentation.	Require graphics talent. Difficult for larger audiences to see. Prepared flipcharts are cumbersome to transport and easily worn with use.
Video 	Gives an accurate representation of the content; strong indication of forethought and preparation.	Creates potential for compatibility issues related to computer video formats. Expensive to create and update.
Props 	Offer a realistic reinforcement of message content. Increase audience participation with close observation.	Lead to extra work and expense in transporting and replacing worn objects. Limited use with larger audiences.

you in selecting the best visual aid for any speaking occasion. Three of the most popular visuals are multimedia slides, overhead transparencies, and handouts.

Multimedia Slides. With today's excellent software programs—such as Microsoft PowerPoint, Apple Keynote, Lotus Freelance Graphics, Corel Presentations, and Adobe Presenter or Adobe Ovation—you can create dynamic, colorful presentations with your PC. The output from these programs is generally shown on a computer monitor, a TV monitor, an LCD (liquid crystal display) panel, or a screen. With a little expertise and advanced equipment, you can create a multimedia presentation that includes stereo sound, videos, and hyperlinks, as described shortly in the discussion of multimedia presentations.

Overhead Transparencies. Student and professional speakers alike still rely on the overhead projector for many reasons. Most meeting areas are equipped with projectors and screens. Moreover, acetate transparencies for the overhead are cheap, easily prepared on a computer or copier, and simple to use. Because rooms need not be darkened, a speaker using transparencies can maintain eye contact with the audience. Many experienced speakers create overhead slides in addition to their electronic slides to have a backup plan in the case of malfunctioning presentation technology. A word of caution, though, when using transparencies: stand to the side of the projector so that you don't obstruct the audience's view.

Handouts. You can enhance and complement your presentations by distributing pictures, outlines, brochures, articles, charts, summaries, or other supplements. Speakers who use presentation software often prepare a set of their slides along with notes to hand out to viewers. Timing the distribution of any handout, though, is tricky. If given out during a presentation, your handouts tend to distract the audience, causing you to lose control. Therefore, you should discuss handouts during the presentation but delay distributing them until after you finish.

To maintain control, distribute handouts after you finish speaking.

Speaker's Notes. You have a variety of options for printing hard-copy versions of your presentation. You can, for example, make speaker's notes, which are a wonderful aid for practicing your talk. Beneath the miniature image of each slide is space for you to key in your supporting comments for the abbreviated material in your slides. You can also include up to nine miniature versions of your slides per printed page. These miniatures are handy if you want to preview your talk to a sponsoring organization or if you want to supply the audience with a summary of your presentation. However, resist the temptation to read from your notes during the slide presentation. It might turn off your audience and make you appear insecure and incompetent.

Designing an Impressive Multimedia Presentation

Few corporate types or entrepreneurs would do without the razzle-dazzle of colorful images to make their point. Electronic slideshows, PowerPoint in particular, have become a staple of business presentations. However, overuse or misuse may be the downside of the ever-present multimedia slideshow. Over the two decades of the software program's existence, millions of poorly created and badly delivered PowerPoint presentations have tarnished PowerPoint's reputation as an effective communication tool. Tools are helpful only when used properly.

PowerPoint has become the business standard for presenting and selling ideas.

Imagine those who sit through the more than 30 million PowerPoint presentations that Microsoft estimates are made each day.[5] No doubt, many of them would say this "disease" has reached epidemic proportions. As a result, PowerPoint is often ridiculed as an ineffective communication tool. PowerPoint, say its detractors, dictates the way information is structured and presented. They say that the program is turning the nation's businesspeople into a "mindless gaggle of bullet-pointed morons."[6] If you looked up "death by PowerPoint" in your favorite search engine, you would score hundreds of thousands of hits. However, text-laden, amateurish slides that distract and bore audiences are the fault of their creator and not the software program itself.

Critics say that PowerPoint is too rigid and produces "bullet-pointed morons."

In the sections that follow, you will learn to create an impressive multimedia presentation using the most widely used presentation software program, PowerPoint. With any software program, of course, gaining expertise requires an investment of time and effort. You could take a course, or you could teach yourself through an online tutorial such as that at **http://office.microsoft.com/en-us/training/default.aspx**. Another way to master PowerPoint is to read a book such as Gilgen's *Absolute Beginner's Guide to Microsoft Office PowerPoint 2003*. If operated by a proficient slide preparer and a skillful presenter, PowerPoint can add a distinct visual impact to any presentation.

Applying the 3-x-3 Writing Process to Creating a Visually Appealing PowerPoint Presentation

Some presenters prefer to create their slides first and then develop the narrative around their slides. Others prefer to prepare their content first and then create the visual component. The risk associated with the first approach is that you may be tempted to spend too much time making your slides look good and not enough time preparing your content. Remember that great-looking slides never compensate for thin content. In the following discussion, we will review the three phases of the writing process and show how they help you develop a visually appealing PowerPoint presentation. In the prewriting phase you analyze, anticipate, and adapt. In the second phase you research, organize, and compose. In the third phase you revise, edit, and evaluate.

Analyzing and anticipating how your audience will react determines your choice of content and design.

Analyzing the Situation.

Making the best content and design choices for your slides depends greatly on your analysis of the presentation situation. Will your slides be used during a live presentation? Will they be part of a self-running presentation such as in a store kiosk? Will they be saved on a server so that those with Internet access can watch the presentation at their convenience? Will they be sent as a PowerPoint show or a PDF document—also sometimes called a "deck"—to a client instead of a hard-copy report? Are you converting PowerPoint slideshows for viewing on video iPods[7] or BlackBerry devices?[8]

If you are e-mailing the presentation or posting it online as a self-contained file, the slides will typically feature more text than if they were delivered orally. If, on the other hand, you are creating slides for a live presentation, your analysis will include answering questions such as these: *Should I prepare speaker's notes pages for my own use during the presentation? Should I distribute hard copies of my slides to my audience?*

Anticipating Your Audience.

Think about how you can design your presentation to get the most positive response from your audience. Audiences respond, for example, to the colors you use. Primary ideas are generally best conveyed with bold colors such as blue, green, and purple. Because the messages that colors convey can vary from culture to culture, colors must be chosen carefully. In the United States blue is the color of credibility, tranquility, conservatism, and trust. Therefore, it is the background color of choice for many business presentations. Green relates to interaction, growth, money, and stability. It can work well as a background or an accent color. Purple can be used as a background or accent color. It conveys spirituality, royalty, dreams, and humor.[9]

Just as you anticipate audience members' reactions to color, you can usually anticipate their reaction to special effects. Using animation and sound effects—flying objects, swirling text, clashing cymbals, and the like—only because they are available is not a good idea. Special effects distract your audience, drawing attention away from your main points. You should add animation features only if doing so helps convey your message or adds interest to the content. When your audience members leave, they should be commenting on the ideas you conveyed—not the cool swivels and sound effects.

Business presentation software is rapidly replacing static visual aids in today's meeting rooms. Microsoft Office PowerPoint transforms routine diagrams and charts into animated graphics. Apple Keynote, which began as a tool to help Apple CEO Steve Jobs make keynote speeches at Macworld conferences, jazzes up proposals with easy-to-create video. GoToMeeting.com publishes computer presentations to the Web, opening up the conference room to partners around the world. What caveats should speakers heed when using presentation software?

© Declan McCullagh / CNET News.com

Adapting Text and Color Selections. Adapt the amount of text on your slide to how your audience will use the slides. As a general guideline, most graphic designers encourage the 6-x-6 rule: "six bullets per screen, max; six words per bullet, max."[10] You may find, however, that breaking this rule is sometimes necessary, particularly when your users will be viewing the presentation on their own with no speaker assistance.

Adapt the colors based on where the presentation will be given. Use light text on a dark background for presentations in darkened rooms. Use dark text on a light background for presentations in lighted rooms. Avoid using a dark font on a dark background, such as red text on a dark blue background. In the same way, avoid using a light font on a light background, such as white text on a pale blue background. Dark on dark or light on light results in low contrast, making the slides difficult to read.

Researching Your PowerPoint Options. You may need to present a complicated idea and will have to learn more about PowerPoint in order to determine the best way to clarify and simplify its visual presentation. Besides using online tutorials and studying books on the subject, be on the lookout as you view other people's presentations to learn fresh ways to illustrate your content more effectively. Chances are you will learn the most from fellow students and team members who have truly mastered the software.

Organizing Your Slides. When you prepare your slides, translate the major headings in your presentation outline into titles for slides. Then build bullet points using short phrases. In Chapter 5 you learned to improve readability by using graphic highlighting techniques, including bullets, numbers, and headings. In preparing a PowerPoint presentation, you will use those same techniques.

The slides you create to accompany your spoken ideas can be organized with visual elements that will help your audience understand and remember what you want to communicate. Let's say, for example, that you have three points in your presentation. You can create a blueprint slide that captures the three points in a visually appealing way, and then you can use that slide several times throughout your presentation. Near the beginning, the blueprint slide provides an overview of your points. Later, it will provide transitions as you move from point to point. For transitions, you can direct your audience's attention by highlighting the next point you will be talking about. Finally, the blueprint slide can be used near the end to provide a review of your key points.

Composing Your Slideshow. All presentation programs require you to (a) create a template that will serve as the background for your presentation and (b) make each individual slide by selecting a layout that best conveys your message. When you craft your template, you can use one of those provided with the program, download one from many Web sites, or create one from scratch.

Novice and even advanced users choose existing templates because they are designed by professionals who know how to combine harmonious colors, borders, and fonts for pleasing visual effects. If you prefer, you can alter existing templates so that they better suit your needs. Adding a corporate logo, adjusting the color scheme to better match the colors used on your organization's Web site, or selecting a different font are just some of the ways you can customize existing templates.

Be careful, though, of what one expert labels "visual clichés."[11] Overused templates and even clip art that ship with PowerPoint can weary viewers who have seen them repeatedly in presentations. Instead of using a standard template, search for *PowerPoint template* in Google or your favorite search engine. You will see hundreds of template options available as free downloads. Unless your employer requires that presentations all have the same look, your audience will most likely appreciate fresh templates that complement the purpose of your presentation and provide visual variety.

PowerPoint comes with the **AutoContent Wizard** feature that can help you through the process of creating a slideshow. The Wizard provides outlines for a variety of types of presentations. Relying only on the Wizard, however, generally leads to text-heavy presentations that lack visual elements. Nevertheless, it's a good start for a PowerPoint newbie. Likewise, you can choose from the layout options in PowerPoint, or you can create a layout from scratch by adding your own elements to each slide.

> Follow the 6-x-6 rule and select background and text colors based on the lightness of the room.

> Overused templates and clip art produce "visual clichés" that bore audiences.

FIGURE 14.4 Revising and Enhancing Slides for Greater Impact

Before Revision

After Revision

Reasons for Selling Online

- Your online business can grow globally.
- Customer convenience.
- Conduct business 24/7.
- No need for renting a retail store or hiring employees.
- Reduce inquiries by providing policies and a privacy statement.
- Customers can buy quickly and easily.

Why You Should Sell Online

- Grow your business globally.
- Provide convenience for customers.
- Conduct business 24/7.
- Save on rent and hiring.
- Provide policies to reduce inquiries.

The slide on the left contains bullet points that are not parallel and that overlap meaning. The second and sixth bullet points say the same thing. Moreover, some bullet points are too long. After revision, the slide on the right has a more convincing title illustrating the "you" view. The bullet points are shorter, and each begins with a verb for parallelism. The photo adds interest.

Figure 14.4 illustrates two of the many layout and design options for creating your slides. You can alter layouts by repositioning, resizing, or changing the fonts for the place-holders in which your title, bulleted list, organization chart, video clip, photograph, or other elements appear. As Figure 14.4 shows, you can experiment with graphic elements that will enhance your presentation by making your slides visually more appealing and memorable. Try to avoid long, boring bulleted lists.

If you look more closely at Figure 14.4, you will notice that the bulleted items on the first slide are not parallel. The slide looks as if the author had been brainstorming or free-writing a first draft. The second and sixth bullet points express the same thought, that shopping online is convenient and easy for customers. Some bullet points are too long. As opposed to that, the bullets on the improved slide are very short, well within the 6-x-6 rule, although they are complete sentences. The photograph in the revised slide adds interest and illustrates the point. You may use stock photos that you can download from the Web for personal or school use without penalty, or consider taking your own pictures if you own a digital camera.

You can add pizzazz to your slides by animating some items and using diagrams from the Diagram Gallery.

Figure 14.5 shows how to add variety and pizzazz to your slides. Notice that the same information that appeared as bullet points in Figure 14.4 now appears as exciting spokes radiating from the central idea: Why You Should Sell Online. This spoke diagram is just one of six common diagram possibilities available in the **Diagram Gallery**. You can also animate each item in the diagram. Occasionally, try to convert pure text and bullet points to diagrams, charts, and other images to add punch to your slideshow. You will keep your audiences interested and help them retain the information you are presenting.

During this composition stage many users fall into the trap of excessive formatting and programming. They fritter away precious time fine-tuning their slides. They don't spend enough time on what they are going to say and how they will say it. To avoid this trap, set a limit for how much time you will spend making your slides visually appealing. Your time limit will be based on how many "bells and whistles" (a) your audience expects and (b) your content requires to make it understandable. Remember that not every point nor every thought requires a visual. In fact, it's smart to switch off the slides occasionally and direct the focus to yourself. Darkening the screen while you discuss a point, tell a story, give an example, or involve the audience will add variety to your presentation.

Create a slide only if the slide accomplishes at least one of the following purposes:

- Generates interest in what you are saying and helps the audience follow your ideas

- Highlights points you want your audience to remember

FIGURE 14.5 Converting a Bulleted Slide Into an Animated Diagram

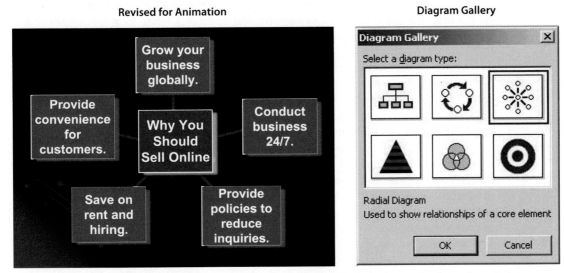

Revised for Animation

Diagram Gallery

The same content that appears in the Figure 14.4 slides takes on a totally different look when arranged as spokes radiating from a central idea. When presenting this slide, you can animate each item and control its appearance, further enlivening your presentation. PowerPoint provides a **Diagram Gallery** with six choices for arranging information.

- Introduces or reviews your key points
- Provides a transition from one major point to the next
- Illustrates and simplifies complex ideas

In a later section of this chapter you will find very specific steps to follow as you create your presentation.

Revising, Proofreading, and Evaluating Your Slideshow.

Use Power-Point's **Slide Sorter View** to rearrange, insert, and delete slides during the revision process. This is the time when you will focus on making your presentation as clear and concise as possible. If you are listing items, be sure that all items use parallel grammatical form. Figure 14.6 shows how to revise a slide to improve it for conciseness, parallelism, and other features. Study the design tips described in the first slide and determine which suggestions were not followed. Then compare it with the revised slide.

FIGURE 14.6 Designing More Effective Slides

Before Revision

After Revision

DESIGN TIPS FOR SLIDE TEXT

1. STRIVE TO HAVE NO MORE THAN SIX BULLETS PER SLIDE AND NO MORE THAN SIX WORDS PER BULLET.
2. IF YOU USE UPPER- AND LOWERCASE TYPE, IT IS EASIER TO READ
3. IT IS BETTER TO USE PHRASES RATHER THAN SENTENCES.
4. USING A SIMPLE, HIGH-CONTRAST TYPEFACE IS EASIER TO READ AND DOES NOT DETRACT FROM YOUR PRESENTATION
5. BE CONSISTENT IN YOUR SPACING, CAPITALIZATION, AND PUNCTUATION.

Design Tips for Slide Text

- Limit: 6 bullets per slide
- Limit: 6 words per bullet
- Upper- and lowercase type
- Concise phrases, not sentences
- Simple typeface
- Consistent spacing, capitalization, and punctuation

The slide on the left is difficult to read and understand because it violates many slide-making rules. How many violations can you detect? The slide on the right illustrates an improved version of the same information. Which slide do you think viewers would rather read?

Notice that both slides in Figure 14.6 feature a blue background, the calming blue serving as the color of choice for most business presentations. However, the background swirls on the first slide are distracting. In addition, the uppercase white font contributes to the busy look, making the slide hard to read. Inserting a transparent overlay and choosing a dark font to mute the distracting waves create a cleaner-looking slide.

As you are revising, check carefully to find spelling, grammar, punctuation, and other errors. Use the PowerPoint spell check, but don't rely on it without careful proofing, preferably from a printed copy of the slide show. Nothing is as embarrassing as projecting errors on a huge screen in front of an audience. Also check for consistency in how you capitalize and punctuate points throughout the presentation.

The final stage in applying the 3-x-3 writing process to developing a PowerPoint presentation involves evaluation. Consider whether you have done all you can to use the tools PowerPoint provides to communicate your message in a visually appealing way. In addition, test your slides on the equipment and in the room you will be using during your presentation. Do the colors you selected work in this new setting? Are the font styles and sizes readable from the back of the room? Figure 14.7 shows examples of slides that incorporate what you have learned in this discussion.

The dark purple background and the green and blue hues in the slideshow shown in Figure 14.7 are standard choices for many business presentations. With an unobtrusive dark background, white fonts are a good option for maximum contrast and, hence, readability. The creator of the presentation varied the slide design to break the monotony of bulleted or numbered lists. Images and animated diagrams add interest and zing to the slides.

A PowerPoint presentation can use dark businesslike colors but enliven the screen with white letters and bright yellow highlights.

FIGURE 14.7 PowerPoint Slides That Summarize and Illustrate Multimedia Presentations

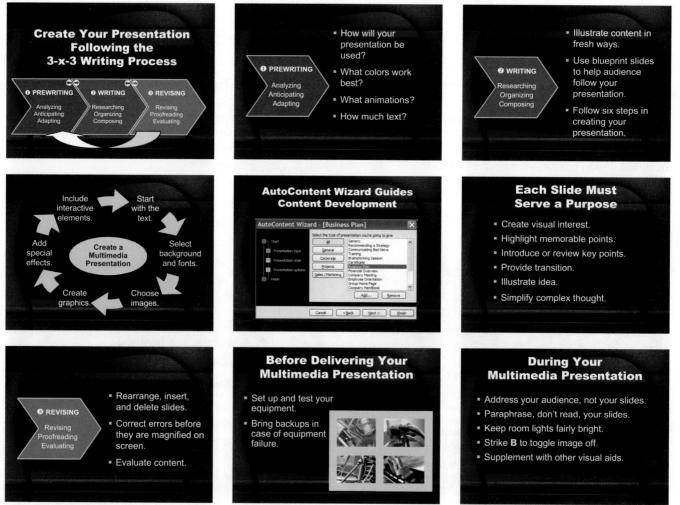

Using PowerPoint Effectively With Your Audience

Many promising presentations have been sabotaged by technology glitches or by the presenter's unfamiliarity with the equipment. Fabulous slides are of value only if you can manage the technology expertly. Apple CEO Steve Jobs is famous for his ability to wow his audiences during his keynote addresses. A *BusinessWeek* cover story described his approach: "Jobs unveils Apple's latest products as if he were a particularly hip and plugged-in friend showing off inventions in your living room. Truth is, the sense of informality comes only after grueling hours of practice."[12] At one of his recent Macworld rehearsals, for example, he spent more than four hours on stage practicing and reviewing every technical and performance aspect of his product launch.

A fabulous slide show can be ruined if you are unfamiliar with the equipment.

Practicing and Preparing

Allow plenty of time before your presentation to set up and test your equipment.[13] Confirm that the places you plan to stand are not in the line of the projected image. Audience members do not appreciate having part of the slide displayed on your body. Make sure that all links to videos or the Web are working and that you know how to operate all features the first time you try. No matter how much time you put into preshow setup and testing, you still have no guarantee that all will go smoothly. Therefore, you should always bring backups of your presentation. Overhead transparencies or handouts of your presentation provide good substitutes. Transferring your presentation to a CD or a USB flash drive that could run from any available notebook might prove useful as well.

Keeping Your Audience Engaged

In addition to using the technology to enhance and enrich your message, here are additional tips for performing like a professional and keeping the audience engaged.

To keep your audience interested, maintain eye contact, don't read from your slides, use a radio remote and a laser pointer, and turn off an image when it has been discussed.

- Know your material. This will free you to look at your audience and gaze at the screen, not your practice notes. Maintain genuine eye contact to connect with individuals in the room.

- As you show new elements on a slide, allow the audience time to absorb the information. Then paraphrase and elaborate on what the listeners have seen. Do not insult your audience's intelligence by reading verbatim from a slide.

- Leave the lights as bright as you can. Make sure the audience can see your face and eyes.

- Use a radio remote control (not infrared) so you can move freely rather than remain tethered to your computer. Radio remotes will allow you to be up to 50 feet away from your laptop.

- Maintain a connection with the audience by using a laser pointer to highlight slide items to discuss. Be aware, however, that a dancing laser point in a shaky hand may make you appear nervous. Steady your hand.

- Don't leave a slide on the screen when you no longer discuss it. In **Slide Show, View Show** mode, strike *B* on the keyboard to turn on or off the screen image by blackening it. Pushing *W* will turn the screen white.

Some presenters allow their PowerPoint slides to "steal their thunder." One expert urges speakers to "use their PowerPresence in preference to their PowerPoint."[14] Although multimedia presentations supply terrific sizzle, they cannot replace the steak. In developing a presentation, don't expect your slides to carry the show. You can avoid being upstaged by not relying totally on your slides. Help the audience visualize your points by using other techniques. For example, drawing a diagram on a white board or flipchart can be more engaging than showing slide after slide of static drawings. Demonstrating or displaying real objects or props is a welcome relief from slides. Remember that slides should be used only to help your audience understand the message and to add interest. You are still the main attraction!

FIGURE 14.8 Creating Visually Appealing Slides That Engage Your Audience

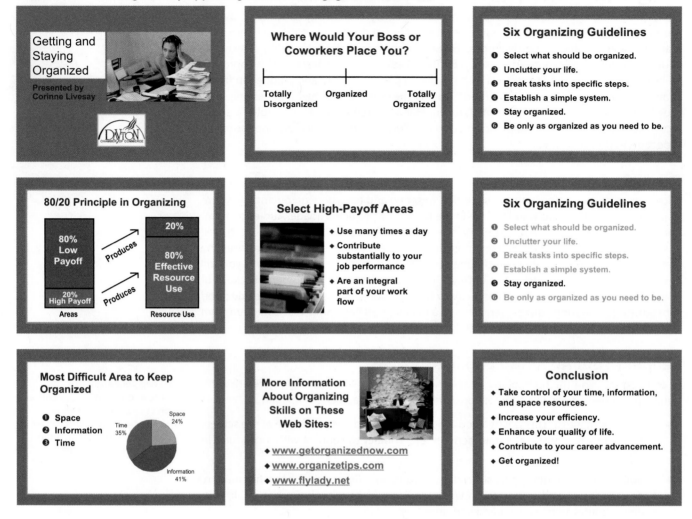

Analyzing an Effective Presentation

As you are reviewing the many tips for crafting successful slide presentations, study the sample slides in Figure 14.8. The nine slides in Figure 14.8 shown in PowerPoint's **Slide Sorter** view are taken from a longer slide presentation. Corinne Livesay, a management training consultant, recently used them during a 2½-hour training session for members of the Dayton Chamber of Commerce. They provide several examples of what you have learned about creating slides.

- The photographs used on Slides 1, 5, and 8 were downloaded from *Microsoft Office Online*. This Web site offers a great variety of royalty-free pictures as opposed to the limited number of images and clip art that ships with the software.

- Slides 2 and 4 were designed using PowerPoint's **Draw** and **AutoShapes** tools. Slide 2 encourages the audience to interact with the speaker and get involved in the topic of discussion. Even though you cannot tell from the image of Slide 4, it is programmed using PowerPoint's **Custom Animation** feature. The presenter brings in elements of the model as they are explained.

- Slides 3 and 6 illustrate how blueprint slides can be used to introduce your main points and later to move from point to point.

- Slide 7 illustrates interactivity with the audience by presenting a polling question. After audience members respond using their handheld devices, the pie chart follows and displays the results.

- Slide 8 illustrates interactivity with the Internet by providing links that can take the audience directly to relevant Web sites.

Eight Steps to Making a Powerful Multimedia Presentation

We have now discussed many suggestions for making effective PowerPoint presentations, but you may still be wondering how to put it all together. Here is a step-by-step process for creating a powerful multimedia presentation:

1. **Start with the text.** The text is the foundation of your presentation. Express your ideas using words that are clear, concise, and understandable. Once the entire content of your presentation is in place, you are ready to begin adding color and all the other elements that will make your slides visually appealing.

2. **Select background and fonts.** Select a template that will provide consistent font styles, font sizes, and a background for your slides. You can create your own template or use one included with PowerPoint. You can also download free templates or pay for templates from many online sites. You can't go wrong selecting a basic template design with an easy-to-read font, such as Times New Roman or Arial. As a general rule, use no more than two font styles in your presentation. The point size should be between 24 and 36. Title fonts should be larger than text font. The more you use PowerPoint and find out what works and does not work, the more you can experiment with bolder, more innovative background and font options that effectively convey your message.

3. **Choose images that help communicate your message.** Images, such as clip art, photographs, and maps, should complement the text. Never use an image that is not immediately relevant. *Microsoft Office Online* is accessed in PowerPoint and contains thousands of clip art images and photographs, most of which are in the public domain and require no copyright permissions. Before using images from other sources, determine whether permission from the copyright holder is required. Bear in mind that some people consider clip art amateurish, so photographs are usually preferable. In addition, clip art is available to any user, so it tends to become "stale" fast.

4. **Create graphics.** PowerPoint includes a variety of tools to help you simplify complex information or transform a boring bulleted list into a visually appealing graphic. You can use PowerPoint's *Draw* and *AutoShapes* tools to create a time line or a flowchart. The **Diagram Gallery** will help you create an organization chart or a cycle, radial, pyramid, Venn, or target diagram as well as over a dozen chart types including line, pie, and bar charts. All of these tools require practice before you can create effective graphics. Remember that graphics should be easy to understand without overloading your audience with unnecessary details or too much text. In fact, put such details in handouts rather than cluttering your slides with them.

5. **Add special effects.** To keep your audience focused on what you are discussing, use PowerPoint's **Custom Animation** feature to control when objects or text appear on the screen. Animate points in a bulleted list to appear one at a time, for example, or the boxes in a radial diagram to appear as each is discussed. Keep in mind that the first thing your audience sees on every slide should describe the slide's content. With motion paths and other animation options, you can move objects to different positions on the slide; or to minimize clutter, you can dim or remove them once they have served their purpose.

   In addition, as you move from slide to slide in a presentation, you can select transition effects, such as *wipe down*. The animation and transition options range from subtle to flashy—choose them with care so that the visual delivery of your presentation doesn't distract from the content of your message. An option at this step is to purchase a PowerPoint add-in product, such as Ovation, that can add professional-looking special effects to your presentation with very little effort.[15]

6. **Create hyperlinks to approximate the Web browsing experience.** Make your presentation more interactive and intriguing by connecting your PowerPoint presentation, via hyperlinks, to other sources that provide content that will enhance

For a powerful presentation, first write the text and then work on templates, font styles, and colors.

Learn to simplify complex information in visually appealing graphics.

Spotlight on Communicators

Novice speakers often speed up their delivery, perhaps out of nervousness or eagerness to sit down. Justice Sandra Day O'Connor, shortly after becoming the first woman on the Supreme Court, revealed a trick she uses when she has important words to speak: "I taught myself early on to speak very slowly—enunciating every word—when I wanted someone's undivided attention."

your presentation. You can hyperlink to (a) other slides within the presentation or in other PowerPoint files; (b) other programs that will open a second window that displays items such as spreadsheets, documents, or videos; and (c) if you have an Internet connection, Web sites.

Once you have finished discussing the hyperlinked source or watching the video that opened in a second window, you close that window and your hyperlinked PowerPoint slide is in view. In this way, you can break up the monotony of typical linear PowerPoint presentations. Instead, your hyperlinked show approximates the viewing experience of a Web user who enters a site through a main page or portal and then navigates at will to reach second- and third-level pages.

7. **Engage your audience by asking for interaction.** When audience response and feedback are needed, interactive tools are useful. Audience response systems may be familiar to you from game shows, but they are also used for surveys and opinion polls, group decision making, voting, quizzes and tests, and many other applications. To interact with your audience, present polling questions. Audience members submit their individual or team responses using handheld devices read by a PowerPoint add-in program. The audience immediately sees a bar chart that displays the response results.[16]

Internet options for slide presentations range from posting slides online to conducting a live Web conference with slides, narration, and speaker control.

8. **Move your presentation to the Internet.** You have a range of alternatives, from simple to complex, for moving your multimedia presentation to the Internet or your company's intranet. The simplest option is posting your slides online for others to access. Even if you are giving a face-to-face presentation, attendees appreciate these *electronic handouts* because they don't have to lug them home. The most complex option for moving your multimedia presentation to the Internet involves a Web conference or broadcast.

Web presentations with slides, narration, and speaker control have emerged as a way for anyone who has access to the Internet to attend your presentation without leaving the office. For example, you could initiate a meeting via a conference call, narrate using a telephone, and have participants see your slides from the browsers on their computers. If you prefer, you could skip the narration and provide a prerecorded presentation. Web-based presentations have many applications, including providing access to updated training or sales data whenever needed.[17]

Some businesses convert their PowerPoint presentations to PDF documents or send PowerPoint shows (file extension *.PPS), which open directly in **Slide Show View**, ready to run. Both types of documents are highly suitable for e-mailing. Among their advantages, they start immediately, can't be easily changed, and typically result in smaller, less memory-hogging files.

Polishing Your Delivery and Following Up

LEARNING OBJECTIVE 5
Specify delivery techniques for use before, during, and after a presentation, and apply reflective thinking skills.

Once you have organized your presentation and prepared visuals, you are ready to practice delivering it. You will feel more confident and appear more professional if you know more about various delivery methods and techniques to use before, during, and after your presentation.

Choosing a Delivery Method

Inexperienced speakers often feel that they must memorize an entire presentation to be effective. Unless you are an experienced performer, however, you will sound wooden and unnatural. What's more, forgetting your place can be disastrous! That is why we don't recommend memorizing an entire oral presentation. However, memorizing significant parts—the introduction, the conclusion, and perhaps a meaningful quotation—can be dramatic and impressive.

If memorizing your business presentation won't work, is reading from a manuscript the best plan? Definitely not! Reading to an audience is boring and ineffective. Because reading suggests that you don't know your topic very well, the audience loses confidence in your expertise. Reading also prevents you from maintaining eye contact. You can't see audience reactions; consequently, you can't benefit from feedback.

Neither memorizing nor reading creates very convincing business presentations. The best plan, by far, is to present *extemporaneously*, especially when you are displaying an electronic slideshow such as PowerPoint. Extemporaneous delivery means speaking freely, generally without notes, after preparation and rehearsing. It means that in your talk you comment on the electronic slideshow you have prepared and rehearsed several times. Remember, PowerPoint and other presentation software have replaced traditional outlines and notes. Reading notes or a manuscript in addition to PowerPoint slides will damage your credibility.

If you give a talk without PowerPoint, however, you may use note cards or an outline containing key sentences and major ideas, but beware of reading from a script. By preparing and then practicing with your notes, you can talk to your audience in a conversational manner. Your notes should be neither entire paragraphs nor single words. Instead, they should contain a complete sentence or two to introduce each major idea. Below the topic sentence(s), outline subpoints and illustrations. Note cards will keep you on track and prompt your memory, but only if you have rehearsed the presentation thoroughly.

> Extemporaneous delivery results in more convincing presentations than those that are memorized or read.

Combating Stage Fright

Nearly everyone experiences some degree of stage fright when speaking before a group. "If you hear someone say he or she isn't nervous before a speech, you're talking either to a liar or a very boring speaker," says corporate speech consultant Dianna Booher.[18] Being afraid is quite natural and results from actual physiological changes occurring in your body. Faced with a frightening situation, your body responds with the fight-or-flight response, discussed more fully in the Career Coach box on page 446. You can learn to control and reduce stage fright, as well as to incorporate techniques for effective speaking, by using the following strategies and techniques before, during, and after your presentation.

> Stage fright is both natural and controllable.

Before Your Presentation

Speaking in front of a group will become less daunting if you allow for adequate preparation, sufficient practice, and rehearsals. Interacting with the audience and limiting surprises such as malfunctioning equipment will also add to your peace of mind. Review the following tips for a smooth start:

- **Prepare thoroughly.** One of the most effective strategies for reducing stage fright is knowing your subject thoroughly. Research your topic diligently and prepare a careful sentence outline. Those who try to "wing it" usually suffer the worst butterflies—and make the worst presentations.

> Thorough preparation, extensive rehearsal, and stress-reduction techniques can lessen stage fright.

- **Rehearse repeatedly.** When you rehearse, practice your entire presentation, not just the first half. In PowerPoint you may print out speaker's notes, an outline, or a handout featuring miniature slides, which are excellent for practice. If you don't use an electronic slideshow, place your outline sentences on separate note cards. You may also wish to include transitional sentences to help you move to the next topic as you practice. Rehearse alone or before friends and family. Also try an audio or video recording of your rehearsals so that you can evaluate your effectiveness.

- **Time yourself.** Most audiences tend to get restless during longer talks. Thus, try to complete your presentation in no more than 20 minutes. Set a simple kitchen timer during your rehearsal to keep track of time. Better yet, PowerPoint offers a function called **Rehearse Timings** that can measure the length of your talk as you practice.

- **Check the room.** If you are using a computer, a projector, or sound equipment, be certain they are operational. Before you start, check electrical outlets and the position of the viewing screen. Ensure that the seating arrangement is appropriate to your needs.

Spotlight on Communicators

To give rhythm and punch to your presentations, says corporate speech consultant Dianna Booher, make ample use of these three techniques: *triads* ("we are one nation—black, white, brown"; "government of the people, by the people, and for the people": "you must have faith, hope, and charity"); *alliteration* ("we wish you health, happiness, and hope"); and *rhyme* ("American business must automate, emigrate, or evaporate").

CAREER COACH

How to Avoid Stage Fright

Ever get nervous before making a presentation? Everyone does! And it's not all in your head, either. When you face something threatening or challenging, your body reacts in what psychologists call the *fight-or-flight response*. This physical reflex provides your body with increased energy to deal with threatening situations. It also creates those sensations—dry mouth, sweaty hands, increased heartbeat, and stomach butterflies—that we associate with stage fright. The fight-or-flight response arouses your body for action—in this case, making a presentation.

Because everyone feels some form of apprehension before speaking, it's impossible to eliminate the physiological symptoms altogether. However, you can reduce their effects with the following techniques:

- **Breathe deeply.** Use deep breathing to ease your fight-or-flight symptoms. Inhale to a count of ten, hold this breath to a count of ten, and exhale to a count of ten. Concentrate on your counting and your breathing; both activities reduce your stress.
- **Convert your fear.** Don't view your sweaty palms and dry mouth as evidence of fear. Interpret them as symptoms of exuberance, excitement, and enthusiasm to share your ideas.
- **Know your topic and come prepared.** Feel confident about your topic. Select a topic that you know well and that is relevant to your audience. Test your equipment and arrive with time to spare.
- **Use positive self-talk.** Remind yourself that you know your topic and are prepared. Tell yourself that the audience is on your side—because it is! Moreover, most speakers appear to be more confident than they feel. Make this apparent confidence work for you.
- **Take a sip of water.** Drink some water to alleviate your dry mouth and constricted voice box, especially if you are talking for more than 15 minutes.
- **Shift the spotlight to your visuals.** At least some of the time the audience will be focusing on your slides, transparencies, handouts, or whatever you have prepared—and not totally on you.
- **Ignore any stumbles.** Don't apologize or confess your nervousness. If you keep going, the audience will forget any mistakes quickly.
- **Feel proud when you finish.** You will be surprised at how good you feel when you finish. Take pride in what you have accomplished, and your audience will reward you with applause and congratulations. Your body, of course, will call off the fight-or- flight response and return to normal!

Career Application

Interview someone in your field or in another business setting who must make oral presentations. How did he or she develop speaking skills? What advice can this person suggest to reduce stage fright? When you next make a class presentation, try some or all of the techniques described here and note which are most effective for you.

- **Greet members of the audience.** Try to make contact with a few members of the audience when you enter the room, while you are waiting to be introduced, or when you walk to the podium. Your body language should convey friendliness, confidence, and enjoyment.

- **Practice stress reduction.** If you feel tension and fear while you are waiting your turn to speak, use stress-reduction techniques, such as deep breathing. Additional techniques to help you conquer stage fright are presented in the accompanying Career Coach box.

During Your Presentation

To stay in control during your talk, to build credibility, and to engage your audience, follow these time-tested guidelines for effective speaking:

- **Begin with a pause.** When you first approach the audience, take a moment to make yourself comfortable. Establish your control of the situation.

- **Present your first sentence from memory.** By memorizing your opening, you can immediately establish rapport with the audience through eye contact. You will also sound confident and knowledgeable.

Eye contact, a moderate tone of voice, and natural movements enhance a presentation.

- **Maintain eye contact.** If the size of the audience overwhelms you, pick out two individuals on the right and two on the left. Talk directly to these people. Don't ignore listeners in the back of the room.

- **Control your voice and vocabulary.** This means speaking in moderated tones but loudly enough to be heard. Eliminate verbal static, such as *ah, er, you know,* and *um*. Silence is preferable to meaningless fillers when you are thinking of your next idea.

- **Skip the apologies.** Don't begin with a weak opening, such as *I won't take much time. I know you are busy.* OR: *I know you have heard this before, but we need to review it anyway.* OR: *I had trouble with my computer and the slides, so bear with me.* Unless the issue is blatant, such as loading all of your slides upside down, apologies are counterproductive. Focus on your presentation. Dynamic speakers never say they are sorry.

- **Incorporate pauses when appropriate.** Silence can be effective especially when you are transitioning from one point to another. Pauses are also effective in giving the audience time to absorb an important point.

- **Put the brakes on.** Many novice speakers talk too rapidly, displaying their nervousness and making it very difficult for audience members to understand their ideas. Slow down and listen to what you are saying.

- **Move naturally.** If you have a lectern, don't remain glued to it. Move about casually and naturally. Avoid fidgeting with your clothing, hair, or items in your pockets. Do not roll up your sleeves or put your hands in your pockets. Learn to use your body to express a point.

- **Use visual aids effectively.** You should discuss and interpret each visual aid for the audience. Move aside as you describe it so that it can be seen fully. Use a pointer if necessary, but steady your hand if it is shaking.

- **Avoid digressions.** Stick to your outline and notes. Don't suddenly include clever little anecdotes or digressions that occur to you on the spot. If it is not part of your rehearsed material, leave it out so that you can finish on time. Remember, too, that your audience may not be as enthralled with your topic as you are.

- **Summarize your main points and arrive at the high point of your talk.** Conclude your presentation by reiterating your main points or by emphasizing what you want the audience to think or do. Once you have announced your conclusion, proceed to it directly.

After Your Presentation

As you are concluding your presentation, handle questions and answers competently and provide handouts if appropriate. Try the following techniques:

- **Distribute handouts.** If you prepared handouts with data the audience will need, pass them out when you finish.

- **Encourage questions.** If the situation permits a question-and-answer period, announce it at the beginning of your presentation. Then, when you finish, ask for questions. Set a time limit for questions and answers.

- **Repeat questions.** Although the speaker may hear the question, audience members often do not. Begin each answer with a repetition of the question. This also gives you thinking time. Then, direct your answer to the entire audience.

- **Reinforce your main points.** You can use your answers to restate your primary ideas (*I'm glad you brought that up because it gives me a chance to elaborate on . . .*). In answering questions, avoid becoming defensive or debating the questioner.

- **Keep control.** Don't allow one individual to take over. Keep the entire audience involved.

- **Avoid *Yes, but* answers.** The word *but* immediately cancels any preceding message. Try replacing it with *and*. For example, *Yes, X has been tried. And Y works even better because. . . .*

- **End with a summary and appreciation.** To signal the end of the session before you take the last question, say something like, *We have time for just one more question.* As you answer the last question, try to work it into a summary of your main points. Then, express appreciation to the audience for the opportunity to talk with them.

> The time to answer questions, distribute handouts, and reiterate main points is after a presentation.

Organizing Team-Based Written and Oral Presentations

LEARNING OBJECTIVE 6
Organize team-based oral presentations and recognize communication tasks in teamwork processes.

Companies form teams for many reasons, as discussed in Chapter 2. The goal of some teams is an oral presentation to pitch a new product or to win a high-stakes contract. Before Apple CEO Steve Jobs and his team roll out one of their hotly anticipated new electronic gadgets, you can bet that team members spend months preparing so that his "stevenotes" presentation flows smoothly.

The goal of other teams is to investigate a problem and submit recommendations to decision makers in a report. At BMW, for example, nimble cross-functional teams excel at problem solving across divisions. Such teams speed innovation and the development of new products such as the electronics that now comprise about 20 percent of a new vehicle's value.[19]

The end product of any team effort is often (a) a written report; (b) a series of self-contained electronic slides, also called a slide *deck*; or (c) an oral presentation delivered live. The boundaries are becoming increasingly blurred between flat, two-dimensional hard-copy reports and multimedia, hyperlinked slideshows. Both hard-copy reports and multimedia presentations are delivered to clients in business today. This is why team writing and speaking appear side by side in this chapter.

Whether your team's project produces written reports, slide decks, or oral presentations, you generally have considerable control over how the project is organized and completed. If you have been part of any team efforts before, you also know that such projects can be very frustrating—particularly when some team members don't carry their weight or when members cannot resolve conflict. On the other hand, team projects can be harmonious and productive when members establish ground rules and follow guidelines related to preparing, planning, collecting information for, organizing, rehearsing, and evaluating team projects.

Preparing to Work Together

Before any group begins to talk about a specific project, members should get together and establish basic ground rules. One of the first tasks is naming a meeting leader to conduct meetings, a recorder to keep a record of group decisions, and an evaluator to determine whether the group is on target and meeting its goals. The group should decide whether it will be governed by consensus (everyone must agree), by majority rule, or by some other method.

The most successful teams make meetings a top priority. They compare schedules in order to set up the best meeting times, and they meet often. They avoid other responsibilities that might disrupt these meetings.

Teams must decide whether they will be governed by consensus, by majority rule, or by some other method.

When teams first organize, they should consider the value of conflict. By bringing conflict into the open and encouraging confrontation, teams can prevent personal resentment and group dysfunction. Confrontation can actually create better final products by promoting new ideas and avoiding groupthink. Conflict is most beneficial when team members can air their views fully. Another important topic to discuss during team formation is how to deal with team members who are not pulling their share of the load. Teams should decide whether they will "fire" members who are not contributing or take some other action in dealing with slackers.

Planning the Document or Presentation

Once teams have established ground rules, members are ready to discuss the target document or presentation. During these discussions, they must be sure to keep a record of all decisions. They should establish the specific purpose for the document or presentation and identify the main issues involved. They must decide on the final format. For a collaborative business report, they should determine what parts it will include, such as an executive summary, figures, and an appendix. They should consider how the report or presentation will be delivered—in person, online, or by e-mail. For a team oral presentation, they should decide on its parts, length, and graphics. For either written or oral projects, they should profile the audience and focus on the questions audience members would want answered.

If the report or presentation involves persuasion, they must decide what appeals would achieve the team's purpose.

Next the team should develop a work plan (see Chapter 11), assign jobs, and set deadlines. If time is short, members should work backward from the due date. For oral presentations, teams must schedule time for content and creative development as well as for a series of rehearsals. The best-planned presentations can fall apart if they are poorly rehearsed.

For oral presentations, all team members should have written assignments. These assignments should detail each member's specific responsibilities for researching content, producing visuals, developing handout materials, building transitions between segments, and showing up for rehearsals. For written reports, members must decide how the final document will be composed: individuals working separately on assigned portions, one person writing the first draft, the entire group writing the complete document together, or some other method.

In planning a team document or presentation, develop a work plan, assign jobs, and set deadlines.

Collecting Information

One of the most challenging jobs for team projects is generating and collecting information. Unless facts are accurate, the most beautiful report or the most high-powered presentation will fail. As you brainstorm ideas, consider cluster diagramming (see Figure 5.2 on page 128 in Chapter 5). Assign topics and decide who will be responsible for gathering what information. Establishing deadlines for collecting information is important if a team is to remain on schedule. Team members should also discuss ways to ensure the accuracy of the information collected.

Unless facts are accurate, reports and presentations will fail.

Organizing, Writing, and Revising

When a project progresses into the organizing and writing stages, a team may need to modify some of its earlier decisions. Team members may review the proposed organization of the final document or presentation and adjust it if necessary. In composing the first draft of a written report or presentation, team members will probably write separate segments. As they work on these segments, they should use the same version of word processing or presentation graphics program to facilitate combining files.

As individuals work on separate parts of a written report, the team should decide on one person (probably the best writer) to coordinate all the parts. The writer strives for a consistent style, format, and feel in the final product. For oral presentations, team members must try to make logical connections between segments. Each presenter builds a bridge to the next member's topic to create a smooth transition. Team members should also agree to use the same template, and they should allow only one person to make global changes in color, font, and other formatting on the slide and title masters.

For team presentations assign one person to coordinate all the parts and make the style consistent.

Editing, Rehearsing, and Evaluating

The last stage in a collaborative project involves editing, rehearsing, and evaluating. For a written report, one person should assume the task of merging the various files, running a spell checker, and examining the entire document for consistency of design, format, and vocabulary. That person is responsible for finding and correcting grammatical and mechanical errors. Then the entire group meets as a whole to evaluate the final document. Does it fulfill its purpose and meet the needs of the audience?

For oral presentations, one person should also merge all the files and be certain that they are consistent in design, format, and vocabulary. Teams making presentations should practice together several times. If that is not feasible, experts say that teams must schedule at least one full real-time rehearsal with the entire group.[20] Whenever possible, practice in a room that is similar to the location of your talk. Consider video recording one of the rehearsals so that each presenter can critique his or her own performance. Schedule a dress rehearsal with an audience at least two days before the actual presentation. Practice fielding questions.

Successful group documents emerge from thoughtful preparation, clear definition of contributors' roles, commitment to a group-approved plan, and a willingness to take responsibility for the final product. More information about writing business reports appeared in previous chapters of this book.

Communicating at Work Part 2

Walt Disney Imagineering

Jon Georges and a Walt Disney Imagineering design team worked intensively on a new creative concept for one of the world's most-visited theme parks, Tokyo Disneyland. However, the entire project would come to a screeching halt without a successful presentation before the owners of Tokyo Disneyland. The Imagineering team had to convince the assembled Japanese that new Winnie the Pooh feature attractions, as well as associated merchandise shops and a major restaurant, would be exciting and profitable additions to the existing theme park.

Understanding the audience and anticipating its reaction were integral parts of Jon's preparation for a presentation. For the Tokyo Disneyland project, Jon and the Imagineering team wanted to present their concepts in broad terms to see whether the financiers liked the total idea. Jon, however, also knew that this audience would be detail oriented. "Japanese businessmen tend to want particulars—like the color of the concrete, the number of restrooms, and the exact location where visitors would exit an attraction."

Other adaptations Jon made for the Tokyo presentation involved choice of language and presentation style. Carefully avoiding Disney and design jargon, he consciously used common words and simple sentences, which the translator had little trouble converting to Japanese. In making his presentation, Jon kept in mind three important elements: organization, visuals, and focus. Although he had thousands of details in mind, he forced himself to keep his presentation logical and simple. He concentrated on one powerful point: convincing his Japanese

© Yoshikazu Tsuno / Staff / AFP / Getty Images

listeners that the new attractions would enhance the value of Tokyo Disneyland and would draw more visitors through the turnstiles.

Critical Thinking
- What questions should Jon Georges have asked himself in anticipating the audience for the Tokyo Disneyland presentation?
- Why is simplicity important in an oral presentation, and why was it particularly important for the Tokyo Disneyland presentation?
- Why are visual aids critical for both local and international audiences?

Adapting Presentations to International and Cross-Cultural Audiences

LEARNING OBJECTIVE 7
Explain effective techniques for adapting oral presentations to cross-cultural audiences, and demonstrate multicultural and diversity understanding.

Every good speaker adapts to the audience, and cross-cultural presentations call for special adjustments and sensitivity. For his presentation in Tokyo, Jon Georges spoke slowly, chose simple English, avoided jargon and clichés, used short sentences, and paused frequently.

Beyond these basic language adaptations, however, more fundamental sensitivity is often necessary. In organizing a presentation for a cross-cultural audience, you may need to anticipate and adapt to different speaking conventions, values, and nonverbal behavior. You may also need to contend with limited language skills and a certain reluctance to voice opinions openly.

Understanding Different Values and Nonverbal Behavior

Addressing cross-cultural audiences requires a speaker to consider audience expectations and cultural conventions.

In addressing cross-cultural audiences, anticipate expectations and perceptions that may differ significantly from what you may consider normal. Remember, for example, that the North American emphasis of getting to the point quickly is not equally prized across the globe. Therefore, think twice about delivering your main idea up front. Many people (notably those in Japanese, Latin American, and Arabic cultures) consider such directness to be brash and inappropriate. Remember that others may not share our cultural emphasis on straightforwardness.[21]

When working with an interpreter or speaking before individuals whose English is limited, you must be very careful about your language. For example, you will need to express ideas in small chunks to give the interpreter time to translate. You may need to slow down as you speak and stop after each thought to allow time for the translation that will follow. Even if your presentation or speech is being translated simultaneously, remember to speak slowly and to pause after each sentence to ensure that your message is rendered correctly in the target language.

The same advice is useful in organizing presentations. Consider breaking your presentation into short, discrete segments. In Japan, Jon Georges divided his talk into three distinct topics: theme park attractions, merchandise shops, and food services. He developed each topic separately, encouraging discussion periods after each. Such organization enables participants to ask questions and digest what has been presented. This technique is especially effective in cultures where people communicate in "loops." In the Middle East, for example, Arab speakers "mix circuitous, irrelevant (by American standards) conversations with short dashes of information that go directly to the point." Presenters who are patient, tolerant, and "mature" (in the eyes of the audience) will make the sale or win the contract.[22]

Match your presentation and your nonverbal messages to the expectations of your audience. In Germany, for instance, successful presentations tend to be dense with facts and precise statistics. Americans might say "around 30 percent" while a German presenter might say "30.4271 percent." Similarly, constant smiling is not as valued in Europe as it is in North America. Many Europeans distrust a speaker who is cracking jokes, smiling, or laughing in a business presentation. Their expectation is of a rational—that is, "serious"—fact-based delivery. American-style enthusiasm is often interpreted abroad as hyperbolic exaggeration or, worse, as dishonesty and can lead to misunderstandings. If an American says "Great job!" to offer praise, a Spanish counterpart might believe the American has approved the project. "When Europeans realize there's no commitment implied," warned an intercultural consultant, "they might feel deceived or that the American is being superficial."[23]

Remember, too, that some cultures prefer greater formality than Americans exercise. Instead of first names, use only honorifics (*Mr.* or *Ms.*) and last names, as well as academic or business titles—such as *Doctor* or *Director*. Writing on a flipchart or transparency seems natural and spontaneous in this country. Abroad, though, such informal techniques may suggest that the speaker does not value the audience enough to prepare proper visual aids in advance.[24]

Adjusting Visual Aids to International and Multicultural Audiences

Although you may have to exercise greater caution with culturally diverse audiences, you will still want to use visual aids to help communicate your message. Find out from your international contact whether you can present in English or if you will need an interpreter. In many countries listeners are too polite to speak up when they don't understand you. One expert advises explaining important concepts in several ways using different words and then requesting members of the audience to relay their understanding of what you have just said back to you. Another expert suggests packing more text on PowerPoint slides and staying closer to its literal meaning. After all, most nonnative speakers of English understand written text much better than they comprehend spoken English. In the United States presenters may spend 90 seconds on a slide, whereas in other countries they may need to slow down to two minutes per slide.[25]

To ensure clarity and show courtesy, provide handouts in English and the target language. Never use numbers without projecting or writing them out for all to see. If possible, say numbers in both languages, but only if you can pronounce or even speak the target language well enough to avoid embarrassment. Distribute translated handouts, summarizing your important information, when you finish.

Whether you are speaking to familiar or cross-cultural audiences, your presentation requires attention to content and strategy. The checklist on page 452 summarizes suggestions for preparing, organizing, and illustrating oral presentations.

Improving Telephone and Voice Mail Skills

One form of business presentation involves presenting yourself on the telephone, a skill that is still very important in today's workplace. Despite the heavy reliance on e-mail, the telephone remains an extremely important piece of equipment in offices. With the addition of today's wireless technology, it doesn't matter whether you are in or out of the office. You can always be reached by phone. This section focuses on traditional telephone techniques and voice mail—both opportunities for making a good impression. As a business communicator, you can be more productive, efficient, and professional by following some simple suggestions.

Ethics Check

The Robot Presenter
In one of your courses, you are witnessing a PowerPoint presentation, during which it becomes obvious that the speaker has completely memorized her talk. However, she stumbles badly a few times, struggling to remember her lines. Worse yet, you perceive her accent as nearly impenetrable. How should the instructor and the class handle the evaluation of such a presentation?

LEARNING OBJECTIVE 8
List techniques for improving telephone and voice mail skills to project a positive image.

Checklist

Preparing and Organizing Oral Presentations

Getting Ready to Speak

✓ **Identify your purpose.** Decide what you want your audience to believe, remember, or do when you finish. Aim all parts of your talk toward this purpose.

✓ **Analyze the audience.** Consider how to adapt your message (its organization, appeals, and examples) to your audience's knowledge and needs.

Organizing the Introduction

✓ **Get the audience involved.** Capture the audience's attention by opening with a promise, story, startling fact, question, quote, relevant problem, or self-effacing joke.

✓ **Establish yourself.** Demonstrate your credibility by identifying your position, expertise, knowledge, or qualifications.

✓ **Preview your main points.** Introduce your topic and summarize its principal parts.

Organizing the Body

✓ **Develop two to four main points.** Streamline your topic so that you can concentrate on its major issues.

✓ **Arrange the points logically.** Sequence your points chronologically, from most important to least important, by comparison and contrast, or by some other strategy.

✓ **Prepare transitions.** Between each major point write "bridge" statements that connect the previous item to the next one. Use transitional expressions as verbal signposts (*first, second, then, however, consequently, on the contrary,* and so forth).

✓ **Have extra material ready.** Be prepared with more information and visuals in case you have additional time to fill.

Organizing the Conclusion

✓ **Review your main points.** Emphasize your main ideas in your closing so that your audience will remember them.

✓ **Provide a strong, final focus.** Tell how your listeners can use this information, why you have spoken, or what you want them to do. As the culmination of your talk, end with a specific audience benefit or thought-provoking final thought (a "take-away"), not just a lame rehash.

Designing Visual Aids

✓ **Select your medium carefully.** Consider the pros and cons of each alternative.

✓ **Highlight main ideas.** Use visual aids to illustrate major concepts only. Keep them brief and simple.

✓ **Try to replace bullets whenever possible.** Use flowcharts, diagrams, time lines, and so forth, to substitute for bulleted lists when suitable.

✓ **Use aids skillfully.** Talk to the audience, not to the visuals. Paraphrase their contents.

Developing Multimedia Presentations

✓ **Learn to use your software program.** Study template and slide layout designs to see how you can adapt them to your purposes.

✓ **Select colors based on the light level in the room.** Consider how mixing light and dark fonts and backgrounds affects their visibility. Use templates and preset slide layouts if you are new to PowerPoint.

✓ **Use bulleted points for major ideas.** Make sure your points are all parallel, and observe the 6-x-6 rule.

✓ **Include multimedia options that will help you convey your message.** Use moderate animation features and hyperlinks to make your talk more interesting and to link to files with related content in the same document, in other documents, or on the Internet.

✓ **Make speaker's notes.** Jot down the narrative supporting each slide and use these notes to practice your presentation. Do not read from notes while speaking to an audience, however.

✓ **Maintain control.** Don't let your slides upstage you. Engage your audience by using additional techniques to help them visualize your points.

Making Telephone Calls Efficiently

Making productive telephone calls means planning an agenda, identifying the purpose, being courteous and cheerful, and avoiding rambling.

Before making a telephone call, decide whether the intended call is really necessary. Could you find the information yourself? If you wait a while, will the problem resolve itself? Perhaps your message could be delivered more efficiently by some other means. Some companies have found that telephone calls are often less important than the work they interrupt. Alternatives to telephone calls include instant messaging, e-mail, memos, or calls to automated voice mail systems. If you must make a telephone call, consider using the following suggestions to make it fully productive.

- **Plan a mini-agenda.** Have you ever been embarrassed when you had to make a second telephone call because you forgot an important item the first time? Before placing a call, jot down notes regarding all the topics you need to discuss. Following an agenda guarantees not only a complete call but also a quick one. You will be less likely to wander from the business at hand while rummaging through your mind trying to remember everything.

- **Use a three-point introduction.** When placing a call, immediately (a) name the person you are calling, (b) identify yourself and your affiliation, and (c) give a brief explanation of your reason for calling. For example: *May I speak to Larry Lopez? This is Hillary Dahl of Sebastian Enterprises, and I'm seeking information about a software program called Power Presentations.* This kind of introduction enables the receiving individual to respond immediately without asking further questions.

- **Be brisk if you are rushed.** For business calls when your time is limited, avoid questions such as *How are you?* Instead, say, *Lisa, I knew you would be the only one who could answer these two questions for me.* Another efficient strategy is to set a "contract" with the caller: *Look, Lisa, I have only ten minutes, but I really wanted to get back to you.*

In making telephone calls, plan a mini agenda, use a three-point introduction, and be brisk if you have little time.

- **Be cheerful and accurate.** Let your voice show the same kind of animation that you radiate when you greet people in person. In your mind try to envision the individual answering the telephone. A smile can certainly affect the tone of your voice, so smile at that person. Keep your voice and throat relaxed by keeping your head straight. Don't squeeze the phone between your shoulder and your ear. Obviously, don't eat food or chew gum while on the phone. Moreover, be accurate about what you say. *Hang on a second; I will be right back* rarely is true. It is better to say, *It may take me two or three minutes to get that information. Would you prefer to hold or have me call you back?*

- **Bring it to a close.** The responsibility for ending a call lies with the caller. This is sometimes difficult to do if the other person rambles on. You may need to use suggestive closing language, such as the following: (a) *I have certainly enjoyed talking with you;* (b) *I have learned what I needed to know, and now I can proceed with my work;* (c) *Thanks for your help;* (d) *I must go now, but may I call you again in the future if I need . . . ?* or (e) *Should we talk again in a few weeks?*

- **Avoid telephone tag.** If you call someone who is not in, ask when it would be best for you to call again. State that you will call at a specific time—and do it. If you ask a person to call you, give a time when you can be reached—and then be sure you are in at that time.

- **Leave complete voice mail messages.** Remember that there is no rush when you leave a voice mail message. Always enunciate clearly and speak slowly when giving your telephone number or spelling your name. Be sure to provide a complete message, including your name, telephone number, and the time and date of your call. Explain your purpose so that the receiver can be ready with the required information when returning your call.

Receiving Telephone Calls Professionally

With a little forethought you can project a professional image and make your telephone a productive, efficient work tool. Developing good telephone manners and techniques will also reflect well on you and on your organization.

- **Identify yourself immediately.** In answering your telephone or someone else's, provide your name, title or affiliation, and, possibly, a greeting. For example, *Larry Lopez, Proteus Software. How may I help you?* Force yourself to speak clearly and slowly. Remember that the caller may be unfamiliar with what you are saying and fail to recognize slurred syllables.

- **Be responsive and helpful.** If you are in a support role, be sympathetic to callers' needs. Instead of *I don't know,* try *That's a good question; let me investigate.* Instead of *We can't do that,* try *That's a tough one; let's see what we can do.* Avoid *No* at the beginning

Receiving productive telephone calls means identifying oneself, acting responsive, being helpful, and taking accurate messages.

of a sentence. It sounds especially abrasive and displeasing because it suggests total rejection.

- **Practice telephone confidentiality.** When answering calls for others, be courteous and helpful, but don't give out confidential information. Better to say, *She's away from her desk* or *He's out of the office* than to report a colleague's exact whereabouts. Also, be tight-lipped about sharing company information with strangers. Security experts insist that employees answering telephones must become guardians of company information.[26]

- **Take messages carefully.** Few things are as frustrating as receiving a potentially important phone message that is illegible. Repeat the spelling of names and verify telephone numbers. Write messages legibly and record their time and date. Promise to give the messages to intended recipients, but don't guarantee return calls.

- **Explain what you are doing when transferring calls.** Give a reason for transferring, and indicate the extension to which you are directing the call in case the caller is disconnected.

Making the Best Use of Voice Mail

Because telephone calls can be disruptive, many businesspeople are making extensive use of voice mail to intercept and screen incoming calls. Voice mail links a telephone system to a computer that digitizes and stores incoming messages. Some systems also provide functions such as automated attendant menus, allowing callers to reach any associated extension by pushing specific buttons.

Voice mail is quite efficient for message storage. Because as many as half of all business calls require no discussion or feedback, the messaging capabilities of voice mail can mean huge savings for businesses. Incoming information is delivered without interrupting potential receivers and without all the niceties that most two-way conversations require. Stripped of superfluous chitchat, voice mail messages allow communicators to focus on essentials. Voice mail also eliminates telephone tag, inaccurate message taking, and time zone barriers.

However, voice mail should not be overused. Individuals who screen all incoming calls cause irritation, resentment, and needless telephone tag. Here are some ways to make voice mail work most effectively for you:

- **Announce your voice mail.** If you rely principally on a voice mail message system, identify it on your business stationery and cards. Then, when people call, they will be ready to leave a message.

- **Prepare a warm and informative greeting.** Make your mechanical greeting sound warm and inviting, both in tone and content. Identify yourself and your organization so that callers know they have reached the right number. Thank the caller and briefly explain that you are unavailable. Invite the caller to leave a message or, if appropriate, call back. Here's a typical voice mail greeting: *Hi! This is Larry Lopez of Proteus Software, and I appreciate your call. You have reached my voice mailbox because I'm either working with customers or talking on another line at the moment. Please leave your name, number, and reason for calling so that I can be prepared when I return your call.* Give callers an idea of when you will be available, such as, *I will be back at 2:30,* or, *I will be out of my office until Wednesday, May 20.* If you screen your calls as a time-management technique, try this message: *I'm not near my phone right now, but I should be able to return calls after 3:30.*

- **Test your message.** Call your number and assess your message. Does it sound inviting? Sincere? Understandable? Are you pleased with your tone? If not, says one consultant, have someone else, perhaps a professional, record a message for you.

This chapter has provided valuable tips for preparing and delivering first-rate oral presentations. You have also learned effective techniques for adapting oral presentations to cross-cultural audiences. Finally, we illustrated techniques for improving telephone and voice mail skills. All of these techniques and tips can help you be a successful business communicator in an increasingly challenging workplace.

Communicating at Work Your Turn

Applying Your Skills at Walt Disney Imagineering

When he was a lead show producer at Walt Disney Imagineering, Jon Georges developed new ideas for theme park attractions. He and other members of Imagineering teams were constantly doing research to gather ideas for new projects or for fleshing out current ideas. Staff members also kept track of what others were doing in the area of themed environments. How are other parks attracting big crowds? What's happening in Las Vegas? What kinds of new themed restaurants are opening—and closing? Imagineering teams "benchmark" (compare) their efforts against those of similar developers of entertainment concepts.

Your Task

Jon Georges asks you and other Imagineering interns to research and locate one or two current theme park innovations or trends.

Prepare an outline of your findings. Then use the outline as the basis for creating a PowerPoint presentation that you will use to inform Jon of your findings.

Summary of Learning Objectives

1 Discuss two important first steps in preparing effective oral presentations. First, identify what your purpose is and what you want the audience to believe or do so that you can aim the entire presentation toward your goal. Second, know your audience so that you can adjust your message and style to its knowledge and needs.

2 Explain the major elements in organizing the content of a presentation, including the introduction, body, and conclusion. The introduction of a good presentation should capture the listener's attention, identify the speaker, establish credibility, and preview the main points. The body should discuss two to four main points, with appropriate explanations, details, and verbal signposts to guide listeners. The conclusion should review the main points, provide a final focus or take-away, and allow the speaker to leave the podium gracefully.

3 Identify techniques for gaining audience rapport, including (a) using effective imagery, (b) providing verbal signposts, and (c) sending appropriate nonverbal messages. You can improve audience rapport by using effective imagery including analogies, metaphors, similes, personal anecdotes, statistics, and worst-case/best-case scenarios. Rapport is also gained by including verbal signposts that tell the audience when you are previewing, summarizing, and switching directions. Nonverbal messages have a powerful effect on the way your message is received. You should look terrific, animate your body, punctuate your words, get out from behind the podium, and vary your facial expressions.

4 Discuss designing visual aids, handouts, and multimedia presentation materials and using presentation technology competently. Use simple, easily understood visual aids to emphasize and clarify main points. Choose multimedia slides, transparencies, flipcharts, or other visuals. Generally, it is best to distribute handouts after a presentation. Speakers employing a program such as PowerPoint use templates, layout designs, and bullet points to produce effective slides. A presentation may be enhanced with slide transitions, hyperlinks, sound, animation, video elements, and other multimedia effects. Speaker's notes and handouts may be generated from slides. Web-based presentations allow speakers to narrate and show slides without leaving their home bases. Increasing numbers of speakers are using the Internet to e-mail or post their slides as electronic shows or report deliverables instead of generating paper copies.

5 Specify delivery techniques for use before, during, and after a presentation, and apply reflective thinking skills. Before your talk, prepare a sentence outline on note cards or speaker's notes and rehearse repeatedly. Check the room, lectern, and equipment. During the presentation, consider beginning with a pause and presenting your first sentence from memory. Speak freely, extemporaneously, commenting on your slides but using no other notes. Make eye contact, control your voice, speak and move naturally, and avoid digressions. After your talk, distribute handouts and answer questions. End gracefully and express appreciation.

6 Organize team-based oral presentations and recognize communication tasks in teamwork processes. In preparing to work together, teams should name a leader and decide how they will make decisions (by consensus, majority rule, or some other method). They should work out a schedule, discuss the benefits of conflict, and determine how they will deal with members who fail to pull their share. They should decide on the purpose, form, and procedures for preparing the final document or presentation. They must brainstorm ideas, assign topics, and establish deadlines. In composing the first draft of a report or presentation, they should use the same software version and meet to discuss the drafts and rehearsals. For written reports, one person should probably compose the final draft, and the group should evaluate it. For group presentations, team members need to work for consistency of design, format, and wording. Several rehearsals, one of which should be videotaped, will enhance the final presentation.

7 Explain effective techniques for adapting oral presentations to cross-cultural audiences, and demonstrate multicultural and diversity understanding. In presentations before groups whose English is limited, speak slowly, use simple English, avoid jargon and clichés, and opt for short sentences. Pause often to allow an interpreter to keep up with you. Consider building up to your main idea rather than announcing it immediately. Also consider breaking the presentation into short segments to allow participants to ask questions and digest small parts separately. Beware of appearing too spontaneous and informal. Use visual aids to help communicate your message, but also distribute translated handouts summarizing the most important information.

8 List techniques for improving telephone and voice mail skills to project a positive image. You can improve your telephone calls by planning a mini-agenda and using a three-point introduction (name, affiliation, and purpose). Be cheerful and responsive, and use closing language to end a conversation. Avoid telephone tag by leaving complete messages. In answering calls, identify yourself immediately, avoid giving out confidential information when answering for others, and take careful messages. For your own message prepare a warm and informative greeting. Tell when you will be available. Evaluate your message by calling it yourself.

Chapter Review

1. Why is it important to know your audience and purpose before you start planning your oral presentation? (Obj. 1)

2. In preparing an oral presentation, you can reduce your fears and lay a foundation for a professional performance by focusing on what five areas? (Obj. 1)

3. In the introduction of an oral presentation, you can establish your credibility by using what two methods? (Obj. 2)

4. Which part of a speech—the introduction, body, or conclusion—will listeners most remember? (Obj. 2)

5. List six techniques for creating effective imagery in a presentation. Be prepared to discuss each. (Obj. 3)

6. Name three ways for a speaker to use verbal signposts in a presentation. Illustrate each. (Obj. 3)

7. Why are visual aids particularly useful to inexperienced speakers? (Obj. 4)

8. Why are transparencies a favorite visual aid? (Obj. 4)

9. Name specific advantages and disadvantages of multimedia presentation software. (Obj. 4)

10. How is the 6-x-6 rule applied in preparing bulleted points? (Obj. 4)

11. What delivery method is most effective for speakers? (Obj. 5)

12. Why should speakers deliver the first sentence from memory? (Obj. 5)

13. Which five issues should be resolved before a team can collaborate productively? (Obj. 6)

14. How might presentations before international or cross-cultural audiences be altered to be most effective? (Obj. 7)

15. How can you avoid telephone tag? (Obj. 8)

Critical Thinking

1. What is extemporaneous speaking, and what makes it the best delivery method for business presentations? (Obj. 5)

2. How can a speaker make the most effective use of visual aids? (Obj. 4)

3. How can speakers prevent multimedia presentation software from stealing their thunder? (Obj. 4)

4. Discuss effective techniques for reducing stage fright. (Obj. 5)

5. **Ethical Issue:** Critics of PowerPoint claim that flashy graphics, sound effects, and animation often conceal thin content.

Consider, for example, the findings regarding the space shuttle *Challenger* accident that killed seven astronauts. Report authors charged that NASA scientists had used PowerPoint presentations to make it look as though they had done analyses that they hadn't. Overreliance on presentations instead of analysis may have contributed to the shuttle disaster.[27] What lessons about ethical responsibilities when using PowerPoint can be learned from this catastrophe in communication? (Objs. 1, 2, and 4)

Activities

14.1 Critiquing a Speech (Objs. 1–4)

Your Task. Search online or your library for a speech that was delivered by a significant businessperson or a well-known political figure. Write a memo report to your instructor critiquing the speech in terms of the following:

a. Effectiveness of the introduction, body, and conclusion

b. Evidence of effective overall organization

c. Use of verbal signposts to create coherence

d. Emphasis of two to four main points

e. Effectiveness of supporting facts (use of examples, statistics, quotations, and so forth)

14.2 Knowing Your Audience (Objs. 1–2)

Your Task. Select a recent issue of *Fortune, Fast Company, BusinessWeek,* or another business periodical approved by your instructor. Based on an analysis of your classmates, select an article that will appeal to them and that you can relate to their needs. Submit to your instructor a one-page summary that includes: (a) the author, article title, source, issue date, and page reference; (b) a one-paragraph article summary; (c) a description of why you believe the article will appeal to your classmates; and (d) a summary of how you can relate the article to their needs.

14.3 Overcoming Stage Fright (Obj. 5)

> Team

What makes you most nervous when making a presentation before class? Being afraid of becoming tongue-tied? Having all eyes on you? Messing up? Forgetting your ideas and looking silly?

Your Task. Discuss the previous questions as a class. Then, in groups of three or four talk about ways to overcome these fears. Your instructor may ask you to write a memo (individually or collectively) summarizing your suggestions, or you may break out of your small groups and report your best ideas to the entire class.

14.4 Investigating Oral Communication in Your Field (Objs. 1, 5)

Your Task. Interview one or two individuals in your professional field. How is oral communication important in this profession? Does the need for oral skills change as one advances? What suggestions can these people make to newcomers to the field for developing proficient oral communication skills? Discuss your findings with your class.

14.5 Outlining an Oral Presentation (Objs. 1, 2)

One of the hardest parts of preparing an oral presentation is developing the outline.

Your Task. Select an oral presentation topic from the list in **Activity 14.10**, or suggest an original topic. Prepare an outline for your presentation using the following format:

Title

Purpose

               I. INTRODUCTION

State your name   A.

Gain attention and involve audience   B.

Establish credibility   C.

Preview main points   D.

Transition

               II. BODY

Main point   A.

Illustrate, clarify, contrast   1.

               2.

               3.

Transition

Main point   B.

Illustrate, clarify, contrast   1.

               2.

               3.

Transition

Main point   C.

Illustrate, clarify, contrast   1.

               2.

               3.

Transition

               III. CONCLUSION

Summarize main points   A.

Provide final focus or "take-away"   B.

Encourage questions   C.

14.6. Creating an Oral Presentation: Outline Your Job Duties (Objs. 1–4)

What if you had to create a presentation for your classmates and instructor, or perhaps a potential recruiter, that describes the multiple tasks you perform at work? Could you do it in a five-minute PowerPoint presentation?

Your instructor, for example, may wear many hats. Most academics (a) teach; (b) conduct research to publish; and (c) provide service to the department, college, university, and community. Can you see how those aspects of their profession lend themselves to an outline of primary slides (teaching, publishing, service) and second-level slides (instructing undergraduate and graduate classes, presenting workshops, and giving lectures under the *teaching* label)?

Your Task. Now it's your turn to introduce the duties of a current position or a past job, volunteer activity, or internship in a brief, simple, yet well-designed PowerPoint presentation. Your goal is to inform your audience of your job duties in a three- to five-minute talk. Use animation features and graphics where appropriate. Your instructor may show you a completed example of this project.*

14.7 Self-Contained Multimedia Activity: Creating a PowerPoint Presentation (No additional research required) (Objs. 2, 3)

You are a consultant who has been hired to improve the effectiveness of corporate trainers. These trainers frequently make presentations to employees on topics such as conflict management, teamwork, time management, problem solving, performance appraisals, and employment interviewing. Your goal is to teach these trainers how to make better presentations.

Your Task. Create six visually appealing slides.* Base the slides on the following content, which will be spoken during the presentation titled "Effective Employee Training." The comments shown here are only a portion of a longer presentation.

Trainers have two options when they make presentations. The first option is to use one-way communication: the trainer basically dumps the information on the employees and leaves. The second option is to use a two-way audience involvement approach. The two-way approach can accomplish many purposes, such as connecting with employees, reinforcing key points, increasing employees' retention rates, changing the pace, and adding variety. The two-way approach also encourages employees to get to know each other better. Because today's employees demand more than just a "talking head," trainers must engage their audiences by involving them in a two-way dialogue.

When you include interactivity in your training sessions, choose approaches that suit your delivery style. Also, think about which options your employees would be likely to respond to most positively. Let's consider some interactivity approaches now. Realize, though, that these ideas are presented to help you get your creative juices flowing. After I present the list, we will think about situations in which these options might be effective. We will also brainstorm to come up with creative ideas we can add to this list.

- Ask employees to guess at statistics before revealing them.
- Ask an employee to share examples or experiences.

- Ask a volunteer to help you demonstrate something.
- Ask the audience to complete a questionnaire or worksheet.
- Ask the audience to brainstorm or list something as fast as possible.
- Ask a variety of question types to achieve different purposes.
- Invite the audience to work through a process or examine an object.
- Survey the audience.
- Pause to let the audience members read something to themselves.
- Divide the audience into small groups to discuss an issue.

14.8 Improving the Design and Content of PowerPoint Slides (Objs. 2, 3)

Your Task. Identify ways to improve the design and content of the three slides presented in Figure 14.9. Classify your comments under the following categories: (a) color choices, (b) font choice including style and point size, (c) 6-x-6 rule, (d) listings in parallel grammatical form, (e) consistent capitalization and punctuation, and (f) graphics and images. Identify what needs to be improved and exactly how you would improve it. For example, if you identify category (d) as an area needing improvement, your answer would include a revision of the listing. When you finish, your instructor may show you a revised set of slides.*

14.9 Researching *Fortune* List Information (Objs. 1–5)

Web

Your Task. Using an electronic database, perform a search to learn how *Fortune* magazine determines which companies make its annual lists. Research the following lists. Then organize and present a five- to ten-minute informative talk to your class.

a. Fortune 500
b. Global 500
c. 100 Best Companies to Work For
d. America's Most Admired Companies
e. Global Most Admired Companies

14.10 Choosing a Topic for an Oral Presentation (Objs. 1–6)

Team

Your Task. Select a topic from the following list or from the report topics at the ends of Chapters 11 and 12. For an expanded list of report topics, go to **www.meguffey.com**. Individually or as

*See the Instructor's Manual and the Instructor's Resource CD.

FIGURE 14.9 PowerPoint Slides Needing Revision

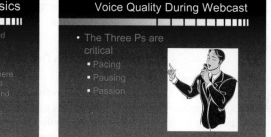

Interactive Learning @ www.meguffey.com

a team, prepare a five - to ten-minute oral presentation. Consider yourself an expert or a team of experts called in to explain some aspect of the topic before a group of interested people. Because your time is limited, prepare a concise yet forceful presentation with effective visual aids.

If this is a group presentation, form a team of three or four members and conduct thorough research on one of the following topics, as directed by your instructor. Follow the tips on team presentations in this chapter. Divide the tasks fairly, meet for discussions and rehearsals, and crown your achievement with a 15- to 20-minute presentation to your class. Make your PowerPoint presentation interesting and dynamic.

a. What are the top five career opportunities for your college major? Consider job growth, compensation, and benefits. What kind of academic and other experience is typically required to apply for each?

b. What information and tools are available at Web job banks to college students searching for full-time employment after graduation? Consider Monster.com and other job banks.

c. How can attendance be improved in a minor sports field (your choice) at your school?

d. What simple computer security tips can your company employ to avoid problems?

e. What is telecommuting, and for what kind of workers is it an appropriate work alternative?

f. What criteria should parents use in deciding whether their young children should attend parochial, private, public, or home school?

g. What travel location would you recommend for college students at Christmas or another holiday or in summer?

h. What is the economic outlook for a given product, such as domestic cars, laptop computers, digital cameras, fitness equipment, or a product of your choice?

i. How can your organization or institution improve its image?

j. What are the Webby Awards, and what criteria do the judges use to evaluate Web sites?

k. What brand and model of computer and printer represent the best buy for college students today?

l. What franchise would offer the best investment opportunity for an entrepreneur in your area?

m. How should a job candidate dress for an interview?

n. What should a guide to proper cell phone use include?

o. Are internships worth the effort?

p. What risks are involved for companies without written rules for e-mail and instant messaging?

q. Where should your organization hold its next convention?

r. What is your opinion of the statement "Advertising steals our time, defaces the landscape, and degrades the dignity of public institutions"?[28]

s. What would you need to know if you were deciding whether to go to the next Olympics?

t. What is the outlook for real estate (commercial or residential) investment in your area?

u. What are the pros and cons of videoconferencing for [name an organization]?

v. What do the personal assistants for celebrities do, and how does one become a personal assistant? (Investigate the Association of Celebrity Personal Assistants.)

w. Can a small or midsized company reduce its telephone costs by using Internet phone service?

x. What scams are on the Federal Trade Commission's List of Top 10 Consumer Scams, and how can consumers avoid falling for them?

y. How are businesses and conservationists working together to protect the world's dwindling tropical forests?

z. Should employees be allowed to use computers in a work environment for anything other than work-related business?

14.11 Consumer: Will Maxing Out My Credit Cards Improve My Credit Rating? (Objs. 1, 2)

Consumer   Web

The program chair for the campus business club has asked you to present a talk to the group about consumer credit. He saw a newspaper article saying that only 10 percent of Americans know their credit scores. Many consumers, including students, have dangerous misconceptions about their scores. Not knowing your score could result in a denial of credit as well as difficulty obtaining needed services and even a job.

Your Task. Using electronic databases and the Web, learn more about credit scores and typical misconceptions. For example, is a higher or lower credit score better? Can you improve your credit score by marrying well? If you earn more money, will you improve your score? If you have a low score, is it impossible to raise it? Can you raise your score by maxing out all your credit cards? (One survey reported that 28 percent of consumers believed the latter statement was true!) Prepare an oral presentation appropriate for a student audience. Conclude with appropriate recommendations.

14.12 Improving Telephone Skills by Role-Playing (Obj. 8)

Your Task. Your instructor will divide the class into pairs. For each scenario take a moment to read and rehearse your role silently. Then play the role with your partner. If time permits, repeat the scenarios, changing roles.

Partner 1

a. You are the personnel manager of Datatronics, Inc. Call Elizabeth Franklin, office manager at Computers Plus. Inquire about a job applicant, Chelsea Chavez, who listed Ms. Franklin as a reference. Respond to Partner 2.

b. Call Ms. Franklin again the following day to inquire about the same job applicant, Chelsea Chavez. Ms. Franklin answers today, but she talks on and on, describing the applicant in great detail. Tactfully close the conversation.

Partner 2

a. You are the receptionist for Computers Plus. The caller asks for Elizabeth Franklin, who is home sick today. You don't know when she will be able to return. Answer the call appropriately.

b. You are now Ms. Franklin, office manager. Describe Chelsea Chavez, an imaginary employee. Think of someone with whom you have worked. Include many details, such as her ability to work with others, her appearance, her skills at computing, her schooling, her ambition, and so forth.

c. You are now the receptionist for Tom Wing, of Wing Imports. Answer a call for Mr. Wing, who is working in another office, at Extension 134, where he will accept calls.

d. You are now Tom Wing, owner of Wing Imports. Call your attorney, Michael Murphy, about a legal problem. Leave a brief, incomplete message.

e. Call Mr. Murphy again. Leave a message that will prevent telephone tag.

c. You are now an administrative assistant for attorney Michael Murphy. Call Tom Wing to verify a meeting date Mr. Murphy has with Mr. Wing. Use your own name in identifying yourself.

d. You are now the receptionist for attorney Michael Murphy. Mr. Murphy is skiing in Aspen and will return in two days, but he doesn't want his clients to know where he is. Take a message.

e. Take a message again.

14.13 Presenting Yourself Professionally on the Telephone and in Voice Mail (Obj. 8)

Practice the phone skills you learned in this chapter. Leave your instructor a professional voice mail message. Prepare a mini-agenda before you call. Introduce yourself. If necessary, spell your name and indicate the course and section. Speak slowly and clearly, especially when leaving your phone number. Think of a comment you could make about an intriguing fact, peer discussion, or your business writing class.

Video Resources

Video Library 1
Effective On-the-Job Oral Presentations
Watch this video to see how businesspeople apply the 3-x-3 writing process in developing a persuasive oral presentation.

Grammar and Mechanics C.L.U.E. Review 14

Total Review

Each of the following sentences has a total of **three** errors in grammar, punctuation, capitalization, usage, or spelling. On a separate sheet, write a correct version. Avoid adding new phrases, starting new sentences, or rewriting in your own words. When finished, compare your responses with the key beginning on page Key-3.

Example: We worried that a list of all our customers names and addresses were all ready released.

Revision: We worried that a list of all our **customers'** names and addresses **was already** released.

1. Even though he was President of the company Mr. Rivera dreaded the 3 presentations he made every year.

2. The companys CPA asked me to explain the principle ways we planned to finance the thirty year mortgage.

3. My team is greatful to be able to give a twenty minute presentation, however, we can emphasize only three or four points.

4. The introduction to a presentation should accomplish three goals, (1) Capture attention, (2) establish credibility, and (c) preview main points.

5. Travis wondered whether focusing on what the audience is to remember, and summarizing main points was equally important?

6. Most novice speakers talk to rapid, however, they can learn to speak more slowly, and listen to what they are saying.

7. A list of suggestions for improving retention of a speakers ideas are found in the article titled "How To Improve Your Listening Skills."

8. The appearance and mannerisms of a speaker definately effects a listeners evaluation of the message.

9. The president of Genesis Enterprises along with other executives of local companies, are promoting overseas' sales.

10. In a poll of three thousand workers only one third felt that there companies valued their opinions.

Interactive Learning @ www.meguffey.com

Unit 5

Employment Communication

Chapter 15
The Job Search,
Résumés, and
Cover Letters

Chapter 16
Interviewing and
Following Up

Chapter 15

The Job Search, Résumés, and Cover Letters

© Photodisc / Getty Images

OBJECTIVES

After studying this chapter, you should be able to

1. Prepare for employment by identifying your interests, evaluating your assets, recognizing the changing nature of jobs, and choosing a career path.

2. Apply both electronic and traditional techniques in a successful job search.

3. Appreciate the need to customize your résumé and know whether to choose a chronological or a functional résumé style.

4. Organize your qualifications and information into effective résumé segments.

5. Describe techniques that optimize a résumé for today's technologies, including preparing a scannable résumé, a plain-text résumé, and an e-portfolio.

6. Write a customized cover letter to accompany a résumé.

Communicating at Work Part 1

Workplace Expert Liz Ryan Shares Job-Search Tips

Job candidates should not spend more than one hour a day trolling for jobs online, says workplace expert Liz Ryan. A former Fortune 500 human resources executive and an expert on the post-millennium workplace, Liz Ryan is recognized as a leader in contemporary job searching. She maintains several blogs, contributes articles to online forums, delivers international keynote speeches, and is a regular columnist for *BusinessWeek Online*.

The Internet has made job searching easier, acknowledges Ryan, but it also can sidetrack candidates who devote all their energies to online searching to the exclusion of other methods that could help them. What job seekers forget, she contends, is that they are vying with hundreds and possibly thousands of other candidates who also saw the same online postings. Instead of spending all their time at online job boards, job candidates should develop their own personal network of friends and acquaintances.[1] As many as 80 percent of jobs are filled through networking. "I believe," says Ryan, "that any new grad can, with sufficient thought, create a list of 100 people that he or she can contact for help, advice, and job leads."[2] Ryan declares that there will never again be as natural an opportunity to ask everyone you know for help.

A résumé, Ryan says, contains two kinds of information. One is facts, including your name, degrees, and experience (companies you worked for, job titles, dates, and so forth). The rest of your résumé is "editorial." If you say you are "proficient in Spanish," you should expect to be able to verify this assertion during your interview. What's more, all of your recommenders should be able to confirm your editorial statements.

For both kinds of information, don't fib or exaggerate. Ryan warns against giving yourself extra credits to gain a degree or saying that you worked full-time when it was a contract or part-time job.

Don't claim a higher title than you actually had. "You know what's bad?" she says. "It's bad to get a job offer, accept it, sign the offer letter, show up on our first day, and get pulled out of New Employee Orientation and dragged into HR to be told you're fired, when you haven't even seen your desk yet. I've seen that happen about six times. It's the worst. Don't fib on your résumé."[3]

Critical Thinking

- Why is searching for a job both exhilarating and intimidating? How can one overcome the feelings of intimidation?
- Is it easier to search for a job by registering at a big job board or by networking? Which method do you think is more successful?
- Do you think companies actually check all the facts in résumés of candidates they interview?

http://www.asklizryan.com

Preparing for Employment

The Internet has definitely changed the way we look for jobs today. As workplace expert Liz Ryan pointed out in the opening case study, the Internet has made job searching easier but also more challenging. Because hundreds and perhaps thousands of candidates may be applying for an advertised position, you must do everything possible to be noticed and to outshine the competition. You must also look beyond the Internet.

The better prepared you are, the more confident you will feel during your search. This chapter provides expert advice in preparing for employment, searching the job market, writing a customized résumé, and developing an effective cover letter. What you learn here can lead to a successful job search and maybe even your dream job.

You may think that the first step in finding a job is writing a résumé. Wrong! The job-search process actually begins long before you are ready to prepare your résumé. Regardless of the kind of employment you seek, you must invest time and effort getting ready. You can't hope to find the position of your dreams without (a) knowing yourself, (b) knowing the job market, and (c) knowing the employment process.

One of the first things you should do is obtain career information and choose a job objective. At the same time, you should be studying the job market and becoming aware of significant changes in the workplace and hiring techniques. You will want to understand how to use the latest Web resources in your job search. Finally, you will need to design a résumé and cover letter that can be customized for small businesses as well as for larger organizations that may be using résumé-scanning programs. Following these steps, summarized in Figure 15.1 and described in this chapter, gives you a master plan for landing a job you really want.

LEARNING OBJECTIVE 1
Prepare for employment by identifying your interests, evaluating your assets, recognizing the changing nature of jobs, and choosing a career path.

Finding a satisfying career requires learning about yourself, the job market, and the employment process.

FIGURE 15.1 The Employment Search

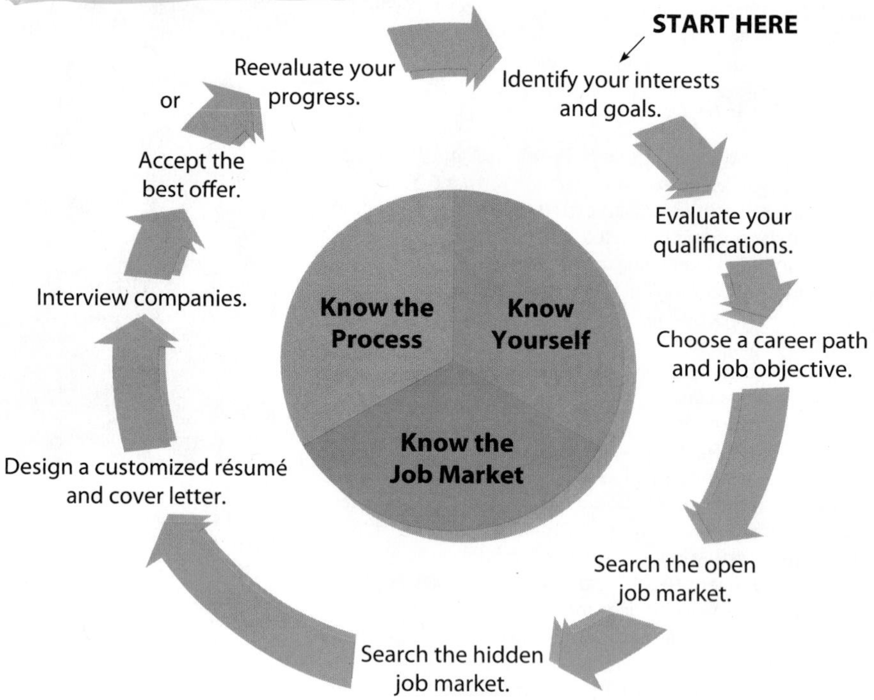

START HERE

Identify your interests and goals.

Evaluate your qualifications.

Choose a career path and job objective.

Search the open job market.

Search the hidden job market.

Design a customized résumé and cover letter.

Interview companies.

Accept the best offer.

or

Reevaluate your progress.

Know the Process

Know Yourself

Know the Job Market

Identifying Your Interests

The employment process begins with introspection. This means looking inside yourself to analyze what you like and dislike so that you can make good employment choices. Career counselors charge large sums for helping individuals learn about themselves. You can do the same kind of self-examination—without spending a dime. For guidance in choosing a field that eventually proves to be satisfying, answer the following questions. If you have already chosen a field, think carefully about how your answers relate to that choice.

> Answer specific questions to help yourself choose a career.

- *Do you enjoy working with people, data, or things?*

- *Would you like to work for someone else or be your own boss?*

- *How important are salary, benefits, technology support, and job stability?*

- *How important are working environment, colleagues, and job stimulation?*

- *Would you rather work for a large or small company?*

- *Must you work in a specific city, geographical area, or climate?*

- *Are you looking for security, travel opportunities, money, power, or prestige?*

- *How would you describe the perfect job, boss, and coworkers?*

Evaluating Your Qualifications

> Decide what qualifications you possess and how you can prove them.

In addition to your interests, assess your qualifications. Employers today want to know what assets you have to offer them. Your responses to the following questions will target your thinking as well as prepare a foundation for your résumé. Remember, though, that employers seek more than empty assurances; they will want proof of your qualifications.

- *What technology skills can you offer?* Employers are often interested in specific software programs.

- *What other skills have you acquired in school, on the job, or through activities?* How can you demonstrate these skills?

- *Do you work well with people? Do you enjoy teamwork?* What proof can you offer? Consider extracurricular activities, clubs, class projects, and jobs.

- *Are you a leader, self-starter, or manager?* What evidence can you offer?

- *Do you speak, write, or understand another language?*

- *Do you learn quickly? Are you creative?* How can you demonstrate these characteristics?

- *Do you communicate well in speech and in writing?* How can you verify these talents?

Recognizing the Changing Nature of Jobs

As you learned in Chapter 1, the nature of the workplace is changing. One of the most significant changes involves the concept of the "job." Following the downsizing of corporations and the outsourcing of jobs in recent years, companies are employing fewer people in permanent positions.

Other forms of employment are replacing traditional jobs. In many companies teams complete special projects and then disband. Work may also be outsourced to a group that's not even part of the organization. Because new technologies can spring up overnight making today's skills obsolete, employers are less willing to hire people into jobs with narrow descriptions. Instead, they are hiring contingency employees who work temporarily and then leave. What's more, big companies are no longer the main employers. People work for smaller companies, or they are starting their own businesses. By 2020 small, privately owned companies are expected to comprise 25 percent of U.S. businesses.[4]

What do these changes mean for you? For one thing, you should probably forget about a lifelong career with a single company. Don't count on regular pay raises, promotions, and a comfortable retirement income. You should also become keenly aware that a career that relies on yesterday's skills is headed for trouble. You are going to need updated, marketable skills that serve you well as you move from job to job. Upgrading your skills and retraining yourself constantly are the best career strategies for the twenty-first century. People who learn quickly and adapt to change will always be in demand even in a climate of surging change.[5]

> People feel less of a sense of job security after downsizing and outsourcing of jobs.

> Jobs are becoming more flexible and less permanent.

Choosing a Career Path

The job picture in the United States is extraordinarily dynamic and flexible. On average, workers between ages 18 and 38 in the United States will have ten different employers, and job tenure averages 6.6 years.[6] Although you may be frequently changing jobs in the future (especially before you reach forty), you still need to train for a specific career area now. In choosing an area, you will make the best decisions when you can match your interests and qualifications with the requirements and rewards in specific careers. Where can you find the best career data? Here are some suggestions:

> Career information can be obtained from campus career centers and libraries, the Internet, classified ads, and professional organizations.

- **Visit your campus career center.** Most have literature, inventories, software programs, and Internet connections that allow you to investigate such fields as accounting, finance, office technology, information systems, hotel management, and so forth. Some have well-trained job counselors who can tailor their resources to your needs. They may also offer job-skills seminars, career days with visiting companies, and mock interviews.

- **Search the Web.** Job-search sites frequently offer career-planning information and resources. One of the best career sites is the Riley Guide (**http://www.rileyguide.com**).

- **Use your library.** Print and online resources in your library are especially helpful. Consult *O*NET Occupational Information Network, Dictionary of Occupational Titles,*

Occupational Outlook Handbook, and *The Jobs Rated Almanac* for information about career duties, qualifications, salaries, and employment trends.

Summer jobs, part-time jobs, and internships are good opportunities to learn about various careers.

- **Take a summer job, internship, or part-time position in your field.** Nothing is better than trying out a career by actually working in it or an allied area. Many companies offer internships and temporary jobs to begin training college students and to develop relationships with them. These relationships sometimes blossom into permanent positions.

- **Interview someone in your chosen field.** People are usually flattered when asked to describe their careers. Inquire about needed skills, required courses, financial and other rewards, benefits, working conditions, future trends, and entry requirements.

- **Volunteer with a nonprofit organization.** Many colleges and universities encourage service learning opportunities. In volunteering their services, students gain valuable experience and nonprofits appreciate the expertise and fresh ideas that students bring.

- **Monitor the classified ads.** Early in your college career, begin monitoring want ads and Web sites of companies in your career area. Check job availability, qualifications sought, duties, and salary range. Don't wait until you are about to graduate to see how the job market looks.

- **Join professional organizations in your field.** Frequently, professional groups offer student membership status and reduced rates. You will receive inside information on issues, career news, and possibly jobs.

Conducting a Successful Job Search

LEARNING OBJECTIVE 2
Apply both electronic and traditional techniques in a successful job search.

Searching for a job today is vastly different as a result of the Internet. Just ten years ago, a job seeker browsed the local classified ads, found a likely sounding job listing, prepared an elegant résumé on bond paper, and sent it out by U.S. mail. All that has changed with the advent of the Internet. The challenge today is realizing how to use the Internet to your advantage. Like other smart job seekers, you can combine both electronic and traditional job-search tactics to land the job of your dreams.

Searching for a Job Electronically

Job boards list many jobs, but finding a job requires more work than merely clicking a mouse.

Searching for a job electronically has become a common, but not always fruitful, approach. With all the publicity given to Internet job boards, you might think that electronic job searching has totally replaced traditional methods. Not so! Although Web sites such as *CollegeRecruiter.com,* and *Yahoo HotJobs.com,* shown in Figure 15.2, list millions of jobs, actually landing a job is much harder than just clicking a mouse.

Both recruiters and job seekers complain about job boards. Corporate recruiters say that the big job boards bring a flood of candidates, many of whom are not suited for the listed jobs. Job candidates grumble that listings are frequently outdated and fail to produce leads. Applicants worry about the privacy of information posted at big boards. Most important, studies have shown that the percentage of hires resulting from job boards is astonishingly low—1.4 percent at *Monster.com,* 0.39 percent at *HotJobs.com,* and 0.27 percent at *CareerBuilder.com.*[7] As workplace expert Liz Ryan says in the opening case study, don't count on finding a job by devoting all your energy to searching online job boards.

The best-known job boards provide job-search, résumé, interviewing, and salary tips.

Despite these gloomy prospects, many job seekers use job boards to gather job-search information, such as résumé, interviewing, and salary tips. Job boards also serve as a jumping-off point in most searches. They can inform you about the kinds of jobs that are available and the skill sets required. With over 40,000 job boards and employment Web sites deluging the Internet, it's hard to know where to start. We have listed a few of the best-known online job sites here:[8]

- **CareerBuilder (http://www.careerbuilder.com)** claims to be the nation's largest employment network. At this writing it lists 1.5 million jobs with over 250,000 client companies posting jobs.

FIGURE 15.2 Job Boards Jump Start a Job Search

Commercial job boards list millions of job openings and also provide excellent tips for conducting job searches, writing résumés, organizing cover letters, and preparing for job interviews.

Source: College Recruiter image courtesy of Collegerecruiter.com. Yahoo image reproduced with permission of Yahoo! Inc. © 2007. YAHOO! and the Yahoo! logo are trademarks of Yahoo Inc.

- **Monster Board (http://www.monster.com)** offers access to information on more than 1.1 million jobs worldwide with 275,000 client companies posting jobs. You may search for jobs by category, city, or nation. Many consider it to be the Web's premier job site.

- **College Recruiter (http://www.collegerecruiter.com)** claims to be the "highest traffic entry-level job site" for students and graduates. It lists over 250,000 jobs from more than 12,500 client companies.

- **CareerJournal (http://www.careerjournal.com)** lists over 125,000 executive positions from 4,468 companies.

- **Yahoo HotJobs (http://www.hotjobs.com)** lists over 150,000 job openings.[9] It says that job seekers voted it the "Best General Purpose Job Board for Job Seekers."

Beyond the Big Job Boards. Disillusioned job seekers may turn their backs on job boards but not on electronic job-searching tactics. Savvy candidates know how to use their computers to search for jobs at Web sites such as the following:

- **Corporate Web sites.** Probably the best way to find a job online is at a company's own Web site. One poll found that 70 percent of job seekers felt they were more likely to obtain an interview if they posted their résumés on corporate sites. In addition to finding a more direct route to decision makers, job seekers thought that they could keep their job searches more private than at big board sites.[10]

- **Association Web sites.** Online job listings have proved to be the single-most popular feature of many professional organizations such as the National Association of Sales Professionals, the Association for Financial Professionals, and the American Chemical

> Job prospects may be more promising at the Web sites of corporations, professional organizations, employers' organizations, and niche fields.

Society. Although you pay a fee, the benefits of joining a professional association in your career field are enormous.

- **DirectEmployers.com.** Several hundred companies now use *DirectEmployers.com* as a gateway to job listings at their own Web sites. This search engine combs over 1,100 corporate sites and links job seekers directly to them, thus bypassing the big commercial job boards. You can enter a job description or job title, and a list of openings pops up. When you click one, you are taken straight to the company's Web site, where you can apply.

- **Niche Web sites.** If you want a job in a specialized field, look for a niche Web site, such as *HealthCareerWeb.com, CareerWomen.com, SixFigureJobs.com,* and so on.

Thousands of job boards listing millions of jobs now flood the Internet. The harsh reality, however, is that landing a job still depends largely on personal contacts. One employment expert said, "Online recruiting is a little like computer dating. People may find dates that way, but they don't get married that way."[11] Another professional placement expert said, "If you think just [posting] your résumé will get you a job, you are crazy. [Electronic services are] just a supplement to a core strategy of networking your buns off."[12] Summing up, a recruiting executive said, "Technology can only bring you so far. At the end of the day, it's about a one-to-one relationship."[13]

Searching for a Job Using Traditional Techniques

Finding the perfect job requires an early start and a determined effort. A recent research study of college graduates revealed that those with proactive personalities were the most successful in securing interviews and jobs. Successful candidates were not passive; they were driven to "make things happen."[14]

Whether you use traditional or online job-search techniques, you should be prepared to launch an aggressive campaign—and you can't start too early. Some universities now require first- and second-year students to take an employment seminar called "Reality 101." Students are told early on that a college degree alone doesn't guarantee a job. They are cautioned that grade-point averages make a difference to employers.[15] They are advised of the importance of experience, such as internships. Traditional job-search techniques, such as those described here, continue to be critical in landing jobs.

- **Check classified ads in local and national newspapers.** Be aware, though, that classified ads are only one small source of jobs, as discussed in the accompanying Career Coach box.

- **Check announcements in publications of professional organizations.** If you do not have a student membership, ask your instructors to share current copies of professional journals, newsletters, and so on. Your college library is another good source.

- **Contact companies in which you are interested, even if you know of no current opening.** Write an unsolicited letter and include your résumé. Follow up with a telephone call. Check the company's Web site for employment possibilities and procedures.

- **Sign up for campus interviews with visiting company representatives.** Campus recruiters may open your eyes to exciting jobs and locations.

- **Attend career fairs.** A recent DirectEmployers Association survey showed that, although career fairs were not the first contact for a candidate, employers considered them important opportunities to meet job seekers.[16]

- **Ask for advice from your instructors.** Your teachers often have contacts and ideas for expanding your job search.

- **Develop your own network of contacts.** Networking still accounts for most of the jobs found by candidates. Therefore, plan to spend a considerable portion of your job-search time developing a personal network. The accompanying Career Coach box gives you advice for traditional networking as well as suggestions for online networking.

Many jobs are posted on the Internet, but most hiring is still done through personal contact.

The most successful job seekers are those who launch aggressive, proactive campaigns.

CAREER COACH

Network Your Way to a Job in the Hidden Market

The "hidden" job market accounts for as many as 75 percent of all positions available.[17] Companies do not always announce openings publicly because interviewing all the applicants, many of whom aren't qualified, is time consuming. What's more, even when a job is advertised, companies dislike hiring "strangers." The key to finding a good job, then, is converting yourself from a "stranger" into a known quantity through networking. You can use either traditional methods or online resources.

TRADITIONAL NETWORKING

- **Develop a list.** Make a list of anyone who would be willing to talk with you about finding a job. List your friends, relatives, former employers, former coworkers, members of your church, people in social and athletic clubs, present and former teachers, neighbors, and friends of your parents. Also consider asking your campus career center for alumni contacts who will talk with students.
- **Make contacts.** Call the people on your list or, even better, try to meet with them in person. To set up a meeting, say, *Hi, Aunt Martha! I'm looking for a job, and I wonder if you could help me out. When could I come over to talk about it?* During your visit be friendly, well organized, polite, and interested in what your contact has to say. Provide a copy of your résumé, and try to keep the conversation centered on your job-search area. Your goal is to get two or more referrals. In pinpointing your request, ask, *Do you know of anyone who might have an opening for a person with my skills?* If the person does not ask, *Do you know of anyone else who might know of someone who would?*
- **Follow up on your referrals.** Call the people whose names are on your referral list. You might say something like, *Hello. I'm Eric Rivera, a friend of Meredith Medcalf. She suggested that I call and ask you for help. I'm looking for a position as a marketing trainee, and she thought you might be willing to spare a few minutes and steer me in the right direction.* Don't ask for a job. During your referral interview ask how the individual got started in this line of work, what he or she likes best (or least) about the work, what career paths exist in the field, and what problems must be overcome by a newcomer. Most important, ask how a person with your background and skills might get started in the field. Send an informal thank-you note to anyone who helps you in

your job search, and stay in touch with the most promising contacts. Ask whether you may call every three weeks or so during your job search.

ONLINE NETWORKING

- **Join a career networking group.** Build your own professional network by joining one or more of the following: http://www.linkedin.com/, http://www.ryze.com, or http://zerodegrees.com/. Some of these sites are fee based, whereas others are free. Typically, joining a network requires creating a password, filling in your profile, and adding your business contacts. Once you connect with an individual, the content of your discussions and the follow-up is similar to that of traditional networking.
- **Participate in a discussion group or mailing list.** Two especially good discussion group resources for beginners are Yahoo Groups (http://groups.yahoo.com) and Google Groups (http://groups.google.com/). You may choose from groups in a variety of fields including business and computer technology.
- **Locate a relevant blog.** Blogs are the latest trend for networking and sharing information. A quick Web search reveals hundreds of career-related blogs and blogs in your field of study. Many companies, such as Microsoft, also maintain employment-related blogs. A good list of career-related blogs can be found at http://www.quintcareers.com/career-related_blogs.html. You can also search a worldwide blog directory at http://www.blogcatalog.com/. Once you locate a relevant blog, you can read recent postings, search archives, and reply to postings.

Career Application

Begin developing your network. Conduct at least one referral interview or join one online networking group. Record the results you experienced and the information you learned from the networking option you chose. Report to the class your reactions and findings.

Creating a Customized Résumé

After using both traditional and online resources to learn about the employment market and to develop job leads, you will focus on writing a customized résumé. This means you will prepare a special résumé for every position you want. The competition is so stiff today that you cannot get by with a generic, all-purpose résumé. Although you can start with a basic résumé, you should customize it to fit each company and position if you want your resume to stand out from the crowd. Include many keywords that describe the skills, traits, tasks, and job titles associated with your targeted job. You will learn more about keywords shortly.

The Internet has made it so easy to apply that recruiters are swamped with applications. As a job seeker, you have about five seconds to catch the recruiter's eye—if your résumé is even read by a person. Many companies use computer scanning technologies to weed out unqualified candidates.[18] Your goal is to make your résumé fit the targeted position and

LEARNING OBJECTIVE 3
Appreciate the need to customize your résumé and know whether to choose a chronological or a functional résumé style.

stand out. Such a résumé does more than merely list your qualifications. It packages your assets into a convincing advertisement that sells you for a specific job.

The goal of a résumé is winning an interview. Even if you are not in the job market at this moment, preparing a résumé now has advantages. Having a current résumé makes you look well organized and professional should an unexpected employment opportunity arise. Moreover, preparing a résumé early can help you recognize weak areas and give you time to bolster them. Even after you have accepted a position, it's a good idea to keep your résumé up-to-date. You never know when an opportunity might come along!

Winning an interview is the goal of a customized résumé.

Choosing a Résumé Style

Résumés usually fall into two categories: chronological and functional. In this section we present basic information as well as insider tips on how to choose an appropriate résumé style, how to determine its length, and how to arrange its parts. You will also learn about adding a summary of qualifications, which busy recruiters increasingly want to see. Models of the résumés in the following discussion are shown in our comprehensive résumé section beginning on page 477.

See our comprehensive collection of résumé models and styles beginning on page 477.

Chronological. The most popular résumé format is the chronological résumé, shown in Figures 15.6 through 15.10 in our résumé collection. It lists work history job by job, starting with the most recent position. Recruiters favor the chronological format because such résumés quickly reveal a candidate's education and experience record. Recruiters are familiar with the chronological résumé, and as many as 85 percent of employers prefer to see a candidate's résumé in this format.[19] The chronological style works well for candidates who have experience in their field of employment and for those who show steady career growth, but it is less appropriate for people who have changed jobs frequently or who have gaps in their employment records. For college students and others who lack extensive experience, the functional résumé format may be preferable.

Chronological résumés focus on job history with the most recent positions listed first.

Functional. The functional résumé, shown in Figure 15.10 on page 481, focuses on a candidate's skills rather than on past employment. Like a chronological résumé, the functional résumé begins with the candidate's name, address, telephone number, job objective, and education. Instead of listing jobs, though, the functional résumé groups skills and accomplishments in special categories, such as *Supervisory and Management Skills* or *Retailing and Marketing Experience*. This résumé style highlights accomplishments and can de-emphasize a negative employment history. People who have changed jobs frequently, who have gaps in their employment records, or who are entering an entirely different field may prefer the functional résumé. Recent graduates with little or no related employment experience often find the functional résumé useful. Older job seekers who want to downplay a long job history and job hunters who are afraid of appearing overqualified may also prefer the functional format. Be aware, though, that online job boards may insist on the chronological format. In addition, some recruiters are suspicious of functional résumés, thinking the candidate is hiding something.

Because functional résumés focus on skills, they may be more advisable for graduates with little experience.

Deciding on Length

Experts simply do not agree on how long a résumé should be. Conventional wisdom has always held that recruiters prefer one-page résumés. A carefully controlled study of 570 recruiters, however, revealed that they *claimed* they preferred one-page résumés. However, the recruiters actually *chose* to interview the applicants with two-page résumés.[20] Recruiters who are serious about candidates often prefer a full picture with the kind of details that can be provided in a two-page résumé. On the other hand, recruiters are said to be extremely busy and prefer concise résumés.

Perhaps the best advice is to make your résumé as long as needed to sell your skills to recruiters and hiring managers. Individuals with more experience will naturally have longer résumés. Those with fewer than ten years of experience, those making a major career change, and those who have had only one or two employers will likely have one-page résumés. Those with ten years or more of related experience may have two-page résumés. Finally, some senior-level managers and executives with a lengthy history of major accomplishments might have résumés that are three pages or longer.[21]

Recruiters may say they prefer one-page résumés, but many choose to interview candidates with longer résumés.

Chapter 15: The Job Search, Résumés, and Cover Letters

Organizing Your Information Into Effective Résumé Categories

LEARNING OBJECTIVE 4
Organize your qualifications and information into effective résumé segments.

Although résumés have standard categories, their arrangement and content should be strategically planned. A customized résumé emphasizes skills and achievements aimed at a particular job or company. It shows a candidate's most important qualifications first, and it de-emphasizes any weaknesses. In organizing your qualifications and information, try to create as few headings as possible; more than six generally looks cluttered. No two résumés are ever exactly alike, but most writers consider including all or some of these categories: main heading, career objective, summary of qualifications, education, experience, capabilities and skills, awards and activities, personal information, and references.

Main Heading

Your résumé, whether it is chronological or functional, should always begin with your name; add your middle initial for an even more professional look. Following your name, list your contact information, including your complete address, area code and phone number, and e-mail address. If possible, include a telephone number where messages may be left for you. The outgoing message at this number should be in your voice, it should mention your full name, and it should be concise and professional. Keep the main heading as uncluttered and simple as possible. Format your name so that it stands out on the page. Don't include the word *résumé* in your main heading. It's like putting the word *letter* above correspondence.

For your e-mail address, be sure it sounds professional instead of something like *toosexy4you@hotmail.com* or *sixpackguy@yahoo.com*. Also be sure that you are using a personal e-mail address. Putting your work e-mail address on your résumé announces to prospective employers that you are using your current employer's resources to look for another job.

Career Objective

Opinion is divided about the effect of including a career objective on a résumé. Recruiters think such statements indicate that a candidate has made a commitment to a career and is sure about what he or she wants to do. Career objectives, of course, make the recruiter's life easier by quickly classifying the résumé. Such declarations, however, can also disqualify a candidate if the stated objective doesn't match a company's job description.[22] A well-written objective—customized for the job opening—can add value to either a chronological or a functional résumé.

A person applying for an auditor position might include the following objective: *Seeking an auditor position in an internal corporate accounting department where my accounting skills, computer experience, knowledge of GAAP, and attention to detail will help the company run efficiently and ensure that its records are kept accurately.*

Also be careful that your career objective doesn't downplay your talents. For example, some consultants warn against using the words *entry-level* in your objective, as these words emphasize lack of experience or show poor self-confidence. If you choose to omit the career objective, be sure to discuss your objectives and goals in your cover letter. Savvy job seekers are also incorporating their objectives into a summary of qualifications, which is discussed next.

> Career objectives are most appropriate for specific, targeted positions; they may limit a broader job search.

> A summary of qualifications section lists your most impressive accomplishments and qualifications in one concise bulleted list.

Summary of Qualifications

"The biggest change in résumés over the last decade has been a switch from an objective to a summary at the top," says career expert Wendy Enelow.[23] Recruiters are busy, and smart job seekers add a summary of qualifications to their résumés to save the time of recruiters and hiring managers. Once a job is advertised, a hiring manager may get hundreds or even thousands of résumés in response. A summary at the top of your résumé makes it easier to read and ensures that your most impressive qualifications are not overlooked by a recruiter, who skims résumés quickly. A well-written summary motivates the recruiter to read further.

Spotlight on Communicators

In her many authoritative books, revered résumé guru Yana Parker strongly advocated lean and focused résumés. Skip the clutter of overly precise dates by listing only years, she said. Short periods of unemployment need not be explained, but longer periods should be accounted for in a positive statement telling what you were doing. "Remember," she advised, "that a résumé is a marketing piece, not an historical document or a confessional." She suggested including a specific job objective, perhaps even a job title. Then, recruiters would not have to guess what you're looking for.

© Courtesy of Yana Parkar

A summary of qualifications should include three to eight bulleted statements that prove you are the ideal candidate for the position. When formulating these statements, consider your experience in the field, your education, your unique skills, awards you have won, certifications, and any other accomplishments that you want to highlight. Include numbers wherever possible. Target the most important qualifications an employer will be looking for in the person hired for this position. Examples of summaries of qualifications appear in Figures 15.6, 15.7, 15.8, 15.9, and 15.11 in the résumé models found in our collection.

Education

The education section shows degrees and GPA but does not list all courses a job applicant has taken.

The next component in a chronological résumé is your education—if it is more noteworthy than your work experience. In this section you should include the name and location of schools, dates of attendance, major fields of study, and degrees received. By the way, once you have attended college, you don't need to list high school information on your résumé. Your grade-point average and/or class ranking may be important to prospective employers. One way to enhance your GPA is to calculate it in your major courses only (for example, *3.6/4.0 in major*). It is not unethical to showcase your GPA in your major—as long as you clearly indicate what you are doing. If your GPA is low, you might choose to omit it. Remember, however, that many employers will assume your GPA is lower than a 3.0 if you omit it.[24]

Under *Education* you might be tempted to list all the courses you took, but such a list makes for very dull reading. Refer to courses only if you can relate them to the position sought. When relevant, include certificates earned, seminars attended, workshops completed, and honors earned. If your education is incomplete, include such statements as *BS degree expected 6/11* or *80 units completed in 120-unit program*. Title this section *Education, Academic Preparation*, or *Professional Training*. If you are preparing a functional résumé, you will probably put the education section below your skills summaries, as Kevin Touhy has done in Figure 15.10.

Work Experience or Employment History

The work experience section of a résumé should list specifics and quantify achievements.

When your work experience is significant and relevant to the position sought, this information should appear before education. List your most recent employment first and work backward, including only those jobs that you think will help you win the targeted position. A job application form may demand a full employment history, but your résumé may be selective. Be aware, though, that time gaps in your employment history will probably be questioned in the interview. For each position show the following:

- Employer's name, city, and state
- Dates of employment (month and year)

Résumés should always be accurate, never misleading or inflated. The consequences of falsifying personal information were illustrated dramatically when the prestigious Massachusetts Institute of Technology (MIT) dismissed former Dean of Admissions Marilee Jones for having fabricated academic degrees from Rensselaer Polytechnic Institute and elsewhere on her résumé. Jones, who had been an outspoken opponent of inflated résumés by teens, said she lacked the courage to correct her résumé throughout her 28 years at MIT. What is the right way to portray limited education on résumés?

© NEAL HAMBERG / Bloomberg News / Landov

- Most important job title

- Significant duties, activities, accomplishments, and promotions

Describe your employment achievements concisely but concretely. Avoid generalities such as *Worked with customers*. Be more specific, with statements such as *Served 40 or more retail customers a day; Successfully resolved problems about custom stationery orders;* or *Acted as intermediary among customers, printers, and suppliers*. If possible, quantify your accomplishments, such as *Conducted study of equipment needs of 100 small businesses in Houston; Personally generated orders for sales of $90,000 annually;* or *Keyed all the production models for a 250-page employee procedures manual*. One professional recruiter said, "I spend a half hour every day screening 50 résumés or more, and if I don't spot some [quantifiable] results in the first 10 seconds, the résumé is history."[25]

Your employment achievements and job duties will be easier to read if you place them in a bulleted list. When writing these bullet points, don't try to list every single thing you have done on the job; instead, customize your information so that it relates to the target job. Make sure your list of job duties shows what you have to contribute and how you are qualified for the position you are applying for. Do not make your bullet points complete sentences, and avoid using personal pronouns (*I, me, my*).

In addition to technical skills, employers seek individuals with communication, management, and interpersonal capabilities. This means you will want to select work experiences and achievements that illustrate your initiative, dependability, responsibility, resourcefulness, flexibility, and leadership. Employers also want people who can work in teams. Thus, include statements such as *Collaborated with interdepartmental task force in developing ten-page handbook for temporary workers* and *Headed student government team that conducted most successful voter registration in campus history*.

Statements describing your work experience can be made forceful and persuasive by using action verbs, such as those listed in Figure 15.3 and illustrated in Figure 15.4. Starting each of your bullet points with an action verb will help ensure that your bulleted lists are parallel.

> **Highlight and quantify your achievements in bullet points that are not complete sentences.**

Capabilities and Skills

Recruiters want to know specifically what you can do for their companies. Therefore, list your special skills, such as *Proficient in preparing federal, state, and local payroll tax returns as well as franchise and personal property tax returns*. Include your ability to use the Internet, software programs, office equipment, and communication technology tools. If you speak a foreign language or use sign language, include it on your résumé. Describe proficiencies you have acquired through training and experience, such as *Certified in computer graphics and Web design through an intensive 350-hour classroom program*. Use expressions such as *competent in, skilled in, proficient with, experienced in,* and *ability to;* for example, *Competent in writing, editing, and proofreading reports, tables, letters, memos, manuscripts, and business forms*.

You will also want to highlight exceptional aptitudes, such as working well under stress, learning computer programs quickly, and interacting with customers. If possible, provide details and evidence that back up your assertions; for example, *Mastered PhotoShop in 25 hours with little instruction*. Search for examples of your writing, speaking, management, organizational, and interpersonal skills—particularly those talents that are relevant to your targeted job. For recent graduates, this section can be used to give recruiters evidence of your potential. Instead of *Capabilities*, the section might be called *Skills and Abilities*.

Those job hunters preparing a functional résumé will place more focus on skills than on any other section. A well-written functional résumé groups skills into categories such as *Accounting/Finance Skills, Management/Leadership Skills, Communication/Teamwork Skills,* and *Computer/Technology Skills*. Each skills category includes a bulleted list of achievements and experience that demonstrate the skill, including specific numbers whenever possible. These skills categories should be placed in the beginning of the résumé, where they will be highlighted, followed by education and work experience. The action verbs shown in Figures 15.3 and 15.4 can also be used when constructing a functional résumé.

> **Emphasize the skills and aptitudes that prove you are qualified for a specific position.**

FIGURE 15.3 Action Verbs

Action Verbs for Powerful Résumés

Communication Skills		Research Skills	Clerical, Detail Skills	Creative Skills	
arbitrated	assessed	evaluated	located	tabulated	overhauled
arranged	assisted	executed	measured	updated	performed
authored	clarified	handled	observed	validated	troubleshooting
clarified	coached	headed	organized		programmed
collaborated	collaborated (with)	implemented	researched	Creative	remodeled
convinced	communicated	improved	reviewed	Skills	repaired
corresponded	coordinated	increased	searched	acted	retrieved
defined	counseled	led	solved	conceptualized	solved
developed	demonstrated	modeled	studied	created	upgraded
directed	demystified	organized	summarized	customized	
drafted	developed	oversaw	surveyed	designed	Financial
edited	enabled	planned	systematized	developed	Skills
enlisted	encouraged	prioritized		directed	administered
explained	evaluated	produced	Clerical,	established	allocated
formulated	expedited	recommended	Detail Skills	fashioned	analyzed
influenced	explained	reorganized	activated	founded	appraised
integrated	facilitated	reviewed	approved	illustrated	audited
interpreted	guided	scheduled	arranged	initiated	balanced
mediated	informed	strengthened	catalogued	instituted	budgeted
moderated	instructed	supervised	classified	integrated	calculated
negotiated	motivated	trained	collected	introduced	computed
participated	persuaded		compiled	invented	developed
persuaded	set goals	Research	edited	originated	forecast
promoted	stimulated	Skills	executed	performed	managed
publicized	teamed (with)	analyzed	generated	planned	marketed
reconciled	trained	clarified	implemented	revitalized	planned
recruited		collected	inspected	shaped	projected
resolved	Management,	critiqued	logged		researched
spoke	Leadership	diagnosed	maintained	Technical	
specified	Skills	evaluated	monitored	Skills	More
suggested	administered	examined	operated	assembled	Accomplishment
summarized	analyzed	experimented	organized	built	Verbs
translated	assigned	extracted	prepared	calculated	achieved
wrote	attained	formulated	processed	computed	expanded
	authorized	gathered	proofread	configured	improved
	chaired	identified	purchased	designed	pioneered
Teamwork,	consolidated	informed	recorded	devised	reduced (losses)
Supervision	contracted	inspected	retrieved	engineered	resolved (problems)
Skills	coordinated	interpreted	screened	fabricated	restored
adapted	delegated	interviewed	specified	installed	revamped
advised	developed	invented	streamlined	maintained	spearheaded
	directed	investigated	systematized	operated	transformed

The **underlined** words are especially good for pointing out accomplishments.

Reprinted with permission from THE DAMN GOOD RESUME GUIDE by Yana Parker, Ten Speed Press, Berkeley, CA. www.tenspeed.com.

Awards, Honors, and Activities

Awards, honors, and activities are appropriate for the résumé.

If you have three or more awards or honors, highlight them by listing them under a separate heading. If not, put them in the education or work experience section if appropriate. Include awards, scholarships (financial and other), fellowships, dean's list, honors, recognition, commendations, and certificates. Be sure to identify items clearly. Your reader may be unfamiliar, for example, with Greek organizations, honoraries, and awards; tell what they mean. Instead of saying *Recipient of Star award*, give more details: *Recipient of Star award given by Pepperdine University to outstanding graduates who combine academic excellence and extracurricular activities.*

It is also appropriate to include school, community, volunteer, and professional activities. Employers are interested in evidence that you are a well-rounded person. This section allows you to demonstrate leadership and interpersonal skills. Strive to use action statements. For example, instead of saying *Treasurer of business club*, explain more fully: *Collected dues, kept financial records, and paid bills while serving as treasurer of 35-member business club.*

FIGURE 15.4 Use Action Verbs in Statements That Quantify Achievements

Identified weaknesses in internships and **researched** five alternate programs

Reduced delivery delays by an average of three days per order

Streamlined filing system, thus reducing 400-item backlog to zero

Organized holiday awards program for 1,200 attendees and 140 workers

Designed three pages in HTML for company Web site

Represented 2,500 students on committee involving university policies and procedures

Calculated shipping charges for overseas deliveries and **recommended** most economical rates

Managed 24-station computer network linking data in three departments

Distributed and **explained** voter registration forms to over 500 prospective voters

Praised by top management for enthusiastic teamwork and achievement

Secured national recognition from National Arbor Foundation for tree project

Personal Data

Today's résumés generally omit personal data, such as birth date, marital status, height, weight, national origin, health, and religious affiliation. Such information doesn't relate to genuine occupational qualifications, and recruiters are legally barred from asking for such information. Some job seekers do, however, include hobbies or interests (such as skiing or photography) that might grab the recruiter's attention or serve as conversation starters. Naturally, you shouldn't mention time-consuming interests or dangerous pastimes (such as rock climbing, scuba diving, caving, bungee jumping, or motorcycle racing). You could also indicate your willingness to travel or to relocate since many companies will be interested.

> Omit personal data not related to job qualifications.

References

Listing references directly on a résumé takes up valuable space. Moreover, references are not normally instrumental in securing an interview—few companies check them before the

> References are unnecessary for the résumé, but they should be available for the interview.

Communicating at Work Part 2

Workplace Expert Liz Ryan Shares Job-Search Tips

When asked about the biggest mistakes job seekers make, workplace expert Liz Ryan says that people applying online tend to "go long." That is, they don't make an effort to be concise because they think that online space is unlimited. Recruiters, however, don't want to read pages and pages of text. Ryan advises keeping your résumé, cover letter, and other messages brief and snappy. Does this mean you should use the abbreviated style of instant messages? Absolutely not! she responds. Use appropriate business language—no abbreviations, no all caps or all lowercase, and no strings of exclamation points.

One big mistake new grads make online is that they fail to look beyond the big boards. She encourages job candidates to focus on smaller, local sites such as CareersColorado (**http://coloradojobing.com**) and JobStar (**http://jobstar.org**). Also check company Web sites because jobs are often listed there before they are posted on the big boards. Even if you don't see exactly the job you want at a company site, you can get a feel for the kinds of positions available. If your skill set doesn't match a particular opening, use that channel to respond. You can say, "I'm not exactly right for this job, but I have this, this, and this, and if something comes along that fits my skills, I'm available."[26]

Ryan encourages job candidates to join e-mail discussion groups (Listservs) such as Craigslist (**http://sfbay.craigslist.org/**). Such groups carry job listings and allow members to post their own messages letting employers and fellow members know they are job hunting.

Another mistake of candidates is not reading job listings carefully. If an ad says, "no phone calls," that means no calls. Some ads say, "When you respond, please comment on our newsletter at this link."[27] Ryan emphasizes that following the directions in the ad is critical.

© IMAGEMORE Co., Ltd. / Getty Images

Critical Thinking
- Compare the advantages and disadvantages of searching for jobs at big board sites, such as *Monster.com*, with searching at company Web sites.
- Why would companies ask job applicants to comment on their newsletter?
- If recruiters are so pressed for time, why don't they appreciate résumés and cover letters written in the abbreviated style of instant messaging?

FIGURE 15.5 Sample Reference List

Provides reference list to be left at interview

References
Casey J. Jepson
1103 Wood Road
Boscobel, WI 53805

Home: (608) 375-1926   Cell: (608) 778-5195   E-mail: cjepson@tds.net

Prints reference list with heading that matches heading on résumé

Lists professional, not personal, references

Mr. Jeff Schmitz
Loan Supervisor
Community First Bank
925 Wisconsin Avenue
Boscobel, WI 53805
(608) 375-4116
jschmitz@commfirstbank.com

Ms. Sue Winder
Work Study Supervisor
Southwest Wisconsin Technical College
1800 Bronson Boulevard
Fennimore, WI 53809
(608) 822-3611, Ext. 1200
swinder@swtc.edu

Lists only people who have given permission

Uses parallel form for all entries

Ms. Sondra Ostheimer
Business/Communication Instructor
Southwest Wisconsin Technical College
1800 Bronson Boulevard
Fennimore, WI 53809
(608) 822-3622, Ext. 1266
sostheimer@swtc.edu

interview. Instead, recruiters prefer that you bring to the interview a list of individuals willing to discuss your qualifications. Therefore, you should prepare a separate list, such as that in Figure 15.5, when you begin your job search. Ask three to five instructors, your current employer or previous employers, colleagues or subordinates, and other professional contacts whether they would be willing to answer inquiries regarding your qualifications for employment. Be sure, however, to provide them with an opportunity to refuse. No reference is better than a negative one.

Do not include personal or character references, such as friends, family, or neighbors, because recruiters rarely consult them. Companies are more interested in the opinions of objective individuals who know how you perform professionally and academically. One final note: most recruiters see little reason for including the statement *References furnished upon request*. It's unnecessary and takes up precious space.

In Figures 15.6 through 15.11, you will find a collection of models for chronological and functional résumés. Use these models to help you organize the content and format of your own persuasive résumé.

Optimizing Your Résumé for Today's Technologies

LEARNING OBJECTIVE 5
Describe techniques that optimize a résumé for today's technologies, including preparing a scannable résumé, a plain-text résumé, and an e-portfolio.

Thus far we have aimed our résumé advice at human readers. However, the first reader of your résumé may well be a computer. Hiring organizations today use a variety of methods to process incoming résumés. Some organizations still welcome traditional print-based résumés that may include attractive formatting. Larger organizations, however, must deal with thousands of incoming résumés. Increasingly, they are placing those résumés directly into searchable databases. So that you can optimize your chances, you may need three versions of your résumé: (a) a traditional print-based résumé, (b) a scannable résumé, and (c) a plain-text résumé for e-mailing or online posting. This does not mean that you have

Courtney Castro used a chronological résumé to highlight her work experience, most of which is related directly to the position she seeks. Although she is a recent graduate, she has accumulated experience in two part-time jobs and one full-time job. She included a summary of qualifications to highlight her skills, experience, and interpersonal traits aimed at a specific position.

Notice that Courtney designed her résumé in two columns with five major categories listed in the left column. In the right column she included bulleted items for each of the five categories. Conciseness and parallelism are important in writing an effective résumé. In the *Experience* category, she started each item with an active verb, which improved readability and parallel form.

Lists most impressive qualifications

Arranges jobs in reverse chronological order

Uses bulleted lists to make résumé easier to read

Shows job titles in bold for readability

Includes detailed objective in response to advertisement

Uses present-tense verbs for current job and past-tense verbs for previous jobs

Specifies relevant activities for targeted position

Provides white space around headings to create open look

Courtney M. Castro
2403 Mira Loma Drive, Costa Mesa, CA 90415   (714) 455-9231   cmcastro@aol.com

OBJECTIVE
Position with financial services organization installing accounting software and providing user support, where computer experience and proven communication and interpersonal skills can be used to improve operations.

SUMMARY OF QUALIFICATIONS
- Over five years' experience in the accounting field
- Experienced in designing, installing, and providing technical support for accounting software, including SAP, Great Plains, Peachtree, and Oracle
- Proficient in Word, Access, PowerPoint, Excel, and QuickBooks
- Skilled in technical writing, including proposals, user manuals, and documentation
- Commended for tactful, professional, and friendly communication skills
- Fluent in speaking and writing Spanish

EXPERIENCE
Accounting software consultant. South Coast Software, Huntington Beach, CA June 2007 to present
- Design and install accounting systems for businesses such as Century 21 Butler Realty, Capital Financial Services, Pacific Lumber, and others
- Provide ongoing technical support and consultation for regular clients
- Help write proposals such as successful $400,000 government contract

Office manager (part-time). Coastal Productions, Fountain Valley, CA June 2006 to May 2007
- Conceived and implemented improved order processing and filing system
- Designed and integrated module code pieces to export and convert data from an inhouse SQL database to QuickBooks format for automated check printing and invoice billing
- Trained three employees to operate QuickBooks software

Bookkeeper (part-time). Home Roofing, Santa Ana, CA August 2002 to May 2006
- Kept books for roofing and repair company with $240,000 gross income
- Performed all bookkeeping tasks including quarterly internal audit and payroll

EDUCATION
Orange Coast College, Costa Mesa, CA
Associate of Arts degree in business administration, June 2006
GPA in major 3.6 (4.0 = A)

Oracle University—currently enrolled in database training seminars leading to Oracle certification

HONORS AND ACTIVITIES
- Dean's list, three semesters
- Elected to Alpha Beta Sigma business student honorary

to write different résumés. You are merely preparing different versions of your traditional résumé. With all versions, you should also be aware of the significant role of résumé keywords. You may decide to create an e-portfolio to showcase your qualifications.

Because résumés are increasingly becoming part of searchable databases, you may need three versions.

Designing a Print-Based Résumé

Print-based résumés (also called *presentation résumés*) are attractively formatted to maximize readability. You can create a professional-looking résumé by using your word processing program to highlight your qualifications. The examples in this chapter provide ideas for

To highlight her skills and capabilities, Casey placed them in the summary of qualifications at the top of her résumé. She used the tables feature of her word processing program to help her format. Because she wanted to describe her skills and experience fully, she used two pages.

Casey J. Jepson
1103 Wood Road
Boscobel, WI 53805

Home: (608) 375-1926   Cell: (608) 778-5195   E-mail: cjepson@tds.net

SUMMARY OF QUALIFICATIONS	• Over three years' experience in administrative positions, working with business documents and interacting with customers • Ability to keyboard (65 wpm) and use ten-key calculator (150 kpm) • Proficient with Microsoft Word, Excel, Access, PowerPoint, FrontPage, and Publisher (passed MOS certification exam) • Competent in Web research, written and oral communication, records management, desktop publishing, computer software troubleshooting, and proofreading and editing business documents • Trained in QuickBooks, Flash, Photoshop, Dreamweaver • Experienced in planning all-day seminars and travel arrangements
EXPERIENCE	**Administrative Assistant, Work Study** Southwest Wisconsin Technical College, Fennimore, Wisconsin, August 2007–present • Create letters, memos, reports, and forms in Microsoft Word • Develop customized reports and labels using Microsoft Access • Maintain departmental Microsoft Excel budget **Loan Support Specialist** Community First Bank, Boscobel, Wisconsin, May 2005–September 2007 • Prepared loan documents for consumer, residential, mortgage, agricultural, and commercial loans • Ensured compliance with federal, state, and bank regulations • Originated correspondence (both oral and written) with customers and insurance agencies • Ordered and interpreted appraisals, titles, and credit reports • Created and maintained paper and electronic files for customers • Protected the confidentiality of all clients **Customer Sales Representative** Lands' End, Dodgeville, Wisconsin, Winter seasons 2005–2007 • Answered phones and assisted customers with orders • Resolved customers' merchandise questions and problems • Entered catalog orders into computer system • Enjoyed working in teams to achieve company goals

Omits objective to keep all options open

Focuses on skills and aptitudes that employers seek

Uses present-tense verbs for current job

Arranges employment by job title for easy recognition

Includes second-page heading

Casey J. Jepson   Page 2

EDUCATION	Southwest Wisconsin Technical College, Fennimore, Wisconsin, Major: Administrative Assistant with Help Desk certificate AA degree expected May 2009. GPA in major: 3.8 (4.0 = A)
ACTIVITIES AND AWARDS	• Assisted state president in all functions and coordinated all activities of the BPA (Business Professionals of America) Torch Awards Program while serving as state vice president • Placed first in state BPA Administrative Assistant competition • Earned second place in Bill Wolfe Writing Contest • Served as SWTC Student Senate Representative for Administrative Assistant program • Nominated for SWTC Ambassador Award (recognizes outstanding students for excellence in and out of classroom)

Combines activities and awards to fill out section

FIGURE 15.8 **Chronological Résumé: Current University Student With Limited Related Experience**

Rick's résumé answers an advertisement specifying skills for a staff accountant. In responding to the ad, he targeted his objective and shaped his statements to the precise job requirements mentioned by the employer.

To produce this attractive print-based résumé, he employed italics, bold, and scalable font features from his word processing program. He realized that this résumé might not be scannable and could not be embedded in an e-mail message. That's why he was ready with a scannable version that shortened the line length and stripped the fancy formatting in case he had to submit it electronically.

Uses italics, larger type size, and bold underline to enhance appearance

RICK M. JAMESON

4938 Mountain Avenue
Sunnyvale, CA 94255
Phone: (408) 479-1982
Cell: (408) 412-5540
E-mail: rmjameson@rrbay.com

Objective: Position as Staff Accountant with progressive Bay Area firm, where my technical, computer, and communication skills will be useful in managing accounts and acquiring new clientele

Responds to specific job advertisement

SUMMARY OF QUALIFICATIONS
Accounting
- Ability to journalize entries accurately in general and specialized journals
- Proficient in posting to general ledger, preparing trial balance, and detecting discrepancies
- Trained in preparing and analyzing balance sheet and other financial statements

Highlights skills named in advertisement

Computer
- Experienced in using Word, Excel, HTML, and Dreamweaver
- Comfortable in Windows and Internet environments
- Able to learn new computer programs and applications quickly, with little instruction

Communication and Interpersonal
- Enjoy working with details and completing assignments accurately and on time
- Demonstrate sound writing and speaking skills acquired and polished in business letter writing, report writing, and speech classes
- Interact well with people as evidenced in my successful sales, volunteer, and internship work; enjoy meeting new people

EXPERIENCE
Tax Preparer, Volunteer Income Tax Assistance program (VITA)
Sponsored by the Internal Revenue Service and California State University, San Jose. Prepare state and federal tax returns for individuals with incomes under $25,000. Conduct interviews with over 50 individuals to elicit data regarding taxes. Determine legitimate tax deductions and record them accurately. (Tax seasons, 2006 to present)

Uses paragraph style instead of bulleted items to pack in more data in a small space

Accounting Intern, Software, Inc., Accounting Department, Santa Clara, CA
Assisted in analyzing data for weekly accounts payable aging report. Prepared daily cash activity report for sums up to $10,000. Calculated depreciation on 12 capital asset accounts with a total valuation of over $900,000. Researched and wrote report analyzing one division's budget of $150,000. (Spring 2006)

Quantifies descriptions of experience

Salesperson, Kmart, Santa Clara, CA
Helped customers select gardening and landscaping supplies. Assisted in ordering merchandise, stocking the department, and resolving customer problems. (Summers 2005, 2006)

EDUCATION
California State University, San Jose. BS degree expected June 2008
Major: Business Administration
Specialization: Accounting Theory and Practice. GPA: 3.2 (A = 4.0)
Participated as member of Accounting Club for two years
San Jose Community College. AA degree June 2006
Major: Business Administration and Accounting. GPA: 3.4 (A = 4.0)
Received Award of Merit for volunteer work as orientation guide and peer tutor

Includes activities and awards with education because of limited space

simple layouts that are easily duplicated. You can also examine résumé templates for design and format ideas. Their inflexibility, however, may lead to frustration as you try to force your skills and experience into a predetermined template sequence. What's more, recruiters who read hundreds of résumés can usually spot a template-based résumé. Instead, create your own original résumé that fits your unique qualifications.

Your print-based résumé should follow an outline format with headings and bullet points to present information in an orderly, uncluttered, easy-to-read format. An attractive print-based résumé is necessary (a) when you are competing for a job that does not require electronic submission, (b) to present in addition to an electronic submission, and

A print-based résumé should be attractive, readable, and outlined with headings in an orderly, uncluttered format.

Because Rachel has many years of experience and seeks executive-level employment, she highlighted her experience by placing it before her education. Her summary of qualifications highlighted her most impressive experience and skills. This chronological two-page résumé shows the steady progression of her career to executive positions, a movement that impresses and reassures recruiters.

RACHEL M. CHOWDHRY
374 Cabot Drive
Thousand Oaks, CA 91359

E-Mail: rchowdhry@west.net
(805) 490-3310

OBJECTIVE Senior Financial Management Position

SUMMARY OF QUALIFICATIONS
- Over 12 years' comprehensive experience in the accounting industry, including over 8 years as a controller
- Certified Public Accountant (CPA)
- Demonstrated ability to handle all accounting functions for large, midsized, and small firms
- Ability to isolate problems, reduce expenses, and improve the bottom line, resulting in substantial cost savings
- Proven talent for interacting professionally with individuals at all levels, as demonstrated by performance review comments
- Experienced in P&L, audits, taxation, interal control, inventor management, A/P, A/R, cash management

Lists most impressive credentials

PROFESSIONAL HISTORY AND ACHIEVEMENT

11/04 to present CONTROLLER
United Plastics, Inc., Newbury Park, California (extruder of polyethylene film for plastic aprons and gloves)
- Direct all facets of accounting and cash management for 160-employee, $3 billion business
- Supervise inventory and production operations for tax compliance
- Talked owner into reducing sales prices, resulting in doubling first-quarter 2007 sales
- Created cost accounting by product and pricing based on gross margin
- Increased line of credit with 12 major suppliers

Uses action verbs but includes many good nouns for possible computer scanning

Explains nature of employer's business because it is not immediately recognizable

1/02 to 10/04 CONTROLLER
Burgess Inc., Freeport, Illinois (major manufacturer of flashlight and lantern batteries)
- Managed all accounting, cash, payroll, credit, and collection operations for 175-employee business
- Implemented a new system for cost accounting, inventory control, and accounts payable, resulting in a $100,000 annual savings
- Reduced staff from 10 persons to 5 with no loss in productivity
- Successfully reduced inventory levels from $1.1 million to $600,000

Emphasizes steady employment history by listing dates FIRST

Describes and quantifies specific achievements

8/00 to 11/01 TREASURER/CONTROLLER
The Builders of Winter, Winter, Wisconsin (manufacturer of modular housing)
- Supervised accounts receivable/payable, cash management, payroll, insurance
- Directed monthly and year-end closings, banking relations, and product costing
- Refinanced company with long-term loan, ensuring stability

Rachel M. Chowdhry   Page 2

4/96 to 6/00 SUPERVISOR OF GENERAL ACCOUNTING
Levin National Batteries, St. Paul, Minnesota (local manufacturer of flashlight batteries)
- Completed monthly and year-end closing of ledgers for $2 million business
- Audited freight bills, acted as interdepartmental liaison, prepared financial reports

ADDITIONAL INFORMATION

Education: BBA degree, University of Minnesota, major: Accounting, 1995
Certification: Certified Public Accountant (CPA), 1997
Personal: Will travel and/or relocate

De-emphasizes education because work history is more important for mature candidates

Recent graduate Kevin Touhy chose this functional format to de-emphasize his meager work experience and emphasize his potential in sales and marketing. This version of his résumé is more generic than one targeted for a specific position. Yet, it emphasizes his strong points with specific achievements and includes an employment section to satisfy recruiters.

The functional format presents ability-focused topics. It illustrates what the job seeker can do for the employer instead of narrating a history of previous jobs. Although recruiters prefer chronological résumés, the functional format is a good choice for new graduates, career changers, and those with employment gaps.

KEVIN M. TOUHY

P.O. Box 341
Monroeville, PA 15146

Phone: (412) 359-2493
Cell: (412) 555-3201

E-mail: ktouhy@aol.com

OBJECTIVE — Position in sales, marketing, or e-marketing in which my marketing, communication, and technology skills can help an organization achieve its goals.

Includes objective that focuses on employer's needs

Uses functional headings that emphasize necessary skills for sales and e-marketing position

SALES AND MARKETING SKILLS
- Developed people and sales skills by demonstrating lawn-care equipment in central and western Pennsylvania
- Achieved sales amounting to 120 percent of forecast in competitive field
- Personally generated over $30,000 in telephone subscriptions as part of the President's Task Force for the Northeastern University Foundation
- Conducted telephone survey of selected businesses in two counties to discover potential users of farm equipment and to promote company services
- Successfully served 40 or more retail customers daily as clerk in electrical appliance department of national home hardware store

Quantifies achievements with specifics instead of generalities

Employs action verbs and bullet points to describe skills

COMMUNICATION AND COMPUTER SKILLS
- Conducted research, analyzed findings, drew conclusions, and helped write 20-page report contending that responsible e-marketing is not spam
- Learned teamwork skills such as cooperation and compromise in team projects
- Delivered PowerPoint talks before selected campus classes and organizations encouraging students to participate in campus voter registration drive
- Earned A's in Interpersonal Communication and Business Communication
- Developed Word, Outlook, Excel, PowerPoint, and Internet Explorer skills
- Commended by instructors for ability to learn computer programs quickly

Calls attention to computer skills

ORGANIZATIONAL AND MANAGEMENT SKILLS
- Helped conceptualize, organize, and conduct highly effective campus campaign to register student voters
- Scheduled events and arranged weekend student retreat for Marketing Club
- Trained and supervised two counter employees at Pizza Planet
- Organized courses, extracurricular activities, and part-time employment to graduate in seven semesters

Highlights recent education and contemporary training while de-emphasizing employment

EDUCATION — Bachelor of Business Administration, Northeastern University, June 2007
Major: Business Administration with e-marketing emphasis
GPA: Major, 3.7; overall, 3.3 (A = 4.0)
Related Courses: Marketing Research; Internet Advertising, Sales, and Promotion; and Competitive Strategies for the Information Age
Associate of Arts, Community College of Allegheny County, 2005
Major: Business Administration with marketing emphasis.
GPA: 3.7

Avoids dense look and improves readability by "chunking" information

EMPLOYMENT — Sept. 2005–May 2007, Pizza Planet, Pittsburgh
Summer 2005, Bellefonte Manufacturers Representatives, Pittsburgh
Summers 2003–2005, Home Depot, Inc., Pittsburgh

(c) to bring with you to job interviews. Even if a résumé is submitted electronically, nearly every job candidate will want to have an attractive printed résumé handy for human readers.

Preparing a Scannable Résumé

A scannable résumé is one that is meant to be printed on plain white paper and scanned by a computer. To screen incoming résumés, many mid- and large-sized companies use automated applicant-tracking software. These systems scan an incoming résumé with optical

Applicant-tracking software scans incoming résumés searching for keywords.

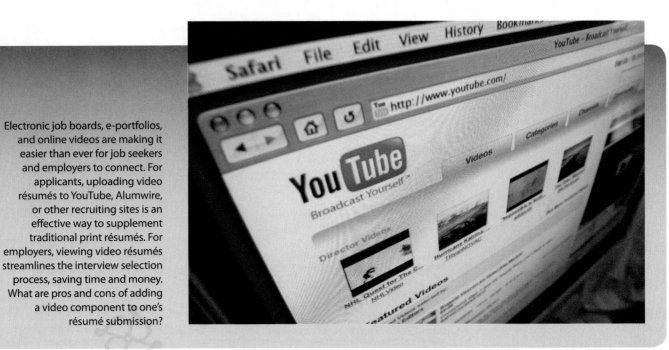

Electronic job boards, e-portfolios, and online videos are making it easier than ever for job seekers and employers to connect. For applicants, uploading video résumés to YouTube, Alumwire, or other recruiting sites is an effective way to supplement traditional print résumés. For employers, viewing video résumés streamlines the interview selection process, saving time and money. What are pros and cons of adding a video component to one's résumé submission?

© Richard Levine / Alamy

character recognition (OCR) looking for keywords. The most sophisticated programs enable recruiters and hiring managers to search for keywords, rank résumés based on the number of "hits," and generate reports. Information from your résumé is stored, usually from six months to a year.

Before sending your résumé, find out whether the recipient uses scanning software. If you can't tell from the job announcement, call the company to ask whether it scans résumés electronically. If you don't get a clear answer and you have even the slightest suspicion that your résumé might be read electronically, you will be smart to prepare a plain, scannable version as shown in Figure 15.11.

Tips for Maximizing Scannability. A scannable résumé must sacrifice many of the graphic enhancements you might have used to make your print résumé attractive. To maximize scannability:

Scannable résumés use plain formatting, large fonts, quality printing, and white space.

- **Use 10- to 14-point type.** Because touching letters or unusual fonts are likely to be misread, using a large, well-known font such as 12-point Times New Roman or Arial is safest. This may mean that your résumé will require two pages. After printing, inspect your résumé to see whether any letters touch—especially in your name.

- **Avoid unusual typefaces, underlining, and italics.** Moreover, don't use borders, shading, or other graphics to highlight text. These features don't scan well. Most applicant-tracking programs, however, can accurately read bold print, solid bullets, and asterisks.

- **Be sure that your name is the first line on the page.** Don't use fancy layouts that may confuse a scanner. Reports generated by applicant-tracking software usually assume that the first line of a résumé contains the applicant's name.

- **List each phone number on its own line.** Your landline and cell phone numbers should appear on separate lines to improve recognition.

- **Provide white space.** To ensure separation of words and categories, leave plenty of white space. For example, instead of using parentheses to enclose a telephone area code, insert blank spaces, such as 212 799-2415. Leave blank lines around headings.

FIGURE 15.11 Scannable Résumé

Leticia P. Lopez prepared this "plain Jane" résumé free of graphics and fancy formatting so that it would scan well if read by a computer. Within the résumé, she included many job titles, skills, traits, and other descriptive keywords that scanners are programmed to recognize. To improve accurate scanning, she avoided bullets, italics, underlining, and columns. If she had had more information to include, she could have gone on to a second page since a résumé to be scanned need not be restricted to one page.

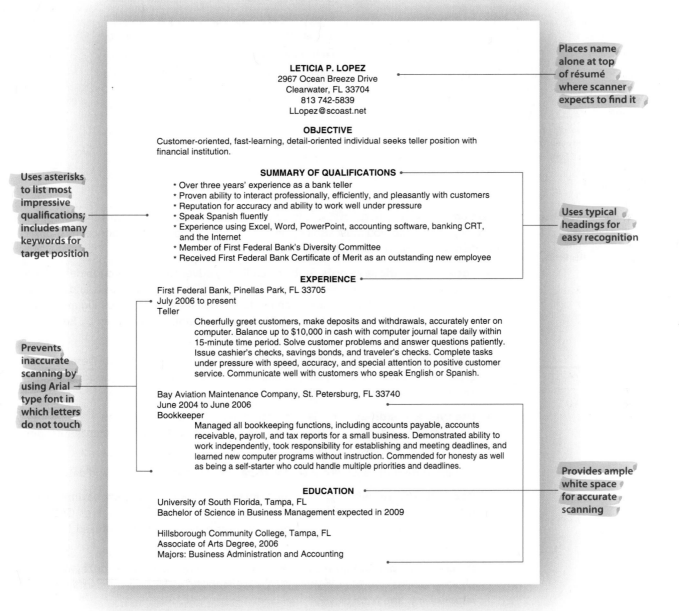

Places name alone at top of résumé where scanner expects to find it

LETICIA P. LOPEZ
2967 Ocean Breeze Drive
Clearwater, FL 33704
813 742-5839
LLopez@scoast.net

OBJECTIVE
Customer-oriented, fast-learning, detail-oriented individual seeks teller position with financial institution.

SUMMARY OF QUALIFICATIONS
* Over three years' experience as a bank teller
* Proven ability to interact professionally, efficiently, and pleasantly with customers
* Reputation for accuracy and ability to work well under pressure
* Speak Spanish fluently
* Experience using Excel, Word, PowerPoint, accounting software, banking CRT, and the Internet
* Member of First Federal Bank's Diversity Committee
* Received First Federal Bank Certificate of Merit as an outstanding new employee

Uses asterisks to list most impressive qualifications; includes many keywords for target position

Uses typical headings for easy recognition

EXPERIENCE
First Federal Bank, Pinellas Park, FL 33705
July 2006 to present
Teller

Cheerfully greet customers, make deposits and withdrawals, accurately enter on computer. Balance up to $10,000 in cash with computer journal tape daily within 15-minute time period. Solve customer problems and answer questions patiently. Issue cashier's checks, savings bonds, and traveler's checks. Complete tasks under pressure with speed, accuracy, and special attention to positive customer service. Communicate well with customers who speak English or Spanish.

Prevents inaccurate scanning by using Arial type font in which letters do not touch

Bay Aviation Maintenance Company, St. Petersburg, FL 33740
June 2004 to June 2006
Bookkeeper

Managed all bookkeeping functions, including accounts payable, accounts receivable, payroll, and tax reports for a small business. Demonstrated ability to work independently, took responsibility for establishing and meeting deadlines, and learned new computer programs without instruction. Commended for honesty as well as being a self-starter who could handle multiple priorities and deadlines.

EDUCATION
University of South Florida, Tampa, FL
Bachelor of Science in Business Management expected in 2009

Hillsborough Community College, Tampa, FL
Associate of Arts Degree, 2006
Majors: Business Administration and Accounting

Provides ample white space for accurate scanning

- **Avoid double columns.** When listing job duties, skills, computer programs, and so forth, don't tabulate items into two- or three-column lists. Scanners read across and may convert tables into nonsensical output.

- **Use smooth white paper, black ink, and quality printing.** Avoid colored or textured paper, and use a high-quality laser or ink-jet printer.

- **Don't fold or staple your résumé.** Send it in a large envelope so that you can avoid folds. Words that appear on folds may not be scanned correctly.

FIGURE 15.12 Interpersonal Keywords Most Requested by Employers Using Résumé-Scanning Software*

Ability to delegate	Creative	Leadership	Self-accountable
Ability to implement	Customer oriented	Multitasking	Self-managing
Ability to plan	Detail minded	Open communication	Setting priorities
Ability to train	Ethical	Open minded	Supportive
Accurate	Flexible	Oral communication	Takes initiative
Adaptable	Follow instructions	Organizational skills	Team building
Aggressive worker	Follow through	Persuasive	Team player
Analytical ability	Follow up	Problem solving	Tenacious
Assertive	High energy	Public speaking	Willing to travel
Communication skills	Industrious	Results oriented	
Competitive	Innovative	Safety conscious	

*Reported by Resumix, a leading producer of résumé-scanning software.
Source: Joyce Lain Kennedy and Thomas. J. Morrow, *Electronic Résumé Revolution* (New York: John Wiley & Sons), 70. Reprinted by permission of John Wiley & Sons, Inc.

Scanners produce "hits" when they recognize targeted keywords such as nouns describing skills, traits, tasks, and job titles.

Tips for Maximizing "Hits." In addition to paying attention to the physical appearance of your résumé, you must also be concerned with keywords that produce "hits" or recognition by the scanner. To maximize hits:

- **Focus on specific keywords.** Study carefully any advertisements and job descriptions for the position you want. Select keywords that describe skills, traits, tasks, and job titles. Because interpersonal traits are often requested by employers, consult Figure 15.12. It shows the most frequently requested interpersonal traits, as reported by Resumix, a pioneer in résumé-scanning software.

- **Incorporate words from the advertisement or job description.** Describe your experience, education, and qualifications in terms associated with the job advertisement or job description for this position.

- **Use typical headings.** Include expected categories such as Objective, Summary of Qualifications, Education, Work Experience, Skills, and Accomplishments. Scanning software looks for such headings.

- **Use accurate names.** Spell out complete names of schools, degrees, and dates.

- **Be careful of abbreviations.** Minimize unfamiliar abbreviations, but maximize easily recognized abbreviations—especially those within your field, such as CAD, JPG, or JIT. When in doubt, though, spell out! Computers are less confused by whole words.

- **Describe interpersonal traits and attitudes.** Hiring managers look for keywords and phrases such as *time management skills, dependability, high energy, leadership, sense of responsibility,* and *team player.*

- **Use more than one page if necessary.** Computers can easily handle more than one page so include as much as necessary to describe your qualifications and maximize hits.

Preparing a Plain-Text Résumé

Employers prefer plain-text documents because they are immediately searchable and they do not require employers to open attachments, which might carry viruses or create software incompatibilities.

A plain-text résumé (also called an *ASCII résumé*) is an electronic version suitable for e-mailing or pasting into online résumé bank submission forms. Employers prefer plain-text résumés because they avoid possible e-mail viruses and word processing incompatibilities. Usually embedded within an e-mail message, a plain-text résumé, shown in Figure 15.13, is immediately searchable. You should prepare a plain-text résumé if you want the fastest and most reliable way to contact potential employers. To create a plain-text résumé, follow these suggestions:

Chapter 15: The Job Search, Résumés, and Cover Letters

FIGURE 15.13 Plain-Text Résumé

To be sure her résumé would transmit well when embedded within an e-mail message, Leticia prepared a special version with all lines starting at the left margin. She used a 4-inch line length to avoid awkward line breaks. To set off her major headings, she used the tilde character on her keyboard. She saved the document as a text file (.txt or .rtf) so that it could be read by various computers. At the end she included a statement saying that an attractive, fully formatted hard copy of her résumé was available on request.

Starts all lines at left margin

LETICIA P. LOPEZ
2967 Ocean Breeze Drive
Clearwater, FL 33704
Phone: 813 742-5839
E-Mail: LLopez@scoast.net

~ ~ ~ ~ ~ ~ ~
OBJECTIVE
~ ~ ~ ~ ~ ~ ~

Customer-oriented, fast-learning, detail-oriented individual
seeks teller position with financial institution.

Shortens lines to avoid awkward line wrapping

~ ~ ~ ~ ~ ~ ~ ~ ~ ~ ~ ~ ~ ~ ~ ~ ~
SUMMARY OF QUALIFICATIONS
~ ~ ~ ~ ~ ~ ~ ~ ~ ~ ~ ~ ~ ~ ~ ~ ~

Sets off headings with the tilde (~) but could have omitted this attempt to improve readability

* Over three years' experience as a bank teller
* Proven ability to interact professionally, efficiently, and
  pleasantly with customers
* Reputation for accuracy and ability to work well under
  pressure
* Speak Spanish fluently
  Experience using Excel, Word, PowerPoint, accounting
  software, banking CRT, and the Internet
* Member of First Federal Bank's Diversity Committee
* Received First Federal Bank Certificate of Merit as an
  outstanding new employee

Creates large empty space that is unavoidable in this format

~ ~ ~ ~ ~ ~ ~ ~
EXPERIENCE
~ ~ ~ ~ ~ ~ ~ ~

First Federal Bank, Pinellas Park, FL 33705
July 2006 to present
Teller
* Cheerfully greet customers, make deposits and withdrawals
* Balance up to $10,000 in cash with computer journal tape
  daily within 15-minute time period
* Solve customer problems and answer questions patiently
* Issue cashier's checks, savings bonds, and traveler's checks
* Complete tasks under pressure with speed, accuracy, and
  attention to positive customer service
* Communicate well with customers speaking English or Spanish

Uses asterisks instead of bullets, which do not scan well

- **Observe all the tips for a scannable résumé.** A plain-text résumé requires the same attention to content, formatting, and keywords as that recommended for a scannable résumé.

- **Reformat with shorter lines.** Many e-mail programs wrap lines longer than 65 characters. To avoid having your résumé look as if a chain saw attacked it, use a short line length.

- **Think about using keyboard characters to enhance format.** In addition to using capital letters and asterisks, you might use spaced equals signs (= = =) and tildes (~ ~ ~) to create lines that separate résumé categories.

- **Move all text to the left.** Do not center items; start all text at the left margin. Remove tabs.

- **Save your résumé in plain-text (.txt) or rich text format (.rtf).** Saving your résumé in one of these formats will ensure that it can be read when pasted into an e-mail message.

- **Test your résumé before sending it to an employer.** After preparing and saving your résumé, copy and paste a copy of it into an e-mail message and send it to yourself. Check to see whether any non-ASCII characters appear. They may show up as question marks, square blocks, or other odd characters. Make any necessary changes.

When sending a plain-text résumé to an employer, be sure that your subject line clearly describes the purpose of your message.

Digitizing Your Qualifications in an E-Portfolio

An e-portfolio offers links to examples of a job candidate's performance, talents, and accomplishments in digitized form.

As the workplace becomes increasingly digitized, you have yet another way to display your qualifications to prospective employers—the digitized e-portfolio. Resourceful job candidates in other fields—particularly writers, models, artists, and graphic artists—have been creating print portfolios to illustrate their qualifications and achievements for some time. Now business and professional job candidates are using electronic portfolios to show off their talents.

An e-portfolio is a collection of digitized materials that provides viewers with a snapshot of a candidate's performance, talents, and accomplishments. It may include a copy of your résumé, reference letters, special achievements, awards, certificates, work samples, a complete list of your courses, thank-you letters, and anything else that touts your accomplishments. An advanced portfolio might include links to electronic copies of your artwork, film projects, blueprints, and photographs of classwork that might otherwise be difficult to share with potential employers. Moreover, you can include attention-getting effects such as color, animation, sound, and graphics.

Job candidates generally offer e-portfolios at Web sites, but they may also burn them onto CDs or DVDs.

E-portfolios are generally presented at Web sites, where they are available around the clock to employers. Some colleges and universities not only make Web site space available for student e-portfolios, but also provide instruction and resources for scanning photos, digitizing images, and preparing graphics. E-portfolios may also be burned onto CDs and DVDs to mail to prospective employers.

E-portfolios have many advantages. At Web sites they can be viewed at employers' convenience. Let's say you are talking on the phone with an employer in another city who wants to see a copy of your résumé. You can simply refer the employer to the Web address where your résumé resides. E-portfolios can also be seen by many individuals in an organization without circulating a paper copy. But the real reason for preparing an e-portfolio is that it shows off your talents and qualifications more thoroughly than a print résumé does.

A video résumé may be useful in applying to a far-off company.

As part of an e-portfolio or as a separate item, you might want to make a *video résumé*. Early video résumés showed candidates in awkward mock interviews or, worse yet, reading their résumés. Today, however, video résumés are short and more professional. They may be useful (a) as a door opener with a few employers you are targeting, or (b) as a distance-reduction technique to get acquainted with a far-off company. It may help you get an in-person interview when other techniques have failed.[28] You can learn more about video résumés by searching the Web.

Applying the Final Touches to Your Résumé

Because your résumé is probably the most important message you will ever write, you'll revise it many times. With so much information in concentrated form and with so much riding on its outcome, your résumé demands careful polishing, proofreading, and critiquing.

As you revise, be certain to verify all the facts, particularly those involving your previous employment and education. Don't be caught in a mistake, or worse, distortion of previous jobs and dates of employment. These items likely will be checked, and the consequences of

Chapter 15: The Job Search, Résumés, and Cover Letters

puffing up a résumé with deception or flat-out lies are simply not worth the risk. The Ethical Insights box on page 489 outlines dangerous areas to avoid.

Polishing Your Résumé

While you continue revising, look for other ways to improve your résumé. For example, consider consolidating headings. By condensing your information into as few headings as possible, you'll produce a clean, professional-looking document. Study other résumés for valuable formatting ideas. Ask yourself what graphic highlighting techniques you can use to improve readability: capitalization, underlining, indenting, and bulleting. Experiment with headings and styles to achieve a pleasing, easy-to-read message. Moreover, look for ways to eliminate wordiness. For example, instead of *Supervised two employees who worked at the counter,* try *Supervised two counter employees.* Review Chapter 5 for more tips on writing concisely.

In addition to making your résumé concise, make sure that you haven't included any of the following information, which doesn't belong on a résumé:

- Any basis for discrimination (age, marital status, gender, national origin, religion, race, number of children, disability)
- A photograph
- Reasons for leaving previous jobs
- The word *résumé*

- Social security number
- Salary history or requirements
- High school information
- References
- Full addresses of schools or employers (include city and state only)

Above all, make sure your print-based résumé looks professional. Avoid anything humorous or "cute," such as a help-wanted poster with your name or picture inside. Eliminate the personal pronoun *I* to ensure an objective style. Use high-quality paper in a professional color, such as white, off-white, or light gray. Print your résumé using a first-rate laser or ink-jet printer. Be prepared with a résumé for people to read as well as one for a computer to scan.

Proofreading Your Résumé

After revising, you must proofread, proofread, and proofread again for spelling, mechanics, content, and format. Then have a knowledgeable friend or relative proofread it yet again. This is one document that must be perfect. Because the job market is so competitive, one typo, misspelled word, or grammatical error could eliminate you from consideration.

By now you may be thinking that you'd like to hire someone to write your résumé. Don't! First, you know yourself better than anyone else could know you. Second, you will end up with either a generic or a one-time résumé. A generic résumé in today's highly competitive job market will lose out to a customized résumé nine times out of ten. Equally useless is a one-time résumé aimed at a single job. What if you don't get that job? Because you will need to revise your résumé many times as you seek a variety of jobs, be prepared to write (and rewrite) it yourself.

Submitting Your Résumé

If you are responding to a job advertisement, be sure to read the listing carefully to make sure you know how the employer wants you to submit your résumé. Not following the prospective employer's instructions can eliminate you from consideration before your résumé is even reviewed. Employers will probably ask you to submit your résumé in one of the following ways:

- **Word document.** Many employers still ask candidates to send their résumés and cover letters by surface mail. They may also allow applicants to attach their résumés as MS Word documents to e-mail messages, despite the fear of viruses.

- **Plain-text, ASCII document.** As discussed earlier, many employers expect applicants to submit résumés and cover letters as plain-text documents. This format is widely used for posting to an online job board or for sending by e-mail. Plain-text résumés may be embedded within or attached to e-mail messages.

Study résumé models for ideas on improving your format.

In addition to being well written, a résumé must be carefully formatted and meticulously proofread.

Send your résumé in the format the employer requests.

- **PDF document.** From a safety perspective, many employers prefer PDF (portable document format) files. A PDF résumé will look exactly like the original and cannot be altered. Newer computers come with Adobe Acrobat Reader for easy reading. Converting your résumé to a PDF file requires Adobe software.

- **Company database.** Some organizations prefer that you complete an online form with your résumé information. This enables them to plug your data into their formats for rapid searching. You might be able to cut and paste your information into the form.

- **Fax.** Although still a popular way of sending résumés, faxing presents problems in blurring and lost information. If you must fax your résumé, use at least a 12-point font to improve readability.

Checklist

Preparing for Employment and Submitting a Customized Résumé

Preparation

✓ **Research the job market.** Learn about available jobs, common qualifications, and potential employers. The best résumés are customized for specific jobs with specific companies.

✓ **Analyze your strengths.** Determine what aspects of your education, experience, and personal characteristics will be assets to prospective employers.

✓ **Study models.** Look at other résumés for formatting and element placement ideas. Experiment with headings and styles to achieve an creative, readable product.

Headings and Objectives

✓ **Identify yourself.** List your name, address, and telephone numbers.

✓ **Include a career objective for a targeted job.** Use an objective only if it is intended for a specific job (*Objective: Junior cost accountant position in the petroleum industry*).

Education

✓ **Name your degree, date of graduation, and institution.** Emphasize your education if your experience is limited.

✓ **List your major and GPA.** Give information about your studies, but don't inventory all your courses.

Work Experience

✓ **Itemize your jobs.** Start with your most recent job. Give the employer's name and city, dates of employment (month, year), and most significant job title.

✓ **Describe your experience.** Use action verbs to summarize achievements and skills relevant to your targeted job.

✓ **Promote your "soft" skills.** Give evidence of communication, management, and interpersonal talents. Employers want more than empty assurances; try to quantify your skills and accomplishments (*Developed teamwork skills while collaborating with six-member task force in producing 20-page mission statement*).

Special Skills, Achievements, and Awards

✓ **Highlight your computer skills.** Remember that nearly all employers seek employees who are proficient in using the Internet, e-mail, word processing, databases, spreadsheets, and presentation programs.

✓ **Show that you are a well-rounded individual.** List awards, experiences, and extracurricular activities—particularly if they demonstrate leadership, teamwork, reliability, loyalty, industry, initiative, efficiency, and self-sufficiency.

Final Tips

✓ **Look for ways to condense your data.** Omit all street addresses except your own. Consolidate your headings. Study models and experiment with formats to find the most readable and efficient groupings.

✓ **Double-check for parallel phrasing.** Be sure that all entries have balanced construction, such as similar verb forms (*Organized files, trained assistants, scheduled events*).

✓ **Make your résumé computer friendly.** If there's a chance your résumé will be read by a computer, be sure to remove graphics and emphasize keywords.

✓ **Consider omitting references.** Have a list of references available for the interview, but don't include them or refer to them unless you have a specific reason to do so.

✓ **Project professionalism and quality.** Avoid personal pronouns and humor. Use quality paper and a high-performance printer.

✓ **Resist the urge to inflate your qualifications.** Be accurate in listing your education, grades, honors, job titles, employment dates, and job experience.

✓ **Proofread, proofread, proofread!** Make this important document perfect by proofreading at least three times. Ask a friend to check it, too.

Submitting

✓ **Follow instructions for submitting.** Learn whether the employer wants candidates to send a print résumé, a plain-text version, a PDF file, or a fax.

✓ **Practice sending plain-text résumés.** Before submitting a plain-text résumé, try sending it to yourself or friends. Perfect your skill in achieving an attractive format.

Ethical Insights

Are Inflated Résumés Worth the Risk?

A résumé is expected to showcase a candidate's strengths and minimize weaknesses. For this reason, recruiters expect a certain degree of self-promotion. Some résumé writers, however, step over the line that separates honest self-marketing from deceptive half-truths and flat-out lies. Distorting facts on a résumé is unethical; lying is illegal. Most important, either practice can destroy a career.

Given the competitive job market, it might be tempting to puff up your résumé. You would not be alone in telling fibs or outright whoppers. One study found that 44 percent of applicants lied about their work histories, 23 percent fabricated licenses or credentials, and 41 percent falsified their educational backgrounds.[29] Although recruiters can't check everything, most will verify previous employment and education before hiring candidates. Over half will require official transcripts.

After hiring, the checking process may continue. If hiring officials find a discrepancy in GPA or prior experience and the error is an honest mistake, they meet with the new-hire to hear an explanation. If the discrepancy wasn't a mistake, they FIRE the person immediately. No job seeker wants to be in the unhappy position of explaining résumé errors or defending misrepresentation. Avoiding the following problems can keep you off the hot seat:

- **Inflated education, grades, or honors.** Some job candidates claim degrees from colleges or universities when in fact they merely attended classes. Others increase their grade-point averages or claim fictitious honors. Any such dishonest reporting is grounds for dismissal when discovered.
- **Enhanced job titles.** Wishing to elevate their status, some applicants misrepresent their titles. For example, one technician called himself a "programmer" when he had actually programmed only one project for his boss. A mail clerk who assumed added responsibilities conferred upon herself the title of "supervisor." Even when the description seems accurate, it's unethical to list any title not officially granted.
- **Puffed-up accomplishments.** Some job seekers inflate their employment experience or achievements. One clerk, eager to make her photocopying duties sound more important, said that she *assisted the vice president in communicating and distributing employee directives.* An Ivy League graduate who

spent the better part of six months watching rented videos on his VCR described the activity as *Independent Film Study.* The latter statement may have helped win an interview, but it lost him the job. In addition to avoiding puffery, guard against taking sole credit for achievements that required many people. When recruiters suspect dubious claims on résumés, they nail applicants with specific—and often embarrassing—questions during their interviews.[30]

- **Altered employment dates.** Some candidates extend the dates of employment to hide unimpressive jobs or to cover up periods of unemployment and illness. Let's say that several years ago Cindy was unemployed for 14 months between working for Company A and being hired by Company B. To make her employment history look better, she adds seven months to her tenure with Company A and seven months to Company B. Now her employment history has no gaps, but her résumé is dishonest and represents a potential booby trap for her.

One of the latest sneaky tricks involves inserting invisible keywords into electronic résumés. To fool scanning programs into ranking their résumés higher, some job hunters use white type on a white background or they use Web coding to pack their résumés with target keywords. However, newer recruiter search tools detect such mischief, and those résumés are tossed.[31]

If your honest qualifications aren't good enough to get you the job you want, start working now to improve them.

Career Application

As a class, discuss the ethics of writing résumés. What's the difference between honest self-marketing and deception? What are some examples from your experience? Where could college students go wrong in preparing their résumés? Is a new employee "home free" if an inflated résumé is not detected in the hiring process? Are job candidates obligated to describe every previous job on a résumé? How can candidates improve an unimpressive résumé without resorting to "puffing it up"?

Creating a Customized Cover Letter

Job candidates often labor over their résumés but treat the cover letter as an afterthought. This critical mistake could destroy a job search. Even if an advertisement doesn't request one, be sure to distinguish your application with a customized cover letter (also called a *letter of application*). It has three purposes: (a) introducing the résumé, (b) highlighting your strengths in terms of benefits to the reader, and (c) gaining an interview. In many ways your cover letter is a sales letter; it sells your talent and tries to beat the competition. It will, accordingly, include many of the techniques you learned for sales letters in Chapter 9, especially if your letter is unsolicited.

LEARNING OBJECTIVE 6
Write a customized cover letter to accompany a résumé.

Recruiting professionals disagree about how long to make a cover letter. Many prefer short letters with no more than three paragraphs. Others desire longer letters that supply more information, thus giving them a better opportunity to evaluate a candidate's qualifications. These recruiters argue that hiring and training new employees is expensive and time consuming; therefore, they welcome extra data to guide them in making the best choice the first time. Follow your judgment in writing a brief or a longer cover letter. If you feel, for example, that you need space to explain in more detail what you can do for a prospective employer, do so.

Regardless of its length, a cover letter should have three primary parts: (a) an opening that introduces the message and identifies the position, (b) a body that sells the candidate and focuses on the employer's needs, and (c) a closing that requests an interview and motivates action. When putting your cover letter together, remember that the biggest mistake job seekers make when writing cover letters is making them sound too generic. You should, therefore, write a personalized, customized cover letter for every position you apply for.

Gaining Attention in the Opening

The opening in a cover letter gains attention by addressing the receiver by name.

Your cover letter will be more appealing, and will more likely be read, if it begins by addressing the reader by name. Rather than sending your letter to the *Hiring Manager* or *Human Resources Department*, try to identify the name of the appropriate individual. Call the organization for the name of the person in charge of hiring for the position. If that fails, says workplace expert Liz Ryan, look on the company Web site under **About Us**. "Either the VP/leader of the function you are interested in (e.g., marketing or engineering)," suggests Ryan, "or the VP/leader of HR is a great person to call or write to."[32] See the accompanying Spotlight feature for additional ways to locate contacts within your target company. If you still cannot find the name of any person to address, you might replace the salutation of your letter with a subject line such as "Application for Position of...."

How you open your cover letter depends largely on whether the application is solicited or unsolicited. If an employment position has been announced and applicants are being solicited, you can use a direct approach. If you do not know whether a position is open and you are prospecting for a job, use an indirect approach. Whether direct or indirect, the opening should attract the attention of the reader. Strive for openings that are more imaginative than *Please consider this letter an application for the position of...* or *I would like to apply for....*

Openers for solicited jobs refer to the source of the information, the job title, and qualifications for the position.

Openings for Solicited Jobs. Here are some of the best techniques to open a cover letter for a job that has been announced:

- **Refer to the name of an employee in the company.** Remember that employers always hope to hire known quantities rather than complete strangers.

  Mitchell Sims, a member of your Customer Service Department, told me that IntriPlex is seeking an experienced customer service representative. The enclosed summary of my qualifications demonstrates my preparation for this position.

  At the suggestion of Ms. Jennifer Larson of your Human Resources Department, I submit my qualifications for the position of staffing coordinator.

- **Refer to the source of your information precisely.** If you are answering an advertisement, include the exact position advertised and the name and date of the publication. For large organizations it is wise to mention the section of the newspaper where the ad appeared:

  The job you advertised in Section C-3 of the June 1 Daily News for an accounting administrator greatly appeals to me. With my accounting training and computer experience, I believe I could serve Quad Graphics well.

  From your company's Web site, I learned about your need for a sales representative for the Ohio, Indiana, and Illinois regions. I am very interested in this position and believe that my education and experience are appropriate for the opening.

Spotlight on Communicators

How can you find a contact person in your targeted company? Career expert Liz Ryan suggests these resources: (a) Use LinkedIn or another networking site and search for the target company name to find people who work there. (b) Search Google with a string such as "Apex+Foods+marketing+director." (c) Use Google's blog-search function to locate people in your target organization. (d) Check the online archive for the local business paper in the city where the company is located. (e) Search the archives at *Yahoogroups.com*. (f) Study the target company's Web site for the names of staffers involved in community and charity work. (g) Search the database of your school's alumni site for graduates who might be employed at the target company.

Courtesy of Liz Ryan

Susan Butler, placement director at Sierra University, told me that DataTech has an opening for a technical writer with knowledge of Web design and graphics.

- **Refer to the job title and describe how your qualifications fit the requirements.** Human resources directors are looking for a match between an applicant's credentials and the job needs:

  Will an honors graduate with a degree in recreation and two years of part-time experience organizing social activities for a convalescent hospital qualify for your position of activity director?

  Because of my specialized training in finance and accounting at Boise State University, I am confident that I have the qualifications you described in your advertisement for a staff accountant trainee.

Openings for Unsolicited Jobs. If you are unsure whether a position actually exists, you might use a more persuasive opening. Because your goal is to convince this person to read on, try one of the following techniques:

Openers for unsolicited jobs show interest in and knowledge of the company, as well as spotlight reader benefits.

- **Demonstrate an interest in and knowledge of the reader's business.** Show the hiring officer that you have done your research and that this organization is more than a mere name to you:

  Because Signa HealthNet, Inc., is organizing a new information management team for its recently established group insurance division, could you use the services of a well-trained information systems graduate who seeks to become a professional systems analyst?

- **Show how your special talents and background will benefit the company.** Human resources managers need to be convinced that you can do something for them:

  Could your rapidly expanding publications division use the services of an editorial assistant who offers exceptional language skills, an honors degree from the University of Maine, and two years' experience in producing a campus literary publication?

In applying for an advertised job, Kendra Hawkins wrote the solicited cover letter shown in Figure 15.14. Notice that her opening identifies the position and the newspaper completely so that the reader knows exactly what advertisement Kendra means. Using features on her word processing program, Kendra designed her own letterhead that uses her name and looks like professionally printed letterhead paper.

More challenging are unsolicited cover letters, such as Donald Vinton's shown in Figure 15.15. Because he hopes to discover or create a job, his opening must grab the reader's attention immediately. To do that, he capitalizes on company information appearing in an online article. Donald purposely kept his cover letter short and to the point because he anticipated that a busy executive would be unwilling to read a long, detailed letter. Donald's unsolicited letter "prospects" for a job. Some job candidates feel that such letters may be even more productive than efforts to secure advertised jobs, since "prospecting" candidates face less competition and show initiative. Notice that Donald's letter uses a personal business letter format with his return address above the date.

Selling Your Strengths in the Body

Once you have captured the attention of the reader and identified your purpose in the letter opening, you should use the body of the letter to promote your qualifications for this position. If you are responding to an advertisement, you'll want to explain how your preparation and experience fill the stated requirements. If you are prospecting for a job, you may not know the exact requirements. Your employment research and knowledge of your field, however, should give you a reasonably good idea of what is expected for this position.

The body of the cover letter promotes the candidate's qualifications for the targeted job.

It's also important to stress reader benefits. In other words, you should describe your strong points in relation to the needs of the employer. Hiring officers want you to tell them what you can do for their organizations. This is more important than telling what courses

FIGURE 15.14 Solicited Cover Letter

Kendra A. Hawkins

1770 Hawthorne Place, Boulder, CO 80304
(303) 492-1244 khawkins@yahoo.com

Uses personally designed letterhead

May 23, 2009

Ms. Courtney L. Donahue
Director, Human Resources
Del Rio Enterprises
4839 Mountain View Avenue
Denver, CO 82511

Addresses proper person by name and title

Dear Ms. Donahue:

Your advertisement for an assistant product manager, appearing May 22 in Section C of the *Denver Post*, immediately caught my attention because my education and training closely parallel your needs.

Identifies job and exact page where ad appeared

According to your advertisement, the job includes "assisting in the coordination of a wide range of marketing programs as well as analyzing sales results and tracking marketing budgets." A recent internship at Ventana Corporation introduced me to similar tasks. Assisting the marketing manager enabled me to analyze the promotion, budget, and overall sales success of two products Ventana was evaluating. My ten-page report examined the nature of the current market, the products' life cycles, and their sales/profit return. In addition to this research, I helped formulate a product merchandising plan and answered consumers' questions at a local trade show.

Relates writer's experiences to job requirements

Intensive course work in marketing and management, as well as proficiency in computer spreadsheets and databases, has given me the kind of marketing and computer training that Del Rio probably demands in a product manager. Moreover, my recent retail sales experience and participation in campus organizations have helped me develop the kind of customer service and interpersonal skills necessary for an effective product manager.

Discusses schooling

Discusses experience

After you have examined the enclosed résumé for details of my qualifications, I would be happy to answer questions. Please call me at (303) 492-1244 to arrange an interview at your convenience so that we may discuss how my marketing experience, computer training, and interpersonal skills could contribute to Del Rio Enterprises.

Refers reader to résumé

Asks for interview and repeats main qualifications

Sincerely,

Kendra A. Hawkins

Kendra A. Hawkins

Enclosure

---

you took in college or what duties you performed in your previous jobs. Instead of *I have completed courses in business communication, report writing, and technical writing,* try this:

> *Courses in business communication, report writing, and technical writing have helped me develop the research and writing skills required of your technical writers.*

Choose your strongest qualifications and show how they fit the targeted job. Remember that students with little experience are better off spotlighting their education and its practical applications, as these candidates did:

> *Because you seek an architect's apprentice with proven ability, I submit a drawing of mine that won second place in the Sinclair College drafting contest last year.*

> *Composing e-mail messages, business letters, memos, and reports in my business communication and office technology courses helped me develop the writing, language, proofreading, and computer skills mentioned in your ad for an administrative assistant.*

FIGURE 15.15 Unsolicited Cover Letter

Uses personal business style with return address above date

2250 Turtle Creek Drive
Monroeville, PA 15146
May 29, 2009

Mr. Richard M. Jannis
Vice President, Operations
Sports World, Inc.
4907 Allegheny Boulevard
Pittsburgh, PA 16103

Dear Mr. Jannis:

Shows resourcefulness and knowledge of company

Today's *Pittsburgh Examiner* reports that your organization plans to expand its operations to include national distribution of sporting goods, and it occurs to me that you will be needing highly motivated, self-starting sales representatives and marketing managers. Here are three significant qualifications I have to offer:

Uses bulleted list to make letter easier to read

- Four years of formal training in business administration, including specialized courses in sales management, retailing, marketing promotion, and consumer behavior

- Practical experience in demonstrating and selling consumer products, as well as successful experience in telemarketing

- Excellent communication skills and a strong interest in most areas of sports (which helped me become a sportscaster at Penn State radio station WGNF)

Keeps letter brief to retain reader's attention

Refers to enclosed résumé

May we talk about how I can put these qualifications, and others summarized in the enclosed résumé, to work for Sports World as it develops its national sales force? I'll call during the week of June 5 to discuss your company's expansion plans and the opportunity for an interview.

Takes initiative for follow-up

Sincerely yours,

Donald W. Vinton

Donald W. Vinton

Enclosure

In the body of your letter, you may choose to discuss relevant personal traits. Employers are looking for candidates who, among other things, are team players, take responsibility, show initiative, and learn easily. Don't just list several personal traits, though; instead, include documentation that proves you possess these traits. Notice how the following paragraph uses action verbs to paint a picture of a promising candidate:

Employers seek employees who are team players, take responsibility, show initiative, and learn easily.

> *In addition to developing technical and academic skills at Mid-State University, I have gained interpersonal, leadership, and organizational skills. As vice president of the business students' organization, Gamma Alpha, I helped organize and supervise two successful fundraising events. These activities involved conceptualizing the tasks, motivating others to help, scheduling work sessions, and coordinating the efforts of 35 diverse students in reaching our goal. I enjoyed my success with these activities and look forward to applying such experience in your management trainee program.*

Finally, in this section or the next, you should refer the reader to your résumé. Do so directly or as part of another statement, as shown here:

As you will notice from my enclosed résumé, I will graduate in June with a bachelor's degree in business administration.

Please refer to the attached résumé for additional information regarding my education, experience, and references.

Motivating Action in the Closing

After presenting your case, you should conclude by asking confidently for an interview. Don't ask for the job. To do so would be presumptuous and naive. In requesting an interview, you might suggest reader benefits or review your strongest points. Sound sincere and appreciative. Remember to make it easy for the reader to agree by supplying your telephone number and the best times to call you. In addition, keep in mind that some hiring officers prefer that you take the initiative to call them. Avoid expressions like *I hope,* which will weaken your closing. Here are possible endings:

This brief description of my qualifications and the additional information on my résumé demonstrate my genuine desire to put my skills in accounting to work for you. Please call me at (405) 488-2291 before 10 a.m. or after 3 p.m. to arrange an interview.

To add to your staff an industrious, well-trained administrative assistant with proven word processing and communication skills, call me at (350) 492-1433 to arrange an interview. I can meet with you at any time convenient to you.

I look forward to the opportunity to discuss my qualifications more fully in an interview. I can be reached on my cell phone at (213) 458-4030.

Next week, after you have examined the enclosed résumé, I will call you to discuss the possibility of arranging an interview.

Sending Your Cover Letter

Many applicants using technology make the mistake of not including cover letters with their résumés submitted by e-mail or by fax. A résumé that arrives without a cover letter makes the receiver wonder what it is and why it was sent. Recruiters want you to introduce yourself, and they also are eager to see some evidence that you can write. Some candidates either skip the cover letter or think they can get by with one-line cover letters such as this: *Please see attached résumé, and thanks for your consideration.*

If you are serious about landing the job, take the time to prepare a professional cover letter. If you're sending your résumé via e-mail, you may use the same cover letter you would send by surface mail but shorten it a bit. As illustrated in Figure 15.16, an inside address is unnecessary for an e-mail recipient. Also move your return address from the top of the letter to just below your name. Include your e-mail address and phone number. Remove tabs, bullets, underlining, and italics that might be problematic in e-mail messages. If you're submitting your résumé by fax, send the same cover letter you would send by surface mail. If you are submitting your résumé as a PDF file, do the same for your cover letter.

Final Tips for Successful Cover Letters

As you revise your cover letter, notice how many sentences begin with *I*. Although it's impossible to talk about yourself without using *I,* you can reduce "I" domination with this writing technique. Make activities and outcomes, and not yourself, the subjects of sentences. For example, rather than *I took classes in business communication and computer applications,* say *Classes in business communication and computer applications prepared me to. . . .* Instead of *I enjoyed helping customers,* say *Helping customers was a real pleasure.*

Like the résumé, your cover letter must look professional and suggest quality. This means using a traditional letter style, such as block. Also, be sure to print it on the same quality paper as your résumé. As with your résumé, proofread it several times yourself; then have a friend read it for content and mechanics. Don't rely on spell check to find all the errors. Just like your résumé, your cover letter must be perfect.

The closing of a cover letter confidently requests an interview and makes it easy to respond.

Ethics Check

Cover Letter Blunders

Advice columns and Internet blogs are teeming with cover letter bloopers. Downright lies aside, some candidates simply need a lesson in selling: *P.S. – I haven't taken a sick day in years – I don't get sick.* Or consider this candid job board posting: *I have a lot of customer service experience, but I am willing to do just about anything. I am in a lot of debt and need a good solid job to help me get out of it.* After reading this chapter, what advice would you give such job seekers?

Serious job candidates send a professional cover letter even if the résumé is submitted online, by e-mail, or by fax.

Look for ways to reduce the overuse of *I.*

A cover letter should look professional and suggest quality.

FIGURE 15.16 E-Mail Cover Letter

Provides complete subject line identifying purpose

```
File  Edit  Mailbox  Message  Transfer  Special  Tools  Window  Help

B  I  U          A  A                          Send

     To:  Courtney L. Donahue <courtney.donahue@delrio.com>
   From:  Kendra A. Hawkins <kendra.hawkins@aol.com>
Subject:  Application for Assistant Product Manager Position Advertised 5-22-09
     Cc:

Dear Ms. Donahue:

Your advertisement for an assistant product manager, appearing May 22 in Section C of
the DENVER POST, immediately caught my attention because my education and training
closely parallel your needs. The advertisement says the job involves coordinating
marketing programs, analyzing sales results, and tracking marketing budgets.


I would like to discuss my qualifications with you and answer any questions you have
about my résumé, which is embedded below. The best way to reach me is to call my
cell at (713) 343-2910 during business hours. I look forward to putting my skills to
work for Del Rio Enterprises.

Sincerely,

Kendra A. Hawkins
1770 Hawthorne Place
Boulder, CO 80304
E-mail: kendra.hawkins@aol.com
Cell: (713) 343-2910

Plain-text résumé embedded below. Attractive print résumé available on request.
```

Addresses proper person by name

Transfers traditional cover letter to e-mail

Calls attention to résumé embedded in same message

Uses signature block for all contact information

Reminds receiver that attractive print résumé is available

Checklist

Preparing and Sending a Customized Cover Letter

Opening

✓ **Use the receiver's name.** Whenever possible, address the proper individual by name.

✓ **Identify your information source, if appropriate.** In responding to an advertisement, specify the position advertised as well as the date and publication name. If someone referred you, name that person.

✓ **Gain the reader's attention.** Use one of these techniques: (a) tell how your qualifications fit the job specifications, (b) show knowledge of the reader's business, (c) describe how your special talents will be assets to the company, or (d) use an original and relevant expression.

Body

✓ **Describe what you can do for the reader.** Demonstrate how your background and training fill the job requirements.

✓ **Highlight your strengths.** Summarize your principal assets in terms of education, experience, and special skills. Avoid repeating specific data from your résumé.

✓ **Refer to your résumé.** In this section or the closing, direct the reader to the attached résumé. Do so directly or incidentally as part of another statement.

Closing

✓ **Ask for an interview.** Also consider reviewing your strongest points or suggesting how your assets will benefit the company.

✓ **Make it easy to respond.** Tell when you can be reached during office hours or announce when you will call the reader. Note that some recruiters prefer that you call them.

Sending

✓ **Include a cover letter with your résumé.** Send your cover letter along with your résumé as a Word attachment, embedded in an e-mail message, as a plain-text attachment, or as a PDF file.

✓ **If you e-mail your cover letter, put your contact information in the signature area.** Move your return address from the top of the letter to the signature block. Include your phone number and e-mail address.

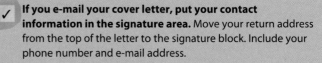

Communicating at Work Your Turn

Applying Your Skills With Liz Ryan

As an intern working with Liz Ryan, you are expected to help her prepare advice articles and interesting blog items. She plans to write an article in the near future about students searching for jobs. She wants you to give her firsthand information. These are some questions she posed:

- What do students fear the most in job searching? Do you have any ideas for overcoming those fears?
- Among your friends, where would most of them go first when they begin a job search?
- How can students begin networking? What would you and your friends do?
- How would you and your friends use the Internet for job searching?

Your Task

In a well-organized e-mail or memo, prepare a short informative report answering the questions listed here. Add any other information or advice that you think would be helpful as advice to students looking for jobs. Arrange your memo as an information report, which was covered in Chapter 12.

© IMAGEMORE Co., Ltd. / Getty Images

Summary of Learning Objectives

1 **Prepare for employment by identifying your interests, evaluating your assets, recognizing the changing nature of jobs, and choosing a career path.** The employment process begins with an analysis of your preferences and your qualifications. Because the nature of jobs is changing, your future work may include flexible work assignments, multiple employers, and constant retraining. You can learn more about career opportunities through your campus career center, the Web, your library, internships, part-time jobs, interviews, classified ads, and professional organizations.

2 **Apply both electronic and traditional techniques in a successful job search.** Electronic job-search techniques include visiting the big commercial sites (such as Monster, Yahoo HotJobs, and College Recruiter) as well as corporations' sites, professional organizations' sites, and niche sites. To establish online networking, job seekers are joining social sites such as LinkedIn and Ryze. Traditional job-search techniques include checking classified ads, studying announcements in professional organizations, contacting companies directly, signing up for campus interviews, attending career fairs, asking for advice from instructors, and developing a personal network of contacts.

3 **Appreciate the need to customize your résumé and know whether to choose a chronological or a functional résumé style.** Because of intense competition, job seekers must customize their résumés for every position sought. Chronological résumés, listing work and education by dates, rank highest with recruiters. Functional résumés, highlighting skills instead of jobs, appeal to people changing careers or those having negative employment histories. Functional résumés are also effective for recent graduates who have little work experience.

4 **Organize your qualifications and information into effective résumé segments.** In preparing a résumé, organize your skills and achievements so that they aim at a particular job or company. Study models to arrange most effectively your main heading, career objective (optional), summary of qualifications, education, work experience, capabilities, awards and activities, personal data (optional), and references (optional). Use action verbs to show how your assets will help the target organization.

5 **Describe techniques that optimize a résumé for today's technologies, including preparing a scannable résumé, a plain-text résumé, and an e-portfolio.** Candidates should consider preparing a scannable résumé that limits line length, avoids fancy formatting, and emphasizes keywords. Keywords are nouns that an employer might use to describe a position and its requirements. Plain-text (also called *ASCII*) résumés are stripped of all formatting and prepared as text files so that they may be embedded within e-mail messages or submitted online. An e-portfolio is a collection of digitized materials that illustrate a candidate's performance, talents, and accomplishments. E-portfolios may be posted at Web sites or burned onto CDs or DVDs.

6 **Write a customized cover letter to accompany a résumé.** Gain attention in the opening by addressing the receiver by name and mentioning the job or a person who referred you. Build interest in the body by stressing your strengths in relation to the stated requirements. Explain what you can do for the targeted company. Refer to your résumé, request an interview, and make it easy for the receiver to reach you. If you send your cover letter by e-mail, shorten it a bit and include complete contact information in the signature block. Remove tabs, bullets, underlining, and italics that could be problematic in e-mail.

Chapter Review

1. How should the job-search process begin? By writing a résumé? (Obj. 1)

2. List five sources of career information. (Obj. 1)

3. Has searching for a job online replaced traditional job-search methods? Explain. (Obj. 2)

4. Using the Web, where should job candidates look in addition to searching the big job board sites? (Obj. 2)

5. What is a customized résumé, and why should a job seeker have one? (Obj. 3)

6. What is a chronological résumé, and what are its advantages and disadvantages? (Obj. 3)

7. What is a functional résumé, and what are its advantages and disadvantages? (Obj. 3)

8. List five tips for writing an effective career objective on your résumé. (Obj. 4)

9. Describe a summary of qualifications, and explain why it is increasingly popular on résumés. (Obj. 4)

10. In addition to technical skills, what traits and capabilities are employers seeking? (Obj. 4)

11. To optimize your résumé for today's technologies, how many versions of your résumé should you expect to make? What are they? (Obj. 5)

12. What changes must be made in a typical résumé to make it effective for computer scanning? (Obj. 5)

13. What are the three purposes of a cover letter? (Obj. 6)

14. What information goes in the body of a cover letter? (Obj. 6)

15. When you send a cover letter within an e-mail message, what changes should you make to the format of the letter? (Obj. 6)

Critical Thinking

1. How has the Internet changed job searching for individuals and recruiters? Has the change had a positive or a negative effect? Why? (Obj. 1)

2. How is a résumé different from a company employment application? (Objs. 1, 2)

3. Some job candidates think that applying for unsolicited jobs can be more fruitful than applying for advertised openings. Discuss the advantages and disadvantages of letters that "prospect" for jobs. (Obj. 5)

4. In regard to hiring, conventional wisdom holds that it's all about whom you know. How can job candidates find an insider to refer them for a job opening? (Obj. 2)

5. **Ethical Issue:** Job candidate Karen accepts a position with Company A. One week later she receives a better offer from Company B. She wants very much to accept it. What should she do?

Activities

15.1 Document for Analysis: Résumé (Obj. 4)

One effective way to improve your writing skills is to critique and edit the résumé of someone else.

Your Task. Analyze the following poorly organized résumé. Discuss its weaknesses. Your instructor may ask you to revise sections of this résumé before showing you an improved version.

Résumé of Brenda Ann Trudell
5349 West Plaza Place
Tulsa, OK 74115-3394
Home: 834-4583 Cell: 594-2985
E-mail: supahsnugglykitty@aol.com

OBJECTIVE: I would like to find an entry-level position with a large corporation that offers opportunity for advancement
SKILLS: Word processing, spreadsheet, QuickBooks, Internet, Excel, Powerpoint, Excel, database.

EDUCATION
Langston University, Tulsa, Oklahoma. Now working on BBA. Major: Accounting. My GPA in major is 3.5. Expected degree date: June 2009. Very interested in forensic accounting. Took courses in: Analysis and Application of Accounting Data and Financial Reporting.

EXPERIENCE

Assistant bookkeeper, 2007 to present. Marsh and McLennan, Inc., Tulsa. I work with many small businesses to keep their bookkeeping records. I have to be accurate, and I get little supervision. I prepare income tax returns, I monitor and update A/R records for Overland Truck Lines. I am responsible for the payroll records at three firms. The owner of Marsh and McLennan said I was reliable and painstaking.

Peterson Controls Inc., Tulsa. I held a data processing internship from July to October 2006. I worked with spreadsheets and also kept information for production uptime and downtime. Prepared graphs, answered phones; helped people with collecting and photocopying their data.

2005–2008. Langston University, Tulsa. I was coordinator of Volunteer Income Tax Assistance Project. I marketed the VITA program to Langston students. I scheduled volunteers, got the supplies, and kept track of all appointments.

Community Service: March of Dimes Drive at Central Park High School; All Souls Unitarian Church, assistant director of Children's Choir.

15.2 Document for Analysis: Cover Letter (Obj. 6)

The following cover letter accompanies Brenda Trudell's résumé (Activity 15.1).

Your Task. Analyze each section of the following cover letter written by Brenda and list its weaknesses. Your instructor may ask you to revise this letter before showing you an improved version.

Dear Human Resources Director:

I would like you to consider me for the accounting position that I saw for Mead Products. I am working part time and trying to finish my degree program, but I think a position at your industry-leading firm would be beneficial and would certainly look good on my résumé.

I have been studying accounting at Langston University for four years, and I have completed 90 units of course work. I have taken courses in business law, management, finance, accounting, and marketing, but I am most interested in my accounting courses, especially in forensic accounting.

I have worked at Marsh and McLennan as an assistant bookkeeper. I should mention that I have had another internship, which was at Peterson Controls. I worked on spreadsheets at Peterson. I also was coordinator of the VITA program at Langston, which helped me develop leadership and interpersonal skills. I think that all of these positions gave me the skills needed to be a good intern for you.

I am a competent, reliable, well-organized person who gets along pretty well with others. I feel that I have a strong foundation in accounting as a result of my course work and my experience. I hope you will agree that, along with my personal qualities and my desire to succeed, I qualify for the open accounting position with your company.

Yours very truly,

15.3 Identifying Your Employment Interests (Obj. 1)

Your Task. In an e-mail or a memo addressed to your instructor, answer the questions in the section "Identifying Your Interests" at the beginning of the chapter. Draw a conclusion from your answers. What kind of career, company, position, and location seem to fit your self-analysis?

15.4 Evaluating Your Qualifications (Objs. 1, 2, and 3)

Your Task. Prepare four worksheets that inventory your qualifications in these areas: employment, education, capabilities and skills, and honors and activities. Use active verbs when appropriate.

a. **Employment.** Begin with your most recent job or internship. For each position list the following information: employer; job title; dates of employment; and three to five duties, activities, or accomplishments. Emphasize activities related to your job goal. Strive to quantify your achievements.

b. **Education.** List degrees, certificates, and training accomplishments. Include courses, seminars, or skills that are relevant to your job goal. Calculate your grade-point average in your major.

c. **Capabilities and skills.** List all capabilities and skills that recommend you for the job you seek. Use words like *skilled, competent, trained, experienced,* and *ability to.* Also list five or more qualities or interpersonal skills necessary for a successful individual in your chosen field. Write action statements demonstrating that you possess some of these qualities. Empty assurances aren't good enough; try to show evidence (*Developed teamwork skills by working with a committee of eight to produce a . . .*).

d. **Awards, honors, and activities.** Explain any awards so that the reader will understand them. List campus, community, and professional activities that suggest you are a well-rounded individual or possess traits relevant to your target job.

15.5 Choosing a Career Path (Obj. 1)

Web

Many people know amazingly little about the work done in various occupations and the training requirements.

Your Task. Use the online *Occupational Outlook Handbook* at **http://www.bls.gov/oco**, prepared by the Bureau of Labor Statistics, to learn more about an occupation of your choice. Find the description of a position for which you could apply in two to five years. Learn about what workers do on the job, working conditions, training and education needed, earnings, and expected job prospects. Print the pages from the *Occupational Outlook Handbook* that describe employment in the area in which you are interested. If your instructor directs, attach these copies to the cover letter you will write in Activity 15.10.

15.6 Locating Salary Information (Obj. 1)

Web

What salary can you expect in your chosen career?

Your Task. Visit America's Career InfoNet at **http://www.acinet .org** and select an occupation based on the kind of employment you are seeking now or will be seeking after you graduate. What wages can you expect in this occupation? Print a copy of the wage information. Click to learn more about this occupation. Take notes on three or four interesting bits of information you learned about this occupation. Bring a printout of the wage information to class and be prepared to discuss what you learned about this occupation.

15.7 Searching the Job Market (Obj. 1)

Where are the jobs? Even though you may not be in the market at the moment, become familiar with the kinds of available positions because job awareness should become an important part of your education.

Your Task. Clip or print a job advertisement or announcement from (a) the classified section of a newspaper, (b) a job board on the Web, (c) a company Web site, or (d) a professional association listing. Select an advertisement or announcement describing the kind of employment you are seeking now or plan to seek when you graduate. Save this advertisement or announcement to attach to the résumé you will write in **Activity 15.9.**

15.8 Posting a Résumé on the Web (Obj. 2)

Web

Learn about the procedure for posting résumés at job boards on the Web.

Your Task. Prepare a list of at least three Web sites where you could post your résumé. Describe the procedure involved in posting a résumé and the advantages for each site.

15.9 Writing Your Résumé (Obj. 4)

Your Task. Using the data you developed in **Activity 15.4,** write your résumé. Aim it at a full-time job, part-time position, or internship. Attach a job listing for a specific position (from **Activity 15.7**). Also prepare a list of references. Revise your résumé until it is perfect.

15.10 Preparing Your Cover Letter (Obj. 6)

Your Task. Write a cover letter introducing your résumé. Again, revise until it is perfect.

15.11 Swapping Résumés (Obj. 2)

A terrific way to get ideas for improving your résumé is seeing how other students have developed their résumés.

Your Task. Bring your completed résumé to class. Attach a plain sheet with your name at the top. In small groups exchange your résumés. Each reviewer should provide at least two supportive comments and one suggestion for improvement on the cover sheet. Reviewers should sign their names with their comments.

15.12 Consumer: Being Wary of Career Advisory Firms With Big Promises and Big Prices (Obj. 1)

Consumer   Web

Not long ago employment agencies charged applicants 5 percent of their annual salaries to find jobs. Most agencies have quit this unethical practice, but unscrupulous firms still prey on vulnerable job seekers. Some career-advisory firms claim to be legitimate, but they make puffed-up promises and charge inflated fees—$4,000 is typical.

Your Task. Using databases and the Web, find examples of current employment scams or danger areas for job seekers. In a presentation to the class or in team discussions, describe three examples of disreputable practices candidates should recognize. Make recommendations to job seekers for avoiding employment scams and disappointment with career-advisory services.

Video Resources

Video Library 1. *The Job Search* illustrates the good and bad job-search tactics of Yolanda and Stephanie. Be prepared to discuss critical-thinking questions your instructor may provide.

Grammar and Mechanics C.L.U.E. Review 15

Total Review

Each of the following sentences has a total of **three** errors in grammar, punctuation, capitalization, usage, or spelling. On a separate sheet, write a correct version. Avoid adding new phrases or rewriting sentences in your own words. When finished, compare your responses with the key beginning on page Key-4.

Example: One West coast company found that e-mail consumed about 24% of staff members workdays.

Revision: One West **Coast** company found that e-mail consumed about 24 **percent** of staff **members'** workdays.

1. The employment process begins with introspection. Which mean looking inside yourself.

2. To find the job of your dreams, you must: (a) Know yourself, (2) know the job market, and (3) know the process.

3. When Marcys job was terminated she applied at 3 online job boards.

4. If you loose your job consider using the internet to find another.

5. Justin wondered whether it was alright to apply at many sights simultaneously?

6. At last months staff meeting team members examined several candidates résumés.

7. Rather then schedule face to face interviews the team investigated videoconferencing.

8. 55 trainees are expected to attend the May 1st meeting, consequently, we need a larger room.

9. Good telephone manners reflects on you and your company, however, to few employees are trained properly.

10. In the last issue of *Newsweek* did you see the article titled "Should a résumé include a Career Objective?"

Chapter 16

Interviewing and Following Up

© Tom Grill / Corbis

OBJECTIVES

After studying this chapter, you should be able to

1 Understand the importance of a job interview, its purposes, and its forms, including screening, hiring/placement, one-on-one, panel, group, sequential, and stress interviews.

2 Describe what to do before an in-person interview, including researching the target company, preparing success stories, and practicing answers to possible questions.

3 Explain how to perform during an interview, including sending positive nonverbal messages and using good techniques in answering questions.

4 Describe how to answer typical interview questions such as those that seek to get acquainted, gauge your interest, probe your experience, explore your accomplishments, look to the future, and inquire about salary expectations.

5 Understand how to close an interview positively, including asking meaningful questions.

6 Outline the activities that take place after an interview, including thanking the interviewer and contacting references.

7 Understand how to complete employment applications and write résumé follow-up, rejection follow-up, job acceptance, and job rejection messages.

Communicating at Work Part 1

Googling for Jobs

Résumés from thousands of prospective Nooglers (new Google employees) arrive at Google's Mountain View, California, headquarters every day. Admired for its technological excellence and nontraditional corporate culture, Google recently topped *Fortune*'s "America's Best Companies to Work For" list. Its growth had been so rapid that Google's employee roster soared from about 1,600 in 2003 to well over 11,000 now. With major offices worldwide, the company typically hires 16 Nooglers a day. It looks for talented, passionate people from a variety of backgrounds. Google seeks enthusiastic candidates who want to make a difference in the world by applying technology to benefit users.

Hiring and retaining the best people are central to Google's continuing success and growth. "It's no accident that my title is Vice-President of People Operations, and not the more traditional description of 'human resources,'" said Laszlo Bock, who had recently joined Google after leaving General Electric. "People are our most vital competitive asset. . . . Our strategy is simple: We hire great people and encourage them to make their dreams a reality."[1]

The uniqueness of the Mountain View Googleplex contributes to employee satisfaction and keeps turnover low—just 4 to 5 percent. Its informal, collaborative work environment has been compared to a university setting. Employees work in small teams that promote creativity and an open exchange of ideas. As the leading Internet search site and advertising giant, Google values out-of-the-box thinking. Managers encourage employees to work on special projects and expand their responsibilities well beyond their original job descriptions.

In addition to encouraging a high-energy atmosphere, Google supports its employees with an exceptional list of benefits. Gourmet meals and snacks, haircuts, car washes and oil changes, gym facilities, sports, language lessons, personal concierge services, day care, running trails, medical and dental care—all these and more are available at the Googleplex.

© ERIN LUBIN / Bloomberg News / Landov

Google's high growth rate places intense pressure on Google's recruiters to fill its many open positions. "As we get bigger, we find it harder and harder to find enough people," said Vice President Bock.[2] Many senior managers were devoting almost one third of their time to interviewing candidates. As a result, one of Mr. Bock's first initiatives was to streamline Google's rigorous hiring processes—while still striking "the right balance between letting candidates get to know Google, letting us get to know them, and moving quickly."[3]

Critical Thinking
- Before you apply for a job, why must you investigate carefully the background of any company that interests you?
- What types of skills and background do you think Google recruiters look for in a candidate?
- How would you craft a résumé and cover letter so that it would stand out when it arrives at Google?

http://www.google.com

The Job Interview: Understanding Its Importance, Purposes, and Types

A job interview, whether at Google or anywhere else, can change your life. Because employment is a major part of everyone's life, the job interview takes on enormous importance. Interviewing is equally significant whether you are completing your education and searching for your first serious position or whether you are in the workforce and striving to change jobs.

Everyone agrees that job interviews are extremely stressful. However, the more you learn about the process and the more prepared you are, the less stress you will feel. It's also important to realize that a job interview is a two-way street. It's not just about being judged by the employer. You, the applicant, will be using the job interview to evaluate the employer. Do you really want to work for this organization?

This chapter will increase your interviewing effectiveness and confidence by explaining the purposes and kinds of interviews and how to prepare for them. You will learn how to gather information about an employer, as well as how to reduce nervousness, control body language, and fight fear during an interview. You will pick up tips for responding to recruiters' favorite questions and learn how to cope with illegal questions and salary matters. Moreover, you will receive pointers on significant questions you can ask during an interview. Finally, you will learn what you should do as a successful follow-up to an interview.

Yes, job interviews can be intimidating and stressful. However, you can expect to ace an interview when you know what's coming and when you prepare thoroughly. It's often the degree of preparation that determines who gets the job.

LEARNING OBJECTIVE 1
Understand the importance of a job interview, its purposes, and its forms, including screening, hiring/placement, one-on-one, panel, group, sequential, and stress interviews.

Purposes of Employment Interviews

An interview has several purposes for you as a job candidate. It is an opportunity to (a) convince the employer of your potential, (b) find out more about the job and the company, and (c) expand on the information in your résumé. This is the time for you to gather information about whether you would fit into the company culture. You should also be thinking about whether this job suits your career goals.

From the employer's perspective, the interview is an opportunity to (a) assess your abilities in relation to the requirements for the position; (b) discuss your training, experience, knowledge, and abilities in more detail; (c) see what drives and motivates you; and (d) decide whether you would fit into the organization.

During job interviews, candidates try to (a) convince an employer of their potential, (b) learn about the job, and (c) amplify résumé information.

Types of Employment Interviews

Job applicants may face a number of kinds of interviews that have different purposes. You must succeed in the screening interview to proceed to a hiring/placement interview.

Screening Interviews. Screening interviews do just that. They screen candidates to filter those who fail to meet minimum requirements. Companies use screening interviews to save time and money by eliminating less qualified candidates before scheduling face-to-face interviews. Although some screening interviews are conducted during job fairs or on campuses, most screening interviews take place on the telephone. See the accompanying Career Coach box to ensure that you can pass the all-important screening interview.

Screening interviews are intended to eliminate those who fail to meet minimum requirements.

Hiring/Placement Interviews. The most promising candidates selected from screening interviews will be invited to hiring/placement interviews. Hiring managers want to learn whether candidates are motivated, qualified, and a good fit for the position. Their goal is to learn how the candidate would fit into their organization. Conducted in depth, hiring/placement interviews may take many forms.

In hiring/placement interviews, recruiters try to learn how the candidate would fit into their organization.

CAREER COACH

Ensuring That You Pass the All-Important Telephone Screening Interview

Job seekers often mistakenly think that telephone interviews are less important and less formal than face-to-face interviews. These screening interviews, however, are the first hurdle in landing a job. If you fail the telephone interview, you won't get a second chance. To increase the odds of passing a screening interview, try these tips:

- Consider using voice mail to screen calls. By screening incoming calls, you can be totally in control when you return a prospective employer's call.
- Tell those who might answer your phone at home about your job search. Explain to them the importance of acting professionally and taking complete messages.
- Prevent children from answering the phone during your job search. Children of all ages are not known for taking good messages!
- If caught off guard by the call, ask whether you can call back in a few minutes. Organize your materials and yourself.
- Avoid using a cell phone. If you have put your cell phone number on your résumé, don't answer your cell phone unless you are in a good location to carry on a conversation with an employer.
- Polish your verbal skills. "Teen speak" and poor grammar are immediate turnoffs. Use a professional tone and businesslike language.

- Be polite and sound enthusiastic as you answer questions and sell your qualifications.
- Have a copy of your résumé available so that you can answer any questions that come up. Also have your list of references, a calendar, and a notepad handy.
- Take good notes during the phone conversation. Obtain accurate directions, and verify the spelling of your interviewer's name. If you will be interviewed by more than one person, get all of their names.
- Ask the employer to send you a copy of the job description and other company information, which you can use to prepare for the interview.
- Before you hang up, reconfirm the date and time of your interview. You could say something like, *I look forward to meeting with you next Wednesday at 2 p.m.*

Career Application

Practice your telephone interviewing techniques with a friend, spouse, or relative. Prepare a set of practice questions and ask your partner to call you so that you can rehearse your answers and develop confidence.

One-on-One Interviews. In one-on-one interviews, which are the most common type, you can expect to sit down with a company representative and talk about the job and your qualifications. If the representative is the hiring manager, questions will be specific and job related. If the representative is from human resources, the questions will probably be more general.

Panel Interviews. Panel interviews are usually conducted by people who will be your supervisors and colleagues. Usually seated around a table, interviewers take turns asking questions. Panel interviews are advantageous because they save time and show you how the staff works together. For these interviews, you can prepare basic biographical information about each panel member. In answering questions, keep eye contact with the questioner as well as with the others. Try to take notes during the interview so that you can remember each person's questions and what was important to that individual.[4]

Group Interviews. Group interviews occur when a company interviews several candidates for the same position at the same time. Some employers use this technique to measure leadership skills and communication styles. During a group interview stay focused on the interviewer, and treat the other candidates with respect.

Sequential Interviews. Sequential interviews allow a candidate to meet with two or more interviewers on a one-on-one basis over the course of several hours or days. You must listen carefully and respond positively to all interviewers. Sell your qualifications to each one; don't assume that any interviewer knows what was said in a previous interview.

Stress Interviews. Stress interviews are meant to test your reactions during nerve-racking situations. You may be forced to wait a long time before being greeted by the interviewer, you may be given a test with an impossible time limit, or you may be treated rudely by one or more of the interviewers. Another stress interview technique is to have interviewers ask questions at a rapid rate. If asked rapid-fire questions from many directions, take the time to slow things down. For example, you might say, *I would be happy to answer your question Ms. X, but first I must finish responding to Mr. Z.* If greeted with silence, another stress technique, you might say, *Would you like me to begin the interview? Let me tell you about myself.* Or ask a question such as, *Can you give me more information about the position?* The best way to handle stress questions is to remain calm and give carefully considered answers. However, you might also reconsider whether you would want to work for this kind of organization.

No matter what interview structure you encounter, you will feel more comfortable and be better prepared if you know what to do before, during, and after the interview.

Various kinds of hiring interviews include one-on-one, panel, group, sequential, and stress.

Before the Interview

Once you have sent out at least one résumé or filled out at least one job application, you must consider yourself an active job seeker. Being active in the job market means that you should be prepared to be contacted by potential employers. As discussed earlier, employers use screening interviews to narrow the list of candidates. If you do well in the screening interview, you will be invited to an in-person meeting.

Researching the Target Company

After scheduling an in-person interview, it's time to begin in-depth research. One of the most important steps in effective interviewing is gathering detailed information about a prospective employer. Never enter an interview cold. Recruiters are impressed by candidates who have done their homework. In an Office Team survey, 47 percent of executives polled said that the most common mistake job seekers make during interviews is having little or no knowledge about the potential employer.[5]

Visit the library or search the Web for information and articles about the target company or its field, service, or product. Visit the company's Web site and read everything. Call the company to request annual reports, catalogs, or brochures. Ask about the organization and possibly the interviewer. Learn something about the company's mission and goals, size, number of employees, customers, competitors, culture, management structure and names of leaders, reputation in the community, financial condition, future plans, strengths, and weaknesses.

LEARNING OBJECTIVE 2
Describe what to do before an in-person interview, including researching the target company, preparing success stories, and practicing answers to possible questions.

Prior to an interview, take time to research the target company and learn about its goals, customers, competitors, reputation, and so forth.

Analyze the company's advertising, including sales and marketing brochures. One candidate, a marketing major, spent a great deal of time pouring over brochures from an aerospace contractor. During his initial interview, he shocked and impressed the recruiter with his knowledge of the company's guidance systems. The candidate had, in fact, relieved the interviewer of his least favorite task—explaining the company's complicated technology.

Talking with company employees is always a good idea, if you can manage it. They are probably the best source of inside information. Try to be introduced to someone who is currently employed—but not working in the immediate area where you wish to be hired. Be sure to seek out someone who is discreet.

Weblogs, or blogs, are also good sources for company research. Many employees maintain both formal and informal blogs, where they share anecdotes and information about their employers. You can use these blogs to learn about a company's culture, its current happenings, and its future plans. Many job seekers find that they can get a more realistic picture of a company's day-to-day culture by reading blogs than they would by reading news articles or company Web site information.[6]

In learning about a company, you may uncover information that convinces you that this is not the company for you. It's always better to learn about negatives early in the process. More likely, though, the information you collect will help you tailor your application and interview responses to the organization's needs. You know how flattered you feel when an employer knows about you and your background. That feeling works both ways. Employers are pleased when job candidates take an interest in them. Be ready to put in plenty of effort in investigating a target employer because this effort really pays off at interview time.

Preparing and Practicing

After you have learned about the target organization, study the job description or job listing. It not only helps you write a customized résumé but also enables you to match your education, experience, and interests with the employer's position. Learning about the duties and responsibilities of the position will help you practice your best response strategies.

The most successful job candidates never go into interviews cold. They prepare success stories and practice answers to typical questions. They also plan their responses to any problem areas on their résumés. As part of their preparation before the interview, they decide what to wear, and they gather the items they plan to take with them.

Prepare Success Stories. To feel confident and be able to sell your qualifications, prepare and practice success stories. These stories are specific examples of your educational and work-related experience that demonstrate your qualifications and achievements. Look over the job description and your résumé to determine what skills, training, personal characteristics, and experience you want to emphasize during the interview. Then prepare a success story for each one. Incorporate numbers, such as dollars saved or percentage of sales increase, whenever possible. Your success stories should be detailed but brief. Think of them as 30-second sound bites.

Practice telling your success stories until they fluently roll off your tongue and sound natural. Then in the interview be certain to find places to insert them. Tell stories about (a) dealing with a crisis, (b) handling a tough interpersonal situation, (c) successfully juggling many priorities, (d) changing course to deal with changed circumstances, (e) learning from a mistake, (f) working on a team, and (g) going above and beyond expectations.[7]

Practice Answers to Possible Questions. Imagine the kinds of questions you may be asked and work out sample answers. Although you can't anticipate precise questions, you can expect to be asked about your education, skills, experience, and availability. Recite answers to typical interview questions in front of a mirror, with a friend, while driving in your car, or in spare moments. Keep practicing until you have the best responses down pat. Consider recording a practice session to see and hear how you answer questions. Do you look and sound enthusiastic?

Clean Up Any Digital Dirt. Many companies that recruit on college campuses are now using Google and Yahoo to screen applicants. The president of a small consulting

---

Blogs can provide authentic information about a company's culture, current happenings, and future plans.

Practice success stories that emphasize your most strategic skills, areas of knowledge, strongest personality traits, and key accomplishments.

Rehearse answers to typical interview questions so that you sound knowledgeable and enthusiastic.

When you prepare for an interview, you must be professional from start to finish. This means removing from the Internet any embarrassing personal information that could end up in the hands of a prospective employer. Tien Nguyen, a UCLA college senior, signed up for job interviews but said he was seldom contacted until he withdrew a satirical online essay titled "Lying Your Way to the Top." Do you think employers are short-sighted or misguided when they judge applicants by what they see in online postings and social networking sites?

company in Chicago was about to hire a summer intern when he discovered the student's Facebook page. The candidate described his interests as "smokin' blunts [cigars hollowed out and stuffed with marijuana], shooting people and obsessive sex."[8] The executive quickly lost interest in this candidate. Even if the student was merely posturing, it showed poor judgment. Teasing photographs and provocative comments about drinking, drug use, and sexual exploits make students look immature and unprofessional. Check out your online presence to see if anything needs to be cleaned up.

Make sure everything posted about you online is professional and positive.

Expect to Explain Problem Areas on Your Résumé.
Interviewers are certain to question you about problem areas on your résumé. If you have little or no experience, you might emphasize your recent training and up-to-date skills. If you have gaps in your résumé, be prepared to answer questions about them positively and truthfully. If you were fired from a job, accept some responsibility for what happened and explain what you gained from the experience. Don't criticize a previous employer, and don't hide the real reasons. If you received low grades for one term, explain why and point to your improved grades in subsequent terms.

If you have gaps or problem areas in your résumé, be prepared to discuss them.

Decide How to Dress.
What you wear to a job interview still matters. Even if some employees in the organization dress casually, you should look qualified, competent, and successful. One young applicant complained to his girlfriend about having to wear a suit for an interview when everyone at the company dressed casually. She replied, "You don't get to wear the uniform, though, until you make the team!" Avoid loud colors; strive for a coordinated, natural appearance. Favorite "power" colors for interviews are gray and dark blue. Cover tattoos and conceal body piercings; these can be a turnoff for many interviewers. Don't overdo jewelry, and make sure that what you do wear is clean, pressed, odor-free, and lint-free. Shoes should be polished and scuff-free. Forget about flip-flops. To summarize, ensure that what you wear projects professionalism and shows your respect for the interview situation.

Gather Items to Bring.
Decide what you should bring with you to the interview, and get everything ready the night before. You should plan to bring copies of your résumé, your reference lists, a notebook and pen, money for parking and tolls, and samples of your work, if appropriate. Place everything in a businesslike briefcase to add that final professional touch to your look.

Ethics Check

Just Looking!
Like all relationships, the job-search process is about two parties looking to find a good match. Filling a position is costly for employers, and candidates likewise invest time and money in their job hunts. Under the circumstances, is it ethical for a job seeker to accept on-site interviews when not genuinely interested in the prospective employer?

During the Interview

On the day of your interview, arrive a little early so that you have time to park and do some last-minute grooming. As you enter the office, be courteous and congenial to everyone. You are being judged not only by the interviewer but by the receptionist and anyone else who sees you before and after the interview. They will notice how you sit, what you read, and even whether you washed your hands after using the restroom. Introduce yourself to the receptionist, and wait to be invited to sit. You may be asked to fill out a job application while you wait. Tips for completing job applications effectively appear later in this chapter.

Sending Positive Nonverbal Messages

You have already sent nonverbal messages to your interviewer by arriving on time, being courteous, dressing professionally, and greeting the receptionist confidently. You will continue to send nonverbal messages throughout the interview. Remember that what comes out of your mouth and what is written on your résumé are not the only messages an interviewer receives from you. Nonverbal messages also create powerful impressions on people. Here are suggestions that will help you send the right nonverbal messages during interviews:

You can send positive nonverbal messages with such actions as controlling your body movements, exhibiting good posture, practicing appropriate eye contact, and listening attentively.

- **Control your body movements.** Keep your hands, arms, and elbows to yourself. Don't lean on a desk. Keep your feet on the floor. Don't cross your arms in front of you. Keep your hands out of your pockets.

- **Exhibit good posture.** Sit erect, leaning forward slightly. Don't slouch in your chair; at the same time, don't look too stiff and uncomfortable. Good posture demonstrates confidence and interest.

- **Practice appropriate eye contact.** A direct eye gaze, at least in North America, suggests interest and trustworthiness. If you are being interviewed by a panel, remember to maintain eye contact with all interviewers.

- **Use gestures effectively.** Nod to show agreement and interest. Gestures should be used as needed, but don't overdo it.

- **Smile enough to convey a positive attitude.** Have a friend give you honest feedback on whether you generally smile too much or not enough.

- **Listen attentively.** Show the interviewer you are interested and attentive by listening carefully to the questions being asked. This will also help you answer questions appropriately.

- **Turn off your cell phone.** Avoid the embarrassment of allowing your cell phone to ring during an interview. Turn it off or leave it at home.

- **Don't chew gum.** Chewing gum during an interview is distracting and unprofessional.

- **Sound enthusiastic and interested—but sincere.** The tone of your voice has an enormous effect on the words you say. Avoid sounding bored, frustrated, or sarcastic during an interview. Employers want employees who are enthusiastic and interested.

- **Avoid "empty" words.** Filling your answers with verbal pauses such as *um, uh, like,* and *basically* communicates that you are unprepared. Also avoid annoying distractions such as clearing your throat repeatedly or sighing deeply.

Projecting a Professional Demeanor

Greet the interviewer confidently, and don't be afraid to initiate a handshake. Doing so exhibits professionalism and confidence. Extend your hand, look the interviewer directly in the eye, smile pleasantly, and say, *I'm pleased to meet you, Mr. Thomas. I am Constance Ferraro.* In this culture a firm, not crushing, handshake sends a nonverbal message of poise and assurance. Once introductions have taken place, wait for the interviewer to offer you a chair. Make small talk with upbeat comments such as, *This is a beautiful headquarters,* or, *I'm very impressed with the facilities you have here.* Don't immediately begin rummaging in your briefcase for your résumé. Being at ease and unrushed suggest that you are self-confident.

© Digital Vision / Getty Images

Poor eye contact, crossed arms, bad posture, gum chewing—these are classic no-nos of interviewing. But a new behavior has joined the list of common interviewing faux pas: failure to turn off cell phones. Though some individuals have a bad habit of taking cell calls at movie theaters, piano recitals, restaurants, and houses of worship, taking a call during an interview can blow one's chances of moving ahead with the interview process. What can job candidates do to evaluate their nonverbal signals prior to interviewing?

The way you answer questions can be almost as important as what you say. Use the interviewer's name and title from time to time when you answer. *Ms. Lyon, I would be pleased to tell you about. . . .* People like to hear their own names. Be sure you are pronouncing the name correctly, and don't overuse this technique. Avoid answering questions with a simple *yes* or *no;* elaborate on your answers to better sell yourself.

During the interview it may be necessary to occasionally refocus and clarify vague questions. Some interviewers are inexperienced and ill at ease in the role. You may even have to ask your own question to understand what was asked, *By _____, do you mean _____?* Consider closing out some of your responses with *Does that answer your question?* or *Would you like me to elaborate on any particular experience?*

Always aim your answers at the key characteristics interviewers seek: expertise, competence, motivation, interpersonal skills, decision-making skills, enthusiasm for the job, and a pleasing personality. Remember to stay focused on your strengths. Don't reveal weaknesses, even if you think they make you look human. You won't be hired for your weaknesses, only for your strengths. Be sure to use good English and enunciate clearly. Avoid slurred words such as *gonna* and *din't,* as well as slangy expressions such as *yeah, like,* and *ya know.*

You cannot expect to be perfect in an employment interview. No one is. However, you can avert sure disaster by avoiding certain topics and behaviors such as those described in Figure 16.1.

How you answer questions can be as important as the answers themselves.

Answering Typical Interview Questions

Employment interviews are all about questions, and many of the questions interviewers ask are not new. You can anticipate a large percentage of questions that will be asked before you ever walk into an interview room. Some questions are meant to help the interviewer become acquainted with you. Others are aimed at measuring your interest, experience, and accomplishments. Still others will probe your future plans and challenge your reactions. Some will inquire about your money expectations. Your interviewer may use situational or behavioral questions and may even occasionally ask an illegal question. To get you thinking about how to respond, we have provided an answer or discussion for one or more of the questions in each of the following groups. As you read the remaining questions in each group, think about how you could respond most effectively.

LEARNING OBJECTIVE 4
Describe how to answer typical interview questions such as those that seek to get acquainted, gauge your interest, probe your experience, explore your accomplishments, look to the future, and inquire about salary expectations.

FIGURE 16.1 Twelve Interview Actions to Avoid

1. **Don't be late or too early.** Arrive five to ten minutes before your scheduled interview.

2. **Don't be rude.** Treat everyone you come into contact with warmly and respectfully.

3. **Don't ask for the job.** Asking for the job is naïve, undignified, and unprofessional. Wait to see how the interview develops.

4. **Don't criticize anyone or anything.** Don't criticize your previous employer, supervisors, colleagues, or job. The tendency is for interviewers to wonder whether you would speak about their companies similarly.

5. **Don't be a threat to the interviewer.** Avoid suggesting directly or indirectly that your goal is to become head honcho, a path that might include the interviewer's job.

6. **Don't act unprofessionally.** Don't discuss controversial subjects, and don't use profanity. Don't talk too much.

7. **Don't emphasize salary or benefits.** Don't bring up salary, vacation, or benefits early in an interview. Leave this up to the interviewer.

8. **Don't focus on your imperfections.** Never dwell on your liabilities or talk negatively about yourself.

9. **Don't interrupt.** Interrupting is not only impolite but also prevents you from hearing a complete question or remark.

10. **Don't bring someone along.** Don't bring a friend or relative with you to the interview. If someone must drive you, ask that person to drop you off and come back later.

11. **Don't appear impatient.** Your entire focus should be on the interview. Don't glance at your watch, which can imply that you're late for another appointment.

12. **Don't act desperate.** A sure way to turn off an interviewer is to act too desperate. Don't focus on why you *need* the job; focus on how you will add value to the organization.

Questions to Get Acquainted

After opening introductions, recruiters generally try to start the interview with personal questions that put you at ease. They are also striving to gain an overview to see whether you will fit into the organization's culture. When answering these questions, keep the employer's needs in mind and try to incorporate your success stories.

1. Tell me about yourself.

   Experts agree that you must keep this answer short (one to two minutes tops) but on target. Use this chance to promote yourself. Stick to educational, professional, or business-related strengths; avoid personal or humorous references. Be ready with at least three success stories illustrating characteristics important to this job. Demonstrate responsibility you have been given; describe how you contributed as a team player. Try practicing this formula: *I have completed a _____ degree with a major in ____. Recently I worked for _____ as a _____. Before that I worked for _____ as a _____. My strengths are _____ (interpersonal) and _____ (technical).* Try rehearsing your response in 30-second segments devoted to your education, work experience, qualifications, and skills.

2. What are your greatest strengths?

   Stress your strengths that are related to the position, such as, *I am well organized, thorough, and attentive to detail.* Tell success stories and give examples that illustrate these qualities: *My supervisor says that my research is exceptionally thorough. For example, I recently worked on a research project in which I. . . .*

3. Do you prefer to work by yourself or with others? Why?

   This question can be tricky. Provide a middle-of-the-road answer that not only suggests your interpersonal qualities but also reflects an ability to make independent decisions and work without supervision.

4. What was your major in college, and why did you choose it?

5. What are some things you do in your spare time? Hobbies? Sports?

> Prepare for get-acquainted questions by practicing a short formula response.

Questions to Gauge Your Interest

Interviewers want to understand your motivation for applying for a position. Although they will realize that you are probably interviewing for other positions, they still want to know why you are interested in this particular position with this organization. These types of questions help them determine your level of interest.

Recruiters want to know how interested you are in this organization and in this specific position.

1. Why do you want to work for (name of company)?

   Questions like this illustrate why you must research an organization thoroughly before the interview. The answer to this question must prove that you understand the company and its culture. This is the perfect place to bring up the company research you did before the interview. Show what you know about the company, and discuss why you want to become a part of this organization. Describe your desire to work for this organization not only from your perspective but also from its point of view. What do you have to offer?

2. Why are you interested in this position?

3. What do you know about our company?

4. Why do you want to work in the _____ industry?

5. What interests you about our products (services)?

Questions About Your Experience and Accomplishments

After questions about your background and education and questions that measure your interest, the interview generally becomes more specific with questions about your experience and accomplishments. Remember to show confidence when you answer these questions. If you are not confident in your abilities, why should an employer be?

1. Why should we hire you when we have applicants with more experience or better credentials?

   In answering this question, remember that employers often hire people who present themselves well instead of others with better credentials. Emphasize your personal strengths that could be an advantage with this employer. Are you a hard worker? How can you demonstrate it? Have you had recent training? Some people have had more years of experience but actually have less knowledge because they have done the same thing over and over. Stress your experience using the latest methods and equipment.

Employers will hire a candidate with less experience and fewer accomplishments if he or she can demonstrate the skills required.

Communicating at Work Part 2

Googling for Jobs

Although Google has improved the efficiency and timeliness of its hiring efforts, the process is still demanding. To sort through the huge volume of résumés quickly without missing qualified applicants, the company developed an online survey with questions about attitudes, work habits, personality, and past experiences. Recruiters use search techniques to identify suitable candidates for a particular job. Then they conduct one or more screening interviews by telephone to get more background on the applicant.

Candidates who meet the hiring criteria then spend a day at the company participating in interviews with an average of five people. "They'll meet the hiring manager, of course, but also a few peers and a few people who would be senior to them, but not direct supervisors," said Judy Gilbert, director of staffing programs.[9] Some interviewees may be asked to perform job-related tasks during the visit.

Interviewers give their feedback to a hiring committee, which evaluates the applicant's skills for the position as well as his or her overall fit into Google's culture and potential future contributions.

Next the executive committee reviews the hiring committee's recommendations. Finally, company founders Larry Page and Sergei Brin themselves sign off on all job offers.[10]

Critical Thinking
- Why are online questionnaires and screening interviews useful tools for Google's recruiters?
- How does thorough preparation help a candidate reduce the stress and butterflies most people feel during an interview?
- How can you prepare in advance for behavioral interview questions?

© ERIN LUBIN / Bloomberg News / Landov

Be sure to mention your computer training and use of the Web. Tell success stories. Emphasize that you are open to new ideas and learn quickly. Above all, show that you are confident in your abilities.

Questions about your experience and accomplishments enable you to work in your practiced success stories.

2. Describe the most rewarding experience of your career so far.

3. How have your education and professional experiences prepared you for this position?

4. What were your major accomplishments in each of your past jobs?

5. What was a typical workday like?

6. What job functions did you enjoy most? Least? Why?

7. Tell me about your computer skills.

8. Who was the toughest boss you ever worked for and why?

9. What were your major achievements in college?

10. Why did you leave your last position? *OR:* Why are you leaving your current position?

Questions About the Future

When asked about the future, show ambition and interest in succeeding with this company.

Questions that look into the future tend to stump some candidates, especially those who have not prepared adequately. Employers ask these questions to see whether you are goal oriented and to determine whether your goals are realistic.

1. Where do you expect to be five (or ten) years from now?

   Formulate a realistic plan with respect to your present age and situation. The important thing is to be prepared for this question. It's a sure kiss of death to respond that you would like to have the interviewer's job! Instead, show an interest in the current job and in making a contribution to the organization. Talk about the levels of responsibility you would like to achieve. One employment counselor suggests showing ambition but not committing to a specific job title. Suggest that you hope to have learned enough to have progressed to a position in which you will continue to grow. Keep your answer focused on educational and professional goals, not personal goals.

2. If you got this position, what would you do to be sure you fit in?

3. This is a large (or small) organization. Do you think you would like that environment?

4. Do you plan to continue your education?

5. What do you predict for the future of the _____ industry?

6. How do you think you can contribute to this company?

7. What would you most like to accomplish if you were to get this position?

8. How do you keep current with what is happening in your profession?

Challenging Questions

Strive to convert a discussion of your weaknesses to topics that show your strengths.

The following questions may make you uncomfortable, but the important thing to remember is to answer truthfully without dwelling on your weaknesses. As quickly as possible, convert any negative response into a discussion of your strengths.

1. What is your greatest weakness?

   It's amazing how many candidates knock themselves out of the competition by answering this question poorly. Actually, you have many choices. You can present a strength as a weakness (*Some people complain that I'm a workaholic or too attentive to details*). You can mention a corrected weakness (*Because I needed to learn about designing Web sites, I took a course*). You could cite an unrelated skill (*I really need to brush up on my Spanish*). You can cite a learning objective (*One of my long-term goals is to learn more about international management. Does your company have any plans to expand overseas?*). Another possibility is to reaffirm your qualifications (*I have no weaknesses that affect my ability to do this job*).

2. What type of people do you have no patience for?

Avoid letting yourself fall into the trap of sounding overly critical. One possible response is, *I have always gotten along well with others. But I confess that I can be irritated by complainers who don't accept responsibility.*

> **Answer challenging questions truthfully but try to turn the discussion into one that emphasizes your strengths.**

3. If you could live your life over, what would you change and why?

4. How would your former (or current) supervisor describe you as an employee?

5. What do you want the most from your job? Money? Security? Power?

6. What is your grade-point average, and does it accurately reflect your abilities?

7. Have you ever used drugs?

8. Who in your life has influenced you the most and why?

9. What are you reading right now?

10. Describe your ideal work environment.

11. Is the customer always right?

12. How do you define success?

Questions About Money

Remember that nearly all salaries are negotiable, depending on your qualifications. Knowing the typical salary range for the target position helps. The recruiter can tell you the salary ranges—but you will have to ask. If you have had little experience, you will probably be offered a salary somewhere between the low point and the midpoint in the range. With more experience, you can negotiate for a higher figure. A word of caution, though. One personnel manager warns that candidates who emphasize money are suspect because they may leave if offered a few thousand dollars more elsewhere. See the accompanying Career Coach for dos and don't in negotiating a starting salary. Here are some typical money questions:

> **Defer a discussion of salary until later in the interview when you know more about the job and whether it will be offered.**

1. How much money are you looking for?

One way to handle salary questions is to ask politely to defer the discussion until it's clear that a job will be offered to you (*I'm sure when the time comes, we will be able*

CAREER COACH

Let's Talk Money: Salary Negotiation Dos and Don'ts

Nearly all salaries are negotiable. The following dos and don'ts can guide you to a better starting salary.

- **Do** make sure you have done your research on the salary you should expect for the position you are seeking.
- **Don't** bring up salary before the employer does. **Do** delay salary negotiation until you know exactly what the position entails.
- **Do** be aware of your strengths and achievements. **Do** be sure to demonstrate the value you will bring to the employer.
- **Do** let the employer make the first salary offer. **Do,** if asked, say you expect a salary that is competitive with the market or give a salary range that you find acceptable.
- **Don't** inflate your current earnings just to get a higher salary offer.
- **Don't** feel obligated to accept the first salary offer. **Do** negotiate salary if the offer made is inadequate.
- **Do** thank the employer for the offer when it is made. **Don't** try to negotiate right after the offer is made. **Do** take the time to consider all factors before making any job offer decisions.
- **Don't** get overly aggressive in negotiating the salary you want.
- **Don't** focus solely on salary. **Do** consider the entire compensation package.

- **Do** try to obtain other concessions (shorter review time, better title, better workspace) or benefits (bonuses, vacation time) if you aren't successful at negotiating a salary you want.
- **Don't** enter salary negotiations as part of an ego trip or part of a game.
- **Don't** agree to the first acceptable salary offer you receive if you are not sure about the job or the company.
- **Do** get the offer in writing.

Career Application

Role-play a situation in which a hiring manager offers a candidate a starting salary of $42,500. The candidate wants $45,000 to start. The candidate responds to preliminary questions and negotiates the salary offer.

to work out a fair compensation package. Right now, I'd rather focus on whether we have a match). Another possible response is to reply candidly that you can't know what to ask until you know more about the position and the company. If you continue to be pressed for a dollar figure, give a salary range with an annual dollar amount. Be sure to do research before the interview so that you know what similar jobs are paying in your geographic region. For example, check a Web site such as **http://www .salary.com**.

2. How much are you presently earning?

3. How much do you think you're worth?

4. How much money do you expect to earn within the next ten years?

5. Are you willing to take a pay cut from your current (or previous) job?

Situational Questions

Questions related to situations help employers test your thought processes and logical thinking. When using situational questions, interviewers describe a hypothetical situation and ask how you would handle it. Situational questions differ based on the type of position for which you are interviewing. Knowledge of the position and the company culture will help you respond favorably to these questions. Even if the situation sounds negative, keep your response positive. Here are just a few examples:

1. You receive a call from an irate customer who complains about the service she received last night at your restaurant. She is demanding her money back. How would you handle the situation?

2. If you were aware that a coworker was falsifying data, what would you do?

3. Your supervisor has just told you that she is dissatisfied with your work, but you think it's acceptable. How would you resolve the conflict?

4. Your supervisor has told you to do something a certain way, and you think that way is wrong and that you know a far better way to complete the task. What would you do?

5. Assume that you are hired for this position. You soon learn that one of the staff is extremely resentful because she applied for your position and was turned down. As a result, she is being unhelpful and obstructive. How would you handle the situation?

Behavioral Questions

Instead of traditional interview questions, you may be asked to tell stories. The interviewer may say, *Describe a time when* or *Tell me about a time when. . . .* To respond effectively, learn to use the storytelling or STAR technique. Ask yourself, what the **S**ituation or **T**ask was, what **A**ction you took, and what the **R**esults were.[11] Practice using this method to recall specific examples of your skills and accomplishments. To be fully prepared, develop a coherent and articulate STAR narrative for every bullet point on your résumé. When answering behavioral questions, describe only educational and work-related situations or tasks, and try to keep them as current as possible. Here are a few examples of behavioral questions:

Spotlight on Communicators

Employers today increasingly rely on behavioral interviews to select the right candidate. Instead of traditional questions, you may be asked to "describe a time when. . . ." Career consultant Daisy Wright advises using the storytelling or STAR technique when responding. Ask yourself what the **S**ituation or **T**ask was, what **A**ction you took, and what the **R**esults were. This method helps you recall specific job-related examples of your skills and accomplishments. Be sure to focus on the successful role you played.

© Courtesy of Daisy Wright

1. Tell me about a time when you solved a difficult problem.

Tell a concise story explaining the situation or task, what you did, and the result. For example, *When I was at Ace Products, we continually had a problem of excessive back orders. After analyzing the situation, I discovered that orders went through many unnecessary steps. I suggested that we eliminate much paperwork. As a result, we reduced back orders by 30 percent.* Go on to emphasize what you learned and how you can apply that learning to this job. Practice your success stories in advance so that you will be ready.

2. Describe a situation in which you were able to use persuasion to successfully convince someone to see things your way.

When answering behavioral questions, describe only educational and work-related situations or tasks.

The recruiter is interested in your leadership and teamwork skills. You might respond, *I have learned to appreciate the fact that the way you present an idea is just as important as the idea itself. When trying to influence people, I put myself in their shoes and find some way to frame my idea from their perspective. I remember when I. . . .*

3. Describe a time when you had to analyze information and make a recommendation.

4. Describe a time that you worked successfully as part of a team.

5. Tell me about a time you dealt with confidential information.

6. Give me an example of a time when you were under stress to meet a deadline.

7. Tell me about a time when you had to go above and beyond the call of duty in order to get a job done.

8. Tell me about a time you were able to successfully deal with another person even when that individual may not have personally liked you (or vice versa).

9. Give me an example of when you showed initiative and took the lead.

10. Tell me about a recent situation in which you had to deal with an upset customer or coworker.

Illegal and Inappropriate Questions

Federal laws prohibit employment discrimination based on gender, age, religion, color, race, national origin, and disability. In addition, many state and city laws exist that prohibit employment discrimination based on such factors as sexual orientation.[12] Therefore, it is inappropriate for interviewers to ask any question related to these areas. These questions become illegal, though, only when a court of law determines that the employer is asking them with the intent to discriminate. Most illegal interview questions are asked innocently by inexperienced interviewers. Some are only trying to be friendly when they inquire about your personal life or family. Regardless of the intent, how should you react?

Candidates who are asked illegal questions must decide whether to answer, deflect the question tactfully, or confront the interviewer.

If you find the question harmless and if you want the job, go ahead and answer it. If you think that answering it would damage your chance to be hired, try to deflect the question tactfully with a response such as, *Could you tell me how my marital status relates to the responsibilities of this position?* or, *I prefer to keep my personal and professional lives separate.* If you are uncomfortable answering a question, try to determine the reason behind it; you might answer, *I don't let my personal life interfere with my ability to do my job,* or, *Are you concerned with my availability to work overtime?* Another option, of course, is to respond to any inappropriate or illegal question by confronting the interviewer and threatening a lawsuit or refusing to answer. However, you could not expect to be hired under these circumstances. In any case, you might wish to reconsider working for an organization that sanctions such procedures.

You may respond to an inappropriate or illegal question by asking tactfully how it relates to the responsibilities of the position.

Here are some inappropriate and illegal questions that you may or may not want to answer:[13]

1. What is your marital status? Are you married? Do you live with anyone? Do you have a boyfriend (or girlfriend)? (However, employers can ask your marital status after hiring for tax and insurance forms.)

2. Do you have any disabilities? Have you had any recent illnesses? (But it is legal to ask if the person can perform specific job duties, such as, *Can you carry a 50-pound sack up a 10-foot ladder five times daily?*)

3. I notice you have an accent. Where are you from? What is the origin of your last name? What is your native language? (However, it is legal to ask what languages you speak fluently if language ability is related to the job.)

4. Have you ever filed a worker's compensation claim or been injured on the job?

5. Have you ever had a drinking problem or been addicted to drugs? (But it is legal to ask if a person uses illegal drugs.)

6. Have you ever been arrested? (But it is legal to ask, *Have you ever been convicted of* _____? when the crime is related to the job.)

7. How old are you? What is your date of birth? When did you graduate from high school? (But it is legal to ask, *Are you 16 years (or 18 years or 21 years) old or older?* depending on the age requirements for the position.)

8. Of what country are you a citizen? Where were you born? (But it is legal to ask, *Are you a citizen of the United States?* or, *Can you legally work in the United States?*)

9. What is your maiden name? (But it is legal to ask, *What is your full name?* or, *Have you worked under another name?*)

10. Do you have any religious beliefs that would prevent you from working weekends or holidays? (An employer can, however, ask you if you are available to work weekends and holidays.)

11. Do you have children? Do you plan to have children? Do you have adequate child-care arrangements? (However, employers can ask for dependent information for tax and insurance purposes after you are hired.)

12. How much do you weigh? How tall are you? (However, employers can ask you about your height and weight if minimum standards are necessary to safely perform a job.)

Closing the Interview

LEARNING OBJECTIVE 5
Understand how to close an interview positively, including asking meaningful questions.

Your questions should impress the interviewer but also provide valuable information about the job.

Once the interview nears conclusion, start thinking about how to end on a positive note. It's easy to become flustered after a challenging interview, so be sure to practice questions that you plan to ask. Also, focus on how to leave a lasting positive impression.

Asking Your Own Questions

At some point in the interview, usually near the end, you will be asked whether you have any questions. The worst thing you can do is say *No,* which suggests that you are not interested in the position. Instead, ask questions that will help you gain information and will impress the interviewer with your thoughtfulness and interest in the position. Remember that this interview is a two-way street. You must be happy with the prospect of working for this organization. You want a position for which your skills and personality are matched. Use this opportunity to learn whether this job is right for you. Be aware that you don't have to wait for the interviewer to ask you for questions. You can ask your own questions throughout the interview to learn more about the company and position. Here are some questions you might ask:

1. What will my duties be (if not already discussed)?

2. Tell me what it's like working here in terms of the people, management practices, workloads, expected performance, and rewards.

3. What training programs are available from this organization? What specific training will be given for this position?

4. Who would be my immediate supervisor?

5. What is the organizational structure, and where does this position fit in?

6. Is travel required in this position?

7. How is job performance evaluated?

8. Assuming my work is excellent, where do you see me in five years?

9. How long do employees generally stay with this organization?

10. What are the major challenges for a person in this position?

11. What do you see in the future of this organization?

12. What do you like best about working for this organization?

13. May I have a tour of the facilities?

14. When do you expect to make a decision?

Ending Positively

After you have asked your questions, the interviewer will signal the end of the interview, usually by standing up or by expressing appreciation that you came. If not addressed earlier, you should at this time find out what action will follow. Demonstrate your interest in the position by asking when it will be filled or what the next step will be. Too many candidates leave the interview without knowing their status or when they will hear from the recruiter. Don't be afraid to say that you want the job!

Before you leave, summarize your strongest qualifications, show your enthusiasm for obtaining this position, and thank the interviewer for a constructive interview and for considering you for the position. Ask the interviewer for a business card, which will provide the information you need to write a thank-you letter, which is discussed later. Shake the interviewer's hand with confidence, and acknowledge anyone else you see on the way out. Be sure to thank the receptionist. Leaving the interview gracefully and enthusiastically will leave a lasting impression on those responsible for making the final hiring decision.

> When you end the interview, summarize your strongest qualifications, thank the interviewer, and ask for the interviewer's card.

After the Interview

After leaving the interview, immediately make notes of what was said in case you are called back for a second interview. Write down key points that were discussed, the names of people you spoke with, and other details of the interview. Ask yourself what went really well and what could have been improved. Note your strengths and weaknesses during the interview so that you can work to improve in future interviews. Next, write down your follow-up plans. To whom should you send thank-you letters? Will you contact the employer by phone? If so, when? Then be sure to follow up on those plans, beginning with writing a thank-you letter and contacting your references.

LEARNING OBJECTIVE 6
Outline the activities that take place after an interview, including thanking the interviewer and contacting references.

Thanking Your Interviewer

After a job interview you should always send a thank-you letter, also called a follow-up letter. This courtesy sets you apart from other applicants, most of whom will not bother. Your letter also reminds the interviewer of your visit as well as suggesting your good manners and genuine enthusiasm for the job. Follow-up letters are most effective if sent immediately after the interview. In your letter refer to the date of the interview, the exact job title for which you were interviewed, and specific topics discussed. Avoid worn-out phrases, such as *Thank you for taking the time to interview me*. Be careful, too, about overusing *I*, especially to begin sentences. Most important, show that you really want the job and that you are qualified for it. Notice how the letter in Figure 16.2 conveys enthusiasm and confidence.

> A follow-up thank-you letter shows your good manners and your enthusiasm for the job.

If you have been interviewed by more than one person, send a separate letter to each interviewer. It's also a good idea to send a thank-you letter to the receptionist and to the person who set up the interview. Your thank-you letter will probably make more of an impact if prepared in proper business format and sent by regular mail. However, if you know the decision will be made quickly, send your follow-up message by e-mail. One job candidate now makes a follow-up e-mail a practice. She summarizes what was discussed during the face-to-face interview and adds information that she had not thought to mention during the interview.[14]

Contacting Your References

Once you have thanked your interviewer, it's time to alert your references that they may be contacted by the employer. You might also have to request a letter of recommendation to be sent to the employer by a certain date. As discussed in Chapter 15, you should have already asked permission to use these individuals as references, and you should have supplied them with a copy of your résumé, highlighted with sales points.

> Thoughtful candidates alert the people who are acting as references so that they will be prepared to be contacted by the target company.

To provide the best possible recommendation, your references need information. What position have you applied for with what company? What should they stress to the prospective employer? Let's say you are applying for a specific job that requires a letter of

FIGURE 16.2 Interview Follow-Up Letter

Christopher D. Wiley

3592 Channel Islands Boulevard, Ventura, CA 90630
(805) 483-6734, cwiley@mail.com

May 28, 2009

Mr. Eric C. Nielsen
Comstock Images & Technology
3201 State Street
Santa Barbara, CA 93104

Dear Mr. Nielsen:

Mentions the interview date and specific job title →

Talking with you Thusday, May 27, about the graphic designer position was both informative and interersting.

Thamks for describing the positionn in such detail and for introdusing me to Ms. Ouchi, the senior designer. Her current project designing an annual report in four colors sounds fascinating as well as quite challenging. ← Pesonalizes the message by referring to topics discussed in the interview

Highlights specific, skills for the job →

Now that I have learned in greater detail the specific tasks of your graphic designers, I'm more than ever convinced that my computer and creative skills can make a genuine contribution to your graphic productions. My training in design and layout using PhotoShop and InDesign ensures that I could be immediately productive on your staff.

Shows appreciation, good manners, and perseverance—traits that recruiters value →

You will find me an enhusiastic and hardworking member of any team effort. As you requested, I'm enclosing additional samples of my work. I'm eager to join the graphics staff at your Santa Barbara headquarters, and I look forward to hearing from you soon. ← Reminds reader of interpersonal skills as well as enthusiasm and eagerness for this job

Sincerely,

Christopher D. Wiley

Christopher D. Wiley

Enclosures

recommendation. Professor Orenstein has already agreed to be a reference for you. To get the best letter of recommendation from Professor Orenstein, help her out. Write a letter telling her about the position, its requirements, and the recommendation deadline. Include a copy of your résumé. You might remind her of a positive experience with you that she could use in the recommendation. Remember that recommenders need evidence to support generalizations. Give them appropriate ammunition, as the student has done in the following request:

Dear Professor Orenstein:

In a reference request letter, tell immediately why you are writing. Identify the target position and company.

Recently I interviewed for the position of administrative assistant in the Human Resources Department of Host International. Because you kindly agreed to help me, I am now asking you to write a letter of recommendation to Host.

The position calls for good organizational, interpersonal, and writing skills, as well as computer experience. To help you review my skills and training, I enclose my résumé. As you may recall, I earned an A in your business communication class; and you commended my long report for its clarity and organization.

Please send your letter to Mr. James Jenkins at Host International before July 1 in the enclosed stamped, addressed envelope. I'm grateful for your support, and I promise to let you know the results of my job search.

Sincerely,

Specify the job requirements so that the recommender knows what to stress.

Provide a stamped, addressed envelope.

Following Up

If you don't hear from the interviewer within five days, or at the specified time, call him or her. Practice saying something like, *I'm wondering what else I can do to convince you that I'm the right person for this job,* or, *I'm calling to find out the status of your search for the _____ position.* You could also e-mail the interviewer to find out how the decision process is going. When following up, it's important to sound professional and courteous. Sounding desperate, angry, or frustrated that you have not been contacted can ruin your chances. The following follow-up e-mail message would impress the interviewer:

Dear Ms. Jamison:

I enjoyed my interview with you last Thursday for the receptionist position. You should know that I'm very interested in this opportunity with Coastal Enterprises. Because you mentioned that you might have an answer this week, I'm eager to know how your decision process is coming along. I look forward to hearing from you.

Sincerely,

A follow-up letter inquires courteously but does not sound angry or desperate.

Depending on the response you get to your first follow-up request, you may have to follow up additional times. Keep in mind, though, that some employers will not tell you about their hiring decision unless you are the one hired. Don't harass the interviewer, and don't force a decision. If you don't hear back from an employer within several weeks after following up, it's best to assume that you didn't get the job and to continue with your job search.

To review the important actions you can take to perform effectively before, during, and after a job interview, see the checklist on the following page.

Other Employment Documents and Follow-Up Messages

Although the résumé and cover letter are your major tasks, other important documents and messages are often required during the employment process. You may need to complete an employment application form and write follow-up letters. You might also have to write a letter of resignation when leaving a job. Because each of these tasks reveals something about you and your communication skills, you will want to put your best foot forward. These documents often subtly influence company officials to offer a job.

LEARNING OBJECTIVE 7
Understand how to complete employment applications and write résumé follow-up, rejection follow-up, job acceptance, and job rejection messages.

Application Form

Some organizations require job candidates to fill out job application forms instead of, or in addition to, submitting résumés. This practice permits them to gather and store standardized data about each applicant. Whether the application is on paper or online, follow the directions carefully and provide accurate information. The following suggestions can help you be prepared:

- Carry a card summarizing vital statistics not included on your résumé. If you are asked to fill out an application form in an employer's office, you will need a handy reference to

When applying for jobs, keep with you a card summarizing your important data.

Checklist

Performing Effectively Before, During, and After a Job Interview

Before the Interview

✓ **Expect to be screened by telephone.** Near your telephone, keep your résumé, a list of references, a calendar, and a notepad. Also have a list of companies where you applied.

✓ **Research the target company.** Once an interview is scheduled, conduct in-depth research about the company's mission, goals, size, customers, competitors, culture, management structure, names of leaders, financial condition, future plans, strengths, and weaknesses. Talk to company employees if possible.

✓ **Prepare success stories.** Organize and practice many success stories with specific examples of your educational and work-related experiences that demonstrate your accomplishments and achievements. Be ready to recite them in 30-second sound bites.

✓ **Practice answers to possible questions.** Recite answers to typical questions in a mirror, with a friend, or in spare moments. Consider recording a practice session to evaluate your performance. Be ready to explain problem areas on your résumé.

✓ **Get ready.** Take a trial trip to locate the employer. Select professional-looking clothes for the interview. Gather items to take with you: copies of your résumé, your reference lists, a notebook and pen, money for parking and tolls, and work samples, if appropriate. Use a presentable briefcase to carry your items.

During the Interview

✓ **Send positive nonverbal messages.** Control your body movements, use good posture, maintain appropriate eye contact, use gestures effectively, smile enough to convey a positive attitude, listen attentively, turn off your cell phone, don't chew gum, sound enthusiastic and interested, and avoid *um, uh, like,* and *ya know.*

✓ **Fight fear.** Remind yourself that you are thoroughly prepared, breathe deeply, know that your fear is typical, and remember that the interviewer has to please you as well.

✓ **Be confident.** Use the interviewer's name, refocus and clarify vague questions, and aim your answers at key characteristics interviewers seek.

✓ **Incorporate your success stories.** As you answer questions, work in your success stories that emphasize your skills and accomplishments. Keep the employer's needs in mind for this particular position.

✓ **Express enthusiasm for working for this company.** Show what you know about the company and explain why you want to become part of this organization.

Closing the Interview

✓ **Ask your own questions.** Be prepared with meaningful, thoughtful questions to help you determine whether this job is right for you.

✓ **End the interview positively.** Summarize your strongest qualifications, show your enthusiasm for the job, and thank the interviewer. Ask for the interviewer's business card. Shake hands, and acknowledge anyone else on the way out.

After the Interview

✓ **Make notes.** Immediately record key points and note what you could improve for your next interview.

✓ **Send a thank-you note.** Thank the interviewer in a message that notes the date of the interview, the exact title of the position, and specific topics discussed. Express your enthusiasm for the job, and thank the interviewer for sharing information about the position and the organization. E-mail notes are increasingly acceptable.

✓ **Contact your references.** Alert your references that they may be contacted by the employer. Provide any additional information that will help them make supportive statements.

---

the following data: graduation dates; beginning and ending dates of all employment; salary history; full names, titles, and present work addresses of former supervisors; full addresses and phone numbers of current and previous employers; and full names, occupational titles, occupational addresses, and telephone numbers of persons who have agreed to serve as references.

- Look over all the questions before starting.

- Fill out the form neatly, using blue or black ink. Many career counselors recommend printing your responses; cursive handwriting can be difficult to read.

- Answer all questions honestly. Write *Not applicable* or *N/A* if appropriate.

- Use accurate spelling, grammar, and punctuation.

- If asked for the position desired, give a specific job title or type of position. Don't say, *Anything* or *Open.* These answers make you look unfocused; moreover, they make it difficult for employers to know what you're qualified for or interested in.

- Be prepared for a salary question. Unless you know what comparable employees are earning in the company, the best strategy is to suggest a salary range or to write *Negotiable* or *Open*.

- Be prepared to explain the reasons for leaving previous positions. Use positive or neutral phrases such as *Relocation, Seasonal, To accept a position with more responsibility, Temporary position, To continue education,* or *Career change.* Avoid words or phrases such as *Fired, Quit, Didn't get along with supervisor,* or *Pregnant.*

- Look over the application before submitting to make sure it is complete and that you have followed all instructions. Sign and date the application.

Application or Résumé Follow-Up Letter

If your résumé or application generates no response within a reasonable time, you may decide to send a short follow-up letter such as the following. Doing so (a) jogs the memory of the personnel officer, (b) demonstrates your serious interest, and (c) allows you to emphasize your qualifications or to add new information.

Dear Ms. Lopez:

Please know I am still interested in becoming an administrative support specialist with Quad, Inc.

> **Open by reminding the reader of your interest.**

Since I submitted an application [or résumé] in May, I have completed my degree and have been employed as a summer replacement for office workers in several downtown offices. This experience has honed my word processing and communication skills. It has also introduced me to a wide range of office procedures.

> **Review your strengths or add new qualifications.**

Please keep my application in your active file and let me know when I may put my formal training, technical skills, and practical experience to work for you.

> **Close positively; avoid accusations that make the reader defensive.**

Sincerely,

Rejection Follow-Up Letter

If you didn't get the job and you think it was perfect for you, don't give up. Employment specialists encourage applicants to respond to a rejection. The candidate who was offered the position may decline, or other positions may open up. In a rejection follow-up letter, it's OK to admit you are disappointed. Be sure to add, however, that you are still interested and will contact the company again in a month in case a job opens up. Then follow through for a couple of months—but don't overdo it. You should be professional and persistent, but not a pest. Here's an example of an effective rejection follow-up letter:

Dear Mr. O'Neal:

Although I'm disappointed that someone else was selected for your accounting position, I appreciate your promptness and courtesy in notifying me.

> **Subordinate your disappointment to your appreciation at being notified promptly and courteously.**

Because I firmly believe that I have the technical and interpersonal skills needed to work in your fast-paced environment, I hope you will keep my résumé in your active file. My desire to become a productive member of your Transamerica staff remains strong.

> **Emphasize your continuing interest.**

I enjoyed our interview, and I especially appreciate the time you and Ms. Goldstein spent describing your company's expansion into international markets. To enhance my qualifications, I have enrolled in a course in International Accounting at CSU.

> **Refer to specifics of your interview.**

Should you have an opening for which I am qualified, you may reach me at (818) 719-3901. In the meantime, I will call you in a month to discuss employment possibilities.

> **Take the initiative; tell when you will call for an update.**

Sincerely,

Job Acceptance and Rejection Letters

When all your hard work pays off, you will be offered the position you want. Although you will likely accept the position over the phone, it's a good idea to follow up with an acceptance letter to confirm the details and to formalize the acceptance.

Dear Ms. Scarborough:

Confirm your acceptance of the position with enthusiasm.

It was a pleasure talking with you earlier today. As I mentioned, I am delighted to accept the position of Web designer with Innovative Creations, Inc., in your Seattle office. I look forward to becoming part of the IC team and to starting work on a variety of exciting and innovative projects.

Review salary and benefits details.

As we agreed, my starting salary will be $46,000, with a full benefits package including health and life insurance, retirement plan, stock options, and three weeks of vacation per year.

Include the specific starting date.

I look forward to starting my position with Innovative Creations on September 15, 2009. Before that date I will send you the completed tax and insurance forms you need. Thanks again for everything, Ms. Scarborough.

Sincerely,

If you must turn down a job offer, show your professionalism by writing a sincere letter. This letter should thank the employer for the job offer and explain briefly that you are turning it down. Taking the time to extend this courtesy could help you in the future if this employer has an opening. Here is a sample job rejection letter:

Dear Mr. Opperman:

Thank the employer for the job offer and decline the offer without giving specifics.

Thank you very much for offering me the position of sales representative with Bendall Pharmaceuticals. It was a difficult decision to make, but I have accepted a position with another company.

Express gratitude and best wishes for the future.

I appreciate your taking the time to interview me, and I wish Bendall much success in the future.

Sincerely,

Resignation Letter

After you have been in a position for a period of time, you may find it necessary to leave. Perhaps you have been offered a better position, or maybe you have decided to return to school full-time. Whatever the reason, you should leave your position gracefully and tactfully. Although you will likely discuss your resignation in person with your supervisor, it is a good idea to document your resignation by writing a formal letter. Some resignation letters are brief, while others contain great detail. Remember that many resignation letters are placed in personnel files. Here is an example of a basic letter of resignation:

Dear Ms. Patrick:

Confirm exact date of resignation. Remind employer of your contributions.

This letter serves as formal notice of my resignation from Allied Corporation, effective Friday, August 15. I have enjoyed serving as your office assistant for the past two years, and I am grateful for everything I have learned during my employment with Allied.

Offer assistance to prepare for your resignation.

Please let me know what I can do over the next two weeks to help you prepare for my departure. I would be happy to help with finding and training my replacement.

Offer thanks and end with a forward-looking statement.

Thanks again for providing such a positive employment experience. I will long remember my time here.

Sincerely,

Communicating at Work Your Turn

Applying Your Skills at Google

With your passion for marketing and technology, you were excited to find a posting for a sales internship at the Google Web site. Interns work on a sales team and assist with industry research, data analysis, advertising strategy, sales administration, and related responsibilities. The requirements for the internship included good organizational and analytical skills, detail orientation, problem-solving abilities, and excellent written and verbal communication skills. You decided to apply for the Google internship, and you sent a cover letter and résumé and filled out the online questionnaire.

Several weeks later, a recruiter called you to chat about your qualifications for the job. You were pleased with how well the screening interview went. The recruiter was too, and she invited you to spend a day at the Googleplex.

Your Task
Using the techniques and resources described in this chapter, prepare for your visit to Google. Research the company and prepare a summary of the company's business philosophy, corporate culture, products, and other topics you consider relevant to the sales internship. Then develop a "cheat sheet" to help you highlight your skills as you answer typical interview questions. Also include questions that you would like to ask the interviewers. Submit your "cheat sheet" to your instructor.

Although the employee who wrote the preceding resignation letter gave the standard two-week notice, you may find that a longer notice is necessary. The higher and more responsible your position, the longer the notice you should give your employer. You should, however, always give some notice as a courtesy.

Writing job acceptance, job rejection, and resignation letters requires effort. That effort, however, is worth it because you are building bridges that later may carry you to even better jobs in the future.

Summary of Learning Objectives

1 **Understand the importance of a job interview, its purposes, and its forms, including screening, hiring/placement, one-on-one, panel, group, sequential, and stress interviews.** Job interviews are extremely important because they can change your life. As a job candidate, you have the following purposes in an interview: (a) convince the employer of your potential, (b) find out more about the job and the company, and (c) expand on the information in your résumé. From the employer's perspective, the interview is an opportunity to (a) assess your abilities in relation to the requirements for the position; (b) discuss your training, experience, knowledge, and abilities in more detail; (c) see what drives and motives you; and (d) decide whether you would fit into the organization. Screening interviews seek to eliminate less qualified candidates. Hiring/placement interviews may be one-on-one, panel, group, sequential, or stress.

2 **Describe what to do before an in-person interview, including researching the target company, preparing success stories, and practicing answers to possible questions.** If you are lucky enough to be selected for an in-person interview, you should research the target company by learning about its products, mission, customers, competitors, and finances. Before your interview prepare 30-second success stories that demonstrate your qualifications and achievements. Practice answers to typical interview questions. Expect to explain any problems areas on your résumé. If you are not sure where the employer is located, take a trial trip the day before your interview. Decide how to dress so that you will look qualified, competent, and professional.

3 **Explain how to perform during an interview, including sending positive nonverbal messages and using good techniques in answering questions.** During your interview send positive nonverbal messages by controlling body movements, showing good posture, maintaining eye contact, using gestures effectively, and smiling enough to convey a positive attitude. Listen attentively, turn off your cell phone, don't chew gum, and sound enthusiastic and sincere. If you feel nervous, breathe deeply and remind yourself that you are well prepared. Tell yourself that you control part of this interview and that interviews are a two-way street.

4 **Describe how to answer typical interview questions such as those that seek to get acquainted, gauge your interest, probe your experience, explore your accomplishments, look to the future, and inquire about salary expectations.** Interviewers often ask the same types of questions. Be prepared to respond to inquiries such as, *Tell me about yourself*. Practice answering questions about why you want to work for the organization, why you should be hired, how your education and experience have prepared you for the position, where you expect to be in five or ten years, what your greatest weaknesses are, and how much money you expect to earn. Be ready for situational questions that ask you to respond to a hypothetical situation. Expect behavioral questions that begin with *Tell me about a time when you. . . .* Think about how you would respond to possible illegal or inappropriate questions.

5 **Understand how to close an interview positively, including asking meaningful questions.** Toward the end of an interview, you should be prepared to ask your own questions, such as, *What will my duties be?* and, *When do you expect to make a decision?* After asking your questions and the interviewer signals the end of the meeting, find out what action will follow. Summarize your strongest qualifications, show your enthusiasm for obtaining this position, and thank the interviewer. Ask for the interviewer's business card. Shake the interviewer's hand with confidence, and acknowledge anyone else you see on the way out.

6 **Outline the activities that take place after an interview, including thanking the interviewer and contacting references.** After leaving the interview, immediately make notes of the key points discussed. Note your strengths and weaknesses during the interview so that you can work to improve in future interviews. Write a thank-you letter including the date of the interview, the exact job title for which you were interviewed, and specific topics discussed. Show that you really want the job. Alert your references that they may be contacted.

7 **Understand how to complete employment applications and write résumé follow-up, rejection follow-up, job acceptance, and job rejection messages.** If you don't hear from the interviewer within five days or at the specified time, call him or her. You could also e-mail to learn how the decision process is going. Sound professional, not desperate, angry, or frustrated. If asked to fill out an application form, look over all the questions before starting. If asked for a salary figure, provide a salary range or write *Negotiable* or *Open*. If you don't get the job, consider writing a letter that expresses your disappointment but your desire to be contacted in case a job opens up. If you are offered a job, write a letter that confirms the details and formalizes your acceptance. Upon resigning a position, write a letter that confirms the date of resignation, offers assistance to prepare for your resignation, and expresses thanks.

Chapter Review

1. What are the purposes of a job interview for a candidate? (Obj. 1)

2. What are the purposes of a job interview for the employer? (Obj. 1)

3. What is a screening interview, and why is it so important? (Obj. 1)

4. What should a job candidate learn about a company before going to a job interview? (Obj. 2)

5. What are *success stories,* and how can they be used? (Obj. 2)

6. How can you send positive nonverbal messages during an interview? (Obj. 3)

7. What should you do if an interview question is vague or unclear? (Obj. 3)

8. What is the best way to answer the question, *Tell me about yourself*? (Obj. 4)

9. How could you respond to the question, *Why should we hire you when we have applicants with more experience or better credentials?* (Obj. 4)

10. What should you do if asked a salary question early in an interview? (Obj. 4)

11. What is the difference between a situational and a behavioral question? (Obj. 4)

12. What kinds of questions should you ask during an interview? (Obj. 5)

13. What should you remember to do at the close of an interview? (Obj. 6)

14. What should be included in a thank-you note after an interview? (Obj. 6)

15. If you are offered a position, why is it important to write an acceptance letter, and what should it include? (Obj. 7)

Critical Thinking

1. Is it normal to be nervous about an employment interview, and what can be done to overcome this fear? (Obj. 1)

2. What can you do to improve the first impression you make at an interview? (Objs. 2, 3)

3. Do you think behavioral questions (such as, *Tell me about a business problem you have had and how you solved it*) are more effective than traditional questions (such as, *Tell me what you are good at*)? Why? (Obj. 4)

4. If you are asked an illegal interview question, why is it important to first assess the intentions of the interviewer? (Obj. 4)

5. **Ethical Issue.** When asked about his previous salary in a job interview, Jeremy boosts his salary a bit. He reasons that he was about to get a raise, and he also felt that he deserved to be paid more than he was actually earning. Even his supervisor said that he was worth more than his salary. Is Jeremy justified in inflating his previous salary? (Obj. 4)

Activities

16.1 Researching an Organization (Obj. 2)

Web

An important part of your preparation for an interview is finding out about the target company.

Your Task. Select an organization where you would like to be employed. Assume you have been selected for an interview. Using resources described in this chapter, locate information about the organization's leaders and their business philosophy. Find out about the organization's accomplishments, setbacks, finances, products, customers, competition, and advertising. Prepare a summary report documenting your findings.

16.2 Learning What Jobs Are Really About Through Weblogs (Obj. 2)

Web

Weblogs, or blogs, are becoming an important tool in the employment search process. By accessing blogs, job seekers can learn more about a company's culture and day-to-day activities.

Your Task. Using the Web, locate a blog that is maintained by an employee of a company where you would like to work. Monitor the blog for at least a week. Prepare a short report summarizing what you learned about the company through reading the blog postings. Include a statement of whether this information would be valuable during your job search.

16.3 Building Interview Skills (Objs. 2, 3)

Successful interviews require diligent preparation and repeated practice. To be well prepared, you need to know what skills are required for your targeted position. In addition to computer and communication skills, employers generally want to know whether a candidate works well with a team, accepts responsibility, solves problems, is efficient, meets deadlines, shows leadership, saves time and money, and is a hard worker.

Your Task. Consider a position for which you are eligible now or one for which you will be eligible when you complete your education. Identify the skills and traits necessary for this position. If you prepared a résumé in Chapter 15, be sure that it addresses these

targeted areas. Now prepare interview worksheets listing at least ten technical and other skills or traits you think a recruiter will want to discuss in an interview for your targeted position.

16.4 Preparing Success Stories (Obj. 2)

You can best showcase your talents if you are ready with your own success stories that show how you have developed the skills or traits required for your targeted position.

Your Task. Using the worksheets you prepared in **Activity 16.3**, prepare success stories that highlight the required skills or traits. Select three to five stories to develop into answers to potential interview questions. For example, here's a typical question: *How does your background relate to the position we have open?* A possible response: *As you know, I have just completed an intensive training program in _____. In addition, I have over three years of part-time work experience in a variety of business settings. In one position I was selected to manage a small business in the absence of the owner. I developed responsibility and customer-service skills in filling orders efficiently, resolving shipping problems, and monitoring key accounts. I also inventoried and organized products worth over $200,000. When the owner returned from a vacation to Florida, I was commended for increasing sales and was given a bonus in recognition of my efforts.* People relate to and remember stories. Try to shape your answers into memorable stories.

16.5 Polishing Answers to Interview Questions (Obj. 4)

Practice makes perfect in interviewing. The more often you rehearse responses to typical interview questions, the closer you are to getting the job.

Your Task. Select three questions from each of these question categories discussed in this chapter: Questions to Get Acquainted, Questions to Gauge Your Interest, Questions About Your Experience and Accomplishments, Questions About the Future, and Challenging Questions. Write your answers to each set of questions. Try to incorporate skills and traits required for the targeted position, and include success stories where appropriate. Polish these answers and your delivery technique by practicing in front of a mirror or by making a recording.

16.6 Learning to Answer Situational Interview Questions (Obj. 4)

Team **Web**

Situational interview questions can vary widely from position to position. You should know enough about a position to understand some of the typical situations you would encounter on a regular basis.

Your Task. Use your favorite search tool to locate typical job descriptions of a position in which you are interested. Based on these descriptions, develop a list of six to eight typical situations someone in this position would face; then write situational interview questions for each of these scenarios. In pairs of two students, role-play interviewer and interviewee, alternating with your listed questions.

16.7 Developing Skill With Behavioral Interview Questions (Obj. 4)

Team **Web**

Behavioral interview questions are increasingly popular, and you will need a little practice before you can answer them easily.

Your Task. Use your favorite search tool to locate lists of behavioral questions on the Web. Select five skill areas such as communication, teamwork, and decision making. For each skill area find three behavioral questions that you think would be effective in an interview. In pairs of two students, role-play interviewer and interviewee, alternating with your listed questions. You goal is to answer effectively in one or two minutes. Remember to use the STAR method when answering.

16.8 Creating an Interview Cheat Sheet (Objs. 2–5)

Even the best rehearsed applicants sometimes forget to ask the questions they prepared, or they fail to stress their major accomplishments in job interviews. Sometimes applicants are so rattled they even forget the interviewer's name. To help you keep your wits during an interview, make a "cheat sheet" that summarizes key facts, answers, and questions. Use it before the interview and also review it as the interview is ending to be sure you have covered everything that is critical.

Your Task. Prepare a cheat sheet with the following information:

Day and time of interview:

Meeting with: (Name of interviewer[s], title, company, city, state, zip, telephone, cell, fax, pager, e-mail)

Major accomplishments: (four to six)

Management or work style: (four to six)

Things you need to know about me: (three or four items)

Reason I left my last job:

Answers to difficult questions: (four or five answers)

Questions to ask interviewer:

Things I can do for you:

16.9 Handling Inappropriate and Illegal Interview Questions (Obj. 4)

Although some questions are considered illegal by the government, many interviewers will ask them anyway—whether intentionally or unknowingly. Being prepared is important.

Your Task. How would you respond in the following scenario? Assume you are being interviewed at one of the top companies on your list of potential employers. The interviewing committee consists of a human resources manager and the supervising manager of the department where you would work. At various times during the interview, the supervising manager asks questions that make you feel uncomfortable. For example, he asks whether you are married. You know this question is illegal, but you see no harm in answering it. But then he asks how old you are. Since you started college early and graduated in three and a half years, you are worried that you may not be considered mature enough for this position. But you have most of the other qualifications required, and you are convinced you could succeed on the job. How should you answer this question?

16.10 Knowing What to Ask (Obj. 5)

When it is your turn to ask questions during the interview process, be ready.

Your Task. Decide on three to five questions that you would like to ask during an interview. Write these questions out and practice asking them so that you sound confident and sincere.

16.11 Role-Playing in a Mock Interview (Objs. 3, 4)

Team

One of the best ways to understand interview dynamics and to develop confidence is to role-play the parts of interviewer and candidate in a mock interview.

Your Task. Choose a partner for this activity. Each partner makes a list of two interview questions for each of the nine interview question categories presented in this chapter. In team sessions you and your partner will role-play an actual interview. One acts as interviewer; the other is the candidate. Prior to the interview, the candidate tells the interviewer the job he or she is applying for and the name of the company. For the interview, the interviewer and candidate should dress appropriately and sit in chairs facing each other. The interviewer greets the candidate and makes the candidate comfortable. The candidate gives the interviewer a copy of his or her résumé. The interviewer asks three (or more depending on your instructor's time schedule) questions from the candidate's list. The interviewer may also ask follow-up questions if appropriate. When finished, the interviewer ends the meeting graciously. After one interview, reverse roles and repeat.

16.12 Videotaping an Interview (Objs. 3–6)

Seeing how you look during an interview can help you improve your body language and presentation style. Your instructor may act as interviewer, or an outside businessperson may be asked to conduct mock interviews in your classroom.

Your Task. Engage a student or campus specialist to videotape each interview. Review your performance and critique it looking for ways to improve. Your instructor may ask class members to offer comments and suggestions on individual interviews.

Interactive Learning @ www.meguffey.com

16.13 Saying Thanks for the Interview (Objs. 6, 7)

You have just completed an exciting employment interview, and you want the interviewer to remember you.

Your Task. Write a follow-up thank-you letter to Ronald T. Ranson, Human Resources Development, Electronic Data Sources, 1328 Peachtree Plaza, Atlanta, GA 30314 (or a company of your choice). Make up any details needed.

16.14 Refusing to Take *No* for an Answer (Obj. 6)

After an excellent interview with Electronic Data Sources (or a company of your choice), you are disappointed to learn that someone else was hired. However, you really want to work for EDS.

Your Task. Write a follow-up letter to Ronald T. Ranson, Human Resources Development, Electronic Data Sources, 1328 Peachtree Plaza, Atlanta, GA 30314 (or a company of your choice). Indicate that you are disappointed but still interested.

16.15 Following Up After Submitting Your Résumé (Obj. 7)

A month has passed since you sent your résumé and cover letter in response to a job advertisement. You are still interested in the position and would like to find out whether you still have a chance.

Your Task. Write a follow-up letter that does not offend the reader or damage your chances of employment.

16.16 Saying *Yes* to a Job Offer (Obj. 7)

Your dream has come true: you have just been offered an excellent position. Although you accepted the position on the phone, you want to send a formal acceptance letter.

Your Task. Write a job acceptance letter to an employer of your choice. Include the specific job title, your starting date, and details about your compensation package. Make up any necessary details.

16.17 Searching for Advice (Objs. 1–7)

> Web

You can find wonderful, free, and sometimes entertaining information about job-search strategies and career tips, as well as interview advice on the Web.

Your Task. Use the Web to locate articles or links to sites with job-search, résumé, and interview information. Make a list of at least five good interview pointers—ones that were not covered in this chapter. Send an e-mail message to your instructor describing your findings, or post your findings to a class discussion board to share with your classmates.

Video Resources

Video Library 1

Sharpening Your Interview Skills

In the video titled *Sharpening Your Interview Skills,* you see the job interview of Betsy Chin. Based on what you learned in this chapter and your own experience, critique her performance. What did she do well? What could she improve?

Grammar and Mechanics C.L.U.E. Review 16

Total Review

Each of the following sentences has a total of **three** errors in grammar, punctuation, capitalization, usage, or spelling. On a separate sheet, write a correct version. Avoid adding new phrases, starting new sentences, or rewriting in your own words. When finished, compare your responses with the key beginning on page Key-4.

1. Before going to a job interview you should research the following—company size, competitors, reputation, strengths and weaknesses.

2. I wonder how many companys use software to scan candidates résumés and search for keywords?

3. Even with the popularity of e-mail most employers' will contact job applicants by telephone to set up there interviews.

4. Initial contacts by employers will usualy be made by telephone, therefore, insure that you keep important information nearby.

5. If you have little experience emphasize your up to date skills, recent training and extraordinary commitment.

6. Interviewees should not criticise anyone or anything and they should not focus on there imperfections.

7. Evan was asked whether he had a Bachelors degree, and whether he had five years experience.

8. If you are hopping to create a good impression be sure to write a thank you letter after a job interview.

9. When Robins interview was over she told friends that she had done good.

10. Robin was already to send a thank-you message, when she realized she could not spell the interviewers name.

Grammar and Mechanics Guide

APPENDIX A

Competent Language Usage Essentials (C.L.U.E.)

In the business world, people are often judged by the way they speak and write. Using the language competently can mean the difference between individual success and failure. Often a speaker sounds accomplished; but when that same individual puts ideas in print, errors in language usage destroy his or her credibility. One student observed, "When I talk, I get by on my personality; but when I write, the flaws in my communication show through. That's why I'm in this class."

How this Grammar and Mechanics Guide Can Help You

This grammar and mechanics guide contains 50 guidelines covering sentence structure, grammar, usage, punctuation, capitalization, and number style. These guidelines focus on the most frequently used—and abused—language elements. Frequent checkpoint exercises enable you to try your skills immediately. In addition to the 50 language guides in this appendix, you will find a list of 160 frequently misspelled words plus a quick review of selected confusing words.

The concentrated materials in this guide help novice business communicators focus on the major areas of language use. The guide is not meant to teach or review *all* the principles of English grammar and punctuation. It focuses on a limited number of language guidelines and troublesome words. Your objective should be mastery of these language principles and words, which represent a majority of the problems typically encountered by business writers.

How to Use This Grammar and Mechanics Guide

Your instructor may give you the short C.L.U.E. language diagnostic test (located in the Instructor's Manual) to help you assess your competency. A longer self-administered diagnostic test is available as part of Your Personal Language Trainer at www.meguffey.com. Either test will give you an idea of your language competence. After taking either diagnostic test, read and work your way through the 50 guidelines. You should also use the self-teaching Trainer exercises, all of which correlate with this Grammar and Mechanics Guide. Concentrate on areas where you are weak. Memorize the spelling list and definitions for the confusing words located at the end of this appendix.

Within these materials, you will find two kinds of exercises for your practice. (1) *Checkpoints*, located in this appendix, focus on a small group of language guidelines. Use them to test your comprehension as you complete each section. (2) *Review exercises,* located at the end of each chapter, help reinforce your language skills at the same time you are learning about the processes and products of business communication.

Many students want all the help they can get in improving their language skills. For additional assistance with grammar and language fundamentals, *Business Communication: Process and Product*, 6e, offers you unparalleled interactive and print resources:

- **Your Personal Language Trainer.** This self-paced learning tool is located at www .meguffey.com. Dr. Guffey acts as your personal trainer in helping you pump up your language muscles. Your Personal Language Trainer provides the rules plus hundreds of sentence applications so that you can test your knowledge and build your skills with immediate feedback and explanations.

- **Speak Right!,** found at www.meguffey.com, reviews frequently mispronounced words. You'll hear correct pronunciations from Dr. Guffey so that you will never be embarrassed by mispronouncing these terms.

- **Spell Right!,** found at www.meguffey.com, presents frequently misspelled words along with exercises to help you improve your skills.

- **Reference Books.** More comprehensive treatment of grammar and punctuation guidelines can be found in Clark and Clark's *A Handbook for Office Workers* and Guffey's *Business English*.

Grammar and Mechanics Guidelines

Sentence Structure

GUIDE 1: Avoid Sentence Fragments.
A fragment is an incomplete sentence. You can recognize a complete sentence because it (a) includes a subject (a noun or pronoun that interacts with a verb), (b) includes a verb (a word expressing action or describing a condition), and (c) makes sense (comes to a closure). A complete sentence is an independent clause. One of the most serious errors a writer can make is punctuating a fragment as if it were a complete sentence.

Fragment	**Improved**
Because 90 percent of all business trans-actions involve written messages. Good writing skills are critical.	Because 90 percent of all business trans-actions involve written messages, good writing skills are critical.
The recruiter requested a writing sample. Even though the candidate seemed to communicate well.	The recruiter requested a writing sample, even though the candidate seemed to communicate well.

Tip. Fragments often can be identified by the words that introduce them—words such as *although, as, because, even, except, for example, if, instead of, since, so, such as, that, which,* and *when.* These words introduce dependent clauses. Make sure such clauses are always connected to independent clauses.

DEPENDENT CLAUSE   INDEPENDENT CLAUSE

Since she became supervisor, she had to write more memos and reports.

GUIDE 2: Avoid Run-On (Fused) Sentences.
A sentence with two independent clauses must be joined by a coordinating conjunction *(and, or, nor, but)* or by a semicolon (;). Without a conjunction or a semicolon, a run-on sentence results.

Run-on	**Improved**
Robin visited resorts of the rich and the famous he also dropped in on luxury spas.	Robin visited resorts of the rich and famous, and he also dropped in on luxury spas.
	Robin visited resorts of the rich and famous; he also dropped in on luxury spas.

GUIDE 3: Avoid comma-splice sentences.
A comma splice results when a writer joins (splices together) two independent clauses—without using a coordinating conjunction *(and, or, nor, but).*

Comma Splice	Improved
Disney World operates in Orlando, EuroDisney serves Paris.	Disney World operates in Orlando; EuroDisney serves Paris.
	Disney World operates in Orlando, and EuroDisney serves Paris.
Visitors wanted a resort vacation, however they were disappointed.	Visitors wanted a resort vacation; however, they were disappointed.

Tip. In joining independent clauses, beware of using a comma and words such as *consequently, furthermore, however, therefore, then, thus,* and so on. These conjunctive adverbs require semicolons.

✓ Checkpoint

Revise the following to rectify sentence fragments, comma splices, and run-ons.

1. Although it began as a side business for Disney. Destination weddings now represent a major income source.

2. About 2,000 weddings are held yearly. Which is twice the number just ten years ago.

3. Weddings may take place in less than one hour, however the cost may be as much as $5,000.

4. Limousines line up outside Disney's wedding pavilion, they are scheduled in two-hour intervals.

5. Most couples prefer a traditional wedding, others request a fantasy experience.

For all the Checkpoint sentences, compare your responses with the answers at the end of Appendix A.

Grammar

Verb Tense

GUIDE 4: Use present tense, past tense, and past participle verb forms correctly.

Present Tense (Today I_____)	Past Tense (Yesterday I_____)	Past Participle (I have_____)
am	was	been
begin	began	begun
break	broke	broken
bring	brought	brought
choose	chose	chosen
come	came	come
do	did	done
give	gave	given
go	went	gone
know	knew	known
pay	paid	paid
see	saw	seen
steal	stole	stolen
take	took	taken
write	wrote	written

The package *came* yesterday, and Kevin *knew* what it contained.

If I *had seen* the shipper's bill, I *would have paid* it immediately.

I *know* the answer now; I wish I *had known* it yesterday.

Tip. Probably the most frequent mistake in tenses results from substituting the past participle form for the past tense. Notice that the past-participle tense requires auxiliary verbs such as *has, had, have, would have,* and *could have.*

Faulty	**Correct**
When he *come* over last night, he *brung* pizza.	When he *came* over last night, he *brought* pizza.
If he *had came* earlier, we *could have saw* the video.	If he *had come* earlier, we *could have seen* the video.

Verb Mood

GUIDE 5: Use the subjunctive mood to express hypothetical (untrue) ideas.
The most frequent misuse of the subjunctive mood involves using *was* instead of *were* in clauses introduced by *if* and *as though* or containing *wish.*

If I *were* (not *was*) you, I would take a business writing course.

Sometimes I wish I *were* (not *was*) the manager of this department.

He acts as though he *were* (not *was*) in charge of this department.

Tip. If the statement could possibly be true, use *was.*
If I *was* to blame, I accept the consequences.

 *Checkpoint*

Correct faults in verb tenses and mood.

6. If I was you, I would have went to the ten o'clock meeting.

7. The manager could have wrote a better report if he had began earlier.

8. When the vice president seen the report, he immediately come to my office.

9. I wish the vice president was in your shoes for just one day.

10. If the manager had knew all that we do, I'm sure he would have gave us better reviews.

Verb Voice

For a discussion of active- and passive-voice verbs, see pages 136–137 in Chapter 5.

Verb Agreement

GUIDE 6: Make subjects agree with verbs despite intervening phrases and clauses.
Become a detective in locating *true* subjects. Don't be deceived by prepositional phrases and parenthetic words that often disguise the true subject.

Our study of annual budgets, five-year plans, and sales proposals *is* (not *are*) progressing on schedule. (The true subject is *study.*)

The budgeted item, despite additions proposed yesterday, *remains* (not *remain*) as submitted. (The true subject is *item.*)

A vendor's evaluation of the prospects for a sale, together with plans for follow-up action, *is* (not *are*) what we need. (The true subject is *evaluation.*)

Tip. Subjects are nouns or pronouns that control verbs. To find subjects, cross out prepositional phrases beginning with words such as *about, at, by, for, from, of,* and *to.* Subjects of verbs are not found in prepositional phrases. Also, don't be tricked by expressions introduced by *together with, in addition to,* and *along with.*

GUIDE 7: Subjects joined by *and* require plural verbs. Watch for true subjects joined by the conjunction *and*. They require plural verbs.

> The CEO and one of his assistants *have* (not *has*) ordered a limo.

> Considerable time and money *were* (not *was*) spent on remodeling.

> Exercising in the gym and jogging every day *are* (not *is*) how he keeps fit.

GUIDE 8: Subjects joined by *or* or *nor* may require singular or plural verbs. The verb should agree with the closest subject.

> Either the software or the printer *is* (not *are*) causing the glitch. (The verb is controlled by the closer subject, *printer*.)

> Neither St. Louis nor Chicago *has* (not *have*) a chance of winning. (The verb is controlled by *Chicago*.)

Tip. In joining singular and plural subjects with *or* or *nor*, place the plural subject closer to the verb. Then, the plural verb sounds natural. For example, *Either the manufacturer or the distributors are responsible.*

GUIDE 9: Use singular verbs for most indefinite pronouns. The following pronouns all take singular verbs: *anyone, anybody, anything, each, either, every, everyone, everybody, everything, neither, nobody, nothing, someone, somebody,* and *something*.

> Everyone in both offices *was* (not *were)* given a bonus.

> Each of the employees *is* (not *are)* being interviewed.

GUIDE 10: Use singular or plural verbs for collective nouns, depending on whether the members of the group are operating as a unit or individually. Words such as *faculty, administration, class, crowd,* and *committee* are considered *collective* nouns. If the members of the collective are acting as a unit, treat them as singular subjects. If they are acting individually, it is usually better to add the word *members* and use a plural verb.

Correct
The Finance Committee *is* working harmoniously. (*Committee* is singular because its action is unified.)

The Planning Committee *are* having difficulty agreeing. (*Committee* is plural because its members are acting individually.)

Improved
The Planning Committee members *are* having difficulty agreeing. (Add the word *members* if a plural meaning is intended.)

Tip. In the United States collective nouns are generally considered singular. In Britain these collective nouns are generally considered plural.

✓ *Checkpoint*

Correct the errors in subject–verb agreement.

11. The agency's time and talent was spent trying to develop a blockbuster ad campaign.

12. Your e-mail message, along with both of its attachments, were not delivered to my computer.

13. Each of the Fortune 500 companies are being sent a survey regarding women in management.

14. A full list of names and addresses are necessary before we can begin.

15. Either the judge or the attorney have asked for a recess.

Pronoun Case

GUIDE 11: Learn the three cases of pronouns and how each is used.

Pronouns are substitutes for nouns. Every business writer must know the following pronoun cases.

Subjective (Nominative) Case Used for subjects of verbs and subject complements	Objective Case Used for objects of prepositions and objects of verbs	Possessive Case Used to show possession
I	me	my, mine
we	us	our, ours
you	you	you, yours
he	him	his
she	her	her, hers

Subjective (Nominative) Case Used for subjects of verbs and subject complements	Objective Case Used for objects of prepositions and objects of verbs	Possessive Case Used to show possession
it	it	its
they	them	their, theirs
who, whoever	whom, whomever	whose

GUIDE 12: Use subjective-case pronouns as subjects of verbs and as complements.
Complements are words that follow linking verbs (such as *am, is, are, was, were, be, being,* and *been*) and rename the words to which they refer.

She and *I* (not *her* and *me*) are looking for entry-level jobs. (Use subjective-case pronouns as the subjects of the verb phrase *are looking.*)

We hope that Marci and *he* (not *him*) will be hired. (Use a subjective-case pronoun as the subject of the verb phrase *will be hired.*)

It must have been *she* (not *her*) who called last night. (Use a subjective-case pronoun as a subject complement.)

Tip. If you feel awkward using subjective pronouns after linking verbs, rephrase the sentence to avoid the dilemma. Instead of *It is she who is the boss,* say, *She is the boss.*

GUIDE 13: Use objective-case pronouns as objects of prepositions and verbs.

Send the e-mail to *her* and *me* (not *she* and *I*). (The pronouns *her* and *me* are objects of the preposition *to.*)

The CEO appointed Rick and *him* (not *he*) to the committee. (The pronoun *him* is the object of the verb *appointed.*)

Tip. When a pronoun appears in combination with a noun or another pronoun, ignore the extra noun or pronoun and its conjunction. Then, the case of the pronoun becomes more obvious.

Jason asked Jennifer and *me* (not *I*) to lunch. (Ignore *Jennifer and.*)

The waiter brought hamburgers to Jason and *me* (not *I*).
(Ignore *Jason and.*)

Tip. Be especially alert to the following prepositions: *except, between, but,* and *like.* Be sure to use objective pronouns as their objects.

Just between you and *me* (not *I*), that mineral water comes from the tap.

Everyone except Robert and *him* (not *he*) responded to the invitation.

GUIDE 14: Use possessive pronouns to show ownership. Possessive pronouns (such as *hers, yours, whose, ours, theirs,* and *its*) require no apostrophes.

All reports except *yours* (not *your's*) have to be rewritten.

The apartment and *its* (not *it's*) contents are *hers* (not *her's*) until June.

Tip. Don't confuse possessive pronouns and contractions. Contractions are shortened forms of subject–verb phrases (such as *it's* for *it is, there's* for *there is, who's* for *who is,* and *they're* for *they are*).

✓ Checkpoint

Correct errors in pronoun case.

16. My partner and me have looked at many apartments, but your's has the best location.

17. We thought the car was her's, but it's license plate doesn't match.

18. Just between you and I, do you think there printer is working?

19. Theres not much the boss or me can do if its broken, but its condition should have been reported to him or I earlier.

20. We received several applications, but your's and her's were missing

GUIDE 15: Use pronouns ending in *self* only when they refer to previously mentioned nouns or pronouns.

The president *himself* ate all the M & Ms.

Send the package to Mike or *me* (not *myself*).

Tip. Trying to sound less egocentric, some radio and TV announcers incorrectly substitute *myself* when they should use *I*. For example, "Jerry and *myself* (should be *I*) are cohosting the telethon."

GUIDE 16: Use *who* or *whoever* for subjective-case constructions and *whom* or *whomever* for objective-case constructions. In determining the correct choice, it is helpful to substitute *he* for *who* or *whoever* and *him* for *whom* or *whomever*.

For *whom* was this software ordered? (The software was ordered for *him*.)

Who did you say called? (You did say *he* called?)

Give the supplies to *whoever* asked for them. (In this sentence the clause *whoever asked for them* functions as the object of the preposition *to*. Within the clause *whoever* is the subject of the verb *asked*. Again, try substituting *he: he asked for them*.)

✓ Checkpoint

Correct any errors in the use of *self*-ending pronouns and *who/whom*.

21. The boss herself is willing to call whoever we decide to honor.

22. Who have you asked to develop ads for our new products?

23. I have a pizza for whomever placed the telephone order.

24. The meeting is set for Wednesday; however, Matt and myself cannot attend.

25. Incident reports must be submitted by whomever experiences a personnel problem.

Pronoun Reference

GUIDE 17: Make pronouns agree in number and gender with the words to which they refer (their antecedents). When the gender of the antecedent is obvious, pronoun references are simple.

One of the boys lost *his* (not *their*) new tennis shoes. (The singular pronoun *his* refers to the singular *One.*)

Each of the female nurses was escorted to *her car* (not *their cars*). (The singular pronoun *her* and singular noun *car* are necessary because they refer to the singular subject *Each.*)

Somebody on the girls' team left *her* (not *their*) headlights on.

When the gender of the antecedent could be male or female, sensitive writers today have a number of options.

Faulty
Every employee should receive *their* check Friday. (The plural pronoun *their* does not agree with its singular antecedent *employee.*)

Improved
All employees should receive *their* checks Friday. (Make the subject plural so that the plural pronoun *their* is acceptable. This option is preferred by many writers today.)

All employees should receive checks Friday. (Omit the possessive pronoun entirely.)

Every employee should receive *a* check Friday. (Substitute *a* for a pronoun.)

Every employee should receive *his or her* check Friday. (Use the combination *his or her.* However, this option is wordy and should be avoided.)

GUIDE 18: Be sure that pronouns such as *it, which, this,* and *that* refer to clear antecedents. Vague pronouns confuse the reader because they have no clear single antecedent. The most troublesome are *it, which, this,* and *that.* Replace vague pronouns with concrete nouns, or provide these pronouns with clear antecedents.

Faulty
Our office recycles as much paper as possible because *it* helps the environment. (Does *it* refer to *paper, recycling,* or *office?*)

The disadvantages of local area networks can offset their advantages. *That* merits further evaluation. (What merits evaluation: advantages, disadvantages, or offsetting of one by the other?)

Negotiators announced an expanded health care plan, reductions in dental coverage, and a proposal of on-site child care facilities. *This* caused employee protests. (What exactly caused employee protests?)

Improved
Our office recycles as much paper as possible because *such efforts* help the environment. (Replace *it* with *such efforts.*)

The disadvantages of local area networks can offset their advantages. That fact merits further evaluation. (*Fact* supplies a concrete noun for the vague pronoun *that.*)

Negotiators announced an expanded health care plan, reductions in dental coverage, and a proposal of on-site child care facilities. *This* reduction in dental coverage caused employee protests. (The pronoun *This* now has a clear reference.)

Tip. Whenever you use the words *this, that, these,* and *those* by themselves, a red flag should pop up. These words are dangerous when they stand alone. Inexperienced writers often use them to refer to an entire previous idea, rather than to a specific antecedent, as shown in the preceding example. You can usually solve the problem by adding another idea to the pronoun (such as *this reduction*).

✓ Checkpoint

Correct the faulty and vague pronoun references in the following sentences. Numerous remedies exist.

26. Every employee must wear their picture identification badge.

27. Flexible working hours may mean slower career advancement, but it appeals to many workers.

28. Any renter must pay his rent by the first of the month.

29. Someone in this office reported that his computer had a virus.

30. Obtaining agreement on job standards, listening to coworkers, and encouraging employee suggestions all helped to open lines of communication. This is particularly important in team projects.

Adjectives and Adverbs

GUIDE 19: Use adverbs, not adjectives, to describe or limit the action of verbs. Use adjectives after linking verbs.

Andrew said he did *well* (not *good*) on the exam. (The adverb *well* describes how he did.)

After its tune-up, the engine is running *smoothly* (not *smooth*). (The adverb *smoothly* describes the verb *is running*.)

Don't take the manager's criticism *personally* (not *personal*). (The adverb *personally* tells how to take the criticism.)

She finished her homework *more quickly* (not *quicker*) than expected. (The adverb *more quickly* explains how she finished her homework.)

Liam felt *bad* (not *badly*) after he heard the news. (The adjective *bad* follows the linking verb *felt*.)

GUIDE 20: Hyphenate two or more adjectives that are joined to create a compound modifier before a noun.

Follow the *step-by-step* instructions to construct the *low-cost* bookshelves.

A *well-designed* keyboard is part of this *state-of-the-art* equipment.

Tip. Don't confuse adverbs ending in *-ly* with compound adjectives: *newly enacted* law and *highly regarded* CEO would not be hyphenated.

✓ Checkpoint

Correct any problems in the use of pronouns, adjectives, and adverbs.

31. My manager and me could not resist the once in a lifetime opportunity.

32. Because John and him finished their task so quick, they made a fast trip to the recently opened snack bar.

33. If I do good on the exam, I qualify for many part time jobs and a few full time positions.

34. The vice president told him and I not to take the announcement personal.

35. In the not too distant future, we may enjoy more practical uses of robots.

Punctuation

GUIDE 21: Use commas to separate three or more items (words, phrases, or short clauses) in a series. (CmSer)

Downward communication delivers job instructions, procedures, and appraisals.

In preparing your résumé, try to keep it brief, make it easy to read, and include only job-related information.

The new ice cream flavors include cookie dough, chocolate raspberry truffle, cappuccino, and almond amaretto.

Tip. Some professional writers omit the comma before *and*. However, most business writers prefer to retain that comma because it prevents misreading the last two items as one item. Notice in the previous example how the final two ice cream flavors could have been misread if the comma had been omitted.

GUIDE 22: Use commas to separate introductory clauses and certain phrases from independent clauses. (CmIntro) This guideline describes the comma most often omitted by business writers. Sentences that open with dependent clauses (often introduced by words such as *since, when, if, as, although,* and *because*) require commas to separate them from the main idea. The comma helps readers recognize where the introduction ends and the big idea begins. Introductory phrases of five or more words or phrases containing verbal elements also require commas.

If you recognize introductory clauses, you will have no trouble placing the comma. (A comma separates the introductory dependent clause from the main clause.)

When you have mastered this rule, half the battle with commas will be won.

As expected, additional explanations are necessary. (Use a comma even if the introductory clause omits the understood subject: *As we expected.*)

In the spring of last year, we opened our franchise. (Use a comma after a phrase containing five or more words.)

Having considered several alternatives, we decided to invest. (Use a comma after an introductory verbal phrase.)

To invest, we needed $100,000. (Use a comma after an introductory verbal phrase, regardless of its length.)

Tip. Short introductory prepositional phrases (three or fewer words) require no commas. Don't clutter your writing with unnecessary commas after introductory phrases such as *by 2006, in the fall* or *at this time.*

GUIDE 23: Use a comma before the coordinating conjunction in a compound sentence. (CmConj) The most common coordinating conjunctions are *and, or, nor,* and *but.* Occasionally, *for, yet,* and *so* may also function as coordinating conjunctions. When coordinating conjunctions join two independent clauses, commas are needed.

The investment sounded too good to be true, *and* many investors were dubious about it. (Use a comma before the coordinating conjunction *and* in a compound sentence.)

Southern California is the financial fraud capital of the world, *but* some investors refuse to heed warning signs.

Tip. Before inserting a comma, test the two clauses. Can each of them stand alone as a complete sentence? If either is incomplete, skip the comma.

Promoters said the investment offer was for a limited time and could not be extended even one day. (Omit a comma before *and* because the second part of the sentence is not a complete independent clause.)

Lease payments are based largely on your down payment and on the value of the car at the end of the lease. (Omit a comma before *and* because the second half of the sentence is not a complete clause.)

Add appropriate commas.

36. Before she enrolled in this class Erin used to sprinkle her writing with commas semicolons and dashes.

37. After studying punctuation she learned to use commas more carefully and to reduce her reliance on dashes.

38. At this time Erin is engaged in a serious yoga program but she also finds time to enlighten her mind.

39. Next fall Erin may enroll in communication and merchandising or she may work for a semester to earn money.

40. When she completes her junior year she plans to apply for an internship in Los Angeles Burbank or Long Beach.

GUIDE 24: Use commas appropriately in dates, addresses, geographical names, degrees, and long numbers. (CmDate)

September 30, 1963, is his birthday. (For dates use commas before and after the year.)

Send the application to James Kirby, 20045 45th Avenue, Lynnwood, WA 98036, as soon as possible. (For addresses use commas to separate all units except the two-letter state abbreviation and the zip code.)

Lisa expects to move from Cupertino, California, to Sonoma, Arizona, next fall. (For geographical areas use commas to enclose the second element)

Karen Munson, CPA, and Richard B. Larsen, PhD, were the speakers. (For professional designations and academic degrees following names, use commas to enclose each item.)

The latest census figures show the city's population to be 342,000. (In figures use commas to separate every three digits, counting from the right.)

GUIDE 25: Use commas to set off internal sentence interrupters. (CmIn) Sentence interrupters may be verbal phrases, dependent clauses, contrasting elements, or parenthetical expressions (also called transitional phrases). These interrupters often provide information that is not grammatically essential.

Harvard researchers, working steadily for 18 months, developed a new cancer therapy. (Use commas to set off an internal interrupting verbal phrase.)

The new therapy, which applies a genetically engineered virus, raises hopes among cancer specialists. (Use commas to set off nonessential dependent clauses.)

Dr. James C. Morrison, who is one of the researchers, made the announcement. (Use commas to set off nonessential dependent clauses.)

It was Dr. Morrison, not Dr. Arturo, who led the team effort. (Use commas to set off a contrasting element.)

This new therapy, by the way, was developed from a herpes virus. (Use commas to set off a parenthetical expression.)

Tip. Parenthetical (transitional) expressions are helpful words that guide the reader from one thought to the next. Here are typical parenthetical expressions that require commas:

as a matter of fact	in addition	of course
as a result	in the meantime	on the other hand
consequently	nevertheless	therefore
for example		

Tip. Always use *two* commas to set off an interrupter, unless it begins or ends a sentence.

 Checkpoint

Insert necessary commas.

41. James listed 1805 Martin Luther King Street San Antonio Texas 78220 as his forwarding address.

42. This report is not however one that must be classified.

43. Employment of paralegals which is expected to increase 32 percent next year is growing rapidly because of the expanding legal services industry.

44. The contract was signed May 15 2006 and remains in effect until May 15 2011.

45. As a matter of fact the average American drinks enough coffee to require 12 pounds of coffee beans annually.

GUIDE 26: Avoid unnecessary commas.
Do not use commas between sentence elements that belong together. Do not automatically insert commas before every *and* or at points where your voice might drop if you were saying the sentence out loud.

Faulty

Growth will be spurred by the increasing complexity of business operations, and by large employment gains in trade and services. (A comma unnecessarily precedes *and*.)

All students with high grades, are eligible for the honor society. (A comma unnecessarily separates the subject and verb.)

One of the reasons for the success of the business honor society is, that it is very active. (A comma unnecessarily separates the verb and its complement.)

Our honor society has, at this time, over 50 members. (Commas unnecessarily separate a prepositional phrase from the sentence.)

 Checkpoint

Remove unnecessary commas. Add necessary ones.

46. Car companies promote leasing because it brings customers back into their showrooms sooner, and gives dealers a steady supply of late-model used cars.

47. When shopping for a car you may be offered a fantastic leasing deal.

48. The trouble with many leases is, that the value of the car at the end of the lease may be less than expected.

49. We think on the other hand, that you should compare the costs of leasing and buying, and that you should talk to a tax adviser.

50. Many American automakers are, at this time, offering intriguing lease deals.

Semicolons, Colons

GUIDE 27: Use a semicolon to join closely related independent clauses.
Experienced writers use semicolons to show readers that two thoughts are closely associated. If the ideas are not related, they should be expressed in separate sentences. Often, but not always, the second independent clause contains a conjunctive adverb (such as *however, consequently, therefore,* or *furthermore*) to show the relation between the two clauses. Use a semicolon before a conjunctive adverb of two or more syllables (such as *however, consequently, therefore,* or *furthermore*) and a comma after it.

Learning history is easy; learning its lessons is almost impossible. (A semicolon joins two independent clauses.)

He was determined to complete his degree; consequently, he studied diligently. (A semicolon precedes the conjunctive adverb and a comma follows it.)

Serena wanted a luxury apartment located near campus; however, she couldn't afford the rent. (A semicolon precedes the conjunctive adverb and a comma follows it.)

Tip. Don't use a semicolon unless each clause is truly independent. Try the sentence test. Omit the semicolon if each clause could not stand alone as a complete sentence.

Faulty	**Improved**
There is no point in speaking; unless you can improve on silence. (The second half of the sentence is a dependent clause. It could not stand alone as a sentence.)	There is no point in speaking unless you can improve on silence.
Although I cannot change the direction of the wind; I can adjust my sails to reach my destination. (The first clause could not stand alone.)	Although I cannot change the direction of the wind, I can adjust my sails to reach my destination.

GUIDE 28: Use a semicolon to separate items in a series when one or more of the items contains internal commas.

Representatives from as far away as Blue Bell, Pennsylvania; Bowling Green, Ohio; and Phoenix, Arizona, attended the conference.

Stories circulated about Henry Ford, founder, Ford Motor Company; Lee Iacocca, former CEO, Chrysler Motor Company; and Shoichiro Toyoda, founder, Toyota Motor Company.

GUIDE 29: Use a colon after a complete thought that introduces a list of items. Words such as *these, the following,* and *as follows* may introduce the list or they may be implied.

The following cities are on the tour: Louisville, Memphis, and New Orleans.

An alternate tour includes several West Coast cities: Seattle, San Francisco, and San Diego.

Tip. Be sure that the statement before a colon is grammatically complete. An introductory statement that ends with a preposition (such as *by, for, at,* and *to*) or a verb (such as *is, are,* or *were*) is incomplete. The list following a preposition or a verb actually functions as an object or as a complement to finish the sentence.

Faulty	**Improved**
Three Big Macs were ordered by: Pam, Jim, and Lee. (Do not use a colon after an incomplete statement.)	Three Big Macs were ordered by Pam, Jim, and Lee.
Other items that they ordered were: fries, Cokes, and salads. (Do not use a colon after an incomplete statement)	Other items that they ordered were fries, Cokes, and salads.

GUIDE 30: Use a colon after business letter salutations and to introduce long quotations.

Dear Mr. Duran: Dear Lisa:

The Asian consultant bluntly said: "Americans tend to be too blabby, too impatient, and too informal for Asian tastes. To succeed in trade with Pacific Rim countries, Americans must become more willing to adapt to native cultures."

Tip. Use a comma to introduce short quotations. Use a colon to introduce long one-sentence quotations and quotations of two or more sentences.

Checkpoint

Add appropriate semicolons and colons.

51. Marco's short-term goal is an entry-level job his long-term goal however is a management position.

52. Speakers included the following professors Rebecca Hilbrink University of Alaska Lora Lindsey Ohio University and Michael Malone Central Florida College.

53. The recruiter was looking for three qualities loyalty initiative and enthusiasm.

54. Microsoft seeks experienced individuals however it will hire recent graduates who are skilled.

55. South Florida is an expanding region therefore many business opportunities are available.

Apostrophe

GUIDE 31: Add an apostrophe plus *s* to an ownership word that does not end in an *s* sound.

> We hope to show a profit in one year's time. (Add *'s* because the ownership word *year* does not end in an *s*.)
>
> The company's assets rose in value. (Add *'s* because the ownership word *company* does not end in *s*.)
>
> All the women's votes were counted. (Add *'s* because the ownership word *women* does not end in *s*.)

GUIDE 32: Add only an apostrophe to an ownership word that ends in an *s* sound—unless an extra syllable can be pronounced easily.

> Some workers' benefits will cost more. (Add only an apostrophe because the ownership word *workers* ends in an *s*.)
>
> Several months' rent are now due. (Add only an apostrophe because the ownership word *months* ends in an *s*.)
>
> The boss's son got the job. (Add *'s* because an extra syllable can be pronounced easily.)

Tip. To determine whether an ownership word ends in an *'s*, use it in an *of* phrase. For example, *one month's salary* becomes *the salary of one month*. By isolating the ownership word without its apostrophe, you can decide whether it ends in an *s*.

GUIDE 33: Use a possessive pronoun or add *'s* to make a noun possessive when it precedes a gerund, a verb form used as a noun.

> We all protested *Laura's* (not *Laura*) smoking. (Add *'s* to the noun preceding the gerund.)
>
> *His* (not *Him*) talking on his cell phone angered moviegoers. (Use a possessive pronoun before the gerund.)
>
> I appreciate *your* (not *you*) answering the telephone while I was gone. (Use a possessive pronoun before the gerund

 Checkpoint

Correct any problems with possessives.

56. Both companies executives received huge bonuses, even when employees salaries were falling.

57. In just one weeks time, we promise to verify all members names and addresses.

58. The manager and I certainly appreciate you bringing this matter to our CPAs attention.

59. All beneficiaries names must be revealed when insurance companies write policies.

60. Is your sister-in-laws job downtown?

Other Punctuation

GUIDE 34: Use one period to end a statement, command, indirect question, or polite request. Never use two periods.

Matt worked at BioTech, Inc. (Statement. Use only one period.)

Deliver it before 5 p.m. (Command. Use only one period.)

Stacy asked whether she could use the car next weekend. (Indirect question)

Will you please send me an employment application. (Polite request)

Tip. Polite requests often sound like questions. To determine the punctuation, apply the action test. If the request prompts an action, use a period. If it prompts a verbal response, use a question mark.

| **Faulty** | **Improved** |
| Could you please correct the balance on my next statement? (This polite request prompts an action rather than a verbal response.) | Could you please correct the balance on my next statement. |

Tip: To avoid the punctuation dilemma with polite requests, do not phrase the request as a question. Phrase it as a command: *Please correct the balance on my next statement.* It still sounds polite, and the punctuation problem disappears.

GUIDE 35: Use a question mark after a direct question and after statements with questions appended.

Are they hiring at BioTech, Inc.?

Most of their training is in-house, isn't it?

GUIDE 36: Use a dash to (a) set off parenthetical elements containing internal commas, (b) emphasize a sentence interruption, or (c) separate an introductory list from a summarizing statement. The dash has legitimate uses. However, some writers use it whenever they know that punctuation is necessary, but they are not sure exactly what. The dash can be very effective, if not misused.

Three top students—Gene Engle, Donna Hersh, and Mika Sato—won awards. (Use dashes to set off elements with internal commas.)

Executives at IBM—despite rampant rumors in the stock market—remained quiet regarding dividend earnings. (Use dashes to emphasize a sentence interruption.)

Japan, Taiwan, and Turkey—these were areas hit by recent earthquakes. (Use a dash to separate an introductory list from a summarizing statement)

GUIDE 37: Use parentheses to set off nonessential sentence elements, such as explanations, directions, questions, or references.

Researchers find that the office grapevine (see Chapter 1 for more discussion) carries surprisingly accurate information.

Only two dates (February 15 and March 1) are suitable for the meeting.

Tip. Careful writers use parentheses to de-emphasize and the dash to emphasize parenthetical information. One expert said, "Dashes shout the news; parentheses whisper it."

GUIDE 38: Use quotation marks to (a) enclose the exact words of a speaker or writer; (b) distinguish words used in a special sense, such as slang; or (c) enclose titles of articles, chapters, or other short works.

"If you make your job important," said the consultant, "it's quite likely to return the favor."

The recruiter said that she was looking for candidates with good communication skills. (Omit quotation marks because the exact words of the speaker are not quoted.)

This office discourages "rad" hair styles and clothing. (Use quotes for slang.)

In *BusinessWeek* I saw an article entitled "Communication for Global Markets." (Use quotation marks around the title of an article; use all caps, underlines, or italics for the name of the publication.)

Tip. Never use quotation marks arbitrarily, as in *Our "spring" sale starts April 1.*

 *Checkpoint*

Add appropriate punctuation.

61. Will you please send your print catalog as soon as possible

62. (Direct quote) Our Super Bowl promotion said the CEO will cost nearly $500,000

63. (De-emphasize) Two kinds of batteries see page 16 of the instruction booklet may be used in this camera

64. Tim wondered whether sentences could end with two periods

65. All computers have virus protection don't they

Capitalization

GUIDE 39: Capitalize proper nouns and proper adjectives. Capitalize the *specific* names of persons, places, institutions, buildings, religions, holidays, months, organizations, laws, races, languages, and so forth. Do not capitalize seasons, and do not capitalize common nouns that make *general* references.

Proper Nouns	**Common Nouns**
Michelle Deluca	the manufacturer's rep
Everglades National Park	the wilderness park
College of the Redwoods	the community college
Empire State Building	the downtown building
Environmental Protection Agency	the federal agency
Persian, Armenian, Hindi	modern foreign languages
Annual Spring Festival	in the spring
Proper Adjectives	
Hispanic markets	Italian dressing
Xerox copy	Japanese executives
Swiss chocolates	Reagan economics

GUIDE 40: Capitalize only specific academic courses and degrees.

Professor Donna Howard, PhD, will teach Accounting 121 next spring.

James Barker, who holds bachelor's and master's degrees, teaches marketing.

Jessica enrolled in classes in management, English, and business law.

GUIDE 41: Capitalize courtesy, professional, religious, government, family, and business titles when they precede names.

Mr. Jameson, Mrs. Alvarez, and Ms. Robinson (Courtesy titles)

Professor Andrews, Dr. Lee (Professional titles)

Rabbi Cohen, Pastor Williams, Pope Benedict (Religious titles)

Senator Tom Harrison, Mayor Jackson (Government titles)

Uncle Edward, Mother Teresa, Cousin Vinney (Family titles)

Vice President Morris, Budget Director Lopez (Business titles)

Do not capitalize a title when it is followed by an appositive (that is, when the title is followed by a noun that renames or explains it).

Only one professor, Jonathan Marcus, favored a tuition hike.

Local candidates counted on their governor, Lee Jones, to help raise funds.

Do not capitalize titles following names unless they are part of an address:

Mark Yoder, president of Yoder Enterprises, hired all employees.

Paula Beech, director of Human Resources, interviewed all candidates.

Send the package to Amanda Harr, Advertising Manager, Cambridge Publishers, 20 Park Plaza, Boston, MA 02116.

Generally, do not capitalize a title that replaces a person's name.

Only the president, his chief of staff, and one senator made the trip.

The director of marketing and the sales manager will meet at 1 p.m.

Do not capitalize family titles used with possessive pronouns.

my mother, his father, your cousin

GUIDE 42: Capitalize the principal words in the titles of books, magazines, newspapers, articles, movies, plays, songs, poems, Web sites, and reports. Do *not* capitalize articles (*a, an, the*) and prepositions of fewer than four letters (*in, to, by, for*) unless they begin or end the title. The *to* in infinitives (*to run, to say, to write*) is also not capitalized unless it appears as the first word of a title or subtitle.

I enjoyed the book *A Customer Is More Than a Name.*

Did you read the article titled "Companies in Europe Seek Executives With Multinational Skills" that appeared in *Newsweek*?

We liked the article titled "Advice From a Pro: How to Say It With Pictures."

Check the "Advice and Resources" link at the *CareerBuilder* Web site.

(Note that the titles of books are underlined or italicized but the titles of articles are enclosed in quotation marks.)

GUIDE 43: Capitalize names of geographic locations. Capitalize *north, south, east, west,* and their derivatives only when they represent specific geographical regions.

from the Pacific Northwest	heading northwest on the highway
living in the West	west of the city
Midwesterners, Southerners	western Oregon, southern Ohio
peace in the Middle East	a location east of the middle of the city

GUIDE 44: Capitalize the main words in the specific names of departments, divisions, or committees within business organizations. Do not capitalize general references.

All forms are available from our Department of Human Resources.

The Consumer Electronics Division launched an upbeat marketing campaign.

We volunteered for the Employee Social Responsibility Committee.

You might send an application to their personnel department.

GUIDE 45: Capitalize product names only when they refer to trademarked items. Do not capitalize the common names following manufacturers' names.

Dell laptop computer	Skippy peanut butter	NordicTrack treadmill
Eveready Energizer	Norelco razor	Kodak color copier
Coca-Cola	Panasonic plasma television	Big Mac sandwich

GUIDE 46: Capitalize most nouns followed by numbers or letters (except in page, paragraph, line, and verse references).

Room 14	Exhibit A	Flight 12, Gate 43
Figure 2.1	Plan No. 1	Model Z2010

✓ Checkpoint

Capitalize all appropriate words.

66. vice president moore bought a new nokia cell phone before leaving for the east coast.

67. when you come on tuesday, travel west on highway 5 and exit at mt. mckinley street.

68. The director of our human resources department called a meeting of the company's building security committee.

69. our manager and president are flying on american airlines flight 34 leaving from gate 69 at the las vegas international airport.

70. my father read a businessweek article titled can you build loyalty with bricks and mortar?

Number Usage

GUIDE 47: Use word form to express (a) numbers *ten* and under and (b) numbers beginning sentences. General references to numbers *ten* and under should be expressed in word form. Also use word form for numbers that begin sentences. If the resulting number involves more than two words, however, recast the sentence so that the number does not fall at the beginning.

We answered *six* telephone calls for the *four* sales reps.

Fifteen customers responded to the *three* advertisements today.

A total of 155 cameras were awarded as prizes. (Avoid beginning the sentence with a long number such as *one hundred fifty-five.*)

GUIDE 48: Use figures to express most references to numbers 11 and over.

Over *150* people from *53* companies attended the two-day workshop.

A four-ounce serving of Haagen-Dazs toffee crunch ice cream contains *300* calories and *19* grams of fat.

GUIDE 49: Use figures to express money, dates, clock time, decimals, and percents.

One item costs only *$1.95*; most, however, were priced between *$10* and *$35*. (Omit the decimals and zeros in even sums of money.)

We scheduled a meeting for May 12. (Notice that we do *not* write May 12th.)

We expect deliveries at 10:15 a.m. and again at 4 p.m. (Use lowercase *a.m.* and *p.m.*)

All packages must be ready by 4 o'clock. (Do *not* write 4:00 o'clock.)

When U.S. sales dropped *4.7* percent, net income fell *9.8* percent. (In contextual material use the word *percent* instead of the symbol %.)

GUIDE 50. Use a combination of words and figures to express sums of 1 million and over. Use words for small fractions.

Orion lost *$62.9* million in the latest fiscal year on revenues of *$584 million*. (Use a combination of words and figures for sums of 1 million and over.)

Only one half of the registered voters turned out. (Use words for small fractions.)

Tip. To ease your memory load, concentrate on the numbers normally expressed in words: numbers *ten* and under, numbers at the beginning of a sentence, and small fractions. Nearly everything else in business is generally written with figures.

✓ *Checkpoint*

Correct any inappropriate expression of numbers.

71. Although he budgeted fifty dollars, Jake spent 94 dollars and 34 cents for his cell phone.

72. Is the meeting on November 7th or November 14th?

73. UPS deliveries arrive at nine AM and again at four fifteen PM.

74. The company applied for a fifty thousand dollar loan at six%.

75. The U.S. population is just over 300,000,000, and the world population is estimated to be nearly 6,700,000,000.

Key to Grammar and Mechanics Checkpoint Exercises in Appendix A

This key shows all corrections. If you marked anything else, double-check the appropriate guideline.

1. Disney, destination

2. yearly, which

3. hour; however,

4. pavilion;

5. wedding;

6. If I *were* you, I would have *gone*. . . .

7. could have *written* . . . had *begun* earlier.

8. vice president *saw* . . . immediately *came*

9. vice president *were*

10. manager had *known* . . . would have *given*

11. time and talent *were* spent [*Note that two subjects require a plural verb.*]

12. attachments, *was* [*Note that the subject is* message.]

13. Each of . . . companies *is* [*Note that the subject is* Each.]

14. list of names and addresses *is* [*Note that the subject is* list.]

15. attorney *has*

16. My partner and *I* . . . but *yours*

17. was *hers*, but *its*

18. you and *me* . . . *their* printer

19. *There's* not much the boss or *I* can do if *it's* broken, . . . reported to him or *me* earlier.

20. but *yours* and *hers*

21. *whomever*

22. *Whom* have you asked. . . .

23. for *whoever*

24. Matt and *I*

25. by *whoever*

26. Every employee must wear *a* picture identification badge, *OR: All employees* must wear picture identification *badges.*

27. slower career advancement, but *flexible scheduling* appeals to many workers. (*Revise to avoid the vague pronoun* it.)

28. Any renter must pay *the* rent. . . . *OR: All renters must pay their* rent. . . .

29. reported that *a* computer. . . . *OR:* reported that *his or her* computer. . . .

30. communication. *These techniques are* particularly important. . . . (*Revise to avoid the vague pronoun* This.)

31. My manager and *I* could not resist the *once-in-a-lifetime* opportunity.

32. John and *he* finished their task so *quickly* (*Do not hyphenate* recently opened.)

33. do *well* . . . *part-time* jobs and a few *full-time* positions.

34. told him and *me* . . . *personally.*

35. *not-too-distant* future

36. class, Erin . . . with commas, semicolons,

37. studying punctuation,

38. program,

39. merchandising,

40. junior year, . . . in Los Angeles, Burbank,

41. Street, San Antonio, Texas 78220,

42. not, however,

43. paralegals, . . . next year,

44. May 15, 2006, . . . May 15, 2011.

45. fact,

46. sooner [*delete comma*]

47. car,

48. is [*delete comma*]

49. think, on the other hand, . . . buying [*delete comma*]

50. automakers are [*delete comma*] at this time [*delete commas*]

51. entry-level job; his long-term goal, however,

52. professors: Rebecca Hilbrink, University of Alaska; Lora Lindsey, Ohio University; and Michael Malone, Central Florida College.

53. qualities: loyalty, initiative,

54. individuals; however,

55. region; therefore,

56. companies' . . . employees'

57. one week's time, . . . members' ·

58. appreciate *your* . . . CPA's

59. beneficiaries'

60. sister-in-law's

61. possible.

62. "Our Super Bowl promotion," said the CEO, "will cost nearly $500,000."

63. Two kinds of batteries (see page 16 of the instruction booklet). . . .

64. two periods.

65. protection, don't they?

66. Vice President Moore . . . Nokia . . . East Coast

67. When . . .Tuesday, . . . Highway 5 . . . Mt. McKinley Street.

68. Human Resources Department . . . Building Security Committee

69. Our . . . American Airlines Flight 34 . . . Gate 69 at the Las Vegas International Airport

70. My . . . *BusinessWeek* article titled "Can You Build Loyalty With Bricks and Mortar?"

71. $50 . . . $94.34

72. November 7 or November 14 (*delete "th"*)

73. 9 a.m. . . . 4:15 p.m. [Note only one period at the end of the sentence.]

74. $50,000 . . . 6 percent.

75. 300 million . . . 6.7 billion

Confusing Words

accede:	to agree or consent	*alright:*	unacceptable variant spelling
exceed:	over a limit	*altar:*	structure for worship
accept:	to receive	*alter:*	to change
except:	to exclude; (prep) but	*appraise:*	to estimate
adverse:	opposing; antagonistic	*apprise:*	to inform
averse:	unwilling; reluctant	*ascent:*	(n) rising or going up
advice:	suggestion, opinion	*assent:*	(v) to agree or consent
advise:	to counsel or recommend	*assure:*	to promise
affect:	to influence	*ensure:*	to make certain
effect:	(n) outcome, result; (v) to bring about, to create	*insure:*	to protect from loss
all ready:	prepared	*capital:*	(n) city that is seat of government; wealth of an individual; (adj) chief
already:	by this time	*capitol:*	building that houses state or national lawmakers
all right:	satisfactory		

cereal:	breakfast food	whole:	complete
serial:	arranged in sequence	imply:	to suggest indirectly
cite:	to quote; to summon	infer:	to reach a conclusion
site:	location	lean:	(v) to rest against; (adj) not fat
sight:	a view; to see	lien:	(n) legal right or claim to property
coarse:	rough texture	liable:	legally responsible
course:	a route; part of a meal; a unit of learning	libel:	damaging written statement
complement:	that which completes	loose:	not fastened
compliment:	(n) praise or flattery; (v) to praise or flatter	lose:	to misplace
conscience:	regard for fairness	miner:	person working in a mine
conscious:	aware	minor:	(adj) lesser; (n) person under age
council:	governing body	patience:	calm perseverance
counsel:	(n) advice, attorney, consultant; (v) to give advice	patients:	people receiving medical treatment
credible:	believable	personal:	private, individual
creditable:	good enough for praise or esteem; reliable	personnel:	employees
desert:	(n) arid land; (v) to abandon	plaintiff:	(n) one who initiates a lawsuit
dessert:	sweet food	plaintive:	(adj) expressive of suffering or woe
device:	invention or mechanism	populace:	(n) the masses; population of a place
devise:	to design or arrange	populous:	(adj) densely populated
disburse:	to pay out	precede:	to go before
disperse:	to scatter widely	proceed:	to continue
elicit:	to draw out	precedence:	priority
illicit:	unlawful	precedents:	events used as an example
envelop:	(v) to wrap, surround, or conceal	principal:	(n) capital sum; school official; (adj) chief
envelope:	(n) a container for a written message	principle:	rule of action
every day:	each single day	stationary:	immovable
everyday:	ordinary	stationery:	writing material
farther:	a greater distance	than:	conjunction showing comparison
further:	additional	then:	adverb meaning "at that time"
formally:	in a formal manner	their:	possessive form of *they*
formerly:	in the past	there:	at that place or point
grate:	(v) to reduce to small particles; to cause irritation; (n) a frame of crossed bars blocking a passage	they're:	contraction of *they are*
		to:	a preposition; the sign of the infinitive
		too:	an adverb meaning "also" or "to an excessive extent"
great:	(adj) large in size; numerous; eminent or distinguished	two:	a number
		waiver:	abandonment of a claim
hole:	an opening	waver:	to shake or fluctuate

160 Frequently Misspelled Words

absence	calendar	decision	envelope
accommodate	canceled	deductible	equipped
achieve	catalog	defendant	especially
acknowledgment	changeable	definitely	evidently
across	column	dependent	exaggerate
adequate	committee	describe	excellent
advisable	congratulate	desirable	exempt
analyze	conscience	destroy	existence
annually	conscious	development	extraordinary
appointment	consecutive	disappoint	familiar
argument	consensus	dissatisfied	fascinate
automatically	consistent	division	feasible
bankruptcy	control	efficient	February
becoming	convenient	embarrass	fiscal
beneficial	correspondence	emphasis	foreign
budget	courteous	emphasize	forty
business	criticize	employee	fourth

friend
genuine
government
grammar
grateful
guarantee
harass
height
hoping
immediate
incidentally
incredible
independent
indispensable
interrupt
irrelevant
itinerary
judgment
knowledge
legitimate
library
license
maintenance

manageable
manufacturer
mileage
miscellaneous
mortgage
necessary
nevertheless
ninety
ninth
noticeable
occasionally
occurred
offered
omission
omitted
opportunity
opposite
ordinarily
paid
pamphlet
permanent
permitted
pleasant

practical
prevalent
privilege
probably
procedure
profited
prominent
quality
quantity
questionnaire
receipt
receive
recognize
recommendation
referred
regarding
remittance
representative
restaurant
schedule
secretary
separate
similar

sincerely
software
succeed
sufficient
supervisor
surprise
tenant
therefore
thorough
though
through
truly
undoubtedly
unnecessarily
usable
usage
using
usually
valuable
volume
weekday
writing
yield

Document Format Guide

APPENDIX B

Business communicators produce numerous documents that have standardized formats. Becoming familiar with these formats is important because business documents actually carry two kinds of messages. Verbal messages are conveyed by the words chosen to express the writer's ideas. Nonverbal messages are conveyed largely by the appearance of a document and its adherence to recognized formats. To ensure that your documents carry favorable nonverbal messages about you and your organization, you'll want to give special attention to the appearance and formatting of your e-mail messages, letters, envelopes, and fax cover sheets.

E-Mail Messages

E-mail messages are sent by computers through networks. After reading e-mail messages, receivers may print, store, or delete them. E-mail is an appropriate channel for *short* messages. E-mail should not replace business letters or memos that are lengthy, require permanent records, or transmit confidential or sensitive information. Chapter 7 presented guidelines on using e-mail smartly and safely. This section provides information on formats and usage. The following suggestions, illustrated in Figure B.1 and also in Figure 7.2 on page 177, may

FIGURE B.1 E-Mail Message

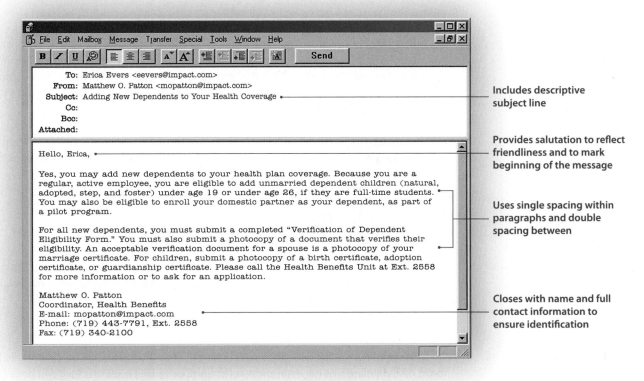

Includes descriptive subject line

Provides salutation to reflect friendliness and to mark beginning of the message

Uses single spacing within paragraphs and double spacing between

Closes with name and full contact information to ensure identification

guide you in setting up the parts of any e-mail message. Always check, however, with your organization so that you can follow its practices.

To Line. Include the receiver's e-mail address after *To*. If the receiver's address is recorded in your address book, you just have to click on it. Be sure to enter all addresses very carefully since one mistyped letter prevents delivery.

From Line. Most mail programs automatically include your name and e-mail address after *From*.

Cc and Bcc. Insert the e-mail address of anyone who is to receive a copy of the message. *Cc* stands for carbon copy or courtesy copy. Don't be tempted, though, to send needless copies just because it is easy. *Bcc* stands for blind carbon copy. Some writers use *bcc* to send a copy of the message without the addressee's knowledge. Writers also use the *bcc* line for mailing lists. When a message is sent to a number of people and their e-mail addresses should not be revealed, the *bcc* line works well to conceal the names and addresses of all receivers.

Subject. Identify the subject of the e-mail message with a brief but descriptive summary of the topic. Be sure to include enough information to be clear and compelling. Capitalize the initial letters of main words. Main words are all words except (a) the articles *a, an,* and *the*; (b) prepositions containing two or three letters (such as *at, to, on, by, for*); (c) the word *to* in an infinitive (*to work, to write*); and (d) the word *as*—unless any of these words are the first or last word in the subject line.

Salutation. Include a brief greeting, if you like. Some writers use a salutation such as *Dear Erica* followed by a comma or a colon. Others are more informal with *Hi, Erica; Hello, Erica; Good morning;* or *Greetings*. See Chapter 7 for a more complete discussion of e-mail salutations.

Message. Cover just one topic in your message, and try to keep your total message under two or three screens in length. Single-space and be sure to use both upper- and lowercase letters. Double-space between paragraphs.

Closing. Conclude an e-mail message, if you like, with *Cheers, Best wishes,* or *Warm regards*, followed by your name and complete contact information. Some people omit their e-mail address because they think it is provided automatically. However, some programs and routers do not transmit the address automatically. Therefore, always include it along with other identifying information in the closing.

Attachment. Use the attachment window or button to select the path and file name of any file you wish to send with your e-mail message. You can also attach a Web page to your message.

Business Letters

Business communicators write business letters primarily to correspond with people outside the organization. Letters may go to customers, vendors, other businesses, and the government, as discussed in Chapters 8, 9, and 10. The following information will help you format your letters following conventional guidelines.

Spacing and Punctuation

For some time typists left two spaces after end punctuation (periods, question marks, and so forth). This practice was necessary, it was thought, because typewriters did not have proportional spacing and sentences were easier to read if two spaces separated them. Professional typesetters, however, never followed this practice because they used proportional spacing, and readability was not a problem. Influenced by the look of typeset publications, many writers now leave only one space after end punctuation. As a practical matter, however, it is not wrong to use two spaces.

Letter Placement and Line Endings

The easiest way to place letters on the page is to use the defaults of your word processing program. In Microsoft Word 2003, default side margins are set at 1¼ inch; in Word 2007 they are set at 1 inch. Many companies today find these margins acceptable. If you want to adjust your margins to better balance shorter letters, use the following chart:

Words in Body of Letter	Margin Settings	Blank Lines After Date
Under 200	1.5 inches	4 to 10
Over 200	1 inch	2 to 3

Experts say that a "ragged" right margin is easier to read than a justified (even) margin. You might want to turn off the justification feature of your word processing program if it automatically justifies the right margin.

Business Letter Parts

Professional-looking business letters are arranged in a conventional sequence with standard parts. Following is a discussion of how to use these letter parts properly. Figure B.2 illustrates the parts of a block style letter. (See Chapter 8 for additional discussion of letters and their parts.)

Letterhead. Most business organizations use 8½ × 11-inch paper printed with a letterhead displaying their official name, street address, Web address, e-mail address, and telephone and fax numbers. The letterhead may also include a logo and an advertising message.

Dateline. On letterhead paper you should place the date two blank lines below the last line of the letterhead or 2 inches from the top edge of the paper (line 13). On plain paper place the date immediately below your return address. Because the date goes on line 13, start the return address an appropriate number of lines above it. The most common dateline format is as follows: *June 9, 2009*. Don't use *th* (or *rd, nd* or *st*) when the date is written this way. For European or military correspondence, use the following dateline format: *9 June 2009*. Notice that no commas are used.

Addressee and Delivery Notations. Delivery notations such as *FAX TRANS-MISSION, FEDERAL EXPRESS, MESSENGER DELIVERY, CONFIDENTIAL,* or *CERTIFIED MAIL* are typed in all capital letters two blank lines above the inside address.

Inside Address. Type the inside address—that is, the address of the organization or person receiving the letter—single-spaced, starting at the left margin. The number of lines between the dateline and the inside address depends on the size of the letter body, the type size (point or pitch size), and the length of the typing lines. Generally, one to nine blank lines are appropriate.

Be careful to duplicate the exact wording and spelling of the recipient's name and address on your documents. Usually, you can copy this information from the letterhead of the correspondence you are answering. If, for example, you are responding to *Jackson & Perkins Company*, do not address your letter to *Jackson and Perkins Corp.*

Always be sure to include a courtesy title such as *Mr., Ms., Mrs., Dr.,* or *Professor* before a person's name in the inside address—for both the letter and the envelope. Although many women in business today favor *Ms.,* you should use whatever title the addressee prefers.

Block style
Mixed punctuation

Letterhead ——————————

Island Graphics
893 Dillingham Boulevard
Honolulu, HI 96817-8817

(808)493-2310
http://www.islandgraphics.com

↓ Dateline is 2 inches from the top or 1 blank line below letterhead

Dateline —————————— September 13, 2009

↓ 1 to 9 blank lines

Inside address —————————— Mr. T. M. Wilson, President
Visual Concept Enterprises
1901 Kaumualii Highway
Lihue, HI 96766

↓ 1 blank line

Salutation —————————— Dear Mr. Wilson:

↓ 1 blank line

Subject line —————————— SUBJECT: BLOCK LETTER STYLE

↓ 1 blank line

This letter illustrates block letter style, about which you asked. All typed lines begin at the left margin. The date is usually placed 2 inches from the top edge of the paper or one blank line below the last line of the letterhead, whichever position is lower.

Body —————————— This letter also shows mixed punctuation. A colon follows the salutation, and a comma follows the complimentary close. Open punctuation requires no colon after the salutation and no comma following the close; however, open punctuation is seldom seen today.

If a subject line is included, it appears one blank line below the salutation. The word *SUBJECT* is optional. Most readers will recognize a statement in this position as the subject without an identifying label. The complimentary close appears one blank line below the end of the last paragraph.

↓ 1 blank line

Complimentary
close —————————— Sincerely,

Mark H. Wong   ↓ 3 blank lines

Signature block —————————— Mark H. Wong
Graphic Designer

↓ 1 blank line

Reference initials —————————— MHW:pil

Modified block style,
Mixed punctuation

In the modified block style letter shown at the left, the date is centered or aligned with the complimentary close and signature block, which start at the center. Mixed punctuation includes a colon after the salutation and a comma after the complimentary close, as shown above and at the left.

In general, avoid abbreviations such as *Ave.* or *Co.* unless they appear in the printed letterhead of the document being answered.

Attention Line. An attention line allows you to send your message officially to an organization but to direct it to a specific individual, officer, or department. However, if you know an individual's complete name, it is always better to use it as the first line of the inside address and avoid an attention line. Here are two common formats for attention lines:

MultiMedia Enterprises
931 Calkins Avenue
Rochester, NY 14301

MultiMedia Enterprises
Attention: Marketing Director
931 Calkins Avenue
Rochester, NY 14301

ATTENTION MARKETING DIRECTOR

Attention lines may be typed in all caps or with upper- and lowercase letters. The colon following *Attention* is optional. Notice that an attention line may be placed two lines below the address block or printed as the second line of the inside address. Use the latter format so that you may copy the address block to the envelope and the attention line will not interfere with the last-line placement of the zip code. Mail can be sorted more easily if the zip code appears in the last line of a typed address. Whenever possible, use a person's name as the first line of an address instead of putting that name in an attention line.

Salutation. For most letter styles place the letter greeting, or salutation, one blank line below the last line of the inside address or the attention line (if used). If the letter is addressed to an individual, use that person's courtesy title and last name (*Dear Mr. Lanham*). Even if you are on a first-name basis (*Dear Leslie*), be sure to add a colon (not a comma or a semicolon) after the salutation. Do not use an individual's full name in the salutation (not *Dear Mr. Leslie Lanham*) unless you are unsure of gender (*Dear Leslie Lanham*).

For letters with attention lines or those addressed to organizations, the selection of an appropriate salutation has become more difficult. Formerly, writers used *Gentlemen* generically for all organizations. With increasing numbers of women in business management today, however, *Gentlemen* is problematic. Because no universally acceptable salutation has emerged as yet, you could use *Ladies and Gentlemen* or *Gentlemen and Ladies*.

Subject and Reference Lines. Although experts suggest placing the subject line one blank line below the salutation, many businesses actually place it above the salutation. Use whatever style your organization prefers. Reference lines often show policy or file numbers; they generally appear one blank line above the salutation. Use initial capital letters for the main words or all capital letters.

Body. Most business letters and memorandums are single-spaced, with double-spacing between paragraphs. Very short messages may be double-spaced with indented paragraphs.

Complimentary Close. Typed one blank line below the last line of the letter, the complimentary close may be formal (*Very truly yours*) or informal (*Sincerely* or *Cordially*).

Signature Block. In most letter styles the writer's typed name and optional identification appear three or four blank lines below the complimentary close. The combination of name, title, and organization information should be arranged to achieve a balanced look. The name and title may appear on the same line or on separate lines, depending on the length of each. Use commas to separate categories within the same line, but not to conclude a line.

Sincerely yours,

Jeremy M. Wood

Jeremy M. Wood, Manager
Technical Sales and Services

Cordially yours,

Casandra Baker-Murillo

Casandra Baker-Murillo
Executive Vice President

Courtesy titles (*Ms., Mrs.,* or *Miss*) should be used before names that are not readily distinguishable as male or female. They should also be used before names containing only initials and international names. The title is usually placed in parentheses, but it may appear without them.

Yours truly,

K. C. Tripton

(Ms.) K. C. Tripton
Project Manager

Sincerely,

Leslie Hill

(Mr.) Leslie Hill
Public Policy Department

Some organizations include their names in the signature block. In such cases the organization name appears in all caps one blank line below the complimentary close, as shown here:

Cordially,
LIPTON COMPUTER SERVICES

Shelina A. Simpson

Ms. Shelina A. Simpson
Executive Assistant

Reference Initials. If used, the initials of the typist and writer are typed one blank line below the writer's name and title. Generally, the writer's initials are capitalized and the typist's are lowercased, but this format varies.

Enclosure Notation. When an enclosure or attachment accompanies a document, a notation to that effect appears one blank line below the reference initials. This notation reminds the typist to insert the enclosure in the envelope, and it reminds the recipient to look for the enclosure or attachment. The notation may be spelled out (*Enclosure, Attachment*), or it may be abbreviated (*Enc., Att.*). It may indicate the number of enclosures or attachments, and it may also identify a specific enclosure (*Enclosure: Form 1099*).

Copy Notation. If you make copies of correspondence for other individuals, you may use *cc* to indicate carbon copy, *pc* to indicate photocopy, or merely *c* for any kind of copy. A colon following the initial(s) is optional.

Second-Page Heading. When a letter extends beyond one page, use plain paper of the same quality and color as the first page. Identify the second and succeeding pages with a heading consisting of the name of the addressee, the page number, and the date. Use the following format or the one shown in Figure B.3:

Ms. Sara Hendricks   2   May 3, 2009

Both headings appear six blank lines (1 inch) from the top edge of the paper followed by two blank lines to separate them from the continuing text. Avoid using a second page if you have only one line or the complimentary close and signature block to fill that page.

Second-page heading → Mr. and Mrs. Tommy Hightower
Page 2
May 14, 2009

↓ 1 inch

↓ 2 blank lines

Kenai Remodeling Solutions has been in business in Alaska for nearly two decades, and we are proud of our reputation for quality work and completion on schedule. If you agree to the terms of the enclosed proposal before May 24, we can begin your job on June 5. Please sign the enclosed contract so that we can order your materials immediately and bring you the remodeled kitchen of your dreams.

↓ 1 blank line

Sincerely,

↓ 1 blank line

Company name → KENAI REMODELING SOLUTIONS

Jeremy M. Marshall

↓ 3 blank lines

Jeremy M. Marshall
President

Reference initials → spt

Enclosure notation → Enclosures: Hightower Proposal and
Contract Remodeling Schedule

Copy notation → *cc:* Mark Hutchinson, Peninsula Contractors, Inc.

Plain-Paper Return Address.

If you prepare a personal or business letter on plain paper, place your address immediately above the date. Do not include your name; you will type (and sign) your name at the end of your letter. If your return address contains two lines, begin typing so that the date appears 2 inches from the top. Avoid abbreviations except for a two-letter state abbreviation.

580 East Leffels Street
Springfield, OH 45501
December 14, 2009

Ms. Ellen Siemens
Escrow Department
TransOhio First Federal
1220 Wooster Boulevard
Columbus, OH 43218-2900

Dear Ms. Siemens:

For letters in the block style, type the return address at the left margin as shown. For modified block style letters, start the return address at the center to align with the complimentary close.

Letter and Punctuation Styles

Most business letters today are prepared in either block or modified block style, and they generally use mixed punctuation.

Block Style.

In the block style, shown in Figure B.2, all lines begin at the left margin. This style is a favorite because it is easy to format.

Modified Block Style. The modified block style differs from block style in that the date and closing lines appear in the center, as shown at the bottom of Figure B.1. The date may be (a) centered, (b) begun at the center of the page (to align with the closing lines), or (c) backspaced from the right margin. The signature block—including the complimentary close, writer's name and title, or organization identification—begins at the center. The first line of each paragraph may begin at the left margin or may be indented five or ten spaces. All other lines begin at the left margin.

Mixed Punctuation Style. Most businesses today use mixed punctuation, shown in Figure B.2. It requires a colon after the salutation and a comma after the complimentary close. Even when the salutation is a first name, a colon is appropriate.

Envelopes

An envelope should be of the same quality and color of stationery as the letter it carries. Because the envelope introduces your message and makes the first impression, you need to be especially careful in addressing it. Moreover, how you fold the letter is important.

Return Address. The return address is usually printed in the upper left corner of an envelope, as shown in Figure B.4. In large companies some form of identification (the writer's initials, name, or location) may be typed above the company name and address. This identification helps return the letter to the sender in case of nondelivery.

On an envelope without a printed return address, single-space the return address in the upper left corner. Beginning on line 3 on the fourth space (½ inch) from the left edge, type the writer's name, title, company, and mailing address. On a word processor, select the appropriate envelope size and make adjustments to approximate this return address location.

FIGURE B.4 Envelope Formats

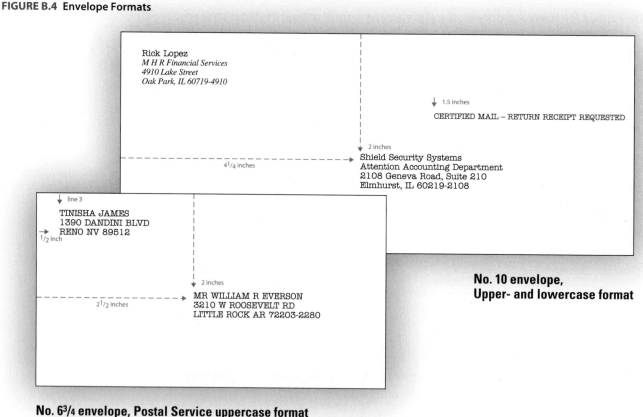

**No. 10 envelope,
Upper- and lowercase format**

No. 6³/₄ envelope, Postal Service uppercase format

Mailing Address. On legal-sized No. 10 envelopes (4⅛ × 9½ inches), begin the address on line 13 about 4¼ inches form the left edge, as shown in Figure B.4. For small envelopes (3⅝ × 6½ inches), begin typing on line 12 about 2½ inches from the left edge. On a word processor, select the correct envelope size and check to be sure your address falls in the desired location.

The U.S. Postal Service recommends that addresses be typed in all caps without any punctuation. This Postal Service style, shown in the small envelope in Figure B.4, was originally developed to facilitate scanning by optical character readers. Today's OCRs, however, are so sophisticated that they scan upper- and lowercase letters easily. Many companies today do not follow the Postal Service format because they prefer to use the same format for the envelope as for the inside address. If the same format is used, writers can take advantage of word processing programs to copy the inside address to the envelope, thus saving keystrokes and reducing errors. Having the same format on both the inside address and the envelope also looks more professional and consistent. For those reasons you may choose to use the familiar upper- and lowercase combination format. But you will want to check with your organization to learn its preference.

In addressing your envelopes for delivery in this country or in Canada, use the two-letter state and province abbreviations shown in Figure B.5. Notice that these abbreviations are in capital letters without periods.

Folding. The way a letter is folded and inserted into an envelope sends additional nonverbal messages about a writer's professionalism and carefulness. Most businesspeople follow the procedures shown here, which produce the least number of creases to distract readers.

For large No. 10 envelopes, begin with the letter face up. Fold slightly less than one third of the sheet toward the top, as shown in the following diagram. Then fold down the top third to within ⅓ inch of the bottom fold. Insert the letter into the envelope with the last fold toward the bottom of the envelope.

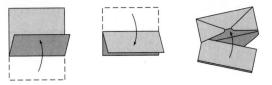

For small No. 6¾ envelopes, begin by folding the bottom up to within ⅓ inch of the top edge. Then fold the right third over to the left. Fold the left third to within ⅓ inch of the last fold. Insert the last fold into the envelope first.

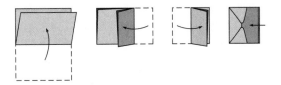

Fax Cover Sheet

Documents transmitted by fax are usually introduced by a cover sheet, such as that shown in Figure B.6. As with memos, the format varies considerably. Important items to include are (a) the name and fax number of the receiver, (b) the name and fax number of the sender, (c) the number of pages being sent, and (d) the name and telephone number of the person to notify in case of unsatisfactory transmission.

When the document being transmitted requires little explanation, you may prefer to attach an adhesive note (such as a Post-it fax transmittal form) instead of a full cover sheet. These notes carry essentially the same information as shown in our printed fax cover sheet. They are perfectly acceptable in most business organizations and can save considerable paper and transmission costs.

FIGURE B.5 Abbreviations of States, Territories, and Provinces

State or Territory	Two-Letter Abbreviation	State or Territory	Two-Letter Abbreviation
Alabama	AL	North Dakota	ND
Alaska	AK	Ohio	OH
Arizona	AZ	Oklahoma	OK
Arkansas	AR	Oregon	OR
California	CA	Pennsylvania	PA
Canal Zone	CZ	Puerto Rico	PR
Colorado	CO	Rhode Island	RI
Connecticut	CT	South Carolina	SC
Delaware	DE	South Dakota	SD
District of Columbia	DC	Tennessee	TN
Florida	FL	Texas	TX
Georgia	GA	Utah	UT
Guam	GU	Vermont	VT
Hawaii	HI	Virgin Islands	VI
Idaho	ID	Virginia	VA
Illinois	IL	Washington	WA
Indiana	IN	West Virginia	WV
Iowa	IA	Wisconsin	WI
Kansas	KS	Wyoming	WY
Kentucky	KY		
Louisiana	LA		
Maine	ME		
Maryland	MD	**Canadian Province**	
Massachusetts	MA	Alberta	AB
Michigan	MI	British Columbia	BC
Minnesota	MN	Labrador	LB
Mississippi	MS	Manitoba	MB
Missouri	MO	New Brunswick	NB
Montana	MT	Newfoundland	NF
Nebraska	NE	Northwest Territories	NT
Nevada	NV	Nova Scotia	NS
New Hampshire	NH	Ontario	ON
New Jersey	NJ	Prince Edward Island	PE
New Mexico	NM	Quebec	PQ
New York	NY	Saskatchewan	SK
North Carolina	NC	Yukon Territory	YT

FIGURE B.6 Fax Cover Sheet

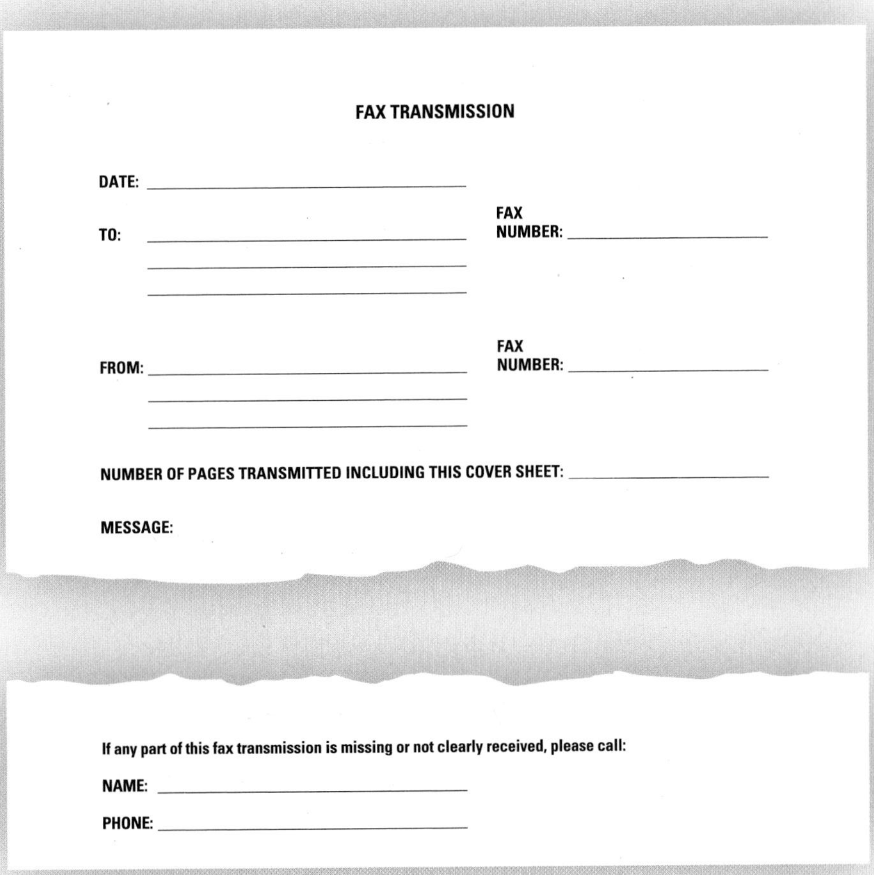

FAX TRANSMISSION

DATE: _____

TO: _____   FAX
                                          NUMBER: _____
_____
_____

FROM: _____   FAX
                                          NUMBER: _____
_____
_____

NUMBER OF PAGES TRANSMITTED INCLUDING THIS COVER SHEET: _____

MESSAGE:

If any part of this fax transmission is missing or not clearly received, please call:

NAME: _____

PHONE: _____

Documentation Guide

For many reasons business writers are careful to properly document report data. Citing sources strengthens a writer's argument, as you learned in Chapter 11. Acknowledging sources also shields writers from charges of plagiarism. Moreover, good references help readers pursue further research.

Before we discuss specific documentation formats, you must understand the difference between *source* notes and *content* notes. Source notes identify quotations, paraphrased passages, and author references. They lead readers to the sources of cited information, and they must follow a consistent format. Content notes, on the other hand, enable writers to add comments, explain information not directly related to the text, or refer readers to other sections of a report. Because content notes are generally infrequent, most writers identify them in the text with a raised asterisk (*). At the bottom of the page, the asterisk is repeated with the content note following. If two content notes appear on one page, a double asterisk identifies the second reference.

Your real concern will be with source notes. These identify quotations or paraphrased ideas in the text, and they direct readers to a complete list of references (a bibliography) at the end of your report. Researchers have struggled for years to develop the perfect documentation system, one that is efficient for the writer and crystal clear to the reader. As a result, many systems exist, each with its advantages. The important thing for you is to adopt one system and use it consistently.

Students frequently ask, "But what documentation system is most used in business?" Actually, no one method dominates. Many businesses have developed their own hybrid systems. These companies generally supply guidelines illustrating their in-house style to employees. Before starting any research project on the job, you will want to inquire about your organization's preferred documentation style. You can also look in the files for examples of previous reports.

References are usually cited in two places: (a) a brief citation appears in the text, and (b) a complete citation appears in a bibliography at the end of the report. The two most common formats for citations and bibliographies in academic work are those of the Modern Language Association (MLA) and the American Psychological Association (APA). Each has its own style for textual references and bibliography lists. The citations in this textbook are based on the APA style, which is increasingly the standard in business communication.

Modern Language Association Format

Writers in the humanities frequently use the MLA format, as illustrated in Figure C.1. In parentheses close to the textual reference appears the author's name and page cited. If no author is known, a shortened version of the source title is used. At the end of the report, the writer lists alphabetically all references in a bibliography called "Works Cited." For more information consult Joseph Gibaldi, *MLA Handbook for Writers of Research Papers*, 6e (New York: The Modern Language Association of America, 2003).

MLA In-Text Format. In-text citations generally appear close to the point where the reference is mentioned or at the end of the sentence inside the closing period. Follow these guidelines:

- Include the last name of the author(s) and the page number. Omit a comma, as (Smith 310).

FIGURE C.1 Portions of MLA Text Page and Works Cited

Peanut butter was first delivered to the world by a St. Louis physician in 1890. As discussed at the Peanut Advisory Board's Web site, peanut butter was originally promoted as a protein substitute for elderly patients ("History"). However, it was the 1905 Universal Exposition in St. Louis that truly launched peanut butter. Since then, annual peanut butter consumption has zoomed to 3.3 pounds a person in the United States (Barrons 46).

America's farmers produce 1.6 million tons of peanuts annually, about half of which is used for oil, nuts, and candy. Lisa Gibbons, executive secretary of the Peanut Advisory Board, says that "peanuts in some form are in the top four candies: Snickers, Reese's Peanut Butter Cups, Peanut M & Ms, and Butterfingers" (Meadows 32).

Works Cited

Barrons, Elizabeth Ruth. "A Comparison of Domestic and International Consumption of Legumes." *Journal of Economic Agriculture* 23 (2006): 45–49.

"History of Peanut Butter." *Peanut Advisory Board.* Retrieved 19 Jan. 2009 <http://www.peanutbutterlovers.com/History/index.html>.

Meadows, Mark Allen. "Peanut Crop Is Anything but Peanuts at Home and Overseas." *Business Monthly*, 30 Sept. 2008, 31–34.

- If the author's name is mentioned in the text, cite only the page number in parentheses. Do not include either the word *page* or the abbreviations *p.* or *pp.*

- If no author is known, refer to the document title or a shortened version of it, as ("Facts at Fingertips" 102).

MLA Bibliographic Format. The "Works Cited" bibliography lists all references cited in a report. Some writers include all works consulted. A portion of an MLA bibliography is shown in Figure C.1. A more complete list of model references appears in Figure C.2. Following are selected guidelines summarizing important points regarding MLA bibliographic format:

- Use italics or underscores for the titles of books, magazines, newspapers, and journals. Check with your organization or instructor for guidance. Capitalize all main words.

- Enclose the titles of magazine, newspaper, and journal articles in quotation marks. Include volume and issue numbers for journals only.

- For Internet citations, include a retrieval date. Although MLA format does not include the words *Retrieved* or *Accessed*, such wording helps distinguish the retrieval date from the document date.

- In citing online documents, list only the search term and main search site page for URLs that are impractically long and complicated (e.g., "Wendy's International," Hoovers .com).

FIGURE C.2 MLA Sample Works Cited

C-3

Works Cited

American Airlines. *2008 Annual Report.* Fort Worth, TX: AMR Corporation. •———————— Annual report

Atamian, Richard A., and Ellen Ferranto. *Driving Market Forces.* New York: •———————— Book, two authors
    HarperCollins, 2007.

Berss, Marcia. "Protein Man," *Forbes* 24 Oct. 2008: 65–66. •———————— Magazine article

Cantrell, Mark R., and Hilary Watson. "Violence in Today's Today's •———————— Magazine article, online, PDF version
    Workplace." PDF version. 10 Jan. 2007 *Office Review:* 24–29.

"Globalization Often Means That the Fast Track Leads Overseas." *The* •———————— Newspaper article, no author
    Washington Post 16 June 2008: A10.

"Information Processing." *Encyclopaedia Britannica.* 2007. Encyclopaedia
    Britannica Online. 19 Oct. 2007. <http://www.britannica.com/eb/ •———————— Encyclopedia, online
    article-61669>.

Lancaster, Hal. "When Taking a Tip From a Job Network, Proceed With •———————— Newspaper article, one author
    Caution." *The Wall Street Journal* 7 Feb. 2008: B1.

Morris, Mark. "Privacy Rules Proposed." *The Washington Post* 14 July 2007. •———————— Newspaper article, online
    July 18, 2007 <http://www.washingtonpost.com>.

Patton, James C., Nicholas P. Vitalari, and Andrew Milner. "Key Trends in
    Systems Development in Europe and North America." *Journal of Global* •———————— Journal article with volume and issue numbers
    Information Management 3.2 (2007): 5–20. ["3.2" signifies volume 3,
    issue 2]

Pinkerton Investigation Services. *The Employer's Guide to Investigation* •———————— Brochure
    Services, 3rd ed. Atlanta: Pinkerton Information Center, 2008.

Procter & Gamble home page. 28 Nov. 2008 <http://www.pg.com>. •———————— Web site

Rivera, Francisco. Personal interview. 16 May 2009. •———————— Interview

"Spam: Eliminate It From the Workplace." *SmartPros.* 8 Aug. 2006. 12 Sept. •———————— Web document, no author
    2008 <http://accounting.smartpros.com/>.

Tillman, Ann. "Avoiding Plagiarism." 9 July 2007. University of British •———————— Web document, with author
    Columbia <http://www.ubc/ca/pbg/plagiarism.htm>.

U.S. Dept. of Labor. *Child Care as a Workforce Issue.* Washington, DC. •———————— Government publication
    Government Printing Office, 2008.

"Wendy's International." *Hoover's Online.* 2008. Hoover's Inc. 9 Nov. 2008 •———————— Database, online
    <http://www.hoovers.com>.

Yellin, Mike. "Re: Managing Managers and Cell Phones." Online posting. 9
    Sept. 2008. 15 Sept. 2008. Message 44 posted to <http://groups.yahoo. •———————— Online forum posting
    com/groups/ecommerce/message44>.

Note 1: Where italics are shown, MLA style originally prescribed the use of underlines. With today's word processors, most writers use italics.

Note 2: To prevent confusion, you might add the words *Accessed* or *Retrieved* preceding the date you accessed an online source.

Note 3: Although MLA style prescribes double-spacing for the works cited, we show single spacing to conserve space and to represent preferred business usage.

FIGURE C.3 Portions of APA Text Page and References

Peanut butter was first delivered to the world by a St. Louis physician in 1890. As discussed at the Peanut Advisory Board's Web site, peanut butter was originally promoted as a protein substitute for elderly patients (History, n.d.). However, it was the 1905 Universal Exposition in St. Louis that truly launched peanut butter. Since then, annual peanut butter consumption has zoomed to 3.3 pounds a person in the United States (Barrons, 2006, p. 46).

America's farmers produce 1.6 million tons of peanuts annually, about half of which is used for oil, nuts, and candy. Lisa Gibbons, executive secretary of the Peanut Advisory Board, says that "peanuts in some form are in the top four candies: Snickers, Reese's Peanut Butter Cups, Peanut M & Ms, and Butterfingers" (Meadows, 2008, p. 32).

References

Barrons, E. (2006, November). A comparison of domestic and international consumption of legumes." *Journal of Economic Agriculture, 23*(3), 45–49.

Meadows, M. (2008, September 30). Peanut crop is anything but peanuts at home and overseas. *Business Monthly, 14,* 31–34.

History of peanut butter (n.d.). Peanut Advisory Board. Retrieved January 19, 2009, from http://www.peanutbutterlovers.com/History/index.html

American Psychological Association Format

Popular in the social and physical sciences, the American Psychological Association (APA) documentation style uses parenthetic citations. That is, each author reference is shown in parentheses when cited in the text, as shown in Figure C.3. At the end of the report, all references are listed alphabetically in a bibliography called "References." For more information about APA formats, see the *Publication Manual of the American Psychological Association,* 5e (Washington, DC: American Psychological Association, 2001) or *Concise Rules of APA Style* (Washington, DC: American Psychological Association, 2005).

APA In-Text Format. Within the text, document each specific textual source with a short description in parentheses. Following are selected guidelines summarizing important elements of APA style:

- Include the last name of the author(s), date of publication, and page number, as (Jones, 2007, p. 36). Use "n.d." if no date is available.

- If no author is known, refer to the first few words of the reference list entry and the year, as (Computer Privacy, 2008, p. 59).

- Omit page numbers for general references, but always include page numbers for direct quotations.

APA Reference Format. List all citations alphabetically in a section called "References." A portion of an APA reference page is shown in Figure C.3. A more complete list of model references appears in Figure C.4. APA style requires specific capitalization and sequencing guidelines, some of which are summarized here:

- Include an author's name with the last name first followed by initials, such as *Smith, M. A.* First and middle names are not used.

FIGURE C.4 APA Sample References

References

American Airlines. (2008). *2008 Annual Report*. Fort Worth, TX: AMR ●————— Annual report
   Corporation.

Atamian, R. A., & Ferranto, E. (2007). *Driving market forces.* ●————— Book, two authors
   New York: HarperCollins.

Berss, M. (2008, October 24). Protein man. *Forbes*, 65–66. ●————— Magazine article

Cantrell, M. R., & Watson, H. (2007, January 10). Violence in ●————— Magazine article, electronic version
   today's workplace [Electronic version]. *Office Review*, 24–29.

Globalization often means that the fast track leads overseas. (2009, June ●————— Newspaper article, no author
   16). *The Washington Post*, p. A10.

Information processing (2007). In *Encyclopaedia Britannica*. Retrieved ●————— Encyclopedia, online
   October 19, 2007, from Encyclopaedia Britannica Online:
   http://www.britannica.com/eb/article-61669>

Lancaster, H. (2008, February 7). When taking a tip from a job ●————— Newspaper article, one author
   network, proceed with caution. *The Wall Street Journal*, p. B1.

Morris, M. (2007, July 14). Privacy rules proposed. *The Washington* ●————— Newspaper article, online
   Post. Retrieved July 18, 2007, from http://www.washingtonpost.com

Patton, J. C., Vitalari, N. P., & Milner, A. (2007, May). Key trends ●————— Journal article with volume and issue numbers
   in systems development in Europe and North America. *Journal*
   of Global Information Management, 3(2), 5–20. [3(2) signifies
   volume 3, series or issue 2]

Pinkerton Investigation Services. (2006). *The employer's guide to* ●————— Brochure
   investigation services (3rd ed.) [Brochure]. Atlanta: Pinkerton
   Information Center.

Procter & Gamble home page. (2008). Retrieved November ●————— Web site
   28, 2008, from http://www.pg.com

Spam: Eliminate it from the workplace. (2006, August 8). *SmartPros*. ●————— Web document, no author
   Retrieved September 12, 2008, from http://accounting.smartpros.com/

Tillman, A. (2006). Avoiding plagiarism. Retrieved July 9, 2007, ●————— Web document, with author
   from University of British Columbia: http://www.ubc/ca/pbg/
   plagiarism.htm

U.S. Department of Labor. (2008). *Child care as a workforce issue.* ●————— Government publication
   Washington, DC: Government Printing Office.

Wendy's International. (2008). Hoover's Inc. Retrieved November 9, ●————— Database, online
   2008, from *Hoover's Online*: http://www.hoovers.com

Yellin, M. (2008, September 9). Managing managers and cell phones. ●————— Online forum or discussion group
   [Msg 44]. Message posted to http://groups.yahoo.com/group/
   ecommerce/message44

- Show the date of publication in parentheses immediately after the author's name, as *Smith, M. A. (2008).*

- Italicize the titles of books. Use "sentence-style" capitalization. This means that only the first word of a title, proper nouns, and the first word after an internal colon are capitalized.

- Do not italicize or underscore the titles of magazine and journal articles. Use sentence-style capitalization for article titles.

- Italicize the names of magazines, newspapers, and journals. Capitalize the initial letters of all main words.

- In citing online documents, list only the search term and main search site page for URLs that are impractically long and complicated.

- To reference a published article that you viewed only in its electronic form, add in brackets after the article title [Electronic version]. Use this form only if the electronic version is identical to the published version.

- To reference an online article that you have reason to believe has been changed (e.g., the format is different from that of the print version or page numbers are not indicated), add the date you retrieved the document and the URL. Do not include a period after a URL that appears at the end of a line.

Correction Symbols

In marking your papers, your instructor may use the following symbols or abbreviations to indicate writing or formatting weaknesses. You will find that studying these symbols and suggestions will help you understand your instructor's remarks. Knowing this information can also help you evaluate and improve your own letters, memos, e-mail messages, reports, and other writing. To improve your command of grammar and mechanics, please review the guides in the Grammar and Mechanics Guide in Appendix A. You can also build your skills by completing the exercises in Your Personal Language Trainer.

Grammar and Mechanics

Act   Use active-voice verbs.

Apos   Use apostrophe correctly.

Art   Use a correct article (*a, an,* or *the*).

Cap   Correct capitalization error.

Cm   Insert a comma.

CmConj   Use a comma before a coordinating conjunction (*and, or, nor, but*) that joins independent clauses.

CmIntr   Use a comma after an introductory clause or a long phrase.

CmSer   Insert commas to separate items in a series.

CS   Correct a comma splice by separating clauses with a period or a semicolon.

DM   Correct a misplaced or dangling modifier by moving the modifier closer to the word it describes or by supplying a clear subject.

Exp   Eliminate expletives (*there is, there are,* and *it is*)

Frag   Revise sentence fragment to express a complete thought.

Num   Express numbers in appropriate word or figure form.

ProAgr   Make pronoun agree in number with its antecedent.

ProCase   Use appropriate nominative, objective, or possessive case.

Ref   Correct vague pronoun reference. Avoid pronoun that refers to a phrase, clause, sentence, or paragraph.

RO   Revise run-on or fused sentence by adding a period or a semicolon to separate independent clauses.

Sp   Correct spelling error.

S/V   Make verbs agree with their subjects.

Vb   Use correct verb tense.

| **V/Shift** | Avoid unnecessary shifts in verb tense. |
| **UnCm** | Eliminate unnecessary comma. |

Content, Organization, and Style

Asgn	Follow assignment instructions.
Awk	Recast to avoid awkward expression.
Ch	Use longer sentences to avoid choppiness. Vary sentence patterns.
Cl	Improve clarity of ideas or expression.
Coh	Develop coherence between ideas. Repeat key ideas, use pronouns, or add transitional expression.
Cop	Avoid copying textbook examples or wording.
DirSt	Start directly with the main idea.
Exp	Expand or explain an incomplete idea.
IS	Use indirect strategy by explaining before introducing main idea.
Log	Reconsider faulty logic.
Neg	Revise negative expression with more positive view.
Ob	Avoid stating the obvious.
Org	Improve organization by grouping similar ideas.
Par	Express ideas in parallel form.
Redun	Avoid redundant expression.
Tone	Use conversational, positive tone that promotes goodwill.
You	Emphasize the "you" view.
WC	Improve word choice.

Format

DS	Insert a double space.
F	Choose an appropriate format for this document.
GH	Use graphic highlighting (bullets, lists, indentions, or headings) to enhance readability.
Mar	Improve margins to fit document attractively on the page.
SS	Insert a single space.
TS	Insert a triple space.

Key to C.L.U.E. Review Exercises

Chapter 1

1. To succeed as a knowledge worker in today's digital workplace, you need highly developed communication skills. [Guide 1, fragment]

2. Companies are looking for individuals with strong writing and grammar skills because employees spend at least 50 percent of their time processing documents. [Guide 1, fragment]

3. Businesses are cutting costs; they are eliminating many layers of management. [Guide 2, run-on]

4. Knowledge workers may be distracted by multitasking; however, clear communication requires shutting out interruptions. [Guide 3, comma splice]

5. Face-to-face conversations have many advantages, even though they produce no written record and sometimes waste time. [Guide 1, fragment]

6. The grapevine can be a major source of information; it is also fairly reliable. [Guide 3, comma splice]

7. Knowledge workers must be critical thinkers; they must be able to make decisions and communicate those decisions. [Guide 2, run-on]

8. Management uses many methods to distribute information downward such as newsletters, announcements, meetings, videos, and company intranets. [Guide 1, fragment]

9. Ethical companies experience less litigation; they also receive less resentment and less government regulation. [Guide 3, comma splice]

10. Horizontal communication starts with coworkers; downward communication starts with decision makers. [Guide 2, run-on]

Chapter 2

1. Our team leader said she **saw** the computer the day before it was stolen. [Guide 4]

2. One of the most frequently requested employment skills **is** writing proficiency. [Guide 6]

3. If I **were** the team leader, I would have gone to the training meeting. [Guide 5]

4. Better decisions and faster response time **explain** why many companies are using teams. [Guide 7]

5. Either the team leader or the manager **is** going to announce the vacation schedule. [Guide 8]

6. Conflict and dissension **are** normal and should be expected in team interactions. [Guide 7]

7. Everything in the meeting minutes and the company records **is** open to public view. [Guide 9]

8. We should have a decision soon because the committee **is** meeting today. [Guide 10]

9. C

10. The appearance of letters, memos, and e-mail messages **has** either a positive or negative effect on receivers. [Guide 6]

Chapter 3

1. Forward the e-mail to the manager and **me** so that he and I can study it. [Guide 13]

2. Just between you and **me**, a new salary schedule will soon be announced. [Guide 13]

3. The software and **its** documentation are difficult to understand. [Guide 14]

4. My friend and **I** could find all of the reports except yours. [Guide 12]

5. Tamara and I want all applications sent to her or **me**. [Guide 15]

6. Every employee should see **his or her** performance review in a timely manner.

   OR: All employees should see **their** performance reviews in a timely manner. [Guide 17]

7. Please deliver the printer supplies to **whoever** ordered them. [Guide 16]

8. Most applications arrived on time, but **yours** and **hers** were not received. [Guide 14]

9. C [Guide 13]

10. **Who** did you say left messages for Jennifer and me? [Guide 16]

Chapter 4

1. Andrea expected to do **well** on the writing exam because she had studied. [Guide 19]

2. Most businesspeople agree that **face-to-face** meetings are better than videoconferences. [Guide 20]

3. The newly redecorated office no longer had **wall-to-wall** carpeting. [Guide 20]

4. If one receives **on-the-job** criticism, it is best to accept it as constructive help. [Guide 20]

5. **Locally installed** online collaboration tools are **easy to use** and inexpensive. [Guide 20]

6. After the technician left, the printer worked **smoothly**. [Guide 19]

7. The **nineteen-year-old** applicant did well in her interview and finished the writing exam more **quickly** than expected. [Guides 19, 20]

8. Business writers strive to use **easy-to-understand** language and familiar words. [Guide 20]

9. The manager told us office workers not to take the CEO's harsh words **personally**. [Guide 19]

10. **Clearly written** safety messages use short words that are quickly understood. [Guide 20]

Chapter 5

1. Informal research methods include looking in the files, talking with your **boss,** and interviewing the target audience. [Guide 21, CmSer]

2. When you prepare to write any **message,** you need to anticipate the audience's reaction. [Guide 22, CmIntr]

3. By learning to distinguish between dependent and independent **clauses,** you will be able to avoid serious sentence faults. [Guide 22, CmIntr]

4. Some business messages require **sensitivity,** and writers may prefer to use passive-voice instead of active-voice verbs. [Guide 23, CmConj]

5. We hired Davida **Rivera,** who was the applicant with the best **qualifications,** as our new marketing manager. [Guide 25, CmIn]

6. Our business was incorporated on August 1, **2003,** in **Phoenix,** Arizona. [Guide 24, CmDate]

7. The new **business,** by the **way,** is flourishing and is expected to show a profit soon. [Guide 25, CmIn]

8. After he **graduates,** Dustin plans to move to Atlanta and find work there. [Guide 22, CmIntr]

9. Last fall our company introduced policies regulating the use of cell **phones,** instant **messaging,** and e-mail on the job. [Guide 21, CmSer]

10. C [Guide 26]

Chapter 6

1. Companies find it difficult to name new **products; consequently,** they often hire specialists. [Guide 27]

2. New product names must be **interesting; however,** most of the best are already taken. [Guide 27]

3. Naming is a costly **endeavor;** fees may range up to $70,000 for a global name. [Guide 27]

4. Expanding markets are in **Paris, France; Beijing, China;** and Dubai **City,** United Arab Emirates. [Guide 28]

5. In regard to naming a fashion product, Jasmine Frank **said:** "If I am launching a new fashion label, the task becomes very difficult. I have to find a name that communicates the creative style that the brand is to embody." [Guide 30]

6. For a new unisex perfume, Ferrari considered the following **names:** Declaration, Serenity, and Earth. [Guide 29]

7. Naming is not a problem for a small **company; however,** it is a big problem for global brands. [Guide 27]

8. C [Guide 29]

9. Attending the conference were James Harper, marketing **director;** Reva Cruz, product **manager;** and Cheryl Chang, vice president. [Guide 28]

10. Distribution of goods has become **global; therefore,** names have to be registered in many countries. [Guide 27]

Chapter 7

1. All **employees'** cars must display a company parking sticker. [Guide 32]

2. Our **company's** health benefits are available immediately. [Guide 31]

3. Will you please send me your latest print **catalog.** [Guide 34]

4. The manager questioned **John's** traveling first class on a recent business trip. [Guide 33]

5. Is the bank open until **6 p.m.?** [Guide 35]

6. You must replace the ink cartridge (**see** page 8 in the **manual)** before printing. [Guide 37]

7. Justin wondered whether all sales **managers'** databases needed to be updated. [Guide 31]

8. (Direct quotation) **"Health** care **costs,"** said the CEO, **"will** increase substantially this **year."** [Guide 38]

9. In just two **months'** time, we expect to interview five candidates for the opening. [Guide 32]

10. The abbreviation GMT means "Greenwich Mean Time," doesn't **it?** [Guide 35]

Chapter 8

1. All **Southwest Airlines** passengers will exit the **plane** at **Gate** 14 when they reach **Ontario International Airport.** [Guides 39, 46]

2. Personal **tax rates** for **Japanese** citizens are low by **international** standards, according to **Professor Yamaguchi** at **Osaka University.** [Guides 39, 41]

3. The vice president of the **United States** said that this country continues to seek **Middle East** peace. [Guides 39, 43]

4. My **father,** who lives in the **Midwest,** has Skippy **peanut butter** and **Coca-Cola** for **breakfast.** [Guides 41, 43, 45]

5. Our **sales manager** and **director** of **marketing** both expected to receive **federal** funding for the project. [Guides 41, 39]

6. Although the **manager** recommended purchasing **Dell** computers, our **vice president** wanted to wait. [Guides 41, 45]

7. Sana Nadir, who heads our **Customer Communication Division,** has a **master's degree** in social psychology from the **University** of **New Mexico.** [Guides 44, 40, 39]

8. Please consult **Figure** 4.5 in **Chapter** 4 to obtain U.S. **Census Bureau** population figures for the **Pacific Northwest.** [Guides 46, 39, 43]

9. Did you see the article in *BusinessWeek* titled, "The **Global Consequences of Using Crops for Fuel**"? [Guide 42]

10. Christian plans to take courses in **marketing, business law,** and English during the **fall.** [Guides 40, 39]

Chapter 9

1. We ordered **three** new computers and **two** printers for our department. [Guide 47]

2. **Thirty-one** candidates applied for the **three** advertised positions. [Guide 47]

3. My company paid **$500** for me to attend the **three**-day workshop. [Guides 49, 47]

4. Our UPS deliveries arrive before **11 a.m.** [Guide 49]

5. Personal income tax returns must be mailed by **April 15.** [Guide 49]

6. We earned 7.5 **percent** dividends on our **$2,000** investment. [Guide 49]

7. Our company applied for a **$100,000** loan at **6 percent.** [Guide 49]

8. A total of **2 million** people attended the World's Fair. [Guide 50]

9. I bought the item on eBay for **$1.50** and sold it for **$15.** [Guide 49]

10. That store offers a **30**-day customer-satisfaction return policy. [Guide 48]

Chapter 10

1. Good listeners absorb facts rather **than interrupting** with frequent questions.

2. Her **principal** reason for declining the invitation was her busy **calendar.**

3. The manager was **conscious** of the navigation problems at the company Web **site.**

4. Because Nedra felt overwhelmed by the **everyday** demands of her job, she sought **advice** from her mentor.

5. Before you **proceed** with the report, check those **embarrassing** statistics.

6. Although we should look into this matter **further,** I am not **surprised** at your report.

7. The judge declared that the comments of **their** attorneys were **irrelevant** to the case at hand.

8. Because the property was **too** difficult to **appraise,** its value was unrecorded.

9. Jordan hoped to **elicit** advice from his counselor, but he was **disappointed.**

10. Is it **necessary** to **compliment** fellow team members when they excel?

Chapter 11

1. **Companies** are looking for individuals with strong writing and **grammar skills** [delete comma] because much time is spent communicating.

2. **Permanent** employees can expect to spend at least **50 percent** of **their** time processing documents.

3. One organization paid **$3,000** each for **12** employees to attend a **one-week** workshop in communication training.

4. Although it cost **$400,** my BlackBerry **allows** my manager and **me** to stay in touch through e-mail.

5. If you work in **an** office with open **cubicles,** it's rude to listen to Web radio, streaming audio, or other **multimedia** [delete comma] without headphones.

6. Bad news is **generally disappointing; however,** the negative feelings can be reduced.

7. On June **1** our company **president** revealed a **$4 million** drop in profits, which was bad news for everyone.

8. Most of us prefer to be let down **gently** [delete comma] when we're being refused **something;** that is why the **reasons-before-refusal** pattern is effective.

9. If I **were you,** I would begin the bad-news message with a **compliment**, not a blunt rejection.

10. Because of rising health **costs,** our **director** of Human Resources announced an increase in **everyone's** contribution.

Chapter 12

1. Reports are a fact of life in **American business; consequently,** business writers must learn to prepare them.

2. **Adrian's** report, which he sent to the manager and **me**, was distinguished by three **characteristics:** clear content, good organization, and correct form.

3. **Six** members of our team will attend the writers' **workshop;** therefore, be sure they **receive** notices.

4. More **than 90** percent of companies now use **e-mail, which** explains why we need an e-mail policy.

5. To search the **Internet,** you need a browser such as Microsoft **Internet Explorer.**

6. Rachel was offered **$400** to complete **Robert's report,** but she said it was too little.

7. The format of a report is determined **by** [delete colon] length, **topic, audience,** and purpose.

8. Our latest press **release,** which was written in our Corporate Communication **Department,** announces the opening of **three** Canadian offices.

9. Letter reports **usually have** side margins of 1¼ inches.

10. The CEO and **manager,** who had **gone** to a meeting in the West, delivered a report to Jeff and **me** when they returned.

Chapter 13

1. The format and organization of a proposal **are important** [delete period] if a writer wants to be taken **seriously.**

2. Our team **members** [delete apostrophe] prepared **two** proposals for the **$3 million** project.

3. Just between you and **me**, we worked **especially** hard to develop a "hook" to capture a **reader's** attention.

4. The manager and **he** realized an item was missing from the **April 2 shipment;** consequently, they sent a claim request.

5. Readers of **business** [delete apostrophe] reports often turn **first** to the conclusions and **recommendations;** therefore, these sections must be written carefully.

6. If a proposal is sent to the **president** or **me,** it should definitely explain the specific credentials and expertise of key **personnel** for the project.

7. Benjamin and **she** wanted to start **their** own **business;** therefore, they wrote a business plan.

8. We invited **75** employees to hear **two** experts **disperse** information about wellness.

9. **Memos** [delete apostrophe] usually contain four necessary **parts:** subject line, opening, **body,** and action closing.

10. Darrin **Jizmejian,** who was recently evaluated, wondered whether his formal report would be presented at the **March 13 meeting.**

Chapter 14

1. Even though he was **president** of the **company,** Mr. Rivera dreaded the **three** presentations he made every year.

2. The **company's** CPA asked me to explain the **principal** ways we planned to finance the **30-year** mortgage.

3. My team is **grateful** to be able to give a **20-minute presentation;** however, we can emphasize only three or four points.

4. The introduction to a presentation should accomplish three **goals:** (1) **capture** attention, (2) establish credibility, and **(3)** preview main points.

5. Travis wondered whether focusing on what the audience is to **remember** [delete comma] and summarizing main points **were** equally **important.**

6. Most novice speakers talk **too rapidly;** however, they can learn to speak more **slowly** [delete comma] and listen to what they are saying.

7. A list of suggestions for improving retention of a **speaker's** ideas **is** found in the article titled "How **to** Improve Your Listening Skills."

8. The appearance and mannerisms of a speaker **definitely affect** a **listener's** evaluation of the message.

9. The president of Genesis **Enterprises,** along with other executives of local companies, **is** promoting **overseas** [delete apostrophe] sales.

10. In a poll of **3,000 workers,** only one third felt that **their** companies valued their opinions.

Chapter 15

1. The employment process begins with **introspection, which means** looking inside yourself.

2. To find the job of your dreams, you **must** [delete colon] (a) **know** yourself, **(b)** know the job market, and **(c)** know the process.

3. When **Marcy's** job was **terminated,** she applied at **three** online job boards.

4. If you **lose** your **job,** consider using the **Internet** to find another.

5. Justin wondered whether it was **all right** to apply at many **sites simultaneously.**

6. At last **month's** staff **meeting,** team members examined several **candidates'** résumés.

7. Rather **than** schedule **face-to-face interviews,** the team investigated videoconferencing.

8. **Fifty-five** trainees are expected to attend the May **1 meeting;** consequently, we need a larger room.

9. Good telephone manners **reflect** on you and your **company;** however, **too** few employees are trained properly.

10. In the last issue of **Newsweek,** did you see the article titled "Should a **Résumé Include** a Career Objective?"

Chapter 16

1. Before going to a job **interview,** you should research the **following:** [delete hyphen] company size, competitors, reputation, **strengths,** and weaknesses.

2. I wonder how many **companies** use software to scan **candidates'** résumés and search for **keywords.**

3. Even with the popularity of **e-mail,** most **employers** [delete apostrophe] will contact job applicants by telephone to set up **their** interviews.

4. Initial contacts by employers will **usually** be made by **telephone;** therefore, **ensure** that you keep important information nearby.

5. If you have little **experience,** emphasize your **up-to-date** skills, recent **training,** and extraordinary commitment.

6. Interviewees should not **criticize** anyone or **anything,** and they should not focus on **their** imperfections.

7. Evan was asked whether he had a **bachelor's degree** [delete comma] and whether he had five **years'** experience.

8. If you are **hoping** to create a good **impression,** be sure to write a **thank-you** letter after a job interview.

9. When **Robin's** interview was **over,** she told friends that she had done **well.**

10. Robin was **all ready** to send a thank-you **message** [delete comma] when she realized she could not spell the **interviewer's** name.

Glossary

abbreviation The shortened form of a word or phrase such as *IRS* or *Dr.*

abstract A brief summary of a proposal's highlights intended for specialists or for technical readers.

abusive language Language that can result in a lawsuit.

academic writing Preparing messages for teachers and professors.

accommodation Making adjustments so that a situation is suitable for those involved.

acquisition When one company acquires possession and control of another company.

acronym A word such as *laser* that is formed by the initial letters of a series of words (*light amplification by stimulated emission of radiation*).

action team A group of people charged with completing a specific task as quickly and efficiently as possible.

actionable Likely to result in a lawsuit.

active voice Sentences in which the subject is the doer of the action (*Brandon sent the message*).

activity reports See "periodic reports."

adaptation The process of creating a message that suits your audience.

adjustment A message that responds favorably to a claim.

advisory team A committee or board appointed to advise management on a specific issue.

age bias Language that seems to exclude or stereotype individuals based on their age.

agenda A list of specific topics to be discussed during a meeting.

alliance An agreement between two or more companies to work together for mutual benefit.

almanac An annual publication containing useful facts and statistics in a specific field or area of interest.

alphanumeric outline An outline that shows major and minor ideas.

alternative A compromise or substitute, often included when delivering negative news.

ambiguous Something that can be reasonably interpreted in more than one way.

American Psychological Association (APA) An organization whose citation method directs readers to sources with parenthetical notes inserted into the text and with a "References" list.

analogy A comparison of similar traits between dissimilar things.

analytical report A report that provides data, analysis, and conclusions and that may also offer recommendations.

ancillary Additional or accompanying material.

anecdote A personal story used to enliven a presentation or to illustrate a point.

anticipating The process of determining who your audience is and what he or she is like.

apology An admission of blameworthiness and regret for an undesirable event.

appendix The part of a proposal, business plan, or report that contains ancillary material of interest.

application follow-up letter A letter sent after your job application generates no responses within a reasonable time.

ASCII A format that offers text only and is readable by all computer programs.

attachment A file attached to an e-mail message or memo.

authority rule with discussion A method of reaching a group decision whereby the leader makes the final decision after listening to members' ideas and discussion.

authorization request The ending of a proposal that requests approval.

AutoContent Wizard A PowerPoint feature that provides outlines for a variety of types of presentations.

averaging A method of reaching a group decision whereby members haggle, cajole, and negotiate to reach a compromise.

background The section of a proposal that identifies the problem and discusses the goals or purposes of the project.

bad news The part of a negative message that provides a clear but understated announcement of the bad news that may include an alternative or compromise.

bar chart A visual aid used to compare related items, illustrate changes in data over time, and show segments as part of a whole.

barrier Anything that disrupts the communication process.

begging the question An error in reasoning that occurs when the idea to be proved is assumed in one of the premises, without providing adequate proof.

behavioral questions Interview questions that require job candidates to tell stories about specific skills and accomplishments.

belief Something held by an individual or group to be true.

bias A preference that leads to impartiality.

bias-free Objective, impartial, nondiscriminatory.

bibliography A list of all sources used that appears at the end of a report.

blanket copies Copies of an e-mail message sent unnecessarily to a large number of recipients.

blind carbon copy (BCC) A copy of a message sent to someone other than the addressee without the addressee's knowledge.

block style A letter style in which all parts of the letter—dateline, inside address, salutation, body, complimentary close, and so on—start at the left margin.

blog A personal online journal in reverse-chronological order that is updated frequently and on which readers can comment. (*See* **weblog**.)

blogosphere The worldwide community of blogs and bloggers.

body The main part of an e-mail message, memo, or letter that explains and discusses the subject logically.

bookmark The process of saving a link to a favorite Web site on a computer so that the site can be revisited easily.

Boolean search strategies Search strategies that use Boolean operators such as AND, OR, NOT, and NEAR.

brainstorming A popular method of generating a wide variety of ideas about a topic or problem.

bribery Offering money or favors in order to gain an advantage or to make someone perform a certain action.

bricks-and-mortar companies Businesses that have a physical presence rather than virtual or online.

broker An individual who helps people buy and sell securities, property, insurance, and other items.

budget The section of a proposal that lists proposed project costs.

buffer A device to reduce shock or pain; opens a negative message with a neutral, concise, relevant, and upbeat statement that makes the reader continue reading.

bullet points Short phrases that are based on your outline in a multimedia presentation.

business plan A report outlining a proposed business that is critical in planning a new venture and securing capital support.

business writing Preparing professional messages that are purposeful, persuasive, economical, and reader oriented.

buyout Purchasing a controlling interest of a company's stock.

buzz Excitement generated by word of mouth.

bypassing When the receiver of a message misunderstands or misses the meaning.

capital Cash or goods owned by a company to generate income.

carbon copy (CC) A copy of a message sent to someone other than the addressee.

card catalog An index of a library's holdings indexed on 3-x-5 cards alphabetized by author, title, or subject.

career fair An event attended by recruiters and job seekers to discuss open positions and career opportunities.

career objective A brief statement on a résumé that summarizes a job seeker's career goal.

career path The defined path a person follows to achieve professional goals.

cell phone A mobile device used for telephone communication.

central selling points One or two features that are emphasized in a sales letter.

channel The medium over which a message is physically transmitted, such as computer, phone, written document, or spoken word.

chronological résumé A résumé that lists work history job by job, starting with the most recent position.

chronology An arrangement of events in the order in which they occurred.

circular reasoning An error in reasoning that occurs when the support given for an argument merely restates the argument.

citation format A method, such as MLA and APA, of directing readers to your sources with parenthetical notes inserted into the text and with bibliographies.

civility Being polite to others.

claim A message written by a customer to identify or correct a wrong.

clarity The quality of being clear and easy to understand.

clause A group of words that has a subject and a verb.

cliché An expression that has been used so frequently that it is no longer meaningful or useful.

clip art Images used to symbolize or illustrate ideas.

closing The end of an e-mail message, memo, or letter that usually contains action information, dates, or deadlines; a summary of the message; or a closing thought.

cluster diagram A process for gathering data or ideas by splitting data into subsets that share common traits.

coercion The act of persuading by using force or power of authority.

coherence Unified writing that occurs when one idea leads logically to the next.

collaboration The process of working together to achieve a goal or to solve a problem.

collaboration tools Tools and technology that make it possible for people to work together when they can't be in the same geographic location.

collaborative software Software that allows people to work together on documents and projects and to engage in team writing.

collectivist Individuals or cultures that emphasize membership in organizations, groups, and teams and encourage acceptance of group values, duties, and decisions.

comma splice A sentence error that results when two sentences are incorrectly joined or spliced together with a comma.

command A sentence beginning with an action verb that tells the audience what to do.

committee A group of people who serve a specific function for a long-term or permanent period of time, such as investigating, discussing, acting upon, or reporting on a matter.

communication The transmission of information and meaning from one individual or group to another.

communication skills Reading, listening, nonverbal, speaking, and writing skills that allow one to communicate effectively with others.

communication style A key dimension of culture that refers to the way an individual communicates with words.

company description The section of a business plan that identifies the form of business and its business type.

complaint A persuasive message that makes a claim about damaged products, mistaken billing, inaccurate shipments, warranty problems, return policies, insurance situation, faulty merchandise, and so on.

complete sentence A sentence that has a subject and a verb and makes sense.

compliance The act of following orders, rules, policies, or procedures.

complimentary closing Words such as *Sincerely, Cheers,* or *Best Regards* that close a message.

component An organizational method that arranges data by components such as location, geography, division, product, or part.

compose The third stage in Phase 2 of the writing process, which involves preparing the first draft of a message.

compound preposition A wordy prepositional phrase that can often be replaced with a single word (*due to the fact that* instead of *because*).

comprehension An understanding of written, oral, or nonverbal communication.

compromise An agreement whereby the parties involved reach a middle ground.

concise Expressing a message in as few words as possible.

conclusion The part of a report that summarizes and explains the findings.

concrete noun Nouns that name objects that can be easily visualized or imagined.

conferencing software Collaboration software that allows individuals who are separated geographically to meet in real time.

confirmation A routine message that records oral decisions, directives, discussions, and IM messages; also called a *to-file report* or an *incident report*.

conflict A state of opposition or disagreement among individuals or groups.

conformity Changing ones views, beliefs, or actions to match those of a group.

consensus A method of reaching a group decision whereby all team members have a chance to air their opinions and, ultimately, agree.

context A key dimension of culture that refers to the stimuli, environment, or ambience surrounding an event.

control group The people who receive no treatment during a scientific experiment and serve as the standard by which experimental observations are evaluated.

controlled variable Independent variable that is selected and controlled by the experimenter to determine its relationship to a dependent variable.

convention An organizational method that arranges data by following a prescribed pattern that all readers understand.

conversational Using an informal instead of a formal, pretentious tone.

copyright A set of exclusive rights granted to the creator of such things as literary works, music, movies, plays, art, software, photos, and intellectual property.

Copyright Act of 1976 Protects authors of published and unpublished works.

copyright infringement Using copyrighted material without a license of permission to do so.

corporation A business that is formed as a legal entity.

correlation A relationship among two or more variables; does not necessarily suggest a cause-and-effect relationship.

corrupt Lacking in integrity or morals.

Corruption Perceptions Index (CPI) An index offered since 1995 by Transparency International that orders the world's countries according to the degree of corruption that is perceived to exist among politicians and public officials.

cover letter A letter used to introduce a résumé to highlight a job seeker's strengths in terms of reader benefits and to gain an interview; also called a *letter of application*.

credibility The quality of being believable or trustworthy.

credit-reporting agency A credit bureau such as Experian, Equifax, or TransUnion that gathers credit information and generates reports for individuals and businesses.

critical listening Listening that enables a person to judge and evaluate what he or she is hearing.

critical thinking The mental process of analyzing and evaluating information, statements, and observations in order to make sound decisions.

cross-functional team A team that has members from various departments within a company or from various organizations.

cross-tabulation A statistical process that allows analysis of two or more variables in a table together.

cultural anthropologist A person who studies cultural systems and human cultural behavior.

cultural diversity Differences in such factors as race, ethnicity, religion, language, and nationality that exist among groups in a community or geographic region.

culture The complex system of values, traits, morals, and customs shared by a society.

customer support team A group of people working together to provide efficient and outstanding support to customers.

customer-centric business A business that has as its ultimate goal the retention of customers over the long term.

damage control An attempt to minimize damage or loss.

dangling modifier A word or phrase that describes or limits a word or words that are missing from a sentence (*Using a search tool, the Web site was finally found*).

data Documented information, statistics, and evidence.

database An organized collection of information.

dateline The part of a letter that identifies the date the letter was written.

decimal outline An outline that shows how ideas relate to one another.

decision matrix A special grid that helps managers make the best choice among complex options.

decoding The act of translating a message from symbol form into meaning.

defamation The legal term for any false statement that harms a person's reputation.

demographics Characteristics of a population such as age, income, gender, education, postal code, and so on.

dependent clause A group of words with a subject and a verb that depends for meaning on an independent clause and, therefore, cannot stand alone.

descriptiveness An attitude that requires one to use concrete and specific feedback to achieve intercultural competence.

design team A group of people who draft product designs, generate prototypes, and perform other similar tasks.

Diagram Gallery A PowerPoint feature that contains six diagrams to insert into presentations including an organizational chart, a cycle diagram, a radial diagram, a pyramid diagram, a Venn diagram, and a target diagram.

diction A writer's choice of words to create meaning.

digital communication technologies Tools such as e-mail, videoconferencing, instant messaging, and Weblogs (blogs) that transmit information in digital form.

digital dirt Web-based information about a job candidate, accessible via sites such as Google or MySpace, that may harm his or her chances during a job search.

digital format A report format the uses digital media to produce and distribute the document in electronic form, not a hard copy.

digression A temporary departure from the main topic of an oral presentation.

direct benefit A benefit that affects the reader directly, such as a tax deduction.

direct claim A claim to which the writer expects the receiver to agree immediately.

direct mail marketing The sale of goods and services through letters, catalogs, brochures, and other messages delivered by land mail.

direct paragraph A paragraph that begins with the main sentence, followed by supporting sentences.

direct pattern Presenting a message with the main idea first, followed by details, explanation, or evidence.

direct reply A message that replies favorably to a request for information or action.

direct report pattern The pattern used when a report opens with an introduction and is followed by the facts and a summary.

direct request *See* **request**.

direct-mail letter A written message sent by land mail that promotes services and products, boosts online and retail traffic, and solicits contributions.

disability bias Language that seems to exclude or stereotype individuals based on the presence of a physical or mental disability.

discrimination Treating a person unfairly or differently due to prejudice.

discriminative listening Listening that is necessary when a person must understand and remember.

discussion board An online bulletin board on which members post and read messages.

disenfranchised An individual or group that has been denied a right given to other individuals or groups.

diversity A wide range of variation in qualities and attributes.

documentation The credit given to information sources.

domestic market The market that exists within a company's own borders.

dovetailing Connecting the idea at the end of one sentence with an idea at the beginning of the next sentence.

downsizing Reducing the number of employees in an organization through layoffs, retirements, and hiring freezes.

downward communication flow A formal channel of communication that exists when information flows downward from managers and decision makers through the chain of command to workers.

dual appeal A persuasive technique that combines rational and emotional appeals.

dynamic Continuously changing.

e-commerce The buying and selling of goods and services on the Web.

electronic address A person's e-mail address.

electronic database A collection of information stored electronically, on a CD-ROM or on the Web, so that it is accessible by computer and is digitally searchable.

electronic handouts Copies of PowerPoint slides and other handouts that are posted to a Web site or sent via e-mail.

electronic index An online index stored in a digital database that helps one locate references, abstracts, and full-text articles from magazines, journals, and newspapers.

e-mail Mail that is composed on and transmitted by a computer system or network.

e-marketing Sales messages delivered by e-mail, Web sites, text message, or fax.

emoticon A word formed from the words "emotion" and "icon"; a text-based symbol use used to convey emotions in electronic messages.

emotional appeal A persuasive technique that is associated with status, ego, and sensual feelings.

emotional interference Emotions such as joy, fear, and anger that can hamper the sending or receiving of messages.

empathy Identifying with another's feelings or situation.

emphatic Being forceful in expression or action.

empty word A word that is unnecessary and adds nothing to a sentence.

encoding The conversion of an idea into words or gestures that convey meaning.

end date A date that identifies a time for completion of an action.

entrepreneur A risk taker who organizes and operates a new business venture.

enunciate To express clearly; to utter articulate sounds.

e-portfolio A collection of digitized materials that provides viewers with a snapshot of a job seeker's performance, talents, and accomplishments.

Equal Credit Opportunity Act A U.S. federal law that gives all consumers an equal opportunity to obtain credit.

ethical Conforming to acceptable conduct or behavior.

ethical code of conduct A written document that outlines a company's values, responsibilities, and ethical obligations.

ethics A set of principles that determines acceptable conduct.

ethnic bias Language that seems to exclude or stereotype individuals based on ethnic identification.

ethnicity A social category based on differences in culture, language, religion, and/or national origin.

ethnocentrism The belief in the superiority of one's own race, which is a natural attitude inherent in all cultures, that causes us to judge others by our own values.

etiquette Rules governing socially acceptable behavior and courtesy.

executive summary A brief, nontechnical summary of the highlights of a proposal, business plan, or report written for managers.

extemporaneously Speaking freely without reading from notes.

external communication Communication that involves exchanging ideas and messages with customers, suppliers, the government, and the public.

eye contact The direct visual contact with the eyes of another person.

factoring Breaking the major investigative problem of a report into subproblems to identify issues to be investigated or possible solutions to the main problem.

facts Statements that are verifiable and often quantifiable.

Fair Credit Reporting Act A U.S. federal law that regulates the collection, distribution, and use of credit information.

fair use A legal concept that limits an individual's right to use copyrighted material without obtaining permission.

fallacy A false or mistaken idea, usually the result of incorrect reasoning or an error in logic.

fax A process of digitally copying a document and electronically transmitting it over telephone lines.

feasibility reports Reports that examine the practicality and advisability of following a course of action.

Federal Trade Commission (FTC) An independent government agency founded in 1915 to enforce consumer protection and antitrust laws.

feedback The verbal and nonverbal responses of the receiver during the communication process.

file sharing Making files available on the Web and over networks for others to download.

filler Excess words that make sentences unnecessarily long (*there is a manager who supervises hiring* instead of *a manger supervises hiring*).

financial analysis The section of a business plan that includes a realistic start-up budget and a projected operating budget.

flabby phrase A phrase that contains more words than are necessary (*at this point in time*).

flat team A team made up of employees at the same hierarchical level within an organization.

flipchart A pad of large blank sheets of paper on a stand for presenting or recording information during an oral presentation or meeting.

flowchart A visual aid that uses standard symbols to illustrate a process or procedure.

font A complete set of alphanumeric characters of a specific design.

footnotes Notes at the bottom of a report pages that are used to cite sources.

Foreign Corrupt Practices Act of 1977 A U.S. act that prohibits payments to foreign official for the purpose of obtaining or retaining business.

foreign investment Purchasing stocks, bonds, or other securities from a foreign company or government.

form letters Letters used to respond to identical requests.

formal channel of communication A communication channel that follows an organization's hierarchy of command.

formal report A report that represents the end product of thorough investigation and analysis and presents ordered information to decision makers in business, industry, government, and education.

formality A key dimension of culture that refers to the emphasis placed on tradition, ceremony, and social rules.

forming The first phase of team development, during which team members get to know one another and discuss fundamental topics.

forwarding Sending an e-mail message to a third party.

fragment An incomplete sentence.

frame of reference A person's preconceived set of ideas or assumptions that determine how a message will be perceived or understood.

free trade Occurs between countries when tariffs and trade restrictions that prevent the free flow of goods and services are eliminated.

freebies Coupons, samples, or gifts sent by companies to restore customer confidence and to promote future business.

Frequently Asked Questions (FAQs) A list of the most commonly asked questions and their answers.

frontloading Another name for the direct method, putting the main idea first.

functional headings Headings used in routine reports that describe functions or general topics, such as *Background* or *Findings*.

functional résumé A résumé that focuses attention on a candidate's skills rather than on past employment.

gender A person's status as male or female.

gender bias Sexist language that seems to exclude or stereotype either gender.

General Agreement on Tariffs and Trade (GATT) An international agreement that promotes open global trade.

gesture A nonverbal form of communication made with a body part, usually the arm or hands.

glass ceiling A term that refers to the idea that an invisible barrier determines how far women and minorities are able to rise in an organization's management structure.

global economy The expansion of economies beyond national borders made possible by reduced trade restrictions, improved communication technologies, and other factors.

global village A term used to describe the fact that media and technology are decreasing time and space barriers, making it possible for people to communicate and interact globally.

globalization The integration of economic, social, and political systems across geographic boundaries, allowing worldwide business and communication.

good-guy syndrome Occurs when we try to make ourselves look better or the receiver feel better when delivering negative news.

goodwill message A message that carries good wishes, warm feelings, and sincere thoughts to friends, customers, and employees.

goodwill A positive feeling a person has toward an individual or an organization.

grapevine An informal communication channel that carries organizationally relevant information, gossip, and rumors.

graphic Graphs, artwork, and other visuals used to clarify and illustrate data.

graphic highlighting A method of using vertical lists, headings, capital letters, underlining, bold type, italics, or blank space to spotlight ideas.

grid A pattern of horizontal and vertical lines on which raw data can be plotted and analyzed.

ground rules The basic rules that all meeting participants are expected to follow during the meeting.

group interview An interview during which an interviewer meets with several candidates for the same position at the same time.

groupthink Faulty decision-making processes by team members who are overly eager to agree with one another.

groupware Software that allows users to share information and documents and to work together on projects.

guide words The *To, From, Date,* and *Subject* lines in an e-mail message or memo.

Gunning Fog Index A well-known formula for measuring readability.

handouts Pictures, outlines, brochures, articles, charts, summaries, or other supplements distributed to listeners during an oral presentation.

hard skills Technical skills such as software competency, accounting knowledge, scientific ability, and equipment operation.

heading A group of words that identifies a section of writing; important tool for highlighting information, improving readability, and organizing material.

hidden job market Jobs that are available but are not advertised in the classifieds or online or listed in job databases.

hierarchical team A group of people organized in a rigid team structure in which each team member reports to a manager and must complete the tasks delegated by that manager.

high-context culture Communicators in these cultures (such as China, Japan, and Arab countries) rely on context (surroundings, situation) to provide meaning; they tend to be intuitive and contemplative.

hiring/placement interview An interview during which a hiring manager determines whether a candidate is motivated, qualified, and a good fit for the position.

hits The number of times scanning software recognizes keywords in a résumé.

hook A clever sentence or paragraph that captures the reader's attention and leaves a lasting impression.

horizontal communication flow A formal channel of communication that exists when information flows among workers at the same level.

hyperlinks "Hot" spots on the screen that allow you to jump instantly to sources outside your multimedia presentation.

hypothesis A tentative assumption that can be tested in an experiment.

hypothetical question A question that makes assumptions and is asked to explore possibilities and test relationships.

icon A visual image that represents an object, word, command, idea, or Web link.

iconography Using symbols, pictures, and images to communicate ideas.

identifying labels Labels such as *Action, FYI, RE, Urgent,* and *REQ* that are added to the subject line of an e-mail message.

idiom An expression that is familiar to native speakers of a language.

idiomatic expression A use of words that is unique to a specific language.

imagery The ability to form mental images.

inbox A folder where incoming e-mail messages are received.

incident report *See* **confirmation**.

inclusive language Language that includes, rather than excludes, and that does not discriminate against individuals or groups based on their gender, ethnicity, disability, age, religion, sexual preference, or other factors.

independent clause A grammatically complete clause that has a subject and a verb and may stand alone.

indirect benefit A benefit that affects the reader indirectly, such as giving back to the community.

indirect paragraph A paragraph that begins with supporting sentences and ends with the main sentence.

indirect pattern Presenting a messages with details, explanations, and evidence first, followed by the main idea.

indirect report pattern The pattern used when a report opens with an introduction and background information and ends with the conclusion and recommendations.

individualism A key dimension of culture that refers to an attitude of independence and freedom from control.

inducement A tool used to encourage a reader to act immediately.

informal channel of communication A communication channel that does not follow an organization's hierarchy of command.

informal research Research (such as looking in files, talking to your boss, interviewing a target audience, and conducting an informal survey) that is often necessary for preparing routine documents and presentations.

information overload Feeling overwhelmed by having too much information, making it difficult to make a decision or keep up-to-date on a topic.

information worker Someone who works with technology for a living.

informational report A report that presents data without analysis or recommendations.

inside address The part of a letter that includes the name and address of the recipient.

instant messaging (IM) Exchanging messages in real time using an instant messaging (IM) service.

intellectual property Information, ideas, and other intangibles that result from one's intellect or creativity.

intercultural competence Understanding the differences that exist between one's own culture and the cultures of others.

interim reports *See* **progress reports**.

internal communication Communication that involves exchanging ideas and messages with superiors, coworkers, and subordinates.

Internet An electronic network of computers that extends across the globe.

Internet job board A site such as Monster.com that posts job listings and career search information.

internship A supervised job, often without pay, that allows a student to gain practical experience in a specific major or field.

interview A tool used to collect primary data by questioning individuals.

interview follow-up letter A brief letter of thanks sent to the interviewer after an interview.

intranet An Internet-like network that belongs to a company and is accessible only to its employees.

investigative reports Reports that deliver data for a specific, nonrecurring situation, without offering interpretations or recommendations.

jargon Specialized or technical vocabulary used by a specific profession, field, or group.

justification/recommendation reports Reports that justify or recommend something.

kaizen A Japanese term that means "continuous improvement" or "change for the better."

keywords Words or phrases that describe the skills, traits, tasks, and job titles that an employer wants.

knowledge worker Someone who works for a living by developing or using knowledge and information.

knowledge-based economy Advanced economies that depend heavily on knowledge, information, and high-level skills.

lag time The time when you are waiting for a speaker's next idea.

leading question A question that that is worded in such a way as to suggest a desired answer.

letter A written document that serves as a primary channel of communication for sending messages outside an organization.

letter of transmittal A letter presenting a proposal, business plan, or report that is addressed to a person outside the organization who is designated to receive the document and who will make the final decision.

letter proposal An informal proposal that is presented in a short (two- to four-page) letter.

liability The legal obligation of responsibility.

libel Written language that harms a person's reputation.

limitations A part of the statement of purpose that presents the conditions that affect the generalizability and utility of a report's findings.

limiting sentence A sentence that opposes the primary idea of a paragraph by suggesting a negative or contrasting thought.

line chart A visual aid used to illustrate trends and changes in data over time.

linear logic A thinking pattern common in low-context communicators, whereby they proceed from Point A to Point B to Point C to arrive at a conclusion.

list of figures A list that includes the titles and page numbers of all tables and figures that appear in a proposal, business plan, or report.

listening The act of hearing with intention.

literature review The part of a formal report introduction that summarizes what other authors and researchers have published on the topic, especially for academic and scientific reports.

litigation A legal proceeding in a court of law.

long lead-in Unnecessary introductory words (*I am writing this letter to inform you that*).

low-context culture Communicators in these cultures (such as North America, Scandinavia, and Germany) tend to rely more on words; they tend to be logical, analytical, and action-oriented.

mailing list A discussion group that operates by having messages delivered to members via e-mail.

majority A method of reaching a group decision whereby group members vote and a majority wins.

management hierarchy Classification of employees within an organization based on their status.

manuscript format An appropriate format for longer, more formal reports.

market analysis The section of a business plan that discusses market characteristics, trends, projected growth, customer behavior, complementary products and services, barriers to entry, customer identification, and strengths and weaknesses of direct and indirect competitors.

mean A statistical term meaning *average* or *arithmetic average*; calculated by adding up all items and dividing by the total number of items.

median A statistical measure that represents midpoint in a group of figures arranged from lowest to highest (or vice versa).

meeting A gathering of people who discuss issues, pool information, solicit feedback, clarify policy, seek consensus, and solve problems.

melting pot A metaphor for the idea that as people from different cultural backgrounds begin to mingle, they lose their unique identities.

memo format An appropriate format for short, informal reports written for circulation within an organization.

memorandum A written document used for informal internal communication.

memory stick A small transportable data storage device.

merge fields Codes that appear in a form letter where information will vary.

merger When two or more companies join together to form a single entity.

metaphor A comparison between otherwise dissimilar things without using the words *like* or *as*.

metasearching An online search tool that combines several powerful search engines into one.

minority A method of reaching a group decision whereby a subcommittee investigates and makes a recommendation for action.

minutes A written record of what took place during a meeting.

misplaced modifier A word or phrase that is unclear because it is not close to the word it describes (*After being in the refrigerator for a week, Lauren said the milk tasted bad*).

mission statement The part of a business plan that describes a business and explains why it will succeed.

mixed message A message that contains both positive and negative elements.

mode A statistical measure that represents the value that occurs most frequently in a group of figures.

Modern Language Association (MLA) An organization whose citation method directs readers to sources with parenthetical notes inserted into the text and with a "Works Cited" list.

morale The attitude workers have toward their jobs and workplaces; the emotional feeling one has toward a situation, task, or function.

multiethnic Involving various ethnic groups.

multimedia slides Computer presentation slides prepared using software such as PowerPoint, Apple Keynote, Lotus Freelance Graphics, Corel Presentations, Adobe Presenter, or Adobe Ovation that contain sound, videos, and hyperlinks.

multinational alliance A formal connection between two or more companies located in different countries that will benefit all parties.

multinational company A company that operates in two or more countries.

multitasking The performance of two or more tasks or activities at the same time.

National Organization of Women (NOW) An organization founded in 1966 to take action to bring equality to all women.

Natural language-processing technology Technology that allows one to ask questions and search for information using standard wording and sentence structure.

netiquette The rules of polite online interaction.

networking Developing lists, making contacts, and following up on referrals during a job search.

newsgroup An Internet-based discussion group that focuses on one topic.

niche A special place within a larger system.

noise Anything in the communication process that interrupts the transmission of a message.

nonjudgmental Avoiding making judgments based on personal opinions or feelings.

nonverbal communication All unwritten and unspoken messages, both intentional and unintentional, including eye contact, facial expressions, body movement, space, time, distance, and appearance.

norming The third phase of team development, during which tensions among team members subside, roles are clarified, and information begins to flow among members.

North American Free Trade Agreement (NAFTA) An agreement that expands free trade among Canada, the United States, and Mexico.

noun conversion Needlessly transforming verbs into nouns.

objective language Language that sounds reasonable, avoids overblown expressions, and does not make preposterous claims.

ombudsman A mediator who hears employee complaints, investigates, and seeks to resolve problems fairly.

one-on-one interview An interview during which the job candidate sits down with a company representative to talk about the job and the candidates' qualifications.

online catalog An automated listing of a library's holdings.

online collaboration tools Tools that support team writing such as e-mail, mailing lists, discussion boards, instant messaging, groupware, portals, blogs, and wikis.

online networking Networking that takes place online via career networking groups, discussion boards, mailing lists, and blogs.

online proposal A proposal that is submitted electronically.

open office An office with flexible workstations and shared conference rooms instead of individual offices and cubicles.

opinions Beliefs that are held in confidence but without substantiation.

optical character recognition (OCR) Technology used to scan text documents.

organization chart A visual aid used to show the line of command and the flow of effective communication from management to employees.

Organization for Economic Cooperation and Development (OECD) A global organization founded in 1961 to help countries that are committed to democracy and a market economy to support economic growth, raise employment and living standards, and maintain financial stability.

outline A tool used to organize ideas into a hierarchy.

outliner A word processing feature that enables writers to divide a topic into a hierarchical order with main points and subpoints.

outsourcing Hiring an outside consultant, an independent contractor, or another company to perform a specific task or job.

panel interview An interview during which the job candidate is interviewed by a panel of two more individuals, usually those who will be the employee's supervisors and colleagues.

paragraph One or more sentences designated as a separate thought group.

parallel construction Balanced sentence structure.

parallelism A writing technique that uses similar grammatical construction to achieve balanced writing (*of the people, by the people, for the people*).

paraphrase To rephrase or summarize a message into your own words, often for the purpose of clarification.

parenthetical citation A reference placed at the end of a sentence in a report that refers to a source listed on a bibliography.

partnership A business owned by two or more persons.

passive voice Sentences in which the subject is acted upon (*The message was sent by Brandon*).

PDF An abbreviation for Adobe Acrobat's *portable document format*.

peer-to-peer tools Networks that rely on the computing power and bandwidth of network participants, usually for sharing content files and digital information.

percentage A portion of a whole, measured in hundredths; calculated by dividing each individual figure by the total figures.

performing The fourth phase of team development, during which information flows freely, deadlines are met, and production exceeds expectations.

periodic (activity) reports Recurring reports written at regular intervals to keep management informed of operations.

periodical A recurrent or periodic publication such as a magazine, pamphlet, and journal.

perk A fringe benefit offered to employees.

personal digital assistant (PDA) A handheld mobile device that has computing, information storage and retrieval, appointment-setting, notetaking, and other capabilities.

persuasion The ability to use argument or discussion to change an individual's beliefs or actions.

persuasive claim A message written by a customer to identify or correct a wrong that requires persuasive techniques; often called a *complaint*.

phonetically Relating to the sounds of words rather than meanings.

phrase A group of words without a subject and a verb.

physical distractions Distractions such as noisy surroundings, extreme temperatures, and inferior acoustics that can disrupt oral communication.

pie chart A visual aid used to show the proportion or parts of a whole.

pilot study A study carried out with a small group of people prior to a large-scale study.

pivoting paragraph A paragraph that starts with a limiting sentence that offers a contrasting or negative idea before delivering the main sentence.

plagiarism The act of using others' ideas without proper documentation.

plain English Using short sentences, simple words, and clear organization to improve clarity.

plain-text résumé An electronic version of a résumé that is suitable for e-mailing or pasting into online résumé bank submission forms; also called an *ASCII résumé*.

podcast A digital audio file that can be downloaded to a portable media player on demand.

polite command A command that is disguised as a question and ends with a period (*Will you please send me your summer catalog*).

portal A Web site that acts as a starting point for using the Internet.

post hoc An error in reasoning that occurs when cause and effect are confused with chronology.

posture The way a person positions or arranges his or her body parts.

prejudice Judgment that forms when a stereotype develops into a rigid attitude and when it's based on erroneous beliefs or perceptions.

presentation software Software such as PowerPoint that is used to create slide shows or multimedia presentations.

press release A written document that announces information about your company to the media.

prewriting The first stage in Phase 1 of the writing process, which includes analyzing, anticipating, and adapting messages to fit their purpose and audience.

primary audience The person(s) for whom a written or oral message is intended.

primary data Data that result from firsthand experience and observation.

primary source An original source (such as a site visit, a traffic count, a questionnaire, an interview, or a focus group) that is used to generate firsthand, primary information.

print index Printed index of periodical titles.

printed forms A report format used to present repetitive data, such as monthly sales reports, performance appraisals, merchandise inventories, and personnel and financial reports.

problem statement A statement that clarifies that task of the report writer.

product liability The responsibility of a manufacturer or company when defective products are made or sold.

professionalism The specific conduct and qualities of a person who is considered to be businesslike and courteous in the workplace.

progress and interim reports Reports that describe the status of a project.

project team A group of people working together under time constraints to complete a specific project.

proofread To correct the grammar, spelling, punctuation, format, and mechanics of a message.

prop A tangible object such as a model used to offer a realistic reinforcement of message content during an oral presentation.

propaganda Information that is created and spread to support a particular cause.

proposal A report written to solve problems, provide services, or sell products; can be solicited or unsolicited, formal or informal.

proprietorship A business owned by one person.

prototype Ideas about people or cultures that are based on objective observations.

public domain Material that is not copyrighted and is available for general public use.

puffery Describing a product or service using exaggerated claims or comments.

pun Using a word or phrase to suggest two or more meanings at the same time, usually for humorous effect.

punitive Inflicting punishment.

purpose statement A statement that defines the focus of a report and provides a standard that keeps the project on focus.

quality control A management process used by a company to ensure proper standards in the goods and services provided to customers.

quality control circle A group of employees with similar positions who meet periodically with management to discuss work-related issues and to offer suggestions for improvement.

quantifiable Able to be counted.

quantitative Measuring quantities or amounts.

query A question or the act of questioning.

questionnaire A written or electronic list of questions designed to gather information from responders on a specific topic.

quota A prescribed minimum or maximum number.

race A category of people that share specific physical traits such as skin color, facial features, or genetics.

racial bias Language that seems to exclude or stereotype individuals based on racial identification.

ragged-right margin Uneven right margin. The opposite of justified or even margins.

range A statistical term that represents the span between the lowest and highest values; calculated by subtracting the lowest figure from the highest figure.

rank A person's status in a company's hierarchy.

rank-and-file employee A lower-level, nonmanagement employee.

rapport A relationship of mutual understanding, harmony, or agreement.

rational appeal A persuasive technique that is associated with reason and intellect.

raw data Data that has not yet been interpreted.

raw materials The unprocessed materials used to create a finished product.

readability A measure of how easily a document can be read.

reader benefit Discussing message elements such as product features from the reader's point of view.

reasons An explanation of the logic behind negative news; uses positive words and shows reader benefits if possible.

receiver The individual in the communication process to whom the message is intended or sent.

recommendation reports See "justification reports."

recommendation Statements that make specific suggestions for actions that can solve a report problem.

recruiter A person in charge of finding qualified candidates for open positions.

recursive A task or process that can repeat itself indefinitely.

red tape A term that describes any procedure that is time-consuming and requires great effort.

redundancy The needless repetition of words with similar meanings (*necessary essentials*).

reference request A letter asking an individual to serve as a reference during an employment search.

references Individuals who are willing to answer questions about a job seeker's qualifications for employment.

rejection follow-up letter A brief letter sent after being rejected for a job.

rejection letter A letter sent to thank an employer for a job offer and to explain briefly why you are turning the offer down.

report A written document that answers questions and solves problems.

report headings Structural clues that highlight major ideas in a report, allowing busy readers to see the big picture at a glance.

report introduction The part of the report that tells the purpose, describes the significance of the topic, and previews the main points.

request for proposal (RFP) A document written to companies to solicit competitive bids.

resale Language that attempts to entice a customer to purchase goods or services from your company again.

resale The process of reassuring customers that their choices were good ones.

research The first stage in Phase 2 of the writing process, which involves collecting needed information.

résumé A document outlining a person's career objective, education, work experience, special skills, and other job-related information.

résumé follow-up letter A letter sent after your résumé generates no responses within a reasonable time.

retention The act of retaining or remembering something.

revise To improve the content and sentence structure of a message.

revising The third stage in Phase 1 of the writing process, which includes revising, proofreading, and evaluating.

routine letters Everyday messages written to suppliers, governmental agencies, other businesses, and customers.

run-on A sentence error that results when two complete thoughts are joined without proper punctuation.

sales message A message used to reach customers and prospects to promote specific products or services.

Sarbanes-Oxley Act (SOX) Legislation passed in 2002 to protect shareholders and the public from accounting errors and securities fraud.

satellite communications A telecommunications system that relies on satellites to relay signals.

saving face Protecting the image a person holds in his or her social or professional network.

scalable font A font that can be printed or displayed in different sizes and styles.

scholarly source Information written by and for experts in a field of study.

scientific experiment A formal experiment or investigation that includes controlled variables.

scope The part of a formal report introduction that clarifies the boundaries of the report, defining what will be included or excluded.

screening interview An interview used to screen candidates to filter those who fail to meet minimum requirements.

search engine An online search tool that uses automated software "spiders" that trawl the vast amount of data on the Web to collect and index their findings.

search tool A computer program such as Google or Ask that is used to search for specific sites and information on the World Wide Web.

secondary audience Others who might see a written message or hear an oral message beyond the primary audience.

secondary data Data that come from reading what others have experienced or observed.

self-identity How a person sees himself or herself.

sender The person or group in the communication process that originates the message.

sentence A group of words with a subject and a verb that expresses a complete thought.

sequential interviews Interviews that allow a candidate to meet with two or more interviewers on a one-on-one basis over the course of several hours or days.

sexism Prejudice or discrimination based on gender.

sexual harassment Requests for sexual favors, unwelcome sexual advances, or any conduct of a sexual nature that creates an intimidating, hostile, or offensive work environment.

shouting Writing an entire e-mail message in all capital letters.

signature block A block of text containing the sender's contact information that is automatically added to the end of an e-mail message.

significance A part of the statement of purpose that states why a topic is worth investigating at this time.

simile A comparison between otherwise dissimilar things that includes the words *like* or *as*.

simple sentence A sentence made up of one independent clause.

situational questions Interview questions related to situations to help employers test a job candidate's thought processes and logical thinking.

6-x-6 rule A rule that says each slide in a multimedia presentation should contain no more than six bullets per screen and no more than six words per bullet.

skim value A quality that allows readers to read a message quickly and grasp main ideas.

slander Spoken language that harms a person's reputation.

slang Nonstandard, informal words used by a particular social group.

slide deck A series of self-contained electronic slides.

slideshow A series of slides shown in consecutive order during a multimedia presentation.

Small Business Administration (SBA) A federal government agency that supports and advocates for small businesses and small business owners.

smart phone A fully functional mobile phone that can also function as a personal computer.

soft skills Nontechnical, personality-related, intangible skills such as communication, leadership, attitude, professionalism, and creativity.

solicited proposal A proposal written when an individual or firm knows exactly what it wants and prepares a request specifying its requirements.

space A form of nonverbal communication in which we communicate to others by the way we arrange things in the space around us.

spam Unsolicited advertisements sent via e-mail.

spam filter A software program that attempts to identify and block junk e-mail messages.

speaker's notes A hard-copy version of a multimedia presentation that includes a miniature image of each slide along with space for supporting comments.

spider Automated software that crawls through the Web at regular intervals to collect and index information from each location visited.

spiral logic A thinking pattern common in high-context communicators, whereby they circle around a topic indirectly and look at it from many tangential or divergent viewpoints to arrive at a conclusion.

sprint writing Recording unedited ideas quickly with revision coming later.

staffing The section of a proposal that describes the credentials and expertise of the project leaders.

STAR technique A technique used to answer behavioral interview questions that involves describing the situation or task, what action was taken, and the results.

steering group A committee that sets agendas and arranges the order of business for a larger body, often a legislative body.

stereotype An oversimplified behavioral pattern applied uncritically to a group.

storming The second phase of team development, during which team members define their roles and responsibilities, decide how to reach their goals, and set governing rules.

streaming video A sequence of moving images that are sent over the Web in compressed form and viewed by the receiver as they arrive.

stress interview An interview meant to test a job candidate's reactions during nerve-racking situations.

subcommittee A small part of a committee assigned to discuss a specific issue and makes a recommendation to the entire committee.

subject directory A commercial or academic online search tool that relies on human editors to sift through Web pages and then organize the information found into subject categories.

subject line The part of an e-mail message or memo that summarizes the central idea, thus providing quick identification for reading and for filing.

subordinate An employee who works under the authority and control of another.

subordinate clause A group of words with a subject and a verb that depends for meaning on an independent clause and, therefore, cannot stand alone.

summary of qualifications A section near the top of a résumé that lists a job seeker's most impressive accomplishments and qualifications in one concise bulleted list.

superlative An exaggerated expression such as *lowest price*, *highest quality*, or *best service in the industry*.

supporting sentence A sentence that illustrates, explains, or strengthens the primary idea of a paragraph.

supportiveness An attitude that requires one to support others positively with head nods, eye contact, facial expressions, and physical proximity.

survey A method of collecting primary data that gathers information from groups of people.

synonym A word that has the same meaning as another word.

syntax The way that words are grammatically arranged in sentences.

synthesize To combine parts into a coherent whole.

systematic Being ordered and planned.

table A visual aid used to present quantitative information in a systematic order of columns and rows.

table of contents The part of a proposal, business plan, or report that shows all headings and their beginning page numbers.

tabulate To place data in a table format.

tact Careful consideration of another's feelings.

talking headings Headings that provide more information and interest than functional headings, such as *Findings Reveal Support for New Parking Rules*.

task force A temporary group of people assigned a specific task, to be completed in a short period of time, such as developing a plan or solving a problem.

team diversity A wide range of variation in the qualities, attributes, ethnicity, and backgrounds of team members.

team-based management A management structure that involves employees at all levels in decision making and communication through their involvement on teams.

telecommuting Using technology to work outside the traditional office or workspace, usually from home.

teleconferencing A real-time connection between three or more people in different geographic locations that involves audio only, usually over a phone line.

telephone tag The result when telephone callers repeatedly miss one another.

templates Professionally designed models that come with a software program such as PowerPoint that contain combinations of harmonious colors, borders, and fonts for pleasing visual effects.

territory The zones of privacy we create around us or the areas we feel are our own.

testimonial A statement of a satisfied customer, often used to effectively create a desire for a product or service.

text messaging Sending or receiving short text messages on a mobile phone.

thesaurus A tool that lists words and their synonyms.

Third World countries Developing countries that have low standards of living, undeveloped industrial bases, and low per-capita income.

thread A sequence of messages sent via e-mail or posted to a discussion board covering a topic of conversation.

3-x-3 Writing Process Systematic plan for developing business communications.

three-point introduction When making a telephone call, this introduction names the person or organization you are calling, identifies yourself and your affiliation, and briefly explains why you are calling.

time orientation A key dimension of culture that refers to the way an individual values or uses time.

title page The part of a proposal, business plan, or report that shows information such as the title, the name of the client organization, the RFP number, the date of submission, the author's name, and the author's organization.

to-file report See **confirmation**.

tolerance Accepting those whose beliefs and actions contradict or differ from one's own.

tone Conveyed largely by the words used, reflects the feeling that people receive upon hearing or reading a message.

tort law Involves wrongful civil acts other than breach of contract.

trade agreement An enforceable agreement between two or more countries related to issues such as free trade and tariffs.

traditional networking Networking that takes place in person, by phone, and in writing.

transition effects A feature that determines the visual delivery of the objects and bullet points in a multimedia presentation.

transitional expression Expressions used to achieve paragraph coherence by acting as verbal signposts to readers and listeners.

transitions Words and phrases such as *however* or *and the same time* that show relationships and help reveal the logical flow of ideas in a document.

transparencies Visual aids prepared on acetate film that are viewed using an overhead projector.

trip, convention, and conference reports Reports that summarize activities or findings from business trips or attendance at conferences or conventions.

trite business phrase A stale expression that has been overused by business writers over the years (*as per you letter*).

unbiased Without prejudice, impartial.

unreceptive audience An audience that will be uninterested in, unwilling to comply with, displeased with, or hostile toward your message.

unsolicited proposal A proposal written when an individual or firm sees a problem to be solved and offers a proposal to do so.

uptalk Making declarative statements sound like questions.

upward communication flow A formal channel of communication that exists when information flows upward from nonmanagement employees to management.

USB flash drive A small, lightweight, removable, transportable storage device.

use policy A policy that covers e-mail and Web use in the workplace.

Usenet An Internet-based worldwide system of discussion groups, bulletin boards, and forums.

values Ideals accepted by an individual or group.

variable A quantity or figure that can assume any of a set of values.

venture capital Money provided by venture capitalists and other investors to help entrepreneurs start or grow business ventures.

verbal signpost A preview, summary, or transition to help audiences recognize the organization and main points in an oral presentation.

video Moving images displayed on a monitor or screen.

videoconferencing A real-time connection between two or more people in different geographic locations that involves audio and video.

vigor A quality that suggests energy and intensity.

virtual community A Internet-based community of individual who share a common interest.

virtual team A geographically dispersed team that uses technology to communicate and collaborate across time and space.

visual aid A tool such as multimedia slides or handouts used during an oral presentation to emphasize and clarify main points and increase audience interest.

voice conferencing A real-time connection between three or more people in different geographic locations that involves audio only, usually over a phone line.

voice mail Links a telephone system to a computer that digitizes and stores incoming messages.

volunteerism The act of performing work or giving time with no financial or tangible gain.

Web conferencing Allows attendees to use their computers to access an online virtual meeting room where they can chat, share documents, and make live presentations and demonstrations.

Web document builder Software such as FrontPage that is used to design and construct Web pages.

webcast Sending live audio or video programming over the Web.

weblog (blog) A personal online journal in reverse-chronological order that is updated frequently and on which readers can comment.

whistleblowing When an individual or group of employees reports a wrongdoing within an organization to the media, the public, or the government.

whiteboard A flat board with a glossy surface on which to write with markers during an oral presentation or a meeting.

Wi-Fi The wireless interface of mobile computing devices such as laptops.

wiki A Web application that allows multiple users to add, edit, and delete content using any Web browser.

wildcard Characters such as an asterisk (*) that are used to represent one or more characters during a Web search.

wireless device A communication device that operates via radio frequency rather than wires.

wireless networking A network that uses high-frequency radio waves instead of wires for communication and data transfer.

word wrap A word processing feature that allows you to continue typing without pressing the ENTER key.

word-of-mouth advertising Informal advertising generated by unpaid endorsers.

work plan A written plan that helps the report writer evaluate resources, set priorities, outline a course of action, and establish a time schedule.

World Trade Organization (WTO) An international organization founded in 1995 that deals with the rules of trade between nations.

World Wide Web(Web or WWW) An enormous collection of specially formatted documents call Web pages located at Web sites around the world. Web offerings include online databases, magazines, newspapers, library resources, job and résumé banks, sound and video files, and many other information resources.

writer's block An inability to write.

yardstick reports Reports that examine problems with two or more solutions using criteria by which to compare the alternatives.

you view Audience-focused perspective that emphasizes receiver benefits.

Notes

Chapter 1

1 Berner, R. (2005, October 31). At Sears, a great communicator; new CEO Lewis will need his people skills to overhaul the giant's hidebound culture. *BusinessWeek*, Issue 3957, 50. Retrieved February 17, 2007, from InfoTrac College Edition database.

2 Lewis, A. (2005). Cougar CEO. Retrieved February 10, 2007, from http://www.mycougarconnection.com/cougar_corner/alywin_lewis.htm

3 Lewis, A. (2005). Cougar CEO. Retrieved February 10, 2007, from http://www.mycougarconnection.com/cougar_corner/alywin_lewis.htm

4 Thomas, J. (2005, Winter/Spring). Kmart CEO leads with passion. Retrieved February 12, 2007, from www.blackmbamagazine.net

5 Double duty for Sears' Lewis. (2005, September 14). Retrieved October 10, 2007, from http://www.businessweek.com/bwdaily/dnflash/sep2005/nf2005914_3914_db008.htm

6 Kinsman, M. (2004, February 1). Are poor writing skills holding back your career? *California Job Journal*. Retrieved February 12, 2007, from http://www.jobjournal.com/article_full_text.asp?artid=1039; Tucker, M. L., & McCarthy, A. M. (2001, Summer). Presentation self-efficacy: Increasing communication skills through service-learning. *Journal of Managerial Issues*, 227–244; Cohen, A. (1999). The right stuff. *Sales and Marketing Management*, 151; and Messmer, M. (1999, August). Skills for a new millennium. *Strategic Finance*, 10–12.

7 Moody, J., Stewart, B., & Bolt-Lee, C. (2002, March). Showcasing the skilled business graduate: Expanding the tool kit. *Business Communication Quarterly*, 65(1), 23.

8 Vance, E. (2007, February 2). College graduates lack key skills, report says. *The Chronicle of Higher Education*, p. A30.

9 Messmer, M. (2001, January). Enhancing your writing skills. *Strategic Finance*, 8. See also Staples, B. (2005, May 15). The fine art of getting it down on paper, fast. *The New York Times*, p. WK13(L).

10 National Commission on Writing. (2004, September 14). Writing skills necessary for employment, says big business [press release]. Retrieved February 12, 2007, from http://www.writingcommission.org/pr/writing_for_employ.html

11 National Commission on Writing. (2004, September 14). Writing skills necessary for employment, says big business [press release]. Retrieved February 12, 2007, from http://www.writingcommission.org/pr/writing_for_employ.html

12 Daniels, C. (2004, June 28). 50 best companies for minorities. *Fortune*, 136.

13 Drucker, P. (1989, May). New realities, new ways of managing. *Business Month*, 50–51.

14 Grimes, A. (2002, June 27). Techno talk. *The Wall Street Journal*, p. B4.

15 Haag, S., Cummings, M., & Phillips, A. (2003). *Management information systems for the information age* (3rd ed.). New York: McGraw-Hill Higher Education.

16 Wessel, D. (2004, April 2). The future of jobs: New ones arise, wage gap widens. *The Wall Street Journal*, p. A1.

17 Fox, W. M., Alm, R., & Holmes, N. (2004, May 13). Where the jobs are. *The New York Times*, p. A27.

18 Thinking for a living. (2006, January 21). *The Economist* (US). Retrieved October 10, 2006, from InfoTrac College Edition database.

19 O'Toole, J., & Lawler, E. E., III. (2006, July). *The New American Workplace*. New York: Palgrave Macmillan, p. 17.

20 Heller, L. (2006, August 7). Customer experience evolves in China. *Retailing Today*, 45(14), 42. Retrieved January 5, 2007 from InfoTrac database.

21 Arvedlund, E. E. (2005, March 17). McDonald's commands a real estate empire in Russia. *The New York Times*, p. C5.

22 Balfour, F., & Kiley, D. (2005, April 25). Ad agencies unchained. *BusinessWeek*, 51.

23 Malone, T. W. (2004). *The future of work*. Cambridge: Harvard Business School Press, p. 32.

24 Team player: No more 'same-ol, same-ol.' (1994, October 17). *BusinessWeek*, 95.

25 Caron, J. R., Jarvenpa, S. L., & Stoddard, D. B. (1994, September). Business reengineering at CIGNA Corporation: Experiences and lessons learned from the first five years. *MISQuarterly*. Retrieved October 4, 2006, from http://www.misq.org/archivist/vol/no18/issue3/sim94/sim94.html#intro

26 Study: Few U.S. workers who could telecommute do so. (2006, July 12). *PC Magazine Online*. Retrieved October 5, 2006, from InfoTrac College Edition database.

27 Karoly, L. A., & Panis, C. W. A. (2004). *The 21st century at work*. Santa Monica, CA: Rand Corporation, pp. 36–39.

28 Shifting workplace demographics and delayed retirement. (2002, May). *Monthly Labor Review*. Retrieved October 11, 2006, from http://www.microsoft.com/enable/aging/references.aspx

29 Hamilton, C., & Parker, C. (1996). *Communicating for results* (6th ed.). Belmont, CA: Wadsworth, p. 7.

30 Sullivan, J., Karmeda, N., & Nobu, T. (1992, January/February). Bypassing in managerial communication. *Business Horizons*, 34(1), 72.

31 McGirt, E. (2006, March 20). Getting out from under: Beset by interruptions, information overload, and irksome technology, knowledge workers need help: A survival guide. *Fortune*, 88.

32 Drucker, P. (1990). *Managing the non-profit organization: Practices and principles*. New York: HarperCollins, p. 46.

33 E-mail becoming crime's new smoking gun. (2005). Retrieved October 11, 2006, from http://www.usatoday.com/tech/news/2002-08-15-email-evidence_x.htm

34 Sims, R. R., Veres, J. G., III, Jackson, K. A., & Facteau, C. L. (2001). *The challenge of front-line management*. Westport, CT: Quorum, p. 10.

35 Burke, L. A., & Wise, J. M. (2003, May/June). The effective care, handling, and pruning of the office grapevine. *Business Horizons*, 71.

36 Goman, C. K. (2006, June). I heard it through the grapevine. Paper presented at the International Association of Business Communicators, Vancouver, Canada. Retrieved October 22, 2006, from http://common.iabc.com/employee/2006/06

37 Karathanos, P., & Auriemmo, A. (1999, March-April). Care and feeding of the organizational grapevine. *Industrial Management*, 41(2), 26. Retrieved January 2, 2007 from InfoTrac College Edition database.

38 Goman, C. K. (2006, June). I heard it through the grapevine. Paper presented at the International Association of Business Communicators, Vancouver, Canada. Retrieved October 22, 2006, from http://common.iabc.com/employee/2006/06

39 Zimmermann, S., Davenport, B., & Haas, J. W. (1996, April). A communication metamyth in the workplace: The assumption that more is better. *Journal of Business Communication*, 33(2), 185–204.

40 Nelson, B. (1997, October). How to energize everyone in the company. *Bottom Line/Business*, 3.

41 Berner, R. (2005, October 31). At Sears, a great communicator; new CEO Lewis will need his people skills to overhaul the giant's hidebound culture. *BusinessWeek*, Issue 3957, 50. Retrieved February 17, 2007, from InfoTrac College Edition database.

42 A year and beyond at Sears Holdings: Aylwin Lewis, CEO. (2006, March 27). *DSN Retailing Today*, 45(6), 33. Retrieved February 11, 2007, from InfoTrac College Edition database.

43 Guy, M. G. (1990). *Ethical decision making in everyday work situations*. New York: Quorum Books, p. 3.

44 Richards, J. I., Andrews, J. C., & Maronick, T. J. (1995, Fall). Advertising research issues from FTC versus Stouffer Foods Corporation. *Journal of Public Policy & Marketing*, 14(2), 301–309.

45 Schroeder, M. (1997, June 18). Get firm "abs" in a few hours? Don't believe it. *The Wall Street Journal*, p. B1.

46 Women entrepreneurs. (2006). Score Association. Retrieved October 14, 2006, from http://www.score.org/women.html

47 Chartered management institute: Checklists: Human resources, training and development. (2006, March). Introducing a whistleblowing policy. Checklist 072. Retrieved January 8, 2007, from InfoTrac College Edition database.

48 Whistleblowing workers: Becoming an endangered species? (2006, June). *HR Focus*, 83(16), 9. Retrieved January 4, 2007, from Business Source Premier (EBSCO) database.

49 Lewis, A. B. (2005, November 2). Speak less, listen more. *The New York Times*, p. BU10.

50 Aylwin Lewis biography. (2005). Retrieved February 12, 2007, from Answers.com at http://www.answers.com/topic/Aylwin-lewis

51 Do your reps' writing skills need a refresher? (2002, February). *Customer Contact Management Report*, 7.

52 Sandberg, J. (2006, September 18). What exactly was it that the boss said? You can only imagine. *The Wall Street Journal*. p. B1.

53 Ahmad, A. (2006, May). To the manner born at the workplace. *The Economic Times*. Retrieved January 7, 2007, from InfoTrac database.

54 The Wall Street Journal ethics quiz. (1999, October 21). *The Wall Street Journal*, p. B1.

55 How to keep your personal information safe. (2006, August 2). *USA Today*, p. 6D; Babbitt, J. (2006, September). Do's and don'ts of protecting

yourself from identity theft. *Information Today*, 60; Chan, S., & Dash, E. (2006, October 31). In new law, residents gain power to freeze credit files. *The New York Times*, p. B3; Correa, B. (2003, October 5). Victims of identity theft can spend years trying to clear up damage. *Knight Ridder/Tribune Business News;* and Black, J. (2003, December 24). How you can thwart ID thieves. *BusinessWeek Online.* Retrieved January 7, 2007, from BusinessWeek Online.

Chapter 2

1 Fackler, M. (2007, February 14). Translating the Toyota way. *The New York Times*, p. C1.

2 Tilin, A. (2005, January/February). The smartest company of the year. *Business 2.0, 6*(1), 67–72.

3 Connelly, J. (2002, Spring). All together now. *Gallup Management Journal. 2*(1), 1+. Retrieved December 30, 2006, from http://www.gallupjournal.com/GMJarchive/issue5/2002315j.asp

4 Discussion of the Toyota Motor Corporation based on Bryant, J. (2007, January 1). Toyota Motor Corporation. *Hoover's Company Records.* Retrieved January 2, 2007, from ProQuest database; About Toyota. Toyota corporate Web site. Retrieved December 31, 2006, from http://www.toyota.com/about/index.html?s_van=GM_TN_ABOUT; Wiser, J. (2006, January 21). Inculcating culture. *Economist, 378(8461),* 11; Wiser, J. (2005, June). Kaizen meets Dewey. *Information Outlook, 9*(6), 27; Liker, A. (2003). The 14 principles of The Toyota Way. *The Toyota Way.* New York: McGraw-Hill, pp. 35–41; and Wigham, R. (2004, June 22). Auto-motivation. *Personnel Today*, 31–33.

5 Brent, P. (2006, November). Soft skills speak volumes. *CA Magazine, 139,* 112. Retrieved December 12, 2006, from Business Source Premier (EBSCO) database.

6 Laff, M. (2006, December). Wanted: CFOs with communications skills. *T & D, 60*(12), 20. Retrieved February 13, 2007, from http://store.astd.org/product.asp?prodid=4282

7 O'Toole, J., & Lawler, E. E., III. (2005). *The new american workplace.* New York: Palgrave Macmillan, p. 20.

8 Mueller, F., Procter, S., & Buchanan, D. (2000, November). Teamworking in its context(s): Antecedents, nature and dimensions. *Human Relations, 53,* 1387. Retrieved December 10, 2006, from Business Source Premier (EBSCO) database.

9 DiSanza, J. R., & Legge, N. J. (2000). *Business and professional communication.* Boston: Allyn and Bacon, p. 98.

10 Ennen, S. (2003, April). Red baron soars with teamwork: New pizza products sate lifestyle needs. *Food Processing, 64,* 40. Retrieved December 10, 2006, from InfoTrac College Edition database.

11 Edmondson, G. (2006, October 16). BMW's dream factory. *BusinessWeek,* 80.

12 Katzenbach, J. R., & Smith, K. (1994). *The wisdom of teams.* New York: HarperBusiness, pp. 68–69.

13 Lipnack, J., & Stamps, J. (2000). *Virtual teams: People working across boundaries with technology* (2nd ed.). New York: Wiley, p. 18.

14 Kiger, P. J. (2006, September 25). Flexibility to the fullest: Throwing out the rules of work—Part 1 of 2. *Workforce Management, 85*(17), 1. See also Holland, K. (2006, December 3).When work time isn't face time. *The New York Times,* p. BU3.

15 Cutler, G. (2007, January-February). Mike leads his first virtual team. *Research-Technology Management, 50*(1), 66. Retrieved February 14, 2007, from InfoTrac College Edition database.

16 Miculka, J. H. (2007). *Speaking for success* (2nd ed.). Cincinnati, OH: South-Western, pp. 96–97.

17 Janis, I. L. (1982). *Groupthink: Psychological studies on policy decisions and fiascoes.* Boston: Houghton Mifflin. See also Miranda, S. M., & Saunders, C. (1995, Summer). Group support systems: An organization development intervention to combat groupthink. *Public Administration Quarterly, 19,* 193–216. Retrieved December 12, 2006, from EBSCO database.

18 Amason, A. C., Hochwarter, W. A., Thompson, K. R., & Harrison, A. W. (1995, Autumn). Conflict: An important dimension in successful management teams. *Organizational Dynamics, 24,* 1. Retrieved December 12, 2006, from InfoTrac College Edition database.

19 Parnell, C. (1996, November 1). Teamwork: Not a new idea, but it's transforming the workplace. *Executive Speeches, 63,* 46. Retrieved December 11, 2006, from InfoTrac College Edition database.

20 Katzennbach J. R., & Smith, K. (1994). *Wisdom of teams.* New York: HarperBusiness, p. 45.

21 Makower, J. (1995, Winter). Managing diversity in the workplace. *Business & Society Review,* 48. Retrieved December 10, 2006, from EBSCO database.

22 Gale, S. F. (2006, July). Commonground. *PM Network,* 48. Retrieved December 5, 2006, from EBSCO database.

23 Bayot, J. (2000, November 8). Developers bet on theaters in glutted L.A. *The Wall Street Journal,* Eastern edition, p. C1.

24 Katzenbach, J. R., & Smith, K. (1994). *Wisdom of teams.* New York: HarperBusiness, p. 50.

25 Connelly, J. (2002, Spring). All together now. *Gallup Management Journal. 2*(1), 1+. Retrieved December 30, 2006, from http://www.gallupjournal.com/GMJarchive/issue5/2002315j.asp

26 Armour, S. (2006, July 6). Some companies aim to tame meetings. *USA Today,* p. 3B.

27 Lancaster, H. (1998, May 26). Learning some ways to make meetings less awful. *The Wall Street Journal,* p. B1.

28 Maher, K. (2004, January 13). The jungle. *The Wall Street Journal,* p. B6.

29 Bruening, J. C. (1996, July). There's good news about meetings. *Managing Office Technology, 41,* 24–25. Retrieved December 4, 2006, from InfoTrac College Edition database.

30 Marquis, C. (2003, July). Doing well and doing good. *The New York Times,* p. BU2.

31 Schabacker, K. (1991, June). A short, snappy guide to meaningful meetings. *Working Women,* 73.

32 Cook, J. K. (1995, April). Try these eight guidelines for more effective meetings. *Communication Briefings,* Bonus Item, 8a.

33 Egan, M. (2006, March 13). Meetings can make or break your career. *Insurance Advocate, 117,* 24.

34 Bulkeley, W. M. (2006, September 28). Better virtual meetings. *The Wall Street Journal,* p. B1.

35 Crockett. R. O. (2007, February 26). The 21st century meeting. *BusinessWeek,* 72.

36 Delio, M. (2005, March 28). Enterprise collaboration with blogs and wikis. *InfoWorld,* 5. Retrieved December 6, 2006, from InfoTrac College Edition database.

37 Robbins, H., & Finley, M. (1995). *Why teams don't work.* Princeton, NJ: Peterson's/Pacesetter Books, p. 123.

38 Pellet, J. (2003, April). Anatomy of a turnaround guru. *Chief Executive,* 41; Mounter, P. (2003). Global internal communication: A model. *Journal of Communication Management, 3,* 265; Feiertag, H. (2002, July 15). Listening skills, enthusiasm top list of salespeople's best traits. *Hotel and Motel Management,* 20; Goby, V. P., & Lewis, J. M. (2000, June). The key role of listening in business: A study of the Singapore insurance industry. *Business Communication Quarterly, 63,* 41–51; Cooper, L. O. (1997, December). Listening competency in the workplace: A model for training. *Business Communication Quarterly, 60,* 75–84; and Penley, L. E., Alexander, E. R., Jerigan, I. E., & Henwood, C. I. (1997). Communication abilities of managers: The relationship to performance. *Journal of Management, 17,* 57–76.

39 Awang, F., Anderson, M. A., & Baker, C. J. (2003, Winter). Entry-level information services and support personnel: Needed workplace and technology skills. *The Delta Pi Epsilon Journal,* 48; and American Management Association. (1999,

August). The challenges facing workers in the future. *HR Focus,* 6.

40 Harris, T. W. (1989, June). Listen carefully. *Nation's Business,* 78.

41 Steil, L. K., Barker, L. I., & Watson, K. W. (1983). *Effective listening: Key to your success.* Reading, MA: Addison-Wesley; and Harris, J. A. (1998, August). Hear what's really being said. *New Zealand Management, 45,* 18.

42 Nelson, E. H., & Gypen, J. (1979, September/October). The subordinate's predicament. *Harvard Business Review,* 133.

43 International Listening Association. (2006). Listening factoids. Retrieved December 3, 2006, from http://www.listen.org/pages/factoids.html

44 Render, M. (2000, September 11). Better listening makes for a better marketing message. *Marketing News, 34,* 22–23. Retrieved December 15, 2006, from Business Source Premier (EBSCO) database.

45 Wolvin, A., & Coakley, C. G. (1996). *Listening* (5th ed.). New York: McGraw-Hill, pp. 136–137.

46 Effective communication. (1994, November). *Training Tomorrow,* 32–33.

47 Wood, J. T. (2003). *Gendered lives: Communication, gender, and culture* (5th ed.). Belmont, CA: Wadsworth, pp. 119–120; Anderson, K. J., & Leaper, C. (1998, August). Meta-analyses of gender effects on conversational interruption: Who, what, when, where, and how. *Sex Roles: A Journal of Research,* 225; and Booth-Butterfield, M. (1984). She hears: What they hear and why. *Personnel Journal, 44,* 39.

48 Tear. J. (1995, November 20). They just don't understand gender dynamics. *The Wall Street Journal,* p. A12; Wolfe, A. (1994, December 12). She just doesn't understand. *New Republic,* 26–34.

49 Burgoon, J., Coker, D., & Coker, R. (1986). Communication explanations. *Human Communication Research,* 463–494.

50 Tarsala, M. (1997, November 7). Remec's Ronald Ragland: Drawing rivals to his team by making their concerns his. *Investor's Business Daily,* A1.

51 Birdwhistel, R. (1970). *Kinesics and context.* Philadelphia: University of Pennsylvania Press.

52 What's A-O.K. in the U.S.A. is lewd and worthless beyond. (1996, August 18). *The New York Times,* p. E7.

53 Zielinski, D. (2001, April). Body language. *Presentations,* 15, 36–42. Retrieved December 14, 2006, from InfoTrac College Edition database.

54 Body speak: What are you saying? (2000, October). *Successful Meetings,* 49–51.

55 Leeds, D. (1995, May 1). Body language: Actions speak louder than words. *National Underwriter,* 18–19. Retrieved December 14, 2006, from InfoTrac College Edition database.

56 Osterman, R. (2006, March 20). Casual loses its cool in business: More employers are trying to tighten up workplace clothing standards. *Sacramento Bee.* Retrieved December 15, 2006, from InfoTrac database; Business casual: out of style? (2005, May). *HR Focus,* 9. Retrieved December 15, 2006, from InfoTrac College Edition database.

57 Wilkie, H. (2003, Fall). Professional presence. *The Canadian Manager,* 14; and Kaplan-Leiserson, L. (2000, November). Casual dress/back to business attire. *Training & Development,* 38–39.

58 Kennedy, M. M. (1997, September-October). Is business casual here to stay? *Executive Female,* 31.

59 Wood, N., & Benitez, T. (2003, April). Does the suit fit? *Incentive,* 31.

60 Business casual out of style. (2005, May). *HR Focus, 82,* 16. Retrieved December 16, 2006, from InfoTrac database; Egodigwe, L. Here come the suits. (2003, March). *Black Enterprise, 33,* 59. Retrieved December 15, 2006, from InfoTrac database; and Summerson, C. (2002, November 18). The suit is back in business. *BusinessWeek,* 130.

61 Chao, L. (2006, January 17). Not-so-nice costs. *The Wall Street Journal,* p. B1.

62 Workplace rudeness is common and costly. (2002, May). *USA Today Magazine,* 9.

63 Wigham, R. (2004, June 22). Auto-motivation, pp. 31–33.

64 Maturo, D. (2005, Winter). Being a technician is not enough: Develop leadership and communication skills. *The Pennsylvania CPA Journal.* Retrieved February 13, 2007, from http://www.picpa.org/asp/Journal/journal_article_details.asp?action=Normal&ID=1294

65 Marquis, C. (2003, July). Doing well and doing good. *The New York Times,* p. BU2.

66 Arrien, A. (2003, March-April). Geese teach lessons on teamwork. *Motion Systems Distributor, 17,* 32. Retrieved December 16, 2006, from InfoTrac College Edition database; and Flying like the geese. (2001, December). *Design Engineering,* 9. Retrieved December 16, 2006, from InfoTrac College Edition database.

67 Adopt active listening skills for better cross-functional team communication. (2002, January). *Inventory Reduction Report,* 9. Retrieved December 16, 2006, from InfoTrac College Edition database.

68 What's the universal hand sign for "I goofed"? (1996, December 16). *Santa Barbara News- Press,* p. D2.

69 Bell, A. H. (1999, September). Using nonverbal cues. *Incentive, 173,* 162. Retrieved December 16, 2006, from EBSCO database.

70 McCarty, M. (2007, January/February). Tattoos: Not just for sailors anymore. *OfficePro,* 26.

Chapter 3

1 Belson, K. (2003, December 14). Wal-Mart hopes it won't be lost in translation. *The New York Times,* Sec. 3, p. 1.

2 Rowley, I. (2006, September 14). Japan: Wal-Mart's looking for a partner—again; slow sales indicate the retailer's style isn't catching on with local consumers. *BusinessWeek Online.* Retrieved January 10, 2007, from InfoTrac College Edition database.

3 Dawson, C., Webb, A., & Zellner, W. (2002, April 1). Will Wal-Mart conquer Japan? *BusinessWeek Online,* Retrieved January 12, 2007, from http://www.businessweek.com/magazine/content/02_13/b3776141.htm

4 Flannery, R. (2004, May 10). China is a big prize. *Forbes, 173*(10), 163. Retrieved January 12, 2007, from InfoTrac College Edition database.

5 Bahree, M. (2006, October 2). The multinational, updated. *Forbes, 178*(6), 173. Retrieved January 11, 2007, from InfoTrac College Edition database.

6 Prior, M. (2006, December 22). P&G's growth plan: Fire on all cylinders. *WWD,* 7. Retrieved January 11, 2007, from InfoTrac College Edition database.

7 Seven-Eleven Japan. (2007). Retrieved January 19, 2007 from http://www.sej.co.jp/english/company/g_stores.html

8 Flannery, R. (2004, May 10). China is a big prize. *Forbes, 173*(10), 163.

9 Holmes, S. (2003, July 21). The real Nike news is happening abroad. *BusinessWeek,* 30.

10 Browning, E. S. (1992, April 23). In pursuit of the elusive Eurocomsumer. *The Wall Street Journal,* p. B1.

11 Stern, G. (1992, November 21). Heinz aims to export taste for ketchup. *The Wall Street Journal,* p. B1.

12 Crabtree, S. (2001). Cultural differences. *Eagle-Tribune.* Retrieved February 13, 2001, from http://www.eagletribune.com/news/stories/19990530/BU-001.htm

13 Brooks, S. (2006, December). Tomorrow, the world. *Restaurant Business, 105*(12), 26–32. Retrieved January 10, 2007, from InfoTrac College Edition database.

14 Adamy, J. (2007, January 17). Dunkin' begins new push into China. *The Wall Street Journal,* p. A4.

15 Creative jobs destruction. (2004, January 6). *The Wall Street Journal,* p. A18.

16 Glater, J. D. (2004, January 3). Offshore services grow in lean times. *The New York Times,* p. B1.

17 Kalin, S. (1997, June 9). Global net knits East to West at Liz Claiborne. *Computerworld,* G4–G6.

18 U.S. Department of Labor. (2007). Futurework: Trends and challenges for work in the 21st century. Retrieved January 12, 2007, from http://www.dol.gov/_sec/gils/records/000187.htm

19 Gleckman, H. (1998, August). A rich stew in the melting pot. *BusinessWeek,* 76.

20 Pollack, A. (1996, December 22). Barbie's journey in Japan. *The New York Times,* p. E3.

21 Chen, G. M., & Starosta, W. J. (1998). *Foundations of intercultural communication.* Boston: Allyn and Bacon, p. 40.

22 Varner, I., & Beamer, L. (2001). *Intercultural communication in the global workplace.* Boston: McGraw-Hill Irwin, p. 18.

23 Hall, E. T., & Hall, M. R. *Understanding cultural differences.* Yarmouth, Maine: Intercultural Press, pp. 183–184.

24 Chaney, L. H., & Martin, J. S. (2000). *Intercultural business communication* (2nd ed.). Upper Saddle River, NJ: Prentice Hall, p. 83.

25 Reardon, K. K. (1987). *Where minds meet.* Belmont, CA: Wadsworth, p. 199.

26 Sheer, V. C., & Chen, L. (2003, January). Successful Sino-Western business negotiation: Participants' accounts of national and professional cultures. *The Journal of Business Communication, 40*(1), 62; see also Luk, L., Patel, M., & White, K. (1990, December). Personal attributes of American and Chinese business associates. *The Bulletin of the Association for Business Communication,* 67.

27 Gallois, C., & Callan, V. (1997). *Communication and culture.* New York: Wiley, p. 24.

28 Jarvis, S. S. (1990, June). Preparing employees to work south of the border. *Personnel,* 763.

29 Gallois, C., & Callan, V. (1997). *Communication and culture.* New York: Wiley, p. 29.

30 Copeland, L., & Griggs, L. (1985). *Going international.* New York: Penguin, p. 94.

31 Copeland, L., & Griggs, L. (1985). *Going international.* New York: Penguin, p. 108.

32 Copeland, L., & Griggs, L. (1985). *Going international.* New York: Penguin, p. 12.

33 Copeland, J. (1990, December 15). Stare less, listen more. American Airlines: *American Way,* 32.

34 Singh, N., & Pereira, A. (2005). *The culturally customized Web site.* Burlington, MA: Elsevier Butterworth-Heinemann, pp. 139–148.

35 Singh, N., & Pereira, A. (2005). *The culturally customized Web site.* Burlington, MA: Elsevier Butterworth-Heinemann, pp. 139–148.

36 French, H. W. (2003, July 25). Japan's neglected resource: Female workers: Can Japan change? *The New York Times,* p. A3. See also DeCrow, K. (2003, August 20). Made in Japan: Outmoded cultural biases regarding women are hard to sink in the land of the rising sun. *Syracuse New Times,* p. 5.

37 Browning, E. S. (1994, May 3). Computer chip project brings rivals together, but the cultures clash. *The Wall Street Journal,* pp. A1, A11.

38 Zimmerman, A., & Fackler, M. (2003, September 13). Wal-Mart's foray into Japan spurs a retail upheaval. *The Wall Street Journal,* p. A1.

39 Belson, K. (2003, December 14). Wal-Mart hopes it won't be lost in translation, p. 12.

40 Belson, K. (2003, December 14). Wal-Mart hopes it won't be lost in translation. *The New York Times,* p. 12.

41 Martin, J. S., & Chaney, L. H. (2006). *Global business etiquette.* Westport, CT: Praeger, p. 69.

42 Hammer, M. R. (1993). Quoted in Chen and Starosta's *Foundations of intercultural communication,* p. 247.

43 Chaney, L. H., & Martin, J. S. (1995). *Intercultural business communication.* Englewood Cliffs, NJ: Prentice Hall Career and Technology, p. 67.

44 Weber, G. (2004, May). English rules. *Workforce Management,* 47–50.

45 *Do's and Taboos Around the World,* (2nd ed.). (1990). New York: Wiley, p. 7l.

46 Martin, J. S., & Chaney, L. H. (2006). *Global business etiquette.* Westport, CT: Praeger, p. 36.

47 Martin, J. S., & Chaney, L. H. (2006). *Global business etiquette.* Westport, CT: Praeger, p. 191.

48 Finney, P. B. (2005, May 17). Shaking hands, greasing palms. *The New York Times,* p. C1.

49 Berenbeim, R. (2000, May). Global ethics. *Executive Excellence,* 7.

50 Dorroh, J., & Saliba, A. (2003, June). Stay out of the shadows: Mexican companies, government move to improve business ethics and values. *Business Mexico, 13*(6), 42. Retrieved January 16, 2007, from InfoTrac College Edition database.

51 Finney, P. B. (2005, May 17). Shaking hands, greasing palms. *The New York Times,* p. C1.

52 Wei, S-J. (2003, March 12). Corruption in developing countries. *Global Economics.* Retrieved January 14, 2007, from http://brookings.org/views/speeches/wei/20030312.htm

53 Alvarez, S. (2006, December). Global integrity: Transparency International's David Nussbaum is fighting for a world that is free of bribery and corruption. *Internal Auditor, 63*(6), 53. Retrieved January 16, 2007, from InfoTrac College Edition database.

54 Hodgson, K. (1992, May). Adapting ethical decisions to a global marketplace. *Management Review,* 56.

55 Solomon, C. M. (1996, January). Put your ethics to a global test. *Personnel Journal,* 66–74. See also Smeltzer, L. R., & Jennings, M. M. (1998, January). Why an international code of business ethics would be good for business. *Journal of Business Ethics,* 57–66. See also Barker, T. S., & Cobb, S. L. (2000). A survey of ethics and cultural dimensions of MNCs [Multinational companies]. *Competitiveness Review, 10*(2), 123. Retrieved January 16, 2007, from InfoTrac College Edition database.

56 Hodgson, K. (1992, May). Adapting ethical decisions to a global marketplace, *Management Review,* 54.

57 Based on 2000 U.S. Census figures, as reported by Little, J. S., & Triest, R. K. (2001). Proceedings from the Federal Reserve Bank of Boston Conference Series. The impact of demographic change on U.S. labor markets. *Seismic shifts: The economic impact of demographic change.* Retrieved January 16, 2007, from http://www.bos.frb.org/economic/conf/conf46/conf46a.pdf

58 Hansen, F. (2003, April). Tracing the value of diversity programs. *Workforce,* 31.

59 Carbone, J. (2005, August 11). IBM says diverse suppliers are good for business. *Purchasing,* 27. Retrieved January 17, 2007, from InfoTrac College Edition database.

60 Neff, J. (1998, February 16). Diversity. *Advertising Age,* S1.

61 Terhune, C. (2005, April 19). Pepsi, vowing diversity isn't just image polish, seeks inclusive culture. *The Wall Street Journal,* p. B4.

62 Andre, R. (1995, June). Diversity stress as morality stress. *Journal of Business Ethics,* 489–496.

63 Based on Basow, S. A., & Rubenfeld, K. (2003, February). Troubles talk: Effects of gender and gender-typing. *Sex Roles: A Journal of Research,* 183. Retrieved January 17, 2007, from InfoTrac College Edition database; Wood, J. T. (2002). *Gendered lives.* Belmont, CA: Wadsworth, p. 119; Tear, J. (1995, November 20). They just don't understand gender dynamics. *The Wall Street Journal,* p. A12; Roiphe, A. (1994, October). Talking trouble. *Working Woman,* 28–31; Stuart, C. (1994, February). Why can't a woman be more like a man? *Training Tomorrow,* 22–24; and Wolfe, A. (1994, December 12). She just doesn't understand. *New Republic, 211*(24), 26–34.

64 Andre, R. (1995, June). Diversity stress as morality stress. *Journal of Business Ethics,* 489–496.

65 Schwartz, J., & Wald, M. L. (2003, March 9). Smart people working collectively can be dumber than the sum of their brains. Appeared originally in *The New York Times.* Retrieved March 6, 2007, from http://www.mindfully.org/Reform/2003/Smart-People-Dumber9mar03.htm

66 Capowski, G. (1996, June). Managing diversity. *Management Review*, 16.

67 Makower, J. (1995, Winter). Managing diversity in the workplace. *Business and Society Review*, 48–54.

68 Simons, G., & Dunham, D. (1995, December). Making inclusion happen. *Managing Diversity*. Retrieved January 17, 2007, from http://www.jalmc.org/mk-incl.htm

69 On the record: Frank Brown. (2007, January 22). *U.S. News & World Report*, 63.

70 Aylwin Lewis biography. (n.d.). Retrieved February 11, 2007, from Answers.com at http://www.answers.com/topic/aylwin-lewis

71 Rothrock, V. (2004, July 16). Culture clash. Retrieved January 23, 2007, from Business Source Premier (EBSCO) database.

72 Examples of cultural blunders made by U.S. businessmen. (1999, May 30). *Eagle Tribune*. Retrieved February 13, 2001, from http://www.eagletribune.com/news/stories/19990530/BU_002.htm

73 Fowler, G. A. (2004, December 7). China bans Nike's LeBron ad as offensive to nation's dignity. *The Wall Street Journal*, p. B4.

74 Cottrill, K. (2000, November 6). The world according to Hollywood. *Traffic World*, 15.

75 Conlin, M. (2007, April 23). Go-go-going to pieces in China. *BusinessWeek*, 88.

76 Thapanachai, S. (2003, October 6). Awareness narrows cross-cultural gap in Thai management training courses. *Bangkok Post*. Retrieved January 22, 2007, from InfoTrac College Edition database.

77 Dawson, D. K. (2005, March). At the top and still climbing. Retrieved January 22, 2007, from http://www.compositesworld.com/hpc/issues/2005/775; and Wucker, M. (1998, December/January). Keep on trekking. *Working Woman*, 32–36.

78 Based on Knotts, R. & Thibodeaux, M.S. (1992). Verbal skills in cross-culture managerial communication. *European Business Review*, 92(2), v–vii.

79 Martin, K., & Walsh, S. M. (1996, October). Beware the Foreign Corrupt Practices Act. *International Commercial Litigation*, 25–27.

80 Makower, J. (1995, Winter). Managing diversity in the workplace. *Business and Society Review*, 48–54.

81 Daniels, C. (2004, June 28). 50 best companies for minorities. *Fortune*, 138.

Chapter 4

1 Fabrikant, G. (2006, March 5). Cleaning up messages, friend to friend [Suze Orman]. *The New York Times*, p. BU5. Retrieved March 10, 2007, from InfoTrac College Edition database.

2 Grainger, D. (2003, June 16). The Suze Orman show. *Fortune*, 147(12), 82–88. Retrieved March 9, 2007, from Business Source Premier (EBSCO) database.

3 Erler, S. (2005, March 31). Suze Orman spills, signs books. *Times* (Munster, Indiana). Retrieved March 7, 2007, from InfoTrac College Edition database.

4 Gallo, C. (2001, June). Best presentations. Suze Orman. *BusinessWeek Online*. Retrieved March 11, 2007, from http://images.businessweek.com/ss/06/01/best_communicators/index_01.htm

5 Powell, E. (2003, November/December). Ten tips for better business writing. *Office Solutions*, 36; and Hay-Roe, H. (1995, January). The secret of excess. *Executive Excellence*, 20.

6 Based on Fichter, D. (2005, July/August). The many forms of e-collaboration: Blogs, wikis, portals, groupware, discussion boards, and instant messaging. *Online*, 29(4), 48–50. Retrieved January 28, 2007, from Business Source Premier (EBSCO) database.

7 Arnold, V. D. (1986, August). Benjamin Franklin on writing well. *Personnel Journal*, 17.

8 Bacon, M. (1988, April). Business writing: One-on-one speaks best to the masses. *Training*, 95. See also Danziger, E. (1998, February). Communicate up. *Journal of Accountancy*, 67.

9 Wallis, C., & Steptoe, S. (2006, January 26). The case for doing one thing at a time. *Time South Pacific* (Australia/New Zealand edition), issue 2, 50. Retrieved March 8, 2007, from Business Source Premier (EBSCO) database.

10 Wallis, C., & Steptoe, S. (2006, January 26). The case for doing one thing at a time. *Time South Pacific* (Australia/New Zealand edition), issue 2, 50. Retrieved March 8, 2007, from Business Source Premier (EBSCO) database.

11 Woolever, K. R. (1990, June 2). Corporate language and the law: Avoiding liability in corporate communications. *IEE Transactions on Professional Communication*, 95–98.

12 Woolever, K. R. (1990, June 2). Corporate language and the law: Avoiding liability in corporate communications. *IEE Transactions on Professional Communication*, 95–98.

13 Newark, N. A. (2005). Avoiding an "implied" employment contract or drafting a favorable one: A primer. *FindLaw*. Retrieved January 29, 2007, from http://library.findlaw.com/2005/Mar/2/157726.html; see also Jenner, L. (1994, March). Employment-at-will liability: How protected are you? *HR Focus*, 11.

14 Walter, R. J., & Sleeper, B. J. (2002, Spring). Employee recruitment and retention: When company inducements trigger liability. *Review of Business*, 17–23.

15 Pickens, J. E. (1985, August). Communication: Terms of equality: A guide to bias-free language. *Personnel Journal*, 5.

16 Armour, S. (2005, June 14). Warning: Your clever little blog could get you fired. *USA Today*. Retrieved January 30, 2007, from http://www.usatoday.com/money/workplace/2005-06-14-worker-blogs-usat_x.htm

17 Templeton, B. (2004, October). 10 big myths about copyright explained. Retrieved February 24, 2007, from http://www.templetons.com/brad/copy-myths.html

Chapter 5

1 O'Donnell, J., & Fetterman, M. (2007, January 24). Can Gap be saved? *USA Today*, B1.

2 O'Donnell, J., & Fetterman, M. (2007, January 24). Can Gap be saved? *USA Today*, B1.

3 O'Loughlin, S. (2006, November 20). Can Gap's ailing Old Navy concept right its ship? Retailer hires turnaround expert to get its 'fash' back on. *Brandweek*. Retrieved February 5, 2007, from InfoTrac College Edition database. See also Lee, L. (2007, February 26). Paul Pressler's fall from the Gap. *BusinessWeek*, 80.

4 Moin, D. (2006, July 12). Old Navy, at crossroads, to lose president. *WWD* [Women's Wear Daily]. Retrieved February 7, 2007, from InfoTrac College Edition database.

5 Merrick, A. (2006, November 27). Gap's crucial Christmas. *The Wall Street Journal*, p. C1.

6 Teschler, L. (2006, August 10). Brainstorming or just hot air? *Machine Design*, 78(15), 8. Retrieved February 7, 2007, from InfoTrac College Edition database. See also Furnham, A. (2000, Winter). The brainstorming myth. *Business Strategy Review*, 21–28.

7 Sutton, R. I. (2006, September 5). The truth about brainstorming. *BusinessWeek*, 17. Retrieved February 7, 2007, from InfoTrac College Edition database.

8 Based on information retrieved February 7, 2007, from http://www.gapinc.com

9 Rindegard, J. (1999, November 22). Use clear writing to show you mean business. *InfoWorld*, 78.

10 Working With Factories. (2007). Gap Inc. Retrieved February 6, 2007, from http://www.gapinc.com/public/SocialResponsibility/sr_fac_wwf.shtml

11 Factory Approval Process. (2007). Gap Inc. Retrieved February 6, 2007, from http://www.gapinc.com/public/SocialResponsibility/sr_fac_wwf_fap.shtml.

See also Merrick, A. (2004, May 12). Gap offers unusual look at factory conditions. *The Wall Street Journal*, p. A1.

12 Booher, D. (2001). *E-Writing*. New York: Pocket Books, p. 126; Elbow, P. (2004). The direct writing process for getting words on paper. In K. J. Harty (Ed.), *Strategies for business and technical writing* (5th ed.). New York: Pearson, Longman, pp. 21–25.

13 Goddard, R. W. (1989, April). Communication: Use language effectively. *Personnel Journal*, 32.

14 Toffler, B. L. quoted in Schmitt, R. B. (2002, November 5). Companies add ethics training; will it work? *The Wall Street Journal*, B1.

15 Mannes, G. (2006, September). Earning a degree in debt. *Money*, 35(9), 98–105. Retrieved February 23, 2007, from Business Source Premier (EBSCO) database. See also Kristof, K. M. (2003, September 14). More grads struggling to repay loans. *Los Angeles Times*, p. C3.

Chapter 6

1 Analysis of Yum! Brands Inc. (2007, February 13). *M2 Presswire*. Retrieved April 8, 2007, from InfoTrac College Edition database.

2 Wheaton, K. (2007, March 5). Yum Brands has a rat problem, but it will have customers, too. *Advertising Age*, 78(1), 4. Retrieved April 8, 2007, from Business Source Premier (EBSCO) database.

3 Lockyer, S. E. (2006, December 18). Yum to expand Taco Bell breakfast test. *Nation's Restaurant News*, 40(51), 3. Retrieved April 8, 2007, from InfoTrac College Edition database.

4 Lockyer, S. E. (2006, December 18). Yum to expand Taco Bell breakfast test. *Nation's Restaurant News*, 40(51), 3. Retrieved April 8, 2007, from InfoTrac College Edition database.

5 Cunneen, D. (2004, January 12). Recipe for success: Fast-food bigwigs vary strategies, menus to make it in 2004 market. *Nation's Restaurant News*, 30. Retrieved April 8, 2007, from http://calbears.findarticles.com/p/articles/mi_m3190/is_2_38/ai_112248145

6 Brumback, N. (1998, September 1). Yo quiero Mexican food. *Restaurant Business*, 43–44.

7 Elbow, P. (1998). *Writing with power: Techniques for mastering the writing process*. Oxford: Oxford University Press, p. 30.

8 Cook, C. K. (1985). *Line by line*. Boston: Houghton Mifflin, p. 17.

9 Dolezalek, H. (2005, September). The clarity challenge: For too long business writing has been a lifeless mass of jargon, obscurity and unnecessary chatter. *Training*, 42(9), 28.

10 Booher, D. (2001). *E-writing*. New York: Pocket Books, p. 148.

11 Neuharth, A. (1990, October 12). Why Washington is lost in the fog. *USA Today*, p. A13.

Chapter 7

1 About Qualcomm. Qualcomm Web site. Retrieved February 2, 2007, from http://www.Qualcomm.com; Qualcomm continues driving wireless innovation as catalyst for the mobile lifestyle. (2007, January 8). Retrieved January 31, 2007, from http://www.Qualcomm.com/press/releases/2007/070108_continues_driving_wireless.html

2 Fjeldheim, Norman. Senior Vice President and CIO, Qualcomm Incorporated (personal communication with Marlene Bellamy, January 30, 2007).

3 Fjeldheim, Norman. Senior Vice President and CIO, Qualcomm Incorporated (personal communication with Marlene Bellamy, January 30, 2007).

4 Sandberg, J. (2006, September 26). Employees forsake dreaded email for the beloved phone. *The Wall Street Journal*, p. B1.

5 Sandberg, J. (2006, September 26). Employees forsake dreaded email for the beloved phone. *The Wall Street Journal*, p. B1.

6 Maney, K. (2003, July 24). How the big names tame e-mail. *USA Today*, p. 2A.

7 Gillette reportedly deleted e-mail evidence: Proofpoint says this is the latest in a series of incidents in which e-mail is a smoking gun. (2005, May 12). *Information Week.* Retrieved May 2, 2007, from InfoTrac College Edition database; E-mail becoming crime's new smoking gun. (2002, August 15). *USA Today Marketplace.* Retrieved July 14, 2004, from http://www.usatoday.com/tech/news/2002-08-15

8 Goldsmith, M. (2007, May 16). Understanding the perils of e-mail. *BusinessWeek.* Retrieved May 20, 2007, from http://www.businessweek.com/careers/content/may2007/ca20070516_392697.htm?chan=rss_topEmailedStories_ssi_5

9 Varchaver, N., & Bonamici, K. (2003, February 17). The perils of e-mail. *Fortune, 147*(3), 66. Retrieved May 2, 2007, from Business Source Premier (EBSCO) database.

10 Employee e-mail use: Big brother may be watching. (2006, October 17). *Mondaq Business Briefing.* Retrieved May 2, 2007, from InfoTrac College Edition database.

11 Zetter, K. (2006, October). Employers crack down on person net use: Misusing e-mail or browsing the wrong sites can cost you your job. *PC World, 24*(10), 26. Retrieved May 3, 2007, from InfoTrac College Edition database.

12 Breaton, S. (2007, January/February). Blogging: Priceless? *CA Magazine,* 13. Retrieved May 2, 2007, from Business Source Premier (EBSCO) database.

13 Employers are cracking down on company e-mail misuse & abuse. (2006, August) *HR Focus,* 9.

14 E-mail policy. (2005, October). *Inc. 27*(10), 119–122.

15 Fjeldheim, Norman. Senior Vice President and CIO, Qualcomm Incorporated (personal communication with Marlene Bellamy, January 30, 2007).

16 Joyce, A. (2004, April 4). Getting the message—pronto. *Washington Post,* p. F06. Retrieved May 5, 2007, from http://www.washingtonpost.com/wp-dyn/articles/A46989-2004Apr3.html

17 Based on Shuit, D. P. (2003, September). Sound the retreat. *Workforce Management,* 39–40.

18 Based on Bee, L. M., & Maatman, G. M., Jr. (2004, January 26). E-mail abuse leaves firms exposed. *National Underwriter,* 27.

19 Lublin, J. S. (2001, March). You should negotiate a severance package—even before job starts. *The Wall Street Journal,* p. B1.

Chapter 8

1 Based on Freese, W. (2006). A letter from our CEO. Ben & Jerry's social environmental assessment report. Retrieved May 27, 2007, from http://www.benjerry.com/our_company/about_us/social_mission/social_audits/2005_sear/sear05_1.0.cfm; Brown, K. (2004, April 15). Chilling at Ben & Jerry's: Cleaner, greener. *The Wall Street Journal,* p. B1; Arnold, M. (2001, May 3). Is Ben & Jerry's losing its Bohemian appeal? *Marketing,* 17; and Ben & Jerry's goes cage-free and expands fair trade. (2006, October 20). *Ice Cream Reporter, 19*(11), 4. Retrieved May 27, 2007, from InfoTrac College Edition database.

2 Forbes, M. (1999). How to write a business letter. In K. Harty (Ed.), *Strategies for business and technical writing.* Boston: Allyn and Bacon, p. 108.

3 Fallows, J. (2005, June 12). Enough keyword searches. Just answer my question. *The New York Times,* p. BU3.

4 Messmer, M. (2001, January). Enhancing your writing skills. *Strategic Finance,* 8–10.

5 Blachly, A., Ben & Jerry's (personal communication with Mary Ellen Guffey, January 12, 1993).

6 Payne, D. R., Parry, B. L., Huff, S. C., Otto, S. D., & Hunt, K H. (2002). Consumer complimenting behavior: Exploration and elaboration. *Journal of Consumer Satisfaction, Dissatisfaction and Complaining Behavior, 15*(3), 128–148.

7 Hershberg, J. (2005, May). It's not just what you say. *Training, 42*(5), 50.

8 Aalberts, R. J., & Krajewski, L. A. (1987, September). Claim and adjustment letters: Theory versus practice and legal implications. *The Bulletin of the Association for Business Communication,* 5.

9 Andrews, M., & Kirshner, J. (2003, August 18). Cancel me! Really! I mean it! *U.S. News & World Report, 135*(5), 58. Retrieved June 3, 2007, from Business Source Premier (EBSCO) database.

10 Mascolini, M. (1994, June). Another look at teaching the external negative message. *The Bulletin of the Association of Business Communication,* 46; Aalberts, R. J., & Krajewski, L. A. (1987, September). Claim and adjustment letters. *The Bulletin of the Association for Business Communication,* 2.

11 Patel, A., & Reinsch, L. (2003, March). Companies *can* apologize: Corporate apologies and legal liability. *Business Communication Quarterly,* 9.

12 Davidow, M. (2003, February). Organizational responses to customer complaints: What works and what doesn't. *Journal of Service Research, 5*(3) 31. Retrieved June 3, 2007, from Business Source Premier (EBSCO) database; Blackburn-Brockman, E., & Belanger, K. (1993, June). You-attitude and positive emphasis: Testing received wisdom in business communication. *The Bulletin of the Association for Business Communication,* 1–5; Goodwin, C., & Ross, I. (1990). Consumer evaluations of responses to complaints: What's fair and why. *Journal of Consumer Marketing* vol.1, 39–47; 7, 39–47; Mascolini, M. (1994, June). Another look at teaching the external negative message. *The Bulletin of the Association for Business Communication,* 46.

13 Liao, H. (2007, March). Do it right this time: The role of employee service recovery performance in customer-perceived justice and customer loyalty after service failures. *Journal of Applied Psychology, 92*(2), 475. Retrieved June 3, 2007, from Business Source Premier (EBSCO) database; Gilbert, P. (1996, December). Two words that can help a business thrive. *The Wall Street Journal,* p. A12.

14 Martin, J. S., & Chaney, L. H. (2006). *Global business etiquette.* Westport, CT: Praeger, p. 150.

15 Haneda, S., & Hirosuke, S. (1982). Japanese communication behavior as reflected in letter writing. *The Journal of Business Communication,* Vol. 1, 29. See also Varner, I., & Beamer, L. (2001). *Intercultural communication.* Chicago: McGraw-Hill Irwin, pp. 131–132.

16 Martin, J. S., & Chaney, L. H. (2006). *Global business etiquette.* Westport, CT: Praeger, p. 159.

17 Loewy, D., German interpreter (personal communication with Mary Ellen Guffey, July 2007).

18 Luciani-Samec, A., French instructor, & Samec, P. French businessman (personal communication with Mary Ellen Guffey, May 1995).

19 Caddell, M. H. (2003, November/December). Is letter writing dead? *OfficePro,* 22.

20 Fallows, J. (2005, June 12). Enough keyword searches. Just answer my question. *The New York Times,* p. BU3.

21 Based on Burbank, L. (2006, March 30). Read cruise lines' fine print. *USA Today,* p. 4D.

22 Based on Scarp, M. J. (1995, October 28). Hotel to cease pigeon poisoning. *Scottsdale Tribune.*

23 Olson, E. (2004, April 22). When the check in the mail is a bill. *The New York Times,* p. C5.

Chapter 9

1 Betancourt, C. M. (1999, November 28). Head of Make-A-Wish chapter is a man with many missions. *The Miami Herald,* p. B1.

2 Morris, P., president and CEO, Hands on Miami (personal communication with Mary Ellen Guffey, August 2, 2006).

3 Hamilton, C. (2005). *Communicating for results* (7th ed.). Belmont, CA: Wadsworth/Thomson, p. 334.

4 Hoar, R. (2005, March 1). Be more persuasive. *Management Today,* 56.

5 Cialdini, R. B. (1993). *Influence: The power of persuasion.* New York: Quill, William Morrow, p. 238.

6 Fracaro, K. E. (2004, August). Managing by persuasion. *Contract Management, 44*(8), 4. Retrieved December 28, 2006, from InfoTrac College Edition database.

7 Newman, R. (2006, September 25). Lessons from the rule breakers. *U.S. News & World Report,* Executive Edition, 4.

8 Pollock, T. (2003, June). How to sell an idea. *Supervision, 64*(6), 15. Retrieved December 28, 2006, from InfoTrac College Edition database.

9 Communicating with the boss. (2006, May). *Communication Briefings,* p. 8.

10 Friesen, P. (2003, October). Customer testimonials. *Target Marketing,* 137.

11 Tyson, E. (2004, February 1). Direct mail success strategies, *Circulation Management, 19*(2). Retrieved December 29, 2006, from InfoTrac College Edition database.

12 McLaughlin, K. (1990, October). Words of wisdom. *Entrepreneur,* 101. See also Wastphal, L. (2001, October). Empathy in sales letters. *Direct Marketing,* 55.

13 Consumer complaints about vital basics—Focus factor. Retrieved September 17, 2006, from http://www.consumeraffairs.com/nutrition/vital.html

14 Loathing of mail and web activity on rise. (2006, April 28). *Precision Marketing,* 2.

15 Suited for employment. (2005, July 15). *The Chronicle of Higher Education,* p. A8.

16 Yancey, K. B. (2006, September 2). Hotels give guests a hand with GPS. *USA Today,* p. 1D.

17 Zbar, J. D. (2001, March). Training to telework. *Home Office Computing,* 72.

18 PDA-based software allows realtors to show homes practically anywhere. Retrieved September 18, 2006, from http://www.pdare.com/vertical/articles/article-460.xml

19 Based on Marquez, J. (2006, January 16). On-site blood testing raises privacy issues. *Workplace Management,* 10.

20 Based on DuFrene, D. D. & Lehman, C. M. (2002, March). Persuasive appeal for clean language. *Business Communication Quarterly, 65*(1), 48–55.

21 Terlep, S. (2005, December 27). Employees told: Lose weight, cash in. *Detroit News Online.* Retrieved September 17, 2006, from http://www.detnews.com/apps/pbcs.dll/article?AID=/20051227/LIFESTYLE03/512270349/1040/LIFESTYLE

22 Based on Yunxia, Z. (2000, December). Building knowledge structures in teaching cross-cultural sales genres. *Business Communication Quarterly, 63*(4), 66–67.

23 Based on Fritscher-Porter, K. (2003, June/July). Don't be duped by office supply scam artists. *OfficePro,* 9–10.

Chapter 10

1 Discussion of Southwest Airlines based on Bailey, J. (2007, March 18). Airlines learn to fly on a wing and an apology. *The New York Times,* p. 1.1. Retrieved from ProQuest database; Marta, S. (2007, March 5) Southwest plumps its image as other airlines cut amenities. *Dallas Morning News.* Retrieved March 7, 2007, from Infotrac database; McGregor, J., Jespersen, F., Tucker, M., & Foust, D. (2007, March 5) Customer service champs. *BusinessWeek, 4024,* 52–64; Miller, L. (2007, March 6). More travelers suffered long runway waits last year. *San Diego Union-Tribune,* p. A5.

2 American Management Association. 2004 Survey on workplace e-mail and IM reveals unmanaged risks. (2004). Retrieved June 10, 2007, from http://www.amanet.org/press/amanews/im_survey.htm

3 McCord, E. A. (1991, April). The business writer, the law, and routine business communication: A legal and rhetorical analysis. *Journal of Business and Technical Communication,* 183.

4 McCord, E. A. (1991, April). The business writer, the law, and routine business communication: A legal

and rhetorical analysis. *Journal of Business and Technical Communication*, 183.

⁵ Shuit, D. P. (2003, September). Do it right or risk getting burned. *Workforce Management*, 80.

⁶ Brodkin, J. (2007, March 19). Corporate apologies don't mean much. *Networkworld*, 24(11), 8. PDF file retrieved June 6, 2007, from Business Source Premier (EBSCO) database.

⁷ Schweitzer, M. E. (2006, December). Wise negotiators know when to say "I'm sorry." *Negotiation*, 4. PDF file retrieved June 6, 2007, from Business Source Premier (EBSCO) database.

⁸ Brodkin, J. (2007, March 19). Rating apologies. *Networkworld*, 24(11), 14. PDF file retrieved June 6, 2007, from Business Source Premier (EBSCO) database.

⁹ Neeleman, D. (2007). An apology from David Neeleman. Retrieved June 10, 2007, from http://www.jetblue.com/about/ourcompany/apology/index.html

¹⁰ Letters to Lands' End. (1991, February). 1991 Lands' End Catalog. Dodgeville, WI: Lands' End, 100.

¹¹ Mowatt, J. (2002, February). Breaking bad news to customers. *Agency Sales*, 30; and Dorn, E. M. (1999, March). Case method instruction in the business writing classroom. *Business Communication Quarterly*, 62(1), 51–52.

¹² Forbes, M. (1999). How to write a business letter. In K. Harty (Ed.), *Strategies for business and technical writing*. Boston: Allyn and Bacon, p. 108.

¹³ Harris, D. (2004, July 5). Court: Dealerships need not repeat a lender's credit rejection notice. *Automotive News*, 78(6101), 18. Retrieved June 10, 2007, from InfoTrac College Edition database.

¹⁴ Mainz, C. (2005, June). Southwest Star of the Month: Fred Taylor. *Spirit*. Retrieved March 8, 2007, from http://www.southwest.com/careers/stars/star_jun05.html; McGregor, J., Jespersen, F., Tucker, M., & Foust, D. (2007, March 5). Customer service champs. Retrieved June 10, 2007, from http://www.businessweek.com/magazine/content/07_10/b4024001.htm

¹⁵ Browning, M. (2003, November 24). Work dilemma: Delivering bad news a good way. *Government Computer News*, p. 41; and Mowatt, J. (2002, February). Breaking bad news to customers. *Agency Sales*, 30.

¹⁶ Browning, M. (2003, November 24). Work dilemma: Delivering bad news a good way. *Government Computer News*, p. 41; and Lewis, B. (1999, September 13). To be an effective leader, you need to perfect the art of delivering bad news. *InfoWorld*, 124.

¹⁷ Gilsdorf, J. W. (1997, June). Metacommunication effects on international business negotiating in China. *Business Communication Quarterly*, 60(2), 27.

¹⁸ Beamer, L., & Varner, I. (2001). *Intercultural communication in the global workplace*. New York: McGraw Hill Irwin, 141.

¹⁹ Conaway, R. N., & Wardrope, W. J. (2004, December). Communication in Latin America. *Business Communication Quarterly*, 67(4), 472.

²⁰ Our involvement with the community. Southwest Airlines corporate Web site. Retrieved March 7, 2007, from http://www.southwest.com/about_swa/share_the_spirit/share_the_spirit.html

²¹ Based on Lee, L. (2007, June 11). A smoothie you can chew on. *BusinessWeek*, 64.

²² Based on Sloan, G. (1996, November 29). Under 21? Carnival says cruise is off. *USA Today*; Sieder, J. J. (1995, October 16). Full steam ahead: Carnival Cruise Line makes boatloads of money by selling fun. *U.S. News & World Report*, 72; and About Carnival Cruise Line. Retrieved July 27, 2004, from http://www.cruisecritic./reviews/cruiseline.cfm?CruiseLineID=9

²³ Based on Burbank, L. (2007, June 8). Personal items can be swept away between flights. *USA Today*, p. 3D.

²⁴ Sorkin, A. R. (1999, November). J. Crew web goof results in discount. *The New York Times*, p. D3.

²⁵ Based on O Harari, H. (1999, July-August). The power of complaints. *Management Review*, 31.

²⁶ Based on SUV surprise. (2004, June 15). *The Wall Street Journal*, p. W7.

²⁷ Osborn, A. (2002, August 24). New from McDonald's: The McAfrika burger (Don't tell the 12m starving). *The Guardian*. Retrieved June 16, 2007, from http://www.guardian.co.uk/famine/story/0,12128,780028,00.html

²⁸ Mishory, J. (2008, June). Don't shoot the messenger: How to deliver bad news and still keep customers satisfied. *Sales and Marketing Management*, 18.

²⁹ Cahill, T. (2002, September 17). Bear Stearns tells employees to dress up—Dot com is over. Bloomberg News Service; Bear Stearns reinstates formal dress code. (2002, September 21). Reuters Business Report; and Dress codes: 'Business conservative' is making a comeback. (2003, March 1). *HR Briefing*, 7.

Chapter 11

¹ Bingham, L. (2004, April 1). Building buzz: Word of mouth a key benefit of experiential marketing. Retrieved November 19, 2006, from http://www.jackmorton.com/360/market_focus/march04_mf.asp

² Lee Jeans One True Fit BzzCampaign: Women declare BzzAgent and Lee Jeans a perfect fit. (2004). Case Study. Retrieved June 28, 2007, from http://www.bzzagent.com/downloads/BzzAgent_Lee_CaseStudy.pdf

³ Gadson, D. (1999-2006). Product review: Lee One True Fit Jeans. *Urban Beauty Online*. Retrieved November 19, 2006, from http://www.urbanbeautyonline.com/product-review-lotfj

⁴ Tischler, L. (2004, May). What's the buzz? *Fast Company*, 76–77.

⁵ D. Balter, CEO, BzzAgent (personal communication with James M. Dubinsky, June 14, 2004).

⁶ D. Balter, CEO, BzzAgent (personal communication with James M. Dubinsky, June 11, 2004).

⁷ Questions for David McCullough. (2006, July 7). *Workforce Management*, p. 9.

⁸ Balter, D. (2004). Honesty. *BzzAgent Welcome Kit*, 6.

⁹ Madden, M. (2006, April). Internet penetration and impact. *Pew Internet & American Life Project*, 1. Retrieved June 26, 2007, from http://www.pewinternet.org/pdfs/PIP_Internet_Impact.pdf

¹⁰ Netcraft, Ltd., *November 2006 Web Server Survey*. Retrieved June 28, 2007, from http://news.netcraft.com/archives/web_server_survey.html

¹¹ Patterson, A. (2005, September 26). We wanted something special for our birthday. Retrieved June 28, 2007, from http://googleblog.blogspot.com/2005/09/we-wanted-something-special-for-our.html; and Google has 24 billion items index, considers MSN Search nearest competitor. (2005, September 27). Retrieved June 28, 2007, from http://www.tnl.net/blog/2005/09/27/google-has-24-billion-items-index-considers-msn-search-nearest-competitor/

¹² Little, L. (2006, March 7). Using a multiple search. *The Wall Street Journal*, p. D1. Retrieved November 23, 2006, from Factiva database.

¹³ Brennan, M., & Holdershaw, J. (1999). The effect of question tone and form on responses to open-ended questions: Further data. *Marketing Bulletin*, 57–64.

¹⁴ Goldsmith, B. (2002, June). The awesome power of asking the right questions. *OfficeSolutions*, 52; and Bracey, G. W. (2001, November). Research-question authority. *Phi Delta Kappan*, 191.

¹⁵ Jameson, D. (1993, June). The ethics of plagiarism: How genre affects writers' use of source materials. *The Bulletin of the Association for Business Communication*, 18.

¹⁶ Bartlett, T. (2006, September 8). Professor faces firing for plagiarism. *Chronicle of Higher Education*, p. 11. Retrieved November 21, 2006, from Academic Search Elite database.

¹⁷ Writing Tutorial Services, Indiana University. *Plagiarism: What it is and how to recognize and avoid it*. Retrieved November 5, 2006, from http://www.indiana.edu/~wts/pamphlets/plagiarism.shtml

¹⁸ Brady, D. (2006, December 4). *!#?@ the e-mail. Can we talk? *BusinessWeek*, 109.

¹⁹ BzzAgents BitLucky & Grace4utwo. (2004). Lee Jeans One True BzzCampaign: Women declare BzzAgent and Lee a perfect fit, 4. Retrieved June 28, 2007, from http://www.bzzagent.com/downloads/BzzAgent_Lee_CaseStudy.pdf

²⁰ Spake, A. (2003, November 17). Hey kids! We've got sugar and toys. *U.S. News & World Report*, 62.

²¹ Iwata, E. (2003, November 20). Blackout report faults Ohio utility. *USA Today*, p. 1A.

²² Hibbard, J. (2006, October 9). How Yahoo! gave itself a face-lift. *BusinessWeek*, 77.

²³ Goldman, A. (2006, December 1). Wal-Mart limps into the holidays. *Los Angeles Times*, p. C4.

²⁴ Edwards, C., & Ihlwan, M. (2006, December 4). Upward mobility. *BusinessWeek*, 68–82.

²⁵ 694 million people currently use the Internet worldwide according to comScore Networks. (2006, May 4). Retrieved June 28, 2007, from http://www.comscore.com/press/release.asp?press=849

²⁶ Naughton, K. (2006, July 3). Corporate giant. *Newsweek*, 74. Retrieved June 28, 2007, from Business Source Premier (EBSCO) database.

²⁷ King, J. E., & American Council on Education. (2006, July). Credit card ownership and behavior among traditional-age undergraduates, 2003-04, 1. Retrieved June 28, 2007, from http://www.acenet.edu/AM/Template.cfm?Section=InfoCenter&CONTENTID=17323&TEMPLATE=/CM/ContentDisplay.cfm

Chapter 12

¹ Case study based on Bramhall, J. (2007, January 1). Starbucks. *Hoover's Company Records*, 15745. Retrieved January 9, 2007, from ProQuest database; Overholt, A. (2004, July). Listening to Starbucks. *Fast Company*, 53; Serwer, A. (2004, January 26). Hot Starbucks to go. *Fortune*, 68; Brown, A. (2004, August). What's brewing at Starbucks? *Black Enterprise*, 25; and ElBoghdady, D. (2002, August 25). The Starbucks strategy? Locations, locations, locations. *The Washington Post*, p. H1.

² Case study based on Wayne, L. (2007, February 24). Starbucks chairman fears tradition is fading. *The New York Times*, p. 3. Retrieved March 4, 2007, from LexisNexis database.

³ Ewing, J. (2007, May 4). First mover in mobile: How Nokia is selling cell phones to the developing world. *BusinessWeek Online*. Retrieved June 5, 2007, from http://www.businessweek.com/

⁴ Woodruff, D. (2007, January 1). FedEx Corporation. *Hoover's Company Records*, 10552. Retrieved January 10, 2007, from ProQuest database; Europe view: Transport a bear for Russia. (2004, April 21). *The Journal of Commerce Online*, 1; FedEx rolls out Europe LTL. (2002, December 18). *The Journal of Commerce Online*, 1; Hawkins, C. (1992, May 25). FedEx: Europe nearly killed the messenger. *BusinessWeek*, 124–126.

⁵ Overholt, A. (2004, July). Listening to Starbucks. *Fast Company*, 50–56.

⁶ Serwer, A. (2004, January 26). Hot Starbucks to go, *Fortune*, 68.

⁷ Tagliabue, J. (2006, December 26). Taking on Starbucks, Italian coffee maker steps up to the bar. *The New York Times*, p. C1.

⁸ Gunderson, L. (2006, September 15). Once feisty Coffee People whipped into Starbucks. *The Oregonian*. Retrieved March 11, 2007, from http://www.oregonlive.com/business/oregonian/index.ssf?/base/business/1158290703132110.xml&coll=7

⁹ Aeppel, T. (2000, November 20). Firestone recall fuels interest in "smart" tires. *The Wall Street Journal*, p. B1.

¹⁰ NissanNews (2007, March 7). New corporate facility to be called Nissan Americas. Retrieved March 23,

2007, from http://www.nissannews.com/corporate/news/current/20070307112818.shtml; Bernard, B. (2005, November 10). Nissan is coming to Tennessee starting next summer: $70 million headquarters on tap for 2008. *Tennessean.com.* Retrieved March 23, 2007, from http://www.tennessean.com/apps/pbcs.dll/article?AID=/20051110/BUSINESS01/51110004

[11] Case based on Kiley, D. (2006, May 1). Howard Schultz looking for his next act: Maybe he's found it at the movies. *BusinessWeek Online.* Retrieved January 13, 2007, from http://www.businessweek.com; Holmes, S. (2005, June 20). Strong lattes, sour notes. *BusinessWeek*, pp. 58–60. Retrieved January 11, 2007, from EBSCO database; Schultz, H. D. (2005, July 4). Readers' report: Starbucks' founder on innovation in the music biz. *BusinessWeek Online.* Retrieved January 13, 2007, from http://www.businessweek.com

[12] Schultz, H. D. (2005, July 4). Readers' Report: Starbucks' founder on innovation in the music biz. *BusinessWeek Online.* Retrieved March 23, 2007, from http://www.businessweek.com

[13] Overholt, A. (2004, July). Listening to Starbucks. *Fast Company*, 50–56.

[14] Red light camera reform (2003, May/June). *WestWays*, 19.

[15] Roberts, D., Engardio, P., Bernstein, A., Holmes, S., & Ji, X. (2006, November 27). Secrets, lies, and sweatshops. *BusinessWeek Online.* Retrieved March 23, 2007, from http://www.businessweek.com

[16] Berenson, A. (2004, June 8). Federal Reserve says banks can continue overdraft plans. *The New York Times*, p. C1.

[17] Based on Witt, B. Ensuring "bounce-proof" overdraft privilege. (2003, May). *Credit Union Magazine*, 84; Webster, W. (2003, July 21). Race to the bottom. *Forbes*, 74; and Cocheo, S. (2003, April). Follow the bouncing check. *ABA Banking Journal*, 32.

[18] This assignment is based on a case study, "Excel Industries, Inc." by James S. O'Rourke, IV, and is used by permission. Copyright: 1995. Revised: 2005. University of Notre Dame. All rights reserved.

Chapter 13

[1] Based on Grinyard, M., Raytheon proposal consultant (personal communication with Mary Ellen Guffey, July 23, 2007).

[2] Piecewicz, M., Hewlett-Packard proposal manager (personal communication with Mary Ellen Guffey, January 12, 1999).

[3] Development of tourism marketing strategy and recommendations for promoting Federal Way as a tourist destination: Request for proposals. (2006, June 2). Retrieved July 2, 2007, from http://www.cityoffederalway.com

[4] Fried, D. M., & Falk, J. S. (2006, December). Toll road update. Chadbourne & Parke LLP. Retrieved July 2, 2007, from http://www.chadbourne.com/

[5] MasterPlans: Professional Business Plan Writers. (n. d.). Rapid development cycle. Retrieved July 12, 2007, from MasterPlans Web site: http://www.masterplans.com

[6] Turner, M. L. (2007). Guide to business plan consultants: Hiring help is the next best thing to writing your plan yourself. Work.com. Retrieved July 3, 2007, from http://www.work.com/business-plan-consultants-880/

[7] Nelson, F. (2004, September 5). Device from UCSB trio ready to take its first breath. *Santa Barbara News-Press*, p. F1.

Chapter 14

[1] Based on combined attendance figures of Tokyo Disneyland and adjacent Tokyo DisneySea as reported in Niles, R. (2007, March 4). 2006 theme park attendance data released (finally!). *Theme Park Insider.* Retrieved July 20, 2007, from http://www.themeparkinsider.com/flume/200704/320/

[2] Georges, J. (personal communication with Mary Ellen Guffey, February 3, 1999). Other information from Ho, D. (2006, February 15). Hong Kong Disneyland. *BusinessWeek Online.* Retrieved July 20, 2007, from http://www.businessweek.com; and Bradsher, K. (2004, October 12). Disney is tailoring new park to fit Hong Kong sensitivities. *The New York Times*, p. W1; Tokyo Disneyland, Disneysea log record visitors in FY03. (2004, April 2). *AsiaPulse News*; Business: Welcome to Bankruptcyland; Theme-parks in Japan. (2003, April 5). *The Economist*, 69; and Emmons, N. (2001, July 18). Tokyo Disneyland offers tix. *Amusement Business*, 23.

[3] Hooey, B. (2005). Speaking for success! Speaking success. Retrieved July 17, 2007, from Toastmasters International Web site http://members.shaw.ca/toasted/speaking_succes.htm

[4] Wharton Applied Research Center. (1981). A study of the effects of the use of overhead transparencies on business meetings, final report cited in Visual Being Blog Archive. (2005, July 14). The 1981 Wharton study. Retrieved July 17, 2007, from http://www.visualbeing.com

[5] Lewis, A. (2005, July 5). So many meetings, so little point, *The Denver Post*, p. C1. Retrieved July 18, 2007, from LexisNexis database; and Paradi, D. (2003). Are we wasting $250 million per day due to bad PowerPoint? Retrieved July 18, 2007, from Think Outside The Slide Web site http://thinkoutsidetheslide.com

[6] Stanford communication professor Clifford Nass quoted in Simons, T. (2001, July). When was the last time PowerPoint made you sing? *Presentations*, 6. See also Geoffrey Nunberg, G. (1999, December 20). The trouble with PowerPoint. *Fortune*, 330–334.

[7] ThinkFree Office 3 and PodPresenter now available online. (2006, March 27). *Market Wire.* Retrieved July 18, 2007, from www.marketwire.com.

[8] Bajaj, G. (2006, November 22). Impatica ShowMate. Retrieved July 18, 2007, from http://www.indezine.com

[9] Booher, D. (2003). *Speak with confidence: Powerful presentations that inform, inspire, and persuade.* New York: McGraw-Hill Professional, p. 126. For more detailed information on the use of color in presentations, go to http://www.indezine.com/ideas/prescolors.html

[10] Bates, S. (2005). *Speak like a CEO: Secrets for commanding attention and getting results.* New York: McGraw-Hill Professional, p. 113.

[11] Bergells, L. (2007, May 2). Top nine visual clichés. *Maniactive.com Blog.* Retrieved July 18, 2007, from http://www.maniactive.com; See also: How to avoid the 7 deadly sins of PowerPoint. (2004, July 30). *Yearbook of Experts News Release Wire,* Retrieved October 11, 2004, from LexisNexis Academic database.

[12] Burrows, P., Grover, R., & Green, H. (2006, February 6). Steve Jobs' magic kingdom. *BusinessWeek*, 62. Retrieved July 18, 2007, from http://www.businessweek.com; see also Gallo, C. (2006, April 6). How to wow 'em like Steve Jobs. *BusinessWeek.* Retrieved July 18, 2007, from http://www.businessweek.com

[13] See the PowerPoint preshow checklist at http://www.tlccreative.com/images/tutorials/PreShowChecklist.pdf

[14] Ellwood, J. (2004, August 4). Less PowerPoint, more powerful points, *The Times* (London), p. 6.

[15] Ozer, J. (2006, January 11). Ovation for PowerPoint. *PC Magazine.* Retrieved July 18, 2007, from http://www.pcmag.com/article2/0,1759,1921436,00.asp; See more information at http://www.adobe.com/products/ovation/

[16] For more information, go to http://www.turningtechnologies.com, http://www.audienceresponse.com, or http://www.optiontechnologies.com

[17] Boeri, R. J. (2002, March). Fear of flying? Or the mail? Try the Web conferencing cure. *Emedia Magazine*, 49.

[18] Booher, D. (2003). *Speak with confidence.* New York: McGraw-Hill Professional, p. 14; and Booher, D. (1991). *Executive's portfolio of model speeches for all occasions.* Englewood Cliffs, NJ: Prentice Hall, p. 259.

[19] Edmondson, G. (2006, October 16). The secret of BMW's success. *BusinessWeek Online.* Retrieved July 17, 2007, from www.businessweek.com

[20] Peterson, R. (n. d.). Presentations: Are you getting paid for overtime? Presentation Coaching Institute. Retrieved July 29, 2007, from http://passociates.com; The sales presentation: The bottom line is selling. (2001, March 14). *Marken Communications.* Retrieved July 29, 2007, from http://www.markencom.com

[21] Schneider, P. (2001, August 12). Scenes from a marriage: Observations on the Daimler-Chrysler merger from a German living in America. *The New York Times Magazine*, 47.

[22] Wunderle, W. (2007, March/April). How to negotiate in the Middle East. The U.S. Army Professional Writing Collection. Retrieved July 20, 2007, from U.S. Army Home Page http://www.army.mil; Dulek, R. E., Fielden, J. S., & Hill, J. S. (1991, January/February). International communication: An executive primer. *Business Horizons*, 23. See also Marks, S. J. (2001, September). Nurturing global workplace connections. *Workforce*, 76.

[23] Brandel, M. (2006, February 20). Sidebar: Don't be the ugly American. *Computerworld.* Retrieved July 20, 2007, from http://www.computerworld.com

[24] Dulek, R. E., Fielden, J. S., & Hill, J. S. (1991, January/February). International communication: An executive primer. *Business Horizons*, 22.

[25] Davidson, R., & Rosen, M. Cited in Brandel, M. (2006, February 20). Sidebar: Don't be the ugly American. *Computerworld.* Retrieved July 20, 2007, from http://www.computerworld.com

[26] Burge, J. (2002, June). Telephone safety protocol for today. *The National Public Accountant*, 35.

[27] Vergano, D. (2004, August 31). Computers: Scientific friend or foe? *USA Today*, p. D6.

[28] Jackson, M., quoted in Garbage In, Garbage Out. (1992, December). *Consumer Reports*, 755.

Chapter 15

[1] Ryan, L. (2007). Online job searching. *BusinessWeek online.* Video interview retrieved July 10, 2007, from http://feedroom.businessweek.com/?fr_story=5e1ec1bacf73ae689d381f30e80dfea30cd52108&rf=rss

[2] Ryan, L. (2007). Ten tips for a new grad's job search. *Ezine Articles.* Retrieved July 13, 2007, from http://ezinearticles.com/?Ten-Tips-for-a-New-Grads-Job-Search&id=116937

[3] Ryan, L. (2007, June 11). Résumé fibs: What's the story? Retrieved July 13, 2007, from LinkedIn at http://linkedin.com/in/lizryan

[4] Jansen, J. (2003). What's keeping you from changing careers? Retrieved July 8, 2007, from http://www.careerjournal.com/jobhunting/change/20030225-jansen.html. Article adapted from Jansen, J. (2003) *I don't know what I want, but I know it's not this: A step-by-step guide to finding gratifying work.* New York: Penguin Books.

[5] O'Connell, B. (2003). *The career survival guide.* New York: McGraw-Hill, pp. 11–12.

[6] Kimmitt, R. M. (2007, January 23). Why job churn is good. *The Washington Post*, p. A17. Retrieved July 14, 2007, from http://www.washingtonpost.com/wp-dyn/content/article/2007/01/22/AR2007012201089.html

[7] Farquharson, L. (2003, September 16). Technology special report: The best way to find a job. *The Wall Street Journal.* Retrieved July 16, 2007, from http://www.taleo.com/news/media/pdf/74En_20030916_WallStreetJournal.pdf

8 Top job boards. (2006, November/December). *Office Pro, 66*(8), 5. Retrieved July 15, 2007, from Business Source Premier (EBSCO) database.

9 Pont. J. (2005, November 7). Leading job boards address challenges of globalization, overabundance of responses. *Workforce Management*, 49.

10 Farquharson, L. (2003, September 16). Technology special report: The best way to find a job. *The Wall Street Journal*. Retrieved July 16, 2007, from http://www.taleo.com/news/media/pdf/74En_20030916_WallStreetJournal.pdf

11 Wells, S. J. (1998, March 12). Many jobs on Web. *The New York Times*, p. A12.

12 Lancaster, H. (1995, February). When taking a tip from a job network, proceed with caution. *The Wall Street Journal*, p. B1.

13 Shedden, M. (2006, September 30). Career fairs still help in the job search. *Tampa Tribune* (Tampa, FL). Retrieved July 15, 2007, from InfoTrac College Edition database.

14 Brown, J., Cober, R. T., Kane, K., Levy, P. E., & Shalhoop, J. (2006). Proactive personality and the successful job search: A field investigation with college graduates. *Journal of Applied Psychology, 91*(3), 717–726. Retrieved July 15, 2007, from Business Source Premier (EBSCO) database.

15 Koeppel, D. (2006, December 31). Those low grades in college may haunt your job search. *The New York Times*, p. 1. Retrieved July 15, 2007, from InfoTrac College Edition database.

16 Shedden, M. (2006, September 30). Career fairs still help in the job search. *Tampa Tribune* (Tampa, FL). Retrieved July 15, 2007, from InfoTrac College Edition database.

17 Wright, C. (2004, September 30). Networking the No. 1 way to find a job. *Chattanooga Times Free Press* (Tennessee), p. E6.

18 Korkki, P. (2007, July 1). So easy to apply, so hard to be noticed. *The New York Times*, p. BU YT 16.

19 Résumé styles: Chronological versus functional? Best-selling author Richard H. Beatty joins in the résumé discussion. (2002, November 5). Retrieved July 21, 2007, from http://www.medzilla.com/press11502.html

20 Blackburn-Brockman, E., & Belanger, K. (2001, January). One page or two: A national study of CPA recruiters' preferences for résumé length. *The Journal of Business Communication, 38*(1), 29–57.

21 Isaacs, K. (2007). How to decide on résumé length. Retrieved July 21, 2007, from http://www.resumepower.com/resume-length.html

22 Hansen, K. (2007). Should you use a career objective on your résumé? Retrieved July 21, 2007, from http://www.quintcareers.com/resume_objectives

.html; and Half, R. (2007). Some résumé objectives do more harm than good. Retrieved July 21, 2007, from http://www.careerjournal.com/jobhunting/resumes/19971231-half3.html

23 Korkki, P. (2007, July 1). So easy to apply, so hard to be noticed. *The New York Times*, p. BU YT 16.

24 Build the résumé employers want. (n.d.). Retrieved July 21, 2007, from http://www.jobweb.com/resources/library/Interviews

25 Washington, T. (2007). Effective résumés bring results to life. Retrieved July 21, 2007, from http://www.careerjournal.com/jobhunting/resumes/20000913-washington.html

26 Ryan, L. (2007). Online job searching. *BusinessWeek online*. Video interview retrieved July 10, 2007, from http://feedroom.businessweek.com/?fr_story=5e1ec1bacf73ae689d381f30e80dfea30cd52108&rf=rss

27 Ryan, L. (2007). Online job searching. *BusinessWeek online*. Video interview retrieved July 10, 2007, from http://feedroom.businessweek.com/?fr_story=5e1ec1bacf73ae689d381f30e80dfea30cd52108&rf=rss

28 The Video Résumé Technique. (2007). Retrieved July 20, 2007, from http://www.collegegrad.com/jobsearch/Guerrilla-Insider-Techniques/The-Video-Résumé-Technique

29 Kidwell, R. E., Jr. (2004, May). 'Small' lies, big trouble: The unfortunate consequences of résumé padding from Janet Cooke to George O'Leary. *Journal of Business Ethics, 51*(2), 175–184.

30 Rigdon, J. E. (1992, June 17). Deceptive resumes can be door-openers but can become an employee's undoing. *The Wall Street Journal*, p. B1. See also Solomon, B. (1998, April). Too good to be true? *Management Review*, 28.

31 Needleman, S. E. (2007, March 6). Why sneaky tactics may not help résumé. *The Wall Street Journal*, p. B8.

32 Ryan, L. (2007). For job-hunters: How to find a contact name inside a target company. Retrieved July 2, 2007, from http://ezinearticles.com/?For-Job-Hunters:-How-to-Find-a-Contact-Name-Inside-a-Target-Company&id=101910

Chapter 16

1 Bock, L. (2007, June 6). Testimony of Google's Laszlo Bock, House Judiciary Subcommittee on Immigration, Citizenship, Refugees, Border Security, and International Law. *BusinessWeek Online*. Retrieved July 8, 2007, from Business Source Premier (EBSCO) database.

2 Hansell, S. (2007, January 3). Google answer to filling jobs is an algorithm. *The New York Times*, p. A1.

3 Delaney, K. (2006, October 23). Google adjusts hiring process as needs grow. *The Wall Street Journal*, p. B1.

4 Panel interview. (2007). Retrieved August 12, 2007, from Job-Employment-Guide.com at http://www.job-employment-guide.com/panel-interview.html

5 Domeyer, D. (2007, January/February). *OfficePro*, 5.

6 Maher, K. (2004, October 5). Job seekers and recruiters pay more attention to blogs. Retrieved August 12, 2007, from http://www.careerjournal.com/jobhunting/usingnet/20041005-maher.html

7 Ryan, L. (2007, May 6). Job seekers: Prepare your stories. Retrieved August 12, 2007, from http://ezinearticles.com/?Job-Seekers:-Prepare-Your-Stories&id=142327

8 Finder, A. (2006, June 11). For some, online persona undermines a résumé. *The New York Times*. Retrieved August 14, 2007, from http://www.nytimes.com/2006/06/11/us/11recruit.html?ex=1307678400&en=ddfbe1e3b386090b&ei=5090

9 Mahoney, S. (2006, September 4). Finding postmodern marketers. *Advertising Age, 77*(36), 15–16. Retrieved July 8, 2007, from Business Source Premier (EBSCO) database.

10 Discussion based on Delaney, K. (2006, October 23). Google adjusts hiring process as needs grow. *The Wall Street Journal*, p. B1; and Hansell, S. (2007, January 3). Google answer to filling jobs is an algorithm. *The New York Times*, p. A1.

11 Wright, D. (2004, August/September). Tell stories, get hired. *OfficePro*, 32–33.

12 Illegal interview questions. (2007). Retrieved August 12, 2007, from FindLaw.com at http://employment.findlaw.com/employment/employment-employee-hiring/employment-employee-hiring-interview-questions.html

13 Illegal interview questions. (2001, January 29). Retrieved August 10, 2007, from USA Today.com at http://www.usatoday.com/careers/resources/interviewillegal.htm; Washington, T. (2007). Advice on answering illegal interview questions. Retrieved August 10, 2007, from http://www.careerjournal.com/jobhunting/interviewing/19971231-washington.htm; Illegal interview questions. (2007). Retrieved August 10, 2007, from FindLaw.com, at http://employment.findlaw.com/employment/employment-employee-hiring/employment-employee-hiring-interview-questions.html

14 Needleman, S. E. (2006, February 7). Be prepared when opportunity calls. *The Wall Street Journal*, p. B4.

Acknowledgments

Chapter 1

p. 4 Spotlight (Aylwin Lewis) based on Double duty for Sears' Lewis. (2005, September 14), Newsmaker Q & A. Retrieved February 16, 2007, from http://www.businessweek.com/bwdaily/dnflash/sep2005/nf20050914_3914db008.htm. Also see Berner, R. (2005, October 31). At Sears, a great communicator; New CEO Lewis will need his people skills to overhaul the giant's hidebound culture. *BusinessWeek*, Issue 3957, 50. Retrieved February 17, 2007, from InfoTrac College Edition database.

p. 5 Spotlight (Oren Harari) based on Harari, O. (1997, November). Flood your organization with knowledge. *Management Review*, 33; Harari, O. (2000, March). Bold visions in the new century. *Management Review*, 25. See also Harari, O. (2006). *Break from the pack: How to compete in a copycat economy.* Upper Saddle River, NJ: FT Press.

p. 8 Photo essay based on Lindsey, C. D., & Krishnan, H. S. (2007, March). Retrieval disruption in collaborative groups due to brand cues. *Journal of Consumer Research, 33*(4), 470–478.

p. 9 Figure 1.3 based on U.S. 2001 Bureau of the Census figures appearing in Karoly, L. A. & Paris, C. W. A. *The 21st century at work.* Santa Monica, CA: Rand Corporation, pp. 36–39.

pp. 10–11 Figure 1.2 based on Chickowski, E. (2006, January 9). Phones offer more than call option; e-mail, text messaging, ability to play music among bells, whistles. *San Diego Business Journal*, p. 17; Quittner, J. (2006, September 4). Wikis offer quick way to collaborate; software acts like intranet, letting widely scattered staffers pool knowledge. *Crain's New York Business*, 34; Blogs, podcasts pushed as enterprise tools. (2006, January 12). *Information Week;* Brandon, J. (2006, June 6). Reworking the office: How will you be working—one, five, twenty years down the road. *PC Magazine*, 97; Open-source VoIP takes a few steps forward. (2006, November 7). *Information Week;* Tricker, J. (2005, September). Office design trends: Bring on the boomerang-shaped table. *Indiana Business Magazine*, 4; Mirel, D. Wide open spaces: Cubicle-ridden offices transition to more open-offices formats, a result of advanced mobile technology and innovative office design. (2006, May–June). *Journal of Property Management*, 30; Held, S. (2006, September). Office tech update: From "print and distribute" to "distribute and print." *Indiana Business Magazine*, 64; Gardyasz, J. (2006, April 24). CustomerVision bringing wikis to business. *Business Record* (Des Moines), 3; The future of tech. (2005, June 20). *BusinessWeek*, 81; Mann, A. (2006, November 1). Enterprise content now encompassing wikis, blogs, podcasts and more. *Network World;* Klein, K. E. (2006, August 21). A company blog keeps people connected. (2006, August 21). *BusinessWeek Online.* Retrieved November 12, 2006, from InfoTrac College Edition database; Brynko, B. (2006, March). Top ten technology trends. *Information Today*, 1; Totty, M. (2005, September 12). Prime time for videoconferences. *The New York Times*, p. R6; and Hof, R. H. (2006, June 19). Web 2.0: The new guy at work. *BusinessWeek*, 58.

Chapter 2

p. 36 Spotlight (Mike Bair) based on Hymowitz, C. (2006, February 13). Rewarding competitors over collaborators no longer makes sense. *The Wall Street Journal*, p. B1.

p. 37 Tech Talk [virtual teams] based on Gordon, J. (2005, June). Do your virtual teams deliver only virtual performance? *Training*, 20; Brown-Johnston, N. (2005, January-February). Virtual teamwork: Smart business leaders are building high-performance virtual teams. *Detroiter*, 55; Managing virtual teams. (2004, March 16). *Info-Tech Advisor Newsletter;* Snyder, B. (2003, May). Teams that span time zones face new work rules. *Stanford Business Magazine.* Retrieved April 15, 2007, from http://www.gsb.stanford.edu/news/bmag/sbsm0305/feature_virtual_teams.shtml; Loudin, K. H. (2003, June). Building bridges: Virtual teamwork in the 21st century. *Contract Management;* and Armstrong, D. (2000, March). Building teams across borders. *Executive Excellence,* 10.

p. 37 Discussion of Tuckman's model based on Robbins, H. A., & Finley, M. (1995). *Why teams don't work.* Princeton, NJ: Peterson's/Pacesetter Books, Chapter 22.

p. 39 Figure 2.2. Portions reprinted with permission of Peterson's, a division of International Thomson Publishing, FAX 800-730-2215. Adapted from *Why teams don't work.* © 1995 by Harvey A. Robbins and Michael Finley.

p. 39 Discussion of conflict and groupthink based on McNamra, P. L. (2003, August/September). Conflict resolution strategies. *OfficePro*, 25; Weiss, W. H. (2002, November). Building and managing teams. *SuperVision*, 19; Eisenhardt, K. M. (1997, July/August). How management teams can have a good fight. *Harvard Business Review*, 77–85; Brockmann, E. (1996, May). Removing the paradox of conflict from group decisions. *Academy of Management Executives*, 61–62; and Beebe, S. A., & Masterson, J. T. (1999). *Communicating in small groups* (New York: Longman), 198–200.

p. 41 Ethical Insights based on Wilson, G. L. (1996). *Groups in context.* New York: McGraw-Hill, pp. 24–27; and Robbins, H., & Finley, M. *Why teams don't work.* Princeton, NJ: Peterson's/Pacesetter Books, pp. 88–89.

p. 52 Spotlight (Oprah Winfrey) based on Marshall, L. (1998, November). The intentional Oprah. *InStyle*, 341.

p. 53 Career Coach box (Listening to Nonnative Speakers) based on Marshall, T., & Vincent, J. Improving listening skills: Methods, activities, and resources," Instructor's Manual, *Business communication: Process and product*, 6e; Varner, I., & Beamer, L. (1995). *Intercultural communication in the global workplace.* (Boston: Irwin, McGraw-Hill), p. 37; and Lee, C. (1993, January). How to deal with the foreign accent. *Training*, 72, 75.

p. 55 Spotlight (Robert Rosen) based on Rosen, R. (2000). *Global literacies.* New York: Simon & Schuster, p. 99.

p. 61 Discussion of etiquette based on Gaining an etiquette edge. (2005, December). *The Office Professional*, 6; and The power of politeness. (2006, August). *Journal of Accountancy.* Retrieved November 30, 2006, from Business Source Premier (EBSCO) database.

Chapter 3

p. 75 Figure 3.1 based on Chaney, L. H., & Martin, J. S. (2000). *Intercultural business communication*, 2e. Upper Saddle River, NJ: Prentice Hall, Chapter 5; J. Chung's analysis appearing in Chen, G. M., & Starosta, W. J. *Foundations of intercultural communication.* Boston: Allyn and Bacon, 1998, 51; and O'Hara-Devereaux, M., & Johansen, R. (1994). *Globalwork: Bridging distance, culture, and time.* San Francisco: Jossey-Bass, p. 55.

p. 77 Tech Talk box based on Singh, N. & Pereira, A. (2005). *The culturally customized Web site.* Elsevier, 2005; Tedeschi, B. (2004, January 12). To reach Internet users overseas, more American Web sites are speaking their language, even Mandarin. *The New York Times*, p. C6; Spethman, M. J. (2003, November). Web site globalization. *World Trade*, 56; Kalin, S. (1997, October 6). The importance of being multiculturally correct. *Computer World*, G16–17; and Morelli, L. (1998, August 17). Writing for a global audience on the Web. *Marketing News*, 16.

p. 83 Figure 3.3 based on Ostheimer, S. (1995, February). Internationalize yourself. *Business Education Forum*, 45. Reprinted with permission of Sondra Ostheimer, Southwest Wisconsin Technical College.

p. 84 Figure 3.4 based on Horton, W. (1993, Fourth Quarter). The almost universal language: Graphics for international documents. *Technical Communication*, 690.

p. 87 Figure 3.6 based on The 2006 Corruption Perceptions Index, Transparency International. Retrieved January 24, 2007, from http://www.transparency.org/policy_research/surveys_indices/cpi/2006

p. 90 Spotlight (J. T. Ted Childs) based on Charles, S. (2003, September 23). Look like your customers: IBM's Ted Childs says diversity good for business. *Wabash College.* Retrieved February 25, 2007, from http://www.wabash.edu/news/displaystory.cfm?news_ID=1186

p. 92 Spotlight (Andrea Jung) based on Byrnes, N. (2007, March 12). Avon: More than cosmetic changes. *BusinessWeek*, 62–63; Avon lady: Ding-dong, opportunity calling. (2003, October). *Cosmo Girl!*, 108; and Andrea calling: This is definitely not your grandmother's Avon. (2002, August). *Institutional Investor International Edition*, 17.

Chapter 4

p. 106 Spotlight (Danny O'Neill) caption based on Stettner, M. (2000, June 15). Experts' tips on writing top-notch memos. *Investor's Business Daily*, A1.

p. 108 Spotlight (Warren Buffett) based on Warren Buffett's remarks appearing in the Preface to *A Plain English Handbook* (1997). Washington, DC: Office of Investor Education and Assistance, U.S. Securities and Exchange Commission. Retrieved November 5, 2004, from http://www.sec.gov/consumer/plaine.htm#A9; and Serwer, A. (2004, January 12). How to play the falling dollar: The world's greatest investor is betting against the greenback. *Fortune*, 143.

p. 111 Spotlight (John H. Johnson) based on Johnson, Ford, Ash cited as greatest entrepreneurs in U.S. history. (February 2004). *Ebony*, 72; and Ebony's John H. Johnson: How he went from a tin-roof shack to the Forbes 400. (1998, March 26). *Investor's Business Daily*, 1.

p. 116 Information on adapting to legal responsibilities based in part on Walter, R. J., & Sleeper, G. J. (2002, Spring). Employee recruitment and retention: When company inducements trigger liability. *Review of Business*, 17; Cordier, P. J. (2003, May). Essentials of good safety communications. (2003, May). *Pulp & Paper*, 25; and Woolever, K. R. (1990, June 2). Corporate language and the law: Avoiding liability in corporate communications. *IEE Transactions on Professional Communication*, 95–98.

p. 116 Ethics Check based on Berner, R. (2006, November 6). Cap One's credit trap. *BusinessWeek*, 35–37.

Chapter 5

p. 127 Spotlight (Gerry Laybourne) based on Founder of Oxygen Media passes along tips for moms who want to be entrepreneurs. (2005, May 7). Retrieved February 23, 2007, from Startup Nation at http:// www.startupnation.com/pages/radio/RD_May7_ 2005_GerryLaybourne.asp; Romano, A. (2003, May 5). Oxygen: It lives! Now can it breathe? *Broadcasting & Cable*; Clemetson, L. (1999, November 15). The birth of a network: With Oxygen Media, Oprah Winfrey and Gerry Laybourne are trying to create TV history. *Newsweek*, 15; Cooper, J. (1998, June 1). Laybourne is born again. *Mediaweek*, 5.

p. 128 Spotlight (Max Messmer) based on Messmer, M. (2004, March). Developing effective performance reviews. *Strategic Finance*, 13; and Messmer, M. (2001, January). Enhancing your writing skills. *Strategic Finance*, 8–10.

p. 137 Spotlight (Bob Knight) based on Guard against five common mistakes. (2007, February). *Writing That Works*, p. 2.

Chapter 6

p. 149 Opening case study based on Lockyer, S. E. (2006, December 18). Yum to expand Taco Bell breakfast test: Potential rollout anchors company's plan to boost core chains' flagging U.S. sales. *Nation's restaurant news*, 40(51), 3. Retrieved April 17, 2007, from InfoTrac College Edition database; Analysis of Yum! Brands Inc. (2007, February 13). *M2 Presswire*. Retrieved April 17, 2007, from InfoTrac College Edition database; Wheaton, K. (2007, March 5). Yum Brands has a rat problem, but it will have customers, too. *Advertising age*, 78(10), 4. Retrieved April 7, 2007, from Business Source Premier (EBSCO) database; and Sharma, S. (2007, January 10). Brand should not get trapped in low-price bracket. *The Economic Times*. Retrieved April 7, 2007, from InfoTrac College Edition database.

p. 150 Spotlight (Colin Powell) based on Quotations from Chairman Powell: A leadership primer. (1996, December). *Management Review*, 36.

p. 155 Spotlight (Arthur Levitt) based on Levitt, A., Jr., & Breeden, R. C. (2003, December 3). Our ethical erosion. *The Wall Street Journal*, p. 16; Carlino, B. (2001, January 8). Industry split on Levitt exit. *Accounting Today*, 1; and Office of investor education and assistance. (1997, January). *U.S. Securities and Exchange Commission: A plain English handbook*.

p. 156 Ethics Check based on Duffy, S. P. (2007, April 23). Attorney hit with $6.6 million malpractice verdict. *The Legal Intelligencer*. Retrieved June 24, 2007, from http://www.law.com.

p. 157 Spotlight (William Raspberry) based on Words to the wise on students' speech. (1998, April). *Writing Concepts*, p. 3.

p. 167 Activity 6.21 based on Pomerenke, P. J. (1998, December). Teaching ethics with apartment leases. *Business Communication Quarterly*, 61(4), 119.

Chapter 7

p. 161 Spotlight (Liz Hughes) based on Hughes, L. (2003, July/August). E-mail etiquette: Think before you send. *Women in Business*, 29, and e-mail communication (July 17, 2007).

p. 173 Photo essay based on Starbucks Gossip Web site. (2007). Starbucks chairman warns of the commoditization of the Starbucks experience. Retrieved June 5, 2007, from http://starbucksgossip .typepad.com/_/2007/02/starbucks_chair_2.html

p. 178 Using E-Mail Smartly and Safely is based on Totty, M. (2007, March 26). Rethinking the inbox. *The Wall Street Journal*, p. R8; Minzesheimer, B. (2007, April 10). Check your e-mail—before you hit send. *USA Today*, p. 1D; Derbyshire, J. (2007, April 21). To: Emailers, Subject: Etiquette. *The Wall Street Journal*, p. 10; Munter, M., Rogers, P. S., & Rymer, J. (2003, March). Business e-mail: Guidelines for users. *Business Communication Quarterly*, 66(1), 26; E-mail acceptable use: An enforceable policy. (2003, September 30). *Info-Tech Advisor Newsletter*; Maney, K. (2003, July 24). How the big names tame e-mail. *USA Today*, p. 1A; Email: The DNA of office crimes. (2003, September/October). *Electric Perspectives*, 4; and Hughes, Liz. (2003, July/August). E-mail etiquette: Think before you send. *Women in Business*, 29.

p. 181 Spotlight (Liz Hughes) based on Hughes, L. (2003, July/August). E-mail etiquette: Think before you send. *Women in Business*, 29.

p. 182 Spotlight (Barbara Hemphill) based on Hemphill, B. (2004, January). Top 10 tips for Managing e-mail more effectively. *Doors and Hardware*, 34.

p. 183 Tech Talk box (Instant Messaging) based on Yahoo Mail offers instant messaging inside e-mail. (2007, February 13). *eWeek*. Retrieved May 5, 2007, from InfoTrac College edition database; Group chat evolving into e-mail. (2006, December 7). *Information Week*. Retrieved May 4, 2007, from InfoTrac College Edition database; McAdams, J. (2007, March 19). IM confidential: Love it or hate it, instant messaging has potential for security problems. *Computerworld*, 32. Retrieved May 4, 2007, from InfoTrac College Edition database; and Malacahy, J. (2007, March 1). Instant access (Instant messaging). *Computing*, 29. Retrieved May 4, 2007, from InfoTrac College Edition database.

Chapter 8

p. 206 Spotlight (Peggy Foran) based on Levitt, A. (2002) *Take on the street*. New York: Pantheon Books, p. 226; Kerins, S. (2004, September 30). Foran supports corporate culture. *The Observer Online*. Retrieved May 27, 2007, from http://media .www.ndsmcobserver.com/media/storage/ paper660/news/2004/09/30/News/Foran.Supports .Corporate.Culture-737240.shtml

p. 208 Ethics Check based on An eagle eye on retail scams. (2005, August 5). *BusinessWeek Online*. Retrieved July 2, 2007, from Lexis-Nexis database.

p. 214 Photo essay based on Zimmermann, S. (2007, June 24). The fixer: Honeymoon glitch—cruising to a solution. *The Chicago Sun-Times*. Retrieved June 29, 2007, from http://www.suntimes.com/news/ zimmermann/440955,CST-NWS-fixer24.article

pp. 214–217 Discussion of claim and adjustment letters based on McCartney, S. (2007, March 20). What airlines do when you complain. *The Wall Street Journal*, p. D5; Liao, H. (2007, March). Do it right this time: The role of employee service recovery performance in customer-perceived justice and customer loyalty after service failures. *Journal of Applied Psychology*, 92(2), 475. Retrieved January 12, 2007, from Business Source Premier (EBSCO) database; Davidow, M. (2003, February). Organizational responses to customer complaints: What works and what doesn't. *Journal of Service Research*, 5(3) 31. Retrieved June 3, 2007, from Business Source Premier (EBSCO) database; Michelson, M. W., Jr. (2003, December). Turning complaints into cash. *The American Salesman*, 22; Torp, J. R. (2003, March/April). In person, by phone, by mail, or online: Managing customer complaints. *ABA Bank Compliance*, 10; Kim, C., Kim, S., Im, S., & Shin, S. (2003). The effect of attitude and perception on consumer complaint intentions. *The Journal of Consumer Marketing*, 20, 352; Lawrence, K. (2000, Fall). How to profit from consumer complaints: Turning problems into opportunities. *Canadian Manager*, 25; David, D., & Baker, M. A. (1994). Rereading bad news: Compliance-gaining features

in management memos. *The Journal of Business Communications*, 267–290; Smart, D. T., & Martin, C. L. (1993, Spring). Consumers who correspond with business: A profile and measure of satisfaction with responses. *Journal of Applied Business Research*, 30–42; and Clark, G. L., Kaminski, P. F., & Rink, D. R. (1992, Winter). Consumer complaints: Advice on how companies should respond based on an empirical study. *Journal of Services Marketing*, 41–50.

p. 219 Spotlight (Andrew S. Grove) based on The fine art of feedback. (1992, February). *Working Woman*, 26.

Chapter 9

pp. 234–237 Effective Persuasion Techniques based on Hoar, R. (2005, March 1). Be more persuasive. *Management Today*, 56; Venter, D. (2006). Negotiation persuasion. Retrieved June 29, 2006, from http://www.calumcoburn.co.uk/articles/ articles-persuasion.html; Muir, G. (2006). *All presenting is persuasive*. *Link&Learn eNewsletter*. Retrieved June 29, 2006, from http://www.linkageinc.com/ company/news_events/link_learn/enewsletter/ archive/2006/01; Master the art of persuasion to boost your managerial effectiveness. (2006, February). *Payroll Manager's Report*, 15; Cialdini, R. B. (2002, April). The science and practice of persuasion. *Cornell Hotel & Restaurant Administration Quarterly*, 40; and Francaro, K. E. (2004, August). Managing by persuasion. *Contract Management*, 4.

p. 238 Spotlight (Margaret Whitman) based on Meyers, W. (2005, October 31). Keeping a gentle grip on power. *U.S. News & World Report*, 139(16), 78; Taylor, C. (2004, April 26). Meg Whitman, *Time*, 74; and Shepard, S. B. (2001, March 19). A talk with Meg Whitman. *BusinessWeek*, 98–99.

p. 240 Spotlight (John W. Thompson) based on Verton, D. (2004, March 29). Frontline defenders. *Computerworld*, 23; Grow, B. (2004, June 21). Symantec: Leading the charge against hackers. *BusinessWeek*, 85; and Hooper, L. (2003, November 17). John Thompson: Chairman and CEO, Symantec. *CRN*, 94.

p. 241 Ethical Insights box based on Troyka, L. Q. (2005). *Simon & Schuster handbook for writers*, 7th ed. Upper Saddle River, NJ: Prentice Hall, pp. 142–145; Crews, F. (1987). *The Random House handbook*. New York: Random House, pp. 76–78; and Downes, S. Stephen's guide to the logical fallacies. Retrieved February 28, 2007, from http:// onegoodmove.org/fallacy/toc.htm

p. 244 Planning and Composing Effective Sales Messages partly based on Benady, D. (2006, August 17). From search box to letterbox. *Marketing Week*, 33; Magill, K. (2006, August 1). E-mail creative: What works and what doesn't. *Multichannel Merchant*, 2(8), 21–22. Retrieved February 25, 2007, from Business Source Premier (EBSCO) database; and Zarwan, J. (2006, August 1). Direct mail delivers. *American Printer*, 123(8), 52–53. Retrieved February 25, 2007, from Business Source Premier (EBSCO) database.

p. 251 Spotlight (Herb Kelleher) based on Krames, J. A. (2003, November). Performance culture. *Executive Excellence*, 16; and Kelleher, K. (1992). Beware the impossible guarantee. *Inc.*, 30.

p. 258 Figure 9.8. Letter adapted from Yunxia, Z. (2000, December). Building knowledge structures in teaching cross-cultural sales genres, Appendix B. *Business Communication Quarterly*, 63(4), 66–67. Permission to reprint granted by Association for Business Communication. Chinese characters provided by Dr. Bertha Du-Babcock.

p. 271 Activity 9.27. Sales letter adapted from Yunxia, Z. (2000, December). Building knowledge structures in teaching cross-cultural sales genres, Appendix A. *Business Communication Quarterly*, 63(4), 66–67. Permission to reprint granted by Association for Business Communication.

Chapter 10

p. 279 Spotlight (Marshall Goldsmith) based on Goldsmith, M., & Reiter, M. (2007). *What got you here won't get you there*. New York: Hyperion Books. Excerpt retrieved June 20, 2007, from http://www .businessweek.com.

p. 280 Ethics Check based on Nifong issues apology to ex-lacrosse players. (2007, April 12). Retrieved June 16, 2007, from http://www.wral.com/news/local/story/1270348/?d_full_comments=1&d_comments_page=2

p. 280 Spotlight (Malcolm Forbes) based on Forbes, M. (1999). How to write a business letter. In K. Harty (Ed.), *Strategies for business and technical writing.* Boston: Allyn and Bacon, p. 108.

p. 295 Ethics Check based on RadioShack uses e-mail to fire employees. (2006, August 30). *Associated Press.* Retrieved July 6, 2007, from http://www.breitbart.com/article.php?id=D8JQV30O1&show_article=1

Chapter 11

p. 319 Spotlight (A. J. Jamal) based on Ehrenfeld, T. (1995, July). Out of the blue. *Inc.,* 70.

p. 320 Spotlight (Peggy Laun) based on Case, J. (1994, January). Total customer service. *Inc.com.* Retrieved June 27, 2007, from http://www.inc.com/magazine/19940101/2715.html

p. 328 Figure 11.9 based on Sullivan, D. (2006, August 21). ComScore media metrix search engine ratings. Retrieved June 28, 2007, from http://searchenginewatch.com/reports/article.php/2156431. During 2005 and 2006, AOL Search has lost percentage points, as did MSN, albeit less significantly than AOL. Yahoo has been hovering at around the 30 percent mark, while Google's popularity continues to rise.

p. 334 Spotlight (Tom Peters) based on Peters, T. (1991). *Thriving on Chaos.* New York: Knopf, pp. 230–231.

Chapter 12

p. 358 Spotlight (Indra Nooyi) based on Levenson, E., & Tkaczyk, C. (2006, October 16). Indra rising—50 most powerful women. *Fortune.* Retrieved July 10, 2007, from http://money.cnn.com/popups/2006/fortune/mostpowerfulwomen/1.html; Kavilanz, P. B. (2006, August 14). PepsiCo names first woman CEO. *CNNMoney.* Retrieved July 10, 2007, from http://money.cnn.com/2006/08/14/news/companies/pepsico_ceo; Bhushan, R., & Chakravarty, C. (2007, July 2). Nooyi's mantra for India: Grab & grow. *India Times.*

p. 366 Career Coach box based on Booher, D. (2001, April). E-writing. *Executive Excellence,* 16; Bernstel, J. B., & Thomases, H. (2001, March). Writing words for the Web. *Bank Marketing,* 16–21; and Graves, P. R., & Murry, J. E. (1990, Summer). Enhancing communication with effective page design and typography. *Delta Pi Epsilon* Instructional Strategies Series.

p. 366 Spotlight (Anthony Miranda) based on Fraser, J. A. (1994, December). He asks to be audited—often. *Inc. Magazine.*

Chapter 13

p. 395 Photo essay based on Mcavoy, A. (2007, May 31). Hawaiian electric talking to Hoku Solar. Associated Press. Retrieved May 30, 2007, from http://biz.yahoo.com/ap/070531/hi_hoku_scientific_solar_power.html?.v=1

p. 399 Spotlight (Tom Sant) based on personal communication with Mary Ellen Guffey, September 16, 2004; and Sant: The proposal experts. Retrieved August 15, from http://www.santcorp.com

p. 403 Photo essay based on Moritz, S. (2007). Clock ticks slowly for XM, Sirius. Retrieved June 11, 2007, from TheStreet.com at http://www.thestreet.com/s/clock-ticks-slowly-for-xm-sirius/newsanalysis/techfocus/10361804.html; and Babington, C. (2007, February 28). House gets first crack at XM-Sirius proposal. *The Washington Post,* p. D01.

p. 422 Figure 13.5 based on Sokuvitz, S., & George, A. M. (2003, June). Teaching culture: The challenges and opportunities of international public relations. *Business Communication Quarterly,* 97; Koh, A. C. (2003). Teaching understanding cultural differ-ences for business in an internet-based economy. *Journal of Teaching in International Business,* 15(2), 27; and Sterkel, K. S. (1988, September). Integrating intercultural communication and report writing in the communication class. *The Bulletin of the Association for Business Communication,* 13–16.

Chapter 14

p. 426 Figure 14.1 based on Elsea, J. G. (1985, September). Strategies for effective presenta-tions. *Personnel Journal,* pp. 31–33 in Hamilton, C. (2001). *Communicating for results.* Belmont, CA: Wadsworth/Thomson Learning, p. 340.

p. 429 Career Coach box based on Booher, D. (2004, May). Selling your ideas. *Executive Excellence,* 27; Gittlen, S. (2004, July 26). The public side of you. *Network World,* 61; Lancaster, H. (1996, January 9). Practice and coaching can help you improve um, y'know, speeches. *The Wall Street Journal,* p. B1; and Decker, B. (1992, February). Successful presen-tations: Simple and practical. *HR Focus,* 19.

p. 427 Spotlight (Howard Schultz) based on Helm, B. (2007, April 9). Saving Starbucks' soul. Retrieved August 3, 2007, from http://www.businessweek.com/magazine/content/07_15/b4029070.htm?chan=search; and Gallo, C. (2006, May 5). Starbucks' secret ingredient. Retrieved August 3, 2007 from http://www.businessweek.com/smallbiz/content/may2006/sb20060505_893499.htm?chan=search

p. 431 Photo essay based on Olesen, A. (2007, June 5). Coca-Cola begins water conservation bid. *Interna-tional Business Times.* Retrieved July 24, 2007, from http://www.ibtimes.com/articles/20070605/china-coca-cola.htm

p. 433 Spotlight (John Chambers) based on Gallo, C. (2007, January 4). The camera doesn't lie. *Busi-nessWeek Online.* Retrieved August 3, 2007, from http://www.businessweek.com/smallbiz/content/jan2007/sb20070103_877305.htm?chan=search

p. 434 Figure 14.3 based on Booher, D. (2003). *Speak with confidence.* New York: McGraw-Hill Professional, pp. 131–143; U.S. Department of Labor (1996, May). Presenting effective presentations with visual aids. Retrieved July 29, 2007, from http://www.osha.gov/doc/outreachtraining/htmlfiles/traintec.html; and McConnon, S. (2002). *Presenting with power.* Oxford: How To Books, pp. 38–43.

p. 441 References to Steve Jobs and his speaking skills based on Gallo, C. (2006, July 6). Steve Jobs' greatest presentation. *BusinessWeek Online.* Retrieved July 17, 2007, from http://www.businessweek.com; and Evangelist, M. (2006, January 5). Behind the magic curtain. *The Guardian.* Retrieved July 17, 2007, from http://technology.guardian.co.uk

p. 444 Spotlight (Justice O'Connor) based on O'Brien, P. (1993, February). Why men don't listen. *Working Woman,* 58.

p. 445 Spotlight (Dianna Booher) based on Booher, D. (2003). *Speak with confidence.* New York: McGraw-Hill Professional, p. 76.

p. 452 Spotlight (Nancy Friedman) based on Fried-man, N. (personal communication with Mary Ellen Guffey, February 2, 1999).

p. 458 Activity 14.7 based on Booher, D. (2003). *Speak with confidence.* New York: McGraw-Hill Professional, pp. 167–172.

Chapter 15

p. 465 Spotlight (Michael Dell) based on Batelle, J., & Dell, M. (2004, May). Still giving 'em Dell twenty years in, Michael Dell's hair is a little grayer—but his taste for beating the competition remains as strong as ever. *Business2.0,* 99; and Turner, N. (1999, March 1). Entrepreneur Michael Dell. *Investor's Business Daily,* p. A8.

p. 466 Searching for a job electronically partially based on Farquharson, L. (2003, September 15). Technol-ogy special report: The best way to find a job. *The Wall Street Journal,* p. R8; Maher, K., & Silverman, R. E. (2002, January 2). Your career matters: Online job sites yield few jobs, users complain. *The Wall Street Journal,* p. A7; and Goodrich, E., & George, M. (2002, February 25). Employer-backed job site lets companies avoid Monster. *Information Week,* p. 24.

p. 469 Networking Career Coach box partially based on Di Meglio, F. (2006, September 19). Netproof-ing your job search. Retrieved July 27, 2007, from http://www.businessweek.com/bschools/content/sep2006/bs20060919_376150.htm; Borzo, J. (2004, September). The job connection: Using online networking, job seekers turn friendship into employment. *The Wall Street Journal,* p. R14; Business: E-schmoozing; business networking. (2004, April 10). *The Economist,* 58; Farr, J. M. (1991). *The very quick job search.* Indianapolis: JIST Works, pp. 50–52; and Rosner, B. (1998, September). What color is HR's parachute? *Workforce,* 50–51.

p. 471 Spotlight (Yana Parker) based on a personal inter-view with Mary Ellen Guffey, 1996. Yana Parker is the author of *Damn Good Résumé* (Berkeley: Ten Speed Press, 1996); and "Hot Tips on Résumé Writing." Her Web site is http://www.damngood.com.

p. 472 Photo essay about Marilee Jones based on Sos, Z., & Davis, D. (2007, April 29). MIT dean resigns in lying scandal. *CNN.* Retrieved July 31, 2007, from http://www.cnn.com/2007/WORLD/americas/04/27/mit.dean/index.html; Bombardieri, M., & Ryan, A. (2007, April 26). MIT dean of admissions resigns for falsifying résumé. *The Boston Globe.* Retrieved July 31, 2007, from http://www.boston.com/news/globe/city_region/breaking_news/2007/04/mit_dean_of_adm.html

p. 476 Optimizing your résumé for today's technolo-gies partially based on the following: All you need to know about the electronic résumé. Retrieved July 27, 2007, from http://www.brooklyn.liu.edu/bbut07/car/career_articles/electronic_resume.html; Scannable résumés. Retrieved July 27, 2007, from http://www.career.vt.edu/JOBSEARC/Resumes/scannable.htm; Wheeler, K. (2006, October 26). The video résumé. Retrieved July 21, 2007, from http://www.ere.net/articles/db/02FEE6D607B142E68D2F80310EDBCCEC.asp; Fisher, A. (2004, June 28). How to ruin an online job hunt. *Fortune,* 43; Conlin, M. (2003, July 14). The résumé doctor is in. *BusinessWeek,* 116; and Hansen, R. (2007). Scannable Résumé Fundamentals: How to write text résumés. Retrieved July 27, 2007, from http://www.quintcareers.com/scannable_resumes.html

p. 482 Photo essay based on Athavaley, A. (2006, December 7). Posting your resume on YouTube to stand out from the competition. *CareerJournal .com.* Retrieved July 31, 2007, from http://www.careerjournal.com/jobhunting/usingnet/20061207-athavaley.html

p. 490 Spotlight (Liz Ryan) based on Ryan, L. (2007). For job-hunters: How to find a contact name inside a target company. Retrieved July 2, 2007, from http://ezinearticles.com/?For-Job-Hunters:-How-to-Find-a-Contact-Name-Inside-a-Target-Company&id=101910

Chapter 16

p. 505 Photo essay (Tien Nguyen) based on Finder, A. (2006, June 11). For some, online persona un-dermines a résumé. *The New York Times.* Retrieved August 14, 2007, from http://www.nytimes.com/2006/06/11/us/11recruit.html?ex=1307678400&en=ddfbe1e3b386090b&ei=5090

p. 507 Photo essay based on Gallo, C. (2007, Febru-ary 8). It's not your mouth that speaks volumes. Retrieved August 3, 2007, from http://www.businessweek.com/careers/content/feb2007/ca20070207_700175.htm?chan=rss_topEmailedStories_ssi_5

p. 511 Career Coach based on Hansen, R. S. (2007). Salary negotiation do's and don'ts. Reprinted with permission of Quintessential Careers. Retrieved August 14, 2007, from http://www.quintcareers.com/salary-dos-donts.html

p. 512 Spotlight (Daisy Wright) based on Wright, D. (2004, August/September). Tell stories, get hired. *OfficePro,* 32–33.

Index

A

A&W All-American Food restaurants, 3
Abbreviations, 83
   of state, territories, and provinces, B-10
   tips for maximizing hits, 484
   using unclear in intercultural messages, 85
Abercrombie & Fitch, 126
Abflex, 23
ABI/INFORM (ProQuest), 126, 324, 325, 328
About, 326, 327, 328
Abstract, 399
Abusive language, 277
Academic documentation, 334–335
Academic Search Elite (EBSCO), 324
Academic writing, 102
Accentuating the positive, 282
Accommodate the reader in organization, tone, and style, 83
Accommodation, 73
Accuracy of Web sources, 329, 330
Acquisitions, 71
Acronyms, 77
Action
   direct requests for, 206–208
   information, close message with, 174
   motivating, 248, 254–255
   of verbs, A-9
   persuasive request for, 240–241, 242–244
   rejecting requests for, 283–286
Action team, 35
Action verbs, in résumés, 474, 475
Actionable, 277
Active voice, 136–137, 141, 407
   verbs, 205–206
Activities, 474
Activity reports. See Periodic reports
Adaptation. See Adapting

Adapting, 102, 109–116, 125, 176, 203, 209, 213, 220, 238, 243, 256, 284, 296, 332, 368, 374, 396
   See also Writing process (3-x-3) phase 1: adapt
Addressee and delivery notations, business letters, B-3
Adidas, 362
Adjectives, A-9
Adjustment, 214
   cultural, 73
   letter of, 214–217
Adopt-a-Pilot program, 298
Adverbs, A-9
Advisory team, 35
Age bias, 113, 116, 206
   See also Diversity; Information age; Workforce diversity
Agenda, 44
   creation of, 126–127
   distributing of, 47
Agreement
   in opening of bad news letter, 278
   of teams, 41, 42
All the Web, 328
Alliances, 71
Almanacs, 126
Alphanumeric outline, 128–131
AltaVista's Babel Fish, 325
Alternative, 276
   bad news letter suggestion of, 282
   businesspeople abroad and, 89
   delivering bad news within organizations, 295
   yardstick reports consider, 377
Alumwire, 482
Ambiguous, 77, 331
American Airlines, 15, 16
American Chemical Society, 467–468
American Express, 235
American Management Association, 180

American Psychological Association (APA), 406, C-1
   format, 337, C-2–C-5
   in-text format, C-4
   reference format, C-4–C-5
   sample references, C-5
   text page and references, portions of, C-4
Analogies, 431
Analysis. See Analyzing
Analytical reasoning skills, 4
Analytical reports, 312, 371–382
   feasibility reports, 377
   indirect pattern, 314–315
   justification/ recommendation reports, 372–376
   memo format, 315
   organizational patterns for, 361
   yardstick reports, 377–381
   See also Reports
Analyzing, 102, 106–108, 125, 172, 176, 203, 209, 213, 220, 237–238, 243, 256, 284, 296, 332, 368, 374, 396
   an effective presentation, 442–443
   three typical audiences, 108–109
   See also Writing process (3-x-3) phase 1: analyze
Ancillary, 399
Anecdote, 431, 432
Announcements, improving downward information flow with, 20
Antecedents
   pronouns agree in number and gender with, A-8
   pronouns it, which, this, and that refer to clear, A-8–A-9
Anthropologie, 242
Anticipating, 102, 108–109, 125, 176, 203, 209, 213, 220, 243, 256, 284, 296, 332, 368, 374, 396

   See also Writing process (3-x-3) phase 1: anticipate
AOL, 326
APA. See American Psychological Association
Apology, 216–217, 279–280, 447
Apostrophe, A-14–A-15
Appearance, 59
   business documents, 58
   cover letter, 489–495
   people, 58–59
   résumé, 469–470, 486–488
   speaker, 432–433
Appendix, 399, 402, 406, 418
Apple, 382, 433, 436, 441, 448
Application follow-up letter, 519
Application form, 517–519
Appreciation
   business letters, 208
   opening of bad news letter, 279
Appreciation message, 219
ASCII, 484
ASCII résumé. See Plain-text résumé
Ash, Mary Kay, 111
Ask, 326, 328
Association for Financial Professionals, 467–468
Association Web sites, 467–468
AT&T, 425
Athanasopoulos, Takis, 5
Attachments, 180, 182, B-2
Attention, gaining of, 239, 251–252
   persuasive messages within organization, 248
   requesting favors and actions, 244
   sales messages should gain, 255
Attention line, business letters, B-5
Attitudes
   glass ceiling as invisible barrier of, 91

Attitudes (*cont.*)
learning new, 79
of culture, 73
Audience analysis
and report organization, 312
issues, 427
Audience benefits, focus on, 116
Audience focus of message, 111
Audiences
adapting message to, 116, 238, 251
anticipating and analyzing, 108–109, 319–320, 418, 436
building rapport, 431–433
diverse workplace, 92
gaining and keeping the attention of, 429
intercultural, 83–84
international and cross-cultural, 450–451
keeping engaged, 441, 442, 444
know your, 426–427
primary, 109
profile your, 109, 116
receptive, 131–133
secondary, 109
spotlighting benefits of, 110–111
unreceptive, 133
using effective imagery, 431–432
using PowerPoint effectively with, 441
writing to general, 108–109
See also Target audience
Audioconferencing, 11, 48
Authority of Web sources, 329, 330
Authority rule with discussion, 40
Authorization, 405
formal proposals, 400
Authorization request, 398–399
AutoContent Wizard, 437
Averaging, 40
Avon, 44, 92
Awards, 474
Axtell, Roger, 82

B

Background, 405
formal report, 412–413
informal proposal, 398
multimedia presentation, 443
problem, purpose, 400
Bad news, 276
applying the 3-x-3 writing process, 276–277

delivering to customers, 288–293
delivering within organizations, 293–297
denying claims, 291
follow-up message, 289, 290
presenting in other cultures, 297–298
presenting the reasons, 280–281
primary and secondary goals in communicating, 275
refusing credit, 291–293
refusing typical requests, 288
strategies for delivering, 274–278
techniques for delivering sensitively, 278–283
See also Messages
Bair, Mike, 36
Baja Fresh, 149
Balmford, Christopher, 150
Balter, Dave, 311, 320, 322, 344
Banana Republic, 124
Bar charts, 338, 339, 340
Barriers, 14, 19
obstruct flow of communication in organizations, 18
Beamer, 74
Begging the question, 241
Behavioral questions, 512–513
Behaviors, learning new, 79
Beliefs, 73
Ben & Jerry's, 201, 203, 218, 223
Benefits, persuasion ties facts to, 236
Best Buy, 36
Best case/worst case, main ideas organized according to, 430
Bias, 74
age bias, 113, 206
disability bias, 113, 206
ethnic bias, 112–113
gender bias, 112, 206
racial bias, 112–113, 206
Bias-free, 112–113
conclusions, 358
Bibliographies, 334
Blachly, Alice, 202, 218
Blame, acceptance of, 82
Blank space, graphic techniques, 155, 156
Blanket copies, 182
Blanket mailings, 251
Blind carbon copy (Bcc), 175, B-2
Block style, 206, 207, B-4, B-7
Blog, 8, 11, 37, 49, 72, 105, 107, 326
avoid getting fired over your Internet use, 180

improving downward information flow with, 20
researching the target company, 504
See also Weblog
Blogosphere, 326
Bloomberg News, 378
BMW, 36, 448
Bock, Laszlo, 501
Body, 174, 177, 204
adjustment letter, 216
business letters, 205, B-5
cover letter, 495
e-mail messages and memos, 174, 191, B-2
formal report, 405, 418
informational reports, 370
oral presentation, 428–430, 452
persuasive request, 239–240
procedural message, 188
request message, 186
response message, 187
résumé cover letter, 490, 491–494
Boeing, 36, 364
Bold type, graphic techniques, 155, 156
Booher, Dianna, 131, 445
Bookmarks, 328, 329
Books, card catalogs and online catalogs for, 324
Boolean search strategies, 327
Brainstorming, 48, 104, 126–127, 238
Brandimensions, 125
Bribery, 86, 88
Bricks-and-mortar companies, 5
Bridgestone/Firestone, 71
Brin, Sergei, 509
BRINT BizTech Network, 328
Broker, 101
Budget, 398, 400
Buffer, 276
delivering bad news within organizations, 295
opening of a bad news letter, 278–279
refusing typical requests, 288
request refusal with compliments, 287
Buffett, Warren, 108
Build on similarities, 92
Bullet points, 437
Bulleted lists, 154–155, 174, 212
Burger King, 149
Burns & McCallister, 78
Business communication ethics, 22–26
functions of, 17
to inform and persuade, primary purpose of, 106

to promote goodwill, secondary purpose of, 106
Business communicators
act as agents of their organizations, 278
adapt to an intercultural workforce and multinational companies, 72
and self examination, 25
being persuasive and ethical, 241–242
making ethical charts and graphics, 343
See also Communicators
Business documents, appearance of, 58, 59
Business etiquette skills, 60–61
Business letters, B-2–B-11
American, 222–223
analyzing, 204–205, 205–206
Chinese, 222
clarify requests, 207–208
foreign letters, 223
formatting—block style, 207
French, 223
German, 222–223
Italian, 222
Japanese, 222–223
show appreciation, 208
understanding the power of, 201–204
See also Adjustment letter; Direct claims; Direct replies; Direct requests; Writing process (3-x-3)
Business organizations, dividends of diversity benefit, 90
Business outlines, 131
Business plan, 401–402
Business practices, 334–335
coping with intercultural ethics, 86–87
Business presentations. *See* Oral presentations; Multimedia presentation
Business reports, 330
Business Source Premier (EBSCO), 126
Business writing, 101–102, 150
express rather than impress, 102, 150
Web search tools for, 328
Business.com, 326, 327, 328
Buy-in, groups and teams have greater, 35
Buyouts, 71
Buzz, 311
Bypassing, 13, 14
BzzAgent, 311, 322, 344

C

Campus career center, 465
Capabilities, 473
Caperton, Gaston, 4
Capital, 4
Capital letters, 182
    graphic techniques, 155, 156
Capitalization, A-16–A-18
Carbon Copy (Cc), 175, B-2
Card catalogs, 126, 324
Career
    building your success with
        communication skills,
        3–4
    taking charge of, 5–6
Career Coach
    casual apparel in the
        workplace, 58
    critical thinking, problem
        solving, and decision
        making, 6
    designing better
        documents, 366
    Fog index to determine
        readability, 157
    gaining and keeping
        audience attention, 429
    gender talk and gender
        tension, 91
    how to avoid stage fright, 446
    listening in the workplace, 53
    network to a job in the
        hidden market, 469
    salary negotiation dos and
        don'ts, 511
    telephone screening
        interview, 502
Career fairs, 468
Career information, preparing
    for employment, 463
Career objective, 471
Career path, 465–466
CareerBuilder.com, 466
CareerJournal, 467
CareersColorado, 475
CareerWomen.com, 468
Careless language, 277
Caribou Coffee, 372
Carnival Cruise Lines, 234, 242
Case sensitivity, 327
Case studies
    Ben & Jerry's, 201, 218, 223
    BzzAgent, 311, 322, 344
    Gap Inc., 124, 133, 141
    Google, 501, 509, 521
    Hands on Miami (HOM), 234,
        242, 261
    Kmart, 3, 22, 26
    Liz Ryan, 463, 475, 496
    Qualcomm, 171, 184, 191
    Raytheon, 394, 400, 419
    Sears, 3

Sears Holdings Corporation,
    3, 22, 26
Sears Roebuck, 3, 22, 26
Seiyu, 70, 80, 93
Southwest Airlines, 274,
    294, 298
Starbucks, 352, 372, 382
Suze Orman, 101, 112, 118
Taco Bell, 149, 158, 160
Toyota, 34, 43, 62
Toyota Disneyland, 425
Toyota Motor Manufacturing
    Canada, 34
Toyota North American
    Parts Center California
    (NAPCC), 34
Wal-Mart, 70, 80, 93
Walt Disney Imagineering,
    425, 450, 455
Cell phones, 8, 11, 17, 60
    as a channel, 13
Central selling point, 251
CEO Express, 328
Ceremony, 76
Chambers, John, 433
Channel, 13, 83, 107–108
Channel noise, 13
    See also Communication
Chao, Elaine, 15
Charts
    bar chart, 339
    line, 340
    making ethical, 343
    organization, 341–342
    pie, 341
    See also Flipcharts; Flowcharts
Check points, A-1
Child labor, intercultural ethics
    of, 88
Childs, J. T. (Ted), Jr., 90
Chipotle, 149
Chronological résumé. See
    Résumé
Chronology, 154, 361
    main ideas organized
        according to, 429
Churchill, Winston, 234
Cigna Corporation, 8
Circular reasoning, 241
Cisco, 433
Citation formats, 337
Cite numbers carefully, 83
Civility, 61
Claim, 208, 291
    denying, 291, 292
    favorable response follow
        direct pattern, 214
    letters, 208–210
    messages, writing
        persuasive, 248–249
    unfavorable response follow
        indirect pattern, 214
    See also Direct claims

Clarity, 150–151
    in written messages, 83
    revise for, 172, 204
Clauses, 135
    and verb agreement, A-4
Cleardocs.com, 150
Clichés, 83, 183, 450
Click-to-call capabilities, 10
Clip art, 134
Closing, 174–175, 204
    adjustment letter, 217
    bad-news messages, 282, 293
    business letters, 205, B-5
    cover letter, 495
    e-mail messages and memos,
        174–175, 191, B-2
    delivering bad news within
        organizations, 295
    indirect pattern for bad
        news, 276
    persuasive messages
        flowing downward, 246
    procedural message, 188
    refusing internal request, 286
    refusing typical requests, 288
    request message, 187
    response message, 187
    résumé cover letter, 494
    See also Conclusions
C.L.U.E. (Competent Language
    Usage Essentials), A-1–A-23
Cluster diagram, 127, 128, 129,
    204, 238, 449
    brainstorming use of, 127
Clusty by Vivisimo, 326
Coca-Cola, 7, 133, 322, 431
Coercion, 235
Cohen, Ben, 201
Coherence, 139–140, 141
    effective paragraphs link
        ideas to build, 138
    transitional expressions to
        build, 140
Colgate-Palmolive, 71
Collaboration, 8, 9, 11, 42, 103
    encouragement of, 42
    resolving conflict through, 39
    technologies: rethinking
        the way we work
        together, 11
    tools for students, 105
    using technology to facilitate,
        48–50
Collaboration tools, 48
Collaborative business report,
    448
Collaborative documents,
    using technology to edit
    and revise, 106
Collaborative software, 37, 134
Colleagues
    listening to, 51
    writing to, 108

Collective nouns, A-5
Collectivist, 76
    view, high-context cultures,
        257
College Board, 4
College Recruiter
    (CollegeRecruiter
    .com), 466, 467
Colons, A-12–A-14
Comedy Channel, 319
Comma splice, 135, A-2–A-3
Command, 360
    language, procedures and
        instructions use, 188
Commas, A-9–A-12
Commercial databases, 325
Committee, 35
Communication, 12
    among diverse workplace
        audiences, 92
    barriers, 14–15, 19
    in organizations, 15–18
    internal and external
        functions, 15–17
    media, 17
    nonverbal, 55–59, 60–61
    of bad news, 275
    overcoming obstacles in, 15
    process of, 12–14
    techniques, 42
    technologies, 10
    See also Oral communication
Communication channels, 107
    downward flow of, 19–20
    formal, 18–21
    horizontal flow of, 21
    upward flow of, 20–21
Communication coaches,
    improving upward
    information flow, 20
Communication process
    feedback travels to sender,
        13–14
    message travels over
        channel, 13
    receiver decodes message, 13
    sender encodes idea in
        message, 13
    sender has idea, 12–13
Communication skills, 3–4, 5,
    6, 35
    cultivation of, 42
    key to your success, 7
    lack of, 20
    writing skills, 4
Communication style, 76–77
Communicators, 3, 4, 5, 24, 36,
    52, 55, 106, 108, 111, 127,
    128, 137, 150, 155, 157, 181,
    182, 183, 206, 219, 238, 240,
    251, 279, 280, 319, 320, 334,
    358, 366, 399, 427, 433, 444,
    445, 453, 465, 471, 490, 512

Communicators (*cont.*)
ask questions to stimulate feedback, 15
cultivating the "you" view, 111
flatter organizations demand skilled, 7
overcome obstacles, 15
See also Business communicators
Company description, 401
Company policy
bad news letter explaining, 281
Internet rules, 180, 183
Comparison/contrast (pro/con), main ideas organized according to, 429
Compensation packages, obstacles to upward information flow, 20
Competition, 42
Competitive edge, 60–61
Complaint, 248–249
Complements, A-6
Complete sentences, 135
e-mail response, 182
in intercultural messages, 85
See also Sentences
Complex documents, proofreading of, 159
Compliance, 237
Compliant messages, 248–249
Complimentary closing, 177, B-5
Compliments
buffer request refusal, 287
opening of bad news letter, 278
Component, 362
of formal and informal proposals, 395
of formal reports, 402, 403–406
of informal reports, 402
Compose, 102, 125, 134–141, 176, 203, 209, 213, 220, 243, 256, 284, 296, 332, 368, 374, 396
creating effective sentences, 135–138
drafting meaningful paragraphs, 138–139
e-mail offline, 180
linking ideas to build coherence, 139–140
See also Writing process (3-x-3) phase 2: compose
Compound modifier, A-9
Compound prepositions, 151, 152
Comprehension, 82
Compromise, 237, 276

bad news letter suggestion of, 282
Computers
as a channel, 13
create better written messages, oral presentations, and Web pages, 134
laptop, 11
Concise, 151–153
Conciseness, 102
revising for, 151–153
Conclusions, 358
analytical reports, 371–382
drawing of, 357–361
formal report, 405–406, 416, 418
informational reports, 370
oral presentation, 430–431, 452
See also Closing
Concrete nouns, 115
Condolences, expression of, 221
Conference
calling, 48
report, 369
Conferencing calling, 11
Conferencing software, 9
Confirmation messages, 188–190
Conflict, 39
confronting, 47
handling in meetings, 47
management of, 42
six-step procedure for dealing with, 39
teams ability to confront, 42
Conformity, 92
Congratulatory note, answering, 221
Consensus, 40, 448
Consumers, dividends of diversity benefit, 89–90
See also Customers
Contact information, e-mail messages conclude with, 177
Contemplation, Asians tend to need time for, 77
Content
business letters, 205–206
notes, C-1
organization, and style, correction symbols for, D-2
organizing for a powerful impact, 427–431
using e-mail smartly and safely, 181
Web sources, 329, 330
Context, 75
Contract, 76
Contractual law, 214

Contradictory messages, nonverbal communication, 55
Control group, 324
Controlled variables, 126
Convention, 362
Conversational, 113–114, 151, 156
but professional, 116
persuasive messages flowing downward should be, 245
Coolidge, Calvin, 50
Cooperation
resolving conflict through, 39
tone of requests invites, 237
Copy notation, business letters, B-6
Copyright, 23, 117–118
Copyright Act of 1976, 117
Copyright infringement, 118
Corporate Average Fuel Economy (CAFE) standards, 323
Corporate blogs, 326
Corporate Services Program, Hands on Miami, 242
Corporate Web sites, 467
Corporation, 401
Correction symbols, D-1–D-2
Correctness
and precision, improving of, 134
proofread for, 204
revise for, 172
using e-mail smartly and safely, 181
Correlations, 355–356
Corrupt, 87
Corruption, global fight against, 88
Corruption Perceptions Index, 87
Cost-cutting measures, obstacles to upward information flow, 20
Courteous language, 114–115
Courtesy copy. *See* Carbon copy
Cover, component of formal report, 403
Cover letter, 489–495
Craigslist, 475
Creative thinking, 5
Credibility, 235, 240, 334
high-context sales letter, 257–258
Credit, refusing of, 291–293
Credit-reporting agency, 291
Creed, Greg, 289
Criteria, ordering information logically by, 362
Critical listening, 51
Critical thinking, 4, 5, 6

Cross-cultural audiences, adapting presentations to, 450–451
Cross-departmental teams, blogs and, 49
Cross-functional teams, 8, 35
Cross-tabulation, 353
Cultural anthropologist, 75
Cultural competence, 79
Cultural differences, 183
Cultural diversity, 72
Culture knowledge and sensitivity, heightened global competition requires, 7
Cultural prejudices, 78
Culture, 73–77, 86
communicating bad news in other, 297
companies must adapt in global markets, 71
dimensions of, 74–77
high-context, 75, 257–259
low-context, 75
Currency of Web sources, 329, 330
Customer letter, 22
adjustment letter, 215
reply letter, 213
response letter, 110
Customer support team, 35
Customer-centric business, 52
Customers
delivering bad news to, 288–293
denying claims, 291
handling problem with orders, 289–291
listening to, 52
refusing credit, 291–293
writing to, 108–109
See also Consumers
Customs, communication skills are key in dealing with different, 7

D

Damage control, 288–289
Damages, recovery of, 214
Dangling modifiers, 137–138
Dash, A-15
Data, 124, 322
analyzing to arrive at conclusions, 358
collection, 406, 418
distinguishing between academic documentation and business practices, 334–335
documenting of, 334–337, 418

electronic research, 329
formats, 83, 337
illustrating of, 337–344
interpreting, 352–357
knowledge workers deal
with, 4
organizing of, 238, 361–365
paraphrasing, 336
primary, 322
report, 323, 333
secondary, 322
Data responses, tabulating
and analyzing, 352–357
Database, 125–126, 488
electronic, 126
Dates, using in intercultural
messages, 85
Dateline, 206
business letters, B-3
Dates, close message with
action information
including, 174
Deadlines, close message
with action information
including, 174
Deceptive or untrue
statements, 23
Decimal outline format,
128–131
Decision makers, writing to,
108
Decision making, 6
Decision matrices, 356–357
Decisions, group and team, 35
Decoding, 13
anticipate problems in, 15
Defamation, 277
lawsuits, 117
Defining the problem,
126–127
Deliberation, Asians tend to
need time for, 77
Delivery of presentation,
444–447
Dell, Michael, 465
Demeanor, during the
interview, 506–507
Demographics, 251
Dependent clauses, 135
Descriptiveness, 81
Design team, 35
Diagram Gallery, 438
Diction, 113
*Dictionary of Occupational
Titles*, 465
Diedrich Coffee, 372
Digital communication
technologies, 5
Digital dirt, 504–505
Digital format, 317
Digression, 447
Direct benefits, 239
Direct claims, 208–210, 211

See also Claim
Direct mail marketing, 249
Direct paragraph, 138, 141
Direct pattern, 131, 212
favorable response to claims
follow, 214
for bad-news letters, 276
for receptive audiences,
131–133
informational reports,
313–314
justification/
recommendation
report, 374
of organizing data, 361
organizational patterns of
reports, 313–314
See also Direct report
pattern
Direct replies, 210–213
Direct report pattern, 313–314,
372–373
See also Direct pattern
Direct requests, 206–208, 209
DirectEmployers Association
(DirectEmployers.com),
468
Direct-mail letters, 202,
249–251
sales letters, 255
Directness
low-context cultures, 79, 259
revising for, 153–154
Disability bias, 113, 116, 206
Discrimination, 90
divisiveness of diversity, 91
suits, 20
Discriminative listening, 51
Discussion boards, 105
Disenfranchised, 91
Disney, 235
Disney/ABC Cable network,
127
Distractions, 14–15
control external and internal,
listening skills, 52
Diversity, 12, 89
dividends of, 89–90
divisiveness of, 91
encouragement of, 42
of teams, 41
See also Workforce diversity
Document format guide,
B–B-11
Document presentation, team-
based, 448–449
Documentation, 334, 335
guide, C-1–C-5
Documents, 366
collaborative, 106
complex, 159
routine, 158–160
team-written, 103–105

Dogpile, 326, 327
Domestic markets, 71
Domino's Pizza, 71
Donation request, refusing,
284
Dovetailing, 140
Downloads, avoid getting
fired over your Internet
use, 180
Downsizing, 20, 171
Downward communication
flow, 19–20
within organizations,
245–246
See also Communication
channels
Drucker, Peter, 5, 15
Dual appeal, 252
Dunkin' Donuts, 71, 372
Dunn, Patricia, 24
Dynamic, 74

E

eBay, 238, 325
E-commerce, 5
Economical, 102
Editing team-based written
and oral presentations,
449
Edmondson, David, 487
Education, 472
Efficiency, North Americans
tend to correlate time
with productivity, 77
Electronic access for formal
research, 125
Electronic address, 175
Electronic databases, 126,
324–325
Electronic handouts, 444
Electronic indexes, 324
Electronic job boards, 482
Electronic job search, 466–468
Electronic presentations, *fig.*, 10
Electronic reports, 311–312
Electronic research data, 329
Electronic slideshows, 435
ELITE (ELIminate The Errors), 36
E-mail, 8, 9, 10, 17, 22, 37, 48,
104, 107, 171
acknowledge receipt of, 182
addresses, 180
applying the writing process
(3 x 3) to, 171–173
as a business document, 58
avoid getting fired over
your Internet use, 180
body, 174
closing, 174–175
content, tone, and
correctness, 181
cover letter, 495

double-check before
sending, 183
getting started, 180
internal communication, 15
messages, B-1–B-2
netiquette, 182
opening, 174
other smart practices, 183
personal use of, 182–183
projecting professionalism,
60
research data, 329
structuring and formatting
of, 173–178
subject line, 173–174
using smartly and safely,
178–183
wireless giant Qualcomm
thrives on, 171, 184
writing typical, 184–191
E-marketing, 249
Emily Post Institute, 279
Emoticons, 178
Emotional appeal, 252
Emotional interference, 14
Empathic communicators, 110
Empathy, 79, 110, 280
Emphatic, 151
Employee morale, 35
flow of information builds,
18
Employment
continual training for
employees, 6
documents and follow-up
messages, 517–521
history, 472–473
interviews, 502–503
letters that deny
applications for, 295
preparing for, 463–466, 488
recommendations, 117
search, 464
Employees, downward flow
of information from
managers to, 19
Empty words, 151, 152–153
Enclosure notation, business
letters, B-6
Encoding, 13
anticipate problems in, 15
End date, 186–187, 205
Enelow, Wendy, 471
English as a second language,
81, 82, 84
Entrepreneurs, 401
Enunciate, 82
Environmental issues,
intercultural ethics of, 88
E-portfolio, 482, 486
Equal Credit Opportunity Act,
291
Equifax, 291

Espressamente, 372
Ethical, 116
  and legal responsibilities, 116–118
  behavior, 23, 88
  business communicators, 23–24
  decisions, 88–89
  insights, 41, 78, 241, 254, 343, 489
  issues, 24–25
  responsibilities, 41, 43
Ethical code of conduct, 86
Ethics, 22–26, 88
Ethnic bias, 112–113
Ethnic makeup of U.S. population, 1980 to 2020, 9
Ethnicity, 9–12, 89
  See also Diversity; Workforce diversity
Ethnocentrism, 78, 86
Etiquette, 61
Evaluate, 102, 125, 149–150, 160–161, 172, 176, 203, 209, 213, 220, 243, 256, 284, 296, 332, 368, 374, 396
  slideshow, 439–440
  team-based written and oral presentations, 449
  See also Writing process (3 x 3) phase 3: evaluate
Envelopes, B-8–B-9
Executive summary, 399, 401, 404, 411, 418
Evidence
  critical thinking and, 5
  effective claim and complaint messages are backed by, 248
Experian, 291
Experimental group, 324
Experimentation, 334
Express rather than impress, goal in business writing, 102
Expressions, avoid ambiguous, 83
Extemporaneous delivery, 444–445
Extemporaneously, 433, 445
External communication, 15, 16
Eye contact, 55, 56, 59, 80–81, 82, 446
  during the interview, 506
  gaining and keeping attention of audience, 429
  keeping your audience engaged by, 441

F
F.U.N. team (Friends Uniting Neighbors), 242
Facebook, 325
Face-to-face, 17
  communicators, 111
  conversation, 107
  meetings, 48, 49, 61, 107
Facial expressions, 56, 59, 80–81, 433
Factiva (Dow Jones), 324, 328
Factoring, 319
Facts, 23, 52, 53
  and sales messages, 252
  in opening of bad news letter, 278
Fair Credit Reporting Act, 291
Fair use, 23, 118
Fallacies, 241
False advertising, marketing information, 117
FAQs (Frequently Asked Questions), 327
FAT™ System, 182
Favor request, 242–244
Favors
  rejecting requests for, 283–286
  thanks for, 219, 220, 222
Fax, 8, 10, 107, 488
  as a channel, 13
  cover sheet, B-9–B-11
Fear of reprisal, obstacles to upward information flow, 20
Feasibility reports, 377, 378
  See also Reports
Federal Trade Commission (FTC), 23, 254
FedEx, 7, 331, 358
Feedback, 13–14, 82, 285
  applying the writing process (3 x 3) to plan for, 173
  communication process, 12, 13–14
  encouragement of, 86
  evaluate messages by, 160
  flows downward from managers to employees, 19
  upward flow of communication, 20
  written communication lacks, 18
Fight-or-flight response, 446
Figures, knowledge workers deal with, 4
File sharing, 9
Fillers, 151, 156
  removing of, 150
Financial analysis, 401–402

Findings, analytical reports, 382
Fireman, Paul, 41, 92
Firestone, 373
First draft, 204
  composing of, 134, 418
  developing a complete message, 175
  partially revised, 161
First Fidelity Trust, 426
Fisher, Sarah, 62
Fjeldheim, Norm, 171, 183, 184
Flabby phrase, 151
Flat team, 35
Flesch-Kincaid Index, 155
Fletcher, Theo, 90
Flexible work schedule, 238
Flexible working arrangements, 9
Flexible workstations, 9
Flipcharts, 434
  brainstorming use of, 127
  See also Charts
Flowcharts, 338, 341, 342
  See also Charts
Fog index. See Gunning's Fog Index
Following up
  after presentation, 444–447
  in writing, 82
Follow-up letter, 289
  application form, 517–519
  application or résumé, 519
  bad news, 289, 290
  employment documents and, 517–521
  job acceptance and rejection letters, 519, 520
  resignation letter, 520–521
Fonts, 443
Footnotes, 118, 334, 375
Foran, Peggy, 206
Forbes, Malcolm, 201, 280, 291
Ford Motor Company, 36, 275
Ford, William, Jr., 275
Foreign Corrupt Practices Act of 1977, 88
Foreign investment, 71
Foreign letters, formatting techniques, 223
Foreign national, 81
Form letters, 286
Formal channel of communication, 18–21
Formal proposals, 394–400
  See also Proposals
Formal reports, 311–312, 402–406, 418
  require all phases of 3-x-3 writing process, 406–417
  work plan for, 321

writing style of, 316
  See also Informal reports; Reports
Formal research, 124, 125–126
  developing ideas for a project by using, 127
  experiment scientifically for, 126
  investigation of primary sources for, 126
  See also Writing process (3-x-3) phase 2: research
Formality, 76
Formats
  alphanumeric outline, 128–131
  APA, 337, 406, 408–417
  correction symbols for, D-2
  data, 83
  decimal outline, 128–131
  digital, 317
  e-mail, 173–178
  envelope, B-8
  letter, 207, 313–314, 316, 371
  manuscript, 316
  memo, 173–178, 315, 316, 368, 369
  MLA, 337, 406
  proofreading for, 158
  reports, 316–317
  scannable résumé, 482
Forming, 37
Forward look, closing bad-news messages, 282
Forwarding, 182
Fragment, 135, A-2
Frame of reference, 12, 14, 20
Franklin, Ben, 110
Free trade, 71
Freebies, 282
Friedman, Nancy, 453
Frito-Lay, 8, 71
Frontloading, 132, 174, 205
Functional headings, 364
Functional résumé. See Résumé
Functional team, 35

G
Gap Inc., 124, 125–126, 127, 133, 141
Gates, Bill, 57, 178
Gender, 9–12, 54, 89, 91
  See also Diversity; Workforce diversity
Gender bias, 112, 116, 206
General Agreement on Tariffs and Trade (GATT), 71
General Electric, 501
General Motors (GM), 36
Generalizations, 74

Geography/space, main ideas organized according to, 429
Georges, Jon, 425, 450, 455
Gerund, A-14–A-15
Gestures, 55, 56, 59, 80–81
    during the interview, 506
    encoding involves, 13
Gift
    intercultural ethics of exchanging, 88
    thanks for, 219, 222
Gilbert, Judy, 509
Gilgen, 435
Glass ceiling, 23, 91
Global competition, 7
Global economy, 70
Global interconnectivity, 72
Global markets
    ethical codes of conduct in, 86
    middle-class growth fuel expansion of, 71
Global treaty banning practice of bribery of foreign government officials, 88
Global village, 70, 71, 325
Globalization, 71–72
Goethe, 322
Goldman Sachs, 394
Goldsmith, Marshall, 279
Good manners, 61
Good news, 214–216
Good wishes, closing bad-news messages, 282
Good-guy syndrome, 277, 278
Goodwill, 61, 115, 171, 206
    basic function of organizational communication, 17
    business communication secondary purpose, 106
    maintaining of when refusing credit, 291
Goodwill messages, 216, 217–222
Goodyear, 373
Google, 105, 260, 326, 328, 437, 490, 501, 509, 521
    Docs & Spreadsheets, 105
    Scholar, 328
GoToMeeting (GoToMeeting.com), 11, 48, 436
GPS devices, 11
Grammar, A-3–A-23
    proofreading for, 157
    use correct, 83
    using correct in intercultural messages, 85
Grammar and mechanics checkpoint exercises, key to, A-19–A-21

correction symbols for, D-1–D-2
    guide, A-1
    guidelines, A-2–A-3
Grammar/style checkers, 159
Grapevine, 21
Graphic technique, 155, 174, 212
Graphics, 134
    formal report preparation of, 418
    illustrating data by matching, 337–342
    in multimedia presentation, 443
    incorporating in reports, 342–344
    making ethical, 343
    See also Charts
Grease payments, intercultural ethics of, 88
Greenfield, Jerry, 201
Greeting, 175–177
Grids, 356
    yardstick report, 379
Grinyer, Dr. Mark, 394, 400, 419
Ground rules, 45
Group decisions, 40
Group interviews, 503
Group sense, valued in high-context cultures, 257
Grouped bar chart. See Bar charts; Charts
Group-oriented cultures, 76
Groups, 35–36
    ethical responsibilities of members and leaders of, 41
    preparing to work with, 35–43
    See also Teams
Groupthink, 39–40, 92
Groupware, 105
Grove, Andrew S., 219
Guffey's 3-x-3 writing process, 102, 125
    See also Writing process (3-x-3)
Guide words, 175
Gunning, Robert, 155
Gunning's Fog Index, 155, 157

H

H. J. Heinz, 71
Hall, Edward T., 57, 75
Hammer, M. R., 81
Handouts, 434, 435, 447
    electronic, 444
Hands on Miami (HOM), 234, 242, 261
    Corporate Services Program, 242

Handwritten note cards, 335–336
Harai, Oren, 5
Hard skills, 3, 34
Hard-copy memos, formatting of, 178, 179
Hard-sell approach, low-context cultures, 259
Harassment suits, obstacles to upward information flow, 20
Hawaiian Electric Co., 395
Headings, 155, 174, 212
    business letters second-page, B-6–B-7
    levels of in reports, 365
    providing reader cues in, 364–365
    tips for maximizing hits, 484
HealthCareWeb.com, 468
Help, 327
Hemphill, Barbara, 182
Hewlett-Packard, 48, 397
Hidden job market, 469
Hierarchical team, 35
High-context cultures, 75, 257–259
    and low-context cultures, use words differently, 76–77
    customize Web content for, 77
    See also Cultures
Hiring/placement interviews, 502–503
Hispanic Association of Colleges and Universities, 298
Hits, 482, 484
Hoku Scientific, 395
Hollister, 124
Honda, 36
Honesty, low-context cultures, 79
Honors, 474
Hook, 397
Horizontal bar chart. See Bar charts; Charts
Horizontal communication flow, 21
    See also Communication channels
Hospitality, thanks for, 219, 222
Hot Topic, 124
How to Search, 327
Hughes, Liz, 181
Human resources information, 117
Hyperlinks, 434, 443–444
    photographs, maps, and illustrations into content, 342

Hyphenation, A-9
Hypothesis, 334
Hypothetical questions, 86
Hyundai Motors, 36

I

IABC Code of Ethics for Professional Communicators, 24
IBM, 72, 79, 90, 319
    Integrated Supply Chain Group, 90
Icon, 77
Iconography, 77
Idea formation, communication process, 12–13
Identifying labels, 182
Idiomatic expressions, 82
Idioms, 83
    in intercultural messages, 85
Illegal questions, 513–514
Illustrations, 338, 342, 418
Illy, 372
Imagery, 431–432
    in multimedia presentation, 443
Immigration, 72
Importance
    main ideas organized according to, 430
    ordering information logically by, 362
Imprecise words, in intercultural messages, 85
Inappropriate questions, 513–514
Inbox, 182
Incentive programs, improving upward information flow, 20–21
Incident reports, 188–190
Inclusive language, 24
Indefinite pronouns, A-5
Independence and freedom from control, low-context cultures value, 75
Independent clauses, 135
    place important idea in, 136
Indirect benefits, 239
Indirect paragraph, 139, 141
Indirect pattern, 131, 242
    for bad news, 276
    for organizing data, 361
    for unreceptive audiences, 133
    handling problems with orders, 289–291
    unfavorable responses to claims follow, 214
    using to prepare the reader, 275–276

Indirect report pattern, 314–315, 373–376
Indirectness
  high-context cultures, 257
  to respect the feelings and dignity of others, 79
Individualism, 75–76
Inducement, 254
Inflated résumés, 489
Inform
  basic function of organizational communication, 17
  business communication primary purpose, 106
InfoMine, 326, 328
Informal channel of communication, 21
Informal proposals, 394–400
Informal reports, 311–312
  components of, 402
  writing style of, 316
  See also Formal reports; Reports
Informal research methods, 124, 126
  conducting an informal survey, 126
  developing ideas for a project by using, 127
  interviewing the audience, 126
  looking in the files, 126
  talking with the boss, 126
Information
  collecting of, 127, 134
  copying and pasting of, 329
  direct requests for, 206–208
  distributing in advance of meeting, 44
  downward flow of, 19–20
  electronic databases, 324–325
  e-mail messages conclude with contact, 177
  formal channels of, 18–21
  horizontal flow of, 21
  improving flow of in organizations, 18–21
  informal channels of, 21
  knowledge workers generate, process and exchange, 5
  logically ordering of, 212, 361–362
  organizing into résumé categories, 471–476
  primary sources of, 330–334
  print resources, 324
  printing of, 329
  rejecting requests for, 283–286

secondary sources of, 322–330
surveys, 330–333
team-based collecting of, 449
upward flow of, 20–21
World Wide Web, 325–330
Information age, 4–6
Information mobility, 326
Information overload, 15
Information technologies, advancement in, 72
Information workers, 5
Informational reports, 312, 313–314, 365–371
  organizational patterns for, 361
  See also Reports
Inform, basic function of organizational communication, 17
InfoSpace, 328
Innovative communication technologies, 8
Inside address, 206, B-3–B-5
Instant communication, 17
Instant messaging (IM), 8, 9, 17, 49, 105, 107, 183
  as a business tool, 184
Instructions
  flow downward from managers to employees, 19
  written in numbered steps, 188
Intel, 219
Intellectual property, 184
Interaction of audience, 444
Interactive communication, 17
Intercultural, 72
  business transactions need special communication training, 7
Intercultural communication, 72
  globalization of markets, 71–72
  intercultural workforce, 72
  recognizing the increasing importance of, 70–72
  technological advancements, 72
Intercultural competence, 81
Intercultural differences, 70
Intercultural environments, 80–86
Intercultural ethics, 86–89
Intercultural letter, 84–85
Intercultural messages, 85
Intercultural proficiency, 78–79, 86
Intercultural workforce, 72
Interest, building of, 239–240
  persuasive messages flowing downward, 246

persuasive messages within organization, 248
requesting favors and actions, 244
sales message, 252, 255
Interest, preparing for employment by identifying your, 464
Interim reports. See Progress reports
Internal communication, 15, 16, 171
Internal persuasive messages, 246
Internal proposals, 372
Internal requests, refusing, 283–286
International Association of Business Communications, 24
International audiences, adapting presentations to, 450–451
International messages, 222–223
Internet, 72, 444
  applying search strategies and techniques, 327–329
  how to avoid getting fired over your use of, 180
  projecting professionalism, 60
  See also World Wide Web
Internet job boards, 466
Internship, 466
Interpersonal communication barriers, overcoming, 14–15
Interpersonal keywords most requested by employers using résumé-scanning software, 484
Interruptions, avoid, 53
Interview, 126, 333
  after, 515–517, 518
  asking your own questions, 514–515
  before, 503–505, 518
  closing, 514–515
  during, 506–507, 518
  See also Employment interviews; Job interview
Interview follow-up letter, 515, 516
Interview questions, 507–514
  about money, 511–512
  about the future, 510
  about your experience and accomplishments, 509–510

behavioral questions, 512–513
challenging, 510–511
illegal and inappropriate questions, 513–514
situational questions, 512
to gauge your interest, 509
to get acquainted, 508
Intimidation, tone of requests avoids, 237
Intranets, 10, 17, 20, 72, 184
  improving downward information flow with, 20
Introduction
  analytical reports, 382
  formal reports, 405,412, 400, 418
  informal proposals, 397–398
  informational reports, 370
  meetings open with brief, 44
  oral presentations, 427–428, 452
  providing reader cues in, 363
Introductory verbal phrases, 137
Investigative reports, 370–371
  See also Reports
Investment information, 116
Invitations, declining, 287
Issues, report should anticipate, 319–320
Italics
  graphic techniques, 155, 156
  tips for maximizing scannability, 482
iTunes, 325

J

Jack in the Box, 3
Jamal, A. J., 319
Janis, Irving, 39
Jargon, 77, 82, 115, 450
JetBlue Airways, 280
Job acceptance letters, 520
Job applicants, saying no to, 295, 297
Job boards, 466–467
Job interview,
  checklist for performing effectively before, during, and after, 518
  understanding its importance, purposes, and types, 501–503
Job objective, preparing for employment, 463
Job placement, importance of communication skills, 3–4
Job plans flow downward from managers to employees, 19

Job search, 466–468
  electronically, 466–468
  using traditional techniques, 468
Jobs
  Googling for, 501, 509
  recognizing the changing nature of, 465
Jobs, Steve, 433, 436, 441, 448
JobStar, 475
Johnson, John H., 111
Jones, Marilee, 472
Journalistic pattern (the six Ws), main ideas organized according to, 430
JSTOR, 328
Judgmentalism, avoiding, 86
Jung, Andrea, 92
Junior Achievement, 298
Junk mail, 250
Justification/recommendation reports, 372–376
  direct pattern, 372–373
  indirect pattern, 373–376
  See also Reports

K

Kaizen, 34
Kane, Joe, 34
Kelleher, Herb, 251, 274
Kerrey, Bob, 4
Keukenhof Gardens, 373
Key idea, 139
  oral presentation focus on, 428
Key terms, definitions of, 405
Keywords, 327, 482
  tips for maximizing hits, 484
KFC, 3, 149
King, Rollin, 274
KISS (Kept It Short and Simple!) principle, 150
Kiuchi, Masao, 80
Kmart, 3, 4, 22, 26
Knight, Bob, 137
Knowledge workers, 4–6
Knowledge-based economy, 7

L

Lag time, 54
Lally, Austin, 253
Lampert, Edward S., 3
Land's End, 108, 109, 251, 281
Language
  avoiding actionable, 291–293
  based on pictographical characters representing meanings of words, 77
  basic expressions in other, 82

courteous, 114–115
  of adjustment letters, 217
  positive and negative expressions, 114
  precise, 115
  simplifying, 115
  skill, lack of, 14
  specialized, 115
  that use letters describing sounds of words, 77
  using bias-free, 112–113
Laptop computers, 11
Laun, Peggy, 320
Laybourne, Gerry, 127
Leadership 2000 initiative, Toyota, 43
Leadership, teams shared, 43
Leading questions, 331
Lee Jeans, 311, 320, 322, 344
Legal and ethical responsibilities, adapting to, 116–118
Legal problems in bad-news messages, 277–278
  abusive language, 277
  careless language, 277
  good-guy syndrome, 278
Letter format, 316
  sends silent but positive messages, 206
Letter of application, 489–495
Letter of transmittal, 399, 401, 403, 409, 418
Letter proposals, 395
Letterhead, business letters, B-3
Letters, 107, 201
  as a channel, 13
  external communication, 15
  of appreciation, 219
  placement, B-3
  styles, B-7–B-8
  that deny applications for employment, 295
Levin, Carl, 323
Levi-Strauss, 36
Levitt, Arthur, 155
Lewis, Aylwin B., 3, 4, 6, 22, 26
LexisNexis, 326
  Academic, 324, 328
Liability, 277, 280
Libel, 277
Librarian's Index to the Internet, 328
Libraries, 126, 465
Lifestyles, communication skills
  are key in dealing with different, 7
Limitations, 318–319
Limiting sentence, 138–139
  See also Sentences

Line charts, 338, 340
  multiple, 340
  segmented, 340
  simple, 340
  See also Charts
Line endings, business letters, B-3
Linear logic, 75
LinkedIn, 490
Linking verbs, A-9
List of figures, 399, 404, 410
Listening, 50–54
  critical, 51
  discriminative, 51
  in the workplace, 50–54
  skills, 14, 50, 52–54
  techniques, 51
  to customers, 51
  without interrupting, 82
Literature review, 405
Litigation, 116
Litigious business environment, 117
Liz Claiborne, 72
Local formats, 83, 86
Logical development, writing persuasive claim and complaint messages, 249
Long John Silver's, 3
Long lead-ins, 151, 156
  deleting of, 151–152
Loss, persuasion recognizes the power of, 236
Low-context cultures, 75, 259
  and high-context cultures, use words differently, 76–77
  customize Web content for, 77
  value individualism, 75
  See also Cultures
Luntz, Frank, 235

M

Magic Johnson Theatres, 41
Mailing address, B-9
Mailing lists, 105, 251
Main heading, 471
Main idea, labeling of, 136
Main sentence, 138–139
  See also Sentences
Majority, 40
  rule, 448
Management
  team-based, 7–8
  selling an idea to, 246
Management hierarchy, 7
Management style
  command and control, 7
  coordination and cultivation, 7
  hamburger, 79

Managers, downward flow of information to employees, 19
Mango, 124
Manners, good, 61
Manual search for formal research, 126
Manuscript format, 316
Maps, 338, 342
MapQuest, 325
Market analysis, 401
Marketing information, 117
Marketing messages, 250
  direct-mail sales letters, 249–251
  planning and composing, 249–256
  sales message, 251–256
Markets, globalization of, 71–72
Marriott Corporation, 358–360
Marriott Hotel, 76, 362
Marshall Fields, 352
Massachusetts Institute of Technology (MIT), 472
Mattel, 7
McCullough, David, 311
McDonald's, 7, 71, 149, 372
Mean, 354–355
Meaning, transmission of, 12
Median, 354–355
Meeting agenda, 44, 45
Meetings, 43–47
  avoiding issues that sidetrack, 46
  deciding necessity of, 44
  distributing advance information for, 44
  ending and following up of, 47
  getting started, 44–45
  handling conflict in, 47
  improving downward information flow with, 20
  planning and participating in productive, 43–47
  selecting participants for, 44
Melting pot, 72
Memo format, 316
Memorandums, 171
  See also Memos
Memory stick, 329
Memos, 107, 189
  body of, 174
  closing of, 174–175
  formatting hard-copy memos, 178
  internal communication, 15
  opening, 174
  subject line, 173–174
  writing typical e-mail, 22, 171–173, 173–178, 184–191

Menu Foods, Inc., 132
Merge fields, 286
Mergers, 71
Message decoding, 12, 13
Message encoding, 12, 13
Message transmission, 7, 12
Messages
    adapting to receiver, 13
    audience focus, 111, 116
    claim and complaint,
        248–249
    contradictory, 55
    developing complete, 175
    direct-mail sales letters,
        249–251
    emphasize the positive in
        mixed, 212
    nonverbal, 13, 55–59
    predicting the effect of, 13
    revising, 156, 176
    sales, 249–256
    sender focus, 111
    verbal, 13
    See also E-mail; Persuasive
        messages
Messmer, Max, 128, 202
Metaphors, 431, 432
Metasearching, 326, 327
Microsoft, 5, 57, 178, 382, 436
    Live Meeting, 11
    Word, 105
Miller, Mark, 426
Mini-agenda for telephone
    calls, 452
    See also Agenda
Minority, 40
    See also Diversity; Workforce
        diversity
Minutes, 45
Miranda, Anthony, 366
Miscommunication, 14
Misplaced modifiers, 137–138,
    141
Mission statement, 401
Misunderstanding, obstacles
    that create, 14–15
Mixed message, 212
Mixed punctuation style, B-8
MLA. See Modern Language
    Association
Mobile communication, 17
Mobile technologies, 9
Mode, 354–355
Modern Language Association
    (MLA), 375–376, 406, C-1
    bibliographic format, C-2
    citation format, 337
    format, C-1–C-2
    in-text format, C-1–C-2
    sample Works Cited, C-3
    text page, portions of, C-2
Modified block style,
    B-4, B-8

Modifiers. See Dangling
    modifiers; Misplaced
    modifiers
Money
    North Americans tend to
        correlate time with
        productivity, 77
    rejecting requests for,
        283–286
Monster Board, 467
Monster.com, 466
Morale, 242, 294
    flow of information builds
        employee, 18
Morris, Pat, 234, 242, 261
Motorola, 104
Mountain View Googleplex,
    501
MSN, 326
Multiethnic, 72
Multifunctional printers, 10
Multimedia presentation,
    435–444, 452
Multimedia slides, 434
Multinational alliances, 70
Multinational companies, 72
Multiple line chart. See Line
    charts
Multitasking, 15, 112
MySpace, 325

N

Names, proofreading of, 157
National Association of Sales
    Professionals, 467–468
National Commission on
    Writing, 4
National Organization for
    Women (NOW), 78
National origin, workforce
    diversity, 89
National Polar-Orbiting
    Operational
    Environmental Satellite
    System, 394
Natural language-processing
    technology, 326
Neeleman, 280
Negative expressions,
    114, 116
Negative language, 217
Negative tactics of persuasion,
    235
Negative team behavior, 38,
    39
Negative words, 216
Nestlé, 372
Netiquette, 182
Networking, 468, 469
New School University, 4
New York NY Fresh Deli, 71
Newell Rubbermaid, 71

News. See Bad news; Good
    news; Press releases
Newsgroups, 325
Newsletters, improving
    downward information
    flow with, 20
Nguyen, Tien, 505
Niche, 468
Nickelodeon, 90
Nickelodeon/Nick at Nite, 127
Nielsen BuzzMetrics, 125
Nifong, Mike, 280
Nike, 7, 71, 362
    advertisements in Japan,
        257
Nissan Motor Company, 377
Noise, 13
Nokia, 71, 104, 358
Nominative case. See
    Subjective-case
Nonjudgmental, 112
Nonjudgmentalism, 81
Nonverbal behavior,
    international and cross-
    cultural audiences,
    450–451
Nonverbal communication,
    55–59, 80
    in intercultural
        environments, 80–81
    forms of, 56–59
    functions of, 55–56
    skills in the workplace, 59
Nonverbal cues, 81, 86
    reinforce spoken words, 56
Nonverbal messages, 13,
    432–433
    communicating through,
        55–59
    forms of, 56–59
    functions, 55–56
    sending positive, during the
        interview, 506
Nooyi, Indra, 358
Norming, 37, 38
North American Free Trade
    Agreement (NAFTA), 71
Notes, take to ensure
    retention, 54
Noun conversion, 153, 156
Nouns, collective, A-5
Number usage, A-18–A-19
Numbered lists, 154–155, 174,
    212
Numbers, proofreading of, 157
Numerical data, 311–312, 352

O

O*NET Occupational
    Information Network, 465
O'Connor, Sandra Day, 444
O'Neill, Danny, 106

Objections, translate into
    selling points, 253
Objective-case, A-6–A-7
    constructions, who/
        whomever, A-7
Objective language, 249
Objectives, illustrating data by
    matching, 337–342
Objects
    of prepositions, A-6–A-7
    of verbs, A-6–A-7
Observation, 334
Obstacles
    overcoming
        communication, 15
    to downward information
        flow, 19–20
    to upward information flow,
        20
Occupational Outlook
    Handbook,
    466
OfficeTeam, 181
Oistamo, Kai, 358
Old boy networks, glass ceiling
    as invisible barrier of, 91
Old Navy, 124, 125–126, 133
Ombudsman, 21
One-on-one interviews, 503
One-to-one relationship, 468
Online catalogs, 324
Online collaboration tools,
    104
Online networking, 469
Online proposals, 399
Online videos, 482
Open Directory Project, 327
Open office, 9, 10
Open-ended questions, 207
Opening, 174, 204
    adjustment letter, 214–216
    bad news letter, 278–279,
        293
    business letters, 205
    cover letters, 490–491, 495
    delivering bad news within
        organizations, 295
    e-mail messages and
        memos, 174, 191
    oral presentations, 427
    persuasive request, 239
    press release, 259–261
    procedural message, 188
    report, 363
    request message, 184
    response message, 187
    sales messages, 251
Operations and management,
    401
Opinions, 23, 52
    critical thinking and, 5
Optical character recognition
    (OCR), 481–482

Oral communication, 15, 17–18
  enhancing in intercultural
    environments, 81–82
  skills, 4
Oral presentations
  adapting to international
    and cross-cultural
    audiences, 450–451
  building audience rapport
    like a pro, 431–433
  checklist for preparing and
    organizing, 452
  computers can help create,
    134
  focus on a few key ideas, 428
  knowing your audience,
    426–427
  knowing your purpose, 426
  nonverbal messages,
    432–433
  organizing content for
    a powerful impact,
    427–431
  organizing team-based,
    448–449
  outline, 428
  planning visual aids
    and multimedia
    presentations, 433–435
  preparing effective,
    425–427
  understanding different
    values and nonverbal
    behavior, 450–451
  using effective imagery,
    431–432
  verbal signposts, 432
Oral reports, 311–312
Orders, problems with
    handling, 289–291
Organization charts, 338,
    341–342
Organization for Economic
    Cooperation and
    Development (OECD), 88
Organizations
  business communicators act
    as agents of, 278
  communicating in, 15–18, 19
  delivering bad news within,
    293–297
  flow of information in,
    18–21
  saying no to job applicants,
    295
  writing persuasive messages
    within, 244–248
Organizational
    communication, basic
    functions of, 17
Organizational success,
    importance of
    communication skills, 3–4

Organize, 102, 125, 127–133,
    176, 203, 209, 213, 220,
    243, 256, 284, 296, 332,
    368, 374, 396, 405
  team-based written and oral
    presentations, 449
  See also Writing process
    (3-x-3) phase 2:
    organize
Organizing data, 238
Oriental Land Company, 425
Orman, Suze, 101, 112, 118
OSRAM, 71
Outline, 128–131, 172, 204,
    238, 407
Outliner, 134
Outsiders, saying no to
    requests from, 283
Outsourcing, 5
Overhead transparencies,
    434–435
Oxygen Media, 127

P

Page, Larry, 509
Pagers, 11
Pampers, 253
Panel interviews, 503
Paragraphs, 138–139
  checklist for composing, 141
  direct paragraph plan, 138
  pivoting paragraph plan,
    139
  use short, 83
Parallel construction, 358
Parallelism, 154, 156, 207, 407
Paraphrase, 54, 335, 336
Parentheses, A-15
Parenthetical citations, 334
Parker, Yana, 471
Parkland Burn Camp, 298
Partnership, 401
Passive voice, 136–137, 141,
    282
Pat on the back, responding
    to, 221
Patience, 79
Patterns, organizing ideas into,
    131
PDAs. See Personal digital
    assistants
PDF, 444, 488
Peer-to-peer tools, 8
People, appearance of, 58–59
People skills, 35
PepsiCo, 7, 90, 358, 372
Pepsi-Cola, 133, 322
Percentage, 353
Performance, importance of
    communication skills, 3–4
Performing, 37, 38
Period, A-15

Periodic (activity) reports,
    366–367, 368
  See also Reports
Periodical indexes, 126
Periodicals, 324
Perks, 352
Personal anecdotes, 431, 432
Personal data, 475
Personal digital assistants
    (PDAs), 8, 10, 11, 326
Personal language trainer,
    A-1–A-2
Personalized statistics, 431, 432
Persuading. See Persuasion
Persuasion, 234–235
  basic function of
    organizational
    communication, 17
  business communication
    primary purpose, 106
  comparing in high- and
    low-context cultures,
    257–259
  effective and ethical use of,
    234–237
  importance of tone, 237
  negative tactics of, 235
  what's fair in, 241
Persuasive, 101
  press releases, 259–261
Persuasive claim, 248–249, 250
Persuasive message, 237–238,
    239–242
  flowing downward, 245–246
  flowing upward, 246–248
  focus on audience needs or
    goals, 238
  internal, 246
  within organizations,
    244–248
Persuasive request, 242–244
  favor requests, 243, 244
  flowing downward,
    245–246
  for action, 236, 242–244
  key components of, 238
Peters, Tom, 334
Pfizer Corporation, 206
Phelps County Bank, 320
Phone call, 107
Phone conferencing, 48
Phonetically, 81
Photograph, 338, 342
Phrases, 135
  and verb agreement, A-4
Physical ability, workforce
    diversity, 89
Physical distractions, 14
Physically challenged
    individuals, 91
  See also Diversity; Workforce
    Diversity
Physical proximity, 81

Pie charts, 338, 341
  See also Charts
Piecewicz, Mary, 397
Pilot study, 333
Pivoting paragraph, 139, 141
Pizza Hut, 3, 149
Plagiarism, 334–335
Plain English, 24, 82, 86
Plain-paper return address,
    business letters, B-7
Plain-text format (.txt), 486
Plain-text résumé. See Résumé
Plan, feasibility reports
    analyze, 377
Planning team, 35
Plural verbs, A-5
Podcasts, 11, 326
Points of Light Foundation,
    242
Policies, flow downward from
    managers to employees,
    19
Polite command, 186, 207
Politeness, high-context
    cultures, 257
Portals, 105
Portland's Coffee People, 372
Positive language, 114, 116
  bad news letter, 281
Positive team behavior, 38, 39
Possessive case, A-7
Post hoc, 241
Post, Emily, 279
Post, Peter, 279
Posture, 56, 59, 80
  during the interview, 506
Powell, Colin, 150
PowerPoint, 435–440, 458
Precise language, 115
Prejudices, 74
  glass ceiling as invisible
    barrier of, 91
Prepositional phrases, revise
    for conciseness, 152
Prepositions, objects of,
    A-6–A-7
Presence, IM's concept of, 49
Presence technology, fig., 11
Presentation software, 134
Presentations, 22
  time-tested guidelines to
    follow during your,
    446–447
  tips for a smooth start
    before your, 445–446
  See also Oral presentations
Press releases, 259–261
Prewriting, 104, 125, 176, 203,
    209, 213, 220, 243, 256,
    276, 284, 296, 332, 368,
    374, 396
  delivering bad news to
    customer, 293

Prewriting (cont.)
  delivering bad news within organizations, 295
  persuasive messages within organization, 248
  phase of 3-x-3 writing process, 102, 172
  phase of composition, 106
  refusing typical requests, 288
  requesting favors and actions, 244
  sales messages, 255
PricewaterhouseCoopers, 90
Primary audience, 109
Primary data, 322
Primary readers, 319
Primary sources, 126
  gathering information from, 330–334
Print indexes, 324
Print resources, 324
Print-based résumé. See Résumé
Printed forms, 317
Printers, multifunctional, 10
Problem or purpose, 405
Problem solving, sharpening your skills for, 6
Problem statement, 318
Problem/solution, main ideas organized according to, 430
Problems with orders, handling, 289–291
Problem-solving meetings, 44
Procedural messages, 187–188
Procedures
  flow downward from managers to employees, 19
  written in numbered steps, 188
Procter & Gamble, 71, 72, 90, 253
Product liability, 116
Product/service description, 401
Productive meetings, planning and participating in, 43–47
Productivity, North Americans tend to correlate time with productivity, 77
Professional direct mailers, 250
Professional image, 113
Professionalism, 60–61
Profiling your audience, 109, 116
Progress and interim reports, 369–370
  See also Reports
Progress report, 22, 369–370, 371

Project team, 35
Pronoun case, A-6–A-7
Pronoun reference, A-8–A-9
Pronouns
  agree in number and gender with antecedents, A-8
  avoid first-person, 407
  ending in self, A-7
  help build coherence and continuity, 139–140
  indefinite, A-5
  it, which, this, and that refer to clear antecedents, A-8–A-9
  objective-case, A-6–A-7
  possessive case, A-7
  subjective-case, A-6
Proofread, 102, 125, 149–150, 157–160, 172, 176, 203, 209, 213, 220, 243, 256, 284, 296, 332, 368, 374, 396, 418
  slideshow, 439–440
  See also Writing process (3-x-3) phase 3: proofread
Propaganda, 330
Proper adjectives, A-16
Proper nouns, A-16
Proposal, 22, 394, 400
  feasibility reports analyze, 377
  formal, 394–400
  informal, 394–400
Proprietorship, 401
Props, 434
Protocol Telecommunications, 366
Prototypes, 74
Psychological compensation, 217
Public Company Accounting Reform and Investor Protection Act of 2002, 23
Public domain, 118
Puffery, 254
Punctuation, A-9–A-12
  business letters, B-2–B-3
  other, A-15–A-16
  proofreading for, 157
  styles, B-7–B-8
Punitive, 281
Puns, 82
Purpose
  analyzing, in persuasive messages, 237–238
  formal report analysis of, 418
  identifying, 106, 116
  knowing, in oral presentation, 426

Purpose statement, 318
Purposeful, 101

Q
Qdoba, 149
Qualcomm, 171, 183, 184, 191
Qualifications, preparing for employment by evaluating your, 464–465
Quality control, 5
Quality control circle, 35
Quantifiable, 331
Quantitative, 353
Query, 327
Question mark, A-15
Questionnaires, 330
Questions
  ask clarifying, 53
  employment interview, 504, 507–514, 514–515
  encourage feedback, 14, 15
  FAQs, 327
  gaining and keeping attention of audience, 429
  hypothetical, 86
  leading, 331
  open-ended, 207
  presentation techniques for handling, 447
  profiling your audience by, 109
Quota, 127
Quotation marks, A-16
Quotations, documenting data, 337

R
Race, 89
  See also Diversity; Workforce diversity
Racial bias, 112–113, 116, 206
Racial makeup of U.S. population, 1980 to 2020, 9
RadioShack Corp., 107, 295, 487
Ragged-right margins, 178, 206
Range, 354–355
Rank, 83
Rank-and-file employees, 171
Rapport, 431
Raspberry, William, 157
Rational appeal, 252
Raw data, 337
Raw materials, 4
Raytheon, 394, 398, 400, 419
Read Across America, 298
Readability, 140, 154–156, 183
  applying the Fog index to determine, 157

measuring formulas for, 155–156
  revise for, 154–155
Reader benefit, 239
  bad news letter citing of, 281
Reader cues, providing, 363–365
Readers' Guide to Periodical Literature, 324
Reading e-mail, 182
Reasoning, analytical reports, 371–382
Reasons, 276
  bad-news letter presentation of, 280–281, 293
  critical thinking and, 5
  delivering bad news within organizations, 295
  refusing typical requests, 288
Reasons-before-refusal pattern, 283, 291
Receiver, 13
Receptive audiences, 131–133
Recommendation reports. See Justification reports
Recommendations, 358–360
  analytical reports, 371–382
  making of, 357–361
  moving from findings to, 360–361
  of formal report, 406, 416, 418
  preparing report, 358–360
Recovery of damages, 214
Recruiters, 466, 509
Recursive, 103
Red Baron, 36
Red tape, 71
Redundancies, 151, 156
  eliminating of, 152
Reebok, 41, 92, 362
Reference books, A-2
Reference initials, B-6
Reference line, B-5
Reference request, 515–517
References, 475–476, C-3
  APA sample, C-5
  citing of, 334
  formal report, 406, 417, 418
  portions of APA text page and, C-4
Refusals
  bad news letter implying, 282
  credit, 291–293
  donation request, 284
  internal requests, 283–286
  invitation, 287
  reasons-before-refusal pattern, 283, 291
  typical requests, 283–288

Rejection follow-up letter, 519
Rejection letters, 520
Relationship appeal, high-context cultures, 257
Religion, 7
   See also Diversity; Workforce diversity
Rensselaer Polytechnic Institute, 472
Reply letters, 213, 218
   that comply with requests, 218
   that make adjustments, 218
Replying to e-mail, 182
Report data. *See* Data
Report headings, 364–365
Report introduction, 363, 405
Reports, 311
   applying the writing process (3 x 3) to, 317–321
   as a channel, 13
   conclusions of, 359–360, 405–406
   electronic, 311–312
   executive summary, 404
   formats of, 316–317, 408–417
   functions of, 312
   incorporating graphics in, 342–344
   letter or memo of transmittal, 403
   list of figures, 404
   management decisions are based on, 311
   or proposal, 107
   oral, 311–312
   organizational patterns, 312–315
   preparing a work plan, 320–321
   recommendations of, 358–360, 406
   understanding basics of, 311–317
   writing style of, 316
   See also Analytical reports; Feasibility reports; Formal reports; Incident reports; Informal reports; Informational reports; Investigative reports; Justification/recommendation reports: Periodic (activity) reports; Progress and interim reports; Progress reports; To-file reports; Trip, convention, and conference reports; Yardstick reports
Request for proposal (RFP), 394, 399

Requests, 184–187, 206
   checklist for writing direct, 210
   declining invitations, 287
   e-mail, 186
   for favors and actions, 242–244
   for information or action, 206–208, 210
   refusing internal, 283–286
   refusing typical, 283–288
   rejecting requests for favors, money, information, and action, 283–286
   saying *no* to requests from outsiders, 283
   using effective persuasion techniques, 235–236
   See also Persuasive request, 238
Resale, 217, 283
Research, 102, 124, 125, 176, 203, 209, 213, 220, 238, 243, 256, 284, 296, 322, 368, 374, 396
   electronic notetaking, 336
   formal research methods, 125–126
   generating ideas by brainstorming, 126–127
   informal methods, 126
   manual notetaking, 335–336
   of product or service, sales messages, 251
   See also Writing process (3-x-3) phase 2: research
Researching. *See* Research
Resignation letter, 520–521
Resistance, 237
   to change, 35
Resistance, reducing of
   high-context sales letter, 258–259
   persuasive messages flowing downward, 246
   persuasive messages within organization, 248
   persuasive request, 240
   requesting favors and actions, 244
   sales message, 252–253, 255
   techniques for, 253
Response, 187
Résumé, 22, 469–470
   action verbs in, 474
   applying the final touches to, 486–488
   chronological, 470, 477, 478, 479, 480
   cover letter to accompany, 489–495
   digitizing in an e-portfolio, 486

   functional, 470, 481
   inflated, 489
   length of, 470
   optimizing for today's technologies, 476–486
   organizing information into categories, 471–476
   posting of, 468
   plain-text, 484–486, 487
   print-based résumé, 477–481
   proofreading, 487
   references, 475–476
   scannable, 481–484, 485
   submitting, 487–488
   video résumé, 486
Résumé follow-up letter, 519
Résumé-scanning software, 484
Retention, 54
Return address, B-8
Review exercises, A-1
Revise, 102, 125, 149–150, 172, 176, 203, 209, 213, 220, 243, 256, 277, 284, 296, 332, 368, 374, 396
   e-mail, 175, 176
   for clarity, 150–151, 172
   for conciseness, 151–153
   for conversational tone, 151
   for readability, 154–156
   for vigor and directness, 153–154
   slideshow, 439–440
   team-based written and oral presentations, 449
   See also Writing process (3-x-3) phase 3: revise
Revising. *See* Writing process (3-x-3) phase 3: revise
Rewriting, phase of 3-x-3 writing process, 102
Riccardi, Toni, 90
Rich text format (.rtf), 486
Riley Guide, 465
Risk, groups and teams have reduced, 35
Robert Half International, 128, 181
Robert's Rules, 45
Ronald McDonald House, 298
Rosen, Robert, 55
Routine documents, how to proofread, 158–160
Routine letters, 202
Routine requests and responses, 204
Royal Caribbean International, 214
Rules
   learn about your company's Internet policy, 180, 183
   of culture, 73

Run-on, 135, A-2
Ryan, Liz, 463, 475, 490, 496

S

Safety information, adapting to legal and ethical responsibilities, 116–117
Salary negotiation dos and don'ts, 511
Sales letters, 256
   analyzing high-context, 257–259
   what's legal and not legal, 254
Sales message, 249–256
   applying the 3 x 3 writing process to, 251
   building interest, 252
   checklist for, 255
   crafting a winning, 251–256
   direct-mail sales letters, 249–251
   gaining attention, 251–252
   high-context culture, 258
   motivating action, 254–255
   planning and composing effective, 249–256
   putting it all together, 255–256
   reducing resistance, 252–253
Sales promotion, 283
Sales report, 22
Salutation
   business letters, B-5
   e–mail, B-2
Sant, Dr. Tom, 399
Sanyo Electric, 395
Sarbanes-Oxley Act (SOX), 23, 25, 88
Satellite communications, 8
Saving face, 79
Saving sources to disk, 329
Scalable fonts, 134
Scannable résumé. *See* Résumé
Schechtman, Morris, 43
Scholarly sources, 330
Schultz, Howard, 173, 352, 372, 382, 427
Scientific experiment, 126
Scope, 318, 405
Scratch list, 128–131
Screening interviews, 502
Sealed Air Corporation, 41
Search, 328
Search engines, 326–329
Search tools, 326–327
Sears, 3, 4
Sears Holdings Corporation, 3, 4, 6, 22, 26
Sears Roebuck, 3, 22, 26

Seattle's Best Coffee, 372
Secondary audience, 109
Secondary data, 322
Secondary readers, 319
Secondary sources, gathering
    information from,
    322–330
    electronic databases,
        324–325
    print resources, 324
    World Wide Web, 325–330
Second-page heading,
    business letters, B-6–B-7
Segmented 100% bar chart.
    See Bar charts
Segmented line (area) chart.
    See Line charts
Seiyu, 70, 80, 93
Self-identity, 74
Selfless, goodwill message
    should be, 218, 222
Semicolons, A-12–A-14
Sender, 12
    cover letter, 495
    encodes idea in message, 13
    feedback travels to, 13–14
    focus of message, 111
    idea formation of, 12–13
Senk, Glen, 242
Sentences, 135
    checklist for composing, 141
    comma-splice, A-2–A-3
    complete, 135
    creating effective, 135–138
    emphasizing important
        ideas, 136
    fragments, A-2
    length of, 83, 155–156
    limiting, 138
    main, 138
    managing active and
        passive voice, 136–137
    place the important idea
        either first or last in, 136
    preferring short, 135–136
    run-on (fused), A-2
    simple, 136
    structure, A-2–A-3
    supporting, 138
Sequential interviews, 503
7-Eleven, 71
Sexism, 91
Sexual harassment, 91
Shared conference rooms, 9
Short, goodwill message
    should be, 219, 222
Short-term goal, low-context
    cultures, 259
Shouting, 182
SideKick Enterprises, 49
Siemens AG, 79
Signature block, 177, B-5–B-6
Significance, 318, 405

Silence, 80
Similes, 431, 432
Simple line chart. *See* Line
    charts
Simple sentence, 136
    See also Sentences
Simple/complex, main ideas
    organized according to,
    430
Sincere, goodwill message
    should be, 219, 222
Singular verbs, A-5
Sirius, 403
Situational questions, 512
6-x-6 rule, 437
SixFigureJobs.com, 468
Size of teams, 41
Skills, 473
Skim value, 154–155, 186, 204
Skype, 48, 183
Slander, 277
Slang, 77, 82, 183
    in intercultural messages, 85
Slide deck, 448
Slides, 437, 438, 439, 442
Slideshow, 437–439
    electronic, 435
    revising, proofreading, and
        evaluating, 439–440
Small Business Administration
    (SBA), 401, 402
Smart phones, 17, 60, 326
Social interaction, 57
Social rules, 76
Soft skills, 3, 34–35
Softphones, 10
Soft-sell approach, high-
    context cultures, 257
Solicited jobs, 490–491, 492
Solicited proposal, 394
Source notes, C-1
Sources and methods, 405
Southwest Airlines, 251, 274,
    294, 298
Space, 56, 59, 80
    desks that save, 9
Spacing, business letters,
    B-2–B-3
Spam, 171, 182
Spam filters, 173
Speak right, A-2
Speakerphones, 37
Speaker's notes, 435, 452
Special effects in multimedia
    presentation, 443
Specialized language, 115
Specific, goodwill message
    should be, 218, 222
Speech habits, projecting
    professionalism, 60
Spell checkers, 159
Spell right, A-2
Spelling, proofreading for, 157

Spiders, 326
Spiral logic, 75
Spontaneous, goodwill
    message should be, 219,
    222
Sprint writing, 134, 135
Staffing, 398, 400
Stage fright, 445, 446
Stanford University, 425
STAR techniques, 512
Starbucks, 71, 173, 352, 353,
    372, 382, 427
Statements in employee
    handbooks, 117
Steering group, 35
Stereotypes, 74, 112
Stop words, 327
Storming, 37
Stouffer Foods, 23
Straightforward claim, 208
Straightforwardness, 76
Streaming videos, 180
Stress interviews, 503
Subcategories, 130
Subcommittee, 40
Subject directories, 326, 327
Subject line, 173–174, 212
    business letters, B-5
    e-mail messages and
        memos, 173–174, 180,
        182, 191
Subject of e-mail message, B-2
Subordinate, 5, 150, 237
Subordinate clause, 281
Subjective-case, A-6
    constructions, *who/whoever*,
    A-7
Subjunctive mood, A-4
Summary
    close message with, 174
    informational reports, 370
Summer job, 466
Suntech Power Holdings, 395
Superiors
    listening to, 51
    writing to, 108
Superlatives, 259
Supplier team, 35
Supporting sentence, 138–139
    See also Sentences
Supportiveness, 81
Survey data, converting into
    finished tables, 354
Surveys, 126, 330–333
Suze Orman Financial Group,
    118
Sylvania, 71
Symantec, 240
Symbols, knowledge workers
    deal with, 4
Sympathy note, 221
Synonyms, 115, 336
Syntax, 329

Synthesize, 104, 335
Systematic, 101

T

Table of contents
    business plans, 401
    formal report, 404, 410, 418
    proposals, 399
Tables, 174, 212, 337–339,
    353–354
Tabulate, 352
Taco Bell, 3, 149, 158, 160, 289
Tact, 137
Talking headings, 364
Tanguay, Ray, 34
Target, 22
Target audience, 126
    press releases, 259–261
    See also Audiences
Task force, 35
Taylor, Fred, 274, 294
TEAM (Together, Everyone
    Achieves More), 40
Team diversity, 40
Team skills, 35
Team-based management,
    7–8
Team-based written and oral
    presentations, 448–449
Teammates, listening to, 51
Teams, 35–36
    acceptance of ethical
        responsibilities in, 43
    agreement in, 41, 42
    analyzing positive and
        negative behavior of, 38
    characteristics of, 40–41
    collaboration ability of, 42
    communication techniques
        of, 42
    conflict in, 42
    development phases of,
        37–38
    effective, 36, 42
    preparing to work with,
        35–43
    shared leadership of, 43
    small and diverse, 41
    virtual, 36–37
Teamwork drives Toyota to
    success, 34
Teamwork skills, 4
Team-written documents,
    103–105
Tech Talk
    computers help create
        better written
        messages, oral
        presentations, and
        Web pages, 134
    customized Web site, 77
    electronic research data, 329

how to avoid getting fired over your Internet use, 180
instant messaging, 183
spell checkers and grammar/style checkers, 159
using technology to edit and revise collaborative documents, 106
using technology to personalize form letters, 286
virtual teams, 37
Technological advancements, 72
Technology
  blogs, 49
  constantly changing of, 6
  instant messaging (IM), 49
  mobile, 9
  using to edit and revise collaborative documents, 106
  using to facilitate collaboration, 48–50
  using to personalize form letters, 286
  videoconferencing, 48
  voice conferencing, 48
  Web conferencing, 48–49
  wikis, 50
Telecommuting, 9
Teleconferencing, 8, 37, 48, 107
Telephone
  as a channel, 13
  improving skills, 451–454
  projecting professionalism, 60
Telephone tag, 453
Telephony: VoIP (Voice over Internet Protocol), 10
Telepresence systems, 48
Template, 437
Temporary workers, obstacles to upward information flow, 20
Territory, 56, 59, 80
Testimonial, 252, 253
Text of multimedia presentation, 443
Text messaging, 8, 9, 17
Thank you message, 219, 220
The Coffee Bean & Tea Leaf, 372
The Jobs Rated Almanac, 466
The Roasterie, 106
The Toyota Way, 34, 62
Thesaurus, 115
Third World countries, 88
Thompson, John W., 240
Thread, 182
3-x-3 writing process. See Writing process (3-x-3)

3M Corporation, 44
Three statistical concepts, mean, median, and mode, 354–355
Three-point introduction, 453
Timberland, 44
Time, 56, 59, 80
  ordering information logically by, 361–362
  limits for brainstorming, 127
  writing tips, 406
Time orientation, 77
Title page, 399, 403, 418
Titles, A-17
  observe, 83
To-file reports, 188–190
Tokyo Disneyland, 425, 450
Tolerance, 79
Tone, 109, 237
  of e-mail, 181
  of goodwill, 206
  of intercultural messages, 84, 85
  of persuasive claim and complaint messages, 249
  of persuasive message flowing upward, 246
  of persuasive messages flowing downward, 245
  of request letters, 208
  revising for conversational, 151
Topic, effective paragraphs focus on one, 138
Topic search, 327
Topic/function/conventional grouping, main ideas organized according to, 429
Top-of-screen test, e-mail, 180
Torrefazione Italia, 372
Tort law, 116, 214
Toshiba Corporation, 79
Toyota, 5, 34, 43, 62
  Institute, 62
  Motor Manufacturing Canada, 34
  North American Parts Center California (NAPCC), 34, 43
Track Changes and Comment feature in Word, 105, 106
Trade agreements, 71
Tradition, 76
Traditional networking, 469
Transition effects, 443
Transitional device, 285
Transitional expressions, 140, 141, 363
  clear business letters feature, 205
Transitions, 363

Transmission of meaning, 12
Transmitting, anticipate problems in, 15
Transparencies, 434
  overhead, 434–435
Transparency International, 87
Transportation technologies, advancement in, 72
TransUnion, 291
Trip, convention, and conference reports, 367–369
  See also Reports
Trite business phrases, 154, 156
Truth telling, 23
Tuckman, B. A., 37
Twain, Mark, 15

U

U.S. Food and Drug Administration, 132
U.S. Securities and Exchange Commission, 155
UCLA, 425
Unbiased, 281
Underdeveloped country, 71
Underlining
  graphic techniques, 155, 156
  tips for maximizing scannability, 482
Unilever, 71, 201
Unreceptive audiences, 133
Unsolicited jobs, 491
  cover letter for, 493
Unsolicited proposal, 394
Uptalk, 60
Upward communication flow, 20–21
  improving, 20–21
  See also Communication channels
Upward flowing persuasive messages within organizations, 246–248
USB flash drive, 441
Use policies, 184
Usenet, 325

V

Value of differences, 92
Values, 73
  adapting presentations to international and cross-cultural audiences, 450–451
Value/size, main ideas organized according to, 430
Variables, 355
Varner, 74

Venture capital, 401
Verb agreement, A-4–A-5
Verb mood, A-4
Verb tense, A-3–A-4
  consistency, 407
Verb voice, A-4
Verbs
  action of, A-9
  linking, A-9
  objects of, A-6–A-7
  plural, A-5
  singular, A-5
Verbal message, 13
Verbal signposts, 432
Vertical bar chart. See Bar charts
Vertical lists, improving skim value by adding, 155
Video, 434
  improving downward information flow with, 20
Video phones, 11
Video résumé, 486
  See also Résumé
Video transmission, 17
Videoconferencing, 8, 11, 17, 37, 48, 107
Vigor, 153–154
Virtual communities, 326
Virtual meetings, 49
Virtual teams, 9, 36–37
Visual aids, 433–435
  adjusting to international and multicultural audiences, 451, 452
  gaining and keeping attention of audience, 429
  oral presentations, 452
  use effectively, 447
Visual clichés, 437
Vivid words, 136
Vivisimo/Clusty, 328
Voice conferencing, 11, 48
Voice mail, 8, 17, 60, 107, 453, 454
  improving skills, 451–454
Voice messages, internal communication, 15
Voice recognition, 10
Volunteering, 466
Volunteerism, 242

W

Wal-Mart, 7, 22, 70, 71, 76, 80, 93
Walt Disney Imagineering, 425, 450, 455
Warnings, written clearly, 116
Web browsing, 10, 443–444
Web conferencing, 11, 48–49

Web document builders, 134
Web pages, computers help create, 134
Web presentations, 444
Web research, 327
    sample business plans, 402
Web search tools, 328
Web sites, 17
    culturally customized global, 77
Web sources
    accuracy of, 329, 330
    authority of, 329, 330
    content of, 329, 330
    currency of, 329, 330
Webcast, 20
WebEx Communications Inc., 11, 46, 48
Weblogs, 8
    researching the target company, 504
    See also Blog
Wendy's, 149
Whistleblowing, 25
White space, 172
    tips for maximizing scannability, 482
Whiteboards, 105, 434
Whitman, Margaret "Meg", 238
Who/whoever, subjective-case constructions, A-7
Whom/whomever, objective-case constructions, A-7
Wi-Fi, 17, 183
Wikipedia, 104, 326, 330
Wikis, 8, 11, 37, 50, 72, 104, 105, 107, 326
Wildcards, 327
Winfrey, Oprah, 52
Wireless devices, 10, 72
Wireless fidelity ("Wi-Fi") networks, 17
Wireless networking, 8, 9
Women, cultural prejudices, 78
Word document, submitting your résumé as, 487
Word length, readability formulas measure, 155–156
Word-of-mouth advertising, 311
Words
    confusing, A-21–A-22
    encoding involves, 13
    frequently misspelled, A-22–A-23
    knowledge workers deal with, 4

languages based on pictographical characters representing meanings of, 77
languages that use letters describing sounds of, 77
low- and high-context cultures different of, 76–77
nonverbal cues reinforce spoken, 56
using precise and vigorous, 115, 116
Word-wrap, 177
Work environments, changing, 6, 9
Work experience, 472–473
Work plan, 317
    reports, 320–321, 418
    team-based written and oral presentations, 449
Work teams, 35, 90
Workforce diversity
    capitalizing on, 89–92
    increasingly diverse, 9–12
    See also Age bias; Diversity; Ethnicity; Gender; Minority; Physically challenged individuals; Race; Religion
Working bibliography, 329
Workplace
    avoid getting fired over your use of Internet, 180
    communication skills in today's, 3–4
    delivering bad news in, 294–295
    expanded team-based management, 7–8
    factors in today's, 7–12
    flattened management hierarchies, 7
    heightened global competition, 7
    increasingly diverse workforce, 9–12
    innovative communication technologies, 8
    new work environments, 9
    nonverbal communication skills in, 59
    perils of casual apparel, 58
    soft skills in today's, 34–35
Workplace listening, 50–54
Works Cited, C-1
    bibliography, C-2
    MLA sample, C-3

portions of, C-2
World Bank, 86
World Trade Organization (WTO), 71
World Wide Web, 72, 77, 325–330, 465
    evaluating sources of, 329–330
    identifying search tools, 326–327
    Internet search strategies and techniques, 327–329
    understanding the vastness and complexity of, 325–326
    See also Internet
World Wildlife Foundation, 431
Worst- and best-case scenarios, 431, 432
Wright, Daisy, 512
Writer's block, 134
Writers
    group similar ideas together to see relationships and follow arguments, 127
    unskilled and unethical, 150
Writing, 102, 104, 125, 172, 176, 203, 209, 213, 220, 243, 256, 277, 284, 296, 332, 368, 374, 396
    skills, 4, 18
    style of a report, 316
    team-based written and oral presentations, 449
    tips, 406–417
    See also Writing process (3-x-3)
Writing plan
    confirmation message, 190
    procedural messages, 188
    request messages, 184
    response messages, 187
Writing process (3-x-3), 102–103
    adapting and altering, 103
    approaching systematically, 101–106
    business writing basics, 101–102
    phase 1
        adapt, 109–116, 172, 202–203, 251, 276–277
        analyze, 106–108, 172, 202–203, 251, 276–277, 317–319, 436

anticipate, 102, 108–109, 172, 202–203, 276–277, 319–320
    phase 2
        compose, 134–141, 172, 204, 277
        organize, 127–133, 172, 204, 277
        research, 124–127, 172, 204, 277, 437
    phase 3
        evaluate, 102, 160–161, 172–173, 204, 277
        proofread, 102, 157–160, 172–173, 204, 277
        revise, 102, 104, 149–156, 176, 204
    recursive nature of, 103
    scheduling the process, 103
    understanding the power of business letters, 201–204
    writing in teams, 103–105
Written communication, 4, 15, 18
Written messages
    computers can help create, 134
    enhancing effectiveness to intercultural audiences, 83–84
Written presentations, organizing team-based, 448–449

X
Xerox, 41
XM, 403

Y
Yahoo!, 181, 326, 327, 328
Yahoo HotJobs (Yahoo HotJobs .com), 466, 467
Yahoogroups.com, 490
Yardstick reports, 377–381
    See also Reports
You view, 110, 111, 206, 212, 259
YouTube, 325, 482
Yum! Brands Inc., 3, 149

Z
Zara, 124
Ziglar, Zig, 252